The Good Pub Guide 1$

The Good Pub Guide 1989

Edited by Alisdair Aird

Assistant editor: Fiona May

Which? BOOKS

PUBLISHED BY CONSUMERS' ASSOCIATION
AND HODDER & STOUGHTON

Which? Books are commissioned and researched by
The Association for Consumer Research
and published by Consumers' Association,
2 Marylebone Road, London NW1 4DX, and
Hodder & Stoughton, 47 Bedford Square,
London WC1B 3DP

Designed by Trevor Vincent and Tim Higgins
Illustrations by Trevor Vincent from photographs by the editor
Cover artwork by Julie Tennent
Maps by Eugene Fleury

The Good Pub Guide.—1989.
    1. Hotels, taverns, etc.—Great Britain—
    Directories   2. Restaurants, lunchrooms etc.
    —Great Britain—Directories
    I. Aird, Alisdair   II. Consumers' Association
    647'.9541'05   TX910.G7

ISBN 0 340 43067 2

Typeset by Gee Graphics Limited
Crayford
Printed and bound in Great Britain by
Hazell Watson & Viney Limited
Member of BPCC plc
Aylesbury, Bucks

Contents

Introduction

In August 1988 the law was changed to allow English and Welsh pubs to stay open all day, except on Sundays. Scottish pubs have been able to do that for more than ten years. By delaying our editorial schedule, we were able to find out what pubs would be doing under the new law. As soon as the change was settled, but before it came into effect, we wrote to each of the pubs included as main entries, asking them about their plans. Many had decided already what they'd be doing. Those that hadn't we telephoned or wrote to again – in August, while the new law was actually coming into operation. This is the first piece of serious research actually to explore on a country-wide basis how the new law is in practice affecting opening times. (Of course we have to admit that the reason we did the work wasn't so much for the sake of the research itself. Its main purpose was to make sure that this new edition has up-to-date information about the opening times of each pub it includes as a main entry.)

In the country as a whole, nearly one in three pubs have decided to stay open all day. In many cases this is (as we predicted last year) on Saturdays only; and all-day opening is more common in the summer than the winter.

Interestingly, we found exactly one in three Scottish pubs – a virtually identical figure – were opening all day when we produced the first edition of this book, which was researched in 1981–2 (their law had been changed not so long before, in 1976). In the six or seven years since then, the proportion of Scottish pubs opening all day has, according to our records, steadily climbed each year. It's now double what it was back then; this year, around two-thirds of all Scottish pubs regularly stay open all day (at least in summer, or at weekends). Obviously, the reason for these pubs staying open through the afternoon when they didn't before is that it makes commercial sense for them to – they profit more, by satisfying a demand which previously they didn't. It's unlikely that these commercial pressures will be wildly different in England and Wales. So the proportion of all-day pubs in England and Wales is likely to climb gradually until, in five to ten years, it reaches the current Scottish proportion – about twice as many pubs opening all day as do now.

In general, as you'd expect, pubs in areas where tourism is important are more likely to stay open all afternoon than pubs elsewhere. And in particular, London pubs are twice as likely to stay open all day as pubs elsewhere. Two-thirds of the London main entries in this book are now opening all day. (As some of these are doing so only on weekdays and closing altogether at the weekend, we have to conclude that a main source of afternoon drinkers in London must be not tourists but people who work locally.)

Elsewhere, it's in the holiday parts of Cornwall, Devon, Wales and, particularly, Cumbria and Derbyshire that the move to all-day opening is strongest; on paper, the same looks true of Norfolk, but the sample of pubs involved there is too small for us to be sure that it's representative of the area. Looking more closely at the figures bears out this general impression that tourism and holiday use is the important factor. The neighbouring counties of Berkshire and Buckinghamshire, for example, share many similarities, with neither really springing to mind as a holiday or day-out destination. But we found nearly twice as high a proportion of Buckinghamshire pubs staying open all day as we found in Berkshire. Close investigation revealed that Buckinghamshire's relatively high showing is due to the fact that many pubs in the Chilterns have decided to stay open on Saturday afternoons to cater for people out walking.

Some parts of the country which are full of holidaymakers have a surprisingly low proportion of all-day pubs. Considering how many people are out and about during the day there – particularly at weekends, and in summer during the week too – we were surprised to find a lower-than-average proportion of all-day pubs in the

Cotswolds and on the Isle of Wight. We'd have expected more pubs to stay open in the Yorkshire Dales and Moors, too; in fact, the proportion's no higher than the national average.

Of course, it's true that, in these areas, the pubs that walkers and other people having a day out are most likely to come across are precisely those very small family-run establishments where all-day opening would be a real administrative headache. And there are many areas where there will be some people around during the afternoon who want refreshment, but not enough to produce a profit for the pubs if they all stay open (with the extra staff costs that entails). As we were doing our research on opening hours, it became clear that many pubs were worrying about this – and, more significantly, worrying about it as a group and not just as individuals. Though publicans are, as a breed, among the most marked individualists in the world, there is in fact a long tradition of mutual co-operation and concerted action between them – particularly within the same area. So, naturally, publicans have been talking to each other about what to do (when it's their decision – the breweries, in general much more bullish about all-day opening than individual publicans, have been pressing those licensees that they control to stay open unless it's clearly uneconomic to). It seems to us that in many areas where there isn't an obvious prospect of profit for all pubs if all stay open, licensees have been inclined to group together and take a joint stand against all-day opening.

That's understandable. If the publicans in the neighbouring villages of Much Messing, Dryhope and Little Luck reckon they'd need, between them, a hundred potential customers coming through their valley in the afternoon to show a profit, and in fact there are only fifty potential customers, no one can blame them for deciding to stay closed. But that still leaves those fifty turned-away customers just as badly off as they were when it was the law that stopped them getting their afternoon refreshments. Indeed, it's precisely in the less visited places that dropping into a quiet pub can be almost the summit of enjoyment – and that finding instead a locked door can be a pitiful disappointment.

So we were particularly interested to find two remote areas – one up in the Lake District, the other a string of downland hamlets along the Wiltshire/Hampshire border – where publicans have been working out a joint rota system. The idea is that, day by day, pubs in the rota should take it in turns to stay open. There are all sorts of practical difficulties, but the principle of this is surely sound. In the many places where there will be some demand for afternoon service in pubs, but not enough demand to keep all or even most of the pubs there open, it must make sense to try to work out a way of satisfying that demand (and profiting from doing so), instead of slamming the door in its face. Broader-based support for this sort of initiative would be welcome, perhaps even aiming for co-operation between breweries: though we can hardly hope that even the most enthusiastic push by a regional tourist authority could bring about the happy situation that all a thirsty afternoon traveller needed to remember was that on Mondays Marstons, Manns and Morlands pubs would be open, on Tuesdays Tetleys, Tollys and Trumans, on Wednesdays Wadworths, Watneys, Websters, Wards and Wethereds, on Thursdays Theakstons and Thwaites, and on Fridays Flowers, Fremlins and Fullers.

This does bring us back to another serious point – information. In our inspection tours this last year, we've kept a tally of which pubs have a notice outside saying when they're open. The proportion is about one in ten. When the new licensing law was being worked out, this *Guide* was not alone in strongly urging the Home Office to require pubs to post a notice of their hours. Nothing was done. Since then, the breweries have been trying to persuade publicans that it does make sense to tell their potential customers when they're open. So far, we've seen little sign of positive action, though. With the new law, clear notices of opening times are doubly important. Before the change in the law, for instance, it was a reasonable assumption in most places that an unfamiliar pub would open at around 6ish. Certainly, in those days no one seeing a locked pub door at 4 in the afternoon would dream of hanging around in case it opened; or wonder whether it would be worth coming by on another afternoon – Saturday, say – in case it was open then. But the new law has opened up exactly those sorts of possibility. It's clear from the opening times quoted in this new edition that there's now tremendous diversity. In the old days, it was a minor annoyance when publicans kept mum about their opening times. Now, it's infuriating. So we ask all those publicans who refuse to put up opening-hours notices: How will you like it when your thwarted customers hammer on your door until you come and tell them just when you are open?

The new law highlights two other problems. First, children. Afternoon opening makes one think of family outings. Yet there are nonsensical variations from area to area in the way that the law about children in pubs is enforced. The law is that children under fourteen are not allowed in that part of a pub in which alcohol is served. In some areas that law is zealously enforced. In others it doesn't seem to be enforced at all. For a family travelling from one area to another, that sort of variation can be embarrassing and disappointing – as indeed it can for the traditional pubgoer who likes to be able to get to the bar counter without stumbling through a knot of nippers. There's the extra difficulty that a law drawn up in the days when 'nice' pubs had lots of little rooms, some with serving-bars and others without, doesn't match up with today, when so many pubs are just one big open-plan area. Absurd rules of thumb then come into play. One publican told us of wielding a tape measure to check on exactly where children sit in his pub; another inch closer to the bar counter, and he reckons he'll be breaking the law.

Then there's the whole question of how pubs are used nowadays. Of course in the last century grave mischiefs befell children in gin parlours. But today it's difficult to imagine anyone seriously suggesting that harm will come to children in any typical or representative pub. And if there are pubs where children under fourteen are running a genuine risk just by being there, then those dire places shouldn't be open at all – they should be closed down.

The only other widely heard argument in favour of the law as it stands is the claim that pubs are nicer places if they don't have children in them. That's surely not a respectable reason for keeping them out by law, though. Indeed, we'd go further and say that the existence of the law in its present form, and the present patchwork of variable enforcement, has actually perpetuated the conflict between the demands of those who want to chat, eat and drink in child-free peace and those who want a place where they can enjoy themselves with their family too. All too often, this particular law has served as an excuse for breweries and publicans. It lets them off the hook when the standard open-plan pub format clearly can't combine under one roof both the cosy adult clubbability which some customers expect and the more elastic style which others are coming to expect. And it's their pat answer when families complain at being relegated to some dismal box-room at the back.

Afternoon opening must surely bring closer a fundamental review of the law about children in pubs.

Another important question is what people now have available to drink in the afternoon. We've been encouraged by the greatly increased proportion of pubs which do decent coffee and even tea without endangering their pubby character. But there are still many publicans – and pub customers – who reserve for the coffee machine and the teapot the same sort of look that the virile young bullock reserves for the vet's knife. That's a missed opportunity for them, and with afternoon opening is a real let-down for many customers.

More seriously, there's the question of the pricing of soft drinks and near-beers – the low-alcohol lagers and beers that are increasingly heavily advertised.

Soft drinks earn the breweries a formidable amount of money. We now spend £3000 million a year on them. In pubs, while people have if anything been buying less beer, spending on soft drinks has been increasing by eight per cent a year, and accounts for about the same proportion of pubs' turnover as wine. The pub pays between 8p and 16p for a typical small soft drink bottle, with a normal price being

11p or 12p; we pay the pub typically 45p – a mark-up of three hundred per cent or more.

The pubs and breweries say that what we're paying for isn't just the drink, it's the service and atmosphere – and of course there's something in that. But it's no coincidence that the great bulk of soft drinks sales in pubs are of Britvic and Schweppes; between them, around ninety per cent of orange juice sales, for instance. The cola market in pubs is similarly dominated by Pepsi Cola and, particularly, Coca-Cola. What one tends to forget is that Coca-Cola and Schweppes both come from the same firm; and what few people realise is that not only do Britvic and Pepsi come from a single firm, but that this firm is ninety per cent owned by a consortium of three of the big five brewers – Bass, Allied (Ind Coope) and Whitbreads. So the soft drinks market is overwhelmingly dominated by two firms – one of which boils down to a consortium of breweries which together owns about a third of Britain's pubs. Though the two soft drinks companies say that they don't influence the pubs' pricing of their products, it would be easier to believe that the pricing was free and fair if this duopoly had a less pervasively powerful grip on the market. Another factor which makes us look askance at soft drinks pricing is the way it appears to be linked almost automatically to the pricing of beer; it's very rare to find soft drinks priced significantly lower than the price of a half-pint of beer, and they're often more expensive – despite the fact that they don't carry the tax burden which beer carries.

Taking account of the point about paying for atmosphere, we think pubs are generally overcharging on soft drinks by 10p a go.

The same sort of argument applies to low-alcohol beers. They typically cost up to around 10p more for a half-pint than the equivalent normal beer. Yet they pay about 9p a pint less in tax. The breweries say that the weak stuff is more expensive to make than the other. But is this sort of pricing – effectively charging twenty per cent extra for something less – really going to help ensure that afternoon pub users aren't just afternoon alcoholics?

Having nagged a bit, it's time to say something positive.

There's been a lot of talk about hooliganism in or connected to pubs. This *Guide* probably gets more direct and independent information about what pubs are actually like than any other organisation. This last year we've had about 20,000 reports from several thousand readers, commenting directly on individuals pubs. They are always quickest to write to us when they have a problem or difficulty or unpleasant experience to tell us about. On the basis of this dense and continuous flow of information about British pubs, we can say with certainty that in the great majority of pubs there is no trace whatsoever of hooliganism – it just doesn't exist as a general problem in pubs. What is equally certain, of course, is that most hooliganism is drinks-related. Our conclusion must be that it's related to drinks either bought in a relatively very few pubs which are quite unrepresentative of pubs generally and should therefore be identifiable, or to drinks not bought in pubs at all. So we'd see the well run typical British pub as, if anything, a restraint on drinks-related hooliganism; a place where drinking is generally responsible.

Alisdair Aird

What is a Good Pub?

The main entries in this book have been through a two-stage sifting process. First of all, some 2000 regular correspondents keep in touch with us about the pubs they visit, and nearly double that number report occasionally. This keeps us up to date about pubs included in previous editions – it's their alarm signals that warn us when a pub's standards have dropped (after a change of management, say), and it's their continuing approval that reassures us about keeping a pub as a main entry for another year. Very important, though, are the reports they send us on pubs we don't know at all. It's from these new discoveries that we make up a shortlist, to be considered for possible inclusion as new main entries. The more people that report favourably on a new pub, the more likely it is to win a place on this shortlist – especially if some of the reporters belong to our hard core of about five hundred trusted correspondents whose judgment we have learned to rely on. These are people who have each given us detailed comments on dozens of pubs, and shown that (when we ourselves know some of those pubs too) their judgment is closely in line with our own.

This brings us to the acid test. Each pub, before inclusion as a main entry, is inspected anonymously by the Editor, the Assistant Editor, or both. They have to find some special quality that would make strangers enjoy visiting it. What often marks the pub out for special attention is good value food (and that might mean anything from a well made sandwich, with good fresh ingredients at a low price, to imaginative cooking outclassing most restaurants in the area). Maybe the drinks are out of the ordinary (pubs with several hundred whiskies, with remarkable wine lists, with home-made country wines or good beer or cider made on the premises, with a wide range of well kept real ales or bottled beers from all over the world). Perhaps there's a special appeal about it as a place to stay, with good bedrooms and obliging service. Maybe it's the building itself (from centuries-old parts of monasteries to extravagant Victorian gin-palaces), or its surroundings (lovely countryside, attractive waterside, extensive well kept garden), or what's in it (charming furnishings, extraordinary collections of bric-à-brac).

Above all, though, what makes the good pub is its atmosphere – you should be able to feel at home there, and feel not just that *you're* glad you've come out but that *they're* glad you've come.

It follows from this that a great many ordinary locals, perfectly good in their own right, don't earn a place in the book. What makes them attractive to their regular customers (an almost clubby chumminess) may even make strangers feel rather out of place.

Another important point is that there's not necessarily any link between charm and luxury – though we like our creature comforts as much as anyone. A basic unspoilt village tavern, with hard seats and a flagstone floor, may be worth travelling miles to find, while a deluxe pub-restaurant may not be worth crossing the street for. Landlords can't buy the Good Pub accolade by spending thousands on thickly padded banquettes, soft music and luxuriously shrimpy sauces for their steaks – they can only win it, by having a genuinely personal concern for both their customers and their pub.

Using the *Guide*

THE COUNTIES

England has been split alphabetically into counties, mainly to make it easier for people scanning through the book to find pubs near them. Each chapter starts by picking out pubs that are specially attractive for one reason or another.

Occasionally, counties have been grouped together into a single chapter, and metropolitan areas have been included in the counties around them – for example, Merseyside in Lancashire. When there's any risk of confusion, we have put a note about where to find a county at the place in the book where you'd probably look for it. But if in doubt, check the Contents.

Scotland and Wales have each been covered in single chapters, and London appears immediately before them at the end of England. Except in London (which is split into Central, North, South, West and East), pubs are listed alphabetically under the name of the town or village where they are. If the village is so small that you probably wouldn't find it on a road map, we've listed it under the name of the nearest sizeable village or town instead. The maps use the same town and village names, and additionally include a few big cities that don't have any listed pubs – for orientation.

We always list pubs in their true locations – so if a village is actually in Buckinghamshire that's where we list it, even if its postal address is via some town in Oxfordshire. Just once or twice, while the village itself is in one county the pub is just over the border in the next-door county. We then use the village county, not the pub one.

STARS

Specially good pubs are picked out with a star after their name. In a few cases pubs have two stars: these are outstanding pubs, really worth going out of your way to find. And just three pubs have three stars – the real aristocrats. The stars do *not* signify extra luxury or specially good food. The detailed description of each pub shows what its special appeal is, and it's that that the stars refer to.

FOOD AWARDS AND STAY AWARDS: ⊗ 🛏

The knife-and-fork symbol shows those pubs where food is a main attraction. The bed symbol shows pubs which are good as places to stay in.

RECOMMENDERS

At the end of each main entry we include the names of readers who have recently recommended that pub (unless they've asked us not to). Important note: the description of the pub and the comments on it are our own and *not* the recommenders'; they are based on our own personal inspections and on later verification of facts with each pub. As some recommenders' names appear quite often, you can get an extra idea of what a pub is like by seeing which other pubs those recommenders have approved.

LUCKY DIPS

At the end of each county chapter we include brief descriptions of pubs that have been recommended by readers, with the readers' names in brackets. They give pointers to thousands of pubs well worth trying, with descriptions often reflecting the balanced judgement of a number of different readers. They haven't usually been inspected by us, unless the recommenders include the initials *LYM* or *BB*. *LYM* means the pub was in a previous edition of the *Guide*. The usual reason that it's no longer a main entry is that although we've heard nothing really condemnatory about it we've not had enough favourable reports to be sure that it's still ahead of the local competition. *BB* means that although the pub has never been a main entry we have inspected it, found nothing against it, and reckon it's useful to know of – and perhaps worth a closer look. In both these cases the description is our own; in others, it's based on the readers' reports.

The flow of these reports has now built up to the point where we are getting hundreds of them each week, many from an inner core of five hundred or so readers whose judgement we have learned to respect particularly highly. So we now reckon this intelligence network has become reliable enough for us to give firm recommendations for some *Lucky Dip* pubs even though we haven't inspected them personally. Such pubs are marked with a ☆. Roughly speaking, we'd say that these pubs are as much worth considering, at least for the virtues described for them, as the main entries themselves.

The *Lucky Dips* (particularly, of course, the starred ones) are under consideration for inspection for a future edition – so please let us have any comments you can make on them. You can use the report forms at the end of the book, the report card included in it, or just write direct (no stamp needed if posted in the UK). Our address is *The Good Pub Guide*, FREEPOST, London SW10 0BR.

MAP REFERENCES

All pubs are given a four-figure map reference. On the main entries it looks like this: SX5678 Map 1. Map 1 means that the town or village is on the first map at the end of the book. SX means it's in the square labelled SX on that map. The first figure, 5, tells you to look along the grid at the top and bottom of the SX square for the figure 5. The *third* figure, 7, tells you to look down the grid at the side of the square to find the figure 7. Imaginary lines drawn down and across the square from these figures should intersect near the pub itself.

The second and fourth figures, the 6 and the 8, are for more precise pinpointing, and are really for use with larger-scale maps such as road atlases or the Ordnance Survey 1:50,000 maps, which use exactly the same map reference system. On the relevant Ordnance Survey map, instead of finding the 5 marker on the top grid you'd find the 56 one; instead of the 7 on the side grid you'd look for the 78 marker. This makes it very easy to locate even the smallest village.

Where a pub is exceptionally difficult to find, we include a six-figure reference in the directions, such as OS Sheet 102 reference 654783. This refers to Sheet 102 of the Ordnance Survey 1:50,000 maps, which explain how to use the six-figure references to pinpoint a pub to the nearest hundred metres.

MOTORWAY PUBS

If a pub is within four or five miles of a motorway junction, and reaching it doesn't involve much slow traffic, we give special directions for finding it from the motorway. And the Special Interest Lists at the end of the book include a list of these pubs, motorway by motorway.

PRICES AND OTHER FACTUAL DETAILS

The *Guide* went to press during the summer of 1988. As late as possible before that, each pub was sent a checking sheet to provide up-to-date food, drink and bedroom prices and other factual information. In the last two or three years we've found that prices tend to increase by about ten per cent over the year – so you should expect that sort of increase by summer 1989. But if you find a significantly different price (with a few pubs this last year, some prices have jumped by over thirty per cent), *please let us know*. Not every pub returned the sheet to us (if it didn't, we don't show a licensee's name after the brewery name at the end of the entry), and in some cases those that did omitted some prices. In such cases we ourselves were often able to gather the information – especially prices – anyway. But where details are missing, that is the explanation. Again, this is something we'd particularly welcome readers' reports on.

Real ale is used by us to mean beer that has been maturing naturally in its cask. We do not count as real ale beer which has been pasteurised or filtered to remove its natural yeasts. If it is kept under a blanket of carbon dioxide ('blanket pressure') to preserve it, we still generally mention it – as long as the pressure is too light for you to notice any extra fizz, it's hard to tell the difference. But we say that the carbon dioxide blanket is there. So many pubs now stock one of the main brands of draught cider that we normally mention cider only if the pub keeps quite a range, or one of the less common farm-made ciders.

Wines and spirits are mentioned only if there's an unusual range, or if we know the quality of wine to be above the general pub average – which is low. (Please let us know if you come across decent wine in a pub.) If we mention country wines, we mean traditional elderberry-type wines.

Meals refers to what is sold in the bar, not in any separate restaurant. It means that pub sells food in its bar substantial enough to do as a proper meal – something you'd sit down to with knife and fork. It doesn't necessarily mean you can get three separate courses.

Snacks means sandwiches, ploughman's, pies and so forth, rather than pork scratchings or packets of crisps. We always mention sandwiches in the text if we know that a pub does them – if you don't see them mentioned, assume you can't get them.

The food listed in the description of each pub is an example of the sort of thing you'd find served in the bar on a normal day. We try to indicate any difference we know of between lunchtime and evening, and between summer and winter (on the whole stressing summer food more). In winter many pubs tend to have a more restricted range, particularly of salads, and tend then to do more in the way of filled baked potatoes, casseroles and hot pies. We always mention barbecues if we know a pub does them. Food quality and variety may be affected by holidays – particularly in a small pub, where the licensees do the cooking themselves (May and early June seems to be a popular time for licensees to take their holidays).

Unless we say otherwise, you can generally assume that bar food is served at normal lunch and supper times (which of course vary from region to region). Though we note days when pubs have told us they don't do food, experience suggests that you should play safe on Sundays and check first with any pub before planning an expedition that depends on getting a meal there. Also, out-of-the-way pubs often cut down on cooking during the week if they're quiet – as they tend to be, except at holiday times. Please let us know if you find anything different from what we say!

Any separate restaurant is mentioned, and we give a telephone number if tables can be booked. We also note any pubs which told us they'd be keeping their restaurant open into Sunday afternoons (when, in England and Wales, they have to close their bars). But in general all comments on the type of food served, and in particular all the other details about meals and snacks at the end of each entry, relate to the pub food and not to the restaurant food.

Children under fourteen are now allowed into at least some part of most of the pubs included in this *Guide* (there is no legal restriction on fourteen-year-olds going into the bar, though only eighteen-year-olds can get alcohol there). As we went to press, we asked pubs a series of detailed questions about their rules. *Children welcome* means the pub has told us that it simply lets them come in, with no special restrictions. In other cases we report exactly what arrangements pubs say they make for children. However, we have to note that in readers' experience some pubs set a time-limit (say, no children after 8pm) that they haven't told us about, while others may impose some other rule (children only if eating, for example). If you come across this, please let us know, so that we can clarify the information for the pub concerned in the next edition. Even if we don't mention children at all, it is worth asking: one or two pubs told us frankly that they do welcome children but don't want to advertise the fact for fear of being penalised. All but one or two pubs (we mention these in the text) allow children in their garden or on their terrace if they have one.

Dogs, cats and other animals are mentioned in the text if we know either that they are likely to be present or that they are specifically excluded – we depend chiefly on readers and partly on our own inspections for this information.

This year, for the first time, you'll see some entries say something like 'on *Good Walks Guide* Walk 22' (or, in the *Lucky Dips*, on 'GWG 22'). This means that the pub is on one of the walks described in *Holiday Which? Good Walks Guide* edited by Tim Locke, also published by Consumers' Association and Hodder & Stoughton (price £8.95).

Parking is not mentioned if you should normally be able to park without difficulty outside the pub or in a private car park. But if we know that parking space is limited or metered, we say so.

Opening hours are for summer weekdays. If these show a pub stays open until 11pm, it will close at 10.30pm in winter unless we say *all year*. And in winter some pubs open an hour or so later, too; we mention this where we know of it. In the country many pubs may open rather later and close earlier than their details show unless there are plenty of customers around (if you come across this, please let us know – with details). Unless we say otherwise for a particular county or pub, pubs generally stay open until 11pm on Friday and Saturday evening. Since summer 1988 pubs in England and Wales have been allowed to stay open all day on Mondays to Saturdays, from 11am (earlier, if the area's licensing magistrates have permitted) until 11pm; Scottish pubs have been allowed to do this since 1976. As late as possible when we went to press, we asked all the main entries if they would actually be staying open in the afternoon. The details show what they told us – but the scheme is so new that, understandably, many warned us they'd have to see how things went over the next year or so (a few simply couldn't make up their minds!); again, we'd be very grateful to hear of any differences from the hours we quote. The new licensing law allows twenty minutes' drinking-up time after the quoted hours (it used to be ten minutes).

Sunday hours are standard for all English and Welsh pubs that open on that day: 12–3, 7–10.30. In Scotland a few pubs close on Sundays (we specify those that we know of), most are open 12.30–2.30 and 6.30–11, and some stay open all day. If we know of a pub closing for any day of the week or part of the year, we say so. The few pubs which we say stay closed on Monday do open on Bank Holiday Mondays.

Bedroom prices normally include full English breakfasts (if these are available, which they usually are), VAT and any automatic service charge that we know about. If we give just one price, it is the total price for two people sharing a double or twin-bedded room for one night. Otherwise, prices before the '/' are for single occupancy, prices after it for double. A capital B against the price means that it includes a private bathroom, a capital S a private shower. As all this coding packs in quite a lot of information, some examples may help to explain it:

> £20 on its own means that's the total bill for two people sharing a twin or double room without a private bath; the pub has no rooms with private bath, and a single person might have to pay that full price
> £20B means exactly the same – but all the rooms have a private bath
> £20(£24B) means rooms with private baths cost £4 extra
> £15/£20(£24B) means the same as the last example, but also shows that there are single rooms for £15, none of which have private bathrooms

If there's a choice of rooms at different prices, we normally give the cheapest. If there are seasonal price variations, we give the summer price (the highest). This winter – 1988–9 – many inns, particularly in the country, will have special cheaper rates. And at other times, especially in holiday areas, you will often find prices cheaper if you stay for several nights. On weekends, inns that aren't in obvious weekending areas often have bargain rates for two- or three-night stays.

Changes are inevitable during the course of the year. Landlords change, and so do their policies. And, as we've said, not all returned our fact-checking sheets. We very much hope that you will find everything just as we say. But if you find anything different, please let us know, using the tear-out card in the middle of the book (which doesn't need an envelope), the report forms at the end of the book, or just a letter. You don't need a stamp: the address is *The Good Pub Guide*, FREEPOST, London SW10 0BR.

Author's acknowledgements

Particular thanks to Bridget Warrington, who joined us in the spring, and Martin Hamilton, who helped out once again with the summer editing crush.

Thanks too to the publicans who have taken such trouble over filling in our very detailed fact sheets – and thanks to them, also, for making and running so many friendly and attractive places.

We owe a great deal to the many hundreds of readers who report, often regularly, on pubs – thanks to you all. Special thanks to the people who have given most help to this new edition (in rough order of volume of reports they've sent us this year): Jon Wainwright, Nick Dowson, Alison Hayward, Wayne Brindle, Roger Huggins, Gwen and Peter Andrews, Roger and Anne Evans, Lyn and Bill Capper, Rob and Gill Weeks, G Gibson, Thomas Nott, S V Bishop, WHBM, Ian Phillips, Derek and Sylvia Stephenson, E G Parish, Mrs Heather Sharland, M A and W R Proctor, Joan Olivier, Phil and Sally Gorton, J S Evans, Richard Sanders, S J A Velate, Gordon and Daphne, Tom McLean, Dave Butler, Lesley Storey, Richard Houghton, BKA, TBB, Pamela and Merlyn Horswell, Dr John Innes, R P Hastings, Brian and Anna Marsden, Frank Cummings, Jenny and Brian Seller, Dr A V Lewis, A T Langton, Len Beattie, Mr and Mrs J H Adam, Simon C Collett-Jones, Dr and Mrs S Donald, Ewan McCall, Roger Taylor, Dr Graham Bush, Peter Corriss, PLC, Alan and Ruth Woodhouse, Michael and Alison Sandy, Sue Cleasby, J C Proud, Patrick Young, David and Flo Wallington, M C Howells, Chris and Shirley Fluck, Stanley Matthews, Peter Griffiths, W P P Clarke, Charles and Mary Winpenny, Joan and John Wyatt, Nigel Paine, Dr and Mrs A K Clarke, H G and C J McCafferty, Mike Hallewell, D L Johnson, Dave Braisted, Lee Goulding, Comus Elliott, W F Leech, Carolyn and Steve Harvey, Joy Heatherley, T D Haunch, Tom Evans.

England

Avon   *see* Somerset
Bedfordshire   *see* Cambridgeshire

Berkshire

Food is often a particular high point of pubs here: the civilised Royal Oak at Yattendon stands out for its remarkable choice of inventive dishes – certainly one of the country's top food pubs. Others to note specially for food include both entries in Aldworth (the helpings at the Four Points so formidably large that regulars enjoy watching newcomers' faces when their plates arrive), the reliable Crown in Bray, the Horns at Crazies Hill (odd to find authentic South-East Asian cooking in such a British pub), the Bird in Hand at Knowl Hill (their buffet is particularly attractive), the Red House at Marsh Benham (imaginative variations on favourite themes), the Little Angel in Remenham (especially for fish), the homely Harrow in West Ilsley (a new entry – simple food, but well done, and good value), the Five Bells at Wickham (our long-standing choice for an off-motorway soup and sandwich), and – for its restaurant, where you can make the most of their fine wine list – the Dundas Arms by the water at Kintbury. Two pubs which have always been popular for their food are showing at least as much promise under new licensees – the Old Boot at Stanford Dingley (a much wider choice than before) and the Slug & Lettuce at Winkfield (taken over by the same small chain that scored high marks with us by leaving our top-rated White Horse near Petersfield in Hampshire as good as ever when they bought it). There are new people too at the Swan in Great Shefford and New Inn in Hampstead

The Crown, Bray

Norreys – preliminary reports suggest that such changes as they've made have won approval; and just as we go to press we hear that the Fox at Hermitage is due to change hands, though major changes in its style seem unlikely. Another change to note is the new Boathouse Bar at the stylish Swan in its lovely gardens by the Thames at Streatley – well worth a visit. Besides the Bell at Aldworth and the Old Boot (both classics of their kind), the county is rich in traditional country pubs, unassuming yet interesting inside, and often in charming settings – such as the cheerful Pineapple on Brimpton Common, the Pot Kiln tucked quietly into a fold of the hills at Frilsham (idyllic in summer, particularly), the little Belgian Arms with its pondside garden at Holyport, the Dew Drop lost in the woods above Hurley, and the quaint Bull just a stroll from the Thames at Sonning. Delving through the Lucky Dips will turn up many more of these Berkshire specialities: our own favourite is probably the Old Hatch Gate at Cockpole Green, though people who might find that too unashamedly basic might prefer instead the altogether more civilised variations on that theme exemplified by the Bell at Waltham St Lawrence (very promising new licensees) or the Plough just outside.

ALDWORTH SU5579 Map 2

Bell ★

The sound of cricket from the nearby playing fields, and seats among roses, mallows and lavender in the quiet side garden make this country pub a peaceful place in summer. It's cosy and warm in winter – and lively, with a cheerful, old-fashioned atmosphere. The small rooms have beams in the shiny ochre ceiling and benches built around the panelled walls and into the gaps left by a big disused fireplace and bread oven (though there's still a wood-burning stove). Perfectly kept Arkells BBB and Kingsdown, Badger Best and Morlands Mild (all on handpump) are handed through a small hatch in the central servery. Fresh hot crusty rolls are filled with Cheddar (50p), ham, pâté or Stilton (55p) and turkey or tongue (65p); darts, shove-ha'penny, dominoes, chess and Aunt Sally (the local single-pin version of skittles). At Christmas time steaming jugs of hot punch and mince pies are handed round after the local mummers perform in the road outside by the ancient well-head (the shaft is sunk 400 feet through the chalk). The path by the pub joins the nearby Ridgeway. *(Recommended by Chris Bourne, Gordon and Daphne, Ian Howard, Stan Edwards)*

Free house Real ale Snacks (not Mon) Children in tap-room Open 11–2.30, 6–11 all year; closed Mon (not bank hols) and 25 Dec

Four Points ⊗

B4009 towards Hampstead Norreys

Dating from 1638, this magnolia-painted thatched pub has simple red leatherette furniture on the red-tiled floor, china in a corner cupboard, a big log fire, vases of flowers, and good croûtons set out on the thick-topped wooden tables. Gargantuan helpings of good food (the menu depends on what the chef fancies cooking that day) include venison, rabbit or steak and kidney pie, liver and bacon or Dover sole (from £5.50), heaped up with lots of different vegetables. Other dishes include sandwiches (from 75p), soup (£1), ploughman's with imaginatively presented salads (£1.95), curried prawn mayonnaise or stuffed tomato, cheese and peppers (£2.25), and avocado cheesy bake salad, ox-tongue and egg pie, or lasagne (£2.70). Well kept Courage Directors, Morlands and Wadworths 6X on handpump, and a thoughtful choice of wines. A partly panelled carpeted side room has sensibly placed darts. The young barman uses a cash register with an odd combination of ancient and modern (a set of cups, one for each denomination of money, with an electronic calculator). Outside, the hanging baskets and flower tubs are very pretty, and the garden across from the pub has tables, climbing-frames, a little-old-lady shoe house and so forth. *(Recommended by John Bell, Dave Braisted, Ian Howard, Gordon and Daphne)*

Free house Licensee John Gillas Real ale Meals and snacks Children welcome Open 11–2.30, 6–11 all year; plans to open summer afternoons, inc Sun for teas

BRAY SU9079 Map 2
Crown ⊗ [illustrated on page 21]

1¾ miles from M4 junction 9; A308 towards Windsor, then left at Bray signpost on to B3028

There's a friendly, relaxed atmosphere in the partly panelled and softly lit main bar of this fourteenth-century timbered pub, and leather-backed seats around copper-topped or wooden tables, low beams, old timbers conveniently left at elbow height where walls have been knocked through, and a cosy winter fire; decorations include caricatures by Spy and his competitors, guns, pistols, and stuffed animals. Good bar food includes sandwiches on request, a choice of well filled rolls (70p), plough-man's (£3.25) and main dishes such as summer salads, cheese and asparagus flan (£3.25), steak and kidney pie, chilli con carne, lasagne or a curry (all £3.55), and popular home-made puddings; vegetables are grown in their kitchen garden; summer Sunday barbecues. Courage Best tapped from the cask, and a fair choice of wines; piped music. There are tables under cocktail parasols here, with more tables and benches on flagstones, shaded by a well trained vine. *(Recommended by JMC, Alison Hayward, Nick Dowson, Jon Wainwright)*

Courage Licensee Hugh Whitton Real ale Meals (not Sat lunchtime, or Sun but see above for barbecues) and lunchtime snacks Children welcome Restaurant tel Maidenhead (0628) 21936; closed Sun Open 10.30–2.30, 5.30–11

BRIMPTON COMMON SU5662 Map 2
Pineapple

B3051, W of Heath End

Standing on the site of a building mentioned in Domesday Book, this thriving, busy country pub has low and heavy black medieval beams, furniture mainly hewn from shiny golden tree-trunks (which suits the quarry-tiled floor and stripped brick and timbering), a rocking-chair by the fire, and wheel-back chairs around neater tables in a side eating area. Bar food includes sandwiches, salads, a very wide range of baked potatoes with enterprising fillings, a choice of several home-made pies, and casseroles such as venison or smoked trout. A lino-floored side area has bar billiards, sensibly placed darts, fruit machine and video pool game, and piped pop music. Well kept Flowers Original, Wethereds and Whitbreads Pompey Royal on handpump; good service. There are lots of picnic-table sets under cocktail parasols on a well hedged side lawn, with swings and a slide. *(Recommended by Neil Lusby, Wg Cdr R M Sparkes; more reports please)*

Wethereds (Whitbreads) Real ale Meals and snacks Open 11–2.30, 6–11 all year

COOKHAM SU8884 Map 2
Bel & the Dragon ★

High Street; B4447

The three communicating lounge rooms in this restful, comfortable old pub have oak panelling, old oak settles and leather chairs, pewter tankards hanging from heavy Tudor beams, and a quietly civilised atmosphere. A gravely friendly red-coated barman behind the very low zinc-topped bar counter serves well kept Brakspears and Youngs tapped from the cask, wines including decent ports and champagne, and all the ingredients necessary for proper cocktails. There are often free peanuts and so forth, as well as home-made soup or quiche (£1.75), home-made pizza (£2.50), slimmer's salad (£3.50), and freshly cut sandwiches to order (prawn £3.75, smoked salmon £4.75; toasties from £1.75). The Stanley Spencer Gallery is almost opposite. *(Recommended by TBB, Mr and Mrs T F Marshall, AE, John Hill, Mike Tucker)*

Free house   Licensee Mr F E Stuber   Real ale   Bar snacks   Restaurant tel Bourne End (062 85) 21263   Children in eating area of bar only   Open 11–2.30, 6–10.30; closed evening 25 Dec

CRAZIES HILL   SU7980   Map 2

Horns ⊗

From A4, take Warren Row Road at Cockpole Green signpost just E of Knowl Hill, then past Warren Row follow Crazies Hill signposts; from Wargrave, take A321 towards Henley, then follow Crazies Hill signposts – right at Shell garage, then left

Simply furnished, this little unspoilt tiled whitewashed cottage has basic beige-cushioned wall benches built into the cream dado, country kitchen chairs, low ceiling, and a cosy brown-wood side alcove. The South-East Asian cooking shows intimate first-hand acquaintance with the real thing: a genuinely Madras lamb curry (£3.95) served with dhal and chopped dry vegetables, say, with side dishes of mango chutney, hot chillies and fresh yoghurt; the samosas and curry puffs are authentic, and Thai prawns (£2.20), nasi goreng (£2.20) or Burmese chicken (£3.25); parties for special South-East Asian or 'six countries' suppers are welcome. There are less exotic dishes too – even sausages or cauliflower cheese (£1.45), ham, celery and Stilton bake (£2.75) and home-made lasagne or moussaka. Besides well kept Brakspears PA and SB on handpump, there's a small but carefully chosen range of decent wines, and a good collection of spirits – as examples, Macallan on optic, and Bunnahabhain (a fine single malt that unaccountably seems appreciated more abroad than in Britain); darts, shove-ha'penny, dominoes and cribbage. There are old-fashioned white garden seats from Lord's Cricket Ground and some picnic-table sets outside, with a side marquee for busy times. *(Recommended by Jane and Calum, Jane Kingsbury, Simon Collett-Jones, Mrs N P North)*

Brakspears   Licensees Andy and Mary Wheeler   Real ale   Meals (limited Sun and Mon evenings) and snacks   Small bistro area tel Wargrave (073 522) 3226   Children in bistro area up to 7.30   Open 11–3 (4pm Sat), 6–11 all year; considering longer afternoon openings

EAST ILSLEY   SU4981   Map 2

Crown & Horns

There are plenty of signs of this lively pub's interest in the surrounding horse-training country – from the racing prints and photographs on the walls in the partly panelled and beamed main bar, and the TV on for the racing in a side bar, to the conversation around you. It's also popular with real ale enthusiasts as there's an excellent and sensibly priced range that at any one time might include Arkells BBB, Morlands, Ruddles, Theakstons Old Peculier and Wadworths 6X, on handpump or tapped from the cask. And there's a fine collection of 170 whiskies from all over the world – Moroccan, Korean, Japanese, Chinese, Spanish and New Zealand. Bar food includes sandwiches (from 85p), soup (90p), ham and egg (£2.75), scampi (£2.95), trout with walnut and celery sauce (£5.75) and steak (£6); friendly service. The public bar has cribbage, and bar billiards, and there is a skittle alley. Fruit machine, juke box and piped music. The pretty paved stableyard has tables under two chestnut trees. Bypassed by the A34, the village is very peaceful. *(Recommended by Joan Olivier, Philip King, I R Hewitt, A M Kelly, C D T Spooner, Derek Stephenson)*

Free house   Licensees Chris and Jane Bexx   Real ale   Meals and snacks   Children in eating area   Open 10.30–2.30, 6–11 all year   Bedrooms tel East Ilsley (063 528) 205; £15/£25

FRILSHAM   SU5473 Map 2
Pot Kiln

From Yattendon follow Frilsham signpost, but just after crossing motorway go straight on towards Bucklebury when Frilsham is signposted right

Perhaps at its most appealing in summer on a quiet weekday, this simple and friendly brick house has sun-trap tables and folding garden chairs surrounded by sheltering woods and peaceful pastures. Inside, the rooms are simply furnished with bare benches and pews, wooden floorboards, a good log fire, and there's a timeless old-fashioned atmosphere. Well kept Arkells BBB, Morlands and Theakstons XB, all on handpump, are served from a hatch in the panelled entrance lobby – which just has room for one bar stool. Generous helpings of good value bar food include filled hot rolls, ploughman's, cottage pie or lasagne, big pizzas, and, in season, pheasant and even rook pie. The public bar has darts, dominoes, shove-ha'penny and cribbage. *(Recommended by Gordon and Daphne, Ian Howard, Stan Edwards, Phil and Sally Gorton)*

Free house   Real ale   Meals (not Sun) and snacks   Children welcome if well behaved   Folk singing Sun   Open 12–2.30, 6–11

GREAT SHEFFORD   SU3875 Map 2
Swan

2 miles from M4 junction 14; on A338 towards Wantage

The friendly atmosphere, good food and the fact that it's close to the M4 make this low-ceilinged pub a popular place for lunch. Bar food includes sandwiches, various ploughman's (£2.25), filled baked potatoes (from £2.25, with prawns, cheese and garlic butter £3.25), and home-made lasagne (£3.25); well kept Courage Best and Directors on handpump. The public bar has darts, pool, cribbage, a fruit machine, juke box and piped music. There are tables on a terrace by a big willow and sycamore overhanging the stream, with more on an attractive quiet lawn with a swing, and summer barbecues. The pub is a base for the local football, cricket and rugby teams, and where the Vine and Craven hunt often meet. *(Recommended by Joan Olivier, John Estdale; more reports on the new regime please)*

Courage   Licensees Judy Bughtman/Lyn O'Callaghan   Real ale   Meals and snacks (not Sun evening)   Children in eating areas   Restaurant tel Great Shefford (048 839) 271 (not Sun evenings)   Open 10.30–2.30, 6–11 all year

HAMPSTEAD NORREYS   SU5376 Map 2
New Inn

Yattendon Road

The fine garden here has well spaced seats among roses, conifers and fruit trees, a sheltered terrace overlooking matured woodlands, and a big lawn with swings, children's play area and goldfish pond with a floodlit waterfall. Inside, the new licensees have added pictures of World War II military aircraft from the local Air Gunners Association to the walls of the comfortable and friendly back lounge (which also have horses and reproduction coaching prints on them), there are horsebrasses on the low black beams, and a log fire. Good value bar food ranges from sandwiches (from 80p, toasties from 85p), soup (90p), ploughman's (from £1.30), home-made cottage pie (£1.35), salads (from £2), plaice dippers (£2.50), and seafood platter (£3.20); in the evening there is a more elaborate menu with dishes such as creamy eggs with smoked salmon (£2.50), chicken Kiev (£4.50) or rump steak (£6.90). Well kept Morlands Mild, Bitter and Best on handpump under light blanket pressure. The lively and simply furnished public bar, decorated with early 1950s local photographs, has darts, dominoes, cribbage, juke box, fruit machine and quiz evenings. (*Recommended by Dave Braisted, A T Langton, Gordon and Daphne, Mrs G K Herbert; more reports please*)

Morlands   Licensees David and Anita Reid   Real ale   Meals and snacks (not Tues evening)   Children may be allowed in at landlord's discretion   Open 11–3, 5–11; 11–2.30, 5.30–11 in winter; open all day Sat   Bedrooms tel Hermitage (0635) 201301; £13/£22

HERMITAGE   SU5073 Map 2

Fox

2½ miles from M4 junction 13: A34 towards Oxford, first right, then left on B4009

After the rush of the nearby motorway, sitting on the terrace here, with your view of the roses and tubs of flowers by a pretty little sloping lawn, is very restorative. Inside, there's a friendly atmosphere, and the prettily decorated lounge bar has soft plush button-back banquettes and stools; the public bar has a fruit machine and juke box. A wide choice of popular bar food has included sandwiches (from 80p; toasties £1.20, club sandwiches from £1.80), with specials such as cottage pie (£2.85) or beef in beer (£2.95). The pub's also been notable for well kept Bass, Charrington IPA, Morlands Bitter and Best, and Wadworths 6X and Farmers Glory on handpump; as we go to press we hear that the owners, having invested in the Old Boot at Stanford Dingley, are planning to sell. (*Recommended by Joan Olivier, Jill and George Hadfield, John Tyzack, John Bell; news of the new regime, please*)

Free house   Real ale   Meals and snacks   Restaurant tel Hermitage (0635) 201545   Open 11–2.30, 6–11

HOLYPORT   SU9176 Map 2

Belgian Arms

1½ miles from M4 junction 8/9; take A308(M) then at terminal roundabout follow Holyport signpost along A308 towards Windsor; in village turn left on to big green, then left again at War Memorial shelter

The walls in the L-shaped bar of this low-ceilinged cottage are decorated with many good prints and framed postcards of Belgian military uniform, there's a china cupboard in one corner, varied homely chairs around the few small tables on the flowery carpet, and a log fire in winter. Good, simple bar food includes sandwiches, plain or toasted (from 80p), ploughman's (from £1.55, with home-cooked ham £2.20), steak in a bun (£1.55), pizzas (£2.20), seafood platter or home-cooked ham and eggs (£3.85) and eight-ounce steak (£6.55). Well kept Brakspears PA and SB on handpump. The garden is delightful, with plenty of tables looking over a flag-iris pond to the green, a climbing-frame and slide, and a pen of goats and hens. (*Recommended by Lyn and Bill Capper, John Day, Richard Houghton, TBB, Mrs G K Herbert*)

Brakspears   Real ale   Meals and snacks (not Fri–Sun evenings)   Open 10.30–2.30, 5.30–11

HUNGERFORD   SU3368 Map 2

Bear ★ 🏠

3 miles from M4 junction 14; town signposted at junction

The spacious main bar in this civilised old coaching-inn – often appreciated most by our older readers – has nice touches like the day's newspapers (including the *FT*, *Sporting Life* and *Herald Tribune*) hanging on reading sticks, spirits served in ¼-gill measures (instead of the usual ⅙-gill) and properly mixed Kirs; there's a huge black and gold wall clock by Marsh of Highworth, and at one end, big French windows open on to a charming enclosed courtyard with a pergola and fountain. Several readers have mentioned the ornate lavatories. Well kept Arkells John's

Bitter (BB) and BBB, and Morlands on handpump. Bar meals are brought to your table by waitresses and include home-made fish soup (£1.55), garlic-fried prawns with crusty bread (£1.95), home-made taramosalata (£2.25), toasted muffin with ham, avocado, poached egg and hollandaise or minute steak in French bread (£4), Alderton ham salad (£4.55), fried market fish (£5.60) and sirloin steak with cafe de Paris butter (£6.75); puddings (£2). There is a pleasantly rambling and well kept garden, with a terrace where the River Dun splashes over a little weir. No dogs. *(Recommended by Sheila Keene, M E Lawrence, J F Estdale, Neville Burke, Ian Phillips, G Berneck, C Herxheimer, Dr and Mrs A K Clarke, E G Parish, L S Manning, I Meredith)*

Free house Licensee Roy Tudor Hughes Real ale Meals and lunchtime snacks Restaurant Children in restaurant Open 10–2.30, 6–10.30 Bedrooms tel Hungerford (0488) 82512; £61B/£71.50B

nr HURLEY SU8283 Map 2

Dew Drop

Just W of Hurley on A423 turn left up Honey Lane – look out for the IGAP sign; at small red post-box after large farm, fork right – the pub is down a right-hand turn-off at the first cluster of little houses

Surrounded by fields and woods, this really secluded brick and flint cottage has a welcoming, characterful landlord, a good mix of customers, simple furnishings and a winter log fire. Generously served and reasonably priced bar food includes sandwiches, good ploughman's, soup, cottage pie, ham and other salads, gammon, egg and chips and seafood platter. Well kept Brakspears PA and Old on handpump and some good malt whiskies; shove-ha'penny. It's a lovely place in summer when you can sit on seats in the attractively wild sloping garden, looking down to where white doves strut on the pub's red tiles, above tubs of bright flowers; there's a children's play area. *(Recommended by Nick Dowson, Simon Collett-Jones, Ian Phillips, John Roué, Ian Meredith, Mary Bates)*

Brakspears Real ale Meals (not Mon evening or Sun) and snacks (not Mon or Sun evening) Open 11–2.30, 6–11

HURST SU7972 Map 2

Green Man

Hinton Road; off A321 Twyford–Wokingham, turning NE just S of filling station in village centre

Once through the low door here, you find black standing timbers, dark oak beams hung with horsebrasses and brass stirrups, lots of alcoves and country pictures, tapestried wall seats and wheel-back chairs around brass-topped tables on the green carpet, and an open fire at both ends (neatly closed in summer by black-and-brass folding doors). The atmosphere is quiet and relaxed, and there are some black japanned milkchurns as seats around the servery, which dispenses well kept Brakspears PA and SB and Old tapped from the cask; gentle piped music (maybe Radio 1). There's a different menu for lunchtime and evening: open sandwiches, burgers (85p), home-made pies like steak and kidney, pigeon or game (£4.75), vegetarian dishes, very original chicken clementine, duck, and steaks (from £5.75); they also do daily specials. Boules, Aunt Sally and a golf society; pleasant back garden. *(Recommended by Caroline Gibbins, Simon Collett-Jones, Nick Dowson, Jane and Calum)*

Brakspears Licensee Allen Hayward Real ale Meals (not Mon evening or Sun) and lunchtime snacks (not Sun) Open 11–2.30 (3 Sat), 6–11 all year

Anyone claiming to be able to arrange or prevent inclusion of a pub in the *Guide* is a fraud. Pubs are included only if recommended by genuine readers and if our own anonymous inspection confirms that they are suitable.

KINTBURY   SU3866 Map 2
Dundas Arms 🛏

Put up in the early nineteenth century for the canal builders, with bedrooms in ex-barge-horse stables, this old-fashioned place is set between a quiet pool of the River Kennet and the Kennet and Avon Canal – there is an attractive lock just the other side of the hump-backed bridge. Food includes sandwiches, home-made soup (£1.15), smoked salmon pâté or crab au gratin (£2), delicious smoked salmon quiche (£2.95), gammon and egg, mixed seafood platter or steak and kidney pie (£3.50), and steak (£5.80); good breakfasts. There's a remarkable collection of blue and white plates on one cream wall in the partly panelled carpeted bar, a juke box with rather a nostalgic repertoire, and a fruit machine. Well kept Adnams Bitter, Huntsman Dorset and Morlands Bitter on handpump. The restaurant has a notable range of wines and has been particularly strong on clarets. Bedrooms have French windows opening on to a secluded waterside terrace. *(Recommended by Capt T J B Cannon, Philip Lewis Williams, AE, J M M Hill, CC, Jenny Seller and others)*

Free house   Licensee David Dalzell-Piper   Real ale   Lunchtime meals and snacks (not Sun)   Restaurant (not Sun)   Children welcome lunchtime   Open 11–2.30, 6–11 all year; closed Christmas to New Year   Bedrooms tel Kintbury (0488) 58263; £40B/£46B

KNOWL HILL   SU8279 Map 2
Bird in Hand ⊗
A4

Though building work on the hotel side was underway as we went to press, business in the bars was carrying on as usual, and generous helpings of good home-made food still includes an excellent buffet (£4.25 for as much as you want), with good cold salt beef, salami, ham, three other cold meats, four or five fish and shellfish dishes, and lots of fresh and imaginative salads such as apple, celery and peanut, or carrot and leek strips in a lemon juice dressing. There are also sandwiches (from £1.25, smoked salmon or prawn open sandwich on home-made brown bread £3.50), Vietnamese spring rolls (£2), filled baked potatoes (from £2), changing daily hot dishes such as steak and kidney pudding, ham shanks, fish pie, half a shoulder of lamb, curry or pasta (£4.25), and good home-made puddings. Well kept Brakspears PA and Old, Courage Directors and Youngs Special on handpump. The spacious main bar has ceiling beams, cosy alcoves, a red Turkey carpet on polished oak parquet, some attractive Victorian stained glass in one big bow window, dark brown panelling with a high shelf of willow pattern plates, and a log fire. A centuries-older, quarry-tiled side bar has darts, and there's a snug well padded back cocktail bar. Efficient, helpful service; a few good malt whiskies, including the Macallan. There are tables in the roomy and neatly kept tree-sheltered side garden. *(Recommended by Nick Dowson, Mrs G K Herbert, John Bell)*

Free house   Licensee Jack Shone   Real ale   Meals and snacks   Children in eating area of bar   Restaurant   Open 11–11   Bedrooms tel Littlewick Green (062 882) 2781; £50B/£70B

MARSH BENHAM   SU4267 Map 2
Red House ⊗
Village signposted from A4 W of Newbury

The two rooms of the comfortable bar in this busy, well kept thatched brick pub are separated by an arch with a fine formal flower arrangement; there are attractive prints (including nice Cecil Aldin village scenes) on the leafy green-and-gold flock wallpaper, deeply carved Victorian gothick settles, with some older ones, and lots of glossily varnished tables set for diners. Imaginative home-made bar food, brought to your table by uniformed waitresses and from a menu that changes daily, includes filled brown or white rolls (£1), soup (£1, roll and butter 30p extra), sandwiches (from £1), lambs' tongues with fresh mint in sherry aspic (£1.50), pies such as savoury goose or steak and kidney (£1.75; £2.25 with salad, £2.50 with vegetables), moussaka (£1.75; with salad £2.25, with vegetables £2.50), good Stilton ploughman's (£2), home-made pâté (£2.50), salads (from £2), home-cooked gammon with fresh pineapple (£3), lobster crêpes with creamy dill sauce (£3.25), smoked salmon cheesecake with prawns (£3.25), Russian blinis with smoked salmon, Danish caviare and so forth (£3.50) and fresh salmon mayonnaise (£4.95); home-made puddings (from £1.50). Well kept Adnams Bitter, Brakspears PA and SPA, Morlands Bitter, Ringwood Fortyniner, and Theakstons on handpump, and good wines by the glass. There's an attractive side garden, with a wooden sun house, a butterfly reserve, and a big model railway that runs every Sunday lunchtime in the summer. (*Recommended by Aubrey and Margaret Saunders, John Bell, Dick Brown, Mrs E M Brandwood, Prof A N Black, Lyn and Bill Capper, Paul McPherson, I Meredith*)

Free house   Licensees Mr and Mrs Bullock   Real ale   Meals and snacks   Restaurant tel Newbury (0635) 41637   Children in restaurant   Open 10.30–3, 6–11 all year

REMENHAM   SU7683   Map 2
Little Angel ⊗

A423, just over bridge E of Henley

There are several special food events here, particularly over Henley Regatta when it's best to book well ahead. The main attraction – not surprisingly – is the wide choice of food, which from the bar menu might typically include home-made soup (£2.50), chicken liver pâté or garlic mushrooms (£3.50), king prawns or jumbo mussels (£4.50), lobster or seafood tagliatelle (£6.50), asparagus hollandaise or 1¼lb Brisham plaice (£6.50), calf's liver and bacon or Scotch smoked salmon (£7), ten-ounce steak (£7.25) and avocado and Cornish crab (£7.25). The restaurant is particularly strong on seafood – they collect from Billingsgate several times a week. The bar has big bay window seats and some built-in cushioned grey walls seats, and the main part has a low ceiling and is decorated in deep glossy red and black, which matches the little tiles of the bar counter and the carpet; this leads through to the Garden Room (and restaurant), with deep pink furnishings, cosy alcoves, candle-light and fresh flowers, which is more given over to eating. The back terrace with tables and pink umbrellas is floodlit at night. Brakspears PA and SB on handpump, a wide range of attractive and reasonably priced wines, and Kirs; piped music. It can get very crowded at peak times (when even the big car park overflows into a tricky narrow side lane); there are some wooden tables and benches outside. (*Recommended by L V Nutton, John Bell; more reports please*)

Brakspears   Licensee Paul Southwood   Real ale   Meals and snacks   Children welcome   Restaurant tel Henley-on-Thames (0491) 574165; open until 4pm Sun   Open 11–3, 6–11 all year

SONNING   SU7575   Map 2
Bull

Off B478, in village

The two communicating rooms of this ancient pub each have an inglenook fireplace, and there are beams in the low ceilings, cushioned antique settles, cosy alcoves and even a penny-farthing. Lunchtime bar food includes a good cold buffet with salads such as pork pie and mixed meats; Flowers Original, Wethereds and SPA on handpump; piped music. The courtyard outside is very attractive with wistaria cascading over the black and white timbered pub, and tubs of flowers and a rose pergola – though unfortunately, at busy times you may find it packed with cars. If you bear left through the churchyard opposite (taken over by Russian ivy), then turn left along the bank of the River Thames, you come to a very pretty lock. (*Recommended by M C Howells, TBB, Ian Phillips, Mrs G K Herbert*)

Wethereds (Whitbread)   Licensee Dennis Catton   Real ale   Meals (evenings, not Sun or Mon) and lunchtime snacks   Restaurant   Children in restaurant   Open 10–2.30, 6–11 all year; closed evening 25 Dec   Bedrooms tel Reading (0734) 693901; £25.30/£50.60

STANFORD DINGLEY   SU5771   Map 2

Old Boot ⊗

In a remote village, this beamed pub has tables outside in front, with more on a secluded back terrace and in its sloping country garden. Inside, it's quietly friendly and neatly kept, with fine old pews, settles, country chairs and tables, bunches of fresh flowers, thoughtfully chosen pictures, attractive fabrics for the old-fashioned wooden-ring curtains, and an inglenook fireplace. A good choice of bar food includes sandwiches, home-made soup (£1.20), garlic mushrooms with bacon and granary toast (£2.50), home-made 8-ounce burgers (from £2.60), chilli con carne (£2.75), Spanish omelette (£2.95), scallops provençale (£3.75), ham and egg (£4.25), lemon sole stuffed with crabmeat (£4.75), changing daily specials and vegetarian dishes. Well kept Arkells BBB, Ind Coope Burton and Tetleys on handpump; piped music. (*Recommended by Calum and Jane, Lyn and Bill Capper, Ian Meredith, Jenny Seller*)

Free house   Licensee Anthony Howells   Real ale   Meals and snacks   Restaurant tel Bradfield (0734) 744292   Children in separate section of bar and in restaurant   Open 10.30–2.30, 5.30–11 all year

STREATLEY   SU5980   Map 2

Swan 🛏

There's a new Boathouse Bar in this substantial Thames-side hotel with a Varsity boating theme and big windows overlooking the river and splendid gardens, where there are barbecues, a children's play area, and outdoor games such as boules. Below the lawns, terraces, and paths winding among rose pergolas and well kept herbaceous borders is a restored Oxford college state barge, tied to the bank and used as a bar – you can also eat light evening meals there (not Sundays). Bar food includes sandwiches, granary rolls (from £1.10), starters such as a hot or cold soup, smoked salmon or mackerel pâté (all £1.45), three or four hot dishes, including home-made pies (all £3.90), a help-yourself buffet with four or five home-cooked meats and seven or eight salads (£3.90) and home-made puddings (£1.80); friendly service. Brakspears PA, Ruddles County and Youngers IPA on handpump; bar billiards, shove-ha'penny, dominoes, cribbage, trivia and piped music. Many of the bedrooms have river views and their own terraces. (*Recommended by K G Young, Michael Langridge; more reports please*)

Free house   Licensee Alan Blenkinsop   Real ale   Meals and snacks   Restaurant   Children welcome   Jazz club Weds evenings   Open 11–10.30   Bedrooms tel Goring-on-Thames (0491) 873737; £60B/£85B

WEST ILSLEY   SU4782   Map 2

Harrow ⊗

Signposted at East Ilsley slip road off A34 Newbury–Abingdon

This homely downland inn has been making many friends among readers. It's a little tiled white house on the edge of a racing village, where something always seems to be happening – the bar was packed with people idly watching a cricket match over the road when we visited, and readers have found it bustling on show days. It's cosy and warmly welcoming inside, simply furnished with red leatherette wall seats and bucket chairs, and decorated with the team and other local photographs that mark a true village pub. Besides snacks and the more usual main dishes such as lasagne, chilli con carne or steak and kidney pie (£2.45), there are things that reflect the area's sporting interests: a good game pie in season, or rabbit off the downs. Vegetables are fresh and nicely cooked. The well kept beer is Morlands Bitter and Old Masters, on handpump; they started brewing in this village before they moved to Abingdon. Darts, juke box. Picnic-table sets and other tables under cocktail parasols look out over the duck pond and cricket green, and a spacious children's garden has a notable play area with a big climber, swings, rocker and so forth – not to mention ducks, fowls, canaries, rabbits, goats and a donkey. There are lots of walks from the village, with the Ridgeway just a mile away. (*Recommended by D Johnson, Mrs M J Dyke, A T Langton, R C Watkins, Mike Tucker*)

Morlands   Licensee Mrs Heather Humphreys   Real ale   Meals and snacks   Children allowed in small restaurant (booking advisable, esp weekends)   Open 11–3, 5–11 all year (opens 6 in winter); 11–11 Sat   Bedrooms tel East Ilsley (063 528) 260; £12/£24

WICKHAM   SU3971 Map 2
Five Bells ⊗ 🛏

3 miles from M4 junction 14; A338 towards Wantage, then first right into B4000

The servery in the long, open-plan carpeted bar of this partly thatched pub extends back into the low eaves, which are hung with all sorts of bric-à-brac: brass blowlamps, an antique muller, copper whisking bowl, old bottles, fox brush, tug-o'-war trophies, even a Saudi camel-goad. At one end (with a stripped brick dado along each side) there are wheel-back chairs around polished tables, and patio doors lead out to the garden, which has plenty more tables, outdoor games and even a swimming-pool. At the other end, beyond brick pillars, there's a huge log fire, with tables set for meals. As most of the pictures demonstrate, the pub is in racing country and there's a separate TV room to keep up with the latest results. Home-made bar food (the prices have hardly changed at all since last year) includes sandwiches (from £1.10), good soup (£1.25), pâté (£1.75), ploughman's (£2.30), jumbo sausages or vegetarian spring roll (£2.75), steak and kidney pie or gammon with egg or pineapple (£4), a choice of salads (from £4.50), grilled steak (£7), daily specials (£4), and a choice of puddings (£1.75). Well kept Ushers Best and Ruddles County on handpump, relatively cheap for the area, with a good choice of spirits; darts, pool-table, dominoes, fruit machine and piped music. (*Recommended by John Bell, TBB; more reports please*)

Ushers (Watneys)   Licensee Mrs Dorothy Channing-Williams   Real ale   Meals and snacks   Children in eating area of bar   Restaurant   Open 10.30–2.30, 5.30–11 all year   Bedrooms tel Boxford (048 838) 242; £25/£33

WINKFIELD   SU9271 Map 2
Slug & Lettuce ⊗

Lovel Road; A330 just W of junction with B3034, turning off at Fleur de Lis towards Winkfield Row; OS Sheet 175 reference 921715

This well kept and popular cottagey pub has been bought by a small chain owning several other free houses – one of them being the White Horse at Petersfield in Hampshire, one of our three-starred pubs. The young and enthusiastic new managers are keen to preserve the pleasant, relaxed atmosphere and to keep the rooms much as they are: herringbone timbered brickwork, a brick-tiled floor, standing black oak timbers, plain wooden chairs and benches by sturdy deal tables, low beams, seascapes, log-effect gas fires, a cosy alcove, and latticed windows; a quiet corner room has tapestried wall benches and a wall of leather book-backs. Good lunchtime bar food includes home-made soup (£1.50), sandwiches (from

£1.75), various ploughman's (from £1.95), home-cooked pizzas, chilli con carne (£3.50), beef and ale pie (£3.95) and roast lunches (from £4.75). Well kept Boddingtons, Brakspears, Courage Best, Theakstons Old Peculier and a regular guest beer on handpump; several wines including a local white one; good service. Dominoes, cribbage and piped music. The Siamese cats are called Theo and Soula, and the black labrador is called Mavros. A seat in front is sheltered by the overhanging upper floor. (*Recommended by Richard Houghton, Nick Dowson*)

Free house   Managers Miss J Dutfield and Mr N Hajigeorgiou   Real ale   Meals and snacks   Restaurant tel Winkfield Row (0344) 883498   Children in restaurant   Open 10.30–2.30, 5.30–11 all year; closed evening 25 Dec

WOKINGHAM   SU8068 Map 2
Crooked Billet

Gardeners Green; from Wokingham inner ring road turn left into Easthampstead Road (just after A329 turn-off to Bracknell); past railway crossing turn right at White Horse, then left into Honey Hill – this avoids the ford which in winter can be quite deep; OS Sheet 175 reference 826668

A lively crowd of mixed customers come to this homely and jolly tucked-away white weatherboarded cottage to enjoy the simple cheap food – filled rolls (from 50p), sandwiches (from 80p), home-made soup (£1), ploughman's (from £1.30), steak and kidney pie (£1.50), omelettes (£1.95) and gammon and egg (£2.20); well kept Brakspears PA, SB, Mild and Old on handpump. The front bar has crooked black joists, plain wooden benches and wall pews on the recently brick-tiled floor, a brick serving-counter, and open fires in winter; darts, cribbage and fruit machine. At the opposite end a communicating carpeted restaurant area (with £6 lunches favoured by management) has some stripped brickwork, but walls are mainly plain cream. There are benches in front, picnic-table sets in a sheltered back rose garden, and swings for children. (*Recommended by JEW, Dr J R Hamilton, Rodney Coe*)

Brakspears   Licensee Graham Hill   Real ale   Meals (not Sun evening) and snacks (limited Sun evening)   Restaurant tel Wokingham (0734) 780438; closed Sun   Children in restaurant   Open 11–11 all year

WOOLHAMPTON   SU5767 Map 2
Rising Sun

A4, nearly a mile E of village

Useful for the A4, this small and friendly pub has a good, regularly changing range of real ales on handpump which might include Archers Best, Arkells BBB, Gales HSB, Morlands, Ringwood Old Thumper, Theakstons XB and Youngers IPA. Good, reasonably priced bar food includes sandwiches, filled baked potatoes (from £1.10), cottage pie (£1.75), home-made pies (from £2.25), cod (£2.45), scampi (£2.85), and vegetarian dishes (from £3.35). The red and black lounge is decorated with small reproduction coaching prints, and the public bar has darts, bar billiards, dominoes, cribbage, fruit machine and piped music. You can sit out behind, where there's a swing. (*Recommended by L G and D L Smith, Ian Howard, John Shirley, John Bell; more reports please*)

Free house   Licensee Peter Head   Real ale   Meals and snacks   Restaurant tel Woolhampton (0734) 712717   Children in restaurant   Open 11.30–2.30, 6–11 all year

YATTENDON   SU5572 Map 2
Royal Oak   ★ ⊗ ⇌

The really special thing in this elegant old inn is the food: the very wide choice changes daily and includes sandwiches or filled rolls (if they're not too busy – they don't like to do them unless they've time to make them really good), home-made soups such as creamy mushroom (£2.50), grilled calves' kidneys and black pudding with green herb mustard sauce or deep-fried brains and sweetbreads with tartare sauce (£3.75), ploughman's with an unusual selection of farmhouse cheeses (£4), crispy duck and salad frisée (£5.75), avocado salad with smoked chicken and prawns (£6.25), shallow-fried large fillet of plaice with herb butter (£7.25), suprême of chicken with oyster mushrooms and creamy curry sauce (£8.25), grilled fillets of Dover sole and John Dory with mussels and shallot sauce (£9.25), and grilled turbot with chive sauce (£10.50); home-made puddings such as apple and raspberry crumble (£3.25) or chocolate and praline ice-cream with butterscotch sauce (£3.50), and good vegetables; to be sure of a table it's best to book. Well kept Adnams Bitter, Bass and Wadworths 6X on handpump; they will also open any bottle of wine on their list and serve half of it for half the price, the rest going to the bar and being sold there by the glass. The stylishly old-fashioned and comfortable lounge and prettily decorated panelled bar have an extremely pleasant atmosphere, and good log fires in winter. The pretty garden is primarily for the use of residents and restaurant guests, but is available on busy days for those in the bar. The village – where Robert Bridges lived for many years – is very attractive. *(Recommended by Wg Cdr R M Sparkes, Mr and Mrs R Griffiths, Alan Wright, Jaine Redmond, A Pearce, S D Samuels, Nancy Witts, Mrs P Clayton, Mrs Jo Corbett, J M M Hill, M H Lloyd Davis)*

Free house   Licensees Richard and Kate Smith   Real ale   Meals and snacks   Children welcome   Restaurant (closed two weeks Jan/Feb)   Occasional jazz evenings   Open 11–3, 6–11 all year   Bedrooms tel Hermitage (0635) 201325; £48B/£58B

Lucky Dip

Besides the fully inspected pubs, you might like to try these Lucky Dips recommended to us and described by readers (if you do, please send us reports):

Ascot [High St; SU9268], *Stag*: Neat and pretty, with good food, friendly welcome and real fire; very busy at lunchtime and packed on race days *(Gary Wilkes, Mrs G K Herbert)*

Aston [Ferry Lane, back road through Remenham; SU7884], *Flower Pot*: Edwardian hotel not far from Thames, taken in hand by new owners who've refurbished the bars (one very smartly, the other welcoming walkers and their dogs – well kept Brakspears); they have considerable plans – a place worth watching; on GWG68 *(John Hayward)*

Beenham [1 mile off A4, half way between Newbury and Reading; SU5869], *Stocks*: welcoming, clean and comfortable small pub in pleasant countryside with good inexpensive food; safe playground *(A L Willett)*

Binfield [SU8471], *Stag & Hounds*: Attractively furnished ancient Courage pub with open fires, relaxed atmosphere and nice collection of rambling low-beamed rooms – the last one of which is a bistro, with quite reasonably priced food *(Nick Dowson, Gordon and Daphne)*; [Terrace Rd North] *Victoria Arms*: Cleverly laid out Fullers pub with good choice of seating areas, well kept real ales, reasonably priced bar food; children's room, summer barbecues in quiet garden *(Dr and Mrs A K Clarke, LYM)*

Bray [SU9079], *Hinds Head*: Smart and beautifully kept – but pricey – with leather armchairs, high-backed settles, early Tudor beams, oak panelling, and handsome upstairs restaurant *(TBB, LYM)*; [High St] *Ringers*: Wide range of straightforward food and good choice of real ales and other beers and lagers in lively low-beamed pub with interesting décor and friendly licensee; seats on back terrace *(Paul Enderby, Nick Dowson, Alison Hayward, TBB)*

Bucklebury [Chapel Row; SU5570], *Blade Bone*: Renovated old pub with red plush settees and stools in lounge, darts and fruit machine in public bar, small restaurant area; sandwiches, ploughman's, salads and hot dishes *(Lyn and Bill Capper)*

Chaddleworth [SU4177], *Ibex*: Comfortably old-fashioned pub in good horse-racing country, popular for quickly served good bar food and well kept courage *(A T Langton, LYM)*

Cheapside [Cheapside Rd; SU9469], *Thatched Tavern*: Friendly low-beamed food pub with well kept Courage ales, smart in spite of its flagstones; good meals rather than snacks *(Mrs G K Herbert)*

☆ **Chieveley** [North Heath, 4 miles from M4 junction 13; A34 N, 1st left in Chieveley, keep on out to B4494, then right; SU4774], *Blue Boar*: Interestingly furnished and prettily preserved thatched sixteenth-century pub in isolated spot, bar area itself not large with rest of space given over to popular bar food (also an attractive oak-panelled restaurant); good choice of drinks including well kept Arkells, comfortable bedrooms; mixed recent reports on atmosphere and welcome – more news particularly on this please *(Mrs Jo Corbett, S Matthews, John Hill, Jill Field, Mrs G K Herbert, Sheila Keene, Mr and Mrs F H Stokes, Robert Kilvington, I Meredith, Ian Phillips, LYM)*

Chieveley [East Lane; in village – these two pubs even handier for M4], *Hare & Hounds*: Cosy low-beamed bar with well kept Ushers, friendly licensee, good helpings of low-priced reliable food from menu changing daily; not far from the Ridgeway *(John Bell, Thomas Newton, John Nash)*; *Red Lion*: Attractive quietly placed village local, clean and comfortable, with wide choice of food (and small restaurant), open fire, good friendly service and excellent real ales such as Wadworths 6X or Thomas Wethered *(Ian Howard, John Bell, Tom Evans, Stan Edwards)*

Cippenham [Lower Cippenham Lane; SU9480], *Kings Head*: Nicely refurbished without killing the atmosphere, good choice of lunchtime food, friendly service, big garden *(R Houghton)*; [Cippenham Lane] *Long Barn*: Classily converted barn by modern housing estate but full of ancient beams; Courage Best on handpump, good atmosphere, restaurant, picnic-table sets outside *(Nick Dowson)*

☆ **Cockpole Green** [SU7981], *Old Hatch Gate*: Remarkable anachronism: genuinely rustic, with very cheap well kept Brakspears PA and SBA in beamed and flagstoned tap-room – the carpeted saloon seems always closed; one for connoisseurs of unspoilt simplicity who won't be put off by rudimentary mod cons (or the huge spider two readers thought must be looking for a cat for supper till the landlord told them it usually lapped up beer spillage from the bar top, but had fallen off one lively night); erratic opening hours; if landlord outside feeding pigs, one of regulars will serve *(Gordon and Daphne, Alison Hayward, Nick Dowson, Simon Collett-Jones, Phil and Sally Gorton, MM, LYM)*

Compton [SU5279], *Swan*: Lively atmosphere and good food under new licensees *(Mrs K Godley)*

Cookham [High St; SU8884], *Royal Exchange*: Wide choice of good food, real ale and decent wines *(P S Yeoman)*

Cookham Rise [SU8984], *Swan Uppers*: Cosy, tastefully decorated pub with lovely timbers and flagstones, Wethereds on handpump and maybe fresh lobster on the menu; noticeable piped music, e.g. Ella Fitzgerald *(Roger Baskerville, TBB)*

Cox Green [not far from M4 junction 9; SU8779], *Barley Mow*: Cottage-style décor in bright, clean, cosy open-plan lounge; reasonably priced food, well kept Trumans

(Mr and Mrs A Collis, Simon Collett-Jones)

Curridge [OS Sheet 174 reference 492723; SU4871], *Bunk*: Popular pub with Morlands, Boddingtons and Arkells, excellent bar food, good value for money (book at weekends); named after local word for railway branch line *(A T Langton)*

East Ilsley [SU4981], *Star*: Character fifteenth-century pub with beams and inglenook log fires, friendly village atmosphere, well kept real ales such as Morlands, Ruddles and Ushers, good range of reasonably priced food using fresh ingredients; bedrooms planned *(Chris and Liz Norman, Lyn and Bill Capper)*

Eton [Bridge St; SU9678], *Watermans Arms*: Well kept Courage in lively neighbourly pub with rowing decorations, close to Thames *(G V Price, LYM)*

Fifield [SU9076], *Hare & Hounds*: Well presented lunches Mon–Sat in nice atmosphere, vegetarian dishes a speciality; keg beers *(David Regan)*

Fifield [Drift Rd; OS Sheet 175 reference 892752; SU8975], *Royal Forester*: Basic Bulmers pub with thatch on edge of bar, three ciders on handpump, fruit machine and juke box *(Nick Dowson)*

☆ **Goring Heath** [Reading Rd (B4526) – OS Sheet 175 reference 664788; SU6579], *King Charles Head*: Very attractive free house nicely off the beaten track in lovely woodland setting, with several well kept real ales such as Adnams, Brakspears and Theakstons XB; wide choice of decent pub food, tables under cocktail parasols, swings, climbing-frames and ladder; nr GWG98 *(Sheila Keene and others)*

Grazeley [The Green; SU6966], *Old Bell*: Extensive range of well kept real ales, large helpings of good home-cooked food and very efficient staff in comfortable friendly pub *(Colyn Nicholls)*

Hampstead Norreys [SU5376], *White Hart*: Very friendly landlord and landlady, open fire and two or three armchairs as well as plenty of tables in spotless lounge, reasonable choice of competitively priced bar food and beers such as well kept Wethereds; small grass playground with slides and swings *(Shirley Fluck, Stan Edwards)*

☆ **Hamstead Marshall** [SU4165], *White Hart*: Friendly country local with cheerful and polite bar staff, variety of well kept beers such as Badger, John Smiths and Wadworths 6X, unusual and interesting bar food (good value), new dining-room; four bedrooms, comfortable and clean, in luxuriously converted barn *(John Tyzack, Chris Ensor)*

Hare Hatch [just N of A4 Reading–Maidenhead; SU8077], *Queen Victoria*: Good local atmosphere in well kept pubby place with lots of games, good value simple food, well kept Brakspears, popular landlord *(Nick Dowson, BB)*

☆ **Hungerford** [Bridge St (A338); SU3368], *John

o' Gaunt: Much altered internally but still has considerable character; interesting range of real ales, good reasonably priced food *(Prof A N Black, John Bell, LYM)*

Hurley [SU8283], *Olde Bell*: Handsome timbered inn with Norman doorway and window, fine gardens, smart if pricey restaurant – formerly popular for its civilised and old-fashioned bar, now part of a small chain including places such as the Bear at Woodstock; bedrooms *(LYM)*

Inkpen [Lower Inkpen; SU3564], *Swan*: Carefully refurbished old-fashioned and heavy-beamed pub, friendly and clean, near village duck pond, picnic-table sets on terrace and in garden, Flowers beer; small helpings of fresh and fragrantly flavoured eastern food have now joined the more usual bar food (not cheap) *(Wg Cdr R M Sparkes, I Meredith; more reports on new regime please)*

Knowl Hill [A4 Reading–Maidenhead; SU8279], *Royal Oak*: Simple friendly pub with excellent service and very good inexpensive home-made steak and kidney pie; spotless gents, good parking *(Brian Barefoot)*; *Seven Stars*: Busy local with wood panelling, separate functions room, good Brakspears *(Nick Dowson, LYM)*

☆ **Littlewick Green** [3¾ miles from M4 junction 9; A423(M), then left on to A4, from which village signposted on left; SU8379], *Cricketers*: runs a couple of teams on the pretty village cricket green opposite, with cricket prints and cartoons in the lounge – as well as the huge clocking-in clock; good range of real ales on handpump, simple range of bar food, notably friendly landlord *(Nick Dowson, TBB, Lindsey Shaw Radley, Greg Parston, LYM)*

Littlewick Green [3 miles from M4 junction 9, following above directions], *Shire Horse*: Worth visiting for Courage's adjoining Shire Horse Centre (which is open Mar–Oct); comfortable open-plan lounge bar, well kept Courage ales, tea house, play area by big side lawn, food, special attention to children *(Mrs P J Bedwell, LYM)*

Maidenhead [High St; SU8783], *Bear*: Young people's pub, vibrant at weekends, with choice of real ales such as Hook Norton and Marstons, and lots of foreign beers; interesting pictures of wartime bomber crews; good food, suits older people at lunchtime *(Paul Enderby)*; [Queen St] *Hand & Flowers*: Friendly atmosphere, good bar food and excellent Brakspears and other beers *(Nick Long)*; [Queen St] *Jack of Both Sides*: Clean place with good, cheap food *(TBB)*; [Pinkneys Green; A308 N] *Golden Ball*: Plushly comfortable Brewers Fayre pub, with touches of original charm in low-ceilinged area and fireplace by bar; well kept Wethereds, friendly courteous staff, traditional pub food, smart lavatories *(Simon Collett-Jones, TBB, Ian Phillips, LYM)*; [Marion Rd; A308 N] *Robin Hood*: Old pub with

low ceilings, excellent service, friendly atmosphere, well kept Courage beer and bar food, garden with slide and swings *(Richard Houghton)*; [Pinkneys Green] *Stag & Hounds*: Rather basic two-room pub with excellent range of simple, home-cooked food, Courage ales and a welcoming atmosphere; children welcome *(Ian Phillips)*

Midgham [Bath rd (A4 – N side); SU5567], *Coach & Horses*: Comfortably refurbished Wethereds pub with wide range of bar food, back garden *(BB)*

Moneyrow Green [B3024 – OS Sheet 175 reference 889768; SU8977], *Jolly Gardener*: Expensively refurbished, pleasant décor, old brick and timber alcoves *(Nick Dowson)*; [OS Sheet 175 reference 892774], *White Hart*: Pleasant, friendly pub; 1930s lounge bar with panelled walls, prints, plates and large mounted butterfly, serving-hatch at one end of bar, Gothick fireplace, sizeable public bar; Morlands ales on handpump *(Alison Hayward, Nick Dowson)*

Newbury [10 Oxford St; SU4666], *Bacon Arms*: Town-centre pub with quite attractive smallish candlelit carvery, good value *(Sheila Keene)*; [Market Pl] *Old Waggon & Horses*: Included for its sunny waterside terrace and perhaps the big family dining bar; popular with young people on weekend evenings *(Paul Corbett, LYM)*; [Stroud Green] *Plough*: Amazingly small and friendly local, full of character – single bar no bigger than a front room; may have peanuts and crisps laid out on tables *(Paul Corbett)*

Oakley Green [B3024; SU9276], *Olde Red Lion*: Pleasant pub with pink button-back banquettes, log-effect gas fire, real ale, separate restaurant *(Alison Hayward, Nick Dowson)*

☆ **Old Windsor** [17 Crimp Hill, between River Thames and Savill Gardens; SU9874], *Union*: Very picturesque outside, oak beams in single bar with tables, settles and stools, piped music and fruit machine; good, friendly service, range of real ales on handpump with good value wine, wide choice of bar food using fresh ingredients, attractive beamed evening restaurant *(H Foster, Lyn and Bill Capper, Mrs Shirley Pielou, MR)*

Old Windsor [Burghfield Rd], *Fox & Castle*: Old, well decorated local with plenty of seats and nice atmosphere; bar food, well kept Courage *(Anon)*; [Straight Rd] *Wheatsheaf*: Recently renovated large pub with conservatory and library areas, bar food, good Ind Coope Burton and Friary Meux and friendly service; soft piped music *(Simon Collett-Jones)*

Pangbourne [Shooters Hill; SU6376], *Swan*: Bar busy at weekends, excellent food and atmosphere in restaurant *(David Jarrett)*

Peasemore [not far from M4 junction 13, via Chieveley; SU4577], *Fox & Hounds*: Pleasantly refurbished, with hunting prints in the clean and friendly lounge bar, good choice of well cooked food – including good ploughman's with real butter; Marstons, Ushers and Wadworths beer, reasonable choice of wines, quick friendly service; looks out over rolling fields (C Matthews)

Reading [35 Blagrave St; SU7272], *Blagrave Arms*: Good atmosphere, well kept Courage ales, Victorian-style refurbishment (Jane and Calum); [Chatham St] *Butler*: Barmen wearing white shirts and brewery ties serving very good Fullers London Pride; tasty food served by ticket number; gets crowded before Reading FC home games (R G Ollier); [Kennet Side] *Fishermans Cottage*: Pretty stone-built Victorian cottage with crenellated front and big conservatory, by Kennet Weir (and new housing estate); pleasant stone snug behind fireplace with wood-burning cast-iron range, brisk efficient service, short but interesting menu, Fullers ales (Ian Phillips); [8 Gt John St] *Retreat*: Epitome of a good, honest, no-nonsense 1960s English pub – narrow benches around genuine old pub tables in two smallish bars with boarded dado and anaglypta walls; warm welcome, plenty of chat and humour, cheap basic food (I D Norris, Ian Phillips)

Remenham [Wargrave Rd; SU7683], *Two Brewers*: Good value food – the sort to treat a bunch of hungry teenagers cheaply – in Braspears pub with consistently warm welcome (Ian Phillips)

Sindlesham [Bearwood Rd; signposted Sindlesham from B3349; SU7769], *Walter Arms*: Dining pub with wide choice of quickly served bar food, well kept Courage Best and Directors; comfortable bedrooms (William Main, LYM)

Slough [Parkstreet; SU9779], *Queen of England*: Back-street town pub with public and lounge bars separated by an arch, giving the feeling of two bars; pleasant welcome and good Wethereds (R Houghton); [Albert St] *Red Cow*: Traditional beamed pub with preservation order, well kept Courage beer, nice friendly atmosphere with pleasant bar staff and very mixed clientele (R Houghton); [Windsor Rd] *Rising Sun*: Long pub with pleasant atmosphere and wide age range of customers; Charrington ale, good choice of bar food, polite service (R Houghton)

Sonning [SU7575], *White Hart*: Spacious Thames-side hotel with oak settles, log fires and bow windows in heavily timbered main bar, expensive sandwiches, other food, lovely riverside lawn and spacious restaurant (Mrs G K Herbert, LYM)

Streatley [SU5980], *Bull*: Thoroughly good bar meals and well kept beer; nr GWG97 (Mike Tucker, E J Cutting)

Tilehurst [Oxford Rd; SU6673], *Roebuck*: Wide choice of well prepared lunchtime bar food, especially specials such as chicken and mushroom pie – good helpings at reasonable prices; overlooks Thames and hills beyond (NHB)

Twyford [A4; SU7876], *Horse & Groom*:

Large, long, old, recently renovated pub with basic good food and Brakspears ales; comfortable and friendly; good parking (Ian Phillips); [Old Bath Rd] *Waggon & Horses*: Recent tasteful renovation, well kept Courage Best and Directors, quiet enough during the week, busy with young people at weekends (Paul Enderby)

☆ **Waltham St Lawrence** [West End – well outside the village; SU8275], *Plough*: Calm old country pub hardly changed since the 1960s, decidedly Beryl's Place, with good Morrells ale, living-room feel, civilised food, devoted customers – some turning up on horseback (Nick Dowson, Sarah and Jamie Allan, LYM)

Waltham St Lawrence [in village; SU8376], *Bell*: Handsome sixteenth-century pub in lovely village setting, with two nicely restored bars, open fires, oak beams, longcase clock and other antiques, open fire, bar food, real ales such as Adnams, Brakspears, Wadworths 6X and Farmers Glory, spirits from small oak kegs; news on the new regime please (Gary Wilkes, JMC, Nick Dowson, LYM); *Star*: Olde-worlde friendly beamed pub with nice fire, good atmosphere, soft lighting and Wethereds ale; attractive rural surroundings (Gary Wilkes)

☆ **Warfield** [Cricketers Lane; SU8872], *Cricketers*: Warm and cosy old-fashioned three-bar pub with at least half a dozen real ales, good choice of food showing novel touches in very pleasantly decorated restaurant, nice garden; popular, can be packed (Simon Collett-Jones, Gary Wilkes); [Church Lane] *Plough & Harrow*: Vivacious landlady who formerly made the Raglan Arms in Wokingham popular, well kept Morlands Best, good value food (Stephen King)

Wargrave [High St; SU7878], *Bull*: Nice low-beamed pub with good open fire, rough wooden benches and tables on covered terrace, well kept Brakspears ales, good bar meals; bedrooms (Peter Gray, Nick Dowson, Jane and Calum, LYM); *St George & Dragon*: Thames-side pub with wide choice of reasonably priced food and ales, décor tastefully blended with surroundings – garden charming for a sunny day (John Bell); [High St] *White Hart*: Spacious but cheerfully bustling low-beamed lounge bar decorated to suit its eighteenth-century character, good value bar food, well kept Whitbreads-related real ale; restaurant (LYM)

Welford [SU4073], *Cricketers Arms*: Nice atmosphere, unpretentious, comfortable; good range of well kept ales (Jon Dewhirst)

Windsor [Thames St; SU9676], *Adam & Eve*: Bustling young people's pub by theatre, lots of actors' pictures, Bass and Charrington IPA, piped music, occasional barbecues in little back yard (C D T Spooner, LYM); [Thames St] *Donkey House*: Unrenovated pub of great potential on riverbank, Friary Meux real ale, usual bar food (Peter Kitson,

Bridgett Sarsby); [Castle Hill, opp Henry VIII Gate] *Horse & Groom*: Well kept Courage ales, helpful staff, good atmosphere and attractively priced imaginative food; pub dates from 1520 *(R J Foreman, Derek Howse)*; [Dedworth Green] *Nags Head*: Comfortably furnished Courage pub with two bars, friendly atmosphere and large garden with Wendy house; piped music, bedrooms *(Simon Collett-Jones)*; [opp stn, nr castle] *Royal Oak*: Pleasant surroundings, friendly staff, good choice of food, nice seating with piped music not too loud *(R Cane, TBB)*; [49 Thames St] *Swan*: Cheerful pub with wide choice of food all week *(Anon)*

Winkfield [SU9272], *Duke of Edinburgh*: Quaint country pub in quiet area with two bars, well kept Arkells, good food and fire; music and slot machine, darts; nice garden *(Gary Wilkes)*; [Church Rd (A330); SU9072] *White Hart*: Attractively modernised Tudor pub with ex-bakery bar and ex-courthouse weekend restaurant, usual bar food, sizeable garden *(Mrs G K Herbert, J W Nice, LYM)*

Winterbourne [not far from M4 junction 13; SU4572], *New*: Generously served and freshly made interesting food in comfortable surroundings; reasonably priced too *(Duncan Bruce)*

Wokingham [Milton Rd, behind theatre; part of Cantley House Hotel; SU8068], *Penguin & Vulture*: Watneys pub in converted stables, genuine low beams, Websters Yorkshire, bar food, separate attractive restaurant, sheltered seating outside *(Ian Phillips)*; [23 The Terrace; in row of cottages on right as you go towards Reading] *Queens Head*: Low-ceilinged warm and friendly Morlands pub *(Dr and Mrs A K Clarke)*; [Peach St – on right as you enter W from Bracknell, opp All Saints Church] *Ship*: Good value daily specials and fine help-yourself salads, Fullers real ales, serving bar leads into high vaulted hall *(Dr and Mrs A K Clarke)*

Yattendon [Burnt Hill; from village centre take Pangbourne rd, then third turn right signposted Bradfield, Burnt Hill; SU5574], *Nut & Bolt*: Generous helpings of good value food and summer barbecues still served by current licensees of this quietly placed country pub; they've wholly refurbished its previously pleasantly idiosyncratic interior so that there's just one open-plan homogeneous bar now, and no longer do bedrooms; more reports on the quality of the several real ales, please *(Jane and Calum, S P Jeffries)*

Buckinghamshire

In contrast with so little uniformity elsewhere, the Chilterns stands out as an area where it's becoming quite the normal thing for pubs to stay open throughout the day on Saturdays, taking advantage of the new Licensing Act. It's also the area where there's the highest concentration of good pubs in the county, many of them notable for good food – such as the well kept Lions of Bledlow with its fine views, the cheery Peacock at Bolter End, the Walnut Tree at Fawley, the Chequers at Fingest (old-fashioned, with a delightful garden), the civilised Yew Tree at Frieth (a new entry – drinks score top marks here, too), the Fox on the common at Ibstone (with a comfortably up-to-date bedroom block), the Rising Sun at Little Hampden (very recently taken over by the people who produce some of the best pub food in the county, at the nearby Plough at Hyde Heath), the White Hart by the woods at Northend, the Old Crown at Skirmett, the Cock & Rabbit at The Lee (decidedly plush now, with good Italian dishes), and the prettily placed Bull & Butcher at Turville. We've got good hopes too for the food under the new regime at the Stag & Huntsman in Hambleden (comfortable bedrooms), and though it's simple fare the honest food is attractively priced at the Red Lion in Whiteleaf near Princes Risborough (another new entry, also with bedrooms). In other parts of the county, places to note for food include the Black Horse in Chesham Vale (its new barn bar is enjoyable), the Ostrich in Colnbrook (with some claim to be among England's oldest pubs), the highly atmospheric Royal Standard of England at Forty Green (not a place to neglect its cheeses), the handsomely restored George in Great Missenden, the rambling low-beamed Swan at Ley Hill (a new entry – thrust straight in with a food award by the immediate success of its new licensees), the ancient Shoulder of Mutton at Little Horwood, the Two Brewers in Marlow, the fine old George & Dragon in West

The Crown, Penn

Wycombe and the engaging White Swan in Whitchurch. Food seems to be becoming more notable than before under the new licensees at the Greyhound in Chalfont St Peter; there are also new licensees at the Ship in Marlow (the food's no longer so outstandingly cheap, but is still fairly priced), and the Swan at Astwood (too soon to tell about the food – but this pub has quite enough virtues to make it well worth a visit anyway). Two other new entries to mention are the Queens Head a little way outside Amersham (nicely unspoilt) and the Pink & Lily at Lacey Green (interesting Rupert Brooke connections, though now most people are there for the food). Particularly promising selections from the Lucky Dip at the end of the chapter include the Bottle & Glass near Aylesbury, Red Lion at Chenies, another Red Lion in Great Missenden, Dog & Badger at Medmenham, Hit or Miss at Penn Street, King William IV at Speen, White Lion at St Leonards and, if it recovers its former poise (it's up for sale as we go to press) Old Swan at The Lee.

ADSTOCK SP7330 Map 4

Old Thatched Inn

Just N of A413, 4 miles SE of Buckingham

The countryside around this pretty village thatched pub is rolling farmland. Inside is cosy and traditional: even the replacement beams come from an ancient barn, and there are stripped joists and standing timbers, and flagstones by the brick and timber bar counter. The furnishings are comfortable, with wheel-back chairs and plush green button-back banquettes in bays in the carpeted areas leading off. Antique hunting prints and some copper and brassware decorate the walls, dried flowers hang from beams, and there's a log-effect gas fire. The wide-ranging, reasonably priced bar food includes open sandwiches (from £1), ploughman's (from £1.75, home-made pâté £2), open prawn sandwiches (£2), cauliflower cheese (£2.50), chilli con carne or chicken tikka (£3) and scampi (£4), with summer salads and a range of daily specials; good friendly service. Well kept Adnams, Marstons Pedigree, Ruddles County and a guest beer on handpump, with Morrells under light blanket pressure – and as a useful alternative as much tea or coffee as you can drink for 50p; piped music. The country noises from the nearby farm often complement the pub talk in the sheltered back garden, which has tables under fruit trees and a sycamore. *(Recommended by Mr and Mrs G D Amos, Lyn and Bill Capper, Miles Galliford, Mark Smith, Miss A Burton, Alison Hayward, Nick Dowson)*

Free house Licensee Ian Tring Real ale Meals and snacks (not Sun evening) Restaurant tel Adstock (029 671) 2584 Children in restaurant Open 12–2.30, 6–11 all year; closed evening 25 Dec

AKELEY SP7037 Map 4

Bull & Butcher

The Square; just off A413

The long open-plan bar in this uncomplicated and friendly village pub has rough-cast walls, comfortable red button-back banquettes below drawings of well known customers, and an interesting exposed curved-beam ceiling at the lower end. In the middle there's a massive stone chimney with a fire on each side (and a third down at one wood-floored end). Well kept Hook Norton Best, Marstons Pedigree and a guest beer on handpump, and good value wines by the bottle; shove-ha'penny, sensibly placed darts, dominoes, cribbage, and bridge club on Sunday evenings; piped music. The small dining-room doubles as a lunchtime buffet with a wide range of decently made help-yourself salads. There's a small selection of main things to go with these, such as cheese, quiche, pie or pâté and ham or beef;

generous baked potatoes with a wedge of granary bread, and good gammon
(around £6) and steak (around £6.50). Pleasant beer garden. *(Recommended by Alison
Hayward, Nick Dowson, Dr J R Hamilton, Mrs M Lawrence, Lyn and Bill Capper, HKR)*

*Free house   Licensee Harry Dyson   Real ale   Meals and snacks (not Mon evening or Sun)
Restaurant tel Lillingstone Dayrell (028 06) 257   Children in eating area   Open 12–2.30
(3 Sat), 6–11 all year; closed evening 25 and 26 Dec*

AMERSHAM   SU9597   Map 4
Kings Arms

High Street; A413

The bar food here is simple and homely, with home-made soup (£1), sandwiches
(£1.35), ploughman's or smoked mackerel pâté (£1.75), filled baked potatoes (from
£1.80), a half-pint of prawns (£2.20), lasagne (£2.50), beef in ale (£3), salads (from
£3) and daily specials. A charming and striking Tudor inn, it has a rambling,
heavily beamed and softly lit bar, with lots of character and a friendly atmosphere.
There are high-backed antique settles and quaint old-fashioned chairs among other
seats on its oak-block floor, a big inglenook fireplace, and plenty of snug alcoves. It
tends to get busy (in a cheerful way) at lunchtime. There's also a very attractive little
flower-filled courtyard and coachyard, beyond which are rustic tables and a
climbing-frame on a tree-sheltered back lawn. Benskins Best and Ind Coope Burton
on handpump, with Ind Coope Bitter tapped from the cask behind the bar counter;
friendly efficient service. *(Recommended by John Tyzack, M C Howells, Lindsey Shaw
Ridley, Simon Collett-Jones, HKR, Nick Dowson, Alison Hayward; more reports please)*

*Benskins (Ind Coope)   Licensee John Jennison   Real ale   Meals and snacks   Restaurant (not
Sun evening or Mon – no pipes or cigars, and they ask other smokers to be considerate) tel
Amersham (0494) 726333   Children in restaurant and eating area   Open 11–2.30, 6–11; all
day Sat (not winter)*

nr AMERSHAM   SU9495   Map 4
Queens Head

Whielden Gate; pub in sight just off A404, 1½ miles towards High Wycombe at Winchmore
Hill turn-off; OS Sheet 165 reference 941957

Monty the Dalmatian's not allowed inside – but on a weekday lunchtime (when it's
usually very quiet out here) he'll probably make a point of welcoming you to this
refreshingly small and simple eighteenth-century country pub. There are low
beams, flagstones by the big inglenook fireplace (which still has the old-fashioned
wooden built-in wall seat curving around right in beside the wood-burning stove –
with plenty of space under the seat for log storage), a stuffed albino pheasant and
old guns. Even the cigarette card collection has a properly rustic theme, with an
interesting Wills series of gardening hints. In winter there's often game on the menu
(bagged by the landlord or by customers); other home-made bar food includes a
pair of warm croissants filled with ham, cheese and mustard (£1.50), ploughman's
(from £1.75), omelettes (from £2), macaroni cheese (£2.25), steak and kidney pie
(£2.50), lasagne (£3.50) and lots of pizzas (from £2.50 to a £6 monster; they also
do these to take away). Well kept Benskins Best and Ind Coope Burton on
handpump; darts, shove-ha'penny, dominoes, cribbage, fruit machine, space game
and on our visit pop music on radio; quizzes in winter. There are often summer
barbecues in the back garden, which has swings and a climber, conifers, and tubs of
flowers on the terrace. *(Recommended by Lyn and Bill Capper, Roger Wilkins, Nick
Dowson)*

*Benskins (Ind Coope)   Licensee Les Robbins   Real ale   Meals and snacks   Children in
family-room   Occasional live music   Open 11–2.30, 6–11 all year; all day Sat*

Sunday opening is now 12–3 and 7–10.30 throughout England.

ASTWOOD SP9547 Map 4

Swan

Main Road; village signposted from A422 Milton Keynes–Bedford

This partly thatched early seventeenth-century pub has a spacious open-plan bar with low oak beams, antique seats and tables, log fires in a fine inglenook, and a pleasantly old-fashioned and friendly atmosphere. There's a decent range of real ales on handpump: Brakspears SB, Flowers Original, Wethereds and Whitbreads Castle Eden, plus a guest beer. Bar food under the new licensees now includes sandwiches, home-made soup (95p), ploughman's (£1.75), pâté (£1.95), quiche (£2.50), vegetable lasagne or harvest pie (£2.80), salads, roast chicken or scampi (£2.95), and steak (£6), with friendly staff; darts, shove-ha'penny, dominoes and maybe unobtrusive piped music. The quiet lawn at the back has tables under old fruit trees, and there are more seats out in front. *(Recommended by Mr and Mrs G D Amos, Mike and Kay Wilson, M P Le Geyt, Mrs M Lawrence, Paul and Margaret Baker)*

Free house   Licensees Paul Cribb, Jim and Diane Niklen   Real ale   Meals and snacks Restaurant   Children in restaurant   Open 11–2.30, 6–11 all year; closed evening 25 Dec Bedrooms tel North Crawley (023 065) 272; £25S/£30S

BLEDLOW SP7702 Map 4

Lions of Bledlow ★ ⊗

From B4009 from Chinnor towards Princes Risborough, the first right turn about 1 mile outside Chinnor goes straight to the pub; from the second, wider right turn, turn right through village

This popular, mossy-tiled pub attracts a fair number of walkers from nearby Bledlow Ridge and the Chilterns, and offers a friendly welcome in its inglenook bar; this has lots of heavy low beams and an old settle. Built into one partly panelled wall there are more modern attractive oak stalls, while the bay windows give marvellous views over a small, quiet green to the plain stretched out below. There are three open fires, though only one is usually lit. At the back a sheltered crazy-paved terrace and a series of small sloping lawns lead on to a track up into the hills and the steep beech woods beyond. Well kept Courage Directors, Wadworths 6X, Wethereds and Youngs on handpump; there's a pool-table and fruit machine in one of the two cottagey rooms opening off the main bar. The small range of decent home-made bar food includes soup (95p), generous open sandwiches (from £1.25), ploughman's (from £1.75), salads (from £2.25), chilli con carne (£2.25), plaice or haddock (£2.50), steak and kidney pie (£2.75), lasagne (£3.25) and scampi (£3.50), with daily specials, including at least one vegetarian dish; there are plenty of tables on the glossily polished antique tiled floor. *(Recommended by Peter Hitchcock, Brian and Rosemary Wilmot, TBB, Simon Collett-Jones, Colin Donald, Maureen Hobbs, HKR, K G Freak, John Nice)*

Free house   Licensee F J McKeown   Real ale   Meals and snacks (not Sun evening) Restaurant (not Sun evening) tel Princes Risborough (084 44) 3345   Children in restaurant and eating area   Open 11–2.30, 6–11 all year; probably all day Sat

BOLTER END SU7992 Map 4

Peacock ⊗

Just over 4 miles from M40 junction 5; A40 to Stokenchurch, then B482

The bar area in this warm and welcoming pub is a rambling series of rooms and alcoves, with rugs on the polished brick and tile floor, and a cheering log fire in winter. The main attraction continues to be the superlative bar food, particularly the range of pizzas; other efficiently served food includes a prawn sandwich or ploughman's (£1.90), giant sausages (£1.80 in French bread, with chips), coq au vin, scampi or home-made pies such as steak and kidney (£3.25), prawn and mushroom provençale served on good Basmati rice (£3.50), salads such as home-cooked ham and melon (£3.25), prawn (£3.95), and good steaks (from twelve-ounce rump, £6.95); the home-made puddings include treacly spotted dick, treacle and walnut tart or chocolate gateau (all £1.40). Very well kept ABC and Bass on handpump, and good cider; darts, dominoes, cribbage, piped music. In summer there are tables on the front grass. *(Recommended by M V Saunders, W A Lund, PLC, HKR, Jane and Calum)*

ABC (Ind Coope)   Licensee Peter Hodges   Real ale   Meals and snacks (not Sun evening) Open 11–2.30, 6–11 all year

CHALFONT ST PETER   SU9990   Map 2
Greyhound
High Street; A413

The new licensees here seem keen to emphasise the friendly and welcoming atmosphere, and early indications are that the food is good, too, with soup (95p), sandwiches (from £1), ploughman's (£1.75), steak and kidney or shepherd's pie, chilli con carne, and gammon (around £3), and daily specials such as seafood platter or lasagne. The low-beamed main bar has an informal feel, with brasses on its dark panelling, a huge winter log fire in a handsome fireplace, and studded blue leatherette armed chairs and stools on the patterned red carpet. The stage-coach in the attractive front courtyard serves as a reminder of the pub's links with the past (which in fact extend back to the fourteenth century). Well kept Courage Best and Directors on handpump, from a good long counter. Outside there are tables among flower tubs, and a climbing-frame and slide on a small lawn by the little River Misbourne. *(Recommended by Monica Robinson, J F and M I Wallington, John Tyzack, Lyn and Bill Capper)*

Courage   Licensee Mr Gilmour   Real ale   Snacks (lunch) and meals   Restaurant   Children in Coach Room and family-room   Open 11–2.30, 5–11 weekdays, 11–11 Fri and Sat, all year; closed evening 25 Dec   Bedrooms tel Gerrards Cross (0753) 883404;£29.50/£39.50

CHESHAM   SP9502   Map 4
Black Horse ⊗
The Vale; leaving Chesham on A416 towards Berkhamsted fork left at Hawridge 3, Colesbury 3½ signpost

This is one of the rare cases where recent extension has actually made a pub seem older than before – the latest addition is a heavy-beamed barn (Grade 2 listed), with the old-fashioned mood heightened by shelves of old books. The small original core has an inglenook fireplace big enough to hold two tables, and it opens into an extension (quite modern-seeming, this one) with lots of heavy dark-lacquered tables, wheel-back chairs and high-backed winged rustic settles; there are little country pictures on the rough-plastered white walls, black beams and joists in the ceiling. Well kept Benskins Best, Friary Meux, Ind Coope Burton and Taylor-Walker on handpump, with lots of pleasant bar staff. Despite its relatively isolated position, it still manages to do close to a thousand meals a week; these are served with friendly briskness, and include sandwiches (from 95p), soup (95p), filled baked potatoes (from £1.95, not Sunday lunchtime), ploughman's (£1.95), salads (from £3.50), plaice or gammon (£3.75), and sirloin steak (£5.75); the popular speciality is a range of half a dozen home-made pies such as steak and kidney, game, pork and apricot or beef with Guinness and orange (all £3.95; not Sunday lunchtime); piped music. There are plenty of well spaced picnic-table sets and a climbing-frame on the big back lawn, with more tables under cocktail parasols in front. *(Recommended by L V Nutton, Doug Kennedy, TBB)*

Benskins (Ind Coope)   Licensee Roger Wordley   Real ale   Meals and snacks   Open 11–3, 6–11 all year; all day Sat

COLNBROOK TQ0277 Map 3
Ostrich ⊗

1¼ miles from M4 junction 5; A4 towards Hounslow, then first right on to B3378 – at start of village where main road bends sharply to right keep straight on into Access Only village High Street

This friendly pub – which has some claim to be Britain's third oldest, though the present building's largely Elizabethan – is popular with overseas tourists (perhaps partly because of its proximity to Heathrow's Terminal Four). It's been with the same family for the past twenty-five years, and a historical feel prevails. That history is sometimes rather chequered – in 1598 a horror-comic printed a tall tale claiming that the original twelfth-century innkeeper had murdered more than sixty travellers here, dropping their stitched-up bodies into the kitchen stock-pot – he was unmasked only when one of their horses escaped to make its riderless way home. In the two carpeted communicating rooms of the heavy-beamed front bar there are wheel-back chairs and red-cushioned winged wall seats around their tables, with big log fireplaces – one with guns and swords above it, the other a reconstructed brick inglenook guarded by a grandfather clock. Old pictures and paintings of the pub hang on the timbered ochre walls. The popular food, efficiently served in both bar and restaurant, includes French onion soup (£1.80), cheese with hot granary bread (£2), stuffed mushrooms (£2.50), salads (from £3.55), vegetarian dishes, seafood Mornay or various home-made pies (from £3.85), sturdier main dishes such as honey-baked poussin (£6.65), roast pork or lamb cutlets (around £7) or steaks (from £8.50); the Courage Best on handpump is a little pricey. Its sign was originally a crane (the bird, that is), repainted as an ostrich when tall tales from Africa became fashionable. There are picnic-table sets under cocktail parasols in the back car park, through the coach entry below the fine jettied upper floor. *(Recommended by Simon Collett-Jones, David Regan)*

Free house   Licensees Derek Lamont and Mervyn Parrish   Real ale   Meals and snacks Restaurant tel Slough (0753) 682628   Children in restaurant   Open 11–2.30, 6–11 all year

FAWLEY SU7586 Map 2
Walnut Tree ⊗

Village signposted off A4155 and off B480, N of Henley

The new licensees in this plain brick pub have now thoroughly confirmed the reputation for good, imaginative food which it won originally under the Hardings. A handsome range of dishes includes deep-fried Camembert (£2.95), baked avocado Mornay or smoked trout (£3.15), chicken Kiev or grilled trout (£5.95), beef Stroganoff (£6.25), baked scallops (£6.95) and Dover sole (£7.75); puddings such as treacle and walnut tart and tangy lemon meringue pie. Well kept Brakspears PA on handpump, and a good range of wines; friendly service, with a warm welcome for ramblers. The décor is simple but attractively so; darts, dominoes, cribbage, fruit and trivia machine, juke box. The big lawn around the front car park has well spaced rustic tables, with some seats in a pleasant sheltered terrace extension with a covered verandah. *(Recommended by Stanley Matthews, Barbara Hatfield, G N G Tingey, R F Neil; more reports please)*

Brakspears   Licensee G W Knight   Real ale   Meals and snacks   Restaurant tel Turville Heath (049 163) 360/617   Children in eating area and restaurant   Open 11–11; closed 2.30–6 in winter

---

Stars after the name of a pub show exceptional quality. One star means most people (after reading the report to see just why the star has been won) would think a special trip worth while. Two stars mean that the pub is really outstanding – one of just a handful in its region. The very very few with three stars are the real aristocrats – of their type, they could hardly be improved.

FINGEST   SU7791   Map 2
Chequers ⊗
Village signposted off B482 Marlow–Stokenchurch

A beamed inner room in this attractively situated pub has eighteenth-century box settles, butterscotch-spiral and other antique seats as well as comfortable more modern ones; there are guns in a rack over the big log fireplace, and lots of figured china – on the mantelpiece, a Delft shelf, and in a corner cupboard. The sunny lounge has comfortable easy chairs, with French windows leading to the garden. The efficiently organised food bar takes orders for sandwiches (from 70p), and serves ploughman's (from £1.75), home-made soup or local spicy sausages (£1.95), steak and kidney pie made with Guinness or chicken and game pie (£3.95), curried prawns, roast lamb or liver and bacon (£4.50), hot avocado and prawns in cheese sauce (£4.95) and poussin stuffed with pâté (£5.50), with a selection of six generous salads. Well kept Brakspears PA, SB and in season Old Ale on handpump; dominoes, cribbage, backgammon. There's a spacious and pretty garden, with lots of tables on quiet lawns among rose and flower beds, and, beyond, pasture slopes up towards the beech woods; it has views right down the Hambleden valley. The unique twin-roofed church tower across the road is early Norman. *(Recommended by HKR, Doug Kennedy, Brian and Rosemary Wilmot, Dr Paul Kitchener)*

Brakspears   Licensee Bryan Heasman   Real ale   Meals and snacks (not Sun evening) Restaurant tel Turville Heath (049 163) 335   Children in eating area and restaurant Open 11–3, 6–11 all year

FORTY GREEN   SU9292   Map 2
Royal Standard of England ⊗
3½ miles from M40 junction 2, via A40 to Beaconsfield, then follow sign to Forty Green, off B474 ¾ mile N of New Beaconsfield

The most attractive part of this ancient, rambling warren of a pub is a room with great black ship's timbers, finely carved antique oak panelling, and a massive settle apparently built to fit the curved transom of an Elizabethan ship. In fact it used to be called the Ship until after the Battle of Worcester in 1651, when Charles II hid in the high rafters of what is now its food bar. Elsewhere there are more oak settles, old rifles, powder-flasks and bugles, ancient pewter and pottery tankards, lots of brass and copper, needlework samplers, stained glass, and fine decorated iron firebacks for the open fires. Your best chance of enjoying this treasure-trove of a pub is at lunchtime, particularly during the week. At other times – even on winter weekends – it can get extremely busy, as it is on the tourist circuit; service can then occasionally be on the brisk side of friendliness. The bar food is expensive but attractive, including home-made soup (£1.25), avocado with fresh crab (£1.35), ploughman's (£2.50, with an uncommonly good choice of cheeses), sausages and chips (£3.25), chicken curry (£4.25), a range of home-made pies such as chicken, beef and kidney, beef and smoked oyster or pigeon (£4.25–£4.50), pork spare ribs, plaice, chicken, scampi, fritto misto or vegetarian flan (all at £4.50). Well kept Brakspears SB, Huntsman Royal Oak and Marstons Pedigree and Owd Rodger (the beer was originally brewed here, until the pub passed the recipe on to Marstons), and another beer brewed for the pub, on handpump. There are seats outside in a neatly hedged front rose garden, or in the shade of a tree. *(Recommended by M C Howells, Ewan McCall, Roger Huggins, Tom Mclean, Lindsey Shaw Radley, George and Chris Miller, Dave Braisted, Nick Dowson, Mike Tucker, Jon Wainwright, C Elliott, AP, Mrs G K Herbert, George Little)*

Free house   Licensees Philip Eldridge and Alan Wainwright   Real ale   Meals and snacks Children in area alongside Candle Bar   Open 10.30–3.30, 5.30–11 all year

FRIETH SU7990 Map 4

Yew Tree ⊗

Village signposted off B482 N of Marlow

The chef/patron has introduced Austrian touches to the bar food here, such as his potato and watercress soup (£1.45), ham and mushroom strudel (£1.95), wiener brathuhn (£4.20) and a dish of the day like stuffed shoulder of veal (around £4), besides vegetarian pancake (£2.45), home-made sausages or spaghetti bolognese (£2.65), fresh skate in cheese sauce (£3.20) and gammon with parsley sauce (£3.25). The civilised and comfortable bar has a patterned carpet on its old brick flooring tiles, with cushioned wall banquettes and armed chairs around the neat dark tables. There are stripped beams and joists, guns over the log fires at each end, china and glass sparkling in corner cupboards, unusual humorous sporting prints and little animal pictures. They take real trouble over the drinks side, with several interesting punches (hot in winter; and the freshly squeezed non-alcoholic fruit punch is something every pub should have), decent wines and coffee, and well kept Arkells, Ruddles County, Theakstons Old Peculier and Websters Yorkshire on handpump. There are tables in front, on the small terrace and neat lawn by a big sculpted yew – with space for tethering horses. (*Recommended by R F Lewellen, V H Balchin*)

Free house Licensee Franz Aitzetmuller Real ale Meals and snacks; also afternoon teas Children welcome Restaurant tel High Wycombe (0494) 882330 Open 10.30–3, 5.30–11 (midnight Sat) all year

GREAT MISSENDEN SP8900 Map 4

George ★ ⊗

The two snug rooms of the bar in this attractive and friendly fifteenth-century pub have heavy beams (beautifully moulded in the main room, with a few pictorial mugs hanging from them), timbered walls decorated with prints, and little alcoves (including one with an attractively carved box settle – just room for two – under a fine carved early seventeenth-century oak panel). There are nicely chosen chairs around a few polished copper and other tables, on rugs and muted red tiles by the fire; the high mantelpiece is decorated with Staffordshire and other figurines. An inner room has a sofa and small settles. The pub food, served in a spaciously comfortable room separate from the bar, continues to enjoy consistent praise from readers. It includes home-made soup (95p), sandwiches (from £1.20, weekday lunchtimes only), ploughman's (£2.25), deep-fried Camembert (£2.25), fresh pasta (£3.25), scampi (£4.20), chicken fillets (£4.45), haddock and cauliflower Mornay (£4.25), gammon or salads (£4.95), a hot beef curry (£5.45) and Scotch rump steak (£6.45). There's also an excellent range of vegetarian dishes such as quiche (£2.95), vegetable puff pastry (£4.25), wheat and walnut casserole (£4.50), and vegetable curry (£4.95); very good puddings; the menu changes frequently. ABC, Bass, Chiltern Beechwood and Everards Tiger on handpump (well kept under a light carbon dioxide blanket), mulled wine in winter, tea, coffee (as much as you can drink for 50p at weekends) and decaffeinated coffee; dominoes, shove-ha'penny, fruit machine and piped light music. (*Recommended by David and Flo Wallington, Stanley Matthews, Mr and Mrs T F Marshall, Lyn and Bill Capper, Pat and Dennis Jones, Alison Hayward, Nick Dowson, Hugh Morgan*)

ABC (Ind Coope) Licensees Guy and Sally Smith Real ale Meals and snacks (not Sun evening) Restaurant Fri–Sat evenings (bookings essential), Sun lunch tel Great Missenden (024 06) 2084 Children welcome Open 11–2.30, 6–11 all year

People named as recommenders after the main entries have told us that the pub should be included. But they have not written the report – we have, after anonymous on-the-spot inspection.

HAMBLEDEN SU7886 Map 2
Stag & Huntsman
Village signposted from A4155

Just as we went to press new licensees took over this pleasant Chilterns pub, so to be on the safe side we are for the moment keeping under suspension its former awards for both food and bedrooms. However, first indications are that the welcoming atmosphere built up by the Vidgens is set to survive. In the busy low-ceilinged lounge there are upholstered bench seats, stools and wooden chairs around the tables on its carpet. The public bar, with shove-ha'penny, dominoes, cribbage and a fruit machine, is attractively simple (and it may be easier to get to the serving-counter from here during busy periods). The country garden, well kept and prettily rearranged, backs directly on to woods. The good choice of home-made bar food, more or less as before, includes soup (£1.20), ploughman's (£2), smoked eel or smoked salmon pâté or Mexican chilli nachos (£2.20), quiches or steak and kidney pie (£3.95), evening steaks from the village butcher (£6.50) and home-made apple pie and ice-cream with walnut purée or fresh fruit in season (£1.20–£1.50). Brakspears PA and SPA, Flowers Original, Huntsman Royal Oak and Wadworths 6X on handpump, with guest beers. *(Recommended by Alison Hayward, Nick Dowson, G B Longden, I Meredith, G V Price, Lyn and Bill Capper, Wg Cdr A B Hughes-Lewis, Margaret and Trevor Errington, Barbara Hatfield, Lindsey Shaw Radley; more reports on the new regime please)*

Free house   Licensees Mike and Janet Matthews   Real ale   Meals and snacks (not Sun evening)   Restaurant   Children in restaurant and eating area   Open 11–2.30 (3 Sun), 6–11 all year   Bedrooms tel Henley (0491) 571227; £22/£30S

HAWRIDGE COMMON SP9406 Map 4
Full Moon
Follow Hawridge signpost off A416 N of Chesham and keep on towards Cholesbury; OS Sheet 165 reference 945062

The snug core of this pleasantly simple little tavern on the common has heavy dark beams, ancient polished flagstones or flooring tiles, shiny black built-in floor-to-ceiling settles, old hunting prints, and on winter evenings a log fire in the inglenook. A couple of more modern little rooms lead off, one with sensibly placed darts, and dominoes, at the back; it can get smoky if it's busy. The unspoilt atmosphere is heightened by the way that it's probably the barmaid herself who'll make up your sandwiches or ploughman's while you wait. The food is simple but wholesome and home made, with pasties (£1), simple salads (from £2.20), or in winter a hearty soup (£1.65), lasagne (£2) and steak and kidney pudding (£2.75). Well kept Wethereds and SPA on handpump, with Winter Royal when it's available; well priced Rombouts coffee, friendly service. Picnic-table sets and rustic seats are set out among fruit trees on a spacious side lawn with roses along its low flint wall. *(Recommended by John Nice, Nick Dowson)*

Whitbreads   Real ale   Meals (weekday lunchtimes) and snacks (lunchtime, not Sun)   Open 11.30–2.30, 6–11 all year

HYDE HEATH SU9399 Map 4
Plough ⊗

As we went to press we heard that the licensee of this pub was relinquishing his interest in it.

IBSTONE SU7593 Map 4

Fox ⊗ 🍴

1¾ miles from M40 junction 5: unclassified lane leading S from motorway exit roundabout; pub is on Ibstone Common

This friendly seventeenth-century inn has recently been refurbished in traditional style. An old kitchen has been incorporated into the lounge bar, which still has its high-backed settles and other country seats under low oak beams, and, in winter, log fires; very old photographs of the village now hang on the walls. The pine settles and tables in the public bar match its wood-block floor; there are still darts, dominoes, cribbage and a fruit machine here. Home-made bar food includes sandwiches (from £1.10), several mammoth ploughman's (£2.25), changing daily specials (from £2.50), fish (from £3.20), home-made pies or vegetarian dishes (from £3.25), lasagne (£3.25), and fresh crab salad (£3.50); in season there are good game dishes (from £4.25 – people particularly like the venison casserole). Puddings include treacle tart, bread-and-butter pudding and chocolate and ginger fudge (around £1.50); very friendly service. The restaurant (in the new bedroom block) is decidedly smart. In summer there are decent cook-it-yourself barbecues in the rose garden, which is particularly fine when lit at night by old lamps. Well kept Brakspears PA and SB, Flowers Original, Wethereds and guest beers on handpump, and in season Winter Royal; very respectable wines by the glass. The pub overlooks the village common and its cricket ground. *(Recommended by HKR, V H Balchin, Mrs M J Dyke, Joan Olivier)*

Free house   Licensees Ann and David Banks   Real ale   Meals and snacks   Restaurant Children in eating area   Open 11–3, 5.30 (5 Sat)–11; 11–2.30, 6–11 in winter Bedrooms tel Turville Heath (049 163) 289; £48S/£60S

LACEY GREEN SP8100 Map 4

Pink & Lily

Parslow's Hillock; from A4010 High Wycombe–Princes Risborough follow Loosley Row signpost, and in that village follow Great Hampden, Great Missenden signpost; OS Sheet 165 reference 826019

Closed for a long while and reopened in 1986 after much rebuilding, this is now a spacious dining pub, popular with lunchers out from High Wycombe. The food's simple but all home cooked, and includes sandwiches (from £1.25), filled baked potatoes (£1.75), salads (from £1.95), ploughman's (from £2.25), chilli con carne (£2.50), lasagne or steak and kidney pie (£2.95) and Indonesian chicken (£3.50); well kept Brakspears PA and SB, Flowers Original, Greene King IPA, Wadworths 6X and Wethereds on handpump; darts, maybe piped music. The main bar is light and airy, with low pink plush seats and steps down to a couple of smaller areas through arches. This was a favourite pub of Rupert Brooke's, and the start of one poem he wrote here, about himself and a hiking friend, suggests quite a deal of liquid inspiration:

> *Never there came to the Pink*
> *Two such men as we think*
> *Never there came to the Lily*
> *Two men quite so richly silly.*

The little tap-room he used has been preserved very much as we remember it before the recent extensions: the broad inglenook with its low mantelpiece, red flooring tiles, built-in wall benches, shove-ha'penny, dominoes and cribbage, the old wooden ham-rack hanging from the ceiling, even the game of ring the bull (the current pub record is 19 out of 21). There are lots of new rustic tables in the sizeable garden (where they play boules in summer). Pub events range from an annual pig roast with jazz band to a Scottish New Year's party with free transport home (they pipe the haggis in on Burns Night, too). *(Recommended by HKR, CGB)*

Free house   Licensees Clive and Marion Mason   Real ale   Meals and snacks   Children in eating area   Open 11–3, 6–11 all year; all day Fri and Sat

LEY HILL   SP9802 Map 4
Swan ⊗

Village signposted from A416 in Chesham

In the very short time they've been here, the Steers have won warm praise from readers for their food, served in big helpings with fresh vegetables. Besides four or five dishes of the day such as cottage pie (£3), chicken and ham pancake (£3.20), smoked halibut with prawns or baked curried crab (£4), it includes home-made French onion soup (£1.20), sandwiches (from £1.25), ploughman's (from £1.85), filled baked potatoes (from £1.95), Stilton and walnut pâté (£2.10), lasagne (£2.65), salads (from £2.95), several pies such as cod with prawns, mussels and crab (£3.25), local trout with mushrooms and walnuts (£4.95) and rump steak (£6.50); puddings (£1.20). There's a small no-smoking eating area with pale wood furniture and a tiled floor. The softly lit main bar is pleasantly rambly, with big black low beams, cushioned window and wall seats or wheel-back chairs around the country tables in its various alcoves, signed cricket bats on the butter-coloured wall by one vast fireplace, and a collection of tobacco pipes by the old kitchen range behind its club fireguard. It's neatly kept, with flowers on the bar and quietly efficient service; well kept Benskins Best, Ind Coope Burton and Youngs on handpump; piped music. There are picnic-table sets among barrels of flowers out on the front terrace and side lawn, looking up to the common. *(Recommended by Lyn and Bill Capper, Mr and Mrs F W Sturch, David Tench, John Tyzack)*

Benskins (Ind Coope)   Licensees Jeff and Sue Steers   Real ale   Meals and snacks (not Sun evening; set Sun lunch)   Children in eating area and restaurant until 7.30   Open 11–3, 6–11 all year; closed evening 25 Dec

LITTLE HAMPDEN   SP8503 Map 4
Rising Sun ★ ⊗

Village signposted from back road (i.e. W of A413) Great Missenden–Stoke Mandeville; pub at end of village lane; OS Sheet 165 reference 856040

The food in this comfortable and isolated Chilterns pub has been simple but good, with fresh cheeses for the ploughman's (£1.80), filled baked potatoes (from £1.80, prawns with seafood sauce £2.75), garlic mushrooms (£2.20), smoked trout (£2.75), plaice (£3), lasagne, moussaka or home-made steak and kidney pie (£3.50 – with excellent pastry), gammon (£4.50), and first-rate eight-ounce fillet steak (£8); puddings are £1.20; on Sundays the bar food may be more limited. The pub's just been taken over by the licensees of the Plough at Hyde Heath; as you can see from our report on that, they've earned a reputation for more distinctive and imaginative food, and we can expect to see their personal style affecting what's on offer here – particularly in the little restaurant, which they plan to reopen. In the quarry-tiled front bar, with its attractive inglenook fireplace, there are plenty of decent-sized tables, as well as in the Turkey-carpeted and pleasantly ventilated modern lounge, and out on the terrace by the sloping front grass. Well kept Adnams, Brakspears SB and Sam Smiths OB on handpump – there may be minor changes or extensions to this range; darts, shove-ha'penny, dominoes and cribbage in the public bar; piped music. At weekends it attracts walkers (as long as they leave their boots outside), who reach it by the tracks leading on through the woods in various directions; the pub's on *Good Walks Guide* Walk 71, which takes in Hampden House and Coombe Hill (National Trust – with fine views). *(Recommended by Peter and Barbara Atkins, Ken and Barbara Turner, Stanley Matthews; more reports on the new regime please)*

Free house   Licensee Rory Dawson   Real ale   Meals and snacks   Open 11.30–2.30, 7–11 all year; may be open all day Sat

LITTLE HORWOOD   SP7930   Map 4
Shoulder of Mutton ⊗
Back road 1 mile S of A421 Buckingham–Bletchley

The furnishings in this half-timbered and partly thatched medieval pub are appropriately simple – pews, sturdy seats, chunky country tables. A large, ancient chimney dominates the T-shaped quarry-tiled bar; and although the room's not actually smoky the huge hearth down at one end has clearly left its blackening mark on the low beamed ceiling and even the walls. The games area has darts, shove-ha'penny, dominoes, fruit machine and juke box. Besides sandwiches and hot light snacks (from £1.30, steak sandwich £1.70), bar food includes a decent ploughman's, lamb cooked in beer, steak and kidney pie, and beef in Guinness with hazelnut-stuffed prunes (main courses £3.85–£5.50) and T-bone steak (£7.25); well kept ABC, Everards Tiger on handpump; pleasant service. In the pub's orchard there are plenty of seats, and a quiet churchyard beside it. *(Recommended by Lyn and Bill Capper, Miss A M Burton, M P Le Geyt)*

ABC (Ind Coope)   Licensee June Fessey   Real ale   Meals and snacks (not Mon, Tues or Sun evenings)   Restaurant tel Winslow (029 671) 2514   Children in eating area   Open 11–3, 6–11 all year; all day Sat

MARLOW   SU8586   Map 2
Ship
West Street (A4155 towards Henley)

The new licensees in this cosy and pleasant pub have extended the range of food (and increased the prices, though they're still very reasonable): it now includes sandwiches (from 85p, toasted 10p extra), ploughman's (from £1.25), filled baked potatoes (from £1.50), home-made lasagne and pizzas (£2.50–£3.50), and steaks (from £4.50); daily specials. Well kept Flowers, Wethereds and SPA on handpump, with Winter Royal in season; fruit machine, piped popular music. The two unusually low-beamed communicating rooms have Windsor armchairs and leatherette seats built into partly panelled walls, a fine collection of warship photographs and various nautical paraphernalia. In a back paved courtyard there are tables among tubs of flowers by a grape vine. *(Recommended by Quentin Williamson, Elaine Kellet, David Regan, H W Wilson; more reports please)*

Wethereds (Whitbreads)   Real ale   Meals and snacks   Restaurant tel Marlow (062 84) 4360   Nearby parking may be difficult in daytime   Open 10.30–2.30, 5.30–11 all year

Two Brewers ⊗

St Peter Street; at double roundabout approaching bridge turn into Station Road, then first right

This friendly pub has a low-beamed but spacious T-shaped bar. There's a good atmosphere here, as well as black panelling and interesting maritime pictures and equipment, including lots of gleaming brassware. Bar food includes sandwiches (£1.20), ploughman's (£2.30), baked potatoes with a choice of fillings which changes each day (£2.60), chilli con carne (£2.90), steak and kidney pie (£3.30), lasagne (£3.50), moules marinière (£3.90) and good salads (from £4.50); pleasant staff; well kept Flowers Original, Wethereds Bitter and SPA on handpump, with related guest beers. It's quietly and attractively placed in a backstreet, and a back courtyard has sturdy rustic seats; benches in front give a glimpse of the Thames. (*Recommended by Colin and Caroline, TBB, Michael and Alison Sandy, Michael O'Driscoll, J P Day*)

Wethereds (Whitbreads)   Licensee F W J Boxall   Real ale   Meals and snacks   Weekend restaurant tel Marlow (062 84) 4140   Children in eating area and area partly set aside for them   Open 11–3, 5.30–11 all year

MARSH GIBBON   SP6423 Map 4

Greyhound

Back road about 4 miles E of Bicester; pub SW of village, towards A41 and Blackthorn

This friendly, ancient pub has a pleasant bar: beams, unusual hexagonal stone flooring tiles, stripped stone walls, comfortable heavy armed seats and a finely ornamented iron stove. Home-made food includes sandwiches, soup (£1.10), salads (from £1.50), ploughman's (from £2.25), Madras curry (£2.95), scampi (£3.50), and vegetarian soufflé or home-made pies (£3.95); well kept Fullers London Pride, Glenny Wychwood Best (from Witney) and Greene King Abbot and IPA on handpump; shove-ha'penny, dominoes, cribbage, piped music. The gardens, very pleasant in summer, have stone-topped tables in the charming little front flower garden, and swings and a climbing-frame on the bigger lawn at the back. The pub was originally Tudor, but largely rebuilt in 1740 after a 'terable fire'. (*Recommended by Ken and Barbara Turner, B P White, Gordon and Daphne, Dr J R Hamilton, B P White, Alison Hayward, Nick Dowson; more reports on the new regime please*)

Free house   Licensee A Carter   Real ale   Meals and snacks (not Sun evening)   Restaurant tel Stratton Audley (086 97) 365   Children welcome   Open 11–3, 6–11 all year

MARSWORTH   SP9114 Map 4

Red Lion

Vicarage Road; follow village signpost off B489 Dunstable–Aylesbury

This friendly and unspoilt cottage pub was built in 1780 at the same time as the Grand Union Canal, which is just down the lane. It's partly thatched, and in the main bar there are pews and tan leatherette seats on the red tiles; a games area divided off by the stripped brick fireplace has bar billiards, darts, shove-ha'penny, dominoes, cribbage, video game and fruit machine; lots of local notices, and an aged curved high-backed settle, as well as more pews and another fire in a big end hearth. The carpeted upper lounge has an attractive china corner cupboard, big pictures of boats (and of an owl), and beige leatherette seats; the serving-hatch here is almost at floor level. There's a little front snug bar, too. On the lower level an ancient tiled-floor lobby takes you through to the back food servery, which does sandwiches (from £1), ploughman's (from £1.50), and salads or a couple of hot dishes, one of which is always a curry (£2.50). Well kept ABC, Bass and Everards Tiger on handpump, and good house wines. There are picnic-table sets in a small but nicely sheltered back garden, with more in front by the lane. The pub is close to some reservoirs and a nature reserve. *(Recommended by Bob Sutherland, Dr Paul Kitchener)*

ABC (Ind Coope)   Licensees Peter and Judy Goodwin   Real ale   Meals and snacks (not evenings or Sun)   Children in public bar extension   Easter Mon bonnet parade and day of folk dance   Open 11–3, 6–11; all day Sat; all year

NORTHEND   SU7392 Map 4

White Hart ⊗

This friendly and snug mossy-tiled pub has an unspoilt partly panelled bar, with Windsor chairs, comfortable window seats, handsomely carved low oak beams, and, in winter, a big log fire in the enormous fireplace. The bar food, all home made and reasonably priced, is excellent and wide-ranging. It includes sandwiches (from 85p) and ploughman's (from £1.70), both with home-made chutney, soup (£1.10), various pâtés (£1.85), and about twelve main courses, such as cauliflower cheese (£2.50), ratatouille crumble (£3.45), savoury pancake with ham and mushroom filling or lasagne (£3.50), fish or steak and kidney pie (£4.25), and beef in Guinness or local venison in red wine (£4.50); also a good selection of puddings, like bread-and-butter pudding, raspberry, apple and almond crumble or nutty meringue sundae (all £1.35). Well kept Brakspears PA on handpump. In summer there's hatch service to the charming garden, sheltered by high hedges as well as by the pub itself, and full of flowers, shrubs and fruit trees; children's play area. The area is popular with walkers. *(Recommended by Caroline Gibbins, Nick Dowson, Alison Hayward, Dr and Mrs E G W Bill, D B S Frost, E Mitchelmore, I Meredith, Lyn and Bill Capper)*

Brakspears   Licensees Gerry and Ann Bean   Real ale   Meals and snacks (not Mon evening)   Children in one room (lunchtime)   Open 11–2.30, 6–11 all year

PENN   SU9193 Map 4

Crown   [illustrated on page 38]

B474

A Chef & Brewer pub (one that's retained a good deal of individuality), this creeper-covered place is on a Chilterns high point: from the tower of the fourteenth-century church opposite, on this ridge over 500 feet high, you are supposed to be able to see twelve counties. The lounge is neat and pleasant, and there are well preserved ancient flooring tiles in one room; the public bar (which was once a coffin-maker's workshop) has a juke box, fruit machine, darts and a pool-table; piped music. Outside there are tables among tubs of flowers on the terraces (with fine views out over rolling pastures), slides, swings, climbing-frames and a wooden horse and cart for children; there's a pretty rose garden in front. Efficiently served bar food includes a choice of main dishes such as chicken chasseur, curry, or salads, and several puddings; the popular carvery serves three-course lunches (not Sunday). Well kept Ruddles County and Websters Yorkshire on handpump. *(Recommended by Mr and Mrs G D Amos, M C Howells, Mr and Mrs F W Sturch, C F Walling, Lindsey Shaw Radley, Nick Dowson, Simon Collett-Jones)*

Trumans (Watneys)   Real ale   Bar meals (not Sat evening)   Restaurant tel Penn (049 481) 2640   Open 11–2.30, 5.30–11 all year

---

Canalside pub theatre Each year from May to September Mikron, a charity theatre company, do a water-borne tour, performing in the evening particularly in or outside canal and other waterside pubs, including twenty or so of those described in this *Guide* – such as the Red Lion mentioned here. For their 1989 itinerary, send a medium-sized SAE to Mikron, 31 Warehouse Hill, Marsden, Huddersfield, West Yorkshire HD7 6AB.

nr PRINCES RISBOROUGH   SP8003   Map 4

Red Lion

Whiteleaf; village signposted off A4010 towards Aylesbury; OS Sheet 165 reference 817040

Tucked up a quiet village lane close to Whiteleaf Fields (National Trust), this simple but spotless inn has cream-painted winged settles and wheel-back chairs in its small low-ceilinged bar, which is decorated with little sporting, coaching and ballooning prints; there are vases of flowers, and a rack of magazines by the log fire. Bar food, at prices keener than most in the Chilterns, includes freshly baked filled rolls (from 75p), filled baked potatoes (from 90p), sausages, ploughman's (from £1.50), burger or chicken nibbles (£1.50), a good steak and kidney pie with fine pastry (£2.85), scampi (£2.95) and eight-ounce rump steak (£6.50). Well kept Brakspears PA and SB, Morlands PA and Hook Norton Best on handpump, with a guest beer such as Morlands Old Masters. Quiet on weekday lunchtimes, the pub's very popular with local people in the evenings – walkers too at weekends. There are a couple of rustic tables on the neat little side lawn. *(Recommended by HKR, Gordon Leighton, Nicolas Walter)*

Free house   Licensees Alan and Cathy Elliott   Real ale   Meals and snacks (not Sun) Restaurant (closed Sun)   Children in eating area and restaurant   Open 11–2.30, 6–11 all year Bedrooms tel Princes Risborough (084 44) 4476; £17.50/£27.50

SKIRMETT   SU7790   Map 2

Old Crown ★ ⊗

High Street; from A4155 NE of Henley take Hambleden turn and keep on; or from B482 Stokenchurch–Marlow take Turville turn and keep on

The friendly new licensees in this simple village inn have very much lived up to the expectations we had of them last year, particularly regarding food. It's good, efficiently served, and includes interesting soups (from £1.35), smoked oysters on toast or hummus (£1.85), deep-fried Camembert (£2.25), ploughman's (from £2.25), well filled baked potatoes (from £3.25), chilli con carne (£4.10), lasagne (£4.30), scampi or steak, kidney and mushroom (£4.50), local rabbit in mustard and tarragon sauce (£4.75), Scotch fillet steak (£8.75), with a range of specials such as savoury vegetable or goulash game pie, and roast pheasant or partridge; a good choice of puddings such as treacle tart (£1.40) or rum and raisin cheesecake (£1.65). It's a delightfully hospitable yet old-fashioned place, with a small central room and a larger one leading off, which have Windsor chairs, tankards hanging from exposed beams, and a large open fire. A small white-painted side room has an old-fashioned settle by its coal fire, and Windsor chairs around trestle tables. Well kept Brakspears PA, SB and Old Ale are tapped from casks in a still-room, and served though a hatch; dominoes, cribbage and Trivial Pursuit. There are old oak casks as seats and tables on a terrace, with half-barrel flower tubs, and picnic-table sets under cocktail parasols on the big back lawn. The alsatian's called Bruno. *(Recommended by Richard Balkwill, Lindsey Shaw Radley, Revd B K Andrews, CG, Alison Hayward, John Bennett)*

Brakspears   Licensees Peter and Liz Mumby   Real ale   Meals and snacks (not Mon) Restaurant (not Mon evening) tel Turville Heath (049 163) 435   Well behaved children in tap-room and restaurant   Live music Tues   Open 10.30–2.30, 6–11 all year

THE LEE   SP8904   Map 4

Cock & Rabbit ⊗

Back roads 2½ miles N of Great Missenden, about 1½ miles E of A413

The attractively served food here is all home made, even down to the sauces and mayonnaise, with produce from the local market. Hence the menu changes throughout the year according to what's in season, but it's likely to include ham or salami rolls (£2.50), fresh sardines and salad (£2.95), pasta of the day (£3.20), lasagne or cannelloni (£4.20), seafood pancakes (£4.25), moussaka or Mediterranean fish and chips (£4.50), and fresh salmon salad (£4.95). On the edge of a quiet village green, this is a stylish and comfortable place, with a carefully decorated lounge: the pink and mauve of its plush seats tone in neatly with the carpets and the big windows' curtains – even the napkins match, and the pine ceiling is an unusual touch. Well kept Flowers, Morlands and Wethereds. The garden is spacious, with seats on terraces, the lawn or sheltered by a verandah. There's an interesting collection of quaint inn signs out here. *(Recommended by Mr and Mrs F W Sturch, Nick Dowson, Alison Hayward; more reports please)*

Free house   Licensees Mirja and Gianfranco Parola · Real ale   Meals and snacks (not Sun or Mon evening)   Restaurant tel The Lee (024 020) 540   Children in eating area and restaurant Open 12–3, 6–11 all year

TURVILLE   SU7690 Map 4
Bull & Butcher ⊗

The motor-racing prints which cover one wall of this lively pub are not just a tribute to the previous licensee's favourite pastime; the vintage Bentley, Jaguar, MG and Lotus owners' clubs still meet here. The comfortable low-ceilinged bar also has some yachting and photography paraphernalia, cushioned wall settles in its two areas, and an old-fashioned high-backed settle by the open fire. The building itself – a picturesque black and white timbered affair – is charmingly set among old cottages, and has tables on a lawn by fruit trees and a neatly umbrella-shaped hawthorn tree. The good, wide-ranging bar food includes baked potatoes with a range of fillings or popular summer salads (from £2.95), chicken and asparagus pasta bake (£3.25), smoked leg of lamb with Stilton sauce (£3.95), beef in ale pie (£4.25) and chicken breast with marmalade and coriander (£4.50); on Monday nights in winter they do a special meal for two (£10, including a bottle of wine). Well kept Brakspears PA, SB and Old Ale on handpump; darts, dominoes, cribbage – with a locals' cards and dice school on Tuesday evenings. A particularly warm welcome is given to walkers from the nearby Chilterns valley. *(Recommended by Ian Phillips, Michael Thomson, HKR, Nick Dowson, Barbara Hatfield, Lindsey Shaw Radley, Martin and Jane Bailey, Brian and Rosemary Wilmot)*

Brakspears   Licensee Peter Wright   Real ale   Meals and snacks   Well behaved children in eating area   Gipsy jazz Thurs evening   Open 11–2.30 (3 or 3.30 Sat), 6–11 all year

WEST WYCOMBE   SU8394 Map 4
George & Dragon ⊗
A40 W of High Wycombe

The quiet modernised bar of this handsome Tudor inn has Windsor chairs and comfortable wall seats around the many wood or copper-topped tables under its massive oak beams, and at least one open fire; Courage Best and Directors on handpump; dominoes, cribbage. The interesting, well served food includes sandwiches (from 75p), soup (£1.20), ploughman's with a choice of cheeses (£1.95), potted Stilton (£2.10), savoury mushrooms and courgettes (£2.65), baked avocado and crab with a cheese sauce (£3.10), interesting home-made pies – very popular with readers – such as Cumberland sweet lamb cooked in beer and rum with apples and dried fruit, or sole and grape in a white wine sauce (£3.25), chicken curry (£3.25) lamb cutlets (£4.45) and sirloin steak (£5.75); puddings might be baked apple with custard or cheesecake with cream (£1.50). The handsome staircase is said to be haunted by the ghostly footsteps of a sixteen-year-old White Lady, and the inn is reputed also to have a mischievous poltergeist who hides things. You can sit in the garden back through the arched and cobbled coach entry: note the magnificent lead inn-sign which dominates the high street of this handsome National Trust village. The pub is on *Good Walks Guide* Walk 70. *(Recommended by Maureen Hobbs, J P Day, Dennis Jones, Mrs M J Dyke, Prof and Mrs Keith Patchett, Lyn and Bill Capper, Mr and Mrs T F Marshall, John Estdale, Nick Dowson, Alison Hayward)*

Courage   Licensee Philip Todd   Real ale   Meals and snacks (not Sun evening)   Children in separate room lunchtime   Open 11–2.30, 5.30–11 all year; all day Sat   Bedrooms tel High Wycombe (0494) 23602; £33B/£43B

WHITCHURCH   SP8020 Map 4
White Swan ⊗

10 High Street; A413 Aylesbury–Buckingham

The animals in this friendly and traditional pub have left their mark for posterity here: the relaxed little beamed front bar is named Sam's after the large golden retriever who gently monopolises much of its space; the other bar – Charlie's – is named after the pub's yellow labrador; while Bertie the budgerigar makes himself heard even from his relatively isolated position in the kitchen. In the odd-shaped saloon there are seats built into squared honey-coloured oak panelling below a Delft shelf, a few venerable leather dining-chairs, a carved Gothick settle and sturdy elm tables, with a longcase clock in one corner and a small open fire; sensibly placed darts, shove-ha'penny, dominoes, cribbage and piped music. The food is wholesome and generous, including soup (85p), a fine choice of well made sandwiches (from 65p, triple-deckers from £1.25, toasted bacon and egg £1.30), ploughman's (from £1.35), salads (from £2), burger (£1.25), omelettes (from £2.25), lasagne (£2.75), farmhouse pie (£3), gammon and eggs (£3.75 – well recommended) and rump steaks (£6.25); the chunky chips are excellent, and waitress service quick yet pleasantly homely. Well kept ABC, Bass and Everards Tiger on handpump, cheap help-yourself coffee. There are picnic-table sets under trees in the informal garden which rambles back behind the car park. *(Recommended by J A Jennings, Dr Paul Kitchener, Lyn and Bill Capper, H Williams)*

ABC (Ind Coope)   Licensees Rex and Janet Tucker   Real ale   Meals and snacks (not Sun evening)   Children in restaurant   Open 11–2.30, 6–11 all year

WINSLOW   SP7627 Map 4
Bell ⊭

Market Square

This is still a real market town, and in the little lanes leading off the main square there are a good many interesting buildings; commanding the square is this elegant black and white timbered inn, mentioned first (in connection with a yeoman's summons to pay ship money) in 1635. Later it was a staging point for the coaching trade; these days it's a comfortably relaxed place, with a snug little tap-room which has dark wood serving-shelves and handpumps against one wall, leather armchairs on oak boards, antique prints, and ancient market documents hanging from the ceiling. In the more spacious, heavy-beamed bar there's a good log fire in winter, and comfortably upholstered settles and stools around neat tables; a third has plush banquettes, with some in a big bow window. Bar food includes soup (£1.10), sandwiches (from £1.25), an excellent ploughman's (from £2.30), filled baked potatoes (from £2.25), main dishes such as pizza (£2.40), quiche (£2.50), basket meals (from £2.85), plaice (£3.25), and daily specials like sweet-and-sour pork (£3.15) or steak and kidney pudding (£3.85); friendly service. Well kept Adnams, Hook Norton Best and Old Hookey, Marstons Pedigree and Sam Smiths OB on handpump; coffee and croissant (90p); fruit machine, piped music. There are pleasant tables on the front terrace. *(Recommended by Lyn and Bill Capper, Mrs M Lawrence, Alison Hayward, KIH, Nick Dowson)*

Free house Licensee William Alston Real ale Meals and snacks (not Sun) Restaurant (including Sun lunch) Children in eating area Open 10.30–2.30, 6–11 all year Bedrooms tel *Winslow (029 671) 2741; £33(£40B)/£45S(£50B)*

Lucky Dip

Besides the fully inspected pubs, you might like to try these Lucky Dips recommended to us and described by readers (if you do, please send us reports):

Amersham [High St (A413); SU9597], *Elephant & Castle*: Pleasant and popular old Wethereds pub, low beams, china, velvet and brasses; piped music; good food (not Sun) *(Nick Dowson, Simon Collett-Jones, LYM)*; [A404] *Saracens Head*: Range of real ales, one changing guest beer, moderately priced bistro; juke box, popular with young people *(LYM)*

Asheridge [SP9404], *Blue Ball*: Excellent play area behind pub; very good food such as chicken curry and lasagne, well kept Brakspears and other real ales, quiet country location; piped music *(Nigel Paine)*

☆ **nr Aylesbury** [Gibraltar; A418 some miles towards Thame, beyond Stone – OS Sheet 165 reference 758108; SP8213], *Bottle & Glass*: Pretty thatched cottage with well spaced tables in several separate areas, low beams, plank-panelled bar with wall benches and old inglenook, good value food including intriguing open sandwiches and enterprising hot dishes from baked potatoes filled with bacon and cream to pork in a prune and cinnamon sauce, homely, comfortable restaurant, fresh flowers, friendly welcome and quick service *(Ian Phillips, John Gagg, HKR, Peter J Powrie)*

Beaconsfield [A40, a mile from M40 junction 2; SU9490], *George*: Civilised old-fashioned inn with tasty food – especially seafood fresh from Yarmouth; well kept Ind Coope real ales; bedrooms *(John Tyzack, LYM)*; *White Hart*: Nice pub part in this hotel – several small areas with fires, comfortable places to sit; very lively and popular, gets very crowded on weekend evenings but still has a cheerful atmosphere; good value interesting restaurant food, excellent salad bar, welcoming service *(L S Radley)*

Bishopstone [SP8010], *Harrow*: Friendly efficient staff and good varied interesting food, with long wine list *(Hugh O'Donnell)*

Botley [Tylers Hill Rd; SP9702], *Five Bells*: Remote and welcoming family-run country pub with inglenook fireplaces and impressive range of real ales; children in eating area *(Alison Hayward, Nick Dowson, LYM)*

Bourne End [Hedsor Rd; SU8985], *Old Red Lion*: Olde-worlde refurbishment, good food in bar and restaurant including vegetarian dishes, Courage real ale *(David Regan, Brian and Rosemary Wilmot)*

Brill [SP6513], *Pheasant*: Perched 600 feet high, by a seventeenth-century windmill, with wide views outside, low beams, open fire and interesting nooks and corners inside; reasonably priced bar meals, seats outside summer *(Joan Olivier)*

Buckingham [Market Sq; SP6933], *White Hart*: THF hotel with small, friendly bar, old Buckingham photographs, Hook Norton Best and Wilsons on handpump; interesting buildings nearby *(Alan Bickley)*

Butlers Cross [SP8406], *Russell Arms*: Small, clean pub, welcoming and efficient staff, consistently good bar food *(Joan Chenhalls)*

Cadmore End [OS Sheet 175 reference 785927; SU7892], *Old Ship*: Unspoilt and old-fashioned simple little country pub *(Phil and Sally Gorton, MM)*

Cadsden [SP8204], *Plough*: Simple little Chilterns pub, a haunt of ramblers, with reasonably priced food, Ind Coope Burton on handpump, tables on green outside; children in adjoining playroom; on GWG 71 *(D C Bail)*

Chalfont St Giles [High St (village signposted off A413); SU9893], *Feathers*: Cosy and cheerful low-beamed local, handy for Milton's cottage, with well kept Whitbreads-related real ales, popular lunchtime snacks, comfortable settees, good open fires, seats outside with pretty flower baskets and boxes *(Alison Hayward, Nick Dowson, Simon Collett-Jones, TBB, LYM)*; [Silver Hill] *Fox & Hounds*: Local with limited range of good value lunchtime food including well filled sandwiches and ploughman's, and atmosphere made by dry-humoured landlord *(Alison Hayward, Nick Dowson)*; [A413] *Pheasant*: Good choice of well cooked and presented simple food lunchtime and evening (not Mon), with excellent fresh vegetables; friendly bar, good service in comfortable dining-room *(Mrs J A King, John Tyzack)*

Chalfont St Peter [Copthall Lane; SU9990], *Waggon & Horses*: Comfortable, spotlessly clean local with well kept beers, food including home-made pastry and home-cooked gammon, pretty terrace *(Anon)*

Chartridge [SP9303], *Bell*: Pleasant bar with cushioned chairs and settles, open fire in winter, bar food including very good omelettes, pool-room, well kept Benskins

Best and Ind Coope Burton *(Lyn and Bill Capper)*

Cheddington [Station Road – by stn, about a mile from village; SP9217], *Rosebery Arms*: Pleasant solid former railway-junction hotel, now a clean and tidy pub/restaurant, sympathetically refurbished somewhat in the style of an Edwardian chop-house, with old pictures, decent bar food including a prize-winning steak and kidney pie, reasonably priced beer and house wine; children welcome *(John Francis)*

☆ **Chenies** [Chesham Rd; TQ0198], *Red Lion*: Friendly landlord, warm welcome, comfortable and tasteful recently refurbished bar with small snug behind, well kept Benskins Best, Ind Coope Burton and Tetleys, good value well presented wholesome bar food; no piped music or fruit machines; handy for Chenies Manor which is open 2–5 Weds, Thurs Apr–Oct *(Mr and Mrs R P Begg, Lyn and Bill Capper, R M Savage)*

Chesham [Waterside; SP9502], *Pheasant*: Well kept beer and good food – deservedly popular *(John Tyzack)*; [Church St] *Queens Head*: Neat, warm local with coal fire in each bar, excellent Brakspears, well presented basic pub food from separate servery *(David and Flo Wallington)*

Colnbrook [High St; near M4 junction 5; TQ0277], *Red Lion*: Terrific atmosphere, welcoming service, good helpings of nicely prepared and reasonably priced food, well kept Courage Best; real log fire in cosy, low-ceilinged bar *(R Houghton)*; [High St] *Star & Garter*: Nicely decorated, cosy, a pleasant welcome and nice atmosphere, particularly well kept Courage; dogs may be sitting on the benches *(Anon)*

Cuddington [5 miles SW of Aylesbury, N of A418; SP7311], *Red Lion*: Outstanding location in quiet village, practical and welcoming landlord, good choice of food including fine seasonal game dishes in bar and separate restaurant (booking needed Sun), real ales; big garden with pets in play area *(I Meredith, HKR)*

Denham [village signposted from nearby M40 junction 1; TQ0486], *Falcon*: One-roomed pub with character and style *(B R Shiner)*; *Swan*: Friendly staff, well kept Courage real ales, bar food often including interesting daily specials, piped music; open fires in neatly renovated bar, extensive flood-lit garden with children's play house *(Simon Collett-Jones, Lyn and Bill Capper, LYM)*

Dinton [Stars Lane; SP7611], *Seven Stars*: Public bar with aged high-backed curved settle, lounge has character too (and no piped music), good, friendly service, simple choice of decent bar food, more choice in pleasant airy restaurant, spotless lavatories, tables in attractive garden; ABC and maybe Tetleys real ales *(Lyn and Bill Capper)*

Dorney [SU9278], *Palmers Arms*: Pleasant pine and stripped-brick décor with large eating area, discreet piped music, friendly and helpful service, well kept Charringtons IPA, good choice of wines, adventurous lunchtime and evening bar food with emphasis on fish, restaurant, garden behind *(Simon Collett-Jones)*

Downley [OS Sheet 165 reference 849959; SU8594], *Le De Spencer*: Unpretentious pub hidden away on common, fairy-lit loggia overlooking lawn, friendly landlord, well kept Wethereds on handpump, snacks *(LYM)*

Easington [off B4011 – OS Sheet 164 reference 687102; SP6810], *Rising Sun*: Tiny but friendly country pub with interesting food (the chilli con carne's particularly good), colourful landlord, ABC and Everards real ales *(Dave Braisted and others)*

Farnham Common [A355 opposite Saab garage; SU9684], *Royal Oak*: Decent Courage pub, quietly comfortable, with good value bar food, large wine list and garden *(R M Savage, Capt F A Bland)*

Flackwell Heath [SU8988], *Green Man*: Popular pub with friendly service (may be slow Sat) and wide choice of good value food – including haddock, plaice or cod and chips to take away; children's room *(Peter Powrie)*

nr **Flackwell Heath** [3½ miles from M40 junction 4; A404 signed High Wycombe, then first right into Flackwell Heath, then right into Sheepridge Lane; SU8988], *Crooked Billet*: Charming flint country pub with pretty garden, good simple food and autumn farm cider as well as Whitbreads real ale *(LYM)*

Fulmer [Windmill Rd; SU9985], *Black Horse*: Simple but remarkably popular three-bar pub with Courage real ales, bar food and small garden; attractive village *(I Meredith)*

Gayhurst [B526; SP8446], *Sir Francis Drake*: Included for the striking incongruity of the building itself – all Gothick traceries and pinnacles; inside, it's cosy, and strong on spirits and cocktails (beers are keg); not cheap *(LYM)*

Great Brickhill [SP9030], *Old Red Lion*: Lawn gives fabulous view over Buckinghamshire and beyond; reports, please, on the major revamp which we understood was planned by Whitbreads; bedrooms *(LYM)*

Great Hampden [on corner of Hampden Common – OS Sheet 165 reference 845015; SP8401], *Hampden Arms*: Very good choice of food (including Sun), good beer, pleasant friendly service, attractive rooms; well placed in the Chilterns *(J Roots, Mr and Mrs F W Sturch)*

Great Horwood [SP7731], *Swan*: Friendly and comfortable old pub doing well under new licensees, good food including notable Stilton ploughman's, steak and kidney pie and chilli con carne *(Mrs M E Lawrence)*

Great Linford [4½ miles from M1 junction 14; from Newport Pagnell take Wolverton Road towards Stony Stratford; SP8542], *Black Horse*: Genuinely pubby atmosphere in spacious rambling pub just below the Grand Union Canal embankment, well kept ABC, Ind Coope Burton and another beer such as Everards Tiger on handpump, bar food, garden including biggish play area; children allowed in restaurant *(M P Le Geyt, LYM)*

☆ **Great Missenden** [62 High St; SP8901], *Red Lion*: Comfortable atmosphere in expensively refurbished low-beamed sixteenth-century inn with dark wooden décor, small bar area and larger area for the well organised bar food, including ploughman's, country soup, sophisticated meat and fish dishes and salads; several changing real ales such as Brakspears, Marston Pedigree and Websters Yorkshire on handpump, good choice of wines, restaurant with no-smoking area; very popular – get there early, and book ahead for Sun lunch; bedrooms (four) *(Alison Hayward, Nick Dowson, Lyn and Bill Capper)*

Great Missenden [Mobwell], *Black Horse*: Excellent Morrells real ale, good mixed grill *(HKR)*; [old London rd 1 or 2 miles E] *Nags Head*: Pleasant and historically interesting pub in lovely country, good choice of food – known locally for excellent steaks, but other dishes good too *(I Meredith)*

Hawridge [The Vale – village signposted from A416 N of Chesham, OS Sheet 165 reference 960050; SP9505], *Rose & Crown*: Around eight well kept real ales on handpump (attracting lots of young people in the evening), masses of whiskies, good value bar food (no evening hot dishes); big log fire in spaciously refurbished open-plan bar, broad terrace with lawn dropping down beyond, play area; children allowed *(T A V Meikle, LYM)*

Hedgerley [One Pin Lane; not far from M40 junction 2; SU9686], *One Pin*: Chairs and tables in front garden of pleasant two-bar pub with good friendly service and consistently well kept Courage ales *(Nick Dowson, Alison Hayward)*

Hedsor [SU9187], *Garibaldi*: Lovely pub, pleasant owner, good food with superb pizzas *(Mrs R Wilmot)*

Holmer Green [SU9097], *Bat & Ball*: Small pub overlooking village green and football pitch; friendly landlord, wide range of excellent bar food, garden *(W A Lund)*

Ivinghoe [SP9416], *Kings Head*: Good food in bar and restaurant of pleasantly placed and well run village inn with polished, friendly service *(K and J M Potter)*

Kingswood [A41; SP6919], *Crooked Billet*: Attractively crooked-looking pub near Waddesdon Manor; low-ceilinged public bar with inglenook, well kept carpeted lounge, restaurant and tables (and swings) out by the pear tree; well kept ABC and maybe Bass, and one reader's party of sixteen turning up unexpectedly were served quickly and smoothly with excellent bar food

(Mrs P J Pearce)

Lane End [SU7991], *Old Sun*: Simple choice of good value bar food such as good-sized BLT sandwich or pasty with sausage roll, chips and beans; Wethereds beers *(Nick Dowson, Alison Hayward)*

Little Horwood [SP7930], *Old Crown*: Welcoming licensee and well kept beer in typical village local *(KIH)*

Little Kingshill [SU8999], *Full Moon*: Pleasantly renovated pub in unspoilt surroundings, with huge log fires and reasonably priced good bar food; the licensees who took over in early 1988 (and previously won a good reputation at the Swan at Ley Hill) are considering converting the adjoining barn into further eating space, with a new kitchen; no food Sunday evening *(Mr and Mrs F W Sturch, I Meredith)*

Little Marlow [off A4155 about 2 miles E of Marlow, pub signposted off main rd; SU8786], *Kings Head*: Wethereds house serving Flowers Original, SPA and Winter Royal; low-beamed, cosy lounge with dark oak panelling, real fire, settles, wooden chairs, brass gongs and keg taps on walls *(Nick Dowson)*

Littleworth Common [Common Lane, off A355 – quite handy for M40 junction 2; SP9487], *Blackwood Arms*: Pleasant surroundings good for walks, rural atmosphere, and several constantly changing real ales such as Arkells, Fullers and Morrells; bar food (but no separate area for diners – and it can get crowded on Sats) *(Nick Dowson, Alison Hayward)*; *Jolly Woodman*: Alone on the edge of Burnham Beeches, beamed and cottagey, popular with young and old, good range of hot and cold bar food including well presented puddings, welcoming efficient service; handy for Cliveden (NT) *(Mr and Mrs F W Sturch, Alison Hayward, Mrs P J Bedwell, LYM)*

Long Crendon [Bicester Road (B4011); SP6808], *Angel*: Partly seventeenth-century, attractively renovated in 1987, with Brakspears, Flowers, Wethereds and Worthington real ales and bar food; ladies' lavatory very Laura Ashley *(Revd Brian Andrews)*; [Bicester Rd] *Chandos Arms*: Small but smart thatched country pub with excellent reasonably priced food – especially the steaks; well kept Wethereds, no hot food Sunday lunchtime *(D S Kennedy, Dave Braisted)*

Longwick [Thame Rd; SP7805], *Red Lion*: Very friendly, well run, huge helpings of fair-priced wholesome food, comfortable bedrooms reasonably priced too *(David Surridge, Hugh O'Donnell)*

Loudwater [quite handy for M40 junction 3; [Derchams Lane; SU8990], *Blacksmiths Arms*: Tiny pub, friendly atmosphere, 1960s piped music, bar food, good barbecues *(Brian and Rosemary Wilmot)*; *General Havelock*: Pleasant little pub with old-fashioned décor, huge helpings of good bar food, lots of nibbles at bar on Sun *(Mrs R Wilmot)*; [London Road (A40)] *White Blackbird*: Carefully thought-out food, super filled rolls, beer well kept, friendly welcome *(John Nice)*

Maids Moreton [SP7035], *Wheatsheaf*: Excellent old pub with cosy lounge, several snugs in public bar, fires in both, good choice of beers and what seems to be the best range of whiskies in Bucks – the landlord's Scottish; weekday lunchtime bar food, separate room for darts and dominoes, well tended back garden with own servery *(John and Vicki Drummond)*

Marlow [SU8586], *Donkey*: Useful for decent food, lots of space and big garden; comfortable modern décor *(Lindsey Shaw Radley)*; [Mill Rd] *Prince of Wales*: Welcoming, recently renovated Wethereds house; comfortable lounge, good, well cooked bar food with dishes of the day and impeccable service, games-bar with pool-table, seats outside *(Ian Phillips)*

Marsworth [Startops Ends; SP9114], *White Lion*: Busy pub by Grand Union Canal, well kept Marstons Pedigree, good food in bar and restaurant including excellent duck and tournedos Rossini; on GWG110 *(Jill Field)*

☆ **Medmenham** [SU8084], *Dog & Badger*: Well served and reasonably priced food – the sandwiches are unusually good – in comfortably modernised Wethereds pub; well kept real ale, welcoming atmosphere, lots of trouble taken over small details, seats on terrace; 10 minutes' stroll from the Thames *(Ian Meredith, Don Mather, BB)*

Mentmore [SP9119], *Stag*: Small but civilised carpeted lounge bar with sturdy green leatherette seats around low oak tables, attractive fresh flower arrangements, open fire, and restaurant leading off; sturdily furnished public bar; good value bar food from sandwiches to main dishes, with wider choice in the evenings; well kept if rather pricey Charles Wells Eagle, polite well dressed staff, charming sloping garden with floodlit pear tree *(Dr and Mrs S L Last, T A V Meikle, BB)*

Milton Keynes [Mount Farm Industrial Est; SP8938], *Beacon*: Overlooking lake with ducks and other waterfowl, this unusual-shaped pub with a mezzanine serves real ale and good value food; children's play area *(E J Alcock)*; [just below the Point, by garden centre] *Old Barn*: Spacious new Beefeater made to look attractively olde-worlde, with big farmhouse tables and conservatory area; real ale, reasonable if rather pricey bar food, restaurant *(Keith Garley)*; [Midsummer Bvd; SP8938] *Point*: Unusual, almost futuristic surroundings, with restaurant, brasserie and bar all open-plan (and leading to cinema and night-club – many customers are film-goers getting discounts on tickets by having receipts from bar); amusement arcade alongside *(Keith Garley)*. *For more Milton Keynes suggestions see Great Linford and Simpson*

Nash [2 Stratford Rd; SP7834], *Old English Gentleman*: Friendly and comfortable, with nice atmosphere – strangers quickly feel really at home; well kept Watneys-related beers, and though range of lunchtime snacks is limited landlady will do other dishes on request; locals say they've seen ghosts here; attractive village of thatched white cottages reflected in tree-surrounded pond *(Lyn and Bill Capper)*

Newton Blossomville [4 miles from M1 junction 14; SP9251], *Old Mill Burnt Down*: Tastefully furnished, wide choice of real ales, good food, welcoming atmosphere; no juke box; comfortable bedrooms *(Alan Phillips)*

Northend [Village Green; SU7392], *Fox & Hounds*: Very welcoming, log fires in both rooms, Brakspears ales and wide range of excellent home-cooked food, very good service, pleasant staff; popular with walkers who leave their muddy boots outside – can get crowded Sunday lunchtime *(Maureen Hobbs)*

Oving [off A413 Winslow rd out of Whitchurch; SP7821], *Black Boy*: 350-year-old pub at end of superb green with panoramic view from terrace over plain towards Buckingham; warm and comfortable atmosphere, well kept Ind Coope Burton, good choice of first-class bar food and separate excellent restaurant *(Brian Law)*

Owlswick [OS Sheet 165 reference 790062; SP7806], *Shoulder of Mutton*: Modernised inn (originally fourteenth-century but much changed over the years) with several real ales such as Bass, Fullers ESB and London Pride, maybe live music Weds; spacious bedrooms are good value *(Alastair Lang)*

Penn [SU9193], *Horse & Jockey*: Pleasant local with fairly varied, good value menu and Ind Coope on handpump; can get quite crowded at weekends *(Mike Tucker)*; [SU9193] *Red Lion*: Famous for Honey, its guard dog, who sniffs out her pet lager, strips off the ring pull, and downs the whole can *(Anon)*

☆ **Penn Street** [SU9295], *Hit or Miss*: Comfortably modernised low-ceilinged, three-room pub with big inglenook fireplaces and own cricket ground; latest news of the new regime is that the food in both bar and restaurant is showing imagination and artistic presentation, the beer is well kept, and service is friendly and efficient – more reports please *(R M Savage, L S Radley, David Gaunt, LYM)*

Preston Bisset [SP6529], *Old Hat*: Lovely unspoilt old thatched village pub, where the first thing you notice is curved back of settle protruding into passage; rather plain room on right, cosy almost parlour-like room on left *(Gordon and Daphne)*

Princes Risborough [Market Sq; SP8003], *Whiteleaf Cross*: Spick-and-span split-level bar in attractively refurbished seventeenth-century house, good range of fairly priced bar food, well kept Morlands, well chosen wines, cosy fire *(HKR)*

☆ **St Leonards** [SP9107], *White Lion*: Splendid

little pub – only significant change in 30 years is that they no longer bring their beer (well kept Benskins and Friary Meux) in jugs from the cellar; lots of beams and atmosphere, simple but attractive food *(D J Wallington)*

Saunderton [SU8198], *Rose & Crown*: Excellent inexpensive bar snacks with special 'snack bar' (rather up-market); Flowers Original, Morlands, Morrells and Wethereds on handpump *(HKR)*

Shabbington [SP6607], *Old Fisherman*: Unpretentious white Morrells pub; clean, comfortable bar with darts, excellent filled cottage rolls, tables on riverside lawn; children 's playground *(Ian Phillips)*

Simpson [SP8836], *Plough*: Small canalside village pub with friendly staff, good imaginative lunchtime food *(E J Alcock)*

Skirmett [SU7790], *Kings Arms*: Inglenook fireplace and log fire in traditionally furnished high-beamed bar, bar food (not Sunday evening) often enterprising, using fresh vegetables and maybe herbs from the garden, and including summer cold buffet in lofty-raftered side room, well kept Brakspears and Whitbreads-related real ales, seats on side lawn, attractive bedrooms; has had jazz Weds; children in eating area and restaurant *(Mr and Mrs T F Marshall, LYM – more reports on the new regime, please)*

Slapton [SP9320], *Carpenters Arms*: Friendly welcome and limited range of good snacks in two bars with different atmosphere and decoration; well kept real ale *(M P Le Geyt)*

☆ **Speen** [Hampden Rd; SU8399], *King William IV*: Bright, clean, warm and comfortable, with a friendly welcome, well kept Ruddles and a good choice of delicious inexpensive food including one or two fine daily specials *(V H Balchin, HKR, Mr Anderson)*

☆ **Speen** [Flowers Bottom Lane; rd from village towards Lacey Green and Saunderton Stn; OS Sheet 165 reference 835995; SU8399], *Old Plow*: Neatly refurbished in a crisply cottagey style, this charmingly placed small country inn earned warm praise in late 1987 and early 1988 for its new owners' interesting food, using fresh ingredients; in summer 1988 they sold it (to open a new place up in Aberfeldy called Farleyer House), and as they had run it in such an individual style we feel it's better in the Dip until reports tell us how it's turned out now *(LYM; up-to-date reports please)*

Stewkley [High St South; junction of Wing and Dunton rds; SP8526], *Carpenters Arms*: Nice old building with jolly little public bar and bookcases and wood-burning stove in more homely lounge, also small restaurant in converted railway carriage; unfortunately the Coles who made it specially worth seeking out for their imaginative freshly prepared food have just moved away *(Margaret and Trevor Errington, Lyn and Bill Capper, AB, LYM)*; *Swan*: Popular local with lots of old

beams and huge open fireplace in spacious open-plan bar, cosily broken up by screens into alcoves; delicious evening bar food, small restaurant, bar billiards and other games, tables in garden *(AB, Stephen and Helen Doole)*

Stoke Goldington [SP8348], *White Hart*: Lively thatched village local with friendly staff, well kept Charles Wells real ale, beamed and quarry-tiled saloon, comfortable plush lounge, games-room off public bar; enterprising choice of drinks, sheltered back lawn *(M P Le Geyt, LYM)*

Stoke Green [1 mile S of Stoke Poges; off B416 signposted Wexham and George Green – OS Sheet 175 reference 986824; SU9882], *Red Lion*: Rambling and interestingly furnished and decorated seventeenth-century former farm, with well kept Bass and Charrington IPA; has now become a Vintage Inn pub-restaurant *(LYM)*

Stoke Hammond [SP8829], *Three Locks*: Neater than many canal pubs, this has one large carpeted bar with lots of tables and waitress-served bar food; restaurant with extensive and reasonably priced menu; garden overlooks a flight of locks on the Grand Union Canal and across to distant fields *(David Crafts)*

Stokenchurch [nr M40 junction 5; SU7695], *Kings Arms*: Popular lounge bar, generous bar snacks throughout opening hours, occasional evening entertainment *(Bob Rendle)*

Stone [Hartwell – A418 SW of Aylesbury; SP7812], *Bugle Horn*: Long low whitewashed stone building with lovely trees in pretty garden leading on to meadows where horses graze; inside, warm friendly atmosphere, open fire, attractively furnished and prettily planted conservatory; bar food, restaurant *(Ian Phillips)*

Stony Stratford [High St; SP7840], *Bull*: Former coaching-inn's basic Vaults Bar has good choice of well kept beer, folk workshops Sunday lunchtime and live music Sunday evening, attracting lively young regulars *(John Clinch, Nick Dowson)*; [72 High St] *Cock*: Plain old coaching-inn with some handsome old oak settles in bar, decent Adnams *(LYM)*; [High St] *George*: Well kept real ale, good food, friendly staff, comfortable and inviting; good value bedrooms *(D K and H M Brenchley)*

The Lee [Swan Bottom, on back rd ¾ mile N of The Lee – OS Sheet 165 reference 902055; SP8904], *Old Swan*: Attractive furnishings in four low-beamed interconnecting rooms, logs burning in cooking-range inglenook, spacious and prettily planted back lawns with play area; has been highly rated in previous editions for cosy and comfortable layout, imaginative food (particularly evening seafood) and interesting choice of well kept real ales – but up for sale spring 1988 after a period of mixed reports; news please *(LYM)*

Thornborough [4 miles E of Buckingham, on A421 outside village – pub named on OS Sheet 165; SP7433], *Lone Tree*: Friendly and pleasant, two smallish clean and tastefully decorated rooms, usual pub food nicely presented, garden with children's play area and occasional evening barbecues, well kept ABC real ales *(M P Le Geyt, Lyn and Bill Capper)*

Twyford [SP6626], *Red Lion*: Very pretty old-fashioned pub where the beer for many years has been beautifully kept; attractively priced and cooked simple food, steaks and so forth, character landlord, lovely garden *(Lance Warrington)*

Wavendon [not far from M1 junctions 13 and 14; SP9137], *Plough*: Pretty pub with foliage-covered walls and interesting painting on garage doors; pleasant atmosphere, imaginative and reasonably priced menu (no food Sun–Tues evenings), clean lavatories *(Rita Horridge)*

Wendover [High St; SP8607], *Red Lion*: Old-fashioned beamed bar with good range of well priced food from soup to steaks and venison, good range of well kept real ales such as Morlands and Youngs, restaurant *(Nick Long)*

Weston Turville [Church Lane; SP8510], *Chequers*: Long black-beamed bar with carpet and flagstones, plates all around walls, friendly and neatly efficient staff, good sandwiches and other food (especially fish), real ales such as Tetleys; restaurant popular with businessmen *(D L Johnson)*

Wheelerend Common [just off A40; SU8093], *Brickmakers Arms*: Rather well done Chef & Brewer, with efficient staff, huge garden with play area and lines of picnic-table sets, upstairs carvery restaurant, Watneys-related beers *(Nick Dowson, Alison Hayward)*

Winchmore Hill [SU9394], *Plough*: Clean and comfortably modernised spacious bar overlooking green, several interconnecting areas, some interesting knick-knacks, piped music, changing well kept real ales such as Theakstons Best and Youngers Scotch and IPA, wide choice of bar food (more reports on this, please), neat and helpful staff, tables on lawn with wishing-well; restaurant named after the landlady, Barbara Windsor *(Lyn and Bill Capper, DCB, Nick Dowson, BB)*

Wooburn Common [SU9387], *Chequers*: Very welcoming, attractive bar with sofas and fire, pleasant licensees *(Brian and Rosemary Wilmot)*; [Wooburn Common Rd] *Royal Standard*: Brightly redecorated pub handy for M40 junction 2, orderly tables, good value lunchtime food pleasantly served, welcoming young licensees, well kept Flowers, Wethereds and a guest such as Brakspears; children welcome *(C J Cuss)*

Wooburn Green [SU9188], *Red Lion*: Formerly an old forge, now a Roast Inn with restaurant; old photographs around bar, well kept beer, pleasant uniformed staff *(Richard Houghton)*

Wooburn Moor [Watery Lane; SU9189], *Falcon*: Lovely little old local with lots of beams, small choice of enjoyable food including super sandwiches and good hot specials, regular old-timers playing dominoes in the corner, friendly landlord *(Brian and Rosemary Wilmot)*

Woughton on the Green [SP8737], *Olde Swan*: Village pub with good value bar food and large garden with play area *(H Rust)*

Worminghall [SP6308], *Clifden Arms*: Pretty sixteenth-century thatched pub with old tools and so forth hanging from beams of small cosy lounge, games-room with pool off public bar, good open fires, Halls Harvest, Ind Coope Burton and Tetleys real ales, good range of hot and cold food; the local rhyme goes 'Brill on the hill, Oakley in the hole, snotty little Ickford and dirty Worminghall' – this really is wellie country in winter *(Lyn and Bill Capper, Gordon and Daphne)*

Cambridgeshire and Bedfordshire

Among new entries to this edition of the Guide, *we'd pick out particularly the Cock at Broom for its combination of a really unspoilt traditional layout with an invigorating approach to cheese as a staple of pub food. This is a real find, and though we heard of it first only a few months ago we'd rate it among the region's very nicest pubs. It's tiny, so if you want to appreciate it at its best go on a midweek lunchtime. Two new Cambridge entries compensate for the loss of the Eagle, submerged (we hope temporarily) under a surrounding rebuilding programme: the Cambridge Blue is an engaging traditional pub where chat comes first, but where both food and drink are a cut above the average; the Old Spring has been prettily revamped – gaslight and all – to evoke the atmosphere of an ancient tavern. Within easy reach of the M11, the Plough at Coton serves reliably good straightforward food. And back in these pages after several years (and a change of licensees) the Locomotive at Deepdale near Sandy is a warmly inviting country pub. Some changes among old favourites include the new brewery added on behind the idiosyncratic Three Fyshes at Turvey, a new landlord for the Racehorse at Catworth, and what amounts to a management buy-out at the stylish Chequers at Fowlmere, so popular for its fine if pricey food. Other pubs where food is a particularly strong point include the Kings Head looking down over the green at Dullingham, the ancient Three Tuns at Fen Drayton with its pretty back garden, the Olde Ferry Boat down by the river near Holywell (even older), the characterful Plough & Fleece at Horningsea, the bustling Bell at Kennett (good for fish), the stylish Pheasant at Keyston, the quiet Queens Head deep in bloodstock country at Kirtling (a nice place to stay at), the attractively simple old Queens Head at Newton and the Olde White Hart on its hill at Ufford (both these two gain our food awards this year, to mark the growing warmth of readers' praise for them), the canalside Anchor at Sutton Gault (determinedly*

The Leeds Arms, Eltisley

*old-fashioned – another pub that's gaslit), the grand old Haycock at Wansford (a
fine if rather expensive place to stay at), the efficiently run and remarkably
low-priced Black Horse at Woburn, and the cheerful Three Blackbirds at
Woodditton. Cheese lovers should also note the handsomely refurbished Bell at
Stilton – where the cheese, which came originally from a very different area, got
its name. The Leeds Arms at Eltisley wins a place-to-stay award this year, and
another good place to stay at is the King William IV at Heydon – its bar an
amazing exercise in fanciful decoration. The Lucky Dip section has grown again
this year – over a dozen entries for Cambridge alone (we can vouch personally for
several of these); elsewhere, the most promising seem to be the Millstone at
Barnack, White Horse in Eaton Socon, George & Dragon at Elsworth,
Exhibition at Godmanchester, and highly individual Tickell Arms at Whittlesford
(many readers' favourite in the area, but with such a strong character it does rub
others up the wrong way).*

BIDDENHAM (Beds)   TL0249 Map 5
Three Tuns
57 Main Road; village signposted from A428 just W of Bedford

Popular at lunchtime with businessmen, this well kept and friendly thatched village
pub has twenty-seven different dishes on the menu: sandwiches (from 75p,
double-deckers 95p), home-made soup (80p; they also do soup and a choice of
sandwich for £1.25 – an idea it would be nice if other pubs copied), salad niçoise or
pâté (£1.20), several ploughman's (£1.30), burgers (from £2), salads (from £2.20),
various hot dishes such as quiche, lasagne or chilli con carne (£2.50), home-made
chicken casserole or steak and kidney pie (£2.80), eight-ounce sirloin steak (£4.95),
and specials such as excellent seafood gratin; children's menu (£1). Well kept
Greene King IPA and Abbot on handpump. The lively public bar may have a
vigorous game of table skittles in progress, as well as darts, dominoes, and fruit
machine. The low-beamed comfortable lounge has country paintings on the walls
and a little jungle of pot-plants in its stone fireplace; piped music. There are doves
and a dovecot in the big garden, which is good for families. (*Recommended by Dr and
Mrs B D Smith, Roger Danes, Pete Storey; more reports please*)

*Greene King   Licensees Alan and Tina Wilkins   Real ale   Meals (not Sun) and snacks (not
Sun evening)   Children in small dining-room   Open 11.30–2.30, 6–11 all year; closed
evening 25 Dec*

BOLNHURST (Beds)   TL0859 Map 5
Olde Plough
B660 Bedford–Kimbolton

The unassuming lounge bar in this five-hundred-year-old squint-walled and
pink-washed cottage – which still has some building work in progress – has a
relaxed and friendly local atmosphere; there are little armchairs around low tables,
a leather sofa in one alcove, a leather armchair by the log fire in the big stone
fireplace, black oak beams in the very low bellying cream ceiling, and timbers in the
ancient walls; in a room leading off here are some dining-tables. Nicely presented
bar food includes home-made soup (95p), burgers (from 99p), toasted French bread
with cheese and herbs (£1.05), ploughman's, moussaka, lasagne, or chicken
chasseur (£1.99), seafood pasta (£2.50), and cod Kiev or gamekeeper's pie (£2.99).
Well kept Nethergate and Paines XXX and EG on handpump. The public bar has
two refectory tables, a pair of settles and other seats, a big wood-burning stove, and
darts, dominoes, cribbage, card games, Trivial Pursuit, pool, hood skittles and fruit
machine; the two friendly cats are called Chubbs and Blacky. The garden is very

pretty, with rustic seats and tables, a long crazy-paved terrace by rose beds, a lawn, and the remains of a moat under trees by a rock bank. *(Recommended by Chris Hill, Roger Danes, Rob and Gill Weeks)*

Free house Licensee M J Horridge Real ale Snacks Children welcome until 9, if well behaved Open 12–2.30, 7–11 all year; closed 25 Dec

BROOM (Beds) TL1743 Map 5
Cock ★ ⊗

From A1 opposite northernmost Biggleswade turnoff follow Old Warden 3, Aerodrome 2 signpost, and take first left signposted Broom

Remarkably unspoilt, this delightful little village pub is ideal for a quick cheese lunch. Though they also serve a good game soup (60p), filled baked potato (65p), meat sandwiches (85p), salads with meat or with hand-raised pork and rabbit or game pie (£2.25), they keep around twenty different cheeses in fine condition – mostly English. These come in sandwiches with thick crusty bread (75p) or in variations on the ploughman's theme, from the simplest (£1.25) to several tailored to the taste of an individual cheese (£1.55–£2.25). Yet this is not the chief attraction here. That is simply the style of the place. Spick and span, it has four small rooms, with antique tile floors, low ochre ceilings, stripped panelling and old-fashioned stripped built-in furnishings – cupboards, uncushioned wall benches, simple latch doors. There are only two or three tables in each room, some with neat gingham tablecloths. A central corridor runs down the middle, with the sink for washing glasses on one side (pewter mugs hang over it) and on the other steps down to the cellar where well kept Greene King IPA and Abbot are tapped straight from the cask – there's no bar counter. Service is most friendly: this is clearly a pub run with real love. There are log fires in winter, hood skittles, darts, shove-ha'penny and dominoes in one front room, unobtrusive piped music. A terrace by the back lawn has some picnic-table sets. Though it's usually very quiet on weekday lunchtimes, weekends can be extremely busy. *(Recommended by G Farmelo, Pete Storey)*

Greene King Licensees Martin and Brenda Murphy Real ale Snacks Children welcome Open 12–2.30, 6–11 (11.30–3 Sat lunchtime) all year; closed evening 25 Dec

CAMBRIDGE TL4658 Map 5
Cambridge Blue

85 Gwydir Street

Run by the same people as our long-standing main entry the Free Press, this has similar virtues, and as it's a free house it has the additional attraction of a range of well kept real ales on handpump – on our visit, Banks & Taylors Shefford and Dark Mild, Elgoods, Nethergate, Tolly and Wadworths 6X. As in the Lloyds' other pub, it's perhaps the atmosphere that counts for most – warm and supportive. The furnishings of the two small rooms, one of them no-smoking, are simple: stripped kitchen chairs and some cushioned built-in wall benches around a medley of tables on dark red linoleum, lots of university sports photographs on the buttery Anaglypta walls, low ceilings (but the big windows brighten it up). French windows open on to a sheltered terrace, with picnic-table sets among some shrubs; in summer they have barbecues and boules. Food includes a good choice of home-made pies and cold meats served with a choice of two salads out of half a dozen (£2.50), soups such as a good fish chowder (90p), and one or two changing hot dishes. The weekly darts match is a great occasion (despite, or maybe because of, the complete absence of a dartboard). *(Recommended by Prof and Mrs Kenneth Rosen,*

Pubs with particularly interesting histories, or in unusually interesting buildings, are listed at the back of the book.

Yvonne Lahaise, Ninka Sharland, John Bromell, Dr John Innes, Alan and Ruth Woodhouse, Catherine Allerton, Gwen and Peter Andrews)

Free house　Licensees Chris and Debbie Lloyd　Real ale　Meals and snacks　Children in snug　Open 12–2.30, 6–11 all year

Free Press ⊗

Prospect Row

Though many pubs in Cambridge sport oars and rowing photographs, this busy, friendly pub has the perfect right to them, as it's the only one here – or indeed anywhere – which is registered as a boat club. It's an unspoilt place, well off the beaten track, and the furnishings are traditional throughout; one room is even served from a hatch. Tasty wholesome bar food includes good soup such as carrot and lemon (£1), filled baked potatoes (£1), cold dishes with interesting salads such as pasta and courgette or beetroot and apple, good smoked ham, and hot dishes like lasagne (£2.60); there's a permanent no-smoking area, and 'No Smoking' signs on the tables where people are eating (get there early if you want a seat). Well kept Greene King IPA and Abbot on handpump; dominoes. *(Recommended by Dave Butler, Lesley Storey, Alan and Ruth Woodhouse, Ninka Sharland, Nicolas Walter)*

Greene King　Licensee C M Lloyd　Real ale　Lunchtime meals　Children in snug　Open 12–2.30, 6–11 all year

Old Spring

Ferry Path (pub's car park is on Chesterton Road)

A charming pastiche of an old country pub, this rambling bare-boarded place has soft gas lighting throughout its bar, and the dimness is accentuated by the earth-coloured rough plaster walls. Electricity's virtually confined to lighting some of the pictures – more interesting than usual, with decent Morland and topographical prints, and an entertaining illustrated song about the death of Tom Moody the whipper-in. Our summer inspection found a new couple just settling in, and already doing promising food including ploughman's (£2.20), meat and other salads from a side counter (£2.50), cauliflower cheese or sausage and tomato pie (£2.95), a selection of Greek dips with pitta bread (£3.10), beef casserole or chilli con carne (£3.45) and a dish of the day such as stuffed shoulder of lamb (£3.75). Furniture matches the décor – cushioned small settles, a pew or two and stools around cast-iron and other traditional tables; there's a couple of open fires. Well kept Greene King IPA and Abbot and Rayments on handpump, two fruit machines, and on our visit piped 1930s jazz. Given the method of lighting, it can get quite hot if crowded. At the time this book comes out, the pub may be closed for the addition of a new conservatory/restaurant; it should reopen early in December. *(Recommended by T E Cheshire, Howard and Sue Gascoyne, R D Norman, Alan and Ruth Woodhouse)*

Greene King　Licensees Adrian and Bernardette Brown　Real ale　Meals and snacks Restaurant (see text) tel Cambridge (0223) 357228　Children allowed if eating Open 11–2.30, 5.30–11 all year

Salisbury Arms

Tenison Road

A dozen or so different real ales attract crowds of customers to the high-ceilinged back lounge here. You can usually find a seat in the calmer side areas, which are decorated with reproductions of old posters relating to beers and brewing, and the much smaller front bar is sometimes a haven of relative quiet. Bar food includes ploughman's with granary bread and a choice of cheeses or pâté, a hot dish such as

---

chilli con carne, and a cold table; darts, dominoes, ring the bull, a pin-table and fruit machine; they also keep farmhouse cider. *(Recommended by Mark Walpole, T Mansell; more reports please)*

Free house   Real ale   Lunchtime snacks   Open 11–2.30, 6–11 all year

CATWORTH (Cambs)   TL0873   Map 5
Racehorse

B660, between A45 (Kimbolton) and A604

This popular pub has lots of photographs and genealogies of Derby winners and flat-racing prints in the spacious well kept lounge, as well as red cloth stools, wall banquettes and small easy chairs. It opens into an airy extension with a rug on its parquet floor. Bar food includes sandwiches, soup (95p), deep-fried mushrooms with garlic (£2.20), ploughman's (from £2.95), lamb moussaka (£3.50), steak, kidney and Guinness pie (£3.75), rump steak (£4.85) and mixed grill (£5.85); the new licensee has introduced a three-course lunchtime special (£3.95; not Sunday). Well kept Adnams and Hook Norton on handpump, a good choice of some seventy whiskies, a log fire and piped music. The red-tiled public bar has sensibly placed darts, table skittles, pool, and fruit machine. There are tables by flowers on a side terrace, with stables behind. *(Recommended by Dr A V Lewis, Rob and Gill Weeks; more reports please)*

Free house   Licensees C R Watson and Kay Owen   Real ale   Meals and snacks   Restaurant tel Bythorn (080 14) 262   Children welcome   Open 11.30–2.30, 6–11 all year

COTON (Cambs)   TL4058   Map 5
Plough ⊗

Under a mile from M11 junction 13; left on to A1303, then village signposted left – once on this side road don't turn off right at the Village, Church signpost; though this junction is exit only northbound and entrance only southbound, you can quickly get back to the motorway by heading straight on past the pub to the nearby junction 12 – which also gives signposted access to the village if you're heading south on the M11

Included for its food, this pub concentrates to some extent on the restaurant which occupies the handsomely beamed front part; the bar is in a spacious modern back extension, with comfortable seats and banquettes around the tables on either side of its arched dividing wall. It's not so much the choice of food as the careful cooking and presentation which wins readers' plaudits, with good fresh ingredients and vegetables done delicately. The bar food includes sandwiches (from £1), decent home-made soups (£1.20), ploughman's (£1.90), smoked mackerel (£2.10), quite a lot of fish such as plaice done with prawns and olives (£3.70), salads (from £3.70), gammon (£4.10) and steaks (from sirloin £7), with specials such as dressed Cromer crab (£4.20). Well kept Flowers Original on handpump; inoffensive piped music. The back garden's attractive, with seats in smallish groups divided by trees and shrubs – and some in a summerhouse. *(Recommended by G F Scott, R C Wiles, Paul and Margaret Baker, G S Cubitt)*

Whitbreads   Licensees Mr and Mrs Barrie Ashworth   Real ale   Meals and snacks Restaurant tel Madingley (0954) 210489   Children welcome   Open 11–2.30, 6–11 all year

DULLINGHAM (Cambs)   TL6357   Map 5
Kings Head ⊗

50 Station Road

There's a cosy, old-fashioned atmosphere in the two connecting carpeted rooms here (except when Newmarket racegoers crowd in): a coal fire at each end in winter, small button-back leatherette bucket seats, Windsor chairs, hunting prints, and some more private booths around sturdy wooden tables. Freshly made bar food – perhaps the feel of the place is more that of a restaurant now – includes sandwiches, home-made soup (70p), home-made pâté (£1.65), ploughman's (from £1.65), potted shrimps (£1.95), filled baked potatoes (from £1.95), lasagne or chilli con carne (£2.35), various omelettes (from £2.35), macaroni cheese (£2.65), grilled ham with two fried eggs (£2.95), steak in Guinness (£3.25), wiener schnitzel (£3.45), and steaks (from £5.45); lots of puddings (from 95p), and children's meals (from £1.35). Well kept Tolly Bitter and Original on handpump; friendly staff. The family/function-room is called the Loose Box. Under fairy lights on the grass above the car park there are sheltered seats, with more on a terrace overlooking the big sloping village green; also swings. *(Recommended by Alison Findlay, Cdr G R Roantree, Frank W Gadbois)*

Tolly   *Licensee Erich Kettenacker   Real ale   Meals and snacks   Restaurant tel Newmarket (0638) 76486; closed Sun   Children in restaurant   Open 11–2.30, 6–11 all year*

ELTISLEY (Cambs)   TL2659   Map 5

Leeds Arms   🛏   [illustrated on page 61]

The Green; village signposted off A45

The friendly beamed lounge bar in this well kept, tall white brick house is basically two rooms knocked together, with red corduroy stools and pew-like cushioned wall benches set around a huge winter log fire; down some steps there's a third room dominated by tables. Good value bar food includes sandwiches (from 80p, not Saturday evenings), home-made soup (90p), ploughman's (£1.50, not Saturday evenings), curry (£2.50), trout (£3), salads (from £3), home-made steak and kidney pie (£3.15), scampi (£3.60), steaks (from £4.75), and lemon sole (£5.75). Well kept Greene King IPA on handpump; good service; darts, a fruit machine sensibly set aside in an alcove, and piped music. There are picnic-table sets, swings and a slide set among the silver birches on the lawn. *(Recommended by M D Hare, G D Howard, Jamie and Sarah Allan, Stephen McKenzie)*

Free house   Licensee George Cottrell   Meals and snacks   Restaurant   Children in restaurant   Open 11.30–2.30, 6.30–11 all year; closed 25 Dec   Bedrooms tel Croxton (048 087) 283; £27.50B/£35B

FEN DRAYTON (Cambs)   TL3368   Map 5

Three Tuns   ⊗

On the banks of the village stream, this pretty thatched pub has a consistently warm welcome and good value, tasty food. There are attractively moulded very heavy early Tudor beams, cushioned settles and an interesting variety of chairs, big portraits and old photographs of local scenes on the timbered walls, old crockery in a corner dresser, and two inglenook fireplaces (one is always alight). Bar food includes sandwiches (not Saturday evening or Sunday lunchtime) with a choice of brown, white or French bread (from 90p), home-made lentil soup (£1.10), home-made chicken liver and bacon pâté (£1.80), ploughman's (from £1.80), various big fluffy omelettes (£2.50), home-made dishes such as vegetable lasagne (£2.70), cottage pie (£2.80) or steak and kidney pie (£2.90), salads (from £2.70), gammon with pineapple (£3.80), breast of chicken pan-fried in garlic butter (£4.20), eight-ounce rump steak (£5.40), and puddings like home-made apple pie or lemon meringue pie (from £1); Sunday roast beef (£3.95), and good garlic bread. Sensibly placed darts, shove-ha'penny, dominoes, cribbage, and fruit machine. Behind the pub, there are tables under cocktail parasols on the neat flower-edged lawn, with apple and flowering cherry trees; also some children's play equipment.

People don't usually tip bar staff (different in a really smart hotel, say). If you want to thank them – for dealing with a really large party say, or special friendliness – offer them a drink.

The inn-sign is unusual – three tiny barrels sitting on a pole. (*Recommended by Alan and Ruth Woodhouse, Rob and Gill Weeks, J Gaudern, M D Hare*)

Greene King   Licensee Michael Nugent   Meals and snacks (not Sun evening)   Children in eating area   Open 11–3, 6.30–11 all year; closed evening 25 Dec

FOWLMERE (Cambs)   TL4245 Map 5

Chequers ⊗

B1368

Civilised and luxuriously restored, this old pub is especially popular with readers for the very good bar food: Normandy onion soup (£2.10), Stilton and walnut pâté with blackberry wine (£2.50), hors d'oeuvre (small £2.80, large £4.50), herring roes, black butter and capers (£2.90), Mexican taco pancake (£3.80), home-made lasagne (£3.90), seafood pancake (£4.20), and a cold buffet with meats on the bone (£6.20); daily specials such as trout escalope (£4.50), and puddings (from £1.90). Besides Tolly on handpump, there is usually a choice of vintage and late-bottled ports by the glass and an excellent range of fine brandies and liqueurs, and they've now installed a Cruover machine so that fine wines can be kept in perfect condition for serving by the glass; freshly squeezed orange juice. The two comfortably furnished communicating bar rooms have a discreet and un-pub-like atmosphere with soft lighting, leather stools and chairs, and upholstered wall banquettes. The lower room has prints and photographs of Spitfires and Mustangs flown from Fowlmere aerodrome, and the upper room has beams, some wall timbering and some notable moulded plasterwork above the fireplace. If you ask, they will point out to you the priest's hole above the bar. Waitress service extends to the white tables under cocktail parasols among the flowers and shrub roses of the attractive and neatly kept garden. (*Recommended by George Little, G and J Halphide, Mr and Mrs R Gammon, David Gaunt, JMC, Barbara Hatfield, John Mitchelmore, Dave Butler, Lesley Storey*)

Tolly Cobbold   Licensee Norman Rushton   Real ale   Meals and snacks   Children welcome   Restaurant tel Fowlmere (076 382) 369   Open 12–2.30, 7–11 all year, though they're considering longer afternoon openings; closed 25 Dec

HEYDON (Cambs)   TL4340 Map 5

King William IV ★ ⇔

Village signposted from A505 W of M11 junction 10; bear right in village

The rambling rooms of this friendly village inn are individually furnished: Liberty-cushioned housekeeper's chairs, carved pews (one with a lectern), and some tables made of great slabs of wood slung on black chains from the ceiling. The dark oak beams, wall timbers and standing props are very nearly covered with plough-shares, yokes, iron tools, cowbells, beer steins, samovars, cut-glass brass or black wrought-iron lamps, copper-bound casks and milk ewers, harness, horsebrasses, smith's bellows, decorative plates, stuffed birds and animals (or rococo full-size models of them). Bar food includes ploughman's or mushrooms in lager butter (£1.75), salads, hot meals such as steak and kidney pie (£2.45), and some vegetarian dishes; well kept Adnams, a Banks & Taylors brew named for the pub (light, quite fragrant, easy to drink), and Greene King IPA and Abbot on handpump; service can be a bit slow; piped Viennese accordion music. The pretty garden has an old farm cart with flowers. Riding and carriage-driving with champion Welsh Cobs and Hackneys can be arranged. The animal sanctuary further along the road is worth a visit. (*Recommended by T D Underwood, T Nott, M C Howells, Joy Heatherley, Alan and Ruth Woodhouse, Gordon Theaker*)

Free house   Licensees Jozsi Hanakamp and John New   Real ale   Meals and snacks   Restaurant   Children in restaurant   Open 12–3, 7–11 all year   Bedrooms tel Royston (0763) 838773; £20B/£29B

HOLYWELL (Cambs)   TL3370 Map 5

Olde Ferry Boat ⊗

Village and pub both signposted (keep your eyes skinned!) off A1123 in Needingworth

Different areas of the rambling beamed bar in this wistaria-covered house are divided by steps, and timbered or panelled walls – each with a distinct character, though all are cosy and old-fashioned; there's a good mix of seats such as a pretty little carved settle, rush ones with big cushions, red leather settees, and river-view window seats, and four open fires – one has a fish and an eel among rushes moulded on its chimney-beam. A stone in the middle marks the site of a nine-hundred-year-old grave, and there's a resident ghost called Juliette. They buy fresh produce from the big London markets every Friday, and bar food includes a daily home-made soup (£1.10), home-made chicken liver pâté (£2.50), sandwiches (from £1.25), ploughman's (£2), omelettes (from £3), sauté of lamb's liver lyonnaise (£3.50), home-made lasagne (£3.95), scampi (£4.40), venison burgers (£4.50), home-made steak and kidney pie (£4.90), smoked wild boar in red wine sauce (£4.95), seafood pilaff (£5.10), chicken Maori (a mild curry with fruit £5.55), escalope of pork (£7.50) and steaks (from £8.50). Well kept Adnams, Bass, Greene King IPA and Abbot and Ruddles Best on handpump; pleasant friendly staff; piped music. On a flower-edged front terrace by the old thatched building there are tables under cocktail parasols, and more on a side rose lawn along the edge of the Great Ouse. (*Recommended by Kelvin Lawton, Sue and Tim Kinning, R Robinson, Paul and Margaret Baker, J C Proud, Alan and Ruth Woodhouse, Kelvin Lawton, Gordon Theaker, I W Bell, Rob and Gill Weeks*)

Free house   Licensee Mrs Joyce Edwards   Real ale   Meals and snacks   Children in lounge area   Restaurant   Open 10.30–2.30, 6–11 all year; closed evening 25 Dec   Bedrooms tel St Ives (0480) 63227; £20(£25B)/£30(£40B)

HORNINGSEA (Cambs)   TL4962 Map 5

Plough & Fleece ★ ⊗

The friendly public bar in this homely village pub has black beams in the red ceiling, butter-yellow walls, high-backed settles and plain seats on the red tiled floor, plain wooden tables – including the regulars' favourite, an enormously long slab of elm (with an equally long pew to match it) – a stuffed parrot, and a lovely log fire; there's also a comfortable lounge. An unusual point about the home-cooked food is that they often use imaginatively recast antique recipes: soup (£1.10), home-made pâté (£1.80), devilled crab (£1.90), cottage pie (£2.25), omelettes (£3), good salads such as home-cooked ham (£2.75), Suffolk ham hot-pot (£3.25), good fish pie (£4), steak, kidney and mushroom pie (£4.50), Romany rabbit (£5), honey-roast guinea-fowl (£5.50), sirloin steak (£7) and beef Wellington (£7.50). In the evenings, when the menu also includes hot garlic cockles (£1.75), a vegetarian dish with asparagus, eggs, cheese and almonds (£4.20) and giant prawns (£5.50), these hot dishes all cost about 80p extra, with extra vegetables. At lunchtimes only there are also sandwiches (from 95p, toasties from £1.10), ploughman's or hot snacks such as sausage and bacon flan (£1.65), and home-cooked ham and egg (£2.50). Good puddings include Norfolk treacle tart or home-made ginger and brandy ice-cream (£1.30) and a potent chocolate pudding (£1.40); efficient service. Well kept Greene King IPA and Abbot on handpump, half a dozen good malt whiskies and a couple of vintage ports. Dominoes and cribbage. There are picnic-table sets (with table service) beyond the car park, and beyond a herbaceous border is a children's play area with a rope ladder climbing into an old pear tree. (*Recommended by Alan and Ruth Woodhouse, Caroline Fisher, Tony Pounder, G L Archer, Mrs Jill Hadfield, Tony Gallagher, Rita Horridge*)

Greene King   Licensee Mr Kenneth Grimes   Real ale   Meals (not Mon evening or Sun) and snacks (not Sun or Mon evenings)   Open 11.30–2.30, 7–11 all year

KENNETT (Cambs)   TL6968 Map 5

Bell ⊗

Bury Road; crossroads B1506/B1085, through Kentford on the Newmarket slip-road just off
A45 Bury St Edmunds–Cambridge

Given the considerable height of its mass of heavy oak beams and the size of its
brick inglenook, this old inn must have been a place of some consequence in Tudor
times. Rambling back behind the freestanding fireplace, the spacious and cheery
Turkey-carpeted bar has plenty of stripped country tables with Windsor armchairs
and cushioned dining-chairs. A wide choice of bar food from an attractive and
efficient servery includes home-made soup (95p), filled baked potatoes (from
£1.25), filled French bread (£1.75), Newmarket jumbo sausage (£1.95), smoked
salmon sandwich (£2.50), ploughman's (from £2.75), a choice of pies (£3.75),
salads (from £3), daily specials such as steak and kidney pie, home-made curry or
lasagne and twice-weekly roasts (from £3.25), and several more expensive dishes
such as steaks (from £7.25) and Dover sole (£9.25). Leading off is a tiled-floor
room serving as a wine and oyster bar where there are occasional 'special' evenings.
Well kept Adnams, Courage Directors, Flowers Original, Nethergate and unobtrusive piped pop music. (*Recommended by G E Oakley, Frank W Gadbois*)

Free house   Licensee C Knighton Hayling   Real ale   Meals and snacks   Restaurant
Children in restaurant at lunchtime   Open 11.30–2.30, 6.30–11 all year   Bedrooms tel
Newmarket (0638) 750286; £22B/£32B

KEYSOE (Beds)   TL0762 Map 5

Chequers

B660

An unusual stone-pillared log fireplace divides the two comfortably modernised,
beamed rooms in this well kept village pub. Straightforward, well cooked food
includes sandwiches (90p), starters (90p–£1.95), lasagne (£2.50), scampi (£3.25),
trout (£3.95), steaks (from £5.95), and puddings (from £1.30); Sunday roast
(£2.75) and children's helpings (from £1.25). Well kept Adnams and guest beers
such as Bass or Batemans XXXB from handpumps on the stone bar counter; darts,
a fruit machine, a space game and piped music. Outside, there's a terrace, and tables
on the small front lawn among flowers, with more on the grass around the car park
behind; swings, a Wendy house, and a fairy-tale play tree. (*Recommended by J K
Clark, Roger Danes and others*)

*Free house   Licensee Jeffrey Kearns   Real ale   Meals and snacks (not Mon)   Children in
eating area   Open 11–2.30, 6.30–11 all year; closed Mon, exc bank hols*

KEYSTON (Cambs)   TL0475 Map 5

Pheasant ⊗

Village loop road

Just off the comfortable and low-beamed main bar in this well kept and relaxing old
village pub is a room that was once the village smithy: high rafters are hung with
heavy-horse harness and an old horse-drawn harrow, and there are leather slung
stools and a heavily carved wooden armchair among the Windsor chairs. The very
popular fresh home-cooked food now includes some filled rolls (from 95p), soup
(£1.25), pâté (£1.95), Paris mushrooms (£2.95), crab Mornay (£3.25), cold ham
salad (£3.95), lasagne (£4.25), tandoori spring chicken or loin of pork with orange
sauce (£4.50), lamb sweetbreads (£4.75), king prawn salad (£5.95), whole grilled
plaice or trout (£4.75), and rump steak (£5.95). In season local pheasant is used in
pâtés and casseroles. Well kept Adnams and Tolly on handpump; friendly, efficient
service. The tables under cocktail parasols in front of this attractive thatched white

house are laid with tablecloths – a pleasant, quiet spot. One of Ivo Vannocci's Poste Hotels. No dogs. *(Recommended by Rita Horridge, C R Cooke, John Baker, Dr A M Evans, G H Theaker, Rob and Gill Weeks, Dr A V Lewis, Joy Heatherley)*

Free house   Licensee William Bennett   Meals and snacks   Children welcome   Restaurant tel Bythorn (080 14) 241   Open 10.30–2.30, 6–11 all year

KIRTLING (Cambs)   TL6857   Map 5

Queens Head ⊗ ⇤

Village signposted off B1063 Newmarket–Stradishall, though pub reached more quickly from Newmarket on the Saxon Street road; OS Sheet 154 reference 690570

When Queen Elizabeth I stayed nearby, this quiet and kindly inn was built to house part of her retinue. The main feature of the pleasantly unassuming little central bar (apart from the informed horse talk which enlivens so many pubs around here) is a huge inglenook fireplace housing all sorts of copper jugs, old farrier's tools, even a cushioned copper kettledrum and a stuffed heron – with a log fire in winter; there are also cushioned wheel-back chairs, mahogany and elm tables, and rugs on its tiled floor. Home-cooked bar food includes sandwiches (from 80p), ploughman's (£2.75), omelettes or filleted trout (£5.75), gammon (£4.50), well hung local steaks (£10.50) and Dover sole (£10); well kept Tolly Mild, Bitter and Original on handpump, farm cider, decent house wines and a good choice of malt whiskies. A more spacious wood-floored bar has darts, dominoes, trivia and juke box. The surroundings are very peaceful, with ducks and uncommon fowls wandering about. *(Recommended by R C Wiles, Frank W Gadbois)*

Tolly   Licensee Ann Bailey   Real ale   Meals and snacks (not Thurs or Sun evenings)   Piano Sat evening   Open 10.30–2.30, 7–11 all year   Bedrooms tel Newmarket (0638) 730253; £14/£30

NEWTON (Cambs)   TL4349   Map 5

Queens Head ⊗

2½ miles from M11 junction 11; A10 towards Royston, then left on to B1368

One reader has several times driven thirty-five miles for the unpretentious and freshly prepared bar food here: a good choice of sandwiches (from 85p for banana, 95p for herb and garlic or Stilton, £1.60 for smoked salmon), superb soup (£1.20) or baked potato (£1.20); in the evening and on Sunday lunchtime they serve plates of excellent quality cold meat, smoked salmon, and cheeses (from £1.80). The rooms have been kept carefully simple with a curved high-backed settle on the yellow tiled floor of the main bar, bare wooden benches and seats built into its walls and bow windows, a loudly ticking clock and paintings on its cream walls. The little carpeted saloon is broadly similar but more cosy. Well kept Adnams Bitter and Broadside tapped from the cask, with Old Ale in winter; efficient service. Darts in a side room, with shove-ha'penny, table skittles, dominoes, cribbage, nine men's morris and a fruit machine. There are seats in front of the pub, with its vine trellis and unusually tall chimney. Belinda the goose, who adopted the pub in summer 1987, still patrols the car park day and night. *(Recommended by Dave Butler, Lesley Storey, Tony Beaulah, Joy Heatherley)*

Free house   Licensee David Short   Real ale   Snacks   Children in games-room Open 11.30 (11 Sat)–2.30, 6–11 all year; closed 25 Dec

nr SANDY (Beds)   TL1749   Map 5

Locomotive

Deepdale; B1042 towards Potton and Cambridge

Particularly handy for people visiting the nearby RSPB headquarters and bird reserve, this friendly, homely pub has an open-plan bar with railway memorabilia all over the walls, cushioned wall banquettes and a big open fire. Good, reasonably priced bar food includes home-made soup (75p), sandwiches (from 75p; toasties from 85p), huge filled 'Loco' rolls (from £1.15), ploughman's (£1.25), salads (from £2.50), scampi (£2.65), roast beef or turkey (£2.95), eight-ounce rump steak (£4.25), and home-made daily specials such as chilli con carne (£2.50) or steak and kidney pie (£2.95). Well kept Charles Wells Eagle and Bombardier on handpump; helpful service; sensibly placed darts, and a fruit machine. Behind the pub, a spacious and attractive garden, floodlit at night, has an outdoor drinks servery, and there are Sunday barbecues in summer, weather permitting. *(Recommended by Edward Barber, Roger Danes, NBM, Rita Horridge, Roy and Barbara Longman)*

Charles Wells Licensee Kenneth Roper Real ale Meals and snacks (not Sun or Mon evenings) Children in eating area Open 11–2.30, 6–11 all year; may stay open longer afternoons in summer if trade demands

SOUTHILL (Beds) TL1542 Map 5
White Horse

The big garden in this pleasantly isolated, popular pub includes a garden shop, a children's games and play area, and, most importantly, a 7¼-inch gauge railway with both steam and diesel engines, bridges and a tunnel. Children's rides are 10p, and steam enthusiasts are encouraged to bring their own locomotives. The comfortable and well kept main lounge has country prints on the cream walls, and the smaller public bar has plain seats and settles in front of a big wood-burning stove, and comic railway pictures and prints among the harness on the terracotta-coloured walls. Bar food includes sandwiches or filled rolls (£1.10), ploughman's (from £2.50), sausages or ham and egg (£2.85), burgers (£3.25), salads (from £3.50), scampi (£3.75), and children's meals (£1.30); they do Sunday roasts. Flowers IPA and Wethereds on handpump. There's an interesting spotlit well in the dining-room; darts, shove-ha'penny, dominoes, cribbage, table skittles, fruit machine and piped music. The pub is handy for the Shuttleworth Collection of old cars and early aeroplanes. *(Recommended by Mr and Mrs G D Amos, Rita Horridge, Lyn and Bill Capper; more reports please)*

Whitbreads Licensee Miss Eileen Herbert Meals and snacks (not Sun evening) Children welcome (not in public bar) Restaurant tel Hitchin (0462) 813364; closed Sun evening Open 11–2.30, 6–11 all year

STILTON (Cambs) TL1689 Map 5
Bell

High Street; village signposted from A1 S of Peterborough

They make quite something of their Stilton in this handsome seventeenth-century stone inn – in their soup, pâté (£1.65), and ploughman's (from £2); the cheese got its name originally from being sold to the inn's coaching customers and thus widely travelled around the country, though until then it had been known as the Quenby cheese and was actually made in Little Dalby and Wymondham up near Melton Mowbray. Other bar food includes sandwiches, poacher's pie (£3.10) and sixteen-ounce rib steak (£6); well kept Greene King Abbot, Marstons Pedigree, Tetleys and guest beers on handpump; friendly staff. The two opened-up rooms of the attractively restored bar have plush-cushioned button-back banquettes built around the walls and bow windows, other sturdy upright wooden seats, big prints of sailing and winter coaching scenes on the partly stripped walls, flagstones, floor tiles, and a large log fire in the fine stone fireplace; shove-ha'penny, dominoes, cribbage and piped music. The sheltered cobbled and flagstoned back courtyard has some tables. There's a fine coach-arch (with distances to cities carved on the courtyard side) and a curlicued gantry for the heavy inn sign, and the rest of the building is being gradually restored by its enthusiastic owners. *(Recommended by Byrne Sherwood, Comus Elliott, Mrs C S Smith, John Roué, Gay Woodland, Quentin Williamson, Rob and Gill Weeks)*

Free house   Licensees John and Liam McGivern   Real ale   Meals and snacks (not Sun evening)   Children in eating area   Restaurant Tues–Sat evenings tel Peterborough (0733) 242626   Folk music Sun evening   Bedrooms planned   Open 11–2.30, 6–11 all year, though will open longer on weekday afternoons if enough customers; open all day Sat

SUTTON GAULT (Cambs)   TL4279 Map 5
Anchor ⊗
Village signposted off B1381 in Sutton

This riverside village pub has three beamed and tiled or carpeted rooms with dining-chairs or kitchen chairs and antique settles (one elaborately Gothick, another with an attractively curved high back), well spaced stripped deal tables, good lithographs and big prints of an avocet, otter and partridges, and a calm, old-fashioned atmosphere. Lighting is by candles and swan's-neck gas lamps, and there's a good log fire in a big brick fireplace. Good home-made bar food includes French onion soup (£1.10), chicken liver and brandy pâté or egg and prawn in garlic mayonnaise (£1.95), vegetarian curried nut loaf with tomato and basil sauce or tagliatelle with bacon, mushrooms and cream (£3.50), seafood pancakes, lasagne or steak and kidney in Guinness (£4.95), and fresh salmon salad with hollandaise (£5.80); home-made puddings such as lemon meringue pie or cheesecakes (£1.50). Well kept Tolly Bitter, Original and XXXX tapped from the cask, and hot punch in winter; they also do freshly squeezed orange juice (90p a glass); friendly service. Shove-ha'penny, dominoes, cribbage, well reproduced pop music or piped Radio 2; there's a rough-haired dachshund. There are tables out by the swans on the Old Bedford River. *(Recommended by S Simon, Michael Thomson, R C Wiles, Dr P D Smart, David Surridge, Roy and Barbara Longman)*

Free house   Licensees A P and J R F Stretton-Downes   Real ale   Meals (not Sun) Restaurant tel Ely (0353) 778537; closed Sun   Children in restaurant until 9   Open 12–2.30, 6–11 all year; closed Mon 1 Oct–30 Apr

SWAVESEY (Cambs)   TL3668 Map 5
Trinity Foot
A604, N side; to reach it from the westbound carriageway, take Swavesey, Fen Drayton turnoff

A wide choice of consistently good and quickly served bar food in this busy but friendly pub includes sandwiches, ploughman's or pâté, plain or curried chicken, lamb cutlets, mixed grill, daily specials which might include oysters as well as steak and kidney pie, and good Sunday roasts; the kitchen staff are particularly helpful. Well kept Wethereds and Flowers Original on handpump; piped music. A good big lawn has a few flowers and roses and a belt of tall trees. *(Recommended by F Oliveira-Pinto; more reports please)*

Whitbreads   Real ale   Meals and snacks (not Sun evening)   Children in eating area   Open 10.30–2.30, 6–11.30 all year; closed 25 and 26 Dec

TURVEY (Beds)   SP9452 Map 4
Three Fyshes
A428 NW of Bedford; pub at W end of village

At the end of 1987, this welcoming pub set up its own brewery (with help from Banks & Taylors) called Nix Wincott, and they now brew their own beer – Two Henrys (OG 1040); other real ales on handpump include Banks and Taylors, Bass, and Marstons Pedigree and Owd Rodger; good country wines. It's determinedly easy-going and traditional inside, with heavy beams, a stone inglenook fireplace, a carpeted and flagstoned floor, and a collection of seats around the close-set tables as well as a large box window seat. A charming squint-walled stone corridor (which has a fruit machine) links this main room up with the cosy flagstoned public bar which has another big inglenook. Food includes good sandwiches (from £1), big crusty rolls (from £1.65; £2.50 for Dynamic – steak with fried egg and cheese – or Thermodynamic – similar, but with ham and pineapple), salads (from £2.95), good aubergine and mushroom lasagne or chilli con carne (£2.95), spicy chicken casserole, and eight-ounce sirloin steak (£5.90). Sensibly placed darts, table skittles, dominoes, cribbage, fruit machine and piped music; several dogs and cats. Close to the River Ouse, there is a room by the small back garden where there are summer barbecues – weather permitting. Well behaved pets welcome. *(Recommended by Mr and Mrs B Amos, Michael and Alison Sandy, Mr and Mrs G D Amos, Virginia Jones, Dennis Royles, Nicholas Walter)*

Free house   Licensee Charles Wincott   Real ale   Meals and snacks   Children welcome Open 11.30–3, 5.30–11 all year; open all day Sat

UFFORD (Cambs)   TF0904   Map 5
Olde White Hart ⊗

In an attractive village – on the only hill for miles – this late seventeenth-century pub was a farm until 1847. A stone chimney divides the well kept and carpeted lounge bar into two, and there are pewter tankards hanging from the beam over the bar counter, wheel-back chairs around dark tripod tables, and Boris the stuffed tarantula. Good substantial home-made food includes very good value rolls (80p), steak and mushroom pie, lasagne or moussaka (£3.75), three lamb chops in mustard sauce (£4.50), and weekly changing specials such as vegetarian tortellini (£4), fresh Cromer crab salad (£3.75) or Mexican tacos (£3.50); on Sunday lunchtime they do hot roast beef rolls (£1.20). Well kept Home Bitter on handpump. Popular with locals, the simple public bar has darts, shove-ha'penny, dominoes and cribbage. There's a sunny terrace with white metal seats and a big, pretty garden with two tethered goats and a children's play area with swings, slides and so forth. *(Recommended by Dr A V Lewis, Tom Evans, Joy Heatherley)*

Home   Licensee Christopher Hooton   Real ale   Meals (not Sun or Mon) and snacks Restaurant tel Stamford (0780) 740250   Children in eating area   Open 10.30–2.30, 6–11 all year

WANSFORD (Cambs)   TL0799   Map 5
Haycock ★ ⊗ ⇤

Heading N on A1, follow village signposts; from other directions follow Elton signpost from village centre

The flagstoned entry hall in this imposing and civilised, yet wholly relaxed, dark golden stone inn takes you back to the seventeenth century with its antique seats and longcase clock; this leads into the lively panelled main bar, which overlooks tables in a charming cobbled courtyard. On the other side of the servery is a quieter lounge with wallpaper to match the long flowery curtains, plush sofas and easy chairs, hunting or steeplechasing prints, and a good log fire in winter. Though you can eat here, it's another lounge, overlooking the attractive and spacious formal garden, which has the buffet table. This, spick and span with gleaming copper on clean white linen, has a good range of cold meats and salads (from £4.95 for home-made turkey and pork pie or vegetarian quiche, £5.95 for fresh roast turkey, £7.65 for poached salmon). Other waitress-served home-made food includes sandwiches to order, soup (£1.95), chicken liver pâté (£2.95), toad-in-the-hole or

---

Pubs with outstanding views are listed at the back of the book.

curried vegetables with rice (£3.95), fresh pasta (£4.25), home-made lasagne, fish stew or steak and mushroom pie (£4.95), and poached fillet of plaice in wine and cheese sauce (£5.45); a good choice of puddings (£2.45) and barbecues (weather permitting, from £4.95). Well kept Bass, Ruddles Best and County and Tolly Original on handpump, with a good range of other drinks extending to properly mature vintage ports by the glass; they've now installed a Cruover machine which allows them to keep a dozen or so decent wines for sale by the glass in perfect condition; courteous service. The old-fashioned and well kept walled garden opens on to its own cricket field by the stately bridge over the River Nene; it also has an extensive pétanque court and fishing (as well as a marquee for weddings and functions). One of Ivo Vannocci's Poste Hotels. *(Recommended by Syd and Wyn Donald, Mr and Mrs B Amos, R C Wiles, E J and J W Cutting, Dave Butler, Lesley Storey)*

Free house   Licensee Richard Neale   Real ale   Meals and snacks   Children welcome Restaurant   Open 10–3, 6–11 all year   Bedrooms tel Stamford (0780) 782223; £59.50B/£75B

WOBURN (Beds)   SP9433 Map 4
Black Horse ⊗

A new garden room has been added to this busy, friendly old pub where the consistently good, reasonably priced bar food is served at lunchtimes (it converts to an evening restaurant): home-made soup (lunchtimes, 65p), sandwiches (from 65p), ploughman's and pâté (lunchtimes, £1.40), pitta bread filled with tuna and egg mayonnaise (£1.70), filled baked potatoes (from £1.90), fisherman's platter (£1.95), quiche (£2), tasty cauliflower cheese with bacon and sweetcorn (£2.10), vegetable lasagne (£2.30), American-style burger (£2.45), salads (£2.50), grilled gammon with pineapple (£2.90), delicious steaks (from £4.15), and a home-made special at lunchtime (£1.90); Sunday lunch. Well kept Banks & Taylors Shefford, Marstons Burton and Pedigree, and Tetleys on handpump, and a range of wines by the glass; pleasant, efficient service. The carefully decorated L-shaped main bar has lots of neat tables and Windsor chairs between the buff walls with their sporting prints and terracotta-coloured half-panelling, and a back room has pine panelling and Liberty prints. Through the coach entry there are several tables in a sheltered garden, looking down to a small lawn and then on to the church. No car park, and parking in the village is limited. The pub is close to Woburn Abbey. *(Recommended by Michael and Alison Sandy, Gordon Theaker, Alison Gurr, J K Clark, Wayne Brindle, Lyn and Bill Capper, Rita Horridge, Mr and Mrs G D Amos, Quentin Williamson)*

Free house   Licensee Thomas Aldous   Real ale   Meals and snacks   Evening restaurant tel Woburn (0525) 290210   Children in eating area and restaurant   Open 10.30–2.30, 6–11 all year

WOODDITTON (Cambs)   TL6659 Map 5
Three Blackbirds ⊗

Village signposted off B1063 at Cheveley

Even when the two snug bars in this pretty thatched village pub do get very busy, service stays friendly and efficient. There are high winged settles or dining-chairs around fairly closely spaced neat tables, cigarette cards, Derby-Day photographs, little country prints, and fires in winter – the room on the left has the pubbier atmosphere. Popular bar food includes sandwiches, home-made soup (£1.10), lunchtime ploughman's (£1.95), potted shrimps (£2.35), home-cooked ham (£3.55), home-made lasagne (£3.75), escalope of pork (£3.95), beef in Guinness or chicken bonne femme (£4.95), seafood gratin (£5.75), and good steaks (from £6.25); puddings (from £1.25) and good three-course Sunday roasts (£7.50) with a choice of rare or well done beef. Well kept Tolly Original on handpump; piped music. The front lawn, sheltered by an ivy-covered flint wall, has flowers, roses, and a flowering cherry, with a muted chorus of nearby farm noises. *(Recommended by Graham and Glenis Watkins, W T Aird, Pamela and Merlyn Horswell)*

Tolly   Licensee Edward Spooner   Real ale   Meals and snacks   Restaurant tel Newmarket (0638) 730811; open Tues–Sat   Children in eating area and restaurant   Open 11–3, 5.30–11 all year

---

Lucky Dip

Besides the fully inspected pubs, you might like to try these Lucky Dips recommended to us and described by readers (if you do, please send us reports):

Abbots Ripton, Cambs [TL2378], *Three Horseshoes*: Delightful thatched inn with well kept Ruddles County on handpump, excellent home-made steak and kidney pie with good vegetables *(AVL)*

Abbotsley, Cambs [High St/St Neots Rd; TL2356], *Jolly Abbot*: Greene King Abbot, Fullers ESB and Ruddles County on handpump in refurbished pub with button-back leatherette settles and rough painted plaster; wide choice of food *(Anon)*

Arrington, Cambs [TL3250], *Hardwicke Arms*: Quaint creeper-covered coaching-inn with simple beamed and panelled lounge, high-ceilinged food bar, Adnams and Greene King real ales, aquariums, games-room, tables outside; next to Wimpole Hall; bedrooms *(Lyn and Bill Capper, LYM)*

Babraham, Cambs [just off A1307; TL5150], *George*: Pleasant old pub with friendly landlord, range of interesting bar food well cooked and served, and favoured restaurant *(Gordon Theaker, Tom, Lorna, Audrey and Alan Chatting)*

Balsham, Cambs [High St; TL5850], *Black Bull*: Welcoming free house with good generous bar snacks, real ale and evening restaurant *(G H Theaker)*

☆ **Barnack**, Cambs [Millstone Lane; TF0704], *Millstone*: Enthusiastic landlord has greatly improved this small village pub, well furnished, with lots of character inside and out, pleasant atmosphere, clean and friendly; good value plain food cooked to order, well kept Adnams, Fullers ESB, and Everards Old Original, Beacon and Tiger *(A V Lewis, Mr and Mrs R H J Wakeling, Steve Coley)*

☆ **Barrington**, Cambs [from M11 junction 11 take A10 to Newton, then turn right; TL3949], *Royal Oak*: Thatched and heavily beamed and timbered Tudor pub on charming cricket green, reasonably priced waitress-served food in rambling modernised bar (not Sun lunchtime), well kept Adnams and Greene King real ales, restaurant, skittle alley; handy for NT Barrington Court *(S A and P J Barrett, Rita Horridge, LYM)*

Bartlow, Cambs [TL5845], *Three Hills*: Excellent rural pub with Greene King IPA and Abbot, decent wines, imaginative choice of good home-cooked food, log fire; very

friendly *(Graham Tuthill and others)*

Bedford [Goldington Rd; TL0449], *Cricketers*: Pleasant two-bar pub with oak panelling, well kept Charles Wells and Greene King Abbot, good bar food, entertaining banter between licensees and locals *(Patrick Godfrey)*; [St Mary's St] *Kings Arms*: Well kept open-plan town-centre pub popular for lunchtime food; Greene King real ales *(LYM)*

Bletsoe, Beds [TL0258], *Falcon*: Pleasant main-road coaching-inn dating from seventeenth century, Charles Wells real ale, sandwiches, bar food and restaurant; big garden, recently reopened after many years, leads down to river *(Keith Garley)*

Boxworth, Cambs [TL3464], *Golden Ball*: Very popular dining pub – booking advisable at weekends – but also worth noting for its ten or so real ales, taken by rotation from a rota of 40; friendly atmosphere, good parking *(E and G Slater)*

Bury, Cambs [TL2883], *White Lion*: Warm and friendly atmosphere in pleasant comfortable lounge, always clean and tidy, genial licensees, good service in good value dining-room, darts, dominoes, pool in bar *(George and Irene Hewitt)*

☆ **Cambridge** [14 Chesterton Rd; TL4658], *Boathouse*: Reopened summer 1987 in the current style of Whitbreads refurbishments – bookcases and so forth; it's the big conservatory, where families are allowed, with its wooden balcony overlooking the river and waterside garden which makes the pub so popular in sunny weather; traditional bar food lunchtime and early evening, Sun lunches, keg Greene King Abbot and Whitbreads *(Howard and Sue Gascoyne, John Bromell, Alan and Ruth Woodhouse)*

Cambridge [by Grafton Centre], *Ancient Druids*: Well designed modern Charles Wells pub with good food and well kept beers – own Kite, Merlin and Druids Special – you can see into the brewhouse from the street; can be very busy at lunchtime *(N and J D Bailey)*; [19 Bridge St] *Baron of Beef*: Busy city pub with unspoilt and unpretentious atmosphere, Greene King ales under pressure from one of longest bars in city, panelled partition divides two bars, sawdust on floor, limited choice of good value food *(Alan and Ruth Woodhouse, Howard and Sue Gascoyne)*; [4 King St] *Cambridge Arms*: Spacious modern conversion of what used to be the Scales Brewery, giving unusual interesting layout; Greene King IPA and Abbot, rather good food, sheltered courtyard, maybe jazz nights *(Stanley Matthews, LYM)*; [Bene't St] *Eagle*: Has been Cambridge's most interesting pub, with sixteenth-century rooms and cobbled and galleried courtyard; sadly closed early 1988, for at least two years, during redevelopment of surrounding buildings *(LYM)*; [Midsummer Common] *Fort St George*: Extended well refurbished Tudor pub in charming waterside position on Midsummer Common, interesting old-fashioned core, Greene King real ales, bistro-style bar food, games in public bar, outside bar serving terrace *(Howard and Sue Gascoyne, LYM)*; [nr Grafton Centre] *Hop Bine*: Well kept Greene King ales including Mild, reasonably priced good food *(Sue and Tim Kinning)*; [King St] *King Street Run*: Simple but pleasant local, included for its well kept Wethereds and Winter Royal and usually fairly quiet – but packed with young people Sat nights *(BKA)*; [205 Milton Rd] *Milton*: Greene King pub, recently extensively refurbished as large open-plan bar with home-cooked food using local produce in eating area, including vegetarian dishes; also restaurant *(Anon)*; *Pike & Eel*: Recently reopened by Greene King after major refurbishment – airy open-plan split-level bar and restaurant with low-key Mississippi theme, overlooking one of the main rowing reaches of the River Cam and grazing cattle and horses on Stourbridge Common; buffet lunches, more substantial evening food, pleasant terrace and garden with play area; jazz some evenings *(Howard and Sue Gascoyne)*; [Thompsons Lane, next to Jesus Common] *Spade & Becket*: New conservatory all way around, with open-air balcony above, overlooks River Cam – as do picnic-table sets on waterside terrace; can get crowded in summer, popular with students *(Anon)*; [Regent St] *University Arms*: Spacious and comfortable hotel bar with windows overlooking cricket pitches on Parker's Piece, good fire in octagonal lounge which serves afternoon teas; good value bar lunches include sandwiches and quite a wide range of meat and other salads; bedrooms *(Liz and Ian Phillips)*; [James St, Newmarket Rd] *Zebra*: Unpromising outside, but comfortable and unprecious inside, Greene King beer, good value food and friendly service *(Tim Locke, T Mansell)*

☆ **Castor**, Cambs [24 Peterborough Rd; TL1298], *Royal Oak*: Good value home cooking, well kept Ind Coope Bitter and Burton, open fires and several small traditional bar areas, in thatched inn; pretty village *(LYM)*

Caxton Gibbet, Cambs [junction A45/A14 –

OS Sheet 153 reference 297607; TL2960], *Caxton Gibbet*: Recently reopened former coaching-inn with well kitted-out bar, open all day (at least for coffee) *(Rob and Gill Weeks)*

Chatteris, Cambs [High St – A141 towards March; TL3986], *Ship*: Unpretentious, with good roaring fires each end of bar, darts and cribbage; lounge bar with flowers on tables and pleasant atmosphere; well kept Adnams and Tetleys on handpump *(Roger Broadie)*

nr **Chatteris**, Cambs [Pickle Fen – B1050 towards St Ives; TL3883], *Crafty Fox*: Welcoming free house, friendly landlord, well kept Adnams and Wadworths 6X, spotless kitchens visible behind bar produce good changing food (chef a retired submariner), big conservatory with vines and barbecue (Fri evening, Sun lunch), spacious dining-room *(Frank Gadbois)*

Clayhithe, Cambs [TL5064], *Bridge*: Pretty garden by River Cam, friendly staff, well kept Everards Tiger, good log fire in beamed and timbered bar; popular buffet; bedrooms in motel extension *(James Douglas, Sue White, Tim Kinning, LYM)*

Conington, Cambs [Boxworth Rd; TL3266], *White Swan*: Friendly pub with wide choice of consistently good food at attractive prices, good atmosphere, Greene King Abbot, big garden with dovecot *(Gordon Theaker, HMT)*

Downham, Cambs [Main St; sometimes known as Little Downham – the one near Ely; TL5283], *Plough*: Superb fenland atmosphere, wide choice of whiskies, good bar food *(John Baker)*

Dunstable, Beds [Watling St – A5, S of town (handy for M1 junction 9); TL0221], *Horse & Jockey*: Plushly comfortable bar with good beer, popular if rather skillet-oriented 'Groaning Board' buttery; though restaurant part is much of bar area, tables there are reserved for diners only when busy; shady back courtyard with picnic-table sets, eight-acre garden with lots of attractions for children *(Michael and Alison Sandy, LYM)*; [also A5 S, by Kensworth turn] *Packhorse*: Good atmosphere in simple but welcoming local *(Margaret and Trevor Errington)*

Duxford, Cambs [Moorfield Rd; TL4745], *John Barleycorn*: Long low-beamed bar, attractively chintzy, with candles and genuine brasses, old oak tables and roaring fire in winter; good beef cobbler, lamb steaks and savoury dishes, barbecues in summer *(Joy Heatherley)*

Earith, Cambs [TL3874], *Riverview*: Excellent reasonably priced food in bar and restaurant, very friendly staff *(E G Passant)*

Eaton Bray, Beds [SP9620], *White Horse*: Has had very good hot food and well kept Benskins, but changed hands spring 1988 *(Michael Back – reports on the new regime please)*

☆ **Eaton Socon**, Cambs [Old Great North Rd – village signposted from A1 nr St Neots; TL1658], *White Horse*: Good value food served quickly in rambling series of well kept low-beamed rooms including one with high-backed traditional settles around fine log fire, several well kept Whitbreads-related real ales on handpump, relaxed chatty atmosphere, play area (maybe with guinea-pigs) in back garden; children in eating areas; bedrooms *(LYM)*

Eaton Socon, *Crown*: Pleasant welcoming atmosphere, good value food, lots of beers *(Rita Horridge)*

☆ **Elsworth**, Cambs [TL3163], *George & Dragon*: Attractively furnished and decorated panelled main bar and quieter back dining area by garden, wide choice of good value food, Tolly real ales, nice terraces, play area in garden, restaurant *(John Branford, Dave Butler, Lesley Storey, LYM)*

Elton, Cambs [TL0893], *Black Horse*: Comfortable low basket chairs in carpeted lounge with bare stone walls, beams and brasses, well kept Sam Smiths OB, bar food, sheep grazing opposite *(Tom Evans)*

Ely, Cambs [Annesdale; TL5380], *Cutter*: Riverside pub with view of moorings and boatyard from narrow terrace and spacious public bar; lounge with tables closely set together, Watneys-related real ales on hand-pump, wide range of bar food from servery shaped like a boat hull *(Howard and Sue Gascoyne)*; [2 Lynn Rd] *Lamb*: Good atmosphere in well kept bar of old inn; bedrooms *(Merlyn Horswell)*

Etton, Cambs [TF1406], *Golden Pheasant*: Nice out-of-the-way country pub with good Ruddles County, good food in bar and big restaurant, fairly busy most evenings; large car park *(Michael Bolsover)*

Eynesbury, Cambs [Coneygear; TL1859], *Coneygear*: Olde-worlde free house with river view, good food at reasonable prices, pleasant atmosphere; excellent for families, with garden and play area; often mid-week bands *(PR)*

☆ **Fen Ditton**, Cambs [High St; TL4860], *Ancient Shepherds*: Small and welcoming well run country pub with excellent food, very comfortable lounge with easy chairs and open fires, small friendly public bar, well kept Tolly on handpump and perfectly served Worthington White Shield; small restaurant *(John Hibbs, J A Jennings)*

Fen Ditton [Green End], *Plough*: Riverside gardens very pleasant in summer, nice walk across meadows from town; recently converted to a Whitbreads Brewers Fayre operation *(LYM)*

☆ **Fenstanton**, Cambs [High St – off A604 near St Ives; TL3168], *King William IV*: Friendly and attractive cottage-style pub with large circular wooden tables, with well kept Tolly ales, wide range of bar food such as excellent beef and oyster pie and enormous ploughman's; portly dog *(Alan and Ruth Woodhouse, David Kirk)*; *King George*: Good beer, friendly bar staff, small warm rooms *(I W Bell)*

Fowlmere, Cambs [High St; TL4245], *Swan House*: Helpful friendly landlord, open fire, excellent bar food (if a bit pricey); separate restaurant *(JB and others)*

Glatton, Cambs [TL1586], *Addison Arms*: Picturesque and characterful old pub with friendly atmosphere and olde-worlde décor; varied menu, good friendly service, cosy restaurant *(G M Heeks)*

☆ **Godmanchester**, Cambs [London Rd; TL2470], *Exhibition*: Excellent help-yourself salad buffet, wide choice of good well presented home-cooked food especially poacher's pie, well kept Watneys-related real ales, interesting décor, no piped music *(Dr A V Lewis, Dr and Mrs R J Ashleigh)*

Gorefield, Cambs [TF4111], *Woodmans Cottage*: Fenland village pub with plenty of beams and fireplaces, lively, well run by welcoming Australian landlady with big smile, recently enlarged; good meals and snacks *(John Honnor)*

Grantchester, Cambs [TL4354], *Green Man*: Attractively laid-out pub in pretty village with individual furnishings, welcoming atmosphere, Tolly real ales *(M C Howells, LYM)*; *Red Lion*: Big food pub with sheltered terrace and good-sized lawn (with animals to entertain the many children); comfortable and spacious, busy good value food counter, restaurant, efficient staff *(Dr and Mrs J D Levi, LYM)*; *Rupert Brooke*: Good atmosphere in busy pub, good range of food including vegetarian dishes served quickly in modern eating area, well kept ales and good value wine, attractive restaurant *(Melvin D Buckner, Alan and Ruth Woodhouse, Gordon Theaker)*

Great Barford, Beds [TL1352], *Anchor*: Reliably good bar food including outstanding French onion soup; Charles Wells ales in fine condition from lovely cellar *(J T Alford)*

☆ **Great Chishill**, Cambs [TL4239], *Pheasant*: Good atmosphere in unassuming but interestingly furnished pub, good food (not Sun lunchtime or Mon), well kept Adnams and Greene King IPA, charming garden; closed Mon lunchtime *(Joy Heatherley, LYM)*

Great Eversden, Cambs [off A603; TL3653], *Hoops*: Country pub with good atmosphere, friendly landlord, pool-table and darts, Charles Wells beers, simple well prepared bar food *(Gordon Theaker)*

Haddenham, Cambs [TL4675], *Three Kings*: Very friendly welcome, good food; children welcome *(R M Williamson)*

Hail Weston, Cambs [TL1662], *Royal Oak*: Friendly old pub with cosy beamed lounge, Charles Wells real ales, good value food *(Margaret and Roy Randle)*

Harston, Cambs [48 Royston Rd (A10); near M11 junction 11; TL4251], *Queens Head*: Friendly and attractively refurbished Greene King pub with nice garden, bar food specialising in home-cooked pies with local fresh vegetables and crisp chips, well kept Greene King ales, decent house wine, efficient service; interesting glass engravers' around the corner *(Joy Heatherley, Jenny Ball)*

Hemingford Abbots, Cambs [TL2870], *Axe & Compass*: Thatched pub with inglenooks, friendly licensees, good food, well kept Watneys-related real ales *(Simon Holmes)*

Henlow, Beds [junction A600/A6001 nr Henlow airport; TL1738], *Bird in Hand*: Very clean, with efficient service and excellent value snacks *(Mrs Shirley Fluck)*

nr **Hexton**, Beds [Pegsdon – B655 a mile E of Hexton; TL1230], *Live & Let Live*: Snug little pub with lovely garden below the Chilterns, two rooms opening off tiled and panelled tap-room, Greene King ales and usual pub food *(LYM)*

Hildersham, Cambs [High St; TL5448], *Pear Tree*: All food freshly cooked and of high quality, service friendly though not speedy *(Anon)*

Houghton, Cambs [TL2872], *Three Horseshoes*: French windows into garden from extended refurbished lounge, locals' bar with black beams and inglenook, well kept Watneys-related real ales, bar food (not Sun evening) including lunchtime cold buffet *(G H Theaker, LYM)*

Houghton Conquest, Beds [3 miles from M1 junction 11; TL0441], *Knife & Cleaver*: Seventeenth-century brick pub opposite attractive church, comfortable restaurant and charming conservatory overlooking garden, uncommonly good food, friendly service, maybe unobtrusive piped classical music *(Eucharis Strong)*

☆ **Huntingdon**, Cambs [TL2371], *Old Bridge*: Quite individual but quite splendid in the Poste Hotels manner, with excellent food including same kind of buffet as at George, Stamford; fine service in comfortable surroundings; bedrooms *(Syd and Wyn Donald, Mrs R Horridge)*

Huntingdon, *Falcon*: Pleasant low-ceilinged room, good simple food reasonably priced, friendly service, well kept beer; some tables outside *(Anon)*; *George*: Elegant and spacious Georgian lounge bar in comfortable THF hotel, popular for bar food; restaurant; bedrooms overlook galleried central courtyard where Shakespeare play performed during last fortnight or so of June *(LYM)*

Isleham, Cambs [TL6474], *Griffin*: Pleasantly served and reasonably priced well cooked food from grill-type menu, well kept Adnams and Greene King real ales, maybe live music Sats *(Pamela and Merlyn Horswell)*

Kimbolton, Cambs [High St; TL0968], *New Sun*: Smart bar, popular with good mix of customers; quality food in bistro-style restaurant *(David Surridge)*

Leighton Bromswold, Cambs [TL1175], *Green Man*: Neatly modernised open-plan village pub with hundreds of good horsebrasses on heavy low beams, bar food, well kept

Tolly Original, sensible games area *(LYM)*

Leighton Buzzard, Beds [Appenine Way, Clipstone Brook estate; SP9225], *Clay Pipe*: Clay pipes and drawings of them on walls, surprisingly good food presented well, friendly and helpful licensee and staff *(D L Johnson)*

Linton, Cambs [TL5646], *Dog & Duck*: Old village local with bustling, homely atmosphere; low-beamed bar, fireplace, old prints and brasses, Greene King on handpump, bar food; pleasant back garden by river and waterfall, lots of tame ducks *(Howard and Sue Gascoyne)*

Luton, Beds [Castle St; TL0921], *Vine*: Good atmosphere in small comfortable lounge, much larger main bar – said to have been the country's first fully computerised pub *(Michael and Alison Sandy)*

☆ **Madingley**, Cambs [TL3960], *Three Horseshoes*: Smartly attractive thatched and beamed pub with comfortable furnishings, efficient service and elegant garden (though not a great many seats out there), pricey food including popular summer buffet, particular emphasis on charcoal-grilled fish; Tolly and Original on handpump; modern restaurant extension built to match; children welcome *(Mary and Edward Fisher, S Lowherd, Peter Hitchcock, LYM)*

March, Cambs [Acre Rd; TL4195], *Acre*: Simply furnished riverside town-centre pub which has been popular for superb value food, friendly and well run, with nice atmosphere – new licensees 1988 come with a good record from Jolly Butchers, Exning *(John Honnor)*; [West End] *White Horse*: Watneys-related ales, good pub food, riverside garden *(E Robinson)*

Melchbourne, Beds [Knotting Rd; TL0265], *St John Arms*: Friendly rambling country pub with bar food, well kept Greene King real ales, peaceful cottagey garden *(LYM)*

Milton, Cambs [TL4762], *White Horse*: Free house with choice of real ales and good atmosphere; good value food *(Sue and Tim Kinning)*

Molesworth, Cambs [TL0775], *Cross Keys*: Busy and friendly pub with well kept Adnams, good service, ample helpings of straightforward but popular food, piped music; bedrooms in attractive back motel unit *(Mrs R Horridge, Dr A V Lewis)*

☆ **Needingworth**, Cambs [Overcote Lane – pub signposted from A1123; TL3472], *Pike & Eel*: Marvellous peaceful riverside location, with spacious lawns and marina; extensive glass-walled restaurant (food confined to this), snugger areas as well as roomy plush bar in original core; provision for children; charming bedrooms *(Gwen and Peter Andrews, Sue and Tim Kinning, Roy and Barbara Longman, LYM)*

Northill, Beds [TL1546], *Crown*: Consistently high standard, welcoming staff, varied and interesting bar food reasonably priced, spacious garden with seats and tables *(P Devitt)*

Odell, Beds [Horsefair Lane; SP9658], *Bell*: Good Greene King beer and excellent good value bar food including home-cooked pies, good range of vegetarian dishes and children's helpings in lovely old pub with garden backing on to River Ouse *(Mr and Mrs Ray)*

Old Warden, Beds [TL1343], *Hare & Hounds*: Cosy and friendly old local with well kept Charles Wells beers and wide choice of well cooked bar food in generous helpings; subdued piped music in comfortable lounge, public bar with darts and fruit machine; separate restaurant, garden with children's play area; close to Old Warden Hall and Shuttleworth Aircraft Museum; live music Thurs *(Lyn and Bill Capper, BMS)*

Old Weston, Cambs [SP7560], *Swan*: Low-ceilinged old pub with big inglenook, Adnams and Greene King real ale, bar food; new licensees early 1988 – reports please *(LYM)*

Ridgmont, Beds [2½ miles from M1 junction 13: towards Woburn Sands, then left towards Ampthill on A418; SP9736], *Rose & Crown*: Open fire in traditional low-ceilinged public bar, smarter lounge, sensible range of good value bar food, warm welcome, well kept Charles Wells Eagle and Bombardier on handpump, games including darts and pool, maybe rabbits in attractive back garden, stables restaurant (not Mon or Tues evenings); children allowed in eating area; bedrooms planned in adjacent cottage *(A T Langton, LYM)*

Riseley, Beds [High St (off A6); TL0362], *Fox & Hounds*: Comfortably refurbished sixteenth-century beamed pub nicely placed in quiet village, nice atmosphere with welcoming licensees, good fresh dining-room food including vegetarian dishes and fish and shellfish straight from Billingsgate *(R Howgego)*

Souldrop, Beds [off A6 Rushden–Bedford; SP9861], *Bedford Arms*: Friendly village pub with large public bar and separate lounge which has tiled floor and a huge central fireplace with crackling log fire in winter; good choice of reasonably priced bar food ranging from chip butty to steak and including excellent mixed grill and home-cooked ham and egg *(Margaret and Roy Randle)*

Stanbridge, Beds [pub signposted off A5 N of Dunstable; SP9623], *Five Bells*: Large low-beamed bar, very comfortable, smart, quiet and friendly, with well kept Charles Wells; though most customers seem to be on their way to the rather nice restaurant, there's just as much welcome for people here for just a drink or two *(Michael and Alison Sandy)*

Stretham, Cambs [from A1123 E of Stretham turn left on to track just after railway – OS Sheet 154 reference 535745; TL5174], *Fish & Duck*: At the confluence of the Cam and the Ouse, so surrounded by water; good basic home-made food in restaurant *(WJGW)*; [off

A10] *Lazy Otter*: Pleasant atmosphere, helpful staff, good beer and imaginative bar and restaurant menus; set by River Cam *(E and G Slater)*

☆ **Studham**, Beds [TL0215], *Red Lion*: Handily placed for Whipsnade Zoo, and in attractive spot with tables in pretty garden looking up to grassy common, this has reopened under new management after plush refurbishment with cheerful modernish décor and good prints; preliminary reports suggest that service is efficient, the lunchtime bar food (not Sun) definitely worth a try, though more expensive, and the range of real ales still interesting, running to Adnams, Hook Norton Best and Old Hookey, Marstons Pedigree, Wadworths 6X and Youngers IPA – more news please *(Michael and Alison Sandy, E G Parish, LYM)*

Stuntney, Cambs [Soham Rd (A142 Ely–Newmarket); TL5578], *Fenlands Lodge*: Warm, friendly atmosphere in lounge bar; well kept Bass on handpump; wide range of bar food at reasonable prices; excellent service from owner; restaurant; luxurious modern bedrooms *(John and Margaret Harvey)*

Sutton, Beds [TL2247], *John o' Gaunt*: Cosy low-beamed bar with easy chairs and low settles around copper-topped tables, enterprising bar food, well kept Greene King IPA; close to fine fourteenth-century packhorse bridge – you have to go through a shallow ford to reach the pub *(Alison Hayward, Nick Dowson, LYM)*

Swaffham Prior, Cambs [B1102 NE of Cambridge; TL5764], *Red Lion*: Good small village pub with welcoming staff, local real ale and good bar food *(K R Harris)*

☆ **Tempsford**, Beds [TL1652], *Anchor*: Extensive road-house yet pleasantly local atmosphere, with lots for children, useful break from A1; big riverside gardens with outdoor chess and draughts, boules, fishing; decent choice of beers and of bar food, restaurant *(Keith Garley, LYM)*

Totternhoe, Beds [SP9821], *Cross Keys*: Very small, friendly bar in old timbered building with lovely garden and views in summer *(Stephen and Helen Doole)*

Trumpington, Cambs [High St; TL4454], *Coach & Horses*: Big helpings of good bar food such as curries, lasagne, moussaka and excellent cold platter selection in large rambling roadside free house with Adnams, Greene King and Marstons Pedigree; very friendly staff, plenty of parking behind *(Alan and Ruth Woodhouse)*

Turvey, Beds [SP9452], *Laws*: Good hotel bar with fine food, especially Sun lunch – reasonable prices *(R H Sawyer)*; [off A428, by church] *Three Cranes*: Tastefully furnished real ale pub with friendly licensees, good food in bar and restaurant *(T L Mathias)*

☆ **Upware**, Cambs [TL5370], *Five Miles From Anywhere, No Hurry*: Spacious modern riverside free house, with friendly and attentive staff, good hot meals even on winter Sun, and atmosphere and décor almost more that of a town hotel than a country pub – even though its name means what it says! Good moorings on River Cam *(R Robinson, LYM)*

☆ **Whipsnade**, Beds [B4540 E; TL0117], *Old Hunters Lodge*: Very good bar food including sandwiches and main dishes – particularly fish, also good restaurant; well kept Greene King Abbot, nice character, not large – and clean; children welcome *(Mr and Mrs G D Amos, D L Johnson)*

☆ **Whittlesford**, Cambs [TL4748], *Tickell Arms*: When this idiosyncratic and flamboyantly theatrical pub was a highly rated main entry in previous editions, there were always some readers who felt uncomfortable (they say they won't have T-shirts or long-haired lefties, and the owner never masks his feelings); now it's in the Dip, readers chorus approval for its exuberant panache, the flower-filled conservatory, formal garden, distinctive food and classical music *(Frank W Gadbois, Peter Hitchcock, AE, GRE, Peter Hall, M A and C R Starling, Barbara Hatfield, George*

Little, Dr P D Smart, LYM)

Wicken, Cambs [TL5670], *Wicken Hall*: Note that this former inn, recommended in previous editions, is now a private house

Wisbech, Cambs [Market Pl; TF4609], *Rose & Crown*: Lovely lounge, smart dining-room, good, well presented food including superb vegetarian dish and roast hare; bedrooms *(Anon)*

Woburn, Beds [SP9433], *Bell*: Well prepared and presented dining-room meals – interesting dishes with excellent sauces and good wine list; bedrooms charming *(P R Lawton)*; [18 Bedford St] *Magpie*: Olde-worlde pub with fine friendly atmosphere, jovial landlord, beautifully prepared reasonably priced food, real ale; bedrooms *(P T Sherring-Lucas, Sue Bourke)*; [Hockcliffe Rd] *Royal Oak*: Very attractive small pub; good beer and simple home cooking, friendly staff *(Nicolas Walter)*

Yielden, Beds [TL0166], *Chequers*: Modernised pub in rather remote village, with decent beer and food, friendly staff; once kept by H E Bates' great-aunt *(Nicolas Walter)*

Cheshire

Something approaching half the main entries for this county have been new-comers to the Guide *either this year or last. Outstanding among them is the Cholmondeley Arms which we've listed under Bickley Moss (the closest place you're likely to find in a road atlas): we were lucky to be able to squeeze in an inspection of this very newly opened pub just as we passed the book for printing in the summer. Otherwise, taking both old and new together, our favourites here include the charmingly old-fashioned White Lion in Barthomley, the traditional Cock o' Barton at Barton, the Stanley Arms snugged into the Macclesfield Forest at Bottom of the Oven, the Bears Head at Brereton Green (particularly as a place to stay), the Pheasant perched on the Peckforton Hills at Higher Burwardsley (another nice place to stay, but good all round), the Holly Bush at Little Leigh, a remarkably untouched farm-cum-pub, the old-world but very civilised Bells of Peover at Lower Peover, the friendly small-roomed Bird in Hand at Mobberley, the traditionally furnished and warmly welcoming Dun Cow at Ollerton, the relaxing Ring o' Bells in Overton, the unpretentious Highwayman looking out over the Cheshire Plain from Rainow, and the Sutton Hall Hotel at Sutton (a very comfortable country hotel, of great character). Many of these have good value food: other pubs where this is a strong point include the Maypole at Acton Bridge, the White Lion at Alvanley, the Birch & Bottle in Higher Whitley, the French-run Roebuck at Mobberley, and the Cheshire Hunt at Pott Shrigley. In the Lucky Dip, pubs to note include the Bickerton Poacher at Bickerton, Broxton Hall Hotel at Broxton (shown on few maps, so we list it under nearby Tattenhall), Telfords Warehouse in Chester, White Horse at Churton, Spinner & Bergamot in Comberbach (perhaps the pick of this bunch), Alvanley Arms at Cotebrook, Unicorn in Dean Row, Cat and Fiddle near Macclesfield (the country's second-highest pub), Whipping Stocks at*

The Bears Head, Brereton Green

Over Peover, Admiral Rodney in Prestbury, Swan in Tarporley, Windmill at Whiteley Green, Crag at Wildboarclough and (among a good many waterside pubs) the Miners Arms at Adlington, unspoilt Bird in Hand at Kent Green, Shady Oak near Tiverton and Ferry Inn outside Warrington.

ACTON BRIDGE   SJ5975   Map 7
Maypole ⊗

Hilltop Road; village signposted down B5153, off A49 in Weaverham; then turn right at Acton Cliff signpost

The spacious and comfortably refurbished beamed lounge bar in this impeccably kept pub has Windsor armchairs, captain's chairs, dark red plush cushioned antique settles, and window seats around the tripod tables on the Turkey carpet, with good coal fires in stripped brickwork at either end. It's decorated with plates set out on a dresser and on a high Delft shelf, and some copper on the swirly plaster. Reliable, good value lunchtime food – popular with older people – includes salads with a wide range of fresh ingredients that have been picked out as good value (around £2.80, fresh salmon when it's available £3.55), though all the food uses good ingredients: home-made soup (85p), sandwiches (from 95p, open sandwiches from £2.20), and daily specials like lasagne (£2.75), steak and kidney or chicken and ham pies (around £2.80), and fresh plaice (£3.20). The friendly licensees feel confident enough about what they serve to come quietly around making sure people have enjoyed their meals; this year they won a brewery food competition. Well kept Greenalls Bitter and Mild on handpump; gentle piped music. The window boxes and hanging baskets are lovely, and there are seats outside, with an orchard behind the simple brick building. *(Recommended by JAH, HLH, R G Ollier; more reports please)*

Greenalls   Licensee David Barker   Real ales   Lunchtime meals and snacks   Open 11.30–3, 5.30–11 all year; closed evening 25 Dec

ALVANLEY   SJ4974   Map 7
White Lion ⊗

2½ miles from M56 junction 14; A5117 towards Helsby, bear left into A56 then quickly turn right, following village signpost; in village, turn right into Manley Road

There are rustic picnic-table sets on the grass by the play area – which has an assault course and sand-floored fortress – and white tables and chairs under cocktail parasols by the black-shuttered white pub, which is prettily decorated with hanging baskets. Inside, the cosy lounge has softly cushioned red plush seats and wall banquettes, beer-steins, pistols, copper jugs and so forth hanging from its nicely moulded black beams, and decorative plates on the white walls; piped music. Generous helpings of well prepared food include soup (90p), sandwiches (from 95p, steak barm-cake £1.40), quite a wide variety of ploughman's (from £1.60), home-made hot-pot or cottage pie (£1.50), and several specials such as roast beef (£2.50), home-made steak pie (£2.75), lamb cutlets (£3.25), gammon and egg (£3.30) and sirloin steak (£5.95). Well kept Greenalls Original on handpump; friendly licensees and staff. The smaller public bar has darts and dominoes. *(Recommended by J J Kennedy, D Storey, R G Ollier, Ernest Lee)*

Greenalls   Licensee Keith Morris   Real ale   Meals and snacks   Children in eating area of bar   Open 11.30–3, 5.30–11 all year

---

Real ale to us means beer which has matured naturally in its cask – not pressurised or filtered. We name all real ales stocked. We usually name ales preserved under a light blanket of carbon dioxide too, though purists – pointing out that this stops the natural yeasts developing – would disagree (most people, including us, can't tell the difference!).

BARTHOMLEY SJ7752 Map 7
White Lion ★

Village link from M6 junction 16, with the completion of the Crewe M-way spur

There's a marvellously friendly atmosphere in this unspoilt, early seventeenth-century pub. The simply furnished main room has attractively moulded black panelling, Cheshire watercolours and prints, heavy oak beams in the low ceiling (one big enough to house quite a collection of plates), an open fire and latticed windows; up some steps, a second room, with more oak panelling, a high-backed winged settle and a paraffin lamp hinged to the wall, and another open fire, has sensibly placed darts, shove-ha'penny and dominoes. Cheap bar snacks include hot pies, well filled ham, beef or cheese salad rolls, and soup at lunchtime; well kept Burtonwood Bitter and Mild on handpump. Tables under the old yew tree beside the pretty black and white timbered and thatched pub or on the front cobbles have a peaceful view of the village and the early fifteenth-century red sandstone church of St Bertiline just opposite. *(Recommended by Wayne Brindle, S D Samuels, Graham Gibson, Jon Wainwright, A M Kelly)*

Burtonwood   Real ale   Snacks (not Sun evening)   Children at lunchtime only Open 11–3, 6–11

BARTON SJ4554 Map 7
Cock o' Barton

A534 E of Farndon

One reader found this well kept, handsome sandstone pub recommended in an 1899 guidebook, and people have actually been coming here for 600 years. The separate snug areas in the more or less open-plan bar have black beams and joists, prints of ornamental fowls and newer ones of game birds on the bobbly white walls, old-fashioned furnishings that include high-backed built-in cushioned settles, log fires, and old carpet squares on the ancient black slate tiles of the older small-roomed part and green Turkey carpet in the most spacious area (closest to the entry); there's a gun above the door and hunting scene prints in the entrance hall. Well kept McEwans 80/- (called Draught here) on handpump, Youngers Scotch on electric; friendly, welcoming service. Good bar food includes home-made soup (95p), sandwiches, ploughman's, cannelloni (£3.50), gammon and eight-ounce rump steak, and at lunchtime on Tuesdays to Fridays a much wider choice including some imaginative main dishes. There are some teak seats by a little lily pool in a dwarf shrubbery; in summer they sell snacks and soft drinks from an outside servery. *(Recommended by Jon Wainwright, Graham Gibson, Laurence Manning, Peter Corris, Lee Goulding)*

Free house   Real ale   Meals and snacks   Open 12–2.15, 7.30–11; closed Mon lunchtime

BICKLEY MOSS SJ5549 Map 7
Cholmondeley Arms ★ ⊗

Cholmondeley; A49 5½ miles N of Whitchurch

The Harrisons, who with their relatives Guy and Carolyn Ross-Lowe opened this in June 1988, previously won great acclaim from readers and from ourselves for the way they developed the Crown at Hopton Wafers in Shropshire – in their days it was the best pub in the region. This new place is very interesting: an inventive conversion of what was formerly a Victorian schoolhouse – so recently, indeed, that on our visit the car park was still marked with the lines of a softball pitch. It's in the new wave of pub design, fresh and airy, yet concentrating firmly on traditional pub virtues: first-class drinks, a wide range of good imaginative food, a warm and friendly atmosphere, and plenty of things to notice. The building is cross-shaped and high-ceilinged, handsome inside, with masses of Victorian pictures (especially portraits and military subjects, but we particularly liked the 1888 painting of Chelsea Reach, on the way to the lavatories). Nice touches include the patterned paper on the shutters, matching the curtains; the interesting furnishings, from cane and bentwood to pews and carved oak; the unobtrusively well reproduced taped music; and the great stag's head over one of the side arches. Besides changing specials, bar food includes soup (£1.25), sandwiches (from £1.25), several children's dishes (£1.50), ploughman's with a choice of cheeses (£2.60), a complicated terrine (£2.75), garlic mushrooms with bacon (£2.75), hot crab pâté (£3), blinis or saffron garlicky prawns (£3.25), omelettes or devilled kidneys (£3.50), gammon or plaice (£4.50), steaks (from £6.80) and grilled king prawns and chicken with satay sauce (£7.50); as people who knew the Crown in their day would expect, there's a very wide choice of home-made puddings (£1.50) and ice-creams (£1.25). Well kept Marstons Burton and Pedigree on handpump, with a guest such as Border; open fire; up over the bar a gantry carries some of the old school desks, but more importantly the old blackboard listing ten or so interesting wines by the glass, including on our visit Domaine Bonnet 1987 (a Chardonnay which had stood out for exceptional value at a London trade tasting we'd been to just the week before) and the champagne which is our own automatic choice on the very rare occasions that we can afford it. There are seats out on a sizeable lawn, and the adjoining school house is being converted to bedrooms. *(Recommended by BOB, Graham Gibson)*

Free house   Licensees Julian and Ginney Harrison   Real ale   Meals and snacks   Children welcome   Open 11–3, 6.30–11 all year; closed 25 Dec   Bedrooms tel Cholmondeley (082 922) 300; £25B/£45B

BOLLINGTON   SJ9377 Map 7

Vale

29 Adlington Road; off B5091 on road heading N by railway viaduct; OS Sheet 118 reference 931781

Down one of the quieter streets in this charming village (which is being well preserved as a conservation area), and close to a bowling-green, cricket field, play-park and tennis courts, this gently modernised, friendly pub has an open-plan bar divided by a couple of big stone supporting pillars with internal arches. There are heavy dark green velvet curtains, brass platters on the end stripped-stone wall, some racehorse prints and 1936 Gallaghers cricketer cigarette cards, and a log fire in the stone fireplace (as well as central heating); also, tapestried wall seats all the way round, wheelback chairs, and tables set with cheery red tablecloths at lunchtime. Food then includes sandwiches, home-made soup (80p), ploughman's (£2.80), home-made dishes such as chilli con carne (£2.80) and steak and kidney pie or lasagne (£3), seafood platter (£3.10), and half a chicken or scampi (£3.50); the beef and ham are home cooked; well kept Thwaites Bitter and Mild on handpump, and maybe Marstons Pedigree, from the substantial heavily timber-topped stone-built corner counter. Fruit machine, good pop music. The garden is a neat little lawn with picnic-table sets, by the edge of a wood, and there are swings, a slide, a rocking-horse, climbing-frame and paddling-pool; handy for start of *Good Walks Guide* Walk 73. *(Recommended by Mr and Mrs A W Hartwell, Dr and Mrs C D E Morris)*

Free house   Licensee Mrs Patricia Capper   Real ale   Lunchtime meals and snacks (not Mon)   Open all day for trial period; closed Mon lunchtime exc bank hols

BOTTOM OF THE OVEN SJ9872 Map 7
Stanley Arms ⊗

From A537 Buxton–Macclesfield heading towards Macclesfield, take first left turn (not signposted) after Cat & Fiddle; OS Sheet 118 reference 980723

Handy for exploring the beautiful Macclesfield forest, this isolated moorland pub has a quiet, friendly atmosphere, little landscape watercolours on the ochre walls, piped Vivaldi, big bunches of flowers in summer, and open fires in winter (enjoyed by the sleek black cat). Two of the three snug rooms, notable for their shiny black lacquered woodwork, have muted red and black flowery plush wall settles and stools and some dark blue seats around the low dimpled copper tables on their grey carpets; the third is laid out as a dining-room, with pretty pastel tablecloths. Bar food served in remarkably generous helpings includes, at lunchtime, sandwiches, home-made soup (£1.10), ploughman's (£2.20), lasagne (£3.40), beef in ale (£3.95), and salads (from £3.95); in the evening there are more substantial dishes such as half a chicken chasseur (£4.95), pork in butter and rosemary (£5.95), halibut steak (£6.80), and half a duckling with orange sauce (£6.95); also, a daily special. Well kept Marstons Burton and Pedigree on handpump, and a good range of spirits. There are some picnic-table sets on the grass behind. Quiet during the week, it can get very busy at weekends. *(Recommended by Lee Goulding, Dr and Mrs R J Ashleigh, Brian and Anna Marsden)*

Marstons   Licensee A J Harvey   Real ale   Lunchtime snacks (not Sun) and meals Restaurant tel Sutton (026 05) 2414   Children in eating area and restaurant   Open 11.30–3, 7–10.30

BRERETON GREEN SJ7864 Map 7
Bears Head ⇚ [*illustrated on page 81*]

1¾ miles from M6 junction 17; fork left from Congleton road almost immediately, then left on to A50; also from junction 18 via Holmes Chapel

The series of well kept, open-plan communicating rooms in this civilised black and white timbered inn – served by two bar counters – have antique panelled settles, big Windsor armchairs and more modern but quite harmonious ladder-back seats, a corner cupboard full of Venetian glass, masses of heavy black beams and timbers, and a large brick inglenook fireplace full of gleaming copper pots (with a coal fire in winter). A section of wall in one room (under glass for protection) has had the plaster removed to show the construction of timber underneath. Bar food (prices have not changed since last year) consists of home-made soup (£1.15), sandwiches (from £1.25, steak £3.95), home-made pâtés – smoked mackerel (£2.75), Stilton (£2.65) or chicken liver (£2.95) – and salads or a hot dish of the day (£3.95), with home-made puddings and ices (£1.75). Bass and Burtonwood Bitter on handpump, well kept in fine deep cellars; courteous service by smartly uniformed staff. Fruit machine, soothing piped music and a pleasantly relaxed atmosphere. A pretty side terrace has white cast-iron tables and chairs under cocktail parasols, big black cast-iron lamp clusters and a central fountain, and is sheltered by a little balconied brick building. *(Recommended by Graham Gibson, AE, Laurence Manning, Charles and Mary Winpenny, E G Parish, GRE)*

Free house   Licensee Roberto Tarquini   Real ale   Meals and snacks (not Sun evening) Children in eating area, restaurant (closed Sun evening), new Italian trattoria (closed Sun and Mon evenings), and residents' lounge   Restaurant   Open 11–3, 6–11 all year; considering longer afternoon opening to meet demand   Bedrooms tel Holmes Chapel (0477) 35251; £39.50S(£41.50B)/£47.50B

Pubs shown as closing at 11 do so in the summer, but close earlier – normally 10.30 – in winter unless we specify 'all year'.

BUTLEY TOWN   SJ9177   Map 7
Ash Tree

A523 Macclesfield–Stockport

The three small, friendly rooms in this white-slated roadside pub (one at the back doesn't have bar service) have drawings of old Cheshire timbered houses, little button-back red leatherette armchairs, more antique panelled settles, old tripod tables, brass and copperware, open fires (one with Delft tiles set into the stonework around it), and even an armour breastplate. They open off a softly lit Turkey-carpeted central corridor with a panelled settle and other cushioned seats, old Schweppes advertisements and a fruit machine. Bar food includes soup (75p), steak barm (95p), sandwiches (from £1), pâté (£1.50), ploughman's or cheese and onion flan (£2), steak and kidney pie (£2.20), an extensive cold buffet (£3.20), gammon with pineapple (£4.35), eight-ounce sirloin steak (£5.85), and daily specials; very well kept Boddingtons Bitter on handpump; darts, dominoes, fruit machine and unobtrusive piped music. (*Recommended by Lee Goulding, Brian and Anna Marsden, Dr and Mrs R J Ashleigh*)

Boddingtons   Licensee Thomas Phoenix   Real ale   Meals and snacks (not Sun, or Mon and Sat evenings)   Restaurant tel Prestbury (0625) 829207; closed Sun   Children in eating area of bar and restaurant   Open 11–3, 5.30–11; opens 6.30 Sat evening

CHESTER   SJ4166   Map 7
Falcon

Lower Bridge Street

The massive stone blocks and the cellars in this splendidly ornamental timbered building go back some 700 years or more, though it mainly dates from around 1600. Inside, it's been sympathetically redecorated with new carpets and uphol-stered seats, and the bar staff now wear uniforms. The airy and quiet upstairs room has a fine range of latticed windows looking over the street (it's available for functions in the early part of the week). Good value food includes open sandwiches (from £1.65), salads such as quiche, ham, prawn, game or turkey and ham pie and smoked mackerel (from £2) and daily hot dishes (from £2.30); well kept Sam Smiths Tadcaster, OB and Museum on handpump; fruit machine, mainstream piped music. It can get very crowded on Friday and Saturday evenings. This whole area of Chester – centring particularly on this handsome pub – has been well restored and brought back to life, earning the city a Europa Nostra civic conser-vation medal. (*Recommended by TPCM, Lee Goulding, Jon Wainwright, RB*)

Sam Smiths   Real ale   Meals and snacks (lunchtime, not Sun)   Parking may be difficult Folk club Weds evening, jazz Thurs evening and Sat lunchtime   Open 11–3, 5.30–11

FULLERS MOOR   SJ4954   Map 7
Copper Mine

A534 Wrexham–Nantwich, just under two miles E of A41 junction

The two low-ceilinged rooms of this friendly and neatly kept place are well broken up into separate seating areas, with soft lighting, stripped beams and timbering, blacked stove doors set into the dividing wall, and masses of copper-mining mementos on the prettily papered walls – blasting explosives and fuses, old lamps, photographic tableaux of more or less tense moments in local mining history. A wide choice of bar food includes soup (90p), pâté (£1.60), pancake rolls (£1.65), smoked trout (£1.95), generous burgers or cottage pie (£3.25), a good few help-yourself salads (from £3.75, ploughman's £3.50), lasagne or honey-grilled

---

'Space game' means any electronic game – even a thoroughly earth-bound one.

pork ribs (£3.95) and steaks (from eight-ounce rump £6.55), with lunchtime children's dishes (from £1.25); well kept Boddingtons Bitter and Mild on hand-pump; juke box, rack of magazines, good open fires. You can watch the house martins nesting in the eaves from the picnic-table sets under cocktail parasols on the side lawn, where they have summer barbecues. *(Recommended by G T Jones, Ned Edwards, Laurence Manning)*

Boddingtons Licensees Dave and Gill Furmston Real ale Meals and snacks Open 11–3, 6–11 all year

GOOSTREY   SJ7870   Map 7

Crown ⊗

111 Main Road; village signposted from A50 and A535

Originally a farmhouse, this comfortable village pub has an attractive new pub sign and there have been plans to change the rooms around. As we went to press, though, things were much the same: a chaise-longue and cushioned settles as well as more conventional seats in the two communicating rooms of the lounge bar, and decorations that include a couple of Lowry prints – not the usual ones. Get there reasonably early to be sure of a place, particularly towards the end of the week. The smaller and brighter tap-room is plain and traditional, with darts, dominoes and cribbage; also pool and piped music. An upstairs room can be booked for dinner parties, preferably not on Saturdays, and is otherwise available for diners. Popular, freshly prepared food includes sandwiches (from 70p, open prawn £2.75; toasties such as ham and pineapple 95p), ploughman's (£1.60), pizza (£1.80), chilli con carne (£2.45), Southern fried chicken (£2.85), and a lunchtime special (£2.50); in the evening there are extra dishes such as Barnsley chop (£4.95) or sirloin steak (£5.25) in the back bistro dining-room. Well kept Marstons Burton, Mild and Pedigree on handpump. Seats on the front terrace face the village road. *(Recommended by Graham Gibson, Wayne Brindle, Jon Wainwright; more reports on the new layout please)*

Marstons Licensee Peter McGrath Real ale Meals and snacks (not Mon, not Sun evening) Restaurant Children in eating area of bar Jazz or folk Sun evening Open 11.30–3, 5.30–11 all year; open all day Sat Bedrooms tel Holmes Chapel (0477) 32128; £12/£18

Olde Red Lion

Main Road; closer to A535

Seafood is a special feature in this comfortably modernised pub, and may include fresh oysters sold singly over the bar as well as prawns by the half-pint or pint, grilled sardines (£2.45), prawn and smoked salmon open sandwich (£3) and fresh plaice (£3.25); other food includes sandwiches, chicken (£3) and beef pie (£3.25). The open-plan bar has red cushioned banquettes built in against the cream swirly plastered walls, dimpled copper tables, and easy chairs at the back. Tetleys and Walkers on handpump; friendly service, and darts, fruit machine and piped music. White tables on a small lawn at the bottom of an attractively planted steep dell make the pretty garden here a popular place in summer. *(Recommended by Wayne Brindle, Jon Wainwright; more reports please)*

Tetleys (Ind Coope) Licensee Peter Yorke Real ale Meals and snacks Children in eating area of bar and restaurant Restaurant tel Holmes Chapel (0477) 32033 Open 11.30–3, 5.30–11 all year

If a service charge is mentioned prominently on a menu or accommodation terms, you must pay it if service was satisfactory. If service is really bad you are legally entitled to refuse to pay some or all of the service charge as compensation for not getting the service you might reasonably have expected.

GREAT BUDWORTH   SJ6778   Map 7
George & Dragon

4½ miles from M6 junction 19; from A556 towards Northwich, turn right into B5391 almost at once; then fork right at signpost to Aston-by-Budworth, Arley Hall & Gardens

The chief appeal of this seventeenth-century beamed pub is in its layout: plenty of nooks and alcoves in a rambling and comfortable panelled lounge. Copper jugs hang from the beams, there's a fine big mirror with horsebrasses on the wooden pillars of its frame, and furnishings such as red plush button-back banquettes and older settles on its Turkey carpet. The lively and simply furnished public bar has darts, dominoes, fruit machine and piped music. Solidly refaced in old-fashioned style in 1875, the pub goes well with the very pretty village, and with the eleventh-century church and village stocks opposite it. Tetleys Mild and Bitter on hand-pump; the usual run of bar food, including a lunchtime cold table on the bar counter. *(Recommended by PAB, Brenda Gentry, Wayne Brindle, AE, GRE, Jon Wainwright, Graham Richardson, N S R Bickers; more reports please)*

Tetleys   Licensee Malcolm Curtin   Real ale   Meals and snacks   Upstairs restaurant tel Comberbach (0606) 891317   Children in eating area at lunchtimes, in restaurant in evenings Open 11.30–3, 7–11 all year; open all day for trial period Thurs–Sat

HIGHER BURWARDSLEY   SJ5256   Map 7
Pheasant 🛏

Burwardsley signposted from Tattenhall (which itself is signposted off A41 S of Chester) and from Harthill (reached by turning off A534 Nantwich–Holt at the Copper Mine); follow pub's signpost on up hill from Post Office; OS Sheet 117 reference 523566

The window with the best view of the Cheshire Plain and the Wirral in this popular seventeenth-century place houses a laconic blue-fronted Amazon parrot, and this faintly seafaring note is underlined by a brass ship's barometer, some ship photographs, and the licensee's own 1958 Merchant Navy apprenticeship papers. Other decorations include foreign banknotes on the beams, large and attractive colour engravings of Victorian officials of the North Cheshire Hunt, a stuffed pheasant (as well as a picture of one), a set of whimsical little cock-fighting pictures done in real feathers, and plates over the high stone mantelpiece of the see-through fireplace – said to house the biggest log fire in the county. There's a tall leather-cushioned fender around this good fire, and the beamed and timbered bar has a fine variety of other seats on its Turkey carpet, ranging from red leatherette or plush wall seats to one or two antique oak settles. Bar food from a constantly changing menu includes home-made soup, sandwiches, ploughman's (£2.20), salads (from £2.50), lasagne or fish pie (£2.75), game, steak and kidney or chicken and ham pies (£3), and chicken and Stilton roulades (£4.30). Well kept Marstons Pedigree and Stones on handpump; fruit machine (not in main bar) and piped music. There are picnic-table sets on a big side lawn that makes the most of this very peaceful spot, with older-fashioned teak seats on a small terrace by a dovecot (with white doves). The bedrooms, all with views, are in an attractively and very comfortably converted sandstone-built barn; there are some self-catering flats as well. The inn is well placed for walks along the Peckforton Hills, and is at the start of *Good Walks Guide* Walk 72; in summer the nearby candle factory is a big draw. *(Recommended by G T Jones, Graham Gibson, Jon Wainwright, C F Walling, Maj M G Huntriss)*

Free house   Licensee David Greenhaugh   Real ale   Meals and snacks   Restaurant Children in restaurant and sun-room lunchtime and early evening   Horses welcomed, and horse-and-trap rides can be arranged   Open 12–3, 6–11 all year; 12–2.30, 7–11 in winter   Bedrooms tel Tattenhall (0829) 70434; £30B/£40

Planning a day in the country? We list pubs in really attractive scenery at the back of the book.

HIGHER WHITLEY   SJ6280 Map 7
Birch & Bottle ⊗
1¼ miles from M56 junction 10; A559 towards Northwich

Interestingly decorated, this spacious and friendly Turkey-carpeted pub has lots of
miniature oil lamps, little country pictures, hunting prints, old engravings, lots of
repoussé brass platters, a stuffed pheasant, guns and even a case of pistols. Surviving sections of knocked-through wall, steps and alcoves break it up into cosier
areas, and there are plenty of dark rustic tables under the heavy beams, with dark
red plush button-back wall settles and wheel-back chairs, and open fires in winter.
Bar food includes home-made soup (85p), sandwiches (from £1.05), ploughman's
(£2.25), cold platters (from £2.75), salads (from £3.25), pan-fried trout or ham
with egg or pineapple (£3.50), breast of chicken chasseur (£4.45), mixed grill
(£5.35), and steaks (from £5.50); daily specials such as pork stuffed with cheese,
puddings such as delicious After Eight delight (£1.75), children's menu (£2), and
Sunday roast lunch (from £3.95). The new dining area is separated from the bar by
attractive leaded-light windows. Very well kept Greenalls Mild, Bitter and Original
on handpump, and fresh orange juice; fruit machine, piped music; they now have
three anti-smoke air-cleaners. They have Fivewin, a 2p seaside glass-cased game
where you try to flick a ballbearing into a winning cup. Outside, there are brick-
built seats and tables on a terrace under an appropriate fairy-lit silver birch.
(Recommended by C F Walling, Lee Goulding, G T Jones, Mr and Mrs Hendry, R G Ollier)

*Greenalls   Licensee Ian Holt   Real ale   Meals and snacks   Restaurant tel Norcott Brook
(092 573) 225   Children in eating area at lunchtime, if eating   Open 11–3, 6–11 all year*

nr LANGLEY   SJ9471 Map 7
Hanging Gate
Higher Sutton; follow Langley signpost from A54 beside Fourways Motel, and that road passes
the pub; from Macclesfield, heading S from centre on A523 turn left into Byrons Lane at
Langley, Wincle signpost; in Sutton (half-mile after going under canal bridge, i.e. before
Langley) fork right at Church House Inn, following Wildboarclough signpost, then two miles
later turning sharp right at steep hairpin bend; OS Sheet 118 reference 952696

First licensed nearly 300 years ago – though it was built much earlier – this friendly
country pub has cosy little low-beamed rooms that look out beyond a patchwork of
valley pastures to distant moors (and the tall Sutton Common transmitter above
them); they are simply furnished with small seats and modern settles by the big coal
fires, a stuffed otter, and some attractive old photographs of Cheshire towns. Down
stone steps an airier garden-room has much the same view from its picture window;
juke box and sitting space game. Reasonably priced bar food includes soup,
sandwiches, and hot food such as steak and kidney, game or cottage pie, chilli con
carne, Spanish-style chicken and curry (all £2.75). Well kept Marstons Pedigree and
Tetleys Bitter on handpump, with mulled wine in winter. The pub is known locally
as Tom Steele's. There is a crazy-paved terrace outside. *(Recommended by Dr and Mrs
R J Ashleigh, J F Derbyshire, M A and W R Proctor, RB, Lee Goulding)*

*Free house   Real ale   Meals and snacks   Children in garden-room or upper small room
Open 12–3, 7–11*

Leathers Smithy
Follow directions from Macclesfield as for previous entry, but keeping on into Langley; in
Langley follow main road forking left at church into Clarke Lane – keep on towards the moors;
OS Sheet 118 reference 952715

This isolated, friendly pub – popular with walkers on the Gritstone Trail – is
backed by the steep mass of Teggs Nose (a country park), and surrounded by rich

upland sheep pastures, hills and pine woods; a couple of benches in front look across to Ridgegate Reservoir. Inside, there are flagstones on the right as you go in, with bow window seats, wheel-back chairs, and a hay basket, gin-traps, farrier's pincers, and other ironwork on the roughcast cream walls, and perhaps the liveliest atmosphere. On the left, there are little country pictures and drawings of Cheshire buildings, Wills steam engine cigarette cards and a locomotive name-plate curving over one of the two open fires, more wheel-back chairs around cast-iron-framed tables on Turkey carpet, and faint piped music. Good, reasonably priced bar food includes sandwiches (£1), beef pie (£1.50), king rib (£1.80), lasagne or moussaka (£2.50), gammon and egg (£3.60), halibut steak (£3.95), and steak (£4.50); also, very good vegetarian dishes like bulghur wheat and walnut casserole (£2.60), tasty steak and kidney pie (£2.60), and delicious puddings such as butterscotch and walnut sponge (£1); well kept Ind Coope Burton, Jennings, and Tetleys Bitter and Mild on handpump, with a decent collection of spirits, including Macallan on optic; dominoes. (Recommended by Lee Goulding, Mr and Mrs J H Adam, Dr and Mrs R J Ashleigh, Brian and Anna Marsden, M A and W R Proctor, Mr and Mrs J H Adam)

Tetleys   Licensee Paul Hadfield   Real ale   Meals and snacks (not Mon evening)   Children in own room Sat and Sun lunchtime only   Open 12–3, 7–11 all year

LITTLE BOLLINGTON   SJ7286 Map 7
Swan With Two Nicks

2 miles from M56 junction 7: A56 towards Lymm from exit junction, then first right at Stamford Arms into Park Lane; note that heading westwards to rejoin the motorway you must take A556 to junction 8

The walls in this unspoilt village inn are decorated richly with superannuated brass fire extinguishers and hose nozzles, horsebrasses, pictures, old photographs of the pub and shelves of china, and the beams are festooned with miners' lamps, brass and copper pots and ornaments. The back room includes antiques such as cushioned oak settles, and the front part has little wheel-back armchairs and upholstered wall seats around its dimpled copper tables and there are lots of snug alcoves; there's a stag's head above the log fire. Good home-cooked lunchtime bar food includes toasted sandwiches (from 75p), farmer's lunch (£2.25), good home-made quiche, plaice (£2.70) and steak and kidney pie (£2.90); well kept Chesters Best, Best Mild and Whitbread Trophy on handpump from the old-fashioned wood-enclosed central servery. On a crazy-paved terrace by the pretty creeper-covered old house, there are traditional white slat seats and tables. The quiet lane past here stops at a footbridge over the River Bollin, for a short walk to Dunham Hall's deer park (National Trust). No dogs (they keep a cat), and plenty of other notices saying what you can and can't do. (Recommended by Jon Wainwright, G T Jones, G Gibson, GRE, AE, Lee Goulding)

Whitbreads   Real ale   Meals and snacks (lunchtime, not Sun)   Open 11.30–3, 5.30–11 all year

LITTLE LEIGH   SJ6276 Map 7
Holly Bush

4½ miles from M56 junction 10: A49 towards Northwich, pub just S of A533 junction

There's a wonderfully unspoilt and old-fashioned atmosphere in this timber-framed thatched cottage, and a friendly welcome from the licensees and the local regulars. The heavy-beamed parlour has varnished wall benches with sloping panelled backs around waxed and polished country tables, a Review of the Fleet 1935 on the wall, and a warm open fire. Well kept Greenalls and Mild (on handpump) is served from the open doorway of a little back tap-room, and there are sandwiches or hot or cold pies with gravy (from 50p); darts, dominoes. A separate overflow room has much more space, less atmosphere; you can also sit outside. *(Recommended by Phil and Sally Gorton; more reports please)*

Greenalls *Licensee Albert Cowap* *Real ale* *Snacks* *Children in separate room, not after 9pm* *Open 12–3, 5.30–11 weekdays, noon–11 Sat, all year*

LOWER PEOVER SJ7474 Map 7
Bells of Peover ★

From B5081 take short cobbled lane signposted to church

This graceful wistaria-covered building has several antique settles and lots of well cushioned seats, including high-backed Windsor armchairs, in the main Turkey-carpeted lounge; also, a large window seat and a brass fender of the sort you can perch on by the fire. There's a substantial dresser filled with china, pictures above the panelling, and a longcase clock. The bar counter, with side hatches, is out in a small tiled room with wall seats under masses of toby jugs and prints from Victorian magazines. Bar food includes soup (£1.20), potted shrimps, whitebait (£2.50), lasagne, and steak and kidney pie with very tender meat. Well kept Greenalls Best on handpump; dominoes. The sheltered crazy-paved terrace in front of the pub faces a beautiful black and white timbered church (mainly fourteenth century, with lovely woodwork inside; the stone tower is sixteenth century). A spacious lawn beyond the old coachyard at the side spreads down through trees and rose pergolas to a little stream. *(Recommended by Tim Halstead, J C Proud, Mr and Mrs J A Hendry, Barbara Hatfield, Simon Turner, Jon Wainwright, G L Archer, M A and W R Proctor)*

Greenalls *Real ale* *Meals and snacks* *Restaurant* tel *Lower Peover (056 581) 2269 (closed Sun evening, Mon)* *Open 11–3, 5.30–11*

LOWER WHITLEY SJ6179 Map 7
Chetwode Arms

2¼ miles from M56 junction 10; village signposted from A49 Whitchurch road

On the right of the small central servery in this traditional country pub is the locals' bar, served by a hatch, with old green-cushioned settles, heavy mahogany tables, and darts and dominoes. By the servery itself there's a snug little room with a settle and some chairs, and two more carpeted rooms lead off, one with a handsome heavy seat built right around its walls. There are little country pictures on the walls, a collection of china teapots and so forth, horsebrasses, some farm equipment such as a miniature harrow and plough, and cosy fires in winter. The hard-working new licensee has introduced a wider range of food: sandwiches, kofta curry (£2.75), fresh fillet of plaice or steak and kidney pie (£2.95), chicken tikka (£3.75), peppered steak provençale (£4.25) and sirloin steak (£5.75); also daily specials; well kept Greenalls Cask Mild and Bitter on electric pump, with Original on handpump; pool, piped music. The bowling-green is beautifully kept. *(Recommended by C F Walling, Graham Gibson, A T Langton, HLH, JAH)*

Greenalls *Licensee R L Southerton* *Real ale* *Meals and snacks* *Children in central lounge area* *Open all day*

MOBBERLEY SJ7879 Map 7
Bird in Hand

B5085 towards Alderley

This partly sixteenth-century building has several atmospheric little low-ceilinged rooms opening through low, wide arches off its friendly central servery. There are small pictures on the attractive Victorian wallpaper, toby jugs and other china on a high shelf, comfortably cushioned heavy wooden seats and so forth, wood panelling in the cosy snug, and a blazing fire in winter. Very well kept Sam Smiths OB and

Museum on handpump; darts, dominoes and fruit machine. The wide choice of good bar food includes home-made soup, sandwiches (from 95p; open sandwiches such as home-cooked ham with peach £2.50 or fresh crab £3), ploughman's or home-made pâté (£2.75), salads (from £3, fresh crab £4), with home-made specials like cheese and ham quiche or chilli con carne (£3.75) or pie of the day and mild chicken curry (£3.90); puddings such as home-made pie or cheesecake (£1.25). The atmosphere is pleasantly relaxed, though it does get crowded. There are seats outside. The inn-sign is most attractive. *(Recommended by AE, GRE, Brian and Anna Marsden, David Waterhouse, Dr David Stanley, Graham Gibson, Lee Goulding, Jon Dewhirst, Jon Wainwright)*

Sam Smiths   Licensee Andrew Bentley   Real ale   Meals (not Mon evening or Sun) and snacks (not Mon or Sun evenings)   Children welcome   Open 11.30–3, 5.30–10.30

Roebuck

Town Lane; down hill from sharp bend on B5085, at E edge of 30mph limit

Run by a French licensee and his Cheshire wife (who does the cooking), this neat and friendly house has a spacious open-plan main room with comfortably cushioned long dark wood pews that were rescued from a redundant Welsh chapel and rich-coloured close-set floorboards that have been recycled from an old mill. Very popular, generously served and reasonably priced home-made bar food includes lunchtime sandwiches (not Sunday), home-made soup (90p), home-made pâtés (£1.90), salads (from £2.10), lasagne, cheese and ham pancake or vegetarian chilli with bulghur wheat and walnuts (£2.75), steak and kidney pie (£3.25), eight-ounce rump steak (£6), and specials like pasta with leeks and cream (£2.75), rare roast beef cooked with garlic (£4.50), and salmon poached in cream (£5.50); puddings like hot banana pancake (£1.30); and Sunday roast lunch (£3.75). Evening food is waitress-served in a separate area. Well kept Websters Choice and Samuel Websters, and Wilsons Bitter from handpumps on the handsome bar counter (which has high stools and a good brass footrail); a wide choice of cocktails; fruit machine and juke box. There is a cobbled courtyard with benches and tables, and, at the back of the pub, an enclosed beer garden with picnic tables – and more by the car park; also a play area for small children with a sandpit and play equipment. The Bulls Head mentioned in the Lucky Dip is just across the quiet lane; a pleasant conjunction on a summer evening when they're playing bowls. *(Recommended by John Derbyshire, Simon Barber; more reports please)*

Wilsons (Watneys)   Licensee Philippe Elissalde   Real ale   Meals and snacks   Restaurant tel Mobberley (056 587) 2757   Children welcome   Open 12–3, 5.30–10.30

OLLERTON   SJ7877   Map 7
Dun Cow

A537 SE of Knutsford

One of those fortunate pubs that embraces you instantly in a warm, timeless welcome, this comfortable place greets you first with the curve of an old-fashioned wooden draught screen sheltering the lounge from the draughty outside world, and then with the contented buzz of idle warm chat. It's a genuine place: people like the corner snug with china ornaments in its cupboard, small pictures, and nice little oak chairs and tables. Our favourite spot in the main room is the little alcove where an oak settle with an unusually broad seat just manages to slot in, but others like the low wicker-seat chair by the fire (like a nursing chair with arms), or the traditional dark wood built-in seats at that end. Things to notice include a couple of longcase clocks, the polished chest by the entry, a couple of large embroidered panels (particularly the one on the way through to the restaurant) and the sawfish snout in the hall. The lounge has not one but two blazing fires in winter. The full range of bar food includes soup (80p), sandwiches (from 90p, lunchtimes only), spare ribs, plaice or steak and kidney pie (all £1.90), and generous evening meals such as gammon or grilled sirloin (£3.50), scampi (£4) and roast duck (£6.50). The small tap-room has darts and dominoes; well kept Greenalls Cask and Original on handpump. There are a few picnic-table sets on the grass under the oak trees in front. *(Recommended by Jon Wainwright, John Broughton, Laurence Manning)*

Greenalls Licensee Geoffrey Tilling Real ale Meals (not Sun, nor Mon–Tues evenings) and snacks (not Sun–Tues evenings) Children in separate room Restaurant tel Knutsford (0565) 3093 Weds–Sat evening Open 11–11 (initially subject to staff availability)

OVERTON   SJ5277   Map 7

Ring o' Bells

Just over 2 miles from M56 junction 12; 2 Bellemonte Road – from A56 in Frodsham take B5152 and turn right (up hill) at Parish Church signpost

Several small cosy rooms ramble around the old-fashioned hatch-like central servery of this early seventeenth-century pub. A couple have red plush seats with windows giving a view past the stone church to the Mersey far below; one at the back has old hunting prints on its butter-coloured walls, some antique settles, and brass and leather fender seats by the log fire; yet another small room, with beams, antique dark oak panelling and stained glass, leads through to a darts room (there's also shove-ha'penny, dominoes and cribbage) liberally adorned with pictures of naked ladies. Waitress-served lunchtime bar food includes sandwiches and home-made steak and mushroom pie, various quiches, chilli or curry (£2.40), prawn-and-mushroom-filled plaice (£2.80), and home-made puddings. Well kept Greenalls Mild, Bitter and Original on handpump; piped music. The cats are called Basil and Blackberry India. *(Recommended by RJH, Jon Wainwright; more reports please)*

Greenalls Licensee Shirley Wroughton-Craig Real ale Lunchtime meals and snacks Children welcome (not in bar) Restaurant tel Frodsham (0928) 32068 Open 11.30–3, 5.30–11 all year

PLUMLEY   SJ7175   Map 7

Golden Pheasant

Plumley Moor Lane; signposted Plumley off A556 by the Smoker – see next entry

This spacious series of comfortably modernised open-plan rooms is noticeable for its ebullient atmosphere. Furnishings are for the most part unremarkable, though the odd sofa is a special draw, there's a nice longcase clock, a couple of elaborate antique flower prints and wooden partitions with stained-glass inserts, and the built-in wall seats are more attractively upholstered than usual. Bar food includes soup (95p), sandwiches (£1.10), chilli con carne or lasagne (£2.75), the day's roast or steak and kidney pie (£3.50), popular specials such as pork jardinière and scampi (£3.95), served by friendly uniformed waitresses; well kept and low-priced Lees Bitter and Mild; open fire; darts, juke box, fruit machine, with pool in a separate games-room. The sizeable garden, which still has a neatly kept bowling-green, has picnic-table sets under cocktail parasols, and a climbing-frame. *(Recommended by Derek Stephenson, J H M Broughton, Lee Goulding, Mr and Mrs J A Hendry)*

Lees Licensee J G Parker Real ale Meals and snacks Restaurant Open 11–3, 6–11 all year Bedrooms tel Lower Peover (056 581) 2261; £33B/£44B

Smoker

2½ miles from M6 junction 19: A556 towards Northwich and Chester

This 400-year-old thatched pub has a cobbled frontage and dismounting block, and the quite spacious side lawn is prettily broken up by roses and flower beds. Inside, the three communicating comfortable rooms have a warm, bustling atmosphere and deep sofas, well cushioned settles, Windsor chairs, some rush-seat dining-chairs and open fires. Decorations include military prints on dark panelling in one room, a glass case containing a remnant from the Houses of Parliament salvaged after it was hit by a bomb in the Second World War, and an Edwardian print by Goodwin Kilburne of a hunt meeting outside the pub. Bar food includes wholemeal sandwiches, lasagne or moussaka (£2.25), kofta curry (£2.50), fresh plaice (£2.95), and home-made steak and kidney pie or scampi (£3.25). Well kept Robinsons Best and Mild on electric pump. *(Recommended by Mr and Mrs J H Adam, W D Horsfield, Simon Barber, Graham Gibson, John Estdale, Jon Wainwright)*

Robinsons   Licensees Ana and Jorge Masso   Meals (not Sat evening or Sun lunchtime) and snacks (sandwiches only Sat evening and Sun lunchtime)   Restaurant tel Lower Peover (056 581) 2338   Children in coffee lounge next to dining-room   Open 11–3, 5.30–11 all year

POTT SHRIGLEY   SJ9479 Map 7
Cheshire Hunt ⊗

At end of B5091 in Bollington, where main road bends left at Turners Arms, fork straight ahead off it into Ingersley Road to follow Rainow signpost, then up hill take left turn signposted Pott Shrigley; OS Sheet 118 reference 945782

Originally an early eighteenth-century farmhouse and then an upland cattle-auction centre, this isolated stone building has several small rooms that ramble up and down steps and are unified by the flowery carpet that spreads throughout. There are spindle-back and wheel-back chairs, solidly built small winged settles, sturdy rustic tables, plates on a high Delft shelf, and beams and black joists. This is a meeting place for the N E Cheshire Drag Hunt, and besides numerous hunt photographs there are hunting-scene curtains, with hunting prints and a hunting crop on the walls. Food is an important draw here, and includes soup (95p), garlic mushrooms (£1.15), seafood pancakes (£2.10 starter, £4.95 main course), steak sandwich (£4), vegetarian bake (£4.95), lots of steaks (from £5.95, twenty-ounce T-bone £9), trout stuffed with celery, walnuts and crab (£6.10), beef Stroganoff (£6.30), with daily specials such as coq au vin (£2.20) or ham in leek sauce (£2.25), and quite a wide choice of puddings (£1.10) including wonderful raspberry Pavlova (£1.40); at lunchtime there are also sandwiches (from 95p), children's dishes (from £1.10), ploughman's (£2.10) and omelettes (from £2.95); get there early if you want a table. Well kept Boddingtons on handpump and electric pump, decent house wines, and lots of liqueurs; courteous service, piped radio music; well dressed customers. Picnic-table sets on a flagstoned terrace look down over the pastures, and there's a children's play area. *(Recommended by Dr and Mrs R J Ashleigh, M A and W R Proctor, Brian and Anna Marsden)*

Free house   Licensee R A Wherity   Real ale   Meals and snacks   Open 11–3, 5.30–11; considering opening all day; closed 25 Dec

RAINOW   SJ9576 Map 7
Highwayman ★

Above village, a mile along A5002 towards Whaley Bridge

Alone on its perch overlooking the Cheshire Plain, this welcoming early seven-teenth-century pub has a series of cosy little rooms, each with its own coal fire in winter. There are low beams, some antique settles as well as simpler cushioned seats around rustic wooden tables, and a high copper-covered bar counter serving well kept Thwaites on handpump. Good value food includes sandwiches and filled barm-cakes, home-made soup, black pudding, savoury pancake rolls, a choice of half a dozen freshly made pizzas, breaded plaice, freshly roasted chicken and scampi; friendly service; darts, fruit machine. From the front terrace, and from the small windows of the pub itself, there are the same marvellous views; on fine summer evenings or weekends it gets quite crowded (when parking nearby may not be easy). *(Recommended by Ian Briggs, Doug Kennedy, M A and W R Proctor, Bob and Val Collman, Dr and Mrs R J Ashleigh, Jon Wainwright, Paul Corbett, Brian and Anna Marsden)*

Thwaites Real ale Meals and snacks Children in snug Open 12–3, 6–11

SANDBACH   SJ7661 Map 7
Old Hall

1¼ miles from M6 junction 17; Sandbach signposted from junction exit; hotel in Newcastle Road just outside centre

The comfortable Jacobean oak-panelled lounge in this handsome black and white timbered hotel has a soft low button-back sofa in front of the handsomely carved fireplace with Staffordshire statuettes on its mantelpiece, wall banquettes and tapestried chairs, black beams, books on the bookshelves, and attractive pictures. A Turkey carpet sweeps through from here into the communicating bar, which has comfortable but more modern furnishings, a cheery atmosphere and piped music. Bar food includes home-made soup (£1.10), sandwiches (£1.20, toasted £1.45), ploughman's or pâté (£2.75), plaice or omelettes (£3.55), brunch (£4.35), pork chop (£4.65) and sirloin steak (£7.15); well kept Boddingtons and Youngers Scotch on handpump or tapped from the cask; friendly service. There are fine carved gable-ends and – for its age, over three centuries – remarkably big windows. The large garden has some tables and chairs. *(Recommended by Brian and Anna Marsden, E G Parish)*

Free house   Licensee Frank Ribeiro   Real ale   Meals and snacks (lunchtime only, not Sun) Handsome Jacobean restaurant (lunchtime only on Sun)   Children welcome   Open all day Bedrooms tel Crewe (0270) 761221; £32.50B/£45B

SUTTON   SJ9271 Map 7
Sutton Hall Hotel ★ ⊗ 🛏

Leaving Macclesfield southwards on A523, turn left into Byrons Lane signposted Langley, Wincle, then just before canal viaduct fork right into Bullocks Lane; OS Sheet 118 reference 925715

Tall black timbers divide the separate areas of the civilised bar in this secluded country hotel, and though furnishings are mainly straightforward ladder-back chairs around sturdy thick-topped cast-iron-framed tables, it gets a good deal of character from several unusual touches. These include the lightly patterned art nouveau stained-glass windows, an enormous bronze bell for calling time, the brass cigar-lighting gas taper on the bar counter itself, antique squared oak panelling, and an open fire, raised a couple of feet, at the end of the bar counter (which is surrounded by broad flagstones – there's carpet elsewhere); also, a longcase clock, a suit of armour by another substantial stone fireplace, and raj fans circling slowly in the lofty ceiling. The atmosphere is warmly welcoming and stylishly pubby. A limited but good range of bar food, kindly served by neatly uniformed waitresses, might include home-made soup (£1.25), open sandwiches (from £1.55), smoked mackerel or chicken liver pâté (£2.75 starter, £3.65 main course), big ploughman's (£3.65), tagliatelle with ham, mushrooms, tomatoes and cream or vegetable kebabs with yoghurt, cucumber and mint dip (£3.95), steak and kidney pie, kebabs or seafood bake (£4.55), and puddings (£1.75). Reliably well kept Bass and Mild, Marstons Burton and Stones Best on handpump; decent wines. There are tables on a tree-sheltered lawn, overlooked by the worn black figures carved into the timbering of one black and white wing – the rest of the house is stone-built. *(Recommended by Laurence Manning, Dr and Mrs R J Ashleigh, Brian and Anna Marsden, M A and W R Proctor)*

Free house   Licensee Robert Bradshaw   Real ale   Meals and snacks   Restaurant   Children welcome weekend and bank hol lunchtimes only   Open all day   Four-poster bedrooms tel Sutton (026 05) 3211; £46.75B/£60B

TARPORLEY   SJ5563   Map 7
Rising Sun ⊗

High Street; village signposted off A51 Nantwich–Chester

Unashamedly a village pub, this is where you'll find the local cricketers or bowls team winding down after a match. There are character seats including creaky nineteenth-century mahogany and oak settles around the well chosen tables, low ceilings with a good few beams (especially in the front room), an attractively blacked iron kitchen range, a big oriental rug in the back room, and sporting and other old-fashioned prints. Lunchtime bar food includes soup (85p), sandwiches or filled baked potatoes (from £1), home-made cottage pie (£2), steak and kidney pie (£2.25), scampi (£2.50), salads (from £2.05), gammon and egg (£2.95) and chicken chasseur (£3.15); the evening sees concentration instead on full meals, with starters such as pâté-stuffed mushrooms (£1.50) and main dishes from home-made lasagne or steak and kidney pie (£2.65) through gammon and egg or a half-chicken (£2.95), to steaks (from eight-ounce sirloin £4.75) and a vigorous mixed grill (£5.25). Well kept Robinsons Best and Mild on handpump, friendly service; fruit machine, maybe unobtrusive background music, three open fires. *(Recommended by Jon Wainwright, Tony Ritson, John Innes, E G Parish, Laurence Manning, Wayne Brindle)*

Robinsons   Licensee Alec Robertson   Real ale   Meals and snacks (not Sun evening) Children in restaurant (lunchtime)   Restaurant tel Tarporley (082 93) 2423   Open 11–3, 5.30–11 all year

WRENBURY   SJ5948   Map 7
Dusty Miller

Village signposted from A530 Nantwich–Whitchurch

The picnic-table sets outside this handsome ten-year-old conversion of an early nineteenth-century mill are on a gravel terrace among rose bushes by the Llangollen Canal; they're reached either by the towpath or by a high wooden catwalk above the little River Weaver which used to drive the mill's side wheel (and before that drove the underpass wheel of a sixteenth-century mill built over the stream for Combermere Abbey). Inside, it's comfortably modern: tapestried banquettes and wheel-back chairs flank dark brown rustic tables in the carpeted main bit, with long low hunting prints on the white walls; a series of tall glazed arches faces the water, with russet velvet curtains. At the back, there's a quarry-tiled standing-only area by the bar counter, which has well kept Robinsons Best and Mild on handpump; piped music. A wide choice of bar food includes soup (85p), open sandwiches (from £1.25), pear with tarragon cream (£1.75), salads (from £2.55), garlic mushrooms (£2.75), chicken (from £3.15), scampi or vegetarian lasagne (£3.95), gammon (£4.75) and steaks (from £6.25); also, daily specials such as game, fish or pork and apricot pies (£4.25) or fresh salmon with hollandaise sauce (£5.95), children's dishes (from £1.45), and home-made puddings. The licensee notches up various awards – including most recently regional Innkeeper of the Year in a trade competition. *(Recommended by Wayne Brindle, CH and others; more reports please)*

Robinsons   Licensee Robert Lloyd-Jones   Real ale   Meals and snacks   Upstairs restaurant tel Nantwich (0270) 780537 (not Sun evening)   Children in restaurant   Open all day in summer, possibly winter too; closed 25 Dec

Lucky Dip

Besides the fully inspected pubs, you might like to try these Lucky Dips recommended to us and described by readers (if you do, please send us reports):

Adlington [Wood Lanes; by Middlewood Way linear park, and Macclesfield Canal – OS Sheet 109 reference 936818; SJ9180], *Miners Arms*: Popular pub with well kept Boddingtons Mild and Bitter, in nice spot by canal; food lunchtime and evening, and new extension relieves pressure on space and the Middlewood Way linear park *(Brian and Anna Marsden)*

Alderley Edge [about 250 yds past Royal Oak, down alley on right; SJ8478], *Moss Rose*: Down an alleyway and extended into the terrace cottages, with its own bowling-green *(Graham Gibson)*

Alsager [SJ7956], *Old Mill*: Friendly welcome, good food lunchtime and evening, relatively quiet lounge with downstairs games-room for younger people, well kept Boddingtons *(Reg Williamson)*; [Sandbach Rd (north)] *Wilbraham Arms*: Good choice of good value food in generous helpings, and very good puddings, in busy and attractive pub with pleasant service *(P C Goodwin and friends)*

Ashton [B5393; SJ5169], *Golden Lion*: Pleasant village pub, well furnished three-tiered lounge with many pictures for sale, well kept Greenalls Original, friendly golden labrador *(Jon Wainwright)*

Astbury [SJ8461], *Egerton Arms*: Charmingly placed pub with lovely views of church in pretty village – spring daffodils on green; bar food including imaginative vegetarian dishes, friendly service, good Robinsons on handpump including Mild; restaurant; bedrooms comfortable *(Sue Holland, Dave Webster)*

Audlem [The Square; junction A529/A525; SJ6644], *Lord Combermere*: Interesting pub full of bric-à-brac; well kept McEwans 70/- on handpump and a good range of spirits *(Graham Gibson)*; [Audlem Wharf – OS Sheet 118 reference 658436] *Shroppie Fly*: Named after the narrowboats using the Shropshire Union Canal, and looking out over one of the long flight of locks here; mainly modern furnishings, one bar shaped like a barge, good canal photographs, collection of brightly painted bargees' china and bric-à-brac, seats on waterside terrace; simple food, friendly service, well kept Boddingtons and Marstons Pedigree on handpump, children in room off bar and in restaurant *(Graham Gibson, Sally Kibble, HLH, JAH, LYM)*

Barbridge [by A51 to Chester, some ¾ miles N of Nantwich; SJ6156], *Barbridge*: Popular with holidaymakers on the canal longboats (which can be moored virtually outside the dining-room), this pub has friendly and cheerful service and good value hot meals with daily specials such as duck soup and venison in red wine; Boddingtons and Hig-

sons on handpump *(E G Parish, Peter Corris)*

Bell O' Th' Hill [signposted from A41 Whitchurch–Chester; SJ5245], *Bluebell*: Comfortable series of rooms in Greenalls pub with one main bar, popular for food lunchtime and evening; pleasant young licensees, cheap house wine, some vegetarian and other interesting dishes *(Jane Kearley)*

☆ **Bickerton** [Bulkeley – A534 E of junction with A41; SJ5052], *Bickerton Poacher*: Attractive sheltered barbecue courtyard (summer Fri and Sat evenings, Sun lunchtime), with lots of live music and special events; traditionally furnished rambling rooms inside, Marstons Pedigree and other real ales – sometimes up to five; bar food; money thrown into the well with the skeleton is collected for charity; skittle alley – rare up here; children welcome; service can be slow *(Jon Wainwright, Graham Gibson, LYM)*

Bollington [SJ9377], *Church House*: Small, friendly pub with well kept Theakstons and Ruddles and good bar food *(Dr and Mrs R J Ashleigh)*

Boothdale [OS Sheet 117 reference 530673; SJ5367], *Boot*: Nice relaxing country pub tucked away on hillside, good views of lush farmland and hedgerows, well kept Greenalls, model of penny-farthing made from pennies set into one wall, bar food *(Jon Wainwright)*

Bosley [Leek Rd (A523); SJ9266], *Harrington Arms*: Spacious and comfortable former Yates wine lodge with Robinsons Best Mild and Best Bitter on handpump, longcase clock, roaring fires, bar food and rock-and-roll nights *(Graham Gibson)*

Buglawton [A54; SJ8763], *Church House*: Agricultural and horticultural theme with scythes and sickles; bar snacks and Robinsons Best Mild and Best Bitter on electric pump; plenty of room outside where a lawn mower is used as a flower box and there are usually doves on the roof *(Graham Gibson)*; *Robin Hood*: Friendly landlord and staff, well kept beer and excellent food from sandwiches to steaks; children in dining-room *(ATC)*

Burleydam [A525 Whitchurch–Audlem; SJ6143], *Combermere Arms*: Rural pub, supposedly 450 years old and haunted; lots of fine woodwork, leaded windows, comfortable wall seating and other chairs and pretty patterned carpet; Bass, Marstons Pedigree, Springfield and Youngers on handpump, bar and restaurant food *(Graham Gibson)*

☆ **Chester** [Tower Wharf, Raymond St – behind Northgate St, nr rly], *Telfords Warehouse*: Attractive open-plan conversion of abandoned warehouse credited architecturally to Thomas Telford, overlooking Shropshire Union Canal basin; pleasing new-wood furniture, well kept Matthew Browns and Theakstons Old Peculier, good lunchtime cheeses and pâtés, loudspeaker food-announcement system; steps down to cellar wine bar, steps up to restaurant area; phone in red telephone box *(Jon Wainwright, Peter Corris, G Gibson)*

Chester [Park St; by Roman Walls, off Albion St], *Albion*: Three rooms, one dominated by wartime advertising plates (including one asking for scrap to make bullets), one with a large mangle and piano, one for darts and TV; open fire, good value food (especially curry), Greenalls Local and well kept Original on handpump; right by Roman Walls, with hypocaust on other side *(Jon Wainwright)*; [Lower Bridge St] *Bear & Billet*: Notable for the fantastic timbering outside; a good deal of potential, and news awaited since Watneys' sale of long lease last year *(Anon)*; [Garden Lane (off A540)] *Bouverie*: Friendly bustling local with narrow tap-room and bigger lounge with prints of old Chester; full range of Greenalls beers on electric pump or handpump, bar food including speciality hot-pot with red cabbage *(Graham Gibson)*; [Foregate St/Frodsham St] *City Arms*: Bright, clean and friendly, set out in three theme areas – bookshop, toys and apothecary/haberdasher's; well kept Greenalls and Davenports, good range of hot and cold bar food at attractive prices *(Mr and Mrs J H Adam, I Brocklehurst, H R Edwards)*; [Bridge St] *Clavertons*: Popular Lees pub/wine bar, nicely furnished, subdued lighting; good lunchtime bar food; busy with young people at night *(Peter Corris)*; [Watergate St] *Custom House*: Plenty of high-backed settles, big wooden tables, curiously mirrored beam, well kept Border Bitter and Marstons Pedigree, reasonably priced lunchtime meals (popular with business folk), very friendly service, good chatty locals – most appealing friendliness with young and old mixing well, unobtrusive piped music; back dining-room crammed with porcelain and brassware *(Jon Wainwright)*; [Westgate Row N] *Deva*: Nicely restored – there's been a pub on this spot since about 1637 *(Wayne Brindle)*; [Lower Bridge St] *Kings Head*: Good food at lunchtime in very old listed building with beams and large fireplace *(I Brocklehurst)*; [Eastgate Row N] *Old Boot*: In Chester's attractive seventeenth-century centre – opens off a first-floor balconied arcade; taken over by Sam Smiths and though the elaborate redevelopments have been taking a long time this is always worth watching – especially its bar down the long entry corridor *(Jon Wainwright, LYM)*; [Northgate St] *Pied Bull*: Quiet, in the heart of the city, and attractive though less old than many pubs in the Rows *(Wayne Brindle)*; [99 Boughton (A51)] *Royal Oak*: Quaint old early eighteenth-century pub with copper-topped tables, tap-room

and lounge with comic hunting scenes, full range of Greenalls beers on handpump, lunchtime sandwiches, juke box, fruit machine, garden *(Graham Gibson)*; [Watergate St] *Watergates*: Wine bar (alas beers are pricey lagers, besides Murphys stout) newly fitted into interesting medieval vaulted cellar formerly used for wines; closed Sun, maybe other times *(Jon Wainwright)*

Christleton [Plough Lane – OS Sheet 117 reference 454653; SJ4466], *Plough*: The atmosphere is the main appeal thanks to lively landlord and landlady, though the older part has interesting window seat, wooden partitioning, hanging kettles, brasses and so forth; Greenalls beers, small beer garden with children's play area *(Jon Wainwright)*; [Laneside (off A41)] *Ring o' Bells*: Pleasantly refurbished big pub with some very comfortable settees and so forth in the lounge, Bass and Stones Best on handpump, old prints, grandfather clock, good range of hot and cold bar food; how nice to find car park spaces reserved for disabled people *(Graham Gibson, Mr and Mrs J H Adam)*

Church Lawton [A34 – OS Sheet 118 reference 828552; SJ8155], *Red Bull*: Seats in garden overlooking lock on Trent and Mersey Canal, cheerful atmosphere in several well set out and well furnished rooms; attractive bar food from hot buffet, Robinsons real ales *(J H M Broughton)*

Churton [Farndon Rd (B5130); SJ4256], *White Horse*: Small village pub with fine atmosphere and friendly service, lots of bric-à-brac especially miners' and other lamps hanging from ceiling, three connecting bars with copper-topped tables, Bass on handpump, lunchtime and evening bar food, pool-table *(Peter Corris, Graham Gibson)*

☆ Comberbach [SJ6477], *Spinner & Bergamot*: Always a good welcome and pleasant service in this bright, cheerful pub – spotless, with three open fires, lots of gleaming brass and flowers inside, flower tubs and hanging baskets out; good varied bar meals – steak and kidney pie and scampi with outstanding home-made batter particularly recommended; well kept Greenalls; own bowling-green *(J H M Broughton, HLH, JAH, Jon Wainwright, D P Manchett, Syd and Wyn Donald)*

Congleton [Willow St (A54); SJ8663], *Grapes*: Small and friendly, Tetleys Bitter and Mild on handpump, bar food; furthest room round to the right of the bar is absolutely festooned with bric-à-brac, and there's an open range where baked potatoes are cooked; pool-room on left, garden; children welcome *(Graham Gibson)*; [outside town, off A34 S] *Great Moreton Hall*: More a hotel and restaurant than pub, but well worth visiting for its setting, grounds and décor – restored to perfection; comfortable bedrooms *(M A and W R Proctor)*

Cotebrook [A49 N of Tarporley – OS Sheet 117 reference 570651; SJ5765], *Alvanley Arms*: Big helpings of reliably well cooked food with fresh vegetables, lunchtime and evening, in two lounge bars and restaurant; prices above many pubs but well worth the extra; pleasant atmosphere, prompt friendly service *(C F Walling, Dr P Webb)*

Crewe [Nantwich Rd (A534), nr rly stn; SJ7056], *Crewe Arms*: Perhaps the town's most attractive building, very ornate inside with marble tables and fireplace surroundings, comfortable furnishings and alabaster naked female figures; meals, Tetleys on handpump; bedrooms *(Graham Gibson)*

Croft [left just after the Noggin, right at next T-junction; SJ6393], *Horseshoe*: Friendly staff, well kept Tetleys and good lunchtime food – especially the fish and chips *(Simon Turner)*

Cuddington [Warrington Rd; SJ6072], *White Barn*: Recently refurbished, pleasant atmosphere and well kept beer *(Neil Allcock)*

Dean Row [SJ8781], *Unicorn*: Comfortable pub with generous helpings of good home-cooked food including fine steak and kidney pie; pleasant staff and particularly well kept Boddingtons beer *(Mr and Mrs A W Hartwell, J Russell)*

Disley [Mudhurst Lane, Higher Disley – off old Buxton rd; SJ9784], *Moorside*: Isolated hotel with superb views across to Stockport and Manchester; tiled bar, fruit machines, compartment seating, Watneys-related beers on handpump, bar food and restaurant; bedrooms *(Graham Gibson)*

Dodleston [turn right on A483 from Chester at Pulford – then 1½ miles; SJ3661], *Red Lion*: A listed building, most attractive inside and out *(Peter Corris)*

Eaton [A536 Congleton–Macclesfield; SU8765], *Plough*: Now the only pub of Clive Winkle (the former brewer); nicely renovated with lead windows and beams; Banks's Best and Mild on handpump and good bar food that includes sirloin steak done in five different ways *(Graham Gibson)*; [Manchester Rd (A34 Congleton–Wilmslow)] *Waggon & Horses*: Roaring log fire, menu chalked up on board and Robinsons Best Mild and Best Bitter on handpump; children's room *(Graham Gibson)*

Farndon [High St (A534 E of Wrexham); SJ4254], *Greyhound*: Bright, clean pub with model ships, open fire, paintings depicting cats as customers and a lovely carpet; Greenalls Best, Mild and Original on handpump and food that may include wild salmon; no meals Sat evening or Sun lunchtime; two cats, two dogs and (in field behind) two donkeys; bedrooms *(Graham Gibson)*

Farnworth [Lunts Heath Rd, nr Black Horse roundabout; SJ5187], *Church View*: Brick and wood bar in attractive pub with nicely varnished beams, log-effect gas fires and brasses; Greenalls Bitter and Mild on handpump *(Graham Gibson)*

Fivecrosses [B5152 Frodsham–Kingsley; SJ5376], *Travellers Rest*: Superb view across the Weaver Valley is the reason for mentioning this pub with nautical theme, ship's wheel hanging from ceiling, two coal fires, dining area, Greenalls Mild and Bitter on handpump *(Anon)*

Gawsworth [SJ8969], *Harrington Arms*: Basic farm pub with tree-trunk tables outside and rudimentary comforts in; the narrow bar room formerly had splendid series of wooden-screened rooms with service through curtained hatch and fine carved bar counter, but though building is listed has been disappointingly opened up, with open fireplaces closed off and considerable loss of character; well kept Robinsons Best and Best Mild on handpump *(Phil and Sally Gorton, Lee Goulding, LYM)*

Glazebury [opp Bents Garden Centre, OS Sheet 109 reference 672976; SJ6796], *Foresters Arms*: Well run spotless local with good snug atmosphere, lots of brass, jugs and so forth, well kept Tetleys, commendably cheap bar meals in spotless surroundings *(G T Jones, Alan and Marlene Radford)*

Grappenhall [Church Lane (off A50); SJ6486], *Rams Head*: One of the most attractive interiors in the county – fine woodwork, leaded windows like those of a church; Greenalls Bitter and Mild on handpump; ornate inn-sign *(Graham Gibson)*

Guilden Sutton [SJ4568], *Bird in Hand*: Recently refurbished Whitbreads village local, tastefully decorated; well kept Castle Eden on handpump and good value bar food; children up to 8pm *(Peter Corris)*

Hartford [opp stn; SJ6472], *Coachmans*: Good food, well kept Greenalls, superbly comfortable refurbishments *(John Renwick)*

Haslington [A534; SJ7456], *Hawk*: On an outside timber of this Tudor pub are the words 'a jug of ale, a whispering word can be found within these walls – the Hawk Inn, be it known of good ale and dry stables'; lots of brasses, two guns behind the bar, some swords, an original door and a log fire; charming low-ceilinged dining-room and bar snacks with lunchtime specials; Robinsons Best and Mild on electric pump *(Graham Gibson)*

Hatchmere [B5152 (off A556 at Abbey Arms); SJ5672], *Carriers*: One of Cheshire's friendliest landlords, always has a pleasant word for both locals and strangers, in pleasantly placed pub with terrace overlooking Hatchmere Lake (noted for pike fishing); tap-room and two-level lounge, Burtonwood Bitter and Mild on handpump, good value Sun lunch, old brewery photographs *(Graham Gibson)*

Heatley [Rushgreen Rd; SJ7088], *Farmers Arms*: Very friendly and well kept, excellent range of cheap bar food *(David and Amanda Watts)*

High Legh [A50; SJ7084], *Bears Paw*: Attractive little country pub with lots of bric-à-brac – plates, bedwarmers, old prints, horns, stuffed fox and so forth; Greenalls Bitter, bar food, open fire; outside drinking area, children's play area *(Graham Gibson)*

Holmes Chapel [19 London Rd (handy for M6 junction 18); SJ7667], *Olde Red Lion*: Welcoming, comfortable and warm pub with home-cooked food and no music *(John Shirley)*; [Station Rd] *Swan*: Bright, clean and comfortable Sam Smiths pub with red plush seating, lots of bric-à-brac including horseshoes, plates, old prints and photographs; well kept OB on handpump and bar food lunchtime and evening, darts *(Graham Gibson, John Hayward, Jon Wainwright)*

Hoo Green [A50, a mile NW of A556; SJ7283], *Kilton*: Well refurbished and nicely kept – particularly good for lunch *(G T Jones)*

Hooton [A41; SJ3678], *Chimneys*: Fine gothic-style hotel, giant fork and spoon hang from beams and clock shaped like key in public bar; Bass, Boddingtons and Stones Best on handpump; grill-room, dining-room; bedrooms £35 *(Graham Gibson)*

Huxley [off A51 SE of Chester; SJ5162], *Farmers Arms*: Pleasant traditional small-roomed beamed pub with friendly landlord and staff, well kept Greenalls, good choice of food – cooked to order, so delays when very busy, but worth waiting for *(Paul Denham)*

Kelsall [SJ5268], *Morris Dancers*: Unspoilt good value pub with a tremendous friendly atmosphere; plain, wholesome food, well kept Greenalls Local and Original, lots of keys hanging from black beams, maybe morris dancers or folk music, darts and pool in back room, dogs and cockatiel *(G T Jones, Jon Wainwright)*

Kent Green [SJ8357], *Bird in Hand*: Little one-room unspoilt – even a bit clannish – local by Macclesfield Canal, beer brought in jug from cellar (though in fact keg Worthington BB), open fire; dominoes and darts *(JRP)*

Knutsford [Tatton St (off A50 at White Bear roundabout); SJ7578], *Lord Eldon*: Unspoilt and attractive, four connecting rooms served by two bars with Websters and Wilsons on handpump, bar food, darts, open fire and toby jugs; used to be called the Duke of Wellington *(Graham Gibson)*

Little Budworth [A54; SJ5966], *Shrewsbury Arms*: Cheerful and welcoming pub with open fire, Robinsons Mild and Bitter, good bar food, restaurant *(J H M Broughton)*

Little Leigh [A49; SJ6276], *Leigh Arms*: Popular mock-Tudor pub in pleasant setting with tasty snacks and country wines *(Wayne Brindle)*

Lower Peover [Crown Lane; SJ7474], *Crown*: Good all-round country pub with very varied choice of delicious and reasonably priced food; comfortable, warm and friendly, with

good mix of visitors and locals – all ages; pleasant piped music *(Yvonne and Don Johnson)*

Lymm [Eagle Brow, nr M6 junction 20; SJ6787], *Spread Eagle*: Pleasantly redecorated village pub with friendly regulars, good range of bar food, Lees real ales, weekly jazz *(G T Jones, David and Amanda Watts)*

nr Macclesfield [A537 Macclesfield–Buxton – OS Sheet 119 reference 001719; SJ9273], *Cat and Fiddle*: Britain's 2nd-highest pub, with splendid views over the surrounding spectacular moorland; sensitively enlarged with spacious and comfortable lounge, roomy public bar, well kept Robinsons real ales, bar food *(Rob and Gill Weeks, John Atherton, Brian and Anna Marsden, Graham Gibson, Ian Briggs, Bob and Val Collman, LYM)*

Malpas [High St; SJ4947], *Red Lion*: Marstons real ales on handpump, pool-room, juke box and even a sauna; bedrooms *(Graham Gibson)*

Marton [Manchester Rd (A34 N of Congleton); SJ8568], *Davenport Arms*: Unpretentious but comfortably modernised Wilsons pub with quite an extensive range of good home-cooked food (done by ex-NHS catering manager) including outstanding omelettes and good apple pie; Watneys-related real ales, open fires, darts, country and western evenings; garden with children's play area *(T P C Mulholland, Gerald Hixon)*

Mickle Trafford [A56; SJ4569], *Shrewsbury Arms*: Pleasant relaxed atmosphere, Whitbreads real ales, real home-cooked hot and cold food lunchtime and evening, large car park and garden *(Andrew Rice)*

Mobberley [Wilsons Mill Lane; SJ7879], *Bulls Head*: Friendly and comfortable low-beamed village pub with soft lighting, well kept Jennings and Tetleys real ale, folk-singing landlord and own immaculate bowling-green *(Jon Wainwright, Lee Goulding, BB)*; [Faulkners Lane – OS Sheet 118 reference 782802] *Frozen Mop*: Notable for the very many reproductions of paintings lining its long walls; good fairly new décor and furniture in this food pub; keg beer *(Jon Wainwright)*; *Plough & Flail*: Good food and well kept Boddingtons and Marstons in well kept friendly pub, attractively extended and refurbished, with extensive gardens *(Neil Alcock, Ian Briggs)*

Moore [Runcorn Rd (A558); SJ5784], *Red Lion*: Nice Greenalls village pub shaded by great beech tree, in attractive Bridgewater Canal village; very popular annual folk day – usually St George's Day (23 Apr) *(Jon Wainwright)*

Mow Cop [Station Rd – OS Sheet 118 reference 854574; SJ8557], *Cheshire View*: What marks out this friendly and simply furnished pub is its tremendous bird's-eye view of the Cheshire Plain; Marstons real ales, bar food *(Jon Wainwright, LYM)*

Nantwich [centre, almost opp W end of church; SJ6552], *Crown*: Striking timbered Elizabethan inn with rambling beamed and timbered bar, comfortably modernised; Ind Coope Burton and Tetleys on handpump, reasonable bar food, quiet at lunchtime but can get very busy with young people in the evenings (when pop music may be loud); restaurant; bedrooms very comfortable and characterful if a bit aged *(Charlie Salt, Jon Wainwright, Wayne Brindle, LYM)*; [Hospital St (by side passage to central church)] *Lamb*: Lovely flower-decked old pub whose pleasantly sedate atmosphere and high standard of service, food in bar and restaurant and drink have – to the personal knowledge of this reader – been hallmarks for over 40 years; previous good licensee moved to Swan at Tarporley late 1987; more news please *(E G Parish)*; *Vine*: Excellent Burtonwood ale, very friendly locals, very hospitable licensees; settles and straight-backed chairs *(Charlie Salt)*

Neston [19 Quayside; SW of town – OS Sheet 117 reference 290760; SJ2978], *Harp*: Great potential, lovely position (despite nearby housing estate) with uninterrupted Dee saltmarsh views to distant mountains, very pleasant licensee, Whitbreads real ale, cheap bar snacks – though interior unremarkable *(Anon)*

Norley [Pytchleys Hollow; SJ5773], *Tigers Head*: Pleasantly restored seventeenth-century country pub with coal fires, tiger's head mounted on wall, and formerly popular for good bar food, with decent wines – but new licensees in 1988, more news please *(Mrs V West, Jon Wainwright, G Gibson)*

North Rode [A536 4m from Macclesfield on a disused loop of road; SJ8966], *Chain & Gate*: Quiet pub with genial landlord and two roomy bars, well kept Marstons including Owd Rodger, good lunchtime food, juke box or maybe hi-fi piped music *(T P C Mulholland)*

Over Peover [Parkgate; SJ7874], *Parkgate*: Cheerful pub with good village atmosphere, good range of bar food – particularly salads *(J Walsh)*; [Stocks Lane (A50) – OS Sheet 118 reference 767746], *Whipping Stocks*: Lots of fine panelling and leaded windows in popular and comfortable country pub with good meals and snacks, well kept Sam Smiths OB on handpump (and freshly squeezed orange juice), fresh flowers, pot plants and brasses; pool-room, children's play area; good walk to Over Peover church and hall *(Graham Gibson, G T Jones, Robert and Claudia Lynch)*

Parkgate [The Parade; SJ2878 – this is the one in the Wirral], *Red Lion*: Old-fashioned pub with charming landlady, well kept Tetleys and Walkers, good bar food; lounge, men's bar and darts-room with fruit machine; hasn't moved with the times – which is part of its charm *(D P Manchett)*

Prestbury [SJ9077], *Admiral Rodney*: Very comfortably and stylishly refurbished, welcoming, with well kept Robinsons ales and good range of bar food *(Mr and Mrs J H Adam, Wayne Brindle)*

Puddington [A540, nr A550 junction; SJ3373], *Yacht*: Nicely decorated with pleasant atmosphere and good choice of beers and food *(Mr and Mrs J H Adam)*

Rainow [SJ9576], *Rising Sun*: Comfortable local with Burtonwood and Marstons on handpump, bar food, low prices *(Simon Turner)*

Risley [Gorse Covert Shopping Precinct – nr M62 junction 11; SJ6592], *Poacher*: Big Tetleys pub useful for good value bar food *(Simon Turner)*

Runcorn [SJ5183], *Prospect*: Well kept Greenalls real ale – a popular ICI lunching haunt *(Anon)*; [Heath Rd South, Weston (off A557)] *Royal Oak*: Another ICI lunching place – this one with well kept Marstons *(Anon)*

Smallwood [SJ8160], *Legs of Man*: Clean, warm and welcoming place with very good value real food cooked by excellent Dutch owner; very pleasant wife and enthusiastic staff in bar *(C A Foden, G Atkinson)*

Stoak [OS Sheet 117 reference 423734; SJ4273], *Bunbury Arms*: Pleasant flagstoned main bar decorated with stuffed fish, good value bar lunches, well kept Boddingtons and Higsons, handy for Chester Zoo *(Jon Wainwright)*

Sutton [Higher Sutton (this is the one nr Macclesfield); SJ9271], *Ryles Arms*: Attractive stone pub by picturesque country lane, variety of comfortable chairs and settees, friendly welcome, very popular range of reasonably priced food; pretty garden *(M A and W R Proctor)*

Swettenham [off A54 Congleton–Holmes Chapel or A535 Chelford–Holmes Chapel; SJ8067], *Swettenham Arms*: Very prettily placed in tucked-away village, behind church; well kept Watneys-related real ales in carefully restored beamed bar with highly polished old-fashioned furnishings, three open fires, and seats outside; may be closed weekday lunchtimes *(Brian and Anna Marsden, Graham Richardson, Jon Wainwright, Graham Gibson, LYM)*

Tarporley [High St; SJ5563], *Swan*: Georgian hotel with engaging traditionally furnished flagstoned bar (formerly the kitchen – there's still a bread over by the log fire); Greenalls Local on handpump, bar food (not Sun lunchtime), restaurant; children in eating area and restaurant; now under new management – more news please *(Wayne Brindle, Laurence Manning, Ian Gordon, Jon Wainwright, LYM)*

nr **Tattenhall** [Whitchurch Rd, Broxton (nr junction A534/A41); SJ4959], *Broxton Hall*: Well run eighteenth-century hotel with pictures depicting the months hanging in the bar, spotless dining-room, comfortable residents' lounge, extensive gardens; good, interesting food, Websters on handpump; bedrooms *(Graham Gibson)*; [Broxton, junction A534/A41 – OS Sheet 117 reference 480532], *Egerton Arms*: Popular black and white pub with good food and beer; cosy atmosphere, excellent restaurant; bedrooms *(E G Parish)*

Tiverton [Wharton's Lock (Bates Mill Lane) – OS Sheet 117 reference 532603; SJ5660], *Shady Oak*: Now a Chef & Brewer pub, with less wide choice of food than when a main entry – but still reasonable; lovely position in open countryside by Shropshire Union Canal, with plenty of seats and good play area in waterside garden and terrace; airy inside, with lounge opening into carpeted conservatory; well kept Websters and Wilsons, fine views of the Peckforton hills; juke box may be rather loud; summer barbecues *(Jon Wainwright, Graham Gibson, LYM)*

Tushingham [old A41; SJ5346], *Blue Bell*: Striking fifteenth-century black and white pub, lots of old beams, Greenalls Original on handpump *(Graham Gibson)*

Walker Barn [A537 Macclesfield–Buxton; SJ9573], *Setter Dog*: Plainly but pleasantly enlarged country pub, Marstons real ale, good open fire to contrast with bleakly windswept view across Macclesfield; more reports on current bar food, please *(J R Pye, M A and W R Proctor)*

Walleys Green [Wimboldsley; A530 Middlewich–Crewe, about 200 yds from main rly line – OS Sheet 118 map reference 684621; SJ6861], *Verdin Arms*: Tastefully modernised country pub with a nice relaxing atmosphere and animal pictures, prints of Chester and a train on the walls; archways lead to different areas; real fires; Robinsons Best Mild and Best Bitter on electric pump and bar food that includes fresh fish *(Graham Gibson)*

Warmingham [Middlewich Rd; SJ7161], *Bears Paw*: Country pub with attractive solid wooden bar and nicely varnished wooden ceiling has switched to keg Whitbreads beers; usual run of pub food *(Anon)*

Warrington [Golden Sq; SJ6188], *Barley Mow*: Lovely timbered and low-beamed fifteenth-century building in new shopping precinct, open all day for coffee, tea and so forth, and a place where a woman on her own can feel quite at home; Tetleys ales, food servery, can get crowded *(G T Jones, Graham Gibson, Peter Corris)*; [Bewsey Farm Cl (off A57/A574)] *Bewsey Farm*: Fairly new pub with very attractive open-plan bar: wall seating, part carpeted and part flagstoned floor, farming pictures, Boddingtons, Higsons and M&B on handpump; darts to one side of bar; outside drinking area *(Graham Gibson)*; [Horsemarket St] *Blue Bell*: Sadly this pub, highly rated in last year's Dip, has been gutted by Greenalls and turned into something more reminiscent of a chrome-and-glass ice-cream parlour, with very high

prices, under the name of T J Appletons Food and Drink Emporium *(Various disappointed readers)*; [Church St] *Ring o' Bells*: Pleasant rambling seventeenth-century pub adjacent to church with low beams, lots of fine panelling, full range of Greenalls ales, friendly atmosphere and good lunchtime bar food; darts, dominoes, juke box *(Graham Gibson, Peter Corris)*

☆ **nr Warrington** [Fiddlers Ferry; leaving Warrington on A562 towards Widnes, keep eyes open as you pass Harris Carpets in Penketh then turn left by Red Lion Cavalier Restaurant (Tetleys); in Tannery Lane turn left again into Station Rd, park by rly and walk across – about 50 yds; OS Sheet 108 reference 560863], *Ferry*: Picturesquely isolated between Manchester Ship Canal and Mersey, with comfortable easy chairs, old-fashioned settle and sofa as well as more modern seats in nautically decorated low-beamed bar, buffet bar food lunchtimes and Fri-Sat evenings, good river views, tables outside; provision for children, well kept Wilsons Original on handpump *(Graham Gibson, Chris Cooke, LYM)*

Weston [handy for M6 junction 16; SJ7352], *White Lion*: Typical seventeenth-century black and white Cheshire inn, expertly managed, with first-class meals in bars and restaurant, excellent service by polite staff, comfortable chairs and settles, pleasant atmosphere only some five mins' drive from M6 now motorway spur finished; recently added bedrooms blend in well *(E G Parish, Joy Heatherley)*

Whiteley Green [OS Sheet 118 reference 924789; SJ9278], *Windmill*: Big lawn prettily planted with shrub and flower borders, summer bar and barbecues – idyllic on a fine afternoon, in attractive countryside; comfortable seats around well spaced tables in spacious lounge with friendly staff, popular lunches in new carvery/bistro (children allowed here, open Sun afternoon too), well kept Boddingtons and Marstons Burton and Pedigree, cappuccino coffee, fruit machine; formerly a silk mill *(Brian and Anna Marsden, Mrs S Corrigan, Paul Corbett, BB)*

Wildboarclough [SJ9868], *Crag*: Sheltered valley pub surrounded by moorland, bar food, restaurant, pretty terrace; changed hands late 1987 – up-to-date news please *(LYM)*; [A54] *Wild Boar*: Very pleasant atmosphere with well kept beer and an excellent selection of home-made hot dishes *(Mr and Mrs J T Grayling, BB)*

Willaston [OS Sheet 117 reference 329777; SJ3378], *Pollards*: Striking building with two sandstone wings, central whitewashed part, biggish lawns and gardens – originally a fourteenth-century farmhouse; stone-floored bar on left has beams and high shelves, nice cushioned wall seats with some stone arm rests, French windows to garden, Greenalls Original on handpump; restaurant on right *(Jon Wainwright)*

Wilmslow [Swan St; SJ8481], *Swan*: Seventeenth-century pub with well kept Boddingtons, lunchtime bar food, evening restaurant meals running to shark and wood pigeon, good friendly service – splendid for an indulgent night out as it's just a stroll from the BR station *(John Gould)*

Wincle [SU9666], *Ship*: Sixteenth-century pub, said to be Cheshire's oldest; name due to local squire who sailed with Shackleton to Antarctic – cosy free house with fine beer such as well kept Marstons Pedigree, good value bar food, coal fire and garden; full at weekends, get there early for a seat or meal; nr start GWG103 *(John Gould, Jon Wainwright, Dr and Mrs R J Ashleigh)*

Winterley [A534; SJ7557], *Foresters Arms*: Pleasant, clean and photogenic pub with one long low-ceilinged room, good value food lunchtime and evening, Tetleys on handpump, good welcome, plenty to look at in the bar *(P Corris)*

Wrenbury [SJ5948], *Cotton Arms*: On Shropshire Canal, popular with narrowboaters; good reasonably priced food and pleasant garden by bowling-green; children's room *(DMM)*

Wybunbury [Main Rd – OS Sheet 118 reference 699499; SJ6950], *Swan*: Fine whitewashed village pub with relaxed, comfortable atmosphere, tasteful décor including ornamented bar, lots to entertain inside; well kept McEwans 80/- and Youngers Scotch; prominent bay window facing church tower (all that's left after storm collapse); comfortable bedrooms *(Jon Wainwright, D P Bagnall)*

Cornwall

The new management's continuing redevelopment of the Devenish brewery chain (which with its rival St Austell dominates the Cornish pub scene) has gone on affecting the county quite markedly. Superficially, the most obvious change this year is the introduction of an attractively packaged range of bottled beers called Newquay Steam (though like the rest of the company's beers they come from Redruth). But they have been experimenting more fundamentally with the relationship between the brewery itself and its pubs. For example, the waterside Shipwrights Arms in Helford (a particular favourite of many readers), which used to be run by tenants, has been sold freehold to a new company run jointly by those former tenants and the brewery – the arrangement seems to be working out well. Unusually, though, it's been among the free houses rather than those tied to any brewery that changes of licensee (with consequent changes of style or character) have been most common here this last year or so. There are new people at the Coachmakers Arms in Callington (warm praise from readers for the new team brings it back into these pages after quite an interval), the Bullers Arms at Marhamchurch (earning it a food award for the first time), the swaggeringly nautical Admiral Benbow in Penzance, and the Blue Peter in Polperro (a very enthusiastic couple – the wife is Burmese – who again have won it its first food award from us). The owners of the Cornish Arms at Pendoggett will probably have sold it by the time this book appears – fingers crossed about whoever takes over this fine old inn. The new man at the very popular Miners Arms in Mithian (a tied house) has kept the atmosphere much as ever, but altered the range of food quite a bit – to readers' initial firm approval; though the management's

The Miners Arms, Mithian

unchanged, the Rising Sun in St Mawes also gets a first-time award from us for its fine food, all fresh. Other important changes to note are the promotion to our main entries of the Fox & Hounds near Lanner and the charming Crows Nest on the edge of Bodmin Moor in the village named after it. And the Trewellard Arms in Trewellard (a former favourite of lovers of the unspoilt) sadly closed down at the start of 1988 – we hope it'll reopen, with a new lease of life. Marking your card for the other main entries, we'd say first of all that the county does in general stand out for value – prices are low indeed compared with most of the rest of England, and beer is for example consistently 6p or 7p a pint less even than in comparable pubs across the Tamar in Devon. A good rule of thumb for finding fine pubs here is often to head for the seashore, where, besides the Blue Peter, Rising Sun and Shipwrights Arms already mentioned, you'll find the thatched Pandora near Mylor Bridge (consolidating its position as readers' favourite Cornish pub), the Old Ferry at Bodinnick, the Heron at Malpas and the Port Gaverne Hotel by a National Trust cove near Port Isaac. The Cobweb in Boscastle, Lamorna Wink at Lamorna, Ship at Lerryn, New in Manaccan and Mill House at Trebarwith are just a stroll from the water, the Logan Rock at Treen is in bracing coastal walking country, and the ancient Bush at Morwenstow is close to some of Cornwall's finest cliffs. Browsing through the main entries, you'll find that the county's certainly got its fair share both of star awards and of awards for food and for places to stay, but what is perhaps most noticeable is the large number of Lucky Dip entries, picked out with their own stars, which readers' reports show are worth special attention. Among these, we'd pick out as particularly promising the Cutty Sark in Marazion, Victoria at Perranuthnoe, and, especially, the Royal Oak at Perranwell Station; in the Scillies, both the Mermaid in Hugh Town and the Turks Head at St Agnes would almost certainly have earned themselves main entries if we'd managed to make the trip there.

BODINNICK   SX1352 Map 1

Old Ferry

Clinging steeply to the hillside above the River Fowey, this old inn actually burrows into rock at one end – a games-room has a stag's head on one wall, and darts, pool (in winter), shove-ha'penny, dominoes, fruit machine and space game. Following the slope down towards the river, the friendly and traditionally furnished public bar has sea photographs on the panelled walls and a very large stuffed salmon. The comfortable lounge bar has a 'Parliament' clock, aquarium, and sea photographs and prints. Bar food includes soup (75p), sandwiches (from 75p, toasties 5p extra), ploughman's (from £1.95, with locally smoked mackerel £2.10, with home-cured ham £2.75) and pâté £2; well kept Flowers Original and St Austell Tinners on handpump (light top pressure may be used). Make sure your brakes work well if you park on the steep lane outside. *(Recommended by Mrs D M Gray, Roger Sherman, Jakki Hewson, G S Miller, Mrs G K Herbert)*

Free house   Licensee Simon Farr   Real ale   Snacks   Evening restaurant (closed Nov–Mar) Children in eating areas   Open 11–2.30, 6–11; open until 3pm Sat   Bedrooms tel Polruan (072 687) 237; £20.50(£23B)/£41(£46B)

BOSCASTLE   SX0990 Map 1

Cobweb

B3263, just E of harbour

The big flagstoned bar of this lively village pub has a log fire in cool weather, two or three curved high-backed winged settles against the dark stone walls, a few leatherette dining-chairs, and hundreds of old bottles hanging from the heavy beams. Good value bar food includes sandwiches (from 80p), soup (90p), plough-man's (£1.50), corned beef salad (£1.60), basket meals (from £1.60), lasagne, moussaka or vegetarian dishes (£2.50), with a daily hot special (from £2). Well kept St Austell Tinners, HSD and Wadworth 6X on handpump, with a guest beer tapped from the cask; pleasant, friendly service; piped music. There's a good juke box, darts, dominoes, pool-table (keen players here), fruit machine, and cards, draughts and chess; the big communicating family-room has an enormous armchair carved out of a tree trunk as well as its more conventional Windsor armchairs, and another cosy fire in winter. Opening off this a good-sized children's room has a second pool-table and more machines. The tiny steeply cut harbour nearby is very attractive, as is the main village climbing up above. *(Recommended by Robin and Bev Gammon, Roger Huggins, J Harvey Hallam, C M Whitehouse)*

Free house   Licensee Alfred 'Ivor' Bright   Real ale   Meals and snacks   Restaurant tel Boscastle (084 05) 278   Children in own room   Folk, country and western or modern music Sat   Open 11–11 weekdays in summer, noon–12 Sat, all year

CALLINGTON   SX3669   Map 1
Coachmakers Arms ⊗ 🛏

Newport Square; A388 towards Launceston

This well kept and friendly seventeenth-century inn has a long irregularly shaped bar with black beams, little winged settles and stools made from polished brass-bound casks, and timbered butter-coloured walls decorated with reproduc-tions of old local advertisements (particularly for coaching and coachbuilding); one more comfortably carpeted end has a log-effect electric fire in its stone fireplace. Good bar food at lunchtime includes sandwiches, home-made pâté (from £1.65, crab or smoked salmon £1.90), ham and eggs (£2.50), cod (£2.75), steak, kidney and mushroom pie cooked in Guinness (£2.95), and scampi (£4.95); in the evening dishes like home-made lamb ratatouille, pork in cider and beef carbonnade. Bass on handpump; good service; fruit machine, euchre and piped music. *(Recommended by John Kirk, Ceri Jarr, Revd Stephen Pakenham, Roy and Barbara Longman)*

Free house   Licensees Jon and Sandy Dale   Meals and snacks   Restaurant   Children in eating area and restaurant   Open 11.30–3, 6.30–11 all year   Bedrooms tel Liskeard (0579) 82567; £20B/£30B

CROWS NEST   SX2669   Map 1
Crows Nest ⊗

Signposted off B3264 N of Liskeard; or pleasant drive from A30 by Siblyback/St Cleer road from Bolventor, turning left at Common Moor, Siblyback signpost, then forking right to Darite; OS Sheet 201 reference 263692

Charmingly old-fashioned but comfortable, this snug stripped stone seventeenth-century pub has lots of stirrups, bits and spurs hanging from its bowed dark oak beams and – among other more orthodox seats around the polished tables – an unusually long black wall settle by the big fireplace. It's decorated with old local photographs, and maybe flowers on the tablecloths, down past the balustered dividing partition. Cheap food includes sandwiches to order, soup (£1.20), ploughman's (£1.80), steak and kidney or rabbit and ham pie (£1.95), beef or vegetable lasagne (£2.20), gammon and egg (£2.45) and daily specials; well kept St Austell Tinners and HSD on handpump; dominoes, euchre, juke box, fruit machine, maybe rather muffled piped radio; quick and pleasant service. There are picnic-table sets out on the terrace by the quiet village lane. *(Recommended by Gill and Ted George, N B Pritchard, Charles Gurney)*

St Austell   Licensee T W C Rosser   Real ale   Meals and snacks   Children in eating area Open 11–11 all year

HELFORD SW7526 Map 1
Shipwrights Arms ★ ⊗

In a lovely waterside position, this very friendly thatched pub has an easy-going
atmosphere, with yachtsmen congregating under the low shiny ochre ceiling by the
bar counter, lots of ship models and navigation lamps, sea pictures, and drawings of
lifeboat coxwains. At the other end there are oak settles and tables in a dining area
with good waitress service; an open fire in winter. Home-made bar food includes
pasties (£1.10), soup (£1.25), ploughman's (from £2.30, with crab £3.95), very
good salads in summer (£3 quiche or mackerel, £4 mixed meat, £4.75 fresh local
crab), and, in winter, a home-made daily special (£3.95), with evening dishes like
mushrooms in garlic butter or pâté (£2), avocado with prawn or crab (£2.25),
lasagne (£3.75), crab salad (£5), beef curry or beef cooked in red wine (£5.25), local
scallops or monkfish provençale in white wine (£6.50), sirloin steak (£6) and
lobster (from £7); home-made puddings (from £1.60). John Devenish and Cornish
Original on handpump. Courteous, efficient staff; dominoes, cribbage, piped
music. On summer evenings you can have eight-ounce burgers, veal chops, fish or
prawns and steaks barbecued out on the terraces – which drop down among
flowers and even palm trees to the water's edge. The top part of the terrace is roofed
over with Perspex. *(Recommended by Roy and Shirley Bentley, Audrey and Alan Chatting,
GB, CH, Gwen and Peter Andrews, Jon Wainwright, Hazel Morgan, R Trigwell, N J Cutter,
Barry and Penny Francis, Ewan McCall, DDC, Mrs C McMahon, R H Cockburn)*

*Cornish Brewery   Licensees Brandon and Susan Flynn   Real ale   Meals and snacks (not Mon
evening in winter, not Sun evening; tel Manaccan (032 623) 235)   Children in eating area
Parking only right outside the village in summer   Open 11–2.30, 6–11 all year, though in
summer they may be open longer in the afternoon, depending on demand*

HELSTON SW6527 Map 1
Blue Anchor

50 Coinagehall Street

A series of small, flagstoned and low-ceilinged rooms opens off the central corridor
in this medieval thatched town pub, mainly popular with locals. There are some
bared stone walls, simple old-fashioned furniture, interesting old prints, and in one
room a fine inglenook fireplace; a family-room has several space games and a fruit
machine. They still use the ancient brewhouse to produce the Medium, Best,
'Spingo' Special and Extra Special ales at very reasonable prices. Past this, and an
old stone bench in the sheltered little garden, is a skittle alley which has its own bar
at busy times. The nearby Cornwall Aero Park has a number of family attractions,
and Godolphin House is well worth visiting. *(Recommended by N W Acton, Phil and
Sally Gorton, MM, KG, Norman England)*

*Own brew   Real ale   Snacks   Children in family-room   Parking sometimes difficult
Open 10.30–2.30, 6–11*

LAMORNA SW424 Map 1
Lamorna Wink

The 'wink' of the name used to be the secret sign you had to give when ordering
drinks if you wanted something stronger than the ale that was all this simply
furnished pub's licence originally covered. It's a neatly kept, beamed place with one
of the best collections of warship mementoes, sea photographs and nautical
brassware in the county; piped music. Bar food includes local pasties (80p),
sandwiches (from 80p), salads (£1.75), and home-made quiche (£2), local crab and
mackerel. Well kept John Devenish tapped from the cask; darts, pool, dominoes,
cribbage, fruit machine, space game, and juke box are in a connected but quite
separate building. Sitting on the front benches outside, you can just hear the sound

of the sea in the attractive sandy cove down the lane, joining the birdsong and the burble of the stream behind – where you can catch trout; near *Good Walks Guide* Walk 3. *(Recommended by Gwen and Peter Andrews, Patrick Stapley, Richard Gibbs, RAB)*

Cornish Brewery   Licensee Bob Drennan   Real ale   Meals and snacks (not Sun evening) Children in eating area of bar   Open all day weekdays; 12–3, 7–10.30 Sat

LANNER   SW7240   Map 1
Fox & Hounds
Comford; junction A393/B3293

Surrounded by hanging baskets and tubs of flowers, this pretty white house has been comfortably modernised inside, with greeny gold plush or deep pink cloth banquettes. But it's kept a good deal of character, rambling around through several red-carpeted areas, with black beams and joists, a wood-burning stove in one granite fireplace and logs burning in another, some stripped stonework and some dark panelling, and comical 1920s prints by Lawson Wood. A good range of bar food, served quickly except at peak times, includes sandwiches, salads (from £2.75, crab in season), half a chicken (£3.75), plaice (£3.95), gammon (£4.75) and sirloin steak (£5.65); a new restaurant area spreads out at the back. Well kept Bass and St Austell BB and HSD tapped from the cask; juke box or piped radio. There are picnic-table sets on the front terrace, with more by swings and a climber on a sheltered and neatly kept back lawn. *(Recommended by Charles and Mary Winpenny and others)*

St Austell   Licensee Coral Snipp   Real ale   Meals and snacks   Restaurant   Children in eating area   Open 11–3, 6–11; all day Sat and Aug, Sept

LANREATH   SX1757   Map 1
Punch Bowl 🛏
Village signposted off B3359

Friendly locals chat in the two-roomed flagstoned Farmers' Kitchen of this early seventeenth-century inn, with its big stone fireplace, built-in red leatherette wall seats and sturdy wooden tables. The Turkey-carpeted Visitors' Kitchen, its atmosphere reminding some of an alpine inn, has some high-backed antique black settles, a couple of flamboyant red velveteen chaises-longues, a Delft shelf above the squared black panelling, and a longcase clock; piped music. Bar food includes sandwiches, ploughman's and well made pies; very well kept Bass and St Austell HSD on handpump. The games-bar has darts, dominoes, pool, fruit machine, space game, trivia and juke box. The tucked-away village has a farm museum and an attractive church with a fine set of bells. *(Recommended by Steve and Carolyn Harvey, J D Mackay, Jakki Hewson, Tony Forbes-Leith, Ilka Nosworthy, G S Miller)*

Free house   Licensee Harvey Frith   Real ale   Meals and snacks   Restaurant   Children in restaurant and family-room   Open 11–11 in summer, 11–3, 6–11 in winter   Bedrooms tel Lanreath (0503) 20218; £16(£19.50)/£32(£39B)

LERRYN   SX1457   Map 1
Ship
Village signposted from A390 in Lostwithiel

Welcoming to visitors and locals alike, and with a range of customers from teenagers to pensioners, this quiet, unpretentious and recently decorated pub is set in a quiet village at the head of a tidal creek off the Fowey Estuary. The open-plan bar (part carpeted, part big slate flagstones) has new furniture, small yachting pictures, brasses on beams, a grandfather clock, and a cheerful local atmosphere. Bar food includes home-made soups (95p), sandwiches (75p), pasty (90p), ploughman's (£2.45), home-made pies (£3.25), scampi, vegetarian dishes, steaks, and specials such as Wiltshire or steak and kidney pies, trout with celery and walnut or celery and blue cheese quiche; children's menu (95p). Well kept Bass, Flowers Original and IPA (known here as Bilge Water) and a guest beer such as Whitbreads Pompey Royal on handpump; sensibly placed darts, pool, dominoes, fruit machines, space game, and piped music. A sheltered back lawn has some picnic-table sets, and there are two more outside the stone building. *(Recommended by Gwen and Peter Andrews, Steve and Carolyn Harvey, J D Mackay, Mr and Mrs D A P Grattan, G S Miller)*

Free house   Licensee Ted Bealey   Real ale   Meals and snacks   Children in eating area of bar   Folk and country and western singers Sat evenings   Open 11.30–2.30, 6–11 all year

LOSTWITHIEL   SX1059 Map 1
Royal Oak
Duke Street; pub easily visible from A390 in centre

Dating from the thirteenth century, this friendly pub has an unusual range of real ales for Cornwall: Bass, Flowers Original and IPA, Fullers London Pride, Hunts-man Royal Oak, Wadworths 6X and guest beers on handpump; they also have a good choice of bottled beers and draught ciders. Generous helpings of bar food (which is served until half an hour before closing) includes sandwiches (from 80p), ploughman's (from £1.80), steak and kidney pie (£2.45) and a good line in steaks (from £6.05), with daily specials (around £2.75) and a weekday lunchtime carvery (£4.10). The well kept lounge has walls stripped back to the old reddish granite, captain's chairs and brown leatherette button-back banquettes on its patterned carpet, and a couple of wooden armchairs by the gas-effect log fire. There's a Delft china shelf, with a small dresser in one inner alcove. The flagstoned back public bar has darts, bar billiards, dominoes, cribbage, fruit machine and juke box, and younger customers. A raised terrace by the car park, lined with cordylines, has picnic-table sets. *(Recommended by Roger Davies, Hon Mrs Fennell, CHC, V and M Rundle, Michael O'Driscoll)*

Free house   Licensees Malcolm and Eileen Hine   Real ale   Meals and snacks Restaurant   Children in restaurant   Open all day in summer; 11–3, 6–11 in winter Bedrooms tel Bodmin (0208) 872552; £18B/£30B

MALPAS   SW8442 Map 1
Heron
Village signposted from A39 at main Truro roundabout

High above a wooded creek, this pub has a friendly and comfortable long rectangular bar with reupholstered seats and carpets, maps and plates on the walls, and log fires in winter. A wide choice of good bar food includes generously filled sandwiches (fresh crab £2.10), home-made steak and kidney pie or cottage pie (£3.25), steak and nuggets (£5.25), and a daily lunchtime special. On Friday and Saturday evening a separate grill-room does trout, large steaks and crab salads (from £5.50). Well kept St Austell Tinners and HSD on handpump; fruit machine, space game, piped music and quiz night on Wednesdays. In summer, much of its appeal lies in the sunny slate-paved front terrace with a good view over the creek. At weekends and in other busy periods, the pub can get exceedingly crowded – when nearby parking may not be easy, but service still copes well. *(Recommended by Roger Mallard, Patrick Young, Margo and Peter Thomas, NWN, D Goodger, Roger Huggins)*

St Austell   Licensee F C Kneebone   Real ale   Meals and snacks   Restaurant (closed Sun) tel Truro (0872) 72773   Children in eating area of bar or grill area on wet days   Ballad/country duo Fri evening   Open 11–3.30, 6–11; 11–2.30, 7–10.30 in winter

It is illegal for bar staff to smoke while handling your drink.

MANACCAN　　SW7625　Map 1
New ★ ⊗

Down hill signposted to Gillan and St Keverne

There's a strong local atmosphere in this cosy little thatched pub with its simply but attractively furnished two-roomed bar: individually chosen chairs, traditional built-in wall seats, tables with heavy embroidered cloths, beam and plank ceiling, and nice touches such as hops around the windows, freshly cut flowers and oriental rugs. Good value bar food concentrates on home-cooked locally caught fish such as plaice, monkfish provençale, scallops, lobster, langoustines and so on (depending on availability, from £5), with home-made soup (£1), home-made pasty (winter only, £1), sandwiches (£1, crab £2), ploughman's (£2), home-made steak and kidney pie or casseroles (£4), and the house speciality, treacle tart (£1.50). Devenish JD tapped from the cask; dominoes, cribbage, euchre, chess, backgammon and yahtzee. A sheltered lawn slopes up behind the pub. (*Recommended by Audrey and Alan Chatting, Clifford Blakemore, C S Trevor, B H Pinsent, Gwen and Peter Andrews, Jon Wainwright, Ewan McCall*)

Cornish Brewery　Licensee Patrick Cullinan　Real ale　Meals and snacks　Children in eating area of bar　Parking may be difficult in summer　Open 10.30–2.30, 6–11

MARHAMCHURCH　　SS2203　Map 1
Bullers Arms ⊗

This big village inn has an L-shaped bar with beams, comfortable little settles forming booths around its walls, local hunting trophies mounted above the stone fireplace, and a pleasant, relaxed atmosphere. The new licensees have introduced a varied bar menu that includes soup (85p), sandwiches (£1, toasties £1.25), ploughman's (from £1.80), omelette (£2.30), vegetarian fruit and nut pilaff (£2.75), lasagne (£2.95), steak and kidney pie (£3.20), ham or chicken salad (£3.50), local Tamar trout (£3.95), gammon (£4) and steaks (from £5.95); pudding of the day (85p) and traditional Sunday roast. Well kept Devenish Cornish Original, Marstons Pedigree, St Austell Tinners, Wadworths 6X and guest beers on handpump or tapped from casks in a back still-room; piped music, cribbage; quick service. Darts and fruit machine in a flagstone-floored back part, and beyond that a separate pool-room. There's now a cocktail bar decorated in 1930s style. Opposite, where the village road joins the A39, a mile-long footpath leads to the cliffy coves just north of Widemouth Sand. (*Recommended by Mr and Mrs J M Elden, Stephen Davies, Charles and Mary Winpenny*)

Free house　Licensees Keith Henry and Christine Nesbitt　Real ale　Meals and snacks Restaurant open Tues–Sun lunch in summer, Thurs–Sun lunch in winter　Children welcome Open all day in summer; 11–2.30, 6–11 in winter　Country, jazz or ballads Thurs and Sat evenings　Bedrooms tel Widemouth Bay (028 885) 277; £13B/£26B

MITCHELL　　SW8654　Map 1
Plume of Feathers

This comfortable and welcoming roadside pub underwent dramatic changes in the summer of 1988. In the large, rambling horseshoe bar the new licensees have uncovered a natural spring well, and stripped the old beams down to their natural state; the enormous open fire at the back once belonged to the old kitchen, which has now been incorporated into the bar – as has the old cellar. There are dark wooden chairs and settles, and plenty of bric-à-brac on the walls, such as kitchen and farm tools. Bar food includes sandwiches (from 90p), a range of ploughman's (from £1.95) and daily specials like home-made steak and kidney pie or casseroles (all at £2.95). Cornish Original and Devenish JD on handpump; darts, pool-table in winter, piped music. The raised lawn at the back has an adventure playground, and lots of farm animals. *(Recommended by R Trigwell, Lyn and Bill Capper, Derek and Jennifer Taylor, Mr and Mrs Pocock, Alan and Julie Wear, John Roué; more reports on the new regime please)*

Cornish Brewery   Licensees Maureen and Peter Fowler   Real ale   Meals and snacks   Children welcome   Open 11–2.30, 6–11 all year

MITHIAN   SW7450   Map 1

Miners Arms   ★ ⊗ *[illustrated on page 104]*

The little back bar in this particularly friendly, well run pub is full of atmosphere, with its wood-block floor, irregular beam and plank ceiling, and bulging squint walls (one has a fine old wall painting of Elizabeth I). A lot of this character spills over into the comfortable and spacious main lounge; there's also a stone-built cellar lounge and darts-room. The new licensees have told us that most of their food is freshly made and they use only fresh vegetables: sandwiches plain or toasted (from 95p), home-made soup with toasted garlic bread (£1.40), burgers (from £1.85), ploughman's (£1.95, with home-cooked ham £2.25), home-made pâté and salad (£2.20), fresh tortatella pasta or beef lasagne (£2.45), Cornish seafood lasagne (£2.65), slices of fresh plaice in breadcrumbs with garlic mayonnaise (£3.10), a seasonal special such as game pie (£3.65) and six-ounce rump steak (£4.50); home-made puddings like traditional English trifle, date and banana cake topped with chocolate cream or apple pie (£1.30); three-course Sunday lunch (booking essential) (£3.85), and afternoon teas with snacks and fancy teacakes. Well kept Cornish Original and Devenish JD on handpump; darts, fruit machine and piped music; good winter fire. There are benches on the sheltered front cobbled terrace. The sherry and glasses in the simple bedrooms are a very nice touch. *(Recommended by D G Nicolson, Mr and Mrs J M Elden, Mr and Mrs G R Salt, Denis Waters, Charles and Mary Winpenny, Roy and Barbara Longman, Barry and Penny Francis, Len Beattie, D Goodger, Ewan McCall, C McMaster-Christie, Hon Mrs Fennell, Alan Phillips, Roger Huggins, Simon Wilmot-Smith)*

Cornish Brewery   Licensee Peter Andrew   Real ale   Meals and snacks   Restaurant   Children in cellar lounge   Open all day June–end Oct; 11–2.30, 7–10.30 in winter   Bedrooms tel St Agnes (087 255) 2375; £12/£18

MORWENSTOW   SS2015   Map 1

Bush   ★

Village signposted off A39 N of Kilkhampton

A ten-minute walk away from one of the grandest parts of the Cornish coast – Vicarage Cliff – with 400-foot precipices, this delightful old-fashioned country pub has a small main bar with ancient built-in settles, a big stone fireplace, and a cosy side area with antique seats, a lovely old elm trestle table, and a wooden propeller from a 1930 De Havilland Gipsy. Well kept St Austell HSD and St Austell Tinners (kept under a light CO2 blanket) on handpump or tapped from a wooden cask behind the wood-topped stone bar counter; pewter tankards line the beams above it. They do sandwiches. An upper bar, opened at busy times, has built-in settles, and is decorated with antique knife-grinding wheels, miners' lamps, casks, funnels and so forth. Darts, fruit machine; the landlord is firmly against piped music. The pub has a strong claim to be one of the very oldest in Britain; part of it dates back just over 1000 years (a Celtic piscina carved from serpentine stone is still set in one wall). Seats outside shelter in the slightly sunken yard. *(Recommended by Jane English, Steve and Carolyn Harvey, Peter Barrett, David and Flo Wallington, Stan Edwards; more reports please)*

Free house   Licensee J H Gregory   Real ale   Meals and snacks (limited in the evening; not Sun, not Mon lunchtime in winter)   Restaurant tel Morwenstow (028 883) 242; advance booking only   Open 11.30–2.30, 7–11 all year; closed Mon lunchtime in winter

nr MYLOR BRIDGE   SW8036 Map 1
Pandora ★ ★ ⊗

Restronguet Passage; from A39 in Penryn, take turning signposted Mylor Church, Mylor Bridge, Flushing and go straight through Mylor Bridge following Restronguet Passage signs; or from A39 further N, at or near Perranarworthal, take turning signposted Mylor, Restronguet, then follow Restronguet Weir signs, but turn left down hill at Restronguet Passage sign

On a relatively remote part of the sheltered tidal waterfront, this beautiful thatched pub has a rambling bar with several interconnecting rooms: cosy alcoves with leatherette benches built into the medieval walls, big flagstones, uneven red tiles and some carpeting on the floor, low wooden ceilings (mind your head on some of the beams), a log fire in a high hearth (to protect it against tidal floods), and a highly polished kitchen range. Lunchtime bar food includes home-made soup such as carrot and orange (60p or 95p), filled baked potato (from £1.25), smoked mackerel pâté (£1.95), sandwiches (from £1.50 for cream cheese, nuts, lettuce, tomato and cucumber, £2.60 for chicken, bacon, lettuce, tomato and mayonnaise with chips, and £3.50 for local crab with cucumber and lettuce), home-made lasagne (£2.75), smoked haddock bake (£2.85), and burger (£2.95), with evening extras such as a superb triple-decker sandwich (£2.60), local lemon sole (£4.50), and char-grilled steak (£5.95); puddings like very good treacle tart (£1.50) and children's menu (from 75p). The restaurant has the same menu at lunchtime, but is à la carte in the evening. There's a floating pontoon where – weather permitting – food and drink are served. Bass, St Austell Tinners, HSD and Bosun on handpump. There are lots of picnic-table sets in front, by a long floating jetty; showers for visiting yachtsmen. Parking is difficult at peak times. (*Recommended by Ted George, R L Turnham, Roger Mallard, J C Proud, Gwen and Peter Andrews, D S Beeson, Charles and Mary Winpenny, Jon Wainwright, H J Stirling, Roger Broadie, Michael Bechley, Stan Edwards, Alan and Audrey Chatting*)

St Austell   Licensee Roger Hough   Real ale   Meals and snacks   Restaurant tel Falmouth (0326) 72678; closed Sun evening   Children in eating area and restaurant   Open 11–5, 6–11 in summer; 11–2.30, 6–11 in winter

PELYNT   SX2055 Map 1
Jubilee ⊗ 🛏

B3359 NW of Looe

An inner area of the lounge in this well kept, comfortable and rather smart old inn is decorated with mementoes of Queen Victoria, whose jubilee its name celebrates; the main part has an early eighteenth-century Derbyshire oak armchair, Windsor armchairs, brown leather and red fabric cushioned wall and window seats, magazines stacked under the oak tables, neatly squared oak beams, and, in winter, a good log fire under a copper hood in the big stone fireplace. An attractively old-fangled glass-paned partition separates it from the flagstoned entry. A green carpet covers most of the handsome flagstones in the lounge itself, but they are left bare in the public bar, which has pool, sensibly placed darts, dominoes, fruit machine, space game and juke box. Good value bar food – served quickly by neat and friendly waitresses – includes a good choice of freshly cut sandwiches (from £1.20, local crab £2.30), home-made soup (£1.20), ploughman's (£1.80), home-baked ham and eggs (£3.60), salads (from £3.95, £5.20 for local crab), steaks (from £6.70), and a daily special such as local scallops, roast beef, fresh plaice or curries (around £3.20); the choice may be different at lunchtime. Well kept Ferguson

---

Ideas for a country day out? We list pubs in really attractive scenery at the back of the book – and there are separate lists for waterside pubs, ones with a really good garden, and ones with lovely views.

Dartmoor Pride (known as Jubilee Original here) on handpump. There is a crazy-paved central courtyard where barbecues are lit six nights a week and on Sunday lunchtime. *(Recommended by Charles Gurney, Mrs Shirley Pielou, Steve and Carolyn Harvey, J D Mackay, G Kahan, Graham Howard, G S Miller)*

Free house   Licensee Frank Williams   Real ale   Meals and snacks   Restaurant   Children welcome   Open 11–3, 6–11 all year; will open longer in the afternoon according to demand by trade   Bedrooms tel Lanreath (0503) 20312; £24.40B/£39.80B

PENDOGGETT   SX0279   Map 1
Cornish Arms ⊗ ⇔
B3314

Sadly, after ten years, the Reverend Alan and Mrs Wainwright and Nigel Pickstone are to sell this comfortable slate-hung house; it has a good deal of underlying character – which we trust will survive any change of ownership, and wish the newcomers well. The big, lively locals' bar has high-backed settles around stripped deal tables, a big wood-burning stove, and darts, dominoes, cribbage, euchre, a fruit machine and maybe a portable television. The two panelled rooms of the front bar have old-fashioned furniture such as high-backed built-in oak settles surrounding solid old wooden tables on the Delabole slate floor, and fresh flowers. At lunchtime there is a good bar buffet with home-made soup (£1.30), a wide choice of salads with meat cut from home-cooked joints of beef, pork, ham, chicken and duck, as well as quiche (from £2.50), a hot dish of the day such as filled baked potatoes, home-made steak and kidney pie or lasagne (£2.50), and home-made fruit pies or treacle tart with clotted cream (£1.20). In the evenings (summer) it's soup, sandwiches (from 85p, local crab £1.50), local plaice (£3.75), crab salad (£3.95), and eight-ounce steak (£5.75); friendly, helpful service. Well kept Bass tapped from the cask, and Pendoggett Special brewed for the pub on handpump. There are tables out on a corner terrace with a sea view down the valley. *(Recommended by W J Hallett, J C Proud, D S Beeson, Mike Hallewell, Stan Edwards, Peter and Rose Flower, Len Beattie)*

Free house   Real ale   Meals and snacks   Restaurant evenings (not 25 or 26 Dec) and trad Sun lunch   Children in eating area at lunchtime, and in restaurant   Old time/country and western/middle of the road music occasionally   Open 11–2.30, 5.30–11   Bedrooms tel Port Isaac (0208) 880263; £24(£26B)/£37(£42B)

PENZANCE   SW4730   Map 1
Admiral Benbow
Chapel Street; turn off top of main street, by big domed building (Lloyds Bank)

The low-beamed upstairs bar here has lots of shiny paintwork, figureheads, fancy carving, elaborate balustered pillars, engine-room telegraphs, model ships in glass cases, wreck charts (including a nice one with Gillespie drawings), navigation lanterns and so forth, with ropes neatly wound in and out all over the place. The various alcoves have red plush seats around the tables, and there are lots of mirrors and plants. A plainer back room – with less atmosphere – has lots of seats. Bar food includes sandwiches, baked potatoes (from 90p), pasty (£1), ploughman's or cottage pie (£2.25), lasagne or plaice (£2.45), chicken curry (£2.95), and home-made steak and kidney pie (£3.25) and other hot dishes such as fresh fish; they stock country wines, and keep Ruddles County and Ushers Best on handpump. Friendly staff; darts, pool, fruit machine and piped music. The pub is popular with young people in the evenings. *(Recommended by Deryck and Mary Wilson, Margo and Peter Thomas, Michael O'Driscoll)*

Free house   Licensee Nicholas Batten   Real ale   Meals and snacks   Restaurant tel Penzance (0736) 63448   Children welcome   Open 10.30–2.30, 5.30–11 all year

We say if we know a pub has piped music.

Turks Head ⊗

Chapel Street (see above)

The busy main bar in this friendly old pub is an atmospheric place with old flatirons, jugs and so forth hanging from the beams, and old pottery above the wood-effect panelling. A wide choice of seafood from a very comprehensive menu includes crab soup (95p), smoked mackerel salad (£2.20), seafood chowder (£2.25), crevettes (from £2.75), mussels in wine, tomato and garlic (£3.25), fisherman's pie (£3.30), crab salad (mixed meat £3.60, white meat £4.20), scallops in wine, cream and garlic (£3.95), cold seafood platter (£4.50), crab and prawn thermidor (£5.50) and whole lobster thermidor (£13.50); there's also plenty of non-seafood variety such as lunchtime sandwiches, filled baked potatoes and ploughman's as well as home-made soup (from 75p), ratatouille topped with cheese (£1.75), chilli con carne (£2.40), lasagne (£3.20), chicken curry (£3.50), gammon steak (£3.60), and very good charcoal-grilled steaks (from £4.90) using English steer beef. Well kept Devenish Royal Wessex, Cornish Original and GBH on handpump; pleasant, helpful service; fruit machine, and a good juke box which attracts a lively young crowd in the evening. There has been a Turks Head here for over 700 years, and though most of the original one was burned down by a Spanish raiding party in the sixteenth century the cellar room has been a bar for several hundred years. The sun-trap back garden has big urns of flowers. (*Recommended by Deryck and Mary Wilson, Roger Chisnall, Audrey and Alan Chatting, Dr and Mrs M F Greaves, Simon Turner, Caroline Bailey, Patrick Stapley, Richard Gibbs, RAB, Michael O'Driscoll*)

Cornish Brewery   Licensee William Morris   Real ale   Meals and snacks   Restaurant tel Penzance (0736) 63093   *Open 11–4.30, 5.30–11 in summer; winter hours will depend on customer demand*

PHILLEIGH   SW8639   Map 1

Roseland ★ ⊗

The furnishings in this spotlessly clean and friendly seventeenth-century pub have been carefully chosen: a solemn old wall clock, lots of old sporting prints and other pictures under its low beams, old-fashioned seats around the sturdy tables on the flagstones, and attractive bunches of fresh flowers; a good fire in winter. Bar food, which changes from day to day, includes sandwiches (from 80p, fresh local crab £2.25), good pasty (85p), steak and kidney pie (£1.20), generous ploughman's (£2.20), tasty seafood Mornay, vegetarian or meat lasagne or avocado and chicken salad (£2.50), egg mayonnaise and prawns with salad or fruity pork curry (£2.75), beef casserole (£3), coquilles St Jacques (£4), and puddings like treacle tart (£1.25) or fresh local strawberries (£1.50). Well kept Devenish JD and Cornish Original on handpump from a temperature-controlled cellar; dominoes, cribbage. The paved courtyard in front of the pub has charming flowers among its attractive tables. The quiet lane leads on to the little half-hourly *King Harry* car ferry across a pretty wooded channel, with Trelissick Gardens on the far side. (*Recommended by Steve and Carolyn Harvey, Dr and Mrs I W Muir, Mrs J H Aston, N C Rose, Patrick Young, Peter Argent, Ian Blackwell, Mrs N W Neill, B H Pinsent, Nick Lyons, Mr and Mrs W W Matthews, Hon Gerald Vane, NWN*)

Cornish Brewery   Licensee Desmond Sinnott   Real ale   Lunchtime snacks (evenings also June–Sept)   Children in lounge   Open 11–3, 6–11 all year; 11–2.30, 7–11 in winter

POLKERRIS   SX0952   Map 1

Rashleigh

The setting here is lovely: an isolated beach and attractively restored protecting jetty, overlooked by tables on the stone terrace (and by the figurehead which presides over it); there are barbecues here in summer. Inside, the stripped-stone front part of the bar is a rather remote (and decidedly more comfortably cushioned) descendant of the humble fisherman's tavern it used to be; there are local photographs on the brown panelling of a more simply furnished back area. Food includes an extensive lunchtime cold buffet; also soup (90p), sandwiches (from £1.10, fresh local crab £2.20, open sandwiches £3.55), ploughman's (£2.65), scampi (£3.85), steak or cottage pies (£4.10), and scampi provençale (£6.05); home-made puddings. St Austell Tinners and HSD on handpump or tapped straight from the cask; good service; dominoes, cribbage, euchre, fruit machine and piped music. This section of the Cornish Coast Path includes striking scenery, and there are safe moorings for small yachts in the cove. No dogs. *(Recommended by Steve and Carolyn Harvey, R Inns, A R Friedl, Charles Gurney, John Parsons, Mrs G K Herbert, NWN, G S Miller)*

Free house   Real ale   Meals and snacks   Restaurant tel Par (072 681) 3991   Pianist Fri evening, accordianist Sat evening   Open 11–2.30, 6–11

POLPERRO SX2051 Map 1
Blue Peter ★ ⊗

The Quay; on the right-hand side as you go round the harbour – a brisk ten-minute walk from the public car park

The new licensees in this cosy, welcoming pub – which overlooks the small working harbour in this picturesque village – bake fresh pizzas every morning (they used to run a pizzeria and wine bar), make their own 100-per-cent-meat burgers, and have introduced curries (the landlady is Burmese); other dishes include sandwiches and baps (from 80p, hand-picked local crab £1.75), pasty (95p), home-made soup (£1), macaroni bake (£1.65), sausage casserole (£1.75), shepherd's pie (£1.95), platters (a mixture between a ploughman's and a salad, from £1.95, home-made pâté £2.20, local crab £3), burgers or pizzas (from £1.95), home-made Rangoon chicken curry (£2.75), deep ocean bake (cod, prawn, tuna and crab in a light cheese sauce topped with potato, £2.85), seafood platter (£5), and specials such as local rainbow trout (£3.15); puddings (from 85p) and children's menu (from 85p). Well kept Courage Best, St Austell Tinners and HSD, and a beer brewed for the pub on handpump. The low-beamed bar has, besides more ordinary seats, a small winged settle, a polished pew, and a seat cut from a big cask; there's a big naval shell by the coal fire, and some boat pictures; one window seat looks down on the harbour, another looks out past rocks to the sea. Darts, bar billiards, fruit machine, space game, trivia and piped music. There are slat seats on the small V-shaped terrace at the top of the flight of steps up to the door. Near *Good Walks Guide* Walk 9. *(Recommended by Colin Gooch, Charles Gurney, Pete Storey, Roger Sherman, J A Hawson, Steve and Carolyn Harvey, G S Miller, Wayne Brindle, Michael O'Driscoll)*

Free house   Licensees Tim Horn and Jennie Craig-Hallam   Real ale   Meals and snacks Restaurant tel Polperro (0503) 72743   Children in restaurant and family-room Light rock/popular '50s, '60s and '70s music Thurs and occasional Sat evenings Oct–May Open all day Easter–1 Nov; 11–3, 6–11 in winter

nr PORT ISAAC SX0080 Map 1
Port Gaverne Hotel ★ ⊗ 🛏

Port Gaverne signposted from Port Isaac, and from B3314 E of Pendoggett

As we went to press, the licensees of this civilised and friendly early seventeenth-century inn were beginning to organise the celebration of their twentieth year here – we hope it went well. The style of the well kept bars fits in aptly here, with low beams, some exposed stone, flagstones where the floors are not carpeted, big log fires, a collection of antique cruets and an enormous marine chronometer. In spring the lounge is filled with pictures from the local art society's annual exhibition in aid of the Royal National Lifeboat Institution (this year they raised £1,500); at other times there are interesting antique local photographs. Very good bar food includes sandwiches (from 90p, crab £1.85), home-made soup (from £1.25, good crab £1.65), home-made pâté (£1.50), ploughman's (from £1.60), fresh home-made cottage pie (£2), Cornish fish pie (£2.25), salads (from £2.95, half a lobster £7.75), and home-made steak and kidney pie or a daily special (£4.25); Sunday roast lunch and, in summer, cream teas. From Spring Bank Holiday until the end of September the food is served buffet-style in the dining-room at lunchtime, and there is the same arrangement for Sunday lunchtime (when food stops at 1.30 sharp) throughout the year, but otherwise it's served in the bar or Captain's Cabin – a little room where everything except its antique admiral's hat is shrunk to scale (old oak chest, model sailing-ship, even the prints on the white stone walls). Besides well kept Flowers IPA and St Austell HSD on handpump, there is a very good choice of whiskies and other spirits such as ouzo, east Friesian schnapps, and akvavit. There's a good wine list, with plenty of half-bottles; dominoes, cribbage, fruit machine. A raised terrace outside has a good sea view (the bar does not). Splendidly unspoilt, the land around the cove a few yards away is owned by the National Trust. *(Recommended by Charles and Mary Winpenny, Tom McLean, Mr and Mrs J M Elden, WHBM, Professor A N Black, Lyn and Bill Capper, Robin and Bev Gammon, D Pearman, Len Beattie, G Kahan, Mr and Mrs J E Rycroft, David and Flo Wallington, Peter and Rose Flower, C M Whitehouse, Howard Mackenzie, Peter Sutton)*

Free house   Licensee Frederick Ross   Real ale   Meals and snacks (see below)   Restaurant (see below)   Children in Captain's Cabin (please reserve) or restaurant   Open all day; closed 7 Jan to 25 Feb   Bedrooms tel Bodmin (0208) 880244; £29.50B/£49B; canine guests £2, food not provided

PORTHLEVEN   SW6225 Map 1
Ship

You have to climb a flight of rough stone steps to get in to this old fisherman's pub – literally cut into the steep rocks over a working harbour. The central bar – with good sea views – has a huge log fire in a big stone fireplace, and preserves what readers still describe as a salty atmosphere. There's also a lounge, and a summer cellar bar. Good bar food includes filled hot crusty bread (£1.05), salads (£1.20), seafood pizza (£2.40), lasagne (£2.75) and pork and leek crumble (£3.25); well kept Courage Best and Directors on handpump. *(Recommended by Patrick Young, Clifford Blakemore, D Pearman, Dr R Scott Watson; more reports please)*

Courage   Licensee Colin Oakden   Real ale   Meals and snacks   Children in family-room Occasional Cornish singing Sun evenings   Parking can be difficult in summer Open 11.30–3.30, 6.30–11; closes 2.30 lunchtimes in winter

ST AGNES   SW7250 Map 1
Railway

Vicarage Road; from centre follow B3277 signs for Porthtowan and Truro

There's a remarkable collection of shoes in this busy little pub – minute or giant, made of strange skins, fur, leather, wood, mother-of-pearl, or embroidered with gold and silver, from Turkey, Persia, China or Japan and worn by ordinary people or famous men. There's also some splendid brasswork, and a notable collection of naval memorabilia from model sailing-ships and rope fancywork to the texts of Admiralty messages at important historical moments. Bar food includes sandwiches (85p), burger or home-made soup (90p), ploughman's (from £1.70), chicken (£2.50), scampi (£3), and a home-made special (£2.50). Well kept Devenish JD, and GBH served from an unusually elaborate handpump beer engine; darts, shove-ha'penny, dominoes, fruit machine and piped music. *(Recommended by Len Beattie, John Roué; more reports please)*

Cornish Brewery   Licensee Christopher O'Brien   Real ale   Meals and snacks   Children in family-room   Open all day

ST EWE   SW9746   Map 1
Crown ⊗

Village signposted from B3287; easy to find from Mevagissey

Warmly welcoming and run by the same licensees for over thirty years, this old-fashioned cottage has traditional furniture including one very high-backed curved old settle with flowery cushions, long shiny wooden tables, sixteenth-century flagstones, and, in winter, a roaring log fire with an ancient weight-driven working spit; shelves beside the fire have plates, a brass teapot and jug. This year, the room opening off the bar and the small dining-room have been opened up, making a much bigger eating area with a burgundy-coloured carpet, velvet curtains, and matching cushions to go on the old church pews. There's a good mix of customers. Quickly served bar food includes traditional and open sandwiches, filled baked potatoes, home-made soup or egg mayonnaise (90p), pâté (£1.50), ploughman's (£1.90), pork chops with apple sauce or scampi (£4), gammon and pineapple (£4.70), tasty steaks (from £5.30), and home-made puddings like banana, mince-meat and brandy pie (90p). Well kept St Austell Tinners on handpump; darts, dominoes, fruit machine, space game and piped music. There are several picnic-table sets on a raised back lawn, with a family-room out at the back too. *(Recommended by D Godden, Mark Evans, Hon Mrs Fennell, Gwen and Peter Andrews, Richard Gibbs, Patrick Stapley, RAB)*

St Austell   Licensee Norman Jeffery   Real ale   Meals and snacks   Restaurant   Children in eating areas and family-room   Open 11–3, 6–11; closed evening 25 Dec   Bedrooms tel Mevagissey (0726) 843322;/£16

ST KEW   SX0276   Map 1
St Kew Inn

Village signposted from A39 NE of Wadebridge

Much grander looking than you'd expect, this rather noble stone building has parking in what must have been a really imposing stableyard. Inside, the friendly bar has an open kitchen range under a high mantelpiece decorated with earthenware flagons, black wrought-iron rings for hanging lamps or hams from the high ceiling, winged high-backed settles and varnished rustic tables on the lovely dark Delabole flagstones, a Windsor armchair, and a handsome window seat. Well kept St Austell Tinners and HSD tapped from wooden casks behind the counter (lots of tankards hang from the beams above it); fruit machine. The local sirloin steaks cooked in the evening (not Sunday) are highly recommended. Picnic-table sets shelter between the wings of the pub, by a stone-trough pump on the front cobbles. *(Recommended by Len Beattie, Roger Huggins, Judy McCluskey, Emma Stops; more reports please)*

St Austell   Real ale   Meals and snacks   Open 10.30–2.30, 5.30–11

ST MAWES   SW8537   Map 1
Rising Sun ⊗ 🛏

The friendly and pubby front bar in this comfortable, carefully refurbished small hotel has a big window seat overlooking the sea; there's also a lounge with antique furniture, royal blue sofas, pale green armchairs and antique prints, and a back cocktail bar. Quickly served home-made bar food (even the bread is home made, and everything is fresh) includes pasties (£1), sandwiches (from 95p, fresh crab £2.25), fresh crab salad (£4.25), filled baked potatoes (from £1.05), good plough-man's (£2.20), interesting quiches or dishes with fresh, home-made pasta (£2.50), salads (home-made pork pie £2.50), prawns with garlic mayonnaise (£3.95), and fresh scallops in a wine and cream sauce (£4.50). Well kept St Austell BB and HSD on handpump; good service, and darts, fruit machine. Outside, there's a crazy-paved harbourside terrace, with sturdy slate-topped tables and a low stone wall to sit on when those are full. *(Recommended by Stephen R Holman, John Tyzack, A J Bright, Mrs N W Neill, Margo and Peter Thomas, G Kahan, CHC, St John Sandringham)*

St Austell   Licensees F N B Atherley and R J Milan   Real ale   Lunchtime meals and snacks Restaurant   Children in eating area   Open 11–4, 6–11; 11–2.30, 6–10.30 in winter Bedrooms tel St Mawes (0326) 270233; £19.50(£24)/£48(£60B)

ST TEATH   SX0680 Map 1

White Hart

Decorations in the main bar of this pleasant village pub include coins embedded in the ceiling over the serving-counter, swords, a cutlass, and sailor hat-ribands and ships' pennants from all over the world; there's a snug little high-backed settle between the counter and the coal fire, and a Delabole flagstone floor. A carpeted room, mainly for eating, leads off, with modern chairs around neat tables, and brass and copper jugs on its stone mantelpiece; gentle piped music in here (in other rooms there's not only a piano but also a venerable harmonium). Simple food in generous helpings includes pasties, pizzas and particularly tender rump steaks, with sandwiches (plain and toasted) and ploughman's (with home-made bread) at lunchtime too; well kept Ruddles County on handpump. The lively games-bar has a good juke box, darts and a well lit pool-table. *(Recommended by John Dewan, Dr and Mrs I W Muir, Len Beattie; more reports please)*

Free house   Meals and lunchtime snacks   Open 10.30–2.30, 5.30–11

TREBARWITH   SX0585 Map 1

Mill House Inn ⊗ 🛏

Signposted from B3263 and B3314 SE of Tintagel

This seventeenth-century converted watermill is idyllically placed in its own wooded valley that runs down to the sea. The welcoming big main bar has pews, handle-back chairs around oak tables, and some stripped pine settles on its Delabole slate floor; an airy communicating extension has pine tables in side stalls. Good bar food includes sandwiches (from 70p), home-made soup (£1.10), basket meals (from £1.30), pâté (£1.65), ploughman's (from £2.20), salads (£3.10), fish platter (£3.30), smoked salmon (£4), gammon (£4.65), and eight-ounce steak (£5.90), with daily specials like pasties (£1.35) and lasagne or steak and kidney pie (£2.95); home-made puddings (£1.25), children's meals (from £1.10). Well kept Flowers IPA and Original on handpump; darts, pool, shove-ha'penny, dominoes, cribbage, fruit machine, ring the bull, draughts and piped music. Outside, an attractively planted flagstoned terrace, on several levels, makes the most of the sun. The beach, a few minutes' walk away, is good for surfing. Dogs accepted with own blanket. *(Recommended by Mr and Mrs D A P Grattan, Mike Hallewell, Doug Kennedy, Jane English, John Roué, Chris Wauton, Alex Mark)*

Free house   Licensee David Liddiard-Jenkin   Real ale   Meals and snacks   Restaurant Children in family-room; accepted for accommodation from 10 years   Probably open all day Sat in summer; the other days will depend very much on trade demand   Bedrooms tel Camelford (0840) 770200; £19.50B/£39B

Please let us know what you think of a pub's bedrooms. No stamp needed: *The Good Pub Guide*, FREEPOST, London SW10 0BR.

TREEN SW3824 Map 1

Logan Rock ⊗

The Logan Rock – which you can walk to from this well run and cosy stone pub, and which like the pub is owned by the National Trust – is an eighty-ton teetering boulder which someone once tipped from its clifftop fulcrum to show off his strength, and then had to pay a small fortune to have it hauled up the cliff again. Old prints telling this story hang on the partly panelled walls of the low beamed bar, and there are high-backed modern oak settles and tables, and a good fire in cold weather. Interesting home-made food includes a wide choice of sandwiches (from 75p, local crab £1.90), big pasties (90p), filled baked potatoes (from £1.25), soup (£1.30), basket meals such as plaice (£2.90) and salads (from £2.75), with hot dishes such as vegetarian quiche (£1.50), lasagne or a popular fish and egg dish they call the Seafarer (£2.75); bookings advisable; except in high summer they do good charcoal-grilled steaks (rump £5.50, T-bone £6.50). They will heat baby foods on request. Well kept St Austell BB, Tinners and HSD on handpump; friendly service. Darts, dominoes, cribbage, piped music, and in the family-room a fruit machine and space game; in winter, a separate pool-room has table skittles. Dogs are allowed in on a lead. There are some tables in a small but attractive wall-sheltered garden, looking over fields, with more in the front court. (*Recommended by Philip Haggar, D G Nicolson, Roger Chisnall, C S Trevor, Tim Locke, Margo and Peter Thomas, D Goodger, Dr Venetia Stent, Ewan McColl, RAB*)

St Austell   Licensees Peter and Anita George   Real ale   Meals and snacks   Winter restaurant tel St Buryan (0736) 810495   *Children in family-room   Open all day in summer,* 10.30–2.30, 6–11 in winter

Lucky Dip

Besides the fully inspected pubs, you might like to try these Lucky Dips recommended to us and described by readers (if you do, please send us reports):

Blackwater [SW7346], *Chiverton Arms*: Friendly country local with U-shaped bar, wood-burning stove, subdued lighting; piped music, fruit machine, space game and darts; consistently well kept Devenish Wessex, Cornish Original and JD on handpump, good lunchtime and evening bar food *(Charles and Mary Winpenny)*

Bolventor [A30 on Bodmin Moor; SX1876], *Jamaica Inn*: In spite of concessions to tourism still has lots of character, much enjoyed by many readers, with friendly helpful staff, reasonable food – particularly the pasties – in quite pleasant added food bar, and Flowers IPA (sold as Stallion) and Original (sold as Jamaica Inn); can get very busy *(Roger Huggins, Tom McLean, John Roué)*

Boscastle [SX0990], *Napoleon*: Small-roomed sixteenth-century pub at top of village, atmospheric and friendly, mainly home-cooked bar food, lots of Napoleon prints, Bass and St Austell real ale, darts, pool, sheltered terrace; in the storms of October 1987 the nearby River Jordan burst its banks and flooded through the pub at shoulder-height; children in eating area *(Gary Scott, LYM)*

Botallack [SW3633], *Queens Arms*: Reasonably priced food – the excellent home-made

pasties seem to get bigger and bigger – in friendly pub with big open fireplace and Devenish beers; darts, fruit machine and beer garden; good walking country along coast and by Cornish mines – nr start GWG4 *(Charlie Salt)*

Botusfleming [SX4061], *Rising Sun*: Entertainingly dilapidated unspoilt free house *(Phil and Sally Gorton)*

Cadgwith [SW7214], *Cadgwith*: Good service and simple bar food in pub full of character, with pleasant terrace; close to beach in pretty village *(Mrs C McMahon)*

Canons Town [A30 Hayle–Penzance; SW5335], *Lamb & Flag*: Very clean and comfortable bars and music-free lounges, gas fires, cheerful welcome, food consistently good value *(P K Hall)*

Carnkie [Piece (nr Redruth); SW6940], *Countryman*: Good cheap food in pub with good atmosphere and pleasant staff; regular music nights *(Mr and Mrs P V Hocking)*

Chapel Amble [village signposted from A39 NE of Wadebridge, and from B3314; SW9975], *Maltsters Arms*: Attractively knocked-together rooms with stripped stone, panelling, big stone hearth, oak joists, heavy furnishings on partly carpeted flagstones; also restaurant and family-room; warm welcome, but mixed reports on food and beer quality (St Austell Tinners) since change of management late 1987, though by summer 1988 things seemed to be settling down – more news please *(Mr and Mrs G R Salt, Dr and Mrs I W Muir, LYM)*

Chilsworthy [OS Sheet 201 reference 415722; SX4172], *White Hart*: Pleasant, well restored village pub with a friendly welcome and good selection of well kept beer – so much a centre of local activity that you may find a knitting class in progress there around the pub *(Phil Gorton)*

☆ **Constantine** [Nancenoy, which is signposted from B3291 Penryn–Gweek; in village turn right just before minimarket (towards Gweek); in nearly a mile pub signposted left – OS Sheet 204 reference 731282; SW7229], *Trengilly Wartha*: The range of real ales – very interesting for the area, and well kept – is the high point of this quietly pleasant small country hotel, with quite a modern feel to its décor, a spacious games-room including darts and pool, a comfortable lounge, and bar food (the summer cold buffet is popular); evening restaurant, provision for children, seats outside, folk music Fri or jazz Sat; bedrooms comfortable and good value; up for sale as we went to press *(J C Proud, Charles and Mary Winpenny, Gwen and Peter Andrews, M P Hallewell, Jon Wainwright, H J Stirling, LYM)*

Crafthole [village signposted off A574; SX3654], *Finnygook*: Much modernised spacious lounge bar with wide choice of good value straightforward food, cheery welcome, pleasant restaurant and nice views from residents' lounge; bedrooms small but very comfortable, warm and attractively priced *(Mrs Shirley Pielou, C G Thompson, BB)*

Cubert [Trebellan; SW7858], *Smugglers Den*: Nicely decorated and picturesque village pub with beams and inglenook, good choice of food, games bar with pool, weekend discos in one bar; crowded in summer, with nearby holiday camp *(Charles and Mary Winpenny)*

Dunmere [A389 W of Bodmin; SX0467], *Borough Arms*: Partly panelled stone walls in long single bar, brown leather banquettes and plush stools around pine tables, wood-burning stove, farm tools, Cornish Original and JD on handpump, good food from sandwiches and ploughman's to main dishes; family-room, tables outside *(Patrick Young)*

☆ **Falmouth** [Custom House Quay; SW8032], *Chain Locker*: Strongly nautical décor and atmosphere, friendly and welcoming bustle, many customers from the inner harbour which it overlooks; well kept Cornish ales, huge good value sandwiches, occasional pianist, seats on waterside terrace; popular new landlord since May 1988 *(Les King, Michael Bechley, Wayne Brindle, Jon Wainwright, LYM)*

☆ **Falmouth** [Church St], *Kings Head*: Well kept Devenish real ales and food such as

ploughman's and pasta in rambling but clean bar engagingly furnished with mixture of hard-backed chairs and soft settees, masses of hat-boxes, old plates and engravings, good log fire, and long efficient servery done out like front of a shop; good reports of new 1988 landlord, with well kept Wessex *(M P Hallewell, Ian Robinson, Roy and Barbara Longman, Jon Wainwright, LYM)*

Falmouth [Prinslow Lane], *Boslowick*: Fine old manor house, recently redecorated with new carpets, new bar, wood panelling, red plush sofas and chairs – and new restaurant; good food, Courage ales; set in modern housing estate *(Jon Wainwright and others)*; [Boslowick Rd] *Clipperway*: Local with character, bar with pool-table, off-licence, large lounge with distinctive fireplace, Ushers *(M P Hallewell)*; [Church St] *Grapes*: Recently renovated and now consists of one large room on two levels with views over the harbour and docks, Cornish beer and Wadworths 6X on tap, pool-table, juke box, bar food *(M P Hallewell)*; [Killgrew St] *Kimberley Arms*: Devenish town-centre pub with cosy atmosphere, low ceiling, stone walls, maritime artifacts, ships' lights, model boats; one room with small bar, good choice of food *(M P Hallewell)*; [The Moor] *Seven Stars*: Warmly welcoming old-fashioned local with well kept Bass, Flowers Original and St Austell HSD straight from the cask, simple snacks, tables on courtyard behind flower tubs; run as it has been for generations – you may even find the barman doing trumpet practice *(J C Proud, BB)*; [Trevethan Hill; from centre follow High St straight on past its end; or entering Falmouth by A39, fork left at Greenbank sign then take first right turn into Old Hill, an excellent short cut into centre – pub then off to your right] *Sportsmans Arms*: If you play euchre you'll be popular in this worthy and relatively quiet local with exceptional harbour views and well kept Cornish ales *(Jon Wainwright, LYM)*; [Killgrew St] *Wodehouse Arms*: Well kept popular St Austell local, warm and cosy, HSD, darts, juke box, bar food *(M P Hallewell)*

Fowey [Esplanade; SX1252], *Ashley House*: Ex-naval chef runs this comfortable hotel; good food and welcome, spotless *(Mr and Mrs A G Smith)*; [Town Quay] *King of Prussia*: Harbour view from bow windows of upstairs bar with St Austell real ales, largely home-cooked food, juke box, maybe rousing company *(Tom Evans, LYM)*; [from town centre follow Car Ferry signs] *Riverside*: Splendid spot with comfortable hotelish lounge overlooking river and boats, more workmanlike streetside public bar; bedrooms comfortable *(BB)*; *Ship*: Interesting building, good service and food that can be enterprising – such as a good lentil and bacon soup *(J D Mackay)*

Fraddon [SW9158], *Blue Anchor*: Standard bar with darts, fruit machine, pleasant lounge, St Austell HSD and Tinners, bar food *(Roger Huggins)*

Gerrans [SW8735], *Royal Standard*: Pleasant friendly pub with cosy and well furnished rambling rooms, Cornish ales and pool-table; opposite church *(Mark Evans)*

☆ **Golant** [SX1155], *Fishermans Arms*: Old-fashioned without being olde-worlde, in quiet spot overlooking beautiful stretch of River Fowey; tourists don't seem to have discovered it, but the stranger isn't an object of suspicion (the landlord comes from Lancashire, so they must be used to them); interesting collection of nautical and other Victoriana, Courage ales, adequate food *(WHBM, Caroline Gibbins)*

☆ **Gunnislake** [The Square; SX4371], *Cornish Inn*: Very good bar service in comfortable inn with generous helpings of good value food such as fresh Newlyn plaice, St Austell beers; bedrooms bright and comfortable *(Alan and Audrey Chatting, J C Proud, Michael O'Driscoll)*

Gunnislake [lower road to Calstock], *Rising Sun*: Lovely unspoilt and simple seventeenth-century pub overlooking upper Tamar Valley, with pretty terraced garden – beautiful and peaceful on a summer's evening; sold early 1988, up-to-date news please *(H G and C J McCafferty)*

☆ **Hayle** [Bird Paradise Park; SW5536], *Bird in Hand*: Good guest beers alongside own-brewed Paradise, Artists and Victory Bobber, in friendly converted stable with alcoves, old photographs and framed hopsacks; decent food, four-table pool-room, garden, play area, summer evening do-it-yourself barbecues; children in food bar and pool-room; open Easter–end Oct, evenings not Sun July–early Sept *(M P Hallewell, Tom McLean, Roger Huggins)*

Hayle [Griggs Quay], *Old Quay House*: Big functional lounge overlooking estuary (popular bird-watching area) with well kept beer, good cheap food in bar and restaurant, efficient staff; jazz club Mon evening *(P and M Rudlin)*

Helford Passage [SW7627], *Ferry Boat*: Big open-plan waterside pub with fruit machine, space games and decent but pricey food, well kept St Austell BB, HSD and Tinners; the location's the best part; afternoon teas *(Margo and Peter Thomas, Les King, BB)*

nr **Helston** [Gunwalloe – signposted off A3083; SW7627], *Halzephron*: Pleasant communicating bars with good log fire and views over clifftop fields to sea and Mounts Bay, well kept Cornish ale, usual run of pub food, outside tables under cocktail parasols; children welcome; bedrooms *(Roger Huggins, Gwen and Peter Andrews, LYM)*

Kilkhampton [SS2511], *New*: Spacious clean local with rambling interconnecting rooms, some traditional furnishings, fine wood-

burner, bar food, well kept Bass; children in good games-room *(LYM)*

☆ **Kingsand** [Fore St, towards Cawsand – OS Sheet 201 reference 434505; SX4350], *Halfway House*: Warm, dimly lit old bar with exposed stonework, heavy beams, central fire and settles – smuggling flavour; Bass and Flowers Original, attractively priced food; darts, juke box, fruit machine; stream in small walled back yard *(Steve and Carolyn Harvey, Gill and Ted George)*

☆ **Lanlivery** [SX0759], *Crown*: Connecting black and white rooms, carpets and flag-stones, church pews, painted settles, armchairs and sofas, ornate stained glass in lounge, cosy atmosphere throughout, Bass and Hancocks HB on handpump, good choice of reasonably priced food with (at 24 hours' notice) whole roast joints; friendly and efficient; bedrooms *(Steve and Carolyn Harvey, Mr and Mrs F G Owen, A J Skull)*

Lanner [SW7240], *Coppice*: Friendly staff go out of their way to be helpful in village pub with play area in garden; bedrooms *(Roger Huggins)*

Liskeard [Church St; SX2564], *Barley Sheaf*: Quiet back-street pub with St Austell real ales, hot and cold food, garden, darts, skittle alley; children in bar *(N B Pritchard)*; [Two Waters Foot (off A38 towards Bodmin)] *Halfway House*: Spacious recently refurbished riverside pub with extensive no-smoking area, wide choice of bar food, well kept Flowers Original and St Austell Tinners, pleasant staff, plenty of seats on terrace; children in family-room *(N B Pritchard, Simon Turner, Caroline Bailey)*; *Red Lion*: Bar with original Victorian carved counter, black and white tiled floor, shelves to ceiling, juke box *(Phil Gorton)*

Lizard [SW7712], *Top House*: Genuine village local, full of nautical relics; food includes good crab sandwiches, ploughman's and rabbit and ham pie; Devenish *(George and Chris Miller, Stephen McNees)*

Longrock [old coast rd Penzance–Marazion; SW5031], *Mexico*: Bustling pub done up in traditional style with open fire, old pine tables and chairs; popular with young people, Bass and St Austell ales, good value food especially 'work and rest' pudding, bold local art on walls *(HEG)*

Looe [Barbican Rd, E Looe; SX2553], *Barbican*: Good value food, helpful staff and good family-room; attractive prices *(P L Schofield)*; *Jolly Roger*: Dimly lit lounge bar, flagstoned floor, pool-table; friendly bar staff, simple bar food *(Steve and Carolyn Harvey)*; [Hannafore, W Looe] *Tom Sawyers*: Bass, Flowers IPA and Original on handpump, good food including home-made pies and Fri/Sat spit-roast, very nice mahogany, no juke box or machines; restaurant; nr GWG9 *(Charles Gurney)*

Mabe Burnthouse [SW7634], *New Inn*: Friendly and informal atmosphere, small public bar, cosy lounge with stone masonry tools and old photographs on the wall; Cornish Original and Newquay Steam Bitter, good choice of reasonably priced bar food (M P Hallewell)

Madron [SW4532], King William IV: Pleasant and cheerful, good food (Alan and Audrey Chatting)

☆ **Marazion** [The Square; SW5231], Cutty Sark: Friendly cheerfully run inn with Theakstons Old Peculier, good reasonably priced food in bar and (more substantially) dining area – fish a speciality; bedrooms good value, superb view of St Michael's Mount from some, with excellent breakfast and evening meal (Michael O'Driscoll, C H Beaumont, C S Trevor)

Mawgan [SW7125], Ship: Simple unspoilt pub, good lunchtime snacks, well kept Cornish ales, children's room near bar(Patrick Young); [at Trelowarren House – off B3293 towards Coverack] Trelowarren Yard Bistro: More wine bar than pub, but Devenish on handpump as well as a good choice of wines including Australian ones; converted stable, with tiled floor, panelled bar, ladder-back chairs, red tablecloths; very good food – light lunches and more ambitious evening meals, with good fresh fish and very frequent menu changes (Patrick Young)

Mawnan Smith [SW7728], Red Lion: Good value simple food served quickly in friendly thatched village pub with warm wood-burning stove in high-ceilinged lounge, spacious public bar, well kept Devenish real ales, tables out by car park; children in big family-room (B H Pinsent, J C Proud, BB)

Menheniot [off A38; SX2862], White Hart: Clean and tidy old pub with pleasant service, good varied food, well kept range of beers (Gill and Ted George)

☆ **Metherell** [Lower Metherell; follow Honicombe sign from St Anns Chapel just W of Gunnislake A390; SX4069], Carpenters Arms: Pleasant atmosphere, friendly landlord and well kept Bass, Flowers Original, Theakstons Old Peculier and Wadworths 6X in heavily black-beamed inn with huge polished flagstones and massive stone walls; from the wide choice of food readers pick out the omelettes and pasta for praise; children welcome, sheltered tables outside; not far from Cotehele; bedrooms (Michael O'Driscoll, Charles and Mary Winpenny, Brian and Anna Marsden, J C Proud, Theo Schofield, J C Braidwood, John Kirk, LYM)

Mevagissey [nr harbour; SX0145], Ship: Recent £100,000 refurbishment, wide range of good cheap food running up to speciality twenty-ounce steak, St Austell ales, friendly service, good atmosphere; children in family area (S J Abrahams)

☆ **Mousehole** [SW4726], Ship: Friendly fishermen's local right by harbour in beautiful village – harbour lights stunning at night, decent bar food, well kept St Austell real ale – terrific New Year's Eve fancy-dress party (RAB, Les King, LYM)

☆ **Mullion** [SW6719], Old: Shipwreck mementoes and crabbing pictures in long lantern-lit bar of sixteenth-century thatched village inn, big inglenook fireplace, well kept Cornish Original and JD on handpump, home-cooked bar food (people like the pizzas and fish pie, though service has been slow at peak times), summer barbecues Tues–Sat, good games area (pool in winter), TV and small aviary in children's room, seats outside; bedrooms and self-catering cottages (Harry Jackson, Clifford Blakemore, D Goodger, Dr Venetia Stott, Alan Sillitoe, G Kahan, R Trigwell, LYM)

Nanpean [SW9656], Grenville Arms: Clean well managed local with warm welcome, photographs of aircraft, good pub meals, quick friendly service (John Roué)

Newlyn [SW4628], Tolcarne: Traditional Cornish local with two rooms; well kept Courage, extensive hot and cold bar food (Clifford Blakemore)

☆ **Padstow** [Lanadwell St; SW9175], London: Friendly and neatly nautical inn with ships' instruments and so forth, near attractive working harbour; bar food including good summer seafood snacks, well kept St Austell BB, Tinners and HSD on handpump, decent choice of whiskies, traditional games and voluble fruit machine; restaurant allowing children until 8.30; bedrooms (not Christmas week) (J C Proud, Dave Butler, Lesley Storey, TBB, LYM)

Padstow [North Quay], Shipwrights:Popular stripped-brick quayside pub with friendly helpful licensees, home cooking, well kept St Austell beers, reasonably priced restaurant (David Dane, Mr Edwicker, LYM)

Par [A3082 towards Fowey; SX0753], Ship: Extensive family pub with two bars, good games-room, good choice of robust well cooked food, St Austell real ale, and service to big garden with amusement area and playthings (Roger Sherman)

☆ **Penryn** [SW7834], Seven Stars: Cosy and friendly Devenish pub notable for its exceptional collection of sparkling-clean brass platters and ornaments – perhaps the biggest in the country (Mr and Mrs L Takkos, BB)

Pensilva [SX2969], Victoria: Unspoilt traditional pub on edge of Bodmin Moor, no music, no food, vast engraving of Queen Victoria on wall of yellowing public bar with cast-iron tables (Phil and Sally Gorton)

Penzance [SW4730], Dock: Typical Cornish coastal pub, lots of nautical memorabilia on walls, warm friendly atmosphere (Ian Robinson); [Barbican – Newlyn rd, opp harbour after swing-bridge] Dolphin: Clean and spacious, with big windows overlooking harbour, maritime theme, friendly staff, quickly served bar food, St Austell ales under light blanket pressure, adjoining family-room and pool-room with juke box etc., terrace tables

(Deryck and Mary Wilson, N R England, LYM)

☆ **Perranuthnoe** [SW5329], *Victoria*: Friendly atmosphere, well kept Courage Best and Directors on handpump, amazing range of excellent reasonably priced home-cooked food in huge helpings, wooden settles – the building dates from the thirteenth century; warm and comfortable family-room with juke box and fruit machines; prices higher than many; a couple of minutes' walk from the sea; bedrooms *(Rod Elwood, Clifford Blakemore, Charlie Salt, Charles Spicer, C N Blakemore)*

☆ **Perranwell** [Perranwell Station – note that this is the Perranwell just off A39 Truro–Falmouth; SW7839], *Royal Oak*: Old-fashioned rookery-nookery atmosphere with low beams, horsebrasses, hunting pictures, old waterpump beside bar, friendly service, unobtrusive piped music – cosy and relaxing; wide choice of good mainly home-made food (fills up quickly – get there early for a table), good friendly service, Devenish JD and Royal Wessex or GBH real ales, good value house wine; tables in garden and front courtyard *(M P Hallewell, C A Foden, G Atkinson, Margo and Peter Thomas, NM)*

Phillack [SW5638], *Bucket of Blood*: Cheerful busy pub with well kept St Austell beers and entertainingly gruesome ghost stories *(Roger Huggins, LYM)*

Pillaton [SX3664], *Weary Friar*: Interesting and attractive twelfth-century village inn which has had its ups and downs and was up for auction in summer 1988 – should be well worth checking out; restaurant, comfortable bedrooms, and it has had well kept Bass and St Austell real ales *(LYM; news please)*

Pityme [Pityme Farm Rd; SW9576], *Pityme*: Former seventeenth-century farmhouse, tastefully extended as free house with bar, restaurant and pool-room; friendly, welcoming and relaxed atmosphere, dartboard and fruit machine, St Austell HSD and Tinners on draught, wide choice of good bar food, pleasant garden with tables and chairs; children welcome *(Peggy and John Tucker)*

Polgooth [SW9950], *Polgooth*: Lively rustic inn with own farmyard, well kept St Austell real ales; bedrooms *(LYM)*

Polruan [SX1251], *Russell*: Warm pub sheltering in a village of closely built cottages; matchboarded walls, coal fire, genial landlord and customers, St Austell Tinners *(J D Mackay)*

Port Isaac [SX0080], *Golden Lion*: Old pub high over harbour in lovely steep village, nice view from seat by the window, snacks, well kept St Austell Tinners *(Roger Huggins, LYM)*

Porthallow [SW7923], *Five Pilchards*: Decent, friendly country pub with good range of lunchtime snacks *(George and Chris Miller)*

Porthleven [Peverell Terrace; SW6225], *Atlantic*: Lovely bar food, especially seafood, and friendly landlord; nice position high on hill overlooking harbour (drive up – there is

parking here); restaurant *(Michael O'Driscoll)*

Portloe [SW9339], *Lugger*: Not really a pub, but a welcome refuge on the Coast Path, with its fine position on a most beautiful cove, good sandwiches – especially crab – and sea views; keg beers, bedrooms *(St John Sandringham, B H Pinsent)*

Portmellon Cove [closed Oct–Mar; SX0144], *Rising Sun*: Small lower bar and big modern upper bar overlooking sandy cove near Mevagissey, bar food, St Austell real ales; open for morning coffee and afternoon cream teas; some live music; children in restaurant and family-room, seats outside *(Jakki Hewson, LYM)*

Portscatho [SW8735], *Plume of Feathers*: Friendly pub with good value food, including takeaways and excellent steaks, from hatch in corner of main bar; small eating area, side locals' bar, well reproduced loudish pop music; very popular *(RAB, Mrs Shirley Pielou, B H Pinsent, LYM)*

Poughill [SS2207], *Preston Gate*: Attractively relaxing partly flagstoned but otherwise modern bar with pews, mahogany tables and log fires in fairly recent conversion of two cottages; reasonably priced bar food, Ruddles County and Ushers Best on handpump, some seats outside; village is pronounced 'Poffle' *(Robin and Bev Gammon, Stephen K McNees, Stan Edwards, LYM)*

Roche [SW9860], *Rock*: Pleasant waitress-service dinner in relatively up-market pub – though not oppressively so; minstrels' gallery, 1547 date on beam *(John Roué)*; *Victoria*: Useful A30 stop with popular food including excellent home-made pasties in softly lit character bar, well kept St Austell ales, panelled children's room, cheery service, restaurant *(John Roué, C A Foden, G Atkinson, LYM)*

Rosudgeon [SW5529], *Coach & Horses*: Busy pub, open fires, wide choice of bar food and separate à la carte menu *(Fiona Carrey)*

Sandplace [SX2456], *Polrean*: Good plentiful bar food in straightforwardly furnished bar of small hotel with Flowers real ale, large terrace and garden; comfortable bedrooms *(P K Hall)*

☆ **Scorrier** [B3298, off A30 just outside Redruth – note that this is different from the nearby pub of the same name in Lanner; SW7244], *Fox & Hounds*: Cosy and relaxing, open fire even in summer, hunting pictures and stuffed fox, wide choice of well presented and reasonably priced food including some imaginative dishes, Cornish and Dry Hop real ales, efficient friendly service *(M P Hallewell)*

Sennen [SW3525], *First & Last*: Small and bustling with tourists, informal atmosphere, reasonable food though service not brisk *(John Roué)*

St Columb Major [Market Sq; SW9163], *Ring o' Bells*: Friendly town pub with simple food in several simply furnished rooms going back from narrow road frontage *(BB)*

☆ **St Dominick** [Saltash; SX3967], *Who'd Have Thought It*: Friendly pub with flock wallpaper, tasselled plush seats, Gothick tables, gleaming pottery and copper, good value bar food, well kept Bass and Courage Directors, engaging Jack Russell terriers, pleasant views *(Gill and Ted George, John Kirk, Alan and Audrey Chatting, LYM)*

St Issey [SW9271], *Ring o' Bells*: Cheerful and well modernised village inn with well kept Courage real ale and good value food; bedrooms *(LYM)*

St Ive [A390 Liskeard–Callington; SX3167], *Butchers Arms*: Old inn set back from main road, first-class Courage Directors, excellent very reasonable meals, large tastefully furnished bar and lounge, friendly staff, big gardens *(Ted George)*

St Just In Penwith [SW3631], *Star*: Well kept and cosy local in centre of wind-swept town not far from Land's End, relaxed atmosphere and really friendly landlord, well kept St Austell real ales and acceptable wine, efficient service, open fire, flagstones; popular with local arts and crafts people *(RAB, LYM)*

St Mawes [SW8537], *Victory*: Lots of sailing and other sea photographs in unpretentious and friendly bar with well kept Devenish JD on handpump, decent straightforward bar food; seats out in the alley, a few steep yards up from the harbour; good value simple bedrooms *(Dr K Bloomfield, LYM)*

St Mawgan [SW8765], *Falcon*: Stone inn with good local real ales and nice garden, in attractive village; bedrooms *(LYM)*

St Neot [SX1867], *London*: Well kept Ushers Best and Founders, hot and cold food including changing daily specials, garden; children in dining area *(N B Pritchard, Mr Edwicker)*

nr **Stithians** [Frogpool – off A393; SW7366], *Cornish Arms*: Good value bar food and steak dinners in friendly village pub with well kept Devenish real ales, cheerful local atmosphere and comfortable sitting areas *(BB)*

Tideford [SX3459], *Rod & Line*: Unspoilt, single-roomed pub with low, bowed, ochre ceiling and Victorian cash register; children allowed *(Phil Gorton)*

Tintagel [High St, Trevenna; SX0588], *King Arthurs Arms*: Large bar with quick service, Flowers Original, reasonably priced food, garden; children in games bar *(N B Pritchard)*; *Min Pin*: Recently converted farmhouse named after the miniature pinschers the licensees breed; their daughter brews own beers, Brown Willy (named after Cornwall's tallest hill) and Legend *(Anon)*

Trebarwith [Trebarwith Strand; SX0585], *Port William*: Unpretentious-looking pub with magnificent sea views, friendly atmosphere and service, good value bar food; self-catering flat upstairs *(Mrs Margaret Dyke)*

Tregadillett [A30; SX2984], *Eliot Arms*: Pleasant Devenish pub, hundreds of horsebrasses on dark oak beams, over twenty

clocks, really good food, nice atmosphere *(C Elliott, Dr and Mrs I W Muir)*

Trelights [signposted off B3314; SW9979], *Longcross*: Pleasant, clean pub behind hotel; lounge with central ornamental fountain, friendly staff, well kept St Austell HSD and Tinners, good value varied bar food, excellent family-room, garden; beautiful surroundings *(Roger Huggins)*

Trelissick [B3291; SW8339], *Punch Bowl & Ladle*: Large pub near lovely Trelissick Gardens, very reasonable food including good value children's menu, family-room, garden, easy parking *(N B Pritchard)*

☆ **Tresillian** [A39 Truro–St Austell; SW8646], *Wheel*: Recognisable for the big wheel in its thatched roof, this smartly renovated but cosy pub has low beams, horsebrasses, rope fancywork and an old ship's wheel dividing two small lounges; Devenish Royal Wessex and reasonably priced bar food – readers praise the ploughman's, gammon, salads and steaks *(Philip King, Jon Wainwright, C A Foden, G Atkinson, BB)*

Trewellard [SW3734], *Trewellard*: Formerly popular for its engagingly laid-back atmosphere in what were somewhat scruffy rambling bars with interesting layout and furnishings; closed start of 1988 after troubled times, then up for sale – news of developments, please; bedrooms *(LYM)*

Truro [Pydar St; SW8244], *City*: Friendly local, jugs and glasses hanging from every hook, notices, photographs and cartoons everywhere, fine Courage Best and Directors, hot nuts, winkles, mulled wine in winter *(Sarah Myners)*; [Lemon St] *Daniel Arms*: Good Victorian prints on cork-lined walls, plush banquettes with upper brasswork, huge foreign coin collection, wide choice of generously served food – especially salads and grills, Cornish Original and GBH; old stone building popular with young businessmen at lunchtime *(Patrick Young)*; [Francis St] *Globe*: Good atmosphere, well kept Devenish JD and Royal Wessex and Marstons Pedigree, wide choice of bar food *(Les King)*; [Lemon Quay – by central car park] *Market*: Radically refurbished last year, with oak-boarded floor, stained oak panelling with inset prints, timbered ceiling with mirror panels, cast-iron-framed oak tables, bentwood chairs – still good for cheap home-made food, with Cornish Original and GBH on handpump *(Patrick Young, LYM)*; [New Bridge St/St Clement St] *St Clement*: Useful pub done up with timbering, pine-fronted bar and brown oak chairs and tables; Bass, Courage Best, St Austell Tinners and Ushers Best tapped from the cask, reasonable bar food *(Patrick Young)*; [Kenwyn St] *William IV*: Newly refurbished large octagonal bar surrounded by slightly secluded raised areas; dark oak panelling, tables and chairs and a comfortable conservatory (children allowed here) and tables outside; lots of

chamber-pots, bottles, scales, ewers and basins; good bar food, particularly the daily specials, and St Austell beers *(Patrick Young)*
Tywardreath [off A3082; SX0854], *New*: Well kept Bass and St Austell ales in friendly pub with nice village setting; bedrooms *(BB)*
Veryan [SW9139], *New*: Traditional village inn, warm and cosy with open fires as well as central heating and fitted carpets, real ale, no piped music, friendly locals, caring licensees, evening meals; good value bedrooms *(G K Litherland, Mrs Shirley Pielou)*
Wadebridge [SW9872], *Molesworth Arms*: sixteenth-century inn with comfortable bedrooms *(HKR)*
Week St Mary [4 Cornish miles off A39; SX2397], *Green*: Excellent choice of bar food, especially mixed grill, well kept beer, friendly licensee, staff and locals; children welcome *(Stan Edwards)*
West Pentire [SW7760], *Bowgie*: Friendly atmosphere, magnificent headland garden with views over Crantock Beach, family-room, games-room, two lounge bars (one with beach view), well kept if pricey Flowers IPA and Original, good value food, friendly service; good play area; bedrooms *(S P Bobeldijk, E G Parish, LYM)*
Zelah [A30; SW8151], *Hawkins Arms*: Welcoming simple local with log fire and good food such as pasties, filled baked potatoes, home-made chilli con carne and cottage pie, appetising puddings; St Austell HSD, Sun lunches, garden; children welcome *(Mr and Mrs Spaull)*
Zennor [SW4538], *Tinners Arms*: St Austells real ales in comfortable stripped-panelling pub near fine part of Coast Path, bar food starting with hardly cheap ploughman's; big new terrace *(Roy and Barbara Longman, LYM)*

SCILLIES

☆ **Hugh Town** [The Quay; SV9010], *Mermaid*: Lovely quayside pub, entertaining surroundings with lots of woodwork and authentic naval artifacts from flags to figureheads, relaxed atmosphere; generous helpings of good reasonably priced food, especially salads and local fish, in upstairs picture-window bar; well kept Devenish JD, Royal Wessex and GBH on handpump, friendly landlord; live music some nights – liveliest on the Fri gig-race evenings *(Graeme Smalley, Steve and Carolyn Harvey, Dave and Angie Parkes, Jon Wainwright, Peter and Rose Flower, Pat and Malcolm Rudlin, Wilfred Plater-Shellard)*
Hugh Town [The Strand], *Atlantic*: Two bars, front one serving simple bar food, back one similarly decorated with pictures of ships that have come to grief on rocks, and sun-trap terrace with views across the bay; well kept Marstons Pedigree *(Jon Wainwright)*
☆ **St Agnes** [The Quay; SV8807], *Turks Head*: Only pub on island, small whitewashed cottage with wonderful views and surroundings, just above the quiet beach; simple inside, with wall benches, low ceilings, nautical prints, photographs and charts; dartboard, piped music, fresh flowers on bar, keg beers; the good value bar food includes outstanding home-made pasties – so famous that if you don't order one when you land you'll find them sold out by midday; Sun evening sing-songs, when a special boat comes from St Marys *(Peter and Rose Flower, Steve and Carolyn Harvey, Pat and Malcolm Rudlin, Angie and Dave Parkes, Wilfred Plater-Shellard)*
St Martins [SV9215], *Seven Stones*: Just to let you know that there is a pub here, with wonderful views – though it's furnished much like a village hall *(Anon)*

Cumbria

Among new entries here this year, the most interesting is the Bay Horse on the coast near Ulverston, which has been reopened under new management (with a prestigious reputation for fine food); unusually for the area, it confines its food to the good restaurant, with none in the attractive pub part. Other newcomers are the old-fashioned Wheatsheaf at Beetham, the Queens Arms at Biggar (tucked away on the interesting Isle of Walney), the Sun in Coniston (good value, honest food and a fine position) and the Kings Arms in Hawkshead; most of these are good to stay at. This year there are new licensees at the quaint and unpretentious Sun in Dent, the comfortable Bower House in Eskdale Green (good reports on their food), the Queens Head in Hawkshead (as good as ever, to eat in or stay at), the interestingly furnished Farmers Arms at Lowick Green, the Middleton Fells Inn alone below the hills at Middleton (they've done lots of work on the pub's layout – and are firmly back to home cooking), and the Beatrix Potter pub at Near Sawrey, the Tower Bank Arms (the new people formerly made a good job of looking after the Lowick Green pub). Sadly, the charming old Swan at Middleton has now closed down. A good many nice places to stay at up here include the old-fashioned and civilised Royal Oak in Appleby, the Barbon Inn at Barbon, the Pheasant at Bassenthwaite Lake (a particularly charming bar), the Hare & Hounds at Bowland Bridge, the charming Britannia by Elterwater, the rather unusual String of Horses at Faugh, the luxurious Wordsworth in Grasmere (really included for its friendly little Dove & Olive Bar), the quaint old Sun in Kirkby Lonsdale, the climbers' favourite, the Old Dungeon Ghyll in Langdale, the Three Shires over at Little Langdale, the matey Hare & Hounds at Talkin, and the handsomely placed Wasdale Head Inn. Most of these are also notable for decent food; others where food is a strong point include the Queens Head at Askham, Pheasant at Casterton, Snooty Fox in Kirkby Lonsdale, Hare & Hounds at Levens, Shepherds up at Melmerby, Kings Head at Ravenstonedale and White Horse at Scales. The Masons Arms on Cartmel Fell still logs the strongest stream of readers' approval as an interesting all-rounder in fine surroundings, with a particularly enthusiastic choice of drinks. One noticeable point is that pubs in the bigger Lakeland towns tend to be rather

The Hare & Hounds, Levens

disappointing – often too little character and too much juke box. The Golden Rule in Ambleside and Dog & Gun in Keswick are worthy exceptions, and you'll find a few others in the Lucky Dips. In the Dips, pubs and inns that currently look specially promising include the Hole in t' Wall in Bowness, Butchers Arms at Crosby Ravensworth, Sawrey Hotel at Far Sawrey, George & Dragon at Garrigill, Bridge at Lanercost, Screes at Nether Wasdale, George in Penrith and Mortal Man at Troutbeck.

AMBLESIDE   NY3804 Map 9

Golden Rule

Smithy Brow; follow Kirkstone Pass signpost from A591 on N side of town

This is one of the most genuinely and unpretentiously pubby places here – and a fine sight in summer, with its window boxes full of colour. The three rooms have built-in leatherette wall seats and cast-iron-framed tables, lots of local country pictures and a few foxes' masks on their butter-coloured walls, lots of horsebrasses on the black beams, and a busy atmosphere. The room on the left has darts, a fruit machine, trivia and dominoes; the one down a few steps on the right is a quieter sitting-room. The golden rule here is a brass measuring yard, mounted over the bar counter where you get your very well kept Hartleys Mild and XB on handpump; sandwiches. The pub sells sweatshirts and belts carrying its image, which go down well with the students and Yorkshire or Lancashire visitors; the pub is near the start of *Good Walks Guide* Walk 130. *(Recommended by Jon Wainwright; more reports please)*

Hartleys   Licensee John Lockley   Real ale   Lunchtime snacks   Children welcome   Nearby parking virtually out of the question   Open all day

APPLEBY   NY6921 Map 10

Royal Oak ⊗ 🛏

Bongate; B6542 on S edge of town

There's a really friendly, homely welcome in this ex-coaching-inn – which includes some remains of the fourteenth-century posting-house which preceded it. The comfortable beamed lounge has a panelling and glass snug enclosing the bar counter, some armchairs and a carved settle, as well as other furniture, old pictures on its timbered walls, and a calm atmosphere. The smaller oak-panelled public bar has had a good open fire. McEwans 70/- and local Yates on handpump; dominoes. Well presented and reasonably priced, the fresh home-made bar food includes very good soup with home-made bread (90p), sandwiches (lunchtime) such as home-cooked ham and beef (85p), terrine, Cumberland sausage or traditional plough-man's (£1.95), potted shrimps (£2.65), vegetarian dishes such as leek and tomato croustade (£2.95) or savoury crumble (£3.45), fresh white fish or salads (from £2.95), fish and meat hors-d'oeuvre or pie of the day (£3.25), local lamb cutlets (£3.95), Loch Fyne langoustines (which they buy fresh from creel fishermen off the West Coast of Scotland, £4.45), and daily specials such as Cevapcici (a Yugoslavian kebab dish in a pitta bread pocket £2.95) or Kotopoulo Kapama (chicken breast in a gently spiced Greek tomato sauce £3.45); puddings (from £1.20), local cheeses (£1.50) and children's meals (from £1.30); the breakfasts are superb. The front terrace has seats among masses of flowers in tubs, troughs and hanging baskets that look over to the red stone church. *(Recommended by Sara Cundy, AHNR, PLC, Carol and Philip Seddon, David and Ruth Hollands, Alan Bickley)*

Free house   Licensees Colin and Hilary Cheyne   Real ale   Meals and snacks   Restaurant Children in eating area   Open 11–3, 6–11 all year; closed 25 Dec   Bedrooms tel Appleby (0930) 51463; £15.50/£31(£38B)

ASKHAM NY5123 Map 9
Punch Bowl

At the bottom of the attractive lower village green, this relaxed pub has some unusual touches like a tribal rug hanging above the cushioned pews, little sprays of flowers decorating nooks in the wall, and an old-fashioned wood-burning stove with a gleaming stainless chimney in the big main fireplace. The rambling beamed main bar has Chippendale dining-chairs and rushwork ladder-back seats around its sturdy wooden tables, an antique settle by an open log fire, and well cushioned window seats in the white-painted thick stone walls. Well kept Whitbreads Castle Eden on handpump; dominoes, and piped pop music, and in the separate public bar darts, pool, fruit machine, trivia and juke box. In late summer 1988, the Zalks, who'd made this unusually decorated pub popular for distinctive food and as a place to stay, sold it. We hope the changes won't be too great. *(Recommended by Roger Stephenson, Jon Wainwright, Ned Edwards, Capt E P Gray, PLC, Alan Franck, M Parsons)*

Whitbreads   Meals and snacks   Restaurant   Children welcome   Open 11–4, 6–11 all year; 11–3, 7–11 in winter; open all day Sat   Bedrooms tel Hackthorpe (093 12) 443; £15/£30

Queens Head ★ ⊗

Outside this well kept, busy and friendly pub, you can sit in an attractive miniature landscape of rocks and shrubs, and watch the elaborate model railway that runs during opening hours. Inside, the main carpeted lounge has two comfortably furnished rooms with some old calico printing blocks on the red flock wallpaper, beams hung with gleaming copper, brass and horsebrasses, and harness, and an open fire. Good waitress-served bar food includes lunchtime sandwiches (£1, smoked salmon £1.75), and excellent soup (£1), cottage pie (£2.55), fish pie (£2.60), very hot chilli con carne (£2.85), salads (from £2.85), and chicken in yoghurt and lime or scampi provençale (£4.75); also daily specials such as meat and potato pie (£2.55), or beef bourguignonne or fish pie (£2.85). Well kept Vaux Samson and Wards Sheffield Best on handpump. The pub is handy for the Lowther Wildlife Park. *(Recommended by T Nott, Jon Wainwright, Syd and Wyn Donald, Brian Randall, J Pearson, Roger Stephenson, R C Wiles, Michael Williamson, John Oliver, Josh Cardy, Miss D A Thain, MGBD, Jon and Heather Cheney)*

Vaux   Licensee John Askew   Real ale   Meals and snacks   Restaurant   Children in back bar   Open all day during school summer holidays; 12–3, 7–11 in winter   Bedrooms tel Hackthorpe (093 12) 225; £20/£36

BARBON SD6385 Map 10
Barbon Inn ★ ⇖

Village signposted off A683 Kirkby Lonsdale–Sedbergh; OS Sheet 97 reference 628826

Several individually furnished and very comfortable small rooms open off the main bar in this quiet, welcoming inn. They are attractively furnished with carved eighteenth-century oak settles, deep chintzy sofas and armchairs, and lots of fresh flowers. Home-made bar food includes soup (95p), sandwiches (from 85p), potted shrimps (£1.80), ploughman's or duck and chicken liver pâté (£1.90), Cumberland sausage (£2.50), steak and kidney pie (£3.25), sirloin steak (£5.95), and puddings like fudgecake (95p); well kept Theakstons Best and Old Peculier on handpump; dominoes. The neatly kept, sheltered garden is very prettily planted and floodlit at night. Tracks and paths lead up to the steep fells above the village. *(Recommended by J E Rycroft, Mr and Mrs D C Leaman, AE, GRE, MGBD, Col G D Stafford, Wayne Brindle)*

Free house   Licensee Keith Whitlock   Real ale   Meals and snacks (not Sat evening) Restaurant   Children welcome   Open 12–3, 6–11 all year   Bedrooms tel Barbon (046 836) 233; £20.90/£39.60

BASSENTHWAITE LAKE NY2228 Map 9
Pheasant ★ ⊗ 🛏

Follow Wythop Mill signpost at N end of dual carriageway stretch of A66 by Bassenthwaite Lake

Beautifully placed in woods below Sale Fell, this charming hotel has a pubby bar with two cosy rooms linked by a fine wood-framed arch: rush-seat chairs, library seats and cushioned settles, hunting prints and photographs on the tobacco-coloured walls, and a low serving-counter, which has a hatch to the entry corridor through a traditional wood and glass partition. A large and airy beamed lounge at the back (overlooking the garden, from which you can walk up into the beech woods) has easy chairs on its polished parquet floor and a big log fire on cool days; there are also attractively chintzy sitting-rooms with antique furniture. Good, freshly made lunchtime bar food includes soup (90p), ploughman's or pâté (£1.95), Cumberland pork and ham pie or vegetable and nut terrine with yoghurt dressing (£2.45), continental meat salad (£2.55), sweet smoked chicken or prawns with lobster sauce (£2.95), crab salad (£3.40) and smoked Scotch salmon (£4.50); they do main dishes in the dining-room (which is non-smoking). Well kept Bass and Theakstons Best on handpump; helpful, friendly service. *(Recommended by Miss A Tress, G Smith, BKA, D Thornton, Syd and Syn Donald, Sue Braisted, Gwen and Peter Andrews, D G Nicolson, Timothy Duke, Brian and Elizabeth Carter, M P W Brown, PLC, Jon Wainwright, K McConnochie, M A and W R Proctor, J E Rycroft)*

Free house   Licensee W E Barrington Wilson   Real ale   Lunchtime snacks   Restaurant Children in lounge (not Sun)   Open 11–3, 5.30–10.30   Bedrooms tel Bassenthwaite Lake (059 681) 234; £33B/£58B

BEETHAM SD5079 Map 7
Wheatsheaf 🛏

Village (and inn) signposted just off A6 S of Milnthorpe

The striking black and white timbered cornerpiece, a glorified two-storey set of gabled oriel windows jettied out from the corner and peeking down what is now the very quiet village street, is both a landmark and a strong hint of what you'll find inside. This is a warmly old-fashioned place, with a comfortably conversational lounge bar – attractive built-in wall settles, tapestry-cushioned chairs, a massive antique carved oak armchair, a cabinet filled with foreign costume dolls, neatly exposed beams and joists, fox mask and brush, and a calm old golden labrador. The one counter serves this, a little central snug, then beyond that there is a tiled-floor bar with darts, dominoes and fruit machine. Bar food includes soup (65p), sandwiches, Cumberland sausage or a choice of quiches (£1.55), chicken and mushroom pie (£2.45) and steak and mushroom casserole or the fresh fish of the day (£2.60); well kept Thwaites Bitter on handpump. *(Recommended by MGBD, A T Langton)*

Free house   Licensee Mrs Florence Miller   Real ale   Meals and snacks   Restaurant   Open 11–3, 6–11 all year   Bedrooms tel Milnthorpe (044 82) 2123; £18(£20.25)/£26.50(£31)

BIGGAR SD1965 Map 7
Queens Arms

On Isle of Walney; follow A590 or A5087 into Barrow-in-Furness centre, then Walney signposted through Vickerstown – bear left on the island

For a stranger, tracking down this pub is an entertaining expedition. The road threads past a series of gigantic shipyard gates, weaves across a couple of great drawbridges, then tracks down the island (more Icelandic-seeming than Cumbrian – neat small houses under a wide sky, and an Atlantic wind smacking freshly across the grassy sand-flats), and finally reaches what looks like a little huddle of black-trimmed white farm buildings. The snug little bar has a good deal of brown varnish, an open fire in its stone fireplace, wheel-back chairs and tapestried built-in banquettes, and a Delft shelf; well kept Hartleys on handpump; piped music. Rustic seats and tables shelter in the yard, and opening off this there's a smallish eating-room with high-backed settles forming booths around the tables (the wide range of bar food from sandwiches to steaks is attractively priced), and a more spacious restaurant. There are broad sandy beaches practically on the doorstep, with a nature reserve to the south (the air's full of the liquid pipings of curlews and wading birds). *(Recommended by Brian Jones, Paul Corbett)*

Whitbreads   Licensee T J Stanley   Real ale   Meals and snacks   Restaurant tel Barrow-in-Furness (0229) 41113   Children in eating-room and restaurant   Open 11–3, 6ish–11 all year

BOOT   NY1701 Map 9

Boot

Village signposted just off the Wrynose/Hardknott Pass road; OS Sheet 89 reference 175010

In a pretty hamlet close to Dalegarth Station (the top terminus of the Ravenglass and Eskdale light steam railway), and to a fine restored cornmill, this friendly, simple inn has a landlord who shepherded for years on these hills, and is expert at suggesting good walks. The surroundings are lovely, with peaceful fells that rise fairly gently at first towards Scafell, and lots of attractive tracks such as the one up along Whillan Beck to Burnmoor Tarn. The beamed and carpeted white-painted bar has an open fire and red leatherette seats; the snug and restaurant can be traced back to 1578. Generous helpings of quickly served bar food includes soup (75p), ploughman's or cheese and onion flan (£2), breaded haddock or cold beef or ham (£2.60), local venison and pheasant pie cooked with fresh herbs, juniper berries, red wine and brandy (£3.70), wienerschnitzel (£4 – the Austrian influence is from Mrs Fosters's mother, who ran the pub for many years until they took it over), sirloin steak (£5.20), and puddings (90p); they grow a lot of the vegetables themselves, and keep hens and pigs. Well kept Jennings on handpump; dominoes, juke box, pool-room. There are seats outside on the sheltered front lawn; near *Good Walks Guide* Walk 125. *(Recommended by Syd and Wyn Donald, Charles and Mary Winpenny, AE, GRE, W P P Clarke, Gwen and Peter Andrews, A Kelly, P Lloyd, Michael and Alison Sandy)*

Free house   Licensee Tony Foster   Real ale   Meals and snacks   Restaurant   Children welcome until 8.45   Open 11–3, 5.30–11 all year   Bedrooms tel Eskdale (094 03) 224; £13.75(£15.25B)/£27.50(£30.50B)

BOWLAND BRIDGE   SD4289 Map 9

Hare & Hounds ⊗ ⇌

Village signposted from A5074; OS Sheet 97 reference 417895

The spacious open-plan lounge bar in this comfortably modernised pub is divided into smaller areas by surviving stub walls, and has ladder-back chairs around dark wood tables on its Turkey carpet; it's decorated with blue and white china, reproduction hunting prints, a stuffed pheasant – and England caps and a Liverpool team photograph (the landlord is the former Anfield favourite and England wing). Besides sandwiches (from £1.20), notably generous helpings of bar food include soup (95p), pâté (£1.85), ploughman's (£2.75), salads (from £2.75), Cumberland sausage (£2.95), roast chicken (£3.75), lasagne or beef Stroganoff (£4.25), and evening steaks (from £7.25); prompt, friendly service; Tetleys on handpump, from a long bar counter with a comfortably cushioned red leatherette elbow rest for people using the sensible backrest-type bar stools; darts, dominoes, pool, fruit machine, space game and juke box in the separate tartan-seated Stable Bar.

(Recommended by J Howard, Jon Wainwright, GAC, Dave Braisted, C F Walling, Mike Suddards)

Free house   Licensee Peter Thompson   Real ale   Meals and snacks   Children welcome   Open 11–3, 6–11   Bedrooms tel Crosthwaite (044 88) 333; £20(£20S)/£33(£33SB)

CARTMEL   SD3879 Map 9
Kings Arms
The Square

At the head of Cartmel's lovely square stands this rather grand little black and white pub. The rambling bar has handsome heavy beams (with foreign banknotes on some of them), a mixture of seats including old country chairs, settles and wall banquettes on the fitted carpet, a fox's mask and small antique prints on the walls, and tankards hanging over the serving-counter (with well kept Hartleys Bitter on handpump). Freshly made bar food includes soup, sandwiches, salads, quiche, home-roast ham, burgers, Cumberland sausage, haddock, roast chicken, scampi and fillet steak; darts, fruit machine, space invaders, unobtrusive piped music. This ancient village has a grand priory church, and close to the pub is a fine medieval stone gatehouse – where there is often an art exhibition; the nearby second-hand bookshop is well worth a look. *(Recommended by A T Langton, AE, GRE, MGDB, Wayne Brindle, Pete Storey)*

Hartleys/Whitbreads   Real ale   Meals and snacks (not Mon evening)   Open 10.30–3, 6–11 all year

CARTMEL FELL   SD4288 Map 9
Masons Arms ★ ★
Strawberry Bank, a few miles S of Windermere between A592 and A5074; perhaps the simplest way of finding the pub is to go uphill W from Bowland Bridge (which is signposted off A5074) towards Newby Bridge and keep right then left at the staggered crossroads – it's then on your right, below Gummer's How; OS Sheet 97 reference 413895

The two stars, putting this isolated Lakeland house into the select company of the country's most interesting pubs, are awarded for an exceptional and imaginative choice of drinks (many of them imported specially by the enthusiastic young landlord), the careful restoration and attractive furnishings that you can find in several of its corners, and the unrivalled fellside setting, looking over the Winster Valley to the woods below Whitbarrow Scar. Food, plentiful though not cheap, is often imaginative, and might include sandwiches, soup (from 95p), ploughman's (£2.95), fisherman's pie or lasagne (£3.75), chicken and mushroom pie (£3.95), beef casserole (£4.95), and specials (with around seven suitable for vegetarians): hummus with pitta bread (£2.25), sweet-and-sour chicken wings (£3), blue cheese and mushroom lasagne (£3.25), tortellini stuffed with ricotta cheese with a fresh tomato and basil sauce (£3.50), baked chicken in a glazed orange sauce (£3.75), rabbit and prune pie or lamb koftas (£3.95), and baked halibut with hollandaise sauce (£4.50). Extensions to the kitchen in early 1988 should overcome some problems reported to us the previous year in busy summer periods (as you'd expect, the pub does attract a great many customers then). There's a tremendous choice of unusual bottled beers (200 or so, with a fine descriptive list, £1; thirty or so are from all over Britain and have their own separate list), and McEwans 80/-, Theakstons Best, Thwaites Bitter and Youngers No 3 on handpump, with guest beers from all over the country (last year they had ninety-seven or so); as we went to press, they were hoping to start work on their own microbrewery, brewing a pale Bitter, eighteen gallons at a time, which should be on handpump by the time this is

---

Bedroom prices normally include full English breakfast, VAT and any inclusive service charge that we know of.

published. Interesting farm ciders and perries, and there are usually country wines. The main bar has low black beams in a bowed ceiling, country chairs and plain wooden tables on polished flagstones, needlework samplers and country pictures, a big log fire, and by it a grandly Gothick seat with snarling dogs as its arms. A small lounge has oak tables and settles to match its fine Jacobean panelling, and a plain little room beyond the serving-counter has more pictures and a fire in an open range. Darts, dominoes, cribbage. The outside has been terraced and there are rustic benches and tables that make the most of the view (which is shared by comfortable self-catering flats in an adjoining stone barn). You can buy a book with walks of varying degrees of time and difficulty, linked on a page with recipes. A new car park is being built. *(Recommended by Miss A Tress, G Smith, Ashley Madden, JH, NIP, J L Thompson, Lynn Stevens, Gill Quarton, Rob and Gill Weeks, S D Samuels, Syd and Wyn Donald, David Gwynne Harper, Mr and Mrs Jon Payne, AE, Ken and Dorothy Worrall, R C Wiles, Margaret and Roy Randle, Wayne Brindle, MGBD, A T Langton, D P Bagnall, Martin Rayner, Caroline Gibbins, Hayward Wane, G C Hixon, Jon Wainwright, W D Horsfield, Dr and Mrs A K Clarke, Col G D Stafford, Philip Denison, C F Walling, Ewan McCall, J E Rycroft, M A and W R Proctor, Laurence Manning)*

Free house   Licensees Helen and Nigel Stevenson   Meals and snacks   Children welcome Open 11–3, 6–11 all year; considering longer afternoon opening Sat Self-catering flats tel Crosthwaite (044 88) 486

CASTERTON   SD6379   Map 7

Pheasant ⊗

A683 about a mile N of junction with A65, by Kirkby Lonsdale

This neatly modernised and well kept village inn has a wide choice of bar food such as sandwiches, home-made soup (£1), Danish herring salad (£1.85), ploughman's, omelettes or hors d'oeuvre (£3), roast chicken or locally smoked salmon (£3.50), steak and kidney pie (£3.75), roast beef salad (£4), gammon with cheese and pineapple or pork skewer (£4.50), seafood platter (£5.50), and eight-ounce minute steak (£5.75). Well kept Jennings, Tetleys, and Thwaites on handpump; friendly staff. The two rooms of the main bar have built-in button-back wall banquettes and red plush stools around the dimpled copper tables on its red carpet, and there's an open log fire in a nicely arched bare stone fireplace; dominoes, piped music. Tables with cocktail parasols shelter in the front L of the white building by the road. There are attractive Pre-Raphaelite stained glass and paintings in the nearby church, built for the girls' school of Brontë fame here. *(Recommended by Wayne Brindle, Jon Wainwright, Mike Suddards, Mrs Margaret Cross, GAC)*

Free house   Licensee David Seed Hesmondhalgh   Real ale   Meals and snacks Restaurant   Children welcome   Open 11.30–2.30, 6–11 all year   Bedrooms tel Kirkby Lonsdale (0468) 71230; £25B/(£37B)

CONISTON   SD3098   Map 9

Sun ⊗ ⏚

Inn signposted from centre

Just above the heart of the village, this substantial stone house looks across its neat tree-sheltered lawn to the spectacular bare fells around. Tracks from the lane lead straight up to the Old Man of Coniston, and the inn serves as a mountain rescue post. Being out of the centre, it's a good deal less touristy than most here. The partly carpeted back bar has handsome polished flagstones, lots of Lakeland colour photographs and some recalling Donald Campbell (this was his HQ during his final attempt on the world water speed record), a small but very warm log fire, and some cask seats (one pair remarkably heavy) as well as cushioned spindle-back chairs and brown plush built-in wall benches around the traditional cast-iron-framed tables. Readers (one, celebrating fifty years of patronage here, reckons the inn is currently right on top of its form) particularly like the chiplessness – so rare in the Lakes – of the bar food. It's all home made, including a soup of the day such as cucumber and mint (£1), sandwiches (from £1), ploughman's, Cumberland sausage or a pair of interestingly filled baked potatoes (£2.50), gammon salad (£3.75), and several dishes of the day such as pork and spinach pâté (£2) and chicken and mushroom pie (£4.20); lots of puddings such as sticky toffee or carrot and cinnamon cake with orange cream icing. The restaurant specialises in local ingredients – Herdwick lamb, Esthwaite trout. Well kept Jennings, Marstons Pedigree and Tetleys on handpump, from the deep sixteenth-century granite cellar; darts, dominoes, unobtrusive piped music. There are white tables out on the terrace, and the big garden runs down to a steep little beck; fishing, riding and shooting can be arranged for residents. *(Recommended by A T Langton, Grahame Archer, Ned Edwards, Linda and Carl Worley, Jon Wainwright)*

Free house   Licensees Joan LeLong and Karen Farmer   Real ale   Meals and snacks Restaurant   Children welcome until 8.30   Open 11–11 all year; closed winter afternoons until 7; closed 25 Dec   Bedrooms tel Coniston (053 94) 41258; £28.50B/£57B

DENT   SD7187 Map 10

Sun

Village signposted from Sedbergh; and from Barbon, off A683

The surrounding high fell scenery brings people to this attractive village with its steep and narrow cobbled lanes, and from the front this little whitewashed inn is one of the prettiest buildings here. Inside, the cheerful modernised carpeted bar still has quite a traditional feel, as well as dark armed chairs, brown leatherette wall benches, some fine old oak timbers and beams (studded with coins), and a coal fire; through the arch to the left are banquettes upholstered to match the carpet (as are the curtains). The walls are decorated with lots of local snapshots and old Schweppes advertisements. Generous helpings of bar food include sandwiches, home-made pasty (£1.95), quiche (£2.25), vegetarian or meat lasagne (£2.55), steak and kidney pie (£2.65), gammon and pineapple (£2.95) and steaks (from £3.45). Well kept Theakstons XB and Youngers Scotch and No 3 on handpump; darts, pool, dominoes, cribbage, fruit machine and piped music. There are rustic seats and tables outside, and barbecues in summer. *(Recommended by Jonathan Williams; more reports please)*

Free house   Licensees Jacky and Martin Stafford   Real ale   Meals and snacks   Children in eating area of bar   Open 11–2.30, 6.30–11; 11–2, 7–11 in winter; open all day Sat Bedrooms tel Dent (058 75) 208;/£22

ELTERWATER   NY3305 Map 9

Britannia Inn   ★ ⊗ 🍴

Off B5343

Unlike many Lakeland places, the traditionally furnished, small beamed bar at the back of this old-fashioned and friendly little inn doesn't turn up its nose at walking-boots. The front bar has settles, oak benches, Windsor chairs and, in winter, coal fires, and a couple of window seats look across the pretty village green to glimpses of Elterwater itself through the trees on the far side (a view shared by seats in the garden above the front of the pub); there's also a comfortable lounge. Good home-cooked bar food includes sandwiches, home-made soup (75p), filled wholemeal baps (95p), filled baked potato (£1), hot potted shrimps on granary roll (£1.70), ploughman's (£2.50), double burger (£2.75), salads (from £3.10), Lancashire hot-pot or vegetable lasagne (£3.25), steak and kidney pie or cheese and broccoli flan (£3.45), and rainbow trout (£4.05); daily specials, puddings (from £1), children's dishes (from £1.20), and good breakfasts. Well kept Bass, Hartleys and Jennings on handpump, several ciders, and country wines; darts, shove-ha'penny, dominoes and cribbage. The pub is well placed for Langdale and the central lakes, with tracks over the fells to Grasmere and Easedale, and is near the start of *Good Walks Guide* Walk 128. It can get quite crowded here in summer, but readers have found the service unruffled even when people flock here to watch morris and step and garland dancers on the green. *(Recommended by JH, J L Thompson, Robert Gartery, Michael Thomson, Wayne Brindle, John Atherton, Jon Wainwright, Gwen and Peter Andrews, John Roué, MGBD, Chris Bourne, S C Beardwell, J Stacey, J L and E B Burns, C M Whitehouse, Capt E P Gray, Peter Race, Simon Bates, A T Langton, Caroline Gibbins, Alun and Eryl Davies)*

Free house   Licensee David Fry   Real ale   Meals and snacks   Restaurant   Summer parking may be difficult   Open all day; closed 25 Dec and evening 26 Dec   Bedrooms tel Langdale (096 67) 210 or 382; £18.75/£37.50(£42.50B)

ESKDALE GREEN   NY1400 Map 9
Bower House ⊗ ⇔

½ mile W of village towards Santon Bridge

This cosy, friendly place has a comfortable lounge bar with cushioned settles and Windsor chairs that blend in well with the original beamed and alcoved nucleus around the serving-counter; there's a good fire in winter too. This opens out on to the very pretty and well kept sheltered lawn and garden – an unusual bonus for the Lake District. Bar food includes sandwiches, pâté (£1.65), beef or ham salad or lasagne (£3.25), steak and kidney or chicken and mushroom pie (£3.40), gammon and egg (£3.85), guinea-fowl in cranberry sauce (£4.35), eighteen-ounce T-bone steak (£7.70), and home-made puddings such as raspberry and ginger russe or cherry pudding (85p). Well kept Hartleys, Theakstons and Youngers on handpump. There's also a separate comfortable lounge with easy chairs and sofas. The current balance of readers' views is that the simple bedrooms in the pub itself seem better value than those in the annexe across the garden – we'd like more views on this. The pub is near *Good Walks Guide* Walk 125. *(Recommended by Miss A Tress, G Smith, Ian Briggs, Mike Muston, Hayward Wane, MGBD, Marcus and Marcella Leith, Dr R Hodkinson, Dr R H M Stewart, Hon Mrs Fennell, Nick Poole, P Lloyd)*

Free house   Licensee D J Connor   Real ale   Meals and snacks   Restaurant   Children welcome   Open 11–3, 6–11   Bedrooms tel Eskdale (094 03) 244; £21.50(£27.50B)/ £30(£43B)

FAUGH   NY5155 Map 9
String of Horses ★ ⊗ ⇔

From A69 in Warwick Bridge, turn off at Heads Nook, Castle Carrock signpost, then follow Faugh signs – if you have to ask the way, it's pronounced Faff

This seventeenth-century inn is pretty outside, with Dutch blinds and lanterns, and more lanterns and neat wrought iron among the greenery of the sheltered terrace. Inside, the cosy, communicating rooms of the open-plan bar have fine old settles and elaborately carved Gothick seats and tables, as well as simpler Windsor and other chairs, heavy beams, and log fires in cool weather (which may even mean a summer evening); decorations include brass pots and warming pans, and some interesting antique prints on the cream walls. Bar food includes sandwiches (from £1.20), prize-winning black pudding or filled baked potato (£1.50), Cumberland sausage (£2.75), a good buffet, chilli con carne (£3.25), home-made steak and mushroom pie (£3.50), salads (from £3.50), gammon with pineapple or fisherman's platter (£3.85), and sirloin steak (£4.95); also, daily specials, and good home-made puddings (£1.50). Evening bar food orders are taken until 10.15pm – unusually late for the area. Piped music. Residents have the use of a jacuzzi, sauna, solarium and small outdoor heated pool. *(Recommended by R Wiles, J H Tate, Nigel Furneaux, Debbie Pratt, Miss D A Thain, G Bloxsom, Mike Lawson, Alan Bickley)*

Free house   Licensee Anne Tasker   Meals and snacks   Restaurant   Children welcome   Occasional music in restaurant Sat   Open 11.30–3, 5.30–11 all year   Bedrooms tel Hayton (022 870) 297 or 509; £43B/£50B

GRASMERE   NY3406 Map 9

Wordsworth ⊗ 🍴

In the village itself

The unpretentious little Dove & Olive Bar – attached to this luxurious hotel, though it has separate staff – is off to the left of the main entrance and has mate's chairs and attractively cushioned built-in seats around cast-iron-framed tables on the slate floor, a good log fire in winter, and a friendly atmosphere; the big bare beams have nice plates, and it's decorated with stuffed fish, foxes' masks and brushes, sea and sporting prints, and photographs of the local fell races. Good value, simple bar food includes generously filled baked potatoes (£1.50), shepherd's pie or potted crab and prawn with toast (£2.50), and at lunchtime home-made soup (90p), filled baps (from £1.10) and ploughman's (£2.50), with a pâté ploughman's (£2.50); well kept Bass Special on handpump. There are sturdy old teak seats in a slate-floored verandah leading out of the cleanly kept bar, and the hotel gardens are very neat; near the start of *Good Walks Guide* Walk 129. *(Recommended by Philip Denison; more reports please)*

Free house   Licensee Robin Lees   Real ale   Meals and snacks (evening food July–Oct only)   Restaurant   Open 11–3, 5.30–11; opens 6 in winter   Bedrooms tel Grasmere (096 65) 592; £39.50B/£71B

HAWKSHEAD   SD3598 Map 9

Kings Arms 🍴

This picturesque old inn has one prize that's at a special premium here, where space is so very tight – a terrace out in the pretty central square, with old-fashioned teak seats and oak cask tables around the roses. The low-ceilinged bar is relaxed and cheerful, with red-cushioned wall and window seats and red plush stools on the Turkey carpet, and most tables of a height to suit drinkers rather than eaters (you can have bar meals at the same price in the restaurant, too). Bar food includes sandwiches (from £1.15), ploughman's (£2.40), vegetarian dishes (from £2.60), Cumberland sausage (£2.75), steak and kidney pie (£3.05), local trout baked with lemon and herbs (£3.55) and eight-ounce sirloin steak (£5.20); well kept Matthew Browns Mild, Tetleys and Theakstons Best on handpump, open fire; darts and dominoes in winter; fruit machine; unobtrusive piped pop music. Some of the bedrooms have ancient coins embedded in the oak beams. *(Recommended by Marcus Leith, Charles and Mary Winpenny, Margaret and Roy Randle, Michael Thomson, Wayne Brindle, AE, GRE)*

Free house   Licensee Lee Johnson   Real ale   Meals and snacks   Restaurant   Children welcome   Open 11–11; may have afternoon rota with other local pubs in winter   Bedrooms tel Hawkshead (096 66) 372; £17.50(£20B)/£28(£35B)

Queens Head ★ ⊗

The new licensees are planning to refurbish the bars here over the next year – we hope without spoiling the special atmosphere, which preliminary reports suggest they have succeeded in preserving. The open-plan bar has red leatherette wall seats and plush stools around heavy traditional tables – most used by diners – on the discreetly patterned red carpet, a few plates decorating one panelled wall, heavy bowed black beams in the low ceiling, and a snug little room leading off. As we went to press in the summer food in the bar and oak-panelled dining-room included home-made soup (£1.10), sandwiches (from £1.10), open sandwiches (from £2.50), ploughman's (£3.25), salads (from £3.25), Cumberland sausage (£3.50), home-made ratatouille, ham, mushroom and cheese quiche or grilled local rainbow trout (£3.95), steaks (from £6.25), and specials like lasagne (£3.95), casseroles (£4.25) or lemon sole (£5.25); some changes in this are likely. Well kept Hartleys Bitter and Mild on handpump; quick, friendly service; dominoes, cribbage, piped classical music. The village is a charming and virtually car-free network of stone-paved alleys winding through huddles of whitewashed cottages. *(Recommended by R H Sawyer, Charles and Mary Winpenny, A T Langton, Brenda Gentry, PAB, M G Hart, Wayne Brindle, AE, GRE, Peter Race, R P Taylor, Miss D A Thain, T Seddon, Colin and Caroline, Dr and Mrs A K Clarke, Mike Lawson, Sue Cleasby, Mike Ledger, J L and E B Burns, Jon Wainwright, D E and A H Clarke, Caroline Gibbins)*

Hartleys   Licensee Tony Merrick   Real ale   Meals and snacks   Restaurant   Children in eating areas   Open all day   Bedrooms tel Hawkshead (096 66) 271; £20(£22.50)/£32(£39B)

nr HAWKSHEAD   SD3598 Map 9
Drunken Duck

Barngates; hamlet signposted from B5286 Hawkshead–Ambleside, opposite the Outgate Inn; OS Sheet 90 reference 350013

The three or four cosy beamed rooms in this old white pub have ladder-back country chairs, blond pews, cushioned old settles, and tapestried stools on fitted Turkey carpet, as well as good fires; also, Cecil Aldin prints, lots of landscapes and a big longcase clock; a new snug attached to the bar has similar furnishings. Popular bar food includes tasty sandwiches (from £1), soup (£1.20), good ploughman's (£2.50), mushroom provençale (£2.75), watercress and mushroom lasagne or vegetable chilli (£3.55), fennel, orange and mushroom bake or moussaka (£3.75), steak and kidney, game or smoked haddock and vegetable pies (£4), and puddings like sticky toffee or jam roly-poly (£1.25); friendly rather than speedy service. Well kept Jennings, Marstons Pedigree, Tetleys Bitter and Theakstons XB and Old Peculier on handpump, with guest beers like Marstons Merrie Monk; a good choice of whiskies (including a couple of Macallans) and good value house wines. Darts, dominoes. There are seats under the bright hanging baskets on the front verandah with views of distant Lake Windermere; to the side there are quite a few rustic wooden chairs and tables sheltered by a stone wall with alpine plants along its top, and the pub has fishing in two private tarns behind. Dogs welcome. *(Recommended by Lynn Stevens, Gill Quarton, Charles and Mary Winpenny, JH, Syd and Wyn Donald, Mike Stables, Mr and Mrs Evelyn Cribb, Mike Muston, Jon Wainwright, Sue Cleasby, Mike Ledger, P Lloyd, K Bamford, Simon Bates)*

Free house   Licensee Peter Barton   Real ale   Meals and snacks   Children welcome (not in bar)   Occasional live music   Open 11.30–3, 6–11; 11.30–2.30, 7–11 in mid-winter; closed 25 Dec   Bedrooms tel Hawkshead (096 66) 347; £15.75 (£18.50B)/£31.50(£37B)

HEVERSHAM   SD4983 Map 9
Blue Bell

A6 (now a relatively very quiet road here)

One reader feels this well kept, civilised place has remained consistently good throughout the seventeen years he's known it. The bay-windowed lounge bar has an antique carved settle, comfortable cushioned Windsor armchairs, and upholstered stools on its flowery carpet, as well as pewter platters hanging from one of the black beams and small antique sporting prints on the partly panelled walls; in cool weather there's an open fire. One big bay-windowed area has been divided off as a children's room, and the long tiled-floor quieter public bar has darts and dominoes. A sensibly short choice of good value bar food includes filled rolls, sandwiches, home-made soup (lunchtime only), locally baked steak and kidney pie, home-made quiche, home-made cottage pie and salads including fresh salmon; well kept Bass, Hartleys XB and Tetleys on handpump; friendly, helpful staff; darts, dominoes and cribbage. *(Recommended by R H Sawyer, Jonathan Williams, Raymond Palmer, MGBD)*

Free house   Licensee John Chew   Real ale   Snacks   Restaurant   Children in eating area of bar   Occasional live music   Open 10.30–3, 6–11 all year; closed 25 and 26 Dec   Bedrooms tel Milnthorpe (044 82) 2018; £28(£37S)/£50B

KESWICK   NY2624 Map 9

Dog & Gun

Lake Road; off top end of Market Square

The Turkey-carpeted main bar in this lively, friendly little tavern has low beams (studded with coins and hung with coloured lanterns), close-set tables with wheel-back chairs and upholstered pews, a slate floor by the bar counter, fires in winter and flickering electric candles. There's a fine collection of striking mountain photographs by the local firm G P Abrahams: big blow-ups in a slate-floored lobby, and mainly smaller ones in a back room with captain's chairs around cast-iron-framed tables on its brown patterned carpet. Good, reasonably priced food, very popular with the friendly locals, includes lunchtime sandwiches, home-made French onion soup (85p), and hot home-roasted ham, fresh Borrowdale trout, home-made Hungarian goulash and hot roast chicken (all £3.60). Well kept Theakstons Best, XB and Old Peculier on handpump; darts, dominoes, cribbage, fruit machine and piped music. *(Recommended by David Gwynne Harper, Rita Horridge, David Millar, Brian and Pauline Fullam, Jon Wainwright, Simon Bates, C Dempsey, Philip Denison)*

Theakstons   Licensee F J Hughes   Real ale   Meals and snacks   Children welcome lunchtime and early evening   Open 11–3, 6–11; closed 25 Dec

KIRKBY LONSDALE   SD6278 Map 7

Snooty Fox ⊗

Main Street (B6254)

This attractively de-modernised, rambling old inn has a healthy mix of visitors and friendly locals, and is especially popular for the good value bar food (get there early, especially on Thursday – market day): home-made soup (£1), filled baked potatoes (from £1.60), mushrooms stuffed with fresh garlic and parsley and topped with cheese sauce (£2.25), Mexican tacos filled with prawns cooked in garlic butter (£2.55), cheese platter (£2.65), filled pancakes (from £2.75), Cumberland sausage with local black pudding and apple sauce (£3.35), a cold platter called Fox's Farmhouse Forage – which also includes a bowl of farmhouse broth (£3.75) – steak and kidney pudding (£3.95), guinea-fowl (£4.75), tagliatelle with shellfish (£4.95), and home-made puddings (£1.65); they use British Charolais beef – excellent – for Sunday lunch and steaks; huge breakfasts. Well kept Hartleys XB and Youngers Scotch on handpump; efficient, friendly service. The various rooms of the bar have flagstones, some oak panelling, one or two high-backed settles, country kitchen chairs, pews, marble-topped sewing-trestle tables, two coal fires and shutters; the bar top in the front bar is made from English oak, and in November the back bar will be repanelled and will also have an English oak bar counter; decorations include stuffed wildfowl and falcons, mugs hanging from beams, mounted badgers' and foxes' masks, guns and a powder-flask, eye-catching coloured engravings, stage gladiator costumes, horse-collars and stirrups and so forth. Dominoes, fruit machine, trivia and good juke box. There are tables out on a small terrace beside the biggish back cobbled stableyard. *(Recommended by Jon Wainwright, Wayne Brindle,*

Hayward Wane, Colin Hall, Professor S Barnett, Tony Pounder, Col G D Stafford, MGBD, Richard G Walz)

*Free house   Licensees Andrew Walker and Jack Shone   Real ale   Meals and snacks
Restaurant   Children welcome   Jazz band third Tues of month   Open all day in summer;
11–3, 6–11 in winter   Bedrooms tel Kirkby Lonsdale (0468) 71308; £15(£25S)/£25(£35S)*

Sun 🛏

Market Street (B6254)

Friendly and relaxing, this old inn – with its unusual pillared porch below an overhanging upper storey – has several neatly kept and comfortably modernised interconnecting rooms. There are maps, old engravings, a large collection of some three hundred banknotes, battleaxes and fancy Pennine walking sticks on the walls – some are stripped to bare stone, others have panelled dados, as well as low beams, green plush cushioned seats, captain's and spindle-back chairs on the red carpet, and fires in winter. They have recently excavated a sixteenth-century arched cellar which will be put to use in the near future. Good value homely bar food includes sandwiches, home-made soup (95p), pâté (£1.75), ploughman's (£2.50), local Cumberland sausage (£2.80), home-made lasagne (£3.25), salads (from £2.95), scampi or home-made steak pie (£3.25), trout (£5.90) and steaks (£5.95); children's menu (£1.75). Well kept Youngers Scotch and No 3, and Theakstons Best on handpump (the stools by the long bar counter in the front room have good back rests); quick, cheerful service; darts (not very well placed), dominoes and piped music. The pub is by a cobbled alley to the churchyard. *(Recommended by Jon Wainwright, Ray and Jenny Colquhoun, R P Begg, G E Hayward)*

*Free house   Licensees Andrew and Belinda Wilkinson   Real ale   Meals and snacks
Restaurant   Children welcome   Open all day   Bedrooms tel Kirkby Lonsdale
(0468) 71965; £15(£17.50B)/£29.50(£32.50B)*

LANGDALE   NY2906 Map 9
Old Dungeon Ghyll 🛏

B5343

A popular meeting-place with walkers and climbers, this friendly pub has a grand view of the Pike of Blisco rising behind Kettle Crag from the window seats cut into the enormously thick stone walls of the simply furnished bar. Good value bar food includes home-made soup and home-made bread (75p), and Cumberland sausage, home-made steak and kidney pie, lasagne or chilli con carne (£2.75); book if you want a full evening meal. They also serve a choice of snuffs – as well as well kept Marstons Pedigree, Theakstons Best, XB and Old Peculier, Yates Bitter, Youngers No 3 and Scotch, and a weekly guest beer on handpump; darts, shove-ha'penny and dominoes. It can get really lively on a Saturday night, when there's a good deal of spontaneous music-making. This splendid spot is surrounded by towering fells, including the Langdale Pikes flanking Dungeon Ghyll Force waterfall (which inspired Wordsworth's poem 'The Idle Shepherd Boys'). *(Recommended by David White, M W Turner, J L and E B Burns, Marcus and Marcella Leith, Dick Brown)*

*Free house   Licensee Neil Walmsley   Real ale   Meals and snacks   Restaurant   Children
welcome   Spontaneous music Weds   Open all day   Bedrooms tel Langdale (096 67) 272;
£16.25(£18.50B)/£33(£37B)*

Bedroom prices normally include full English breakfast, VAT and any inclusive service charge that we know of. Prices before the '/' are for single rooms, after for two people in double or twin (B includes a private bath, S a private shower). If there is no '/', the prices are only for twin or double rooms (as far as we know there are no singles). If there is no B or S, as far as we know no rooms have private facilities.

LEVENS   SD4886 Map 9
Hare & Hounds ⊗ [*illustrated on page 126*]

Village signposted from A590; since completion of dual carriageway link, best approach is
following route signposted for High Vehicles

Smartened up since last year, without spoiling its friendly atmosphere or character,
this village pub has good value simple food that includes soup (70p), sandwiches
(from 75p, toasties from £1, shrimp open sandwich £1.90), filled baked potato
(80p), ploughman's (£1.70), plaice (£2.35), flan (£2.55), beef or scampi (£2.75),
properly served, delicious Morecambe Bay shrimps, and in the evening six-ounce
steak (£3.45) and grilled ham (£4.40). Well kept Vaux Samson and Bitter and
Wards on handpump and electric pump. The low-beamed, carpeted lounge bar
angles around the servery, and on its sloping floor there is a wicker-backed
Jacobean-style armchair and antique settle, as well as old-fashioned brown
leatherette dining-seats and red-cushioned seats built into the partly panelled walls.
The snug front public bar, with a shelf of gamebird plates above its serving-counter,
has darts, dominoes, cribbage and a fruit machine. A separate pool-room, down
steps, has golden oldies on its juke box. (*Recommended by A T Langton,
Peter Race, H B Smith, MGBD, Jon Wainwright, Dave Braisted*)

*Vaux   Licensee Jim Stephenson   Real ale   Meals and snacks Easter–end Oct; no food
Sun or Mon evenings Nov–Easter   Children in lounge bar beyond dining-room
lunchtime only   Open 11.15–3, 6–11 all year; considering afternoon opening if enough
customers*

LITTLE LANGDALE   NY3204 Map 9
Three Shires ⊗ 🛏

From A593 3 miles W of Ambleside take small road signposted The Langdales, Wrynose Pass,
then bear left at first fork

The carefully extended back bar in this very friendly and comfortable stone-built
house has antique oak carved settles and country kitchen chairs and stools on its big
dark slate flagstones, with local photographs on the walls and a coal fire in cool
weather. Ruddles and Websters Yorkshire on handpump; good service; darts,
dominoes. Good value, generously served bar food at lunchtime includes soup
(95p), sandwiches (from 95p), excellent ploughman's or salads (from £2.55),
Cumberland pie or sausage (£3), home-made steak and kidney pie (£3.50), grilled
lamb chops or local trout (£4.50), and sirloin steak (£6.25); in the evening, dishes
are slightly more expensive, and include prawns in garlic (£2.50) and a vegetarian
dish (£3.60); children's menu (from £1.40), and daily specials. There are seats on
the verandah with a lovely view out over the valley to the partly wooded hills below
Tilberthwaite Fells, with more seats on a well kept lawn behind the car park,
backed by a small oak wood. The pub is on *Good Walks Guide* Walk 128.
(*Recommended by TOH, Peter Race, Martin Howell, Dr Stewart Rae, MGBD, CSS,
R C Watkins*)

*Free house   Licensee Neil Stephenson   Real ale   Meals and snacks   Restaurant   Children
in eating area and restaurant until 9   Open 10.30–3, 5–11 all year; 12–2, 8–11 in winter;
closed 25 Dec   Bedrooms tel Langdale (096 67) 215; £19/£38(£46B)*

LOWESWATER   NY1222 Map 9
Kirkstile

From B5289 follow signs to Loweswater Lake; OS Sheet 89 reference 140210

Surrounded by striking peaks and fells, and close to Loweswater and Crummock
Water (where there is fishing), this friendly country inn has a carpeted main bar
with low beams, partly stripped stone walls, comfortably cushioned small settles
and pews, and a big log fire. Home-baked rolls filled with cheese, pasties, and

salads with various meats are served in here. An adjoining room with big windows looking on to the beck and the fells has a much wider choice of bar food, including sandwiches (from 85p), home-made soup (£1.10), burgers, ploughman's (£2.20), omelettes, Cumberland sausage (£3), home-made pizzas (£4.10), haddock and steaks (£7.70); good breakfasts. Well kept Jennings on handpump, and a good choice of malt whiskies. Darts, dominoes and a slate shove-ha'penny board; a side games-room called the Little Barn has pool, fruit machine, space game and juke box. *(Recommended by C M T Johnson, C A Hood, I C Kinloch, Simon Bates, Jacob and Elsebet Holm)*

Free house Real ale Meals and snacks Restaurant Children welcome Open all day Bedrooms tel Lorton (090 085) 219; £22(£29B)/£29(£36B)

LOWICK GREEN   SD2985 Map 9
Farmers Arms
A595

Behind a massive wooden door several centuries old, the heavy beamed public bar of this rambling old hotel has huge flagstones and a handsome fireplace with a big open fire; some seats are in cosy side alcoves. Bar food includes soup (70p), sandwiches (from £1), ploughman's (£2.50), home-made pâté (£1.50), haddock (£2.80), home-made steak and kidney pie in stout (£2.95), half a chicken (£3.25), scampi (£3.45), gammon (£3.75), and specials such as lasagne, chilli con carne, chicken curry or fresh salmon (from £2.95). Well kept Youngers Scotch and No 3 on handpump, and a good choice of wines by the glass; a computerised till displays a list of purchases, prices and even the barmaid's name on a VDU above the bar; dominoes, fruit machine, trivia, juke box, and piped music (may be loud); also pool-room and darts alley. Across the courtyard, the hotel – which has new licensees – is attractively furnished, and has its own plusher lounge bar, as well as a preserved spinning gallery. Coniston Water is not far away. *(Recommended by Brian Jones, A T Langton, Mike Muston, Simon Bates, M A and W R Proctor, Dr Pete Crawshaw)*

Scottish & Newcastle Licensee Alan Lockwell Real ale Meals and snacks Restaurant Children welcome Open all day Bedrooms tel Greenodd (022 986) 376; £18.50(£26B)/ £40B

MELMERBY   NY6237 Map 10
Shepherds ⊗
A686

Looking across the green of the unspoilt red sandstone village, with the Pennines climbing immediately behind, this spacious pub has a friendly atmosphere as well as cushioned wall seats, sunny window seats, sensible tables and chairs, light panelling, lots of pot plants, and an open fire. A wide choice of good, popular, home-made food (using local produce where possible, and local butchers) is brought to your table: sandwiches, home-made rolls to order, home-made pasties (70p), soup (£1), pork and port pâté (£2), ploughman's with some fourteen good cheeses to choose from – the mature Cheddar is *really* mature – or home-cooked ham (£2.20), plaice (£2.85), Cumberland sausage and egg or salads (£3), grilled halibut steak (£3.20), chicken curry, lasagne, steak and kidney or very good ham and mushroom pie (£3.50), spiced lamb or game hot-pot (£4), chicken breast Leoni (£4.10), beef goulash (£4.30) and rump or sirloin steak (£6); lots of daily specials, vegetarian dishes such as chestnut and mushroom pie or hot-pots (around £3.50), surprise starters like chicken wings in sherry and ginger, Sunday roast lunch (£3.40) and home-made puddings (£1.20). Very well kept Marstons Burton, Pedigree, Merrie Monk and Owd Rodger on handpump. A games-bar has darts, pool, table skittles, shove-ha'penny, dominoes, cribbage and fruit machine. Hartside Nursery

Garden, a noted alpine plant specialist, is just over the Hartside Pass. *(Recommended by Comus Elliott, Grahame Archer, Dewi and Linda Jones, R C Wiles, Dr Stewart Rae, Gwen and Peter Andrews, Ian Clay, Mrs T Frank, Dr R U Watson, EHS, RMS)*

Marstons Licensee Martin Baucutt Real ale Meals and snacks Children in eating area Open 10.30–4, 6–11 all year; 11–2.30 in winter; closed 25 Dec

MIDDLETON SD6397 Map 10
Middleton Fells
A683 Kirkby Lonsdale–Sedbergh

As we went to press, the new licensees told us that several alterations would be taking place over the next six months or so; this will include knocking through to an existing barn where they will put a pool-table, changing the present restaurant into a lounge bar where bar food and Sunday lunches will be served, and installing inside lavatories. Home-made, popular bar food from a menu that changes weekly includes soup (95p), warm French crusty bread with various fillings (from £1.25), a selection of starters (from £1.50), lasagne or spicy chicken and vegetable curry (£3), fisherman's pie (£3.45), beef bourguignonne or steak in ale pie (£3.50), ten-ounce gammon (£3.95) and sirloin steak (£5.95); Sunday roast lunch (£3.50 main course, £5.25 three courses. Service is friendly; well kept Tetleys Bitter and Mild, and Youngers on handpump; darts, pool, dominoes, fruit machine and juke box. The neatly kept and attractive garden has pretty shrub and flower borders with sturdy old-fashioned teak benches and more modern tables and seats out on the back terrace. The pub is surrounded by the quiet countryside of the Lune valley below the great fells that lead up to Calf Top. *(Recommended by MGBD, Col G D Stafford, Wayne Brindle; more reports on the new regime please)*

Free house Licensee John O'Neill Real ale Meals and snacks Children welcome until 8.30 Open 12–3, 7–11; opens 11.30 and 6 Sat

NEAR SAWREY SD3796 Map 9
Tower Bank Arms ⊗
B5285 towards the Windermere ferry

New licensees here don't seem to have changed the good natured, relaxed atmosphere in this country inn, owned by the National Trust and backing on to Beatrix Potter's farm. The traditionally furnished main bar has a big cooking-range with a lovely log fire, high-backed settles on the rough slate floor, a grandfather clock, local hunting photographs under the low beams, and maybe Maxwell or Nelson the pub's black labradors. Good lunchtime bar food includes sandwiches (from £1, lunchtime only), brown rolls (from £1), home-made soup (£1), good ploughman's (from £2.30), pâté (£3.10), home-made quiche (£3.25), home-made pie or chicken (£3.50), and daily specials (from £3); the larger evening menu has extra dishes like potted shrimps (£2.50), salad with home-cooked ham (£3.75), local trout (£4.25), gammon and egg (£4.50), steaks (from £6.25), and specials; very good breakfasts. The dining-room is no-smoking. Well kept Matthew Browns Mild, Theakstons Best and XB, and Youngers Scotch and No 3 on handpump; darts, shove-ha'penny, dominoes and cribbage. Seats outside the quaint black and white cottage have a view of the wooded Claife Heights. It does get crowded in summer. *(Recommended by Wayne Brindle, Miss A Tress, G Smith, Michael and Alison Sandy, Simon and Sally Boxall, Brian Jones, A T Langton, Margaret and Roy Randle, Hayward Wane, Jon Wainwright, Dr Pete Crawshaw)*

Free house Licensee P J Broadley Real ale Meals and lunchtime snacks Restaurant Children in restaurant, in eating area of bar lunchtime Open all day Bedrooms tel Hawkshead (096 66) 334; £20S/£30S

RAVENSTONEDALE   NY7204 Map 10
Kings Head ⊗

Village and pub signposted off A685 W of Kirkby Stephen

Attractive rolling moorland pasture surrounds the village here, and the quiet and friendly black-beamed inn has tables outside that include some over the quiet lane beside Scandal Beck. Inside, the two well kept rooms of the bar are divided by a sturdy stone chimney with good log fires; one side has built-in button-back banquettes and a couple of tables, the other more tables with tapestried dining-chairs. But it's the good value food (with prices almost unchanged since last year) that people like most: home-made soup (70p), sandwiches (80p, toasties 90p), ploughman's (£2), home-made shepherd's pie (£2.50), haddock or good fresh plaice (£2.60), hot roasts (£2.80), scampi or chicken (£3.20), ham and egg (£3.60), and cold meats or seafood from a buffet in summer (£3.95). Very well kept Tetleys and Jennings on handpump. The games-room has sensibly placed darts, pool and fruit machine; also dominoes and piped music. *(Recommended by Mike Tucker, Stephanie Sowerby, AE, GRE, M L Tucker, Dave Braisted, MGBD, Tony Pounder, John and Heather Cheney, R Davies)*

Free house   Licensees C and M Porter   Real ale   Meals and snacks   Restaurant   Children welcome   Open 12–3, 6.30–11 all year   Bedrooms tel Newbiggin-on-Lune (058 73) 284; £13B/£26B

SCALES   NY3427 Map 9
White Horse ⊗

A66 1½ miles E of Threlkeld: keep your eyes skinned – it looks like a farmhouse up on a slope

This popular, friendly place has an eating area with a large oak table in what used to be the old kitchen. Local produce is used in the cooking as much as possible – no chips or convenience foods – and at lunchtime (when it's best to get there early) this includes home-made tomato and orange soup (£1), cottage pie, broccoli and cheese flan or Scotch egg with cranberry sauce (£2.95), prawn open sandwich (£3.25), potted shrimps with hot garlic bread (£3.35), Waberthwaite Cumberland sausage with mushrooms (£3.95) and Waberthwaite dry-cured ham with two eggs (£4.75); puddings such as Blencathra plum pudding (from £1.75). In the evenings (when booking is essential – Threlkeld (059 683) 241) there are dishes like poached Borrowdale trout (£5.50), pork fillet with sherry and mushroom sauce (£6.75) and steaks (from £6.95); in the afternoons in summer they will serve sandwiches, savouries and home-made cakes, scones and strawberry sundaes. Jennings on handpump, dominoes. The spotlessly clean, beamed bar has a growing range of attractive locally mounted animals and birds native to the area, as well as Windsor chairs on the red carpet, local hunting cartoons, an unusual textured wall hanging showing a white horse on the fells, and warm fires in winter; there's also a cosy little snug (in what used to be the dairy). From this isolated cluster of pub and farm buildings, tracks lead up into the splendidly daunting and rocky fells around Blencathra – which have names like Foule Crag and Sharp Edge. *(Recommended by Miss A Tress, G Smith, V P Prentice, BKA, H A R Saunders, Andy Tye, Sue Hill, Hayward Wane, Miss D A Thain, Roger Sherman, Ken and Dorothy Worrall, Ian Clay, M D Jones, K McConnochie, Philip Denison)*

Jennings   Licensee Laurence Slattery   Real ale   Meals and lunchtime snacks; evening meals Sat only Nov–Mar; no food lunchtime 25 Dec   Children in eating area   Open 11–5, 6–11 in summer; winter hours will be more restricted

---

The initials GWG – mentioned, for instance, as 'on GWG 22' – stand for our companion Consumers' Association's book *Holiday Which? Good Walks Guide*, and show that the pub is on or near the walk numbered.

STAINTON NY4928 Map 9
Kings Arms

1¾ miles from M6 junction 40: village signposted from A66 towards Keswick, though quickest to fork left at A592 roundabout then turn first right

The open-plan bar in this comfortably modernised old pub has leatherette wall banquettes, stools and armchairs, wood-effect tables, brasses on the black beams and swirly cream walls. Good value bar food includes soup (65p), sandwiches (from 80p, toasties from 70p), filled baked potato or burger (90p), home-made steak and kidney pie (£1.80), salads (from £2.20), home-roast ham (£2.50), local trout (£2.80), gammon with egg or pineapple or spinach and walnut lasagne (£2.90) and sirloin steak (£4.50); children's menu (£1.10). Whitbreads Castle Eden on handpump; pleasant staff. Sensibly placed darts, dominoes, fruit machine, fairly quiet juke box. It's fairly quiet on weekday lunchtimes, though more lively in the evenings when it's full of local people and visitors. There are tables outside on the side terrace and a small lawn. (*Recommended by H A R Saunders, Neil and Angela Huxter, Sue Braisted, L D Rainger, Dick Brown, Wayne Brindle*)

Whitbreads   Licensee Raymond Tweddle   Real ale   Meals and snacks (not winter weekday evenings)   Children welcome until 9.30   Country and western Sun evening   Open 10.30–3, 6–11 all year, though considering all day opening in July and Aug

TALKIN NY5557 Map 10
Hare & Hounds ★ ⌂

Village signposted from B6413 S of Brampton

The welcome at this well kept, small eighteenth-century village inn is unusually warm, friendly and personal: the licensees put you on first-name terms with the staff and perhaps other guests. The two knocked-through rooms, one black-beamed and timbered, the other with a shiny white plank ceiling, have settles, wicker armchairs and red-cushioned country chairs around the close-set dark elm rustic tables, big antique prints over the two open fires, a fine longcase clock (made in Bampton), and stained-glass municipal coats of arms over the serving-counter. Big helpings of good food includes soup (70p), baked potatoes with six interesting fillings (from 80p), burgers (95p), double-decker sandwich (£1.50), and steak sandwich (£1.95), with main dishes such as plaice with ratatouille (£3), scampi (£4.75), good local fillet steak (£5.75); home-made specials such as lasagne (£1.95), and beef in beer, steak and kidney pie or minty lamb pie (£2.45), puddings (from 80p), and cheap children's dishes (under £1). Tables in the main bar – which can be booked – may all be reserved for diners, so you might find yourself in a quieter back room with stalls around rustic tables. Well kept Hartleys XB and Theakstons Best, XB and Old Peculier on handpump; darts and dominoes; no dogs. There are a few tables on a gravel side terrace, and they have acquired a red telephone box for the use of customers – it was in the village for forty-five years before being replaced by a more modern one. You can walk straight from the small village into fine countryside (Talkin Tarn is a lovely spot for boating, fishing or just sitting, and there's a golf course virtually on the doorstep, which has reduced green fees for residents). The RSPB have designated an area of 90,000 acres nearby as a Bird Reserve. (*Recommended by John Townsend, Lynn Stevens, Gill Quarton, Mrs J Frost, Mrs B M Kinnell, R Wiles, Mrs M Wettern, P H S Wettern, G Bloxsom, Jon and Fiona Mutch, SS, Alan Bickley, Dr R U Watson*)

Free house   Licensees Les and Joan Stewart   Real ale   Meals and snacks (see note below) Children in family lounge   Open 12–3, 7–11 all year, but closed weekday lunchtimes (exc mid-July to end Aug)   Bedrooms tel Brampton (069 77) 3456; £15(£18B)/£25(£27B)

Food details, prices, timing, etc. refer to bar food – not to a separate restaurant if there is one.

THIRLSPOT   NY3217   Map 9
Kings Head
A591 Keswick–Ambleside, by Thirlmere

This long, low, white seventeenth-century building stands alone by the road below Helvellyn. The recently refurbished bar, also long, has an interesting series of photographs showing Wythburn village before the valley was flooded to help supply Manchester with water, as well as the dam being built, and the top-hatted Mancunian dignitaries formally opening it; there's a lounge bar as well. Generous helpings of bar food includes weekday sandwiches, home-made soup (£1), a variety of lunchtime help-yourself salads (from £2.95, game pie £3.25, roast rib of local beef £4.50), ploughman's or scampi (£3.25), and charcoal grills such as local pork chop (£4.25), steaks (from £6.25), and specials. Welcoming service (even for booted hikers). Well kept Marstons Pedigree and Yates on handpump; games end with darts, pool, and dominoes; piped music. Perversely (in view of the unpropitious terrain) this is the HQ of the Cumberland County Cricket Club, as well as the area's hound trailing association. There are picnic-table sets on the tarmac forecourt and in a well walled sunken garden; the hotel part is quite separate from the bar. *(Recommended by N Burrell, N B Pritchard)*

Free house   Licensee Brian Pattinson   Real ale   Meals and snacks   Restaurant   Children welcome   Open 11–3, 5.30–11 all year; closes 2 in winter   Bedrooms tel Keswick (076 87) 72393; £20B/£31(£36B)

ULVERSTON   SD2978   Map 7
Bay Horse ⊗
Canal Foot; in Ulverston follow Industrial Estate signpost off A596 and keep on down North Lonsdale Road, bearing left at T-junction and skirting vast Glaxo plant – the pub's name is painted in huge letters on its slate roof; OS Sheet 96 reference 314777

Reopened in 1988 after refurbishment by its new owners (who run an outstanding restaurant at their Miller Howe hotel on Windermere), this combines a charmingly renovated real pub with a conservatory bistro where the short choice of imaginative food, changing weekly, has won immediate praise from many readers. We should stress that this is restaurant food (none is served in the bar itself). On our summer visit it included five starters such as chilled cucumber soup with chives and brandied sultanas (£1.80), a poached peach stuffed with herby cream cheese and flavoured with lightly curried mayonnaise and toasted coconut (£2.80) and a fine richly crab-filled pastry (£3.20), and five main courses such as saddle of hare with beetroot and a chestnut sauce (£8.50) and duck with pickled kumquats and bacon and sage stuffing (£9.50); the puddings (£1.75) are sumptuous. The smallish bar is civilised but pubby, with attractive wooden armchairs, glossy hardwood traditional tables, some pale green plush built-in wall banquettes, black beams and props with lots of horsebrasses, and blue plates on a Delft shelf, with a huge but elegant stone horse's head – oddly reminiscent of the monuments at Persepolis – in the corner. Besides well kept Mitchells Best on handpump, there's a decent choice of spirits, with a wine list that's not long but full of interest (we can firmly recommend the Morris Old Liqueur Muscat from Australia as a sweet wine, by the glass). Magazines are dotted about, there's a handsomely marbled green granite fireplace, and well chosen decently reproduced piped music. A small room by the entrance has a pool-table, with dominoes. The windows (and particularly the conservatory) give a marvellous view across Morecambe Bay, and there are picnic-table sets out on the terrace. *(Recommended by GRE, AE, Martin Rayner, Mrs L Huddart and others)*

Mitchells   Licensee Robert Lyons   Real ale   Meals (not Sun evening or Mon)   Children welcome (but not in bistro under 12 years old)   Open 11–3, 6–11 all year

WASDALE HEAD NY1808 Map 9

Wasdale Head Inn ★ ⇐

This gabled old hotel makes an excellent base for walking and climbing as it's well away from the main tourist areas and surrounded by steep fells; Wastwater itself – the most severely grand of all the lakes – is nearby, surrounded by towering screes. The big main bar has a polished slate floor, high ceilings, shiny panelling, cushioned settles, a log-effect gas fire, pool-table, and an excellent atmosphere that conjures up the days when this was a centre for pioneer rockclimbers – there are fine George Abraham photographs of that period on the walls. There is also a panelled and comfortably old-fashioned residents' bar and lounge. Good home-made bar food includes soup (95p), filled baked potato (£1.20), home-made pâté, locally potted shrimps or cheese and onion flan (£1.90), ploughman's (from £2.50), steak and kidney pie (£2.45), chicken casserole (£2.90) and mixed locally smoked meat salad (£3.80); also daily specials. Well kept Jennings, Theakstons Best and Old Peculier and Yates on handpump; pool, dominoes, cribbage. The main bar is named after the inn's first landlord, Will Ritson, who for his tall stories was reputed to be the world's biggest liar, and in his memory they still hold liar competitions here towards the end of November. There's a self-catering cottage and two flats in converted inn buildings nearby. (*Recommended by Heather Sharland, R H Sawyer, Gary Wilkes, Tony Pounder, Gwen and Peter Andrews, Ewan McCall, C M Whitehouse, C F Walling*)

Free house   Licensee Jasper Carr   Real ale   Meals and snacks   Restaurant   Children in fire room   Open all day, though during the periods mentioned below bar open only Fri evening–Sun lunchtime   Bedrooms (they only do dinner, bed and breakfast; no accommodation mid-Nov–mid-Mar (exc New Year period) tel Wasdale (094 06) 229; £37B/£68B

Lucky Dip

Besides the fully inspected pubs, you might like to try these Lucky Dips recommended to us and described by readers (if you do, please send us reports):

Ambleside [NY3804], *Sportsman*: Despite unpubby exterior, cosy and quite pubby inside, with lots of photographs; ; nr start GWG130 (*John Roué*); [Market Pl] *White Lion*: Good atmosphere in spacious town pub with unobtrusive piped music, wide choice of food in generous helpings, Bass and Stones ales, friendly staff; bedroooms (*Brian and Pauline Fullam, Gwen and Peter Andrews*) nr **Ambleside** [A592 Troutbeck–Patterdale; NY4009], *Kirkstone Pass*: Remote mountain inn with wide choice of whiskies, lively amusements, all-day summer cafe, fine surrounding scenery; bedrooms (*Michael Craig, LYM*)
Appleby [Boroughgate; NY6921], *Crown & Cushion*: Unpretentious town pub, very reliable for cheap lunch; Jennings and Tetleys on handpump (*D Stokes*); *Gate*: Good food very pleasantly served, comfortable tables and chairs, excellent ambience (*Theresa Frank, D Tinbergen*)
Arnside [SD4678], *Albion*: Lovely in good weather, with broad view across estuary to Lakeland hills from outside tables and from main bar (which has no juke box); nr start GWG124 (*MGBD*)
Askham [outside village (precise location not

known – information please!); NY5123], *Gate*: Tiny place with good beer and atmosphere, open fires – a real local (*Capt E P Gray*)
Bampton [NY5118], *St Patricks Well*: Excellent food and quick, friendly service; bedrooms (*Mrs P Cardy*)
Bampton Grange [NY5218], *Crown & Mitre*: Elegant small white house with portico and balcony above, spacious through lounge, pleasant chatty landlady, usual range of food and drink; useful for Haweswater, and – with the church opposite – worth the small detour (*Anon*)
Bardsea [SD3074], *Bradylls Arms*: Popular and pleasant extended village pub overlooking Morecambe Bay, bar food, well kept Hartleys, French windows to terrace and good garden with play area (*AE, GRE, MGBD*)
Bassenthwaite [NY2228], *Sun*: Very good food and service (*L D Rainger*)
☆ **Bowness on Windermere** [SD4097], *Hole in t' Wall*: Ancient pub with farm tools, smith's bellows, ploughshares and so forth in slate-floored lower bar, handsome panelled upper room with fine plaster ceiling, simple lunchtime food, Hartleys XB on handpump; nice flagstoned courtyard (*Ewan McCall,*

A J Foote, Jon Wainwright, LYM)

Bowness on Windermere [Queens Sq], *Albert*: Busy tourist pub with popular dining-lounge and big clean bedrooms *(A J Hartley)*; [Helm Rd] *Crag Brow*: Very good food and service and nice wine list in reasonably priced small hotel *(Capt E P Gray)*; [Rayrigg Road] *John Peel*: Decent food at fair prices in spacious pub with dark stone walls and dim lighting, pleasant service, Theakstons Old Peculier, juke box (not too obtrusive), upstairs pool-room *(Mrs Pamela Roper, C Dempsey, Jon Wainwright)*

Brampton [A69 ½ mile SW of village; NB this is the Brampton at NY5361, E of Carlisle], *End of Lane*: Original and strikingly clean interior with various objects related to 1960s–70s cars, good cheap food, friendly atmosphere and staff *(J H Watson)*; [Market Pl] *Nags Head*: Attractive frontage, obliging and prompt service, good bar food including huge salads, conventional décor *(Anon)*

☆ **Brampton** [NB this is the smaller Brampton – home of the Appleby gipsy horse fair in 2nd week of June – N of Appleby at NY6723], *New Inn*: Friendly oak-beamed and flagstoned country pub, snug and welcoming bar with original cooking-range fireplace, good cheap bar food from sensibly short menu (pastry particularly good), excellent restaurant, well kept Youngers Scotch; bedrooms *(Gwen and Peter Andrews, Anon (Dartford))*

Brigsteer [OS Sheet 97 reference 481896; SD4889], *Wheatsheaf*: Whitbreads house with well kept Castle Eden, good bar food – especially soups *(A T Langton)*

Brough Sowerby [NY7913], *Black Bull*: Very pleasant welcome, good hot food, very clean *(J E Rycroft)*

Broughton in Furness [Princes St; SD2187], *Black Cock*: Pleasantly unpretentious and old-fashioned pub with thick stone walls and blazing log fire in winter; well kept Watneys-related beers on handpump, good food; bedrooms *(GRE, AE)*; [Foxfield Rd] *Eccle Riggs*: Well run hotel (once the home of a Victorian Home Secretary), under new management; Whitbreads Castle Eden on handpump, bar food and extensive Sun lunchtime buffet – children can use heated indoor swimming-pool free if they have a bar meal; also nine-hole golf course *(GRE, AE)*; [A595 towards Millom] *High Cross*: Hilltop food pub with splendid view over the Duddon estuary and neighbouring fells; changed hands early 1988; bedrooms *(GRE, AE)*; [Church St] *Old Kings Head*: Attractive whitewashed building, colourful with hanging flower baskets in summer, comfortably refurbished inside with soft pink lights, log-effect fire in stone fireplace, piped music, chintz and knick-knacks; well kept Hartleys on handpump, wide choice of food including children's dishes and masses of puddings in dining area; bedrooms *(Raymond Palmer)*

☆ **Buttermere** [NY1817], *Bridge*: Robust if not cheap lunchtime bar food in plainly refurbished but comfortable lounge bar of extended stone hotel, well kept Theakstons Best, XB and Old Peculier on handpump, tables on flagstoned terrace; handy for Crummock Water and Buttermere – the village fills with walkers in summer; evening restaurant; nr start GWG135 *(TOH, Gwen and Peter Andrews, D Rowlatt, C M T Johnson, Miss A Tress, G Smith, LYM)*

Buttermere, *Fish*: Basic inn with good value food, relatively cheap Theakstons, bedrooms; at start of GWG135 *(C A Hood)*

Cark in Cartmel [SD3776], *Engine*: Friendly, clean and comfortably modernised Bass pub with good range of whiskies, well kept real ale, good fire, piped music; tables out by little stream *(A T Langton, Pete Storey, LYM)*

Carlisle [Lowther St; NY4056], *Pippins*: Efficient service and enormous reasonably priced ploughman's, good filter coffee; can get rather crowded *(J A V Rose)*; [Lowther St] *Post*: Large Victorian-style pub in former post office building, full of mahogany and stained-glass dividers between banquettes; helpful cheerful staff, wide choice of good food, Matthew Browns John Peel and Theakstons Old Peculier; can be very busy at lunchtime *(Raymond Palmer)*; [St Nicholas St] *Theakston*: Rather basic town pub with open fires, well kept Matthew Browns Mild and remarkable value food *(Mr and Mrs Hendry)*

Cartmel [off main sq; SD3879], *Cavendish Arms*: Large, dark and cosy interior, well kept Bass, good bar food including cheap sandwiches and all different cuts of real Aberdeen Angus steaks, helpful service *(Pete Storey)*; *Pig & Whistle*: Stone exterior, long bar with old photographs of interesting local scenes; pleasant landlord, well kept Hartleys, good coffee, occasional sessions by local folk musicians *(Pete Storey)*; *Royal Oak*: Roomy, good atmosphere, friendly staff, local paintings, well kept Whitbreads Castle Eden *(Pete Storey)*

Chapel Stile [B5343; NY3205], *Wainwrights*: Generous helpings of good value food including lasagne, scampi and children's dishes, served quickly by landlady; well kept Theakstons XB and Old Peculier on handpump, good friendly atmosphere *(N B Pritchard, N F Doherty)*

Cockermouth [Main St; NY1231], *Globe*: Building dates from 1750; bars (the main one has big marble tables) and restaurant decorated with old music-hall posters; about 20 malt whiskies; bedrooms *(Dave Braisted)*; [Station St] *Tithebarn*: Friendly town pub with cheap well kept Jennings beer *(BB)*; [centre] *Trout*: Chintz and red plush in comfortable bar of solid old hotel, good snacks, well kept restaurant, garden by River Cocker; bedrooms *(BB)*

Coniston [SD3098], *Black Bull*: Less touristy than most pubs here; nr start GWG126 *(MGBD)*; [towards Broughton] *Ship*: Nice old pub, welcoming landlord, friendly labradors, well kept Hartleys on handpump; Morecambe Bay shrimps on toasted muffins before a big open fire a real treat after a wintry walk on Coniston Old Man *(GRE, AE)*

☆ **Crosby Ravensworth** [NY6215], *Butchers Arms*: Very good English country cooking including wonderful sticky puddings, friendly landlord, well kept Marstons Pedigree and Youngers on handpump, pleasant relaxed atmosphere, children and dogs welcome; delightful unspoilt village *(Penelope Willink, Martin Rayner)*

Dalton in Furness [Goose Green; SD2273], *Brown Cow*: Matthew Browns ales in small and friendly country inn run by young couple; excellent value bar food, children welcome, seats on terrace *(Mrs L Huddart)*; [Market St] *Red Lion*: Hospitable family, well kept Tetleys beer, spirits the cheapest we found in the area, good food quickly served, breakfasts enormous; neat and tidy bedrooms *(Robin and Carole Smith)*

Dean [just off A5086 S of Cockermouth; NY0825], *Royal Yew*: Comfortable, pleasantly furnished, village free house with good evening atmosphere, Theakstons and Youngers beers, good reasonably priced bar food; plans for extension *(R D Norman)*

Dockray [NY3921], *Royal*: Has been improving, above-average food in bar and separate lounge; darts; beautiful setting; bedrooms *(Peter Race)*

Eaglesfield [just off village road, on right coming from A5086; NY0928], *Blackcock*: Simple locals' village pub, spick and span, with cheap Jennings real ales and uncommon version of ring the bull *(LYM)*

Eamont Bridge [NY5328], *Beehive*: Eighteenth-century pub with excellent, homely service, Whitbreads ales, varied and interesting bar food (special prices for OAPs and children), dogs welcome; children's play area *(E R Thompson)*

☆ **Far Sawrey** [SD3893], *Sawrey*: Interesting Claife Crier stable bar with wooden stalls dividing tables and harness on rough white walls, good simple food including wide choice of sandwiches and fine ploughman's, well kept Jennings and Theakstons real ales, good friendly service; seats on lawn look up to Claife Heights, which have good views of Lake Windermere; bedrooms *(Ewan McCall, Peter Race, Gwen and Peter Andrews, Jon Wainwright, N Burrell, AE, GRE, Hayward Wane, LYM)*

Flookburgh [SD3676], *Hope & Anchor*: Large relaxing pub in small, pleasant village with friendly landlord, darts, pool, well kept Hartleys Mild and Bitter *(Pete Storey)*

☆ **Garrigill** [NY7441], *George & Dragon*: Seventeenth-century pub on no-through road

in beautiful scenery, 2½ miles from the source of the Tyne; big flagstoned bar with cheerful informal welcome, well kept beer and good value imaginative pub food, with unexpectedly wide choice in partly panelled stone-walled dining-room; bedrooms small but comfortable – good value *(Mr and Mrs C R Bryant, Mrs T Frank, R A Hall)*

Glenridding [back of main car park, top of road; NY3917], *Travellers Rest*: Generous helpings of good food at reasonable prices, lunchtime and evening, in comfortable hospitable pub; very popular in summer, and ramblers welcome all year, but not too touristy; wonderful view of fells across Ullswater from terrace; nr start GWG138, nr GWG132 *(Yvonne and Don Johnson, Charles and Mary Winpenny)*

☆ **Gosforth** [off A595 and unclassified rd to Wasdale; NY0703], *Gosforth Hall*: Lovely Jacobean building with fine plaster coats of arms over bar mantelpieces, good bar food, attentive service; bar customers as well as residents can use the heated pool in the sun-trap garden; comfortable bedrooms *(Gwen and Peter Andrews, AE, GRE)*

Gosforth [A595 just N of sign to Wasdale; NY0703], *Red Admiral*: Spotlessly clean Matthew Browns pub, smiling welcome, good coffee, real ales, wide choice of lunchtime bar food, roast Sun lunches; children welcome *(Gwen and Peter Andrews)*

☆ **Grasmere** [main bypass rd; NY3406], *Swan*: Good home-made bar food and sandwiches in relaxing and attractively old-fashioned lounge of spacious and comfortable THF hotel where Sir Walter Scott used to nip in for his meridian when staying with the abstemious Wordsworths in nearby Dove Cottage; darts in small public bar, friendly service; a comfortable base for the fells which rise behind *(G C Hixon, Wayne Brindle, Jon Wainwright, Stephen R Holman, Laurence Manning, Col G D Stafford, LYM)*

Grasmere [main bypass road], *Travellers Rest*: Wide choice of usual bar food and well kept Watneys-related real ales in main-road pub, fitted carpet stretching from games-room through plainly furnished lounge to family dining-room, piped music, tables in small area outside; bedrooms; nr start GWG129 *(S Godfrey, BB)*; [in village] *Tweedies*: Young theme bar named after local character, very friendly welcome even for bedraggled hikers; large games-room, lots of chatter – it's assumed you'll join in *(David Gwynne Harper)*

Hawkshead [SD3598], *Red Lion*: Comfortably modernised inn with well kept Watneys-related real ales, old-fashioned touches, lively atmosphere, restaurant; bedrooms *(K Clapp, Wayne Brindle, A T Langton, Charles and Mary Winpenny, LYM)*

High Newton [just off A590 – coming from Leven turn right in village; SD4082], *Crown*: Very good Sunday lunch, quick service

(S Braisted, A T Langton)
Hoff [NY6718], *New Inn*: Friendly straight-forward pub with good value bar food; children welcome; bedrooms *(Anon (Dartford))*
Ireby [NY2439], *Sun*: Plentiful helpings of wholesome food including very filling mixed grill; out-of-the-way village on fringe of the northern fells *(N J Neil-Smith)*
Kendal [SD5293], *Globe*: Popular for quiet morning coffee and other drinks; pleasant décor, bar food and upstairs dining-room where children welcome; livelier in the evenings, when piped music may be loud – with live jazz and folk music twice a week *(MGBD)*
☆ **Keswick** [St John's St; NY2624], *George*: Attractive black-panelled side room where the poet Southey used to wait for Wordsworth to arrive from Grasmere, also open-plan main bar with old-fashioned settles and modern banquettes under Elizabethan beams; bar food (may be served in music-free comfort in the restaurant), good choice of well kept real ales, trout fishing; bedrooms comfortable *(EHS, RMS, Jon Wainwright, Simon Bates, LYM)*
Keswick [Lake Rd], *Four in Hand*: Ex-coaching-inn with cosy old panelled back lounge, warm and friendly, with fire in winter, hunting pictures and old photographs; good food lunchtime and evening (not Sun in winter); popular with locals and visitors *(Yvonne and Don Johnson)* [off Market Sq; NY2624] *Lake Road Vaults*: Attractive whitewashed building with well kept Jennings, good relaxed and very friendly atmosphere, nice snug back corner *(Jon Wainwright)*; [off Market Sq, behind Lloyds Bank] *Pack Horse*: Snug and likeable low-beamed town pub in attractive alley courtyard, friendly landlord, well kept Jennings Bitter and Mild, and Tetleys *(C Dempsey, LYM)*; [Crosthwaite Rd] *Pheasant*: Welcoming and agreeably furnished one-room Jennings local, with nice touches such as dried flower arrangements *(Jon Wainwright)*; [off Market Sq] *Queen*: Tucked away off an alley; comfortable seats down the sides of a large, long, dimly lit lounge with good fire in impressive fireplace, interesting upstairs games-room with pool *(Jon Wainwright)*
nr Keswick [Newlands Valley – OS Sheet 90 reference 242217; NY2624], *Swinside*: Friendly and unpretentious country inn in quiet valley, surrounded by marvellous crags and fells – tables outside, and picture-window upstairs dining-room, make the most of the view of Causey Pike and Stile End Barrow; modest bar food in immodestly big helpings, Jennings Mild and Bitter; good value bedrooms *(Philip Denison, Rita Horridge, R D Norman, Dave and Sue Braisted, D Pearman, LYM)*
☆ **Kirkby Stephen** [NY7808], *Kings Arms*: Solid comfort in cosy oak-panelled lounge bar,

darts and dominoes in easy-going and friendly public bar, bar food may include enterprising evening dishes, restaurant allowing children, well kept Whitbreads real ale; bedrooms *(W D Horsfield, Tony Pounder, LYM)*
Kirkoswald [NY5641], *Fetherston Arms*: Good food in clean stripped-stone lounge bar and second picture-window bar, well kept Theakstons, no pressure to hurry; bedrooms *(Gwen and Peter Andrews)*
☆ **Lanercost** [NY5664], *Bridge*: Well converted old hay barn with lots of character, attached to New Bridge Hotel; friendly smart staff, Theakstons beers and superb lunches – all fresh vegetables and original recipes; lovely situation; bedrooms *(Robert and Susan Phillips)*
Levens [on new cut-off from A590, nr junction with A5074 – OS Sheet 97 reference 472854; SD4886], *Gilpin Bridge*: Well kept Matthew Browns and Theakstons, good food *(Dave Braisted)*; [Sedgwick Rd, nr entrance to Sizergh Castle – OS Sheet 97 reference 500872] *Strickland Arms*: Comfortable, well kept Theakstons ales, excellent bar food *(A T Langton)*
Lindale [OS Sheet 97 reference 419805; SD4280] *Lindale Inn*: Real ale, good bar food *(A T Langton)*
Loweswater [unclassified Loweswater rd off B5289 Cockermouth–Buttermere; NY1421], *Scale Hill*: Peaceful hotel where non-residents welcome; entrance lounge with comfortable sofas and armchairs, old-fashioned fireplace and inviting snug; drinks served through small hatch, bar food *(AE, GRE)*
Middleton [A683 Kirkby Lonsdale–Sedbergh; SD6386], *Swan*: Sadly this quaint little inn – one of very few licensed to sell stamps, and much appreciated by readers for its homely charm, well kept beer and interesting food – closed down in 1988 *(LYM)*
Moresby [attached to Rosehill Theatre, though run separately; NX9921], *Rosehill*: Though it's a small restaurant rather than a pub, this recently opened and extremely friendly place serves highly praised snacks in the bar too *(Syd and Wyn Donald)*
Mungrisdale [2 miles N of A66 Keswick–Penrith – OS Sheet 90 reference 363302; NY3731], *Mill*: Recently renovated retaining character, warm welcome, well kept Theakstons and Youngers beers, good plentiful bar food at reasonable prices including good cold table choice and admirable puddings with lots of cream; clean, excellent service even when busy; good value bedrooms *(Dick Brown, David Heath)*
☆ **Nether Wasdale** [between Gosforth and Wasdale Head; NY1808], *Screes*: Cosy inn with friendly, relaxed atmosphere, good food, good range of reasonably priced malt whiskies, well kept Hartleys Mild and XB, Robinsons Old Tom, Theakstons Best and

Old Peculier, local customers and people from the nearby Youth Hostel – also a very friendly placid Great Dane; nice position in spectacular valley, off the usual tourist track; five bedrooms *(Rob and Gill Weeks, A Kelly, MGBD)*

Nether Wasdale, *Strands*: Pleasant pub in lovely setting, comfortable lounge, simpler back bar popular with campers, well kept Hartleys and Robinsons, good range of well cooked food; bedrooms *(Mr and Mrs C France, P Lloyd, K Bamford)*

Newby Bridge [SD3786], *Newby Bridge*: Good atmosphere in large bar of rambling eighteenth-century inn with cosy nook and big open fireplace *(John Roué)*

Oxenholme [SD5389], *Station*: Nice Whitbreads country pub, quiet at lunchtime, spotlessly clean; excellent home-made soups, no music in lounge, Whitbreads house – same landlord for many years *(MGBD)*

Patterdale [NY3916], *White Lion*: Small but lively Lakeland bar, usual food, basic bedrooms – handy for GWG132 *(John Roué)*

☆ **Penrith** [NY5130], *George*: Well run and substantial hotel with old-fashioned lounge hall – oak panelling and beams, handsome plasterwork, big bow-window seats, oak settles and easy chairs around good open fire; lunchtime bar food, friendly service, well kept Marstons Pedigree, lively back bar *(Heather Sharland, CG, LYM)*

Piel Island [accessible by ferry from Roa Island, nr Rampside SE of Barrow; SD2364], *Piel Island Inn*: Unique island setting, shared with castle ruins – sparsely decorated, ideal for unusual evening; hosts finish of annual coastal raft race *(Paul Corbett)*

Ravenglass [SD0996], *Ratty Arms*: Ex-railway bar (terminus for England's oldest narrow-gauge steam railway) with pool-table in bustling public bar, good value restaurant *(LYM)*

☆ **Ravenstonedale** [just off A685 Kirkby Stephen to M6 junction 38; NY7204], *Black Swan*: Rather sombre hotel bar, usually very quiet and peaceful at lunchtime, with comfortable seats, open fire, polished copper-topped tables, some stripped stonework and panelling-effect wall finish, tables in tree-sheltered streamside garden over road; quickly served bar food, Youngers No 3 on handpump; comfortable bedrooms *(Dr A B Clayton, Tim Brierly, HNJ, CAE, BB)*

Rydal [NY3706], *Glen Rothay*: Small hotel with boats for residents on nearby Rydal Water, comfortable armchairs around fire in beamed hotel bar, seats in pretty garden, and Badger Bar with bar food, Bass and Hartleys XB on handpump, piped music; comfortable bedrooms; nr GWG129 *(E J Cutting, LYM)*

☆ **Sandside** [B5282 – OS Sheet 97 reference 478808; SD4780], *Ship*: Extensive modernised pub with glorious view over the broad Kent estuary to the Lakeland hills; good value bar food, friendly efficient service, well kept Youngers real ales, summer barbecues, unusually good children's play area – and children allowed in eating area at lunchtime; bedrooms good, warm and nicely furnished, with good breakfast *(Dave Braisted, Eithne McGourty, Matthew Waterhouse, Comus Elliott, Brian Jones, Mike Suddards, LYM)*

☆ **Seathwaite** [Duddon Valley (i.e. *not* Seathwaite in Borrowdale); SD2396], *Newfield*: Friendly welcome in good unspoilt local, popular with walkers – the only place of refreshment in the 12-mile long valley; Wordsworth wrote 35 sonnets to the river, and stayed here; good value food, open fires, striking slate-paved floor, real ale, friendly atmosphere, no-smoking dining-room, tables in garden; children until 8pm *(GRE, AE, Mrs P Brown, Dr Pete Crawshaw)*

Seatoller [NY2414], *Yew Tree*: More restaurant than pub – though the back bar does serve well kept Jennings; lovely low-ceilinged seventeenth-century dining-room with pictures, old photographs and cigarette cards; outstanding food such as sea-trout and venison at restaurant prices, also simpler lunches; nr start GWG134 *(Dick Brown)*

Sedbergh [Main St; SD6692], *Dalesman*: Well renovated attractive bar, good service, friendly staff, good choice of well prepared bar food; nice well equipped bedrooms at low rates *(DJF, Col G D Stafford)*; [Finkle St (A683)] *Red Lion*: Cheerful local bar with stuffed gamebirds and sporting dog prints, Marstons Mild, Burton and Pedigree on handpump, decent straightforward bar food; bedrooms *(Mr and Mrs N Mitchell, BB)*

nr Sedbergh [A683 half way between Sedbergh and Kirkby Stephen; SD6692], *Fat Lamb*: Alone on the moors, pews and piped music in two-room bar with some red flock wallpaper and brightly patterned carpet, but also open fire in traditional black kitchen range and good photographs of steam trains and local beagles; filling bar food, restaurant, seats outside by sheep pastures, bedrooms *(BB)*

Staveley [SD4798], *Eagle & Child*: Good value simple food including cheap steak in a bun and nice home-cooked ham or Cumberland sausage – generous helpings; bright but comfortable little modern front lounge and more spacious carpeted bar; well kept, with small neat garden; bedrooms quite cheap *(BB)*

☆ **Talkin** [Talkin Tarn; NY5557], *Tarn End*: Nineteenth-century farmhouse on banks of Talkin Tarn, with two boats for residents; unusual dishes in bar and evening restaurant such as venison sausages, mussels and scallops, excellent puddings; particularly good family service, warm welcome for children; afternoon teas; bedrooms well equipped and good value *(E R Thompson, Nigel Furneaux, Debbie Pratt, Alan Bickley)*

Talkin, *Blacksmiths Arms*: Warm and

friendly welcome in bright, airy pub with cosy comfortable atmosphere, cheerful service and good bar food; dogs welcome; bedrooms well appointed *(Mr and Mrs R G Ing, Mr and Mrs L D Rainger)*

Tebay [A685 N of village, nr M6 junction 38; NY6204], *Barnaby Rudge*: Large pub on two levels including restaurant, Victorian décor, friendly service, separate pool-room, good bar food *(M V Fereday)*

Temple Sowerby [NY6127], *Kings Arms*: Comfortable and quite cosy hotelish lounge in handsome red sandstone inn, also bigger L-shaped lounge bar with lots of window seats; bedrooms *(LYM)*

Threlkeld [NY3325], *Horse & Farrier*: Typical seventeenth-century Lakeland village pub below Blencathra, no fancy trimmings, main bar and pool-room; decent sandwiches *(Yvonne and Don Johnson)*; [old main rd, bypassed by A66] *Salutation*: Friendly local popular with fell-walkers; open fire, cards and dominoes; massive helpings of good food, well kept Matthew Browns and Old Peculier on handpump *(Simon Barber)*

Tirril [3½ miles from M6 junction 40; A66 towards Brough, A6 towards Shap, then B5320 towards Ullswater; NY5126], *Queens Head*: Still a core of low beams, black panelling, old-fashioned settles and inglenook fireplace, but the atmosphere's mainly much more modern – there's even a pizzeria besides more standardised bar food; Matthew Browns and Theakstons on handpump, noticeable fruit machine and juke box, has had live entertainment Thurs; bedrooms *(Gwen and Peter Andrews, Martin Ragg, Gary Wilkes, Wayne Brindle, Simon Bates, LYM)*

Torver [SD2894], *Wilsons Cottage*: Period furniture, roaring log fires, helpful licensees, well kept Tetleys, excellent food; bedrooms comfortable and well equipped, at low rates *(Phil Ridgewell)*

☆ **Troutbeck** [NY4103], *Mortal Man*: Friendly up-market comfortable hotel serving above-average lunches in pleasant main bar with open fire, also sandwiches and restaurant meals; quick service, Youngers Scotch; on GWG130 (with a welcome for hikers); bedrooms *(MGBD, Eileen Broadbent, John Roué, Mr and Mrs David M Jones, K W Schofield, JH, Col G D Stafford, Syd and Wyn Donald)*

Troutbeck [NY4103], *Queens Head*: Lots of oddities (even a massive Elizabethan four-poster as bar counter) in popular tourists' pub with lively atmosphere, antique carvings, rambling alcoves, heavy beams; fine views from seats outside, Watneys-related real ales, bar food (not cheap); nr GWG130 *(G Cooper, Len Beattie, Jon Wainwright, Simon Bates, LYM)*

Ulpha [SD1993], *New Field*: Clean pub, warm welcome, excellent service, good bar food, first-class steak; good value bedrooms *(Peggie Ellwood)*

Ulverston [King St; SD2978], *Rose & Crown*: Interesting old building with a wide choice of food and well kept beer *(Mrs P Brown, AE, GRE)*

Warwick on Eden [2 miles from M6 junction 43; A69 towards Hexham, then village sign-posted; NY4657], *Queens Arms*: Well kept Tetleys and decent solid pub food (not Sun evening) in friendly two-room bar with good log fires, lots of model cars, trains, vintage car pictures and the like; seats in attractive garden with good play area; children welcome, restaurant, occasional live music; bedrooms *(Syd and Wyn Donald, T A Hoyle, Dick Brown, J F M West, Alan Bickley, Richard Dolphin, Jon Wainwright, LYM)*

Winton [just off A683; NY7810], *Bay Horse*: Friendly little local in lovely moorland setting, two low-ceilinged bar rooms decorated with Pennine photographs and local fly-tying, good value bar food, McEwans, Youngers and guest real ales; pool in games-room; bedrooms *(LYM)*

Derbyshire and Staffordshire

One of Britain's most idiosyncratic pubs – and most interesting – is the Yew Tree at Cauldon, packed with all sorts of unusual things. And it's an outstanding example of the area's generally attractive pricing of both food and drinks. A good many other pubs in the area stand out for character, including the George at Alstonefield, the Meynell Arms at Ashley, the little Coopers Tavern in Burton-on-Trent (new licensees have resisted the temptation to bring it much further into the twentieth century), the rambling Black Lion in Butterton (a nice place to stay at), the Bull i' th' Thorn that we list under Buxton (for lack of anywhere nearer this striking Tudor outpost), the decidedly unpretentious Black Lion hidden away in a lonely canal valley near Consall, the civilised Chequers on Froggatt Edge, the spick-and-span Old Bulls Head at Little Hucklow (with its fine collection of agrricultural machinery outside), the handsome – even grand – Peacock at Rowsley (a splendid place to stay at), the Malt Shovel at Shardlow (a canalside ex-maltings, with some of the best value food in this bunch), and that remarkable farm pub, the Three Stags Heads at Wardlow. Character's a strong point too at all the new entries included in this edition – the Cavalier at Grindon (already excellent, though the current licensees came only in 1988), the cottagey Pack-horse at Little Longstone (both these first two have good food), the Greyhound at Penkhull (a real village pub in the heart of the Potteries), the Rising Sun at Shraleybrook (one of the best ranges of real ales in the area), and the Little Mill at Rowarth (back in these pages after some time in the Lucky Dip). Other pubs to note for good food include the Druid at Birchover, the Royal Oak at Millthorpe,

The Black Lion, Consall

the Holly Bush at Seighford, the Castle Hotel in Castleton, the Maynard Arms in Grindleford, and the Lathkil at Over Haddon (these last three are good places to stay at). As you can see from the stars scattered liberally through them, a good few of the Lucky Dip entries at the end of the chapter have notable attractions. Among them, the Goats Head in Abbots Bromley, the Devonshire Arms at Beeley, the Burton Bridge Brewery in Burton-on-Trent (the tap for the brewery of that name), the Worston Mill at Little Bridgeford, the Red Lion at Litton (excluded from the main entries simply because it's now so much more restaurant than pub) and the Olde Dog & Partridge at Tutbury look specially promising.

ABBOTS BROMLEY (Staffs)   SK0724 Map 7
Crown 🛏

Set in the attractive village centre, this friendly and unpretentious inn has been refurbished recently; the lounge bar is softly lit and carpeted, with comfortable plush button-back banquettes and modern panelling, and fresh flowers. In the public bar there are darts, dominoes, cribbage and a fruit machine; piped music. The good value bar food includes soup (70p), big helpings of sandwiches, a few daily specials, and steaks (rump £6.50); the breakfasts are generously served. Well kept Bass on electric pump. (*Recommended by S M Shaw, M J How, John Atherton, Lyn and Bill Capper, Mrs M M Harding*)

Bass   Licensee Clifford Lewis   Real ale   Meals and snacks   Children welcome   Open 11–3, 6–11 all year; all day Sat   Bedrooms tel Burton-on-Trent (0283) 840227; £14.50/£26

ALREWAS (Staffs)   SK1714 Map 7
George & Dragon 🛏
High Street; bypassed village signposted from A38 and A513

This welcoming, busy village inn has been in the same family for over forty years – hence the family photographs hanging above the remarkably long inglenook mantelpiece. The warm, low-beamed rooms leading off the central servery are furnished in a simple but homely way, with flagstones and a large number of brass candlesticks; the large room at one side has a splendid collection of commemorative Royal china. Bar food includes sandwiches (from 65p), ploughman's (£1.50), a wide choice of hot dishes such as omelettes (from £2), home-made pies (£2.20), salads (£2.40), vegetarian dishes (from £2.40), cold meat with crusty bread (£2.50), gammon with egg or pineapple (£4.10) and sirloin steak (£6.30), with a choice of baked potatoes or chips; friendly, efficient service. Well kept and very reasonably priced Marstons Burton and Pedigree on handpump; dominoes, cribbage, fruit machine, piped music. The attractive garden has a terraced area and lots of good things for children – a swing, playboat and aviary with cockatiels and other birds, white doves strutting along the tops of the walls and roofs, and a play elephant called Eric. The modern bedrooms are in a separate block. (*Recommended by Tim and Lynne Crawford, Pamela and Merlyn Horswell, Mandy and Michael Challis*)

Marstons   Licensees Ray and Mary Stanbrook   Real ale   Meals and snacks (not Sun) Restaurant (evenings)   Children in eating area   Open 11–2.30, 6–11 all year Bedrooms tel Burton-on-Trent (0283) 790202; £25B/£35B

ALSTONEFIELD (Staffs)   SK1355 Map 7
George
Village signposted from A515 Ashbourne–Buxton

The welcomingly snug sixteenth-century inn in this stone-built hamlet has a low-beamed bar, with darkening cream walls, a fine collection of old Peak District photographs and drawings, a collection of foreign banknotes, pewter tankards hanging by the copper-topped bar counter and a good fire in winter. In the spacious family-room there are lots of wheel-back chairs around tables. The pretty rockery in the sheltered and spacious back stableyard has picnic seats, and beneath the inn sign at the front there are some stone seats. Darts, dominoes, shove-ha'penny, cribbage, fruit machine. The Ind Coope and Burton are well kept on handpump, and the simple food is good value, including soup, sandwiches, an excellent ploughman's, home-made Spanish quiche, meat and potato pie, plaice and smoked trout; friendly service. The area has many good walks. *(Recommended by Jenny Seller, Dr and Mrs R J Ashleigh, BKA, Lee Goulding, D Stephenson, M A and W R Proctor, Brian and Anna Marsden)*

Free house   Real ale   Meals and snacks   Open 10.30–2.30, 6–11 all year; opens 7 in winter; closed 25 Dec

ASHLEY (Staffs)   SJ7636 Map 7
Meynell Arms
Village signposted from A53 NE of Market Drayton

This quiet and welcoming village pub (situated in a quiet backwater down narrow lanes) serves decent bar food, including sandwiches (80p), lasagne, scampi or cheese and walnut salad (£2.50), specials such as home-made curry with poppadums (£3) and steaks (from £4.25). The lounge bar is old-fashioned and atmospheric, with deep sofas and plush bucket seats and an old-fashioned cast-iron stove. One wall is stone-faced, others have some panelling or oak timbers in gently ageing plaster. In the carpeted public bar there are sensibly placed darts, bar billiards, dominoes, table skittles, cribbage, fruit machine and juke box. Well kept Bass on handpump. *(Recommended by Laurence Manning, D P Bagnall)*

Bass   Licensee Veronica Foley   Real ale   Meals and snacks   Children in eating area   Open 12–3, 7–11 all year

BAMFORD (Derbys)   SK2083 Map 7
Derwent ⊗ 🛏
Main Street (A6013)

All the indications are that the new licensees are continuing to justify the awards we've given this friendly and welcoming pub. The good bar food now includes sandwiches (from £1), soup (£1.20), ploughman's, filled Yorkshire puddings or burgers (£2.50), barbecued chicken or steak and kidney pie (£2.95), lasagne (£3), chicken breast in a wine sauce (£4.25) and steaks (£5.25); home-made puddings (95p). The rambling layout is quite unusual: the servery is in a central carpeted hall, from where several rooms lead off. One of these has an airy feel, with lots of wooden tables, big pictures on its wood-effect panelling, and big sunny windows; another has an old-fashioned green plush wall seat curving all around it (including two more bay windows), and its partly panelled walls are hung with yokes, heavy-horse harness and trace shafts; there are usually lots of fresh flowers and potted plants – the spacious layout means that the atmosphere is particularly relaxed. The charming little dining-room has stripped-pine panelling. The games-bar (with its local team photographs) has darts, table skittles, pool, fruit machine, shove-ha'penny, cribbage, shut-the-box, Connect-4 and Trivial Pursuit; piped music. Well kept Stones Best, Wards Sheffield Best and a guest beer on handpump; seats in the garden. *(Recommended by Brian and Anna Marsden, W P P Clarke, Michael Lloyd, KC, T Houghton)*

Free house   Licensees David and Angela Ryan   Real ale   Meals and snacks   Children welcome   Restaurant   Probably open 11–11   Bedrooms tel Hope Valley (0433) 51395; £19.50/£28.50(£34B)

BIRCHOVER (Derbys) SK2462 Map 7
Druid ⊗
Village signposted from B5056

A strange cave among the beech trees sprouting from the Row Tor, behind this off-the-beaten-track pub, reputedly inspired the pub's name during the eighteenth-century craze for druids (and indeed the pub dog still has a suspiciously druidical look). The simplicity of the bar – with green plush-upholstered wooden wall benches, small dining-chairs and stools around simple tables and a little coal fire – belies its unusually wide range of very interesting food, which includes soups (£1.30), fillet of herring in sour cream sauce or walnut pâté (£2.20), prawns in hot garlic butter with apple and celery or melon filled with prawns and mayonnaise (£2.50) and a generous three-cheese ploughman's (£3.20); main courses can include such dishes as steak and mussel pie (£3.60), lasagne, Greek moussaka or spaghetti bolognese (£3.90), grilled pork chop with chilled cream, apple and French mustard or lamb curry with yoghurt, a dish of nuts, mango chutney and a poppadum (£4.80), lamb cooked Turkish-style with apricot, almonds, cumin, cardamom, garlic and yoghurt or chicken cooked in lemon, lime, ginger and banana (£5.90), sirloin steak (from £6.20), and chicken Kiev (£6.40); there's also a good range of vegetarian dishes like casserole with red kidney beans (£3.40), fruit and vegetable curry or steamed Chinese vegetables in a sweet-and-sour sauce (£4.20) and almond risotto (£4.40); enterprising puddings range from brandy snaps to chocolate roulade (all at £1.80); half-price helpings for children. Such dishes have resulted in the chef/patron Brian Bunce being repeatedly shortlisted in cooking competitions run by the trade paper *Pub Catering*. In the spacious and airy two-storey dining extension, candlelit at night, there are pink plush seats on olive-green carpet and pepper-grinders and sea salt on all the tables. Well kept Marstons Pedigree on handpump and a good collection of malt whiskies; a small public bar has darts, dominoes, cribbage and fruit machine; piped classical music. There are picnic-table sets in front of this creeper-covered gritstone house. (*Recommended by David Hooley, Roger Broadie, Eve Prugar, Mrs P Cardy, Dr and Mrs R J Ashleigh, Miss A Robinson, K G A Lewis, Oliver Howes, Angie and Dave Parkes, AE, Dr and Mrs K J Baxter, Paul and Margaret Baker, Dorothy and Ken Worrall*)

Free house Licensees Brian Bunce and Chris Rose Real ale Meals and snacks Bookings tel Winster (062 988) 302 Children in bar until 8 Open 12–3, 7–11 all year

BIRCH VALE (Derbys) SK0287 Map 7
Sycamore ⇄
From A6015 take Station Road towards Thornsett

The wide choice of efficiently served bar food in this family pub includes soup (£1), stuffed pepper (£1.50), ploughman's (£2.15), open sandwiches (from £2.70), steak sandwich (£2.70), cannelloni, chilli con carne or vegetarian moussaka (£3.25), home-made steak pie (£3.45), fresh plaice or mixed grill (£6.50) and eight-ounce steak (£7.25), with children's dishes (from £1.25) and lots of rich puddings (from £1.50). The main bar area upstairs is primarily for eaters (you can book except on Saturday evening and Sunday lunchtime, and there's a sensible table-queue system with a 'waiting board' for busy times), the downstairs one for drinkers; well kept, very reasonably priced Marstons Burton and Pedigree on handpump (and a good choice of strong bottled beers); there's an indoor fountain down here. Four warmly welcoming connecting carpeted rooms have some stripped brick walls, and a variety of seats including wheel-back chairs, pews, button-back red plush wall banquettes, mate's chairs, high seats by eating-ledges, and settees; fruit machine and piped music. The pub also has its own sun and sauna fitness room. Below the pub (where you can also find the main car park), there are some attractively spacious valley gardens by a stream; these have good solid swings, seesaw, and a climbing-frame made of trunks and logs, a play-tree, canaries in an aviary, and rabbits; also a summer drinks and ice-cream bar. There are do-it-yourself summer barbecues on a terrace up above. (*Recommended by Lee Goulding, Derek Stephenson, David Waterhouse, Brian and Anna Marsden*)

Free house   Licensees Malcolm and Christine Nash   Real ale   Meals and snacks   Children in eating areas until 7.30   Open 12–3, 5.30–11 all year; all day Sat   Bedrooms tel New Mills (0663) 42715; £26.50B/£40.50B

BURTON-ON-TRENT (Staffs)   SK2423 Map 7
Coopers Tavern

Cross Street; off Station Street but a No Entry – heading N down High Street then Station Road from centre, pass Bass brewery and turn left into Milton Street (from which the pub has a back entrance)

As we went to press the new licensees in this friendly locals' pub were intending to transform the old-fashioned and unspoilt back room into more of a Victorian parlour, in line with the pub's showpiece, the ancient gas meter (which they've managed to hold on to despite the East Midland Gas Board's modernising plans). The front bar is simple and carpeted, and has darts, dominoes, table skittles and a fruit machine; piped music. Good cheap food includes soup, filled cobs (45p), sausage or bacon 60p), toasties (60p), hot pork stuffing and apple sauce baps (65p), pie and chips (£1.40) and salads (£1.60). The museum in the nearby gleaming Bass brewery is well worth a visit. (*Recommended by Rob and Gill Weeks, Angus Lindsay, A V Lewis, Richard Sanders, Pete Storey*)

Bass   Licensees Helen and Terry Knight   Real ale   Meals and snacks (not Sun lunchtime) Children in front lounge   Open 11–2.30, 5–11; opens 7 Sat

BUTTERTON (Staffs)   SK0756 Map 7
Black Lion ★ 🛏

Village signposted from B5053

Bar food in this unspoilt eighteenth-century stone village inn, close to the Manifold Valley, includes sandwiches (85p), ploughman's or salads (£2.50), roast chicken or steak and kidney pie (£2.75), lasagne, moussaka or vegetarian curry (£2.95), liver, bacon and onions (£3), beef in red wine (£3.65) and rump steak (£4.75). The layout of the several rooms is interestingly rambling: one with a low black beam and board ceiling has a fine old red leatherette settle around its good log fire, well polished mahogany and other tables, and comfortable old bar stools with back rests. An inner room (with a lively parakeet) has a Liberty-print sofa and an old kitchen range. A third has red plush button-back banquettes around sewing-machine tables; the dining-room has a good log fire. There are attractive Victorian prints throughout. Well kept McEwans 70/- and 80/- and Youngers No 3 on handpump, with Theakstons Best occasionally; darts, shove-ha'penny, dominoes, table skittles, pinball, juke box, space game, fruit machine, and a separate well lit pool-room; piped music. Picnic-table sets and rustic seats on a prettily planted terrace have a quiet view of the surrounding hills. The local church, with its tall and elegant spire, is nearby. (*Recommended by Laurence Manning, AHNR, BKA, Nick Dowson, Alison Hayward, M A and W R Proctor, Lee Goulding, Joy Heatherley, Michael Bolsover*)

Free house   Licensees Ron, Derek and Marie-Pierre Smith   Real ale   Meals and snacks (not Weds lunchtime)   Restaurant   Children welcome   Open 11–11, subject to demand, all year   Bedrooms tel Onecote (053 88) 232; £17.25B/£27.60B

Stars after the name of a pub show exceptional quality. But they don't mean extra comfort – and though some pubs get stars for special food quality, it isn't necessarily a food thing either. The full report on each pub should make clear what special quality has earned it.

nr BUXTON (Derbys)   SK0673 Map 7

Bull i' th' Thorn ★

Ashbourne Road, Hurdlow Town; A515 a few miles S of Buxton; OS Sheet 119 reference 128665

The lively carvings over the main entrance of this very attractive, roadside Tudor inn include one of the bull caught in the thornbush that gives the pub its name; there are others of an eagle with a freshly caught hare, and some spaniels chasing a rabbit. The interior very much lives up to the expectations aroused by the exterior: the main bar is a striking Tudor hall, dating from 1472, full of oak beams, joists, and squared panelling. The furnishings and decorations are in historical character, with ancient carved and panelled seats cut into the thick walls, longcase clock, armour, swords, blunderbusses and so forth, and old flagstones stepping shallowly down to a big open fire. Bar food is straightforward and good value: soup (60p), sandwiches (from 50p), ploughman's (£1.50), hot dishes such as sausages (£1.20), cottage pies and peas (£1.70), steak and kidney pie, roast beef or plaice (£2.30), scampi (£2.50), prawn salad (£3) and sirloin steak (£4.25); children's dishes (£1) and a Sunday roast lunch (£2.75); friendly service. An adjoining room has darts, pool, dominoes and a juke box; cheap, well kept Robinsons Best on handpump. The family-room opens on to a terrace and big lawn, with swings, and there are more tables in a sheltered angle in front. *(Recommended by Mr and Mrs Burton-Johnson, J E Rycroft, R F Moat, Frank Cummins, Dave and Angie Parkes, Lee Goulding, Jon Wainright, M A and W R Proctor)*

Robinsons   Licensees Bob and Judith Haywood   Real ale   Meals and snacks   Children in family- and games-rooms   Open 11–11 in summer (subject to demand); 11–3, 5.30–11 in winter   Two bedrooms tel Longnor (029 883) 348; £9/£18

CASTLETON (Derbys)   SK1583 Map 7

Castle Hotel ⊗ 🛏

High Street at junction with Castle Street

This welcoming Peak District inn has quite a strong pagan history: a woman is said to have been buried under its threshold – a throwback to pagan rites designed to bring prosperity to a new building; and on 29 May a colourful band and horseback procession moves from pub to pub, ending at the maypole; reputedly it celebrates Charles II's escape, but the custom's probably a good deal older. The atmosphere inside complements this sense of history: the plush bars have stripped stone walls with built-in cabinets, an open fire, finely carved early seventeenth-century beams and, in one room, ancient flagstones. Generously served bar food includes soup or Yorkshire pudding with onion gravy (75p), fresh crudités (£1.45), club sandwich (£1.75), ploughman's or vegetable lasagne (£1.95), whole cauliflower cheese (£2.15), stuffed pancakes (£2.25), Madras curry (£2.75), gammon (£3.25) and steak (£4.95). Stones on handpump; darts and a fruit machine; there are some seats outside. The village is just below the ruins of Peveril Castle and handy for some of Derbyshire's most spectacular caves; on *Good Walks Guide* Walk 71. *(Recommended by Alistair Campbell, Brian and Anna Marsden)*

Bass   Licensee Jose Rodriguez   Real ale   Meals and snacks   Restaurant   Children in their own area   Open 11–3, 5.30–11 all year; may open longer in afternoon   Bedrooms tel Hope Valley (0433) 20578; £35B/£45B

Children welcome means the pub says it lets children inside without any special restriction. If it allows them in, but to restricted areas such as an eating area or family-room, we specify this. Places with separate restaurants usually let children use them; hotels usually let them into public areas such as lounges. Some pubs impose an evening time-limit – let us know if you find this.

CAULDON (Staffs) SK0749 Map 7
Yew Tree ★ ★ ★

Village signposted from A523 and A52 about 8 miles W of Ashbourne; OS Sheet 119 reference 075493

The very high award here, ranking the pub as one of the most interesting in Britain, is for the remarkable collection of treasures which Alan East has squirreled away into these old-fashioned and cluttered rooms, lit dimly by lamps hanging from the exposed beams. So don't expect much in the way of creature comforts, nor anything great in the food line – unless it's the remarkably low prices for the hot sausage rolls (20p), big pork pies (35p), big filled baps (from 55p) and large pasties up from St Austell (60p). What does far exceed the hopes of most readers who've managed to track down this otherwise very basic pub (sometimes from very far-flung corners of the globe) is the contents – above all, on the musical side. Besides the pianola which Mr East is always happy to get his feet into, there's a remarkable collection of working Polyphons and Symphonions (towering nineteenth-century developments of the musical box, with all sorts of sound effects); even readers who've gone well stocked with the 2p pieces they sometimes take get so engrossed they run out. Some ancient musical instruments include a medieval leathern serpent, and the radio's a 1955 valve set (the telephone has a crank handle). On the hour, the dominant sound is the chorus of longcase clocks which stand sentinel around an upper gallery. As well as all that, there are lots of eighteenth-century plain or elaborately carved settles (besides some pleasantly soggy old sofas), old guns and pistols, a couple of pennyfarthing cycles propped casually, as if the riders had just dismounted, swordfish blades, old rocking-horses, and some notable early Staffordshire pottery in an attractive marquetry cabinet. Every time you go there seems to be some new little bits and bobs. The atmosphere is exceptionally friendly, and the drinks – now including well kept Bass, Burton Bridge and M&B Mild on handpump or tapped from the cask – are uncommonly cheap; darts, shove-ha'penny, table skittles, dominoes and cribbage. It's easy to miss the old brick pub: as you go between the huge quarry and the multi-coloured cement works which threaten to gobble it up, keep your eyes skinned for the big yew tree which it hides behind. Not far from Dovedale and the Manifold Valley. (*Recommended by Angus Lindsay, Nick Dowson, Alison Hayward, BKA, Laurence Manning, Dr Aristos Markantonakis, Jenny Seller, Rob and Gill Weeks, John Vereker, Jon Wainwright, C Elliott, James Cain, Virginia Jones, Wayne Brindle, Derek Stephenson, C D T Spooner, Michael Cooke, Mr and Mrs P Burton-Johnson, A V Lewis, Dr John Innes, Michael Craig*)

Free house   Licensee Alan East   Real ale   Snacks   Children in Polyphon room   Open 11–3, 6–11 all year

CHEDDLETON (Staffs)   SJ9651 Map 7
Boat

Basford Bridge Lane; off A520

Handy for the North Staffordshire Steam Railway museum, this pub reflects the canal area it's situated in: inside it's long and narrow, with low plank ceilings to match. The furnishings are simple, with upholstered wall benches and wooden tables at one end, copper ones at the other – which is decorated with masses of local motor-cycling trophies. It has good moorings for barges, and is close to the little Caldon Canal – attractive for its brightly painted boats. Bar food includes sandwiches, basket meals, home-made cottage pie or steak and kidney pie, gammon and egg and steak, with a choice of chips or jacket potatoes. Very well kept Marstons Burton and Pedigree on handpump; darts, dominoes, space game, maybe piped music. There are benches at the front, and tables and seats under a Perspex roof; also a couple of swings. *(Recommended by Dr R Hodgkinson, Andrew McKeand, Janet Williams; more reports please)*

Marstons   Real ale   Meals and snacks (not Tues evening; sandwiches only Tues and Sun lunchtime)   Children in eating area   Open 11–2.30, 6–11 all year; opens 7 in winter

CONSALL (Staffs)   SJ9748 Map 7
Black Lion   [illustrated on page 151]

Consallforge; from A522 just S of Wetley Rocks (which is E of Stoke-on-Trent) follow Consall turn-off right through village, then turn right into Nature Park, with easy access to the pub from its car park; OS Sheets 118 and 119 reference 000491

The simple and slightly down-at-heel atmosphere in this unspoilt canalside pub is all part of its charm; there are cafe seats and Formica tables on the tiles, plain brick walls, a good coal fire on cool days, and straightforward bar food. The welcome – from the strong-minded landlady or her sons – is warm and friendly. It's attractively situated near the Caldon Canal and the weir on the River Churnet, and, although it no longer has its distinctive sense of isolation in this deep wooded valley, it's still pleasantly remote; the two traditional walks to it – from the footpath sign just past the Old Hall on the village road, or along the canal from Cheddleton – are still well worth making. Well kept, reasonably priced Marstons Pedigree and Ruddles County on handpump; sensibly placed darts at one end; also table skittles, dominoes, cribbage, maybe piped music. Watch out for the lively pub goat. *(Recommended by G C Hixon, Andrew McKeand, E J Alcock, Dr R Hodgkinson)*

Free house   Real ale   Meals and snacks   Children welcome   Occasional live music   Open 10.30–2.30, 6–11 all year

nr FOOLOW (Derbys)   SK1976 Map 7
Barrel

Bretton; signposted from Foolow which itself is signposted from A623 just E of junction with B6465 to Bakewell

The bar food in this cheerful and traditional pub is simple but welcoming, including sandwiches (from 70p), ploughman's (£1.50) and open prawn baps or poacher's pie (£1.90). The bar area is a series of knocked-through rooms divided by the stubs of massive knocked-through stone walls; there's a variety of seating, including some old barrels, a Delft shelf has lots of old glass and china bottles, and the cream walls are decorated with local maps, an aerial photograph, a rack of clay pipes, and poems about the pub. The far end of the beamed bar is very snug, with a leather-cushioned settle and built-in corner wall bench by an antique oak table in front of the open fire (the cats' favourite spot). Well kept Stones and Bass Mild on electric pump, and a good choice of whiskies. There are fine views, particularly from the breezy front terrace, to the pastures below this high ridge. *(Recommended by Keith and Sheila Baxter, Jon Wainwright, Mr and Mrs P Burton-Johnson)*

Bass   Licensee Edward Walsh   Real ale   Snacks (not Thurs evening)   Children in eating area   Open 12–3, 6.30–11 all year

FROGGATT EDGE (Derbys)   SK2477 Map 7
Chequers

B6054, off A623 N of Bakewell; OS Sheet 119 reference 247761

Close to a striking Peak District edge, and looking out over an attractive valley, this old-fashioned and comfortable inn has antique prints on its white walls (partly stripped back to big dark stone blocks), a big solid-fuel stove and library chairs or small high-backed winged settles on its well waxed floorboards. There's a big grandfather clock in one corner and a nicely carved oak cupboard in another; the

LITTLE HUCKLOW (Derbys)   SK1678   Map 7
Old Bulls Head ★
Pub signposted from B6049

In its quietly traditional village, surrounded by upland sheep pastures, this immaculate little pub slots comfortably into the relaxed and never-changing way of life. The two small oak-beamed rooms have interesting collections of locally mined semi-precious stones and of antique brass and iron household tools; the built-in settles are comfortably cushioned, and there's a coal fire in a neatly restored stone hearth. One is served from a hatch, the other over a polished bar counter. They have a splendid collection of well restored and attractively painted old farm machinery, outside among lovely flower beds and neat dry-stone walls. Well kept Wards Sheffield Best on handpump; bar snacks are simple, consisting of freshly cut sandwiches (80p) and ploughman's (£1.80); good coffee. There may be well reproduced Beethoven, Bach, Mozart, Chopin or Mahler. *(Recommended by Brian and Anna Marsden, Derek Stephenson, M A and W R Proctor, John Derbyshire, Michael Bolsover, Mr and Mrs P Burton-Johnson, Jon Wainwright, S Hampson, Lee Goulding, C D T Spooner)*

Free house   Licensee D G Hawketts   Real ale   Snacks (lunchtime)   Children welcome Occasional folk groups   Open 12–3, 7–11 all year; closed weekday lunchtimes in winter

LITTLE LONGSTONE (Derbys)   SK1971   Map 7
Packhorse ⊗
Monsal Dale and Ashford Village signposted off A6 NW of Bakewell; follow Monsal Dale signposts, then turn right into Little Longstone at Monsal Head Hotel

Cosy and snug in its village terrace, this sixteenth-century cottage has been transformed during the Lythgoes' three years here into the epitome of a traditional village tavern. The two small rooms have open fires, beam and plank ceiling, simple furnishings from country-kitchen chairs and cloth-cushioned settles to an odd, almost batwinged corner chair, and decorations that are distinctive but discreet – attractive landscape photographs by Steve Riley, blow-ups of older local photographs, prettily hung decorative mugs, the odd cornet or trumpet, and a collection of brass spigots. Bar food includes soup (85p), sandwiches (85p), baps spread with dripping and generously filled with hot well hung beef (85p) or with hot pork, apple sauce and stuffing (95p), aubergine and bean bake or ploughman's (£2.25), meat salad or chilli con carne (£2.55), steak and kidney pie (£2.85) and casseroles (around £3). Well kept Marstons Burton and Pedigree on handpump; darts, dominoes, cribbage, and a fine relaxed local atmosphere – almost deceptively so, as in a quiet break you may find Mr Lythgoe skating through one of the weightier papers' crosswords in about five minutes. In summer the steep little informal garden has a shifting population of lambs, goats and rabbits. *(Recommended by Derek Stephenson, Lynda Brown and others)*

Marstons   Licensees Sandra and Mark Lythgoe   Real ale   Meals and snacks   Children in eating area until 8   Open 11–3, 5–11 (opens 6 Mon) all year; open all day Sat

nr MELBOURNE (Derbys)   SK3825   Map 7
John Thompson
Ingleby; village signposted from A514 at Swarkestone

This pub is unique for being named after the man who both owns it and brews its very popular beer; there's also Marstons Pedigree on handpump. The lounge is big and modernised, with button-back leather seats, sturdy oak tables, some old oak settles and antique prints and paintings, and a log-effect gas fire; a couple of smaller cosier rooms open off. Bar food consists of sandwiches (nothing else on Sundays), soup, a cold buffet, hot roast beef (£3.50, not Monday) and puddings. In summer the surroundings are an obvious draw: there are beautifully kept lawns and flower beds running down to the rich watermeadows along the River Trent, with lots of tables on the upper lawn, and a partly covered outside terrace with its own serving-bar. *(Recommended by R Hazzard, Dr A V Lewis, Dave Butler, Lesley Storey, Pete Storey)*

Own brew   Licensee John Thompson   Real ale   Meals (lunchtime, not Sun; cold buffet only, Mon) and snacks   Children in separate room   Open 10.30–2.30, 7–11 all year

MILLTHORPE (Derbys)   SK3276   Map 7
Royal Oak ⊗
B6051

The main room of this intimate seventeenth-century stone inn has robust furnishings, with old oak beams, bare stone walls, a warm fire in winter and lots of character. It opens into a small, more comfortable and quieter lounge. The food is all home made by the friendly and welcoming licensees and includes sandwiches and filled rolls (from 80p – the toasted ham and cheese and black pudding and bacon are particularly recommended, £1–£1.15), pork pie and salad (£1.50), cottage pie (£2), a wide choice of ploughman's (£2–£2.20), chilli con carne (£2.20), lasagne or chicken curry (£2.35) and seafood Mornay (£2.50), with Cumberland sausage (£2.50) and mixed grill or eight-ounce steak (£3.95) on winter evenings. Well kept and well priced Darleys Thorne and Wards Sheffield Best on handpump. There are picnic-table sets on a crazy-paved terrace, partly shaded by hawthorn, ash and other trees, and up on a side lawn. *(Recommended by Jon Wainwright, Sue Cleasby, Mike Ledger, W P P Clarke, P R E McGhee)*

Free house   Licensees Harry and Elaine Wills   Real ale   Meals and snacks (not Sat–Sun evenings)   Open 11.30–3, 5.30–11; closed Mon lunchtime in winter

MONSAL HEAD (Derbys)   SK1871   Map 7
Monsal Head Hotel
B6465

The layout of this beautifully placed inn has changed somewhat in the last year. What used to be the back walkers' bar is now a Victorian dining-room. In its place, the former stables have been turned into an all-day bar – a lively flagstoned room with cushioned oak pews around flowery-clothed tables in the stripped timber stalls that used to house the horses which lugged people and their luggage up from the station deep down at the end of the valley viaduct; it's decked out with harness and horsy brassware, and they've put a big wood-burning stove into the inglenook. Steps lead up into a crafts gallery, and tables out in the yard look over the road to the steep and spectacular dale. The spacious high-ceilinged main front bar has big windows on the same view, and is set out more as a wine bar, with dining-chairs around big tables; it's partitioned off from the restaurant area. Simple bar food includes soup (85p), sandwiches (from 85p), and ploughman's (£2), with several lunchtime hot dishes such as steak and kidney pie, chicken chasseur, Lancashire hot-pot or aubergine and mushroom lasagne (all £2.50) and roast beef or pork (£3.45); some of these are also served in the evening (about 70p more). The Sunday lunch is good value. Well kept John Smiths, Theakstons Best and Old Peculier and a regularly changing guest beer on handpump; also tea and decent coffee; darts, table skittles, dominoes and cribbage. There's a back garden with a play area and

---

The Post Office makes it virtually impossible for people to come to grips with British geography by using a system of post towns which are often across the county boundary from the places they serve. So the postal address of a pub often puts it in the wrong county. We use the correct county – the one the pub is actually in. Lots of pubs which the Post Office alleges are in Oxfordshire are actually in Berkshire, Buckinghamshire, Gloucestershire or the Midlands.

animals. Trout fishing on the Wye for residents. *(Recommended by Derek Stephenson, PS, Simon Holmes, G C Davenport, Kirsten Hoffman; more reports please)*

Free house   Licensee Nicholas Smith   Real ale   Meals and snacks   Restaurant   Children in eating area and restaurant   Open 11–3, 6–11 all year; opens 7 in winter; closed 25 Dec; Stable Bar open all day   Bedrooms – not 24–25 Dec – tel Great Longstone (062 987) 250; £15(£17.50B)/£25(£30B)

NEWBOROUGH (Staffs)   SK1325 Map 7
Red Lion

B5234

This is a simple and unpretentious place, facing on to the quiet village square; the modernised carpeted lounge has dove-coloured comfortable banquettes and stools around copper-topped cast-iron tables, and a log fire in winter. There are two fruit machines, darts and dominoes in the cheerful lino-floored public bar; piped music. The home-cooked food is attractive for its simplicity, including filled cobs (from 50p), sandwiches (from 70p, home-cooked gammon 85p), soup (80p), plough-man's (from £1.80), hot dishes such as steak and kidney pie (£3), quiche (£3.15), plaice (£3.40), scampi or seafood pasta (£3.75), meat salads (from £4) and steaks (from £5.20). Well kept Marstons Burton and Pedigree on handpump. There are some tables and a swing at the back, fenced off from the car park. *(Recommended by Dr C D E Morris; more reports please)*

Marstons   Real ale   Meals and snacks   Children in eating area   Open 10.30–2.30, 6.30–10.30; opens 7 in winter

OVER HADDON (Derbys)   SK2066 Map 7
Lathkil ⊗ 🍺

Village and inn signposted from B5055 just SW of Bakewell

The bar food here is served in the spacious and sunny family dining area on the left (which doubles as a restaurant in the evenings); it includes home-made soup or filled cobs (£1.10), smoked mackerel salad (£2.80), home-made quiche (£3.10), lamb curry (£3.15), lasagne (£3.30), good steak and kidney pie or beef and mushroom casserole (£3.40), excellent smoked local trout (it's also supplied to the Dorchester in London), and a help-yourself cold buffet (£3.20); home-made sweets (£1.10). The pleasant and welcoming room on the right has black beams, big windows, a cheery fire in the attractively carved fireplace, leatherette seats, old-fashioned settles, a Delft shelf of blue and white plates on one white wall, original prints and photographs. Well kept Darleys Thorne and Wards Sheffield Best on handpump; piped jazz or classical music, shove-ha'penny, dominoes, cribbage. It's a very popular place with walkers, who are enticed off Lathkill Dale and the moors by the pub's friendly and informal atmosphere – there's even a place in the lobby to leave boots, though the muddiest pot-holers stay sitting out on the long stone ledge and the low wall along the front of the pub. *(Recommended by A D Lealan, C F Walling, Patrick Young, Dr and Mrs R J Ashleigh, P and H B, R A Hutson, Dr John Innes, R F Moat, Jon Wainwright, Anthony Lowe, D J Milner, Paul and Margaret Baker, Dr and Mrs B D Smith)*

Free house (part tied to Wards)   Licensee Robert Grigor-Taylor   Real ale   Meals and snacks (lunchtime)   Evening restaurant (not Sun)   Children in eating area (lunchtime; evening if dining in restaurant with adults)   Open 11–3, 6–11 all year; closed evening 25 Dec   Bedrooms tel Bakewell (062 981) 2501; £27.50B/£50B

We checked prices with the pubs as we went to press in summer 1988. They should hold until around spring 1989 – when our experience suggests that you can expect an increase of around 10p in the £.

PENKHULL (Staffs)   SJ8644   Map 7
Greyhound

Leaving Newcastle centre on A34 for Stafford, look out for the first left turn after two hospital signposts and a stretch of parkland; turn into this Newcastle Lane to find village centre at top of hill; pub in Manor Court Street, opposite church; OS Sheet 118 reference 868448

Though surrounded by the urban heart of the Potteries, this is a genuine – and genuinely friendly – little village, with its pub to match. It's a pretty building, very traditional inside: one room with red plush seats around massive old-fashioned gilt tables, tiny pictures on its white walls, a neat and cosy inglenook fireplace, another with seats built into its darkening Anaglypta walls, elaborate gas-style wall lamps, a piano with placards perched along its top, dark panelling elsewhere – very much, you feel, what the 1940s should have been like, but sadly never really were. Simple cheap bar food includes filled baps (50p), soup (70p), ploughman's (£1.35), lasagne, curry or chilli con carne (£1.75) and home-made pies (£1.95) – if lobby's on the menu, go for it; well kept Ansells Bitter and Mild and Ind Coope Burton on handpump; table skittles, darts. A couple of picnic-table sets on the front pavement face the churchyard, with more behind. (*Recommended by Alison Hayward, Nick Dowson, D P Bagnall*)

Ansells (Ind Coope)   Licensees Mr and Mrs John Chadwick   Real ale   Meals and snacks Children in lounge and food serving-room   Open 12–3, 7–11 all year

ROWARTH (Derbys)   SK0189   Map 7
Little Mill

Turn off A626 at Mellor signpost (in steep dip at Marple Bridge); fork left at Rowarth signpost, then follow Little Mill signpost; OS Sheet 110 reference 011889

This comfortable pub stands out as an oasis of bustling activity in an otherwise remote and seemingly deserted area, and the welcome you should receive is more than adequate compensation for the perseverance required to find it. When it is quiet, the atmosphere is calm and relaxing in the open-plan Turkey-carpeted bar, which has stub walls, bare brick pillars, little settees and armchairs. Popular bar food includes the usual run of steak and kidney pie, grills or fried foods with chips and so forth. Well kept Boddingtons, Robinsons Bitter and Best Mild and Ruddles County on handpump; darts, pool, dominoes, cribbage, fruit machine and two space games in one of several alcoves; unobtrusive juke box. Tubs of flowers, roses and honeysuckle decorate the front terrace, and there are little lawns with ash trees, seats, swings, and a climbing-frame in this steep little dell by a millstream. The Pullman railway dining-car, which they've somehow managed to haul up here, dates from 1932. The area is good for walks. (*Recommended by David Waterhouse, Michael Craig, Lee Goulding, GP*)

Free house   Real ale   Meals and snacks   Upstairs restaurant   Children welcome   Open 11.30–3, 5.30–11 all year   Bedrooms tel New Mills (0663) 43178; £32 (they may let out the twin room as a single if it's quiet)

ROWSLEY (Derbys)   SK2566   Map 7
Peacock 🏨

A6 Bakewell–Matlock

This is a civilised, refined place, and the people who come here tend to be smartly dressed; although it's more of a hotel than a pub, it's well worth a visit, both for its gardens running down to the River Derwent and for its home-made marmalade with rum flavour, which they also sell at reception. The softly lit inner bar has an old-fashioned feel, with oak beams, stripped stone walls, a copper-topped bar counter, antique settles, a nineteenth-century cockfighting chair (with an arm swollen into a little table, like a fiddler crab's fat claw), and an alcove seat for the red-coated lounge waiter. The lounge is quiet and spacious, with comfortable Windsor chairs and more antique settles; there's a help-yourself lunchtime buffet here (£4, not Sundays), and snacks like courgette and potato soup with croûtons (£1.60), sandwiches (from £1.75), ploughman's (£2.80), and a main dish such as braised minute steak in onion gravy (£4); puddings (£1.65). Well kept Ind Coope Burton on handpump; morning coffee served from 9.30; also afternoon teas. It was originally built as a dower house for Haddon Hall in 1652, and became an inn in 1828. Good trout fishing is available; near *Good Walks Guide* Walk 79. *(Recommended by Miles Kington, Mr and Mrs M C Jaffé, R A Hutson)*

Embassy Hotels (Allied Lyons – the parent company of Ind Coope)   Licensee G M Gillson Lunchtime bar food (not Sun)   Restaurant   Children may be allowed under certain circumstances   Open 11–3, 6–11 all year   Bedrooms tel Matlock (0629) 733518; £30(£48B)/£39(£55B)

SANDONBANK (Staffs)   SJ9428   Map 7
Seven Stars

4½ miles from M6 junction 14; A34 link road towards Stone but at first roundabout continue on A513 ring road, then turn left on to B5066; alternatively, from A51 in Sandon follow signpost B5066, Stafford

The open-plan bar in this comfortable white house has several cosy corners, little country prints, lots of polished brass, and good fires in winter, with plenty of blue plush stools and cushioned captain's chairs on a sweep of carpet. Steps lead down to a lower lounge, popular with families; well kept Burtonwood and Dark Mild on handpump; piped music. Outside there are picnic-table sets at the front, and a swing on the grass at the back. The bar food, served efficiently by waitresses, includes ploughman's (£1.85, lunchtime only), home-made steak and kidney or chicken and mushroom pie (£3.20, also lunchtime only), plaice (£3.20), beef curry (£3.45), aubergine lasagne or vegetable pie (£3.95), scampi (£4.20), gammon and eggs, chicken Kiev or turkey Cordon Bleu (£4.25), beef Stroganoff (£4.50) and rump steak (£7). The credit-card signs outside don't apply to bar meals. *(Recommended by Brian and Anna Marsden, AMcK; more reports please)*

Burtonwood   Licensee Ron Roestenburg   Real ale   Meals and snacks   Restaurant tel Sandon (088 97) 316   Children welcome   Open 11–3, 6.30–11 all year

SEIGHFORD (Staffs)   SJ8725   Map 7
Holly Bush ⊗

3 miles from M6 junction 14: A5013 towards Eccleshall, left on to B5405 in Great Bridgeford, then first left signposted Seighford

The spacious and airy black-beamed bar in this charming place is extremely clean, and has big windows, ivy-leaf chintz curtains, and light modern prints of poppies and landscapes; the varnished rustic tables – it's very much a country pub – have wheel-back chairs and comfortable settles around them. There's an ever-expanding collection of antique bric-à-brac, brass cooking instruments and foreign coins – these are stuck on the mirrors around the attractively carved inglenook fireplace. Well kept Tetleys on handpump, and good ports, brandies and after-dinner malt whiskies, as well as an above-average selection of non-alcoholic drinks; darts, piped music. The enterprising range of bar food includes soup (85p, seafood or French onion £1.20), Gruyère and Edam cheese fritters (£1.75), devilled whitebait (£1.85), ploughman's or hot brioche with mushroom sauce (£1.95), open sandwiches (from £2.50), devilled lambs' kidneys with rice (£2.85), vegetarian lasagne or home-made chilli con carne (£2.95), smoked haddock in cheese sauce (£3.25), salads (from £3.45), scampi or pork chop in cider (£3.45), chicken Kiev (£4.45), gammon

(£4.50), and steaks (from £5.65); there are puddings like sherry trifle or home-made bread pudding (90p), strawberry mallow (£1.25), raspberry Pavlova (£1.35) and hot figs in brandy (£1.65). In early 1988 not all reports were as warmly enthusiastic about the food as we're used to, and people found that service could be slow. This coincided with the time that the owners were putting a good deal of energy into opening a new venture – the Radbrook Manor at Preston on Stour, a renovated country house with a poolside bar, restaurant and lots of leisure facilities. We hope that things will be back to normal by the time this edition is published. The neat back rose garden has seats on a terrace, in a vine arbour, and on the spacious lawn. (*Recommended by TBB, W D Horsfield, K and R Markham, Mr and Mrs B Amos, G Bloxsom, Dick Brown, Mr and Mrs Ken Turner, Peter Leverkus, Wayne Brindle, Len and Sue Beattie, A Duff, Laurence Manning*)

Ansells (Ind Coope)   Licensee Mrs Louise Fowden   Real ale   Meals and snacks   Restaurant tel Seighford (0785) 75280   Children welcome   Open 12–3, 7–11 all year

SHARDLOW (Derbys)   SK4330 Map 7
Malt Shovel ⊗

3½ miles from M1 junction 24; A6 towards Derby, then in Shardlow turn down Wilne Lane, then left after crossing canal

The bar food in this interesting eighteenth-century canalside pub remains popular with readers, who are attracted both by its consistency and its good value; it includes sandwiches (from 55p), soup (65p), ploughman's (£1.50), basket meals (from £1.50), sausage and egg (£1.80), steak and kidney pie or beef casserole (£2.25), meatballs in a rich oxtail sauce (£2.70), chicken and ham pie (£2.90), salads (from £2.95), ham and pineapple (£3.25), a hot-pot of cod and mushrooms topped with a cheese sauce or chopped lamb, bacon and apple wrapped in pastry (£3.95), and steaks (from £4.50); puddings (85p). There's lots inside to keep the eye occupied, such as brewery and tobacco mirrors and advertisements, cigarette cards, cartoons, and other pictures, jugs, mugs, plates and swords. The atmospheric bar has an interesting layout, all odd angles and varying ceiling heights; good log fire in winter. Well kept Marstons Pedigree and Mercian Mild on handpump, and a wide choice of wines; piped music. Good window seats overlook the busy Trent and Mersey Canal, with more tables out beside it. The nearby marina has a museum of canalboat life, and the Castle Donington collection of historic racing cars is not far. No motor-cyclists. (*Recommended by RJH, Derek and Sylvia Stephenson, T Houghton, Tim and Lynne Crawford, Dr and Mrs B D Smith, Rob and Gill Weeks, Dave Butler, Lesley Storey*)

Marstons   Licensee Peter Morton-Harrison   Real ale   Meals and snacks (lunchtimes, not Sun)   Children welcome   Open 11–11 all year; closed evening 25 and 26 Dec

SHRALEYBROOK (Staffs)   SJ7850 Map 7
Rising Sun

3 miles from M6 junction 16; from A500 towards Stoke take first right turn signposted Alsager, Audley; in Audley turn right on the road still shown on many maps as A52, but now in fact a B, signposted Balterley, Nantwich; pub then signposted on left (at the T-junction look out for the Watneys Red Barrel)

Outside you can hear the rush of the nearby motorway; inside it seems a hundred miles away, with the shiny black paintwork of the panelling, beams and timbers in the ochre walls, the gentle lighting, the red leatherette seats tucked into cosy alcoves, and the warm open fire. There's a fine relaxed and friendly atmosphere – epitomised in Zoot, the pub's cocker spaniel. They have seven well kept real ales on handpump, constantly changing among the thirty or so they cellar; Marstons Pedigree is more or less a fixture, and on our visit the others were Merrie Monk, Midsummer Ale (brewed by Burton Bridge for the small independent chain of pubs of that name), Ruddles Best and County, Theakstons Best and Unicorn Hellgate (from an own-brew pub at Ketley, near Telford). A wide choice of bar food includes soup (80p), sandwiches or burgers (80p), filled baked potatoes (£1), smoked cod or breaded plaice (£2.75), specials such as lasagne (£2.75), lots of vegetarian dishes (£3.25) and chicken Kiev or sirloin steak (£5). *(Recommended by Sue Holland, Dave Webster, D P Bagnall)*

Free house   Licensee Mrs G M Holland   Real ale   Meals and snacks   Children welcome Open 12–3, 6.30–12 all year; open all day Sat

WARDLOW (Derbys)   SK1875   Map 7
Three Stags Heads
Wardlow Mires; A623 by junction with B6465

The atmosphere in this little white-painted slate cottage – where, it seems, nothing ever changes – is particularly charming. The small parlour bar is warmly welcoming, with a couple of antique settles with flowery cushions, two high-backed Windsor armchairs, old leathercloth seats and simple oak tables on the lino, a double rack of willow-pattern plates, and a grandfather clock; an overflow room has plainer, more modern furnishings. The cast-iron kitchen range, kept alight in winter, has a gleaming copper kettle. Very well kept Youngers Scotch on handpump. Watch out for the petrified cat in its glass case – though some readers are uncertain whether to regard it as an attraction or not. The front terrace outside looks across the main road to farmland rising gently into the distant hills. Walkers – and their boots – are welcomed. *(Recommended by P and H B, Keith and Sheila Baxter, Tim and Lynne Crawford, Geoffrey Cleaver)*

Free house   Real ale   No food (and no real car park)   Open 11–3, 6–11 all year

WETTON (Staffs)   SK1055   Map 7
Olde Royal Oak
Set in National Trust country (with places like Wetton Hill and the Manifold Valley nearby), this simple and very friendly village pub has a log fire in the stone fireplace of its original core; also black beams supporting white ceiling-boards, and an oak corner cupboard. In the small dining-room there are chairs and built-in wall settles around its rustic tables. It extends into a more modern-feeling area, with another fire and a door into a carpeted sun lounge, which looks on to the small garden. The range of bar food includes sandwiches (from 80p), soup (£1), ploughman's (from £2 – the cheese for the Stilton version is made in nearby Hartington), omelettes (£2), and main dishes (for which they allow twenty-five minutes' cooking time) like home-made steak and kidney pie (£3), veal Cordon Bleu (£3.25), grilled fresh trout (£4), rump steak (£4.75), whole lemon sole (£5.25) and duck à l'orange (£5.50); three-course roast Sunday lunch (£4.75); well kept Ruddles Best and County and Theakstons XB on handpump; darts, dominoes, cribbage and, they say, regular toe-wrestling. The stone platform outside the white-painted and shuttered house serves as a handy seat for walkers. *(Recommended by Jenny Seller, Geoffrey Cleaver, Lee Goulding)*

Free house   Licensees Roger and Trisha Probert   Real ale   Meals and snacks   Children in sun lounge   Open 11.30–3, 6.30–11; 11.30–2.30. 7–11 in winter

WHITMORE (Staffs)   SJ8141   Map 7
Mainwaring Arms ★
3 miles from M6 junction 15; follow signs for Market Drayton, Shrewsbury, on to A53

Opposite the lovely village church, this exceptional Staffordshire stone pub has a charming series of interconnecting oak-beamed rooms, rambling up and down and in and out. Throughout there are some old-fashioned settles among comfortable more modern seats, with reproduction memorial brasses on the walls. The big open fire in the lower room's capacious stone fireplace, backed up by a couple of others elsewhere, tries its best to combat the cold weather. Bar food includes sandwiches, a buffet set out with salads and a choice of meats including reliable roast beef and pies (around £2.50), and hot dishes such as ham and broccoli or chicken and sweetcorn flans, chilli con carne, chicken curry and moussaka (all around £3); well kept Boddingtons, Davenports and Marstons Pedigree on handpump. It's named after the family that has owned it and most other things around here for some nine hundred years; the local hunt may use it for gatherings. Seats outside. (*Recommended by R G Ollier, C F Walling, J L Thompson, Andor Gomme, L S Manning, GRE, AE, D P Bagnall, John Innes*)

Free house   Real ale   Meals and snacks (not Sun evening)   Children in eating area   Open 11–2.30, 5.30–11 all year

---

Lucky Dip

Besides the fully inspected pubs, you might like to try these Lucky Dips recommended to us and described by readers (if you do, please send us reports):

☆ **Abbots Bromley**, Staffs [SK0724], *Goats Head*: Appealing old pub, attractive outside and pleasant in, with character and big cosy inglenook; good reasonably priced bar food, well kept Ind Coope Burton (*Lyn and Bill Capper, John Atherton, Jon Wainwright, M A and W R Proctor*)
Abbots Bromley, Staffs [High St], *Coach & Horses*: Attractive low-beamed bar with warm welcome, friendly atmosphere, wide range of customers; lunchtime food, well kept Ind Coope Burton; three comfortable bedrooms (*HRH*); [High St] *Royal Oak*: Interior belies very ordinary exterior – most attractive bar with well kept real ales such as Wadworths 6X, good value imaginative food in bar and restaurant, efficient service; garden (*HRH, Fiona Carrey*)
☆ **Alstonefield**, Staffs [Hopedale; SK1355], *Watts Russell Arms*: Simple welcoming pub with friendly service, open fire, well kept Marstons Pedigree on handpump, usual range of bar food decently prepared, piped radio, tables on small terrace by quiet lane; handy for Dovedale and Manifold Valleys (*Douglas Bail, Brian and Anna Marsden, Mr and Mrs K J Baxter, BB*)
Amington, Staffs [Shuttington Rd; SK2304], *Pretty Pigs*: Warm and friendly welcome in bar and lounge with lots of exposed beams, wide choice of good food including children's dishes, well kept M&B Brew XI, piped music, fruit machine; handy for Alvecote Nature Reserve and ruined Priory, in rural setting; children in lounge and carvery (*Colin Gooch*)
Anslow, Staffs [Bramhill Rd; SK2125], *Brickmakers Arms*: Small, unpretentious, friendly pub, well kept Marstons Pedigree, generous and good value food well prepared and presented (*Eric Locker*)
Ashbourne, Derbys [Ashbourne Green – top

of hill on way to Matlock; SK1846], *Bowling Green*: Excellent varied bar snacks including vegetarian dishes, Bass in fine condition, committed owners (*G C Hixon*); [St Johns St] *Smiths*: Sixteenth-century beamed pub with homely atmosphere, attractive décor, welcoming young licensees, well kept Marstons and fine choice of malt whiskies; good well presented home-made food, live music Fri (*J Yorke, Mr and Mrs L J Songhurst*)
Ashford in the Water, Derbys [SK1969], *Devonshire Arms*: Stone pub (with Stones on handpump too) in picturesque village with trout in nearby stream, village cricket (*Jon Wainwright, BB*)
Ashley, Staffs [SJ7636], *Peel Arms*: Well run pub with interconnecting rooms, totally refurbished under new licensees – plush seating and big black range fire; well kept Marstons Pedigree, lovely garden, pretty village (*Laurence Manning*)
Bakewell, Derbys [Market Pl; SK2168], *Peacock*: Clean, bright, cheerful and comfortable modernised pub; Wards ales (*R A Hutson*); [Market Pl] *Red Lion*: Panelled lounge with atmosphere of market-town pub; excellent Marstons Pedigree (*R A Hutson*); [The Square] *Rutland Arms*: A pub in a hotel – superb plush refurbishment, good service, fine reception and hospitality; varied choice of excellent food and drinks; bedrooms (*G C Hixon, BB*)
Bamford, Derbys [Taggs Knoll, A625; SK2083], *Anglers Rest*: Extensive menu, service always very quick (*T Houghton*); [A625] *Marquis of Granby*: Derwentside garden and cocktail bar furnished with sumptuous panelling, etc. salvaged from *Titanic*'s sistership distinguish this old inn; spacious bedrooms (*Gwen and Peter Andrews, LYM*)
Barlaston, Staffs [just off A34; SJ8938], *Duke of York*: Homely country pub, well run and

popular – a home from home *(D P Bagnall)*

Barton Under Needwood, Staffs [Main St; SK1818], *Red Lion*: Small friendly Marstons pub, well kept Pedigree on handpump, bar meals, cosy lounge, more spacious public bar with darts and dominoes, upstairs pool-room *(B M Eldridge)*; [The Green] *Royal Oak*: Marstons house with recently refurbished church pews around walls, original stained glass in partitions, ceiling and supporting beams from old sailing-ship, scrubbed tables; well kept Pedigree on handpump, friendly service; children's room *(B M Eldridge)*

Baslow, Derbys [SK2572], *Devonshire Arms*: Good home-cooked food, excellent ploughman's, quiche and steak sandwich, pleasant ambience, kind and friendly people; close to Chatsworth, and this is a pleasant Peak District town *(Dora Leat)*; [High St] *Prince of Wales*: Good value food and well kept Wards beer *(N F Doherty)*; *Rutland Arms*: Refurbished, and more restaurant than pub, but very pleasant and efficient *(P and HB)*

☆ **Beeley**, Derbys [SK2667], *Devonshire Arms*: Black beams and stripped stonework in spacious pub handy for Chatsworth, with Theakstons and Wards real ales, big log fires, enjoyable food including children's dishes in bar and nice restaurant *(Michael Bolsover, Mark and Shirley Elvin, Brian and Anna Marsden, Derek and Sylvia Stephenson, R A Hutson, Dr A V Lewis, Jon Wainwright, LYM)*

Belper, Derbys [OS Sheet 119 reference 350485; SK3447], *Grapes*: Excellent family-run local with big collection of brass blow-lamps, good friendly atmosphere, well kept Marstons Pedigree *(Michael Bolsover)*

Betley, Staffs [OS Sheet 118 reference 753486; SJ7548], *Black Horse*: Friendly old-fashioned stone-floored pub with Boddingtons on handpump, basic bar food and good value Sun lunches, efficient service; restaurant; children welcome if eating *(D P Cartwright, G C Hixon)*

Bradley, Staffs [SJ8718], *Red Lion*: Friendly welcome at sixteenth-century pub with excellent food and drink *(Derrick Turner)*

Bradwell, Derbys [Smalldale – off B6049; SK1781], *Bowling Green*: Good views from terrace outside much-modernised village pub with lots of malt whiskies *(LYM)*

☆ **Brassington**, Derbys [SK2354], *Olde Gate*: Attractively olde-worlde seventeenth-century pub with big kitchen range in public bar, real ale, good daily changing choice of tasty, reasonably cheap and often unusual food, friendly licensees, good atmosphere, family-room; in a nice setting – the village is handy for Dovedale and Tissington walks *(Alastair Campbell, Tim and Lynne Crawford)*

Brassington, Derbys, *Miners Arms*: Friendly reception, good meals, well kept Marstons Pedigree; big clean bedrooms, good value, with excellent breakfast *(R Eddington)*

Brown Edge, Staffs [SU9053], *Varsovia Lodge*: Excellent bar food in smart downstairs lounge bar – also restaurant *(AMcK)*

Burbage, Derbys [SK0473], *Duke of York*: Family-run pub with good value lunchtime food, hard-working and enthusiastic licensee *(Rita Landless)*

☆ **Burslem**, Staffs [Newcastle St – quite handy for M6 junction 15; SJ8749], *Travellers Rest*: Imaginative home-cooked food including good vegetarian dishes, choice of well kept real ales (sadly the pub's own Titanic brewery went into liquidation in spring 1988), friendly landlord and staff, lively atmosphere, good mix of customers, jazz Mon and Tues evenings *(Peter Griffiths, Sue Holland, Dave Webster, Jon Wainwright)*

☆ **Burton-on-Trent**, Staffs [Bridge St (A50); SK2423], *Burton Bridge Brewery*: Pub attached to brewery doing excellent Burton Bridge XL, Bridge, Porter and Festival – has guest beers too; cheap bulk supplies can be ordered 24 hours ahead – Burton-on-Trent (0283) 36596; filled rolls, skittle alley with weekly folk night, view into brewery on way to gents *(A V Lewis, Colin Dowse, Iain Anderson)*

Burton-on-Trent, Staffs [Shobnall Rd – by A38 flyover, nr Marstons Brewery], *Albion*: Tastefully modernised, large two-roomed pub with conservatory off lounge; well kept Pedigree, wide range of hot and cold lunchtime bar food including hot beef rolls and daily roast; juke box, pool-table and darts; well kept garden with swings for children and a fenced stream *(Richard Sanders, Colin Gooch)*; [349 Anglesey Rd] *New Talbot*: Friendly Marstons pub with well kept Pedigree on handpump, wide range of bar food, piped music in lounge, pool-table and juke box in public bar, organ singalong Sat evening *(B M Eldridge)*

☆ **Buxton**, Derbys [High St; SK0673], *Cheshire Cheese*: Pleasant, open pub, interesting décor, stained-glass panelling, well kept Hardys & Hansons, warm welcome and gourmet cooking by landlord in bar and restaurant *(Nick and Jean Norton, Jon Wainwright)*

Buxton, Derbys [Bridge St], *Railway*: Very clean and comfortable, good hot and cold food, excellent wine, good service *(H R Edwards)*

S of Buxton, Derbys [Hurdlow; A515 Ashbourne Rd, about half a mile from the Bull i' th' Thorn], *Duke of York*: Friendly, helpful landlord, food including excellent soup, good melon, very good steak sandwich, children's dishes; Robinsons beer *(Ian D Coburn)*

Castleton, Derbys [SK1583], *Olde Cheshire Cheese*: Two comfortable communicating bar areas in slated white timbered pub; well kept Wards real ale, sensibly placed darts, leatherette seats around wooden tables, popular with young people; bedrooms *(BB)*; [Cross St] *Olde Nags Head*: Village hotel recently renovated to preserve character, small bar with open fire, good bar food and service, separate restaurant; bedrooms comfortable *(J J Hansen)*

Cheslyn Hay, Staffs [Moon Lane; SJ9706], *Mary Rose*: Small country pub with nautical décor, well kept beer, excellent value bar meals, friendly speedy service *(M V Fereday)*

Chesterfield, Derbys [Lond Shambles; SK3871], *Royal Oak*: Friendly, welcoming pub with tiny medieval high-ceilinged lounge and more basic bar; Stones on handpump, good value lunchtime bar food *(Richard Sanders, G P Dyall)*

Clayton, Staffs [Westbury Rd, Westbury Park; very near M6 junction 15; SJ8542], *Westbury*: Excellent beer and food choice in clean, homely and comfortable pub with friendly staff *(Martin Degg, D P Bagnall and friends)*

☆ **Clifton Campville**, Staffs [SK2510], *Green Man*: Spick-and-span fifteenth-century village pub with low beams, inglenook and chubby armchair in public bar, airy lounge, kind service, well kept Ind Coope Bitter and reasonably priced bar meals; children in snug and family-room, garden with donkeys, rabbits, fish pond, aviary and swings; only reason it's not a main entry is mystifying absence of recent reports *(LYM)*

Combs, Derbys [SK0478], *Beehive*: Big old pub in lovely dale village with stream running through garden; main bar has a huge fireplace, rugs on the wooden floor, and Wilsons ales; generous helpings of interestingly varied home-cooked food in neatly ordered dining-room; bedrooms *(Doug Kennedy)*

Cowers Lane, Derbys [junction A517/B5023; SK3047], *Railway*: Wide choice of unusual bar food – well cooked, well presented and reasonably priced; Ind Coope beers, comfortable furnishings, polite service *(Tim and Lynne Crawford)*

Derby [Harington St – nr Baseball Ground; SK3435], *Baseball*: Pleasant atmosphere with friendly locals, good value food and drink *(Ekbal Rai)*; [Railway Terr] *Brunswick*: Corner pub with flagstone floor, well kept Batemans, Burton Bridge, Hoskins and Timothy Taylors real ales, lunchtime food *(R A Sanders)*; [Queen St] *Olde Dolphin*: In shadow of cathedral, said to be Derby's oldest pub (dating from 1530); basic bar, neat and cosy lounge, memorabilia from former local brewery, tea-rooms upstairs; well kept Bass beers, wide choice of good bar food, friendly service *(Richard Green)*; [St Thomas Rd] *Vulcan Arms*: Popular with businessmen for good value food and drink; efficient French chef *(Ekbal Rai)*

☆ **Dovedale**, Staffs [Thorpe–Ilam rd; Ilam signposted off A52, Thorpe off A515, NW of Ashbourne; SK1452], *Izaak Walton*: Low-beamed bar with some distinctive antique oak settles and chairs and massive central stone chimney for the good log fire; Ind Coope Burton on handpump, good service,

bar food and restaurant, morning coffee and afternoon tea; seats outside; this quite sizeable hotel has to itself a fine position on the peaceful sloping pastures of Bunster Hill; nr start GWG84; bedrooms comfortable *(AE, LYM)*

Draycott in the Clay, Staffs [SK1528], *Roebuck*: Simple roadside Marstons pub with big inglenook and good atmosphere; well kept real ales *(BB)*; *Swan*: Basic village local, friendly staff, well kept Ind Coope from cask *(Jon Wainwright)*

Edale, Derbys [SK1285], *Old Nags Head*: Popular walkers' pub with substantial basic cheap food, open fire, real ales (recently Marstons and Youngers); children in airy back family-room; out of season may not open evenings until 7ish; nr start GWG83 *(W P P Clarke, E J Alcock, Mike Muston, LYM)*

Ellastone, Staffs [SK1143], *Duncombe Arms*: Nice enough small village pub *(Anon)*

Elvaston, Derbys [5 miles W of M1 junction 24, ½ mile N of A6; SK4132], *Harrington Arms*: Friendly country pub with good real ale, good value bar food from simple menu, separate eating-rooms *(Mandy and Mike Challis)*

☆ **Etruria**, Staffs [Etruria Rd; SJ8647], *Rose & Crown*: Friendly local constantly improving; lots of naval connections, and full of period knick-knacks giving bar a warm Edwardian feel, lounge bar with tables covered in gingham tablecloths, well kept beer and reasonably priced bar food *(M A and W R Proctor, Dr and Mrs A K Clarke)*

☆ **Eyam**, Derbys [Water Lane; SK2276], *Miners Arms*: Cheerful and helpful service and nice atmosphere in village inn that deliberately avoids olde-worlde clutter, good value pleasant and unhurried set lunch; dark wood, red curtains and carpets, rather upmarket feel; bedrooms *(Dr and Mrs J W McClenahan, R A Hutson, LYM)*

Flash, Staffs [A53 Buxton–Leek; SK0267], *Travellers Rest*: Isolated hill pub on main road included for its ranking as Britain's third highest; astonishing array of beers with probably the largest number of pumps and taps in the country (most keg, not all on); loud juke box, ditto décor, no shortage of amusement machines; nice views from back terrace, simple snacks *(LYM)*

Foolow, Derbys [SK1976], *Lazy Landlord*: Very old, popular pub with cosy bar and open fire; good range of bar food, attractive small restaurant; gliding nearby *(Norman Battle)*

Glascote, Staffs [B5000; SK2203], *Anchor*: Friendly and comfortable pub by Coventry Canal, usual range of bar food (with shellfish seller visiting most evenings), well kept Springfield, juke box, fruit machine; can get very busy *(C P Gooch)*

Glossop, Derbys [Arundel St (off A57); SK0394], *Friendship*: Pleasant and lively atmosphere, friendly welcoming landlord

(R A Hutson); [Milltown (off High St East)]
Prince of Wales: Fine modernisation –
retains 1940s atmosphere but matches
demands and fashions of the 1980s
(R A Hutson)

Hartington, Derbys [The Square; SK1360],
Devonshire Arms: Large pub in two adjoining buildings, one stone/brick, the other rendered; snug beamed lounge with real fires,
popular with locals, food served in more
spacious second lounge, well kept Ind Coope
Burton; seats outside looking over
village square; nr start GWG77 *(Lee
Goulding)*

Hartshill, Staffs [296 Hartshill Rd; SJ8545],
Jolly Potters: Smashing little pub with cosy
atmosphere in lots of little rooms, well kept;
real ale in good condition *(Dr and Mrs
A K Clarke)*

Hassop, Derbys [SK2272], *Eyre Arms*: Stone
exterior covered in climbing plants; pleasant
interior with coal fire, exposed beams and
wooden-backed benches; friendly bar staff,
well kept beer, bar food; in good walking
area *(M A and W R Proctor)*

Hathersage, Derbys [SK2381], *George*: Substantial old inn, comfortably modernised and
a nice place to stay at – they look after you
well; popular lunchtime bar food, smart barman, neat flagstoned back terrace by rose
garden; nr start GWG80; bedrooms quieter
at the back *(Peter Walker, Mr and Mrs
M C Jaffé, LYM)*; [Sheffield Rd] *Millstone*:
Well kept pub with good atmosphere, locally
renowned for meat and potato pie, good
chipsteak *(T Houghton)*

nr **Hathersage**, Derbys [A625 2½ miles E of
village – putting the pub itself just over the S
Yorks border; SK2680], *Fox House*: Handsome eighteenth-century stone moorland pub
with cheap food, piped Sinatra, simple
furnishings; popular with walkers *(BB)*

Hayfield, Derbys [Church St; SK0387],
George: Unspoilt, very accommodating
landlord, lots of interesting mementoes
(Dr and Mrs A K Clarke); [off A624 Glossop–
Chapel-en-le-Frith] *Pack Horse*: Handsome
stone-built pub full of antique and repro
brasses and pottery, dark wood panelling;
good range of drinks including John Smiths
on handpump, wide choice of popular bar
food, upstairs restaurant (open for food all
day Sun); pub well kept, can get very busy
(N Hesketh); [Kinder Rd, outside village]
Sportsman: Solid comfortable olde-worlde
atmosphere in spacious bar with fine stone
fireplaces, in quietly beautiful wooded Sett
Valley below Kinder Scout; Thwaites on
handpump, bar food, piped music, traditional Sun lunch (open all day for food then);
children welcome, no car park *(John Gould)*

nr **Hayfield**, Derbys [Little Hayfield, A625
N; SK0388], *Lantern Pike*: Small and friendly
village inn, cosy and homely with chatty
locals; bar food lunchtime and evening, fine
views of hills from back garden; good value

bedrooms *(Yvonne and Don Johnson)*

High Offley, Staffs [Grub Street Village;
SJ7825], *Royal Oak*: Old building modernised in and out, lovely country setting;
excellent traditional English fare in restaurant including good Sun lunches, and it
must be admitted that the bar's really meant
for pre-meal drinks – though a few locals use
it too; very quiet mid-week lunchtimes, busy
weekends *(M V Fereday)*

Hoar Cross, Staffs [SK1323], *Meynell Ingram
Arms*: Fine old local in marvellous spot – big
windows look on to surrounding countryside; fires in public bar and lounge and a
friendly, relaxed atmosphere; well kept
Marstons Pedigree and simple food; popular
with locals *(Angus Lindsay)*

☆ **Holmesfield**, Derbys [Lydgate – B6054
towards Hathersage; SK3277], *Robin Hood*:
Wide choice of popular food (not Sun evening) and well kept Wards Sheffield Best and
Darleys Best in friendly and well kept rambling moorland pub with open fires, beams,
flagstones, plush banquettes, and a high-
raftered restaurant with big pictures; piped
music, stone tables out on cobbled front
courtyard *(M L Tucker, James Walker,
LYM)*

☆ **Hope**, Derbys [Edale Rd; SK1783], *Cheshire
Cheese*: Little up-and-down oak-beamed
rooms in sixteenth-century stone-built village
pub with lots of old local photographs and
prints, abundant coal fires, well kept Wards
Sheffield Best and Darleys Best; has had
decent wines and other drinks and popular
home cooking; children allowed in eating
area; nr start GWG81 *(Brian and Anna
Marsden, P and H B, Jon Wainwright, Dr R V
Watson, Mr and Mrs P Burton-Johnson, David
and Valerie Hooley, C D T Spooner, LYM –
though more recent reports have been mixed;
more news please)*

Hope, Derbys [Castleton Rd], *Poachers
Arms*: Excellent restaurant, but meals in the
several attractively decorated bars so competitive that these are often preferred, good
quantity and quality including adventurous
vegetarian dishes; very welcoming atmosphere, good service; children welcome, good
bedrooms *(Dorothy and Ken Worrall and
others)*

Hopwas, Staffs [SK1704], *Chequers*: Big helpings of good simple food in friendly well kept
local near canal, Courage Directors in good
condition, frequent discos and live music
(E J Cutting, LYM)

Horse Bridge, Staffs [Denford (off A53
Stoke–Leek); SJ9553], *Holly Bush*: Canalside
Ansells pub with log fires, well kept ales and
bar food including regional dishes
(G C Hixon)

Horsley, Derbys [Church St; SK3744], *Coach
& Horses*: Welcoming and spotless pub with
about a dozen good home-cooked dishes,
well kept Marstons Pedigree and Merrie
Monk, cosy beamed lounge, modest snug;

tables in big garden with swings, attractive village *(P W Peck)*

Hulme End, Staffs [SK1059], *Manifold Valley*: Well kept Darleys and Wards real ales, generous helpings of usual pub food, plain but comfortable furnishings; fine setting *(Brian and Anna Marsden, BB)*

☆ **Ipstones**, Staffs [B5053]; village signposted from A52 from A523; SK0249], *Red Lion*: Gentle colour scheme and comfortable seats in well run modernised pub overlooking valley, well kept Burtonwood Best on handpump, reliably good value bar food, friendly landlord, games area, piped music *(Nick Dowson, Alison Hayward, G C Hixon, Mike Tucker, Wayne Brindle, M A and W R Proctor, AMcK, LYM)*

Ivetsey Bank, Staffs [A5, 5 miles from M6 junction 12; SJ8311], *Bradford Arms*: Friendly pub with excellent range of food and well kept M&B beers *(G H Theaker)*

Kings Bromley, Staffs [SK1216], *Royal Oak*: Basic but cosy bar with very enjoyable atmosphere, pleasant dining-room and good choice of food – nothing fancy, but well prepared and agreeably presented; two donkeys at back of garden *(E J Alcock)*

Kings Newton, Derbys [SK3826], *Sir Francis Burdett*: Good choice of real ales on handpump, good food, friendly welcome, nice atmosphere, garden with children's play area *(A G Taylor)*

Kinver, Staffs [A449; SO8483], *Whittington*: Striking black and white timbered Tudor house built by Dick Whittington's family, fine garden with pétanque, old-fashioned bar, usual range of bar food *(LYM)*

Kirk Ireton, Derbys [SK2650], *Barley Mow*: Unusual, notable for its difference from fancy-frills pubs – very basic series of interconnecting rooms, lots of woodwork, well kept choice of real ales tapped from the cask *(Tim Crawford)*

Knockerdown, Derbys [1½ miles S of Brassington; SK2352], *Knockerdown*: Pleasant pub with well kept Marstons Pedigree – popular in the evening with the local farming community *(Alastair Campbell)*

Ladybower Reservoir, Derbys [A57 Sheffield–Glossop, at junction with A6013; SK1986], *Ladybower*: Hardy stone pub nestling in sharp-sided valley with menacing boulders perched above; smartly comfortable open-plan bar with popular food in eating area, well kept Tetleys, Theakstons and Wilsons; stone settles outside, good views of reservoir and surrounding moorlands (many walks nearby) *(Lee Goulding, J L Thompson)*

Lane Head, Derbys [junction of A623/B6044 – OS Sheet 119 reference 160764; SK1676], *Anchor*: Pleasant pub with good welcoming staff, friendly atmosphere, Robinsons ales and very good choice of reasonably priced bar food *(Mr and Mrs P Burton-Johnson)*

Lea, Derbys [SK3357], *Coach House*: Enthusiastic chef in cosy converted coach-house with fire in old cooking-range, lots of old harness and so forth; simple informal and friendly atmosphere, nicely presented straightforward food; close to Lea rhododendron gardens *(Dr and Mrs J W McClenahan)*

Leek, Staffs [Ball Haye Rd; SJ9856], *Ball Haye*: Welcoming atmosphere, most congenial landlord and excellently kept beer *(J P Swinbourne)*

Lichfield, Staffs [Greenhill; SK1109], *Duke of York*: Beamed public bar and smart, comfortable Victorian-style lounge; Davenports ales, bar food *(C J Dyall)*; [Market St – one of the central pedestrian-only streets] *Scales*: Old-fashioned two-room pub with big etched window, Delft shelf over dark oak panelling, Bass and M&B Springfield on electric pump, attractively planted sun-trap back courtyard; bar food (lunchtime, not Sun) has been efficiently and kindly served, with attractive cold table and good coffee – we'd like more news, please; small restaurant; children welcome *(Wayne Brindle, LYM)*; [London Rd] *Shoulder of Mutton*: Striking neo-Victorian décor, with book-lined library, fireplace and newspapers such as FT; good atmosphere, excellent bar food, unusually friendly *(Sue Cleasby, Mike Ledger)*

☆ **Little Bridgeford**, Staffs [nr M6 junction 14; turn right off A5013 at Little Bridgeford; SJ8727], *Worston Mill*: Fine building – carefully and cleverly converted former watermill, with wheel and gear still preserved, ducks on millpond and millstream in spacious garden with play area, attractive conservatory; bar food with something of an American slant, piped music, Whitbreads-related real ales, restaurant; children welcome *(William Meadon, Richard Steel, Wayne Brindle, Roger Taylor, R P Taylor, Dave Braisted, Marcus and Marcella Leith, David Young, LYM)*

☆ **Litton**, Derbys [SK1675], *Red Lion*: Food is the main thing at this cosy and pretty partly panelled village pub almost wholly given over to close-set bookable tables (reservations Tideswell (0298) 871458 – not open weekday lunchtimes); snug low-ceilinged front rooms with open fires, bigger back room with stripped stone and antique prints *(Gordon Theaker, Lynda Brown, R A Hutson)*

Lower Penn, Staffs [Greyhound Lane; SO8696], *Greyhound*: Old country inn with a wide-ranging menu including vegetarian section, good Bass *(Peter and Davina Whitehead)*

Lullington, Derbys [SK2513], *Colvile Arms*: Excellent atmosphere and good beer in unspoilt bar and lounge of characterful pub set in delightful village *(David Gaunt)*

Makeney, Derbys [Holly Bush Lane; SK3544], *Holly Bush*: A fine stone-built free house in quiet village with interesting inn sign, stone floors and open fire; beer served from foaming jugs; back terrace, little games-room *(Jon Wainwright)*

Marchington, Staffs [Church Lane; SK1330], *Dog & Partridge*: Attractive setting in peaceful village; long, handsome building by brook, small simple bar and traditional lounge; well kept Ind Coope Burton *(Jon Wainwright)*

Marston, Staffs [SJ8514], *Fox*: Low-ceilinged old pub with good choice of real ales – and in adjoining barn a choice of 11 different ciders *(E J Alcock)*

Matlock Bath, Derbys [Main St; SK2958], *Princess Victoria*: Looks more like a cafe than a pub, but has well kept range of real ales (mainly from Vaux/Wards); good value bar food with home-made daily specials and choice of vegetables; upstairs restaurant; parking difficult; nr GWG78 *(Dave and Angie Parkes)*

Melbourne, Derbys [SK3825], *White Swan*: Interesting old pub carefully restored to show ancient structure, friendly staff, good service and Sun lunch – especially puddings; pleasant narrow garden; children welcome *(Virginia Jones, LYM)*

Millers Dale, Derbys [SK1373], *Anglers Rest*: Marvellous riverside setting, old stone building (though not a truly pubby atmosphere), pleasant family service, bar food, John Smiths and Marstons Pedigree on handpump, good choice of whiskies; nr GWG82 *(Patrick Young)*

Moorwood Moor, Derbys [SK3656], *White Hart*: Good cheap Home ales, fairly wide choice of good pub food, swing in garden *(Charlie Salt)*

Morley, Derbys [SK3940], *Rose & Crown*: Pleasant country setting, good ploughman's *(HKR)*

Muckley Corner, Staffs [A5/A461; SK0806], *Muckley Corner*: Tidy, clean and well decorated, friendly atmosphere, efficient service, pleasant décor, sensibly priced food in bar and restaurant, well kept beer; children in dining area *(M V Fereday)*

Mugginton, Derbys [SK2843], *Cock*: Friendly place with good beer and food, cheerful service; honest good value *(D P Cartwright)*

Newcastle under Lyme, Staffs [Gallowstree Lane (off Keele Rd, a mile W of centre); SJ8445], *Dick Turpin*: Welcoming, busy pub with pleasant atmosphere, spacious modern lounge with mock windows of highway scenes, beams, dark wheel-back chairs, thick carpets; well kept Bass, reliably good home-cooked hot and cold lunchtime bar food including vegetarian dishes and lots of salads with good home-made mayonnaise *(Laurence Manning, Andor Gomme)*; [High St] *Stones*: New pub, popular with people in their twenties in the evening; covered back courtyard with Victorian street scene and trees; good choice of food, Bass real ale *(D P Bagnall)*

Norbury Junction, Staffs [SJ7922], *Junction*: Picturesquely placed with relaxing canalside garden; clean and friendly, excellent beer, good value bar food; very popular *(Paul and Margaret Baker)*

Oaken, Staffs [A41 just E of A464 junction; SJ8502], *Foaming Jug*: Interesting interior with variety of jugs, fireplace, Bass Springfield and Highgate *(Dave Braisted)*

Old Glossop, Derbys [SK0494], *Wheatsheaf*: Pleasant and efficient service in Whitbreads pub, in conservation village, with big helpings of good value food – they really make an effort *(R Hutson)*

Onecote, Staffs [SK0555], *Jervis Arms*: Neat riverside garden including good play area outside small two-room pub with plush-cushioned traditional seating, open fire, Bass, McEwans and Theakstons Best and XB on handpump, quickly served bar food (not winter weekday lunchtimes) *(Derek Stephenson, LYM)*

Osmaston, Derbys [off A52 SE of Ashbourne; SK1944], *Shoulder of Mutton*: Warm welcome, good choice of beers and comfortable rooms *(Alan Robertson)*

Owler Bar, Derbys [A621 2 miles S of Totley; SK2978], *Peacock*: Moorland setting a main attraction at this well kept pub; wide choice of popular reasonably priced food, keg beers *(George Curley)*

Padfield, Derbys [SK0396], *Peels Arms*: Stone village pub with split-level lounge, cosy public bar, three real fires, games-room, well kept Youngers real ales; if you can crawl through the hole in the lounge wall you get a free pint *(Lee Goulding)*

Parwich, Derbys [SK1854], *Sycamore*: Cosy and friendly village pub with three rooms, open fires, Bass, darts, pool, attractive food; tables made from copper milk-churns, collection of wooden Shrove Tuesday 'footballs' from Ashbourne *(Ned Edwards)*

Renishaw, Derbys [A616 Sheffield rd, 2 miles from M1 junction 30; SK4578], *Sitwell Arms*: Food in comfortable high-ceilinged bar, restaurant, comfortable hotel extension behind *(LYM)*

Rugeley, Staffs [Lichfield Rd; SK0418], *Eaton Lodge*: Wide choice of imaginative reasonably priced food using local ingredients in bar and restaurant, menu changing daily; well kept bar, good service, comfortable bedrooms *(G C Hixon)*

Rushton Spencer, Staffs [Congleton Rd; off A523 Leek–Macclesfield at Ryecroft Gate; SJ9462], *Crown*: Friendly simple local in attractive scenery, with busy front snug, bigger back lounge, games-room, home-made food, Youngers real ales *(Pat Woodward)*

Ryecroft Gate, Staffs [Congleton Rd, off A523 in village – OS Sheet 118 reference 923618; SJ9461], *Fox*: Cosy pub with real fire, comfortable chairs and sofas in small, partitioned areas; well kept Ind Coope Burton *(Jon Wainwright)*

Salt, Staffs [signposted S of Stone on A51; SJ9527], *Holly Bush*: Food good to excellent, drinks well kept, service excellent and very friendly; children welcome *(M V Fereday)*

Sawley, Derbys [Trentlock (off B6540, not far from M1 junction 25 via Long Eaton slip road – OS Sheet 129 reference 490313); SK4731], *Steamboat*: Character pub, popular (very much so on summer weekends) for its position at junction of canal and river; huge log fireplace, wide choice of bar food *(Andrew Stephenson)*

Shardlow, Derbys [London Rd – A6 about ½ mile E; SK4330], *Cavendish Arms*: Wards, Darleys and Vaux, bar food *(Dave Braisted)*; [London Rd] *Hoskins Wharf*: One of Hoskins' small chain, and carefully converted from an eighteenth-century canal warehouse in a picturesque setting, with reasonably priced beer and bar food; reached by drawbridge from car park *(Quentin Williamson, Stewart Argyle)*

Shenstone, Staffs [Birmingham Rd; SK1004], *Bulls Head*: Drinks well kept, good value food in bar and restaurant *(M V Fereday)*

Somercotes, Derbys [Nottingham Rd (B600); SK4253] *Royal Tiger*: Friendly pub, Hardys & Hansons real ales, good choice of bar food, snooker and other pub games *(Ian Crickmer)*

South Normanton, Derbys [a mile from M1 junction 28, on B6019; SK4457], *Hawthorne*: Happily extended and refurbished in summer 1987, with very popular carvery *(T Houghton)*

Sparrowpit, Derbys [nr Chapel-en-le-Frith; SK0980], *Wanted Inn*: New licensees doing good home-produced food, in what's always been a nice pub *(P and H B)*

Stableford, Staffs [A51 towards Nantwich; SJ8138], *Cock*: Real olde-worlde beamed country pub in pleasant surroundings; excellent facilities, good beer and wines, restaurant, garden *(D P Bagnall)*

Stafford, Staffs [Mill St; SJ9223], *Bird in Hand*: Popular town-centre pub, well kept Courage Directors, games- and snooker-room, good range of bar food, garden with plenty of sheltered seating *(Paul and Margaret Baker)*; [A34/A449 central roundabout – take Access Only rd past service stn] *Malt & Hops*: Lively rambling pub with real ales such as Holdens, Marstons Pedigree and McEwans 80/-, busy at lunchtime for low-priced food, often crowded with young people in the evenings – especially the Thurs-Sat discos when it stays open until 1am (midnight other nights); provision for children *(LYM)*; [Forebridge (Lichfield rd, opp Borough Library)] *Sun*: Newly refurbished rambling low-beamed pub, good Bass on handpump, excellent choice of changing good value food in bar and restaurant *(Paul and Margaret Baker, G C Hixon)*

Stone, Staffs [21 Stafford St; A520; SJ9034], *Star*: Canal photographs and exposed joists in intimate public bar, snug lounge and family-room of simple, friendly eighteenth-century pub in attractive canalside setting; well kept Bass and M&B Springfield, open fire, basic food *(AMcK, Jill Hadfield, Tony Gallagher, Maureen Hobbs, Leith Stuart, LYM)*

Stourton, Staffs [Bridgnorth Rd; SO8585], *Fox*: Clean warm modernised pub with unusually good food for this area; Banks's ales *(Brian Green)*

Sudbury, Derbys [off A50; SK1632], *Vernon Arms*: Pleasant seventeenth-century free house almost opposite Sudbury Hall with Marstons beers and good poacher's pie; hollows in high brick wall opposite were worn by its former stableboys kicking their heels as they waited for the coaches *(Dave Braisted)*

Swinscoe, Derbys [SK1348], *Dog & Partridge*: Seventeenth-century moorland pub with lovely views from good value restaurant; bedrooms in motel wing *(P Wayne Brindle)*

Swynnerton, Staffs [SJ8535], *Fitzherbert Arms*: Welcoming bar in hotel set in beautiful country village; at-home feeling, good food and facilities *(D P Bagnall)*

Tamworth, Staffs [Church St; SK2004], *Manhattan*: Spaciously plush split-level bar with good range of beers, wines, spirits and cocktails, wide choice of reasonably priced food, friendly quick service *(Colin Gooch)*

Tansley, Derbys [A615 Matlock–Mansfield; SK3259], *Royal Oak*: Well kept Hardys & Hansons, limited choice of excellent value plain and unpretentious food in comfortable lounge bar of stone-built pub with lounge and family-room *(Dr and Mrs B D Smith, Gwen and Peter Andrews)*

Thulston, Derbys [B5010, off A6 towards Elvaston Castle; SK4031], *Harrington Arms*: Long series of neatly furnished and well kept black-beamed rooms with Marstons Pedigree and Sam Smiths in good condition on handpump, good value and reliable straightforward bar food, evening restaurant; juke box and fruit machine down at one end, maybe local honey for sale *(J T Murfin, Frank Cummins)*

Ticknall, Derbys [B5006 towards Ashby-de-la-Zouch; SK3423], *Chequers*: Good fire in the enormous inglenook fireplace of this recently renovated sixteenth-century pub with well kept Bass tapped from the cask, unusual spirits, good value bar food (not Sun), sizeable garden *(Dave Butler, Lesley Storey, Angus Lindsay, LYM)*

Tideswell, Derbys [SK1575], *George*: Old coaching-inn with particularly good bar food, spacious main bar with lots of prints and watercolours on painted panelling, old settles and oak chairs and tables on the carpet, Hardys & Hansons Best on handpump; pool-room, small locals' bar; bedrooms *(Patrick Young)*

nr Trentham, Staffs [A34 about 5 miles S; SJ8640], *Yesterdays*: Comfortable, well refurbished and tastefully cluttered pub set on large traffic island with good selection of bar meals, handy for Trentham Gardens *(E J Alcock)*

☆ **Tutbury**, Staffs [SK2028], *Olde Dog & Partridge*: Stylish Tudor coaching-inn, quaint but imposing building, with lots of rooms including carvery and nice bar (if a bit crowded with diners waiting for good but pricey restaurant); well kept Bass tapped from the cask, friendly staff; bedrooms very comfortable, with good breakfasts *(Graham Bush, Angus Lindsay, Mike Suddards)*

Uttoxeter, Staffs [Dove Bank (A518); SK0933], *Roebuck*: Reasonable, snug pub with well kept Burton Bridge *(Jon Wainwright)*

nr **Uttoxeter**, Staffs [Stowe-by-Chartley; SK0027], *Cock*: Strangely shaped free house with excellent choice of food and Ind Coope Burton, Tetleys and maybe ABC on handpump *(Ned Edwards)*

Wardlow, Derbys [B6465; SK1874], *Bulls Head*: Lots of olde-worlde bric-à-brac and open stonework in attractively furnished pub with open fires, good choice of reasonably priced well cooked food including fine charcoal-grilled steaks, well kept Wards on handpump *(John Firth, Tim and Lynne Crawford)*

☆ **Warslow**, Staffs [SK0858], *Greyhound*: Small, welcoming pub with settles and elegant furniture in surprisingly spacious bar with log fire, Marstons ales in excellent condition; good range of well prepared home-cooked bar food; beautiful walking country; good, clean bedrooms *(Gerald Hixon, Mrs A Trustman)*

☆ **Wessington**, Derbys [The Green; SK3758], *Three Horseshoes*: Good view over village green, comfortable lounge used for good value bar lunches in big helpings, restaurant, Hardys & Hansons beer, friendly service *(Dave and Angie Parkes, Wayne Brindle, George Curley)*

Whittington, Staffs [this is the one nr Lichfield; SK1608], *Dog*: Pleasant, rambling building, friendly service, Ind Coope ales, bar food *(Dave Braisted)*

Whittington Moor, Derbys [Sheffield Road (off A61) – this is the one 1½ miles N of Chesterfield centre; SK3873], *Derby Tup*: Friendly no-frills basic drinking establishment with small snug and large lounge, and emphasis on wide range of real ales such as Batemans XXXB, Ruddles County, Timothy

Taylors Landlord, Tetleys, Theakstons Best or XB and Old Peculier, Wards Sheffield Best and Whitbreads Castle Eden – somehow, they manage to keep all these in good condition; range of pub games, but no food *(Dave and Angie Parkes, Richard Sanders)*

Windley, Derbys [Nether Lane (B5023); SK3045], *Puss in Boots*: Isolated olde-worlde pub with low beams, brasses, two open fires, sandwiches, Bass on handpump, hot punch, home-made chutney sold; seats outside, with good children's play area *(Tim and Lynne Crawford)*

Winster, Derbys [A5012 / B5056; SK2460], *Miners Standard*: Cosy and friendly seventeenth-century coaching-inn, tastefully refurbished, good choice of snacks and meals, well kept Marstons Pedigree and Theakstons XB, lots of mining photographs and memorabilia; summer flat to let *(Ned Edwards)*

Wirksworth, Derbys [Market Pl; SK2854], *Hope & Anchor*: Comfortable lounge bar with excellent Home ales, splendid Jacobean wooden fireplace and unspoilt atmosphere; in conservation town *(R A Hutson)*; [Cromford Rd] *Lime Kiln*: Tastefully decorated local with Bass on handpump and big helpings of food – great value Sun lunch *(David Stonier)*

Woolley, Derbys [White Horse Lane (off B6014, Woolley Moor); SK3661], *White Horse*: Friendly inn in quiet country handy for Ogston Reservoir, good views and children's playground; Bass and Springfield Bitter on handpump, with occasional guest beers in summer; extensive home-cooked menu (not Sun evening) *(Angie and Dave Parkes)*

Wrinehill, Staffs [SJ7547], *Crown*: Pleasant country pub with good value food, excellent beer and relaxing atmosphere *(D P Bagnall)*

Wyaston, Derbys [OS Sheet 119 reference 184426; SK1842], *Shire Horse*: Excellent atmosphere, ale and food *(R H Petherick)*

Yarnfield, Staffs [SJ8632], *Labour in Vain*: Very well run, with good décor, M&B on handpump, popular food *(Anon (Gosport))*

Yoxall, Staffs [Main St; SK1319], *Crown*: Marstons house, recently refurbished; large bar with pool-table, small, cosy lounge, large fireplace with log-effect gas fire, separate raised dining-room; well kept Pedigree on handpump, wide choice of bar food, friendly service *(B M Eldridge)*

Devon

Among new entries this year, the ancient Church House at Stoke Gabriel stands out as so exceptional that we have, straight off, awarded it a star. Several other newcomers come in with an immediate food award: the quaint Exmoor-edge Poltimore Arms at Brayford, the cheerful Butterleigh Inn at Butterleigh, the Pyne Arms with its unusual upper gallery at East Down, the interestingly restored old Barn Owl at Kingskerswell, the Golden Lion at Tipton St John (simple but comfortable bedrooms) and, particularly, the cosy New Fountain in Whimple. The London Hotel in Ashburton is notable for its own-brewed beers; the Durant Arms at Ashprington is good to know for its warm welcome, as is the Kingfisher at Colyton; the Royal Castle in Dartmouth combines a lively harbourside bar with the solid virtues of a very long-established and comfortable hotel. Changes among entries that have been in before include the Manor House Hotel in Cullompton being sold to a small chain that includes other pubs much enjoyed by readers, particularly for food; our visit shortly after the takeover detected little change yet. Similarly, we found the same interesting range of food, especially fine fish dishes, at the ancient Cherub in Dartmouth, though that too has new licensees. The Swans Nest at Exminster, remarkably interesting and full of character for a place that is probably the busiest food pub in the county, has joined the stable of the Major family (who already own two or three other pubs, in other counties, that are proving at least as popular as ever in their hands). New licensees at the Church House in Holne are proving so popular with readers that we've restored the pub to the main entries, after a gap of some years. There are also promising new licensees at the Ring of Bells in North Bovey and the Tower at Slapton – both of them attracting warm notice from readers. We also have to welcome new licensees at the New Inn in Coleford, the George in Hatherleigh, the Seven Stars at South Tawton, the Tradesmans Arms at Stokenham and the

176

Kingsbridge in Totnes: as we go to press it's still too soon to be sure how these attractive pubs will rank, particularly for food quality. Readers' top-rated pubs in the county are the Nobody Inn at Doddiscombsleigh (remarkable all round – and outstanding for wines), the Elephants Nest tucked away up on Dartmoor at Horndon, and the Masons Arms at Knowstone (a little delight, on the edge of Exmoor). Other favourites are the quaint Olde Globe at Berrynarbor, the very civilised Masons Arms at Branscombe, the idiosyncratic Double Locks on the edge of Exeter and the more airy Turf down at Exminster (both of them on the old ship canal, and both under the same ownership), the White Hart in Exeter (one of the warmest-hearted hotel bars we know of, and a very pleasant place to stay at), the Rock at Haytor Vale (a cosy refuge from Dartmoor), the ancient Royal at Horsebridge (brewing its own fine beers), the unusual little Old Rydon at Kingsteignton (particularly interesting food), the individual Castle at Lydford (good food, a pleasant place to stay at), the busy Who'd Have Thought It down off the moor in Miltoncombe (again, good food) the Peter Tavy Inn up on Dartmoor (notable vegetarian food, in charming surroundings), the delightfully friendly Blue Ball at Sidford (good simple food, comfortable bedrooms), the extraordinary and exuberant Highwayman at Sourton, the remarkable old Oxenham Arms at South Zeal (good food, comfortable bedrooms), the Bridge at Topsham (a marvellous range of real ales, in quaint little rooms), the waterside Start Bay at Torcross (where the licensee catches much of the fish with his bare hands – he's a skindiver) and the Diggers Rest at Woodbury Salterton (the traditional virtues of a fine village pub). Among the mass of promising Lucky Dip entries at the end of the chapter, we'd pick out as particularly promising the Watermans Arms at Ashprington, Drakes Manor at Buckland Monachorum, Anglers Rest at Drewsteignton, Black Horse in Great Torrington, Church House at Harberton, Tally Ho in Hatherleigh, Warren House near Postbridge and Old Smithy at Welcombe.

ASHBURTON   SX7569 Map 1

London Hotel

11 West Street

The beers they brew here – Bitter and IPA – are distinctive and good value (in Plymouth you can try them at the Mutton Cove, which Mr Thompson took over not long ago). This imposing old three-storey coaching-inn – no bedrooms, despite its name – is a very different place from most own-brew pubs. The lounge is spacious and Turkey-carpeted, with little brocaded or red leatherette armchairs as well as other seats around the copper-topped casks they use as tables; it spreads back into a softly lit dining area with one wall curtained in red velvet, and on our visit the piped music was of the sweeping strings variety. The clean white walls are largely stripped back to stone, and there's a central fireplace. Bar food includes original soups (£1), sandwiches, ploughman's (from £1.50), shepherd's pie (£2.75), omelettes (from £3), whole plaice (£5), Dart salmon (£7), steaks (from eight-ounce sirloin £7) and chicken Cordon Bleu (£7.40). They keep a choice of farm ciders; fruit machine. *(Recommended by John Roué, Philip and Trisha Ferris, David Fisher, Dr and Mrs R Wright, B Chapman, SC)*

Own brew   Licensee D F Thompson   Real ale   Meals and snacks   Restaurant   Children welcome   Open 11–11 all year

You are now allowed twenty minutes after 'time, please' to finish your drink – half an hour if you bought it in conjunction with a meal.

ASHPRINGTON   SX8156 Map 1
Durant Arms
Village signposted off A381 S of Totnes; OS Sheet 202 reference 819571

Currently readers' favourite pub in the vicinity, this pretty cottage of a pub with its traceried gable ends has a friendly village atmosphere. The well equipped games bar's simply furnished, with white-painted rough stone and cob walls; the carpeted lounge has been noted for its idiosyncratic cutaway barrel seats and the flowery-cushioned bay window overlooking the village street – we hope that extensions put in hand by the new licensees as we went to press won't spoil the old-fashioned style and cosiness. Bar food includes sandwiches (80p), home-made soup (£1), vegetarian dishes (from £1.75), ploughman's served with real butter (£2), steak and kidney pie (£2.75), fresh fish brought up from Plymouth each day (£3.30) and salads (from £3.50). Well kept Halls Harvest tapped from the cask (it's been labelled Durant Bitter), Ind Coope Burton on handpump, Churchward's cider and a choice of reasonably priced wines; tables in the sheltered back garden; the black labrador's called George. They no longer do bedrooms. *(Recommended by J G Everton, Mr and Mrs G W Keddie, S V Bishop, Brian Marsden, D B S Frost, David and Flo Wallington, Jon Wainwright; more reports on the new regime please)*

Free house   Licensees Jill and John Diprose   Real ale   Meals and snacks   Children welcome in eating area   Open 11–2.30, 6–11 all year

BANTHAM   SX6643 Map 1
Sloop ⊗ 🛏

The chequered history of this old village inn stretches back to the sixteenth century; it has long associations with local smuggling, and indeed was once owned by John Widdon, one of the more notorious smugglers and wreckers of the South Hams. These days the licensees are more respectable, and have created an enjoyable and lively atmosphere in the black-beamed and flagstoned bar, which has stripped stone walls, country chairs around wooden tables, and easy chairs in a quieter side area – this part has quite a nautical atmosphere, with lots of varnished marine ply. The Bass, Palmers IPA and Ushers Best are very well kept (on handpump), as is the local Hill's cider – not always the case elsewhere; decent wines. The wholesome and wide-ranging bar food includes home-made soup (95p), granary-bread sandwiches (from £1.10, fresh crab £1.95), an excellent ploughman's (from £1.80), good fresh local seafood such as crab claws (£2.40), moules marinière (£2.50), sole (£4.20), plaice or skate (£4.40) and twelve-ounce rump steak (£6.95); puddings like raspberry Pavlova (£1.30) or hot chocolate fudgecake (£1.40). Darts, dominoes, cribbage, table skittles, fruit machine, space and trivia games, piped music. The sandy beach – one of the best for surfing on the South Coast – is only a few hundred yards over the dunes; the Coast Path runs past here. They provide good rooms and hearty breakfasts, and there are seats around a wishing-well in the yard behind. *(Recommended by Ian and Daphne Brownlie, F A and J W Sherwood, W C M Jones, Brian and Anna Marsden, David and Ann Stranack, J C Tyzack, A R Tingley, Simon Levene, Grahame and Brenda Blair)*

Free house   Licensee Neil Girling   Real ale   Meals and snacks   Restaurant   Children welcome   Open 11–2.30, 6–11; opens 6.30 in winter   Bedrooms tel Kingsbridge (0548) 560489; £18(£18.50B)/£32(£33B)

If you have to cancel a reservation for a bedroom or restaurant, please telephone or write to warn them. A small place – and its customers – will suffer if you don't.

Pubs are not allowed to advertise the fact that they are included in *The Good Pub Guide* – for example, on their menu or brochure. Please let us know of any that infringe this rule.

BERRYNARBOR SS5646 Map 1
Olde Globe ★
Village signposted from A399 E of Ilfracombe

Set in a pretty little higgledy-piggledy village, this seventeenth-century inn (converted from three thirteenth-century cottages) has much to occupy the attentive observer: genuinely old local pictures, a rustic profusion of sheep shears, thatchers' knives, priests (fish-coshes), gin-traps, pitchforks, antlers, copper warming pans and lots of cutlasses, swords, shields and fine powder flasks. The bar area consists of a selection of dimly lit and low-ceilinged homely rooms and alcoves, which ramble through bulging uneven and even curved walls darkened to a deep ochre. The floors are of flagstones or of ancient lime-ash (with silver coins embedded in them); there are old high-backed oak settles (some carved) and red leatherette cushioned cask seats around antique tables; log fires in winter. Outside, the crazy-paved front terrace has old-fashioned garden seats, with an attractive garden beside it. Bar food includes sandwiches (from 60p), pasties, steak and kidney pie (£1.50), ploughman's (£1.70), pizza (£2), lasagne (£2), salads (from £2.50), lasagne or spaghetti bolognese (£2.50), plaice (£2.60), scampi (£2.95), gammon (£3.70) and eight-ounce rump steak (£4.70), with children's meals (£1.25); traditional Sunday lunch (you have to book). Well kept Ushers Best on handpump, and cheap own-label house wines; reasonably priced locally caught trout often for sale; sensibly placed darts, skittle alley, pool-room, dominoes, cribbage, fruit machine, piped music. The pub's terrier, Lucy, makes sure there's no after-hours drinking: ringing the time-bell is traditionally her responsibility. (*Recommended by David and Flo Wallington, Steve and Carolyn Harvey; more reports please*)

Free house   Licensees Lynne and Phil Bridle   Real ale   Meals and snacks   Gaslit restaurant tel *Combe Martin (027 188) 2465   Children in eating area, restaurant and skittle alley Children's night Thurs   Open 11–2.30, 6–11 all year; opens 7 in winter*

BLAGDON SX8960 Map 1
Barton Pines
Blagdon Road, Higher Blagdon; pub signposted with Aircraft Museum on right, leaving Paignton on A385 Totnes road

There's an attractive range of bar food in this Elizabethan-style Victorian mansion; it includes home-made soup (90p), generously garnished sandwiches (£1.45 for home-cooked meats, local crab £2.25), home-made pâté (£1.65), pasty (£1.95), sausages and egg (£2.10), vegetable lasagne (£2.50), home-made steak, kidney and Guinness pie or roast chicken with barbecue sauce (£2.95), scampi, plaice or cod in cheese sauce (£3.30), gammon steak (£3.95), salads (from £3.95) and steak (£5.75), with additional evening dishes such as local rainbow trout (£4.75), a large mixed grill (£5.85), and half a roast duckling in an orange and Gran Marnier sauce (£7.95); several children's dishes (from £1.25) and puddings (from £1.20). The interior is spacious; on the left-hand side of the lounge bar there are oak window seats in the tall stone-mullioned windows, squared oak panelling, a coffered ceiling, and a handsome stone fireplace with a grandiose carved chimney-piece; the right side is more modern, and has dominoes, darts and a fruit machine, and other rooms include a simpler picture-window family extension and (in the rambling back area) a carpeted pool-room with pin-table, juke box and space game, and a children's room with a couple more space games and a grabber game. The large garden has a series of stepped lawns, old pines and plenty of flowers; it looks down over the sea beyond Paignton, and over the countryside to Dartmoor, and includes a heated outdoor swimming-pool, skittle alley, and a play area (with a tractor to scramble over). Halls Harvest on handpump, piped music. It's right next to the museum,

Pubs brewing their own beers are listed at the back of the book.

which has an extensive model railway and fine rose garden. (*Recommended by Brian and Anna Marsden, Dr Nicola Hall; more reports please*)

Free house   Licensees Mr and Mrs Peter Devonshire   Real ale   Meals and snacks   Restaurant tel Paignton (0803) 553350   Children in restaurant, pool-room, functions room   Live music Fri and Sat in summer   Open 12–3.30, 6.30–1am; 12–2.30, 7–11 in winter   Self-catering flats

BRANSCOMBE   SY1988   Map 1

Masons Arms   ★ ⊗ ⇐

Village signposted S of A3052 Sidmouth–Lyme Regis

The welcoming low-beamed main bar here rambles about – like the creepers on its medieval exterior – in a pleasantly old-fashioned way, with chairs and cushioned wall benches, and a grandfather clock; there are settles on the flagstones around the massive central hearth, with its roaring log fire, which is used on Thursday lunchtimes, and on request in the evenings, to spit-roast joints. Outside, the quiet flower-filled front terrace has tables with little thatched roofs, extending into a side garden. Lunchtime bar food includes soup (95p), sandwiches (from £1, fresh crab £1.60) and nicely presented open wholemeal specials (from £1.80), ploughman's (from £2.10), baked eggs (£2.20), salads (from £2.80), omelettes using herbs from the pub's garden (from £1.90), chicken kebab (£3.60), grilled lamb cutlets with garlic and herbs (£3.80), and lots of local fish (£1.90–£4.80); evening bar meals have half a dozen main dishes such as quiche (£2.40), chicken curry with a poppadum (£3.20), local crab au gratin or rainbow trout (£3.60), and venison and mushroom pie (£3.80). Recent reports have suggested that service, when under pressure, hasn't always been up to its usual standards, and we'd like more information on this front. Well kept Bass, Badger Best and Tanglefoot on handpump, good Inch's cider; darts, shove-ha'penny, dominoes, fruit machine. The sea is half a mile down the lane, and the village is surrounded by little wooded hills; it's near the Donkey Sanctuary. (*Recommended by Wayne Brindle, R D Jolliff, DMF, G and M Brooke-Williams, William Rodgers, P Conrad Russell, J F Estdale, WFL, Gwen and Peter Andrews, S M L Armstrong, Mrs J M Aston, John Knighton, G D Howard*)

Free house   Licensee Mrs Janet Inglis   Real ale   Meals (not Sun lunchtime) and snacks   Restaurant   Open 11–11 all year   Bedrooms (some in cottage across road) tel Branscombe (029 780) 300; £19(£32.50B)/£38(£49B)

BRATTON FLEMING   SS6437   Map 1

White Hart ⊗

This is a welcoming and at times bustling place, with a traditionally furnished rambling low-ceilinged bar. This is divided into several cosy nooks and alcoves by steps, corners, and even the pillars protected by draymen's leather aprons; there are robust cushioned chairs and wooden stools on flagstones or parquet floors, with a refectory table in one area, and lots of cartoons and Guinness advertisements as decoration. The big stone inglenook has a fine log fire. The home-made food is unpretentious and attractively priced: toasted sandwiches (£1), cottage pie (£1.75), steak and kidney pie (£1.95), and a selection of pasta, vegetarian dishes and puddings. Well kept Bass and Flowers IPA on handpump, draught cider from a big earthenware jug (drinks prices generally are cheap here). The selection of games is good, with shove-ha'penny, dominoes, cribbage, darts, pool, fruit machine, space game and juke box in one side section. There is a separate skittle alley, a small flagstoned courtyard with seats, and a useful evening takeaway stall. The village is pleasantly situated in the hills above the River Yeo. (*Recommended by Christopher and*

We mention bottled beers and spirits only if there is something unusual about them – imported Belgian real ales, say, or dozens of malt whiskies; so do please let us know about them in your reports.

Heather Barton, D B Delaney, Jack Taylor, Frank Cousins, Steve and Carolyn Harvey, Mr and Mrs R Tame)

Free house   Licensees Timothy Nicholls and M Doyle   Real ale   Meals and snacks (not Sun lunchtime)   Children in eating area, restaurant and skittle alley   Open 11–2.30, 5–11 all year

BRAYFORD   SS6834   Map 1
Poltimore Arms ⊗

Yarde Down – three miles from village, towards Simonsbath; OS Sheet 180 reference 724356

On the edge of Exmoor, this friendly little pub has strong horsy and hunting connections, with stuffed foxes' heads, a deer's head, photographs of hunt meetings, hunting cartoons – even the menu shows the hunt meeting under the antlers outside the pub's front door. The main bar has old leather-seated chairs with carved or slatted backs, wooden wall settles with flowery cushions, a little window seat, old sewing-machine and other interesting tables, a beam in the slightly sagging cream ceiling with another over the small serving-counter, and an inglenook fireplace with a wood-burning stove, old saws and a kettle; there are copper jugs and kettles on the mantelpiece. The lounge bar – full of diners on our visit – has a small brick open fire, a mix of chairs and a settle, Guinness and Fry's Chocolate prints, plants, and wildlife drawings for sale; a plainly decorated games-room has pool, darts, two fruit machines, trivia and juke box. Good bar food includes tasty home-made soup (70p), sandwiches (from 70p, toasties 10p extra), good curried eggs, omelettes (£1.25), ploughman's (from £1.80), home-made steak and kidney pie or lasagne (£1.80), vegetarian nut croquette (£2.25), salads (from £2.50) and tender steaks (from £4.80), with extra evening dishes such as their speciality noisettes of lamb (£4), fresh fish (from £4) and mixed grills (£5.50). Well kept Ushers and Websters Yorkshire on handpump, Cotleigh Tawny tapped from the cask. A side garden has picnic-table sets and a grill for barbecues. *(Recommended by Steve and Carolyn Harvey, Patrick Stapley, RAB, Colin Humphreys, H Butterworth)*

Free house   Licensees Mike and Mella Wright   Real ale   Meals and snacks   Children's room   Open 11.30–2.30, 6–11 all year

BUCKLAND BREWER   SS4220   Map 1
Coach & Horses

The cosy bar in this homely thatched house has heavy beams, antique settles, and attractive furnishings, with logs burning in the big stone inglenook fireplace; the extension at the back, which serves as a family-room, is new. Home-cooked bar food includes sandwiches (90p, French sticks £1), soup or pasty (95p), a generous ploughman's (from £1.50), with main dishes like chilli con carne (£2.25), scampi, chicken or cod (£2.50), beef curry (£2.95), salads (from £2.75), local trout (£3.25), well cooked and presented gammon (£3.25), a daily vegetarian dish, and steak (£5.50). On Sundays there's a set roast lunch in winter, with salads in summer. Well kept Flowers IPA on handpump; darts, dominoes, shove-ha'penny, cribbage, euchre, fruit machine, space game and juke box. There's a stone-walled terrace at the front, and a pretty little garden at the side, with tables, swings and slides. *(Recommended by Peter Cornall, J E F Rawlins, David and Flo Wallington, Charles and Mary Winpenny, Sue Cleasby, Mike Ledger, Steve and Carolyn Harvey)*

Free house   Licensees Ken and Susan Wolfe   Real ale   Meals (not Mon) and snacks Restaurant tel Horns Cross (023 75) 395   Children in bar extension (young children until 7, others 8) and restaurant   Open 11–2.30, 5–11 all year; closed evening 25 Dec

---

Meal times tend to vary from day to day and with the season, depending on how busy the pub hopes to be. We don't specify them as our experience shows you can't rely on them. Avoid the disappointment of arriving just after the kitchen's closed by sticking to normal eating times for whatever area the pub is in.

BURGH ISLAND   SX6443   Map 1
Pilchard

Park in Bigbury-on-Sea and walk about 300 yards across the sands, which are covered for between six and eight hours of the twelve-hour tide; in summer use the Tractor, a unique bus-on-stilts which beats the tide by its eight-foot-high 'deck'

It's this pub's location that makes it so special; once safely inside the small L-shaped bar, and protected by the thick-walled embrasures and the storm-shuttered windows, it can be quite satisfying to watch the tide inch across the sands to cut you off. It's lit by big ships' lamps hanging from the beam and plank ceiling, has lots of bare wood and stripped stone, with low chairs, settles edged with rope, others with high backs forming snug booths, and a good – though not always lit – log fire. Bar food might include soup (75p), home-made pasties (90p), filled baked potatoes (£1.10), open sandwiches (from £2.25), and salads (from £2.95, prawn £3.95, smoked salmon £5.75); Palmers IPA, Ruddles County and Ushers Founders on handpump, farm cider; maybe piped music. The white-plastered back bar has darts, shove-ha'penny and dominoes. It can seem quite basic on an off day out of season, when food and service can be lacking. Agatha Christie was a regular visitor to the adjacent 1929 art-deco hotel. (*Recommended by Dennis Jones, Graeme Smalley, Jon Wainwright, P J Hanson, Peter Hood, KG*)

Free house   Licensee Tony Porter   Real ale   Meals and snacks   Evening seafood and salad bistro, bookings only tel Kingsbridge (0548) 810344   Children in back bar and bistro   £1 car parking in Bigbury   Open 11–11

BUTTERLEIGH   SS9708   Map 1
Butterleigh Inn ⊗

Village signposted off A398 in Bickleigh; or in Cullompton take turning by Manor House Hotel – it's the old Tiverton road, with the village eventually signposted off on the left

Warmly welcoming and convivial, this unpretentious but interestingly furnished village inn has several little rooms: old dining-chairs around country kitchen tables in one, sensibly placed darts and an attractive elm trestle table in another, prettily upholstered settles around the four tables that just fit into the cosy back snug. Plates hang by one big fireplace, there are topographical prints and watercolours, pictures of birds and dogs, and a fine embroidery of the Devonshire Regiment's coat of arms. The atmosphere's pleasantly chatty and local, with unobtrusive piped pop music. Bar food includes sandwiches (70p), home-made burgers (£1.90), interesting pâtés (£1.95), salads (£2.25), two or three dishes of the day such as vegetarian chilli (£2.50) and lamb steak (£4.25), egg and hot chilli sausages (£2.75), fresh fish such as sole (£4.50), sirloin steak glazed with honey and mustard (£6.20) and a formidable mixed grill (£6.95); well kept Cotleigh Tawny, Kingfisher and Old Buzzard on handpump. There are tables on a sheltered terrace and neat small lawn with a log cabin for children. We'd expect this to be a nice place to stay, though readers have not yet reported on this aspect. (*Recommended by Mr and Mrs C France, Giles Bullard*)

Free house   Licensees Mike and Penny Wolter   Real ale   Meals and snacks   Open 12–3, 6–11 all year   Bedrooms tel Bickleigh (088 45) 407; £14.50/£21; also cottage sleeping four, £200 a week

CHERITON BISHOP   SX7793   Map 1
Old Thatch ⊗

Village signposted from A30

The rambling bar in this welcoming sixteenth-century pub has a very relaxed atmosphere; the wide range of bar food is generously served, and includes home-made soup (80p), sandwiches, imaginative starters such as prawns, tomato and egg in cheese sauce served in a scallop shell (£1.50), ploughman's (£1.80), salads (from £2.75), and good hot dishes like cauliflower moussaka or steak and kidney pudding (£2.80), a daily curry (£3.10), scampi (£3.30), jugged rabbit (£3.50), sole Véronique or chicken breast with white wine, red peppers, olives and orange (£4.20), stuffed pork fillet (£4.50), wiener schnitzel (£4.90), steaks (from £5.75), and enterprising puddings: Cointreau lemon sorbet (95p), spiced bread pudding (£1) and peach trifle (£1.15). Ruddles County and Ushers Best on handpump, and local cider; dominoes, cribbage, piped music. It makes for an attractive detour from the A30. *(Recommended by Roy and Barbara Longman, D Godden, Mrs G K Herbert, S Godfrey, J S Meadow)*

Free house   Licensee Brian Edmond   Real ale   Meals and snacks
Open 12 (11.30 Sat)–2.30, 6–11 all year; opens 7 in winter   Bedrooms tel Cheriton Bishop (064 724) 204; £17.50(£24.50B)/£25(£35B)

CHITTLEHAMHOLT   SS6521   Map 1
Exeter Inn   ⊗   ⇤

Village signposted from A377 Barnstaple–Crediton and from B3226 SW of South Molton

The beamed main bar in this very welcoming sixteenth-century thatched inn has cushioned mate's chairs and stools, settles, a couple of big cushioned cask armchairs by the open wood-burning stove in a huge stone fireplace, and a collection of matchboxes and foreign coins. In the side area there are seats set out as booths around the tables under the sloping ceiling. The attractive bar food includes soup (85p), sandwiches (from 80p, local sausage in French bread £1.25), hogg pudding (Devon's answer to haggis – £2.20), ploughman's with home-made bread (from £1.80), basket meals (£2), home-made steak and mushroom pie (£3.25), local trout (£3.50) and steak (£4.75); roast Sunday lunch (£3.95); friendly service. Well kept Ushers Best and Websters Yorkshire on handpump, local farm cider; darts, shove-ha'penny, dominoes, cribbage, fruit machine, and juke box or piped music. It's on the old Barnstaple packhorse road, and close to Exmoor National Park. *(Recommended by Peter Cornall, Mrs J M Scott, J S Evans, Steve and Carolyn Harvey, Mr and Mrs R J Welch)*

Free house   Licensees Norman and Kim Glenister   Real ale   Meals and snacks
Restaurant   Children in eating area   Open 11–2.30, 6–11 all year; may open longer in afternoon if trade demands   Bedrooms tel Chittlehamholt (076 94) 281; £15.60B/£26.40B

CHURCHSTOW   SX7145   Map 1
Church House   ⊗

A379 NW of Kingsbridge

The thirteenth-century arch of the main door dates back to the time when this atmospheric pub was a Benedictine hospice; the current licensees are maintaining the tradition of hospitality, particularly with the generous bar food, served at the curtained-off end of the bar. It's earned the unanimous praise of readers, and includes pasty (70p), sandwiches (from 75p, crab £1.75), soup (75p; the carrot is recommended), ploughman's (from £1.45, with a generous ham one), basket meals (from £1.35), home-made dishes such as cottage or fish pie (£2.25) and devilled chicken or sweet-and-sour pork (£2.45), salads (from £2.75), trout (£3.45), mixed grill (£4.25), and eight-ounce rump steak (£5.65); puddings (from £1.10); the carvery – fine roasts, help-yourself vegetables – is good value (£5.25 including home-made puddings). The bar itself has plenty of character, with low and heavy black oak beams, a great stone fireplace with a side bread oven, and stripped stone walls with cushioned seats cut into the deep window embrasures. The long, cosy room is neatly kept and comfortable, with an antique curved high-backed settle as well as the many smaller red-cushioned ones by the black tables on its Turkey carpet, and a line of stools – each with its own brass coathook – along the long glossy black serving-counter. Well kept Bass and Ushers Best and Founders on handpump; dominoes, cribbage, fruit machine. There are seats outside. *(Recommended by Jon Wainwright, Margaret and Trevor Errington, Sue Cleasby, Mike Ledger, Mrs Carol Mason, Derek McGarry, A J Triggle, Liz and Ian, Alan and Ruth Woodhouse, Ken and Barbara Turner, Mrs A Hossack, Dr N M Hall)*

Free house   Licensee H (Nick) Nicholson   Real ale   Meals and snacks (not 25 or 26 Dec) Carvery Weds–Sat evenings, Sun lunch tel Kingsbridge (0548) 2237   Children welcome Open 11–2.30, 6–11 all year; closed evening 25 Dec

COCKWOOD   SX9780 Map 1
Anchor ⊗

Off, but visible from, A379 Exeter–Torbay

In this cheerful local there's a very attractive emphasis on fish dishes, which could hardly be fresher, sometimes including shellfish from the River Exe just a couple of hundred yards away. The fish soups are enterprising – crab and brandy (£2.50) or seafood chowder (£3.25); other seafood includes prawns with a dip (£2.95), crab cocktail (£3.25), grilled plaice (£4.25), crab salad (£6.50), king prawns (£9.50), local scallops (£9.95) and a plate of mixed shellfish (£10.50). There are also crusty bread sandwiches (from 90p, crab £1.10), ploughman's (£2.55) and hot dishes (mainly at £3.35, except cottage or steak and kidney pie at £3.60) and ten-ounce fillet steak (£9.25). The bar is a series of communicating small rooms, with low ceilings, black panelling, good-sized tables in various alcoves, and a cheerful local atmosphere even at busy holiday times. Well kept Bass, Flowers IPA and Original and Huntsman Royal Oak on handpump, with quite a few wines by the glass; darts, shove-ha'penny, dominoes, cribbage, fruit machine, maybe piped music. Tables on a sheltered verandah look over a quiet lane to yachts and crabbing boats in the landlocked harbour. The pub can get very busy in season, when nearby parking may be difficult. *(Recommended by Tom Evans, Jon Wainwright, S Matthews, Gwen and Peter Andrews, Alan and Audrey Chatting)*

Heavitree (who no longer brew)   Licensees J D Enacott and P Reynolds   Real ale   Meals and snacks   Restaurant tel Starcross (0626) 890203   Children in restaurant   Open 11–2.30, 6–11 all year

COLEFORD   SS7701 Map 1
New Inn ⊨

Just off A377 Crediton–Barnstaple

The new licensees in this fourteenth-century thatched inn are keen to maintain the well established, warm and welcoming atmosphere. The only thing that's changed is the range of food, which now includes ploughman's (£1.75), home-made curry, chilli, lasagne and pies (£2.95), plaice (£4.50), haddock or trout (£4.75), home-made specials like lamb or beef in wine or meats in various sauces (£4.95–£5.50), steaks (from £6.80), and puddings (from £1); Sunday roast in winter. The spaciously rambling bar has a considerable amount of character: in the central servery there are modern settles forming stalls around tables on the russet carpet, and a solid-fuel stove. The four areas that spiral around this have an interesting variety of furnishings and seats, including settles ancient and modern, spindle-back chairs, low dark green velour armchairs and plush-cushioned stone wall seats. There are some character tables – a pheasant worked into the grain of one – carved dressers and chests, paraffin lamps, antique prints and old guns on the white walls, landscape plates on one of the beams and pewter tankards hanging from another. Well kept Flowers IPA and Original and Wadworths 6X on handpump; fruit machine (out of the way up by the door) and piped music. They still have the parrot (a manic blue-fronted Amazon), which continues to lend its non-stop stream of scatty pub chatter and hilarity to the general atmosphere. The ducks on the stream outside are a somewhat quieter variety of bird. *(Recommended by Theo Schofield, Kay and Bill Waggoner; more reports on the new regime please)*

Free house   Licensee Paul Butt   Real ale   Meals and snacks   Children in eating area   Open 11.30–2.30, 6–11 all year   Bedrooms tel Copplestone (036 34) 242; £20(£24B)/£26(£28B)

COLYTON   SY2493   Map 1
Kingfisher

Dolphin Street; village signposted off A35 and A3052 E of Sidmouth, in village follow Axminster, Shute, Taunton signpost

It's increasingly rare to find a pub where a stranger's warmly welcomed by a solid core of local regulars, drawn from right across the social spectrum. That's certainly one of this village pub's marked virtues. The well kept beers are another – Badger Best, Flowers IPA, Huntsman Royal Oak and a guest such as Wethereds SPA on handpump; they also have Farmer John's cider, from along the Exeter road a bit (the cider farm's open for visits). There are blue plush cushioned window seats, stools, sturdy elm wing settles and rustic tables, and glasses slotted into the two waggon-wheels hanging above the bar swing in unison when someone upstairs walks above the beamed ceiling. The walls are stripped back to stone, and there's a big open fireplace. Bar food includes sandwiches (from 75p, local crab £1.80), filled baked potatoes (from £1.50), ploughman's (from £1.60), plaice (£2.75) and gammon (£2.95), with children's dishes (£1.50); sensibly placed darts, dominoes, cribbage, fruit machine, and skittle alley; dogs on leads allowed. The back terrace has tables under cocktail parasols. *(Recommended by Bryan Petts, Mr and Mrs C France, DMF, Dr D M Forsyth)*

Free house   Licensees Graeme and Cherry Sutherland   Real ale   Meals and snacks Children in family-room   Open 11–2.30, 5.30–11 all year

COMBEINTEIGNHEAD   SX9071   Map 1
Coombe Cellars

Pub signposted off B3195 Newton Abbot–Shaldon

More than £400,000 has been spent in completely gutting and renovating this popular estuary pub. The long main bar now has very large windows along its left-hand side, offering a superb view up the River Teign; it's also decorated with nautical bric-à-brac and captain's chairs, with compasses set into the couches. There's a family area off one end, three fire-effect gas fires and lots of patio area outside. The decent range of bar food includes home-made soup (95p), open sandwiches (from £1.75), ploughman's (from £1.95), home-made vegetable lasagne (£3.25), fresh fish (from £3.25), and steaks (from five-ounce sirloin £4.50). Courage Best and Directors on handpump; fruit machine and piped music. When the tide's out the area's a naturalist's delight, with innumerable busy wading birds joining the shelducks, mergansers, herons, cormorants and gulls to pick over the shiny mudflats. There's a play area outside, and lots of water-sports facilities – the pub is the base for the South Devon Water Sports Association, and has its own landing-stage. *(Recommended by E G Parish, C A Foden, G Atkinson, Ian Bampton)*

Free house   Licensee Peter Uphill   Real ale   Meals and snacks   Children in eating area and restaurant   Open 11–11 all year

The letters and figures after the name of each town are its Ordnance Survey map reference. *How to use the Guide* at the beginning of the book explains how it helps you find a pub, in road atlases or large-scale maps as well as in our own maps.

COUNTISBURY   SS7449 Map 1
Exmoor Sandpiper ⊗ 🍺

A39, two or three miles E of Lynton on the Porlock road

This charming low white inn stands out for the ham it serves: it's smoked on the premises in the chimneys of the four log fires – look in particular for the ones hanging among the pots, cauldrons and kettles of the great central fire. The ham features prominently in the salads (£1.95–£2.35); other dishes include soup (90p), ploughman's (from £1.60), jumbo sausage (£1.80), chicken (£2.95), seafood platter (£5.95) and lobster (£7.95). The friendly and relaxing bar consists of four or five cosy rooms, which have ancient bumpy plaster walls, low ceilings, some heavy black beams, as well as antique dining-chairs and settles with well made more modern ones (some forming stalls around tables). The selection of paraphernalia includes an interesting and wholly addictive antique fortune-telling machine, badger and fox masks and paperbacks to borrow; darts, pool, fruit machine in the games area; piped music. Well kept Bass and Charringtons IPA on handpump, and a good range of unusual whiskies. Tucked into the hillside opposite a moorland church, it's well placed for Exmoor and the National Trust Watersmeet estate; on *Good Walks Guide* Walk 22. It's still known to many as the Blue Boar – a name it carried for more than three hundred years. *(Recommended by Wayne Brindle, Lynne Sheridan, Bob West, Wilfred Plater-Shellard, Steve and Carolyn Harvey, Dick Brown)*

Free house   Licensee A Vickery   Real ale   Meals and snacks   Book-lined restaurant   Children in eating area   Open 11–11 (12–3, 7–10.30 Sat) all year   Bedrooms tel Brendon (059 87) 263; £25.30B/£50.60B

CULLOMPTON   ST0107 Map 1
Manor House 🍺

½ mile from M5 junction 28: enter town and turn left at T-junction; pub is on right

When we heard in summer 1988 that this spacious hotel had changed hands (bought by the owners of the Carpenters Arms in Stanton Wick, whose growing stable of pubs includes the Ashcott Inn in Somerset – a popular resort of many readers), we hot-footed it down there to see how it had changed. Initially at least, the answer's very little: it still has its relaxing and stately L-shaped lounge bar, with the carefully restored Adam moulded plaster ceiling; there's some early seventeenth-century oak panelling here, and a locally made grandfather clock stands over the well spaced tables, together with a range of antiques and old prints. The lively coach house bar still has well kept Flowers Original on handpump, and darts, dominoes, cribbage, pool, juke box and fruit machine. Bar food includes sandwiches, salads including home-cooked ham and local beef, hot dishes such as seafood or chicken and mushroom pie, and puddings, with a traditional roast lunch (and limited menu) served in the restaurant on Sundays. *(Recommended by Ian Blackwell, Gabriele Berneck, Christine Herxheimer, M P Hallewell, B H Pinsent, Alan and Audrey Chatting; more reports on the new regime please)*

Free house   Licensee Stephen Hordacre   Meals and snacks   Restaurant   Children in restaurant   Open 11–3, 5–11 all year   Bedrooms tel Cullompton (0884) 32281; £24.50B/£38.50B

DARTINGTON   SX7762 Map 1
Cott ⊗ 🍺

In hamlet with the same name, signposted off A385 W of Totnes opposite A384 turn-off

This archetypal local Devonshire inn can lay two claims to fame: it's one of the oldest in the country (it got its first licence in 1320), and reputedly has the longest continuous thatch (183 feet) in the South of England. Both factors contribute to the never-changing atmosphere, particularly in the communicating rooms of the heavy-beamed bar, which have big open fires, some flagstone flooring and sturdy high-backed settles, some elaborately carved. Most readers still reckon that the food (not that cheap by West Country standards) is good stuff; it includes soups, pâté or ploughman's (£1.25–£2.25), and an attractive lunchtime buffet, with salads (£2.95–£4.50); also half a dozen changing hot dishes which might be home-made steak and kidney pie, rabbit casserole, local cod in parsley sauce, lamb chops in claret or roast pork with apple sauce and stuffing (all £3.75). They stick to fresh vegetables – no chips – and serve gooey home-made puddings (£1.60). Service is quick (and you can book tables for the same food in the restaurant part). In the evenings you can get a salad in the bar, and hot dishes like pancakes with seafood filling (£3.95) or pork in cider (£4.25), but most eating is then a restaurant affair, with freshly cooked main meals such as guinea-fowl with redcurrant jelly gravy or fresh salmon hollandaise (two courses £12.50). Well kept Bass and Halls Harvest on electric pump, Hill's cider, a good range of wines by the glass. You can sit out on the big lawn beside the long, low house, and there are good walks through the grounds of nearby Dartington Hall. The area is good for visits – particularly the popular Dartington craft centre, the Totnes–Buckfastleigh steam railway and one of the prettiest towns in the West Country, Totnes. *(Recommended by J M Soanes, George and Chris Miller, Simon Turner, JAH, CED, J C Braidwood, AJH, GDH, S V Bishop)*

Free house   Licensees Stephen and Gillian Culverhouse   Meals and snacks (lunchtime) Evening restaurant   Children in restaurant   Open 11–2.30, 6–11 all year Bedrooms tel Totnes (0803) 863777; £20/£37

DARTMOUTH   SX8751 Map 1

Cherub ⊗

Higher Street

For the second time in three years this charming little place has changed hands, but again we feel confident that it can more than justify itself as a main entry. Reports suggest that the new range of food is well up to the previous high standards, now including sandwiches, soup (£1, French onion £1.25), filled baked potatoes (from £1.25), smoked haddock baked in white wine and cheese sauce (£1.50), pâté (£2), an excellent ploughman's (from £2), spaghetti bolognese or smoked prawns (£2.75), celery hearts baked with ham in a cheese sauce, chilli con carne or ratatouille (£2.95), tagliatelle (£3.25), smoked chicken with leeks and ham (£3.50), seafood pasta (£4.20), fresh scallops (£4.95), and speciality fish – fresh-tasting dishes such as fillet of sole stuffed with lemon and prawns (£5.75), poached brill with a dill and cucumber sauce (£6.50) and grilled halibut with a chive sauce (£6.95). The building itself was originally a fourteenth-century wool merchant's house, and has shown a resilient attitude to the progress of time: it survived an 1864 fire which destroyed the southern end of the street, and the Second World War bombing which destroyed the north side; hence it's the oldest building around here, and one of very few British pubs listed officially as Grade I. In traditional style each of the two heavily timbered upper floors jut further out than the one below; inside, the bar is snug, warm and welcoming, with tapestried seats under creaky heavy beams, red-curtained leaded-light windows and an open stove in the big stone fireplace. Well kept Bass, Blackawton and Flowers IPA and Original on handpump, and a fine collection of malt whiskies; the upstairs evening restaurant concentrates on fresh local ingredients, especially fish, with game in season. *(Recommended by AE, GRE, David and Ann Stranack, C A Foden and G Atkinson, Jon Wainwright, R Sinclair Taylor, Simon Turner, Paul and Margaret Baker, Mr and Mrs*

People don't usually tip bar staff (different in a really smart hotel, say). If you want to thank a barman – dealing with a really large party, say, or special friendliness – offer him a drink. Common expressions are: 'And what's yours?' or 'And won't you have something for yourself?'

A Holman Dunn, Liz and Ian, S V Bishop, J F Derbyshire, Mr and Mrs D G Austin, Miss L C Mee, CED, Miss J Wakeham, J Walsh)

Free house   Licensees Craig Carew-Wootton and Bob Bennett   Real ale   Meals and snacks   Restaurant tel Dartmouth (080 43) 2571   Children in restaurant   Open 11–11 June–Sept; 11–3, 6–11 Oct–May

Royal Castle 🛏

11 The Quay

Behind its stately Regency façade, this harbourside hotel dates back over three hundred years; the bar on the left is a lively local place, with country kitchen chairs, mate's chairs and a couple of interesting old settles around a mix of tables, from scrubbed deal through traditional cast-iron-framed ones to polished mahogany. One wall is stripped to the original stonework, there's a big log fire, and decorations include navigation lanterns, glass net-floats and old local ship photographs. Big windows overlook the inner harbour and beyond to the bigger boats in the main one. On the right, there's a more sedate beamed bar with plush furnishings and Turkey carpet. A wide choice of bar food includes soup (£1.10), filled baked potatoes (from £1.75), half a pint of prawns (£2.75), steak and kidney pie (£3.75), trout (£4.25) and rump steak (£5.85), with sandwiches (from 95p) and ploughman's (from £2.25) at lunchtime. Well kept Bass and Courage Best on handpump; darts, fruit machine, trivia machine, maybe unobtrusive piped music. (*Recommended by J E F Rawlins, Jon Wainwright, Pamela and Merlyn Horswell*)

Free house   Licensees Mr and Mrs Nigel Way   Real ale   Meals and snacks   Restaurant Children in eating areas   Open 11–11 all year   Bedrooms tel Dartmouth (080 43) 4004; £32.95B/£57.50B

DITTISHAM   SX8654   Map 1
Ferry Boat

Follow Ferry sign (*sharp* right turn), park in main car park and walk down narrow steep lane to water's edge; or at low tide keep straight on past Ferry sign, park down by playing-fields and walk along foreshore to pub; or even come up on the little passenger ferry from Dartmouth

There's a pleasantly nautical atmosphere in this simple pub, with a ship's bell (there's another outside which you can use to call the ferry to take you across the river to Dartmouth) and other brass gear including a ship's clock over the coal fire, ships' badges over the serving-counter, and photographs of boats and ships; they chalk the tide times on the wall. Simple seats include some in the big picture window, and there are others outside. Its position is particularly idyllic, at the bottom of the quiet thatched village, and looking out over the boats on the wide river. Bar food includes a summer cold table with mussels in garlic, home-cooked joints, pies, quiche, shellfish, fresh Dart salmon; also home-made puddings and, in the evening, hot dishes such as casseroles and curries. In winter they do soup, filled rolls, filled baked potatoes, seafood bakes and other hot dishes; well kept Courage Best and Directors on handpump; shove-ha'penny, dominoes, cribbage. (*Recommended by K and R A Markham, Jon Wainwright, Margaret and Trevor Errington, David and Ann Stranack, S V Bishop*)

Courage   Real ale   Meals (not Tues in winter) and snacks   Open 10.30–2.30, 5.30–11 all year

DODDISCOMBSLEIGH   SX8586   Map 1
Nobody Inn ★ ★ ⊗ 🛏

Village signposted off B3193, opposite northernmost Christow turn-off

Readers are almost unanimous in their praise for this very attractive and welcoming sixteenth-century village inn; the lounge bar is particularly atmospheric:

in its two rooms there are carriage lanterns hanging from the beams (some of which are original), some handsomely carved antique settles, Windsor and wheel-back chairs, red leatherette benches and a Turkey carpet, with guns and hunting prints decorating a snug area by one of the big inglenook fireplaces. The standard of the bar food remains consistently high, with a wide range of things, including sandwiches (from 85p, made to order), a richly spicy home-made soup (£1.10), coarse home-made calf's liver pâté (£1.20), hot smoked mackerel or sausage and mash (£1.90), pitta salad (£2), butter-bean casserole (£2.30), and lasagne with a lamb sauce or vegetable pie (£2.80), with specials like beef in beer (£2.20) or venison casserole (£2.50); the rich puddings include ice-cream sprinkled with raisins and marinated in Australian Muscat wine (£1.20), fruit flan (£1.60), chocolate fudgecake (£1.90) and an interesting selection of six local cheeses (£2); friendly, helpful service. They also sell local honey (£1.90 a pound) and clotted cream (65p a quarter-pint). It also has the distinction of being probably the best pub for wines in the country, with a remarkable choice of over six hundred well cellared wines by the bottle, a good range by the glass, properly mulled wine in winter, and tutored twice-monthly winter tastings (they also do a retail trade, and the good tasting-notes in their fat list are worth the £1.50 it costs – anyway refunded if you buy more than £10-worth). To add to the feeling of alcoholic gourmandise there's a choice of some two hundred whiskies; the accompanying tasting notes encourage adventure, with half a dozen each of the Macallan and Smiths Glenlivet, a dozen or so more than thirty years old, and even an Indian malt. There's well kept Bass, Charringtons IPA, Huntsman Royal Oak and guest beers like Bagers Best, Golden Hill Exmoor and Marstons Owd Rodger on handpump or tapped straight from the cask. There are picnic-table sets in the charming garden, with views of the surrounding wooded hill pastures. The medieval stained glass in the local church is some of the best in the West Country. *(Recommended by M W Barratt, David and Flo Wallington, Roger and Kathy, Alan and Ruth Woodhouse, TBB, WFL, Mrs E M Brandwood, CED, Tom Evans, W C M Jones, Stephen McNees, Richard Balkwill, S Matthews, Mr and Mrs J C Dwane, J C Proud, Gwen and Peter Andrews, WHBM, D Russell, Prof and Mrs Keith Patchett, J C Tyzack, R S Fuller, Sally Watson, Verney and Denis Baddeley, Elizabeth Kemp, Dave Butler, Lesley Storey, Mr and Mrs D F Fowler, Chris Needham, Sara Heel)*

Free house Licensees Nicholas Borst-Smith and Philip Bolton Real ale Meals and snacks Restaurant (closed Sun) Children in restaurant Open 11–2.30, 6–11 all year; closed evening 25 Dec Bedrooms (some in distinguished 18th-century house 150 yds away) tel Christow (0647) 52394; £12/£20(£35B)

DREWSTEIGNTON SX7390 Map 1
Drewe Arms

The reason this pub is still so small, basic and unaffected by the passage of time is that the landlady Mabel Mudge has for many decades set herself against modernisation – it remains, as ever, a thatched village local alehouse in pre-war style, where basic built-in wooden benches face each other across plain tables, ochre walls have local team photographs and advertisements tacked to them, and there's no serving-counter – the well kept Wadworths 6X, Whitbreads and draught cider are drawn in a back room. Note the herringbone-pattern Elizabethan brick floor. Though nearby Castle Drogo (open for visits) looks medieval, it was built earlier this century. *(Recommended by Phil Gorton, Mrs Thompson, WFL, Sally Watson)*

Free house Real ale Snacks Open 10.30–2.30, 6–11 all year

EAST DOWN　SS5941　Map 1

Pyne Arms ⊗

Off A39 Barnstaple–Lynton; OS sheet 180 reference 600415

The beamed and dimly lit L-shaped bar of this popular food pub has a very high-backed curved settle by the door (and more ordinary pub seating), and horseracing prints and Guinness and Martell placards on the red walls; there's a wood-burning stove with horse harness and farm tools on the wall above it, some copper jugs, and big barrels standing around. Up some steps is a small galleried loft with more tables and chairs. A flagstoned games area has pine-plank wall benches, a shelf with old soda syphons, handbells, and a clock, some swan-necked wall lamps, antlers, racing and hunting prints and a piano; pool-table, darts and fruit machine. Very generous helpings of food include home-made soup (85p), filled rolls and sandwiches (from 85p), ploughman's (£1.65), home-made pâté (£1.75), home-cooked ham and egg (£2.25), salads (from £2.35), good shellfish such as mussels au gratin in spicy garlic sauce (£3.75), beef Stroganoff or steaks (from £5.45) and several veal dishes (£5.45), with several specials and home-made puddings; it's best to get there early for a table. Well kept Flowers IPA on handpump, several wines by the glass or bottle. The young, boisterous Dobermann is not allowed in, but on our visit showed it knew how to open doors. There's a pretty garden, and Arlington Court is close by. (*Recommended by Alan Symes, Wayne Brindle, Steve and Carolyn Harvey, Wilfred Plater-Shellard, Colin and Ginny Humphreys, Patrick Stapley, RAB*)

Free house　Licensees Mr and Mrs Kemp　Real ale　Meals and snacks　Children in small eating area　Open 11–2.30, 6–11 all year

EXETER　SX9292　Map 1

Double Locks ★ ⊗

Canal Banks, Alphington; from A30 take main Exeter turn-off (A377/396) then next right into Marsh Barton Industrial Estate and follow Refuse Incinerator signs; when road bends round in front of the factory-like incinerator, take narrow dead-end track over humpy bridge, cross narrow canal swing bridge and follow track along canal; much quicker than it sounds, and a very worthwhile diversion from the final M5 junction

The food in this remote but charmingly placed (on the ship canal) pub is very good value, including sandwiches (from 65p), soup (80p), unusual side-salads (90p, with raw mange-tout and exotic fruits), filled baked potatoes (from £1.25), ploughman's (£1.60), garlic mushrooms (£1.70), with good hot dishes (£1.50) such as lasagne or several vegetarian dishes, and salads (£2.50); home-made puddings like carrot cake (80p) or ice-creams (£1.10); weekend barbecues. The atmosphere is outstandingly relaxed and easy-going in the bar, which somewhat resembles the interior of a retired seafarer's cottage, with nautical impedimenta including ship's lamps and model ships. The well kept Gibbs Mew Bishops Tipple, Golden Hill Exmoor, Huntsman Royal Oak, Marstons Pedigree and Owd Rodger and Wadsworth 6X are all tapped from the cask, with Everards Old Original on handpump; darts, shove-ha'penny, chess, draughts, backgammon, dominoes and cribbage in the main bar, bar billiards in another. Under the same ownership as the Turf further down the canal at Exminster, it's probably the oldest canal lockhouse in the country. There are picnic-table sets and a play area, with an old steam train and swings, out on the grass. (*Recommended by Byrne Sherwood, Jon Wainwright, Ruth Humphrey, Patrick Young, Serena Hanson, WHBM, JDL, J Figueira, B G Steele-Perkins, D Pearman, Hugh Butterworth*)

Free house　Licensee Jamie Stuart　Real ale　Meals and snacks　Children welcome Occasional folk music or jazz (outside if warm)　Open 11–11

White Hart ★ 🏠

South Street; 4 rather slow miles from M5 junction 30; follow City Centre signs via A379, B3182; straight towards centre if you're coming from A377 Topsham Road

This fine, well kept fourteenth-century inn is exceptionally atmospheric, particularly in the rambling main bar, where the walls are decorated with pictorial plates, old copper and brass platters (on to which the antique lantern lights glisten), silver and copper in a wall cabinet, and long-barrelled rifles above the log fire in one great fireplace. There are big Windsor armchairs and built-in winged settles with latticed glass tops to their high backs around oak tables on the bare oak floorboards (carpet in the quieter lower area); big copper jugs hang from heavy bowed beams in the dark ochre terracotta ceiling; and a set of fine old brass beer engines resides in one of the bay windows. From the latticed windows, with their stained-glass coats of arms, one can look out on to the cobbled courtyard, a lovely sight when the wistaria is flowering in May. It's very much the sort of place, one feels, where the city's people have congregated for generations – and no doubt for centuries. The Tap Bar, across the yard, is furnished sturdily after the style of an old-fashioned alehouse and serves soup (95p), sandwiches (from £1.20), plate of prawns (£1.95), cold-table meats (from £3.20), chicken and chestnut pie (£4.15) or a large steak and kidney pie (£4.35) and twelve-ounce rib steak (£5.95). The candlelit bare-stone-and-sawdust wine bar serves much the same food, with additional dishes like bacon and eggs (£3.15) or beef and oyster pie (£4.15); there's a respectable range of Davy's wines here, and more unusual touches like pint jugs of vintage port from the wood or tankards of bucks fizz; on Sundays both these bars are closed. Well kept Bass and Davy's Old Wallop on handpump; friendly, efficient service. The very comfortable and well equipped modern bedroom block doesn't at all diminish the old-fashioned character of the original building. *(Recommended by Jon Wainwright, Dr J R Hamilton, Serena Hanson)*

Free house   Licensee Brian Wilkinson   Real ale   Meals (not Sun) and snacks (not Sun evening)   Restaurant   Children welcome   Open 11–2.30, 5–11 all year   Bedrooms tel Exeter (0392) 79897; £25(£36B)/£53.50B

EXMINSTER   SX9487   Map 1

Swans Nest ★ ⊗

Pub signposted from A379 S of village

The new licensees in this genuine character place have made a successful effort to maintain its highly deserved reputation as a food pub. Even under pressure, particularly on a Saturday – when there can be anything up to a 1000 hungry mouths to feed – service stays both friendly and efficient; the carvery, introduced last year, continues to be popular (£4.95, evenings £5.50, with help-yourself vegetables), and there's a good choice of other food from the no-smoking servery, including sandwiches (from £1.45, crab £1.60 – not Saturday evening or Sunday lunchtime), soup (95p), lunchtime specials like home-made steak, kidney and mushroom pie, coq au vin or ham omelette (£3.50), a good choice of salads (from £3.25 – seafood £6.70, made up as you watch) from the new salad bar, and chef's specials such as fresh scampi in a wine and cream sauce or veal escalope (£5.95), and fillet steak or Norfolk duckling (£7.50). All meats are fresh, not frozen. There is a wide choice of rich ice-creams, puddings and sundaes (from £1.60). The layout of the relaxed and softly lit bar is decidedly rambling, and indeed at first you wonder where it's going to end; under the heavy beams there are groups of sofas and armchairs, some carved old-fashioned settles, lots of wheel-back chairs, high-backed winged settles (upholstered in button-back green leather or flock red plush, and set out as booths around the tables), grandfather clocks, high shelves of willow-pattern platters and so on. Well kept Bass and Flowers Original on handpump; piped music. There's a non-smoking area and air-conditioning throughout. In the vast but charmingly landscaped car park they ask you to drive forwards into the bays, to prevent exhaust damage to their fine shrubs. *(Recommended by Mr and Mrs Jon Payne, Gordon Hewitt, Harry Robinson, M P Hallewell, D T Taylor, Alan and Audrey Chatting)*

Free house   Licensees the Major family   Real ale   Meals and snacks   Dance-music trio Thurs–Sat evenings, piano Sun   Open 11–11 all year

Turf ★ ⊗

Continue past the Swans Nest (see previous entry) to end of track, by gates; park, and walk right along canal towpath – nearly a mile

The food in this isolated waterside inn is simple but generous and fresh, including pasties (70p), soup (80p), sandwiches (from 70p, toasted from 80p), filled baked potato (£1.10), cottage pie (£1.20), ploughman's (from £1.65), ham and eggs (£1.80), salads (£2.20) and puddings (from 70p); in summer there's a well run cook-yourself barbecue; friendly service. From the bay windows there's a fine sea view out to the mudflats at low tide, full of gulls and waders. The connected series of airy high-ceilinged rooms is furnished with flagstones or broad bare floorboards, a wood-burning stove, fresh flowers on low varnished tables, canal photographs and big bright shorebird prints by John Tennent on the white walls. Well kept Flowers IPA and Huntsman Royal Oak on handpump or tapped from the cask, and Inch's cider; darts, shove-ha'penny, dominoes, cribbage, piped music. Behind the pub, the canal basin is full of sizeable boats. Below, on the big lawn running down to the shore, you can play boules; there are also log seats, picnic-table sets and a beached cabin-boat for children to play in. It's possible to reach it by a twenty-minute saunter along the ship canal from the Double Docks at Exeter (owned by the same licensees), or by a forty-minute boat ride from Countess Wear (bar on board; £2 return, charter for up to 56 people £75 – the pub, which runs the boat, will quote for a full run from Exeter Maritime Museum). *(Recommended by P J Bevan, Phil and Sally Gorton, Jon Wainwright, B G Steele-Perkins, D Pearman, Alan and Audrey Chatting)*

Free house   Licensee Kenneth William Stuart   Real ale   Meals and snacks   Children welcome   Open 11–11; 11–2.30, 6–11 in winter   Bedrooms tel Exeter (0392) 833128; £11/£22

HATHERLEIGH   SS5404 Map 1

George ⊗ 🛏

The good bar food in this warmly welcoming thatched fifteenth-century inn includes sandwiches (£1), ploughman's (£1.50), fry-ups (£2.10), steak and kidney pie (£3), excellent lasagne or ratatouille, salads (from £3.25), grills (£4.95), with puddings like chocolate marquise, meringue glacé or peach brûlée (all £1.75). The main bar was built from the wreck of the inn's old brewhouse and coachmen's loft; it's a spacious L-shaped affair, with beams, a wood-burning stove and antique settles around sewing-machine treadle tables; a quieter extension, with more modern furnishings, leads off this. The little front bar – mainly for residents – in the original part of the inn has easy chairs, sofas and antique cushioned settles, an enormous fireplace, tremendous oak beams and stone walls two or three feet thick. Across the corridor from this there's an even smaller and very simple bar, which is only open on market day (Tuesday). The pleasant courtyard has hanging baskets and window boxes on the black and white timbering, and rustic wooden seats and tables on its cobblestones. Well kept Bass, Flowers Original, Wadworths 6X and a

---

Bedroom prices normally include full English breakfast, VAT and any inclusive service charge that we know of.

guest beer on handpump; darts, cribbage, pool. One disabled reader found both staff and customers exceptionally obliging. Outside by the car park (but well screened) is a small heated swimming-pool. *(Recommended by J Harvey Hallam, Juliet Streatfield, Neil Evans, Dexter Masters, David Sawyer, Mrs Pamela Sawyer, Jill Hadfield, Tony Gallagher, Steve and Carolyn Harvey, Stan Edwards)*

Free house   Licensees Veronica Devereux and John Dunbar-Ainley   Real ale   Meals and snacks   Restaurant   Children in lower room of main bar   Acoustic music once a month, maybe folk once a week   Open 10.30–2.30, 6–11   Bedrooms tel Okehampton (0837) 810454; £23.50(£30.75B)/£30.75(£40.75B)

HAYTOR VALE   SX7677 Map 1
Rock   ★ ⊗ 🛏

Haytor signposted off B3344 just W of Bovey Tracey, on good moorland road to Widecombe

The wide choice of waiter-served bar food in this civilised and friendly Dartmoor inn includes sandwiches (from £1, toasted from £1.55, not Sunday lunchtimes), home-made soup (£1.15), filled baked potato (£1.95), omelettes made with local free-range eggs (£2.65), ploughman's (£2.75), vegetarian dishes (from £2.75), curries (£3.65), rabbit and cider casserole (£3.95), local trout (£5.95) and steaks (from eight-ounce sirloin £5.95). The welcoming bar is partly panelled, and has polished antique tables, easy chairs, oak Windsor armchairs and high-backed settles. The two communicating rooms have flowers in summer, good log fires in winter (the main fireplace has a fine Stuart fireback), and old-fashioned prints and decorative plates on the walls; well kept Bass, Huntsman Dorchester, Dorset and Royal Oak, and Devon cider. The big garden is pretty and well kept, with good views of the surrounding moors, and in summer has a help-yourself lunchtime buffet. The winter Friday-night breaks – you pay for a meal for two in the restaurant and get free overnight accommodation – is still very good value. *(Recommended by William Rodgers, David and Flo Wallington, SC, Mr and Mrs P W Dryland, Roger Huggins, Tom McLean, Ewan McCall, Paul and Margaret Baker, Cynthia McDowell, Michael O'Driscoll, Richard Davies, Alan and Audrey Chatting; more reports please)*

Free house   Licensee Christopher Graves   Real ale   Meals and snacks   Restaurant (residents only Sun)   Children in family-room   Open 11–2.30, 6–11 all year   Bedrooms tel Haytor (036 46) 305/465; £20(£25.50B)/£37(£40B)

HOLNE   SX7069 Map 1
Church House

The friendly new licensees in this medieval Dartmoor pub have very much brought it back into the reckoning as a main entry this year; the lower bar has been redecorated to good effect, with stripped pine panelling, while the old atmosphere of the charming carpeted lounge bar continues to thrive; the ancient heavy oak partition is sixteenth century, the curved elm settle eighteenth. There are fine moorland views from the pillared porch (popular with regulars). Bar food includes sandwiches (from £1.15), ploughman's (from £1.85), omelettes (£2.50), lasagne (£2.75), steak and kidney or chicken and ham pie (£3.25), chicken breasts in mushroom sauce or hot roasts (£3.75), and grills (from £4.25); Blackawton Headstrong and Burtons on handpump, local cider, and a good range of traditional country wines. The public bar has darts, dominoes and cribbage, and there is a family-room. The village is surprisingly untouristy; perhaps the nicest way of getting here is the quarter-hour walk from the Newbridge National Trust car park, and there are many other attractive walks nearby, up on to Dartmoor as well as along the wooded Dart valley. Like so many others in Devon, the pub got its name from the fact that it grew up hand in glove with the church, originally brewing church ale on feast days such as Whitsun. *(Recommended by David and Flo Wallington,*

Philip and Trisha Ferris, Jon Wainwright, P J Hanson, D I Baddekey, A N Martin, Wendy Amos, WHBM, Mrs J A Trotter, Pat and Malcolm Rudlin, Prof A N Black)

Free house   Licensees N E and W J Bevan   Real ale   Snacks (not evening) and meals Restaurant   Children in dining-room   Occasional local musicians   Open 11–2.30, 6–11; 12–2.30, 7–10.30 in winter   Bedrooms tel Poundsgate (036 43) 208; £11.50(£13.50B)/£23(£27B)

HORNDON   SX5280 Map 1
Elephant's Nest ★ ★ ⊗

If coming from Okehampton on A386 turn left at Mary Tavy inn, then left after about ½ mile; pub signposted beside Mary Tavy Inn, then Horndon signposted; on the Ordnance Survey Outdoor Leisure Map it's named as the New Inn

The homely bar food in this sixteenth-century isolated Dartmoor pub includes home-made soup (95p), filled rolls, ploughman's (£1.90), salads, home-made lasagne (£2.75), curry (£4.25), chicken Kiev or local river trout (£4.50) and eight-ounce steak (£5.95). The cushioned stone seats built into the bar's windows look out on the moor, and there are big flagstones, captain's chairs around the tables, large rugs, a beam and board ceiling, and a good log fire on cool days – much enjoyed by the resident, and rather portly, Jack Russells. Well kept Palmers IPA, Ruddles Best and County and St Austell HSD on handpump; sensibly placed darts and fruit machine. Though you can walk from here straight on to the moor or Black Down, a better start (army exercises permitting) might be to drive past Wapsworthy to the end of the lane, at OS Sheet 191 reference 546805. There are white tables and chairs on its spacious flower-bordered lawn. The pub's name *doesn't* come from its entertaining elephant mural, but in fact derives from a previous licensee's nickname. *(Recommended by Simon Turner, Dennis Heatley, Caroline Bailey, Dr G M Stephenson, R C Vincent, Jill Hampton, Mr and Mrs G J Packer, Verney and Denis Baddeley, J C Braidwood, Nigel Acton, Steve and Carolyn Harvey)*

Free house   Licensees Owen and Dave Phillips   Real ale   Meals and snacks   Local fiddling group occasionally   Children in restaurant   Open 11.30–2.30, 6.30–11

HORSEBRIDGE   SX3975 Map 1
Royal ★

Village signposted off A384 Tavistock–Launceston

The bridge from which the village takes its name is a fine thing, with remarkably exact unmortared masonry; it was the first bridge over the Tamar, built by monks in 1437 – not long before they built this inn, which is about fifty yards away. It's a cordially welcoming place, with a simple and old-fashioned bar; you get the impression that it can't have changed much since Turner slept on a settle in front of the fire so that he could slip out early to paint the bridge. The room on the right has vertically panelled cushioned stall seats around neat old tables, some mate's chairs and wheel-back chairs, and harness and brasses on its stripped stone walls. The one on the left, with lots of farm tools on its partly panelled walls and beams, has cushioned casks and benches around three tables on the slate floor, and dominoes, sensibly placed darts and bar billiards; log fires, unobtrusive piped music. There's another small room for the overflow at busy times (they call it the Drip Tray). Besides Tamar, Horsebridge Best and the power-packed Heller (all brewed on the premises), they keep Bass, Hancocks HB, Huntsman Royal Oak and a changing guest beer on handpump. The wide choice of ploughman's comes with home-made herby bread (£1.80), and other dishes include pot meals like moussaka or lasagne (£2), salads (from £2.50), half a smoked chicken, venison in port or chicken with Stilton stuffing (£3–£4); a good range of vegetarian dishes and a mass of puddings such as pineapple Pavlova (£1.10). It was originally called the Packhorse, and got

its present name for services to Charles I (whose seal is carved in the doorstep).
(Recommended by Simon Turner, Caroline Bailey, WFL, Betsy and David White, Phil and Sally Gorton)

Own brew   Licensees T G and J H Wood   Real ale   Snacks (not lunchtimes) and meals (not Sun evenings)   Open 12–2.30, 7–11 (10.30 Mon–Thurs); closed evening 25 Dec

KINGSKERSWELL   SX8767   Map 1
Barn Owl ⊗

Aller Road; just off A380 Newton Abbot–Torquay – inn-sign on main road opposite RAC post

The owner, from New Zealand, has devoted his three years with this seventeenth-century former farmhouse to bringing out the best of its ancient features, and adding new points of interest. Two rooms have been stripped back to low black oak beams, with polished flagstones and a kitchen range in one; a third room with an elaborate ornamental plaster ceiling has been fitted with antique dark oak panelling, including a very decorative wooden chimney-piece. This room has the grandest furnishings, including a couple of carved oak settles and old-fashioned dining-chairs around the handsome polished tables on its flowery carpet; the others have a variety of more simple furniture, including monks' chairs, a high-backed built-in settle, window seats in the white stone walls and scrubbed kitchen farmhouse tables. A wide choice of bar food using fresh local supplies includes soup (90p), sandwiches (from £1.35), filled baked potatoes (from £1.65), whitebait (£1.75), fresh plaice (£3.25) and sole (£3.50), salads such as home-boiled ham (£3.75), lamb chops (£4) and rump steak (£6.25), with lots of specials such as cauliflower and spinach flan (£3) and tarragon chicken (£3.20). Well kept Courage Directors and Janners on handpump; log fires throughout (they've uncovered all the old fireplaces); on our visit piped instrumental music, though they tell us they don't normally have this. There are picnic-table sets in a small sheltered garden.
(Recommended by RH, Mrs B G Francis, Peter Lanceley, Mr and Mrs Glendinning, GHM, Elisabeth Kemp)

Free house   Licensees Derek and Margaret Warner   Real ale   Meals and snacks   Restaurant Mon–Sat evenings and Sun lunchtime tel Kingskerswell (080 47) 2130   Children in restaurant   Open 11–2.30, 7–11 all year

KINGSTEIGNTON   SX8773   Map 1
Old Rydon ★ ⊗

From A381 Teignmouth turning off A380, take first real right turn (Longford Lane), go straight on to the bottom of the hill, then next right turn into Rydon Road following Council Office signpost; pub at end of straight part of this lane; OS Sheet 192 reference 872739

The snug and alcovey little bar in this tucked-away farmhouse pub has a good atmosphere, as well as a heavy beam and plank ceiling with lots of beer mugs hanging from them, a big log fire in winter in a raised fireplace, and cask seats and upholstered seats built against the white-painted stone walls. There are a few more seats in an upper former cider loft, now a gallery facing the antlers and antelope horns on one high white wall. Well kept Bass, Janners Devon Special (called Old Rydon Ale here) and Wadworths 6X on handpump; occasional piped music. The food comes as something of a surprise, particularly for its cosmopolitan flavour; the menu changes daily depending on what fresh ingredients they've bought, but it might include soup (85p), an interesting Mexican avocado dip with tortilla chips (£1.45), duck and orange pâté (£1.45), with main dishes like cauliflower and prawn Mornay (£2.95), chicken and duck chow-mein or rabbit casserole or half a roast chicken (£3.25), beef and mushroom pie in Stilton and port sauce (£3.40) and marinated red mullet, crab claw and Norwegian prawns (£5.25); local game and fresh mussels in winter; good puddings, all with clotted cream (£1.25). There are seats on a covered side terrace and in a nice biggish sheltered garden, which has a swing. *(Recommended by Alan Sillitoe, Gordon Hewitt, CED, Jon Wainwright, S Bird)*

Free house   Licensees Hermann and Miranda Hruby   Real ale   Meals and snacks Restaurant tel Newton Abbot (0626) 54626   Children in restaurant lunchtime, upstairs until 8   Open 11–3, 6–11 all year; closed 25 Dec

KINGSTON   SX6347   Map 1
Dolphin ⊗

The wide range of food in this pretty yellow-shuttered sixteenth-century house includes crab sandwiches (£1.75), a good ploughman's (£2.25), eight-ounce Cumberland sausage with garlic bread (£2.95), home-made chicken curry (£3.65), home-made steak and kidney pie (£3.75), charcoal-grilled chicken breast (£4.95) or steak (£6.50), with very good home-made puddings like treacle tart or raspberry Pavlova (£1.75); children's helpings (£1.20). The bar consists of a series of knocked-through beamed rooms, with rustic tables and cushioned seats and settles around their bared stone walls; the atmosphere is cheerful and informal; well kept Courage Best and Directors on handpump. Outside, just below the imposing village church, are tables, swings, a children's summer snack bar, and summer barbecues. Half a dozen tracks lead down to the sea, and unspoilt Wonwell Beach, about a mile and a half away. *(Recommended by Sue Cleasby, Mike Ledger, Ian and Daphne Brownlie, J M Soanes, Jon Wainwright, Mr and Mrs J C Dwane)*

Courage   Licensees Barry and Dee Fryer   Real ale   Meals and snacks   Restauant tel Bigbury-on-Sea (054 881) 314   Children in family-room and on end of bar   Open 11–11 (closed afternoon weekdays in winter)

KNOWLE   SS4938   Map 1
Ebrington Arms (⊗)
Pub signposted just off A361, in village two miles N of Braunton

Though the new licensees have smartened up this pub, they've retained much of its atmosphere and character; the carpeted lounge (actually two rooms opened together) still has red plush stools around low tables, some pews, and cushioned seats built into its stripped-stone outer walls (the inner ones are white); the copper on the chimney-breast is new. The walls and black joists are decorated with lots of brass, prints, plates and pewter mugs; a candlelit bistro area is up one or two steps at one end. A snug bar (very much the haunt of the regulars) has darts, table skittles, shove-ha'penny, cribbage, space game and a fruit machine ; separate pool-room. The bar menu has changed but remains popular, with filled baked potatoes (95p), soup (£1), ploughman's (from £2.15), chilli con carne or cottage pie (£2.15), leek, ham and cheese gratin (£2.50), smoked trout or vegetable Strogonoff (£2.95), steak and mushroom casserole in Guinness and crevettes with garlic bread (£4.95); in the evening bistro they serve their speciality, beef Zingo (£6.25), which when on form is excellent. Bass on handpump; juke box and piped music. *(Recommended by David and Flo Wallington, Chris Fluck, Steve and Carolyn Harvey; more reports on the new regime please)*

Free house   Licensees Alex and Nancy Coombs   Real ale   Meals and snacks   Bistro tel Braunton (0271) 812166   Children in eating area and restaurant   Open 11–2.30, 6–11 all year

KNOWSTONE   SS8223   Map 1
Masons Arms ★ ★ ⊗ ⌂

One of the main attractions in this thatched thirteenth-century stone inn is its unpretentious traditionally furnished bar, where the atmosphere is pitched at just the right level. The small main room is stone-floored, with wall settles and benches around slab-top tables, farm tools on the walls, ancient bottles of all shapes and sizes hanging from the heavy medieval black beams, and a fine open fireplace with a big log fire and side bread oven. A small lower sitting-room has cosy easy chairs, bar billiards and table skittles. The personal attention you get from the owners is very much in line with this – friendly and old-fashioned; Mr Todd in particular continues to earn readers' praise for his helpful advice about interesting places to go to and so forth. A third attraction is the good and often imaginative bar food, which has a very genuine farmhouse flavour and presentation; it includes home-made soup (95p), home-made pâté (£1.35), ploughman's (from £1.25), home-made pies like cheese and leek or rabbit and venison or chicken curry (£2.65), meat salads (£2.75), fritto misto (£4.55) and puddings (£1.25); the breakfasts for residents are particularly generous. Badger Best, Boddingtons Bitter and Wadworths 6X tapped from the cask, and a potent dry farm cider; several snuffs on the counter; darts, dominoes, cribbage, shut-the-box, board games and jigsaws. The engaging bearded collie is called Charlie (incidentally, dog-owners recommend the ground-floor annexe rooms if you're staying); as we went to press two kittens – a ginger and a tabby to be christened Rob and Flora respectively – were set to join him. It tends to be more popular with tourists – attracted by its lovely quiet position, just opposite the church, and by the views from its garden over the hilly pastures leading up to Exmoor – than with locals. (*Recommended by Brian and Anna Marsden, Nigel Paine, Dennis Jones, Pat and Malcolm Rudlin, Peter Cornall, Simon Townend, Paul McPherson, Della Thomson, Wayne Brindle, E Mitchelmore, Sally Watson, Ned Edwards, Anthony Sargent, Frank Cousins, Steve and Carolyn Harvey, D P Hearsum, R J and F J Ambroziak, Joyce and Geoff Tomlinson, Judy McCluskey, Emma Stops, G P Hewitt, Dr and Mrs L A Branda*)

Free house   Licensees David and Elizabeth Todd   Real ale   Meals and snacks   Restaurant   Children in eating areas   Open 11–2.30, 6–11; opens 7 in winter; closed evening 25 Dec   Bedrooms tel Anstey Mills (039 84) 231; £16.50(£20S)/£33(£40S)

LUSTLEIGH   SX7881   Map 1

Cleave ⊗

Village signposted off A382 Bovey Tracey–Moretonhampstead

Set in an attractive out-of-the-way village, this friendly thatched white fifteenth-century inn has a cosy low-ceilinged lounge bar, with fresh flowers in summer and big log fires in winter, and an attractive antique high-backed settle as well as the pale leatherette bucket chairs, red-cushioned wall seats and wheel-back chairs around the tables on its patterned carpet. A traditionally furnished second bar has darts, pool, dominoes, euchre and a fruit machine. Well kept Bass, Flowers IPA and Original on handpump. The good bar food includes, at lunchtime, soup (£1.30), large baps (£1.95), ploughman's (from £2.30), home-made cheese and onion flan (£2.40), home-cooked ham (£2.50) and coq au vin (£3.10), with additional dishes like home-made steak, kidney and Guinness pie (£4.75) in the evening. The evening restaurant is distinctly good, with an undertone of *nouvelle cuisine* about it. There's a neat and pretty sheltered garden where you may meet strolling peacocks; near *Good Walks Guide* Walk 18. (*Recommended by Alan and Ruth Woodhouse, Philip and Trisha Ferris, Mrs E M Brandwood, G and M Stewart, C A Foden, G Atkinson, S Matthews, Eileen Broadbent, David and Ann Stranack, Dr K Bloomfield*)

Heavitree (who no longer brew)   Licensees A and A Perring   Real ale   Meals and snacks; afternoon teas from 3 (not Tues)   Restaurant   Open 11–11 (closed Tues and winter afternoons)   Parking may be difficult   Bedrooms tel Lustleigh (064 77) 223; £15/£28

If a pub is on or near one of the walks described in *Holiday Which? Good Walks Guide*, also published by Consumers' Association, we mention this – giving the walk's number.

Pubs with attractive or unusually big gardens are listed at the back of the book.

LUTTON SX5959 Map 1
Mountain ⊗

Pub signposted from Cornwood–Sparkwell road

The efficiently served bar food in this welcoming Dartmoor pub is simple but good – readers praise in particular the French bread filled generously with beef and ham (£2.80) or crab (£3.50); they also serve pasties and pies (65p), sandwiches (£1.30), chilli con carne or curries (£2), soup with cheese and a roll (£2.20) and ploughman's (£2.80). The rustic beamed bar has a window seat, rugs on the flagstones, some walls stripped back to the bare stone, and a high-backed settle by the log fire, with Windsor chairs around old-fashioned polished tables in a larger connecting room. Well kept Burton Ind Coope, Butcombe, Fergusons Dartmoor (from a new micro-brewery), Golden Hill Exmoor on handpump, and local farm cider (they'll make you a cup of tea if you want); darts, dominoes, fruit machine. From the seats at the front there are fine views of the lower slopes of Dartmoor. *(Recommended by Dr and Mrs D N Jones, R Sinclair Taylor, Roger Mallard)*

Free house   Licensees Charles and Margaret Bullock   Real ale   Meals and snacks   Children in eating area   Open 11–3, 6–11 all year

LYDFORD SX5184 Map 1
Castle ★ ⊗ 🍺 [illustrated on page 176]

The old-fashioned charm of this pink-washed Tudor inn is best experienced in the twin rooms of the bar, which have old captain's chairs, country kitchen chairs and high-backed winged settles around mahogany tripod tables on big slate flagstones; the stripped stone walls are decorated with Hogarth prints, sentimental engravings, local 1850s livestock auction notices and above all masses of brightly decorated plates. There are unusual stained-glass doors, and an attractive grandfather clock; the seven pennies near the serving-counter were hammered out in the old Saxon mint in the reign of Ethelred the Unready in the tenth century. Well kept Courage Best on handpump; sensibly placed darts, shove-ha'penny, dominoes, cribbage, piped music. The imaginative lunchtime cold buffet table has a wide choice of salads with the meats, home-made pies and Scotch eggs, salmon, trout, cold tandoori chicken and so forth; other bar food, which changes daily, might typically include corned beef hash (£3), chicken provençale or lasagne (£3.75) and an attractive seafood risotto, with puddings such as creamy apple crunch or brown-bread ice-cream. A Bernese mountain dog has taken over the amiable role of the late retriever Gilbey, and there are a couple of cats (Harvey and JR). The beautiful wooded river gorge running past the village is owned by the National Trust. The well kept garden has an adventure playground and barbecue area, and seats looking up at the daunting ruined medieval tower after which the inn is named. The village was one of the four strongpoints developed by Alfred the Great as a defence against the Danes. *(Recommended by Janet and Paul Waring, Philip and Trisha Ferris, Brian and Genie Krakowska Smart, WFL, Verney and Denis Baddeley, Mr and Mrs H Perry, Jill Hampton, P and M Rudlin, Doug Kennedy, Mrs J Green)*

Free house   Licensees David and Susan Grey   Real ale   Meals and snacks   Restaurant   Children welcome   Open 11–3 (4 Sat, 3 in winter), 6–11 all year   Bedrooms   tel Lydford (082 282) 242; £20(£25B)/£30(£35B)

LYNMOUTH SS7249 Map 1
Rising Sun 🍺

Mars Hill; down by harbour

Well placed for the fine stretch of coast (with Foreland Point in the distance), and for the lovely steep walk up the Lyn valley to Watersmeet (National Trust) and

Exmoor, this beautiful, thatched fourteenth-century inn has a modernised panelled bar, with stripped stone at the fireplace end, black beams in its white ceiling, leatherette stools and cushioned built-in stall-seats, and latticed windows facing the harbour. Bar food includes sandwiches (from £1, crab £1.45), home-made soup (£1), ploughman's (£2.25), lasagne (£2.35), fisherman's pie (£2.65) and salads (from £3.55). Perhaps the best bet for food is the small oak-panelled dining-room, which serves good dinners and breakfasts. The bedrooms – most of which are in the adjoining cottages that ramble up the hill – have been refurbished in the last couple of years to a very high standard. The terraced garden behind the pub (for residents) is most attractive. Near *Good Walks Guide* Walk 20; parts of *Lorna Doone* were written here. (*Recommended by P Bacon, W A Harbottle, Mr and Mrs Darlow, J C Smith, John Durham, Sue Cleasby, Mike Ledger, Michael and Alison Sandy*)

Free house   Licensee Hugo Jeune   Meals and snacks   Restaurant   Children in restaurant Open 11–2.30, 5.30–11 all year   Bedrooms tel Lynton (0598) 53223; £29.50B/£51B

MILTONCOMBE   SX4865 Map 1

Who'd Have Thought It ★ ⊗

Village signposted from A386 S of Tavistock

Handy for the lovely gardens of the Garden House at Buckland Monachorum and for Buckland Abbey, this bustling, friendly pub has a lot of character, with cushioned high-backed winged settles around a wood-burning stove in the big stone fireplace, colourful plates on a big black dresser, and rapiers and other weapons on its walls; two other rooms have seats made from barrels. Well kept Golden Hill Exmoor, Huntsman Royal Oak, Palmers IPA, Ushers Best and Wadworths 6X on handpump, with a choice of draught ciders; friendly service; darts, dominoes, cribbage, fruit machine. The bar food is good value and efficiently served, including granary bread sandwiches (from £1; the crab, when available, are recommended), soup (£1.20), generous ploughman's (from £2), chicken (£2.80), mixed seafood (£3.30), salads (from £3.75) and steaks (from eight-ounce sirloin £6.75), with a dozen or so good home-made daily specials and lots of puddings. There are picnic-table sets on a small terrace by the swift little stream that runs down this steep valley. (*Recommended by Chris Hill, H F and J Hobbs, Elisabeth Kemp, George and Jill Hadfield, David Shillitoe, P and M Rudlin, Tom Evans, Ted George*)

Free house   Licensees Keith Yeo and Gary Rager   Real ale   Meals (restricted to basket meals Sun lunchtime and bank hols) and snacks   Folk club Sun evening   Open 11.30–2.30, 6.30–11 all year

MORETONHAMPSTEAD   SX7585 Map 1

White Hart 🛏

This meticulously kept friendly old inn is a comfortable place to stay for Dartmoor, with particularly well appointed bedrooms. In the spacious Turkey-carpeted lounge bar there are armchairs, plush seats, stools and oak pews from the parish church; the hall has a splendidly large-scale 1827 map of Devon by Greenwood; the lively public bar has leatherette seats and settles under a white beam and plank ceiling; darts, shove-ha'penny, dominoes and fruit machine. Bar food includes soup (£1.50), hot dishes such as quiche or home-cooked ham (£2.35), home-made chicken and ham pie (£2.95), salads (£3.50) and scampi (£3.85); at lunchtime there are also pasties (£1), sandwiches (from £1.25, prawn £2.25) and various ploughman's (£2.35); several puddings such as good treacle tart with clotted cream (£1.40); no bar meals after 8pm. Well kept Bass and Flowers IPA on handpump, farm cider. You can sit on a pew among the flowers in the small back courtyard.

(Recommended by Bernard Phillips, G and M Stewart, Sue Jenkins, Robert Olsen, B C Head, Alan and Audrey Chatting, S V Bishop)

Free house   Licensee Peter Morgan   Real ale   Meals and snacks; afternoon cream teas Restaurant and evening grill-room   Children welcome   May have to park in the public car park a short walk away   Open 11–3, 6–11 all year   Bedrooms tel Moretonhampstead (0647) 40406; £27.50B/£45.50B

MORTEHOE   SS4545   Map 1

Ship Aground

Village signposted with Woolacombe from A361 Ilfracombe–Braunton; free parking by church

The open-plan bar in this warm village pub has red leatherette wall seats and mate's chairs around massive tree-trunk sections mounted on cask bases, with sea pictures (for sale) and quite a bit of nautical brassware – shell-cases, a binnacle, porthole surrounds, bronze propeller; sweet-smelling beech logs may be burning in the big stone fireplace; well kept Flowers Original, Golden Hill Exmoor and a guest ale on handpump. Bar food includes good sandwiches (from 80p, crab £1.80), soup (90p), ploughman's (£1.40), steak and kidney pie (£3.15), curry (£3.30), vegetarian dishes (from £2.95) and haddock served with prawns, cockles and mussels (£6); tea or coffee. Dominoes, cribbage, fruit machine, piped music. There are a few tables in front, with more in a small sheltered back courtyard under a fairy-lit vine. There are good walks in National Trust country around here – to Morte Point and on round to Bull Point and Lee, or, southwards, to Woolacombe Warren. *(Recommended by D Godden, David and Flo Wallington, Steve and Carolyn Harvey; more reports please)*

Free house   Licensee Roger McEvansoneya   Real ale   Meals and snacks   Restaurant tel Ilfracombe (0271) 870856   Children in restaurant and games-room   Open 11–11; afternoon opening in winter according to demand

nr NEWTON ABBOT   SX8671   Map 1

Two Mile Oak ⊗

A381 Newton Abbot–Totnes, 2 miles S of Newton Abbot

Generous helpings of good food in this very friendly local include soup (80p), large wholemeal rolls (from £1.20), ploughman's with local cheeses (from £2.10), cod and prawn Mornay (£2.60), scampi or smoked ham (£3.90) and rump steak (£5.50). The beamed lounge has a handsome old settle, romantically secluded candlelit alcoves and a roaring log fire in winter. The beams of the black-panelled and traditionally furnished public bar are decorated with old beer mats and lots of horsebrasses; this too has a good log fire on cool days, and darts, cribbage, fruit machine; well kept Flowers IPA on handpump, Bass and Huntsman Royal Oak tapped from the cask. The family dining-room was once the stables. There are seats on a back terrace, with more on a sheltered lawn broken up by tubs of flowers and well grown shrubs. *(Recommended by Charlie Salt, CED, Jon Wainwright)*

Heavitree (who no longer brew)   Licensee Helen Peers   Real ale   Meals and snacks Children away from main rooms   Open 11–2.30, 6–11 all year; closed 25 and 26 Dec evening

NEWTON ST CYRES   SX8798   Map 1

Beer Engine

Sweetham; from Newton St Cyres on A377 follow St Cyres Station, Thorverton signpost

The main reason for including this bustling ex-station pub is its beers; these are brewed on the premises (still fairly unusual around here): you can see the stainless brewhouse – which turns Rail Ale, Piston, and the very strong Sleeper – from the cellar bar. The spacious main bar has partitioning alcoves, Windsor chairs and some button-back banquettes around dark varnished tables on its red carpet; darts, shove-ha'penny, dominoes and cribbage; fruit machine and space game in the downstairs lobby. The simple range of food includes filled baked potatoes, a range of speciality sausages, chilli con carne, salads, steaks and so forth. There's a terrace and a little sheltered verandah outside. Twice a night (except Sunday) there's a real ale/real train linkup with Exeter. (*Recommended by Charlie Salt; more reports please*)

Own brew   Licensee Peter Hawksley   Real ale   Meals and snacks   Children in eating area   Live music Fri and Sat evenings, occasional Sun lunchtimes   Open 11.30–2.30 (3 Sat), 6–11 all year (cellar bar open to midnight Fri and Sat)

NORTH BOVEY   SX7483 Map 1
Ring of Bells ⊗

Early reports on the change of ownership of this friendly medieval village inn suggest that things are as good as ever, particularly on the food side; this now includes a traditional ploughman's served with home-made soup (£2), main dishes like rabbit casserole, lasagne and curry (around £3.50), a summer help-yourself salad bar (£2–£4) and occasional summer evening barbecues. The simply furnished carpeted main bar has bulgy white walls and horsebrasses on its beams, and a good range of real ales tapped from the cask or on handpump: Bass, Fergusons Dartmoor, Halls Plympton Best, Wadworths 6X and regular guest beers; darts, cribbage, pool in winter, fruit machine and piped music. It's set back from the village green – a lively place during the traditional mid-July Saturday fair – and has seats on a terrace and lawn that are well sheltered by the mossily thatched white buildings around it, and prettily bordered with flowers and shrubs. There's a good children's play area outside; fishing, shooting and pony-trekking can be arranged for guests, and the inn is well placed for some of the most interesting parts of Dartmoor. (*Recommended by P A King-Fisher, Shirley Allen, Mrs Pamela Roper, Paul and Margaret Baker, Pete Bolsover, Mrs Joan Harris; more reports on the new regime please*)

Free house   Licensee Anthony P Rix   Real ale   Meals and snacks   Restaurant   Children in lounge (lunchtimes) and eating area   Open 11–11; closed 3–5 in winter   Bedrooms tel Moretonhampstead (0647) 40375; £16B/£32B

PAIGNTON   SX8960 Map 1
Inn on the Green
27 Esplanade Road

The very wide choice of bar food in this airy and well kept family place includes soup (95p), sandwiches (from £1.65), filled baked potatoes (£1.65), ploughman's (from £2.15), home-made jumbo sausages (£2.25), cockle and bacon pie (£3.25), a range of fish dishes like cod Mornay (£3.80) or local poached halibut (£4.95), several vegetarian dishes such as mung-bean and mushroom biriani (£3.45), charcoal grills (from £3.95, steaks from £5.95); Sunday carvery; there are children's dishes, and puddings served with clotted cream (£1.60). The lounge bar spreads spaciously around the enormously long serving-counter through a succession of arches, where lots of blond cane chairs and cane-framed tables match the soft colour-scheme of peachy beige plush banquettes, pink and buff swagged curtains in the many bay windows, and gently marbled creamy-yellow wallpaper. Seats on the front terrace among cordylines, pampas-grass and hydrangeas look out over the green towards the sea. Ushers Best on handpump, tea by the pot and good coffee; good service; well reproduced piped music. The family-room has a free-play juke box and small dance-floor, as well as darts, pool, space game; fruit machine in lobby. (*Recommended by Brian and Anna Marsden, M Harris, Mrs M F Jennings*)

Free house   Licensee Brian Shone   Real ale   Meals and snacks   Restaurant Children in eating area and family-room   Live music nightly (George Melly to Acker Bilk) Open 11–midnight all year   Self-catering apartments tel Paignton (0803) 557841; from £8.50 a night

PETER TAVY   SX5177 Map 1

Peter Tavy ★ ⊗

This pub has the relative disadvantage of being both very small and very popular, so it does fill up quickly; when it's quieter it's a particularly atmospheric place, with high-backed settles on the black flagstones by the big stone fireplace (which usually has a good log fire on cold days), smaller settles in stone-mullioned windows, entertaining DIY graffiti on the low beams, and a snug side dining area; darts. The good range of real ales changes as a cask is finished, typically including Bass, Butcombe Bitter, Courage Best, Fergusons Dartmoor, Huntsman Royal Oak and Wadworths 6X. The bar food is uncommonly good, too, particularly on the vegetarian side, with dishes like creamy cashew-nut fingers (£1.05), pancakes stuffed with spinach and garlic (£2.20) and cauliflower croustade (£3.15), with a choice of unusual salads; on the meat side there's ham (£1.80 a helping), beef (£2 a helping) and beef pepper pot (£4.15). They use only fresh ingredients, and encourage you to come into the kitchen to pick and choose or even see your food being prepared. Picnic-table sets among fruit trees in a small raised garden have peaceful views of the moor rising above nearby pastures. A track opposite the church leads straight on to the moor, and another past the pub leads down to the River Tavy. (*Recommended by Ceri Jarr, J D Mackay, Mr and Mrs D A P Grattan, Alan and Ruth Woodhouse, R C Vincent, Cynthia Pollard, Jutta Brigitta Whitley, J M Soanes, Doug Kennedy, P and M Rudlin, Sally Watson, Wg Cdr R M Sparkes, Gill and Ted George, John Milroy*)

Free house   Licensees P J and J Hawkins   Real ale   Meals and snacks   Children in side room   Nearby parking often difficult   Open 11.30–3, 6.30–11; closed evening 25 Dec

RATTERY   SX7461 Map 1

Church House

Village signposted from A385 W of Totnes, and A38 S of Buckfastleigh

This welcoming pub can lay claim to being one of the oldest in Britain – some parts probably date from around 1030 (though the ancient-looking flight of spiral stone steps behind a little stone doorway on your left as you go in is fourteenth-century). There's a pleasant atmosphere in the two interesting bar rooms, which have massive oak beams and standing timbers, large fireplaces (one with a little cosy nook partitioned off around it), Windsor armchairs, comfortable leather bucket seats and window seats, and prints on the plain white walls. Well presented bar food includes home-made soup (£1.45), filled granary rolls (£2), ploughman's (£2), grilled plaice (£3.50), smoked chicken (£3.75), steak and kidney pie (£4), seafood lasagne (£4.95), steaks (from six-ounce rump £5.50), with local fish and game and fresh vegetables; good value four-course meal on Friday evenings (£7.50). Well kept Courage Best and Directors and a weekly guest beer on handpump, wines, quite a few malt whiskies, farm cider; cribbage. Outside, there are peaceful views of the partly wooded surrounding hills from picnic-table sets on a hedged courtyard by the churchyard – the building has always been connected with the Norman church, and may have housed the craftsmen who built it. (*Recommended by Colin Way, Philip and Trisha Ferris, J C Proud, Charles Gurney, Neville Burke, S V Bishop, Mrs T Salisbury, Steve and Caroline Harvey, Andy Tye and Sue Hill, Jon Wainwright, Theo Schofield, David and Flo Wallington, Liz and Ian, Mr and Mrs N S J Rich, Sally Watson, Charles Gurney, J G S Widdicombe, Pat and Lee Crosby, Desmond Simpson*)

Free house   Licensees D E and J J Winzer   Real ale   Meals and snacks   Tables can be booked tel Buckfastleigh (0364) 42220   Children (over five lunchtimes, over ten evenings) in eating area   Open 11–2.30, 6–11 all year; closed evening 25 and 26 Dec

Tipping is not normal for bar meals, and not usually expected.

SAMPFORD PEVERELL ST0214 Map 1
Globe

1 mile from M5 junction 27; village signposted from Tiverton turn-off

The spacious bar in this comfortably modernised place has green plush built-in settles and wheel-back chairs around heavy cast-iron tables, a log fire and some stripped stone; Flowers Original and IPA and a guest beer on electric pump (unusual for here); piped music; sensibly placed darts, dominoes, cribbage, draughts, juke box and two fruit machines in the public bar; also a pool-room with two space games, and a full skittle alley. The wide range of food includes sandwiches (from 80p), hot pies (£1.10), ploughman's (from £1.80, with a good selection of local cheeses), salads (from £2.40), smoked chicken (£2.75), omelettes or a big fry-up (£2.75), whole plaice (£4.25) and a generous mixed grill, with roast Devon beef and Yorkshire pudding for Sunday lunch (£3 – as it can get very crowded then they recommend booking). There are picnic-table sets in front by the quiet road. (*Recommended by Gwynne Harper, Wendy Healiss, Richard Dolphin, Wayne Brindle, S V Bishop, Philip and Hazel John, P J Derrington, C A Gurney, David and Flo Wallington, Simon Turner, Caroline Bailey, T H G Lewis, K R Harris, Liz and Ian, Roger Price*)

Whitbreads   Licensees D and A R Trevelyan   Real ale   Meals and snacks   Bookings tel Tiverton (0884) 821214   Children in eating area and family-room   Open 11–11 all year

SHEEPWASH SS4806 Map 1
Half Moon ⊗ 🛏

This buff-painted and civilised inn takes up one whole side of the colourful village square – blue, pink, white, cream and olive thatched or slate-roofed cottages. The unusually attractive inn-sign (a curving salmon neatly interlocking with a crescent moon) hints at the inn's fishing reputation: it can arrange salmon or trout fishing on the Torridge for non-residents as well as residents, and there are lots of fishing pictures in the beamed and carpeted main bar. It's a warmly welcoming place, with white walls, solid old furniture and a big log fire fronted by slate flagstones. Lunchtime bar food includes sandwiches or pasty (£1), soup (£1.10), ploughman's (£2.25), a hot dish (£2.75) and good, fresh salads (£3). Bass and Courage Best on handpump (kept well in a temperature-controlled cellar), a fine choice of spirits, a big earthenware keg of amontillado sherry and good coffee; darts, and a separate pool-room. (*Recommended by Mrs Pamela Roper, David Sawyer, Mrs N Lawson, D B Delany, Dr John Innes*)

Free house   Licensees Benjamin Robert Inniss and Charles Inniss   Real ale   Snacks (lunchtime)   Evening restaurant (must book)   Children in games-room   Open 11.30–2.30 (3.30 Sat), 6–11 all year   Bedrooms tel Black Torrington (040 923) 376; £19.50(£21.25B)/ £38(£41B)

SIDFORD SY1390 Map 1
Blue Ball ★ ⊗ 🛏

A3052 just N of Sidmouth

This unpretentious thatched village inn, run by the same family for some seventy-five years, is very genuinely welcoming, with a lovely winter log fire in the stone fireplace of its partly panelled lounge bar; it has Windsor chairs and upholstered wall benches around the tables under its low and heavy fourteenth-century beams. Extensive refurbishment in the summer of 1988 has left the atmosphere and character of the bar untouched (beyond a new carpet and a spot of paint), but a new food area has been added (converted from the two old kitchens at the back); there's lots of food enticingly displayed here, particularly fresh local fish on crushed ice. A new lobby has been built at the front, beamed and decorated in keeping with the rest of the building. Good value bar food includes sandwiches (from 90p, crab £1.60), an enormous ploughman's (from £2), cheese and asparagus flan (£2.75), home-made steak and kidney pie (£3.25), salads (from £2.75, home-cooked gammon £3.85) and steaks (from eight-ounce rump £5.75). Devenish JD and Royal Wessex on handpump, kept well in a temperature-controlled cellar; a plainer public bar has darts, dominoes, cribbage and a fruit machine, and there's a family-room. Tables on a terrace look out over a colourful walled front flower garden, with more on a bigger back lawn where there are occasional summer barbecues. *(Recommended by Jane and Calum, DMF, E G Parish, Stephen R Holman, Mr and Mrs Jon Payne, WFL, Derek McGarry, G Kahan)*

Devenish   Licensees F H and R H Newton   Real ale   Meals and snacks   Children in eating area   Open 11–11; closed afternoons in winter   Bedrooms tel Sidmouth (039 55) 4062; £16/£24

SLAPTON   SX8244 Map 1

Tower

Aa we went to press four new licensees were in the process of taking over this fine fourteenth-century inn, and all the early signs are that its charm remains as unaffected as ever. Carrying on the tradition of fine ales here, they've expanded the range to ten now, typically including Badger Tanglefoot, Blackawton, Gibbs Mew Bishops Tipple, Exe Valley, Golden Hill Exmoor, Huntsman Royal Oak, Palmers IPA, Ruddles County and Best and Wadworths 6X. The flagstoned and low-ceilinged bar, warmed on cool days by a wood-burning stove as well as by the log fire in one stripped stone wall, has small armchairs, low-backed settles and some furniture made from casks. Bar food includes pasties (75p), sandwiches (from 90p), filled baked potatoes (from £1.25), ploughman's (£2), seafood au gratin (£2.90), salads (prawn £3.60, crab £4.20), and an evening buffet (from £2.50); puddings (from £1.35). A carpeted side games-room has darts, pool, shove-ha'penny, dominoes, fruit machine and space game. There are picnic-table sets on the quiet back lawn, which is overhung by the ivy-covered ruin of a fourteenth-century chantry; you reach the inn by a tortuous narrow lane at the top of this hill village. *(Recommended by David and Ann Stranack, St John Sandringham, J Coles, B Richardson, J Overton, A Mitchell, Jon Wainwright, Sue Cleasby, Mike Ledger, Ruth Humphrey, G F Couch, Tom Evans, C Elliott; more reports on the new regime please)*

Free house   Licensees Keith and Kim Romp, Jan Khan, Carlo Cascianelli   Real ale   Meals and snacks   Children in games-room and dining-room   Open 11–11; closed afternoons in winter   Bedrooms tel Kingsbridge (0548) 580216; £15/£30

SOURTON   SX5390 Map 1

Highwayman ★

A386 SW of Okehampton; a short detour from the A30

Nothing in print can do justice to the sheer eccentricity of this place, and nothing can prepare you for the sensation of a first visit to it. The porch – a pastiche of a nobleman's carriage – leads into an extraordinary fantasy located somewhere between Treasure Island and Middle Earth: a warren of dimly lit stonework and flagstone-floored burrows and alcoves which is richly fitted out with red plush seats discreetly cut into the higgledy-piggledy walls, elaborately carved pews, a leather porter's chair, Jacobean-style wicker chairs, and seats in quaintly bulging small-paned bow windows. The ceiling in one part gives the impression of being underneath a tree, roots and all, and in the mysterious lighting it's quite hard to tell the real cat from the stuffed sleepy-looking badgers. The separate Rita Jones' Locker is a make-believe sailing galleon, full of intricate woodwork and splendid timber baulks, with red-check tables in the embrasures that might have held cannons; its bar counter is beautifully made from dragon-shaped Dartmoor bog oak. All of this is the creation of Mr Jones, who is now turning his attentions to the exterior – the tables, lighting and playthings for children echo the style of the inn itself, with little black and white roundabouts like a Victorian fairground, a fairy-tale pumpkin house and an old-lady-who-lived-in-the-shoe house. The food is confined to delicious pasties made by Mrs Jones, and, though they don't serve real ale, the traditional farm cider (which you can also take away by the bottle) is very good. There's a penny fruit machine, and above-average piped music. *(Recommended by J C Proud, Gwynne Harper, J Overton, A Mitchell, Charlie Salt, Patrick Young, Michael O'Driscoll, JDL)*

Free house   Licensees Buster and Rita Jones   Snacks   Open 10–2, 6–10.30   Bedrooms tel Bridestowe (083 786) 243; £12/£24

SOUTH POOL   SX7740 Map 1
Millbrook

The licensees, whom we welcomed as new in last year's *Guide*, have gone from strength to strength in this delightfully diminutive pub – its one of the smallest we know of – earning readers' praise both for the overall character of the place and for the standard of the food. The cosy little back bar – more like a private sitting-room – is particularly welcoming, with a chintz easy chair, handsome Windsor chairs, fresh flowers, a coal fire, and drawings and paintings (and a chart) on its cream walls. The small public bar, with flowery cushions on its old-fashioned settle, has darts; well kept Bass tapped from the cask, and Churchward's cider; piped music. Bar food includes home-made soup (90p), pasties (90p), sandwiches (from 90p, excellent crab £2.25), cottage pie (£1.65), quiche (£1.75), salads such as smoked mackerel (£1.75) or prawn (£2.80), and ploughman's (from £2), with filled baked potatoes and toasted sandwiches in winter, and for pudding apple cider cake (75p). There are seats out in front, on a sheltered flowery terrace just a few moments' stroll from the brook which gives the pub its name; you can get here in forty-five minutes by hired boat from Salcombe. It can get very crowded at weekends. *(Recommended by Jon Wainwright, ACMM, David and Ann Stranack)*

Free house   Licensees Michael and Christine Jones   Real ale   Snacks   Children in front bar   Open 11–3, 6 (6.30 in winter)–11; may open longer to cover high tide

SOUTH TAWTON   SX6594 Map 1
Seven Stars
Village signposted (with South Zeal) from A30 at E end of Sticklepath

This is one of those pubs that seems to be able to survive changes of licensee with scarcely a flicker – there have been several this decade, with another this last year. Everything seems much as before, with good helpings of food still, such as sandwiches (from 80p), soup (80p), filled baked potatoes (from £1.05), ploughman's (£1.25), vegetarian dishes (£1.80), steak and kidney pie or chilli con carne (£2.50), with roasts on Sunday (£2.95, three courses £5); puddings (80p); Burton Ind Coope and Palmers on handpump, Wadworths 6X tapped from the cask and scrumpy from the barrel. There's an unpretentious village atmosphere in the Turkey-carpeted lounge bar, which has blue and white plates on the mantelpiece over its coal fire, blow-ups of old local photographs, and captain's chairs with the built-in red leatherette wall seats around its rustic tables; darts, pool, dominoes, cribbage, euchre, fruit machine, piped music. They have two dogs, a collie (Sandy) and a retriever (Tanya). You have to thread your way through narrow country

---

Pubs staying open all afternoon are listed at the back of the book.

lanes to reach this tucked-away village. *(Recommended by P and H B, K G Freak; more reports on the new regime please)*

Free house   Licensee L D Lockett   Real ale   Meals and snacks   Restaurant (closed Sun and Mon evenings in winter)   Children welcome   Dartmoor Folk Club last Sun in month   Open 11–2.30, 7–11

SOUTH ZEAL   SX6593   Map 1
Oxenham Arms   ★ ⊗ 🛏

Village signposted from old A30 near Sticklepath

This inn has developed gently over the centuries from the Norman monastery which was built here to surround and to defuse the pagan power of the neolithic standing stone that you can still see forming part of the wall in the family TV-room behind the bar. The part that shows, incidentally, is only the very tip: there's some twenty feet of it below that; other details include stretches of fine polished granite stonework, elegant mullioned windows, Stuart fireplaces, and handsome antique furnishings. The generous bar food ranges from sandwiches (from £1), home-made soup (95p) and ploughman's (£1.75), through fish and chips (from £2.25), home-made steak, kidney and mushroom pie (£2.75), salads (from £2.50), grilled trout (£3.50), to daily specials such as duck and orange or fish pot pie (£3.15); service, though always polite, can be on the slow side. The stately exterior of this grand building makes the welcoming homeliness of the beamed and partly panelled bar something of a surprise; it has Windsor armchairs around low oak tables, St Austell Tinners and HSD tapped from the cask, local cider, and darts, shove-ha'penny, dominoes and cribbage; there may be unobtrusive piped music. Imposing curved stone monastery steps lead up to the garden, and a sloping spread of lawn. *(Recommended by Roy and Shirley Bentley, R H Inns, Elisabeth Kemp, Sally Watson; more up-to-date reports please)*

Free house   Licensee James Henry   Real ale   Meals and snacks   Restaurant   Children in separate room near bar   Open 11–2.30, 6–11 all year   Bedrooms tel Okehampton (0837) 840244; £24(£30B)/£32(£40B)

STOKE GABRIEL   SX8457   Map 1
Church House   ★

Village signposted from A385 just W of junction with A3022, in Collaton St Mary; can also be reached from nearer Totnes; nearby parking not easy

Probably built not long after 1300 to house men repairing the village church, this is still owned by the Church of England. It has an exceptionally attractive medieval beam and plank ceiling in the neatly kept carpeted lounge, which still has a black oak partition wall, and where the huge fireplace is still used in winter to cook the stew. It's simply furnished, with window seats cut into the thick butter-colour walls, a couple of high-backed traditional settles, and decorative plates and vases of flowers on a dresser (one is stripped back to bare stone). Most generously priced and served bar food includes soup (80p), sandwiches (from 85p, steak cob £1.10), filled baked potatoes (£1.10), ploughman's in variety (£1.80), home-made cottage or steak and kidney pie (£2.25) and Dart salmon caught by the licensee's son-in-law (£4.50); summer afternoon cream teas with home-made scones. Many readers have noted the fine quality of the Bass on handpump, which is fed unusually from a temperature-controlled cellar at a higher level. The little public bar has darts; also dominoes, cribbage, euchre, fruit machine, and on our visit unobtrusive piped music. They display a mummified cat, probably about two hundred years old, recently found during restoration of the roof space in the verger's cottage three doors up the lane – one of a handful found in the West Country and believed to have been a talisman against evil spirits. There are picnic-table sets on the little terrace in front of the pub, prettily hung with a mass of hanging baskets; the River Dart is just below the village. *(Recommended by Hugh Patterson, John and Margaret Harvey, Pamela and Merlyn Horswell, Graham and Glenis Watkins)*

Bass   Licensee G W Bradford   Real ale   Meals and snacks   Open 11–11 all year, at least for trial period

STOKENHAM   SX8042   Map 1
Tradesmans Arms
Just off A379 Dartmouth–Kingsbridge

The beamed and carpeted bar in this pretty thatched cottage has a solid-fuel stove in its big fireplace, neat little Windsor chairs around its many sturdy antique tables, and red leatherette window seats looking across a field to the village church; there are more tables up a step or two at the back. Well kept Bass, Ushers Best and guest beers like Adnams, Badger Tanglefoot and Wadworths 6X on handpump, and a fine range of some 120 malt whiskies; piped classical music. Bar food includes sandwiches, ploughman's, honey-baked gammon (£4.20), hot Madras curry (£5.50), chicken liver pâté, haddock (£3.50), lemon sole (£4.25) and halibut (£4.75) (all the fish is delivered fresh from Plymouth's Barbican fish market), and Tamar salmon (£6.95), grilled or poached (with hollandaise), or cold – perhaps as a sandwich (£2.50). Picnic-table sets outside are flanked by some carefully chosen shrubs. *(Recommended by Sue Cleasby, Mike Ledger, G F Couch, David and Ann Stranack, P J Hanson, Ian and Daphne Brownlie, J C Braidwood, Dave Braisted, Sally Watson; more up-to-date reports please)*

Free house   Licensee P A Henderson   Real ale   Meals and snacks   Restaurant tel Kingsbridge (0548) 580313   Open 11–3, 6–11; 12–2.30, 7–11 in winter

TIPTON ST JOHN   SY0991   Map 1
Golden Lion ⊗ ⇄
Pub signposted off B3176 Sidmouth–Ottery St Mary

Comfortably refurbished, this small village inn has cheerful service and a pleasantly relaxed atmosphere, with soft lighting and on our visit gentle Dylanesque piped music. Besides wheel-back chairs and red leatherette built-in wall banquettes there's an attractive gothick carved box settle, a comfortable old settee, a carved dresser and a longcase clock. It's been liberally decorated with guns, little kegs, a brass cauldron and other brassware, bottles and jars along a Delft shelf, and in summer plenty of fresh flowers. A wide choice of home-cooked bar food includes soup (85p – crab £1), sandwiches (from £1.50), filled baked potato (£1.75), ploughman's (from £2), quiche or lasagne (£2.65) and salads (from £3.25), with grills (not Sunday lunchtime) such as gammon (£4.95) and eight-ounce rump steak (£5.95); well kept Bass and Flowers IPA and Original on handpump; dominoes, open fire. There are a few picnic-table sets on the side lawn. *(Recommended by Harry Jackson, H Mayhall, DMF, JH, Gordon Smith, Aileen Stone)*

Heavitree (who no longer brew)   Licensees Colin and Carolyn Radford   Real ale   Meals and snacks   Small restaurant (not Sun evening), best to book   Open 11–2.30, 6–11 all year   Two bedrooms tel Ottery St Mary (040 481) 2881; £15.52/£28.75

TOPSHAM   SX9688   Map 1
Bridge ★

2¼ miles from M5 junction 30: Topsham signposted from exit roundabout; in Topsham follow (A376) Exmouth signpost

The layout and character of this old-fashioned sixteenth-century ex-maltings are a delight, bordering for some readers on the eccentric. The walls are decorated with a booming grandfather clock, crossed guns, swords, country pictures and rowing cartoons, and mugs hanging from the beams. But the main attraction continues to be the real ales – a remarkable range of sixteen, all in very good condition, particularly the less common strong and old ales: Blackawton Headstrong, Gibbs Mew Bishops Tipple, Marstons Owd Rodger, Theakstons Old Peculier, Wadworths Old Timer and Wiltshire Old Devil, besides Badger Best and Tanglefoot, Bass, Blackawton, Courage Directors, Golden Hill Exmoor, Huntsman Royal Oak, Marstons Pedigree, Uley Old Spot and Wadworths 6X. The ales are tapped by Mrs Cheffers from casks in a cosy inner sanctum where the most privileged regulars sit, and passed through a hatch into a cosy little parlour, partitioned off from the inner corridor (with leaded lights let into the curved high back of one settle). At busy times a bigger room across the corridor is opened. Food is confined to sandwiches, ploughman's and excellent pasties. It's positioned just above the river. *(Recommended by Jon Wainwright, Denis Heatley, P J Bevan, Phil and Sally Gorton)*

Free house   Licensee Mrs Phyllis Cheffers   Real ale   Snacks   Children in room across corridor   Open 12–2, 6–10.30 (11 Sat)

Globe ★

In Topsham, keep straight on into Fore Street, where the inn has a small car park

Good value bar food in this handsome sixteenth-century coaching-inn includes sandwiches (from £1.20), ploughman's (£1.75), whitebait, home-made pies, pork with cider or bacon, egg and kidneys (£2.75) and home-made puddings (from £1); beside the main restaurant there's a snug little eating-room with its own fire; friendly service. The heavy-beamed bar has red leatherette seats around the big bow window, and traditional décor including a big panel-back settle, heavy wooden armchairs, ships' badges above the serving-counter, and good sporting prints on the dark oak panelling, with an open fire under the attractive wooden mantelpiece. Bass and Ushers Best on handpump; dominoes, cribbage and piped classical music. There are seats out in a small sheltered and partly covered courtyard. The inn is very much the traditional meeting-place of this pretty little waterside town. *(Recommended by Jon Wainwright, E G Parish, AE; more reports please)*

Charringtons   Real ale   Meals and snacks   Restaurant   Children in eating area   Open 11–11   Bedrooms tel Topsham (039 287) 3471; £26B/£35B

Passage ⊗

In Topsham, turn right into Follett Road just before centre, then turn left into Ferry Road

This lively place is decorated in a traditional but cheerful style which emphasises its age; electrified oil lamps hang from big black oak beams in the ochre ceiling, and there are plank panelling and crazy-paving flagstones in one room, with leatherette wall pews and bar stools. The front courtyard has benches and tables. A wide choice of bar food includes soup (95p), lunchtime sandwiches (from 95p, crab £2.75), ploughman's with a good chunk of cheese (£1.75, lunchtime), four-ounce steak sandwich (£2.70 – particularly good value), salads (such as crab £3.95, Exe salmon or mixed seafood £6.95), gammon, egg and sausage (£4.95) and a range of steaks (from four-ounce rump £4.75); friendly service. Well kept Bass and Flowers IPA and Original on handpump; fruit machine in the public bar. It does look down to the estuary, though for a real view over the water you should try the seats down on the quiet shoreside terrace. They have a small car park. *(Recommended by Jon Wainwright, P J Bevan, Serena Hanson, B G Steele-Perkins)*

Heavitree (who no longer brew)   Licensees R G and D R Evans   Real ale   Meals and snacks (not Sun evenings)   Restaurant tel Topsham (039 287) 3653   Children in restaurant   Open 11–11 all year

If you stay overnight in an inn or hotel, they are allowed to serve you an alcoholic drink at any hour of the day or night.

TORBRYAN   SX8266 Map 1
Old Church House
Most easily reached from A381 Newton Abbot–Totnes via Ipplepen

The bar on your right as you go in is the pride of this white twelfth-century thatched pub, with benches built into Tudor panelling as well as the red plush cushioned high-backed settle and leather-backed small seats around its big log fire. On the left there is a series of comfortable and discreetly lit lounges, one with a splendid deep Tudor inglenook fireplace with a side bread oven; darts, dominoes and euchre; maybe piped music. But perhaps the most notable feature is the range of real ales – anything up to twenty or so, typically including Badger Best, Cotleigh Tawny and Old Buzzard, Flowers Original, Gibbs Mew Bishops Tipple, Golden Hill Exmoor Dark, Janners Bitter, Old Original and (carrying the name of the pub here) Devon Special, Marstons Merrie Monk, Pedigree and Owd Rodger, Palmers Tally Ho, Wadworths Farmers Glory and Wiltshire Weedkiller. Bar food includes sandwiches (from £1), ploughman's (£1.60), pies (£3.25), curries and various salads (from £3.25, with a very generous chicken one), and trout (£3.80). There's a hillock of lawn between the pub and the church (which has a notable 1430 carved screen). *(Recommended by Phil Gorton, Jon Wainwright, R H Inns, Gwen and Peter Andrews, P J Bevan)*

Free house   Real ale   Meals and snacks   Restaurant (evening) tel Ipplepen (0803) 812372   Children in restaurant and family-room   Open 11–2.30, 5.30–11 all year; opens 7 in winter

TORCROSS   SX8241 Map 1
Start Bay ★ ⊗
A379 S of Dartmouth

This relaxing fourteenth-century thatched seafront pub is very much a food place; readers continue to praise the unusually fresh and generous helpings of seafood, in particular the whitebait, plaice or haddock, with a medium–large helping at £2.90 and a jumbo – in fact gargantuan – one at £3.60; other food includes sandwiches (from 95p, fresh crab or prawn £2.10), home-made vegetarian lasagne (£2.50), gammon (£3.50), fish pie or scampi (£3.85), and a gigantic seafood platter heaped with prawns, shrimps, cockles, mussels and smoked mackerel (£5.20); children's helpings. In the carpeted main room there are wheel-back chairs around plenty of dark tables or (around a corner) back-to-back settles forming booths, country pictures and some brasses on its cream walls, a coal fire in winter; a small chatty drinking area by the counter has a brass ship's clock and barometer. There's more booth seating in a family-room with sailing-boat pictures, and a good games-room with pool, darts, shove-ha'penny, dominoes, cribbage, and two space games; well kept Whitbreads PA and a guest beer such as Flowers Original on handpump; fruit machine in the lobby, maybe piped music. Picnic-table sets on the terrace look out over the pebble beach, and the wildlife lagoon of Slapton Ley is just behind the pub. Though the sea wall cuts off much of the view from the pub, it seems worth it for the protection against the excesses of the sea it's suffered in the past – as some of the photographs on the walls testify. It tends to get very busy even out of season. *(Recommended by CED, Eileen Broadbent, Verney and Denis Baddeley, Brian and Anna Marsden, S V Bishop, Alan and Ruth Woodhouse, David and Ann Stranack, R R Veale)*

Heavitree (who no longer brew)   Licensee Paul Stubbs   Real ale   Meals and snacks Children in eating-room   Open 11–2.30, 6–11 all year; opens 11.30 in winter; closed 24 Dec; no food and open only 11.30–1.30 25 Dec

Children – if the details at the end of an entry don't mention them, you should assume that the pub does not allow them inside.

TOTNES   SX8060   Map 1

Kingsbridge

Leechwell Street; going up the old town's main one-way street, bear left into Leechwell Street
approaching the top

The new licensees here have made some changes – such as removing the bar and
serving-counter upstairs – but have maintained the charm that makes it popular
with readers. The little rambling rooms of the bar still have their individual appeal,
with broad stripped plank panelling, bare stone or black and white timbering, low
heavy beams in a dark ochre ceiling, and comfortable peach plush seats around
rustic tables on the dark carpet. There's an elaborately carved bench in one intimate
little alcove, a miniature waterfall and rockery in another, an antique water pump
and a log-effect gas fire; Burton Bridge and Courage Best on handpump. Bar food
includes home-baked filled rolls (from 75p), soup (95p), filled baked potatoes (from
£1.50), ploughman's (from £1.80), steak and kidney pie (£2.65), curry (£3) and
steaks (£6.25). It's Totnes' oldest pub, with parts of it dating from the ninth
century, and it gets a mention in the Domesday Book. *(Recommended by Ceri Jarr, SC,
Jon Wainwright, AE, Mrs Joan Harris, S V Bishop; more reports on the new regime please)*

*Free house   Licensees Timothy and Susan Langsford   Real ale   Meals and snacks   Children
in eating area and restaurant   Jazz various nights   Bedrooms planned, tel Totnes
(0803) 863324   Open 11.30–2.30, 6–11 all year*

UGBOROUGH   SX6755   Map 1

Anchor

On B3210; village signposted from Ivybridge (just off A38 E of Plymouth)

Set in an attractive village – unusual for its spacious central square – this well kept
pub serves good value, straightforward food such as sandwiches, ploughman's
(£1.75), basket meals (from £1.60), salads (from £3), gammon (£3.20), seafood
platter (£3.50) and steaks (from £5.95), with vegetarian dishes; good service. The
oak-beamed public bar has wall settles and seats around the wooden tables on the
polished wood-block floor, and a log fire in its stone fireplace. The comfortable
carpeted lounge has Windsor armchairs; well kept Bass and Wadworths 6X tapped
from the cask; darts, bar billiards, dominoes, fruit machine and piped music.
(Recommended by J S Evans, H E and J Hobbs, Jon Wainwright, Lynne Sheridan, Bob West)

*Free house   Licensee Mrs M M Baker   Real ale   Meals and snacks   Open 11–2.30,
5.30–11 all year*

WHIMPLE   SY0497   Map 1

New Fountain ⊗

Village signposted off A30 Exeter–Honiton

This pub has a remarkable dual personality. By day it's very much the simple village
pub, with bar food such as sandwiches (£1), soup (£1.15), ploughman's (from
£1.75), venison sausages (£2.95), lasagne (£3.50), steak and kidney pie (£3.95) and
eight-ounce Aberdeen Angus sirloin steak (£6.95); in the evenings (not Sunday) it
turns into a serious restaurant, serving starters such as deep-fried Brie (£2.50) and
game pâté (£2.70), and main courses such as freshly made tortellini (£5.20) and
duck and bacon pie or honey-roast poussin (£6.25). Some of the evening virtuosity
does spill over into the lunchtime specials and the interesting puddings (£1.50). We
inspected just a few weeks after the present licensee took over, and the other
customers' pleasure was clear. The atmosphere in the small carpeted lounge bar is
civilised and snug, with simple chairs around the sturdy wooden tables, fresh
flowers, a collection of Dickens cigarette cards from Players and a log-effect gas

fire. Besides well kept Devenish Royal Wessex on handpump, they keep an interesting range of wines; inoffensive piped music. There are some tables in the garden, where we found a couple of angora rabbits (the cats you may meet are Corky and Felix). *(Recommended by M E Dormer, David and Flo Wallington; more reports on the new regime please)*

Devenish   Licensee Patrick Jackson   Real ale   Meals and snacks (not Sun evening); booking advised Fri/Sat evenings, essential Sun lunch tel Whimple (0404) 822350   Open 11–2.30ish, 6–11 all year

WINKLEIGH SS6308 Map 1
Kings Arms

Off B3220, in village centre

This old-fashioned pub, on the edge of the village square, has an unspoilt beamed bar, with some old-fashioned built-in settles as well as scrubbed pine tables and benches on its flagstones, a big log fire in winter, and subdued lighting by little fringed wall lamps. It opens out on one side into an area with a neat row of more modern tables and booth seating. There are a couple of picnic-table sets under cocktail parasols in the small front courtyard, sheltered by large shrubs. The good food includes vegetable soup, crab pâté, steak and kidney pie and cold beef. Well kept Ushers Best on handpump, maybe piped music. It has a couple of large aquariums – an unusual feature. *(Recommended by J and A Thurston, Mrs Thompson, P G Spencer, David and Flo Wallington; more up-to-date reports on the food please)*

Free house   Meals (lunchtime, not Mon) and snacks (not Mon)   Restaurant Tues–Sat evenings, Sun lunch   Children in eating area   Open 11–2.30, 6–11 all year; has been closed Mon exc bank hols

WOODBURY SALTERTON SY0189 Map 1
Digger's Rest ★

3½ miles from M5 junction 30: A3052 towards Sidmouth, village signposted on right about ½ mile after Clyst St Mary; also signposted from B3179 SE of Exeter

Many years ago a wandering Australian came to roost as landlord of this friendly thatched Tudor pub – hence the name. They serve good value bar food, including home-made soup (95p), sandwiches (local crab £1.45), ploughman's (from £1.80, hot turkey pie or home-cooked gammon (£2.90), salads (from £3.95) and a daily special (around £2.80); puddings (around £1.10); friendly service. The carpeted main bar has comfortable old-fashioned country chairs and settles around polished antique tables under its heavy black oak beams, a grandfather clock, plates decorating the walls of one alcove, a log fire at one end, and an ornate solid-fuel stove at the other. Well kept Bass, Flowers IPA and a guest beer pulled by ancient and unusual handpumps, and farmhouse cider; sensibly placed darts, and dominoes, in the small brick-walled public bar. The terrace garden has views of the countryside. Families are well catered for in a room at the end of the bar behind a fine dark oak Jacobean screen, and there's a big skittles and games-room. *(Recommended by Pamela and Merlyn Horswell, B G Steele-Perkins; more reports please)*

Free house   Licensee Sally Pratt   Real ale   Meals and snacks   Children in family-room Open 11–2.30, 6.30–11

Lucky Dip

Besides the fully inspected pubs, you might like to try these Lucky Dips recommended to us and described by readers (if you do, please send us reports):

☆ **Alswear** [A373 South Molton–Tiverton; SS7222], *Butchers Arms*: Impressive clean simplicity; uncluttered public bar has exposed stone walls, flagstones, beams and brasses, chiming grandmother clock, huge log fire in inglenook, fruit machine and sensibly placed darts; plusher cosy lounge with another log fire; pool-room with juke box and fruit machine, skittle alley, small restaurant; bar food including generously filled lean ham sandwiches and hot dishes, friendly service, local atmosphere, well kept Bass and Flowers on handpump; bedrooms *(Steve and Carolyn Harvey, M J Lovett)*

☆ **Ashprington** [Bow Bridge (towards Tuckenhay), OS Sheet 202 reference 819571; SX8156], *Watermans Arms*: Efficient new management in idyllically placed pub with waterside tables over the road; high-backed settles in flagstoned front area, comfortable oak-beamed part behind, bar food and restaurant (used also for family bar lunches); good farm cider but beer is keg *(Ken and Barbara Turner, Tom Evans, David and Flo Wallington, Jon Wainwright, S V Bishop, Pamela and Merlyn Horswell, LYM)*

Avonwick [B3210 ½ mile from A38; SX7157], *Mill*: Attractive free house with huge helpings of popular straightforward food, friendly service, delightful surroundings – peacocks outside, and children's area (it's a shame they've filled in the moat); Bass on handpump *(C G Thompson, PEG, J S Evans)*

Axmouth [SY2591], *Ship*: Attractive garden (a sort of convalescent home for owls and other birds from Newbury Wildlife Hospital); warm and comfortable inside, with log fires, pleasant service, Devenish real ales and local cider, bar meals, evening buttery bar concentrating on fish *(J E Bland, Mrs A Roberts, LYM)*

Aylesbeare [A3052 Exeter–Sidmouth, junction with B3180; SY0392], *Halfway Inn*: Very friendly with good, quickly served bar snacks and restaurant area; marvellous views westwards *(Michael Thomson)*

Barnstaple [off High St, S end; SS5533], *Golden Lion*: Dark rambling place with many relics of yesteryear, serving smart food; worth knowing if you're in the area *(David and Flo Wallington)*; [The Strand; centre, opp bus stn] *Inn on the Strand*: Useful for lunch – good helpings, quick efficient service, reasonable prices; Flowers real ale, raised platform decked out as an old library, piped music *(Steve and Carolyn Harvey)*; *Tavern in the Town*: An olde-worlde conversion, well done with old iron ranges and prison doors on the loos; useful and comfortable meeting-place, with Whitbreads real ales

(David and Flo Wallington); *Three Tuns*: Its claim to fame (and reason for inclusion) is that it's the oldest pub in the oldest road in the oldest borough in Britain *(Anon)*

Belstone [SX6293], *Tors*: Enjoyable country pub on Dartmoor edge; good food, local atmosphere *(H and P B)*

Bickington [SX7972], *Dartmoor Half Way*: Warm welcome, good Flowers, wide range of bar food *(J S Evans)*

Bickington [SS5332], *Old Barn*: Good atmosphere, clean and efficient, good value bar meals *(David Gaunt)*

☆ **Bickleigh** [A396, N of junction with A3072; SS9407], *Trout*: Comfortable and individual furnishings in remarkably spacious dining lounge with wide choice from efficient food counter, including good help-yourself salads; well kept Bass and Courage Directors, restaurant, tables on pretty lawn, provision for children; under promising new management from late 1987, bedrooms being equipped with own bathrooms *(Mrs Anne Fowler, PHF, Verney and Denis Baddeley, P Bromley, C Parry, LYM)*

nr **Bigbury** [St Ann's Chapel – B3392 just inland; SX6544], *Pickwick*: Main bar with traditionally rustic feel, pool, real ales such as Bass and Flowers, usual bar food, big newish family extension, restaurant; mixed reports since change of management a year or so ago, more news please *(Mr and Mrs J C Dwane, Jon Wainwright, John Drummond, Mr and Mrs G J Lewis, Ian and Daphne Brownlie, R J Whitney, LYM)*

Bishops Tawton [A377 S of Barnstaple; SS5630], *Chichester Arms*: Clean, comfortable and homely thatched village pub; Ushers ales and good range of food *(K R Harris)*

Blackawton [SX8050], *Normandy Arms*: Free house with plenty of character in pretty village; traditional décor, Second World War memorabilia (this was where they practised for D-Day), real fire, well kept Blackawton ales, outstanding bar food and separate restaurant featuring local seafood; bedrooms *(Allan Wright)*

Bovey Tracey [SX8278], *King of Prussia*: Good old-fashioned English pub with very friendly landlady, excellent Bass; lounge and public bar *(Charlie Salt)*

Bow [SS7201], *Kings Arms*: Interesting historic building, friendly and enthusiastic licensee; good farm cider, darts, pool *(Kay and William Waggoner)*

Brandis Corner [A3072 Hatherleigh–Holsworthy; SS4103], *Bickford Arms*: Good well run pub with reasonably priced good food, choice of real ales, friendly staff; garden behind *(Keith Houlgate, Derek Godfrey-Brown)*

Branscombe [SY1988], *Fountainhead*: Fourteenth-century flagstoned country pub on approach to picturesque thatched village, two bars, friendly licensee, well kept Badger, good value bar food including local seafood, children's room *(E G Parish)*; [A3052] *Three Horseshoes*: Wide choice of good food, good service, family-room and play area for children; bedrooms very clean, reasonably priced *(Denise Saunders)*

Braunton [A361; SS4836], *Agricultural*: Big roadside pub known as the Aggi, with leather sofa and armchairs making series of small intimate areas in comfortable beamed lounge, open fire, farm tools, pots, jugs and prints; good value food quickly prepared, generous helpings, Bass, staff jolly even under pressure; largely popular with young people, skittle alley *(Steve and Carolyn Harvey, Chris Fluck)*; [South St] *Mariners Arms*: Decent pub with good food (including excellent chips), shove-ha'penny, open coal fires, own football team *(Steve and Carolyn Harvey)*; *New Inn*: Small pub in pretty part of village with helpful service, well kept Ushers and good bar food *(Chris Fluck)*

Brendon [OS Sheet 180 reference 767482; SS7748], *Staghunters Arms*: Glorious spot with riverside garden; Golden Hill Exmoor and bar food in hotel bar, restaurant; surrounded by NT land *(Lynne Sheridan, Bob West)*

Bridestowe [A386 Okehampton–Tavistock; SX5189], *Fox & Hounds*: Simple red leatherette bar in roadside Dartmoor pub, open fires, good value food, games-room, skittle alley; children and animals welcome; bedrooms good value *(Mr and Mrs C F J Aburrow, Christine and Kevin Shults, BB)*

Brixham [OS Sheet 202 reference 904564; SX9255], *Churston Court*: Good food in bar, including well filled good sandwiches – except Sat and Sun lunchtimes when it's too busy; bedrooms *(Peter Lanceley)*

Broadclyst [SX9897], *New Inn*: Especially good bar food such as chicken and mushroom pancakes served with tomato stuffed with Stilton and garlic *(J D Acland)*

☆ **Broadhembury** [ST1004], *Drewe Arms*: Unpretentious fifteenth-century village inn separated from the quiet village's church (and its sonorous clock) by a flower-filled lawn; well kept Bass, simple food, basic bedrooms, friendly local atmosphere *(D I Baddeley, Mrs Pamela Roper, K R Harris, WFL, LYM)*

Buckfast [SX7467], *Black Rock*: Good real ale and home-cooked food served by obliging staff in small but friendly hotel bar with pleasant terrace overlooking the River Dart; afternoon cream teas, Halls Harvest, children welcome in dining area, companionable dalmatian and Jack Russell; bedrooms *(N F Calver, Brian and Anna Marsden)*

Buckfastleigh [SX7366], *Dartbridge*: Excellent family facilities, indoors and out,

and has had good food and resident harpist; opposite Dart Valley Rly and not far from abbey, so gets very popular in summer; ten letting chalets, swimming-pool; being sold summer 1988 *(Rodney Coe)*

☆ **Buckland Monachorum** [SX4868], *Drakes Manor*: Lovely well kept and cosy old country pub with well kept Courage ales, good cider, simple but tasty home-cooked food at attractive prices, open fire, friendly staff, efficient service; plain public bar with friendly locals and juke box, homely traditional lounge bar, restaurant with good value Sun roast; very handy for the lovely nearby Garden House *(P and H B, Helen Crookston, Jutta Brigitta Whitley)*

Budleigh Salterton [Chapel St; SY0682], *Salterton Arms*: Well kept comfortable L-shaped bar with upper gallery (where children allowed), wide choice of food including marvellous crab sandwiches, quick friendly service, real ales *(Jim Matthews)*

Burlescombe [A38 some way E of village turning; ST0716], *Poachers Pocket*: Simple food in quiet and comfortably modernised lounge bar of well kept inn, handy for M5 junction 27, with children's dishes, well kept Ushers Best, restaurant, skittle alley *(Alan Carr, LYM)*

Chagford [Mill St; SX7087], *Bullers Arms*: Old-fashioned local atmosphere, good value simple food in unpretentious pub with three changing real ales, log fires, a collection of militaria and summer barbecues *(Harry Jackson, LYM)*

☆ **Challacombe** [OS Sheet 180 reference 695411; SS6941], *Black Venus*: Under same ownership as Pyne Arms, East Down (see main entry); broadly similar food, layout and atmosphere; darts, pool and juke box in side room, Flowers IPA and Original; bedrooms *(Steve and Carolyn Harvey)*

Chardstock [off A358 Chard–Axminster; ST3004], *George*: Superb country free house with plenty of olde-worlde charm, very good Sam Whitbreads and piped music mainly jazz; outside servery for small well kept garden; restaurant *(Ted George)*

Cheriton Bishop [SX7793], *Sir John Devenish*: New licensees have divided the bar into two, added a children's room, replaced the pool-table with bar billiards, and are now serving excellent food including a good value Sun lunch; well kept Boddingtons, Exe Valley, Marstons Pedigree and Wadworths real ales, decent house wines *(CS)*

Cheriton Fitzpaine [The Hayes; SS8706], *Ring of Bells*: Fourteenth-century thatched country pub with open log fires in winter, old oak settles, well kept real ales, good choice of bar food, small restaurant; comfortable well equipped bedrooms and self-catering holiday flat *(Simon Boulter)*

☆ **Christow** [Village Rd; SX8385], *Artichoke*: Thatched village local with flagstone floors and log fire in simple unspoilt interior, well kept real ale, good home-cooked food, fruit machine; bedrooms comfortable *(Alan Robertson, Charlie Salt)*

Chudleigh [B3344, off A38; SX8679], *Highwaymans Haunt*: Popular carvery for evening and Sun lunch (subject to seasonal change), bar snacks at other times, courteous cheerful staff, comfortable restaurant; no children under seven *(K Peet)*

Chudleigh Knighton [SX8477], *Clay Cutters Arms*: Big helpings of simple food in thatched village local with big log fires in winter, Flowers IPA and Huntsman Royal Oak, popular games area, seats on side terrace and in orchard; basic but warm bedrooms *(St John Sandringham, LYM)*

Chulmleigh [South Molton Rd; SS6814], *Fortescue Arms*: Home-made food including local fish and game in season (service may not be the briskest), in fishing inn with simple, pleasant bar, well kept Bass, dining-room; bedrooms *(BB)*

Churston Ferrers [SX9056], *Churston Court*: Atmosphere, good wide range of food cooked only when ordered (which compensates for slow service) *(Verney and Denis Baddeley)*

Clayhidon [ST1615], *Harriers*: Friendly pub, good range of local real ales, good bar food, large garden; in good area for picnics and walks *(K R Harris)*

Clyst Hydon [B3176, not far from M5 junction 28; ST0301], *Five Bells*: Very friendly atmosphere in secluded pub with good bar lunches and restaurant, good service, well kept Badger and (particularly) Bass *(E G Parish, D T Taylor)*

Clyst St Mary [Sidmouth Rd; SX9790], *Cat & Fiddle*: Wide variety of attractively priced hot and cold food including cheap well served curry, good service, comfortable lounge eating area; children in play room *(Denise Saunders, DMF)*

Coffinswell [SX8968], *Linhay*: Excellent Devon longhouse with first-class food in bar and restaurant *(GHM)*

Combe Martin [SS5847], *Dolphin*: Large cosy front lounge bar overlooking bay, with big lanterns and ships' wheels on walls; excellent value food including children's dishes, served quickly by pleasant staff; space games and pool in back room *(Derek and Jennifer Taylor)*; *Old Sawmill*: Pleasant outlook to stream, small bar with well kept Exmoor ale, good though not cheap bar food in generous helpings, restaurant *(Steve and Carolyn Harvey)*

☆ **Cornworthy** [SX8255], *Hunters Lodge*: Largely bypassed by tourists, this genuine old village local serves an astonishing range of really good interesting food including their own delicious home-made Dart salmon gravadlax; sweet-and-sour duck, stir-fried prawns and chicken, grilled plaice and mussels and prawns with garlic are also

recommended, and vegetables and salads are excellent; friendly Alsatian (and staff), comfortable furnishings, well kept Ushers Best and Ruddles County on handpump *(S V Bishop, Brian and Anna Marsden)*

Crediton [High St; SS8300], *Swan*: Jolly market-town pub, good beers, extensive lunchtime and evening menus, skittle alley; has won a breakfast-of-the-year award *(Charlie Salt)*; [High St] *White Swan*: Very friendly and amusing staff, warm atmosphere, delicious Sun traditional meals with excellent beef – very popular locally so must book *(Kay and William Waggoner)*

☆ **Croyde** [SS4439], *Whiteleaf*: Not a pub but a guest house – included here because it's where readers have been glad to track down the Wallingtons, who previously made the Rhydspence at Whitney on Wye (Hereford & Worcester) outstandingly popular for civilised character and interesting food, using prime ingredients; they're doing the same sort of thing here – a place to go if you want to be pampered for a few days, comfortable and well fed, with all fresh food and a good wine list; dogs accepted *(Mike Ledger, Sue Cleasby, Miss J A Harvey)*

Croyde [SS4439], *Manor*: New licensees are serving a wider range of food than before in this friendly local, popular with families in summer – well kept Flowers, bar billiards, darts, shove-ha'penny, skittles and nice terraced garden *(David and Flo Wallington)*; *Thatched Barn*: Extended thatched inn near fine surfing beach, interesting original features still to be found in rambling largely modernised bar, well kept Courage ales, largely home-made bar food including local fish and good puddings, provision for children, morning coffee served from 10am, restaurant *(Dr and Mrs B D Smith, J Pearson, Liz and Ian, LYM)*

☆ **Dalwood** [a mile N of A35 Axminster–Honiton; ST2400], *Tuckers Arms*: Seventeenth-century thatched pub in quiet village with a typical 'village local' flagstoned bar floor, inglenook fireplace with bread ovens and a nicely furnished lounge; well kept real ales including Courage Best and Directors and Marstons Pedigree, good food especially steaks and Sun lunches, singalongs *(W L B Reed, Ted George)*

☆ **Dartmouth** [Smith St – up hill off Fairfax Pl, which leads off corner of inner harbour; SX8751], *Seven Stars*: Good atmosphere in long black-beamed oak-panelled bar with leatherette settles around rustic elm tables, well kept Courage Best and Directors, piped pop music and fruit machine; upstairs restaurant, children's room, efficiently served and well priced popular food; bedrooms *(David and Ann Stranack, Paul and Margaret Baker, Jon Wainwright, John and Alison Logan, J S Evans, D N and K A Jones, BB)*

Dartmouth [Sandquay], *Floating Bridge*: Lovely view of harbour and steam railway from big windows of friendly pub with generous helpings of good value food (good choice), well kept Ushers, pleasant, airy atmosphere, efficient service; children in family-room *(Jon Wainwright, Pat and Lee Crosby)*; [Mayors Ave] *George & Dragon*: Cosy pub with naval theme and young licensees; Bass and Flowers Original, bar snacks and meals, children – and fishing parties – catered for; comfortable well equipped bedrooms *(Leslie Campbell)*; [Henborough Post; B3207 3 miles outside] *Sportsmans Arms*: Recently extended, with pleasant atmosphere, imaginative and extensive bar menu, well kept Bass *(Dr and Mrs D N Jones)*

Dawlish [Beach St; SX9676], *Exeter*: Tucked away down small alley near railway station, lively local, long and narrow with well kept Huntsman Royal Oak and various local ciders *(Jon Wainwright)*; [Strand] *Prince Albert*: Good, warm, friendly local serving well kept Bass and Flowers IPA; locally known as Hole in the Wall *(Jon Wainwright)*

Denbury [SX8268], *Union*: Good, clean, welcoming village pub with well kept Flowers and Whitbreads, excellent value home-cooked food including unusual puddings; recently refurbished to show the fifteenth-century granite masonry, extending the bar and dining area; live folk and pop music twice a week, piano player on Sat; big garden *(J Rachkind, Mrs S Higgins, W H Anderson)*

Devonport [main rd; SX4555], *Brown Bear*: Excellent food, with home-made pies, chilli con carne and so forth at lunchtime, steaks and three-course meals in the evening; Courage real ale *(Charles Gurney)*

Dittisham [The Level; SX8654], *Red Lion*: Pleasant village local overlooking Dart, good bar food (especially steak sandwich, local salmon and sticky puddings), well kept Bass and Ushers or maybe Plympton Pride; two comfortable bedrooms *(Jon Wainwright, AE, Tony Forbes-Leith, Ilka Nosworthy)*

Dog Village [B3185; SX9896], *Hungry Fox*: Large, efficiently run mock-Tudor pub with friendly service, Flowers beer, reasonable value wine, good choice of simple food, big log-effect gas fire *(Theo Schofield)*

Dolton [SS5712], *Union*: Comfortable lounge bar with log fire and beautiful mahogany bar front; public bar with darts, music and fruit machine, pool-room; has been immaculate, with well kept Exe Vale and Ushers, and good steaks in the evening – but up for sale spring 1988 *(Anon)*

☆ **Drewsteignton** [Fingle Bridge – OS Sheet 191 reference 743899; SX7390], *Anglers Rest*: Sprucely airy and spacious bar in outstanding scenery – picturesque wooded valley by sixteenth-century packhorse bridge; reliable pub food, well kept John Smiths and Wadworths 6X, brisk summer business in tourist souvenirs; winter opening times more restricted; lots of good walks nearby, including GWG19 *(Prof and Mrs Keith Patchett, Verney and Denis Baddeley, LYM)*

Dunsford [OS Sheet 191 reference 813891; SX8189], *Royal Oak*: Good value bar food including choice of vegetarian dishes in light and airy lounge bar of village inn, well kept Ushers real ales, games in public bar, small restaurant, provision for children, Fri barbecues on terrace, pretty walks along the River Teign, down the lane; good value bedrooms *(M E Walters, LYM)*

East Budleigh [SY0684], *Sir Walter Raleigh*: Beautiful thatched Devon pub, pleasant licensee, friendly atmosphere, very clean, reasonable bar snacks *(E G Parish, AE)*

East Prawle [SX7836], *Pigs Nose*: Very cheerful welcome, good beers, open fire and better-than-average pub food in Devon's most southerly pub, with an interesting 'piggy' theme; new licensees 1987; nr start GWG12, in nice village setting off lovely stretch of Devon Coast Path; family-room *(Sue Cleasby, Mike Ledger, Dr Nicola Hall, D Pearman)*

Ermington [SX6353], *Crooked Spire*: Attractive, clean and well organised pub in well kept village; good if somewhat pricey food *(E L Lawson)*

Exbourne [SX6002], *Red Lion*: Good friendly pub with original furniture, no plastic beams, very good West Country beer; pleasant surroundings in small village, a nice place to stay at *(V and D Sage)*

Exeter [59 Magdalen St, opposite eye hospital; SX9292], *Milestone*: Said to be Britain's first no-alcohol pub, a cellar bar furnished as a pub, with pub food and amusements including darts and pool, alcohol-free beers and wines as well as soft drinks, frequent live music *(Steve Harvey)*; [The Quay] *Prospect*: Originally two seventeenth-century cottages, adjoining Maritime Museum by waterside and used in filming the *Onedin Line* TV series; frequent evening live music *(JO)*; [St Martin's Lane] *Ship*: Photogenic fourteenth-century pub just off Cathedral Close, with well kept Bass, Flowers IPA and Original and Sam Whitbreads on handpump, fish including good Torbay sole, slick service *(Pamela and Merlyn Horswell, LYM)*; [High St North] *Turks Head*: City-centre Beefeater pub, long two-level modernised lounge bar with bookshelves, polite staff, Flowers Original on handpump, wide choice of bar food, restaurant *(E G Parish)*; [The Close] *Well House*: Haven of peace on busy shopping expeditions, in tasteful premises in Cathedral Close; good Exe Valley beer, pleasant restful atmosphere *(R H Inns)*

Exminster [SX9487], *Stowey Arms*: Good English food from the couple who formerly did so well at the Anchor in Cockwood, including seafood from Exe estuary; cooking all fresh, so not quick; real ale *(Anon)*

Filleigh [just off A361 Barnstaple–South

Molton; SS6627], *Stags Head*: Sixteenth-century thatched pub by lake, single heavy-beamed bar with one side devoted to generous helpings of notable bar food, often unusual; old-fashioned furnishings, efficient service, Bass and Websters Yorkshire, picnic-table sets outside; good value bedrooms *(Steve and Carolyn Harvey)*

Folly Gate [A386 Hatherleigh–Okehampton; SX5797], *Crossways*: Good reasonably priced food, friendly staff and atmosphere, well kept real ale *(Keith Houlgate)*

Fremington [SS5132], *New Inn*: Good value tasty food *(John Naylor)*

Galmpton [Maypool – off A3022 at Greenway Quay signpost, then bear left to Maypool; SX8856], *Lost & Found*: Not strictly a pub (drinks served only if you eat) but well worth knowing for its idyllic setting overlooking Torbay Steam Railway, and its fine food including superb sandwiches and seafood; Flowers real ale, restaurant with dining terrace; comfortable bedrooms *(Pamela and Merlyn Horswell, S V Bishop, A J Triggle)*; [OS Sheet 202 reference 889563] *Manor*: Friendly local with excellent food, especially fish from Brixham; neatly and attractively presented at reasonable prices; spacious new restaurant area *(Verney and Denis Baddeley, Liz and Ian)*; [Churston Bridge, Dartmouth Rd] *Weary Ploughman*: Food and beer of high standard, beautiful carvings of large scenes in both main rooms of bar; bedrooms excellent *(D Clarke)*

Georgeham [Rock Hill, above village – OS Sheet 180 reference 466399; SS4639], *Rock*: Simple basic family-run local with well kept Ushers Best, good choice of reasonably priced food including steaks, low beams, partly pine-panelled walls, old photographs of pub and village; old brass milk churns made into bar stools; separate dining-room; fruit machine, piped music, garden *(Steve and Carolyn Harvey)*

☆ **Great Torrington** [The Square; SS4919], *Black Horse*: Interesting heavily beamed fifteenth-century inn with solid furniture and Civil War connections; attractive and well run; good atmosphere, friendly staff, well kept Ushers Best; generously served well cooked good value bar food, panelled dining-room; comfortable bedrooms *(K R Harris, D J Wallington, Miss J Metherell, A R Gale, L J Nichol)*

☆ **Harberton** [SX7758], *Church House*: Ancient pub in attractive steep village, with antique furnishings including lots of settles, flagstones, medieval oak panelling and beams; promising reports since sale early 1988 of warm welcome, good friendly service, good value food and well kept Courage Best and Directors; family-room *(K Peet, Jon Wainwright, LYM)*

Hartland Quay [SS2522], *Hartland Quay*: Very simple but warmly welcoming, with good cider, very reasonable bar snacks *(Anon)*

☆ **Hatherleigh** [Market St; SS5404], *Tally Ho*: Decorative plates on walls, log fires, friendly welcoming atmosphere, Huntsman Royal Oak, IPA and Dorchester and Wadworths 6X real ales, good meals in bar and dining-room extension; the courteous and attentive Italian owners make sure there's a good choice of Italian wines; children welcome, pleasant garden; three cosy Laura Ashley-esque bedrooms with own bathrooms *(Juliet Streatfield, Neil Evans, Verney and Denis Baddeley, Mrs Pamela Roper, Mrs M Charlton)*

Haytor Vale [SX7677], *Moorlands*: Excellent friendly Agatha Christie bar, beautiful dining-room overlooking south-facing gardens and extensive views beyond; opposite open moor and path to Haytor; good food, comfortable bedrooms *(Philip and Trisha Ferris)*

Hemborough Post [SX8352], *Sportsmans Arms*: Pleasant, welcoming stop *(Jon Wainwright)*

Hemyock [ST1313], *Catherine Wheel*: Pleasantly appointed, with wide choice of good food *(Mrs Shirley Pielou)*

Hennock [SX8380], *Palk Arms*: Gorgeous views over Teign valley from picture-window lounge with good value and comprehensive salad buffet, other bar food, well kept Ushers, cosy front bar with fishing talk, seats on lawn, provision for children; bedrooms *(LYM)*

Hexworthy [village signposted off B3357 Tavistock–Ashburton, 3¾ miles E of B3212; SX6572], *Forest*: Extensive knocked-together lounge with separate quite distinctively furnished seating areas, walkers' bar, sheltered tables outside; children welcome, restaurant; previously praised for attractively priced Bass, straightforward food and good value simple bedrooms, but since late 1987 reports have been very mixed; main attraction is undoubtedly the location, isolated in the middle of Dartmoor, with fishing available on the Dart; nr GWG17 *(LYM)*

Holbeton [Fore St; SX6150], *Dartmoor Union*: Traditional village pub, tastefully modernised, excellent fresh fish delivered daily from Plymouth and other home-cooked dishes *(J J Hansen)*

Honiton [Fenny Bridges (A30); SY1198], *Greyhound*: Big thatched Chef & Brewer roadhouse, droves of red plush dining-chairs and banquettes in its heavily beamed rambling bar, and a deliberately old-fashioned style; quickly served food, separate carvery with generous helpings, Ushers on handpump, comfortable well equipped games-room, big garden; bedrooms *(Dr D M Forsyth, Patrick Young, LYM)*

Hope Cove [SX6640], *Hope & Anchor*: Simple welcoming seaside local, good open fire, straightforward filling food and cheap bedrooms *(Leslie Dawes, Liz and Ian, P A*

King-Fisher, LYM); *Lobster Pot*: Recently transformed under new regime of local coast-guard family; pleasant, comfortable atmosphere, good cheap food *(W M Sharpe)*

Horns Cross [A39 Clovelly–Bideford – OS Sheet 190 reference 385233; SS3823], *Hoops*: Ancient thatched inn, neatly kept and popular with older people, with home-made bar food, Flowers IPA and Original, logs burning in big inglenook fireplaces of oak-beamed main bar; neatly refurbished to cope with many diners; bedrooms *(Wayne Brindle, Shirley Allen, Mr and Mrs J M Elden, LYM)*

Horrabridge [SX5169], *Leaping Salmon*: Good lunchtime food attractively served in generous helpings – and they keep Mild ale *(C G Thompson)*

☆ **Iddesleigh** [SS5708], *Duke of York*: Rough pine tables and benches in flagstoned bar of rambling thatched village pub dating from thirteenth century; pleasant fire in inglenook (newly chopped wood stacked outside), well kept Bass, new licensees from spring 1988 doing promising food with interesting Italian and Greek influences *(David and Flo Wallington)*

Ilfracombe [Broad St (by harbour); SS5147], *Royal Britannia*: Well placed above the harbour, in the quaint part of town; warm atmosphere in clean and comfortable lounge, tub chairs around copper tables, hunting prints on dark panelling; well kept Courage, several cocktails, friendly staff, bar food including fresh local fish and home-made cottage pie; tables on terrace; bedrooms *(D J Wallington, Michael and Alison Sandy)*

Instow [SS4730], *Quay*: Generous single-bar waterfront pub looking up Torridge estuary to Bideford, well kept Flowers Original and a guest such as Fullers, good freshly caught plaice and generous helpings of other good simple bar food including wide range of home-made pizzas *(Hugh Butterworth, Richard Fawcett)*

Ipplepen [Poplar Ter; SX8366], *Plough*: Lively, friendly village local with interesting photographs, modernised building, well kept Halls Harvest on handpump *(Jon Wainwright)*

Ivybridge [Western Rd; SX6356], *Imperial*: Courage Best and Directors, excellent bar food at reasonable prices including steak, seafood and a fine curry with poppadums and side dishes; small but busy (it tends to get crowded), friendly staff, garden behind; children welcome *(R J Whitney, Peter and Sue Darling)*

Kenn [not far off A38; SX9285], *Ley Arms*: Dark, cosy old pub in quiet, attractive village; more modern eating area with carvery and good choice of reasonably priced hot and cold food, friendly efficient service *(WAG, Mrs Joan Harris)*

Kennford [off A38 – if coming from Plymouth, turn off at top of Haldon Hill; SX9186], *Anchor*: Mock-Tudor-faced main-road pub of character, which has been well run, with a good choice of bar food and of drinks; but being sold summer 1988 *(More news please)*

Kentisbeare [ST0608], *Wyndham Arms*: Comfortable pub with welcoming new landlord since 1987, doing good beer and food *(David Gaunt)*

Kilmington [A35; SY2797], *Old Inn*: Friendly and welcoming thatched inn with character bar, comfortable inglenook lounge, good value food in bar and restaurant, traditional games and skittle alley, tables in good garden with children's play area, seats outside *(David Gaunt, Peter Gray, Mrs A Roberts, R D Jolliff, LYM)*

Kings Nympton [SS6819], *Grove*: Simple village inn with cream teas, bar food, Tues fish-and-chips night, well kept Ushers Best and Founders, lots of games and skittle alley; provision for children *(LYM)*

Kingsbridge [edge of town; SX7344], *Crabshell*: Delightful riverside position, very good value ploughman's *(R J Whitney, David and Ann Stranack)*; [Fore St] *Kings Arms*: Very friendly much-modernised coaching-inn (it even has a little swimming-pool), popular food, decent wines, good service; bedrooms big and comfortable *(Pat and Lee Crosby)*

Kingskerswell [SX8767], *Hare & Hounds*: Whitbreads pub extended to house a carvery and dining-room; good wide menu; it's geared mainly to food and gets busy – best to book *(M P Hallewell)*

Kingsteignton [below A38; SX8773], *Passage House*: On a creek of the River Teign, this friendly pub has a two-tiered bar with a relaxed atmosphere and lots of comfortable chairs; food pricey in restaurant *(M P Hallewell)*

Landscove [OS Sheet 202 reference 778661; SX7766], *Live & Let Live*: Unassuming village pub with homely open-plan bar, popular food, well kept Courage Best and Flowers IPA, country wines, tables in small orchard *(P and K McAteer, LYM)*

Lapford [SS7308], *Maltscoop*: Very friendly local with kitchen bar full of character, comfortable lounge bar and good plain food *(RH)*

Lee [SS4846], *Grampus*: Attractive four-teenth-century pub with nice quiet garden, just a stroll up through the village from the sea *(Sue Cleasby, William Ledger, LYM)*

Lifton [SX3885], *Arundell Arms*: Comfortable fishing hotel with 20 miles on the Tamar and its tributaries – can also arrange shooting, deer-stalking and riding; rich but not too up-market décor; very good cold buffet in hotel bar and exceptional English cooking for evening restaurant meals, especially fish, meats and elaborate puddings; bedrooms *(Patrick Young, William Richards)*

Littleham [SS4323], *Crealock Arms*: Well kept modern pub with good, friendly service and wide choice of bar food

(Anon of Colchester)
Littlehempston [A381; SX8162], *Pig & Whistle*: Comfortable and attractive old pub with wide range of bar food, friendly service and Bass and Wadworths 6X and Farmers Glory on handpump *(J Walsh, Mr Edwicker)*

Lower Ashton [SX8484], *Manor*: Austere but homely Teign Valley village pub with open fires, friendly dog and shove-ha'penny; Bass and good home-cooked food, reasonably priced *(Charlie Salt)*

Luppitt [OS Sheet 192 reference 169067; ST1606], *Luppitt Inn*: Two rooms in farmhouse, by the kitchen – one quite cosy, the other a spartan games-room; real ale tapped from the cask; lavatories across farmyard *(Phil Gorton, MM)*

Lustleigh [SX7881], *White Hart*: Large friendly thatched pub in pretty village, with good food *(P Baguley)*

Lynmouth [SS7249], *Rock House*: Small, cosy hotel bar open to non-residents with lots of nautical memorabilia; friendly, efficient bar staff and good choice of standard bar food; piped music; bedrooms *(Wilfred Plater-Shellard)*

Lynton [North Walk; SS7149], *Lynton Cottage*: Not really a true pub, more of a hotel, but nice and plushly comfortable inside, and terrace with magnificent view of coast; limited choice of acceptable bar food; bedrooms *(Wilfred Plater-Shellard)*

☆ *nr* **Lynton** [Martinhoe, towards Heddon's Mouth – OS Sheet 180 reference 654482], *Hunters Inn*: Well kept Exmoor Vale and Huntsman Dorset beer, bar meals (rather than snacks) including good help-yourself salads, cheery service even when busy; peacocks in garden; at start of GWG21 *(Mrs Jenny Seller, Lynne Sheridan, Bob West)*

☆ *nr* **Lynton** [Rockford, towards Brendon – OS Sheet 180 reference 755477], *Rockford Inn*: Attractive old inn in the heart of Doone country, with lovely Exmoor walks and scenery; very friendly, good service, particularly good beer and traditional country cooking by the owners who took over in 1987; nearly two miles of fishing on the River Exe, handy for the Watersmeet and Glenthorn fisheries; on GWG22; six comfortable bedrooms *(Mr and Mrs J R Aylmer)*

Manaton [SX7581], *Kestor*: Gorgeous spot, spacious and pleasant bar, sun lounge, varied bar food, garden with tables and chairs; children welcome *(Mrs Shirley Pielou)*

Mary Tavy [A386; SX5079], *Mary Tavy*: Free house with genial licensee and friendly atmosphere, good bar food including help-yourself buffet, good choice of beer including Bass and St Austell HSD; open-plan lounge bar free from juke box and fruit machines, restaurant, children's room with video *(R C Vincent, N F Calver)*

Meavy [SX5467], *Royal Oak*: Friendly local, uniquely owned by the parish – attractive

spot on green of Dartmoor village, comfortable L-shaped main bar with rustic tables, smaller attractively traditional public bar, simple food served cheerfully, Bass and Ushers Best on handpump; popular with walkers *(W M Sharpe, Simon Turner, LYM)*

Merrivale [SX5475], *Dartmoor Inn*: Good fire in heavy-beamed bar, Courage Best and Directors and Wadworths 6X on handpump, efficient service, maybe open early morning for coffee; at start of GWG15 *(Margaret and Trevor Errington)*

Molland [SS8028], *London Inn*: Long white pub by church on edge of Exmoor, in the same family for ages; specialist appeal to connoisseurs of the unspoilt who prefer their pubs almost literally redolent of age – interesting pictures, but little light to see them by other than from the roaring log fire; flagstones, basic country furniture, small pretty garden *(JRP, Steve and Carolyn Harvey)*

☆ **Monkton** [A30 NE of Honiton; ST1803], *Monkton Court*: Imposing stone house, handy for the trunk road, with extensive beamed main bar, snug little inner bar (not always open), usual bar food, restaurant, Courage real ales, games-room; provision for children, spacious relaxing garden *(S A and P J Barrett, LYM)*

☆ **Muddiford** [SS5638], *Muddiford Inn*: Cosy sixteenth-century village pub with log fire, darts, bar billiards, fruit machine and space game in low-beamed main bar, separate food counter in back dining-bar, Ushers tapped from the cask, very friendly cheerful service, unhurried congenial atmosphere; restaurant, picnic-table sets on small terrace, children's play area *(Steve and Carolyn Harvey, Prof and Mrs Keith Patchett)*

Newton Abbot [East St; SX8671], *Olde Cider Bar*: Only pub in Devon licensed solely for the sale of cider; choice of farmhouse ciders from 40-gallon wooden barrels behind the bar; totally unspoilt *(David Fisher)*

Newton Ferrers [Riverside Road East; SX5448], *Dolphin*: Nice location overlooking harbour, friendly atmosphere, Bass and Worthington real ale, garden *(Pat and Lee Crosby)*

No Mans Land [SS8313], *Mountpleasant*: Warm welcome, good choice of beers and wines, excellent food served in bar and Old Forge restaurant *(Colin Williamson)*

☆ **Noss Mayo** [SX5447], *Old Ship*: Picturesque pub with good village view in lovely harbourside setting, waterside tables, quick cheerful service, wide choice of good bar food – especially the toasted bacon and mushroom sandwiches and steak and kidney pie, well kept Bass and Courage on handpump; attractive upstairs restaurant overlooking harbour; children's bar *(G S and W P Pocock, Pat and Lee Crosby)*

Parkham [SS3821], *Bell*: Comfortably refurbished thatched village pub with good freshly cooked food and choice of real ales *(LYM)*

Plymouth [behind Theatre Royal; SX4755], *Bank*: Renovated Lloyds bank full of mahogany and brass; well kept beer, popular cheap food; best pub in central Plymouth *(W M Sharpe)*; [Barbican] *Distillery*: Previous gin distillery, nicely converted to slick modern town pub with wrought iron and palm trees in the main bar, children welcome in more rustic stone-floored entrance area, good basic pub food *(H G and C J McCafferty)*; [Mutley Plain] *Fortescue*: More character than most here – with 'London' atmosphere at lunchtime in the lounge bar, good food in bar and dining-room *(Peter Skinnard)*; [Southside St, Barbican] *Queens Arms*: One-room pub in Plymouth's old fishing-port area; very popular at lunchtime, particularly for its notable fresh sandwiches; great mix of customers *(Peter Skinnard)*; [West Hoe Rd, corner of Millbay Rd] *Sippers*: Friendly Whitbreads pub close to centre, on three levels; quick service, straightforward bar food, juke box (not too loud), space game and fruit machine; gets its name from the naval way of drinking rum *(Colin Gooch)*; [Dockside] *Swan*: Traditional dockside pub with good murals in the gents *(KG)*

Postbridge [B3212; SX6579], *East Dart*: Chummy roadside family bar in central Dartmoor hotel which has some 30 miles of fishing, efficiently served bar food; choice of real ales on handpump, farm cider, children welcome; bedrooms *(LYM)*

☆ **nr Postbridge** [B3212 1¾ miles NE; SX6780], *Warren House*: Superb position quite alone on Dartmoor, lovely views over moor, Ushers pub with maybe a guest beer such as Gibbs Mew Bishops Tipple, Grays farm cider (from Devon's longest-standing cider-makers), traditional furnishings, promptly served bar food, fire burning since 1845, home-brewed electricity; an old-fashioned moorland local out of season, often quite crowded with tourists in summer; good children's room *(Helen Crookston, H and P B, Alan and Ruth Woodhouse, JDL, P and M Rudlin, Wg Cdr R M Sparkes, LYM)*

Poundsgate [SX7072], *Tavistock*: Unspoilt friendly local, good value snacks, well kept Courage Best on handpump, quick service *(B G Steele-Perkins, Philip and Trisha Ferris)*

Princetown [SX5873], *Devils Elbow*: Welcoming landlord, pool-table, Bass, Courage Best and Directors, bar food *(Simon Turner)*; *Prince of Wales*: Good value food at candle-lit tables, cheerful warders from Dartmoor Prison chatting and joking, huge fires in two rooms, Flowers and Ruddles on handpump; can't be accused of skimpy decoration, with all those rugs draped on the walls *(GB, CH, Simon Turner, BB)*

Rackenford [SS8518], *Stag*: Friendly atmosphere, well kept real ale, farm cider and interesting layout, with thick thirteenth-century walls *(C M Tyrwhitt Jones, BB)*

☆ **Ringmore** [SX6545], *Journeys End*: Interesting old-fashioned furnishings in panelled lounge of friendly and unusual partly medieval inn with wide range of bar food, evening restaurant, good choice of well kept real ales and farm cider, helpful service, charming flower garden; not far from the sea; bedrooms comfortable and well equipped *(W C M Jones, Jon Wainwright, JAH, LYM)*

St Budeaux [Saltash Passage; SX4458], *Royal Albert Bridge*: Breathtaking views of railway and road bridges over Tamar in lounge with nautical theme; good bar food, well cooked and presented; high hygiene standards *(A R Prout, M Hunt)*

St Giles in the Wood [SS5319], *Cranford*: Pleasant staff and good nicely served food *(John Naylor)*

Salcombe [off Fore St nr Portlemouth Ferry; SX7338], *Ferry*: It's the terrific setting which earns a place for this pub, whose tiers of stripped-stone bars rise steeply from sheltered flagstone waterside terrace; well kept Palmers real ales, bar food, restaurant, games bar – and of course holiday crowds, which can slow food service and tax the ventilation system *(J S Evans, P J Hanson, Jon Wainwright, LYM)*; [Fore St] *Shipwrights*: Good town-centre pub, long and thin with strong nautical theme, clean and tidy, good service, well kept Courge Best, good value bar food, table skittles, pleasant back courtyard with hanging baskets *(Jon Wainwright)*; *Victoria*: Decent Bass on electric pump, satisfactory lunch *(Pamela and Merlyn Horswell)*

Sampford Courtenay [A3072 Crediton–Tavistock; SS6301], *New Inn*: Charming sixteenth-century pub with three comfortable bars, settles, good range of real ales, reasonably priced buffet and other straightforward bar food; children's room *(Charlie Salt, K R Harris)*

☆ **Sandy Park** [SX7189], *Sandy Park Inn*: Small but friendly little country pub with good choice of beers from cask as well as the potent bottled Crippledick, excellent home-cooked food, big log fire *(Charlie Salt, Martin and Rob Jones)*

Scorriton [SX7068], *Tradesmans Arms*: Pronounced local atmosphere in attractively placed pub overlooking moors, Ushers Best on handpump and local farm cider, bar food, simple children's room; bedrooms, and caravan to let *(Pat and Lee Crosby)*

☆ **Shaldon** [SX9371], *Ness House*: Elegant colonial-style nineteenth-century hotel in lovely spot on Ness headland giving attractive views, fine furnishings, Bass, Flowers and Huntsman Royal Oak on handpump, good bar food, faultless service; restaurant; comfortably refurbished bedrooms *(E G Parish, C G Thompson)*;

Shaldon [Ringmore Road (B3195 to Newton Abbot); SX9272], *Shipwrights Arms*: Friendly village local, with good value food under new management; good chatty atmosphere, well kept Courage Best, river views from back garden *(LYM)*

Shebbear [SS4409], *Devils Stone*: Friendly though maybe rather noisy country village pub with well kept Flowers Original; bedrooms simple, but good value at their low price *(Dr John Innes, Peter Cornall, LYM)*

Sidmouth [ST1386], *Anchor*: Delightful old pub, well kept beer and good, unusual food *(Elizabeth Lloyd)*

☆ **nr Sidmouth** [Bowd Cross; junction B3176/A3052], *Bowd*: Thatched pub with one of the best gardens in this part of Devon, clean, warm and comfortable inside, with soft lighting, an expanse of Turkey carpet, soothing piped music and nice family-room; well kept Devenish and a guest beer such as Marstons Pedigree, plenty of space for diners and a more up-market feel than many Devon pubs; some interesting furnishings, though character is not now its strong suit *(C A Foden, G Atkinson, E G Parish, P Gillbe, LYM)*

Silverton [SS9502], *New Inn*: High standards in warm, welcoming pub with good modestly priced food and Wadworths 6X, friendly service *(Cdr G F Barnett)*

Slapton [SX8244], *Queens Arms*: Good friendly service, Badger Best on handpump, small garden *(Jon Wainwright)*

Sourton [SX5390], *Bearslake*: Good food in attractive restaurant with decent range of wine, reasonable choice of beer in pleasant bar, nice friendly atmosphere *(V and D Sage)*

South Brent [Exeter Rd; SX6960], *London*: Reliably good well priced food, well kept Courage, young friendly licensees, strongly local atmosphere; bedrooms quiet, clean and comfortable – excellent value *(Pat and Malcolm Rudlin, Alan Carr)*; [Plymouth Rd] *Pack Horse*: Pleasant interior, friendly service, well kept Flowers IPA on handpump *(Jon Wainwright)*

Starcross [SX9781], *Atmospheric Railway*: Friendly local with railway on other side of road (can be exhilarating standing outside when 125 train hurtles past), and Exe estuary beyond; good atmosphere, Huntsman Royal Oak on handpump, generous ploughman's, toasted sandwiches and main dishes such as gammon or steak and kidney pie; nearby museum devoted to Brunel's original 1830s atmospheric railway, drawn by pumping stations every few miles – there's a working model *(Mrs Joan Harris, Jon Wainwright, Mr and Mrs G H Rosenthal)*

☆ **Staverton** [SX7964], *Sea Trout*: Cleanly kept comfortable inn with wide choice of good food, well kept Bass and Golden Hill Exmoor, cheerful polite service, no piped music in plush lounge; juke box and pool in locals' bar; bedrooms *(S V Bishop, C G Thompson, Charlie Salt, LYM)*

Sticklepath [SX6494], *Devonshire*: Busy sixteenth-century thatched village inn with

big log fire in friendly beamed bar, easy chairs in cosy sitting room, well kept Courage and Ushers real ale with a guest such as Wadworths 6X, traditional games, usual bar food served quickly, restaurant, provision for children; bedrooms *(Len Beattie, Mayur Shah, LYM)*

Stockland [ST2404], *Kings Arms*: Old pub in delightful village with attentive service and superb, well presented food, decent wine; extensive refurbishments under way summer 1988 *(Mr and Mrs F E Dethridge)*

Stoke Fleming [SX8648], *London Inn*: Good pasties and other more unusual food at reasonable prices in nice surroundings, efficient service; children liked the friendly dog and pet duck *(Sue Jenkins)*

Stoke Gabriel [SX8457], *Victoria & Albert*: Good value food including salmon and crab, well kept Whitbreads beers, children allowed in upstairs functions room; very attractive Dart-edge village *(S V Bishop)*

Stokenham [opposite church, N of A379 towards Torcross; SX8042], *Church House*: Main draw is good food in bar and dining-room, especially excellent local fish, shellfish and steaks; happy atmosphere, well kept Flowers Original *(Ian and Daphne Brownlie, A R Tingley, Derek McGarry)*

Tamerton Foliot [Seven Stars Lane; SX4761], *Seven Stars*: Rambling old pub with climbing roses and trees in tubs in its walled courtyard, small public/food bar with flagstones and upholstered window seats; big helpings of good value food such as chilli con carne *(Mrs Pamela Roper)*

Tedburn St Mary [village signposted from A30 W of Exeter; SX8193], *Kings Arms*: Line of knocked-together rooms form long cosy open-plan bar with big log fire, eating area at one end (no bar food Sun evening), games area around corner at other end, well kept Bass and another real ale, local cider, friendly welcome; children allowed in eating area; bedrooms *(Charlie Salt, RT, Ian and Daphne Brownlie, Hope Chenhalls, LYM)*

Teignmouth [Quay Side; SX9473], *Newquay*: Friendly well decorated pub with good beer and food *(G A Hannam)*

☆ **Thelbridge Cross** [OS Sheet 180 reference 790120; SS7912], *Thelbridge Cross*: Cosy and tastefully traditional old pub with half a dozen well kept ales tapped from the cask, Inch's farm cider, home-made food from a changing menu, log fire, lots of local customers *(John Dubarry, Mr and Mrs L Takkos, Mrs A Byles, Rowland Bultitude, Mrs L Tompkins)*

Thorverton [SS9202], *Ruffwell Arms*: Excellent food, marvellous value for money *(Tom Gondris)*

Thurlestone [SX6743], *Village Inn*: Interesting building with several homely, friendly rooms; inventive menu with home-made puddings; good wine *(Sue Cleasby, Mike Ledger)*

Topsham [SX9688], *Lighter*: Spacious and
well kept comfortably refurbished pub with
red plush seats, efficient food bar and good
Badger real ales, by waterside; good choice
of board games; bedrooms *(BB)*; [High St]
Lord Nelson: Delightful atmosphere, attentive service, excellent good value food *(Jim
Beesley)*; [68 Fore St] *Salutation*: Excellent
value home-made hot chicken curry with
brown rice, large crusty roll, side dishes of
coconut and mango chutney – big helpings
(Mr and Mrs P A Jones); [Monmouth Hill]
Steam Packet: Attractive old-world restoration with flagstones, scrubbed boards,
panelling, stripped stonework and brick, bar
food; has had well kept Bass, Flowers
Original and Whitbreads, but lease on
market summer 1988; on boat-builders'
quay *(LYM; more news please)*
Torquay [Pavilion; SX9264], *Boulevard*:
Cafe/bar/restaurant in upmarket redevelopment of Victorian Assembly Rooms with
opulent décor, bijou shops on ground floor
and really huge helpings of very good low-
priced food; efficient, interested and swift
service; children in restaurant and on terrace
(Sue Jenkins); [Park Lane] *Devon Arms*:
Bustling little pub up a short steep hill, away
from the main shopping area; well kept beer,
straightforward pub food tasty and well
presented – not expensive *(Colin Gooch)*;
[Pimlico] *Pickwick*: Warm friendly town
pub, generous helpings of very good value
food, well kept Courage Directors
(G Upham)
Totnes [SX8060], *Bull*: Pleasant and well kept
– worth knowing *(S V Bishop)*; [Fore St, The
Plains] *Royal Seven Stars*: Good food and
service in vibrant and likeable former
coaching inn, well kept Courage and Ushers
Best; bedrooms *(Jon Wainwright,
W A Lund)*
Trusham [signposted off B3193 NW of
Chudleigh – 1½ very narrow miles; SX8582],
Cridford: Roses round door of charmingly
cottagey pub with excellent reasonably
priced food from sandwiches up, Bass tapped
from the cask, old-world atmosphere and
picnic-table sets on terrace *(WHBM)*
Tuckenhay [SX8156], *Maltsters Arms*:
Included for its position by peaceful wooded
creek, with picture windows, Courage Best
and Directors, Churchwards cider, friendly
staff; best tables set aside for diners, more
out on terrace; children welcome (dartboard
in family area) *(Brian and Anna Marsden, Jon
Wainwright, Pamela and Merlyn Horswell,
LYM)*
Two Bridges [B3357/B3212 across Dartmoor; SX6175], *Two Bridges*: Delicious thick
home-made soup and very good ploughman's with excellent brown bread; bedrooms
(J E F Rawlins)
Tytherleigh [A358 Chard–Axminster;
ST3103], *Tytherleigh Arms*: Good relaxing
food pub with big fireplace in comfortable

bar, attentive host, wide choice of bar food
especially local fish, well kept Huntsman
Dorset on handpump, small restaurant doing
English cooking – often quite unusual *(Ted
George)*
Upottery [ST2007], *Sidmouth Arms*: Very
pleasant and friendly pub with good choice
of tasty food, all home cooked, including
sandwiches, soup, cottage or steak and
kidney pie, lasagne and so forth; a choice of
potatoes *(Mrs Shirley Pielou)*
☆ Welcombe [SS2218], *Old Smithy*: Pretty
thatched country pub with charming garden
– a good choice for meals outside on a sunny
day; carefully served if not cheap bar food
including good home-made pasties, well kept
Cornish ales, comfortable open-plan bar
with log fires, juke box and so forth; the
landlord's humour may take some getting
used to – most readers enjoy it; nearby
Welcombe Mouth is an attractive rocky
cove; very good modern bedrooms, reasonably priced *(W A Harbottle, Stan Edwards,
Mr and Mrs G J Lewis, Peter Cornall, JDL,
Wilfred Plater-Shellard, C H Beaumont,
LYM)*
West Alvington [SX7243], *Ring o' Bells*:
Good food and service, chatty teetotal
landlord, well kept Bass *(Pamela and Merlyn
Haswell, Mr and Mrs R H Door)*
Westleigh [½ mile off A39 Bideford–Instow;
SS4628], *Westleigh Inn*: Village pub included
for the gorgeous views down over the
Torridge estuary from its neatly kept
garden; straightforward bar food, well
kept Ushers Best *(LYM)*
☆ Widecombe [SX7176], *Olde*: Lovely old pub,
comfortably refurbished, with good friendly
service, good beer (especially the Widecombe
Wallop), interesting reasonably priced food
including enormous salads, Mexican beef,
lamb in gin sauce, vegetarian and children's
dishes; good garden; the beauty-spot village
is a magnet for visitors, so in summer the
pub's very busy indeed – best out of season,
when the lovely open fire's an added
attraction *(Pat and Malcolm Rudlin, Sue and
John Brumfitt, B C Head, LYM)*
Widecombe [OS Sheet 191 reference
720765], *Rugglestone*: Quite unspoilt alehouse, no spirits licence, two very traditionally furnished rooms, no bar counter –
just a half-door in the tap-room *(Phil and
Sally Gorton)*
Winkleigh [SS6308], *Winkleigh Inn*: Varied
choice of food, well prepared and presented
and pleasantly served *(W A Lund)*
Woodland [signposted off A38 just NE of
Ashburton; SX7968], *Rising Sun*: Nicely kept
food pub in isolated country setting *(Ian
Robinson, LYM)*
Woolacombe [Ossaborough – unclassified rd
signposted off B3343 and B3231; SS4543],
Mill: Seventeenth-century flagstoned mill
barn with potential – two bars separated by
big wood-burning stove; well kept Courage

Directors, generous bar food served
efficiently, pool-table, piped music which
can be loud; tables in walled courtyard
(M W Barratt, Steve and Carolyn Harvey)
Wrafton [A361 just SE of Braunton; SS4935],
Williams Arms: Spacious and comfortably
furnished main bar, busy on summer evenings, in thatched sixteenth-century pub with
Bass and plenty of good value bar snacks;
log-effect gas fire, separate restaurant (Steve
and Carolyn Harvey, Chris Fluck)
☆ **Yelverton** [by roundabout on A386 half-way
between Plymouth and Tavistock; SX5267],

Rock: Really smashing beer – loony-juice
with a great taste; excellent courteous bar
staff, comfortable surroundings with pub
characters in every corner, attractive food
including enormous puddings (not served
earliest part of evening); bedrooms (Simon
Turner, P and M Rudlin)
Yeoford [SX7898], *Mare & Foal*: Friendly
Edwardian-looking pub with wide choice of
beer, reasonable sandwiches, good value
steak, comfortable lounge, parquet-floored
games bar, good log fires, upstairs sauna;
good parking (BB)

Dorset

The most important change in our Dorset chapter this year is the addition of quite a clutch of new main entries – the White Lion at Bourton (attractive inside, with good food), the small-roomed old Greyhound, very much the centre of Corfe Castle, the Sailors Return at East Chaldon (extensively but successfully extended in an old-fashioned style), the Weld Arms at East Lulworth (a good deal of character both in its furnishings and in its food), the Avon Causeway at Hurn (spacious and quite modern, with genuinely interesting and unusual railway connections), the comfortably well run Angel in Poole and the unspoilt but civilised Tigers Head at Rampisham (good food and a nice place to stay – probably our favourite of all these, though it's difficult to choose). We've been getting promising reports too on quite a few new licensees here – at the White Hart in Bishops Caundle (still tipped for good food), both contrasting entries in Cerne Abbas (the New Inn, with comfortable bedrooms, seems to have had the edge so far for food – but it's early days yet), the Elm Tree in Langton Herring (another where food's decidedly the main thing), the Pilot Boat in Lyme Regis (considerable changes here, under the people who previously made the Ilchester Arms at Symondsbury a favourite with many readers), the big and busy Bakers Arms near Lytchett Minster (the same family now owns the Swans Nest in Exminster, Devon, and Old Beams at Ibsley, Hampshire – similarly big and thriving), and the New Inn at Stoke Abbott (yet another pub where food's been a particular draw). Other pubs we'd currently pick out for food in the county include the Spyway at Askerswell (a character pub alone in the hills, though quite near the coast), the civilised George in Bridport (its local eel dishes are popular – though we have to admit to a personal inability to understand this particular taste), the Winyard's Gap Inn with its terrific view near Chedington, the welcoming old Fox at Corscombe, the well kept Fleur-de-Lys in Cranborne (a

*nice place to stay – as both Thomas Hardy and Rupert Brooke knew too), the
Acorn in Evershot (another comfortable Thomas Hardy inn), the Blackmoor
Vale in Marnhull (Hardy described this one as Rollivers in Marlott), the Marquis
of Lorne at Nettlecombe (a pleasant place to stay), the pretty Shave Cross Inn at
Shave Cross (particularly notable for its honest ploughman's), the bustling Elm
Tree at Langton Herring, the Manor Hotel looking down to the sea in West
Bexington (this comfortable place has added a spacious new conservatory), and
the thatched Castle just a stroll from the sea at West Lulworth (a good place to
stay). The county's best pub food, at a price, is now to be found at the Three
Horseshoes in Powerstock – outstanding fish, and its fine hors-d'oeuvre trolley is
an idea worth copying. For quaintness, top contenders include the ancient Fox in
Corfe Castle, the Smiths Arms at Godmanstone (with a claim to be the country's
smallest pub) and the very staunchly local Square & Compass at Worth
Matravers, looking out to sea from its perch on the Isle of Purbeck. Besides other
main entries, the county's Lucky Dip entries at the end of the chapter include
many so promising that we've marked them with a star – particularly well
recommended among these are the Anchor near Chideock, Fiddleford Inn at
Fiddleford, Hambro Arms at Milton Abbas, Brace of Pheasants at Plush, Digby
Tap in Sherborne, Ilchester Arms at Symondsbury, Rose & Crown at Trent and
Ship at West Stour.*

ABBOTSBURY   SY5785 Map 2
Ilchester Arms
B3157

This handsome old inn – in a lovely golden stone village – has three cosy main areas
in its rambling beamed bar; there's a friendly, relaxed atmosphere (though it does
get busy in summer), lots of pictures in which swans figure strongly – hundreds nest
at the nearby swannery (which is closed for visits during the nesting season), and
red plush button-back seats around cast-iron-framed tables on the Turkey carpet.
Bar food includes soup (95p), a good choice of ploughman's with several pickles
(from £2.50), haddock (£2.75), seafood platter (£3.45), salads (from £3.45),
scampi (£3.75), sirloin steak (£7.95) and a daily special (£3.50). Well kept Devenish
JD and Cornish Original and Wadworths 6X on handpump; pleasant service;
maybe piped music. You can see the sea from the windows of the comfortable and
attractive back bedrooms, and lanes lead from behind the pub into the countryside
– the nearby abbey and its subtropical gardens are worth visiting. *(Recommended by
John Nash, I R Hewitt, Derek and Sylvia Stephenson, Heather Sharland, J H C Peters)*

*Devenish   Real ale   Meals and snacks   Restaurant   Children in eating area   Open
10.30–2.30, 6–11 all year   Bedrooms tel Dorchester (0305) 871243; £28B/£34B*

ASKERSWELL   SY5292 Map 2
Spyway ★ ⊗
Village signposted N of A35 Bridport–Dorchester; inn signposted locally; OS Sheet 194
reference 529933

The friendliness in this well run pub is not just the more effusive substitute you find
in more touristy pubs, and goes deeper – while the landlord's dry sense of humour
keeps the locals' banter in check. Very good value home-cooked food includes club
sandwiches (£2.20), a good choice of ploughman's such as generous helpings of
good quality ham and sweet pickle or locally made sausage (from £1.40), three-egg
omelettes (£1.50), plaice or haddock (£1.95), good quiche salad (£2.10), venison
with Cumberland sauce (£2.10), seafood platter (£2.75), and evening grills such as

lamb cutlets (£3.50), gammon (£3.80), and steaks (£5.25); there are daily specials like chilli con carne, ratatouille, lasagne or home-made pies (£2.10), good puddings such as pineapple cheesecake (£1), and children's dishes. Well kept Ruddles County, Ushers Best, and Websters Yorkshire on handpump; country wines. The nicest and most cosy of the small carpeted bars has old-fashioned high-backed settles, a grandfather clock, rows of delicately made cups and plates, and old printed notices and local bills on its ochre walls; another has cushioned seats built into its walls, an attractive window seat, beams, and a milkmaid's yoke and harness. Darts, shove-ha'penny, table skittles, dominoes and cribbage. Outside, there's a quiet and neatly kept garden, with a small duck pool, pets' corner, swings and climbing-frame. The views over these steep downs just in from the coast are lovely, and the lane past the pub opens on to many paths and bridleways (not to mention badger tracks). (*Recommended by Peter and Rose Flower, Richard Cole, R D Jolliff, Peter Hitchcock, Gwen and Peter Andrews, Mrs E B Robinson, John and Joan Nash, J S Clements, Dr A V Lewis, Mr and Mrs B E Witcher, C R and M Southcombe, Mr and Mrs A F Walker, Mr and Mrs Jon Payne, P J Hanson*)

Free house   Licensees Don and Jackie Roderick   Real ale   Meals and snacks   Children in family-room   Open 11–2.30, 6–11 all year; closed evening 25 Dec

BISHOPS CAUNDLE   ST6913 Map 2
White Hart ⊗
A3030

New licensees have swept into this popular food pub with a new broom – the big irregularly shaped lounge bar has been redecorated and refurbished with dark wood furniture and deep red curtains, though still keeping its low beams (some attractively moulded) and very old black panelling. Bar food includes sandwiches (from 80p), filled French sticks (jumbo sausage and onions £1, four-ounce sirloin steak and onions £2.15), several ploughman's (mostly £1.80), salads (from £2.60), lasagne (£2.75), home-made cheese and onion quiche (£2.80), local ham and egg (£2.90), speciality pies such as ham, leek and cider with a cheesy topping (£2.95), gammon steak with egg or pineapple (£4.75), steaks (from £4.75) and specials like Dorset trout with prawns, mushrooms and a cream sauce (£5.25); children's meals (from £1.05). Well kept Badger Best and Tanglefoot on handpump; dominoes, cribbage, fruit machine, alley skittles and piped music. The garden – floodlit at night – has a children's play area. (*Recommended by John Kirk, Nigel Paine, Mark Walpole, Melanie White, Lyn and Bill Capper, Alan and Audrey Chatting*)

Badger   Licensees Stephen and Denise Symonds   Real ale   Meals and snacks   Children in eating area of bar   Open 11–2.30 (3 Sat), 6.30–11 all year

BOURTON   ST7430 Map 2
White Lion ⊗
Pub signposted off A303

Partially covered with climbing roses and clematis, this old stone pub draws warm plaudits for its friendly and relaxed atmosphere – as one reader puts it, old-fashioned in the best sense of the word. The landlord is notably friendly, the locals are jolly. The beamed and flagstoned main bar has a door into the garden, and also opens into an attractive room with Turkey rugs on its old stone floor, a curved bow-window seat, a longish settle by the old oak table in front of the big fireplace. Across the entrance corridor a tiny bar, popular with locals, has military hats on the ceiling, cushioned wall seats, wheel-back chairs around nice old tables, and yet another open fire; up a couple of steps, a top room is set out for eating with built-in wooden plank settles and a medley of tables and chairs. Good bar food (they use fresh local produce where possible) includes sandwiches (from 85p), home-made soup (£1), burger (£1.95), ploughman's (from £1.95), good home-cooked ham and egg (£2.55), home-made steak and kidney or pork and apple pie (£2.95), a daily curry (from £2.95), vegetarian dishes like spinach and walnut lasagne or beans and peppers simmered in a coconut spicy sauce (£3.25), game pie (£3.45), outsize salads (from £3), gammon steak with egg and pineapple (£3.75), and fresh local trout (£4.50); also, daily specials and puddings such as jam roly-poly (90p); excellent three-course Sunday roast lunch (£5.50), booking advisable. Well kept Ruddles Best and County and Ushers Best on handpump; darts, shove-ha'penny, dominoes, cribbage, fruit machine, trivia and quiet piped music. In front of the pub there are a couple of picnic-table sets, with two more in a small enclosed garden across the lane; the back garden has a two-tiered lawn, trees and shrubs, a thatched well with water pump, a swing and a couple more picnic-table sets; there are fortnightly barbecues. Stourhead is a few minutes away. (*Recommended by Cdr F A Costello, John Nash, Mr and Mrs B E Witcher, Patrick Stapley, RAB, Richard Gibbs, Martin and Rob Jones, David Allsop*)

Free house   Licensee C M Frowde   Real ale   Meals and snacks   Restaurant tel Gillingham (0747) 840866   Children in eating areas (until 7.30 unless over 12)   Open all day in summer; 10.30–2.30, 6–11 winter weekdays

BRIDPORT   SY4692   Map 1
George ⊗
South Street

This consistently friendly, old-fashioned town local has a good atmosphere and interesting home-made food cooked by the licensee: soup (£1), sandwiches (from 90p, toasted bacon and mushroom £1.50), ploughman's (with local farm Cheddar, Blue Cheddar, Blue Shropshire or Stilton, £1.85), crudités (£1.75), pâté (£1.95), Welsh rarebit (£1.50), a choice of omelettes (£1.85), home-made seasonal pies (fish, game, rabbit from £2), kipper (£2.25), home-cooked ham or beef (£2.25 for a small helping, £4.50 for large one, salad £1 extra), sauté kidneys (£3.50), curry (£3.50), popular local eel fried in garlic and white wine (£3.50) or stewed (£4), Finnan haddock (£4.50), entrecôte steak (£6), and they nearly always have fresh fish – plaice (£3.50), lemon sole (£6.50). Well kept Palmers Bridport, IPA and Tally Ho on handpump; freshly squeezed orange or grapefruit juice (70p) and apple juice from a local cider farm (60p); an ancient pre-fruit machine ball game and Radio 3 or maybe classical or jazz tapes. There are country seats and wheel-back chairs set around the sturdy wooden tables on the flowery carpet, upholstered seats in knobby green cloth built against the gold and green papered walls, and, in winter, a log fire. (*Recommended by Jim Matthews, Gary Scott, R H Inns, Tim Locke*)

Palmers   Licensee John Mander   Real ale   Meals and snacks (not Sun lunchtime, bank hol Mon or 25–26 Dec)   Children in dining-room   Open all day in summer; 10–2.30, 6.30–11 in winter; closed evening 25 Dec (also open for continental breakfast 8.30–11.30) Bedrooms tel Bridport (0308) 23187; £15/£30

CERNE ABBAS   ST6601   Map 2
New Inn ⊗ ⇚
14 Long Street

Seats in the mullioned windows of the L-shaped lounge bar here overlook the main street of this pretty village; it's a comfortable and well kept place (even the lavatories are attractive), with oak beams in its high ceiling, chatty locals, and generous helpings of good food: home-made soup (95p), sandwiches (from 99p, toasties £1.50), French bread with meats from the carvery (£1.50), home-made quiche (from £1.50), ploughman's (£1.90), Dorset pâté or burger (£1.95), sausages and egg (£2.10), three-egg omelette (from £2.45), meats, fish and cheese from the cold carvery and help-yourself salads (£3.99), pan-fried trout (£4.95), grilled gammon with egg or pineapple (£5.25), steaks (from £7.50), and two daily specials. Well kept Huntsman Dorset and Royal Oak on electric pump, kept under light blanket pressure; piped music. Past the old coachyard (which still has its pump and mounting block) is a sheltered back lawn; a good track leads up on to the hills above the village, where the prehistoric (and rather rude) Cerne Giant is cut into the chalk, and the pub is on *Good Walks Guide* Walk 29. *(Recommended by Mea Horler, Peter and Rose Flower, Wayne Brindle, WFL, Pamela and Merlyn Horswell, Paul Marsh, Mr and Mrs P W Dryland, DK, Alan and Audrey Chatting, John Roué, Mrs L Coleridge)*

Huntsman   Licensee P D Edmunds   Real ale   Meals and snacks   Children in eating area of bar   Open all day   Bedrooms tel Cerne Abbas (030 03) 274; £17.50/£30

Royal Oak

Long Street

At the beginning of 1988 new licensees took over this Tudor inn with its very steep stone slab roof and three attractive communicating rooms; early reports on the new regime have been encouraging – mentioning especially the warm and friendly welcome. There are flagstones by the long serving-counter, which has a useful foot rail, black oak beams, lots of dark panelling, stripped stonework, farm tools, old photographs of the village and, in winter, good log fires. Generous helpings of popular bar food includes soup (£1), filled rolls (from £1.35), garlic mushrooms (£1.25), cod (£3), plaice (£3.15), scampi (£3.60), steaks (from £6), and daily specials like tasty steak and kidney pie, lasagne or macaroni cheese (from £2.75); Sunday roast lunch (£3.25). Well kept Devenish JD and Royal Wessex, and Marstons Pedigree on handpump. Darts, dominoes, cribbage and piped music. There are seats outside. The pub is on *Good Walks Guide* Walk 29. *(Recommended by A and K D Stansfield, John Nash, Gordon and Daphne, Mr and Mrs P W Dryland, John Roué)*

Devenish   Licensee Barry Petterson   Real ale   Meals and snacks   Open 11–2.30, 6–11 all year; closed evening 25 Dec

CHEDINGTON   ST4805 Map 1

Winyard's Gap ⊗

A356 Dorchester–Crewkerne

There's a marvellous view (described at length in Thomas Hardy's *At Winyard's Gap*) over the little rolling fields far below, from window seats inside this comfortably furnished and modernised old inn. There are beams, plenty of seating, brasses and copper and lots of pottery. Bar food includes sandwiches (from 90p, steak £2.40, toasties from £1.20), home-made soup (95p), ploughman's (from £1.90), filled baked potatoes (from £2), curries (from £2.80), kedgeree (£2.95), several pies (from £3.85 for fish with egg and mushroom, £5.50 for steak and oyster in Guinness), local trout stuffed with almonds (£4.25), pork chop with orange and cranberry sauce (£3.90), and steaks (from £5.90); also, vegetarian dishes, with daily specials and puddings chalked up on a blackboard, and Sunday roast lunch (£3.25). They use locally made pottery to serve real butter and cream. Well kept Bass, Golden Hill Exmoor, Huntsman Dorchester, and a guest ale on handpump; pleasant staff. Darts, pool, a spacious and comfortably furnished skittle alley, fruit machine and piped music. Outside, the terrace has cast-iron furniture, and there's an attractively planted garden. The old barn has been converted into two self-catering flats. Behind the pub, there's a nice walk to the monument, then through the woods to Chedington village (where there is a farm nature trail). *(Recommended by Heather Sharland, J L Simpson, Nigel Paine, Mr and Mrs David Chapman)*

Free house   Licensees Alan and June Pezaro   Real ale   Meals (not Sun evening) and snacks Restaurant   Children in skittle alley   Live music Sun evenings   Open 11.30–2.30, 6.30 (7 in winter)–11 all year

CHESIL   SY6873   Map 2
Cove House

Entering Portland on A354, bear right: keep eyes skinned for pub, up Big Ope entry on right

This typical Devenish pub has a magnificent position overlooking the sea and Chesil Beach. It's simply though comfortably furnished, and the room on the right has dark settles and benches on the polished boards, little lantern lights strung along its beams, and darts, dominoes, cribbage and a fruit machine; the room on the left past the servery has photographs of local shipwrecks and Chesil Beach storms, and blue plush chairs and modern settles around tables on the carpet. Reasonably priced bar food chalked up on blackboards at both ends of the bar includes prawn or crab sandwiches (£1.25), ploughman's (£1.95), fresh baked mackerel (£2.60), lasagne, pork and plum or turkey and leek pie (£2.95), savoury baked crab or smoked turkey and avocado salad (£3.95), and fresh crab salad (£4.25). Well kept Devenish JD and Royal Wessex on handpump; friendly, helpful service; piped music. There are seats and parasols on the promenade, with the pebble beach curling away for mile after mile on your right. *(Recommended by Jack Taylor, D Pearman, Dr A V Lewis, K and D E Worrall)*

Devenish   Licensee S D Durkin   Real ale   Meals and snacks   Restaurant tel Portland (0305) 820895; open until 4 Sun   Children in eating area and restaurant   Open all day in summer; 11–2.30, 6–11 in winter

CHIDEOCK   SY4292   Map 1
George

A35 Bridport–Lyme Regis

This busy 300-year-old thatched inn has a dark-beamed lounge bar with pewter tankards hanging from the mantelpiece above the big fireplace (with good log fires in winter), boat drawings and attractively framed old local photographs on its cream walls, a collection of over 250 foreign banknotes donated by customers, and high shelves of bottles, plates, mugs and so forth. There are comfortable red plush stools and wall and window seats. Good value bar food from a wide menu includes soup (70p), sandwiches (from 85p), omelettes (from £1.10), pâté (£1.20), various ploughman's (from £1.35), salads (mostly £2.50), scampi (£2.65), gammon with pineapple and egg (£3.20), and steaks (from £5.35); puddings (mostly 75p), specials such as chicken curry (£2.70), half a honey-roast duck (£5.15), or beef bourguignonne (£4.45), and children's meals (from 65p). Well kept Palmers BB, IPA and Tally Ho on handpump; unobtrusive piped music, some road noise. The neatly kept carpeted games-bar has darts, well lit pool, shove-ha'penny, dominoes, table skittles, two fruit machines and a juke box. There are picnic-table sets and stone tables in the back garden – where Georgian coins have been found – and a small pond. The car park has been made bigger and there are still plans for a new cellar, lavatories and a family/functions-room; near *Good Walks Guide* Walk 23. *(Recommended by Ted George, Mr and Mrs J Wilmore, R F Davidson; more reports please)*

Palmers   Licensee Michael Tuck   Real ale   Meals and snacks   Restaurant tel Chideock (0297) 89419; open until 3.30 Sun   Children in restaurant and family-room   Open all day; 11–2.30, 6–11 in winter

nr CHRISTCHURCH   SZ1696   Map 2
Fishermans Haunt 🛏

Winkton: B3347 Ringwood road nearly 3 miles N of Christchurch

Close to weirs on the River Avon, this creeper-covered pub has a variety of furnishings and moods in its modernised and extended series of interconnecting bars: stuffed fish and fishing pictures, oryx and reindeer heads, and some copper, brass and plates; at one end of the chain of rooms big windows look out on the neat front garden, and at the other there's a fruit machine and a space game. Good value bar food includes soup (£1), sandwiches (from £1.10, toasted £1.45, fresh crab £1.65), ploughman's (from £1.75), home-made fisherman's pie, ham and cheese quiche or chilli con carne (£2.20), fried fish (from £2.65), chicken (£2.75), scampi or seafood platter (£3.30), and puddings like home-made mixed fruit crumble (£1.10). Well kept Bass, Courage Directors and Ringwood Fortyniner on hand-pump, cheerful staff; piped music. At night the hotel is decked with fairy lights, and by day you can sit on the back lawn among shrubs, roses, other flowers and a swing. (*Recommended by Dr James Haworth, Ken and Dorothy Worrall, Richard Cole, Tony Bland, Tom Evans*)

Free house   Licensee James Bochan   Real ale   Meals and snacks   Restaurant   Children in eating area and restaurant   Open all day in summer; will close afternoons in winter unless trade demands otherwise   Bedrooms tel Christchurch (0202) 484071; £19(£26B)/£37(£40B)

COLEHILL   SU0201 Map 2

Barley Mow

Village signposted from A31 E of Wimborne Minster, and also from Wimborne Minster itself; in village take Colehill Lane opposite big church among pine trees; OS Sheet 195 reference 032024

As this unpretentious thatched building is one of the better country pubs within easy reach of Bournemouth, it does get so busy at weekends that you have to be prepared for a wait for service. The main bar is comfortably carpeted and furnished, with some nicely moulded oak panelling, old beams, Hogarth prints on the walls, and, in winter, a fire in the huge brick fireplace. The usual range of bar food, at normal prices. Badger Best, Hectors and Tanglefoot on handpump; darts, pool, dominoes, fruit machine, space game, juke box and maybe piped music. There are tables among the tubs of flowers in front, or on the back grass (sheltered by oak trees). (*Recommended by Dr James Haworth, PJP; more reports please*)

Badger   Real ale   Meals and snacks   Children in family-room   Open 11–2.30, 6–11

CORFE CASTLE (Isle of Purbeck)   SY9681 Map 2

Fox

West Street, off A351; from town centre, follow dead-end Car Park sign behind church

The tiny front bar in this delightfully unspoilt and warmly welcoming old pub scarcely has room for its single heavy oak table and the cushioned wall benches which surround it; among other pictures above the ochre panelling is a good old engraving of the ruined castle, and the room is lit by one old-fashioned lamp. It is served by a hatch, though like other pubs round here many people just stand in the panelled corridor to get their well kept Fremlins tapped from the cask; good dry white wine. A back lounge is more comfortable, though less atmospheric. Generous helpings of good value bar food include sandwiches (from 90p), ploughman's (£1.80), spinach and sweetcorn or Stilton and celery quiche (£2) and fresh crab when available. Extended this year, the attractive sun-trap garden at the back is reached by a pretty flower-hung side entrance, and has good views of the ruined castle; the surrounding countryside is very fine and the pub is on *Good Walks Guide* Walk 25. There's a local museum opposite. (*Recommended by Alan and Ruth Woodhouse, Phil and Sally Gorton, Peter Hitchcock, Gwen and Peter Andrews, KG, Heather Sharland*)

Whitbreads   Licensee Graham White   Real ale   Lunchtime snacks   Open 11–2.30, 6–11; opens 7 in winter; closed 25 Dec

Greyhound

A351

In the middle of the village and just below the castle, this old-fashioned place has a main bar that is divided into three small low-ceilinged areas with mellowed oak panelling and old photographs of the town on the walls; the recently refurbished family area is no-smoking. Fresh local seafood is the speciality here: Poole cockles (£1), Mediterranean prawns sauté in garlic (£3.20), fresh crab salad (£5), fresh lobster and prawn salad or mixed seafood platter (£7); other bar food includes large filled rolls (from 60p, local crab £1.80), a good choice of filled baked potatoes (from £1.50) ploughman's (from £1.70), lasagne or steak and kidney pie (£2.50), and salads (from £3); daily specials and seafood are chalked up on a blackboard. Well kept Flowers Original, Whitbreads Strong Country and a guest beer on handpump; friendly service; darts sensibly placed in the back room; pool, fruit machine, juke box and piped music. There are benches outside. *(Recommended by Alan and Audrey Chatting, A P Carr, Wayne Brindle, Dr R Fuller, Heather Sharland, D Pearman)*

Whitbreads   Licensee R A Wild   Real ale   Meals and snacks   Children in family area Open 11–2.30, 6–11 all year

CORSCOMBE   ST5105 Map 2
Fox ★ ⊗

On outskirts, towards Halstock

This cosy, friendly and well kept thatched pub has one small room with dark flagstones, traditional black built-in high-backed settles, a spinning-wheel in the big fireplace, and antlers and whips for decoration; a second, similarly old-fashioned but carpeted room has some china on the white walls – which have been stripped back in one place to show the old stone – a high-backed elm settle by the fire, with lower ones under the beams. The tables (with small bowls of pansies) are made by the licensee, complete with carved fox heads, and this year Mrs Marlow had made new seat covers and curtains. Good value lunchtime food, freshly cooked to order (don't expect instant fast food here), includes soup, sandwiches, ploughman's with local farmhouse Cheddar or home-made pâté, beef and Guinness pie (£2.65), haddock and cauliflower Mornay (£3.25), omelettes with fresh garden herbs, pork and apricots in cider (£4.25), locally farmed trout with seafood sauce (£4.95), hot or cold fresh salmon (in summer, £5.75), puddings such as cherry and almond meringue (£1) or exotic fruit and ice-cream concoctions (£1.75). In the evening they concentrate more on main courses, and can also cater for vegetarians and people on diets. Devenish JD and Huntsman Dorset on handpump; darts, table skittles, shove-ha'penny, dominoes, cribbage. You can sit across the quiet village lane, on a lawn by the little stream which just down the road serves an unusual moated farmhouse. *(Recommended by Gary Scott, Heather Sharland, Peter and Rose Flower, Mr and Mrs D E Salter, H and P B, Pamela and Merlyn Horswell, Nigel Paine, Gordon and Daphne, C R and M S, JK, Alan and Audrey Chatting)*

Free house   Licensee Stephen Marlow   Real ale   S.acks (not Mon lunchtime, though see below) and evening meals   Open 11.30–2.30, 7–11 all year; will stay open longer in afternoon if trade demands; closed Mon lunchtime except bank hols

CRANBORNE   SU0513 Map 2
Fleur-de-Lys ⊗ ⌷

B3078 N of Wimborne Minster

From one end of the attractively modernised, oak-panelled lounge bar in this busy, friendly pub you can get sandwiches (from £1.05, toasties 20p extra), home-made soup with home-made wholemeal roll (£1.15), ploughman's (from £1.95, ham cooked in cider and honey £2.25), basket meals (from £1.95), smoked trout or mackerel (£2.45), vegetarian dishes (£3.15), home made steak pie (£3.45), salads (from £3.75; the mayonnaise, cocktail sauce and tartare sauce are all home made and free from additives and preservatives), grilled local trout (£5.30), grilled gammon with egg or pineapple (£5.45) and eight-ounce rump steak (£6.85); there are home-made puddings such as blackcurrant cheesecake or raspberry Pavlova (from £1.20), daily specials, and in the evening they also do a special three-course meal (£8.65 which includes wine and coffee). Well kept Badger Best and Tanglefoot on handpump. The simply furnished beamed public bar has darts, shove-ha'penny, dominoes, cribbage, fruit machine and juke box. There are swings and a slide on the lawn behind the car park. The attractive rolling farmland round the village marks its closeness to the New Forest with occasional ancient oaks and yews. Thomas Hardy stayed in the inn for part of the time that he was writing *Tess of the d'Urbervilles*, and if you fork left past the church you can follow the downland track that Hardy must have visualised Tess taking home to 'Trentridge' (actually Pentridge) after dancing here. *(Recommended by E G Parish, E V Palmer-Jeffery, Steve Dark, C Williams, Nigel Paine, P J and S E Robbins, WFL, Roy McIsaac, Mr Moody, Dorothy and Kenneth Worrall)*

Badger Licensee Charles Hancock Real ale Meals and snacks Restaurant Children in eating area Open 10.30–3, 6–11 all year Bedrooms tel Cranborne (072 54) 282; £17(£21B)/£27.50(£35B)

EAST CHALDON SY7983 Map 2
Sailors Return

Village signposted from A352 Wareham–Dorchester; from village green, follow Dorchester, Weymouth signpost; note that the village is also known as Chaldon Herring; OS Sheet 194 reference 790834

This old pub was extensively renovated in 1985, and naturally readers who previously particularly admired its small size and very simple old-fashioned atmosphere were worried about the outcome. It is indeed very much more spacious now, but the extensions have been kept carefully in line with the original interior – that low-ceilinged stone-floored core now serves as a coffee house. The new part has open beams showing the roof above, with furnishings kept uncompromisingly plain and simple, and old notices for decoration, and the dining area has solid old tables in nooks and crannies. We're sorry we can't give any up-to-date food information as the licensee not only didn't return our fact checking sheet, but peremptorily told us they had no time to help us when we rang – fortunately ordinary customers seem to have come across no sign of this attitude, reporting friendly, pleasant service. They may do afternoon cream teas. Well kept Flowers, Wadworths 6X, Whitbread Strong Country and guest beers. Benches, picnic-table sets and log seats on the grass in front look down over cow pastures to the village, which is set in a wide hollow below Chaldon Down: a very pretty, peaceful spot, and from nearby West Chaldon a bridleway leads across to join the Dorset Coast Path by the National Trust cliffs above Ringstead Bay. *(Recommended by Mrs K Cooper, P and M Rudlin, J Roots, Mr and Mrs C France, WHBM, Jon Johnson; more reports please – particularly about food prices)*

Whitbreads Real ale Snacks Open 11–2.30, 6.30–11

EAST LULWORTH SY8581 Map 2
Weld Arms ⊗

B3070

Nautical charts, newspaper sailing clippings, yacht pennants behind the bar and the ensigns which drape the yellowing ceiling reflect the licensee's enthusiasm – he's a single-handed Transatlantic man. The homely and relaxed main bar has big oak tables, with a couple of long oak-panelled settles, a pair of pews and some assorted easy chairs up by the fireplace, as well as more regular seats; in winter you may be able to roast your own chestnuts, and in summer there are likely to be fresh flowers from the rambling garden. Lunchtime bar food includes home-made soup (90p), burgers (£1.10), home-made cottage pie (£1.60), steak rolls (£1.60), usually prawn or crab sandwiches (£1.70), steak and kidney pie (£2.10) and smoked trout salad (£3); when we went, the changing but distinctive evening menu included mushroom fritters (£1.90), pheasant pieces casseroled in red wine (£2.20), avocado and prawns (£2.30), nut roast (£4.90), plaice niçoise (£5.60), lamb noisettes in a creamy crème de menthe sauce (£5.90) and sea-trout (£6.90). Well kept Devenish JD and Royal Wessex on handpump, decent unobtrusive piped music. There's a smaller, snugger bar on the left (not always open) and a back family-room, with darts, shove-ha'penny, dominoes, table skittles, cribbage, fruit machine and juke box. There are picnic-table sets behind the thatched white house. (*Recommended by Mr and Mrs C France, J F Pritchard, Mr and Mrs D G W Reakes, Dr R B Crail, R Inns, Barry and Anne*)

Devenish Licensee Peter Crowther Real ale Meals and snacks Children in garden-room Open 11–2.30, 6.30–11 all year; opens 7 in winter Bedrooms tel West Lulworth (092 941) 211; £12/£21

EVERSHOT ST5704 Map 2

Acorn ⊗ 🛏

Village signposted from A37 8 miles S of Yeovil

Copies of this warm and friendly village inn's deeds going back to the seventeenth century are hung on the partly hessian-covered bare stone walls in the comfortable L-shaped lounge bar, which also has tapestry-covered wooden benches, and two fine old fireplaces. The carpeted public bar has sensibly placed darts, pool, shove-ha'penny, table skittles, dominoes, cribbage, fruit machine, space game and juke box; the beamed skittle alley – with tables and chairs as well – opens off here and runs alongside the new terrace with its dark oak furniture. Very good, home-made bar food includes a daily home-made soup (£1), sandwiches (from £1.05, £3.25 smoked salmon; toasties 25p extra), burger (£2.45), various ploughmans (from £2.50), salads (from £3.50, home-cooked ham £3.95), lasagne (£3.95), steak and kidney pie or fresh breaded seafood platter (£4.50), and steaks (from £7.50); they specialise in fresh fish, with deliveries three times a week, and have changing daily specials like curries, Somerset pork chops, several vegetarian dishes such as stuffed aubergines or baked egg custard, fish crêpes and fresh game in season (all from about £4.25). Children's meals are available (£1.75); very good breakfasts, and hard-working, polite staff. Well kept Batemans XXXB, Greene King Abbot, Marstons Pedigree, Palmers IPA and Youngs Special (some are kept under light blanket pressure), with weekly changing guest beers; a decent wine list; maybe piped music. A nice village to stay in, 600 feet up in real Hardy country – the inn was the model for Evershead's Sow and Acorn in *Tess of the d'Urbervilles*. There are lots of good walks around. (*Recommended by Peter and Rose Flower, Jack Taylor, Mea Horler, M S Hancock, A Cook, Heather Sharland, D Pearman, A and K D Stansfield, John Nash, P H S Wettern, Ted George, N D Paine, M D Hare*)

Free house Licensees Keith and Denise Morley Real ale Meals and snacks Restaurant Children in refurbished skittle alley and restaurant Open 11–2.30, 6.30–11 all year Bedrooms tel Evershot (093 583) 228; £21B/£28B

Children welcome means the pub says it lets children inside without any special restriction. If it allows them in, but to restricted areas such as an eating area or family-room, we specify this. Places with separate restaurants usually let children use them; hotels usually let them into public areas such as lounges. Some pubs impose an evening time-limit – let us know if you find this.

GODMANSTONE   SY6697 Map 2
Smiths Arms   [illustrated on page 223]
A352 N of Dorchester

This pretty thatched flint building is billed as 'England's smallest inn'. The little bar has high leather bar stools with comfortable back rests, some antique waxed and polished small pews around the walls, one elegant little high-backed settle, National Hunt racing pictures, and a warm atmosphere. Well kept Devenish JD and Royal Wessex Best tapped from casks behind the bar; polite, helpful staff; darts, dominoes, cribbage, backgammon and maybe piped music. Food includes sandwiches, country cottage pie, lasagne, cod and prawn pie and bread pudding and cream. You can sit outside on a crazy-paved terrace or on a grassy mound by the narrow River Cerne – and from here you can walk over to Cowdon Hill to the River Piddle, one of the rivers the devil is supposed to have pissed around Dorchester. *(Recommended by Wayne Brindle, Peter and Rose Flower, John Roué, Paul S McPherson, Roy and Barbara Longman, G Cooper)*

Free house   Licensee John Foster   Real ale   Meals and snacks (not Mon evening in winter) Open all day in summer; 10–2.30, 6.30–11 in winter

HURN   SZ1397 Map 2
Avon Causeway ⊗ 🍺
Hurn signposted off A338, then at Hurn roundabout follow Avon, Sopley, Mutchams singpost

Originally a station on LSWR's Ringwood, Christchurch and Bournemouth line until it was abandoned in 1935, when this first became a pub it used old railway coaches. Those days are long past: it's now virtually entirely rebuilt, with an expansively comfortable and spacious lounge bar. Sturdy pale wood tables are divided into several separate rambling areas by the layout of the button-back plush seats, with softly glowing substantial standard-lamp globes standing sentinel here and there. It's interestingly decorated with scale drawings of steam locomotives and old local timetables, posters, uniforms and photographs, and spreads into an airy Moroccan-theme family-room complete with palm trees. There's a fine range of well kept real ales on handpump – up to eleven, including on our visit Adnams, Marstons Pedigree, Merrie Monk and Owd Rodger, Ringwood Best, Fortyniner and Old Thumper, Wadworths 6X and Farmers Glory and Youngers IPA. Generous helpings of bar food include sandwiches (from 95p), filled baked potatoes (£1.65), basket meals (from £1.75), ploughman's (from £1.95), salads (from £2.85, crab £3.95), fish from cod (£2.95) to salmon (£4.95), steak and kidney pie (£3.25), home-cooked ham and egg (£3.45), weekend roasts (£3.50), steaks (from £6.15) and children's dishes (£1.25). Unobtrusive piped music, fruit machine, space game, trivia. Outside (surrounded by quiet woodland) is fun: they've kept the old platform, with its traditional toothed-edge canopy supporting bright hanging baskets, where sturdy old mahogany station seats face a Pullman carriage (by the time this book is published it should be opened as a restaurant). There are also lots of picnic-table sets under cocktail parasols. *(Recommended by WHBM, Hazel Morgan)*

Free house   Licensees John Ricketts and Paul DuBock   Real ale   Meals and snacks Children in family-room, eating area and restaurant   Open 11–11; 11–2.30, 6–10.30 in winter   Bedrooms tel Christchurch (0202) 482714; £30B/£40B

LANGTON HERRING   SY6182 Map 2
Elm Tree ⊗
Village signposted off B3157

This attractive and very popular food pub still has a wide choice of home-made, often inventive specials under its new licensees, and the food is still that of a pub rather than of a restaurant. It includes sandwiches (from 85p), home-made soup (£1.20), ploughman's (from £2), sausages (£2.50), salmon and prawn pâté (£2.75), bean and pasta bake (£3.25), Danish mushroom and herb cake (£3.50), bacon and apple roll (£3.85), home-made quiches (£3.95), prawn-stuffed garlic bread (£4.10), salads with home-cooked ham or beef (from £4.25), pork and apple curry (£4.65), mixed grill (£5.25), steaks (from £5.50), and home-made ice-creams (from £1.10). The two main carpeted rooms have cushioned window seats, red leatherette stools, Windsor chairs, lots of tables, and beams festooned with copper and brass; there is a central circular modern fireplace in one room, an older inglenook (and some old-fashioned settles) in the other. Devenish Royal Wessex on handpump kept under light top pressure, and a good choice of cocktails listed sensibly, with succinct descriptions; piped music. There are tables out in the pretty flower-filled sunken garden, and a track leads down to the Dorset Coast Path, which here skirts the eight-mile lagoon enclosed by Chesil Beach. (*Recommended by Peter and Rose Flower, Robin Armstrong, Gary Scott, John and Joan Nash, W J Wonham, P J Hanson, J Webb, R D Jolliff, Heather Sharland, W A Rinaldi-Butcher, P J Hanson, K and D E Worrall*)

Devenish   Licensees Anthony and Karen Guarraci   Real ale   Meals and snacks   Open 11–2.30, 6.30–11

LYME REGIS   SY3492   Map 1
Pilot Boat ⊗

Bridge Street

We've always liked this pub, and towards the end of 1987 it got a new boost – in the arrival of the Wiscombes, who previously made the Ilchester Arms at Symondsbury so popular with readers. Mrs Wiscombe was delighted to find, in the notable collection of sailors' hat ribands in the bar, one from her own father's old ship. They've made the bar much lighter and more airy, with more of a dining atmosphere, and comfortable blue plush seating. But besides the ribands, they've kept the local pictures, navy and helicopter photographs, lobster-pot lamps, sharks' heads and the interesting collection of local fossils, and been lent a model of one of the last sailing-ships to use the harbour. Bar food is chalked up on blackboards and changes daily, and includes lots of fish bought fresh every morning from the fishmonger across the road: seafood lasagne (£3.75), skate wings (from £3.75), crab salad (£4.95), seafood salad (£5.50), red mullet, turbot and so forth. Also sandwiches (from 80p, crab £1.25), home-made soup (95p), huge ploughman's or a popular Norwegian mushroom dish (£1.95), steak and kidney pie or vegetable moussaka (£3.95), steaks, puddings such as lemon meringue pie, treacle tart or bread pudding (£1.35), and a children's menu. Palmers Bridport, IPA and Tally Ho on handpump. Darts, dominoes, cribbage. (*Recommended by Peter and Rose Flower, Stan Edwards, Alan and Ruth Woodhouse, Peter Lake, E G Parish, Mrs R Thornton, Derek and Sylvia Stephenson*)

Palmers   Licensee W C Wiscombe   Meals and snacks   Restaurant tel Lyme Regis (029 74) 3157   Children in eating areas   Occasional live entertainment   Open 11–3, 4–11 May–Sept; 11–2.30, 7–11 in winter

LYTCHETT MINSTER   SY9593   Map 2
Bakers Arms

Dorchester Road

This friendly thatched pub – popular with families – is a delight for people with the magpie instinct: army badges, some antique Dorset buttons, cigarette cards, models, watches, holograms, a good collection of English stamps, and a run of annual statistics on some sixty items from 1900 onwards; also birds' eggs (shown with pictures of the birds), and even a glass beehive with working bees. The walls show a complete set of £5, £1 and 10/- English notes and of English silver and copper coins since 1837. The roomy open-plan bar has plenty of comfortable seats and tables on the Turkey carpet, and video displays tell you when you can collect your order from the efficient food counter: home-made soup (90p), ploughman's (from £1.65), three pâtés (from £1.75), basket meals (from £1.85), a range of help-yourself salads (from £3, home-cooked meats from £4.25), home-made steak and kidney pie (£3.50), grilled local trout (£3.95), gammon and pineapple (£4.25), a carvery (from £4.75), and eight-ounce rump steak (£5.75); also daily specials, vegetarian dishes and puddings like home-made applecake (£1). Well kept Flowers Original and Wadworths 6X; fast, efficient service; piped music, fruit machine, trivia, space game and communicating skittle alley. Behind the pub, with tables beside it, is an adventure playground. *(Recommended by Clifford Blakemore, Ken and Dorothy Worrall, WHBM, Tom Evans)*

Free house (part tie to Whitbreads) Licensee Roy Forrest Real ale Meals and snacks Children in eating area Open all day; closed 25 Dec

MARNHULL ST7718 Map 2

Blackmore Vale ⊗

Burton Street; quiet side street

Readers still call this friendly pub Rollivers – the one which Hardy modelled on it in *Tess of the d'Urbervilles*. The carpeted and comfortably modernised lounge bar has cushioned wrought-iron and wooden seats built out from the stripped stone wall at the end that has the log fire; it's decorated with a gun, keys, a few horsebrasses and old brass spigots on the beams. Bar food, brought to your table, includes a range of several home-made pies (from £2.20) including an unusual crab pie done with whisky, cheese and cream (£4.45), and a wide choice of other bar food includes home-made soup (75p), sandwiches (from 85p), ploughman's (from £1.75), lasagne (£2.50), vegetarian dishes like mushroom and nut fettuccine or country lentil crumble (£2.60), home-cooked ham and egg (£2.75), lambs' kidneys in rich sherry sauce with Lincolnshire cocktail sausages and mushrooms (£3.95), gammon and pineapple (£4.25), and steaks (from £6); also children's dishes. Well kept Badger Best and Tanglefoot and Gales BBB on handpump; darts, cribbage, fruit machine, piped music, a skittle alley and boules; a friendly sheepdog. An extensive range of purpose-built wooden children's play equipment was being added as we went to press. *(Recommended by Lyn and Bill Capper, J P Copson, Nigel Paine, Mr and Mrs P W Dryland, CRS, MS)*

Badger Licensees Rodney and Claire Brough Real ale Meals and snacks (not evening 26 Dec) Children in family-bar – if not booked for occasional functions Open 11–2.30, 6–11 all year; will probably stay open longer Sat afternoon; closed 25 Dec

Crown ⇔

B3092

Old settles and elm tables on the huge flagstones of the oak-beamed public bar, with window seats cut into thick stone walls, and logs burning in a big stone hearth, seem like something out of Thomas Hardy, and indeed this was 'The Pure Drop' at 'Marlott' in *Tess of the d'Urbervilles*. The small and comfortable lounge bar has more modern furniture. Good, reasonably priced bar food includes sandwiches (from 75p, toasties from £1), ploughman's or a choice of home-cooked pâtés (from £2), generous omelettes (from £3), scampi, chicken, gammon or steak (from £3), puddings (from £1), and about three daily set lunches (from £2.50); Sunday roast lunch with a choice of two roasts. Well kept Badger Best and Tanglefoot and Worthington Dark on handpump or tapped from the cask – appropriately enough, a stuffed badger lurks half way up the stairs to the bedrooms. Darts, a skittle alley, and fruit machine. You can sit outside by the rose-covered lichened walls looking across to the church or at picnic-table sets on the lawn (where there's a swing). *(Recommended by Roger Huggins, WFL, David Evans, J L and H M B Evans, Mr and Mrs P W Dryland)*

Badger   Licensee Thomas O'Toole   Real ale   Meals and snacks   Restaurant   Children in eating area and restaurant   Open 11–3, 6–11 all year; closed 25 Dec   Bedrooms tel Marnhull (0258) 820224; £14/£28

NETTLECOMBE   SY5195   Map 2
Marquis of Lorne   ⊗ 🛏

Close to Powerstock and can be found by following the routes described under the entry included for that 6illage – see below

In a lovely unspoilt position, this very friendly sixteenth-century inn remains especially popular with readers for its good food: sandwiches (from 90p), home-made soup such as lemon and lentil (£1.30), filled, deep-fried mushrooms with mayonnaise dip (£1.50 starter, £2.50 main course), filled baked potatoes (from £1.95), pâté (£2.25), ploughman's (from £2.25), basket meals (from £2.15), home-cooked ham and egg (£2.95), chicken in barbecue sauce (£3.25), chicken Kiev (£5.25), vegetarian moussaka (£5.95), sirloin steak (£6.50), half a honey-roasted duck (£6.95), and salads in summer; superb Sunday lunch (three courses £6.50). Well kept Palmers Bridport and IPA on handpump; darts, shove-ha'penny, dominoes, liar dice, table skittles and piped music. The main bar has green plush button-back small settles and round green stools by highly varnished tables on a flowery blue carpet, and a log fire; a similar side room decorated in shades of brown opens off it. The big garden has masses of swings, climbing-frames and so forth among the picnic-table sets under its apple trees. Very good value winter weekdays bed and breakfast. *(Recommended by Peter and Rose Flower, Mr and Mrs F W Sturch, Jon Dewhirst, Gordon and Daphne, John Clements, Derek and Sylvia Stephenson, Roger and Kathy, C R and M S, D J Ferrett, Mrs L Coleridge)*

Palmers   Licensee Robert Bone   Real ale   Meals and snacks   Restaurant   Children in eating area and restaurant   Open 10.30–2.30, 6–11 all year; closed 25 Dec   Bedrooms tel Powerstock (030 885) 236; £13.50(£15B)/£27(£30B)

POOLE   SZ0190   Map 2
Angel   ⊗

28 Market Street; opposite Guildhall which is signposted off A348 in centre – parking at the pub

One reader reckons he must have tried Poole's pubs, all of them (are there really fifty-one?), in the wrong order, as he's only just found this soothingly refurbished and well run place. The spacious relaxed lounge has cushioned banquettes forming bays around pale wood tables, with a couple of sofas, and its walls, carefully decorated in shades of green, are hung with turn-of-the-century prints, magazine covers and advertisements including ones by Toulouse-Lautrec and Mocha, as well as naughty 1920s seaside postcards and some interesting old local photographs. Bar food from a separate efficient servery includes sandwiches, cauliflower and almond au gratin (£2.50), several hot dishes such as fisherman's pie, pork chop in cider or home-made steak and kidney pie (£2.95) and various salads (from £2.95), with children's helpings at half-price as well as a separate menu for them (around £1.25). There are picnic-table sets in the back courtyard, with summer barbecues and (often on Saturdays) pig roasts, perhaps with live music. Well kept Ushers Best and Ruddles Best and County on handpump (with spirits half-price 6–7 except Sunday); fruit machine, trivia, piped music, Sunday quiz league in winter; besides various fancy-dress party nights, they have an August charity fete, cricket team, football team and Thursday disc jockey. The handsome eighteenth-century Guild-hall is a museum of the town's development. *(Recommended by WHBM)*

Ushers (Watneys)   Licensees A A Gray and D McGuigan   Real ale   Meals and snacks
Children in new family-room   Open 11–11 all year

POWERSTOCK   SY5196 Map 2
Three Horseshoes ⊗ 🍺

Can be reached by taking Askerswell turn off A35 then keeping uphill past the Spyway Inn, and bearing left all the way around Eggardon Hill – a lovely drive, but steep narrow roads; a better road is signposted West Milton off the A3066 Beaminster–Bridport, then take Powerstock road

On the neat lawn perched steeply above this secluded stone and thatch pub there are charming views, as well as swings and a climbing-frame. Inside, the comfortable L-shaped bar has country-style chairs around the polished tables, pictures on the stripped panelled walls and warm fires. Good bar food concentrates on fresh local fish, such as a properly made fresh fish soup or moules marinière (£3.50), prawns (half-pint £3.95, pint £4.95), fresh crab (from £4), wing of skate with black butter (£4.75), good grilled Lyme Bay plaice (£5), scallops in lovely sauce (£7.50); other food includes French onion soup (£1.60), an interesting hors d'oeuvre trolley with sixteen different things such as three sorts of salami, smoked mackerel and trout, fresh mussels, several salads, green, black or stuffed olives, taramosalata, asparagus and so forth (single items £2, vegetarian plate £3, mixed plate £3.75), ploughman's with interesting cheeses (£3.25), wholewheat pancakes with spinach and cheese sauce (£2.75), roast rack of local lamb and sirloin steak (£6.50); Sunday roast (£5.25). Well kept Palmers Bridport and IPA on handpump; good service. *(Recommended by J Roots, Philip and Trisha Ferris, D Pearman, Derek and Sylvia Stephenson, R D Jolliff, Mr and Mrs T Dawson, HEG, Nancy Brien, Mr and Mrs C France, David Mortimer, Peter and Rose Flower)*

Palmers   Licensee P W Ferguson   Real ale   Meals (not Sun or Mon evenings in winter without prior booking) and snacks   Restaurant   Well behaved children welcome
Open all day in summer according to demand by trade; 10.30–2.30, 6–11 in winter
Bedrooms tel Powerstock (030 885) 328; £16/£37.50B

RAMPISHAM   ST5602 Map 2
Tigers Head ⊗ 🍺

Pub (and village) signposted off A356 Dorchester–Crewkerne; OS Sheet 194 reference 561023

Built in 1915 to replace an earlier pub which had burned down, this can't have changed much since – as indeed the local landowners who still let the pub are careful to ensure. The most important consequence is that the atmosphere has a delightful flavour of the past that in our experience is now almost unique: this is where people from all walks of life in this pretty valley village catch up on each other's news (and jokes), and are punctilious about making sure strangers don't feel excluded. Two little rooms have comfortable old settles and a sofa, and hunting prints of all ages that are clearly a careful personal choice; countless competition award rosettes above the bar confirm that riding's a particular interest of the licensees (Mrs Austin judges at horse shows, too), who with notice can arrange riding, clay-pigeon shooting or fishing for residents. Bar food, all home made and largely using local ingredients and fresh vegetables, includes sandwiches (80p), steak and kidney pie, rabbit pie or a range of vegetarian dishes (£3.25), venison casserole (£5.25) and steaks up to a twenty-four-ounce rump (£11.90); well kept Bass, Butcombe and Wadworths 6X tapped from casks behind the bar on our visit, though you may find Marstons Pedigree or Palmers IPA instead; local farm cider. There are darts, shove-ha'penny, dominoes, table skittles and a skittle alley; a friendly Burmese cat wanders in and out, though customers' favourite is Gladys the bulldog (a seasoned TV personality). An attractive sheltered back garden has picnic-table sets; this is pleasant walking country. (*Recommended by John Roué, Heather Sharland, Bill Hendry, Peter and Rose Flower, Angie and Dave Parkes*)

Free house   Licensees Mike and Pat Austin   Real ale   Meals and snacks   Children's room Restaurant   Open 11–3, 7–11 all year   Two bedrooms tel Evershot (093 583) 244; £15/£30

SHAFTESBURY   ST8622 Map 2
Ship

Bleke Street; you pass pub on main entrance to town from N

The main bar counter in this unpretentious and traditionally furnished seventeeth-century pub has a striking old oak staircase climbing up behind it, and seats built into the snug black-panelled alcove facing it; on the left is a panelled but similarly furnished room, and, down on the right, a more modern room with pool and darts. Well kept Badger Best and Tanglefoot on handpump; cribbage, fruit machine and juke box. Bar food includes soup (95p), toasted sandwiches (£1.20), ploughman's (£1.50), open prawn sandwich (£1.75), pizza or Wiltshire home-cured ham (£2.95), chicken or scampi (£3.50) and steaks (£6.50). Outside this handsome old building, there's a small beer garden. They no longer do bedrooms. (*Recommended by Barry and Anne, Hope Chenhalls, Gordon and Daphne*)

Badger   Licensee Ronald May   Real ale   Meals and snacks   Children in eating area   Open 10.30–2.30, 6.30–11 all year

SHAVE CROSS   SY4198 Map 1
Shave Cross Inn ★ ⊗

On back lane Bridport–Marshwood, signposted locally; OS Sheet 193 reference 415980

Several very strong attractions to this civilised cottagey pub include the beautiful surrounding countryside of the Marshwood Vale, friendly, polite staff, and an excellent ploughman's (£1.25). The original timbered bar is a lovely flagstoned room with an enormous inglenook fireplace with plates hanging from the chimney breast, one big table in the middle, a smaller one by the window seat, and a row of chintz-cushioned Windsor chairs. The larger carpeted side lounge has modern rustic light-coloured seats making booths around the tables, and a dresser at one end set with plates. Good bar food includes soup (40p), pâté (£1.55), basket meals (from £1.95), daily specials like lamb and apricot pie, lasagne or pork and apple in cider (£2.75), salads that include fresh crab or lobster (from £2.75), puddings such as Dorset applecake, and children's meals (from £1.25). Well kept Badger Best, Bass and Huntsman Royal Oak on handpump; darts, table skittles, dominoes, cribbage and space game. The pretty flower-filled garden, sheltered by the thatched partly fourteenth-century pub and its long skittle alley, has a thatched wishing-well and a goldfish pool. There's a children's adventure playground, and a small secluded campsite for touring caravans and campers. (*Recommended by Gordon and Daphne, Peter and Rose Flower, J E F Rawlins, A and K D Stansfield, Mrs Joan Harris, Paul and Margaret Baker, Derek and Sylvia Stephenson, Mrs A Roberts, E A George*)

Free house   Licensees Bill and Ruth Slade   Real ale   Meals and snacks (not Mon, except bank hols)   Children in two family-rooms   Open 11–3 (2.30 in winter), 7–11 all year; closed Mon (exc bank hols)

STOKE ABBOTT   ST4500 Map 1
New Inn ⊗

Village signposted from B3162 and B3163 W of Beaminster

We haven't heard whether the new licensees have kept the good matchbox collection behind the serving-counter in the black-beamed carpeted bar of this well kept inn; a settle is built into a snug stripped-stone alcove beside the big log fireplace, there are wheel-back chairs and cushioned built-in settles around its simple wooden tables, and old coins framed on the walls. Bar food includes ploughman's or basket meals (from £1.95), home-made pizza or quiche (£2.75), salads or vegetarian dishes (from £2.95), plaice or chicken curry (£3.25), excellent home-made steak and kidney pie (£3.50), ten-ounce sirloin steak (£7.15), mixed grill (£7.25), home-made puddings (£1.20), and daily specials. Well kept Palmers Bridport, IPA and Tally Ho on handpump kept under light blanket pressure; table skittles, romantic piped music (an enormous choice of tapes), and pleasant, friendly service. The well kept garden – with soporific views of sheep grazing on the sides of the peaceful valley – shelters behind a golden stone wall which merges into attractively planted rockery; there are swings and long gnarled silvery logs to sit on, as well as wooden benches by the tables. (*Recommended by D G Nicolson, Gordon Lane, Paul McPherson*)

Palmers   Licensee Graham Gibbs   Real ale   Meals and snacks   Children in dining-room Open 12–2.30, 7–11 all year; they may open longer in afternoon if trial period is successful Bedrooms tel Broadwindsor (0308) 68333; £12/£20

TARRANT MONKTON   ST9408 Map 2
Langton Arms ⊗

Village signposted from A354, then head for church

This welcoming and pretty seventeenth-century thatched pub has special food themes on most evenings – Chinese, French, pizzas and curry, as well as minestrone or lentil and onion soup (£1), pâté or salmon mousse (£1.75), good value ploughman's (£1.75), steak and kidney pudding, chilli con carne, or mushroom florentine (£2.40), salads (£2.50), plaice (£4), gammon (£4.25) and steaks (from £5.50); also daily specials such as Italian fennel casserole, cauliflower and ham Mornay or pork suprême (£2.40) and puddings such as filled pancakes or chocolate mousse (£1). To be sure of a table, it's best to get there early. The main bar has window seats and another table or two at the serving end where the floor's tiled, and settles forming a couple of secluded booths around tables at the carpeted end. The public bar, with a big inglenook fireplace, has darts, shove-ha'penny, dominoes, cribbage and juke box, while a skittle alley with its own bar and more tables has a space game and fruit machine. Well kept Adnams Bitter, Bass, Wadworths 6X and guest beers on handpump or tapped from the cask; piped music. There's a barbecue in the pretty garden. On the end of the building, they have opened a village/craft/delicatessen shop. To get to the pub – by the village church – you drive through a shallow ford, and the surrounding countryside is attractive, with tracks leading up to Crichel Down above the village. Badbury Rings, a hill fort by the B3082 just south of here, is very striking. (*Recommended by Charles and Mary Winpenny, Bernard Phillips, Richard Cole, David Jones, Alison Kerruish, Roger and Kathy, Roy McIsaac, Mrs A Roberts, CG, Margaret Drazin, Paul McPherson, Brigid Avison, Mrs L Coleridge, Gwen and Peter Andrews*)

Free house   Licensees Chris and Diane Goodinge   Real ale   Meals and snacks   Restaurant Children welcome   Occasional live music   Open 11.30–2.30, 6–11 all year   Bedrooms tel Tarrant Hinton (025 889) 225; £23B/£35B

WEST BEXINGTON   SY5387 Map 2
Manor Hotel ⊗ 🛏

Village signposted off B3157 SE of Bridport, opposite the Bull in Swyre

A handsome Victorian-style conservatory with airy furnishings and lots of plants has been added on to this small and well kept hotel. The popular, pubby Cellar Bar is reached down a flight of steps from the handsome flagstoned and Jacobean carved-oak-panelled hall: soft lighting, heavy harness over the log fire, small country pictures and good leather-mounted horsebrasses on the walls, black beams and joists, and red leatherette stools and low-backed chairs (with one fat seat carved from a beer cask). A good choice of bar food includes home-made soup (£1.25), sandwiches (from £1.45, very fresh crab £2.35), ploughman's (from £2.25), smoked mackerel pâté (£2.45), salads (from £2.95, crab £4.95), fresh sardines in garlic butter (£3.35), home-made steak and kidney pie, casserole of guinea-fowl or chicken in cider with mushrooms (£4.25), whole local plaice (£5.95), scallops (£6.95), poached salmon, steaks, and puddings like sherry trifle or fresh fruit salad (£1.55); they also have daily specials, vegetarian dishes and children's specials. Well kept Huntsman Royal Oak, Palmers Bridport (which here carries the pub's name) and Wadworths 6X on handpump; smiling, efficient service; skittle alley, trivia and piped music. The spreading south-sloping garden has picnic-table sets on a small lawn with flower beds lining the low sheltering walls, and a much bigger side lawn with a children's play area. A smashing place to stay or visit, and just a stroll (past the bungalows which make up most of this village) to the sea. *(Recommended by Ian Phillips, Alan and Ruth Woodhouse, Jon Dewhirst, Heather Sharland, John and Joan Nash, Mrs M C Gray, Derek and Sylvia Stephenson, Gwen and Peter Andrews)*

Free house   Licensee Richard Childs   Real ale   Meals and snacks   Restaurant Well behaved children in eating area of bar and conservatory   Open 11–2.30, 6–11 all year; closed evening 25 Dec   Bedrooms tel Burton Bradstock (0308) 897616; £27.95B/£49B

WEST LULWORTH   SY8280   Map 2
Castle ⊗ ⇌
B3070

The cosy if modern-feeling lounge bar in this warmly friendly little thatched inn is comfortably furnished with blue banquettes under the countryside prints on the walls, and pewter tankards hanging from one beam; the lively public bar has polished flagstones and button-back leatherette seats forming a maze of booths around the tables. Quickly served and geared to tourists, the popular bar snacks include sandwiches, generous filled rolls (from 90p), soup, a choice of ploughman's (£2.40 – the ham is good), local fish, sweet-and-sour pork or chicken (£3), salads (crab £5, prawn £6), and daily specials; excellent breakfasts. Well kept Devenish JD, Royal Wessex and GBH on handpump; darts, shove-ha'penny, table skittles, dominoes, cribbage, fruit machine, trivia and piped music. There is a large barbecue area in the garden on the lawn above steeply terraced rose beds behind the thatched white house. Best to walk down to Lulworth Cove from here, as the car park at the bottom is expensive; there are lots of fine walks in the area, usually with splendid views. *(Recommended by Ian Phillips, Alan and Ruth Woodhouse, Barry and Anne, D Pearman, Heather Sharland, Mr and Mrs P W Dryland, P J Hanson, Tim Locke, Mr and Mrs A F Walker)*

Devenish   Licensee G B Halliday   Real ale   Meals and snacks   Restaurant   Open all day in summer; 11–2.30, 7–11 in winter; closed 25 Dec   Bedrooms tel West Lulworth (092 941) 311; £15(£18B)/£25(£30B)

WORTH MATRAVERS (Isle of Purbeck)   SY9777   Map 2
Square & Compass
At fork of both roads signposted to village from B3069

People looking for unruffled relaxation really enjoy this defiantly traditional pub. It's been in the Newman family for eighty years, and the old-fashioned main bar has interesting local pictures under its low ceilings, and wall benches around the elbow-polished old tables on the flagstones. Whitbreads Pompey Royal and Strong Country are tapped from a row of casks behind a couple of hatches in the flagstoned corridor (local fossils back here, and various curios inside the servery), which leads to a more conventional but very rarely opened summer bar; friendly service. Darts, shove-ha'penny, dominoes, bar snacks such as home-made pasties or filled rolls and ploughman's. There are seats outside on a side lawn that look down over the village rooftops to the sea showing between the East Man and the West Man (hills that guard the sea approach); on summer evenings you can watch the sun set beyond Portland Bill. The pub is at the start of an OS Walkers Britain walk and on *Good Walks Guide* Walk 25. (*Recommended by Peter Hitchcock, Phil and Sally Gorton, C Gray, D Pearman, Alan and Audrey Chatting, Barry and Anne, Roy McIsaac, Jane and Calum, Steve and Carolyn Harvey, Jon and Ros MacKenzie*)

Whitbreads   Real ale   Snacks   Children in eating area and small children's room   Open 10.30–3, 6–11 all year; closes 2.30 in winter

Lucky Dip

Besides the fully inspected pubs, you might like to try these Lucky Dips recommended to us and described by readers (if you do, please send us reports):

Almer [just off A31; SY9097], *Worlds End*: Charming fifteenth-century thatched pub with beautifully renovated red tiles, horse-brasses, wide choice of good value food in eating area decorated with straw hats and fans (children allowed here), Badger Best and a beer brewed for the pub, friendly atmosphere; tables out in former sheep pen, play area (*Gwen and Peter Andrews, Mark Walpole, Melanie White*)

☆ **Ansty** [Higher Ansty; NB not to be confused with the Ansty in Wilts; ST7603], *Fox*: After hiccups in service and food quality (and a price hoik) during 1987, most recent indications are that this intriguingly decorated place is again giving more general satisfaction – and it has been smartened up; there's a fantastic collection of toby jugs and of colourful plates, and a well equipped children's bar; the countryside is most attractive; bedrooms (*Steve Dark, Dr R B Crail, R Sinclair Taylor, Dr K Bloomfield, LYM – more reports please*)

Bere Regis [West St; SY8494], *Royal Oak*: Very friendly family-run Whitbreads pub, good meals in dining-room at very reasonable prices; family-room, cheap bedrooms with good breakfasts (*Peter Davies*)

Bournemouth [SZ0991], *Broadway*: The old gentleman in the corner, Snowy, has reputedly been in here *every* day since the pub opened in 1935 (*WHBM*); [423 Charminster Rd] *Fiveways*: A good example of refurbishment, interesting but not too effusive, with pleasant atmosphere, wide range of good food including children's dishes (they even heat your baby food), three Huntsman beers on handpump, good games-room with two pool-tables and efficient built-in ventilation; no-smoking area (*Jack Rayfield, WHBM*)

Bradford Abbas [ST5814], *Rose & Crown*: Well managed and clean, with pleasant service, good food and Huntsman ales; bedrooms (*John Roué*)

Branksome [Pinewood Rd; SZ0590], *Inn in the Park*: Converted Victorian house in

classy residential suburb of Bournemouth, clean and well run, with well kept Ringwood and reasonably priced bar food – useful for the area; bedrooms (*Bernard Phillips, WHBM, John Knighton*)

Buckhorn Weston [ST7524], *Stapleton Arms*: Spacious and friendly, piped classical music, good choice of well kept real ales, reasonably priced bar food, garden (*Nigel Paine*)

Burton Bradstock [SY4889], *Anchor*: Big helpings of good food, excellent puddings (*Mr and Mrs J Holden*); *Three Horseshoes*: Attractive thatched inn with comfortable carpeted lounge, Palmers real ales, ploughman's and good range of hot and cold dishes including children's ones, nice atmosphere with no piped music, restaurant, bedrooms; pleasant shingle beach a few minutes' drive away (*Lyn and Bill Capper*)

Cattistock [SY5999], *Fox & Hounds*: Good value food in beamed character bar with decorative hunt theme; some readers have found good service, others not (*D C Jacobs, CRS, MS, LYM*)

Cerne Abbas [ST6601], *Red Lion*: Cosy, picturesque and friendly, with real ale, good food and real oak beams; licensee ex-Dorchester Regiment (*WFL, John Roué*)

Charlton Marshall [A350 Poole–Blandford; ST9004], *Charlton*: Attractive refurbished country-style bars with friendly, obliging staff, wide choice of good value and generously served food, unobtrusive piped music, Badger Best and Tanglefoot (*Richard Burton*)

Charmouth [SY3693], *Charmouth House*: Warm welcome, good food, wide choice of beers; bedrooms very comfortable (*Mr and Mrs J E Short*); *Royal Oak*: Cheerful public bar with good service and beer, quick food, tranquil lounge bar (*Mr Savage*)

Chesil [SY6873], *Little Ship*: Friendly local with Huntsman beers and bar food (*T R G Alcock*)

Chetnole [ST6007], *Chetnole Arms*: Well kept real ale in quiet, comfortable and pleasant village pub owned by very pleasant teetotal ex-Australian policeman; no piped music *(Mrs K C Livingstone-Joyce, Capt Joyce)*

Chickerell [SY6480], *Lugger*: Pleasant welcome from new landlord, down from London *(Peter and Rose Flower)*

Chideock [SY4292], *Clock*: Engaging mix of styles and furnishings in open-plan bar with feminist Amazon parrot, aquarium, popular food, well kept Devenish Wessex, table skittles, brightly lit pool-table; restaurant, simple bedrooms; nr GWG23 *(BB)*

☆ nr **Chideock** [Seatown, which is signposted off A35; SY4291], *Anchor*: This little pub, isolated in a lovely setting by the sea, is quite a favourite in winter with its quiet welcome, well kept Palmers beer, and roaring log fires and sundry cats and dogs; in summer, when it can be crowded, it's most appreciated by families who enjoy the fried fish and so forth – there's a good family-room, with picnic-table sets outside; nr GWG23 *(Mrs H M Martin, Tim Locke, R H Inns, Mrs A Roberts, Steve and Carolyn Harvey, HEG, LYM)*

☆ **Child Okeford** [on lane entering village from A357 Sturminster Newton–Blandford; ST8312], *Union Arms*: Has been a favourite with readers who like little unchanged village pubs, with Hook Norton Best and summer guest beers, good value lunchtime snacks, high-backed wooden settles huddled around big open fire, traditional games; but we've had no news of the new owner who took over at the end of 1987 – except for hearing that he was even considering changing the pub's name *(Gordon and Daphne, LYM; reports please, particularly on changes to furnishings and style)*

Christchurch [Walkford Rd – OS Sheet 195 reference 222943; SZ1593], *Amberwood Arms*: Large, warm and comfortable, excellent range of imaginative bar meals, well kept Huntsman ales, ring the bull, good value restaurant; children welcome *(M V Beiley)*; [Church St] *Castle*: Friendly pub near the Priory, plush seats and stools, carpet, unobtrusive piped music, fine range of real ales including Bass or Worthington, Ringwood Best, Fortyniner and Old Thumper, and a guest such as Felinfoel; usual pub food, upstairs folk nights; Norman wall, once part of castle, forms part of back kitchen; very busy July–Aug *(Lyn and Bill Capper, G S Crockett, Roger and Kathy)*; *Royalty*: Large, clean, modern pub; Flowers Original, Wadworths 6X and Whitbreads Pompey Royal, wide choice of filled baked potatoes and puddings *(John Hayward)*

Church Knowle [SY9481], *New*: Stripped stone and high rafters in leather-seated pub with children's bar, well kept Devenish beers, restaurant (with some concentration on fish), pub games; breakfast 8.30–11, takeaway picnics; can get very busy in summer *(Mrs Margaret Branney, S J A Velate, Heather Sharland, Dr R F Fletcher, LYM)*

Dorchester [Monmouth Rd; SY6890], *Bakers Arms*: Friendly licensees, still has previous bakers' ovens in one tiled wall, good, simple home-made food, Huntsman ales *(Ian Phillips)*; [High East St] *Kings Arms*: Smart old-fashioned hotel with well kept Huntsman IPA and Bitter and wide choice of freshly prepared and reasonably priced bar food including plenty of vegetarian dishes, in comfortably refurbished lounge bar; close associations with Nelson and Hardy's *Mayor of Casterbridge*; bedrooms *(D Pearman, LYM)*; [High East St] *Tom Browns*: Pleasant and unpretentious, brewing its own Goldfinch Tom Brown and Flashmans Clout *(Stan Edwards)*; [A352 towards Wareham] *Trumpet Major*: Big pub in spacious grounds with good play area, wide choice of food including mixed grill, well kept beer, dining area off sporting-theme public bar, restaurant off lounge; children welcome *(Stan Edwards)*; [53 High East St] *White Hart*: Friendly pub on edge of town centre, well kept Badger Tanglefoot, good value bar food, wide variety of pub games, singing and juggling landlord *(S M House)*

Farnham [ST9515], *Museum*: Cosily renovated bar with inglenook, real ales, excellent food and house wines; four good value bedrooms *(John Kirk)*

Ferndown [SZ0700], *Fox & Hounds*: Good value traditionally prepared bar food in very pleasant refurbished pub *(C G Stephens)*

☆ **Fiddleford** [A357 Sturminster Newton–Blandford Forum; ST8013], *Fiddleford*: Too soon to give a clear verdict on the new owners who took over in autumn 1987, but the real ales are interesting, the food attractively varied if not cheap, and the atmosphere in the nicely furnished bar with its vast flagstones usually warmly friendly; good garden with play area; bedrooms comfortable *(WHBM, Mrs V Borski, LYM)*

Gillingham [off B3081 at Wyke 1 mile NW, pub 100yds on left; ST8026], *Buffalo*: Good local with lovely cheap seafood specials and first-class home-made minestrone; friendly customers and landlord *(Nigel Paine, Mea Horler)*; [in village] *Red Lion*: Good helpings of reasonably priced food, well cooked and presented; friendly atmosphere *(Mr and Mrs A F Walker)*

Gold Hill [ST8313], *Saxon*: Friendly, comfortable and cosy with a good choice of tasty food; log fire and wood-burning stove *(Mrs Sybil Baker)*

Hinton St Mary [ST7816], *White Horse*: Excellent fish such as fresh mackerel pâté and local trout, wide choice of other fresh food such as pheasant casserole, in small simple lounge bar; Wadworths 6X, darts in larger public bar, no piped music; superb manor house and medieval tithe barn in beautifully quiet village *(Lyn and Bill Capper, Michael Revell)*

☆ **Horton** [SU0207], *Drusillas*: Friendly staff, good food such as steak and kidney or cod and prawn pie, well kept beer; pleasant atmosphere, nice dining-room *(John Kirk, JMW)*

Kingstag [ST7210], *Green Man*: Very friendly unpretentious pub, generous helpings of tasty well presented home-made food including excellent venison sausages *(Mrs L Coleridge, Mea Horler)*

☆ **Kingston** [B3069; SY9579], *Scott Arms*: General agreement on the superb view of Corfe Castle from the garden, and on the good family-room, and the rambling layout is interesting; best food value is usually the steak and kidney pie; Devenish beers; too much of a commercial tourist operation to please everyone, though; efficient service even when busy (which it is in summer – can be very quiet in winter), bedrooms comfortable; on GWG25 *(A P Carr, Mr and Mrs G J Lewis, Phil and Sally Gorton, Dr A V Lewis, R Inns, RH, Roy McIsaac, P J Hanson, LYM)*

Langton Matravers [SY9978], *Kings Arms*: Popular village local with fine marble fireplace in simple beamed main bar, friendly customers and staff, good pub games including splendid antique Purbeck longboard for shove-ha'penny; children's room, seats outside; bedrooms *(Phil and Sally Gorton, LYM)*; [B3069 nr junction with A351] *Ship*: Robust basic locals' pub with lively Purbeck longboard, shove-ha'penny and very cheap bedrooms *(LYM)*

Longham [A348 Ferndown–Poole; SZ0698], *Angel*: Spacious pub, based on much smaller original core; open fires, nooks and corners, well kept Badger ales, reasonably priced home-made food (not Mon evening), collection of famed banknotes, well equipped play area in big garden – even trampolines; children in family eating room *(WHBM)*; [Ringwood Rd] *Bridge House*: Real ale, good value snacks and carvery meals, friendly service, garden *(Ken and Dorothy Worrall, P Gillbe)*

Lyme Regis [The Cobb; SY3492], *Cobb Arms*: Harbourside pub with very good atmosphere, well kept beer, lots of maps of wrecks *(Dr and Mrs A K Clarke)*; [Broad St] *Royal Lion*: Old-fashioned many-roomed bar with well kept if pricey Hancocks ale, food, games-room, restaurant; comfortable bedrooms *(Prof S Barnett, LYM)*; [Broad St] *Three Cups*: Interesting upgraded pub with stained-glass panels above the bar and other wall decorations *(Dr and Mrs A K Clarke)*; [top of Broad St (A3052 towards Exeter)] *Volunteer*: Dozens of chamber-pots and so forth in cosy low-ceilinged bar, good value simple food, well kept Hancocks HB; ebullient landlord is a town crier *(Bob Smith, LYM)*

Maiden Newton [Main St; SY5997], *Chalk & Cheese*: Recently refurbished pub with new, attentive, hard-working licensees; well kept Devenish beers, usual bar food, skittle alley *(Bill Hendry)*

Marshwood [SY3799], *Bottle*: Simple country pub with well kept Ushers, traditional games and skittle alley; usually has reasonably priced bar food and is handy for pretty walking country *(Gordon and Daphne, WHBM, LYM)*

Melplash [SY4898], *Half Moon*: Good value lunches, excellent evening choice, caters for vegetarians *(Mrs R Thornton)*

Middlemarsh [A352 Sherborne–Dorchester; ST6607], *White Horse*: Decent food in dining area by bar and in bright and clean recently opened restaurant, attentive service; bedrooms *(Anon)*

☆ **Milton Abbas** [ST8001], *Hambro Arms*: Like the beautifully landscaped village, this pretty inn is a powerful draw in the tourist season, and still favoured by most readers after a change of management and the opening up of the bar (many consider the alterations attractive); we'd like their opinion confirmed by others, please, before reinstating this as a main entry; well kept Devenish on handpump, decent bar food; on GWG24; neat bedrooms *(Derek and Sylvia Stephenson, WHBM, A Cook, Roy and Barbara Longman, Tom Evans, P R Slater, Tim Locke, LYM)*

☆ **Mosterton** [High St; ST4505], *Admiral Hood*: Ancient stone building that's survived fire (and alterations) unscathed – lovely open fireplace with blocked-off stone stairs behind in large L-shaped bar, nice friendly landlord; some concentration on big helpings of good food with fresh vegetables, though still used by the locals; good beer; lavatories get top marks; children welcome in dining area *(Gordon and Daphne, Mrs J B Eveleigh, Nigel Paine)*

☆ **Mudeford** [beyond huge seaside car park at Mudeford Pier – OS Sheet 195 reference 182916; SZ1891], *Haven House*: Quaint old heart to much-extended seaside pub with well kept Devenish ales and good value snacks and lunchtime meals; family cafeteria, tables on sheltered terrace; touch of authenticity given by red telephone on bar counter For Lifeboat Crew Only; you can walk for miles eastwards along the foreshore from here *(P Gillbe, WHBM, Mike Matthews, LYM)*

☆ **Osmington Mills** [SY7381], *Smugglers*: Good bar food from ploughman's, deep-fried garlicky mushrooms filled with pâté or hot avocado and crab, to swordfish steak, monkfish, or mixed grill; well kept Courage and Ringwood (but cellar so far from bar that they have to use a lot of pressure), good house wine; licensees previously won high rating from us when they ran the Black Dog at Broadmayne *(John Kirk, WHBM and others)*

Piddlehinton [SY7197], *Thimble*: Comfortable thatched picture-postcard inn with welcoming atmosphere, decent bar food and real ale; homely good value bedrooms, good varied breakfasts *(Mr and Mrs A Court, WHBM)*

Piddletrenthide [SY7099], *Poachers*: Convenient, attractive setting, big riverside garden, good range of traditional food in pleasant oak-beamed bar with dining area, also restaurant; bedrooms *(HRH, Jim Matthews)*

Pimperne [off A354; ST9009], *Anvil*: Friendly locals and welcoming staff in pleasant beamed bar, but hotel licence, so customers can have alcoholic drink only with food – such as good plaice or baked Dorset crab; comfortable bedrooms *(JMW, Michael Bolsover)*

Plush [village signposted from B3143 N of Dorchester at Piddletrenthide; ST7102], *Brace of Pheasants*: On form, this charmingly placed thatched pub is so delightful that it's hard to beat, with a good deal of character in its comfortable beamed bar, well kept Bass and Hancocks HB, and good-sized garden and play area; food usually interesting and good value, service variable; children in restaurant and family area *(Mea Horler, Wayne Brindle, Dr A V Lewis, Cdr F A Costello, R B Crail, Gwen and Peter Andrews, HRH, J E F Rawlins, K and D E Worrall, Heather Sharland, A J and R A Buchan, J M Watkinson, LYM)*

Poole [Sandbanks Rd, Lilliput; SZ0190], *Beehive*: Old stripped beams imported into large suburban family pub with no-smoking area, Huntsman Dorset and Dorchester on handpump, bar food; terrace with cook-it-yourself barbecues, big play area *(Jack Rayfield, S J A Velate)*; [Harbour] *Jolly Sailor*: Lovely atmosphere and unusual dishes including fresh scampi in garlic sauce *(The Edwickers)*; [Quayside] *Poole Arms*: Magnificent green-tiled façade of waterfront tavern looking across harbour to Brownsea Island; handy for Poole Aquarium *(LYM)*

Portland [Grove Rd; SY6876], *Clifton*: Good well kept beer, big helpings of good food at low prices, A1 staff *(A Atkins)*; [Reforne] *George*: Low beams and fine old Portland stone in ancient pub mentioned by Thomas Hardy and reputed to have smugglers' tunnels running to the cliffs, massive helpings of good value food, Cornish Original, Royal Wessex and Websters Yorkshire *(WHBM, J A Harrison)*; [Portland Bill] *Pulpit*: Refurbished, piped music, Gibbs Mew beers, restaurant *(T R G Alcock)*

Pymore [SY4694], *Pymore*: Unpretentiously clean and smart with a friendly welcome and very good home-cooked food *(Jean and Roger Skipper)*

Sandbanks [73 Haven Rd; SZ0387], *Harbour Heights*: Attractive hotel busy at lunchtime for reasonably priced bar food, stunning views from window tables *(B J E Phillips)*

☆ **Sandford Orcas** [ST6220], *Mitre*: Remote and delightful old village pub; landlord, a vintage motor-cycle enthusiast, and wife give spinning demonstrations using wool from their own sheep; very good reasonably priced food served in stone-flagged dining-room, well kept Bass, wood-burning stove – with up to

five whippets and two cats snuggled in front of it; children welcome *(John Nash, Nigel Paine)*

Shaftesbury [The Commons; ST8622], *Grosvenor*: Pleasant wistaria-covered former coaching-inn with small fish pond in front, now a THF hotel; public bar used by locals, serving cheap bar food including large ploughman's with endless 'ready-cooked' bread and help-yourself salad *(Heather Sharland)*; [High St] *Mitre*: Lovely view from cosy lounge bar of well kept inn with good bar food, decent wines and well kept Huntsman real ales; bedrooms *(JMW, LYM)*; [Cheap St] *Cross Keys*: Pleasant clean Huntsman pub with attractively decorated lounge and public bar, close to east end of abbey *(John Roué)*

☆ **Sherborne** [Cooks Lane; ST6316], *Digby Tap*: Good traditional pub in side street near abbey, simple but with lots of character and busy unspoilt atmosphere, pub games, good variety of well kept real ales and farm cider; good value food, seats outside *(Mr and Mrs C France, A J Ritson, D Pearman)*

Sherborne [Swan Passage], *Swan*: Long, low-beamed historic pub with pleasant and relaxed atmosphere, real ales, good food, friendly service *(Anon)*

Southbourne [Broadway – OS Sheet 195 reference 155914; SZ1591], *Saxon King*: Spacious pub, not old, with Huntsman ales and good atmosphere; locally useful, for walks on Hengistbury Head *(Anon)*

Stratton [SY6593], *Bull*: Friendly beamed local with well kept Huntsman Dorchester and good range of bar food, restaurant *(Paul and Margaret Baker)*

☆ **Studland** [SZ0382], *Bankes Arms*: Modest inn with simple, friendly bar and excellent views of Poole Harbour and Bournemouth Bay from garden; well kept beer, huge quantities of good, plain food, pleasant atmosphere; attractive surroundings at start of south-western Coast Path, also nr start GWG26; bedrooms *(DCB, Alan and Audrey Chatting, Paul and Margaret Baker)*

Studland [Beech Rd], *Manor House*: Operates under restaurant licence, so hardly qualifies for the *Guide*, but bar meals are first class and service polite and cheerful in this lovely old manor house from which King George VI and Montgomery watched the invasion fleet rehearse; bedrooms *(E G Parish)*

Sturminster Marshall [SY9499], *Black Horse*: Comfortable pub with good bar food, pleasant atmosphere, cheerful service; handy for NT Kingston Lacey *(W J Wonham, JMW)*

☆ **Sturminster Newton** [A357; ST7814], *Red Lion*: Delightful small and cosy pub with welcoming atmosphere and friendly landlord, good reasonably priced food from sandwiches to steaks, log fire under central copper canopy, service unhurried but good *(Mr and Mrs P W Dryland, Anna Weeden)*

Sutton Poyntz [SY7083], *Springhead*: Stunning views from wonderfully placed big and airy pub with welcome lack of dark-brown-wood and dark-red-furnishings syndrome, good food well presented *(Mrs L Coleridge)*

Swanage [Durlston Rd; SZ0278], *Durlston Castle*: Engagingly unusual design like a bar put together in a tea-room, in 1890 turreted 'castle' overlooking the Needles and sea, friendly landlord, dungeon lavatories; children in separate games-room *(Jonathan Warner, WHBM)*; [Ulwell Rd] *Ferryboat*: Warm welcome in tidily refurbished pub with excellent view across bay *(Mike Matthews)*; [Burlington Rd] *Grand*: Good food, prompt friendly staff and good atmosphere in comfortable lounge of large hotel; a good place to stay *(Brian Smith, Alan and Audrey Chatting)*; [1 Burlington Rd], *Pines*: Good choice of very good value simple lunchtime food and good range of beers in spotless, spacious and comfortable hotel bar – get there by noon for a table; bedrooms with superb views *(Mike Matthews, B J E Phillips)*; [High St] *Purbeck*: Friendly welcome in warm stone-walled pub – dark, but invitingly so *(Mike Matthews)*; [The Square] *Ship*: Good if pricey choice of real ales in spacious maritime-theme plush bar, traditional bar food, separate games-room; bedrooms *(LYM)*

Swyre [B3157; SY5288], *Bull*: Comfortable and friendly, with bar, dining area – good food including local plaice and sole – children's room, open-air swimming-pool and play area *(Stan Edwards)*

☆ **Symondsbury** [village signposted from A35 just W of Bridport; SY4493], *Ilchester Arms*: Attractive old thatched inn with inglenook in pine-furnished open-plan bar, skittle alley, streamside garden, good value bedrooms; the licensees who made it so highly rated in previous editions, and served refreshingly different home-made food, moved in December 1987 to the Pilot Boat in Lyme Regis; since then there have been some uncertainties, but as 1988 progressed there were signs that these were being ironed out, with readers particularly enjoying the fish (brought to the table for inspection shortly after arriving from the harbour), the decent choice of wines, and usually the welcome – we hope further readers' reports will confirm that the pub does indeed merit both main-entry status and its former food award; friendly Great Dane and a couple of Burmese cats, children welcome *(Peter and Rose Flower, Freddy Costello, Jim Matthews, Gordon and Daphne, LYM)*

Tarrant Gunville [ST9212], *Bugle Horn*: Sensibly refurbished village free house with touch of luxury, pleasant young manager, Wadworths 6X and good range of food; same owners as Fleur-de-Lys, Cranborne (see main entries); bedrooms *(WHBM)*

Three Legged Cross [SU0805], *Old Barn*

Farm: Former early eighteenth-century thatched farmhouse with covered-over well in the open-plan lounge, choice of real ales, wide choice of food, servery to big garden with barbecue terrace; children in family-room *(Anon)*

☆ **Trent** [ST5918], *Rose & Crown*: Delightful converted farmhouse by beautiful old country church where Archbishop Fisher lies at rest; civilised, relaxed atmosphere, books over the fire and growing corn waving at the window; well kept Hook Norton and Wadworths 6X, interesting wines, charming licensee and American wife, wide choice of reasonably priced food including imaginative puddings *(Michael Andrews, W L Sleigh, Nigel Paine, JEFR)*

Uploders [SY5093], *Crown*: Smallish cosy bar on right opens on to small back lawn; good atmosphere makes you quickly feel at home *(Gordon and Daphne)*

Wareham [South St; SY9287], *Bridge House*: Good food and beer, friendly service *(P Gillbe)*; [41 North St (A351, N end of town)] *Kings Arms*: Flagstoned central corridor to back serving-counter divides the two traditional bars of this thatched local; Whitbreads Strong Country and Pompey Royal well kept, reasonably priced bar food (not Fri–Sun evenings), back garden *(LYM)*; [Quayside] *New*: Well run town pub in idyllic quayside setting, welcoming atmosphere, decent bar food, excellent Whitbreads Strong Country *(Andy and Colleen Auton, T R Espley)*; [High St] *Red Lion*: Welcoming and well kept, good value food and bedrooms *(C G Stephens)*

West Bay [SY4590], *Bridport Arms*: Good bar food (served late at lunchtime) and very friendly service – the public bar's the one to go for; bedrooms *(Dr and Mrs A K Clarke)*; *George*: Overlooking the harbour, with well kept Palmers ales on handpump, good bar food including well filled crab sandwiches, nice mix of locals and holidaymakers *(David Fisher)*

☆ **West Stour** [ST7822], *Ship*: Small, clean and friendly eighteenth-century local, big log fire, Bass and Wadworths 6X, attentive service; good reasonably priced food in bar and recently added intimate and tasteful split-level restaurant, ample parking across road; bedrooms comfortable *(D A Ash, Nigel Paine)*

Weymouth [85 The Esplanade; SY6778], *Cork & Bottle*: Deceptively large cellar bar, well kept Devenish, Marstons Pedigree and Wadworths 6X, good low-priced bar food from sandwiches to steaks, live bands Sun *(S M House)*; *Golden Lion*: Fairly modern pub with friendly landlord, well kept Devenish, Marstons and Wadworths real ales, clean and tidy, good bar food *(J B Tippett)*; [Barrack Rd] *Nothe Tavern*: Large, lively local with sea views from back lawn, popular bar food and well kept Huntsman real ales *(Mr and Mrs I M Howden, LYM)*; [7 Ridgeway, Upwey] *Ship*: Warm friendly out-of-the-way pub, wide choice of food, nice ale *(A Atkins)*; [The Quay – note that this is quite a different pub, in spite of the same name] *Ship*: Spacious waterfront pub with attractive harbour views from modernised nautical-theme open-plan bar and upstairs steak bar; good bar food including local crab; provision for children; Badger real ales *(Keith Garley, Stan Edwards, LYM)*

☆ **Wimborne Minster** [Corn Market – pedestrian precinct nr N door of minster], *White Hart*: Interesting listed seventeenth-century building, on a decided upswing under new management; old-fashioned, low-beamed bar with two alcoves, separate public area, well prepared and presented food from sandwiches or ploughman's to scampi cooked with cream and brandy, well kept Huntsman IPA, Dorchester and Royal Oak on handpump, speciality cocktails, friendly welcome *(WHBM)*; [High St] *Albion*: Typical town pub with good home-cooked meals, even on Sun – big helpings *(Dorothy and Ken Worrall)*; [The Square] *Kings Head*: Decent bar in THF hotel with lunchtime bar food; comfortable bedrooms *(WHBM)*; [2 Church St] *Odd-fellows Arms*: Minute pub – get there by opening (noon) to get a seat; very good value food, pleasant landlord *(K and D E Worrall)*; [East St (A31)] *Rising Sun*: Efficient pub with clean recent renovations, big black-leaded kitchen range along one wall of comfortable lounge, Badger Best, wide range of bar food from sandwiches and filled baked potatoes to steaks, riverside terrace *(Ian Phillips, BB)*

Wimborne St Giles [SU0212], *Bull*: Good food, well kept beer and charming service in comfortable pub with big garden; interesting village *(JMW, Mrs P Adams)*

Winkton [OS Sheet 195 reference 166962; SZ1696], *Lamb*: Otherwise plain pub notable for its rotating choice from among fourteen well kept real ales, and for its unusually efficient clean-air system *(WHBM)*

Winterborne Whitechurch [SY8399], *Milton Arms*: Lovely bright and cosy public bar with genuinely friendly licensees, good beer and food; pleasant bedrooms *(D Sibley)*

Yetminster [ST5910], *White Hart*: Popular, well run rural pub with well kept Bass and Oakhill Farmers, attractive exterior, seats outside *(A J Ritson)*

Durham and Northumberland (including Cleveland and Tyne & Wear)

A good few changes in the area include new licensees at the well kept Granby in Longframlington and at the Linden Pub, attached to the Linden Hall country-house hotel at Longhorsley (in both cases, readers report well on the new regimes), and also at the Masons Arms at Rennington (it's too early to judge yet whether their food will match up to the high standards of their predecessors). The popular waterside Chain Locker in North Shields has opened a new dining-room and enlarged the bar a bit, and a new fish-and-chip restaurant is a useful addition to the Cooperage near the water in central Newcastle. Changes have been most extensive at the George at Piercebridge – running even to a new ballroom bar; readers have been most enthusiastic (it also gains a food award this year). But perhaps there'll be most welcome for the real ales which have been introduced at the Olde Ship in Seahouses: many people have felt that this has been the one thing missing from what is otherwise the most engaging pub in the North-East. Two new entries, more or less at opposite ends of the area, are the stylish and interesting old Morritt Arms at Greta Bridge (good food and a comfortable place to stay at) and the Warenford Lodge at Warenford (also good food, very handy for the A1). Other pubs notable for food here include the comfortable Blue Bell in Belford, the Fox & Hounds in Cotherstone (try the local cheese – other good food has helped to earn the pub a star award this year), the

The Lord Crewe Arms, Blanchland

*Three Tuns in the attractive village of Eggleston, the Waterford Arms in Seaton
Sluice (ace fish and chips), and the warm-hearted Wooden Doll with its terrific
view over Tynemouth harbour. Among the Lucky Dip entries, some promising
possibilities include the Lord Crewe Arms at Bamburgh, both contrasting
Beamish entries, the Swan & Three Cygnets in Durham, the Tankerville Arms at
Eglingham, the Grotto cut into the cliffs on the edge of Marsden, the Jolly Sailor
near Moorsholm, the Horseshoes at Rennington and the Seven Stars at Shincliffe.
For Kielder Water, try the entries under Bellingham, Falstone and Stannersburn.*

BELFORD (Northumberland)   NU1134 Map 10

Blue Bell ⊗ 🛏

Market Place

The lounge bar in this relaxing and welcoming inn makes for quite a luxurious
refuge from the A1 (which bypasses what has now become a quiet village), with
gold-tinted flowery wallpaper, matching fabric for the comfortable seats, thick
carpet and Audubon bird prints. The good value bar food includes starters such as
soup (95p), a weight-watcher's salad (£1.30) or garlic mushrooms (£1.60),
ploughman's (£1.90), and main dishes like omelettes (£2.90), home-made steak and
kidney pie (£2.95), a selection of four casserole dishes (£4), mixed grill (£4.50) and
rump steak (£5), with good fresh vegetables – some of which come straight from the
hotel's own attractive and spacious garden. (*Recommended by T Nott, John Oddey,
Gordon and Daphne*)

*Free house   Licensee Carl Shirley   Meals and snacks   Restaurant   Children in restaurant
Open 11–3, 6–11 all year   Bedrooms tel Belford (066 83) 543; £30B/£52B*

BLANCHLAND (Northumberland)   NY9750 Map 10

Lord Crewe Arms ★ [illustrated on page 247]

The star award is for this well kept inn's remarkable architecture, partly Norman
and – like the rest of the village – hardly touched in the last two centuries. It was
originally part of the guest house of a monastery, part of whose cloister still stands
in the neatly terraced gardens, and one bar is down in a crypt – simply furnished,
with pews against massive stone walls under a barrel-vaulted ceiling. The building
was sold in 1704 to the formidable old Bishop of Durham, Lord Crewe, who had
married a Forster some forty years younger than him. When her Jacobite nephew
Tom escaped from prison in London, he hid in a priest's hole which you can still see
by a great thirteenth-century fireplace. People say that the ghost of his sister
Dorothy – who never saw him again, after arranging his escape to exile in France –
still asks visitors to take a message to him there. Upstairs, the Derwent Room has
old settles, low beams and sepia photographs on its walls. Simple bar food includes
soup (95p), good sandwiches (£1.10), ploughman's (£2.15), salads (£2.75), fish and
chips (£3.20) and gammon (£3.55); Vaux Samson on handpump; friendly service.
The village is in a magnificent moorland setting, near the Derwent Reservoir; it can
get very busy. (*Recommended by TRA, MA, Sue Cleasby, Mike Ledger, Chris and Sandra
Taylor, R F Moat, Kenneth Finch, Warwick Peirson, HKR*)

*Free house   Real ale   Meals and snacks (lunchtime)   Restaurant   Children welcome   Open
11–11 all year   Bedrooms tel Blanchland (043 475) 251; £38.90B/£55.80B*

If you report on a pub that's not a main entry, please tell us any lunchtimes or evenings when it
doesn't serve bar food.

Most pubs kindly let us have up-to-date food prices as we went to press in summer 1988; with
those that didn't – normally recognised by the absence of a licensee's name – we've assumed a
10 per cent increase.

COTHERSTONE (Durham)   NZ0119 Map 10
Fox & Hounds ★ ⊗

B6277 – incidentally a good quiet route to Scotland, through interesting scenery

The neat and comfortable L-shaped beamed bar in this old white-painted stone house has a good winter open fire, thickly cushioned wall seats in its various alcoves and recesses, local photographs and country pictures, and simple wooden chairs around the many tables. The star is earned largely for the carefully prepared bar food, which continues to earn readers' praise for its imaginative use of good fresh ingredients. It includes sandwiches (from 95p), a meat and vegetable broth (£1.15), ploughman's with local cheese (£2.25), steak and kidney pie (£3.50), chicken pieces with pineapple and walnuts in a light curry mayonnaise or vegetarian pancake (£3.95), and specials like local plaice (fresh from the East Coast) in prawn sauce (£4.95) or wild Scottish salmon salad (£5.95); game in season; puddings (from £1.50). The same menu – with the same prices – is used in the restaurant. Well kept John Smiths on handpump; tea or coffee (from Taylors of Harrogate). It's attractively placed on the edge of the little village green. *(Recommended by Stephanie Sowerby, Dr P D Smart, TRA, MA, RAMS, SS, Patrick Young, Jon Wainwright, John Oddey)*

Free house   Licensees Patrick and Jenny Crawley   Real ale   Meals and snacks   Restaurant tel Teesdale (0833) 50241   *Children in eating area   Open 11.30–2.30 (3 Sat), 6.30–11* *Self-catering holiday cottage*

CRASTER (Northumberland)   NU2620 Map 10
Jolly Fisherman ★

Off B1339 NE of Alnwick

The original bar – particularly the snug by the entrance – in this welcoming local is very atmospheric, and there are good sea views from the big picture window in the airy extension; the front turf which you can see from here leads on to a splendid clifftop walk – *Good Walks Guide* Walk 145 – to Dunstanburgh Castle. It's an unpretentious place, with many regulars from the kippering shed opposite and the working harbour just below; Tetley Bitter on handpump. Bar food includes hot pies, pasties, toasted sandwiches and beefburgers (65p), home-made pizzas (75p), and good local crab and salmon sandwiches (95p); wine from the wood; darts, shove-ha'penny, dominoes, cribbage, juke box, fruit machine and space game; pleasant service. *(Recommended by Sue Cleasby, Mike Ledger, Michael Thomson, SS, G L Archer, M S Hancock, F A Noble, S V Bishop)*

Tetleys (Ind Coope)   Licensee A George   Real ale   Snacks   Children welcome   Open 11–11 in summer; 11–3, 6–11 in winter

EGGLESTON (Durham)   NY9924 Map 10
Three Tuns ⊗

Close to some fine moorland roads (the B6282, B6278 and B6279), this very friendly stone-built country pub has a beamed bar with old oak settles on its carpet, one with amusingly horrific Gothick carving, as well as Windsor armchairs and the like, and maybe a log fire; dominoes. From the back buttery bar, big windows look out past the terrace and garden to open fields, maybe with rabbits. The good home-made food includes soup (90p), cheese rolls (80p), ploughman's (£1.85), pâté (£2.05), cottage pie (£2.25), omelettes (£2.75, with their own free-range eggs), trout (£3.50), duck (£4.25), eight-ounce sirloin steak (£5.45) and puddings (£1.25).

Children welcome means the pub says it lets children inside without any special restriction. If it allows them in, but to restricted areas such as an eating area or family-room, we specify this. Some pubs may impose an evening time-limit.

It faces on to the broad village green, and is handy for the Bowes Museum. *(Recommended by W A Harbottle, Hayward Wane, G Bloxsom, Jon Wainwright, Margaret and Roy Randle)*

Whitbreads   Licensees James and Christine Dykes   Meals and snacks (not Mon, not Sun evening)   Restaurant Sun lunch and Tues–Sat evenings, bookings only by previous day, tel Teesdale (0833) 50289   Children in eating area and restaurant   Open 11.30–2.30, 7–11; closed Mon (exc bank hols) and 25 Dec

ETAL (Northumberland)   NT9339 Map 10
Black Bull

Off B6354, SW from Berwick

A two-hundred-yard stroll through this pleasant and very well kept village brings you to the bare ruins of a castle on the banks of the River Till, and it's well placed for Heatherslaw's working watermill (where you can buy flour ground on the premises) and the restored Ford Castle. The pub itself is a handsome white-painted and thatched affair; its roomy and friendly lounge bar is smartly modernised and has glossily varnished beams and Windsor chairs set neatly around the tables on its carpet. Good value bar food includes filled rolls and sandwiches (from 60p), home-made soup (70p), ploughman's (£1.60), vegetarian choices like pizza, lasagne or curry (from around £2.50), haddock (£2.50), farm-cured gammon (£4), and Tweed salmon salad (£5.10); well kept Lorimers Scotch on handpump; darts, dominoes, cribbage, fruit machine. There's a quoits pitch in front. The village's offspring, New Etal, a diminutive hamlet across the river, was originally conceived to replace Etal when it was destroyed by Border marauders. *(Recommended by T Nott, Hope Chenhalls, SS; more reports please)*

Vaux   Licensee T Hails   Real ale   Meals and snacks   Children in eating area only, away from the bar   Open 12–3, 7–11; 12–4, 6–11 Sat

GRETA BRIDGE (Durham)   NZ0813 Map 10
Morritt Arms ⊗ 🛏

Hotel signposted off A66 W of Scotch Corner

The Dickens Bar of this well kept and polished old-fashioned hotel has a wonderfully lively lifesize Pickwickian mural, well lit and running right the way around the room, done in 1946 by J V Gilroy (famous for the old Guinness advertisements – there are three here, signed by him). This civilised high-ceilinged room has sturdy green-plush-seated oak settles and big Windsor armchairs around traditional cast-iron-framed tables, with big windows looking out on the extensive lawn. An adjacent room, darkly green, is decorated with a stag's head and a big case of stuffed black game. Good bar food includes sandwiches (from 90p), soup (£1.15), home-made pâté or ploughman's (£2.75) and salads from smoked mackerel (£2.75) to salmon (£5.20), with two or three hot dishes such as lasagne (£3.50) and steak and mushroom pie (£4). Well kept Theakstons Best on handpump; good open fires; dominoes and shove-ha'penny, with darts, pool and a juke box in the wholly separate public bar. There are picnic-table sets and swings at the far end, and teak tables in a pretty side area look along to the graceful old Dairy Bridge by the stately gates to Rokeby Park. One of the brothers who bought the hotel a couple of years ago previously worked for ten years in the Middle East – ending with a spell in a Saudi jail for making his own home-made wine (it says a lot for his temperament that he can still smile at jokes about the move from behind bars to behind bars). *(Recommended by Jon Dewhirst, John Oddey)*

Free house   Licensees David and John Mulley   Real ale   Meals and snacks (lunchtime; sandwiches in evening)   Restaurant   Children welcome   Open 12–3, 6–11 all year Bedrooms tel Teesdale (0833) 27232; £23(£31B)/£38(£48B)

HEDLEY ON THE HILL (Northumberland) NZ0859 Map 10
Feathers

Village signposted from New Ridley, which is signposted from B6309 N of Consett; OS Sheet 88 reference 078592

The Turkey-carpeted bar in this well run pub is a relaxing place, with beams, stripped stonework, solid brown leatherette settles, wood-burning stoves, and country pictures. A side lounge is decorated in similar fashion, with a flowery carpet. Officially, they serve basic food only at the weekends (and more in the evening than at lunchtime), but they'll rustle up some welcoming dish for the foot-weary traveller pretty much at any time. They do generously filled sandwiches (from 60p), home-made soup (90p), ploughman's (£1.45) and in winter a beef casserole (£2.95). As with last year, we've found that the lack of food has more to do with local demand than the licensees' willingness. Well kept Theakstons Best and XB and a fortnightly guest beer on handpump; darts, shove-ha'penny, table skittles, dominoes, space game in children's room. *(Recommended by John Oddey; more reports please)*

Free house   Licensees Marina and Colin Atkinson   Real ale   Snacks (Sat and Sun evenings, but see above)   Children in small room off lounge   Open 6–11 (all day Sat) all year

HIGH FORCE (Durham)   NY8728 Map 10
High Force Hotel 🛏

B6277 about 4 miles NW of Middleton-in-Teesdale

Positioned on a track leading straight up beyond the pine woods to the high moors, this inn doubles as a mountain rescue post; it's also suitably welcoming to those in need of other forms of sustenance. The snug and cheerful public bar has robustly simple furniture on its wood-block floor, piped music, darts and dominoes; the lounge and other rooms are comfortable. The wide choice of bar food includes sandwiches and toasted sandwiches (from 65p), soup (85p), ploughman's (£2, lunchtime only), good home-made steak and kidney pie (£3, lunchtime only), salads (from £3, very generous prawn at £4.50), trout or scampi (£3.50) and steaks (£5.75); friendly service; good malt whiskies. It's named after England's biggest waterfall: within earshot, and just a short stroll away on the other side of the road. The best, if most precipitous, views of the fall are from the opposite side of the River Tees. *(Recommended by Joy Heatherley, Jon Wainright, Malcolm Steward, Margaret and Roy Randle)*

Free house   Licensees Barrie and Lilian Hutchinson   Meals and snacks (not Mon evenings, except June–Sept)   Children welcome at lunchtime, eating areas only at other times   Open 11–3, 6–11; opens 7 in winter   Bedrooms tel Teesdale (0833) 22222/22264; £14/£24

LONGFRAMLINGTON (Northumberland)   NU1301 Map 10
Granby ⊗ 🛏

A697

Though the licensee is new here, this small inn's main attraction remains its food – people tend to come here to eat rather than to drink. The wide choice of food includes soup (£1.05, not evenings), deep-fried Camembert (£1.75), garnished sandwiches (from £1.75, steak £1.95), grilled asparagus topped with cheese (£2.35), home-made steak and kidney pie (£3.25, lunchtime only), a good range of seafood from cod (£3.05) to lobster (£14.50), salads (from £4.25, poached salmon £5.25), saddle of lamb (£5.45) and steaks (from £6.25); generous breakfasts for residents. The two rooms of the white-walled bar are comfortably modernised, with a patterned carpet, red upholstered stools matching the wall banquettes around the walls and in the bow windows, lots of oak tables, a copper-covered fireplace in one room, and copper and stone jars hanging from the black beams; piped music. There are seats outside. *(Recommended by R H Martyn, R A Hall, E R Thompson, TBB)*

Bass Licensee Anne Bright Meals and snacks Restaurant Open 11–3, 6–11; closed 25 Dec Bedrooms tel Longframlington (066 570) 228; £17.50(£18.50B)/£35(£37B)

LONGHORSLEY (Northumberland) NZ1597 Map 10
Linden Pub ★ ⊗ 🛏

Part of Linden Hall Hotel; down long drive, and past the hotel itself

Attached to a handsomely restored country-house hotel, this hospitable pub is attractive in its own right, particularly on the food side: the wide range, changing daily and served from a side counter, typically includes a couple of soups (95p), sandwiches (£1.25), ploughman's (£2.75), salads with a choice of pâté or four meats (£2.95), nine or ten hot dishes such as steak pie, chicken Kiev, Northumberland sausage, leek and ham crumble, fisherman's pie or vegetarian lasagne (from £3.25), and steak (£4.95); puddings (from 75p); helpful service. The building's actually an ex-granary, and has an airy feel on its two levels; the red-carpeted bar has lots of light-coloured woodwork, and a notable collection of enamel advertising signs on its largely stripped stone walls, with stairs to the galleried upper part. Well kept Ruddles County, Theakstons Best, Websters Best and a guest beer on handpump or tapped from the cask; darts, pool (both sensibly placed), dominoes, cribbage, fruit machine and piped music; log-effect gas fire in a large round central hearth. You can sit in the flagstoned yard, where some tables shelter under a Perspex roof, and there are barbecues in good weather. Quoits and garden draughts are played out here, and there is a good outdoor games area in the spacious and attractively planted grounds of the hotel, as well as the play area by the pub. Popular with families at weekends. *(Recommended by Sue Cleasby, Mike Ledger, TBB; more reports please)*

Free house Licensees Jon Moore and Rod Tait Real ale Meals and snacks Children upstairs Open 11–3, 6–11; closes 10.30 in winter exc Fri and Sat Bedrooms and restaurant in the hotel tel Morpeth (0670) 516611, Telex 538224; £59.50B/£69.50B

NEWCASTLE UPON TYNE (Tyne & Wear) NZ2266 Map 10
Bridge Hotel

Castle Square (in local A–Z street atlas index as Castle Garth); right in centre, just off Nicholas Street (A6215) at start of High Level Bridge; only a few parking meters nearby, but evening parking easy

This well preserved Victorian pub, by the remains of the city wall, has a neatly kept and decorous lounge, with high ceilings, a massive mahogany carved fireplace, a bar counter equipped with unusual pull-down slatted snob screens, tall mirrors, and green plush banquettes and elegant small chairs on its brown carpet. In the public bar, which has some cheerful stained glass, there's a good juke box, pool, darts, dominoes and fruit machine (there's a second in the lounge lobby). Well kept Marstons Pedigree, Sam Smiths OB, Theakstons Best and XB on handpump; simple bar snacks include meat pie and peas (55p), toasted sandwiches (65p) and stottie cakes with meat and salad (70p). A few picnic-table sets on the flagstoned back terrace of this Grade II listed building have a fine view down over the Tyne and the bridges. *(Recommended by Perry Board and Andrew O'Doherty, Dave Butler, Lesley Storey; more reports please)*

Free house Real ale Snacks Blues Tues, folksong and ballads Thurs Open 11–3, 6–10.30; closed 25 Dec, 1 Jan

Cooperage

32 The Close, Quayside; immediately below and just to the W of the High Level Bridge; parking across road limited lunchtime, easy evening

One of the city's oldest buildings, this wonky timbered Tudor house (where, as its name implies, casks were indeed once made) makes a fine contrast to the cluster of bridges which stride over it so loftily. A quick turnover keeps the real ales really fresh; as well as Ind Coope Burton, Marstons Owd Rodger, Tetleys and Wards Sheffield Best, they have three regularly changing (and sometimes unusual) guest beers such as Everards Old Original, Fullers ESB, Greene King Abbot, Marstons Pedigree, Ruddles County and Websters Choice; also Coates farm cider. The bustling bar has heavy Tudor oak beams and exposed stonework, and there's extra seating in the lounge area by the pool-room. The reasonably priced bar food includes fresh grilled grapefruit (35p), home-made vegetable soup (45p), steak sandwich with mushrooms and chips (£1.10), fish pie (£1.85), roast chicken (£2.35), a good range of fish (from £2.40), and fillet steak (£4.35). Fruit machine, space game, juke box and darts area. There's a new restaurant, serving generous helpings of fish and chips. (*Recommended by Michael Bolam, Comus Elliot; more reports please*)

Free house   Licensee Michael Westwell   Real ale   Meals and snacks (not Sun evening) Restaurant tel Newcastle (091) 232 8286   Children in restaurant and eating area Open 11–11 all year; closed 25 Dec

NORTH SHIELDS (Tyne & Wear)   NZ3468 Map 10

Chain Locker ⊗

New Quay

The bar menu in this turn-of-the-century pub relies heavily on the nearby North Shields Fish Quay and changes daily; typically it might include pâté (£1.50), ploughman's (from £1.50), cod and mushroom bake (£1.95), steak and kidney pie (£2.10), fish pie (£2.40), and seafood salad (£2.50); friendly service. The atmosphere in the bar – which has been enlarged recently – is unassuming, with a lofty wooden ceiling, open fire, navigational charts and nautical pictures on the walls, local literature and arts information, and stools and wooden wall benches around small tables – the one on your left as you go in, built over a radiator, is prized in winter. Well kept Theakstons Best, XB and Old Peculier, Youngers No 3 and a guest beer on handpump; dominoes, fruit machine, and a friendly cat. The separate dining-room is new. It's tucked into a corner of the restored Tyne pedestrian ferry landing area and right by the river. (*Recommended by John Oddey, GB, Grahame Archer; more up-to-date reports please*)

Free house   Licensees Sue and John Constable   Real ale   Meals (not Sun evening) and snacks (lunchtimes, not Sun)   Children in eating area   Quiz evening Weds, folk Fri   Open 11.30–3, 5.30–11; may open longer afternoons

PIERCEBRIDGE (Durham)   NZ2116 Map 10

George ⊗

B6275 just S of village

Since taking over this former coaching-inn in 1987, the licensee has changed both its décor and its atmosphere for the better; perhaps the most impressive innovation is the Ballroom Bar – just that, a bar inside a fully fitted ballroom. If you come at the right time – it's open only for special functions or during barbecues – it's well worth a visit. In the three other bars there are plates, pictures and old farming equipment on the walls, solid wood furniture, and Chesterfields in the lounge (which overlooks the river); there are no fewer than five open fires in one room or another. There's a wide range of food, too, with a hot and cold lunchtime buffet serving five or six starters and seven or eight main dishes, including a tasty chicken basquaise (£2.95) and a hot joint (£3.95); other lunchtime food includes soup (95p) and sandwiches (£1.25). In the evening they do six fish dishes (£3.75–£5.95, with good trout) and five pasta dishes (£1.45–£4.25); steaks (from £6.95) and puddings (from £1.75). John Smiths on handpump; dominoes, games box, fruit machine and piped music. The garden running down to the River Tees is attractive. The existence of this inn is yet another reason for taking this scenic road as an alternative to the A1 between Scotch Corner and Edinburgh. (*Recommended by Clare Greenham, TRA, MA, Bev Prentice, Bill Russell, Tony Gayfer, G Blease*)

Free house   Licensee Jezz Brannigan   Real ale   Meals and snacks   Restaurant tel Piercebridge (032 574) 576   Children in separate room   Open 11–11 all year

RENNINGTON (Northumberland)   NU2119 Map 10
Masons Arms

Stamford Cott; B1340 NE of Alnwick

Friendly new licensees in this coastal place are keen to maintain its atmosphere as a welcoming family inn. The comfortable lounge bar has a solid-fuel stove at one end and a gas fire at the other, green leatherette stools and russet wall banquettes on the brown carpet, local newspapers set out to read, and photographs of heavy horses (and a locally beached whale) on the cream walls above the brown panelled dado. Bar food includes home-made soup (65p), pâté (£1.50), chicken or vegetarian lasagne (£2.50), steak sandwich (£2.85), gammon (£3.25), steaks (from £5.50) and three daily specials; children's dishes from £1.10. Marstons Pedigree on handpump, piped music; juke box, darts, dominoes, cribbage and fruit machine on the public side. There are sturdy rustic tables among lavender and other flowers on the small front terrace. The quiet lane past here was – as you can see from murals in the snug little dining-room – once the pre-A1 Great North Road. (*Recommended by John Oddey, David Waterhouse, Mr and Mrs M D Jones, Sue Cleasby, Mike Ledger, Gill and Neil Patrick; more reports on the food under the new regime please*)

Free house   Licensees George and Patricia Beattie   Real ale   Meals   Restaurant   Children welcome   Open 11–11 all year   Bedrooms tel Alnwick (0665) 77275; £12/£24

ROMALDKIRK (Durham)   NY9922 Map 10
Rose & Crown ★ 🛏

Just off B6277

Standing on a particularly fine village green, this comfortable old coaching-inn has a snug and traditionally furnished front bar, with cream walls decorated with lots of gin-traps, some old farm tools and a large chiming clock, and old-fashioned seats facing the fireplace; the atmosphere has a certain timeless appeal, perhaps at its best in winter, when there are warm fires inside and rooks in the bare trees outside. Most of the bar food is smartly served in quite a spacious and airy room, and includes salads (from £1.95), fresh sardines or deep-fried squid (£3.95), lamb cutlets (£4) and spicy chicken wings (£4.25); there are also soup (£1), sandwiches (£1.25) and ploughman's (£1.95); reduced price menu for pensioners. Matthew Browns and Theakstons XB or perhaps Old Peculier on handpump; dominoes, maybe piped music. (*Recommended by E R Thompson, H Bramhall, Jon Wainwright, Margaret and Roy Randle, Dave Braisted, Alan Hall, Mrs E Brown*)

Free house   Real ale   Meals and snacks   Restaurant   Children welcome   Open 11–11 all year   Bedrooms tel Teesdale (0833) 50213; £35B/£46B

If you enjoy your visit to a pub, please tell the publican. They work extraordinarily long hours, and when people show their appreciation it makes it all seem worth while.

SEAHOUSES (Northumberland)   NU2232 Map 10

Olde Ship ★ ★ ⊗ 🛏

B1340 coast road

Readers praise this nautical harbourside inn's ability to combine a friendly attraction to visitors with a local village community atmosphere, with sailors (who assiduously add to the bar's décor) as many of the regulars. It's a treasure-trove of sparkling ship's brassware and other instruments and equipment; most of the windows have stained-glass sea pictures, and the one that's clear looks out over the harbour to the Farne Islands, but if you're not lucky enough to get a seat by it – the pub is very popular – you can pay to watch the fishing-boats coming in on radar (proceeds to charity). The poop deck area has recently been carpeted, and contrasts with the bare floors elsewhere (it's actually ship's decking, and they may close for a day or two in early spring for sanding and rewaxing); besides good sea pictures there are some good ships' models including a fine one of the North Sunderland lifeboat, and a new knotted anchor made by local fishermen. There is another low-beamed snug bar, and a back room with stuffed seabirds. Throughout, teak and mahogany woodwork, shiny brass fittings and small rooms feel almost more like a ship than a building. There are pews around barrel tables in the back courtyard, and a battlemented side terrace with a sun lounge looks out on the harbour. Bar food (served from 11.30 or earlier in the morning) includes home-made soup such as cream of carrot or crab (80p), filled rolls and sandwiches (from 75p, local fresh crab 90p), ploughman's (£1.40) and salads, with three or four lunchtime hot dishes such as beef stovies, fish stew, beef and Guinness casserole or lamb goulash (around £2–£2.75); no chips. There are sandwiches and teas in the afternoon, and the hotel dining-room does a Sunday roast lunch (as well as good meals in the evening, when only sandwiches are served in the bar). An added bonus this year has been the introduction of real ales – McEwans Scotch and 80/- on handpump; also unusual blended whiskies, some uncommon bottled beers, and in winter mulled wine. Open fire, pool (in winter), dominoes, fruit machine and space game; piped music. The boat trip to the Farne Islands is well worth while (you may see seals and puffins), and there are bracing coastal walks – Bamburgh Castle is about an hour. *(Recommended by Robert and Vicky Tod, T Nott, GP and NP, R F Moat, Sue Cleasby and Mike Ledger, Dave Butler, Lesley Storey, S V Bishop, SS, G Bloxsom, Lee Goulding, G L Archer, John Oddey, Michael Craig)*

Free house   Licensees Alan and Jean Glen   Real ale   Meals (lunchtime) and snacks (evenings sandwiches only)   Restaurant   Children in restaurant   Open 11–11; 11–3, 6–11 in winter   Bedrooms tel Seahouses (0665) 720200; £17(£19B)/£34(£38B)

SEATON SLUICE (Northumberland)   NZ3477 Map 10

Waterford Arms ⊗

Just off A193 N of Whitley Bay

Well placed close to the sea, with the small fishing-harbour just down beyond the grass on the far side of the road, this modernised pub is comfortably furnished, with spacious green plush banquettes in roomy bays, and bright paintings in one high-ceilinged room, and brown plush furnishings and a big children's rocking-machine in another. The main attraction remains its profusion of local fish, served in vast helpings. Priced according to size – small, medium or large – this includes lemon sole (£2.95–£5.25), cod and haddock (£3.25–£7.95) and a generous seafood platter (£7.35). The wide choice of other food includes sandwiches (from 90p), soup (£1), sausage and mash (£2.75), leek and mince pudding (£3.10), home-made steak and kidney pie (£3.50), ploughman's (£3.95) and steaks (from twelve-ounce sirloin £6.80); large breakfasts, with home-made jams, for residents. Well kept Vaux Samson on handpump; dominoes, cribbage, piped music, and a fruit machine in the back lobby. *(Recommended by Richard Dolphin, GB, John Oddey; more reports please)*

Vaux   Licensee Mrs Patricia Charlton   Real ale   Meals and snacks (not Sun evenings in winter)   Children in eating area   Open 11–4, 6.30–11 all year   Bedrooms tel Tyneside (091) 237 0450; £17.50S/£35S

TYNEMOUTH (Tyne & Wear)　NZ3468　Map 10
Tynemouth Lodge

Tynemouth Road (A193); a few minutes' walk from the Tynemouth Metro station

This clean little pub, on the edge of Northumberland Park, has copper-topped cast-iron tables, and button-back green leatherette seats built against the walls (which have stylish bird-of-paradise wallpaper); in winter there's a coal fire in the neat Victorian tiled fireplace. The selection of very well kept real ales is surprisingly wide-ranging, with Belhaven 80/-, Hartleys XB, Marstons Pedigree, Robinsons Best Bitter, Theakstons Best and Wards Sheffield Best on handpump. Bar food includes stottie sandwiches (65p) and pot meals such as chilli con carne with pitta bread or lamb hot-pot (£1.70); Sunday lunch. No dogs. There are tables beyond the car park; slightly masculine atmosphere. *(Recommended by Grahame Archer, G Bloxsom, Jon Dewhirst; more reports please)*

Free house   Licensee Hugh Price   Real ale   Meals and snacks (lunchtime, not Sun) Live music most nights   Open 11–11 all year

Wooden Doll ★ ⊗

103 Hudson Street; from Tyne Tunnel, follow A187 into town centre; keep straight ahead (when A187 turns off left) until, approaching the sea, you can see the pub in Hudson Street on your right

The fresh bar food in this thriving yet unassuming place includes filled rolls (60p), soup (80p), half a pint of prawns (£1.75), ham salad (£2.70), chilli con carne (£2.75), fish pie (£2.95), and seafood salad (£3.95); efficient, friendly service. The range of real ales is unusually extensive, with ABC Bitter, Halls Harvest, Ind Coope Burton, Ruddles County, Tetleys Bitter and Mild, Youngers No 3 and Theakstons Best and Old Peculier as guest beers, on handpump. The friendly, relaxed atmosphere inside belies its rather severe exterior; the bar consists of two simply furnished rooms (brown and green leatherette chairs, a brown plush long settle, Formica-topped cast-iron tables) connected by a long spiral corridor, with open fires in winter. The walls may be decorated with paintings for sale, or good local photographs. Shove-ha'penny, dominoes, fruit and trivia machines and piped music. There's a fascinating seagull's-eye view down over the bustling boats and warehouses of the Shields Fish Quay immediately below, harbour derricks and gantries beyond, and then the sweep of the outer harbour with its long piers, headlands, and low Black Middens rocks. There's also a covered glassed-in verandah. *(Recommended by Grahame Archer, Sue Cleasby, Mike Ledger, John Oddey)*

Free house   Licensee Mrs Pat Jones   Real ale   Meals and snacks (not Sun)   Children in eating area until 7   Classical quartet Sun evening, jazz trio Mon evening, quiz night Tues, piano Weds–Fri evenings and all day Sat   Open 11–11; closed winter afternoons (exc Sat) and evening 25 Dec

WARENFORD (Northumberland)　NU1429　Map 10
Warenford Lodge ⊗

Just off A1 Alnwick–Belford, on village loop road

Unusual home-cooked food, consistently well prepared and attractively presented, brings many readers to this usefully placed pub: the wide choice includes soup (95p), chilli bean pancake (£1.20), potted trout (£1.80), grilled mussels or a plate of hors-d'oeuvre (£2.50), creamy cannelloni or ham with pease pudding (£3.10), beef and pigeon stew, a Northumbrian version of bouillabaisse or poached salmon with lime butter (£4.90) and an enormous sirloin steak (£7.50). Down by the bar counter, there are brocaded wall seats and stools around wooden tables, with some walls stripped back to bare stone and a coal fire in the big stone fireplace. An upper level has neat blond pine tables and armed benches, but also easy chairs and settees around lower tables, and a big solid-fuel stove. *(Recommended by A E Jenkinson, Dr J R Backhurst, T Nott, Dr P D Smart and others)*

Free house   Licensee Raymond Matthewman   Meals and snacks (not Mon lunchtime) Restaurant tel Belford (066 83) 453   Children in restaurant   Open 12–2, 7–11 all year; closed Tues–Weds lunchtime and all day Mon Oct–Easter

Lucky Dip

Besides the fully inspected pubs, you might like to try these Lucky Dips recommended to us and described by readers (if you do, please send us reports):

Acklington, Northumberland [NU2302], *Railway*: Old stone railway pub, recently completely renovated, with interesting railway photgraphs and relics; good food and service in attractive restaurant and bar *(G L Archer)*

Acomb, Northumberland [NY9366], *Miners Arms*: Small, friendly pub serving excellent home-made bar food and well kept beer; children in dining-room *(Matthew Waterhouse)*

Allendale, Northumberland [NY8456]: Keen competition among the five pubs and two inns around the square ensures a choice of good bar food *(Adrian Dodd-Noble)*

Alnmouth, Northumberland [Northumberland St; NU2511], *Red Lion*: Consistently good McEwans 80/- on handpump in warm and friendly unspoilt pub with decent bar food including good seafood platters; restaurant Tues–Sat evenings; children welcome lunchtime (and in evening restaurant) *(Tony Ritson, John Taylor)*

Alnwick, Northumberland [Narrowgate; NU1913], *Olde Cross*: Interestingly old, with ancient bottles in low window and story to suit, picturesque locals keen to display skill at dominoes, good beer on handpump, low-priced bar food – friendly, unpretentious and fun *(WFL)* [Market St]; *Queens Head*: Unpretentious, but roomy and dignified, with good real ale and good value food, very friendly staff taking much trouble; bedrooms good value *(WFL)*

Bamburgh, Northumberland [NU1835], *Lord Crewe Arms*: Relaxing and comfortable inn, beautifully placed in charming coastal village below magnificent Norman castle; most interesting bar is the back cocktail one, full of entertaining bric-à-brac, with log fire in winter; bar food and grill-room, children in side bar; bedrooms comfortable *(Gordon and Daphne, LYM)*

Barlow, Tyne & Wear [NZ1661], *Black Horse*: Welcoming pub on hill, canny landlord, tree-trunk stools, authentic décor, open fire, Theakstons ales, separate area for diners in lounge *(Andrew and Sean O'Doherty, Perry Board)*

Barnard Castle, Durham [Market Pl; NZ0617], *Golden Lion*: Lovely old warm and comfortable pub with excellently kept ale; good, reasonably priced food – fresh fried plaice – and well stocked bar *(SS)*; [by Market Cross] *Kings Head*: Welcoming, pleasant, cheerful atmosphere, three-sided lounge, well kept John Smiths, good choice of well presented bar food *(Mr and Mrs J H Adam)*; [Startforth; Bowes rd, signposted to A67] *White Swan*: Dramatic setting on rocks above River Tees, opposite castle ruins; straightforward inside *(Margaret and Roy Randle, LYM)*

☆ **Beamish**, Durham [NZ2254], *Shepherd & Shepherdess*: Handy for open-air museum – welcoming brightness in big L-shaped bar split into sections, with big helpings of excellent food, obliging service, well kept Vaux real ale; seats outside in wood *(Mr and Mrs J H Adam, Dr J K McCann, GB)*

☆ **Beamish**, [actually in Museum – shares its opening hours], *Sun*: Rescued in 1985 from Bishop Auckland and reconstructed here as re-creation of Victorian north-eastern pub; atmospheric and authentically basic, interesting collection of pub mirrors and early 1900s furnishings; run by McEwans/Youngers, who stable their Clydesdale horses behind the pub; well kept real ale *(Alan Bickley, G L Archer, Jon Dewhirst)*

Belford, Northumberland [A1; NU1134], *Black Swan*: Small friendly pub, nothing fancy, a good place to meet the locals; well kept real ale, lively pool-room *(Gordon and Daphne)*

Bellingham, Northumberland [Greystead; towards Kielder Water, past Birks – OS Sheet 80 reference 768856; NY8483], *Moorcock*: Plain country pub on way to Kielder Water, welcoming landlord, well kept beer, short choice of excellent food – all home-cooked *(John Oddey)*; *Riverdale Hall*: Victorian hotel on River North Tyne, nearby salmon fishing, cheerful welcome, reasonably priced bar food changing daily, tables overlooking swimming-pool and cricket field, also out on lawn *(E R Thompson)*

Belsay, Northumberland [NZ1079], *Highlander*: Comfortable, with pleasant décor, consistently good bar food including excellent puddings, separate evening restaurant *(Ken Smith)*

Berwick upon Tweed, Northumberland [A1 N of town; NU0053], *Meadow House*: Excellent reasonably priced food in simple but spacious eating area, and Vaux Lorimers Scotch on handpump *(David Waterhouse)*; [Tweed St, near rly stn] *Tweed View*: Hotel converted from convent, with excellent bar food in lounge overlooking Tweed's magnificent bridges (as does terrace) *(Hope Chenhalls)*

Bishop Auckland, Durham [Canney Hill (A688 towards Spennymoor); NZ2130], *Sportsman*: Very well kept Camerons and Everards Old Original on handpump and good food; three rooms, with open fire in cosy little snug *(Ned Edwards)*

Bowes, Durham [NY9914], *Ancient Unicorn*: Comfortably modernised open-plan bar, good bedrooms in well converted stable-block, in coaching-inn with Nicholas Nickleby connection; bedrooms *(LYM)*

Chatton, Northumberland [NU0628], *Percy Arms*: Welcoming helpful hosts, real fire (in cool July), good bar food; comfortable bedrooms, good breakfasts *(M Thomas, A Matheson, T Nott)*

Chollerford, Northumberland [NY9372], *George*: This hotel's setting is its attraction, with immaculate gardens running down to Upper Tyne; the pubby part is the Fisherman's Bar in what was the original smaller stone inn – plain food, pool, darts, etc. (closed winter mornings); children welcome; bedrooms comfortable *(LYM)*

Coatham Mundeville, Durham [off A68, ¼ mile A1(M); NZ2920], *Foresters Arms*: Useful break – good pub lunches including delicious ham sandwiches, real ale *(Carol Boothby)*; [part of Hallgarth Hotel; from A1(M) turn towards Brafferton off A167 Darlington rd on hill] *Stables*: Converted from stone outbuildings with high ceilings, lots of seating, well kept McEwans 80/- and Theakstons Best, Old Peculier and XB, bar food, Sun lunches, separate no-smoking eating area at back, conservatory at side for families; bedrooms in hotel *(Michael and Alison Sandy)*

nr Corbridge, Northumberland [about 3 miles N, at junction A68/B6318; NY9964], *Errington Arms*: Landlord and staff most welcoming and friendly, good bar food including attractive cold table, well organised, pleasant atmosphere *(Derek and Maggie Washington)*

☆ **Durham** [Elvet Bridge; NZ2743], *Swan &*

Three Cygnets: Pleasantly restored without being overdone, very friendly relaxed atmosphere, well kept Sam Smiths, generous helpings of good lunchtime food including vegetarian dishes *(Jon Dewhirst, Dave Braisted, T J Maddison, Wayne Brindle)*

Durham [N of Nevilles Cross on A167; NZ2541], *Duke of Wellington*: Big pub with several bars, one in elaborate Spanish style; main draw is varied, substantial and cheap food, including good choice of vegetarian dishes, excellent value Sun lunch (when it's busy); bedrooms comfortable *(Philip Haggar, T J Maddison)*; [Old Elvet] *Dun Cow*: Engaging traditional town pub in pretty black and white timbered cottage; good value cheap snacks, well kept Whitbreads Castle Eden; children welcome *(G Bloxsom, LYM)*; [2 Sherburn Rd, Gilesgate Moor; NZ2942] *Queens Head*: Range of real ales on handpump, good bar food, friendly staff, nice warm fire, often folk group Thurs in one of the rooms off the beam-effect bar; bedrooms good value, with own bathrooms *(WFL)*; [Sadler St (between Market Sq and cathedral] *Shakespeare*: Small, cosy and unpretentious old pub with a good range of beers such as McEwans 80/- and Youngers No 3, all well kept; back room and snug tend to be popular with students in the evening; main front bar always welcoming *(T J Maddison, Philip Haggar)*

Eastgate, Durham [signposted from A689 W of Stanhope; NY9638], *Horsley Hall*: Lovely old manor house-type building with comfortable, modern bar and beautiful original restaurant; huge helpings of good value food, caring owner, two lovely well fed St Bernards and live piranha *(Shaun Burnley)*

☆ **Egglescliffe**, Cleveland [663 Yarm Rd (A67); NZ4213], *Blue Bell*: Good value simple lunchtime bar food (not Sun) and friendly service in spacious bar with big windows looking down on River Tees, seats on terrace by goat-cropped grass sloping down to the water giving fine view of the great 1849 railway viaduct, restaurant; children welcome *(F A Noble, TAB, TRA, MA, LYM)*; *Pot & Glass*: Pleasant atmosphere, nice setting, decent food, well kept Bass *(Jon Dewhirst)*

☆ **Eglingham**, Northumberland [B6346 Alnwick–Wooler; NU1119], *Tankerville Arms*: Under friendly new owners, this olde-worlde village pub is warm, charming and characterful; good value bar food, attractive restaurant (evening, Sat and Sun lunches), Stones ale; special prices for children, who are welcome *(John Oddey, Richard Davies, E R Thompson, Matthew Waterhouse)*

Falstone, Northumberland [NY7287], *Blackcock*: Very friendly unspoiled pub near Kielder Water; real ale, attractive old-fashioned fireplaces; good value bedrooms *(David Bolton)*

Fatfield, Tyne & Wear [Bone Mill Lane; NZ3054], *Havelock Arms*: Homely pub by

River Wear with pleasant welcome from licensees, well kept Vaux Lorimers Scotch and Samson, good choice of home-made bar food *(E R Thompson)*

☆ **Fir Tree**, Durham [A68; NZ1434], *Duke of York*: Clean, very comfortable bar in former stables fitted out by 'mouseman' Thompson, friendly polite service and super food; decorated with Stone Age flints, African spears and hunting rifles, standing in extensive grounds *(Mrs Sue Johnson, Mr and Mrs D B Allan)*

Gateshead, Tyne & Wear [Eighton Banks; NZ2758], *Ship*: Excellent licensee, good beer and food *(George Butler)*

Great Stainton, Durham [NZ3422], *Kings Head*: Good local beer and excellent value food in cheerful and friendly pub; comfortable chairs, stools and settles around wooden tables in large saloon bar, busy restaurant, public bar with darts and so forth *(Doug Kennedy)*

☆ **Great Whittington**, Northumberland [NZ0171], *Queens Head*: Good atmosphere and friendly service – a pub that's on the up and up; village won county's best-kept village award *(G Bloxsom, Drs S P K and C M Linter)*

Guisborough, Cleveland [Bow St (between A171 and A173, E of centre); NZ6016], *Fox*: Comfortable open-plan bar in modernised coaching inn recently refurbished as one of Newcastle Breweries, Chandlers food pubs; children welcome; bedrooms *(LYM)*

Haltwhistle, Northumberland [Rowfoot, Featherstone Pk; OS Sheet 86 reference 683607; NY7164], *Wallace Arms*: Handsomely refurbished, caring licensees, four well kept real ales, food in bar and restaurant; bedrooms *(John Oddey)*

Haverton Hill, Cleveland [NZ4923], *Queens Head*: Well run, with competitive prices and very civil clientele *(F E M Hardy)*

Haydon Bridge, Northumberland [NY8464], *General Havelock*: Behind pub is friendly and pleasant stripped-stone dining-room (open Weds–Sun, not Sun lunch) overlooking garden, River Tyne and hill sheep pastures; good value food showing really careful cooking of fresh ingredients, obliging service *(Alun Moore, Michael Herbert)*

Heighington, Durham [West Green; NZ2522], *Bay Horse*: Seventeenth-century pub in pleasant surroundings, very good choice of food, well kept beer, quick pleasant service, spacious straightforwardly comfortable lounge; popular at lunchtime with businessmen from nearby Newton Aycliffe new town *(RAMS)*

Hexham, Northumberland [Priestpopple; E end of main st, on left entering from Newcastle; NY9464], *County*: Pleasant straightforward lunchtime bar food served quickly in lounge bar of town hotel *(Anon)*; [Battle Hill] *Globe*: Hospitable licensees serving good value lunchtime sandwiches (especially

prawn) and McEwans/Youngers beers in small town bar, in Grade II listed building; unusual curved counter in front bar, also back room; décor blues and greys, with dark wood seat backs, stools and tables *(GB)*

Holmside, Durham [NZ2249], *Wardles Bridge*: Remarkable collection of whiskies in friendly country pub *(LYM)*

Holy Island, Northumberland [NU1343], *Crown & Anchor*: Excellent beer and quickly served crab sandwich in busy pub with cheerful landlord, good décor and succulent beef sandwiches; interesting rope fancy-work *(Kenneth Finch)*

Holystone, Northumberland [NY9503], *Salmon*: Comfortably furnished Coquet Valley local, good value simple food and lively pool-room; in attractive countryside close to Holy Well *(LYM)*

Hurworth, Durham [NZ3110], *Otter & Fish*: Attractive position, very good choice of well prepared food *(RAMS)*

Knarsdale, Northumberland [NY6854], *Kirkstyle*: Very friendly village pub, simple but nice, with good beer and good value food *(R A Hall)*

nr Langley on Tyne, Northumberland [A686 S; NY8361], *Carts Bog*: Quickly served bar food and well kept Tetleys and Theakstons Best in cosy beamed bar and lounge with pool and other games; summer weekend barbecues out by the moors; children in back lounge; may be closed weekday lunchtimes *(E and T G Preston, LYM)*

Longframlington, Northumberland [Wheldon Bridge; NU1301], *Anglers Arms*: Imaginative lunchtime food including good helpings of excellent chicken Kiev and fresh local fish; good table service *(M D Jones)*

Lowick, Northumberland [NY0239], *Black Bull*: Well kept McEwans on handpump, nice quiet back snug, lively locals' bar, friendly landlord; very good local salmon *(Mr and Mrs M D Jones)*

☆ **Marsden**, Tyne & Wear [signposted passage to lift in car park on A183, just before entering Marsden coming from Whitburn; NZ4164], *Grotto*: Partly built into cliff caverns; you go down in a lift to the two floors – upper pink plush, lower brown varnish; good food including beautifully cooked fresh vegetables, Vaux Samson real ale, popular restaurant *(John Oddey, Philip Haggar)*

Marske by the Sea, Cleveland [NZ6423], *Mermaid*: Plush and spaciously comfortable modern Bass Charrington estate pub with good bar food, conservatory family area, friendly atmosphere; keg beer *(Alison Hayward, BB)*

Matfen, Northumberland [NZ0372], *Black Bull*: Country pub in idyllic surroundings facing village green; welcoming new owners, promising food *(D G Malkin)*

Middleton in Teesdale, Durham [Market Pl; NY9526], *Teesdale*: Warm welcome in clean, comfortable and well furnished pub with good food including pasta in variety and poached salmon; unobtrusive piped music (mainly Viennese), well kept Tetleys, restaurant; comfortable bedrooms *(Stephanie Sowerby)*

Middleton One Row, Durham [NZ3612], *Devonport*: View from lounge bar over green and down to Tees valley, excellent sandwiches and choice of hot and cold dishes; the people who took over in 1987 are working hard to make this a success; bedrooms *(Mrs Shirley Pielou, John Oddey)*

☆ **Moorsholm**, Cleveland [A171 nearly a mile E of Moorsholm village turnoff; NZ6914], *Jolly Sailor*: Cosy little booths in long beams-and-stripped-stone bar with generous helpings of good value home-made bar food, quick service, good juke box, tables and play area looking out to the surrounding moors, restaurant; closed Mon lunchtime (except bank hols) and winter weekday lunchtimes; children welcome *(TAB, LYM)*

Netherton, Northumberland [OS Sheet 81 reference 989077; NT9807], *Star*: A museum-piece in totally original condition, Whitbreads Castle Eden tapped from barrel on kitchen drainer and served through hatch *(Anon)*

Newcastle upon Tyne [Broad Chare (by river); NZ2266], *Baltic Tavern*: Spacious and comfortably converted warehouse, lots of stripped brick and flagstones or bare boards (as well as plusher carpeted parts) in warren of separate areas, good value bar food, well kept Whitbreads Castle Eden *(LYM)*; [City Road (nr quayside)] *Barley Mow*: Good choice of beers, attentive bar staff, entertainment, interesting clientele *(D J Chesham)*; [Westmoreland Rd (nr Central Stn)] *Dog & Parrot*: Brews own Wallop, friendly staff and good if not authentic atmosphere *(D J Chesham)*; [off Bigg Mkt] *Duke of Wellington*: Very lively, well kept ales including Marstons Pedigree, Tetleys and Theakstons; horseshoe bar with small tables, red-upholstered seats, interesting nineteenth-century documents and prints – many referring to the duke *(Doug Kennedy)*; [Shields Rd, Byker; NZ2764] *Tap & Spile*: Popular Camerons theme pub with multi-roomed local feel; wide range of well kept real ales including own-brewed Gladiator *(Jon Dewhirst)*; [Percy St] *Three Bulls Heads*: Busy, well laid out pub with central bar, well kept Bass and Stones, lunchtime bar food, wide range of customers *(John Thorndike)*

Newton, Cleveland [A173; NZ5713], *Kings Head*: Spruce, attractive and carefully restored, with lots of alcoves in nicely furnished spacious lounge; good value food, especially club sandwiches, casseroles and the three-course midweek lunches (half-price for children); below Roseberry Topping, a beauty-spot for walks *(Eileen Broadbent, E R Thompson)*

Newton by the Sea, Northumberland [Low Newton; NU2426], *Ship*: Down the little dead end connecting High Newton to Low Newton is this little group of cottages around a grassy green near the sea – and one's a pub; nothing fancy, just a knocked-through bar, but in a lovely position *(Gordon and Daphne)*

Newton on the Moor, Northumberland [NU1605], *Cook & Barker Arms*: Unpretentious locals' pub, a short detour from A1, with plain good value simple snacks, well kept McEwans 80/- and Youngers No 3, piped music (which may be loud); children in eating area *(John Oddey, Mrs Sue Johnson, LYM)*

Otterburn, Northumberland [NY8992], *Tower*: Decent bar meals and morning coffee or afternoon tea in plush lounge of sprawling 1830s castellated hotel built around original thirteenth-century peel tower; well kept public bar, stately grounds, own fishing on 3½ mile stretch of River Rede; bedrooms comfortable *(Robert Mitchell, LYM)*

Ovington, Durham [NZ1415], *Four Alls*: Good choice of bar food including fine steak and kidney pie, pleasant cosy atmosphere, well kept real ale, rewarding weekend carvery; an honest-to-goodness country pub *(Linda Tarren)*

Ovington, Northumberland [signposted off A69 Corbridge–Newcastle; NZ0764], *Highlander*: Good food using fresh ingredients and herbs from garden in pleasant and unostentatious dining-room of refurbished old village pub, warm welcome, relaxing atmosphere, calmly efficient service; seats on sloping lawn *(Miss E G Tweddle)*

☆ **Rennington**, Northumberland [NU2119], *Horseshoes*: Super country pub with flagstones, friendly locals and remarkably warm welcome; good freshly cooked food *(John Oddey, Mrs M Ryan)*

Saltburn by the Sea, Cleveland [A174 towards Whitby; NZ6722], *Ship*: Magnificent position right on the beach with splendid sea views from original nautical-style black-beamed bars and big plainer summer dining-lounge; bar food, restaurant, children's room, seats on terrace by the beached fishing-boats *(LYM)*

Seahouses, Northumberland [above harbour; NU2232], *Bamburgh Castle*: Hotel superbly sited above harbour, looking out to sea and islands; friendly, good beers on handpump, good bar food, big warm fires, shelves of books; bedrooms comfortable and inexpensive *(WFL)*; *Lodge*: Welcoming bar in Scandinavian-style hotel with nice atmosphere, bar snacks based on seafood and restaurant; bedrooms *(Sue Cleasby, Mike Ledger)*

☆ **Shincliffe**, Durham [A177 a mile S of Durham; NZ2941], *Seven Stars*: Quiet atmosphere in comfortable and homely pub with friendly staff, good substantial food in bar and restaurant and Vaux real ales; one half of bar traditionally furnished, the other has a remarkable fireplace; amicable pug dog; lovely in summer, with some outside seats – it's won lots of awards for its flower-decked exterior; good value bedrooms *(T J Maddison, Patrick and Carole Jones, A P Hudson, Philip Haggar)*

Shotley Bridge, Durham [NZ0953], *Raven*: New multi-level pub with valley views from picture windows – such a nice change from the basic pubs which seem to predominate around Consett *(E J Alcock)*

Slaley, Northumberland [NY9858], *Rose & Crown*: Friendly new owners, well kept McEwans/Youngers ales, home-made food – with growing concentration on this *(John Oddey)*

South Shields, Tyne & Wear [Mill Dam; NZ3766], *Steamboat*: Old-fashioned nautical pub full of photographs and ship models, plenty of authentic atmosphere, Vaux ales, bar food *(John Oddey)*

Stannersburn, Northumberland [NY7286], *Moorcock*: Welcoming, friendly pub, bar food, children truly welcomed; handy for Kielder Water *(Matthew Waterhouse, David Bolton)*

Stannington, Northumberland [NZ2279], *Ridley Arms*: Spacious open-plan bars with cosy furnishings, efficient food counter serving huge helpings, well kept Whitbreads Castle Eden *(John Oddey, LYM)*

Stockton on Tees, Cleveland [Hartburn Village; NZ4218], *Masham Arms*: Black and gold flock wallpaper in one room, panelling in the next, flamboyant paintwork in the next – chandeliers everywhere; well kept Bass, always busy, good atmosphere *(Doug Kennedy)*

Summerhouse, Durham [B6279 7 miles NW of Darlington; NZ2019], *Raby Hunt*: Pleasantly decorated pub in small village, comfortable and welcoming, with excellent home-cooked bar lunches served with four or five genuinely fresh vegetables; nice people *(J S Ellis, RAMS)*

Tantobie, Durham [NZ1855], *Oak Tree*: Excellent atmosphere, good unobtrusive service, very good food and decent range of wines *(Jon Silkin)*

Thropton, Northumberland [NU0302], *Three Wheat Heads*: Three-hundred-year-old pub with good views from garden, friendly and homely atmosphere, lovely fires in bar and lounge, excellent service, good bar food – especially local game; adventure playground; good value bedrooms *(E R Thompson, Richard Davies)*

Thropton, *Cross Keys*: Traditional three-bar village pub, handy for Cragside and the Coquet Valley *(LYM)*

Trimdon, Durham [NZ3734], *Bird in Hand*: Very warm friendly atmosphere, pleasant staff, good bar meals and excellent restaurant; entertainment Fri *(Kieron Hall)*

Ulgham, Northumberland [NZ2392], *Forge*:

Good range of food in comfortable and airy lounge opening on to terrace and sheltered neat lawn with croquet, quoits and play area; cheery high-ceilinged public bar used to be the village smithy *(T Nott, LYM)*

Upsall, Cleveland [NZ5616], *Cross Keys*: Appetising good value home cooking in friendly open-plan Scottish & Newcastle pub with well stocked bar; good evening restaurant; children welcome at lunchtime *(Mrs Trudi Tilley)*

Waldridge, Durham [off A167; NZ2550], *Waldridge*: Country pub with welcoming fire in lounge, soft piped music, no juke box or fruit machines, excellent service, Vaux beers, good range of well served bar food *(E R Thompson)*

Wall, Northumberland [NY9269], *Hadrian*: Cosy, comfortable atmosphere in Jacobean-style bars of sixteenth-century hotel with Vaux beers, good food and service; restaurant; bedrooms *(Ken Smith)*

Wark, Northumberland [NY8677], *Battlesteads*: Very friendly and cosy, with large fire in cocktail bar and nice atmosphere; bedrooms *(John Oddey)*

Warkworth, Northumberland [Castle St; NU2506], *Hermitage*: Friendly and comfortable, bar food and small restaurant *(BB)*

West Woodburn, Northumberland [NY8987], *Bay Horse*: Comfortable bedrooms in refurbished inn with bustling unpretentious atmosphere in bar; new licensees early 1988 *(S C Beardwell, J Stacey, LYM)*

West Wylam, Tyne & Wear [off A695; NZ1163], *Falcon*: Attractive, modern pub with olde-worlde charm, pleasant lounge, no piped music; well kept Whitbreads Castle Eden, excellent varied bar food, Roast Inn dining-room, Postman Pat menu for children (who are welcome), helpful service, special terms for OAPs *(E R Thompson)*

☆ **Witton le Wear**, Durham [just E of A68, 5 miles N of West Auckland; NZ1531], *Victoria*: Comfortable, warm and well kept, good welcome, quick friendly service, varied choice of good value food *(Dr Peter Smart, W M Tomlinson)*

Wolviston, Cleveland [NZ4526], *Wellington*: Pleasant local with good atmosphere, well kept Bass *(Jon Dewhurst)*

Wooler, Northumberland [High St; NT9928], *Black Bull*: Simple old town hotel with straightforward lunchtime bar food in season, McEwans real ale, games in public bar, quieter high-ceilinged knocked-through main bar; bedrooms *(LYM)*; [High St] *Red Lion*: Characterful, friendly pub with extensive pizza menu and well kept real ales; bare stripped walls, half-panelling, beams and open fireplaces; lively bar and relaxing lounge/eating area; pool and darts in secluded corner *(Lee Goulding)*; [Ryecroft Way, off A697] *Ryecroft*: Rather stretching a point to include this well run family hotel as a pub, but it does have a busy lounge bar, popular

with locals as well as visitors; Lorimers 70/-
and 80/-, Marstons Pedigree and Yates
Bitter, open fire; imaginative set menu in
restaurant; handy for Cheviots and
Northumberland coast where there's
good walking and birdwatching; bedrooms
(Angie and Dave Parkes, Lee Goulding)

Yarm, Cleveland [NZ4213], *George &
Dragon*: Included as the place where the
Stockton & Darlington Railway Co first
met, to start modern mass transport;
comfortably modernised; quickly served bar
food *(LYM)*

Essex

Changes in the county include new licensees at the cosy Half Moon tucked away in Belchamp St Paul, the Compasses in the countryside outside Coggeshall (they're putting a lot of energy into refurbishments), the Swan by the river at Henny Street near Great Henny, and the Dolphin at Stisted. The quality of food in the county's pubs continues the improvement we detected last year. In this new edition we've granted a food award to the picturesque old Bell at Castle Hedingham with its unusually big garden; it joins the distinctively furnished Axe & Compasses in Arkesden (many readers' favourite Essex food pub), the comfortable Swan at Chappel (with its riverside garden and pretty dining courtyard), the cheerful Anchor in Danbury, the fine old Marlborough Head in Constable's Dedham, the busy Black Bull in Fyfield, the spick-and-span old Bell in Horndon-on-the-Hill, the Gardeners Arms in Loughton (an unexpectedly picturesque and old-fashioned pub for this area), the handsomely timbered Eight Bells in Saffron Walden (particularly for seafood), and the Green Man at Toot Hill (it takes more interest in its wines than most pubs in the area). Many would add to this list the ancient Cock & Bell in High Easter, and on a simpler level there's good food value to be had at the Generals Arms in Little Baddow, the Green Man in Little Braxted, the quaint Rainbow & Dove at Hastingwood and the rambling Duck at Newney Green. One of this year's new entries stands out for good value food – the charmingly placed Three Horseshoes on Bannister Green. Among the other new entries, the Crooked Billet in Leigh on Sea earns its place primarily through its delightfully old-fashioned character, so well matching its position overlooking the harbour still used by the cockle-boats. The Old Dog at Herongate's got a good deal of character, too – and with Greene King taking it in hand themselves now, we suspect they'll be exploiting an obvious opportunity on the food side. The fourth newcomer, the Hoop in the attractive village of Stock, is a really happy place – not least because of its tremendous changing range of real ales, which makes it the best choice in the area for the beer lover (and they by no means neglect other drinks). Particularly promising Lucky Dips include all the Coggeshall entries, the Old Anchor in Kelvedon and the Red Lion at Lamarsh – and we've labelled a good few others with the star that suggests above-average appeal.

ARKESDEN   TL4834 Map 5
Axe & Compasses ★ ⊗

Village signposted from B1038 – but B1039 from Wendens Ambo, then forking left, is prettier; OS Sheet 154 reference 482344

This distinctively furnished, thatched pub – in a pretty village – is a well run place with a particularly friendly welcome and good value, generously served lunchtime food: very good home-made soup such as tomato or minestrone (80p), generous wholemeal sandwiches (from 90p), various ploughman's (£1.75), sausages, fish and grills with good, big chips, and home-made daily specials which the licensee and the chef dream up as they drive in to the pub each day – steak and kidney pie, beef and mushroom hot-pot, a different roast three times a week, and so forth, and puddings that include moist chocolate rum gateau, lovely lemon soufflé or home-made ice-cream specialities (£1.60). Each evening there's a different 'theme': on Tuesday, fresh fish and scampi from Lowestoft (from £3.50); Wednesday, a £6.95 meal with steak or plaice as the main course, including a glass of wine or a pint of bitter; Thursday, traditional English cooking – sausages, cottage pie, steak and kidney pie or lamb cutlets (from £2.50); Fridays and Saturdays a grander range of full meals (£13) as well as bar snacks; Sundays, roast lunches (£7.50) and evening pasta (£3.50). You can eat in the carpeted saloon bar, which rambles comfortably up and down, with cushioned oak and elm seats, quite a few easy chairs, old wooden tables, lots of brasses on the walls, and a bright coal fire; the smaller public bar, with cosy built-in settles, has sensibly placed darts, shove-ha'penny, dominoes, cribbage and a fruit machine. Well kept Greene King Abbot, BBA ('Rayments'), and IPA, and good house wines; part of the bar is set aside for non-alcoholic drinks. There are seats outside on a side terrace with colourful hanging baskets; there's a popular barbecue here too on Saturday and Sunday lunchtimes, on Sunday evening and Bank Holidays – weather permitting (95p–£4.25). *(Recommended by Joy Heatherley, Q Williamson, G A Farmer, Gwen and Peter Andrews, S J A Velate, Miss D A Thain, G N G Tingey, R F Neil, R L and A V Roberts)*

Greene King   Licensee Jerry Roberts   Real ale   Meals and snacks (not Mon evening) Restaurant tel Clavering (079 985) 272   Children in restaurant   Open 11–2.30, 6–11 all year

BANNISTER GREEN   TL6920   Map 5

Three Horseshoes ⊗

Village signposted with Felsted from A131 Chelmsford–Braintree opposite St Annes Castle pub; also signposted from B1417, off A120 Dunmow–Braintree at Felsted signpost

With tables out on the big, quiet village green, this low dormer-windowed tiled white local is covered with flowers in summer. There's a big fireplace and a collection of pewter mugs hanging over the counter in the tiny, chatty saloon bar on the right. The bar on the left has dark plush ribbed wall banquettes and spindle-back chairs around neat tables, lots of brass and a musket decorating its fireplace, a high brown panelled dado, and a low seventeenth-century beam and plank ceiling. The atmosphere's warm and relaxing. Dishes particularly recommended by readers include the pâté (£1.50), beef ploughman's (£1.90), ham and egg (£1.90), fisherman's pie, seafood platter (£2.40), gammon (£3.85) and chicken Kiev (£5.50); well kept Ridleys on handpump, decent wines by the glass and a good choice of whiskies; darts, shove-ha'penny, dominoes, cribbage, ring the bull (rare in Essex), fruit machine, and on our visit unobtrusive piped late-1970s pop music. The neat side garden has more picnic-table sets under cocktail parasols among fruit trees, with a summer weekend soft-drinks bar. The friendly licensees, who took over late in 1987, are planning an additional dining area for 1989 – we'd guess they'll need the space. *(Recommended by Gwen and Peter Andrews)*

Ridleys   Licensees John and Marcina Coward   Real ale   Meals and snacks (not Sun–Tues evenings)   Children in eating area   Occasional pie mash and pianist nights   Open 10–11, probably closing 2.30–6 Mon–Thurs in winter; closed evening 25 Dec

BELCHAMP ST PAUL   TL7942   Map 5

Half Moon

Cole Green; Belchamp St Paul is on good back road Great Yeldham–Cavendish; the Belchamps are quite well signposted within the Sudbury–Clare–Sible Hedingham triangle

New licensees have redecorated this pretty white thatched pub inside and out, adding new carpets and mirror-tiling the area behind the bar. The neat lounge area

---

has Elizabethan beams in its cream ceiling (steeply sloping under the low eaves), cushioned built-in wall benches and Windsor chairs on the dark red carpet, a glass-fronted solid-fuel stove, and a snug cubby by the serving-counter. Good food includes sandwiches with thick-cut fresh local bread (from 80p), home-made soup (95p), sausage (£1.75), ploughman's (from £2), home-made cottage pie or scampi (£2.75), home-made chilli or lasagne (£2.95), breaded chicken stuffed with prawns and lobster (£5.95), and steaks (from £6.95); puddings include good home-made fruit pie; friendly service. Well kept Greene King IPA and Abbot, Nethergate and Ruddles Best on handpump from the temperature-controlled cellar. The lively locals' bar has darts, dominoes, cribbage, two fruit machines, trivia, and piped music. In summer, a bar in the back beer garden serves soft drinks and so forth. The broad village green is very attractive. (*Recommended by Gwen and Peter Andrews, J S Evans, NBM, Miss A Findlay, R L and A V Roberts*)

Free house Licensees B R and C J Searles Real ale Meals and snacks (limited Tues and Thurs evening) Restaurant tel Clare (0787) 277402 Children in eating area; not Sat evening Open 11–2.30, 7–11 all year; closed evening 25 Dec

BURNHAM-ON-CROUCH TQ9596 Map 5
White Harte
The Quay

Popular with locals and boating people, this old inn has a good view of the yachting estuary of the River Crouch from seats on the private jetty overhanging the water, and from the window seat in the front bar. The atmosphere is hearty and there are old-fashioned, comfortably cushioned seats around oak tables on the polished parquet floor, and other traditionally furnished, high-ceilinged rooms with sea pictures decorating the panelled or stripped brick walls. Attractively priced bar food consists of a very good choice of sandwiches or filled rolls (from 70p; toasties from £1, steak £2.50, giant steak £4.50), and seafood platter with local fresh fish (£1.75). Well kept Adnams and Tolly on handpump; dominoes. (*Recommended by Dave Butler, Lesley Storey, Graham Bush, Marcus Leith, Quentin Williamson*)

Free house Licensee John Lewis Meals (not Mon–Thurs evening, Sat evening, Sun lunchtime) and snacks Restaurant Children in eating area of bar Open 11–3, 6–11 all year Bedrooms tel Maldon (0621) 782106; £17.50(£23B)/£31.50(£39B)

CASTLE HEDINGHAM TL7835 Map 5
Bell ⊗
B1058 towards Sudbury

The rather neutral-looking exterior gives little hint of the friendly, beamed and timbered saloon bar inside this busy, rambling pub – let alone the extensive garden behind it. The bar is furnished with Jacobean-style seats and Windsor chairs around oak tables, and up some steps beyond standing timbers left from a knocked-through wall there's a little gallery; a good mix of customers and maybe Lucia the Great Dane. Bar food includes Stilton ploughman's or sausage huffer (£1.50), mushrooms in garlic butter (£2), fresh mussels in garlic butter (£2.40), chicken and mushroom pancake or lasagne (£2.50), good trout meunière (£3.95), sirloin steak (£5.50), and puddings like good treacle tart (£1.40). Well kept Greene King IPA and Abbot tapped from the cask; brisk service; piped pop music. A games-room behind the traditionally furnished public bar has cribbage and space game. Behind the pub there's a fine big walled garden – an acre or so, with grass, trees and shrubs, and

---

If you book a bedroom, you should ask for written confirmation – this last year or two a small but disturbing number of readers have found they've been double-booked, or the pub has denied all knowledge of their booking.

seats on a small terrace in the car park. The twelfth-century castle keep is very striking. *(Recommended by Gwen and Peter Andrews, Tony Beaulah, Heather Sharland, J S Evans, Q Williamson, Jenny Cantle)*

Grays (who no longer brew) Licensee Mrs Sandra Ferguson Real ale Meals and snacks (not Mon evening exc bank hols) Children welcome (not in public bar) Folk club every first Sat in the month in winter Open 11.30–2.30, 6–11 all year; considering opening all day Sat

CHAPPEL TL8927 Map 5
Swan ⊗

Wakes Colne; pub visible just off A604 Colchester–Halstead

This rambling, timbered fourteenth-century pub has a well kept, spacious carpeted lounge with low dark beams, standing oak timbers dividing off side areas, banquettes around lots of dark tables, red velvet curtains on brass rings hanging from wooden curtain rails, and one or two swan pictures and plates on the white partly panelled walls; above the very big fireplace (log fires in winter, lots of plants in summer) there are a few attractive tiles. Bar food includes home-made ham and tomato or leek and potato soup (£1), sandwiches (from £1), filled French rolls (£1.20), ploughman's (from £1.75, with a little steak £2.95), basket meals or home-cooked ham (£2.50), home-made steak and kidney pie or fresh cod (£2.95), cold rare Scotch beef (£4.95), steak (£5.50), and king-size mixed grill (£7.45). Ingredients come fresh from the London markets. Well kept Greene King IPA and Mauldons Special on handpump, and a good selection of wines by the glass; faint piped music; pool, dominoes, cribbage, fruit machine, space game, trivia and juke box in the biggish well furnished public bar. The very sheltered sun-trap cobbled courtyard has a slightly continental flavour with its big tubs overflowing with flowers, parasols and French street signs; it's flanked on one side by the glass wall of the restaurant extension. The River Colne runs through the garden and below a splendid Victorian viaduct (which carries the Colne Valley Steam Railway, and steam enthusiasts will find the Railway Centre only a quarter of a mile away). The garden itself has picnic-table sets on grass stretching away from the big car park. *(Recommended by Gwen and Peter Andrews, Quentin Williamson, Heather Sharland, Jenny Cantle)*

Free house Licensees Terence and Frances Martin Real ale Meals and snacks (not 25 or 26 Dec) Restaurant (no bookings) Children in eating areas of bar, restaurant and courtyard Open 11–3, 6–11 all year; midnight supper licence Sat; closed evening 25 Dec

nr COGGESHALL TL8522 Map 5
Compasses

Pattiswick; signposted from A120 about 2 miles W of Coggeshall; OS Sheet 168 reference 820247

Surrounded by farmland, this secluded country pub has been heavily refurbished and redecorated by the new licensees. The bars have kept the beams, tiled floors and brass ornaments, and the restaurant has been smartened up. Bar food includes lunchtime snacks like soup (80p), filled baked potatoes (£1), sandwiches (from £1 for toasties), ploughman's (£1.95), cottage pie (£2.29) and cold ham (£2.50); also, steak and kidney pie (£3.50), salads (from £3.50), meat or vegetable lasagne (£3.75), gammon steak (£4.35), and breadcrumbed chicken stuffed with a tangy pineapple and cream-cheese filling (£4.20). Well kept Greene King IPA and Abbot and Mauldons Bitter (called Compass here) on handpump, kept under light blanket pressure; darts, table skittles, shove-ha'penny, dominoes, cribbage, draughts, fruit

---

Most pubs in this book sell wine by the glass. We mention wines only if they are a cut above the – generally low – average. Please let us know of any good pubs for wine.

machine and piped music. Outside there are lawns (which will be landscaped in the future), a children's play area and an orchard. *(Recommended by Miss A Findlay; more reports please)*

Free house   Licensee G F Heap   Real ale   Lunchtime snacks and meals (not Mon or Tues)   Restaurant tel Coggeshall (0376) 61322   Children welcome (not in bar)   Open 11–2.30 (3 Sat), 6.30 (6 Sat)–11 all year

DANBURY   TL7805   Map 5
Anchor ⊗

Runsell Green; just off A414 Chelmsford–Maldon

The more or less open-plan bar in this rambling, largely fifteenth-century pub has comfortable plush settles and stools around simple modern oak tables, masses of brass and copper around its fireplaces (including an engaging clock with a tinkling chime), decorative plates on the cream walls, and heavy black oak beams and sturdy standing timbers. There's a new conservatory/family-room that also converts to an evening restaurant. Big helpings of bar food include sandwiches (95p), soup (£1.25), ploughman's (£2.10), home-made chicken liver pâté with brandy (£2.25), pan-fried mussels in garlic butter or devilled whitebait (£2.50), hot Cromer crab Italian-style (£3.50), scampi (£4.25), steak, kidney and mushroom pie in Guinness or lamb cutlets grilled with Stilton (£4.95), steaks (from £5.95), Highland venison steak in a port and blackberry sauce (£7.75), and home-made puddings like blackberry and apple crumble (£1.65). Well kept Bass and Charrington IPA on handpump, and more malt whiskies than usual for the area; efficient service, and a pleasantly lively and chatty atmosphere (it can get crowded in the evening); fruit machine and space game in a side room, maybe unobtrusive piped music. There are picnic-table sets on a raised front lawn with hollyhocks, roses and so forth, and swings behind. *(Recommended by Roger Broadie, Gwen and Peter Andrews, Jenny Cantle)*

Charringtons   Licensees C L and W E Abbott   Real ale   Meals and snacks (not Sun or Mon evenings)   Evening restaurant tel Danbury (024 541) 2457   Children in restaurant   Open 11–2.30, 6–11 all year

DEDHAM   TM0533   Map 5
Marlborough Head ⊗

This old timbered building was built a year or two after the discovery of America for a local cloth merchant, and became an inn in 1704. The two most interesting rooms are the central lounge – with a wealth of finely carved woodwork – and the refurbished beamed and timbered Constable Bar – popular for eating with many tables in wooden alcoves around its plum-coloured carpet. Bar food includes excellent soup (£1), sandwiches (from £1, £1.65 for sweet-cure ham with cream cheese, walnuts and onion), filled baked potato (£1.30), ploughman's with home-made chutney (£1.50), smoked salmon pâté (£2.25), bacon, mushroom and tomato quiche (£3.25), chickpeas and nuts in espagnol sauce (£3.50), home-made Scotch egg (£3.75), turkey curry or sweet-and-sour pork (£4.25), Aga-roasted back bacon steak with peaches or poached monkfish with potted prawn sauce (£4.50), English lamb chops (£4.75) and sirloin steak (£7.50); puddings – such as home-made treacle tart (£1.60) – are popular; get there early if you want a table; good value Sunday roast. Well kept Ind Coope and a guest beer on handpump; smiling, willing service, and a cheerful atmosphere. There are seats in the garden behind. Constable's old school is opposite. Dogs welcome. *(Recommended by J S Evans, Andy Tye, Sue Hill, Robert and Vicky Tod, Peter Griffiths, B K Scott, Gwen and Peter Andrews,*

Most pubs in the *Guide* sell draught cider. We mention it specifically only if they have unusual farm-produced 'scrumpy' or specialise in it. Do please let us know about any uncommon draught cider you find in a pub.

Alison Findlay, PLC, Margaret and Roy Randle, Dr and Mrs J Levi, Toby and Doreen Carrington, Patrick Young, Rob and Gill Weeks, Jenny Cantle, Dr Paul Kitchener, Cdr and Mrs E St Leger Moore)

Ind Coope   Licensee Brian Wills   Real ale   Meals and snacks   Children in family-room and Royal Square Room   Open 11–2.30, 6–11 all year; closed 25 and 26 Dec   Bedrooms tel Colchester (0206) 323250; £23S/£41S

FYFIELD   TL5606   Map 5
Black Bull ⊗

B184, N end of village

This busy, rural listed building is particularly popular at lunchtime with business-men and older people for its wide choice of good value food: guacamole (£1.75), fiery chicken wings (£1.85), chicken tikka (£2.25), barbecued spare ribs (starter £1.75, main course £2.95), lasagne (£2.35), steak and kidney pie (£2.85), chilli con carne (£3), shark steak or pork in chilli sauce (£4), lamb cutlets in lemon and mint (£5), and steaks (from £5.50), with lunchtime extras like taramosalata (£1.60), ploughman's (from £1.95, mixed fish £2.95), ratatouille (£2) and filled baked potatoes (from £1.60). There's a buoyant atmosphere in the several communicating but separate areas of the more or less H-shaped layout, with low ceilings, big black beams, standing timbers, and cushioned wheel-back chairs and modern settles on the muted maroon carpet. Well kept Bass and Charrington IPA on handpump, piped music (unobtrusive, under the buzz of conversation), fruit machine; efficient service. By the car park, an aviary just past a group of white tables under a fairy-lit arbour has budgerigars and cockatiels, and there are a few picnic-table sets on a stretch of grass further back. *(Recommended by Alan and Ruth Woodhouse, Dorothy and Jack Rayner, Rosemary Cladingbowl, SJC)*

Charringtons   Licensee Alan Smith   Real ale   Meals and snacks   Open 10.30–2.30, 6–11

nr GREAT HENNY   TL8738   Map 5
Swan

Henny Street; A131 from Sudbury, left at Middleton road at foot of Ballingdon hill; OS Sheet 155 reference 879384

In countryside right by a weir on the River Stour, this small pub was once a barge-house. The L-shaped lounge has well cushioned seats, military prints on the timbered walls, and a big fireplace with a coal-effect gas fire. Bar food includes sandwiches (from 85p), good home-made soup (95p), pâté (£1.80), scampi (£3.95), sole or trout (£5.90), steaks (from £6.25), half a roast duck (£6.50), pheasant (in season, £8), and daily specials like home-made steak and kidney pie, moussaka, crab salad, lamb curry or guinea-fowl (from £2.50). Well kept Greene King IPA and Abbot on handpump; maybe Radio Chiltern. Outside, there are pretty hanging baskets, a flower-edged terrace, and a delightful riverside lawn with rustic benches among the willows; fishing permits are available. *(Recommended by J S Evans, Alison Findlay, Jenny Cantle, Lt Cdr and Mrs St Leger Moore, TA)*

Greene King   Licensee P A Underhill   Real ale   Meals (not Sun evening) and snacks Restaurant tel Twinstead (078 729) 238   Children in eating area and restaurant Open 11–3, 6–11 weekdays; all day Sat

GREAT SALING   TL7025   Map 5
White Hart

Village signposted from A120

The attractive timbered lounge bar of this flower-decked Tudor pub has Windsor chairs on its antique tiles, guns hanging behind the bar, and a stairway up to a little gallery with roughly timbered walls and easy chairs on its wide oak floorboards. The generous giant huffer sandwiches have been a long-standing speciality here, and there are also rollmops, home-made pâté and more conventional sandwiches. Well kept Adnams Extra and Ridleys on handpump; darts, dominoes and a fruit machine in the public bar. You can sit outside either on the bench built right around the trunk of a fine lime tree or at picnic-table sets. *(Recommended by Gwen and Peter Andrews; more reports please)*

Ridleys   Real ale   Snacks   Open 11–3, 6–11 all year

HASTINGWOOD   TL4807 Map 5
Rainbow & Dove

¼ mile from M11 junction 7; Hastingwood signposted from exit roundabout

Three small low-beamed rooms open off the bar area in this rose-covered sixteenth-century cottage. The one on the left is particularly snug and beamy, with old golf clubs, brass pistols and plates, and the lower part of the wall stripped back to bare brick; decorations elsewhere include lots of big brass platters, brass horseshoes and so forth, with horse-collars, the odd halberd and boomerang, and even a collection of garden ornaments in one fireplace. Simple bar food (popular with older people at lunchtime) includes sandwiches (from 80p), soup (£1), ploughman's (£1.90), ham and egg (£2.40), pizza (£2.45), smoked haddock and prawn pasta (£2.75) and eight-ounce rump steak (£7.40); it gets busy at weekends; maybe piped radio. Picnic-table sets under cocktail parasols, on a stretch of grass hedged off from the car park, are bordered by an eighteen-hole putting course and a paddock; there may be a children's summer bar out here at busy times, and there are Sunday evening barbecues in summer. *(Recommended by Alan and Ruth Woodhouse, Jenny Cantle, Joy Heatherley)*

Ind Coope   Licensee A R Bird   Meals (not Mon evening, not Sun) and snacks (not Mon evening)   Children in eating area of bar   Open 11–3, 6–11 all year; closed evening 25 Dec

HERONGATE   TQ6391 Map 5
Old Dog

Dunton Road; turn off A128 Brentwood–Grays in village, at big sign for Boars Head

Attractively weatherboarded, this largely seventeenth-century pub has a long main bar with the dark-beamed ceiling showing the pitch of the roof at the sides. A line of black-lacquered tables faces the long bar counter, and down at the end a small separate area is partitioned off as 'the dog house'. There are open fires in here and in the varnished brick fireplace of the smaller Turkey-carpeted public bar, which has darts, a fruit machine and juke box. There's been a very traditional relaxed atmosphere (even when it gets busy – as it can do), and a good range of real ales on handpump – Adnams Extra, Greene King IPA and Abbot, Ridleys and Ruddles County. As this edition of the *Guide* was being printed, Greene King was taking over what had until now been a free house. To counterbalance a possible contraction of the range of beers, we'd expect some expansion on the food side; there's clearly scope for that, with the range until now having been fairly simple, and bar food service confined to lunchtimes (only sandwiches and ploughman's at weekends). There are picnic-table sets on the front terrace, and in a neat sheltered side garden. *(Recommended by E J Cutting, Graham Bush, Dave Butler, Lesley Storey, Jenny Cantle)*

Greene King   Real ale   Meals and snacks (see above)   Restaurant   Open 10–2.30, 6–11 all year

Please tell us if any Lucky Dips deserve to be upgraded to a main entry – and why. No stamp needed: *The Good Pub Guide*, FREEPOST, London SW10 0BR.

HIGH EASTER   TL6214 Map 5
Cock & Bell
The Easters are signposted from the Rodings, on B184/A1060

At its best, the food in this warmly welcoming pub wins national awards. Generously served and good value, it includes burgers (£1.05), sandwiches (from £1.10), pâté (£1.60), sirloin steak in French bread (£1.80), ploughman's (£1.90), eggs caviare, lasagne or super home-made wholemeal quiche (£2.45), pasta or bread, cheeses served with a glass of claret or home-cooked ham salad (£2.70), home-made steak and mushroom pie (£3), scampi (£3.10), a cold plate of meat, cheese and fish (£5.45), and suprême of chicken poached in white wine and herbs with Stilton and brandy sauce; home-made puddings like scrumpy apple pie (£1.35) and children's dishes (from £1); good value Sunday lunch. They have occasional Dickensian evenings in winter and Elizabethan spit-roast evenings in summer. Well kept Ruddles on handpump; a good choice of house wines; piped music. The carpeted lounge bar has comfortably cushioned Windsor chairs, massive oak beams and vases of fresh flowers. The cheerful public bar has the oldest dragon-beam ceiling in Essex, a log fire, and darts, table skittles, and fruit machine. Outside this heavily timbered black and white house is a terrace and garden with a play area. *(Recommended by E J Cutting, Jack and Dorothy Rayner, Alan and Ruth Woodhouse, Gwen and Peter Andrews, NBM, Roger Danes, Mr and Mrs J Turnbull)*

Trumans (Watneys)   Licensee Barrie Day   Real ale   Meals and snacks   Children welcome   Restaurant   Classical guitar quartet second and third Sun evening of month   Open 12–2.30, 7–11 all year   Bedrooms tel Good Easter (024 531) 296;/£25B

HORNDON-ON-THE-HILL   TQ6683 Map 3
Bell ⊗
There's an intimate, almost Northern feel to this friendly, partly medieval country pub. The busy open-plan bar has some antique high-backed settles, plush burgundy stools and benches, flagstones or highly polished oak floorboards, timbering and panelling, and seats in a bow window at the back of the open-plan bar with views over the fields; the fossilised objects hanging from the ceiling are hot-cross buns – collected, one a year, since 1900, though perhaps the wood carvings hanging from a block on the panelling and collected over much the same period are more edifying. Good bar food – served from an upstairs room that's furnished without compromise for eating – includes home-made soup (£1.10), ploughman's (known as 'tafs' here, £1.45), chilli con carne or moussaka (£2.50), country pie (£2.95), spaghetti carbonara (£3), and beef and pork with mushrooms (£3.40). Charrington IPA on handpump with Bass tapped from the cask. There are picnic-table sets in the sheltered back yard (with pretty hanging baskets and old mangles used as flowerpots). They very much go in for sport; they have a ski club, a team in the London to Brighton cycle ride and they take part in the *Sunday Times* Fun Run at Hyde Park. *(Recommended by Anne Heaton, Graham Bush, E G Parish, Peter Griffiths)*

Charringtons   Licensee John Vereker   Real ale   Meals (not Sun lunchtime) and snacks (not Sun)   Restaurant (closed 25 Dec–30 Dec)   Children in eating area and restaurant   Open 10–2.30, 6–11   Bedrooms in house two doors away tel Stanford-le-Hope (0375) 673154; /£45.50B

LEIGH ON SEA   TQ8385 Map 3
Crooked Billet
51 High Street; from A13 follow signpost to station, then cross bridge over railway towards waterside

Up steps from the narrow street, the lounge bar of this unspoilt pub has cushioned seats built in around its walls and its two big bay windows – facing into the room rather than sets of chairs opposite them, they add to the sense you get here of being part of a community. The shiny yellowing walls are decorated with photographs of local cockle smacks, and there are more in the lino-floored public bar on the left – which has sensibly placed darts, shove-ha'penny, cribbage, dominoes, and a huge log fire rather than the other room's solid-fuel stove. Well kept Ind Coope Burton, Taylor-Walker, Tetleys and now Youngs on handpump; filled rolls (from 75p), cheese-filled baked potatoes (£1.20), giant sausage in French bread (£1.35), ploughman's (£2.10) and four hot dishes changing daily, such as pies (£2.50) or Lancashire hot-pot (£3). They have picnic-table sets and long stoutly painted tables and benches out on a big terrace by the ancient wooden salt store and the sea wall – which itself is a nice place to sit on, looking down on the shellfish boats in the old-fashioned working harbour. Out here, they don't mind you eating cockles, shrimps or jellied eels from Ivy Osborne's marvellous stall, just down the lane (it shuts at 10pm). *(Recommended by Pat and Lee Crosby, Graham Bush, R Inns)*

Ind Coope   Licensee A C Downing   Real ale   Meals and snacks (lunchtime, not Sun and quiet evenings)   Folk club upstairs Tues   Open 12–11 all year, weather permitting

LITTLE BADDOW   TL7807 Map 5
Generals Arms

The Ridge; minor road Hatfield Peverel – Danbury

Well run and friendly, this pub has attractively exposed brickwork and original beams in its three rooms; the central snug has red plush button-back wall banquettes and dimpled copper tables, the left-hand bar – set for food at lunchtime – is packed with antique military tunics, and the other has a very big collection of sailor hat ribands; log-effect gas fires. Good value simple food includes giant rolls (from 85p), jumbo sausages (£2.20), well grilled rainbow trout (£2.85), and good lemon sole or scampi (£3.05). Well kept Bass and Charrington IPA on handpump; darts, dominoes, cribbage and fruit machine. There are picnic-table sets among neatly kept rose beds and three fine old holly trees on the big side lawn, and a children's play area with swings, climbing-frame and slide. *(Recommended by Gwen and Peter Andrews)*

Charringtons   Real ale   Meals (lunchtime, not Sun) and snacks   Open 11.30–2.30, 6–11 all year

LITTLE BRAXTED   TL8314 Map 5
Green Man

Kelvedon Road; village signposted off B1389 by NE end of A12 Witham bypass – keep on patiently

Mr MacGregor has run this cosy and pretty tiled brick house for twenty years, and the small traditional lounge has a quiet, friendly atmosphere, a lovely copper urn, an open fire and a collection of two hundred horsebrasses and some harness, as well as mugs hanging from a beam. Good value bar food includes sandwiches (from 70p), filled baked potatoes or hot locally baked French bread filled with ham off the bone, sardines, liver sausage, chicken, turkey, beef or even meaty haggis brought from Scotland (from £1), pâté (£1.50), ploughman's (from £1.95), lasagne, beef curry, moussaka or a very hot chilli con carne (£2.60), and big salads (from £4). Well kept Ridleys is dispensed from handpumps in the form of fifty millimetre brass cannon shells; piped music. The tiled public bar leads to a games-room with darts, shove-ha'penny, dominoes, cribbage, a fruit machine and space game. The pub stands on a very quiet lane, and there are picnic-table sets in the sheltered back garden. *(Recommended by Roger Huggins, Peter Griffiths, Gwen and Peter Andrews, Hope Chenhalls, Alison Findlay, A V Chute)*

Ridleys   Licensee Eion MacGregor   Real ale   Meals and snacks (not Mon evening) Children in eating area of bar   Open 11–3, 6–11 all year; opens 7 in winter; closed 25 Dec

LOUGHTON TQ4296 Map 5
Gardeners Arms ⊗

2¼ miles from M11 junction 5; in Loughton, turn left on to A121, then right at war memorial
and Kings Head on right; 103 York Hill

On one of the highest hills in Essex, this partly sixteenth-century pub has an
open-plan bar that spreads quite spaciously around the central servery; the
atmosphere manages to stay relatively intimate – perhaps because the windows are
mainly opaque, and both lighting and ceilings are low (except in one place, where it
soars up to the full height of the pitched roof). It's decorous and old-fashioned, with
an aged kitchen clock, two or three Delft shelves, some figured plates on the walls,
good prints, engravings and pencil drawings of this and other picturesque old inns
(including some by Cecil Aldin), and a couple of open fires. Appealing bar food
includes sandwiches (from 90p, toasties (from £1, steak £2.95), Scotch broth, a
choice of ploughman's (£1.95), omelettes (£2.25), crudités (£2.45), lasagne or chilli
con carne (£2.85), salads with home-cooked meats (from £3.20), steak, kidney and
mushroom pie (£3.75), seafood pancake (£4.25), good liver and bacon, lamb
cutlets (£4.75), mixed grill, steaks (from £6.25), and daily specials; as it's all freshly
cooked, they warn of delays of twenty to thirty minutes with some dishes. Well kept
Ruddles County, Best and Websters Yorkshire on handpump; efficient friendly
service; fruit machine, maybe piped music. Outside this tiled and weatherboarded
house there are spreading views that include parts of Epping Forest from the
picnic-table sets on the side terrace. (*Recommended by Steve Evans, Stanley Matthews,
Robert Mitchell, Mr and Mrs G T Hunt*)

*Watneys Licensee Robert Worrell Real ale Lunchtime meals and snacks (not Sun)
Restaurant tel 01-508 1655; closed Sun evening Open 10.30–2.30, 6–11 all year*

MILL GREEN TL6400 Map 5
Viper

Highwood Road; from Fryerning (which is signposted off *north-east bound* A12 Ingatestone
bypass) follow Writtle signposts; OS Sheet 167 reference 640019

The garden of this homely cottage is lovely – masses of nasturtiums, foxgloves,
geraniums and lathyrus around the tables on a neat lawn, with honeysuckle and
overflowing hanging baskets and window boxes on the pub itself. The parquet-
floored tap-room (where booted walkers are directed) has simple shiny wooden
traditional wall seats, and leads to a further room with country kitchen chairs and
sensibly placed darts. The two little rooms of the lounge have spindle-back seats,
armed country kitchen chairs, and tapestried wall seats around neat little old tables,
vases of flowers in summer, pale hessian walls (the log fireplace is in a stripped
brick wall), and a low ochre ceiling. Bar snacks include sandwiches (85p, toasties
from 95p), soup (95p), Hawaiian toast (£1.50), chilli con carne (£1.95), and
ploughman's (from £2). Well kept Trumans, Ruddles Best and Websters Yorkshire
on handpump from the oak-panelled bar counter; shove-ha'penny, dominoes,
cribbage, table skittles and a fruit machine. The pub is idyllically set in an oak
wood, with a bank of sweet chestnuts behind it, which makes it popular with
walkers. (*Recommended by Dave Butler, Les Storey, Dora Leat*)

Trumans Licensee Fred Beard Real ale Snacks Open 10–11 all year

NEWNEY GREEN TL6507 Map 5
Duck

Village signposted off A414 W of Chelmsford

There's an old-fashioned, almost cosy feel in this attractive and well run country
pub, even though it spreads extensively enough to cope with very considerable

numbers of people. Some of the many tables are tucked between high-backed booth seats, though most have wheel-back chairs, and there are one or two interesting seats such as the great curved high-backed settle in one of the alcoves. In a big two-faced brick fireplace draped with hop-bines, there's a coal-effect gas fire, the beams and joists are dark, the partly dark-panelled and partly timbered walls are hung with ancient-looking pictures and old farm and garden tools, and there's a wind-up gramophone. Food from a servery by the bar includes filled baps (£1.10) and Stilton ploughman's with a good garnish (£1.90 – both these at lunchtime only); also turkey and mushroom pie or vegetarian quiche (£3.55), gammon, veal Cordon Bleu or seafood platter (£4.40), sole stuffed with prawns, a daily special (around £3.85), and Sunday roast (£4.95); you're given a big wooden duck with your number on when you order. Adnams, Crouch Vale Woodham and Greene King Abbot on handpump; quick, polite service. The garden by the huge car park has tables under cocktail parasols, lit by old streetlamps; there are two big lily ponds (with anti-heron defences for the goldfish) in a rockery, and a hollow play tree for children, with swings, a slide and a treehouse. (*Recommended by Dave Butler, Lesley Storey, NBM, Gwen and Peter Andrews, P J and S E Robbins, Alan and Ruth Woodhouse*)

Free house   Real ale   Lunchtime snacks (not Mon) and meals (not Sun evening or Mon) Open 10.30–2.30, 6–11

PELDON   TL9916 Map 5

Rose

B1025 Colchester–Mersea, at junction with southernmost turn-off to Peldon

One or two standing timbers in this big, popular seventeenth-century pub support the low ceiling with its dark bowed oak beams, the cream walls are timbered, and there are chintz curtains in the leaded-light windows. Brass and copper decorate the mantelpiece of the gothick-arched brick fireplace, and there may be bunches of flowers. The atmosphere is cosy and relaxed, and though the tables – mostly antique mahogany, and sometimes rather creaky – are quite close together, people don't feel on top of each other because they are a good size. A new garden room/conservatory overlooks the biggish duck pond. The food servery, beside a stripped pine dresser on an old-fashioned brick floor, does Dutch pea soup, sandwiches, plaice (£2.90), beef curry (£3.05), lasagne (£3.25), goulash and steak and kidney pie (£3.45); other alcovey areas lead off here. Well kept Adnams on handpump, attentive service – and a golden labrador and black and white cat, both plump and placid. There are good teak seats outside the pink-washed house, and the garden has a swing and seesaw. (*Recommended by D R Linnell, B J E Phillips, Alison Findlay, P J and S E Robbins, A F Murray-Johnson*)

Free house   Licensees Ariette and Alan Everett   Real ale   Meals and snacks   Restaurant; only Fri and Sat and lunchtime Sun   Children in eating area of bar and garden-room   Open 11–2.30, 5.50–11 all year   Bedrooms tel Peldon (020 635) 248; £20/£28

PURLEIGH   TL8401 Map 5

Bell

Seats in the front bow window of this welcoming, homely old pub – set on the only hill for miles (with New Hall Vineyard just below) – look out over hedged flatlands to the Blackwater Estuary. The rambling main bar has cushioned wall banquettes and Windsor chairs on the carpet, heavy black beams and timbers, a huge log fire, and a warm atmosphere. Good simple food is made by the landlord's mother: sandwiches (from 80p, toasties 10p extra), pizza (£1.50), ploughman's or giant sausage and egg (£1.60), ham and egg (£2), salads (from £2.30), plaice (£2.60) and scampi (£3). Well kept Ind Coope and Adnams on handpump (the landlord encourages moderate drinking for drivers); dominoes, cribbage, fruit machine.

Inside lavatories were under construction as we went to press. Picnic-table sets on the side grass have estuary views. George Washington's great-great-grandfather was rector in the neighbouring church until, in 1642, he was turned out for spending too much time in taverns. *(Recommended by Graham Bush, Dr Paul Kitchener, John and Helen Thompson, Alison Findlay, Dave Butler, Les Storey)*

Ind Coope   Licensee Robert A Cooke   Real ale   Meals (not Sun, nor Fri–Sat evenings) and snacks   Open 11–3, 6–11 all year

SAFFRON WALDEN   TL5438   Map 5
Eight Bells ⊗

Bridge Street; B184 towards Cambridge

The busy and neatly kept open-plan bar here is full of people enjoying the seafood, mostly fresh from Lowestoft, such as mussels marinière (£2.95), prawns (£2.55), good grilled fresh plaice or scampi (£4.25), baked fresh cod with cream, dill and lemon (£3.75), baked devilled crab (£4.95) and fresh skate or prawns thermidor (£4.95, also available as a vegetarian dish with mushrooms instead of prawns) both with garlic bread. Other dishes include omelettes (£3.50), home-made lasagne (£3.95), tasty cheese and vegetable pie with crisp pastry, home-made steak and kidney pie (£4.50), good beef carbonnade, mixed grill (£4.95) and charcoal-grilled steaks (from £6.50); there's a popular summer cold buffet, lunchtime snacks such as home-made soup (£1.20), ploughman's (from £2.25), home-made pâtés (from £1.95), and fresh wholemeal pasta noodles with cream, mushrooms and garlic (£2.45), home-made puddings (from £1.50), and daily specials. A good children's menu (from £1.20, including a drink, and quite a few things on the main menu are served in half-portions). The bar is divided up by the old timbers of a knocked-through wall, and has modern oak settles forming small booths around its tables; there's a family-room in the tiled-floor tap-room. Well kept Adnams, Benskins and Ind Coope Burton on handpump; fruit machine. The restaurant, in a splendidly timbered hall with high rafters, has high-backed settles forming booths, and a very long refectory table. There are seats in the garden behind the handsomely timbered black and white Tudor building. Nearby Audley End makes a good family outing, and the pub is near the start of *Good Walks Guide* Walk 107. *(Recommended by Tom, Lorna, Audrey and Alan Chatting, G and J Halphide, Gordon Theaker, Gwen and Peter Andrews, N and J D Bailey, Quentin Williamson, Dave Braisted)*

Ind Coope   Licensee Robin Moore   Real ale   Meals and snacks   Restaurant   Children in family-room and restaurant   Open all day; closed 25–26 Dec   Bedrooms tel Saffron Walden (0799) 22790;/£31

STISTED   TL7924   Map 5
Dolphin

A120 E of Braintree

Mr Brown who left this pub in 1987 was such a popular landlord that the many readers with a soft spot for this friendly place were keeping their fingers firmly crossed to see how the new landlord would work out. So far, things seem to be working out quite well. There's still a country-pub atmosphere, and one heavily beamed and timbered room has comfortable banquettes on the black wood floor, an open fire, soft lighting, piped music – and darts, dominoes, cribbage, fruit machine, juke box and piped music; the other has a collection of chamber-pots. Bar food includes sandwiches, cottage pie (£1.50), prawn curry (£2.15), home-made steak pie or roast beef (£2.50), plaice or chicken (£4.50), and puddings like strawberry cheesecake. Well kept Adnams Extra, Ridleys PA and XXX Mild are tapped from wooden casks behind the bar. The garden has been made bigger, there are self-service barbecues, an aviary with rabbits and cockatiels, and a well equipped children's play area. *(Recommended by Aubrey Saunders, Gwen and Peter Andrews, Miss A Findlay)*

Ridleys   Licensee John French   Real ale   Meals and snacks   Children in eating area of bar Open 11–3, 5–11 all year; open all day Sat

STOCK   TQ6998   Map 5
Hoop

B1007; from A12 Chelmsford bypass take Galleywood, Billericay turn-off

It's the beer which makes this small and friendly pub so popular. They normally have Adnams Bitter and Mild, Boddingtons, Hook Norton Old Hooky, Marstons Pedigree and Owd Rodger, Nethergate, Theakstons Old Peculier and Wadworths 6X on handpump or more likely tapped from the cask, with Timothy Taylors Landlord every fortnight, and two or three guest beers – on our visit, Brains Red Dragon, Robinsons Mild and Palmers Tally Ho, though on the May Day weekend they have a hundred (and pray for fine weather). It's cosy and chatty, with brocaded wall seats around dimpled copper tables on the left, and a cluster of brocaded stools on the right – where there's a coal-effect gas fire in the big brick fireplace. Bar food includes sandwiches (from 60p), home-made soup (85p), ploughman's (£1.50), quiche (£2), chicken curry (£3), braised oxtail, prawn and trout pie or steak and kidney pie (£3.50); sensibly placed darts (the heavy black beams are studded with hundreds of darts flights); farm cider, decent wines by the glass. There are lots of picnic-table sets in the big sheltered back garden, which is prettily bordered with flowers and where they have occasional summer barbecues and maybe croquet (or boules on the front gravel). They say that Misty the dog gets his nature from the advanced age of his unexpected parents; Thomas the cat adds to the confusion – he's a lady. *(Recommended by Dave Butler, Lesley Storey, Graham Bush, Gwen and Peter Andrews, David Fowles)*

Free house   Licensee Albert Kitchin   Real ale   Meals and snacks   Open 10–11 all year

TOOT HILL   TL5103   Map 5
Green Man   ⊗

Village signposted from A113 in Stanford Rivers, S of Ongar; and from A414 W of Ongar

The real attraction of this village pub is the food – and drink. Well chosen wines from five different wine merchants include forty different champagnes by the bottle (many pinks, including their *doyenne*, Veuve Clicquot), with one sold by the glass; it's freshly opened, and the brilliantly clean glasses, without any trace of soap residue, let the *mousse* work really well; there are also Beaujolais tastings. As well as sandwiches, good soup and ploughman's (£1.75), the home-cooked food might include mussels with white wine (£2), grilled herrings in oatmeal or avocado in Stilton sauce (£2.50), pork fillet with Stilton sauce or pink trout (the fish is fresh and delivered daily), lemon sole (£6.90), game pies and fresh vegetables; Sunday roast lunch (£3.95), and there may be Cheddar and cheesy biscuits at the bar. Well kept Ruddles Best and Websters Yorkshire on handpump; friendly service. A smallish and simply furnished area by the bar has mushroom plush chairs and pale mustard leatherette stools and settles, one or two hunting prints above the dark varnished wood dado, brass platters on a shelf just below the very dark grey-green ceiling, and an open fire. Darts around the other side, shove-ha'penny, dominoes, cribbage and maybe piped Radio 1. The main emphasis is on the long dining-lounge a step up from here, with candlelit tables, fresh flowers, and attractively figured plates on a Delft shelf. In the evenings they take bookings for tables in here, but only for 7.30; after that, when you turn up they put you on a queue for tables that come free. In summer, there's a lovely mass of colourful hanging baskets, window boxes and flower tubs (for which they've won floral competitions), prettily set off by the curlicued white iron tables and chairs. Many more picnic-table sets on the grass behind have a fine view over the quiet rolling fields and woods to North Weald. *(Recommended by Alan and Ruth Woodhouse, Dave Butler, Lesley Storey, Joy Heatherley, Mr and Mrs Darlow, Roger Broadie, Gwen and Peter Andrews, G L Archer, D French)*

Watneys   Licensee P Roads   Real ale   Meals and snacks   Restaurant tel North Weald (037 882) 2255   Children in restaurant, and if over 10 in eating area of bar   Open 11–3, 6–11 all year

WOODHAM WALTER   TL8006 Map 5
Bell

There's a warm welcome and a homely atmosphere in the well kept, quiet lounge bar of this lovely tiled and timbered Elizabethan building, as well as old timbers and beams, little alcoves, comfortable seats and a log fire. Good bar food includes toasted sandwiches (from 80p, cheese with bacon £1.20, steak £1.95), soup or giant sausage in French bread or cheeseburger (£1.20), ploughman's (from £1.45), salads (from £3.20), scampi (£4.20) and daily specials such as liver and onion (£2.95), good home-cured ham (£3.15), and steak and kidney pie (£3.30), with rump steak (£6.25); there is a prettily decorated dining-room in a partly panelled gallery up steps from the main bar. Well kept Ind Coope Burton on handpump. *(Recommended by Dave Butler, Lesley Storey, Alison Findlay, C Neville Smith)*

Ind Coope   Real ale   Meals (not Sun) and snacks   Children welcome   Restaurant tel Danbury (024 541) 3437   Open 10.30–2.30, 6–11 all year

Cats
On back road to Curling Tye and Maldon, from N end of village

The well kept garden, looking out over quiet fields, makes this pretty cottage – its roof decorated with prowling stone cats – an attractive place in summer. Inside, the rambling traditional bar is welcoming whatever the weather, with its black beams and timbering set off well by neat white paintwork, button-back red leatherette seats, bow windows and collection of china cats on the mantelpiece over the open fire. The food is very simple and straightforward, and the Adnams, Greene King IPA and Abbot and Mauldons on handpump particularly well kept; they have another real ale, brewed specially for them, called Cats Piss. *(Recommended by Gwen and Peter Andrews, Jenny Cantle)*

Free house   Snacks   Real ale   Open 10.30–2, 6.30ish–11 all year

Lucky Dip

Besides the fully inspected pubs, you might like to try these Lucky Dips recommended to us and described by readers (if you do, please send us reports):

Abridge [Market Pl; TQ4696], *White Hart*: Well kept beer, good value food *(Anon)*
Althorne [TQ9199], *Huntsman & Hounds*: Popular country pub, friendly staff, good bar food and garden *(Alison Findlay, LYM)*
Ardleigh [Harwich Rd (A137 – actually towards Colchester); TM0529], *Wooden Fender*: Comfortably modernised open-plan beamed bar with usual pub food, well kept Adnams, Greene King IPA and Abbot and Marstons Pedigree on handpump, good log fire, piped music (can be obtrusive); restaurant allowing children, a pool in back garden *(Gwen and Peter Andrews, LYM)*
Battlesbridge [TQ7894], *Hawk*: Pleasantly

renovated – light and airy, with comfortable seats; garden in front, village attractive now it's bypassed, with antique centre, old mills and sailing-barge moored on river *(Jenny Cantle)*
Beaumont [byroad B1035–B1414; TM1724], *Swan*: Small pub in nice spot off beaten track, reasonable bar food, Adnams real ale *(T Nott)*
Birchanger [nr M11 junction 8 – right turn off A120 to Bishops Stortford; TL5022], *Three Willows*: Pleasant pub in small village; cricketing theme, well kept real ales including Greene King Abbot, decent choice of food (not Sun) including good

ploughman's *(Frank Williams, T Nott)*
Blackmore [nr church; TL6001], *Bull*:
Included for the attraction of the building
and the surrounding village – and the beer's
well kept; food not cheap, atmosphere rather
that of a chain restaurant *(Dave Butler, Les
Storey)*; [The Green] *Prince Albert*: Attractive
pub with log fires, friendly landlord and
staff, good bar food including vegetarian
dishes and baked pots with toppings named
after eminent Victorians *(NBM)*
Bradfield [TM1430], *Lamb & Hoggit*:
Trumans Best on handpump, good bar food
such as gammon, ham and eggs, steak,
garden with waterfall, pond and fenced play
area *(P J and S E Robbins)*
Bradwell [A120 Braintree–Colchester;
TL8022], *Swan*: Attractive inside, unusual
décor, antique furniture, well kept Greene
King IPA and Abbot *(Jenny Cantle)*
Bradwell on Sea [Waterside; TM0006], *Green
Man*: Interestingly furnished flagstoned
fifteenth-century pub with games-room and
garden, close to sea *(LYM)*; *Kings Head*:
Nice, cosy, well furnished pub, fairly
spacious and very clean, with friendly and
obliging staff and very good value food;
good children's play area *(Miss A Findlay)*
Braintree [Bradford St, Bocking; TL7524],
Old Court: Nice atmosphere in former sixteenth-century weavers' hall, tables in lovely
garden, very friendly service, good food
including some unusual items such as carrot
and fennel soup, and nice beer too; pleasant
garden; a Chef & Brewer pub, but good for
all that *(J S Evans)*
Brentwood [Ongar Rd; TQ5993], *Old
Victoria*: Popular, open-plan and much
modernised pub near the town centre
with Greene King ales *(Graham Bush)*
Buckhurst Hill [5 Queens Rd; TQ4193],
Railway: Friendly local with several steam
railway prints, real ales on handpump,
games-room *(Robert Lester)*
Bulphan [TQ6485], *Harrow*: Excellent beer,
good simple bar food, very comfortable bars;
restaurant *(E J Cutting)*
Bumbles Green [TL4004], *King Harolds
Head*: Truly local local, said to date back to
eleventh century; Courage ales, great chips
(EDVM)
Canewdon [TQ9094], *Anchor*: Smashing very
old busy pub, beams, open fire, brass, etc. in
cosy bars with separate eating area (Sun
carvery), well kept Ruddles County and
Websters Yorkshire, good views over fields
to R Crouch, or south to Southend, nice
walks; children allowed in good family-room
and restaurant *(Jenny Cantle)*; *Creeksea
Ferry*: Completely rebuilt after predecessor, a
bit to the side, burned down twice: well laid
out, attractively furnished, good value food,
Greene King Abbot and Tolly on handpump,
riverside restaurant; very busy at weekends,
especially for family Sun lunches; pleasant
riverside walks *(Jenny Cantle)*

Canfield End [TL5821], *Lion & Lamb*:
Welcoming pub, well kept Ridleys, good bar
food, especially huffers, separate restaurant,
efficient service *(S J Curtis, T G Saul)*
Chelmsford [A130; TL7006], *Bell*: Popular
main-road pub with friendly atmosphere and
staff *(Bernita Bramley)*; [Moulsham St] *Black
Horse*: Well kept Charrington on handpump, sandwiches and simple lunches at
check-clothed tables in carpeted bar *(E J
Cutting)*; [Roxwell Rd] *Horse & Groom*:
Popular mock-Tudor pub, friendly and busy
but relaxed, good reasonably priced food
including lots of salads (not Sun), Trumans
and Websters real ale, good furnishings
and décor, benches outside *(Gwen and Peter
Andrews)*; [Lower Anchor St] *Partners*: Well
kept Adnams, Greene King, Ridleys and
maybe guest beers; near county cricket
ground – its popularity with players and
aficionados gives it rather an unusual sports-
club atmosphere sometimes *(Ian Clark)*;
[Victoria Rd (nr cattle mkt)] *Springfield Mill*:
Excellent tasteful conversion of previously
derelict seventeenth-century weatherboarded
watermill; bar on lowest floor still has some
of the mill machinery – bar snacks, real ales,
restaurants *(Elaine Kellet)*
nr **Chelmsford** [Cooksmill Green – A414
5 miles W; TL6306], *Fox & Goose*:
Spaciously extended well kept pub with lots
of tables, lively but not boisterous evening
atmosphere, well kept Trumans, bar food,
friendly efficient service *(LYM)*
Chignall Smealy [TL6711], *Pig & Whistle*:
Relaxed welcoming atmosphere in L-shaped
bar of country local, brasses and farm tools,
well kept Adnams and a guest such as
Harveys or Youngs Special on handpump,
good but limited bar food (not Sun), no
music, tables outside *(Gwen and Peter
Andrews)*
Chigwell [TQ4693], *Kings Head*: Attractive
seventeenth-century building with Dickens
connections, antique furniture, picturesque
village location; can get crowded
(G L Archer)
Clavering [B1038 Newport–Buntingford,
Newport end of village; TL4731], *Cricketers*:
Enormous L-shaped bar with comfortable
seats in sixteenth-century pub, Wethereds on
handpump, good bar food, restaurant, tables
outside *(Gwen and Peter Andrews,
Mrs B M Palmer)*
☆ **Coggeshall** [7 West St; TL8522], *Cricketers*:
Cosy and homely with attractive L-shaped
bar, friendly and welcoming staff, log fire,
generous helpings of good value bar food,
Trumans Best and Websters Yorkshire on
handpump, good wine by the glass, good
coffee *(Alison Findlay, Peter Andrews)*
☆ **Coggeshall** [West St, towards Braintree],
Fleece: Handsome Elizabethan pub next to
Paycocke's (lovely timber-framed house open
pm summer Weds, Thurs and Sun); grand
fireplace, finely carved beams, well kept

Greene King IPA and Abbot on handpump, decent wine, straightforward pub food (not Tues evening), play area in spacious sheltered garden; provision for children *(Gwen and Peter Andrews, LYM)*

☆ **Coggeshall**, *White Hart*: Good atmosphere in bar of fine fifteenth-century inn incorporating former guildhall, well kept Adnams, freshly squeezed orange juice and decidedly above-average house wines, good bar food with fish and seafood (including their own smoked salmon) often predominating; some women readers would appreciate warmer treatment, but apart from that this is probably now the pick of the town's several really good pubs; restaurant; bedrooms comfortable *(Gwen and Peter Andrews, Brian Wood, AE)*

☆ **Coggeshall** [91 Church St], *Woolpack*: Handsome timber-framed Tudor inn with good log fires in attractive period lounge; the most recent reports from readers suggest that friendly new licensees who formerly ran the Hole in the Wall in Colchester are reviving the pub's reputation for good value home cooking, well kept Ind Coope ales and other decent drinks; children welcome; bedrooms comfortable *(Gwen and Peter Andrews, D Jackson, LYM)*

☆ **Colchester** [East St; TM0025], *Rose & Crown*: Timbered and jettied Tudor inn carefully modernised, parts of a former jail preserved in its rambling beamed bar, good value bar food, Tolly real ale; bedrooms comfortable *(Marcus and Marcella Leith, JJM, LYM)*

Colchester [Lexden Rd], *Hospital Arms*: Very friendly atmosphere in cricket- and rugby-orientated pub with well kept Tolly; always packed, nicknamed Ward 9 as opposite eight-ward hospital *(Philip Blaxill)*; [High St] *Red Lion*: Vestiges of former Tudor grandeur survive in what is now a businessman's comfortable central hotel, with Greene King ales and a popular variety of eateries from coffee shop through burger and pizza bar to steakhouse *(LYM)*; [North Hill] *Wig & Pen*: Pleasant pub with Greene King IPA and good selection of bar snacks; excellent staff; restaurant *(JJM)*

Coopersale Common [TL4702], *Garnon Bushes*: Large helpings of food from wide choice; you might see a mortar bee here *(Geo Rumsey)*

Cressing [TL7920], *Willows*: Good atmosphere in attractive black and white pub with snug Toby bar and larger, lighter, country bar with unusual brasses and russet-brown upholstery; friendly locals, well kept Adnams Southwold and Extra, attentive service, excellent food, live music Thurs; pretty flower boxes outside *(Gwen and Peter Andrews)*

Dedham [TM0533], *Sun*: Comfortably refurbished Tudor inn with modern furnishings and décor but nicely carved

beams and panelling, popular with locals – darts and cribbage team; friendly, attentive bar staff, good choice of bar food from doorstep sandwiches to steak and chips, Tolly ale; attractive back lawn *(E J Cutting, G B and J E Halphide, Toby and Doreen Carrington, LYM)*

Duton Hill [pub signposted off B184 Dunmow–Thaxted, 3 miles N of Dunmow; TL6026], *Rising Sun*: Typical of Ridleys pubs in being genuinely unspoilt, apart from quiet piped music – traditional village local with tables in L-shaped bar, darts at one end and maybe regulars playing cards on a green baize table at the other, Ridleys PA on handpump, bar food (only basket meals in the evening) *(Gwen and Peter Andrews)*

☆ **Easthorpe** [village signposted from A12; TL9121], *House Without A Name*: Heavy standing timbers and low beams in lively but cosy Tudor bar with good choice of real ales including Mauldons (sold under the pub's name), log fire, usual pub food, restaurant, seats in small garden; piped music may be loud; provision for children *(J S Evans, Alison Findlay, Jenny Cantle, Quentin Williamson, R Houghton, LYM)*

Eastwood [Eastwood Rd; TQ8488], *Bellhouse*: Courage pub/restaurant, warm and inviting, in beautiful building reached by small bridge over moat, surrounded by floodlit trees *(Jenny Cantle)*

Epping [High St; TL4602], *Duke of Wellington*: Friendly, comfortable one-bar local with brass plates and good atmosphere *(Robert Lester)*; [High St, nr police stn] *George & Dragon*: Four-hundred-year-old pub with welcoming atmosphere, can get crowded in evening *(Robert Lester)*; [Ivy Chimneys; TL4500] *Spotted Dog*: Friendly and quite spacious, bar food and restaurant, garden *(Robert Lester)*; [Bell Common; TL4401] *Forest Gate*: Large simple one-bar pub with variety of customers, well kept Adnams, good home-cooked bar food; may have local fruit and veg for sale *(Alan and Ruth Woodhouse)*

Epping Forest [High Beech, Lippitts Hill – OS Sheet 166 reference 396970; TQ3997], *Owl*: Worth knowing for its superb forest views and (usually) McMullens real ale; rebuilt completely in early 1970s, routine food *(R P Hastings)*

Fairstead [The Green; TL7616], *Square & Compasses*: Decidedly on the up and up, under friendly landlord – folk music buff, so piped music more interesting and specialised than usual, and regular morris dancing; well kept Ridleys, excellent position on Essex Way *(Ian Clark)*

Feering [TL8720], *Anchor*: Large, well kept, busy pub, good bar food, restaurant *(Alison Findlay)*

Felsted [TL6721], *Chequers*: Family-run pub with superb service, good local ale and warming atmosphere *(B J Collins)*

Finchingfield [TL6832], *Fox*: The splendid pargeting makes this late eighteenth-century inn by the well kept Green one of the best sights in this touristy picture-book village; warm welcome, good atmosphere, spacious beamed bar with alcoves, coal fire and impressive display of tankards; Charringtons IPA, Ruddles County and Bitter on hand-pump, good bar food, restaurant *(Gwen and Peter Andrews)*

Frating [TM0822], *Kings Arms*: Warm welcome in seventeenth-century pub with very obliging staff, good value varied plough-man's (food served until closing time), well kept Ruddles County, warm red furnishings *(Peter Griffiths)*

Frinton [The Triangle; TM2319], *Essex Skipper*: Well kept Greene King, good choice of food especially boiled ham prepared by landlady, good service and excellent licensees – Yorkshire-born landlord was a professional footballer (Sheffield Utd) and cricketer *(J J Merrett)*

Fuller Street [off A131 Chelmsford–Braintree, towards Fairstead; TL7416], *Square & Compasses*: Lovely, rural spot; genuine old converted cottage with real ales, excellent food; landlord a real character, occasional folk music *(R Clark)*

Furneux Pelham [TL4327], *Brewery Tap*: Well kept Greene King and Rayments BBA (alas, no longer from the little brewery opposite, which Greene King closed in late 1987); tasty reasonably priced bar food *(Adrian Kelly)*

Gestingthorpe [OS Sheet 155 reference 813375; TL8138], *Pheasant*: Simple country pub with attractive old-fashioned furnishings, popular and often interesting lunchtime food, Adnams, Greene King and a beer from Sudbury brewed for the pub *(Gwen and Peter Andrews, G N G Tingey, R F Neil, LYM)*

☆ Gosfield [TL7829], *Green Man*: Most welcoming and attractive, partly sixteenth-century but not twee, good plain English cooking from sandwiches to grills, including a popular cold table and deliciously gooey puddings; Greene King IPA and Abbot on handpump, good coffee with real cream, sensible choice of wines, pleasant garden run by John and Betty Arnold *(Aubrey and Margaret Saunders, FA)*

Gosfield [A1017 Braintree–Halstead], *Kings Head*: Extraordinary collection of police uniforms on full-size dummies, truncheons, handcuffs, and so forth; popular pub with good food and coffee; good value bedrooms *(Tim Baxter)*

Great Bardfield [TL6730], *Vine*: Pleasantly efficient staff, Ridleys PA and Adnams Extra (and decent coffee), good value straightfor-ward bar food; children allowed if eating *(Gwen and Peter Andrews)*

Great Stambridge [TQ9091], *Cherry Tree*: Gigantic terrarium as dining-room, like a bit of Kew Gardens tacked on to side of old pub, good food including baked avocado with prawns and crispy cheese topping, chunky steak and kidney pie, gigantic burgers; Trumans Sampson *(Peter Griffiths)*

Great Wakering [TQ9487], *Exhibition*: Friendly staff and good value simple food in Watneys pub with Websters Yorkshire on handpump; family-room; small garden with plastic ducks, gnomes and waterfall for pond *(Jenny Cantle, Roger Huggins)*; [High St; TQ9487] *White Hart*: Nice split-level bar with antique furniture, beautiful huge round glass table with ship's wheel, really hot open fire, Watneys-related real ales, popular food in side eating area, pretty floodlit garden with children's playhouse *(Jenny Cantle)*

Great Waltham [A130, about ¾ mile from Ash Tree Corner junction with A131; TL6913], *Free House*: Cosy and relaxed, with plenty of seats and standing room in lounge bar with unusual choice of well kept real ales including ones that are really rare around here; impressive display of pistols over fireplace; large pool-table in cellar bar; snacks weekday lunchtimes *(Gwen and Peter Andrews)*; [Howe St] *Green Man*: New owners have knocked a wall down making one long L-shaped bar which has increased the pubby classless atmosphere; well kept Ridleys, restaurant/carvery Tues–Sat evenings, Sun lunchtime *(Gwen and Peter Andrews)*; *Windmill*: Very attractive, feels like a small country hotel inside rather than a pub, with armchairs and pretty wallpaper; interesting if pricey food in restaurant, well kept Adnams *(Dave Butler, Les Storey)*

Great Warley Street [TQ5890], *Thatchers Arms*: Picturesque pub beside village green, recently brightened up without spoiling its character; well kept beer, good food, tree-shaded courtyard *(Quentin Williamson)*

Great Yeldham [A604; TL7638], *White Hart*: Striking old timbered hotel (Pepys is said to have endorsed its original application for a licence) with tastefully subdued rather than pubby atmosphere, large, comfortable beamed and panelled lounge, well kept Adnams on handpump, carvery, extensive lawns with lots of crab-apple trees, tables outside *(Howard and Sue Gascoyne)*

Hadstock [B1052; TL5544], *Kings Head*: Unpretentious and friendly village local with well kept Tolly beers, beautifully prepared home-made food including excellent vegeta-rian dishes as well as pies, fry-ups, grills and so forth *(Alan and Ruth Woodhouse, Stuart Watkinson)*

Harwich [Kings Quay St; TM2632], *Ship*: Good honest food in up-market cafe-style atmosphere, seafaring paintings on walls – more restaurant and coffee-house than pub *(Roy Cutting)*

Hatfield Broad Oak [TL5416], *Dukes Head*: Interesting and unusual food in old pub with friendly atmosphere; close to Hatfield Forest

— and Stansted Airport *(Gordon Theaker)*

☆ **Hatfield Heath** [TL5215], *White Horse*: Friendly three-bar sixteenth-century village pub on famously large green; well kept Greene King Abbot and Rayments on hand-pump, decent wines by glass, solid wooden benches and a mix of interesting tables, good food especially gammon, lemon sole and mixed grill in dining area which opens on to nice garden *(Gwen and Peter Andrews, Alan and Ruth Woodhouse)*

Hempstead [TL6337], *Rose & Crown*: Comfortably modernised low-beamed pub with good choice of real ales and bar food – Dick Turpin was in real life brought up here, as his father was the landlord *(LYM)*

Henham [Chickney Rd; TL5428], *Cock*: Pleasantly placed family pub/restaurant, heavily timbered, with friendly landlord and staff, very good reasonably priced fresh food, real ales *(DJT)*

Herongate [A128 S of Brentwood; TQ6391], *Bear*: Pub with fourteenth-century origins and good short choice of freshly cooked food, full of Ford staff on weekday lunchtimes, very busy too on Sun *(E J Cutting)*; [pub signposted off A128] *Boars Head*: Beautiful setting in pretty village with seats by large duck pond; four Tudor cottages knocked together and georgianised, lots of exposed beams and brickwork, big bay windows facing pond; Chef & Brewer pub, very busy with Ford office staff Mon – Fri lunchtime *(E J and J W Cutting, GPB, Jenny Cantle)*

Heybridge Basin [Basin Rd; TL8707], *Jolly Sailor*: Good value lunchtime food, nice position on River Blackwater, though sea wall hides estuary views *(N J Ransdale)*

High Roding [The Street (B184); TL6017], *Black Lion*: Attractive building with friendly atmosphere, interesting menu and landlord who cares about his beer *(Dave Butler, Lesley Storey)*

Hockley [Main Rd; TQ8293], *Bull*: Attractive weatherboarded and beamed local near Hockley Woods, well thought out, extension in character with real well and low slanting roof, wide choice of beers and whiskies, food, jolly licensee; can get packed with families, youngsters and dogs in the evening; spacious garden with own servery, pond animals and enormous play boot *(Jenny Cantle, Bernita Bramley)*

Horndon-on-the-Hill [TQ6683], *Swan*: Comfortable and sedate Ind Coope pub, with bar billiards – rare in Essex; unobtrusive service, tasty food, discreet piped music *(E G Parish)*

Horsley Cross [B1036; TM1227], *Hedgerows*: Free house with good choice of home-cooked food and of beers and wines, reasonable prices; children allowed by arrangement *(C H Fewster)*

Howe Street [TL6914], *Green Man*: Attractive beamed lounge, well kept Ridleys, decent bar food, help-yourself carvery Thurs – Sat

evening and Sun lunchtime; slides, swings and pets corner in garden *(Gwen and Peter Andrews)*

Ingatestone [TQ6499], *Bell*: Stylish building in attractive village, well kept Charrington IPA, popular with younger people as the evening wears on and perhaps at its best when less busy *(Dave Butler, Les Storey, GB, NBM)*

☆ **Kelvedon** [TL8618], *Old Anchor*: Large and popular pub dated 1592, two well polished bars with open fire, green plush banquettes, brassware and copper, beams decorated with Ipswich Town FC programmes, matchboxes, calling cards, postcards, even cuddly toys behind the bar, well kept Watneys-related real ales, decent malt whiskies, wide choice of reasonably priced food including good help-yourself salads, friendly staff, restaurant *(Jenny Cantle, Heather Sharland, Brian Wood)*

☆ **Lamarsh** [TL8835], *Red Lion*: Attractive and friendly heavily beamed pub with cosy church pews, bar made from Edwardian decorative pulpit; well kept Flowers IPA and Original and Greene King IPA, good value food, lovely raftered restaurant, children welcome; amusing cats owning the place; good views from pretty sloping garden filled with amusements for children, including animals in paddock; river not far away *(Jenny Cantle, Michael Thomson, NBM)*

Little Hallingbury [TL5017], *Sutton Arms*: Spacious two-bar pub in lovely countryside, comfortable old sofas and chairs, large gardens, excellent value traditional food such as steaks *(Alan and Ruth Woodhouse)*

Little Walden [B1052; TL5441], *Crown*: Popular free house with good choice of well kept beers, nicely placed in peaceful area, straightforward if somewhat pricey bar food *(Alan and Ruth Woodhouse, T G Saul)*

Loughton [Baldwins Hill; TQ4296], *Foresters Arms*: Cosy local near forest, Ind Coope Bitter and Burton on handpump, small garden *(Robert Lester)*

Maldon [Silver St; TL8506], *Blue Boar*: Our recommendation is for the attractive Harness Bar – real pubby atmosphere, with coal fire, friendly staff, well kept Adnams tapped from the cask, darts, fruit machine; a THF hotel, usual THF bar snacks *(Gwen and Peter Andrews)*; [High St] *Kings Head*: Rather nice old pub with exposed beams and attentive staff; bedrooms *(Brian and Rosemary Wilmot)*

Manuden [TL4926], *Yew Tree*: Refurbished free house dating back over 500 years with black and white mural of village street, pleasant service, good bar food, evening restaurant; two bedrooms with own bathrooms in converted adjoining forge *(J G Saul)*

Matching Tye [TL5111], *Fox*: Seventeenth-century country village local with nice paintings and photographs of foxes, good choice of reasonably priced food such as home-made pies and popular ploughman's; log fire, good welcome – even for children, hikers and motor-cyclists; an Ind Coope pub *(Alan and Ruth Woodhouse, F W Folley)*

Monk Street [TL6128], *Greyhound*: Successfully refurbished open-plan pub with red carpet throughout, matching plush upholstery and beams decorated with brasses; friendly landlord, well kept Adnams Southwold, Greene King IPA and Abbot, vintage port decanted, nibbles of cheese and olives on bar on Sun, wide range of bar food (not Sun evening) *(Gwen and Peter Andrews)*

Moreton [TL5307], *Moreton Massey*: Numerous good value bar snacks – it's best to get there early *(Geo Rumsey)*

Mountnessing [TQ6297], *Prince of Wales*: Real pub with Ridleys beer, small but unusual selection of malt whisky; good value food from well placed servery *(Dr G P Bush)*

Navestock [Horsemans Side, off B175; TQ5397], *Alma Arms*: Popular, comfortable, low-beamed free house serving Adnams Southwold, Greene King IPA and Abbot, Rayments BBA and Youngs Special; good lunchtime bar food *(Robert Lester, M A Cott)*; [Sabines Rd, Navestock Heath] *Plough*: Friendly free house with Adnams Extra, Crouch Vale SAS, Greene King Abbot and Rayments BBA on handpump; country and western music first Weds of month, occasional beer festivals; children welcome *(Robert Lester)*

Navestock Side [TQ5697], *Green Man*: Pleasant village pub opp cricket green; friendly landlady, Ind Coope Burton *(Robert Lester)*

North Fambridge [TQ8597], *Ferryboat*: Small old building by the river, often flooded in wet weather; intimate and very local atmosphere, stone floor, beams, old benches, friendly people, well kept Ind Coope beers; does Sun lunches *(Graham Bush)*

North Weald [TL4904], *Queens Head*: Included for its friendly atmosphere and attractive conservatory, though refurbishment has lost it the log fire; bar food, Watneys-related real ales on handpump *(Pat and Lee Crosby)*

☆ **Nounsley** [Sportsman Lane (back road between those from Hatfield Peverel to Little Baddow); TL7910], *Sportsmans Arms*: The new landlord has created a welcoming atmosphere of quiet contentment in this long one-bar family country pub, with good bar food (not Sun), well kept Ind Coope ales on handpump; children welcome, big garden with climbers *(Gwen and Peter Andrews, Jenny Cantle)*

Old Harlow [Market St; TL4712], *Chequers*: Very friendly old town pub, good value lunchtime meals and snacks, particularly well kept Courage Directors; very busy weekend evenings *(Alan and Ruth Woodhouse)*

Paglesham [TQ9293], *Plough & Sail*: Good value Watneys food pub, quick helpful service, attractive building in pleasant location, garden *(Anon (Southend), Gordon Smith)*

Pilgrims Hatch [Ongar Rd; TQ5895], *Black Horse*: Plain good value food and good Charrington IPA on handpump in very old pub with good atmosphere, garden *(N J Ransdale)*

Pleshey [TL6614], *White Horse*: Attractively refurbished fifteenth-century free house in delightful village; friendly service, good local atmosphere, good value bar food including spicy chicken wings (£1.80) and lamb with lemon and redcurrant jelly (£6.60); evening restaurant; pétanque pitch and patio *(G H Theaker, Shirley Pielou, Gwen and Peter Andrews)*

Ramsey [TM2130], *Castle*: Spacious and pleasant well kept pub, popular for reasonably priced good food *(Miss A Findlay)*

Rayleigh [High St; TQ8190], *Paul Pry*: Busy but cosy family pub with Watneys-related real ales *(Graham Bush)*; [The Chase (off A1015)] *Rayleigh Lodge*: Interesting multi-level building that appears to be a small, converted stately home, now a Watneys pub/restaurant; large gardens, barbecues; bedrooms *(Graham Bush)*

Rettendon [Southend Rd (A130); TQ7698], *Plough & Sail*: Small but very friendly and popular pub, lovely in the summer; good reasonably priced restaurant, indoor glass-enclosed barbecue *(Bernita Bramley)*

☆ **Rickling Green** [B1383 Stansted–Newport; TL5029], *Cricketers Arms*: Well kept Greene King and Rayments ales tapped from the cask in attractively refurbished pub on village green; interesting reasonably priced food in bar and restaurant; friendly atmosphere *(Adrian Kelly, Alan and Ruth Woodhouse, Graham Bush)*

☆ **Rochford** [North St; TQ8790], *Golden Lion*: Varied choice of excellent real ales including a guest beer in friendly and peaceful no-frills local *(D Fowles, Graham Bush)*

Roydon [High St (B181); TL4109], *White Hart*: Pleasant, cosy bar with Greene King Abbot and Rayments BBA on handpump *(Robert Lester)*

Saffron Walden [10 – 18 High St; TL5438], *Saffron*: Former coaching-inn, unashamedly modern inside – very comfortable and well decorated (if you like aeroplanes); wide choice of good waitress-served bar food, tables on terrace; bedrooms *(K Howard)*

☆ **Shalford** [TL7229], *George*: Village local with beams, real fires and friendly welcome; well kept Flowers Original and good wine by the glass; well cooked and generously served straightforward food at reasonable prices *(Gwen and Peter Andrews)*

South Weald [off A12; TQ5793], *Tower Arms*: Good Sun lunches, well kept Adnams, Greene King IPA and Abbot, Youngs Special; separate family-room, garden *(M A Cott)*

Southminster [2 High St; TQ9599], *Kings Head*: Many well kept beers, friendly helpful licensee, tasty home-made pizzas cooked to

order; children welcome *(D Fowles)*
Stanford Rivers [Toot Hill Rd; TL5300], *Drill House*: Super salads in summer – when there are tables in the garden *(GR)*
Stanway [London Rd; TL9324], *Swan*: Unusually warm, with friendly management and staff, lots of oak beams, big open fire; excellent bar snacks, good restaurant which allows children *(Mr and Mrs P N Waller)*
Stapleford Abbotts [Oak Hill Rd (B175); TQ5096], *Royal Oak*: Popular, especially in summer; good atmosphere *(Robert Lester)*
Stapleford Tawney [TQ5098], *Mole Trap*: Tiny country pub, miles from anywhere, pretty out and cosy in, with McMullens Best and Mild, a few tables and benches, lovely unspoilt atmosphere, fantastic views all round – a little gem *(Jenny Cantle)*
Steeple [TL9302], *Star*: Trim and cosy village pub with family atmosphere, L-shaped bar with bookable tables, log fire, alcoves with exposed brickwork and local pictures; usual bar food, and readers' reports point to Greene King IPA as the wise drink *(Gwen and Peter Andrews)*
Steeple Bumpstead [TL6841], *Fox & Hounds*: Attractive pub, comfortable lounge with hunting pictures, friendly landlord, good bar food *(Mr and Mrs J Wilmore)*
☆ **Stock** [The Square (just off village street); TQ6998], *Bear*: Small, attractive front bar with lots of character and sporting links including associations with Essex CCC; friendly landlord, well kept Ind Coope beers; very food-orientated, but the restaurant doesn't dominate the pub – which is older than it looks; readers like the 'late breakfast' on the bar lunch menu *(Dave Butler, Lesley Storey, Graham Bush, Michael Thomson)*
Stock [Common Rd, just off B1007 Chelmsford–Billericay], *Bakers Arms*: Smiling landlord, cosy but roomy L-shaped bar with Trumans on handpump, decent wines by glass, good value quickly served bar food and Sun lunch in restaurant; pleasant garden; parking limited *(Gwen and Peter Andrews, Graham Bush)*
Thaxted [TL6130], *Star*: Cheerful pub with good service, wide choice of good food – generous helpings and cheap *(Tom, Lorna, Audrey and Alan Chatting)*; [Bullring] *Swan*: Dates back to late fifteenth century, with four gables, beams everywhere, large inglenook fireplace in big open-plan bar with central servery, separate cellar bar; has been a busy local, with Greene King Abbot, Rayments and guest beers – changed hands spring 1988 for close to £500,000 *(Quentin Williamson, Gwen and Peter Andrews – up-to-date reports please)*
Thorpe le Soken [High St; TM1922], *Crown*: Excellent value home-cooked bar meals; small restaurant for evenings or parties (bookings only), children's games-room at back *(C H Fewster)*
Threshers Bush [spelled Thrushesbush on some maps – OS Sheet 167 reference 501092; TL5009], *John Barleycorn*: Main attraction is lovely garden with big pond; very smart inside with well kept Courage beers, bar snacks, and small side bar with pool-table; very isolated and peaceful *(Alan and Ruth Woodhouse)*
Tilbury [follow road to Tilbury Fort; TQ6475], *Worlds End*: Unspoilt seventeenth-century waterside pub with interesting views of Gravesend across the water and of the docks up river; three fireplaces, original flagstones throughout, Bass and Charrington IPA, very lively in the evening with darts, bar billiards and piped music; climbing-frame, slides and so forth in small garden behind, with cattle and horses wandering around or trying the taste of car aerials *(Jenny Cantle)*
Tiptree [TL8916], *Maypole*: Welcoming Ind Coope local, lounge bar with coal fire, brasses over fireplace, hanging plants and local radio discreetly playing; public bar with pool-table; reasonably priced bar food *(Gwen and Peter Andrews)*
Toppesfield [TL7337], *Chestnut*: Friendly, pleasantly decorated free house with good choice of real ales *(B Cook)*
Upshire [Horseshoe Hill; TL4100], *Horseshoes*: Friendly, comfortable local dating from 1800s, McMullens Bitter and AK Mild on handpump, garden *(Robert Lester)*; [Paternoster Hill] *Queens Head*: Young person's pub with plush lounge bar and impressive public bar; McMullens AK Mild and Bitter on handpump *(Robert Lester)*
Waltham Abbey [Honey Lane; handy for M25 junction 26 – via A121; TL3800], *Woodbine*: Big pub with comfortable banquettes in U-shaped lounge, small bar, some prints, coal-effect gas fire, usual bar food from sandwiches or filled baked potatoes to steaks; family conservatory with Epping Forest views *(A A Worthington, Ian Phillips)*
Westcliff on Sea [West Cliff Parade; TQ8685], *West Cliff*: Large well placed hotel overlooking Thames Estuary, extensively renovated in early 1988 – warm comfort, excellent service, very good bar meals, Youngers IPA on handpump, tables on terrace; nice bedrooms *(E G Parish)*
Wicken Bonhunt [TL4933], *Coach & Horses*: Partly thatched country pub with unusual inn-sign and home-cooked food *(Anon)*
☆ **Widdington** [High St; TL5331], *Fleur de Lys*: Pleasant, friendly and very clean pub serving generous helpings of well cooked bar food using fresh produce; reasonably priced, good interesting choice; well kept beers *(Alan and Ruth Woodhouse, Mrs A Dobson)*
Willingale, *Bell*: Sadly, this simple country pub, facing the two Norman churches of Willingale Doe and Willingale Spain which uniquely share the same churchyard, closed in spring 1988, to become a private house *(LYM)*

Witham [Newland St; TL8214], *Spread Eagle*: Well kept Ind Coope beer on handpump, simple food cooked to order; bedrooms *(E J Cutting)*

Wivenhoe [TM0321], *Rose & Crown*: Very friendly, with good river views – great sitting out on the quayside; landlord's special cocktail is excellent *(Colin and Caroline)*

Woodham Mortimer [Hidden up a track; TL8104], *Hurdlemakers Arms*: Quiet tucked-away local looking like a cosy house, open fire in simply furnished flagstoned lounge with cushioned settles, low ceiling and timbered walls; Greene King IPA and Abbot, good darts alley in public bar, picnic-table sets well spaced among trees and shrubs outside *(J L Thompson, BB)*

Writtle [Highwood Rd, Edney Common; TL6504], *Green Man*: Spacious free house with low ceiling, Greene King Abbot, Trumans Best and Websters Yorkshire on handpump *(Robert Lester)*

Gloucestershire

Good food's a major attraction at several of the new entries for this edition: the staunchly old-fashioned little Golden Heart at Brimpsfield, the Bakers Arms at Broad Campden (serving it in summer all through the day), the Seven Springs at Coberley (an interesting entirely new pub – the licensees have a fine track record), the pretty little Olde Inne at Guiting Power, the Weighbridge just outside Nailsworth (perhaps the nicest of all this year's new entries here), the Black Horse at Naunton (sophisticated rusticity), the naval-minded Crown at Shuthonger and the stylishly old-world Ram at Woodchester. This and the Golden Heart both have a particularly interesting range of real ales. Other new entries to note particularly include the Horse & Groom at Bourton on the Hill (a tantalisingly foreign atmosphere, and a comfortable place to stay at), the neatly stone-stripped Lygon Arms in Chipping Campden, the unpretentious Plough at Cold Aston and the friendly Queens Head at Stow-on-the-Wold. One or two notable changes include the big new bedroom block at the popular Crown of Crucis in Ampney Crucis, new licensees at the Crown at Frampton Mansell, the Trout near Lechlade and the delightfully placed Mill Inn at Withington; connoisseurs of the unusual will want to know of the Celtic coffin lid acquired by the George at St Briavels. On the negative side, we have to report the closure for redevelopment of both the New Inn at Coln St Aldwyns and the George at Winchcombe – notable inns which it's sad to lose. But of course most of the old favourites are still thriving. A shortlist of 'specials' would have to include the increasingly civilised Crown at Blockley, the imaginatively refurbished Slug & Lettuce in Cirencester, the quaint Green Dragon near Cowley, the lively Plough at Ford, the rambling Hunters Hall at Kingscote, and the New Inn hidden away in the countryside near North Nibley (fine real ales). The Fossebridge Inn at Fossebridge is doing very well indeed

284   *The Gardeners Arms, Alderton*

under its newish owners – well in line for a star award; the Gardeners Arms at Alderton has also been winning warm praise recently. A rising star among the Lucky Dips is the Ragged Cot at Hyde.

ALDERTON SP0033 Map 4
Gardeners Arms ⊗ [illustrated on page 284]
Village signposted from A438 Tewkesbury–Stow-on-the-Wold

The food award for this thatched and timbered black and white Tudor house really reflects readers' pleasure in the evening restaurant, which specialises in local game and good meats – a reflection on the landlord-chef's years in the meat trade. But the lunchtime bar snacks are very good too, with sandwiches (from 95p), soup (£1.50), ploughman's (from £1.75), pâté (£2.25) and salads (from £2.95); friendly service. The stylishly old-fashioned L-shaped bar is appropriately furnished with high-backed antique settles and other good solid seats around the tables, old mugs and tankards hanging from its sturdy beams, and a fine collection of interesting nineteenth-century prints on its cream walls – sporting, political and scurrilous French literary ones by J-J Granville; fresh flowers, and a good log fire in winter. The simpler public bar has sensibly placed darts, shove-ha'penny, dominoes, cribbage, fruit machine and juke box. Well kept Whitbreads PA and Flowers Original on handpump. There are tables outside, where a partly covered crazy-paved back courtyard and a second terrace open on to a well kept garden. *(Recommended by Dr F Peters, B Walton, PADEMLUC)*

Whitbreads   Licensee Jack Terry   Real ale   Meals (Sun lunch only) and snacks (lunchtime, not Sun)   Evening restaurant tel Alderton (024 262) 257   Children welcome Singer-guitarist Thurs   Open 10.30–2, 6.30–11 all year; closed evening 25 Dec

AMPNEY CRUCIS SP0602 Map 4
Crown of Crucis ⊗
A417 E of Cirencester

As with last year's edition we can again report substantial structural changes here; the twenty-two-bedroom block is now open, and as we went to press the bar and restaurant were about to undergo refurbishment (to be completed by Christmas); but we feel confident that the busy, friendly and local atmosphere will survive unscathed in the enlarged environment. The bar food – popular at lunchtime with older people and business people from Cirencester – is attractive for both its price and quality, including sandwiches (from 70p, lunchtime), home-made soup (75p), ploughman's (£1.50, lunchtime), basket meals (from £1.50), with main dishes like fried plaice (£1.85), pancakes filled with mushrooms, spinach and nuts (£2.50), home-made beef curry (£2.60), salads (from £2.90), lamb kebabs (£2.90), steak and kidney pie (£2.90, evenings), gammon (£3.05) and steak (from £4.40); children's dishes (from £1); the service, from a sprucely decorated side area, is friendly and efficient. Well priced Archers Village, Courage Directors and Marstons Pedigree on handpump. There are lots of tables on the grass at the back, by a stream with ducks and maybe swans. The pub gets very busy at weekends, especially for Sunday lunch. *(Recommended by Michael and Alison Sandy, Alison Hayward, Nick Dowson, Lyn and Bill Capper, Ewan McCall, Roger Huggins, Tom McLean, D W Davison, Dorothy and Ken Worrall)*

Free house   Licensee R K Mills   Real ale   Meals and snacks   Restaurant   Children welcome   Bedrooms tel Poulton (028 585) 403; £38.50B/£49.50B   Open 10.30–3.30, 6–11 all year; closed 25 Dec

BARNSLEY   SP0705 Map 4
Village Pub ⊗
A433 Cirencester–Burford

This well laid out and friendly pub serves good homely food, including sandwiches (from £1.30, prawn or smoked salmon £2.25), ploughman's (from £2.25), salads (from £3.20), half a chicken (£3.95), kebabs (£4.25), local pink trout (£4.50), ten-ounce charcoal-grilled sirloin steak (£6.75) and daily specials (around £4; the recipe for the house special, creole curry, came with the landlord's wife from the Seychelles); puddings (from £1.20); polite service. In the low-ceilinged communicating rooms there are comfortable plush chairs, stools and window settles around the polished tables on the carpet; the walls (some stripped back to bare stone) are decorated with gin-traps, scythes and other farm tools; several log fires in winter. Well kept Flowers IPA and Wadworths 6X on handpump, and a range of country wines; dominoes, piped music. The sheltered back courtyard has plenty of tables and its own outside servery. *(Recommended by V W Bankes, Aubrey and Margaret Saunders, Michael and Alison Sandy, Joan Olivier, John Broughton, Tom McLean, Ewan McCall, Roger Huggins)*

Free house   Licensees Tony and Marie-Anne Baker   Real ale   Meals and snacks Restaurant   Children welcome   Bedrooms tel Bibury (028 574) 421; £20B/£30B Open 11.30–2.30 (3 Sat), 7–11 all year

BLEDINGTON   SP2422 Map 4
Kings Head ⊗ 🛏
B4450

Quiet on a weekday lunchtime, this friendly fifteenth-century Cotswolds inn transforms into a busy restaurant pub in the evenings; though they sensibly reserve one end of the beamed bar for drinkers (and in fact you can book a table here), some readers feel that it can create cramped conditions. As we went to press the licensees were about to expand the building, creating an enlarged garden-room and restaurant. They're also planning a new car park at the back, next to the landscaped garden (which has a children's play area). But the warm atmosphere of the main bar will remain; it has high-backed wooden settles, gate-leg or pedestal tables and some beams, including a heavy vertical one next to the serving-counter; there's a cheering log fire in the stone inglenook, in which hangs a big black kettle. The bar food changes weekly, typically including sandwiches (hot roast beef with salad £2.95), soup (£1.10), vegetarian pancake (£2.50), lasagne or spare ribs (£3.50), and in the evening deep-fried aubergine and garlic (£2.95), vegetarian walnut bake (£3.75) and pork fillet in sherry (£5.25); a cold table operates in summer, and roast Sunday lunch from October to May. A good choice of malt whiskies and country wines from the barrel, as well as well kept Hook Norton, Tetleys and Wadworths 6X, on handpump from the antique bar counter; piped music. The public bar has darts, pool, bar billiards, dominoes, fruit machine and space game, with Aunt Sally in the garden. There are tables on terraces at the front, looking over the attractive village green with its ducks and stream. In summer months morris dancers regularly perform in the courtyard. *(Recommended by Simon Velate, Robert Olsen, John and Joan Wyatt, D Stephenson, A J Hughes, Bridget Carter, David Gittins, Leith Stuart, L S Manning, Michael O'Driscoll, Dave Loukidelis, Lyn and Bill Capper, S V Bishop)*

Free house   Licensees Michael and Annette Royce   Real ale   Meals and snacks (not Sun evening)   Restaurant   Children in garden-room   Open 10.30–2.30, 6–11 all year Bedrooms tel Kingham (060 871) 365; £24B/£39B

The details at the end of each main entry start by saying whether the pub is a free house or if it's tied to a brewery (which we name).

Offa's Dyke Path and the Devil's Pulpit, with views over the Wye and Tintern Abbey. *(Recommended by Keith and Sheila Baxter, Julian Proudman, Michael and Alison Sandy, Tom Evans)*

Free house   Licensee George Jones   Real ale   Meals and snacks   Children in eating area Open 12–3 (11.30–4 Sat), 7–11 all year   Bedrooms tel Tintern (029 18) 548; £15/£28

CHIPPING CAMPDEN   SP1539 Map 4
Lygon Arms

Interesting wines by the glass included on our visit a very respectable Crozes-Hermitage, and they keep Donnington SBA, Hook Norton Best, Ruddles Best, Wadworths 6X and a guest beer on handpump. The bar's not large, with a variety of horse photographs and hunting plates on its stripped stone walls, stripped high-backed settles and green plush stools around the dimpled copper tables on the flowery carpet, and a curious stone-slate roof over the stone-built bar counter. Bar food includes filled rolls (from 55p), sandwiches (from 90p, steak £3.75), salads (from £2.75), gammon and egg (£3.80), home-made lasagne (£4) and steaks (from eight-ounce rump £6.25). Darts in the back area, on our visit unobtrusive piped salsa. A few white cast-iron tables are set out in the sheltered inner courtyard. *(Recommended by Aubrey and Margaret Saunders, E V Walder, Rob and Gill Weeks)*

Free house   Licensee I G Potter   Real ale   Meals and snacks   Raftered steak-and-wine bar (not Sun lunchtime)   Children in family-room   Folk music Sun evening   Open 11–2.30, 6–11; open all day in summer   Bedrooms tel Evesham (0386) 840318; £15/£24

Noel Arms ⊗ 🛏

Reputedly licensed since 1360, this quiet old stone hotel has a fine atmospheric bare-stone bar decorated with casks hanging from its beams, and farm tools, horseshoes and gin-traps; there are attractive old tables, seats and settles among the Windsor chairs, and a coal fire; the lounge areas are comfortable and traditionally furnished. Bass and Flowers Original on handpump. Bar food includes sandwiches (from £1.20), ploughman's (£2.50), filled baked potatoes (£2.95), lasagne verde (£3.25), black pudding with mustard sauce or coq au vin (£3.50), steak and kidney pie (£3.75) and steak (£4.95). The hall has a fine clock, Jacobean oak chairs and a wall hung with armour. You can sit outside in the coachyard. Charles II is said to have stayed here on his flight after the Battle of Worcester. *(Recommended by S V Bishop, Dr W Davison, George Jonas, J S Evans, NWN, Lyn and Bill Capper, Gill and Ted George)*

Free house   Licensee R P Sargent   Real ale   Meals and snacks (lunchtime)   Restaurant Children in lounges and restaurant   Open 11–3, 5.30–11 all year   Bedrooms tel Evesham (0386) 840317; £37.50B/£48.75B

CIRENCESTER   SP0201 Map 4
Slug & Lettuce ★ ⊗
West Market Place

Good bar food in this laid-back place includes home-made liver and brandy pâté (£2.50), good value and well cooked sardines in garlic (£2.75), tagliatelle (£2.95), generous eggs, bacon and black pudding (£3), home-made salmon fishcake (£3.25), ham salad (£4.50) and lambs' kidneys with mustard sauce (£5.25); they take table bookings. The atmosphere is old-fashioned in a deliberately re-created way, with a lot of stripped pine, stonework and flagstones, large rugs on bare boards, long cushioned pews or country kitchen chairs as well as a superannuated consulting-couch, an enormous banqueting-table and a grand piano, big log fires, shelves and cases filled with books, and old wine bottles or labels, claret case ends and vineyard charts (they keep decent wines). It's spacious and well kept, with several communicating areas and cosier side alcoves. Well kept Courage Best and Directors on handpump, lively piped music. There are tables in a well protected central courtyard. It was actually called the Crown until recently. *(Recommended by Maggie Jo St John, Tony Dudley Evans, Joy Heatherley, Mike Hallewell, S V Bishop, Gill and Rob Weeks, Ewan McCall, Roger Huggins, Tom McLean)*

Courage   Licensee Ian MacKenzie   Real ale   Meals and snacks   Bookings tel Cirencester (0285) 3206/2454   Children welcome   Open 11–3, 5.30–11 all year; closed 25 Dec

COATES   SO9700 Map 4
Tunnel House

Village signposted off A419 W of Cirencester; in village follow Tarlton signposts, turning right then left; pub up track on right just after railway bridge; OS Sheet 163 reference 965005

There's a lively atmosphere in this isolated and handsome bow-fronted Cotswold-stone house, created for the most part by the large lurcher, alsatians, parrot and garrulous students from the nearby Royal Agricultural College. There's plenty to occupy the attentive observer, with a well carved wooden fireplace for one of the several open fires, a haphazard mixture of easy chairs, a sofa, little spindle-back seats, massive rustic benches and seats built into the sunny windows, and lots of dried flowers, enamel advertising signs, race tickets and air travel labels hanging from its beams; there's also a (usually dormant) python in a vivarium by the bar. Bar food includes cheeseburger (£1.70), ploughman's or sausage and mash (£2.20), spaghetti bolognese (£2.50) and lamb cutlets (£2.70). Well kept Archers Best, Flowers and a guest beer on handpump; darts, space game, fruit machine and nostalgic juke box in a separate area at one end, with maybe unobtrusive piped pop music (there may be a TV on). The disused canal here plunges from its deep wooded cutting into an elaborate stone arch below, which was built originally for the tunnel workers; the tunnel is derelict now, but once carried the old Thames and Severn Canal two and a quarter miles to Sapperton. A companion pub there, the Daneway (see Sapperton, below), also served the 'leggers' who worked the barges through the tunnel. *(Recommended by Rob and Gill Weeks, Julie Vincent, Patrick Freeman, Alison Hayward, Nick Dowson, Aubrey Saunders)*

Free house   Real ale   Meals and snacks   Children welcome   Open 11–11 in summer, 11–2.30, 7–11 in winter

COBERLEY   SO9516 Map 4
Seven Springs ⊗

A436 Brockworth–Andoversford, just SW of junction with A435 Cheltenham–Cirencester

Opened in late 1987 by the licensees who had previously made first the Boat at Redbrook and then the Green Dragon near Cowley so popular with our readers, this is on an altogether different scale from those cosy pubs. It's an imaginative reworking of what must have been a cavernously large barn, without the self-conscious rusticity that often marks such places. This, by contrast, is neat and clean – almost streamlined. By the serving-counter it's quite cosy and low-ceilinged, with country kitchen chairs around scrubbed tables, a log fire even during the only warm week of August, small pictures on white walls, rugs on polished floorboards. Down a step or two is the main lofty-ceilinged area, overlooked by a side gallery, with a good deal of stripped brickwork, many more orthodox pub tables among rugs on dark flagstones, and another log fire. A pleasantly light and airy L-shaped side room opens off, with Lloyd-Loom-type chairs around modern tables and crisp photographic posters. It overlooks sloping grass, with lots of picnic-table sets above a big duck pond; they play boules outside in summer. Bar food includes soup (£1.50), ploughman's (from £1.50), several quiches (from £2.50), fresh grilled pilchards (£2.50), vegetable kebabs in sweet-and-sour sauce (£3.45), suprême of chicken in a wine and grape sauce (£3.95), pork fillet (£4.95) and steaks (from eight-ounce sirloin £5.95); well kept Boddingtons, Courage Directors, Hook Norton Best, John Smiths, Wadworths 6X and maybe a guest beer on handpump, with decent wines by the glass, half-bottle and bottle; newspapers set out, fruit machine, unobtrusive lunchtime piped pop music in the upper part; pleasant tidy staff. (*Recommended by John and Joan Wyatt*)

Free house   Licensees Chris and Jenny Phillips   Real ale   Meals and snacks   Children welcome until 8   Pianist nightly   Open 11–11 all year

COLD ASTON   SP1219   Map 4
Plough

Village signposted from A436 and A429 SW of Stow-on-the-Wold; beware that on some maps the village is called Aston Blank, and the A436 called the B4068

A huge sycamore dominates this quiet village, and the seventeenth-century pub has Virginia creeper scrambling up its heavy stone slates. Small enough already inside, it's divided into even snugger areas by standing timbers and by one built-in white-painted traditional settle facing the stone fireplace. There are simple old-fashioned seats on the flagstone and lime-ash floor, and low black beams. Generous helpings of bar food include filled rolls (from 95p), ploughman's (from £1.75), nicely filled baked potatoes (from £1.90), cheese and onion quiche (£2.50), spring vegetables in cheese sauce or lasagne (£2.75) and home-baked ham salad (£3.25); well kept Wadworths 6X and a beer brewed for the pub on handpump, with Norburys farm cider; darts, table quoits and on our visit nostalgic piped pop music. Service is friendly, the atmosphere gentle; small side terraces have picnic-table sets under cocktail parasols. (*Recommended by Ian Howard, G Wolstenholme, Craig and Suzanne Everhart*)

Free house   Licensee J A King   Real ale   Meals and snacks   Children in eating area   Open 11–2.30, 6.30 (6 Sat)–11 all year

nr COWLEY   SO8319   Map 4
Green Dragon   ★   ⊗

Cockleford; pub signposted from A435 about 1½ miles S of junction with A436; OS Sheet 163 reference 969142

Praise for the food in this friendly and prettily restored stone-fronted pub has been virtually unanimous from readers; the extensive menu changes weekly, but may include tomato and Stilton soup or apple and tuna quiche (from £1.50), home-cooked ham, vegetarian quiche or a choice of generous ploughman's (£1.95), cold beef (£2.50), spicy curry or excellent sliced breast of duck in a light sherry sauce (£4.25), char-grilled steaks (from £5.95), and puddings like banoffi pie (£1.50); it fills up quickly so it's best to get there early for a table. The bar has country kitchen chairs and tables, big flagstones as well as some red carpet, a growing collection of foreign banknotes pinned to some of the beams, logs burning all year in a spacious stone fireplace, and a wood-burning stove in a big stone fireplace. Well kept Hook Norton Best on handpump, and Adnams, Bass, Butcombe, Theakstons Best and Old Peculier, and Wadworths 6X tapped from the cask; fruit machine, and a skittle alley (used as an overflow for weekend lunchers); efficient, helpful service (they ask customers to dress decently). There are seats outside on the terrace opposite the car park. (*Recommended by GCS, John and Joan Wyatt, Jill and Howard Cox, Graham and Glenis Watkins, Catherine Steele-Kroon, Simon Velate, Joy Heatherley, I D Shaw, Michael and Harriet Robinson, Mrs M E Lawrence, Roger Huggins, Tom McLean, Ewan McCall, Dave Braisted, Oliver Howes, Pamela and Merlyn Horswell, PLC, Robert and Vicky Tod, JF, Frank Cummins, A Saunders*)

Free house   Licensee Barry Hinton   Real ale   Meals and snacks   Children in restaurant Jazz Mon, folk Weds evenings   Open 11–3, 6–11 all year

nr ELKSTONE   SO9610   Map 4
Highwayman

Beechpike; A417 6 miles N of Cirencester (though we list this under Elkstone as it's the closest place marked on most road maps, that village is actually some way off)

Unremarkable from the outside, this roadside pub has an interesting interior – a rambling warren of low beams, stripped stonework, small-paned bay windows, cushioned antique settles (as well as wheel-backs and Windsor armchairs around the tables), and heartening log fires; there's a water-buffalo head on the wall in the back carpeted room. Arkells BB, BBB and Kingsdown on handpump, and friendly service; piped classical music at lunchtime, with more variety in the evening. Bar food includes soup (£1), sandwiches (from £2), ploughman's (£2.30), avocado pear with various fillings (£2.75), home-made pizzas (from £3), steak (£5.95), with salads in summer and in winter filled baked potatoes (from £2.50) and home-made chilli con carne (£3.50); there are children's dishes (£1.95) and puddings such as home-made treacle tart (£1.20). The sheltered back rose lawn has picnic-table sets, a good climber, slide and swings among young conifers. It's a handy break from the busy trunk road. *(Recommended by Simon Velate, Miss J A Harvey, Dr J R Hamilton, Donald Godden, Frank Cummins, Wayne Brindle, Derek Stephenson)*

Arkells   Licensees David and Heather Bucher   Real ale   Meals and snacks   Restaurant tel *Miserden (028 582) 221   Children in two family-rooms   Open 11–2.30, 6–11.30 all year*

EWEN   SU0097   Map 4
Wild Duck ⊗ ⇔

Village signposted from A429 S of Cirencester

As we went to press this small hotel had just gone on the market; but if it is sold its old-fashioned atmosphere is unlikely to change substantially. Its high-beamed main bar has attractive seats and tables among the rugs on a parquet floor, old guns, swords, horsebrasses and duck pictures on the walls, and a fine longcase clock. In winter there's an open fire in the handsome stripped stone fireplace. Bar food should include soup (£1.25), ploughman's (£2.40), lasagne (£2.65), home-made steak and mushroom pie with cauliflower cheese (£3.95), and steak (£7). Bass Light, Ruddles County, Websters Yorkshire and Wadworths 6X on handpump, shove-ha'penny, gentle piped music, courteous service. There are teak tables and chairs in the sheltered and well kept garden – always up among the leaders in a national pub garden competition. Quietly placed on the edge of a peaceful village, the inn is handy for Cirencester. *(Recommended by Gordon Theaker, Nigel Williamson, Aubrey Saunders, Colin Meredith, Alison Hayward, Nick Dowson)*

Free house   Licensee Kevin Shales   Real ale   Meals and snacks   Restaurant   Children in eating area   Open 10.30–2.30, 6.30–11 all year   Bedrooms tel *Kemble (028 577) 364; £43.50B/£58B*

FORD   SP0829   Map 4
Plough ★ ⊗

B4077

The bar in this former courthouse is a lively and rambling place, and has beams, bare stone walls, log fires, and old settles and benches around the big tables on its uneven flagstones; there are oak tables in a snug alcove. They serve good asparagus feasts (April to June, £7), and other bar food like soup (£1), sandwiches (from £1), mushrooms or beans on toast or a fruity ploughman's (£2.25), home-made pies (£4.75), and generous pheasant (£6.95), with salads on request and seafood every other Thursday evening; at busy times one or two readers have felt that the table-cleaning routine needed tightening up. Well kept Donnington BB and SBA on handpump, and farm cider; darts, shove-ha'penny, dominoes and cribbage. There are benches in front, with rustic tables and chairs on grass by white lilacs and fairy lights. The pub's cellar used to be the jail for the area. *(Recommended by M A and C R Starling, Mrs M J Dyke, Simon Velate, Hazel Church, Rob and Gill Weeks, Alan Mosley, PLC, Liz and Tony Hall, Leith Stuart, Paul McPherson, A T Langton, Mr and Mrs Ken Turner, Wayne Brindle)*

Donnington   Real ale   Meals and snacks   Children welcome   Frequent pianist – golden oldies   Open 10.30–2.30, 5.30–12 all year

FOSSEBRIDGE   SP0811 Map 4

Fossebridge ⊗ ⇔

A429 Cirencester–Stow-on-the-Wold

The original core of this Tudor inn is an architectural delight; the two bars here, linked by arches, have dark brown limestone walls and beams on the sloping ceiling, with simple but effective furnishings: Oriental rugs on flagstones, traditional wooden chairs, wall benches and tables. There are prints, reproductions of old maps, decorative plates and copper pans on the walls, and a fine log fire up at the waist-high level of the original floor. A more modern area, with an attractive restaurant, leads off. The bar food continues to earn readers' consistent praise; it's an attractive combination of more standard pub meals – steak and kidney pie (home made, £4.25), chilli con carne – and serious restaurant food: good soups, such as an excellent celery (£1.20), duck pâté (£2.25), spinach and Gruyère crêpe (£3.50), lamb (£4.50), chicken breast with forest mushrooms (£5.25), warm salad of smoked pheasant (£5.75) and fresh scallops and bacon salad (£7.25); freshly baked baguettes (from £1.95). Well kept Marstons Burton and Pedigree on handpump, and a useful choice of good malt whiskies and reasonably priced wines; sensibly placed darts and shove-ha'penny. There are tables out on the streamside terrace and a spacious lakeside lawn. It's close to Denfurlong Farm Trail, and not far from the Chedworth Roman villa (you can walk all the way from the inn along the pretty river valley). *(Recommended by BKA, Mrs Margaret Dyke, Catherine Steele-Kroon, Alastair Campbell, Alun Davies, Mr and Mrs Wyatt, H G Bown, S N Hancock, S V Bishop, Mrs Jo Corbett, Mr and Mrs WWM, Harriet and Michael Robinson, Dr and Mrs A K Clarke)*

Free house   Licensees Hugh and Suzanne Roberts   Real ale   Meals and snacks Restaurant   Children welcome   Open 11–3, 5.30–11 all year   Bedrooms tel Fossebridge (028 572) 721; £35B/£55B

FRAMPTON MANSELL   SO9102 Map 4

Crown

Village signposted off A419 Cirencester–Stroud

The bar food in this simple Cotswold village inn is served by uniformed waitresses from a cold buffet; there's a range of salads, from ham or chicken (£3) to beef (£4.50), as well as soup (£1) and ploughman's (£1.60). The main bar has stripped stonework, a dark beam and plank ceiling, little mullioned windows, a traditional settle alongside more up-to-date cushioned wall benches and ladder-back rush seats on the patterned carpet; there's a simpler public bar. Well kept Archers Village and Wadworths 6X on handpump, decent wine, piped music; friendly service. Good teak seats outside look out over the roofs to the steep wooded valley beyond. *(Recommended by NIP, Ewan McCall, Roger Huggins, Tom McLean, Alison Hayward, Nick Dowson; more reports on the new regime please)*

Free house   Licensee Mr Sykes   Real ale   Meals and snacks   Restaurant Open 11–3, 6–11 all year; closed 25 Dec   Bedrooms tel Frampton Mansell (028 576) 601; £35B/£50B

GREAT BARRINGTON   SP2013   Map 4
Fox

Village signposted from A40 Burford–Northleach; pub between Little and Great Barrington

For one reader the meat and vegetable soup they serve in this Cotswold riverside inn is more like a heart-warming stew, and at 85p it's exceptionally good value; other food includes sandwiches (80p), popular toasted sandwiches (£1.10), ploughman's or pâté (from £1.60), salads, and hot dishes such as ham, chicken, fish or scampi and pies (£2–£2.75). The bar has an unpretentious and unchanging atmosphere, with low ceilings, stripped stone walls, good log fires, and rustic wooden chairs, tables and window seats, bare stone walls and warm fires in winter. Well kept Donnington BB, SBA and XXX Mild on handpump; friendly service; sensibly placed darts, dominoes, cribbage, fruit machine, and a skittle alley out beyond the sheltered yard. There are seats on the concrete terrace by the quiet River Windrush. (*Recommended by Graham Tayar, Simon Velate, Ewan McCall, Joan Olivier, Mr and Mrs Peter Gordon, Caroline Raphael, D Stephenson, G Shannon*)

Donnington   Licensee F W Mayer   Real ale   Meals (not Sun) and snacks   Open 11–2.30, 6.30–11 all year   Bedrooms tel Windrush (045 14) 385; £14/£27

GREAT RISSINGTON   SP1917   Map 4
Lamb ⊗ 🛏

This partly seventeenth-century Cotswold inn has a cosy carpeted two-room bar, with wheel-back chairs grouped around polished tables on the carpet, and a log-effect gas fire in the stone fireplace; it's decorated with plates, pictures and an interesting collection of old cigarette and tobacco tins. Home-cooked bar food includes soup (£1.25), home-made pâtés (£2.25), with main dishes like seafood platter or mild chicken curry (£4.95), home-made steak and Guinness pie or plaice stuffed with prawns (£5.25), grilled trout (£5.50), sirloin steak (£6.55) and duck and orange (£7.50). Well kept Boddingtons, Flowers Original and Wadworths 6X on handpump; piped pop music. The neat and sheltered hillside garden looks over the village to the hills opposite, and has a play area and aviary. One of the chintzy bedrooms in the warren of small stairs and doors has a four-poster carved by the landlord; there's an indoor swimming-pool. (*Recommended by Sarah and Jamie Allan, Simon Velate, RKA, Leith Stuart, Malcolm Steward, Peter Griffiths, Mr and Mrs P W Dryland Patrick and Mary McDermott, Liz and Tony Hall, Ned Edwards*)

Free house   Licensees Richard and Kate Cleverly   Real ale   Meals and snacks Restaurant   Children welcome   Open 11–2.30, 6–11 all year   Bedrooms tel Cotswold (0451) 20388; £19.50(£25S)/£28(£34S)

GUITING POWER   SP0924   Map 4
Olde Inne ⊗

Village signposted off B4068 SW of Stow-on-the-Wold (still called A436 on many maps)

Some call this pub Th'Ollow Bottom; it's snug and gently lit inside, with attractive built-in wall and window seats (including one, near the serving-counter, that's the height of the bar stools) and small brocaded armchairs. In winter logs burn in an unusual pillar-supported stone fireplace. Turkey carpet sweeps from here into a more spacious dining-room with winged settles and wheel-back chairs around neat tables. The public bar, with flagstones and stripped stone masonry but furnished like the main bar, has sensibly placed darts, pool, dominoes and cribbage. Besides sandwiches including home-cooked ham (from 75p), soup (£1.20), ploughman's (from £1.60), haddock or home-made lasagne (£2.95), steak and kidney pie (£3.50 and scampi (£3.65), bar food includes a few dishes from the landlady's home country – marinated herrings with a home-made Danish sauce (£1.65) or frikadelmer (meat rissoles – £3.50); steaks are served on fat wooden platters. Well kept Hook Norton Best and Wadworths 6X on handpump. Tables on a strip of gravel in front of the stone pub (very pretty with its creeper, hanging baskets and tubs of flowers) look over the quiet lane to a gentle slope of field. *(Recommended by Simon Velate, Denis Waters)*

Free house   Licensee Chris Hilterman   Real ale   Meals and snacks (not Mon exc bank hols)   Children in dining-room if well behaved   Open 11.30–2.30, 5.30–11 all year; closed 25 Dec

KINGSCOTE   ST8196   Map 4

Hunters Hall ★ ⊗

A4135 Dursley–Tetbury

The great attraction in this busy Tudor pub is the series of elegant high-beamed connecting rooms, which have a comfortable miscellany of easy chairs, sofas and a fine old box settle as well as some more elementary seats, velvet curtains, exposed stone walls and good log fires in winter; there's more space to eat in the Gallery upstairs. The lower-ceilinged public bar has sturdy settles and oak tables on the flagstones in front of another big log fire. Bass, Charrington IPA and Hook Norton on handpump. Bar food includes sandwiches, mussels in white wine, smoked trout, steak and kidney pie (£2.75), generous turkey and ham pie (£3.25), seafood pancakes or crumble (£3.25), lamb kebabs (£4.25), salads such as rare beef or mixed meats (£4.25) and maybe sea-trout, salmon, or local trout (£4.65), duck with interesting sauces such as honey and chestnut (£5.75) and charcoal-grilled steaks (from £6.25). It's served chiefly from an appetisingly presented buffet, set out in an airy end room. Shove-ha'penny and sensibly placed darts. The big garden has weekend summer barbecues. It gets crowded very early at weekends. *(Recommended by Dr James Haworth, Alison Hayward, Nick Dowson, J V Hayward, S Matthews, Alastair Campbell, Frank Cummins, Roger Huggins, Gwen and Peter Andrews, N W Kingsley, Tim Locke, Wilfred Plater-Shellard, Aubrey Saunders, S Matthews)*

Free house   Licensee David Barnett-Roberts   Real ale   Meals and snacks   Restaurant tel Dursley (0453) 860393   Children in eating and gallery area and restaurant   Open 11–3, 6–11; opens 7 in winter; closed 25 Dec

nr LECHLADE   SU2199   Map 4

Trout

St John's Bridge; 1 mile E of Lechlade on A417

In 1220 this pub's predecessor was founded as an almshouse to accommodate workmen building a new bridge across the Thames, and, though the main priory was dissolved by Edward VI in 1472, the almshouse continued as an inn known as 'Ye Sygne of St John the Baptist's Head'; the name changed to the Trout in 1704. In keeping with this the low-beamed and partly panelled bar is decorated with trout, as well as stuffed pike. A wrought-iron screen separates a carpeted eating area (with leatherette bucket seats around copper-topped tables) from the flagstoned part by the serving-counter, which has Courage Best and Directors on handpump; friendly efficient service; dominoes, cribbage, maybe piped music. Bar food includes home-made soup, ploughman's, basket meals, scallops in a prawn and mushroom white wine sauce, pizza, home-made pies, a very good seafood crumble and steaks, with daily specials, several puddings and children's dishes; in summer there are salads. There are plenty of tables by the old walnut tree which presides over this pub's spacious lawn by a broad, still stretch of the upper Thames – under an ancient royal charter the pub has two miles of coarse-fishing rights. There is a summer bar and family marquee out here, with barbecues on fine summer Sunday lunchtimes; and it's worth sparing a moment for the view from the gate opposite, over the meadows towards Lechlade. The pub was due to change hands just as this edition was at the printers, so there may be some changes. *(Recommended by Frank Cummins, Lyn and Bill Capper, Mr and Mrs H W Clayton, Jon and Joan Wyatt, Leith Stuart, E Kinnersly, Alastair Campbell, Mr and Mrs R Densley)*

Courage   Real ale   Meals and snacks   Restaurant tel Faringdon (0367) 52313   Children in eating area and (at lunchtime, or if it's not being used) in restaurant   Open 10.30–2.30, 6–11 all year; opens 7 in winter; closed 25–26 Dec

LITTLE WASHBOURNE   SO9933   Map 4
Hobnails ⊗

A438 Tewkesbury–Stow-on-the-Wold

The snug little front bar in this attractive old place (some of it is five hundred years old) has old wall benches by a couple of tables on its quarry-tiled floor, under low sway-backed beams hung with pewter tankards. There's more space in the carpeted back bar – more modern, with comfortable button-back leatherette banquettes. Readers' enthusiasm for the fresh soft baps remains undiminished; these are enormous, in size and range, and generously filled, ranging from fried egg (50p), through sausage and grilled ham (£2.25), to steak with egg and mushrooms (£3.85), burgers (from £1.60); the tossed salad filling is very good value at 95p. There's also a choice of soups (£1.30) and other starters, and a wide range of home-made puddings including several based on liqueurs (around £1.55–£2.10); friendly service. Well kept Flowers IPA and Original and Whitbreads PA on handpump; darts, shove-ha'penny, fruit machine, piped music. A separate skittle alley (for hire Monday to Friday evenings) has more tables. A terrace between the two buildings, and beside a small lawn and flower bed, has good tables. It's been with the same family for over two hundred and forty years. *(Recommended by Frank Cummins, Catherine Steele-Kroon, PAB, Chris Cooke, B K Scott, Dr J R Hamilton, PLC, Leith Stuart)*

Flowers (Whitbreads)   Licensee Stephen Farbrother   Real ale   Snacks   Restaurant tel Alderton (024 262) 237   Children in eating area, restaurant and skittle alley when free   Open 10.30–2.30 (3 Sat), 6–11 all year; closed 25 and 26 Dec

LOWER SWELL   SP1725   Map 4
Golden Ball

B4068 W of Stow-on-the-Wold (sometimes still called A436 on maps)

The neat and simple bar of this seventeenth-century village inn has a friendly local feel. Behind the fireplace (which has a cheering log fire in winter) there are tables on the edge of the games area (sensibly placed darts, shove-ha'penny, dominoes, cribbage, fruit machine and juke box). Generously served bar food includes soup (£1.10), ploughman's (from £2), a good choice of filled baked potatoes (from £1.10), scampi (£3.25), home-made cottage or steak and kidney pie (£3.50) and trout or steak (£4.95); friendly licensees. Well kept Donnington BB, SBA and XXX Mild on handpump – the brewery, one of the prettiest in England, is only about twenty minutes' walk from here. There's a pleasant garden at the back, by the little stream; they have occasional barbecues, and play Aunt Sally and quoits out here. *(Recommended by Simon Velate, Derek and Sylvia Stephenson, Mr and Mrs M V Cook, PADEMLUC, Michael and Alison Sandy, Ted George, John and Joan Wyatt, C F Walling)*

Donnington   Licensees Steve and Ness Aldridge   Real ale   Meals and snacks (not Sun evening)   Evening restaurant (not Sun), bookings only   Open 11–2.30, 6–11 all year; opens 6.30 in winter   Bedrooms tel Cotswold (0451) 30247; £12.50/£22.50

If you see cars parked in the lane outside a country pub have left their lights on at night, leave yours on too: it's a sign that the police check up there.

NAILSWORTH   ST8499 Map 4
Weighbridge ⊗
B4014 towards Tetbury

It's the pies that readers go for here – especially the two-in-one with steak on one side and cauliflower cheese on the other (£3.30 large, £2.20 small), also shepherd's (£2.20), steak and mushroom or turkey and sweetcorn (£2.30); other bar food includes sandwiches (from 85p), filled baked potatoes (from 95p), ploughman's (from £1.95), lasagne (£2.30) and salads (from £2.40). Three chatty little downstairs rooms all have log fires, with attractive antique settles and small country chairs, and walls either crisply white or stripped to bare stone; the one on the left has its black beam and plank ceiling thickly festooned with black ironware – sheepshears, gin-traps, lamps, cauldrons, bellows. Steps lead up to a raftered loft with candles in bottles on an engaging mix of more or less rustic tables, and you can step straight out into the sheltered garden rising behind the pub, with swings and picnic-table sets under cocktail parasols. Well kept Adnams, Badger Best, Wadworths Farmers Glory and 6X on handpump, with Old Timer in winter; friendly staff. *(Recommended by Frank Cummins, Tim Locke, DE, Roger Huggins, Patrick Freeman, Steve Breame, E A George)*

Free house   Licensee G F Reece   Real ale   Meals and snacks   Children welcome   Open 11–2.30, 7 (6.30 Sat)–11 all year; closed 25 Dec

NAUNTON SP1123 Map 4
Black Horse ⊗ 🛏
Village signposted from B4068 (shown as A436 on older maps) W of Stow-on-the-Wold

The physical trappings of this small village inn are very much in the pleasantly unpretentious Donnington style: flagstones and flooring-tiles, black beams and some stripped stonework, simple country-kitchen chairs and built-in oak pews, polished elm cast-iron-framed tables, a big wood-burning stove. The atmosphere though is a good deal more sophisticated than that of a rustic local. Bar food includes soup (£1.25), salads (from £3.50), home-baked ham (£4), succulent gammon (£5.50) and Scotch steak (£7.50), with specials such as marinated herring (£2), flavoursome casseroles like beef carbonnade (£4), and Barnsley chop (£5); well kept Donnington BB and SBA, sensibly placed darts, fruit machine and juke box. Some tables shelter in the L of the building, by the quiet village lane. *(Recommended by Joy Heatherley, Ned Edwards, Jill Field, Simon Velate, Dr J M Jackson, L S Manning, Dr F Peters)*

Donnington   Licensees Adrian and Jenny Bowen-Jones   Real ale   Meals and snacks Restaurant   Open 11–2.30, 6–11 all year; closed evening 25 Dec   Two bedrooms tel Guiting Power (045 15) 378;/£25

NORTH CERNEY SP0208 Map 4
Bathurst Arms
A435 Cirencester–Cheltenham

The new chef in this extremely pink old Cotswold inn has already earned readers' praise for his cooking; bar meals, served in the communicating area behind the main bar, include tagliatelle with cream and garlic, lasagne, chilli con carne and chicken Kiev (all around £3.50), and good peppered steak (£6.25); three-course Sunday lunch (£6.25). The beamed and black-panelled bar has a relaxed atmosphere, with high-backed antique settles and nice window seats, Windsor chairs on the Turkey carpet, and a splendid stone fireplace with good log fires in winter. Pewter tankards hang above the bar counter, which has Courage Best, Flowers Original, Gibbs Mew Bishops Tipple, Hook Norton Best, Ind Coope Burton,

Wadworths 6X and Wethereds Winter Royal on handpump. The quite separate Stables Bar has shove-ha'penny, cribbage and dominoes. There are tables outside on a creeper-clad porch and pretty front lawn by the little River Churn, with summer barbecues most weekends, lunchtime and evening. They can arrange weekend ballooning, shooting and fishing. *(Recommended by Pamela and Merlyn Horswell, Mike Muston, Joy Heatherley, Alison Hayward, Nick Dowson, S V Bishop, Peter Wade, Mr and Mrs J M Elden, L S Manning, Aubrey Saunders, Mr and Mrs J P Camilleri, Jon Wainwright)*

Free house   Licensees Mr and Mrs F A C Seward   Real ale   Meals and snacks Restaurant   Children welcome   Open 11–11 all year   Bedrooms tel North Cerney (028 583) 281; £25B/£30B

NORTH NIBLEY   ST7496 Map 4

Black Horse

B4060

The black-beamed bar in this lively inn is partly divided by standing timbers and surviving stub walls, and has some stripped stonework (including one particularly handsome fireplace with a wood-burning stove), wheel-back chairs and red cloth built-in wall and window seats around very sturdy rustic tables. It's decorated with black iron farm tools, heavy-horse harness and copper pans. The generously served bar food includes sandwiches or filled rolls, soup (90p), hot pitta bread filled with steak (£1.50, prawn £2), salads (from £2.25), plaice or scampi (£2.95), chilli con carne (£3.25), gammon (£3.50) and steak (£6.50); puddings (from £1). Well kept Flowers Original and Whitbreads PA on handpump, with a guest beer; friendly service. Darts, dominoes and fruit machine over on the right; piped music. There are some picnic-table sets on the terrace in front of the stone-roofed building, with more on the grass behind, looking up to a steep wooded knoll and the Italianate monument on its crest. *(Recommended by Dr and Mrs A K Clarke, Frank Cummins, Paul McPherson, Mrs Maureen Hobbs)*

Whitbreads   Licensee Rod Hamston   Real ale   Meals and snacks   Restaurant (Tues–Sat evenings)   Open 11–2.30, 6 (5.30 Sat)–11 all year   Bedrooms tel Dursley (0453) 46841; £22(£24.50B)/£31.50(£35B)

New Inn ★ ⇔

Waterley Bottom, which is quite well signposted from surrounding lanes; inn signposted from the Bottom itself; one route is from A4135 S of Dursley, via lane with red sign saying Steep Hill, 1 in 5 (just SE of Stinchcombe Golf Course turn-off), turning right when you get to the bottom; another is to follow Waterley Bottom signpost from previous main entry, keeping eyes skinned for small low signpost to inn; OS Sheet 162 reference 758963

The warmth of the welcome here is in inverse proportion to the remoteness of its location; once you've found it it's worth a decent stay to savour the peacefully rural atmosphere. The cosy and cheerful carpeted lounge bar has cushioned Windsor chairs and varnished high-backed settles against its partly stripped stone walls, a fine collection of breweriana – particularly antique-handpump beer engines – and piped music. Picture windows look out on to a beautifully kept rose terrace and attractive garden below the slopes of the hillside; there are swings and slides in a small orchard. The simply furnished public bar has sensibly placed darts, dominoes, shove-ha'penny, cribbage and quiz games. There's a good range of well kept real ales on handpump, including Cotleigh Tawny, Greene King Abbot, Smiles Best, Theakstons Old Peculier, and WB (a bitter brewed for the pub by Cotleigh), quite a number of unusual bottled beers, and good ciders. Bar food, all home made, includes sandwiches, pâté (£1.80), lasagne (£1.85), chilli con carne (£1.95), chicken and mushroom pie (£2.20), and beef or ham salad (£3.50); puddings like a good peach and banana crumble (95p). To stay here (it's pleasant walking country) you have to book a long way ahead; and it's probably best to arrive outside normal opening hours. (*Recommended by M E Dormer, Sue Cleasby, A C Watson and C J Lindon, Mike Ledger, Dr and Mrs A K Clarke, Alastair Campbell, N P Gibney, Margaret and Douglas Tucker, Roger Huggins, D Stephenson, Julian Jewitt, Brian and Anna Marsden, Gill and Rob Weeks, SJC, Tim Halstead*)

Free house   Licensee Ruby Sainty   Real ale   Meals and snacks   Open 12–2.30, 7–11 all year; closed evening 25 Dec   Two bedrooms tel Dursley (0453) 3659; £12/£24

PAINSWICK   SO8609   Map 4

Royal Oak ⊗

St Mary's Street

There hasn't been a bad word from readers about the food in this friendly local; praise has come in particular for its homeliness and the generous portions. It ranges from home-made soup (85p), good sandwiches or large filled rolls (from £1), and ploughman's (from £1.10), through home-made pâté (£1.50) and salads (from £2.65), to an enterprising range of hot dishes, changing every day, but typically including home-made lasagne, lamb cutlets, kidneys and bacon, and towards the end of the week local fish (around £2–£5); attentive service. The lounge bar is divided in two by a massive chimney (with an open fire in winter), and has some walls stripped back to silvery stone, seats and copper-topped tables made from barrels, an elegant oak settle, and a lovely panelled oak door leading to a second bar on the left; well kept Flowers Original and Whitbreads PA on handpump. A small sun lounge faces a sheltered sun-trap courtyard with wistaria and colourful pots of geraniums and calceolarias. It's well positioned in the centre of this charming small hillside town of old stone buildings (many of them now antique shops) in narrow alleys, and handy for St Mary's churchyard with its ninety-nine yew trees. (*Recommended by Ted Denham, G C Calderwood, C and J Cadbury, E J Alcock, Nigel Williamson, Tom Evans*)

Flowers (Whitbreads)   Real ale   Meals and snacks (not Sun)   Children welcome   Nearby parking may be difficult   Open 11–3, 6–11 all year; closed evening 25 Dec

REDBROOK   SO5410   Map 4

Boat

Pub's inconspicuously signed car park in village on A466 Chepstow–Monmouth; from here 100-yard footbridge crosses Wye (pub actually in Penallt in Wales – but much easier to find this way); OS Sheet 162 reference 534097

The main thing in this relaxed riverside pub is the notable range of well kept real ales, tapped straight from casks behind the long curved bar counter. There are usually three guest beers, as well as the regular Bull Mastiff Best, Fullers London Pride, Greene King Abbot, Marstons Pedigree, Theakstons Best, XB and Old Peculier, Timothy Taylors Landlord and Wadworths 6X. Bar food includes filled baked potatoes (£1.20), ploughman's (£1.70), steak bap (£2.15), pasta with black olives (£2.50), some vegetarian dishes (from £2.50), seafood pancakes (£2.65), lasagne (£2.70), chicken curry (£2.85) and smoked salmon salad (£3.60); service is particularly efficient and friendly. The bar's stripped-stone décor is spartan, but pleasantly so; dominoes and a space game. The walk over what was once a light railway bridge over the swirling river makes for the most unusual approach to any pub in this part of England; there are splendid views of the river and the Wye Valley from the steep terraced garden, which has tables among little waterfalls, and a pond cut into the rocks. (*Recommended by Barry and Anne, Maggie Jo St John, Dudley Evans,*

Though we don't usually mention it in the text, lots of pubs will now make coffee – always worth asking. And some – particularly in the North – will do tea.

M A and W R Proctor, Gwynne Harper, Mr and Mrs G J Packer, Dominic Williams, Paul Duncan, Dr Paul Kitchener, Karen Bettesworth, Roger Entwistle)

Free house   Licensee Brian Beck   Real ale   Meals and snacks   Children in family-room
Folk music Tues, trad jazz Thurs   Open 11–3, 6–11 all year

ST BRIAVELS   SO5605   Map 4

George 🛏

The welcoming three-roomed rambling bar here has toby jugs and antique bottles on black beams over the servery, green-cushioned small settles, old-fashioned built-in wall seats, some booth seating, and a large stone open fireplace. A Celtic coffin lid dating from 1070, discovered when a fireplace was removed, is now permanently mounted next to the bar counter. Bar food includes sandwiches (from 80p) and ploughman's (from £1.50; prior arrangement needed for both of these in the evening) as well as hot dishes such as cheese and broccoli flan (£2.50), lasagne (£2.90) and home-made steak and kidney pie (£3.50); their speciality is what they call an oriental steampoat (at twenty-four hours' notice). Well kept Adnams, Marstons Pedigree and Wadworths 6X on handpump; darts, cribbage, fruit machine. At Whitsun, after evensong, a forester standing on the wall outside the neighbouring church throws bits of bread and cheese down – people catching them have the right to collect wood and graze in the woods that stretch to the west of the village (a forest trail through them passes ancient earthworks). Outside the pub there are tables among roses, decorative shrubs, a Robinia tree and an outdoor chess and draughts board; tables on a flagstoned terrace at the back overlook a grassy former moat to a silvery stone twelfth-century castle built as a fortification against the Welsh, and later used by King John as a hunting-lodge (the castle buildings within the ruined walls now house a Youth Hostel). *(Recommended by Nick Dowson, Barry and Anne, M A and W R Proctor, Col G D Stafford, R A Corbett)*

Free house   Licensee M E Day   Real ale   Meals and snacks   Open 11–11 all year
Bedrooms tel Dean (0594) 530228; £15/£25

SAPPERTON   SO9403   Map 4

Daneway

Village signposted from A419 Stroud–Cirencester; from village centre follow Edgeworth, Bisley signpost; OS Sheet 163 reference 939034

The pub was built originally for the tunnel workers, who lived here in the four years in the 1780s that the tunnel of the Thames and Severn Canal (about five hundred yards away) was being quarried through the stone, up to two hundred and fifty feet below ground. It then became a popular bargees' pub, frequented particularly by 'leggers', men who lay on top of the canal-boats and pushed them through the two-and-a-quarter-mile tunnel, using their legs against the tunnel roof. The heavy-horse harness and brasses in the traditionally furnished lounge recall those days – the canal fell into disuse around 1930, though it's now being partially restored by a canal trust. There's also a remarkably grand and dominating fireplace, elaborately carved mahogany from floor to ceiling, and racing and hunting prints on the attractively papered walls. Bar food includes filled rolls (from 65p, not Sundays), ploughman's (from £1.50), filled baked potatoes (from £1.65), nut roast or chilli con carne (£2.60) and steak, kidney and Guinness pie (£3.95); well kept Archers Best and a beer brewed for the pub (which has been coming from the Cirencester Brewery) on handpump and electric pump, Wadworths IPA on handpump, and 6X tapped from the cask, also regular guest beers; darts, dominoes and cribbage in the public bar, which has a big inglenook fireplace (no dogs in here); friendly, attentive service. Lots of picnic-table sets on a sloping lawn bright with flower beds and a rose trellis look down over the remains of the canal and the valley of the little River Frome. The pub's car park is built over what used to be one of its locks – you can still see the cornerstone of the lock gates. It's on *Good Walks Guide* Walk 89. *(Recommended by Alison Hayward, Nick Dowson, Mr and Mrs J G Simpson, Frank Cummins, Tom McLean, Ewan McCall, Roger Huggins)*

Free house   Managers Liz and Richard Goodfellow   Real ale   Meals and snacks   Children in small family-room off lounge   Open 11–4.30, 6.30–11

SHUTHONGER   SO8834 Map 4
Crown ⊗

A38 two miles N of Tewkesbury, on W side of road (car park opposite)

The range of food here is straightforward, but the choice of ingredients and cooking are particularly careful – main dishes come with several good fresh vegetables which might include fennel or baby beetroot in a creamy sauce, and soups (£1.50) are interestingly nourishing. The choice includes charcoal-grilled burgers (£1.50), ploughman's (£2.25), black pudding down from Thornleys (£2.75), steak bap (£2.95), salads with home-made mayonnaise, home-baked ham (£3.95) and charcoal-grilled steaks such as eight-ounce sirloin (£6.50). Furnishings are simple and modern, and there's quite a bit of nautical brassware against the plain cream walls – an Aldis lamp, engine-room telegraph, even two porthole hatches from the *Ark Royal*. Well kept Banks's, Bass and Wadworths 6X or a guest beer on handpump, as is Weston's Old Rosie cider; trivia machine. *(Recommended by John and Joan Wyatt, Mr and Mrs Devereux, B Walton)*

Free house   Licensee Emma Bezani   Real ale   Meals and snacks   Restaurant tel Tewkesbury (0684) 293714   Children in restaurant   Open 11–2.30ish, 6–11 all year; closed 25 Dec

SOUTHROP   SP1903 Map 4
Swan ⊗

Village signposted from A417 and A361, near Lechlade

This creeper-covered stone-tiled pub serves surprisingly enterprising and sophisticated home-made food; the choice on the monthly changing menu is widest in the evening, when it might include Stilton and onion soup (£1.80), venison and claret pâté, deep-fried Camembert with cranberry and orange sauce or smoked quails' eggs (£2.30), and a wide range of main dishes such as chicken and ham buckwheat pancakes (£5.25), pork and apricot casserole (£5.50), and fillet steak, ham and Stilton in puff pastry (£6.50); at lunchtime they serve ploughman's (£2.25), and a selection of the evening dishes at markedly lower prices; sandwiches on request; friendly staff. The low-ceilinged front lounge – increasingly popular with eaters – has cottagey wall seats and chairs, and log fires in winter. It leads through to a spacious stripped-stone-wall skittle alley, well modernised, with plenty of tables on the carpeted part, and its own bar service at busy times. Well kept Morlands PA and Wadworths 6X on handpump; darts and juke box. There are tables in the sheltered garden behind. *(Recommended by Wg Cdr R M Sparkes, Ewan McCall, Roger Huggins, Tom McLean, Paul S McPherson, Roy McIsaac)*

Free house   Licensee Patrick Keen   Real ale   Snacks (not lunchtimes) and meals   Restaurant tel Southrop (036 785) 205   Children welcome   Open 12–3, 7–11 all year

STANTON   SP0634 Map 4
Mount

Village signposted off A46 SW of Broadway; Old Snowshill Road – take no through road up hill and bear left

The most atmospheric area of this attractive stone Cotswold pub is its original central core; this has cask seats on big flagstones, a big fireplace in which a tree-trunk lies smouldering, black beams, heavy-horse harness and racing photographs. There are also big picture windows in a spacious extension with comfortable oak wall seats, cigarette cards of Derby and Grand National winners, and an aquarium of goldfish and angelfish; cheap well kept Donnington BB on handpump, farm cider, and mulled wine in winter. Good bar food includes sandwiches (£1, not evenings; toasted £1.75), ploughman's (from £2.20), steak and kidney pie, or ratatouille lasagne (£3), with extra dishes in the evening like chicken curry (£2) and sirloin steak (£4). The pub is particularly well positioned – up a steep, quiet lane looking back down over the lovely golden stone village. On a clear day you can see across to the Welsh mountains; the view is particularly fine from lots of seats around barrel tables on the terrace and grass outside. Darts, dominoes, shove-ha'penny, cribbage, piped music; fruit machine in extended porch, and boules outside. (*Recommended by PADEMLUC, A C Watson and C J Lindon, Ian Blackwell, Wayne Brindle, Mrs E M Lloyd, Rob and Gill Weeks, Robert and Vicky Tod, Leith Stuart, G N G Tingey, R F Neil, Alan Mosley*)

Donnington   Licensee Colin L Johns   Real ale   Meals and snacks (not Thurs evening)   Children welcome if well behaved   Open 11–11; 11–2, 7–11 in winter; closed 25 Dec

STOW-ON-THE-WOLD   SP1925 Map 4

Queens Head

The Square

This town is full of charming buildings (and with its climbing rose and hanging baskets this old stone house fits in well); it's also full of pubs, and this is probably the best. The stripped-stone front lounge, packed with small tables, little Windsor armchairs and brocaded wall banquettes, is friendly and cosy, with an elderly golden labrador threading his way carefully through. There's more space, and a more local atmosphere, in the flagstoned back bar, which has a couple of attractive high-backed settles as well as its wheel-back chairs, lots of beams, and a big log fire in the stone fireplace; piped music in here (not in front), darts and fruit machine. Bar food includes sandwiches (from £1.10), soup or filled baked potatoes (£1.50), broccoli flan (£2), ploughman's (£2.25), chilli con carne or faggots (£2.75) and sirloin steak (£6.50); Donnington BB and SBA are particularly well kept. There are some white tables in the back courtyard, and a green bench in front looks across the square (bustling with tourists by day, but very peaceful in the evenings). (*Recommended by Leith Stuart, Wayne Brindle, Mike Hallewell*)

Donnington   Licensee Timothy Eager   Real ale   Meals and snacks (not Sun)   Children welcome   Occasional jazz Sun, sometimes guitarist in week   Open 11–2.30ish, 5.30 (6 Sat)–11 all year; closed 25 Dec, evening 26 Dec

nr STOW-ON-THE-WOLD   SP1925 Map 4

Coach & Horses

Ganborough; A424 2½ miles N of Stow; OS Sheet 163 reference 172292

The main bar area in this friendly local is decorated with good wildlife photographs and coach-horns on its ceiling-joists, and has leatherette wall benches, stools and Windsor chairs on the flagstone floor, and steps up to a carpeted part with high-backed settles around the tables. In winter there's a log fire in the central chimney-piece; darts, fruit machine, space game and juke box. Donnington XXX, BB and SBA, from the nearby brewery, is well kept on handpump. The decent range of food includes game soup (£1.10), toasted sandwiches (£1.30), basket meals (from £1.85), filled baked potatoes (£1.90), ploughman's (from £2.20), good omelettes (£2.95), local trout (£4.40) and sirloin steak (£5.95); puddings (from £1.10). There are seats outside on a terrace and a narrow lawn. The firemen here, from the nearby college, are out to quench more than fires. *(Recommended by Joan Olivier, Simon Velate, James D Ruth, Dr J R Hamilton; more reports please)*

Donnington   Licensees A V and S H Morris   Real ale   Meals and snacks (not Sun evening)   Children in eating area   Open 11–2.30, 6–11 all year; may be all day Sat

WITHINGTON   SP0315 Map 4
Mill Inn ★

Village signposted from A436, and from A40; from village centre follow sign towards Roman villa (but don't be tempted astray by villa signs *before* you reach the village!)

For the second time in as many years this beautifully isolated mossy-roofed pub has changed its licensees, but not at the expense of its unique atmosphere and charm. The site of the original mill from which it takes its name is now an island in the garden, connected by a stone bridge. The garden itself is neatly kept, with plenty of tables, and a children's bar in summer, and it's from here that you can best appreciate the pub's position – virtually cut off in a little valley surrounded by beech and chestnut trees and a rookery. The rambling carpeted bar is an atmospheric place, full of little nooks and corners, with antique high-backed settles and big cut-away barrel seats under its beams, an attractive bay window seat, old china and pewter on a high Delft shelf, and good log fires in its stone fireplace (much of the masonry here came from the former Northleach House of Correction); little side rooms open off it. Bar food includes ploughman's (£2), basket meals (from £2.30), and main dishes like grilled trout, beef Stroganoff and curries (around £3–£5.50) and steaks (from £5.50); children's dishes (from £1). Well kept Sam Smiths OB and Museum on handpump; darts, Trivial Pursuit and other board games, as well as a fruit machine and space game in the quarry-tiled public bar. On fine weekends even in winter the pub does get very busy. There are plenty of walks nearby. They no longer do bedrooms. *(Recommended by S J Edwards, Ewan McCall, Roger Huggins, Tom McLean, Leith Stuart, Prof A N Black, Dr A Y Drummond; more reports on the new regime please)*

Free house   Licensee David Foley   Real ale   Meals and snacks   Restaurant   Children in side rooms and restaurant   Open 11–11; may close afternoons in winter

WOODCHESTER   SO8302 Map 4
Ram ⊗

South Woodchester, which is signposted off A46 Stroud–Nailsworth

Picnic-table sets on the terrace by tubs of flowers and an unusually big hibiscus look out past the villagers' neat vegetable plots to the steep and pretty valley. Inside, the tidy L-shaped bar has a nice combination of crisp white walls with some neatly stripped stonework; there are country-kitchen chairs and several cushioned antique panelled settles around a variety of country tables on the broad polished floorboards, with carefully built-in wall and window seats. Enterprising bar food includes beef roll (£1.35), ploughman's (from £1.95), home-cooked pizza (£2.25), steak and kidney pie (£2.35), cottage pie (£2.50), prawn and crab tart or baked avocado with Stilton (£3.50), nut roast with chilli relish (£3.95) and a couple of specials such as suprême of chicken stuffed with a prawn and crab mousse in lobster and brandy sauce (£5.95). The range of well kept real ales on handpump is equally enterprising – Archers Village, Boddingtons, Holdens, Hook Norton Old Hookey and the local Uley Hogshead and Old Spot, with a guest beer such as Fullers London Pride; decent wines by the glass; three log fires in winter; sensibly placed darts, table skittles, fruit machine. *(Recommended by Mr and Mrs Wyatt, Catherine Steele-Kroon, Patrick Freeman, Jonathan Williams)*

Free house   Licensee Stuart Gallaway   Real ale   Meals and snacks   Children in eating area   Impromptu piano   Open 11–2.30, 6–11 all year; closed evening 25 Dec

Lucky Dip

Besides the fully inspected pubs, you might like to try these Lucky Dips recommended to us and described by readers (if you do, please send us reports):

Aldsworth [A433 Oxford–Cirencester; SP1510], *Sherborne Arms*: Away from tourists, ample helpings of good value food, well kept real ale and excellent draught French wine, friendly locals; good service, garden; handy for Bibury and Burford (*Mrs L Brightmore, K R Harris*)

Alvington [SO6001], *Blacksmiths Arms*: Local free house with good range of beers and cider, friendly helpful staff, freshly prepared good value food including vegetarian dishes and good range of barbecued steaks; small candlelit dining-room (booking advised); gardens, children's play area (*John Blake*)

Amberley [SO8401], *Amberley Arms*: Good food and beer, real atmosphere in public bar (*Patrick Freeman*) *Black Horse*: Attractive free house with good range of well kept beers, wide range of above-average bar food (excellent value), perceptive helpful licensee; in delightful Cotswolds village (*Ivor Jarvis*)

Ampney Crucis [turn left at the Crown of Crucis and veer left at the triangle – OS Sheet 163 reference 069024; SP0602], *Butchers Arms*: Two rooms knocked into one bar, with good simple food, well kept Flowers IPA and Original and a guest beer on handpump, friendly licensees, decidedly local atmosphere, peaceful tables outside; rumours of possible closure circulating, summer 1988 (*Ewan McCall, Roger Huggins, Tom McLean, Alison Hayward, Nick Dowson*)

Andoversford [SP0219], *Royal Oak*: Old stone building with two large connected bars divided by open fireplace, back room with pool-table and seating area rather like a first-floor gallery; well kept Whitbreads beers, imaginative choice of food including chinese dishes, simple bench seating, juke box; tables on terrace (*Maureen Hobbs, Ewan McCall, Roger Huggins, Tom McLean*)

Apperley [SO8628], *Farmers Arms*: Well run pleasant old Cotswold family pub with wide choice of food, beams, open fire, garden; children welcome (*John Lewis*)

☆ **Awre** [off A48; SO7108], *Red Hart*: Charming new licensee in warm, welcoming, traditional pub; good food in bar and restaurant, log fire, good atmosphere; delightful remote site in quiet and pleasant riverside village (*Patrick Freeman, E A George*)

☆ **Berkeley Road** [A38; SO7200], *Prince of Wales*: Well run and comfortable inn with good food in bar and carvery restaurant (not cheap but good value); bar full of Prince of Wales memorabilia has real ales such as Marstons Pedigree, Theakstons Best, Wadworths 6X and Whitbreads PA; good service, piped music; attractive big garden; bedrooms comfortable – good value (*S V Bishop, Miss E R Bowmer, Jenny Ball, Jill Field*)

Berry Hill [SO5713], *Pike House*: Good home-cooked bar food and Sun lunches in country pub with Flowers Original and Whitbreads PA on handpump, friendly service (*Anon*)

☆ **Bibury** [SP1106], *Catherine Wheel*: Friendly atmosphere in cosy village pub with small dining area – generous helpings of excellent home-cooked food, good choice of imaginative dishes, fresh vegetables, attentive service, well kept Courage Directors, roaring log fire; pretty garden; handy for walks along River Coln (*John Lewis, Ewan McCall, Roger Huggins, Tom McLean, Martin and Debbie Chester*)

Bibury, *Swan*: Beautiful bar with big log fire, efficient service (empties collected as soon as put down), good bar food; bedrooms (*L S Manning*)

☆ **Birdlip** [A417/A436 roundabout; SO9214], *Air Balloon*: Whitbreads pub with multi-level bar and Flowers Original and IPA on handpump; well cooked food from a varied menu, good service and two garden areas, one with goats and rabbits; children welcome (*Aubrey and Margaret Saunders, Dr J M Jackson*)

☆ **Bisley** [SO9005], *Old Bear*: Very interesting and welcoming new landlord, excellent atmosphere, good beer; superb sixteenth-century building in very pretty village (*Lady Quinny, Neville Burke*)

Bourton-on-the-Water [SP1620], *Duke of Wellington*: Food not traditional but rather good in pub with bar, garden and wine-bar/dining-room, beers and décor good (*G C Hixon*)

Bream [Forest of Dean; SO6005], *Cross Keys*: Old-fashioned pub with charm and character, well kept beers, wholesome food, traditional décor (*John Holmes*)

Broadoak [SO7013], *White Hart*: Severn-side pub with windows overlooking water, oak and red plush, food counter with good strong Cheddar in ploughman's, turkey and ham or pork and cheese pie with generous salad, quiches and hot dishes; friendly and efficient service, beers include Flowers and Welsh Bitter; unobtrusive piped music, fruit machine (*Anne Morris, E A George*)

Broadwell [off A429 2 miles N of Stow-on-the-Wold; SP2027], *Fox*: This would have been a prominent new main entry in this edition if a change of licensees – with consequent refurbishments (a good point previously was the wealth of antiques) and diminished food choice hadn't put some previous supporters back on the fence; it's a pleasant village pub attractively placed opposite a large village green, with well kept

Donnington ales and real cider; two comfortable double bedrooms *(Angie and Dave Parkes, Rob and Gill Weeks, Paul McPherson, Simon Velate)*

☆ **Brockhampton** [the one between Andoversford and Winchcombe – OS Sheet 163 reference 035223; SP0322], *Craven Arms*: Pleasant and comfortable seventeenth-century pub with several rooms, low beams, tiled floors, wall settles, tub chairs and thick stone walls; efficient and cheerful service, good atmosphere, well kept Butcombe and Hook Norton or Wadworths 6X on hand-pump, good bar food; doing well under new management in 1988 *(Frank Cummins, PADEMLUC)*

Brockworth [A46; SO8816], *Brewers Fayre*: Friendly staff, extensive choice of well cooked food, Whitbreads ales, tables outside; children allowed in separate dining area *(Mrs B E Asher)*

Cam [High St; ST7599], *Berkeley Arms*: Welcoming, friendly landlord, excellent service with good choice of beers *(Julian Jewitt)*

Cambridge [3 miles from M5 junction 13 – A38 towards Bristol; SO7403], *George*: Roomy and comfortable, with several cosy separate galleries, well kept Flowers Original, interesting framed cartoon graffiti in gents, collection of matchboxes and cigarette packets, friendly staff and well kept Flowers Original; but set out largely as a restaurant (the food's good value); handy for Slimbridge Wildfowl Trust *(Tom Evans, Joy Heatherley, ATC, Jill Field)*

Camp [B4070 Birdlip–Stroud, at junction with Calf Way – OS Sheet 163 reference 914114; SO9109], *Fostons Ash*: Pleasant country pub with welcoming atmosphere, well kept Flowers Original and Whitbreads PA on handpump; good value simple food, gin-traps and man-trap over bar, fruit machine, darts and nickelodeon, pleasant small back garden *(Frank Cummins, J H C Peters)*

Chaceley Stock [SO8530], *Yew Tree*: Spacious river-view dining-room in rambling country pub with choice of real ales and lots of different bar areas including skittle alley with three pool-tables; well kept Brains ale, attractive waterside lawns, Severn moorings *(John and Joan Wyatt, PADEMLUC, LYM)*

Charlton Kings [London Rd; SO9620], *London*: Good atmosphere in unpretentious local festooned with flowers; large public bar with darts and quoits, small lounge bar, very lively helpful staff; good bar snacks and Flowers IPA and Original on handpump; quiet courtyard garden with parasols; restaurant; bedrooms *(JH)*

Chedworth [OS Sheet 163 reference 052121; SP0511], *Seven Tuns*: Remote pub attractively set in delightful valley; quick, friendly service; Courage Directors, original and varied bar food, pleasant lounge bar; some tables outside at the front with more across

the road and up a bank beside a tumbling stream; Courage Best and Directors on hand-pump; games-room for children; at start of GWG86 *(Simon Velate, Ewan McCall, Roger Huggins, Tom McLean, Dick Brown)*

☆ **Cheltenham** [Portland St; SO9422], *Cotswold*: Handsome Regency pub, tastefully and comfortably furnished, with Victorian prints on the flock wallpaper; well kept Wadworths IPA, 6X and Farmers Glory on handpump, good food and service *(Simon Velate, PADEMLUC)*

Cheltenham [North Pl], *Duck & Pheasant*: Good choice of well cooked and attractively presented hot food *(S Procter)*; [Portland St] *Evergreen*: Light and airy town bar with good food in bar and restaurant, good beer on handpump and a quiet back courtyard garden with tables under cocktail parasols; bedrooms *(JH)*; [St James' Sq] *Gas*: Interestingly laid out cafe-bar with good American food, fine atmosphere *(Simon Reynolds)*; [Leckhampton Rd] *Malvern*: Suburban pub with one spacious bar, Flowers Original on handpump, good omelettes *(Mr and Mrs J H Wyatt)*; [37 High St] *Old Swan*: Comfortable Victorian pub, nicely furnished, with own brew as well as Flowers, Marstons Pedigree and Wadworths 6X; wide range of good value and rather unusual food in back area up three steps where children allowed *(Michael and Alison Sandy)*; [High St] *Restoration*: Good helpings of excellent reasonably priced food, good atmosphere and furnishings; keg beers *(Mary and Patrick McDermott)*; [Montpellier Walk] *Rotunda*: Simply furnished public bar with sawdust on floor and colourful T-shirts and caps on walls and ceiling; also a separate (undecorated) area with basic seats and tables and panelled walls; six real ales that include Ind Coope Burton, Smiles and Wadworths; burgers and pizzas in evening; lively atmosphere with quite loud music *(Simon Velate)*

Cherington [ST9098], *Cherington*: Good food in pleasant surroundings, well kept Courage Directors, hard-working licensees, very quiet small village – thoroughly enjoyable *(Aubrey and Margaret Saunders)*

Chipping Campden [SP1539], *Kings Arms*: Formerly highly rated for friendly service, imaginative food and old-fashioned atmosphere in comfortable (if often crowded) bar with log fire; became food-and-bedrooms only, and then 1987–8 taken over by a small chain, becoming less personal – though food still good; said to be changing hands again summer 1988; bedrooms stylish and comfortable *(LYM – news please)*

Cirencester [Castle St; SP0201], *Black Horse*: Comfortable lounge bar in partly fourteenth-century pub saved by local campaign from plan to turn it into an estate agent's; four bedrooms *(Roger Huggins)*; [Dollar St/Gloucester St] *Corinium Court*: Hotel of character, with good range of beers including

Hook Norton and Wadworths 6X; bedrooms (*Ewan McCall, Roger Huggins, Tom McLean*); [Market Pl] *Fleece*: Flagstones and stripped wood in Shepherds food and wine bar, plusher hotel bar; bedrooms (*Keith Garley, BB*); [Gloucester St] *Nelson*: Friendly, lively and comfortable, with ship theme in lounge, Flowers IPA and Original (*Ewan McCall, Roger Huggins, Tom McLean*)

☆ **Clearwell** [B4231; SO5708], *Wyndham Arms*: Hook Norton Best in stylish and carefully renovated beamed bar, with seats on neat terraced lawns – but has subordinated its bar snacks (none now in the evening, just a lunchtime hors-d'oeuvre trolley) to its popular restaurant meals; bedrooms comfortable, attractive countryside near Wye and Forest of Dean (*Michael and Alison Sandy, E J Knight, Mrs Eileen Webb, R A Corbett, LYM*)

Clearwell, *Lamb*: Useful alternative to the other entry here, with decent bar food lunchtime and evening (*Maggie Jo St John, Dudley Evans*)

Coleford [Joyford; Joyford signposted off B4432 at Globe and Home Centre in Five Acres – OS Sheet 162 reference 579133; SO5813], *Dog & Muffler*: Remote, hospitable free house with bar food, garden and eighteenth-century cider press; children's play area (*Maggie Jo St John, Dudley Evans*)

Colesbourne [A435; SO9913], *Colesbourne Inn*: Relaxed and homely olde-worlde pub with log fires, oak tables, pleasant and efficient waitress service, cosy and hospitable atmosphere, good value home cooking (*J Greenwood*)

Coln St Aldwyns, *New*: Sadly this prettily placed Cotswold inn, very popular indeed with many readers for its snug series of sixteenth-century rooms and comfortable bedrooms, has just been bought by a property developer who plans to close it and turn it into flats (*LYM*)

Cranham [SO8912], *Royal William*: Large busy Brewers Fayre food pub catering for families, well kept Flowers and Whitbreads ales, Bulmers cider (*N W Kingsley*)

Ebrington [SP1840], *Three Oaks*: Well kept Hook Norton in fine pub with good well cooked food in small restaurant, darts, dominoes and cribbage; bedrooms very clean, personal and private, huge breakfast – good value (*Angus Panton*)

Fairford [Market Pl; SP1501], *Bull*: Very friendly, good value food, great location near fifteenth-century church and river walk; occasional live entertainment; bedrooms very comfortable (*M J Masters*); *Lamb*: Service alert but not intrusive, ambience excellent, food imaginative and delicious; reliably high standards (*A M Kimmins*); *White Hart*: This charming fifteenth-century building, carefully refurbished and previously popular with readers for its good food, relaxing atmosphere and well kept beers including a

potent home-brew, was sold in 1988 for conversion into flats

Glasshouse [by Newent Woods; first right turn off A40 going W from junction with A4136 – OS Sheet 162 reference 710213; SO7122], *Glasshouse*: Carefully preserved and cleanly kept as basic country tavern, with decorative plates, fine British Match poster, scrubbed tables and open fires in cavernous hearth of little kitchen bar, well kept changing real ales such as Butcombe and Flowers, Theakstons or even Morrells tapped from a rack of casks, seats on grass outside; fine nearby woodland walks (*Phil and Sally Gorton, LYM*)

Gloucester [100 Westgate St; SO8318], *Dick Whittingtons House*: Grade I listed building, largely fourteenth century and timber framed behind its early Georgian façade, though the connection with Dick Whittington is very tenuous; at least four real ales on handpump or tapped from the cask, some unusual furniture, log fire, friendly and helpful bar staff, fresh mainly home-made bar food generously served; separate downstairs bar, garden with barbecues (*Alastair Campbell*); [A40 1 mile W of Gloucester; SO8119] *Dog at Over*: A handy stop, much older and more interesting than it looks from the outside; also tables on a side lawn; plain but reasonably priced bar food, now has real ale; piped music (*John and Joan Wyatt, Ken and Barbara Turner, LYM*); [Bristol Rd; SO8318] *Linden Tree*: What a surprise – a country pub in the city, super inside, excellent beer, very friendly staff (*Dr and Mrs A K Clarke*)

Guiting Power [SP0924], *New Inn*: Pleasant lunchtime atmosphere, well kept Donnington beer, good and reasonably priced bar food (*Dr A Y Drummond*)

Hardwicke [Sellars Bridge; SO7912], *Pilot*: Pleasantly furnished with solid chairs, fine pot plants, framed prints on walls (huntin', fishin') and various knick-knacks; well kept beer maybe including Whitbreads Pompey Royal, wide choice of bar food including good value steak and kidney pie; overlooks canal lock (*Tom Evans*)

nr Horsley [A46 2 miles S of Nailsworth; ST8397], *Tipputs*: Very wide choice of food, especially fish, and good choice of real ales including Hook Norton, Ruddles and Tetleys, in biggish open-plan bar with unobtrusive piped music (*Andor Gomme*)

☆ **Hyde** [Burnt Ash; Nailsworth–Cirencester rd, at Tetbury turn-off – OS Sheet 162 reference 886012; SO8801], *Ragged Cot*: Lovely setting, real friendly welcome, excellent reasonably priced home-made food, efficient waitress service, wide choice of well kept beers including Brains SA, Youngers IPA and local Uley Old Spot, pleasant atmosphere; recent refurbishment has improved décor with big log fires at each end of beamed L-shaped bar, no-smoking area now set aside for meals, and first-class modern lavatories; seats out under chestnut trees and in pavilion-like summerhouse *(Mrs Sybil Baker, DMJ, Frank Cummins, Ewan McCall, Roger Huggins, Tom McLean, John Broughton)*

Kempsford [SU1597], *Axe & Compass*: Very pleasant atmosphere, excellent value bar food, well kept Courage ales *(Christopher Fluck)*

☆ **Kineton** [village signposted from B4068 and B4077 W of Stow-on-the-Wold; SP0926], *Halfway House*: Well kept and attractively priced BB and SBA from nearby Donnington brewery, limited choice of good value simple bar food and ancient farm tools in unpretentiously plain and traditional but welcoming bar; tables and swings on sheltered back lawn overlooking steep valley; restaurant; provision for children, at least at lunchtime; the pub dog tolerates the cats, but doesn't take kindly to visiting pets; bedrooms *(Simon Velate, G N G Tingey, R F Neil, J C Carter, LYM)*

Lechlade [SU2199], *Red Lion*: Attractive village, pleasant and spacious oak-beamed bar with well kept real ale, good value bar food, obliging service; on noisy corner of lorry route to Swindon *(John and Joan Wyatt, Christopher Fluck)*

Leighterton [off A46 S of Nailsworth; ST8291], *Royal Oak*: Old, charming free house in beautiful countryside under new regime; good, simple bar food at reasonable prices, good choice of real ales including own brew *(Helen Maddison, R G Cadman)*

Little Barrington [A40 W of Burford; SP2012], *Inn For All Seasons*: Carefully preserved eighteenth-century coaching-inn with open fires, period furniture, flagstone floor in bar; very comfortable, good food, welcoming licensees, beautiful gardens; comfortable bedrooms *(Stuart Taylor)*

✗ **Longhope** [Ross Road (A40); SO6919], *Farmers Boy*: Very pleasant new owners doing well in comfortable old pub with nice choice of good food, decent wines and beer, room for teenagers *(B Walton, John Miles, Sybil Baker)*; [Ross Rd] *Nags Head*: Reasonable food at very low prices, including first-class French onion soup, in modest unpretentious pub; car park difficult *(Roy and Pamela Wade)*

Lower Lydbrook [SO5916], *Courtfield Arms*: Friendly roadside pub on banks of River Wye, well kept Bass, superb value food in wide range *(SJC)*; [Ventian Lane] *Royal Spring*: Sixteenth-century free house in beautiful setting, enthusiastic and welcoming young licensees, good food and beer, wood-burning stove *(Sybil Baker)*

Lower Swell [SP1725], *Old Farm House*: Not strictly a pub, but lunchtime bar snacks are excellent; pleasant peaceful atmosphere *(S V Bishop)*

Lower Wick [ST7196], *Pickwick*: Fairly simple and traditional country pub with large lino-tiled public bar and Butcombe,

Theakstons and a changing guest beer; freshly cooked food *(Nigel Cant)*

Mickleton [SP1543], *Butchers Arms*: Welcoming, comfortable pub with good atmosphere and in pleasant surroundings, well kept Flowers IPA and good range of bar food; fruit machine in bar *(PADEMLUC)*; *Kings Arms*: Delightful Cotswold-stone pub with good atmosphere, friendly service, well kept Whitbreads and home-baked rolls; gets busy in summer *(Robert and Vicky Tod)*; [Chapel Lane (A46, at junction with Pebworth rd)] *Three Ways*: Excellent large hotel, very efficiently run; good spacious bar, helpful staff, food exceptional for quality and quantity – breakfast keeps you going for most of the day; entertainment Fri; bedrooms comfortable *(W J Wonham, Paul McPherson)*

☆ **Minchinhampton** [Minchinhampton Common; Nailsworth–Brimscombe – on common fork left at pub's sign; SO8600], *Old Lodge*: Partly sixteenth century, superbly placed on high National Trust commons (nearby tump is consecrated as a place of worship), with a good range of interesting real ales including local Uleys, friendly service from diligent new licensee, bar food *(Patrick Freeman, Wilfred Plater-Shellard, Tom Evans, Margaret and Douglas Tucker, LYM)*

Miserden [OS Sheet 163 reference 936089; SE9308], *Carpenters Arms*: Cotswold stone pub in attractive estate village; lots of wood inside; popular lunchtime food bar on right (including good value help-yourself buffet in summer), drinks on left (including well kept Flowers Original, Whitbreads PA and Wethereds Winter Royal in season); in the evenings the atmosphere is more restaurant, with all tables set for meals (main courses and puddings only – no cooked food Mon or Tues evenings) *(Frank Cummins, John and Joan Wyatt, Tom McLean)*

Moreton in Marsh [High St; SP2032], *White Hart Royal*: Very comfortable partly fifteenth-century THF hotel with an old 'inn bar' – you can just imagine the stage-coach stopping outside; one part, with main bar, has a small open fire, but the room off has a real roaster in winter in a large inglenook fireplace; Bass tapped from the cask, bar food, nice place for morning coffee; bedrooms good, though expensive *(Rob and Gill Weeks)*

Newent Woods [SO7122], *Yew Tree*: Comfortable well laid out pub, well off the beaten track with excellent bar food, good beer and friendly service; fine restaurant *(Roy Clark)*

Newland [SO5509], *Ostrich*: Beautiful seventeenth-century pub in most picturesque village close to River Wye (the church is the 'cathedral' of the Forest of Dean), friendly landlord, good mix of locals, choice of ales from four breweries, big log fire, tasty food, comfortable settles and wooden benches, Sun newspapers *(Revd I A Watson, M A* *and W R Proctor)*

Nympsfield [SO8000], *Rose & Crown*: Pub well placed for walkers, with very welcoming landlord, good reasonably priced home-cooked food (faggots recommended), bar games *(Mrs Maureen Hobbs)*

Oakridge Lynch [SO9102], *Butchers Arms*: Attractively modernised mainly eighteenth-century building in picturesque hillside village; real ale and outstandingly good food at reasonable prices; up-market regulars, often smoking at bar *(John and Joan Wyatt)*

Oddington [Upper Oddington – OS Sheet 163 reference 222257; SP2225], *Horse & Groom*: Straightforward bar food, well kept Wadworths 6X, open fire; friendly service and enormous helpings in little restaurant; bedrooms (winter breaks good value) *(BKA)*

Overbury [SO9537], *Star*: Attentive licensees, well kept Flowers ales, good value food including particularly attractively priced steaks; bedrooms comfortable *(Ian Robinson)*

Parkend [SO6208], *Woodman*: Whenever we go walking or mushrooming in the Forest of Dean we make a point of eating here – good atmosphere, warm welcome, well kept beers, delicious food, usually interesting company; bedrooms *(Prof and Mrs Keith Patchett)*

Perrotts Brook [A435; SP0105], *Bear*: Improving Courage pub, friendly staff; recent alterations include very wide doors which would allow wheelchair access *(Ewan McCall, Roger Huggins, Tom McLean)*

Prestbury [Mill St; SO9624], *Plough*: Unspoilt thatched pub with well prepared lunches, good choice of Flowers and Whitbreads ales, attractive antique furnishings (but clean modern kitchen and lavatories) *(N W Penney)*

Quedgeley [Bristol Rd; SO8014], *Little Thatch*: One of oldest buildings in Gloucestershire, excellent choice of food *(Julian Jewitt)*

Rodborough [Rodborough Hill; SO8404], *Albert*: Very friendly pub with the highest bowling-green in England; close to Rodborough Common *(Roger Entwistle)*

Sapperton [OS Sheet 163 reference 948033; SO9403], *Bell*: Well kept Courage Directors, Flowers Original and Whitbreads PA and reasonably priced bar food in unpretentious roomy bar with wall and window settles and Windsor chairs; good games area, tables on small front lawn, fine walks from here – it's on GWG89 *(Frank Cummins, Aubrey Saunders)*

☆ **Sheepscombe** [village signposted from B4070 NE of Stroud and A46 N of Painswick; SO8910], *Butchers Arms*: Cheerful atmosphere and low prices in simple village inn with well kept Flowers Original and Whitbreads PA under light carbon dioxide blanket, simple lunchtime bar food, fine views from bay windows and seats outside; the carved inn-sign is rather special; bedrooms (not heated) *(A C Watson, C J Lindon, J Knight, LYM)*

Shipton Oliffe [SP0318], *Frogmill*: Two or three bar areas including one with water-wheel inside, in lovely Cotswold manor setting with very pretty large gardens (and big play area); has been popular for good choice of quickly served bar food at reasonable prices, serving Whitbreads ales and welcoming children, but under new ownership summer 1988, and evidently trying to expand the hotel/motel bedroom side *(John Miles)*

Siddington [Ashton Road – OS Sheet 163 reference 034995; SU0399], *Greyhound*: Wadworths pub (unusual in this area) under efficient new licensees, large renovated brick-floored lounge, good atmosphere in public bar, well kept IPA, 6X and winter Old Timer, good well presented bar food *(Aubrey and Margaret Saunders)*

☆ **Snowshill** [SP0934], *Snowshill Arms*: Well kept Donnington ales, open fire, efficiently served popular food (including Tannoy system for back garden, which has a good play area); more airy inside than many Cotswold pubs, with modern furniture and relatively high ceilings – and charming village views from bow windows; cheery atmosphere; children welcome if eating *(Aubrey and Margaret Saunders, Michael and Alison Sandy, PAB, LYM)*

Staunton [A4136, Forest of Dean; SO5513], *White Horse*: Reasonable food in pub with impressive 1½-mile walk down to the Wye through woods; also on GWG199; under current licensees no longer has bedrooms *(Dr Paul Kitchener)*

Stow-on-the-Wold [The Square; SP1925], *Old Stocks*: Good value bedrooms in well run simple hotel with small comfortable bar, seats on pavement and in sheltered garden *(Wayne Brindle, BB)*; [The Square] *White Hart*: Cheery atmosphere (it's next to the YHA) in front bar with heavy rustic furniture, some easy chairs, and log-effect gas fire; green plush seats in plainer back lounge with tables set for bar lunches; clean and well kept; bedrooms *(Lyn and Bill Capper, G S Burrows)*

Stroud [Nelson St; top of town, turn off before Police Stn; SO8504], *Duke of York*: Local atmosphere in unpretentious town pub with good range of well kept real ales and unsurprising food *(Jonathan Williams, BB)*; [Selsey Hill] *Ram*: Superb view of valley, excellent choice of real ales, bar food *(J C and D Aitkenhead)*

Tetbury [Market Pl; ST8893], *Crown*: Welcoming friendly staff, good atmosphere, log fire, well kept Whitbreads beers, interesting food with good daily special, individual furnishings with odd chairs around big wooden tables *(Ewan McCall, Roger Huggins, Tom McLean, Alison Hayward, Nick Dowson)*; [Long St] *Gentle Gardener*: Good choice of well kept real ales, excellent lunchtime bar food, restaurant, local atmosphere, good service, no games machines; bedrooms *(Gary*

Moyler, A Saunders); [London Rd] *Priory*:
Tastefully decorated new pub with warm
welcome, good bar food with different specials each day and separate à la carte menu,
well kept beer; comfortable bedrooms *(Mrs
S Curnock, Dr and Mrs A K Clarke)*; [A433
towards Cirencester], *Trouble House*: Low-
ceilinged lounge, popular at lunchtimes and
in evenings; basic bar, reasonable food,
Wadworths beers *(Roger Huggins)*

☆Tewkesbury [52 Church St; SO8932], *Bell*:
Comfortable plush bar, very clean and tidy,
with some neat William and Mary oak
panelling, black oak timbers, medieval leaf-
and-fruit frescoes and armchairs by big log
fire; popular and efficient lunchtime food
counter, good choice of ales, garden above
Severnside walk; bedrooms *(L S Manning,
BB)*

Tewkesbury [High St], *Black Bear*: Quiet
and rambling heavy-beamed rooms off
black-timbered corridors, largely home-
made simple food, well kept Flowers real
ales, riverside lawn *(A M Kelly, Quentin
Williamson, Andrew Ludlow, LYM)*; *Swan*:
Very pleasant pub with well kept Flowers,
excellent service, reasonably priced good
meals *(M R S Bennett)*

Twyning [SO8936], *Village Inn*: Pleasant pub,
fine atmosphere, interesting locals, imaginative food with very good vegetables or salad,
first-rate service, reasonable prices *(Barry and
Anne, Mrs J Donald, J C Proud)*

Uley [The Street; ST7898], *Old Crown*: New
owners doing remarkably cheap food, with
well kept Flowers; simple furnishings, darts
area, popular with young people at weekends
(Alastair Campbell); *Upper Crown*: Pleasant,
clean and well furnished with good choice of
about ten hot dishes; opposite church on the
green, useful for walks *(Miss E R Bowmer)*

Up Hatherley [Alma Rd; SO9120], *Bass
House*: Food very good – must book Fri and
Sat evening, often crowded in evening;
friendly modern estate pub *(Nicholas
Kingsley)*

Wanswell Green [SO6901], *Salmon*: Good
atmosphere, obliging staff, generous helpings
of very well prepared food – good value *(Mr
and Mrs R W J Oswell)*

Westbury-on-Severn [Grange Ct, off A48;

SO7114], *Junction*: Good choice of real ales
and excellent bar lunches at reasonable
prices, in what used to be the railway pub for
a now-defunct station – lots of railwayana in
spacious bar *(John and Joan Wyatt)*

Whitminster [A38 1½ miles N of M5 junction 13; SO7708], *Forge*: Friendly welcome
and service in pleasant unpretentious pub,
imaginative bar food attractively served,
reasonable prices *(D H and M C Watkinson)*

Winchcombe [High St; SP0228], *Corner
Cupboard*: Pleasantly welcoming old pub in
Cotswold stone, bar food including excellent
ploughman's, decent Flowers and Wethereds
real ale *(AE)*; [High St], *George*: Sixteenth-
century black and white timbered inn, noted
for its remarkable Elizabethan galleried
courtyard; sadly closed in May 1988 *(LYM)*;
[37 North St] *Old White Lion*: Open, light,
pleasant décor in what is basically a
restaurant, but does have a bar *(Paul
McPherson)*

Woodchester [North Woodchester; SO8302],
Royal Oak: Good beer and generous helpings of well cooked food at reasonable prices
from extensive menu in free house with
friendly staff and atmosphere; beautiful
setting *(JMR)*

Woodmancote [Stockwell Lane; SO9727],
Apple Tree: Well kept Whitbreads and good
food in comfortable and welcoming pub,
though not everyone agrees about the
modernisation and extension; playground
and barbecue area outside *(M J R Cooper)*

Woolaston [ST5999], *Blacksmiths Arms*:
Nice olde-worlde pub with happy atmosphere, good quick service and reasonably
priced generously served food *(L J and
C A Wood)*

☆Woolaston Common [off A48 at Netherend
signpost – OS Sheet 162 reference 590009;
SO5900], *Rising Sun*: Very friendly rural pub
on fringe of Forest of Dean, good lunchtime
bar food, well kept Hook Norton, Marstons
Pedigree and Theakstons, lovely window
boxes, good garden and children's play
equipment *(John and Joan Wyatt, John
Wolfenden)*

Wotton-under-Edge [Haw St; ST7593], *Royal
Oak*: Split-level pub, good toasted sandwiches, garden with play area *(Joan Olivier)*

Hampshire

Two of the new entries here are particularly noteworthy. The beautifully placed Montagu Arms at Beaulieu has developed its separate Wine Press bar into a delightfully relaxed and well decorated place – with really good wines by the glass as well as decent food and ale. And Whitbreads get full marks for their sensitive conversion of Luzborough House outside Romsey into a charming and most interestingly laid out pub. Other notable places, either wholly new main entries or coming back into the Guide *after an absence, include the bouncy old Hobler at Battramsley and its more decorous neighbour the Filly at Setley (both of them New Forest pubs – the Hobler's garden in summer has the edge for families), the carefully kept Fox at Bramdean (another with a fine garden for families – it even has a trampoline), the rambling old-fashioned George at East Meon, the High Corner near Linwood (deep in the New Forest – yet again, an outstanding garden), the unspoilt Chequers, a former salt exchange down by the coast at Pennington, and the George at Vernham Dean (where new licensees have started doing food again, and are trying a weekday rota for all-day opening with pubs in a couple of nearby villages – a good idea for pubs where the volume of trade is a bit marginal for all-day opening). Virtually all of these have specially good food. A lot's been happening at other main entries, too – apart from the experiments many are making with all-day opening. There are new licensees at the Horse & Groom in Alresford, the Fox & Hounds at Crawley (a new chef and new menu, too), the Jolly Sailor near Fawley (sadly no more open fires – but in other respects this waterside pub is doing as well as ever), the Yew Tree at Highclere, the Angel in Lymington (as we publish, work's just about to start on refurbishment) and the Tichborne Arms at Tichborne. In all of these, preliminary reports suggest that everything's well up to standard still. Though new licensees at the Rose & Thistle at Rockbourne are determined to keep up the pub's reputation for fine fish dishes, earliest reports have been rather mixed and we'd be particularly grateful for your views. Many readers will be pleased to hear that the White Horse near Petersfield – in most people's view the county's finest pub, and one of the best anywhere –*

The Boot, nr Vernham Dean

has started doing a few hot dishes. The Editor has mixed feelings about the new furniture at another of the county's favourite pubs, the Wykeham Arms in Winchester: ancient desks from his old school, so painful memories. At the end of the chapter, stars show that many of the Lucky Dip entries are well worth watching – particularly the Queens Head at Burley, Fox & Hounds at Bursledon, Red Lion at Chalton, Queens Head at Dummer, Royal Oak at Fritham, Calleva Arms at Silchester, Grapes in Southampton and (though it's too restaurantish now for a main entry) the Three Lions at Stuckton.

ALRESFORD   SU5832 Map 2

Horse & Groom ⊗

Broad Street; on corner of A31

Early reports on the new licensee here suggest that, though there have been some changes on the food side, standards are as good as ever; the range now includes sandwiches (from £1.05), soup (£1.50), ploughman's (from £2), sausages (£2.75), a half-pint of prawns (£2.95, when available), with main dishes like home-cooked gammon (£3), home-made steak and kidney pie (£3.25), local trout (£5.50), and pork fillets in wine (£6.25). Although the comfortable bars are open-plan, there are lots of pleasant nooks and crannies to give them a rambling and secluded feel; perhaps the nicest tables are those in the three bow windows in the right-hand bar, looking out over the wide street; there are plenty of others, with neat settles, Windsor chairs and round stools under the black beams, old local photographs on the partly stripped timbered brick walls, shelves of earthenware jugs and bottles, and a coal-effect gas fire. Well kept Flowers Original, Whitbreads Strong Country and guest beers on handpump; fruit machine. *(Recommended by BKA, Dr John Innes, J Nicholson, John Roué, Steve and Carolyn Harvey)*

Whitbreads   Licensee Robin Howard   Real ale   Meals and snacks   Daytime parking nearby may be rather difficult   Open 11–2.30, 6–11; closes 10.30 in winter

BATTRAMSLEY   SZ3099 Map 2

Hobler ⊗

A337 a couple of miles S of Brockenhurst; OS Sheet 196 reference 307990

Four hundred years old, this quaint pub has been given a bouncy new lease of life by its young landlord. Décor and furnishings are old-fashioned and cosy – black beams and joists supporting shiny ochre planks (one part filled with ancient saws to underline the New Forest connection), a black-panelled dado, red leatherette bucket seats, pews, little dining-chairs, a cushioned bow-window seat, one snug book-shelved area, and guns and blue plates on the walls. But the atmosphere's lively and jaunty. Bar food includes well filled baked potatoes or garlic bread with cheese (from £1.25), ploughman's (from £1.75), steak and kidney pie (£2.95), beef ragout, gammon, nut and mushroom Stroganoff or pork hock in a bitter-orange sauce (£3.95), trout or salmon (£4.95) and steaks (from ten-ounce sirloin £5.95); vegetables are fresh and nicely cooked. Well kept Flowers Original, Gales HSB (called Hobler Special here), Wethereds SPA and a guest beer on handpump, with Winter Royal tapped from the cask in winter, and a decent range of whiskies and wines (including some expensive bargains by the bottle); on our visit piped Joan Armatrading; friendly golden labrador. There are picnic-table sets out on a big lawn by the woods, beside a paddock with ponies, donkeys and hens; as well as big swings and a splendid children's tumbler-room, there's also a summer bar and marquee out here. *(Recommended by Daphne and Gordon Merrifield, Calum and Jane, Jon Payne, Philip and Trisha Ferris)*

Whitbreads   Licensee Peter Stevens   Real ale   Meals and snacks   Children in outside games-room   Jazz Tues (maybe Sun in summer)   Open 11–11 all year; closed 2.30–6 in winter; closed evening 25 Dec

BEAULIEU   SU3802 Map 2

Montagu Arms ⊗ 🛏

The Wine Press bar to one side of this decorously well kept and civilised small hotel is a marvellous innovation. It's spacious and relaxing, cool in summer, with a soothing colour-scheme of dark and pale greens (on our visit even the Huntsman beermats matched) offset by black and blond tables and neat black bentwood Deco cafe-chairs on the maroon carpet, and by the attractively patterned brocade of the wall banquettes. Brick arches and low partitions topped with curtains on brass rails divide it into quiet separate areas, and it's decorated with little local landscapes by Stanley Orchart and a big Cecil Aldin hunting print. Quickly served bar food includes soup (£1.30), ploughman's with a good choice of cheeses (from £1.95), several vegetarian dishes (from £1.95), open sandwiches (from £2.85), cottage pie (£3), Lancashire hot-pot or steak and kidney pie (£4) and chicken in a tomato and tarragon sauce (£4.25); help-yourself salads (from £4.10) are attractive, with clever home-made dressings. Besides well kept if not cheap Courage Directors, Ruddles Best and Wadworths 6X on handpump, a Cruover machine allows half a dozen unusually interesting wines by the glass (around £2); unobtrusive and thoughtfully chosen piped pop music. If they could replace the loudspeaker food announcements with a more appropriate service system, we'd rate this uncommon place very highly indeed (though we'd not recommend eating at the tempting picnic-table sets in the front courtyard – donkeys may make a really determined effort to share your meal). The Palace gates are almost opposite, and there's a pretty lake just past the inn. *(Recommended by Patrick Young, David Bland, H G and C J McCafferty, B W B Pettifer)*

Free house   Licensee N Walford   Real ale   Meals and snacks   Restaurant   Children welcome at lunchtime   Open 11–11 all year; closed evening 25 Dec   Bedrooms tel Beaulieu (0590) 612324; £45B/£60B

BEAUWORTH   SU5726 Map 2

Milbury's ⊗

Turn off A272 Winchester/Petersfield at Beauworth ¾, Bishops Waltham 6 signpost, then continue straight on past village

Perhaps the most striking attraction in this remote late-seventeenth-century pub is its three-hundred-feet-deep well; it's in a side room overlooked by a little timber gallery, and was probably dug six hundred years ago. Its depths are carefully spot-lit, and if you drop an ice cube through the safety grid you can count off nearly five seconds before it reaches the water. The massive treadwheel beside it used to be worked by a donkey; in the war, when the landlord had to give up the donkey, he found it took him 678 paces to wind up the original eighteen-gallon water cask. The rest of the carefully restored rambling bar has broad flagstones, sturdy beams, gnarled rustic tables with good cushioned seats built into the stripped brick walls, and, in winter, log fires in massive open fireplaces (one with a deep bread oven). Bar food, largely home made with fresh local ingredients, includes sandwiches (from 90p), soup (£1.10), a choice of ploughman's (£1.95), prawn, spinach and cheese-filled pancake (£3.50), salads (from £3.45), lasagne or nut cutlet (£3.50), gammon (£3.95), and steak (from £6.30), with daily specials and children's dishes (from £1.50), a good choice of home-made puddings (from 95p) and Sunday roasts; they serve a Sunday brunch (9.30–11.30), complete with Sunday papers.

Well kept Flowers Original, Gales HSB and Hermitage and a beer brewed for the pub on handpump, and lots of liqueurs and whiskies. There are weekend summer barbecues out in the garden, where rustic seats have quite a view; the pub is surrounded by the Millbarrow Bronze Age cemetery (most visible over to the east), which gave the pub its present name – originally a nickname when it was the Fox & Hounds. *(Recommended by W J Wonham, E U Broadbent, MBW, JHW, A R Lord, E Manley, Keith and Sheila Baxter, WHRM, Michael Bechley, A V Chute, Aubrey and Margaret Saunders, J E Figueira, Dr and Mrs A K Clarke)*

Free house   Licensees Mr and Mrs L G Larden   Real ale   Meals and snacks   Restaurant Children in well-room and gallery   Open 10.30–2.30, 6–11; closed 1 Jan

BENTLEY   SU7844 Map 2
Bull

A31 Farnham–Alton, W of village and accessible from both directions at W end of dual carriageway Farnham bypass

The bar food in this friendly tiled white cottage is all freshly prepared, which can mean delays; it includes sandwiches (from 95p), soup (£1.05) and other starters such as garlic mushrooms (£2.15), filled baked potatoes (from £1.10), ploughman's (from £1.80), filled pancake or Spanish omelette (£2.75), lasagne (£3.25), steak and kidney pie (£3.55), gammon (£3.85) and rump steak (£6.25), with puddings such as home-made apple pie (£1.65); roast Sunday lunch. The two-room bar has a relaxing atmosphere, as well as tapestried wall seats and stools, low black beams and joists, small windows, and stripped brick and timber work. Besides country and Old Master prints, there are several comical pre-war Bonzo prints – particularly in the left-hand room, which has a dimly lit back alcove with a tapestried pew built around a nice mahogany table, and a log-effect gas fire in a big old fireplace. Well kept Courage Best and Directors on handpump; darts, shove-ha'penny, dominoes, cribbage, fruit machine. The side terrace has picnic-table sets by a fairy-lit Wendy house on stilts. It's under the same management as the Hen & Chicken down the road at Froyle, and is well placed for Alice Holt Forest. *(Recommended by Dr John Innes, E G Parish, Roger Lamble; more reports please)*

Courage   Real ale   Meals and snacks   Restaurant tel Bentley (0420) 22156   Children in restaurant   Open 11–3, 5–11

BOLDRE   SZ3298 Map 2
Red Lion ★ ⊗

Village signposted from A337 N of Lymington

The décor in two of the four communicating rooms in this welcoming New Forest pub consists predominantly of masses of chamber-pots hanging from black beams; there are also flagstones, log fires in big fireplaces, big blue and white trenchers, fat urns, flagons and copper saucepans, heavy-horse harness, farm tools, gin-traps and man-traps, landscapes and needlework pictures, and seats varying from orderly tables and chairs to pews and snugger seats in alcoves. Bar food remains popular, with sandwiches (from £1.20), soup (£1.20), ploughman's (£2), avocado pear with prawns (£2), smoked trout (£2.80), and salads (from £3.50); basket meals go well beyond the standard range of fried food, and include marinated pork chops (£3.80), and half a duck with fresh orange soaked in wine (£4.10); friendly, efficient service. Well kept Huntsman Dorchester and Royal Oak on handpump.

Real ale may be served from handpumps, electric pumps (not just the on-off switches used for keg beer) or – common in Scotland – tall taps called founts (pronounced 'fonts') where a separate pump pushes the beer up under air pressure. The landlord can adjust the force of the flow – a tight spigot gives the good creamy head that Yorkshire lads like.

On the edge of the New Forest, with its front flower beds a blaze of colour in summer, the pub is also handy for the Lymington River. *(Recommended by Clifford Blakemore, M C Howells, Jon Payne, Drs S P K and C M Linter, Mr and Mrs K J Baxter, B J E Phillips, JAH, Ken and Barbara Turner)*

Huntsman   Licensees A E Fenge and J Bicknell   Real ale   Meals and snacks   Restaurant tel Lymington (0590) 73177   Open 10–3, 6–11 all year

BRAMDEAN   SU6128   Map 2

Fox ⊗

A272 Winchester–Petersfield

The spacious open-plan brown-carpeted bar is simply and neatly furnished with cushioned wall pews and wheel-back chairs; some of its black beams are hung with whisky-water jugs, and besides a big painting of a fox and the famous fox mask which inspired a song by Peter Warlock and Bruce Blunt there's a collection of plates decorated with foxes and hunting scenes over the brick fireplace, with more decorative china on Delft shelves. Carefully done and rather individual bar food includes sandwiches (from £1.50), particularly good soup (£1.95), ploughman's (from £2.25), deep-fried Camembert or ham and egg pie (£2.50), game pie (£2.75), cauliflower cheese with bacon or steak and kidney pie (£4.25), fillet of fresh sole with crab (£4.95) and beef Stroganoff (£5.25). In the evening the menu changes, to steaks, fresh local fish and elaborate meat dishes. Well kept Marstons Burton and Pedigree on handpump, decent coffee, friendly service; sensibly placed darts in the games-room, fruit machine, very unobtrusive piped music. There are picnic-table sets under cocktail parasols on a spreading lawn among fruit trees, with swings, a seesaw and even a well kept trampoline, with a tidy hen-run alongside; weekend barbecues in summer. *(Recommended by F N Clay, DMG, J A Calvert, Gordon Smith, Anthony Willey)*

Marstons   Licensee Mrs Jane Inder   Real ale   Meals and snacks   Open 10.30–2.30, 6–11 all year; closed 25 Dec

BURSLEDON   SU4809   Map 2

Jolly Sailor

From A27 follow Bursledon Station signpost, keeping left into Lands End Road

This old-fashioned riverside pub has a light and airy front bar, with ship pictures, shells in a net strung from the ceiling, and Windsor chairs and settles on the oak floor; maybe piped music. Its bow windows give a lovely view across the yacht anchorage. A more traditional beamed and flagstoned back bar has pews and settles by a huge fireplace; darts and dominoes here. Bar food includes sandwiches (from £1), filled rolls (£1.40), ploughman's (from £1.75), salads (from £2.95), and hot dishes like lasagne, steak and kidney or chicken and mushroom pie and chilli con carne (around £3.20); well kept Badger Best, Courage Directors, Gales HSB and Wadworths 6X on handpump, with Old Timer in winter. The waterside garden, which has a children's bar at busy times, has old-fashioned wooden seats and tables under a big yew, and more tables on its jetty. It has the distinction of being featured in a BBC TV series. *(Recommended by Keith Garley, H G and C J McCafferty, SJC, Gwen and Peter Andrews, Ian Phillips, Mr and Mrs Jon Payne)*

Free house   Real ale   Meals and snacks   Restaurant tel Bursledon (042 121) 5557 Children in eating area and restaurant   If parking in lane is full use station car park and walk Open 11–2.30, 6–11

The initials GWG – mentioned, for instance, as 'on GWG 22' – stand for our companion Consumers' Association's book *Holiday Which? Good Walks Guide*, and show that the pub is on or near the walk numbered.

CHERITON   SU5828 Map 2
Flower Pots

Pub just off B3046 (main village road) towards Beauworth and Winchester; OS Sheet 185 reference 581282

This simple and homely village local got its name from the retired head gardener from nearby Avington Park who built it in 1840. The atmosphere in its two rooms is very unspoilt; the quiet and comfortable little room on the left has pictures of hounds and ploughmen on its striped wallpaper, bunches of flowers, and a horse and foal and other ornaments on the mantelpiece over its small log fire. Behind the servery there's disused copper distilling equipment, and lots of hanging gin-traps, drag-hooks, scaleyards and other ironwork; well kept Flowers Original and Whitbreads Strong Country tapped from the cask. Snacks include toasted sandwiches (from 80p) and ploughman's (£1.40); darts in the neat plain public bar; also cribbage, shove-ha'penny, dominoes and fruit machine. There are old-fashioned seats on the front grass. The village regularly wins Best Kept in County competition, and was the site of one of the last Civil War battles, in 1644. *(Recommended by Phil and Sally Gorton; more reports please)*

Whitbreads   Real ale   Snacks   Open 11–2.30, 6–11; closed evening 25 Dec   Bedroom tel Bramdean (096 279) 318; £11.50/£23

CRAWLEY   SU4234 Map 2
Fox & Hounds

Village signposted from A272 Winchester–Stockbridge and B3420 Winchester–Andover

New licensees in this civilised pub have expanded the range of bar food; it now includes sandwiches, smoked trout pâté (£1.75), ploughman's (£1.75), seafood pastries or beef curry (£3.25), steak and kidney pie (£3.45), lamb kebab (£3.75), and king prawns (£3.95); they still do the popular Sparsholt Smokie, and serve a full breakfast throughout the day (£2.95). From the outside it's a striking sight, with each timbered upper storey successively jutting further out, lots of pegged structural timbers in the neat brickwork (especially around the latticed windows), and elaborately carved steep gable-ends. Inside there are small easy chairs on the oak parquet floor of the lounge, a log fire, latticed windows, and an elegant black timber arch leading through to the refurbished restaurant. The main beamed bar is carpeted, with panelled black wall benches and wheel-back chairs around polished copper tables, country pictures and prints of Old Masters, a log-effect gas fire and darts. Well kept Flowers Original, Gales HSB, Wadworths 6X and Whitbreads Strong Country on handpump. The village has fine old houses and a pretty duck pond. *(Recommended by Dr R Fuller, Kate and Russell Davies, Mark Walpole, Melanie Byrne, Michael Lane; more reports on the new regime please)*

Free house   Licensee Peter Morgan   Real ale   Meals and snacks (not Sun or Mon evenings) Restaurant   Children in restaurant and eating area   Open 11.30–3, 6–11 Bedrooms tel Sparsholt (096 272) 285; £25B/£35B

EAST MEON   SU6822 Map 2
George ✗

Church Street; village signposted from A272 about 4 miles W of Petersfield, and from A32 Alton–Fareham in West Meon

Unusually, the spotlessly tiled stainless-steel kitchen is part of this friendly and relaxed bar, down at one end. It serves ploughman's (from £2), hot dishes such as burgers, gammon and egg and cod Kiev (£3.50), pork chop (£4) and charcoal-grilled steaks (£8), with half a dozen interestingly flavoured dishes of the day such as Stilton and asparagus quiche, chicken curry, lamb stew with rosemary, prawn and mushroom lasagne and pheasant pie (all £3.50); there's a battery of crisp help-yourself salads. The bar rambles around a central brick servery: furnishings include massive curving slabs of raw wood, scrubbed deal country-kitchen tables and chairs, and attractive open fireplaces, with candles in bottles, a few timber props and beams in the ochre ceiling, and some (but not too much) saddlery and harness on the cream walls. Well kept Gales BBB and HSB, Ind Coope Bitter and Burton and maybe a guest beer on handpump; fruit machine, friendly and helpful service. There are some picnic-table sets behind by the car park, and in front alongside the quiet and pretty village street, looking along to the church which stands on the lowest slope of steeply rounded Park Hill. No dogs. *(Recommended by Mrs Shirley Fluck, Charles Turner, HEG, Colin Gooch, Yvonne Healey, A R Lord, MCG, Peter Davies, SJC)*

Free house Licensees Jake and Barbie Cable Real ale Meals and snacks Charming candlelit restaurant tel East Meon (073 087) 481 Children in restaurant Open 11–11 all year; closed evening 25 and 26 Dec

EMERY DOWN SU2808 Map 2
New Forest Inn ⊗ 🛏
Village signposted off A35 just W of Lyndhurst

The large open-plan bar here has small seats, mate's chairs, russet plush settles and wall seats on the green carpet, antlers above one of the log fires, and a cabinet of china forest animals. The good choice of food, efficiently and cheerfully served on wooden platters, includes soup (£1.25), a selection of ploughman's (from £1.75), crab pâté (£1.75), Cumberland sausages (£2.25), a good creamy lasagne or curry (£3.25) and salads (from £3.75), with specials like jumbo prawns wrapped in bacon, cheese and garlic or shark steaks in Cajun sauce, and extra evening dishes such as escalope of veal in sherry and cream or freshly cut gammon and egg (£5.25) and steaks (from £6.25); good coffee. Flowers Original, Whitbreads Strong Country and a guest beer on handpump, under a light carbon dioxide blanket; darts, shove-ha'penny, fruit machine. The sloping woodside garden has a wooden and brick porch, as well as white rabbits, a pony looking over the post-and-rails fence, and maybe lambs or kids bleating in the side stables. It's attractively positioned in the New Forest, but welcomingly uncrowded. The pub's Old English sheepdog now has three daughters to keep her company. *(Recommended by Nigel Williamson, Roger Broadie, Heather Sharland, DCB, Nick Dowson, Alison Hayward, Dr John Innes, Andy Tye, Sue Hill, C Williams, Roy McIsaac, Roger and Cathy, Clifford Blakemore)*

Whitbreads Licensees Sue and Nick Emberley Real ale Meals and snacks Children welcome Summer string quartets in garden, morris dancing Open 11–2.30, 6–11; closed 10.30 in winter Bedrooms tel Lyndhurst (042 128) 2329; £15/£30

nr FAWLEY SU4503 Map 2
Jolly Sailor
Ashlett Creek; from A326 turn left into School Road, signposted Fawley ½; at Falcon pub crossroads take Calshot road, then fork left almost at once

Not far from the magnificent Rothschild rhododendron gardens at Exbury, this pub is attractively positioned by the waterside. The wood-ceilinged bar has soft banquettes on its carpet, and red velvet curtains, with photographs of Southampton liners on its rough plaster and dark oak walls; the central open fire has been replaced by a flame-effect one. The bar opens into a restaurant which has big windows overlooking the busy shipping channel, where curlews and sandpipers strut at low water. Decent bar food includes soup (95p), open baps or sandwiches (from £1.95), ploughman's (from £1.95), plaice (£2.85), Cumberland sausage or burger (£2.95), salads (from £3.25), gammon (£3.95) and rump steak (£5.65).

Flowers Original and Whitbreads Strong Country on handpump; shove-ha'penny, cribbage, fruit machine, piped music. There are picnic-table sets out on a long side lawn by a dinghy park and the tidal saltings. (*Recommended by David Crafts, Dr R F Fletcher, Blair and Dinah Harrison, Roy McIsaac*)

Whitbreads Licensee J P Orritt Real ale Meals and snacks Evening restaurant tel Fawley (0703) 891305 Children in restaurant and eating area Guitar duo Sun evenings Open 11–2.30 (3 Fri and Sat), 6.30–11 all year

FROYLE SU7542 Map 2
Hen & Chicken
A31 Alton–Farnham

There's a strong emphasis on bar food in this welcoming pub, and many of the tables are set out for eaters; the range includes sandwiches (from £1.20), filled baked potatoes (from £1.75), ploughman's (from £1.80), omelettes (from £2.95), salads (from £3), lamb curry (£3.50), steak and kidney pie (£3.95), roast of the day (£4.25) and rump steak (£6.25); very good service. The open-plan bar has more modern seats among the antique settles and oak tables in front of the huge fireplace (which still has the rack used for messages in coaching days above it), and several old coaching prints. Brakspears SB, Courage Directors, Flowers Original, Gales HSB, King and Barnes Festive, and Ruddles on handpump, and a good choice of ciders; piped music. Seats on a terrace face the road, with more in the garden behind, which has boat swings, a climbing-frame and slide trampoline. In the last century the local squire got so cross with crowds of rowdy horse-dealers outside here blocking his way to church that the pub lost its licence for Sunday opening and didn't get it back until 1955. It's under the same management as the Bull at Bentley. (*Recommended by Martin, Jane, Simon and Laura Bailey, R H Sawyer, KC, E G Parish, W A Gardiner*)

Free house Licensees Peter and Mary Holmes Real ale Meals and snacks Panelled restaurant tel Bentley (0420) 22115 Children welcome Jazz Mon evenings Open 11–2.30 (3 Sat), 5–11 all year

HAMBLE SU4806 Map 2
Olde Whyte Harte
3 miles from M27 junction 8; on B3397 (High Street)

Very popular with yachtsmen and watermen, this genuinely ancient pub can get extremely busy at weekends. The white-panelled bar has settles and Windsor chairs on the flagstones, a fine inglenook fireplace, old maps and charts, rope fancywork, mugs and copper pans. The building's listed officially as having special architectural interest: points to notice are the low beams in the bar, which are original Tudor ships' timbers, and still have some of their old fastenings; the fireback, which carries Charles I's coat of arms; and the three-foot-thick back wall, which may be even older than the rest of the building – perhaps forming part of the nearby Norman Benedictine priory. Good value cheap bar food includes sandwiches and toasties (from 65p), shepherd's pie (£1), ploughman's (£1.30), omelettes and salads (from £1.30), curry or chilli con carne (£1.45), fish (£1.90) and scampi (£2.20); Gales BBB and HSB and XXX Mild on handpump, with XXXXX in winter; dominoes, shove-ha'penny, cribbage, fruit machine, maybe piped music. Besides barrel seats on the small front terrace, there is a back terrace by the sheltered lawn and garden. (*Recommended by MBW, JHW, Mr and Mrs Wilkins; more reports please*)

Gales Licensee Colin Partridge Real ale Meals and snacks Children in snug bar Open 11–11 all year

If you know a pub's ever open all day now that the licensing laws have changed, please tell us.

HECKFIELD   SU7260 Map 2
New Inn ⊗

B3349 Hook–Reading – still called A32 on many maps

The range of food in this low-beamed pub is simple and good value, including sandwiches (from £1.20, toasties from £1), ploughman's (from £1.95), eight-ounce burgers (from £3.55), salads, lasagne (£3.95), lamb cutlets (£5.20), mixed grill (£5.75) and steak (from £6.45 for eight-ounce rump); friendly service. In the rambling open-plan bar there are lots of well spaced tables with cushioned wheel-back chairs and round stools in its various carpeted bays, alcoves and extensions. There's some traditional furniture as well, including an attractively carved early eighteenth-century settle, and a couple of good log fires. The garden has a sizeable terrace. Well kept Badger Best and Tanglefoot and Courage Best on handpump; piped music. *(Recommended by KC, Ian Howard, Dr R Fuller, E Kinnersly; more up-to-date reports please)*

Free house   Licensees B and A Francis   Real ale   Meals and snacks   Restaurant (not Sun) Open 10.30–2.30, 6–11 all year   Bedrooms tel Heckfield (0734) 326374; £58B(£40B weekends)/£68B(£50B weekends)

HIGHCLERE   SU4360 Map 2
Yew Tree 🛏

Andover Road; A343 S of village

New licensees in this seventeenth-century, white cottagey inn have done some modest refurbishment, but in general the atmosphere seems as comfortable as before (though we'd appreciate reports confirming this). The bar has three green and brown carpeted areas, with green plush button-back banquettes and mate's chairs around dark brown tables, and green velvet curtains swagged back from the windows. On the right, under beams and joists, there are more tables and chairs by a big log fire; another big fireplace decorated with sheep shears and some other country tools divides off the far end. The range of home-made bar food now includes soup (£1.50), pâté (£2), ploughman's (£2.25), burgers (£3), lambs' kidneys in port (£3.50), steak and kidney or chicken and ham pie (£4), half a shoulder of lamb (£4.95), and sirloin steak (£7.50); puddings. Flowers Original, Fremlins and Wadworths 6X on handpump. *(Recommended by M Tuohy, Ian Howard, John Bell; more reports on the new regime please)*

Free house   Licensees Jean and David Marshall   Real ale   Meals and snacks   Small restaurant   Children in area off bar   Open 12–2.30, 6–11 all year; closed 25 Dec Bedrooms tel Highclere (0635) 253360; £30B/£36B

IBSLEY   SU1509 Map 2
Old Beams ⊗

A338 Ringwood–Salisbury

The atmosphere in this large, thatched and friendly pub at times seems to border on that of a restaurant, such is the number of customers enthusiastically appreciating the well presented and efficiently served food. There's an extensive cold buffet (from £3.75; cold meats £4.75 for three slices) as well as soup (80p), sandwiches (from £1.40), ploughman's (from £1.80), home-made steak and kidney pie (£4.45), a daily roast (£4.75), good Scotch steak (from £6.95), and anything up to fifteen daily specials; puddings (from £1). The olde-worlde-style oak-beamed main room, divided by a wood screen and canopied log-effect gas fire, has an expanse of varnished wooden tables and country kitchen chairs. The U-shaped bar servery has

We say if we or readers have seen dogs or cats in a pub.

Ind Coope Burton, Gibbs Mew Bishops Tipple, Huntsman Royal Oak, Ringwood Best, Tetleys and Wadworths 6X. In the back garden, partly shaded by trees, there are picnic-table sets. *(Recommended by Roger and Kathy, Donald Godden, Tom Evans, S White, T Kinning, J Walsh, H B Smith)*

Free house   Licensees D W and R Major   Real ale   Meals and snacks   Restaurant tel Ringwood (0425) 473387   Children in eating area   Open 10–11; closes 10.30 in winter

KINGS WORTHY   SU4933 Map 2
Cart & Horses ⊗
A3090 E of Winchester, just off A33

Lots of rustic tables in the comfortably furnished and spacious lounge are set for good value food, which includes filled French bread or large soft baps (from £1), soup (£1.05), filled baked potatoes (£1.50), a handsome choice of help-yourself salads (from £2.25), vegetarian dishes (around £3.50), home-made steak and kidney pie (£4.25), lasagne (£4.25) and local trout (£4.95). The public bar, decorated with old enamel advertising placards and softly lit at night, has cushioned settles and some milk churn seats in its various rambling alcoves, with bar billiards, fruit machine and juke box – there's also a separate skittle alley. Well kept Marstons Burton and Pedigree on handpump, Owd Rodger tapped from the cask, and farm cider; friendly, efficient service. Besides heavy wooden tables in front of the picturesque building (which is attractively decorated with window boxes), there are more in the sheltered garden behind, which has barbecues in summer, and a play area including several trampolines, a seesaw and a Wendy house. *(Recommended by S Punchard, W J Wonham, H G and C J McCafferty, Alan Vere, J B Tippett, WHBM)*

Marstons   Licensee David-Lee Smith   Real ale   Meals and snacks   Restaurant tel Winchester (0962) 882360   Children in eating area, restaurant and conservatory   Open 11–3, 5.30–11 in summer; 11–4, 7–11 in winter; may open longer in afternoon; open all day bank hol Sat and Mon; closed evening 25 and 26 Dec

LINWOOD   SU1810 Map 2
High Corner
Linwood signposted via Moyles Court from A338 (and also from A31); follow road straight up on to heath and eventually pub signposted left down a gravelled track; OS Sheet 195 reference 196107

Several rooms ramble off beyond the main serving-bar in this remote New Forest pub, including a comfortable low-ceilinged inner room with an aquarium, another bar with rustic tables and chairs up some steps in a beamed extension, and a family-room between; there's even a sun lounge. Well kept Flowers Original, Wadworths 6X and Whitbreads Pompey Royal on handpump; darts, dominoes, cribbage, pinball, fruit and trivia machine, space game, piped music. Good food includes home-made soup (£1.10), sandwiches (from £1.15), ploughman's (from £1.85), sausages (from £1.85) and main dishes like chicken (£2.95), plaice (£3.15), home-made steak and kidney pie (£3.95), trout (£4.35) and a choice of steaks (from £6.95); children's dishes (from £1.45); in summer they have cook-yourself barbecues (though they'll cook it for you at a discretionary charge); a separate stable bar here may be open in summer. It can get very busy in summer, even in the big wood-side lawn, with its well spaced picnic-table sets and children's play area. There's a squash court, and it's near *Good Walks Guide* Walk 40. *(Recommended by Steve and Carolyn Harvey, Jill Cox, H G and C J McCafferty, Tim Locke, Dr James Haworth)*

Free house   Licensees Roger Karnan and Nigel Brunner   Real ale   Meals and snacks Restaurant tel Ringwood (0425) 473973   Children in eating area   Open all day in summer; 11–2.30, 6–10.30 in winter; may open longer afternoons

LONGPARISH SU4344 Map 2
Plough ⊗

For some readers this is more of a restaurant than a pub – the pubby part is reduced to a minimum, and the rambling open-plan lounge (which has some comfortable easy chairs) is mainly set for food; nonetheless the quality of both the food and the service is an overriding factor for most, even though it's normally best to book. The wide choice includes watercress soup (£1.15), starters such as smoked trout pâté, ploughman's (£2.15), and hot dishes such as chicken casserole or steak and kidney pie, gammon or baked trout (£5.25) and rump steak (£6.95); puddings (£1.45). On Sunday there's either a three-course roast lunch (£7.25) or ploughman's. Well kept Flowers Original, Whitbreads Strong Country and a guest on handpump. There are plenty of tables under cocktail parasols in the big garden; various notices out here have strictures against dogs, coaches, picnics, ball-games and so forth. It's usefully placed on good B roads that, depending on where you were heading, could be a relaxed alternative to either the A34 or the A30. *(Recommended by Doug Kennedy, Mr and Mrs Markham, Roy McIsaac, Ian Howard; more up-to-date reports please)*

Whitbreads Licensee Trevor Colgate Real ale Meals and snacks (not Sun evening) Restaurant tel Andover (0264) 72358 Children in restaurant Open 11–2.30, 6–11 all year; closed evening 25 and 26 Dec

LYMINGTON SZ3295 Map 2
Angel
High Street

Bar food (much of it home made) in this ex-coaching-inn includes sandwiches (from £1), soup (£1.10), filled baked potatoes (from £1.60), basket meals (from £1.85), ploughman's (from £1.95), omelettes (from £2.35), salads (from £2.75), steak and kidney pie (£3.25), and vegetable Stroganoff (£3.35). The main bar is comfortable, spaciously modernised, and decorated with yachting pictures; it's particularly popular with visiting yachtsmen; a good atmosphere. The foundations reputedly go back to 1250, and in the seven hundred years since it's collected no fewer than three ghosts – including, unsurprisingly, one of the very few known naval ones. Huntsman Dorchester, Dorset and Royal Oak on handpump. The new licensee is planning a major refurbishment at the end of the year, so things may change. *(Recommended by WFL, Andy and Colleen Auton, E G Parish; more reports on the new regime please)*

Huntsman Licensee Tony Marks Real ale Meals and snacks Children in Tuck bar Open 10.30–11; closes 10.30 Mon–Thurs in winter Bedrooms tel Lymington (0590) 72050; £18.50/£32.50

MINLEY SU8357 Map 2
Crown & Cushion
From A30 take B3013 towards Fleet, then first left turn signposted Minley, Cove, Farnborough

The name of this tiled and timbered pub commemorates the closest that anyone has come to stealing the Crown Jewels – Colonel Blood from nearby Minley Warren was caught here in 1671 with the jewels in his saddlebags, after a subtle raid on the Tower of London. The 'Meade Hall' behind it is perhaps its most attractive feature, an engaging pastiche of a Cromwellian or older feasting-place; the rafters and timbers are draped with scythes, pitchforks and other rustic hardware, and there are two very long and convivial communal tables stretching along the flagstones, smaller candlelit ones in more intimate side stalls, and a huge log fire; the piped music and slot machines seem rather out of character here. A quick-service food counter does a wide choice of home-cooked meats and good fresh salads (around £2.50–£13.50), ploughman's (from £1.70), lunchtime roasts (not Sunday), two lunchtime hot dishes such as steak and kidney pie or lasagne (£2.70–£3.20), with a wider choice of evening hot dishes such as basket meals (from around £2.80), gammon or plaice (£3.25), and steak (£4.90); filled baked potatoes (from £1.90) on Sundays. Gales HSB, Ruddles County and Websters Yorkshire on handpump, with country wines, mead and a couple of draught ciders. The original sixteenth-century low-beamed pub itself has sandwiches, darts, dominoes, cribbage and a fruit machine. The yew tree outside – if you look hard enough – is cut in the shape of a cushioned crown. Picnic-table sets overlook the wood-side cricket pitch. *(Recommended by Ian Phillips, Ray Challoner, Alison Hayward, Nick Dowson, J P Berryman)*

Phoenix (Watneys)   Real ale   Meals (not Sun) and snacks   Open 10.30–2.30, 5.30–11; Meade Hall opens noon and 7

MORTIMER WEST END   SU6363 Map 2
Red Lion ⊗

From Mortimer–Aldermaston road take turn signposted Silchester 1¾

This attractive and welcoming country pub has stripped black beams on the walls and ceiling of the big carpeted main room, as well as panelling, timber and brickwork; there's a good log fire in winter, and plenty of tables (with upholstered stools); piped music. The largely home-made food (they use a public address system to announce your number) includes soup (£1.25), ploughman's (from £2.25), beef casserole (£3.85), scampi (£4.50), home-made pies (£4.95), chicken wings, prawn and asparagus (£5.25) and sirloin steak (£6.25). A good choice of well kept real ales includes Brakspears PA, Fullers London Pride, Huntsman Royal Oak, Palmers IPA and Wadworths 6X on handpump, and they keep farm cider. There are sheltered old-fashioned teak seats outside. *(Recommended by Mayur Shah, KC, Ian Howard; more reports please)*

Free house   Licensee Peter Neal   Real ale   Meals and snacks   Restaurant (closed Sun) tel Silchester (0734) 700169   Children in eating area and restaurant (not Fri or Sat evening) Open 12–3, 6–11 (12–11 Sat) all year; closed 25 Dec

OVINGTON   SU5531 Map 2
Bush ★ ⊗

Village signposted from A31 on Winchester side of Alresford

Though many readers are attracted by the food, the atmosphere here is decidedly that of a particularly fine old-fashioned rural pub. The bar is dimly lit, but its liveliness (particularly on a crowded summer weekend) prevents any sense of sombreness. There are cushioned high-backed settles here, and pews and kitchen chairs around the elm tables, deep green walls packed with old pictures in heavy gilt frames, a large stuffed bat and stuffed fish in cases, lots of greenery in the windows, and an open fire at one end, an antique solid-fuel stove at the other. Well kept Flowers Original, Gales HSB, Wadworths 6X, Whitbreads Strong Country and Adnams as a guest beer on handpump; a good selection of wines. Bar food includes home-made soup, filled wholemeal baps or sandwiches (from £1.40), ploughman's (from £1.95), taramosalata (£1.95), garlic toast with chopped savoury-dressed beef (£2.75), mushroom and Stilton curry or home-made chilli con carne (£3.50), salads (from mixed cheese and fruit at £3.50, to a seafood platter of smoked salmon, oysters, prawns, cockles, mussels, lumpfish roe and smoked mackerel for £6.95), trout (£4.50) and steak (£5.95); children's lunches (£1.95) and a roast Sunday lunch (when the choice of other dishes may be more limited). Tucked away down a leafy lane, it's very peaceful outside, with white wrought-iron furniture on a pergola

---

If you stay overnight in an inn or hotel, they are allowed to serve you an alcoholic drink at any hour of the day or night.

dining terrace by a good-sized fountain pool, and quiet walks along the River Itchen. *(Recommended by H G and C J McCafferty, Michael and Harriet Robinson, Dr John Innes, BKA, Sue Cleasby, Mike Ledger, H E G, Gwen and Peter Andrews, Mr and Mrs Mouncey, J M M Hill, A V Chute, Mrs Margaret Branney, Roy McIsaac, A Foley, Ian Howard, Mr Moody, Prof A N Black)*

Free house   Licensees Mr and Mrs Geoffrey Draper   Real ale   Meals and snacks   Evening restaurant (not Sun) tel Alresford (0962) 732764   Children in eating area (lunchtime) and restaurant   Open 11–2.30, 6–11

OWSLEBURY   SU5124   Map 2

Ship

The knocked-through bar here has a genuinely pubby atmosphere, with its well worn flagstones by the entrance, its simple furnishings of built-in cushioned wall seats and wheel-back chairs around shiny wooden tables, modern ship prints, and flowers on the tables. Varnished black oak seventeenth-century ships' timbers serve as beams and wall props, and in winter there's a fire in the big central hearth. Bar food includes sandwiches and toasties (from £1.10), ploughman's (from £1.65), a variety of starters such as deep-fried mushrooms (£1.65), basket meals (from £1.65), home-made lasagne (£4.25), seafood platter (£4.35) and eight-ounce sirloin steak (£6.55), with lunchtime daily specials; on Sundays only filled rolls are available. Well kept Marstons Burton, Merrie Monk and Pedigree on handpump; sensibly placed darts, shove-ha'penny, dominoes, cribbage, fruit machine. It's flanked by two high downland gardens; from one side, on a clear day the picnic-table sets give a view right across the Solent to the Isle of Wight, and from the other, which has swings, a climber and a slide, you look down over the fields towards Winchester; there are occasional barbecues out here in summer. Handy for Marwell Zoo. *(Recommended by MBW, JHW, J E Figueira, Yvonne Healey; more reports please)*

Marstons   Licensee Robert O'Neill   Real ale   Meals (not Sun) and snacks   Children in comfortable family dining-room   Open 11–2.30, 6–11; closes 10.30 in winter

PENNINGTON   SZ3194   Map 2

Chequers ⊗

Ridgeway Lane; marked as dead end at A337 roundabout in Pennington W of Lymington, by White Hart

Tucked away on the quiet lane down to the salt marshes, this isolated and unspoilt sixteenth-century white cottage is visited only by those in the know – yachtsmen, often. The well laid out bar has wall pews and simple chairs around wooden or cast-iron-framed tables on neat quarry tiles or well polished boards; there are some Thelwell yachting cartoons and little local landscapes and townscapes by Rachel Long above the dark red-stained panelled dado. Bar food, changing daily, is often interesting, and besides soup (£1), filled baked potatoes (£1.50) and ploughman's (£1.95) might include garlic prawns, chilli con carne or lasagne (£1.50), a half-pound burger (£2.75), stuffed peppers (£2.95) and fresh scampi (£4.75). Well kept Flowers Original, Wadworths 6X and Whitbreads Strong Country on handpump; well chosen and reproduced piped pop music, darts and fruit machine. There are picnic-table sets in a neat and sheltered garden, with teak tables on a terrace below, and more tables in the inner courtyard. *(Recommended by H G and C J McCafferty, R H Inns, Patrick Young, Tim Locke)*

Free house   Licensees Michael and Maggie Jamieson   Real ale   Meals and snacks Restaurant tel Lymington (0590) 73415   Children in restaurant   Open 11–2.30ish, 6–11 all year; 11–11 Sat

It's very helpful if you let us know up-to-date food prices when you report on pubs.

nr PETERSFIELD SU7423 Map 2
White Horse ★ ★ ★

Priors Dean – but don't follow Priors Dean signposts: simplest route is from Petersfield, leaving centre on A272 towards Winchester, take right turn at roundabout after level crossing, towards Steep, and keep on for four miles or so, up on to the downs, passing another pub on your right (and not turning off into Steep there); at last, at crossroads signposted East Tisted/Privett, turn right towards East Tisted, then almost at once turn right on to second gravel track (the first just goes into a field); there's no inn sign – it's often called the Pub With No Name; alternatively, from A32 5 miles S of Alton, take road by bus lay-by signposted Steep, then, after 1¾ miles, turn off as above – though obviously left this time – at East Tisted/Privett crossroads; OS Sheet 197 coming from Petersfield (Sheet 186 is better the other way) reference 715290

The great charm and attraction of this remote two-roomed seventeenth-century country pub is the continuity in its unhurried, contented atmosphere. Though its reputation is such that it attracts people from many miles around, it remains unaffectedly local and genuine, refusing to succumb to the artificialities that all but destroy so many places. One result of this policy is that it's decidedly not a smart place; some of the furnishings have seen better days, but their charming individuality is undeniable, particularly the antique oak settles, drop-leaf tables and chairs, longcase clock, and rugs in the beamed main bar; there are old pictures, stuffed antelope heads and farm tools on the walls here, and good log fires. It comes into its own when its quiet is disturbed by nothing much more than the crackle of the log fire and maybe the snoring of a dozing dog; though there are times (not always predictable, with Sundays – even in winter – often busier than Saturdays) when it does get packed. This year Jack and Margaret Eddleston, who have run it for the past sixteen years, have extended the range of food (until now basic but very homely) to cope with the increasing demand; they now serve two home-made hot dishes most days, from a wide repertoire of pies such as steak and kidney, beef and ale, fish, or chicken and mushroom (all £3.25), as well as Lancashire hot-pot or chicken Masala (from £2.75); other food includes sandwiches (from 65p, prawn £1.95), home-made soup (recommended), ploughman's (from £1.80) and salads (from £2.75). There's a welcoming range of well kept real ales, a dozen or so, including their own very strong White Horse No Name, as well as Badger Best, Ballards, Bass, Boddingtons, Courage Best, Gales HSB, Huntsman Royal Oak, King and Barnes Mild and Bitter, and Whitbreads Royal Oak; a fine choice of country wines, tapped from small china kegs; shove-ha'penny, dominoes, cribbage. You can usually buy local eggs, including organic free-range ones, and in season pheasants, but EEC milk quota regulations have now put paid to the fresh cream they have sold in the past. In summer you can sit outside on rustic seats or chunks of treetrunk; as this is one of the highest spots in the county it can be quite breezy. The large fields that surround the pub are now being put to more active use, and they're available for bookings for outdoor activities (Pony Club and Trap meets, say). *(Recommended by Stuart Watkinson, TOH, Simon Collett-Jones, Alan Franck, Alison Hayward, Dennis Jones, Roger Mallard, Richard Houghton, John Payne, Peter Bligh, Ian Phillips, R H Inns, S F James, Wendy Arnold, Mrs H M T Carpenter, Chris Fluck, Steve and Carolyn Harvey, Heather Sharland, A V Chute, C Elliott, Annie Taylor, WHBM, Prof A N Black)*

Free house Licensees Jack and Margaret Eddleston Real ale Meals (not Fri–Sat evenings or Sun) and snacks (not Sun evening) Open 11–3, 6–11; may open longer in afternoon if trade demands

ROCKBOURNE SU1118 Map 2
Rose & Thistle

Village signposted from B3078 Fordingbridge–Cranborne

Smart and comfortable, this seventeenth-century thatched pub is strong on fresh seafood such as taramosalata (£2), prawns and king prawns, fresh or smoked salmon, daily fresh sea fish such as lemon or Dover sole (particularly recommended for its taste and size), Dorset crab and lobster (around £7–£9); there's also home-made soup (85p), sandwiches (from £1), pâté (£1.55), and in winter fish pie (£2.75), mussels (£2.95), and steak and kidney pie (£4.20). The lounge bar, recently re-carpeted and re-upholstered, has prettily upholstered stools and small settles, a shiny white plank ceiling, old engravings on the walls, quite a lot of polished brass, and in winter a good log fire. The public bar's seating is more in the style of booths. Well kept Whitbreads Strong Country and Pompey Royal on handpump; good service; piped music. There are tables in the neat front garden, beside a thatched dovecot. We heard as we went to press that there was a new licensee, and although, as we've said, the pub is strong on fish we'd like more news on this, and on the situation in general. The charming village has the excavated remains of a Roman villa. (*Recommended by Dr R A L Leatherdale, Gordon Leighton, Hazel Ricketts, J M Watkinson, Oliver Howes*)

Whitbreads Licensee Norman Toombs Real ale Meals and snacks Open 10.30–2.30, 7–11; closed lunchtime 25 Dec

ROMSEY SU3720 Map 2
Luzborough House ⊗

3 miles from M27 junction 3; A3057 towards Romsey, but turn right at A27

This is an exceptionally sympathetic conversion and extension of an old and interesting house: it has sustained the character of the original building without slavishly following an old-world style – indeed, the spacious main area is quite modern in many ways. Though there's a low plank ceiling by the serving-counter, most of this area has pitched high rafters; there are high-backed stools by ledges around stripped-brick pillars, floral-print wall seats with a variety of other chairs around the many tables, and in one corner a sofa and easy chairs. Most people head off for the more individual areas which ramble off from here; a low-beamed sixteenth-century country kitchen with a huge wood-burning stove in its inglenook fireplace, a snug and narrow side room up some steps, a little family-room, an elegant cream-panelled eighteenth-century dining-room decorated with attractive landscapes, and beyond that a neat conservatory with white cast-iron tables. Throughout, careful attention's been paid to the lighting. A spacious walled lawn has well spread picnic-table sets under cocktail parasols, with a slide and sprung rockers, and there are more picnic-table sets in front. Bar food quickly served by neat staff includes soup (95p), pâté (£1.45), sandwiches (from £1.75), ploughman's (from £2.25), salads (from £2.50), steak and kidney pie (£3.25), sirloin steak (£5.95), grilled salmon with a prawn sauce (£6.95) and a substantial mixed grill (£7.25). Well kept Flowers Original, Whitbreads Strong Country and Pompey Royal on handpump, fruit machine, unobtrusive piped music. (*Recommended by Joseph Figuera, C G Stephens, Mr and Mrs J Townsend*)

Whitbreads Licensee J Orritt Real ale Meals and snacks Children in family-room/conservatory Open 11–2.30, 6–11 all year

ROTHERWICK SU7156 Map 2
Coach & Horses ⊗

4 miles from M3 junction 5; follow Newnham signpost from exit roundabout, then Rotherwick signpost, then turn right at Mattingley, Heckfield signpost; village also signposted from A32 N of Hook

Popular bar food in this white, partly creeper-covered sixteenth-century village house includes sandwiches (from 80p, steak £2.45), ploughman's (from £1.70), burger or home-made pâté (£1.90), a variety of home-made pizzas (from £2.15),

---

Pubs in outstandingly attractive surroundings are listed at the back of the book.

cold pork with bubble and squeak (£3), gammon and egg (£3.35) and mixed grill or rump steak (£6.50). The fine choice of well kept real ales on handpump typically includes Arkells Kingsdown, Badger Best, Fullers London Pride, Huntsman Dorset and Royal Oak, Marstons Pedigree, Palmers BB, Ringwood Old Thumper, Ruddles County and Theakstons Old Peculier; decent wines. Two small beamed front rooms, one carpeted and the other with neat red and black flooring-tiles, and each with a stripped brick open fireplace, open off the parquet-floored inner serving area. Interesting furnishings include some nice oak chairs and a giant rattan one, and a fine assortment of attractive pictures include Alken sporting prints, Tudorici Pickwickian ones, and others in similar vein. The atmosphere is quietly welcoming. There are no games, machines or sounds of modernity. The façade is bright with tubs and baskets of flowers in summer, and there are rustic seats and picnic-table sets under cocktail parasols outside. They have a resident Siamese cat, Cleo. *(Recommended by KC, Joy Heatherley, R C Vincent, S Griffin, Mark Walpole and Melanie Byrne, Gary Wilkes)*

Free house Licensee Mrs Terry Williams Real ale Meals and snacks (carvery only, Sun lunchtime) Weekend carvery tel Rotherwick (025 672) 2542 Children welcome Open 11–2.30, 5.30–11 all year

SETLEY SU3000 Map 2
Filly ⊗

A337 Brockenhurst–Lymington

Neatly well run, this New Forest pub's a good deal bigger inside than you'd imagine from the road. Two spacious rooms have beams liberally decorated with horse-brasses, little wooden kegs, cork and glass net-floats, tackle blocks and antlers. Dark red walls, dark ochre ceilings, dim lighting and capacious fireplaces make for a warm feel; one carpeted room has spindle-back chairs around oak tables with a couple of cosy alcoves, the other has long cushioned antique settles and built-in pews, with some flagstones by the brick and timber bar counter. Bar food includes sandwiches (from 90p, triple-deckers from £1.85), pâté (£1.25), four-ounce burgers (£1.50), garlic mushrooms or other vegetables (£1.65), smoked trout (£1.75), chicken kebab or filled baked potatoes (£2.25), a wide choice of vegetarian dishes from a veggieburger (£1.50) to cashew nutlets in mushroom sauce (£3.95) and specials such as plaice florentine (£5.95); the prize-winning Ringwood Old Thumper, Wadworths 6X and a guest beer such as Palmers on handpump, well kept; quite a good collection of whiskies; maybe unobtrusive piped music, with a loudspeaker food-announcement system. The alert alsatian's called Tess. There are a few picnic-table sets on tidy grass at the back. *(Recommended by Clifford Blakemore, H G and C J McCafferty, Gary Wilkes)*

Free house Licensees Tony and Lynn Bargrove, Manager Mark Fishwick Real ale Meals and snacks Children in back bar Open 11–2.30, 6–11 all year; closed 25 and 26 Dec

SOPLEY SZ1597 Map 2
Woolpack

B3347 N of Christchurch; village signposted off A338 N of Bournemouth

The open-plan bar in this thatched village pub has a rambling atmosphere, with red leatherette wall seats and wooden chairs, a case of fishing dry flies and old village photographs on the ochre walls, banknotes on beams, a wood-burning stove and a small black kitchen range. Bar food includes sandwiches (from 85p), filled baked potatoes (from £1.50), ploughman's (from £1.85), cottage pie (£2.15), prawn and cod pasta (£2.50), home-made curry (£2.60), pizza or various home-made casseroles (£2.85) and scampi (£3); well kept Whitbreads Strong Country and Pompey Royal on handpump, and a collection of unusual foreign beers; darts, dominoes, cribbage, juke box, space game, fruit machine, unobtrusive piped music. As we were going to press an all-weather conservatory was being added at the back, by the little chalk stream with its weeping willows and spring-time daffodils. Over a little bridge out here there's a grassy children's play area with a swing and climbing-frame. *(Recommended by Roger and Kathy, WHBM; more reports please)*

Whitbreads   Licensees Lez and Helen Pine   Real ale   Meals and snacks   Children in eating area and family-room   Open 11–11; may close afternoons in winter

SOUTHAMPTON   SU4212 Map 2
Red Lion

55 High Street; turning off inner ring road, in S of city

This popular pub is included above all for its historical interest, seen particularly in its lofty medieval hall, with dark Tudor panelling and a creaky upper gallery running around the timbered walls below steeply pitched rafters. There's a tradition (upheld chiefly by the building's age and stature) that it was here that Henry v, before sailing for Agincourt, sentenced to death Lord Scrope and his own cousin Richard Earl of Cambridge for plotting against him. Among arms and armour hangs a flag reputed to have been presented to Southampton by Elizabeth i in 1585. Standard pub food, served in the lower-ceilinged back bar, includes filled rolls (from 45p) and sandwiches (from 55p), ploughman's (from £1.45), basket meals (from £1.75), lasagne (£2.25), salads (from £2.45), cod (£2.65), home-made steak and kidney pie (£2.65), scampi (£3.95) and steak (from eight-ounce rump, £5.75); Ruddles Best and County and Websters Yorkshire on handpump; fruit machine and trivia game, piped music. *(Recommended by Ben Wimpenny; more reports please)*

Phoenix (Watneys)   Licensee I J Williams   Real ale   Meals (not Sun lunchtime) and snacks Restaurant tel Southampton (0703) 333595   Children in restaurant   Daytime parking nearby difficult   Open 11–11 all year; closed 25 Dec

STEEP   SU7425 Map 2
Harrow   ⊗

Village signposted from A325 and A3 NE of Petersfield; then take road signposted Steep Church, then continue past church

Good home-made food in this peaceful local village tavern includes Scotch eggs (80p), sandwiches (from 90p), soup (£1.20), ploughman's (from £2.10, home-cooked ham £3.60), lasagne or cauliflower cheese (£3) and salads (from £3.60 for an excellent home-made meat loaf). The little public bar has built-in wall benches around scrubbed deal tables on its tiles, with a good log fire in the big inglenook in winter, and flowers on the tables in summer; both bars have recently been stripped back to their original pine wallboards. Well kept Flowers Original, Whitbreads Strong Country and Sam Whitbread are tapped from casks behind the counter; traditional cider, and strong country wines. At weekends or other busy holiday times it gets full to bursting, and it's really too small to cope with droves of outsiders, though there are plenty of tables in the big flower-filled garden, or in front, by the quiet lane. Note that they don't take children. *(Recommended by Jane Palmer, Dr and Mrs A K Clarke, Wendy Arnold; more reports, particularly on service, please)*

Whitbreads   Licensee Edward McCutcheon   Real ale   Meals and snacks   Open 10.30–3, 6–11; closes 10.30 in winter

---

The Post Office makes it virtually impossible for people to come to grips with British geography by using a system of post towns which are often across the county boundary from the places they serve. So the postal address of a pub often puts it in the wrong county. We use the correct county – the one the pub is actually in. Lots of pubs which the Post Office alleges are in Oxfordshire are actually in Berkshire, Buckinghamshire, Gloucestershire or the Midlands.

STOCKBRIDGE SU3535 Map 2
Vine ⊗

High Street; A30

The relaxed and welcoming main bar here has button-back banquettes and
Windsor chairs around its many tables, red velvet curtains, and a Delft shelf of
china and pewter. There's a strong emphasis on fish on the bar menu, not least
because a branch of the bounteous River Test runs along its back garden; as well as
the regular fresh grilled sardines (£3.50), trout (from £3.60) and Poole Bay plaice
(£3.95), they have seasonal fish specials; other food includes sandwiches (from £1;
open £2.65), soup (£1.10), ploughman's (from £2.25), omelettes (from £2.60),
quiche (£2.95), lasagne verde (£3.25) and gammon and egg (£3.50). Flowers
Original and Whitbreads Pompey Royal and Strong Country on handpump are
kept under a light carbon dioxide blanket. (*Recommended by G A Gibbs, John Calvert,
Mrs D A Biggs, Col E Richardson, R D Jolliff, H B Smith*)

*Whitbreads   Licensees Michael and Vanessa Harding   Meals and snacks (not Sun
evening)   Restaurant   Children welcome   Open 11–3.30, 6–11 all year   Bedrooms tel
Andover (0264) 810652; £15/£25*

White Hart ⊗ 🛏

Bottom end of High Street; junction roundabout A272/A3057

The dark-beamed bar of this friendly old coaching-inn has old small prints on the
walls, a collection of shaving mugs hanging over the bar counter, oak pews,
wheel-back chairs and low rustic elm stools. Its irregular shape and the brick pillars
supporting its low ceiling divide it into plenty of separate little areas. Bar food
includes sandwiches (from 90p), daily specials like lasagne or bacon pie (£2.50),
ploughman's or pâté (£2.80), smoked local trout (£3), home-made pies (£3; cottage
£2.50), steaks and several puddings; good Sunday lunches, and cook-it-yourself
summer barbecues. Bass and Charringtons IPA on handpump, Flowers Original
and Wadworths 6X tapped from cask heads let into the back of the bar, and a range
of country wines; shove-ha'penny. There's also a back wine bar; a jolly local
atmosphere. Front benches shelter under the unusually deep overhang of the
pillared upper storey. (*Recommended by J H C Peters, Gary Scott, Alan Bickley, Harriet
and Michael Robinson*)

*Free house   Real ale   Meals and snacks   Restaurant (not Mon)   Children in restaurant
Open 11–11 all year; closed 25 Dec evening   Bedrooms tel Andover (0264) 810475;
£18(£28.50B)/£34(£40B)*

TICHBORNE SU5630 Map 2
Tichborne Arms ⊗

Village signposted off A31 just W of Alresford

New licensees in this attractive thatched pub have quickly established a strong
reputation of their own (taking up where the last owners left off), particularly on
the food side; the decent range (with more emphasis on snacks than hot main
dishes) includes sandwiches (from 90p, bacon and local watercress £1.20, toasties
from £1), home-made soup (£1), liver and bacon nibbles with a home-made dip
(£1.10), ploughman's (from £1.80), baked potatoes with a fine range of fillings
(from £2.60), salads (from £3.25), and a good selection of home-made puddings
such as golden syrup sponge with custard and fudge and walnut flan with cream
(£1.25); friendly service. The square-panelled room on the right has wheel-back
chairs and settles (one very long), flowery curtains for the latticed windows, fresh
flowers on the tables, and a log fire in an attractive stone fireplace. It's decorated
with pictures and documents relating to the Tichborne Case – when this estate was
claimed by a fat fraudulent 'heir from the colonies'. On the left, a larger and livelier

room, partly panelled and also carpeted, has sensibly placed darts, shove-ha'penny, cribbage and a fruit machine. Well kept Bass, Courage Best, Flowers Original and Wadworths 6X tapped from the cask. There are picnic-table sets in the big well kept garden outside the pub. (*Recommended by Keith and Sheila Baxter, Michael and Harriet Robinson, G B Longden, MBW, JHW, G and M Stewart, J and J Measures, Steve and Carolyn Harvey, Gwen and Peter Andrews, GBH*)

Free house   Licensees Chris and Peter Byron   Real ale   Meals and snacks   Open 11.30–2.30, 6–11; all day Sat

TIMSBURY   SU3423   Map 2
Bear & Ragged Staff

Michelmersh; on A3057 Romsey–Stockbridge, 1¼ miles on Stockbridge side of Timsbury

This friendly and comfortable country pub has an extensive well kept bar, with flowers on its heavy elm tables and brasses on the black beams and cross-joists in its red ceiling; it's partly brick-tiled, partly carpeted, and has a big log fire in winter. There are two serving-counters, with a third doing food including sandwiches (from £1), ploughman's (from £1.70), and main dishes like plaice or cod (£2.50), ratatouille (£2.70), chilli con carne (£3.25), gammon (£4.60) and rump steak (£6.25); there's also a help-yourself salad bar (from £2.85). Well kept Flowers Original, Whitbreads PA and Strong Country, and a guest beer on handpump; fruit machine. Tables on the front terrace include some under a white awning, and there are more in a fairy-lit side garden with swings and hollow play trees. The local pumpkin show is held here in September. (*Recommended by John Nash, H G Allen; more reports please*)

Whitbreads   Licensee Tony Cavalier   Real ale   Meals and snacks (not Sun evening)   Live music every other Fri   Open 10.30–2.30, 6–10.30 (11 Fri and Sat); closed 25 Dec evening

TURGIS GREEN   SU6959   Map 2
Jekyll & Hyde ⊗

A33 Reading–Basingstoke

The good food in this sixteenth-century, rambling main-road pub includes sandwiches (from 95p, steak £3), home-made soup (£1), ploughman's (from £1.75), spinach and bacon Mornay (£2.45), filled baked potatoes (from £2.85), lasagne (£3.45), charcoal-grilled sardines (£3.55), salads (from £3.55), a range of daily specials such as game in season or a Dover sole, which for one reader approached the quality you'd expect in a top fish restaurant (around £5–£8), steaks (from eight-ounce sirloin £7.85, thirty-two-ounce T-bone £17.95), and sticky puddings (£1.60); efficient waitress service. A spread of muted brown carpet unifies the various areas opening off each other; there are black beams and joists, wheel-back chairs around rather rustic oak tables, and cream-painted walls, with some stripped brickwork – for instance, a big fireplace filled in summer with copper pans and brass platters. Well kept Adnams (rare away from Suffolk), Badger Best and Tanglefoot and Wadworths 6X on handpump; fruit machine, piped music. A back room with big Morland and Landseer prints, and a fine high-backed stripped settle by a nicely waxed kitchen table, has patio doors opening on to the attractive garden. Out here are plenty of picnic-table sets under cocktail parasols among shrubs and chubby conifers, with swings, a slide and a climber behind. (*Recommended by Roger Huggins, KC, Gary Wilkes, John Bell, Mark Walpole, Melanie White*)

Free house   Licensees Ian and Christine Sorrell   Real ale   Meals and snacks   Restaurant tel Basingstoke (0256) 882442   Children welcome   Open 11–2.30, 6–11 all year

Bedroom prices normally include full English breakfast, VAT and any inclusive service charge that we know of.

VERNHAM DEAN SU3456 Map 2

George

Friendly new licensees in this old-fashioned downland village pub have restored the lunchtime bar food; it includes a range of ploughman's (from £1.60), salads (from £2.50) and hot dishes like kebab or vegetarian crumble (£2.50) and chicken tikka (£2.60); but in the evenings it's primarily a drinking-house to relax in. The series of rambling bars has been replaced by an open-plan layout; large log fires in winter. The smooth curve of the tiles over the first-floor windows gives the old timbered brick and flint building a raised-eyebrows look. Well kept Marstons Burton and Pedigree on handpump; darts, shove-ha'penny, cribbage, dominoes, fruit machine; a sleepy-village atmosphere. They alternate all-day opening with two other pubs just across the border in Wiltshire, advising customers to try the Hatchet at Lower Chute or the Crown at Upton on the afternoons of Tuesday, Wednesday and Friday. The garden at the back is attractive. (*Recommended by Gordon and Daphne, Neville Burke, Dr Paul Kitchener*)

Marstons   Licensees Trilby and Philip Bond   Real ale   Meals and snacks (lunchtimes) Open 11–3, 6–11 Tues, Weds and Fri; 11–11 Mon, Thurs and Sat (see above); all year Bedrooms tel Andover (0264) 87279; £14/£20

nr VERNHAM DEAN SU3456 Map 2

Boot ⊗ [*illustrated on page 310*]

Littledown; follow signs to Vernham Street from Vernham Dean–Upton road

The original low-beamed white-panelled core of this isolated downland flint cottage is very small – just a couple of tables by the attractive inglenook fireplace, with a fine collection of model boots and shoes in a corner cupboard – but there's more room in a plainer extension, and also a conservatory (not really suitable for winter use) with darts, dominoes, cribbage and shove-ha'penny. The limited range of bar food includes sandwiches (from £1), ploughman's (from £1.75), a half-pint of prawns (£3.25), seafood platter or scampi (£4.25) and steak (from £7.25, not evenings); puddings (from £1, not evenings). There's a more elaborate choice in the small evening restaurant. Badger Best, Marstons Burton and Pedigree, and Wadworths 6X tapped from the cask, and lots of malt whiskies; friendly efficient service. A terrace leads into the attractive garden, which has a climbing-frame and horse-drawn caravan. (*Recommended by Gordon and Daphne, F N Clay, Michael Thomson, Mr and Mrs R Griffiths, Dr Paul Kitchener*)

Free house   Licensees John Paul Edward and Janet Ann Aldham   Real ale   Meals and snacks (not Mon)   Restaurant (not Mon) tel Linkenholt (026 487) 213   Children in restaurant and conservatory   Open 12–2.30 (3 Sat), 6–11; opens 7 in winter; closed Mon exc bank hols

nr WHERWELL SU3941 Map 2

Mayfly

Testcombe; B3420 SE of Andover

This lovely spot by the River Test, with lots of riverbank tables, is a sure pull in summer. You queue at a food bar for a wide choice of good cheeses with crusty home-baked wholemeal bread, quiche or cold meats with salads, and a hot dish such as tandoori chicken. The big bow-windowed and beamed carpeted bar has Windsor chairs around lots of tables, two wood-burning stoves, and fishing pictures and bric-à-brac on the cream walls above its dark wood dado. Flowers Original and Whitbreads Strong Country on handpump. (*Recommended by WHBM, A T Langton, Mrs G K Herbert, Mike Corser, Mary Redgate, Mark Walpole, Melanie Byrne*)

Whitbreads   Licensees Barry and Julie Lane   Real ale   Meals and snacks   Children in eating area   Open 10.30ish–2.30, 6ish–11

WINCHESTER   SU4829 Map 2
Wykeham Arms ★ ⊗ ⇐

75 Kingsgate Street (corner of Canon Street)

This charmingly restored small inn has a central bar area served by an attractive series of rooms around it, each with its own log fire. The wall banquettes have recently been replaced by sixteen nineteenth-century oak and cast-iron school desks from Winchester College, many with initials and inscriptions carved into them, and with fresh flowers in each inkwell; there are also kitchen chairs, stripped tables decorated with flowers (and candles at night), interesting prints, a reading shelf, and a piano decorated with houseplants. The no-smoking room at the other side has a twelve-foot carved pew from Winchester Chapel, and a framed set of Ronald Searle 'Winespeak' prints. There's an uncommonly good range of more than twenty wines by the glass, which are very popular, accounting for more than thirty per cent of their alcohol sales. The well kept Huntsman Dorchester, IPA and Royal Oak on handpump (kept under a light carbon dioxide blanket) are very popular too. Changing home-made bar food includes sandwiches (from £1, lunchtime only), soup (£1.25), ploughman's (from £1.80), with changing evening dishes like pork medallions in cider sauce or grilled local trout (£5.25), beef and Guinness casserole, calf's liver in orange sauce or rump steak (£5.95) and rack of lamb (£6.95); puddings such as honey and walnut tart (£1.65). There are tables on a covered back terrace, with more out on the grass. Residents have the use of a sauna; the inn is very handy for the cathedral. (Recommended by Barbara Hatfield, R G Ollier, GRE, AE, Patrick Young, Phil and Sally Gorton, Roger Davison, Alison Hayward, P J Kitson, B A B Scarsby, Dr John Innes)

Huntsman   Licensees Mr and Mrs Graeme Jameson   Real ale   Meals and snacks (not Mon evening or Sun)   Children in area partly set aside   If the small car park is full local parking may be difficult   Open 11–11 all year   Bedrooms tel Winchester (0962) 53834; £27.50(£37.50B)/£37.50(£47.50B)

Lucky Dip

Besides the fully inspected pubs, you might like to try these Lucky Dips recommended to us and described by readers (if you do, please send us reports):

Alresford [Broad St (extreme lower end); SU5832], Globe: Well kept Watneys-related real ales, decent food, photographs of old Alresford, interesting history of the pub and neighbouring twelfth-century ponds – especially nice on a summer's day (BKA, John Roué); [East St (A31)] Peaceful Home: Very friendly and chatty local with good choice of well kept real ales (John Roué)

Alton [Church St; SU7139], Eight Bells: Knowledgeable landlord keeps his beers, rotating monthly, in excellent condition, including interesting guest beers (Olav Larsen)

Ampfield [A31 Winchester–Romsey; SU4023], Potters Heron: Good value bar food in comfortably done-up pub (Tim Powell)

Andover [Weyhill Rd; SU3645], Railway: Lively pub given spirit by the enthusiastic landlord (Dr and Mrs A K Clarke)

Avon [B3347 – OS Sheet 195 reference 147986; SZ1399], New Queen: Effusively welcoming licensee, well kept Bass and Ringwood, attractive two-level bar, riverside garden, fishing rights, play area; bedrooms (WHBM); Tyrrells Ford: Good food served at a relaxed pace in bar and comfortable restaurant of country-house hotel; pleasant owner; bedrooms (B J E Phillips)

☆ Ball Hill [Hatt Common; leaving Newbury on A343 turn right towards East Woodhay – OS Sheet 174 reference 423631; SU4263], Furze Bush: Clean and airy décor, pews and pine tables, usual bar food, well kept Bass, Border Mild and Marstons Pedigree on handpump, decent wines by the bottle, tables on terrace by good-sized sheltered lawn with play area, restaurant; has had jazz Sun; well behaved children allowed, no-smoking area in dining-room (LYM)

Bashley [SZ2497], Plough: Away from the crowded New Forest area, this rustic pub has good beer, reasonably priced food and big back garden; not smart but good value (Bernard Phillips)

Basing [The Street; SU6653], Bolton Arms: One tidy quiet bar, another so busy and lively it's like another pub altogether; friendly welcoming service, well kept Courage *(Geoff Kellett)*; [Bartons Lane (attached to Bartons Mill Restaurant)] *Millstone*: Old converted building nicely placed by the River Loddon, with ducks and swans; friendly service, dry-humoured licensee, Gibbs Mew Salisbury, Wadworths 6X and other real ales tapped from the cask, good atmosphere, lots of chat *(Geoff Kellett)*

Basingstoke [Winton Sq; SU6352], *Wheatsheaf*: Recently refurbished with nice décor (if you can overlook the plastic plants), good atmosphere, very nice cottage-kitchen nook if you're early enough to get a seat in it; Bass, weekday food *(Geoff Kellett)*; [NB different from the above pub – A30 just W, and visible from M3] *Wheatsheaf*: Up-market refurbishment of a Georgian coaching-inn with panelled walls, red patterned carpet, beams and oak furniture and a huge fireplace; shotguns, whips, lanterns, etc. on the walls; Wadworths 6X and Wethereds on handpump; food bar is an old cast-iron range – filled brown rolls, various ploughman's, basket meals, steaks and a daily roast; comfortable bedrooms in recently added wing *(Patrick Young)*; [opp police stn] *White Hart*: Friendly local, lots of merriment, good food, well kept Courage *(Adrian Smith)*

Binsted [SU7741], *Cedars*: Lively local with big public bar (and huge boar's head), quieter sitting-roomish lounge bar, well kept Courage ales, good freshly prepared food *(BB)*

Bishops Sutton [A31 Alton side of Alresford; SU6031], *Ship*: Cosy main-road pub with bar food *(LYM)*

Bishops Waltham [The Square; SU5517], *Crown*: Large, well run period Whitbreads pub with relaxed atmosphere, good service and good choice of food; children in restaurant area *(R A Abbott, MBW, JHW)*

Bishopstoke [SU4619], *River*: Spacious pub with bric-à-brac on the walls and ceiling, including a replica of the Crown Jewels *(Ben Wimpenny)*

Blacknest [OS Sheet 186 reference 798416; SU7941], *Jolly Farmer*: Enjoyable bar food, well kept Badger beer, tables outside *(E U Broadbent)*

Botley [The Square; SU5112], *Bugle*: Well refurbished as half-pub, half-restaurant; well kept Flowers and Whitbreads Strong Country on handpump, good bar food *(A R Lord)*

Braishfield [SU3725], *Dog & Crook*: Charming country pub with good range of well kept Whitbreads ales, in lovely countryside *(Joseph Figueira)*

☆ **Bransgore** [Highcliffe Rd; SZ1897], *Three Tuns*: Small thatched and oak-beamed village pub with good home-cooked food, friendly rather than swift service, well kept beer, log fire and separate dining-room; very characterful *(G W Simpson, Gary Wilkes)*

Bransgore [Burley Rd], *Carpenters Arms*: Pleasant staff, good food and tables well spaced or in alcoves *(NIH)*

Brockenhurst [Lyndhurst Rd; SU2902], *Snakecatcher*: Friendly local, Huntsman Royal Oak and IPA, decent bar food with daily specials, garden with ancient yew *(WHBM)*

Bucklers Hard [SU4000], *Master Builders House*: Ideal location just above the water in carefully preserved village (part of the Montagu estate); beamed and timbered bar with big log fire, adjoining buffet bar – mixed recent reports on atmosphere, service and food, more news please; bedrooms in substantial hotel complex behind *(Keith Garley, TRA, MA, Peter Hitchcock, LYM)*

Burghclere [off A34; SU4761], *Carpenters Arms*: Well kept, delightful pub, friendly welcome, unobtrusive piped music, fruit machine, Watneys-related real ales, big helpings of reasonably priced bar food including vegetarian dishes, small evening restaurant; garden *(Pat and Dennis Jones)*

☆ **Buriton** [OS Sheet 197 reference 205735; SU7420], *Five Bells*: Very wide choice of interesting unusual home-made bar food such as wholemeal spaghetti with courgettes and blue cheese dressing, very reasonable prices; service may not be speedy *(Steve and Carolyn Harvey, A Banister, Glyn Edmunds)*

☆ **Burley** [back rd Ringwood–Lymington; SU2003], *Queens Head*: Tudor pub with flagstones, low beams, timbering, panelling, good log fire and a swarm of bric-à-brac from assegais to divers' helmets and bespectacled animals' heads; usual bar food (not winter evenings), well kept Flowers Original and Whitbreads Strong Country on handpump, maybe piped music; gift/souvenir shop in courtyard – pub can get packed in summer as this village is Hants' answer to Widecombe-in-the-Moor; provision for children *(Gwen and Peter Andrews, Roger and Kathy, John Innes, LYM)*

☆ **Bursledon** [Hungerford Bottom; SU4809], *Fox & Hounds*: Popular for handsomely rebuilt ancient Lone Barn behind – long oak-trunk table, lantern-lit side stalls, jolly rustic atmosphere, food bar, well kept Gales HSB, Ushers Best and Websters Yorkshire, seats out in sheltered flagstone courtyard; games and juke box in main pub; children in Lone Barn *(Patrick Young, H G and C J McCafferty, Prof A N Black, LYM)*

Cadnam [by M27, junction 1; SU2913], *Sir John Barleycorn*: Good food in attractive pub with beams, log fires (which can smoke), friendly service; barbecue in garden *(The Edwickers)*

☆ **Chalton** [SU7315], *Red Lion*: The county's oldest pub – thatched, timbered and jettied; inside has high-backed settles, elm tables, heavy beams, panelling; Gales ales on handpump, and food side (not Fri–Sun evenings) being developed by new licensees, who came from the Old House at Home, Havant; more news of the new regime, please *(AJVB, Phil and Sally Gorton, Mark Walpole,*

Melanie White, LYM

Chilbolton [OS Sheet 185 reference 394398; SU3939], *Abbots Mitre*: Clean and comfortable village pub with attractive raised brick fireplace, friendly atmosphere, good-sized garden, good beers, Whitbreads-related and guest real ales; nice Test Valley walks nearby *(S A Lovett)*

Crawley [A272 Stockbridge–Winchester, about 5 miles N of Winchester; SU4234], *Rack & Manger*: Well kept Marstons real ales, large helpings of good value bar food, play area *(Mark Walpole, Melanie White)*

Crookham [OS Sheet 186 reference 792518; SU7852], *Chequers*: Badger and Courage real ales in well polished bar with fresh flowers on big mahogany table, half-octagon cushioned settle around huge curtained bay window, lots of pot plants, panelled bar counter with ancient till and stuffed heron behind; room on left with cushioned seats, tables and darts; third room sometimes open with armchairs or basket chairs, stuffed fish, piano; eggs from landlady's own chickens *(Phil and Sally Gorton, KG)*

Denmead [Worlds End; SU6312], *Chairmakers Arms*: Wide choice of bar food and well kept Gales ales in comfortably knocked-together rooms of popular pub surrounded by paddocks and farmland *(Colin Gooch, LYM)*; [Southwick Rd, Bunkers Hill; SU6511] *Harvest Home*: Delicious home-made food, service always polite and friendly in pretty and well decorated country pub with good-sized garden *(Alan and Sharron Todd)*

Downton [SZ2793], *Royal Oak*: Good home-cooked food such as hunter's pie, well kept ales, good wine by the glass and family atmosphere in well run pub, free from juke box and fruit machines *(John Kirk)*

Droxford [SU6018], *Hurdles*: Friendly service, well kept beer and good choice of food at reasonable prices in bustling fast-food pub, small share-a-table bar, separate restaurant *(TRA, MA)*; *White Horse*: Though the furnishings and atmosphere in this rambling old inn aren't what they used to be, the good choice of real ales is well kept, there is still a log fire and the food's good value; close to pleasant country walks; bedrooms *(V M J Sage, LYM)*

☆**Dummer** [½ mile from M3 junction 7; SU5846], *Queens Head*: Fine choice of well kept beers and generous good value food such as goulash, marinated venison kebabs and quite magnificent well filled sandwiches; quite pleasantly enlarged and though it can be packed with businessmen on weekday lunchtimes it's comfortable and cosy, with welcoming efficient staff; children allowed in restaurant areas *(Joy Heatherley, Mrs C A B Johnson, WHBM, KG)*

Dundridge [Dundridge Lane; off B3035 towards Droxford and Swanmore, then right at Bishops Waltham 3¾ signpost – OS Sheet 185 reference 579185; SU5718], *Hampshire*

Bowman: Simple isolated downland pub with good Gales ales, straightforward food, friendly welcome, big lawn *(LYM)*

Durley [Heathen St – OS Sheet 185 reference 516160; SU5116], *Farmers Home*: Comfortable old-fashioned free house with Whitbreads, very large and well equipped children's play area *(MBW, JHW)*

☆**East Stratton** [SU5439], *Plough*: Lovely old-fashioned and undeveloped country pub, well kept real ales, limited bar food using fresh vegetables from own superbly kept gardens, friendly atmosphere, loud juke box, darts, fruit machine; children's room, skittle alley, beautiful green opposite *(G L Archer, Doug Kennedy, GSS)*

East Tytherley [SU2929], *Star*: Lots of ambience and good food in quaint restaurant *(Ian Scrivens)*

Easton [SU5132], *Chestnut Horse*: Said to date from sixteenth century, with beams, open fires, and licensee with an exuberant sense of humour *(GSS)*

Emery Down [SU2808], *Green Dragon*: Busy pub with pleasantly mixed bag of customers, well kept beer, interesting bar, food, quick service, garden *(Philip and Trisha Ferris)*

Emsworth [Main street; SU7406], *Ship*: Good value simple food and well kept Bass in plain but comfortable well kept pub *(LYM)*

Eversley [SU7762], *White Hart*: Good atmosphere and beer and good traditional crowd including the 'old boy' *(Sarah and Jamie Allan)*

Eversley Cross [SU7861], *Chequers*: Comfortably modernised (though in fact partly fourteenth century); Watneys pubs with quickly served bar food *(LYM)*

Everton [SZ2994], *Crown*: Attractive and hospitable Whitbreads village pub with good range of drinks including real ales on handpump, good bar lunches in adjacent eating area, very good service, licensee with nice sense of humour *(E G Parish)*

Ewshot [A287 Farnham–Odiham; SU8149], *Queens Arms*: Attractive bar with lovely coal fires and good atmosphere, excellent service from licensee; good, well presented bar snacks, restaurant (not Sun lunchtime) *(Mrs J Ward)*

Exton [SU6121], *Shoe*: Included for pleasant riverside garden, pub well kept inside with Friary Meux and Ind Coope Burton on handpump *(Roger Lamble)*

Fareham [Trinity St/West St; SU5706], *Daniels*: Spacious, clean and efficiently run pub, good pastiche of 1930s cocktail bar with chrome bar stools, mirrors and elegant, comfortable sofas and banquettes in pastel colours; Whitbreads ales, well cooked and presented burgers, prompt service *(Ian Phillips)*; [Funtley Rd] *Miners Arms*: Tastefully decorated, pleasant licensees, well kept Gales ales and country wines, good filling bar food such as baked potatoes, lasagne, generous omelettes – full of locals every lunchtime *(J A Barker)*

Farnborough [Rectory Rd; SU8753], *Prince of Wales*: Dedicated real-ale pub with good range of beers such as Badger Best and Tanglefoot, Fullers London Pride, Huntsman Royal Oak, King and Barnes and Wadworths 6X, good helpings of adequate food in support, friendly staff *(R J Walden, KC)*

☆ **Fordingbridge** [High St; SU1414], *George*: Good choice of generously served food, well kept Flowers Original and Wadworths 6X and decent wine and coffee, cheerful atmosphere, nice riverside terrace *(P J and S E Robbins, JMW, Gwen and Peter Andrews)*

☆ **Fritham** [SU2314], *Royal Oak*: Thatched New Forest pub, Flowers and Strong Country tapped from the cask for two quite unspoilt and decidedly basic bars, one with high-backed settles and stairs, pots and kettles hanging from old wide chimney of original fireplace; outside seats, tables, climbers and two very friendly sheep, with cows, ponies and even pigs wandering nearby; no food beyond pickled eggs, but you are welcome to take your own sandwiches; children in back room; at start of GWG40 *(Roger and Kathy, Phil and Sally Gorton, Roy McIsaac, LYM)*

☆ **Grateley** [SU2741], *Plough*: Attractive old pub in quiet village with pleasant, friendly staff, big log fire, good choice of local ales, games in separate public bar, and very good food served in candlelit dining area *(Mr and Mrs W C Waggoner, Mark Spurlock, Dr I C Perry)*

Hambledon [SU6414], *Bat & Ball*: Good food, well kept Ind Coope real ales, relaxing atmosphere, interesting china and long cricketing history – lots of memorabilia in the restaurant which now dominates the pub; very busy weekend lunchtimes *(David Gaunt, LYM)*; [West St] *Vine*: Pleasant roomy pub with emphasis on food – chicken, grills, steaks and so forth; good range of beers, busy in spite of not being easy to find *(J W Anderson)*

Havant [South St; SU7106], *Old House at Home*: Carefully enlarged Tudor pub, much modernised inside (electronic games, etc.); has been popular for lunchtime food and well kept Gales BBB and HSB, but licensees moved start of 1988 to Red Lion, Chalton; more views on the new regime, please *(LYM)*

Hawkley [Pococks Lane; SU7429], *Hawkley*: Interesting little pub, difficult to find and even to get into (as under its new licensees it's quite the 'in' place now); very friendly, with well kept Wiltshire Stonehenge Best; décor could be bettered *(Richard Houghton, John Innes)*

Hayling Island [OS Sheet 196 reference 689000; SU7201], *Ferry Boat*: Uncrowded comfort by the sea – in bad weather the spray hits the window; reasonable food, well kept Friary Meux Best and Ind Coope Burton, pool in separate bar with juke box; old bus with slide for children *(Gary Wilkes)*

Hazeley Heath [SU7459], *Shoulder of Mutton*: In summer concentrates mainly on restaurant, in winter is more pubby – warm and welcoming *(Ian Phillips)*

Heckfield [SU7260], *Hatchgate*: Good varying food at a price in attractive restaurant of free house with Courage and Huntsman ales, good service *(P D Finch)*

Highcliffe [SZ2193], *Globe*: Wide choice of good food from sandwiches to steaks, with daily specials and Sun roasts – all freshly cooked, meat and vegetables bought locally; comfortable bar, family dining area, screened-off restaurant, unobtrusive juke box, fruit machine and space game; fair choice of well kept beers, garden *(Patrick and Mary McDermott)*; [Walkford Rd], *Walkford*: Good food, char-grilled in front of you in well run pub with excellent service *(C G Stephens)*

☆ **Hill Head** [Hill Head Rd; SU5402], *Osborne View*: Decently refurbished, with friendly staff, relaxed atmosphere, well prepared and generously served bar food that includes enormous omelettes, full range of Badger beers; superb views over Solent and Isle of Wight, beach garden where you can even swim in summer *(Michael Bechley, SJC)*

Hill Top [B3054 Beaulieu–Hythe; SU4003], *Royal Oak*: Pleasant Whitbreads country local with bare brickwork, split pine logs on walls and bar front, roaring fire; Flowers Original and Whitbreads Strong Country on handpump, straightforward home-made food *(Patrick Young)*

Hinton [A35 4 miles E of Christchurch; SZ2095], *East Close*: Large, friendly pub with variety of local beers including Ringwood Best and Bishops Tipple and large choice of hot and cold bar food, big helpings, cheaper children's dishes, children's area *(Dr R B Crail)*

Horndean [London Rd; SU7013], *Ship & Bell*: A town rather than a country pub; virtually the tap to Gales Brewery and a well run place with genuine working landlord; bedrooms *(WHBM)*

Hursley [A31 Winchester–Romsey; SU4225], *Dolphin*: U-shaped bar in low-beamed village local with good Flowers Original, Wadworths 6X and Whitbreads Strong Country on handpump; stuffed pheasants, lots of fish prints, big garden behind *(Mark Walpole, Melanie White)*

Hurstbourne Tarrant [A343; SU3853], *George & Dragon*: Coaching-era reminders in low-beamed lounge bar of simple inn with well kept Courage Directors, bar food with meat from good local butcher, games in public bar, children allowed in eating area and restaurant; bedrooms *(LYM)*

Hythe [Waitrose shopping centre, first floor; SU4207], *Mariner*: The magnificent Solent view is what distinguishes this place, otherwise much what you might expect from the first floor of a modern shopping centre –

though it has Badger ales and satisfactory food *(Patrick Young)*

Keyhaven [SZ3091], *Gun*: Wide choice of simple good value bar food and choice of Whitbreads beers in small and therefore often crowded pub overlooking boatyard; garden, good walk along spit to Hurst Castle with Isle of Wight views *(Jenny Cantle, H G and C J McCafferty)*

Kingsclere [SU5258], *Crown*: Long comfortable partly panelled lounge with central log fire, Courage real ales, games in simpler public bar, pleasant atmosphere; very popular for somewhat pricey home cooking; children in family-room; comfortable bedrooms *(J P Berryman, Dr and Mrs M Rayner, LYM)*; [A339 outside] *Star*: Attractive food, good quick service, nicely arranged refurbished bars – a popular busy main-road pub *(G B Pugh, Mr and Mrs J G Simpson)*

☆ **Langstone** [SU7105], *Royal Oak*: Charmingly placed on edge of landlocked natural harbour, with fine views from waterside benches and seats in bow windows; attractive building, with worn flagstones, two open fires, appropriately simple furnishings, well presented bar food, efficient friendly bar staff in smart uniforms; a Whitbreads pub with well kept Badger too; may be dogs or cats in eating area *(Richard Houghton, J F Reay, WHBM, Charles Turner, LYM)*

Langstone [A3023], *Ship*: Large busy waterside pub with reasonably priced food bar, friendly service and well kept Gales *(JH, AJVB)*

Lasham [SU6742], *Royal Oak*: Very pleasing, warm atmosphere, beam hung with toby jugs and steins, mantelbeam above open fire with rack of pipes and horsebrasses, glowing wall lamps; good food and beer, seats on lawn *(Prof and Mrs Keith Patchett)*

nr **Liphook** [B3004 towards Alton; SU8331], *Passfield Oak*: Fine setting backing on to National Trust woodland, tables on front lawn and in big back garden, cheery bustling bar with simple rooms off, several real ales such as Ballards and Bunces, simple bar food, children's room *(J Walsh, LYM)*

Liss [A325; SU7728], *Spread Eagle*: Pleasant country pub overlooking square, friendly service in lounge bar, plain public bar with pool-table *(Dr John Innes)*

Liss Forest [SU7829], *Temple*: Recently refurbished local with friendy atmosphere, pool-table, well kept Gales HSB, reasonably priced bar food, good garden; children's room, play area and tree house in garden *(D C Bail)*

Longstock [SU3536], *Peat Spade*: Extensively renovated though still straightforward old pub with good Gales HSB, BBB and XXX and well priced seafood and steaks *(Mark Walpole, Melanie White)*

Lower Farringdon [Gosport Road (A32); SU7035], *Royal Oak*: Fast, friendly service, Courage beer, reasonably priced bar food in

otherwise unremarkable main-road pub *(Anon)*

Lower Froyle [SU7544], *Anchor*: Pleasant pub with friendly atmosphere; piped music in brightly lit bar, good range of beers, separate restaurant *(Dr John Innes)*

Lower Wield [SU6340], *Yew Tree*: Varied choice of good food, particularly fish, and good choice of real ales including rarities; friendly landlord *(Peter Bligh)*

Lymington [High St; SZ3295], *Red Lion*: Small pub with bare floorboards, wooden chairs and a nice atmosphere; very good beer and superb mussels *(H G and C J McCafferty)*

Marchwood [SU3810], *Pilgrim*: Immaculately sprightly décor in smart thatched pub with Huntsman beers and lunchtime snacks; neat garden *(LYM)*

Mattingley [SU7358], *Leather Bottle*: Good real ales tapped from the cask by very welcoming staff, nice log fire, decent food in bar and restaurant, old oak beams; justifiably busy, get there early *(Tony Witt, KC)*; [B3011] *Shoulder of Mutton*: Popular pub well off beaten track, impeccable service, well kept Courage, good if somewhat pricey food; get there early for a table *(Richard Houghton)*

Meonstoke [SU6119], *Bucks Head*: Clean place with a friendly welcome – especially from the landlord – and good wholesome food *(Roger Mallard)*

Milford on Sea [SZ2891], *Red Lion*: Great local atmosphere, especially on a Fri night, and good beer; garden *(H G and C J McCafferty)*

Nether Wallop [village signposted from A30 or B2084 W of Stockbridge; follow sign for church but turn right just before you actually reach the church; SU3036], *Five Bells*: Simple village pub with long cushioned settles and good log fire in beamed bar, cheap bar food, well kept Marstons real ales on handpump including Mild, and billiards and other traditional games in locals' bar, small restaurant, seats outside, provision for children *(John Tyzack, LYM)*

Newtown [A34/A339 2 miles S of Newbury; SU4764], *Swan*: Very handy pub with good food and service – waitresses in Beefeater costumes *(John Robinson)*

Oakhanger [off A325 Farnham–Petersfield; SU7635], *Red Lion*: Small, cosy lounge with brasses and large log fire, well kept Directors, good interesting food, friendly service and separate dining area *(John Atherton)*

Odiham [High St; A287; SU7450], *George*: Well kept Courage real ales and food in old-fashioned bar; bedrooms *(LYM)*

Pennington [Milford Rd; SZ3194], *White Hart*: Friendly, jolly landlord, good atmosphere, well kept beer, bar food, garden and terrace *(Philip and Trisha Ferris)*

☆ **Petersfield** [College St; SU7423], *Good Intent*: Welcoming sixteenth-century pub, probably best in winter, with log fires and spotlessly clean lavatories; it's modestly sized, so on a warm summer evening can become a bit airless; small restaurant at one end; also well cooked and presented bar food and good range of beers *(Gwen and Peter Andrews, Canon G Hollis, BJP)*

Portsea [The Hard; SU6400], *Ship Anson*: Comfortably refurbished pub with good food (not Sun evening), Flowers Original, Wetbreads and Whitbreads Strong Country; good service – very polite *(Keith Douglas)*

Portsmouth [High St; SU6501], *Dolphin*: Spacious pub in Old Portsmouth with Wadworths 6X and Whitbreads Strong Country on handpump, wide range of hot and cold bar food *(AE)*; [Portsdown Hill Rd, Widley; SU6706] *George*: Whitbreads pub with wonderful views of Hayling Island, Portsmouth, Southsea and Isle of Wight from terrace; hunting décor with guns, cartridges and stuffed birds; friendly, helpful service, real ale, bar food *(Ian Phillips)*; [High St] *Sallyport*: Wall panelled to resemble a boat's bows, lots of brass ship's lanterns with flickering electric candles, electric fire – but welcoming staff, warm atmosphere, Marstons Pedigree, good value bar food; bedrooms spotless and very reasonably priced *(Mrs Nedelev, Ian Phillips)*; [Bath Sq] *Still & West*: Included for its marvellous waterside position, with upstairs windows and terrace seeming almost within touching distance of the boats and ships fighting the strong tides in the narrow harbour mouth; Gales real ales on electric pump, basic pub food (lunchtime, not Sun), plain side family-room, bland décor *(MBW, JHW, Colin Gooch, LYM)*; [Surrey St, town centre] *Surrey Arms*: Good value lunches – big helpings of good food; Flowers, Wetbereds and Wadworths 6X; bedrooms comfortable *(Keith Douglas, H G and C J McCafferty)*; [off Grand Parade, Old Town] *Wellington*: Well kept Friary Meux, lovely fish and chips – especially swordfish steak *(A J Triggle)*

Poulner [SU1606], *London*: Nice quiet one-bar village local, relaxed and friendly *(John Roué)*

Ringwood [A31 W of town – OS Sheet 195 reference 140050; SU1505], *Fish*: Comfortably modernised and friendly main-road Whitbreads pub with properly pubby atmosphere in clean and pleasant bar, plain eating area where children allowed, lawn by River Avon; reasonably priced straightforward food; a useful stop for travellers, though not worth a special trip *(WHBM, K and D E Worrall, LYM)*; [by back of Woolworths] *Inn on the Furlong*: Ringwood Brewery's only tied house, carefully renovated with attractive pine and brick interior *(R H Inns)*

Rockford [OS Sheet 195 reference 160081; SU1608], *Alice Lisle*: Open-plan bar with Bass and Ringwood real ales, limited choice of good food including charcoal-grilled steaks, evening restaurant, Wendy house

with games in garden; on New Forest green *(H G and C J McCafferty, BB)*

☆ **Romsey** [Middlebridge St, nr W end of bypass; SU3521], *Three Tuns*: Reliably good modestly priced home-cooked food and quick service from experienced staff in very old and cosy pub, three Whitbreads ales on handpump *(A E Wildash, WHBM)*

Romsey [Church Rd], *Abbey*: Pleasant central pub with good choice of hot and cold food, interesting décor, Courage Directors on handpump; children welcome in dining area, jazz Sun evening; garden with stream *(Mr and Mrs J Townsend)*; *Old House At Home*: Good Gales ales, good food in warmly welcoming pub, partly thatched; near town centre *(R J Foreman)*

Ropley [SU6431], *Chequers*: Superb imaginative home cooking including extensive cold food display, big helpings, most reasonable prices; cosy atmosphere, waitress service, cheerful licensee *(A E Wildash)*

☆ **Sarisbury** [Sarisbury Green; nr M27, between junctions 8 and 9; SU5008], *Bat & Ball*: Whitbreads pub which has made a speciality of appealing to familes with children and providing really well for them; good menu and efficient service, friendly bar staff, Sam Whitbread and Strong Country *(J P Copson, Anon of Gosport)*

Selborne [SU7433], *Queens*: Useful small hotel in Gilbert White's village; comfortable simple lounge bar, lively public bar, well kept Courage Best and Directors, friendly owners, buttery bar open for snacks all day; bedrooms good value, with decent breakfasts *(Gwen and Peter Andrews, Roy McIsaac, Cdr G R Roantree, LYM)*; *Selborne Arms*: Improving village local with friendly service, well kept Courage, decent straightforward food *(Anon)*

Sherborne St John [SU6255], *Swan*: Thatched pub with attractive conservatory, terrace and big garden – good for families; meals centre round the barbecued meats which are served with home-made chips or jacket potato and salad; several wines available *(Stephen Coverly)*

Sherfield on Loddon [SU6857], *Four Horseshoes*: Delightful atmosphere, friendly licensee, well kept Courage, blazing fire *(Geoff Kellett)*; *White Hart*: Interesting relics of coaching days, including message rack over big inglenook fireplace and attractive bow-window seat where the ostlers and coachmen used to sit; but rather a regulars' pub now, Courage, though well kept, not cheap, and can be smoky – more news please *(Ian Phillips, LYM)*

☆ **Silchester** [Silchester Common – OS Sheet 175 reference 625625; SU6262], *Calleva Arms*: Attractive and popular, with friendly polite staff, well kept Gales ales, good atmosphere, unobtrusive piped music; lunchtime food brings many customers; well kept and attractive garden with good play area *(Colyn Nicholls, TOH, Ian Howard)*

☆Soberton [SU6116], *White Lion*: Character retained under new regime, but with enlarged eating area and tables in back yard; good atmosphere, friendly service and eight types of pasta *(MBW, JHW and others)*

☆Southampton [Oxford St; SU4212], *Grapes*: Lovely ornately Victorian atmosphere and décor, waiters and barman in bowler hats, self-playing pianola with dummy pianist in tails, roaring log fire, small round tables with red-fringed tablecloths to the floor, collection of chamber-pots, food that includes good value daily specials, well kept Flowers Original, quick pleasant waitresses *(JKW, Tom Evans, Joseph Figueira, Ian Phillips)*

☆Southampton [Town Quay; by Mayflower Park and IOW ferry terminal], *Royal Pier*: Lofty conversion of previously derelict pier building, upper floor reached by spiral staircase; relaxed atmosphere, well kept Flowers, good range of reasonably priced bar food, efficient and helpful service; sheltered suntrap terrace, ample parking; children welcome; live jazz or rock at weekends, very much a young person's pub in the evening *(Ian Phillips, Mark Spurlock, A J Triggle)*

Southampton [33 Canute Rd; OS Sheet 196 reference 428110], *Frog & Frigate*: Spit-and-sawdust with regular boisterous singsongs; has been popular for home-brewed ales with guest beers such as Ringwood and Youngers, but for sale late 1987 *(C J Dyall)*; [Adelaide Rd] *Nellies Nob*: Downstairs bar with bare floorboards, wooden tables, chairs and pews and smaller upstairs bar with armchairs; Frog & Frigate beers (same company) as well as guest beers *(C J Dyall)*; [Park Rd, Fremantle] *Wellington Arms*: Worth the (short) walk from the city centre for this cosy pub with a wide range of beers *(Ben Wimpenny)*

Southsea [Eldon St; SZ6498], *Eldon Arms*: Very good beer and atmosphere, good food in small back restaurant; popular with polytechnic students *(Charles Turner)*

Sparsholt [SU4331], *Plough*: Comfortable lounge popular at lunchtime (including Sun) for consistently tasty food including good ploughman's and chicken in basket, well kept Flowers; children welcome *(Prof A N Black, John Calvert)*

St Mary Bourne [SU4250], *Coronation Arms*: Friendly village local with welcoming landlord and Marstons real ale *(BB)*

Steep [Church Rd; Petersfield–Alton, signposted Steep off A32 and A272; SU7425], *Cricketers*: Warm welcome in main bar with light panelling, brass rails, biscuit-coloured upholstery and green carpet; back bar has unusual rotating pool-table and darts – it may soon be a restaurant; busy at lunchtime for good food, particularly well kept Gales on handpump and decent malt whiskies; good service; piped music, garden; families welcome; handy for walkers – steeply wooded hangers, good views from Edward

Thomas Memorial *(HEG)*

Stockbridge [High St; SU3535], *Grosvenor*: Hotel with friendly bar service and good well served food; no piped music; bedrooms *(Roy McIsaac, BB)*

Stratfield Saye [SU6861], *New Inn*: Very friendly unspoilt pub with good choice of beers *(S Griffin)*

☆Stuckton [village signposted S of Fordingbridge, by A338/B3078 junction; SU1613], *Three Lions*: Pub-restaurant with wide choice of interesting and unusual food, good wines and well kept Halls Harvest, Ind Coope Burton and Wadworths 6X on handpump; the general feeling is that this is now best thought of as a restaurant rather than a pub – which is why we no longer include it as a main entry – but there is a neat and airy bar with lots of fresh flowers, and a good choice of lunchtime snacks (not Mon) *(P H F Hampson, P L Leonard, R Reid, Francis Morris, R C Watkins, LYM)*

Swanmore [Hill Grove – OS Sheet 185 reference 582161; SU5716], *Hunters*: Fast-food pub with wide choice of good value food from sandwiches to steaks; particularly liked by families with children *(Steve and Carolyn Harvey)* [Chapel Rd] *New Inn*: Cosy low-ceilinged bar with lots of bric-à-brac – it's had well kept Marstons and a wide choice of good value food, but the landlord who's been responsible for its success left in late summer 1988; pretty garden with play area *(Reports on the new regime please)*

Sway [SZ2798], *Hare & Hounds*: Well spaced tables in comfortable bar and lounge of agreeable New Forest pub at edge of village, with pleasant atmosphere, real ales, decent food and service, big garden and ample parking *(E G Parish, WHBM)*

Tangley [Tangley Bottom; towards the Chutes – OS Sheet 185 reference 326528; SU3252], *Cricketers Arms*: Has been popular as village local with good cricketing prints and fine fireplace in stylishly simple small original bar, and well kept Flowers Original and Whitbreads Strong Country on handpump; from late 1987 it's been under new licensees (who previously ran a modern London pub), and considerable developments afoot on the food side – so the character isn't the same *(LYM – more news please)*; *Fox*: Well kept ale, good moderately priced bar food, popular restaurant with pleasant ambience and a choice of wines that reflects the new licensees' keen interest in this *(Dr A Y Drummond, Wg Cdr R M Sparkes)*

Thruxton [just off A303 – village signposted from flyover (both these pubs are good long-journey breaks); SU2945], *George*: Very good varied lunchtime food, brisk service; pub in very pleasant village *(Mr and Mrs J Wilmore)*; *White Horse*: Useful food bar, good welcome and well kept beer in clean pub with sun-trap garden *(I Meredith)*

Totford [B3046 Basingstoke–Alresford;

SU5738], *Woolpack*: Pleasant and interesting pub in nice isolated spot with rambling, comfortable bar with nooks and corners; Gales and Palmers real ales, plain bar snacks, more interesting restaurant-style menu for full meals *(J and M Walsh)*

Twyford [High St; SU4724], *Phoenix*: Friendly pub with really good plain food, quick drinks service (including well kept beer), friendly busy licensee *(J L Oliver)*

☆ **Upham** [Shoe Lane; SU5320], *Brushmakers Arms*: Old, unspoilt pub decorated with brooms and brushes; pleasant, scrubbed tables, friendly service by new licensees, well kept Bass and Youngs, impressive range of malt whiskies, proper coffee and good food in spacious new wing; said to be haunted *(Tim Powell, JKW, Mrs J Fellowes)*

Upton [the one near Hurstbourne Tarrant; SU3555], *Crown*: Spick-and-span comfortable country pub with flock wallpaper, dolls and china collection, home-cooked bar food and well kept Gibbs Mew ales; piped music *(BB)*

Upton Grey [SU6948], *Hoddington Arms*: Traditional local with good log fire, friendly welcome, good value home cooking – especially fish, brought fresh from Portsmouth each Thurs; restaurant area may spill over into bar on busy evening – booking advised Fri and Sat *(Mary Redgate)*

Wallington [Wallington Shore Road (nr M27 junction 11); SU5806], *Cobb & Pen*: Reasonably priced good food from extensive menu, in generous helpings, and well kept real ale; plain but comfortable place with a very relaxed atmosphere, big garden with some shade *(Gwilym and Joey Jones)*

Warnford [A32; SU6223], *George & Falcon*: Very popular locally for its generous helpings of good food; Huntsman Dorchester, Dorset and Royal Oak on handpump; hard to find parking space on Sat evening *(KIH)*

Warsash [Fleet End Road – OS Sheet 196 reference 509062; SU4906], *Jolly Farmer*: Friendly landlord, well kept beer and wide choice of food in olde-worlde place with ancient farming tools hanging from beams; outside seating surrounded by flowers in the front, huge adventure playground behind *(J A Hawson)*; *Rising Sun*: Two-storey Whitbreads pub overlooking river, with best views upstairs; bright décor, well kept beer, wide range of bar food *(Gwen and Peter Andrews, SJC)*

Waterlooville [London Road (Old A3); SU6809], *Wellington*: Enlarged to include adjacent church hall, with good décor, well kept Bass on handpump, good bar food, unobtrusive juke box; use nearby large public car park *(Keith Houlgate)*

☆ **Well** [from A31 best approach is through Froyle – OS Sheet 186 reference 761467; SU7646], *Chequers*: Character low-beamed bar with antique settles, comfortable country seats, snug alcoves and log fires; formerly

very popular for authentic French food and wines, but the French licensee sold his lease in 1987; news of the new regime, please – which we hear is friendly, not significantly changing the interior, and serving well kept Whitbreads and other ales; children in front conservatory *(Phil and Sally Gorton, Gary Wilkes, Dr John Innes, LYM)*

West End [High St; SU4614], *Sportsman*: Recently modernised pub with friendly staff and nice food; particularly good facilities for children *(Joseph Figueira)*

☆ **West Meon** [SU6424], *Thomas Lord*: Friendly licensee in attractive village local with very good reasonably priced food from sensibly short menu; Flowers and Whitbreads Strong Country real ales, cricketing theme *(KIH, C D Kinloch, Mr and Mrs Whatley, Mr and Mrs C Knight)*

West Wellow [nr M27 junction 2, on A36 2 miles N of junction with A431; SU2919], *Red Rover*: Good range of real ales and food *(K R Harris)*

Weyhill [A303; SU3146], *Weyhill Fair*: Lively local popular for its changing choice of well kept real ales and swiftly served good value food; easy chairs around wood-burner, other solid furnishings, prints of stamp designs, old advertisements and poster for eponymous fair; pleasant atmosphere, friendly speedy service, good food and excellent changing choice of beers *(B H Pinsent, BB)*

Wherwell [OS Sheet 185 reference 390410; SU3941], *White Horse*: Good food including some imaginative specials in well kept Whitbreads pub, in picturesque village near though not on the River Test; licensees previously made the Royal Oak at Langstone popular *(WHBM)*

Whitchurch [Bell St; SU4648], *Bell*: Friendly pub with basic, brightly lit bar, large open fire in nice back lounge bar, and steps up to attractive beamed room *(Gordon and Daphne)*;

Whitchurch [SU4648], *Red House*: Ancient flagstones under heavy beams by inglenook fireplace, simple bar food, well kept Halls Harvest and Ind Coope Burton, very friendly staff, games and juke box in saloon, sheltered seats outside; children in eating area and saloon *(Gary, LYM)* *White Hart*: Fine family-run local, food excellent especially the family Sun lunch; big following for trad jazz first Fri in month *(Mr and Mrs J G Simpson)*

Whitsbury [SU1219], *Cartwheel*: Good atmosphere and food in remote village pub with horseracing connections; free house, at start of GWG37 *(R H Inns)*

Wickham [Wickham Sq; SU5711], *Kings Head*: Gales ales and over 130 whiskies in two main bars, with an extra one behind by the skittle alley; good bar food – not many tables, so get there early *(Keith Houlgate)*; [Station Rd] *White Lion*: Warm and friendly atmosphere behind Victorian exterior, good food from sandwiches and super soup to hot dishes such as home-made pie served with lots of vegetables *(J A Barker)*

Wildhern [Charlton Down; SU3550], *Hare & Hounds*: Rather isolated one-bar regulars' pub with predominantly Greek food in dining-room – kavouras, moussaka and sofritto recommended *(Anon)*

☆ **Winchester** [off 22 High St (down passage to right of Barclays Bank); SU4829], *Bakers Arms*: Off the tourist beat, full of regulars with their dogs, lots of stuffed fish on one wall; interesting menu with pizzas, burgers and ploughman's (lack of puddings), Gales HSB, Websters Yorkshire; fruit machines all down one end of the bar, tables out in the alley; warm friendly atmosphere, helpful staff *(Alison Hayward, RAB, R E White)*

☆ **Winchester** [The Square; between High St and cathedral], *Eclipse*: Picturesque partly fourteenth-century pub with heavy beams, timbers and oak settles, very handy for the cathedral; new licensees keep their Whitbreads Strong Country and Pompey Royal well, but we've yet to have readers' approval for their new food – views please *(D L Johnson, Dr John Innes, A J V Baker, LYM)*

Winchester [Wharf Hill; from bottom of High St follow road round to right signposted Southampton, Portsmouth, then take first right turn], *Black Boy*: Has been popular for wide range of real ales including interesting guest beers, and generous helpings of usual bar food at lunchtime, with good juke box making it lively in the evening; bays of button-back banquettes in main L-shaped bar, separate rustic barn bar open busy evenings, seats outside; some suggestion end 1987/early 1988 that it was not on top form, though seemed to be recovering by summer 1988 – news please *(Heather Martin, LYM)*; [34 The Square] *Old Market*: Good food and drink promptly served in pleasant Whitbreads corner pub

with soft piped music; handy for cathedral *(LYM)*; [Little Great Minster St] *Old Vine*: Quite smart Courage pub, convenient for cathedral – gets crowded with tourists *(Alison Hayward)*; [14 Bridge St; continuation of High St, over river] *Rising Sun*: Friendly split-level low-beamed bar in timber-framed Tudor pub whose cellar was once a jail; generous helpings of food including steak pie, basket meals and T-bone steak, well kept Courage Best and Directors, games-room with two pool-tables; has its own football team; one bedroom *(BKA, Dr and Mrs A K Clarke, Mark Walpole)*; [St Peters St] *Royal*: Up-market hotel bar and lounge, very relaxing after major refurbishment, good lunchtime bar food, spacious walled garden; bedrooms *(Keith Garley)*; [Royal Oak Passage (off pedestrian part of High St)] *Royal Oak*: Olde-worlde furniture in brick and panelled bar, Flowers and Wadworths 6X, small stage for live music three nights a week (otherwise piped music), busy with young people at lunchtime and often packed with them at night, fruit machines; the special feature is the no-smoking cellar bar, sadly often closed in the evening, with massive twelfth-century beams – and a Saxon wall which gives it some claim to be the country's oldest drinking spot *(Alison Hayward, Mark Walpole, LYM)*; [The Square] *Spys*: Decent beer, lovely view of cathedral, comfortable bar downstairs *(Tim Powell)*

Winchfield [Vale Farm; SU7654], *Plane Tree Barn*: Tastefully furnished balconied and high-beamed barn of a farmhouse, at the end of a long drive among fields; good food, choice of real ale, open fire, not too loud video juke box; own trout lake and club *(Gary Wilkes)*

Woodgreen [OS Sheet 184 reference 171176; SU1717], *Horse & Groom*: Pleasant, cosily refurbished pub with food served in new eating area off lounge bar; real ale *(Phil and Sally Gorton)*

Hereford & Worcester

Several changes in the area include new licensees for the White Hart at Aston Crews (the new landlord already owns places in Gloucester and Tenbury Wells; he's keeping on the same staff), the idiosyncratic Little Pack Horse in Bewdley (little evident change – apart from the new children's sweetie-box), the Green Dragon at Bishops Frome (as popular as ever with readers; the new people have grafted on an extension that fits in well), the charming Cottage of Content at Carey and (sadly no longer brewing its own beer) the Swan in Upton upon Severn. Improvements elsewhere include the integration of the adjacent pretty cafe-restaurant (previously owned and run separately) with the Hope & Anchor by the river in Ross on Wye, the careful refurbishment of the riverside bar at the Swan in Upton upon Severn and the restoration of the previously hidden inglenook fireplace in the Anchor at Wyre Piddle (its waterside garden is floodlit now, too). Among entirely new entries, perhaps the most unusual is the Monkey House outside Defford – licensed only to sell cider, and scarcely recognisable as a pub. If that's carrying traditionalism almost too far for comfort, the Three Kings at Hanley Castle is a fine choice for the discerning yet comfort-minded traditionalist, while the cosily modernised Fox & Hounds in Bredon goes one step further up the comfort ladder (with good food, too). A high proportion of the pubs we list as main entries here are extra-special by any standard: the elegant and superior old Lygon Arms in Broadway, the charmingly furnished Loughpool at Sellack, the Butchers Arms out in the country below Woolhope, the ancient Rhydspence on the Welsh border at Whitney on Wye, and above all the

The Cottage of Content, Carey

Fleece in Bretforton – a remarkable old place, full of antiques, and one of Britain's top three pubs. In the Lucky Dip section at the end of the chapter, ones to note particularly include the Gate at Bournheath, the March Hare at Broughton Hackett, the Pandy at Dorstone, the Broad Oak at Garway, the Swan in the Herefordshire Kington, the Feathers at Ledbury, the Royal George at Lyonshall, the Boot at Orleton and the Ancient Camp at Ruckhall.

ASTON CREWS   SO6723   Map 4
White Hart
Off B4222; village signposted off A40 at Lea

Early reports suggest that this hilltop village pub has survived a second change of ownership in as many years, keeping its previous friendly and attentive staff and attractive layout. There are easy chairs and a long built-in upholstered settle in the low-beamed sloping main bar, which is dominated by an enormously wide stone fireplace with a log-effect gas fire; two small rooms lead off, one much like the main bar, another with green-cushioned settles back to back around tables. As we went to press the kitchen was being altered, so the menu may well expand; at present it includes home-made dishes like lasagne and steak and kidney or lamb and apricot pie (£2.95). Banks's Bitter and Wadworths 6X on handpump; darts, pool, shove-ha'penny, dominoes, table skittles, cribbage, fruit machine, piped music. Rustic tables shelter in a little sunken court outside, with more tables in a pretty garden. *(Recommended by Mr and Mrs Wyatt, Patrick Freeman, Roy and Pamela Wade; more reports on the new regime please)*

Free house   Licensee Trevor Bufton   Real ale   Meals and snacks   Restaurant tel Lea (098 981) 203   Children in restaurant   Open 10.30–3, 6–11 all year

BEWDLEY   SO7875   Map 4
Little Pack Horse ★
High Street; no nearby parking – best to park in main car park, cross A4117 Cleobury road, and keep walking on down narrowing High Street

The most straightforwardly pubby of Mr O'Rourke's small new chain of normally more eccentric Little pubs, this is to our mind also the best. It's the epitome of an old-fashioned traditional pub: low black beams, small rooms, lots of old photographs, advertisements, clocks and wood-working tools on the roughly plastered white walls, pews, red leatherette wall settles and a mixed bag of tables on the red-tiled floor, transfer-printed china pub's tankards hanging above the bar counter, a wood-burning stove, and above all a fine atmosphere, carefree and amiably chatty. Good value bar food includes sandwiches (from £1, weekdays only), soup (£1.05), filled baked potatoes (from £1.90), vegetarian samosa (£2.15), quiches (from £2.50), prawns (half-pint £2.65), lasagne or omelettes (£2.75), the daunting but very popular Desperate Dan pie (£3.25) and eight-ounce sirloin steak (£5.50). Well kept Ind Coope Burton on handpump, and the good value Lumphammer ale that's brewed for the chain; darts, dominoes and a fruit machine in the end room, as well as an idiosyncratic game that involves using a weighted string to knock a coin off the ear or snout of a wall-mounted wooden pig's mask. Dogs allowed (Pepper the good-natured alsatian cross who seems to think he lives there is actually just a visitor). The new licensee keeps a special sweet-box for children. The mosaic wall of the entrance corridor is interesting, and this quiet riverside town is full of attractive buildings. *(Recommended by Dave Braisted, David Burrows, Gordon and Daphne, Rob and Gill Weeks, E J Alcock, Dr Iain McColl, Paul Denham, J M Steward, Miss E L Rogers)*

Free house   Licensee Peter L D'Amery   Real ale   Meals and snacks   Children very welcome Live entertainment Tues evening   Open 11–11 all year

BISHOPS FROME SO6648 Map 4

Green Dragon ★ ⊗

This cosy and cheerful pub, under welcoming new licensees, has a traditionally furnished bar, with heavy sway-backed beams, old pews, settles and high-backed chairs on its polished flagstones and red tiles, and a big log fire; benches are built into the walls below electric coach-lamps, and the clock over the bar has as its face a section of tree-trunk; piped music. There's an impressive range of real ales: Courage Directors, Fullers ESB, Hook Norton and Old Hookey, Robinsons and Old Tom, Ruddles Best, Theakstons Best and Old Peculier, and Timothy Taylors Bitter and Landlord. Bar food includes sandwiches (from £1, steak £2.60), eight or nine starters (from around £1), ploughman's (£1.85), omelettes (from £2.40), salads and hot dishes from burgers (£1.50) through curries (£3.25) to steaks (£7.95). A new extension has a pool-table and darts; also dominoes, cribbage, pinball, fruit machine and space game. There are a few tables on a small raised side lawn, with herbaceous borders and apple trees. *(Recommended by Jason Caulkin, Gordon and Daphne, Alan and Audrey Chatting, Tom Rhys, PADEMLUC, David Gittins, HRH)*

Free house   Licensees John and Anna Maria Pinto   Real ale   Meals and snacks   Restaurant tel Munderfield (088 53) 607   Children in restaurant   Open 12ish–2.30, 6.30–11 (all day Sat) all year

BREDON SO9236 Map 4

Fox & Hounds ⊗

4½ miles from M5 junction 9; A438 to Northway, left at B4079, then in Bredon follow To church and river signpost on right

Neatly thatched and prettily decorated with hanging baskets, this friendly pub has quite a spacious lounge bar with dark red plush cushioned dining-chairs around its well polished mahogany or cast-iron-framed tables, carpet on flagstones, stripped oak beams and timbers, and etched glass swan's-neck wall lamps. The side bar has red leatherette wall seats, with more in its inglenook. Popular bar food includes ploughman's (from £2.25), savoury mushrooms (£2.65), a half-pint of prawns, chicken or cottage pie (£2.95), chilli con carne (£3.25) and smoked haddock (£3.65), or anything from the wide choice of restaurant dishes – steak and kidney pie (£3.65), say, pigeon braised in port (£5.50 – two for £6.75), or steak with Stilton sauce (£7.95); puddings are good. There's a popular Sunday lunch (£7.75, children £4.95). Well kept Flowers IPA and Original and maybe a guest beer on handpump; prompt service; piped music, darts, dominoes, cribbage, fruit machine, trivia machine and a quoits board. There are picnic-table sets, some under Perspex, in a side garden with a barbecue and thatched Wendy house. Dogs allowed. *(Recommended by Robert and Vicky Tod, Lyn and Bill Capper, PADEMLUC, M E A Horler)*

Flowers (Whitbreads)   Licensee Michael Hardwick   Real ale   Meals and snacks (not Sat or Sun evenings)   Restaurant   Children welcome   Open 11–11 at least for trial period, all year   Two bedrooms across road tel Bredon (0682) 72377; £17.50/£25

BRETFORTON SP0943 Map 4

Fleece ★ ★ ★

B4035 E of Evesham: turn S off this road into village; pub is in centre square by church; there's a sizeable car park at one side of the church

Until 1977, when it was bequeathed to the National Trust, this charming antique of a pub had belonged to the same family for centuries, and all of the furnishings are original, many of them heirlooms, such as the great oak dresser in the back parlour, holding a virtually priceless forty-eight-piece set of Stuart pewter trenchers; other furnishings here include a curved high-backed settle with drawers below, a rocking-chair and an inglenook fireplace with a deeply polished chimney beam and a rack of heavy pointed iron shafts, probably for spit-roasting. The main room has another curved high-backed settle where the long-standing regulars still warm themselves at the big log fire, if they're not sitting on the old wooden chairs snugged into its inglenook fireplace. There are massive beams and exposed timbers, worn and crazed flagstones (scored with marks to keep out demons), and many more antiques, such as the huge cheese-press weighted by a great cube of stone. An interesting leaflet sold here explains the uses of the more esoteric objects. It's perhaps because of its genuine place in antiquity that it manages to preserve such an unspoilt character, despite being visited by so many people. In summer the extensive grounds help to take off the pressure, of course, with plenty of seats on the goat-cropped grass which spreads around a splendidly restored thatched and timbered barn and among fruit trees (some strung prettily with fairy lights); there are more at the front by a stone pump-trough. They have barbecues out here, and on the first weekend in July a Friday-to-Sunday festival with bands, a children's bouncing castle, pony rides and up to thirty real ales. Simple food includes sandwiches (from 80p), ploughman's (from £1.90), chilli con carne or Gloucester sausages (£2.20), home-cured ham (£2.60), steak and kidney pie (£2.95) and locally cured gammon (£3.75). It's ordered from a hatch and served pleasantly – and usually quickly, though they warn of delays at busy times. Well kept Hook Norton Best, M&B Brew XI, Uley Pigs Ear and a guest beer often from a small independent brewer on handpump, and a choice of farm ciders and country wines, with mulled wine or hot toddy in winter, and a chilled punch in summer; darts, dominoes, cribbage, shove-ha'penny and quoits. On the Sunday before the Spring Bank Holiday Monday they hold an auction of the choicest local asparagus, with proceeds to the village Silver Band – who play throughout the evening. On the Bank Holiday itself morris men perform at lunchtime, and there are quite a few other occasional events. When Lola Tappin, who had run the pub single-handedly since the war, bequeathed it to the National Trust, she stipulated that no crisps, peanuts and so forth should be sold. (*Recommended by Dennis Jones, Jason Caulkin, Martin and Debbie Chester, Andrew Ludlow, Aubrey and Margaret Saunders, WHBM, Bernard Phillips, Wayne Brindle, Laurence Manning, A Royle, PADEMLUC, G Bloxsom, S and S PH, Nick Dowson, Gill and Ted George, Gill and Rob Weeks, Leith Stuart, Rita Horridge, Alan Mosley, A Royle, Peter Hitchcock, S V Bishop, George Jonas, Jon Wainwright, Tim Locke, C Elliott*)

Free house   Licensees Dan and Nora Davies   Real ale   Meals and snacks   Children in both inglenook rooms   Open 11–11; may close afternoons in winter

BROADWAY   SP0937 Map 4
Lygon Arms ⊗ 🏠
A44

This is admittedly not a true pub – it's an extremely smart hotel owned by the Savoy group, with prices to match. Yet it preserves so many of the best virtues of a traditional inn, and is such a splendidly handsome old place, that it would be a shame to miss it. For us, of course, the excuse for including it is the civilised cocktail bar – the sort of place where barmen remember you after just one visit, and do mix proper cocktails. In here they now serve snacks including an excellent ploughman's at lunchtime – but don't expect much change from £10 for a couple of beers and a plate of sandwiches. It has handsome oak panelling and partly bared stone walls, a collection of antique drinking-glasses and wine jugs, and backgammon and chess on hand. Among the many other rooms which ramble through this historic house is a cosy beamed lounge with easy chairs in front of the massive inglenook fireplace; it used to be the kitchen. An adjoining wine bar, Goblets, serves imaginative food, and sandwiches are available all day in the lounges. In summer you can sit in the courtyard, surrounded by trees and shrubs, and the neatly kept hotel gardens are very attractive. *(Recommended by Mr and Mrs W H Crowther, M A and C R Starling, Peter Hitchcock, Mrs G K Herbert, Brian and Rosemary Wilmot)*

Free house Licensee Kirk Ritchie Meals and snacks Restaurant Children welcome exc in bar Open 11–11; 10.30–2, 6–10.30 in winter Bedrooms tel Broadway (0386) 852255; £70B/£105B

CAREY SO5631 Map 4
Cottage of Content [illustrated on page 339]
Village, and for most of the way pub itself, signposted from good road through Hoarwithy

New licensees have won readers' praise for maintaining the cosy charm of this truly cottagey little medieval inn. The dark-beamed and partly panelled lounge bar has comfortable leather seats, an antique settle in one alcove, wooden benches built into its timbered panelled walls, rugs on the bare boards, and fresh flowers and plants. There's another antique settle in an alcove on the way through to the public bar, which has a winged high-backed settle in one snug corner, and some more conventional seats. Bar food includes soup (£1), sandwiches (from £1), mussels in garlic butter (£1.85), ploughman's (from £1.85), and hot dishes such as plaice (£2.50), lasagne (£2.85), scampi or pie of the day (£3.50) and ten-ounce rump steak (£6.75), though not all the dishes listed on the blackboard menu may be available. Well kept Hook Norton Best and Old Hookey, Marstons Pedigree and Border Mild and Wethereds on handpump, with fine farm ciders including Stourford Press; darts, dominoes, cribbage and a fruit machine in the public bar. Tables on a back terrace look up to a steep expanse of lawn beyond a rock wall, and there are a couple more on the flower-filled front terrace, facing the very quiet village lane. *(Recommended by M D Hare, M A and W R Proctor, Patrick Freeman, Richard Gibbs, Jason Caulkin, John Hill, Gordon and Daphne, Col G D Stafford, RH, John Estdale, A P Hudson; more reports on the new regime please)*

Free house Licensees M J Wainford and G T Johns Real ale Meals and snacks Restaurant Children welcome Open 11.30–2.30, 6.30 (6 Sat)–11; opens 7 in winter Bedrooms tel Carey (043 270) 242; £22.50B/£30B

DEFFORD SO9143 Map 4
Monkey House
Woodmancote; A4104 towards Upton – immediately after passing Oak public house on right, there's a small group of cottages, of which this is the last

Quite unmarked by any inn-sign, this is a really traditional cider house. It's only once you start walking up the garden path that you see a board on the pretty little black and white thatched cottage saying that it's licensed to sell cider (and tobacco). There isn't even a bar. You stand outside a hatch while Bulmer's Medium or Special Dry tapped from wooden barrels is poured by jug into pottery mugs; it's very cheap. If it's too wet or cold to stay out among the hens and cockerels that wander in from the collection of caravans and sheds that they share with ponies and horses, there is a little raftered outbuilding with a couple of plain tables, a settle and an open fire. *(Recommended by Alan Mosley, Phil and Sally Gorton, Gill and Rob Weeks)*

Free house Licensee Graham Collins Open 11–2.30, 6–10.30 (11 Sat); closed Mon evening, Tues

---

Stars after the name of a pub show exceptional quality. One star means most people (after reading the report to see just why the star has been won) would think a special trip worth while. Two stars mean that the pub is really outstanding – one of just a handful in its region. The very very few with three stars are the real aristocrats – of their type, they could hardly be improved.

FOWNHOPE SO5834 Map 4
Green Man ⊗ 🛏
B4224

There's a decent range of bar food in this striking black and white Tudor inn, with home-made soup (£1), sandwiches (from 85p, including home-cooked beef with a generous salad), ploughman's (from £1.85), local chicken (£2.40), steak sandwich or home-cooked ham or beef salad (£2.45), lasagne (£2.75), trout with almonds (£3.65) and rump steak (£5.50); hot Sunday roasts. The impressive lounge bar has comfortable armchairs under its high oak beams, bench seats set into tall latticed windows, and cushioned settles against the timbered ochre walls, which are decorated with brasses and small pictures. It's named after Tom Spring, the champion bare-knuckle pugilist who was born in the village in 1795 – though it should really be called the Winter Bar as that was his real name, and it does have a fine log fire. A second bar, similar but smaller and named after the judges who used this as their Petty Sessions court, has darts, dominoes, cribbage and a fruit machine. Well kept Hook Norton Best, Marstons Pedigree and Sam Smiths OB on hand-pump; efficient service. In fine weather they serve morning coffee and afternoon tea as well as bar meals out on the big back lawn, which has robust benches and seats around slatted tables among trees and flower beds, and a play area. It's only half a mile from the River Wye, and was originally (in 1485) called the Naked Boy. Popular with village locals. (*Recommended by Patrick Freeman, Hope Chenhalls, Dr R Fuller, Elizabeth Lloyd, Mike Muston, John Blake, Dennis Jones, Gordon and Daphne, M A and W R Proctor, Gordon Leighton, Jane Thomas, E Kinnersly, John Innes*)

Free house   Licensees A F and M J Williams   Real ale   Meals and snacks   Two restaurants   Children in eating area and restaurant   Open 11–2.30, 6–11 all year Bedrooms tel Fownhope (043 277) 243; £26B/£34B

HANLEY CASTLE SO8442 Map 4
Three Kings
Pub signposted (not prominently) off B4211 opposite castle gates, N of Upton upon Severn

Facing a great cedar and close to the striking brick and stone church, this picturesque pub combines a quaint black and white half-timbered cottage with another faced in Georgian brick. As you go in there's a little tiled-floor bar on the right with a comfortable bow-window seat and a great built-in winged settle facing a cavernous inglenook fireplace, which has a case of stuffed birds over it; there's just a small serving-hatch. On the left, another small room with chairs around its wall, another bay-window seat and lots of small locomotive pictures has darts and cribbage, with pool in a room beyond. There's a separate entrance to the peaceful lounge bar, which has little leatherette armchairs and spindle-back chairs, another antique big winged settle, some timbering exposed, and a neatly blacked kitchen range. Good value bar food includes soup (50p), sandwiches (from 50p), omelettes (£1), ploughman's (from £1.25), pork chop or gammon and egg (£3.25) and hefty steaks (£6.75), with specials which may take quite a bit longer to prepare such as salmon en croûte; well kept and low-priced Butcombe, Theakstons and Wadworths 6X tapped from the cask, with a guest beer such as Smiles Best or Boddingtons Mild, and Weston's Old Rosie cider. The front terrace has old-fashioned wood and iron seats. (*Recommended by PADEMLUC, Gordon and Daphne, John Barker*)

Free house   Licensee George Roberts   Real ale   Meals and snacks   Children in side room Singing duo Sun evening   Open 11–2.30, 6–11 all year

---

Pubs shown as closing at 11 do so in the summer, but close earlier – normally 10.30 – in winter unless we specify 'all year'. Often, country pubs don't open as early as we say at quiet times of the year.

INKBERROW   SP0157 Map 4

Old Bull

A422 Worcester–Alcester; set well back down quiet side road, but visible from main road

This fine black and white Tudor timbered inn has been the model not only for the Bull at Ambridge, in the BBC *Archers* radio serial, but also (as readers with a keen eye may have noted) the front cover of the first edition of this *Guide*. There are plenty of Archers photographs and clippings on the timbered walls, and something of the rustic atmosphere you'd expect from the connection. The flagstoned lounge bar has been modified slightly of late, with the servery moved back to give more space; but the good atmosphere remains, and there are partly stripped stone walls, old-fashioned settles, rustic chairs, big log fires in huge inglenooks at each end, a high-raftered pitched ceiling (with posthorns and copper kettles decorating the cross-beams – they no longer need the swinging bale of hay that kept the air sweet in smokier days) and regimental crests. Home-made bar food includes filled rolls (£1), ploughman's (£1.95), bacon, sausage and egg or chilli con carne (£1.75), smoked trout fillets and salad, omelettes or lasagne (£2.25), beef curry (£2.65), and steak and kidney pie, prawn stir-fry or gammon and egg (£2.95); afternoon teas. Well kept Flowers IPA and Original on handpump, and lots of ciders; darts, cribbage and fruit machine. There are tables on a flagstoned terrace out by the great sheltering yew tree. (*Recommended by A Royle, Bernard Phillips, Dr J R Hamilton, PADEMLUC, Rob and Gill Weeks*)

Flowers (Whitbreads)   Licensee S G Pitcher   Real ale   Meals and snacks (lunchtime)
Children in eating area   Open 11–11 in summer, 10.30–2.30, 6–11 in winter

KIDDERMINSTER   SO8376 Map 4

Little Tumbling Sailor ⊗

Mill Street, which is signposted off ring road by A442 Bridgnorth exit – then fork right at General Hospital

With a pervading and very entertainingly executed maritime theme, this probably has the best food of any of the refreshing local chain of Little pubs (see our Bewdley entry for another, perhaps less eccentric, example). Charmingly served, and cooked visibly in a side kitchen, it includes filled baked potatoes (from £1.95), pâté or whitebait (£2), vegetarian dishes (from £2.10), omelettes (from £2.85), enterprising pies including a vegetarian one (from £2.75; the steak and kidney – the Desperate Dan – is big enough for two), trout or fresh plaice (£3.55), salmon (£3.75) and one-pound steak (£5.45). The pub meanders right the way around a central servery, with its navy-blue walls almost a solid mass of ship pictures, including a fine collection of naval photographs (each ship carrying the relevant sailor's hat riband). There are plenty of cast-iron-framed tables (the tops given appropriate pokerwork emblems) with red and blue leatherette seats. Any gap in the pictures, and most of the ceiling, is filled with nautical bric-à-brac – ships' badges, floats, hammocks, a risqué figurehead, brassware, ships in and out of bottles, rope fancywork. Outside, there's even a mock-up of a lighthouse, in the little sheltered garden which for children has a trawler's deckhouse and a beached whaler (called *Lucia and Mapp*). Well kept Ansells Mild, Ind Coope Burton and the chain's own Lumphammer on handpump, a good range of rums, fruit machine, trivia machine, piped pop music. They sell their own pink seaside rock. (*Recommended by P J Hanson, Dave Braisted, E J Alcock, Rob and Gill Weeks*)

Free house   Licensee F Trick   Real ale   Meals and snacks   Children welcome   Music night
Mon (from '50s and '60s to folk and Irish)   Open 11–2.30, 6–10.30; closed evening 25 Dec

---

If you have to cancel a reservation for a bedroom or restaurant, please telephone or write to warn them. A small place – and its customers – will suffer if you don't.

KNIGHTWICK   SO7355   Map 4
Talbot ⊗ 🛏
Knightsford Bridge; B4197 just off A44 Worcester–Bromyard

This fourteenth-century inn has an uncommonly enterprising range of food (the same as is served in the small restaurant), including sandwiches, pheasant eggs Florentine (£1.95), carrot and gammon pâté (£2.25), vegetarian dishes like mild-curried beans with coconut cream (£2.75) or mushroom Stroganoff (£3.50), and liver and bacon (£3.95), honey-cured chicken salad (£4.25), chicken and coriander pie or sweetbreads gratiné (£4.50), lemon sole in prawn sauce (£5.50), duck in pepper sauce or monkfish and lemon cream (£6.25), guinea-fowl (£6.50) and salmon steak hollandaise (£6.75); puddings like orange and cashewnut ice-cream or baked rum banana (£1.50). Charmingly placed by the old bridge over the River Teme, it has a spacious civilised lounge with a large central stone fireplace – containing a truly enormous wood-burning stove. There are very heavy black beams, humorous Cecil Aldin coaching prints and *Jorrocks* paintings by John Leech on the butter-coloured walls, and seats of considerable character, including winged settles in the bow windows that look out to the humpy wooded hills. The well furnished back public bar has darts, pool on a raised side area, fruit machine, space game and juke box; well kept Banks's, Bass and Flowers IPA and Original on handpump; well behaved dogs welcome. There are some old-fashioned seats outside, in front, with more on a spacious lawn over the lane (they serve out here too). *(Recommended by PADEMLUC, Dave Braisted, M A and W R Proctor, Verney and Denis Baddeley, Jill and George Hadfield, Dr John Innes, Dave and Valerie Hooley, Tony Gayfer, John Barker, Gordon Leighton, Joy Heatherley, PLC)*

Free house   Licensee Derek Hiles   Real ale   Meals and snacks (limited Sun evening) Restaurant   Children welcome if well behaved   Open 10.30–2.30, 6–11 all year Bedrooms tel Knightwick (0886) 21235; £16(£18.50B)/£27.50(£37B)

OMBERSLEY   SO8463   Map 4
Crown & Sandys Arms ⊗
It may save time searching to know that, coming into the village from the A433, you turn left at the roundabout, into the 'Dead End' road

It's chiefly the food that attracts readers to this pretty Dutch-gabled white house; home made, it includes soup (£1), sandwiches (from £1, dressed crab £1.85), ploughman's (from £1.85), several starters like chicken liver pâté (£1.60), quiche (£3.25), chilli con carne (£3.45), daily specials, with two or three vegetarian ones, steak and kidney pie (£3.85), gammon (£4.50) and ten-ounce local sirloin steak (£6.75), with children's dishes (£1.25); very good puddings; they can arrange special restaurant menus for parties. The black-beamed bar has brocade-cushioned Windsor armchairs and settles and plush built-in wall seats on the carpet over its dark flagstones, and old prints and maps on its timbered walls. There are a couple of easy chairs with a high-backed traditional settle in a cosy alcove by the inglenook fireplace, which has the royal arms on its impressive iron fireback. Well kept Hook Norton Best and a range of guest beers like Adnams, Badger Tanglefoot, Bass and Hook Norton Old Hookey on handpump; friendly service, coping calmly even at busy times; dominoes, cribbage. The garden has picnic-table sets looking up to the sheep-cropped slopes behind. There is an antique shop and picture framer's in the back stables – Tuesday, Friday and Saturday. *(Recommended by Mr and Mrs W H Crowther, Frank Cummins, T H G Lewis, Dr John Innes, Mrs Z A Fraser, David and Ruth Hollands, A Royle, Mike Tucker, GB, Dr and Mrs M Rayner, PLC)*

Free house   Licensee R E Ransome   Real ale   Meals and snacks   Restaurant tel Worcester (0905) 620252   Well behaved children (not in prams or push-chairs) until 8 in eating area and restaurant   Open 11–2.30, 6–11 all year; closed 25 Dec

Kings Arms ⊗

The wide choice of enterprising home-made bar food in this comfortable, rambling Tudor pub includes sandwiches (from £1, lunchtime), soup (£1), pâtés including a vegetarian one (£2.10–£2.65), and main dishes like salad (from £1.95; cold meat £3.95), fish kedgeree (£3.45), macaroni cheese with walnuts, peppers, tomatoes and onions (£3.65), steak and kidney pie or beef chowder (£3.75), crab and asparagus quiche (£4.25), seafood crumble (£4.75), and sirloin steak (£5.95), with quite a few puddings (£1.10); fast and friendly service. The black-beamed, timbered and quarry-tile-floored bar has cosy corners – one with a polished brick inglenook fireplace, and smaller nooks and crannies decorated with stuffed animals and birds, rustic yokes and pots; two open fires. One room has Charles II's coat of arms moulded into its decorated plaster ceiling (this is reputed to have been his first stop, fleeing after the Battle of Worcester). Bass on handpump; no dogs. There are tables under cocktail parasols in an attractive courtyard sheltered by yew, laurel and ash trees. *(Recommended by M A and W R Proctor, David and Ruth Hollands, J Keppy, Graham and Glenis Watkins, Chris Cooke, Pamela and Merlyn Horswell, Dr and Mrs John Deller, Robert and Vicky Tod, PADEMLUC, Quentin Williamson, Elaine Kellet, Frank Cummins, PLC)*

Mitchells & Butlers (Bass)   Licensees Chris and Judy Blundell   Real ale   Meals and snacks   Children over six in eating area, up to 8   Open 11–2.30 (3 Sat), 6–11 all year

PEMBRIDGE   SO3958 Map 6

New Inn

Market Square; A44

The massive stones below the black and white timbered walls of this inn date back some seven hundred years, and it used to house the Petty Sessions court and jail. Inside is warm, cosy and friendly, with heavy ceiling beams, timber-framed walls, ancient latch doors and worn flagstones in front of the big log fire, with a curved settle said to have come originally from a cockfighting pit. Tables on the cobbles behind look across to a charming little open-stage sixteenth-century wool market. Bar food includes sandwiches, garlic mushrooms, pitta bread filled with garlicky minced lamb, herring in oatmeal, crunchy aubergines, filled pancakes, home-made pies, pork fillet in cider and apples, and puddings. Flowers IPA and Original and a guest beer on handpump, under light top pressure, and farm cider; darts, shove-ha'penny, dominoes, cribbage and quoits. The delightful black and white town has an unusual fourteenth-century detached bell tower by the church. The licensee is the sister-in-law of the licensee at one of our Somerset entries, the Notley Arms at Monksilver. *(Recommended by Alan and Audrey Chatting, Elizabeth Lloyd, PLC, JAH, Mike Suddards, C P Scott-Malden; more reports please, particularly on the food)*

Whitbreads   Licensee Jane Melvin   Real ale   Meals and snacks   Evening restaurant Children in eating area   Open 11–5, 6–11; closed afternoons in winter Bedrooms tel Pembridge (054 47) 427; £12/£24

ROSS ON WYE   SO6024 Map 4

Hope & Anchor

Riverside; entering town from A40 W side, first left turn after bridge

Included chiefly for its fine riverside position, with prettily planted lawns, this cheery pub's main downstairs bar has recently been refurbished; it still has its boating theme, with photographs of river life on the Wye at the turn of the century, and boat paraphernalia, as well as a good coal fire, built-in wall seats, some varnished panelling, and arches separating the various areas – including a small but airy extension. The upstairs bar is a pleasant pastiche of an old parlour, with comfortable armchairs and old church pews, Victorian prints on the walls, and an old mahogany shop counter as the serving-bar. The little dining-room that it leads to is decorated in Victorian style too, with a period open fireplace, more pews and dark captain's chairs, long Jacquard curtains, shell lamps and shelves of books and bric-à-brac. Bar food includes soup (£1.45), basket meals (from £2.20), ploughman's (£2.75), vegetable lasagne (£3.75), beef and Guinness pie (£4.20) and smoked haddock pasta with prawns and mushrooms (£4.30). Well kept M&B Springfield and Marstons Pedigree on handpump; darts and fruit machine. There's a quite separate conservatory-style restaurant, with a downstairs wine bar, and marble and cast-iron tables, herringbone pavers, pale beams and a cast-iron staircase. *(Recommended by Wayne Brindle, Byrne Sherwood, R W Clifford, SJC)*

Free house Licensee John Gardner Real ale Meals and snacks Parlour restaurant tel Ross on Wye (0989) 63003; Conservatory restaurant tel 66184 Children in eating area Silver band Sun evening mid-May–Aug Open 11–3 (4 Sat), 6–11 all year

SELLACK SO5627 Map 4

Loughpool ★ ⊗

Back road Hoarwithy–Ross on Wye; OS Sheet 162 reference 558268

Remote though it is, this beautifully placed black and white cottage attracts a great many warmly favourable reports from readers – though it can get busy, the licensees are so attentive that service is always quick and smooth. A particularly appealing point is the way that the food they serve embraces both simple pubby tastes and more exacting palates, including home-made soup (£1.25), pâté (from £1.45), sausage and chips (£2.50), scampi and bacon in a white wine sauce with a crumble topping or chicken (£2.75), chilli con carne (£3.25), curried vegetable risotto or pasta with ham and garlic cheese (£3.75), seafood lasagne (£5.05) and trout with lemon butter (£5.50); flavours often reflect the use of uncommon herbs and spices. The beamed and largely flagstoned central room has a log fire at each end, cushioned window seats and kitchen chairs around plain wooden tables, sporting prints on the cream walls, and traditional air sweeteners – hanging bunches of dried flowers, hay and hops. Other rooms lead off, with attractive individual furnishings and nice touches like the red-patterned plates on one wall dresser. Well kept M&B Springfield and Wye Valley Hereford on handpump. There are plenty of picnic-table sets around the great millstone on the well kept lawn in front. *(Recommended by Phil and Sally Gorton, Richard Gibbs, Miss J A Harvey, Graham and Glenis Watkins, Lynda Cantelo, Gordon and Daphne, E M Atkinson, Pamela and Merlyn Horswell, M W Barratt, GAC, MJC, PLC, PADEMLUC, Lyn and Bill Capper, B H Stamp, Harry Jackson, E Kinnersly, B Walton, Miss D A Thain, JHW)*

Free house Licensees Paul and Karen Whitford and June Fryer Meals and snacks Restaurant tel Harewood End (098 987) 236 Well behaved children in restaurant Open 12–2.30, 7–11.30 all year

UPTON UPON SEVERN SO8540 Map 4

Olde Anchor

High Street

Though the new licensees no longer brew this Severn-side pub's own beer, they serve well kept Ruddles County and Websters on handpump. The lively U-shaped carpeted bar in this sixteenth-century black and white timbered building has lots of sparkling copper and brass (including an unusual copper mantelpiece), old-fashioned settles and Windsor chairs around oak tables, old black timbers propping up its low ceiling, and timber-framed windows looking out on the street. There's an extensive range of reasonably priced bar food, with daily specials like cauliflower cheese (though we can't be more specific as the licensees haven't sent us up-to-date prices!); friendly service. Dominoes, cribbage, fruit machine, space game, piped music. There's an attractive summer servery on the back terrace. (*Recommended by Gordon and Daphne, P G Giddy, Gill and Rob Weeks, Alan Mosley, Mrs Jo Corbett, Col G D Stafford; more reports on the new regime please*)

Free house Real ale Meals and snacks Children in family-room Live music weekends Open 11–2.30, 6–11 all year

Swan

Riverside

Food is the chief attraction in this civilised and attractively restored seventeenth-century Severn-side pub. Served in the comfortable beamed lounge and a next-door food bar, it isn't cheap, but it is attractive, including smoked haddock in a cream and cheese sauce (£3.50), home-made lasagne (£3.75), baked trout or home-made quiche (£3.95), ham salad or home-made lamb and apricot pie (£4.25), home-cured gravadlax with mustard dill sauce or roast duckling (£4.95), king prawns in garlic butter (£5.25) and steaks (from sirloin with anchovies and capers, £5.95, to pan-fried fillet, £8.25). The recently refurbished riverside bar has fine views, as well as antique settles, easy chairs, sofas, Windsor chairs and a big open fire at one end. Well kept Butcombe and Wadworths 6X on handpump, and decent wines; piped music. There's waitress service to tables outside, and the pub has its own moorings by a lawn across the quiet lane. (*Recommended by J H C Peters, PADEMLUC, Alastair Lang, M A and W R Proctor, Col G D Stafford, Margaret and Douglas Tucker, Gill and Rob Weeks*)

Free house Licensees Peter and Sue Davies Real ale Meals and snacks (not Sat evening or Sun and Mon, and in evenings served in bistro instead tel Upton upon Severn (068 46) 2601 Open 11.30–2.30, 6.30–11 all year; closed Mon lunchtime exc bank hols

WEATHEROAK HILL   SP0674 Map 4
Coach & Horses

Between Alvechurch and Wythall: coming S on A435 from Wythall roundabout, filter off dual carriageway so as to turn right about 1 mile S, then in Weatheroak Hill village turn left towards Alvechurch

Generously served, simple and reasonably priced food in this out-of-the-way pub includes filled rolls (around 50p), soup (60p – or a large helping of main-course onion soup, £1.50), ploughman's (£1.40), home-made pies (£2.20), gammon (£2.40), lasagne, chilli con carne or moussaka (£2.70) and home-made fruit pies (£1.10). There's also a fine choice of real ales on handpump: Banks's Bitter, Davenports, Everards Old Original, Flowers, Holdens Mild and Special, Hook Norton Old Hookey and Sam Smiths. The two-level beamed and carpeted lounge is simply furnished with plush wall seats, chairs and stools; it's clean, airy and usually quiet – though it gets busy at weekends. The public bar has sensibly placed darts, dominoes, cribbage and a fruit machine (there's another in the lounge); maybe piped music. There's a big peaceful garden, with an assortment of elderly seats, and newer ones on a neat terrace. (*Recommended by Mr and Mrs W H Crowther, E J Alcock, Rob and Gill Weeks, Andor Gomme; more reports please*)

Free house Licensee Phil Meads Real ale Meals (not Sun, not Sat evening, until 8.30 other evenings) and snacks Children in eating area Open 11–11; may close afternoons in winter

WHITNEY ON WYE   SO2747 Map 6
Rhydspence ★ ⊗ ⟐

Pub signposted off A438 about 1½ miles W of Whitney

This is a striking ancient timbered building oozing character and atmosphere. It's a civilised, relaxed and pleasantly old-fashioned place, with old library chairs and cushioned benches built into the heavily timbered walls of the rambling beamed rooms, a fine big stone fireplace in the central bar, and magazines and newspapers set out on a table in the hall. Food is served at the same price in the bar and in a charmingly cottagey dining-room, and includes soup (£1.25), a good ploughman's with a relish of damsons and cloves (from £2.40), farmhouse sausages (£3.25), vegetarian dishes, Mediterranean prawns in garlic and white wine (£3.75), home-baked ham (£4.50), steak and kidney pie (£5.50), well hung local steaks (from £5.75 for five-ounce rump), spit-roast Norfolk duckling and good (and sometimes unusual) specials. Well kept Robinsons Best and Wem Best on handpump, and Dunkerton's farm cider; very friendly service. Darts, dominoes and cribbage; no dogs. The tables on the terraces outside and on the sloping lawn have a fine view of the Wye Valley and the hills beyond; the Welsh border follows the line of the little stream running past. *(Recommended by Doug Kennedy, Dennis Jones, Mr and Mrs W H Crowther, A Cook, Jonathan Williams, P and L Russell, Frank Cummins, Gordon and Daphne, Mrs Joan Harris, John Milroy, Mr and Mrs W Smurthwaite, PLC, Robert and Vicky Tod, Mrs Jo Corbett, Miss D A Thain, JAH)*

Free house   Licensees Peter and Pamela Glover   Real ale   Meals and snacks   Restaurant Children welcome (not evenings)   Open 11–2.30, 7–11 all year   Bedrooms tel Clifford (049 73) 262; £18B/£36B

WINFORTON   SO2947 Map 6
Sun ⊗

Mrs Hibbard does the cooking in this friendly and spotless pub, and, besides sandwiches, there's a decent choice of often original dishes such as devilled crab au gratin (£2.75), deep-fried Camembert with fruit coulis (£2.95), spicy pork casserole (£3.85), oxtail braised in cider (£4.70), guinea-fowl with walnuts, apples and a wine sauce (£5.20) and interesting puddings (£1.35). There are comfortable country chairs around individually chosen wooden tables, vases of fresh flowers, gleaming brass platters and horsebrasses (on the original harness), haycutters and other old farm tools on the walls (mainly stripped masonry), old beams and some wooden pillars, and a good wood-burning stove. Well kept Felinfoel and Wadworths 6X on handpump; sensibly placed darts, dominoes and table quoits. There's a good timbery children's play area in the nicely kept garden, with some tables in a sheltered area. *(Recommended by Alan and Audrey Chating, C R Cooke, D J Wallington, JAH)*

Free house   Licensees Brian and Wendy Hibbard   Real ale   Meals and snacks   Children in eating area   Open 11–2.30ish, 6.30–11 (though may open longer afternoons) all year; closed Tues Nov–May

WOOLHOPE   SO6136 Map 4
Butchers Arms ★ ⊗ ⇔

Signposted from B4224 in Fownhope; carry straight on past village

This delightful fourteenth-century inn is down a country lane through a gentle wood-rimmed valley, and has sliding French windows opening on to a charming terrace with wooden seats, roses, tubs of flowers and a rockery built around a millstone. Fields stretch away beyond the tiny stream which runs by, under willows, ash trees and poplars. Home cooking with good fresh ingredients includes lunchtime sandwiches (from £1), interesting home-made soups such as coconut (£1.25), ploughman's (from £1.95 – the apple and ginger chutney is home made, they pickle the onions each autumn, and cook their own smoked ham), vegetarian lasagne (£3.35), mushroom biriani, rabbit and bacon or steak and kidney pie (£3.75), salads (from £3.55), specials such as tuna pasta with mushrooms and cream (£3.35), evening grills (gammon £4.55, local rump steak from £6.55) and puddings such as damson and almond strudel (£1.35 – not Friday or Saturday evenings). The welcoming beamed twin bars have padded benches built into the walls, Windsor armchairs, log fires and old pictures and monochrome engravings (including ones of the pub); well kept Hook Norton Best and Old Hookey and Marstons Pedigree on handpump, local farm cider, Rombouts coffee; generous breakfasts; no dogs. It makes for a pleasant base from which to explore the Hereford countryside. *(Recommended by Mike Muston, J S Evans, M A and W R Proctor, Gordon Leighton, Mrs E M Lloyd, John Blake, Gordon and Daphne, Keith and Sheila Baxter, Andrew Green, JAH, Tony Dudley-Evans, Maggie Jo St John, Patrick Freeman, Rob and Gill Weeks, J H C Peters, Grahame Archer, Elisabeth Kemp, PLC, John Milroy, John Tyzack, John Innes, E Kinnersly, B Walton, P W Barratt)*

Free house   Licensees Mary Bailey and Bill Griffiths   Real ale   Meals and snacks   Restaurant (Weds–Sat evenings)   Children in bar (lunchtime only) and restaurant (when open)   Open 11.30–2.30, 6–11 all year; opens 7 in winter   Bedrooms tel Fownhope (0432 77) 281; £19.50/£31

WORCESTER   SO8555   Map 4
Farriers Arms ⊗

Fish Street; off pedestrian High Street, just N of cathedral

This most enjoyable town pub can get very busy, though in fine weather the outside terrace with its separate serving area is a great help. The welcoming seventeenth-century black-beamed lounge bar is decidedly snug, and has some attractive old seats among the copper-topped tables, and a grandfather clock carved with writhing lizards. Reasonably priced, attractive home-made food includes soup (75p), pasty (85p), hummus with hot pitta bread (£1), ploughman's (£1.50), a vegetarian dish such as leek, potato and tomato bake or brown rice nut risotto (from £1.50), lasagne, quiche, pizza or their own-recipe pies (£1.95p) and a daily special (from £1.85); puddings such as tipsy trifle (75p) and treacle tart flavoured with lemon and ginger (85p); well kept Courage Best and Directors on handpump. The simple rambling public bar has sensibly placed darts, shove-ha'penny, dominoes, cribbage, an old penny arcade machine (which works with 2p pieces), a fruit machine, trivia game and juke box; dogs allowed. The licensee sells (and signs) her book on pressed flowers here, and the pub is very handy for the cathedral. *(Recommended by Byrne Sherwood, W L Congreve, A Royle, C D T Spooner, Robert and Vicky Tod)*

Courage   Licensee Nona Pettersen   Real ale   Meals and snacks   Open 11–11; closed afternoons in winter exc Sat

WYRE PIDDLE   SO9647   Map 4
Anchor ⊗

B4084 NW of Evesham

The spacious steep lawn with flower-lined steps down to the River Avon, and peaceful fields stretching away opposite, is a particular summer attraction in this relaxing seventeenth-century pub. The view takes in the Vale of Evesham as far as the Cotswolds, the Malverns and Bredon Hill, and in summer barges tying up alongside and ducks scuttling about on the water – not to mention the cheerful staff whisking food down to the tables – give plenty of foreground action, even in the evenings, now that the garden is floodlit. Good value simple home-made food includes sandwiches, substantial soup (£1), an honest ploughman's (£1.75), omelettes (from around £3), locally smoked chicken, plaice or gammon (£3.15), and home-baked honey-roast ham or Scotch beef salad (£3.15); their bread is supplied from the bakery across the road, and the puddings, particularly the home-made meringue concoctions, are popular. There's a snug little dark green lounge with just a couple of tables, upholstered chairs and settles, regimental badges over the inglenook (now restored to its original state), two beams in its shiny deep red ceiling, and a hop-bine strung above the bar. For the views, choose instead the airy side room with red leatherette banquettes and big wildfowl prints. Well kept Flowers Best and Original and Whitbreads PA on handpump; occasional unobtrusive Radio 2, dominoes, cribbage. *(Recommended by GB, Frank Cummins, Kit Read, Roger Taylor, Wayne Brindle, PLC)*

Free house   Licensee G N Jordan   Real ale   Meals and snacks (not Sun evening)   Riverview lunchtime restaurant tel Pershore (0386) 552799   Children in eating area and restaurant Open 11–2.30, 6–11 all year

---

Lucky Dip

Besides the fully inspected pubs, you might like to try these Lucky Dips recommended to us and described by readers (if you do, please send us reports):

Abberley [SO7667], *Manor Arms*: Well kept and comfortable hotel bar with open fires, very friendly, helpful service and good, tasty bar food with unusual things like quails' eggs as well as salads, steak and kidney pie and so forth; lovely new Laura Ashley-esque bedrooms with fresh fruit and flowers *(Mrs D M Hacker, Mrs N W Neill)*
Abbey Dore [SO3839], *Neville Arms*: Pleasant countryside location, good lunchtime bar food including dishes for vegetarians *(B Ratcliffe)*
Alvechurch [Red Lion St; SP0272], *Red Lion*: Pleasant friendly bar with good range of bar food and separate restaurant *(Sue Braisted)*
Ashton under Hill [OS Sheet 150 reference 997378; SO9938], *Star*: Village pub with pleasant bars and a good atmosphere; food good for range but adequate for quality; well kept Flowers IPA; no machines *(PADEMLUC)*
Aston Crews [SO6723], *Penny Farthing*: Lovely spot, slightly up-market pub with well spaced dimpled copper tables and log fire; well kept Hook Norton and Bass on draught, nibbles on bar, extensive good value bar food including masses of filled baked potatoes; children allowed in top bar *(Maggie Jo St John, Dudley Evans, John Miles)*
Badsey [2 miles E of Evesham on B4035; SP0743], *Round of Gras*: Plain pub with modern furnishings, Flowers real ale, log fire and locally popular food – the name stresses connection with local asparagus growing, and a visit in May or June will make the most of this; much as ever under new management *(PLC, BB)*
Barnards Green [SO7945], *Blue Bell*: Pleasant old-fashioned pub with a limited range of good quality food and good Marstons Pedigree; welcoming atmosphere and although busy at lunchtime wasn't too noisy *(PADEMLUC)*
Beckford [SO9735], *Beckford*: Friendly, hardworking landlord, a good selection of unusual, very generously served and excellently prepared food and large range of

beers; skittle alley, steak restaurant *(Anon)*
Belbroughton [near M5 junction 4; A491 towards Stourbridge; SO9277], *Bell*: Handsome and interesting old building with striking stone inglenook in plushly comfortable lounge bar and fine split-level barn of a restaurant with a central log fire; closed in summer 1988 with plans to reopen early winter as Toby pub/restaurant *(LYM – news please)*; [High St (off A491)] *Queens*: Excellent spaghetti bolognese, superb fruit crumble, wide choice of other food; well kept Marstons Pedigree, comfortable, good service *(M B P Carpenter, EJ)*; [also in village] *Talbot*: Dark, cool interconnecting rooms, well kept Hansons beer, good bar food, friendly and helpful staff, pleasant garden, decent range of well priced bar food *(Ian Phillips, EJ)*
Berrow [junction A438/B4208; SO7934], *Duke of York*: Friendly pub, older than it looks from outside, with Flowers real ales, popular food, log fire in winter and big lawn for summer; pleasant efficient service *(B Walton, BB)*
Bewdley [50 Wyre Hill, off A456; SO7875], *Black Boy*: Small unpretentious pub in row of cottages; pleasant, friendly landlady, well kept Banks's beer including Mild served alongside cups of tea, no piped music, pleasant garden *(Gordon and Daphne, EJ)*; [A456 towards Kidderminster, just past railway arch] *Great Western*: Recently redecorated with railway pictures, imaginative use of wall tiles and balcony, Banks's and Hansons ales; convenient for Severn Valley Railway *(Dave Braisted)*
Birtsmorton [off B4208; SO7935], *Farmers Arms*: Attractive black and white timbered village pub with outside skittle pitch, well kept real ale, limited but reasonable bar food, very low beams inside; decidedly a local *(B Walton, BB)*
Bishops Frome [B4214; SO6648], *Chase*: Friendly and attractively decorated bar, limited range of home-made traditional bar food; also restaurant; comfortable

bedrooms *(HRH, Dave Braisted)*

Bishopstone [Bridge Sollers, A438 about 6 miles W of Hereford; SO4142], *Lord Nelson*: Comfortable roadside pub with helpful staff, straightforward bar food and Sun roast lunch, some ceiling stripped away to show old timbers and pitched rafters, lots of tables by biggish side lawn; children allowed in restaurant, has had country and western music Thurs, closed Mon lunchtime in winter *(Roger and Jenny Huggins, LYM)*

Bliss Gate [signposted off A456 about 3 miles W of Bewdley; SO7572], *Bliss Gate*: New, young, enthusiastic tenants have taken over this small village inn and have totally redecorated it; small, cosy lounge bar with wood-burning stove and larger, tiled public bar; landlord's interest is in aeroplanes and there are lots of paintings on the walls as well as local artists' work; excellent Marstons Burton and Pedigree and plans for more adventurous food; very good value sandwiches and Sun lunch *(Paul and Nicola Denham)*

Bodenham [just off A417 at Bodenham turn-off, about 6 miles S of Leominster; SO5351], *Englands Gate*: Good welcome, excellent food and local beer *(J H C Peters)*

Bournheath [Dodford Road – OS Sheet 139 reference 935735; SO9474], *Gate*: Well kept beers including Flowers IPA and Theakstons Old Peculier, excellent and expanding range of home-cooked bar food including superb mixture of steak with garlic butter and chilli, in charming pub of genuine character and history; friendly service; can get very busy, especially in summer and on Sat evening; restaurant; seats and tables on back lawn *(Brian Jones, J T C Heslop, Colin Hall)*

Bransford [SO7852], *Fox*: Generous helpings of good straightforward food at attractive prices, and jokey friendly service, in pub refurbished in 1970s *(Anon)*

Bretforton [Main St; SP0943], *Victoria Arms*: Excellent choice of well presented reasonably priced food in warm and cordial surroundings *(Mr and Mrs Spragg)*

Brimfield [off A49 near junction with A456; SO5368], *Roebuck*: Stunning choice of home-cooked food in cosy beamed lounge bar with high shelf of willow-pattern plates and Ansells Bitter, or in adjoining restaurant (not Mon lunchtime or Sun); well worth the extra price – family connections with Walnut Tree at Llandewi Skirrid; perhaps best thought of now as a restaurant with bar *(PLC, T Nott)*

Broadway [Collin Lane; marked Gt Collin Farm on OS Sheet 150 at reference 076391 – follow Willersey sign off A44], *Collin House*: Small hotel with well kept Donnington, good lunchtime bar food – everything fresh; small restaurant open in evenings *(M A and C R Starling)*

Broughton Hackett [A422 Worcester–Alcester – OS Sheet 150 reference 923543; SO9254], *March Hare*: Friendly family pub

with small public bar, larger beamed lounge with Windsor and ladder-back chairs, chintz armchairs and sofas, wall settles, snugs opening off, pleasant peaceful atmosphere; good varied food promptly served, separate restaurant, keg beers, decent wines; tables on terrace with barbecue in summer, and on back lawn *(D S Foster, Chris Cooke, A J Hill, FC)*

Callow Hill [Elcocks Brook – OS Sheet 150 reference 010645; SP0164], *Brook*: Good food and friendly service in well kept pub *(A Royle)*

Castlemorton [Castlemorton Common; SO7937], *Farmers Arms*: Country pub with some terrific throat-stripping farm cider *(Alan Mosley)*; [B4208, 1¼ miles S of Welland crossroads] *Robin Hood*: Attractively beamed welcoming pub with good reasonably priced bar food, small summer restaurant, very clean well arranged lavatories, adequate parking *(Dr J M Drew)*

Chaddesley Corbett [SO8973], *Fox*: Pleasant, friendly staff, good food in bar and carvery with crispy Yorkshire puddings and fresh vegetables *(Mrs N W Neill)*

☆ **Claines** [3 miles from M5 junction 6; A449 towards Ombersley – leave dual carriageway after nearly 3 miles, at second exit for Worcester; village signposted from here, and park in Cornmeadow Lane; SO8558], *Mug House*: Ancient place accurately known as The Pub In The Churchyard, decidedly plain and simple décor, well kept cheap Banks's Bitter and Mild, basic snacks (not Sun), sizeable garden merging into farmland with view of the Malvern Hills; children allowed in snug away from servery *(Phil and Sally Gorton, GB, LYM)*

Clent [SO9279], *Fountain*: Useful for the Clent Hills – nineteenth-century village pub with low beams, period décor, electric fires, straightforward bar food *(C M Whitehouse)*

Clifford [B4350 N of Hay on Wye; SO2445], *Castlefield*: Beautifully positioned pub with a friendly welcome, lovely atmosphere, good beer and food and log fire; children welcome *(Mrs Sybil Baker)*

Clows Top [Tenbury Road (A456); SO7172], *Colliers Arms*: Tastefully modernised with open fire, Ansells beer, good food with excellent dish of the day and pleasant service *(BJT)*

Colwall [SO7342], *Horse & Jockey*: Extremely friendly village pub with real fire, pool-table; Ansells and Ind Coope Burton, bar food and small restaurant *(Alastair Lang)*

Conderton [southern slope of Bredon Hill – OS Sheet 150 reference 960370; SO9637], *Yew Tree*: We've had no news of this since it came up for sale in summer 1987, but it's been popular for a fine unspoilt interior with stone floors, beams and so forth *(Phil and Sally Gorton)*

Craswall [SO2736], *Bulls Head*: Very remote,

unspoilt inside with ancient settles and chairs on the stone floor of the one small low-beamed room, several sentimental Victorian prints – which have obviously never seen the inside of an antique shop – above the Victorian cast-iron stove, draught cider and keg beer served through a hole in the wall; only modern touch a fruit machine *(Phil and Sally Gorton)*

Crowle [SO9256], *Old Chequers*: Comfortable, with good service by welcoming new licensees from the Eagle & Sun in Droitwich; well kept Tetleys, good range of well prepared bar food *(PADEMLUC, H E Panton)*

Cutnall Green [SO8768], *Live & Let Live*: Converted from row of old cottages; long narrow bar invariably packed with people eating excellent value meals; tables in garden *(EJ, NWN); New Inn*: Friendly village pub with good beer and a variety of bar snacks; separate eating area *(A Royle)*

Defford [SO9143], *Defford Arms*: Typical friendly and homely country village pub with well kept Davenports and substantial good value bar food *(Dr Rob Horam)*; [A4104 towards Upton] *Oak*: Well kept and reasonably priced Bass, good range of food (mainly Italian – like the owners), reasonably comfortable; small and pleasant, and the pizza parlour attached will appeal to some *(PADEMLUC)*

☆ **Dorstone** [pub signposted off B4348 E of Hay on Wye; SO3141], *Pandy*: Cosy bar with worn flagstones, massive open fire, timbered walls and snug alcoves, generously served food running up to sea-trout or Wye salmon, good range of drinks including well kept Bass, Springfield and a guest beer such as Theakstons XB, pool in side games-room; children welcome, tables outside; Herefordshire's oldest inn, dating back some 800 years – we wish more readers visited it! *(LYM)*

Drakes Broughton [A44 Pershore–Worcester; SO9248], *Plough & Harrow*: Large rambling lounge with lamps, flowers, settees, good choice of beer, extensive bar menu including good sandwiches, friendly service *(Laurence Manning)*

Drayton [SO9076], *Robin Hood*: Good value well kept pub *(A Royle)*

Droitwich [Hanbury Rd, 1½ miles out on B4090; SO9063], *Eagle & Sun*: Canalside pub which has been popular for friendly and efficient service and good food, but the licensees have now moved to the Old Chequers at Crowle; [off B4090 on outskirts] *Himbleton Arms*: Big helpings of good food, often interesting – their paella beats Spanish ones *(Dr and Mrs John Deller)*

Dunhampstead [OS Sheet 150 reference 919600; SO9160], *Firs*: Excellent home cooking, very good choice lunchtime and evening, friendly quick service, tables outside near canal *(RLN, NWN)*

Eardisland [A44; SO4258], *Cross*: Friendly family-run simple old inn with simple food; bedrooms *(LYM)*; [A44] *White Swan*: Fine good value food, really pleasant friendly welcome in lovely pub; pleasant interior, polite and attentive licensee, well kept Marstons, log fire *(John Hicks, Jane and Jerry Bevan, Peter Hitchcock)*

Eardiston [SO6968], *Nags Head*: Modest, well kept, friendly, good beer, excellent food *(Anon)*

Eckington [B4080; SO9241], *Anchor*: Very good value bar snacks and well kept real ales such as Banks's and Hansons *(Mr and Mrs Devereux)*

Elmley Castle [Mill Lane; village signposted off A44 and A435, not far from Evesham; SO9841], *Old Mill*: Former mill house in pleasant surroundings, with tables on well kept lawn looking over village cricket pitch to Bredon Hill; neat L-shaped lounge, well kept Flowers IPA and Original and Wadworths 6X on handpump, mainly older customers but children allowed in eating area; food quality and service often good but not consistently so – maybe teething troubles under newish management, more news please *(Gordon Leighton, Mr and Mrs W H Crowther, Lesley and Paul Compton, Frank Cummins, H Bramhall, Robert and Vicky Tod, LYM); Plough*: Very basic cider house with very cheap own-brewed cider and M&B real ales *(Jason Caulkin, Gill and Rob Weeks); Queen Elizabeth*: Ancient pub with local atmosphere in decidedly old-fashioned tap-room, in pretty village below Bredon Hill; well kept Marstons real ale *(LYM)*

Finstall [34 Alcester Rd; SO9869], *Cross*: Pine-panelled lounge and small timbered snug in local perched high above road, with good value bar food and well kept Flowers real ales; seats on sheltered lawn *(A Royle, LYM)*

☆ **Garway** [SO4522], *Broad Oak*: Charmingly renovated seventeenth-century pub with very good food, well kept Bass, Marstons Pedigree and Wadworths 6X on handpump, and big garden *(B H Stamp, J H C Peters)*

Grimley [A443 5 miles N from Worcester, right to Grimley, right at village T-junction; SO8360], *Camp House*: Remote and basic Severn-side pub with excellent atmosphere, farm cider and bar food *(HDC)*

Hadley [SO8664], *Bowling Green*: Comfortable pub with good beer and first-class food *(A Royle)*

Hanbury [SO9663], *Eagle & Sun*: Good choice of home-cooked food, with good range of salads in summer *(RLN, NWN)*; [part of craft centre, closed Mon and Tues – OS Sheet 150 reference 962649] *Jinney Ring*: Though not a pub (part of local craft centre) has extensive range of good value snacks and meals in imaginative surroundings; wines and spirits licence *(Mr and Mrs W H Crowther)*

Harvington [SO8774], *Dog*: Excellent food and beer – not cheap, but comfortable and spacious village pub *(A Royle)*

Hoarwithy [SO5429], *New Harp*: Darts and fruit machine, well kept Flowers, good reasonably priced bar food – the home-cured ham's recommended, pleasant atmosphere and small garden *(Richard Gibbs, J H C Peters)*

Holy Cross [SO9278], *Bell & Cross*: Basic unspoilt country tavern with M&B real ale *(Anon)*

Howle Hill [coming from Ross, fork left off B4228 on sharp right bend, then turn left at X-roads after phone box – OS Sheet 162 reference 608207; SO6121], *Crown*: White-painted, beamed old ramblers' pub, bought by previous owners of Wye Hotel; it has been recently, but simply, renovated and is well kept and clean; excellent pub lunches from a wide menu, well kept real ale, darts, cribbage, skittles; chairs outside for meals overlooking the hillside and grazing sheep *(Ikka Boyd, Sara Nathan)*

Kemerton [Bredon–Beckford; SO9437], *Crown*: Pleasant eighteenth-century pub with L-shaped lounge bar, panelled benches, horseracing photographs and paintings, good atmosphere, friendly and obliging land-lady; well kept Flowers and fresh sandwiches attractively served *(Robert and Vicky Tod)*

Kidderminster [Comberton Hill – in Severn Valley Rly Stn; SO8376], *King & Castle*: Wide range of real ales, and varied range of interesting bar snacks in clean and atmospheric place with railway memorabilia – the steam-railway-station location is an attraction *(SP, Tony Tucker)*

☆ **Kington** [The Bourne; note this is the Worcs Kington, at SO9855], *Red Hart*: Comfortable and well kept, with very good lunchtime food from well garnished sandwiches to main courses such as pheasant and partridge in season; good atmosphere, well kept Bass *(T H G Lewis, PADEMLUC)*

Kington [High St – the Worcs one still], *Lamb*: Sixteenth-century pub reopened late 1987 after complete refurbishment, some concentration on food – all home cooked; real ale, Australian and Californian as well as French wines *(Anon)*

☆ **Kington** [Church St (A44) – note this is the Herefs Kington at SO3057], *Swan*: Border-town inn with ceiling-fans in attractively redesigned airy bar overlooking square and main street; efficient and welcoming service, good value food (including well filled toasted sandwiches and excellent ploughman's), well kept Ansells and Tetleys, good evening restaurant; children welcome; at start of GWG93; bedrooms *(JAH, John Evans, J H C Peters)*

Kington [Herefs again], *Royal Oak*: Wide choice of good value food in both bar and restaurant; bedrooms adequate *(Graham and Sharon Hughes)*

Kinnersley [off A4112; SO3449], *Kinnersley Arms*: Choice of good real ales on handpump; games-room, bar meals, tiny restaurant, gardens; children welcome *(Dr and Mrs C D E Morris)*

Kinnersley [SO8643], *Royal Oak*: Tastefully decorated and furnished – very clean, with warm friendly atmosphere *(G Wolstenholme)*

☆ **Ledbury** [High St (A417); SO7138], *Feathers*: Elegantly timbered sixteenth-century inn – a nice place to stay – with character seats by fire of civilised and high-beamed central lounge, livelier panelled public bar, new lunchtime food bar, restaurant; Bass and M&B Brew XI on electric pump, children allowed in lounge; nr start GWG91; reports as the new food operation settles in, please *(J H C Peters, Col G D Stafford, LYM)*

Ledbury [New St], *Olde Talbot*: Old building – an inn since 1595 – with cheerful atmosphere, real fire, good beer and cider, standard bar food; bedrooms *(Tony Dudley-Evans, Maggie Jo St John, BB)*; [down narrow passage to church from Town Hall] *Prince of Wales*: From outside looks deceptively small, but once inside the pleasant rooms – nicest at front – seem to stretch back for miles; friendly Scottish landlord *(Gordon and Daphne)*; [Southend] *Royal Oak*: Good friendly atmosphere, well kept Gibbs Mew Wiltshire and Ind Coope Burton real ales, excellent choice of tasty and well prepared bar food *(J H C Peters)*; [High St] *Seven Stars*: Fun, homely, old-fashioned, attractively hig-gledy-piggledy pub with three small rooms, real fire in public bar; friendly service and good food from Eileen's kitchen; outside courtyard; full marks for not overpricing their tea *(Tony Dudley-Evans, Maggie Jo St John)*

Leigh Sinton [SO7750], *Somers Arms*: Excel-lent food and a couple of good local ciders in fairly small pub with family-room and seats in garden, popular with people from Great Malvern; frequent jazz *(Alan Mosley)*

Lingen [SO3767], *Royal George*: Clear, reasonably priced menu of home-made specialities; first-class alpine plants nursery nearby *(Mr and Mrs C Crosthwaite)*

☆ **Lyonshall** [SO3355], *Royal George*: Six-teenth-century oak-beamed bar, always bright, clean and cheerful – excellent layout, with three bars opening off central servery; well kept Flowers beer, farm cider, big helpings of well garnished good food, particularly the well chosen fish and meats; no-smoking dining area, no music *(Freddie Else, D J Wallington, B S Bourne)*

Malvern [SO7845], *Kings Head*: Interesting small pub of character tucked away behind courtyard; real ale, restaurant *(Grahame Archer)*; [British Camp, Wynds Pt; SO7641] *Malvern Hills*: Comfortable oak-panelled lounge, real ale, open fire, excellent lunchtime buffet and superb location; good bedrooms *(Grahame Archer)*; *Morgan*:

Interesting for its associations with the locally made Morgan car; real ale, satisfactory food *(Grahame Archer)*

Malvern Wells [Wells Rd; A449 Malvern –Ledbury – OS Sheet 150 reference 772438; SO7742], *Railway*: Marstons Pedigree and Border Mild on draught, separate skittles hall, pool-table, bar food and separate restaurant *(Alastair Lang)*

Martin Hussingtree [A38 towards Droit-wich; SO8860], *Copcut Elm*: Spacious and very comfortable main-road pub with good choice of lunchtime food, good beer *(Arthur Royle)*

☆ **Mathon** [SO7345], *Cliffe Arms*: Archetypal black and white timbered village pub with cosy low-beamed tiny rooms full of nooks and crannies – spotless, everything shines; open fires, pool, well kept Flowers, Hook Norton and Marstons Pedigree, worthwhile cider, good food, streamside garden, jolly landlord *(Paul and Joanna Pearson, Jason Caulkin)*

Much Marcle [SO6633], *Royal Oak*: Very pleasant roadside country inn with a good selection of beers and other drinks; well furnished with quite a large lounge bar and dining area; quite extensive menu of well cooked food (lunchtime and evening) at reasonable prices; clean and tidy *(CEP)*; *Slip*: Enjoyable and well managed, with good food and drink *(Mr and Mrs W H Crowther)*

nr **Newnham** [A456 towards Tenbury Wells; SO6368], *Peacock*: Pleasant old pub – beamed bar, tables in nice side garden, well kept Flowers and Marstons, excellent ploughman's, window seats, variety of tables and chairs *(Robert and Vicky Tod)*

Newtown Cross [A417, junction with A4103; SO6245], *Newtown Inn*: Very popular locally for food, very welcoming, real ale; can get very crowded *(Tim Locke)*

Oddingley [Smite Hill; near M5 junction 6 – A4538 towards Droitwich, then first right; OS Sheet 150 reference 901589; SO9059], *Pear Tree*: Reliably good bar meals in pleasant surroundings, service pleasant and good, piped music not intrusive *(Mr and Mrs W H Crowther)*

Old Swinford [Hagley Rd; SO9283], *Crown*: Interesting exterior, cosy if not cramped interior in Victorian style with lots of bric-à-brac and large collection of hats and ties displayed on walls, good bar food *(E J Alcock)*

☆ **Orleton** [SO4967], *Boot*: Comfortable old black and white building, picturesque with-out being twee, with wide choice of excellent value freshly prepared food, both traditional and more unusual – puddings extra special, particularly the home-made ices; good service, pleasant garden; the outbuildings and car park could be improved *(Chris Cooke, G Bloxsom, Lesley and Paul Compton, Mr and Mrs R Tod)*

Penalt [SO5729], *British Lion*: Unspoilt

throwback to 1950s on country lane, old wood-burning stove, well kept real ales, pretty side garden, campsite; friendly; bedrooms *(BB)*

Pensax [B4202 Abberley–Clows Top; SO7269], *Bell*: Consistently well kept Timothy Taylors and good interesting bar food under cheerful new licensee *(PLC)*

Pershore [High St; SO9445], *Angel*: Good value bar snacks even Sun evening – handy for area; bedrooms *(Dave Braisted)*; *Millers Arms*: Friendly, spacious but cosy old beamed bar – a young person's pub, particu-larly in the evening; well kept real ales such as Hook Norton Old Hookey, Wadworths Farmers Glory and 6X, generous helpings of good bar food especially the home-made steak and kidney pie; seats on terrace *(Jilly Mills, Andrew Ludlow)*

Pixley [SO6639], *Trumpet*: Pleasant old pub, popular at lunchtimes, with attractive timbers, rambling bars, bar food *(Gordon and Daphne)*

Redditch [Birchfield Rd; SP0467], *Foxlydiate*: Large pub on fringe of town with good value food and good beer *(A Royle)*

☆ **Romsley** [B4551 towards Halesowen; SO9679], *Sun*: Particularly attractively priced food, well kept Banks's and friendly atmosphere; well placed for walks in Clent Hills *(E J Alcock, Roger Huggins)*

Romsley [Bromsgrove Rd; B4551], *Manchester*: Popular main-road pub with good food and beer *(A Royle)*

Ross on Wye [Edde Cross St; SO6024], *King Charles II*: Huge helpings of well cooked food, very well kept beer, piped light music, children's room *(J G Stacey)*; [High St] *Kings Head*: Full of character; hot lunchtime bar food including vegetarian dish *(B Ratcliffe)*; *White Lion*: Very comfortable riverside pub, on the bank opposite the town, with seats on riverside lawn; wide choice of bar food, friendly staff *(Tim Brierly)*

☆ **Ruckhall Common** [from Hereford on A465 SW, right at Belmont Abbey – pub later signposted; SO4539], *Ancient Camp*: Very pretty old inn in idyllic spot looking down on a peaceful stretch of the Wye; exceptionally reasonably priced food in bar and restaurant, well kept real ale, lots of atmosphere in comfortable bar, fine but unobtrusive service from genial new licensees, seats on terrace among flowers; bedrooms (two doubles, one twin) pretty, comfortable and well equipped *(Dr F E McAllister, RLB)*

St Johns [Hylton Rd; SO8353], *Crown & Anchor*: Friendly local atmosphere in comfortable pub with Marstons beers including good Merrie Monk *(P Gisborne)*

St Margarets [SO3533], *Sun*: Good local beer and cider in isolated rural setting, next to one of Betjeman's favourite churches and over-looking the Black Mountains *(N J Neil-Smith)*

Severn Stoke [A38 S of Worcester; SO8544], *Rose & Crown*: Low-beamed main parlour with spacious inner room; Marstons, Ansells and Banks's beers, good home-cooked bar food; by green, play area for children *(P Giddy, Dave Braisted)*

Shenstone [off A450; SO8673], *Plough*: Real country pub with Bathams beer and friendly service even at busy times; good value food *(John Baker)*

Shrawley [SO8064], *Lenchford*: Friendly, helpful staff and good food in the bar of this riverside hotel, ideal in summer; bedrooms *(Mrs N Neill)*

Stoke Lacy [A465 Bromyard–Hereford, just N of village; SO6249], *Plough*: Good value interesting home-made food including gravadlax and intensely flavoured ices in modern main-road pub next to Symonds Cider Shop; skittle alley, quiet restaurant, keen and friendly young owners *(Catherine Steele-Kroon)*

Stoke Works [Shaw Lane; 1 mile from M5 Junction 5 – OS Sheet 150 reference 938656; SO9365], *Bowling Green*: Attractive building with extensive garden, very handy for Worcester–Birmingham Canal (and only slightly spoiled by adjacent railway); limited choice of exceptional value lunchtime food, very well cooked and presented, very friendly landlord, Banks's beer; it does indeed still have its own bowling-green, open to visitors for a very small fee *(Dr R Hodkinson, Dave Braisted)*

Symonds Yat [Symonds Yat West; SO5616], *Old Ferre*: Lively and attractive pub overlooking river, real ale, good value restaurant meals – order mixed grill only if you are very hungry!; nr start GWG90 *(John and Lynn Massam)*; [Symonds Yat West; B4164] *Wye Knot*: Lovely old-world pub with friendly atmosphere, quick service with a smile, plentiful country-style food – good value *(L J and C A Ward)*

Tenbury Wells [A4112 just outside; SO5968], *Fountain*: Good food in attractive bar and restaurant, well kept real ales, properly chilled white wine, pleasant and efficient licensees; well equipped adjacent playing-field for children *(Ronald Wheeldon, John Nicholson)*

Tenbury Wells [Worcester Rd; A456 about 2 miles E], *Peacock*: Friendly new landlord, lovely lounge with big windows and fireplace, side bar with pool-table, well kept Bass and Marstons Pedigree on handpump, lunchtime and evening bar food, small restaurant, garden overlooking road *(A Cook, SP)*; [High St] *Ship*: Lots of dark wood, Ansells bitter, good range of good reasonably priced bar meals concentrating on seafood, rather nice semi-separate dining-room (smarter yet more intimate); back bar with pool and so forth; bedrooms comfortable *(Michael and Alison Sandy)*

Tibberton [Plough Rd; near M5 junction 6, off A4538; SO9057], *Speed the Plough*: Pleasantly modernised old pub just beyond the canal bridge, good welcome, comfortable and not too noisy, well kept Banks's ales and good bar food *(PADEMLUC, Dave Braisted)*

☆ **Upper Wyche** [Chase Rd, off Jubilee Dr (B4218 Malvern–Colwall – take 1st left after hilltop heading west); SO7643], *Chase*: Small country pub nestling on western side of Malvern Hills with good views from charming lounge, well kept Donnington BB and SBA, very good value bar food ranging from rolls through omelettes to steaks, open fire *(Nigel Winters, B Walton)*

Upton Snodsbury [A422 Worcester–Stratford; SO9454], *Royal Oak*: Charming Ansells pub with chute-cum-Wendy house in trellised garden; hot dishes and good choice of cold food; handy for Spetchley Park gardens; also has Rafters wine bar *(Hope Chenhalls)*

Upton upon Severn [SO8540], *Kings Head*: Pleasant riverside pub, well kept Flowers, good bar food and friendly service *(Robert and Vicky Tod)*; *White Lion*: Good food in popular hotel lounge with warm and lively atmosphere, comfortable sofas, stag's head and old prints; bedrooms *(BB)*

☆ **Wadborough** [Station Rd; SO9047], *Masons Arms*: Friendly and unpretentious village pub with good food including fine sandwiches – roast beef still warm from the oven, generous thick ham off the bone, thick farmhouse bread; well kept Banks's beers *(J S Walmsley, Michael Lee, PADEMLUC)*

Welland [On A4104; SO7940], *Marlbank*: Small clean unpretentious pub, good bar food, seats and play area outside, spacious car park *(Gordon Leighton)*

☆ **Weobley** [SO4052], *Red Lion*: Striking fourteenth-century black and white timbered and jettied inn, separated from graceful village church by bowling-green; easy chairs, sofas, high-backed winged settles and huge stone fireplace in civilised heavily beamed lounge bar, well kept Flowers Original; lovely village; some concentration on pricey restaurant, though they do serve bar food in the simple flagstoned back bar; bedrooms comfortable *(Anna Weeden, G G Calderwood, Eileen Broadbent, J N Fiell, LYM)*

☆ **Whitney on Wye** [SO2747], *Boat*: Spacious, clean and well furnished, warm and friendly place; on banks of River Wye with large windows and lovely views; consistently good food, with all puddings home made; bedrooms *(Mrs B M Matthews, Peter Davies)*

Woolhope [just up the road from the Butchers Arms; SO6136], *Crown*: Has been popular for friendly atmosphere, good service, good value food and well priced wine, with simple but comfortable bedrooms, but we've heard nothing since it was taken over late 1987 by people from the Cottage of Content at Carey *(News please)*

Worcester [SO8555], *Bird in Hand*: Good ploughman's *(Prof A N Black)*; [Hylton Rd] *Crown & Anchor*: Friendly landlord and landlady, relaxed atmosphere and cheap, well kept ale especially Marstons Merrie Monk *(J G Wherry)*; [London Rd] *Mount Pleasant*: Delicious food, well presented and very good value *(Miss A Robinson)*; [12 Cornmarket] *Slug & Lettuce*: Most friendly staff, good food, well kept beer *(N and J D Bailey)*; [8–10 Barbourne Rd, The Tything] *Talbot*: Good comfortable atmosphere, genial licensee, well kept Courage Directors, no-nonsense food at reasonable prices; bedrooms *(P Gisborne, Roy Clark)*

Wychbold [A38 towards Bromsgrove; part of Webbs Garden Centre – open 10–5 – OS Sheet 150 reference 929670; SO9265], *Thatch*: Good range of well cooked and presented snacks and meals in pleasant surroundings; though not a pub (part of Webbs Garden Centre, with wines licence) is worth noting for value for money *(Mr and Mrs W H Crowther)*

Yarpole [SO4765], *Bell*: Pleasant pub in lovely village with Woods beer, bar food and attractive garden; there are riding-stables for the disabled behind, and many disabled people use the pub as there's good access for them; children's play area *(Lynne Sheridan, Bob West)*

Hertfordshire

This year we've awarded a star to the George & Dragon at Watton at Stone in recognition of its combination of inventive food with a splendidly pubby atmosphere, in surroundings of considerable character. The other starred pubs in the county are the lively Fox & Hounds at Barley (where the food's simpler but also good – it's a pub full of energy, brewing its own beer and getting top marks from us for its get-you-home-safely minibus), and the Brocket Arms at Ayot St Lawrence (pleasantly idiosyncratic old-fashioned character – a real favourite of those who like this type of pub). Several changes in the area include new licensees for the quaint low-beamed Elephant & Castle in Amwell with its pretty garden, the buoyant old Countryman in Chipping (another nice garden here, too), and the Barley Mow at Tyttenhanger Green outside St Albans (concentrating now on freshly made food in comfortable surroundings, rather than its former eclectic choice of real ales). New entries are the rambling White Hart at Puckeridge (its food – particularly the seafood – earns praise; it's not been in these pages for some years), the Bull in Much Hadham (lively and interesting, with good value food) and the distinctively traditional Sow & Pigs on the A10 just outside Wadesmill (fine sandwiches). The first two of these have gardens of quite some character – which seems to be quite a speciality of pubs in this area. The most stylish garden here is probably the one at the Green Man in Great Offley (a good choice of real ales, decent food, and notably well run). Surprisingly often here (the Lucky Dip section at the end of the chapter is full of examples), attractive village greens seem to sprout good pubs alongside them – such as the cottagey Three Horseshoes in Letchmore Heath, the civilised Two Brewers at Chipperfield (a nice place to stay at), and the Three Horseshoes near Harpenden (more of a common than a green, here – it's quite a surprise to find the pub tucked away in its depths). Record-hunters should note the claim to very great age of the Fighting Cocks in St Albans – which has no shortage of fine pubs. Among the Lucky Dips,

The Fox & Hounds, Barley

some pubs that stand out include the Two Bridges at Croxley Green, the Horns near Datchworth, the Candlestick at Essendon, the Green Dragon in London Colney and the Coach & Horses at Newgate Street; the two attracting the warmest praise from readers are the Cabinet at Reed and, particularly, the Garibaldi in St Albans.

ALDBURY   SP9612   Map 4
Valiant Trooper ⊗
Trooper Lane (towards Aldbury Common)

This partly white-painted tiled brick building is well kept and friendly, and has black beams in the lively red and black tiled room, a wood-burning stove in its inglenook fireplace, and small dining-chairs, a pew and built-in wall benches around the attractive country tables. The brown-carpeted middle room has spindle-back chairs around its tables, and some exposed brickwork, and the far room – quiet even at weekends when young people crowd into the tiled part – has a brick fireplace and nice country kitchen chairs around individually chosen tables; decorations are mostly antique prints of cavalrymen. The changing choice of bar food, though not wide, is good value – good home-made soup, ploughman's or filled baked potatoes (£1.80), liver and bacon casserole or pork chop in a red wine sauce (£2.80), fresh trout (£3.20), and mixed grill (£3.50). Well kept Fullers ESB and London Pride, Greene King Abbot, Marstons Pedigree and Morrells Varsity on handpump; darts, shove-ha'penny, dominoes, cribbage. There are some tables in the small garden behind the pretty village house, which has attractive front flower beds; on *Good Walks Guide* Walk 109. *(Recommended by BKA, Mrs M E Lawrence, M P Le Geyt)*

Free house   Licensee Dorothy Eileen O'Gorman   Real ale   Meals (not Mon or Sat evening, not Sun) and snacks (not Mon, Sat or Sun evening)   Restaurant tel Aldbury Common (044 285) 203   Children in coffee area Sat lunch and in front porch   Open 11.30–3 (2.30 in winter), 6–11; open all day Sat for trial period

AMWELL   TL1613   Map 5
Elephant & Castle
Village signposted SW from Wheathampstead

Outside this prettily restored, ancient pub a neat and secluded back garden is kept free from dogs and children, and on the sweeping front lawn – floodlit at night – there are seats spaced well apart among fruit trees and a weeping willow. Inside, the main bar has a 200-foot well shaft as well as an inglenook fireplace, low beams, some panelling (other walls stripped to the timbered brick), and low leatherette-cushioned stalls and high-backed bucket seats on the red and black tiled floor. Good, simple lunchtime bar food includes sandwiches, good soup, ploughman's (£1.90), individual home-made dishes such as cottage pie, macaroni cheese or chilli con carne (£2), scampi (£2.75) and rump steak (£5.20); well kept Benskins, Ind Coope Burton and two guest beers on handpump. *(Recommended by Stanley Matthews; more reports please)*

Benskins (Ind Coope)   Licensees Stewart and Anne Willett   Real ale   Meals and snacks (not Sun)   Restaurant tel Wheathampstead (058 283) 2175; closed Sun   Children in eating area of bar   Open 11–3, 5.30–11 all year

AYOT ST LAWRENCE   TL1916   Map 5
Brocket Arms ★
Not far from George Bernard Shaw's home and close to the romantic ivy-hung ruins of a medieval church, this fourteenth-century tiled house is a very relaxing,

friendly place. The two old-fashioned rooms (cosy enough to get crowded at times) have a long built-in wall settle in one parquet-floored room, orange lanterns hanging from the sturdy oak beams, a big inglenook fireplace and a wide choice of piped music from Bach to pop. Bar food includes ploughman's or pâté (£2.50), scampi (£3), and coq au vin, tagliatelle or fish pie (£3.80); Sunday roast lunch in winter. Well kept Adnams, Greene King IPA and Abbot, Timothy Taylors Landlord, and Wadworths 6X tapped from the cask; darts and dominoes. The licensee has spent some time improving the walled gardens behind the white-painted brick house, which are especially safe for children; on *Good Walks Guide* Walk 108. *(Recommended by Andy Blackburn, A J and M Thomasson, D L Johnson, G L Tong, Mr and Mrs R J Welch, C Elliott, Dave Butler, Lesley Storey)*

Free house   Licensee Toby Wingfield Digby   Real ale   Meals and snacks (not Sun or Mon evenings)   Restaurant   Children welcome   Open 10.30–2.30 (11–3 Sat), 6–11   Bedrooms tel Stevenage (0438) 820250; £30B/£35

BARLEY   TL3938   Map 5

Fox & Hounds ★ ⊗ *[illustrated on page 359]*

An inn since 1797 and before that used by James I when hunting from Royston, this solid old place has several low-ceilinged, thoughtfully furnished rambling rooms with an enjoyable country atmosphere; there's an assortment of simple but comfortable furniture in the various alcoves – one of the stripped wood tables has a brightly painted cast-iron base which used to be a wringer – and there are substantial log fires on both sides of a massive central chimney. The dining area, with its odd-shaped nooks and crannies, was until last year the kitchen and cellar, and as we went to press they were adding a conservatory. A big bonus is the fact that they brew their own beer: Nat's P and slightly stronger Hogshead (summer only) as well as Flowers IPA and Original, and five guest beers from a very wide range of sources; good house wine. Bar food from a huge menu of seventy mostly home-made dishes ranges from sandwiches, ploughman's, vegetarian and slimmers' dishes, lasagne or moussaka (£2.95), whole plaice stuffed with prawns and mushrooms (£4.35), steaks (£5.45), and pies such as lamb and apricot or beef and venison with good pastry; quite a range of seafoods and puddings; service is efficient and friendly even when pushed. An excellent range of games includes darts (two league darts teams), bar billiards, shove-ha'penny, dominoes (two schools), cribbage; fruit machine and juke box. The pub also has a league football team. There are swings, a slide and climbing-frame as well as picnic-table sets on grass around the car park, and a cook-your-own barbecue area (food is bought over the counter). They have a minibus which offers a pick-up and get-you-home service. *(Recommended by R Wiles, Gordon Theaker, W H Cleghorn, Joy Heatherley, S Matthews, Jenny Ball, Alan and Ruth Woodhouse, M J Williamson)*

Own brew   Licensee Rita Nicholson   Real ale   Meals and snacks   Children in eating area of bar   Occasional live entertainment   Open 11.30–2.30, 6–11 all year

CHIPPERFIELD   TL0401   Map 5

Two Brewers

This neatly kept and well run inn overlooks the pretty tree-flanked village cricket green – with pleasant walks in the woods beyond. The main bar has dark beams, cushioned antique settles, some early nineteenth-century prints of bare-knuckle pugilists (a reminder that Jem Mace, Bob Fitzsimmons and others trained in the back club-room), and a relaxed and genuinely pubby atmosphere. Lunchtime bar food is served in the comfortable bow-windowed room: home-made soup (£1.20), duck liver pâté or local baked ham and savoury bacon quiche (£2.65), a good choice of ploughman's or a daily hot dish (£2.95), and Hertfordshire tea cup trifle (£1.05p). Tables in this room are spread with linen cloths at lunchtime and there are easy chairs and sofas. Well kept Bass, Courage Best, Greene King IPA and Abbot, Marstons Pedigree and Ruddles Best on handpump, and (uncommon around here) maybe a Mild ale. *(Recommended by Lyn and Bill Capper, GP, Mr and Mrs Ken Turner)*

Free house (THF)   Real ale   Snacks (lunchtime, not Sun)   Restaurant   Children in lounge and restaurant   Open 10.30–2.30, 5.30–11 all year; open all day Sat   Bedrooms tel Kings Langley (092 77) 65266; £61.95B/£77.90B

CHIPPING   TL3532 Map 5
Countryman
A10

A high Delft shelf with a frieze of gundogs and horses, and gin-traps, ancient sickles and billhooks by the worn old wall timbers, support the name of this beamed seventeenth-century pub, under new ownership. It's a busy place with a pleasant atmosphere, comfortable traditional-style settles, and a cosy fire. Bar food includes baked potatoes (from 85p), sandwiches (from £1), various ploughman's (from £1.50), and home-made specials such as sausage, egg and bacon pie, lasagne, curry, chilli con carne and shepherd's pie (from £2); Sunday roast lunch (main course £3.25), children's helpings available. Well kept Adnams Bitter, Courage Best, and Ruddles County from the elaborately carved bar counter; piped music. Walled off from the car park, there's a terrace with benches leading to a big garden with flower beds and a fish pond – which should be pleasantly quiet now that the Buntingford bypass has been opened. *(Recommended by Dave Butler, Lesley Storey, J Millbank)*

Free house   Licensees D A and R D Carney   Real ale   Meals (not Sun lunchtime) and snacks   Restaurant tel Royston (0763) 72616   Children in restaurant   Open 11.30–2.30, 5.30–11; open all day Sat in summer

GREAT OFFLEY   TL1427 Map 5
Green Man ⊗
Village signposted off A505 Luton–Hitchin

A couple of our most enthusiastic reader-reporters feel that this is the best larger pub they've come across for some time, and we can understand their reaction. The attractive rambling bars – which quickly fill up with diners at lunchtime – have lots of antique farm-tool illustrations, wheel-back and spindle-back chairs around simple country tables, stripped brick, low moulded beams, and a wood-burning stove and fruit machine on the left; the larger and more airy right-hand room has lots of little countryside prints and one or two larger pictures, a cabinet of trophies, cushioned built-in wall seats as well as the chairs around its tables, and another big wood-burner (with a row of brass spigots decorating the chimneypiece) and fruit machine. The quickly served food includes soup (95p), generous sandwiches and large filled rolls (from £1.25), filled baked potatoes (from £1.50), ploughman's (from £1.95), cottage or chicken and mushroom pie (£3.25), a good lunchtime spread of help-yourself salads (from £4), half a chicken (£4.50) and gammon (£4.75); well kept Flowers IPA and Original, Ruddles County, Websters Yorkshire and (unusual down here) Whitbreads Castle Eden on handpump, a decent choice of wines by the glass; cheerful, efficient service. You can step out on to the flagstoned terrace (overlooked by a high-pillared comfortable restaurant), where curlicued iron tables and chairs have a grand view, beyond the lawn with its rockery, pond and little waterfall, of the flatter land below, stretching for miles to the east. There's a mass of flowers, with lots of hanging baskets and tubs of flowers, and a couple of ponies may be stretching their necks over the stile at the end of the lawn. Children

---

By law pubs must show a price list of their drinks. Let us know if you are inconvenienced by any breach of this law.

are asked to sit out in front instead, where there are swings and a slide.
(Recommended by Rita Horridge, Lyn and Bill Capper, Michael and Alison Sandy, D L Johnson)

Free house   Licensees R H and M A Scarbrow   Real ale   Meals and snacks   Restaurant tel
Offley (046 276) 256   *Children welcome   Open all day; closed evening 25 and 26 Dec*

nr HARPENDEN   TL1314   Map 5
Three Horseshoes ⊗

East Common; from A1081 about 600 yds S of the S edge of Harpenden, follow sign towards
Ayres End, Amwell, then turn left at Harpenden Common sign; OS Sheet 166 reference 144120

Divided up by the timbers and beams of a partly knocked-through wall, the
open-plan modernised bar of this friendly, rather genteel pub is a comfortable place
with popular home-made food: good soup, sandwiches (hefty club sandwich
£1.70), baked potatoes, ploughman's, salads, cod or plaice (£2.50), scampi (£2.90)
and daily specials such as steak and kidney pie (£2.50), lasagne or quiche (£2.75) or
generously served chilli con carne. Well kept Brakspears, Flowers IPA and
Wethereds on handpump. There are some snug alcoves, cushioned rustic-style seats
and stools around the many dark wood tables, horsebrasses, and inglenook
fireplaces with open fires in winter; sensibly placed darts, dominoes, cribbage, fruit
machine and piped music. Tables on the side lawn and the terrace in front of the
building (which has a newer brick front wing) are surrounded by a quiet common,
with tracks off through it and a right of way over the golf course that's on the other
side of the lane. *(Recommended by John Atherton, J F Estdale, Stanley Matthews, Mrs
M Lawrence, John Townsend, D L Johnson)*

*Whitbreads   Licensee Ronald Shaw   Real ale   Lunchtime meals and snacks (not Sun)
Children in side room   Jazz Tues evening   Open 10.30–2, 5.30–11; open all day Sat*

LETCHMORE HEATH   TQ1597   Map 5
Three Horseshoes ⊗

2 miles from M1 junction 5; A41 towards Harrow, first left signposted Aldenham, right at
Letchmore Heath signpost

In genuinely rustic surroundings – opposite the duck pond on a serenely tree-shaded
village green – this well kept cottagey local is quite a find for this part of the world.
There's a good mix of customers in the tiny, low-ceilinged and carpeted main
lounge, which has an old panelled settle as well as green-patterned plush cushioned
wooden wall seats (some in a big bay window etched with the pub's name and
emblem), horsebrasses on the beams, a few olde-worlde prints on the walls, and an
open fire. A wide choice of bar food includes nicely made sandwiches (from 70p),
ploughman's and a good many variants (from £1.60), hot snacks such as seafood
pasta or turkey and ham hash (around £2.10) and changing dishes such as liver and
bacon or chicken and leek pie (£2.85), with lots of vegetables or salad. Well kept
Benskins Best and Ind Coope Burton on handpump; darts, shove-ha'penny,
dominoes, cribbage and maybe faint piped pop music. There are a good many white
tables on a side terrace beside the attractive house (covered in summer with pretty
hanging baskets and window boxes), with more on the lawn; pretty quiet, except
for birdsong and the occasional scream of a neighbouring peacock. *(Recommended by
Dr John Innes, M C Howells, Stanley Matthews, D L Johnson)*

*Benskins   Licensee Ann Parrott   Real ale   Lunchtime meals and snacks (not Sun)   Open
11–3, 5.30–11 all year*

If a service charge is mentioned prominently on a menu or accommodation terms, you must pay
it if service was satisfactory. If service is really bad you are legally entitled to refuse to pay some
or all of the service charge as compensation for not getting the service you might reasonably
have expected.

MUCH HADHAM TL4319 Map 5
Bull ⊗
B1004

The warmest atmosphere (with some extra food bargains) is to be found in the public bar – a simple place, with cafe seats and tables, but also a timber-propped inglenook and a beam so low that it surely added bruises on that notorious day in 1813 when the licensee locked the doors while two of his customers fought to the death in here. This room has sensibly placed darts, dominoes, fruit machine and a decent juke box. Food here includes generous filled French sticks (95p), a choice of ploughman's (£1.50), chilli con carne (£2) and gammon or steak and kidney pie (£2.25); on the other side, a much wider choice includes sandwiches (from 80p), soup (95p) with lots of other starters such as devilled mushrooms (£1.80), ploughman's (from £1.75), lasagne (£2.95), chicken and ham pie (£3.20) or steak and kidney pie (£3.45), salads (£3.50), fish pie or fresh poached haddock (£3.85) and steaks (£6.25), with rich puddings and children's helpings at half-price. The carpeted lounge bar has comfortable brocaded wall banquettes around neat tables, and is decorated with big blow-ups of old local photographs; it's supplemented by a cosy back family dining-room with brocaded seats around closer-spaced tables, and one or two old enamel advertising placards on its timbered white walls. Well kept Benskins Best and Ind Coope Burton on handpump. There are rustic seats dotted around in the big informal back garden, where hens scratch about in the long grass (and there may be more of a menagerie). *(Recommended by Alan and Ruth Woodhouse, R C Vincent, SJC)*

Benskins Licensee Mike Wade Real ale Meals and snacks Children in dining-room Jazz fortnightly Open 11–2.30, 6–11 all year; closed evening 25 Dec

PUCKERIDGE TL3823 Map 5
White Hart ⊗
Village signposted from A10 and A120

This large, rambling pub is comfortably and interestingly furnished, though for most people the main attraction is the good value food – especially seafood, fresh daily: crab sandwich (£1.50), prawns (from £1.75, Mediterranean prawns from £4.25), insalata di mare (octopus, squid, prawns and mussels) or spicy crab pâté (both £1.95), dressed crab (£2.75), whole baked plaice stuffed with prawns (£5.25), and seafood platter (£5.50). Other food includes sandwiches (from 95p), ploughman's (from £1.60), home-made ratatouille (£1.65), ham off the bone (£4.25), fresh oven-roasted turkey (£4.50), lots of vegetarian dishes like home-made tomato pancakes with thermidor sauce (£4.75) or butter-bean and vegetable gratin (£4.95), home-made lasagne or gammon with pineapple (£4.95), and steaks (from £6.95); there's also a children's menu; best to book on Saturday evenings. Under the heavy beams of the spreading bar is a medley of wooden armchairs, wheel-back chairs and button-back banquettes; the fireplace has a massive carved mantelbeam, and traditional decorations include pewter tankards, horsebrasses and coach horns. Well kept McMullens Country and AK Mild on handpump; dominoes, cribbage, fruit machine, trivia and piped music. There are seats and swings in the floodlit garden by a paddock with chickens, roosters, ducks, goats, rabbits, sheep and ponies, and more under a thatched shelter built around a spreading tree. *(Recommended by H Paulinski, Dave Wright, Alan and Ruth Woodhouse, D L Johnson)*

McMullens Licensee Colin Boom Real ale Meals and snacks Restaurant tel Ware (0920) 821309 Children in eating area of bar Open 11–2.30, 5.30–11; closed evening 25 and 26 Dec

Please let us know of any pubs where the wine is particularly good.

ST ALBANS TL1507 Map 5
Fighting Cocks

Off George Street, through abbey gateway (you can drive down, though signs suggest you can't)

There has been some sort of building here since 795 when the abbey was founded, and by Norman times it served as a battlemented gatehouse (the upper fortifications were demolished in 1300); it was first opened as an alehouse in 1600 and was known as the Round House due to its almost circular shape and quaintly conical tiled roof. Perhaps the most notable feature in the modernised bar is the small area down steps which used to be part of the Stuart cock-fighting pit which gave the pub its modern name. There are some pleasant window alcoves, other nooks and corners, heavy low beams, and a good log fire in the inglenook fireplace. Good helpings of straightforward lunchtime bar food include rolls (85p), sandwiches (£1), burgers (£1.20), ploughman's (from £1.65), fresh roast chicken or sausage and egg (£2.65), roast Shetland lamb (£2.75), home-cooked gammon and egg (£2.80), home-made hunter's pie or scampi (£2.95) and trout (£3.20); well kept Benskins Best, Ind Coope Burton and Tetleys on handpump; shove-ha'penny, fruit machine and piped music. The surroundings are very attractive: seats in the garden, then beyond that lots of ducks on the River Ver, a lakeside park, and the Roman remains of Verulamium. *(Recommended by Michael and Alison Sandy, Wayne Brindle, TBB; more reports please)*

Benskins (Ind Coope)   Real ale   Lunchtime meals and snacks (Sun only in summer)
Children in family-room   Open 11–3, 6–11

Goat

Sopwell Lane; a No Entry beside Strutt and Parker estate agents on Holywell Hill, the main southwards exit from town – by car, take the next lane down and go round the block

Since last year, this busy old pub has been completely refurbished, but has kept a good range of real ales: Adnams, Greene King Abbot, Hook Norton Best and Old Hookey, Marstons Pedigree, Wadworths 6X, and a guest winter ale all on handpump; cocktails (£1.75), Pimms and sangria in summer, mulled wine in winter. Bar food includes sandwiches, cauliflower soup, chicken liver pâté, filled baked potatoes, home-made pies, burgers, tagliatelle carbonara, pork or veal, steaks and daily specials. Dominoes, cribbage, fruit machine, trivia and piped music. Tables on the neat lawn-and-gravel back yard are sheltered by what, two hundred years ago, used to be the most extensive stables of any inn here. *(Recommended by D C Bail, Nick Dowson, Stanley Matthews, Michael and Alison Sandy, Jill Hadfield, Tony Gallagher, Chris Fluck)*

Free house (though now owned by Inn Leisure/Devenish)   Licensee Anthony Ginn   Real ale
Meals and snacks   Children in eating area of bar   Jazz Sun lunchtime   Nearby parking may be rather difficult   Open 11–3, 5.30–11 all year; open all day Sat; closed evening 25 Dec

Rose and Crown ⊗

St Michaels Street; from town centre follow George Street down past the abbey towards the Roman town

Well worth the short trip out from the centre, this attractive and civilised old pub, hidden behind its elegant Georgian façade, is a homely, well kept place with a friendly welcome. There are unevenly timbered walls, old-fashioned wall benches, a pile of old *Country Life* magazines, and black cauldrons in the deep fireplace. Bar food includes plain or toasted sandwiches, home-made soups (in winter, £1.10), poacher's pie (£1.50), cheese, onion and potato pie (£1.75), quiches, omelettes, home-made casseroles or beef, bean and vegetable hot-pot (£1.95), and salmon and cucumber pie (£2.25); unusual crisps. Well kept Benskins, Ind Coope Burton and Tetleys on handpump; farm ciders, country wines, and hot punch in winter. Darts (placed sensibly to one side), shove-ha'penny, dominoes, cribbage, fruit machine, trivia, juke box and piped music. There's always a selection of books for sale – proceeds go towards buying guide dogs (they've bought sixteen so far). (*Recommended by BKA, Sonia Elstow*)

Benskins (Ind Coope)   Licensees John and Paula Milligan   Real ale   Lunchtime snacks Folk music Thurs   Open 11 (11.15 Sat)–2.30, 5.30 (6 Sat)–11 all year

nr ST ALBANS   TL1805   Map 5
Barley Mow

Tyttenhanger Green; from A405 just under 2 miles E of A6/A1081 roundabout, take B6426 singposted St Albans, then first left turn

This last year, this busy and popular pub has changed hands, with several significant consequences. One that will be regretted by many people is that its former eclectic range of real ales has been replaced by a clutch of Watneys-related ones (Ruddles Best and County, Trumans Best and Websters on handpump, still well kept). But to redress the balance the food is now all home made, using fresh ingredients, and a lot of effort has gone into refurbishing the spacious bar, with its sunny window alcoves. So, though it's still too early for us to have had any real volume of reports from readers on the changes, our provisional view is that this pub is still well worth knowing. Bar food includes cauliflower cheese (£1.75), ratatouille with melted Mozzarella (£2.20), lasagne or steak and kidney pie (£2.25), and cold roast beef salad or chicken curry (£2.50). Outside, plenty of picnic-table sets and rustic seats overlook the paddocks. (*Recommended by Mrs J Jelliffe and family, BKA, Dave Butler, Lesley Storey*)

Watneys   Licensee John Tweed   Real ale   Lunchtime meals and evening snacks   Children welcome   Open all day if trade demands

WADESMILL   TL3517   Map 5
Sow & Pigs

Thundridge; A10 just S of Wadesmill, towards Ware

They really know how to make sandwiches in this warmly traditional pub; from the wide choice (from 95p) people pick out the roast beef done with dripping, the smoked salmon (£1.45) and the steak (£2.25). Other well priced bar food includes soup (75p), ploughman's (£1.35), cottage or steak and kidney pie (£2.15), and a bargain three-course steak lunch (£4.50). The central serving-bar's a snug little place, with dark glossy plank-panelling, a collection of military badges, a rustic cask-supported table in the bay of the comfortable window seat, and an attractive wall clock. It opens on either side into more spacious rooms, with cosy wall seats and little spindle-back chairs around massive rustic or traditional cast-iron tables, big copper urns hanging from dark beams, antlers and prints above the dark dado – and, throughout, the buzz of chatter and quiet enjoyment that marks a good, well run pub. Well kept Benskins Best, Ind Coope Burton and Tetleys on handpump. There are picnic-table sets under cocktail parasols, with their own service hatch, on a smallish fairy-lit grass area behind by the car park, sheltered by tall oaks and chestnut trees. (*Recommended by HGM, D L Johnson, EDVM*)

Benskins   Licensee W S Morgan   Real ale   Meals and snacks   Children in dining-room Open 10.30–2.30, 6–11 all year; closed evening 25 Dec

---

Meal times are generally the normal times at which people eat in the region. But they tend to vary from day to day and with the season, depending on how busy the pub hopes to be. We don't specify them as our experience shows you can't rely on them.

Bedroom prices are for high summer. Even then you may get reductions for more than one night, or (outside tourist areas) weekends. Special rates are common in winter, and many inns cut bedroom prices if you have a full evening meal.

WATTON-AT-STONE TL3019 Map 5
George & Dragon ★ ⊗
High Street

Readers who feel this comfortable, very well run village pub is the best within twenty miles of Bishops Stortford can't be alone: locals and visitors alike praise the fresh, imaginative food such as good home-made soup (£1), sandwiches (from £1), ploughman's (£2.25), good pâté (£3), flaked smoked haddock and tomato concasse in a ramekin with browned cheese and served with fingers of brown-bread toast and salad, or Corsican fish soup (highly spiced and poured over toasted croûtons which are covered with garlic, chilli and tomato sauce and grated cheese, both £2.75), deep-fried Brie with apricot sauce (£3), salads (from £3), smoked salmon cured in the village or cocktail of flaked fresh salmon and prawns covered with lemon mayonnaise and garnished with kiwi-fruit (£4.50), fillet steak in a bread roll (from £5), and a really hefty fish hors-d'oeuvre (£6.75); there are also daily specials – at lunchtime (£3) and in the evening (£2.50), and a wide choice of puddings (£1.50); proper napkins and good house wines by half-pint or pint carafes. The Greene King beers are kept under pressure. The carpeted main bar has dark blue cloth-upholstered seats in its bay windows, country kitchen armchairs around attractive old tables, an interesting mix of antique and modern prints on its partly timbered ochre walls, and a big inglenook fireplace. A quieter room off, with spindle-back chairs and wall settles cushioned to match the green floral curtains, has a nice set of Cruikshank anti-drink engravings above its panelled dado, and beyond that there are picnic-table sets in a small shrub-screened garden. Service is friendly and efficient and daily papers are set out to read at lunchtime. They like you at least to wear shirts with sleeves. The pub is handy for Benington Lordship Gardens. *(Recommended by Harold Glover, Hope Chenhalls, Mr and Mrs S Pollock-Hill, Mr and Mrs A R Walmsley, Rita Horridge, Stanley Matthews, C P Harris)*

Greene King   Licensee Kevin Dinnim   Meals and snacks (not Sun)   Restaurant tel Ware (0920) 830285; closed Sun evening   Children in restaurant   Open 10–2.30, 5.30–11 all year; closed 25 and 26 Dec

WESTMILL TL3626 Map 5
Sword in Hand
Village signposted W of A10, about 1 mile S of Buntingford

This is one of the most attractive buildings in a particularly pretty village: rows of tiled or thatched cottages, some timbered and others – including the pub – colour-washed. On weekday lunchtimes it's a peaceful place with comfortably cushioned seats on the Turkey carpet or parquet floor, country prints on the black and white timbered walls, murmured conversations in quiet corners, and a cat snoozing by the log fire. Bar food ranges from toasted sandwiches and soup through ploughman's to lasagne, steaks and so forth; well kept Benskins and Ind Coope Burton on handpump or tapped from the cask; friendly staff. Darts, shove-ha'penny, dominoes, cribbage, fruit machine, trivia and piped music. There are tables on a partly crazy-paved sheltered side garden under the pear tree. *(Recommended by Peter Storey, Wayne Brindle, Mrs P J Pearce)*

Benskins (Ind Coope)   Licensee Alan Perry   Real ale   Meals and snacks   Restaurant tel Royston (0763) 71356   Children in eating area of bar   Open 11–2.30, 6–11

Lucky Dip

Besides the fully inspected pubs, you might like to try these Lucky Dips recommended to us and described by readers (if you do, please send us reports):

Aldbury [SP9612], *Greyhound*: Simple old pub with Georgian refacing, by village duck pond below Chilterns beech woods; on GWG109 *(LYM)*

Ashwell [beside church; TL2639], *Bushel & Strike*: Excellent food served efficiently in nice Charles Wells pub, in attractive village *(N and J D Bailey)*; [69 High St] *Rose & Crown*: Home-cooked food such as soups, curries and pies in earthenware bowls, summer salad bar, very good quick service and friendly welcoming atmosphere, open fire, attractive garden *(Anon)*

Barkway [TL3835], *Chaise & Pair*: Plushly modernised small pub with bar food from sandwiches to steaks, real ale, restaurant *(LYM)*

Bedmond [Bedmond Rd; TL0903], *Bell*: Good reasonably priced lunches in spotless attractive bar – can get crowded Sat lunchtime; garden, good car park *(Rowna and Jack Saunders)*

Belsize [OS Sheet 176 reference 034009; TL0309], *Plough*: Pleasant country pub, central bar, barn-like lounge with open fire, wooden beams, bench seats and stools, darts, fruit machine; good, friendly service, Benskins Best and Ind Coope Burton on handpump, good value lunchtime bar food, unobtrusive piped music, picnic-table sets in garden *(Lyn and Bill Capper, Mr and Mrs F W Sturch)*

Benington [just past Post Office, towards Stevenage; TL3023], *Bell*: Smallish lounge bar, bigger public bar with inglenook, darts, juke box; four real ales, good food *(D L Johnson)*

Berkhamsted [Winkwell; SP9807], *Three Horseshoes*: Pretty sixteenth-century canal-side pub with dark low-beamed intimate bars; busy in summer *(Chris and Jacqui Chatfield)*

☆ **Bishops Stortford** [Waterside; TL4820], *Five Horseshoes*: Attractive and friendly tiled-roof beamed pub overlooking cricket pitch, picnic-table sets in lovely walled garden – quiet country location; Benskins ales, good food including filled interesting freshly baked croissant-type rolls and spicy sausages *(S Pollock-Hill and others)*

Bishops Stortford [Bedlars Green – just off A120 by M11 junction 8; pub itself actually in Essex; TL5220], *Hop Poles*: Small, friendly, village pub close to National Trust-owned, extensive Hatfield Forest; Benskins Best, Friary Meux and Ind Coope Burton on handpump *(Robert Lester)*

Boxmoor [TL0306], *Fishery*: Big-windowed and airy open-plan upstairs bar has fine view of canal with brightly painted barges, as do waterside tables; usual bar food, Ind Coope real ales, maybe loud disco music evenings *(LYM)*

Breachwood Green [TL1521], *Red Lion*: Very friendly Greene King pub with warm red décor for soft seats, carpet and half the walls; log fire, sandwiches and good simple food *(D L Johnson)*

Bricket Wood [School Lane – nr M1 junction 6; TL1202], *Old Fox*: Small, friendly, comfortable pub with well kept beers, farm cider and excellent food; children welcome, good walking nearby *(Hugh Geddes)*

Bushey [42 Sparrows Herne; TQ1395], *Royal Oak*: Excellent menu with several daily specials and steaks; Charles Wells and Marstons Burton and Pedigree; small play area for children in garden *(Stan Edwards)*; [25 Park Rd – off A411] *Swan*: Homely atmosphere in rare surviving example of single-room back-street terraced pub, reminiscent of 1920s *(LYM)*

☆ **Chandlers Cross** [TQ0698], *Clarendon Arms*: Good atmosphere in large bar with plenty of tables, friendly staff and locals, cheap bar food (not Sun) lunchtime – when it may be full of young people; Ruddles County, Websters Yorkshire, Wethereds Winter Royal and Whitbreads, help-yourself coffee; good setting, with pleasant – if sometimes noisy – covered verandah; watch the step at the side entrance! *(BKA, Lyn and Bill Capper, D L Johnson)*

Charlton [TL1727], *Windmill*: Pleasant setting with seats out by duck pond, comfortable seats, good choice of reasonably priced hot and cold food including a choice of ploughman's *(Lyn and Bill Capper)*

Cheshunt [Turnford; TL3502], *Old Anchor*: Friendly modernised pub with well kept McMullens Country Bitter *(John Baker)*

Chipperfield [Tower Hill; TL0401], *Boot*: Charming exterior and immaculate interior, with fascinating regalia all over the place, open fires, fresh flowers, Benskins Best, Friary Meux and Ind Coope Burton on handpump; limited adequate food, no puddings, local atmosphere *(D L Johnson, BKA, Lyn and Bill Capper)*; *Windmill*: Simple pub, no piped music, well kept Ind Coope Bitter and Burton, good, plain, cheap bar food *(Dr M Quinton)*

Chorleywood [Artichoke Dell, Dog Kennel Lane, the Common; TQ0295], *Black Horse*: Unpretentious building in pleasant walking country, nice seating under low dark beams in attractively divided room with open fire and children's area, good food including generously filled buns and sandwiches, salads and home-made hot dishes, Benskins Best and Ind Coope Burton *(Hugh Wilson)*; *Garden Gate*: Food served from noon to

9.30 in pub handy for walkers on well wooded common nearby; well kept Benskins Best and Ind Coope Burton on handpump; children welcome *(LYM)*; [Long Lane, Heronsgate – which is signposted from M25 junction 17; TQ0294] *Land of Liberty, Peace & Plenty*: Friendly landlord in well kept refurbished pub with spotless glasses and good range of bar food (especially lunchtime); well kept Courage beers, coffee, maybe unobtrusive piped music; children's play area off car park; several pub dogs *(Lyn and Bill Capper)*; [Long Lane] *Stag*: Modest, unpretentious pub with open fire, good value home-cooked bar food with fresh vegetables (not Sun evening), friendly service *(Mr and Mrs F W Sturch)*; [A404 just off M25 junction 18] *White Horse*: Lots of atmosphere in ancient beamed pub; warm welcome, well kept Greene King IPA and Abbot, varied lunchtime bar food at reasonable prices including omelettes with a choice of fillings *(R M Savage)*

Codicote [High St; TL2118], *Bell*: Comfortable old Whitbreads house, completely modernised; lounge bar with upholstered chairs, banquettes, polished wood tables and brass fans, back patio bar, smart restaurant; well kept Flowers and Wethereds on handpump, unobtrusive piped music, fruit machine, good bar food with daily specials and salad bar; bedrooms *(Lyn and Bill Capper)*; *Goat*: Plushly renovated rambling old Benskins pub with full meals and smartly uniformed bar staff *(LYM)*

Cole Green [TL2811], *Cowper Arms*: Excellent food; bedrooms comfortable and well designed *(Lorna Smith)*

Colney Heath [TL2005], *Crooked Billet*: Good range of well kept real ales and lots of unusual bottled beers in traditional tiled bar and comfortably modernised lounge, straightforward bar food, summer barbecues, pets' corner in garden, maybe children's ponies to ride in summer; roofed-over terrace *(LYM)*

Colney Street [Radlett Rd; TL1502], *Black Horse*: Licensee 27 years in Navy, and his son 15 years – naval crests and pictures, Falklands mementoes in bright and breezy no-nonsense pub; very pleasant staff, Benskins Best, basic food *(D L Johnson)*

Cottered [TL3129], *Bell*: Restful lighting in long bar with dining area at one end, fruit machine at the other; welcoming licensee, unobtrusive piped music, Benskins Best and Ind Coope Burton on handpump, very friendly atmosphere *(Gwen and Peter Andrews)*; *Bull*: Good simple food, soft piped music in lounge, darts and fruit machine in public bar; attractive village *(Lyn and Bill Capper)*

☆ **Croxley Green** [Rickmansworth Rd (A412) at junction with Watford Rd and Baldwins Lane – OS Sheet 176 reference 087959; TQ0795], *Two Bridges*: Handsomely reno-

vated roadhouse, with feel of well heeled and relaxing solidity in the several decently and interestingly furnished areas of its spacious bar, and when it first opened quite a landmark in its attractive muted décor, sofas, easy chairs, books and so forth, with well kept Ind Coope-related real ales and maybe a guest such as Youngs; in the last year or so, though, the food seems more ordinary, and service and atmosphere perhaps less welcoming *(Ian Phillips, Mr and Mrs F W Sturch, BKA, TBB, Mr and Mrs F H Stokes, Lyn and Bill Capper, LYM – more reports please)*

Croxley Green [The Green], *Artichoke*: Friendly and skilfully restored double-fronted pub on village green, beams, open fires, gas lighting, parrot, dogs allowed; food in bar, well kept Trumans Sampson and Websters Yorkshire *(John and Denise Keable)*

Dane End [Great Munden; from Dane End go 2 miles past the Boot – OS Sheet 166 reference 352234; TL3321], *Plough*: Included for the unique full-size Compton theatre organ in the comfortable and lofty lounge extension that's been built specially to house it; otherwise, usual bar food, well kept Greene King IPA and Abbot and Rayments, local atmosphere *(D L Johnson, LYM)*

Datchworth Green [1 Watton Rd; TL2718], *Inn on the Green*: Large well refurbished lounge bar, plenty of room for eating in another bar; very good food, good choice of real ales such as Adnams, friendly atmosphere and good service *(D L Johnson, M Draper)*; *Plough*: Simple friendly pub with well kept Greene King real ales *(LYM)*

☆ **nr Datchworth** [Bramfield Rd, Bulls Green; TL2717], *Horns*: Pretty fifteenth-century country pub decorated interestingly to show its age, with attractive rugs on patterned brickwork floor, big inglenook, low beams or high rafters, seats out on the crazy paving among roses; decent pub food, well kept Flowers Original and Wethereds on handpump, good cider and coffee; not all readers, however, have found the friendliness that welcomed us – more reports on this please *(Philip Haggar, Tony Semark, Rachel Britton, D Johnson, LYM)*

Eastwick [village signposted from A414; TL4311], *Lion*: Friendly village pub in pleasant rural surroundings, good atmosphere, well kept McMullens ales, tidy gardens *(Alan and Ruth Woodhouse)*

☆ **Essendon** [West End Lane; TL2708], *Candlestick*: Friendly isolated local with generous helpings of low-priced food from varied menus lunchtimes and Tues–Fri evenings, well kept McMullens ales, log fires in comfortable lounge and public bar with darts and fruit machine, friendly service, flower-bordered terrace; food service can be slow when busy – it's popular at lunchtime with BT staff and older people *(Robert Young, D L Johnson, Mr and Mrs BPS, Lyn and Bill Capper)*

☆Flaunden [Hogpits Bottom; TL0100], *Bricklayers Arms*: Cottagey and low-beamed, interesting choice of real ales, old-fashioned peaceful garden *(LYM)*

☆Flaunden, *Green Dragon*: Neat and comfortably refurbished partly panelled pub with well kept Marstons Pedigree and Merrie Monk and Taylor-Walker on handpump, bar food (note that prices may not include VAT, and service has sometimes been slow); charmingly well kept garden with summerhouse and aviaries *(LYM)*

☆Frithsden [TL0110], *Alford Arms*: A Whitbreads pub, brewing its own Cherry Pickers and other real ales in tiny brewhouse (worth a look in daylight), and stocking well kept Brakspears, Flowers Original and Wethereds; simple bar food, attractive country surroundings, local atmosphere – a fine summer pub *(Nick Long, BKA, LYM)*

Ganwick Corner [TQ2599], *Duke of York*: Good fillet steaks and salads, well kept beer, very good service – a Berni house *(Anon)*

Graveley [TL2327], *George & Dragon*: Good range of interesting inexpensive food in generous helpings at lunchtime – popular then with men working nearby; boules and small play area in big garden, special-event evenings *(Peter Briercliffe, D L Johnson)*

Great Offley [TL1427], *Crusty Loaf*: Relatively short choice of very good food in small pub with restaurant *(Phil Mollicone)*; *Red Lion*: Good bar food, particularly prawns in garlic butter, small restaurant has excellent value set price menu including fine steaks *(Phil Mollicone)*

Hailey [TL3710], *Galley Hall*: Warm, friendly atmosphere, well kept Benskins Best and Ind Coope Burton, good value food lunchtime and evenings *(Dave Wright)*

Harpenden [469 Luton Rd, on edge of town; 2¼ miles from M1 junction 10 – A1081 (ex-A6) towards town; TL1314], *Fox*: Extremely friendly local, well kept beer and good food *(Douglas and Lorna Collopy)*; [main st] *Harpenden Arms*: Clean, comfortable pub with superbly kept Fullers, interesting bar food; parking can be a problem *(John Baker)*; [Marquis Lane] *Marquis of Granby*: Welcoming, pleasant atmosphere, good food *(Mr and Mrs F E M Hardy)*

nr Hemel Hempstead [Briden's Camp; leaving on A4146, right at Flamstead/Markyate signpost opp Red Lion – OS Sheet 166 reference 044111; TL0506], *Crown & Sceptre*: Character pub with roaring fire, old-fashioned style, good range of real ales – more reports please on how it's been doing since sold by Banks & Taylors in 1987 *(Stephen King, LYM)*; [Piccott's End; by roundabout on new northerly route of A4147] *Marchmont Arms*: Heavy ornate mirrors and oil paintings on yellowed walls, some chaises-longues – mixed with machine with flashing lights, big vending machines on walls, electronic scorer for darts; very helpful

licensee and attractive staff; wide choice of sandwiches, rolls, hot dishes and salads *(D L Johnson)*

☆Hertford [Fore St; TL3212], *Salisbury Arms*: The incongruity of a sedate English country hotel concealing a full-blown Chinese restaurant – the place is Chinese-run, and very well, too – almost justifies an entry in itself; three very comfortable rooms – cocktail bar, public bar with machines, darts, and so forth, and lounge with lots of tables; well kept McMullens Bitter and AK Mild; waitress-served excellent value food, fine sandwiches with meat carved in front of you *(Revd Ian Watson, Ian Phillips)*

Hertford [The Folly], *Old Barge*: Comfortably renovated canalside pub with well kept Benskins real ale, popular with young people *(D L Johnson, LYM)*

Hitchin [Stevenage Rd; TL1929], *Orange Tree*: Good local music, friendly atmosphere, well kept McMullens *(Adrian Smith)*; [Bucklersbury (just off Market Sq)] *Red Hart*: May be town's oldest building – pretty little courtyard, well kept Greene King IPA and Abbot, simple bar food, comfortably modernised *(LYM)*; *Sailor Boy*: Quite large Whitbreads pub with food counter, help-yourself salads, wide choice of very good chips-ish food, friendly Beefeater-style atmosphere; conservatory-like family annexe *(D L Johnson)*

Hoddesdon [Spitalbrook; TL3709], *George*: Recently modernised roadside pub with coal fire, friendly, attentive staff, Benskins Best on handpump and freshly cooked food including good range of toasted sandwiches as well as more substantial dishes *(Mr and Mrs S Pollock-Hill)*

Ickleford [TL1831], *Old George*: Rambling beamed Tudor pub by churchyard, good value bar food and Greene King beers *(LYM)*

Kings Langley [A41 N of town; TL0702], *Eagle*: The Canadian licensee who lifted this simply furnished but friendly Benskins local out of the ordinary left in autumn 1987; lunchtime bar food, Ind Coope-related real ales, good outside areas with playground, maybe occasional jazz; bedrooms *(LYM)*

Knebworth [(just outside); TL2520], *Lytton Arms*: Has had very friendly and helpful casually dressed staff, good choice of bar food, good real ales and attractive wines by the glass; but being sold by Banks & Taylors in 1988 – latest news, please *(D L Johnson, Rodney Coe)*

☆Lemsford [A6129 towards Wheathampstead; TL2111], *Crooked Chimney*: Very energetic licensee who previously made Fox at Harpenden popular for unusually wide range of food, especially seafood; doing well in this smartly refurbished open-plan bar around central chimney, with well kept Ind Coope real ales, but little seating space for bar meals and there may be a charge if you sit in restaurant; garden by fields, friendly service *(D L Johnson, LYM)*; *Sun*: Cheerful Courage pub close to River Lea, lots of beams and timbers, good filled rolls; where Joseph Arch's pioneer Agricultural Labourers Union used to meet *(LYM)*

Leverstock Green [TL0806], *Leather Bottle*: Old-world cosy beamed pub facing green, open fires at each end of bar, good collection of antique leather bottles; popular, but quick and efficient service; varied and reasonably priced bar food, Ind Coope Burton on handpump *(Miss C S Pedder, T J Maeer, D L Johnson)*; *White Horse*: Plushly refurbished modern pub on different levels with conservatory-style extension – rather like a nightclub without the dance floor; excellent décor and atmosphere, cosy settees, subtle lighting, good range of beers and other drinks, good lunchtime food, piped pop music; always very busy *(Miss C S Pedder, T J Maeer)*

Lilley [TL1126], *Lilley Arms*: Good food and service from pleasant people in very old pub, being extended *(MR)*

Little Gaddesden [village signposted from B4506; SP9913], *Bridgewater Arms*: Included in previous editions for its cheerful combination of own-brewed beer with civilised but unpretentious comfort; sadly, it has changed hands and no longer has the own-brewed beer *(LYM)*

☆ **Little Hadham** [TL4422], *Nags Head*: Well kept Greene King and Rayments real ales and good food using fresh ingredients such as locally caught trout and Cromer crab in sixteenth-century country local – the puddings are specially good *(Alan and Ruth Woodhouse, LYM)*

Little Wymondley [TL2127], *Bucks Head*: Handy for A1(M), chintzy and friendly with well kept Wethereds beer; attractive garden *(LYM)*

☆ **London Colney** [Waterside (just off main st by bridge at S end); TL1704], *Green Dragon*: A dearth of reports recently on this immaculately kept pub, with lunchtime bar food (not Sun), friendly staff, well kept Benskins, lots of beams and brasses, tables outside by quiet riverside green; no children *(Dave Butler, Lesley Storey, S Matthews, Mr and Mrs Ken Turner, D R Shillitoe, LYM)*

Long Marston [38 Tring Rd – OS Sheet 165 reference 899157; SP8915], *Queens Head*: ABC pub with log fire in olde-worlde flagstoned bar, ABC Bitter, Bass, Everards Tiger and Ind Coope Burton, wide range of bar food, small garden, children's room *(Phil Cook)*

Markyate [TL0616], *Sun*: Low-beamed old Benskins pub with inglenook log fire and garden *(LYM)*

☆ **Newgate Street** [a mile N of Cuffley; TL3005], *Coach & Horses*: Not many recent reports on this civilised old country pub with mellow mix of wall settles, carpet, flagstones and pair of open fires; bar food (not Sun) from sandwiches – including popular heavy-duty

toasted ones – to home-made specials such as pork and apples in cider, well kept Benskins Best and Ind Coope Burton on handpump, seats outside and on sheltered lawn; good walks nearby; children in club-room *(Mr and Mrs M J Leith, Gwen and Peter Andrews, Dave Butler, Les Storey, R P Hastings, LYM)*

Nuthampstead [TL4034], *Woodman*: Very warm welcoming atmosphere, first-class ham and egg (almost too big a helping), a jug of real cream with the coffee, good puddings; Adnams, Boddingtons and Greene King IPA, clean and comfortable bar *(SAL)*

Oxhey [Upper Paddock Rd; TQ1195], *Haydon Arms*: Pleasant friendly small back-street pub with something of a country-pub air, tables on small terrace behind white-painted fence, little public bar, L-shaped lounge with wood-boarded ceiling, Benskins Best and Ind Coope Burton *(Stan Edwards)*; [108 Villiers Rd (which runs between Pinner Rd nearly opp Bushey & Oxhey Stn and Watford–Bushey rd] *Villiers Arms*: Old pictures and maps on walls of Benskins single-bar town pub, comfortably carpeted, will turn down piped music on request; bar food *(Lyn and Bill Capper)*

Perry Green [TL4317], *Hoops*: Wide choice of food until 9pm and very friendly staff in attractively renovated McMullens pub, nice gardens *(Philip Haggar, Tony Semark, Rachel Britton)*

Pirton [TL1431], *Cat & Fiddle*: Homely pub facing village green, well kept Charles Wells real ales, bar food, swing on back lawn *(LYM)*

Potten End [TL0109], *Red Lion*: Reliably good bar food at reasonable prices *(Mr and Mrs F W Sturch)*

Potters Crouch [TL1105], *Holly Bush*: Attractive whitewashed Benskins pub with marvellous highly polished biggish tables, walls covered with pictures, plates, brasses and antlers, reasonable simple food, Benskins Best, Ind Coope Burton, coffee; large garden *(D L Johnson)*

Puckeridge [High St; TL3823], *Crown & Falcon*: Pepys stayed here in 1662 – steep-roofed and friendly old inn, comfortably modernised; bar food, restaurant, good Sun lunch with big helpings, well kept Benskins Best and Ind Coope Burton; children in eating area; bedrooms *(H Paulinski, LYM)*

Radlett [14 Cobden Hill (Watling St); TL1600], *Cat & Fiddle*: Well kept Trumans Bitter and first-class lunchtime home cooking using quality ingredients *(C M Tyrwhitt Jones)*

Redbourn [nr M1 junction 9; TL1012], *Chequers*: Chef & Brewer pub with good food in bar and restaurant – mostly fresh and home cooked, including vegetarian dishes; comfortable beamed bar with Watneys-related real ales; large garden *(P C Marsh)*

☆ **Reed** [High St; TL3636], *Cabinet*: Friendly and relaxed tiled and weatherboarded house, a pub for centuries; parlourish inside (though with large lounge extension), nice garden out, wide choice of real ales such as Adnams, Greene King Abbot, Hook Norton Best, Mauldons and Nethergate tapped from the cask, reasonably priced bar food, children's summer bar *(Dave Butler, Lesley Storey, Alan and Ruth Woodhouse, LYM)*

Rickmansworth [High St; TQ0594], *Coach & Horses*: Old-fashioned low-ceilinged pub with warm local atmosphere, open fire, well kept Greene King on handpump, popular darts in bar (which often has Sun entertainment) *(L Baker, L Good)*

Ridge [Crossoaks Lane; TL2100], *Old Guinea*: Small friendly local, well kept Benskins Best on handpump, excellent fish (fresh daily) and good steak *(Paul Marsh)*

☆ **Rushden** [village signed off A507 about 1 mile W of Cottered; TL3031], *Moon & Stars*: Unspoilt and cottagey, with low heavy beams, big white-panelled inglenook fireplace, Windsor chairs around long scrubbed table, sandwiches and home-cooked hot dishes (not Sun), Greene King keg beers, playthings and tables in back garden – the bustling little dog's called Sheba *(Charles Bardswell, LYM)*

Sandridge [High St; TL1610], *Rose & Crown*: Old pictures and horsebrasses in Whitbreads pub with Flowers real ale; good choice of excellent if not cheap food, good service *(D L Johnson, T R Espley)*

Sarratt [The Green; TQ0499], *Boot*: Attractive early eighteenth-century tiled local facing green, cosy rambling rooms, nice inglenook fireplace, well kept Benskins and Ind Coope real ales, good lunchtime food *(LYM)*; [Church End – a pretty approach is via North Hill, a lane N off A404, just under a mile W of A405; TQ0398] *Cock*: Country pub in attractive setting, unusual traditional two-room layout, inglenook fireplace and so forth; nearby church well worth a visit *(BKA, LYM)*; [The Green] *Cricketers*: Very popular, facing green with tables outside, quick service in comfortable low-beamed lounge bar's well laid out eating area, good bar food from crusty rolls to salads and hot dishes; Courage and Websters Yorkshire, darts, fruit machines, no piped music *(Lyn and Bill Capper)*

☆ **Sawbridgeworth** [8 Vantorts Rd, Far Green; TL4814], *King William IV*: Small and welcoming, with enterprising food and well kept Courage real ales; friendly staff, no coin machines or loud music *(N and J D Bailey)*; [West Rd] *Three Horseshoes*: Well kept McMullens, good if slow bar food at reasonable prices, outside tables and play area *(R C Vincent)*

☆ **St Albans** [61 Albert St; left turn down Holywell Hill past White Hart – car park left at end; TL1507], *Garibaldi*: A current favourite of this town's notably choosy beer-lovers (and its radicals): cleanly refurbished by Fullers to give an almost Tardis-like impression, with Shakespearian prints, conservatory-like no-smoking bar and separate serving-bar; enthusiastic young licensees, imaginative good value food using real ingredients (trout with a mussels and orange stuffing, for instance), with superb fresh vegetables and no chips; convivial atmosphere, well kept Chiswick, London Pride and ESB, seats on terrace, occasional barbecues *(Andy Blackburn, Michael and Alison Sandy, Keith Ogden, John Baker, David Mabey)*

☆ **St Albans** [Holywell Hill], *White Hart*: Friendly hotel with long and entertaining history, comfortable open-plan bar with antique panelling, fireplaces and furnishings; bar food and accommodating restaurant, Benskins and Ind Coope Burton on handpump *(Jon Dewhirst, Wayne Brindle, LYM)*

St Albans [Adelaide St (off High St on W side by Texas Homecare shop)], *Adelaide Wine House*: Notable for staying open until very late Fri and Sat, this three-floor pub has a simply furnished upstairs bar with lunchtime food, downstairs wine bar and restaurant, real ale, and top-floor discos and live bands *(LYM)*; [corner main st and Hatfield Rd] *Cock*: Comfortably modernised town pub with interesting history – it once had a floor of human bones, probably from second Battle of St Albans in 1461 *(LYM)*; [French Row] *Fleur de Lys*: Historic medieval building, though the best parts of it are now in a museum and it's been comfortably modernised *(LYM)*; [36 Fishpool St] *Lower Red Lion*: Lots of old beams in very comfortable plush lounge; also attractive brick and beams public bar; wide choice of well kept real ales such as Fullers, Greene King and Youngs, good value simple lunchtime bar food *(Michael and Alison Sandy)*; [6 London Rd] *Peahen*: Comfortably furnished and welcoming McMullens hotel, decent bar food (not Sun), well kept real ale *(Anon)*; [St Michaels] *Six Bells*: Comfortably well kept low-beamed Benskins pub with bar food and well kept real ales *(LYM)*

Stevenage [Old Town; TL2324], *Marquis of Lorne*: Friendly pub with good beer and food, exemplary lavatories, tables outside *(P Gillbe)*

Thorley Street [A1184 Sawbridgeworth–Bishops Stortford; TL4718], *Coach & Horses*: Recently extended and tastefully furnished dining area in keeping with rest of pub; homely atmosphere, busy but cosy and very friendly; good value food including reasonably priced carvery, Benskins beer and generous glasses of decent wine *(Alan and Ruth Woodhouse)*

Tring [London Rd (A41); SP9211], *Cow Roast aka Drovers Rest*: Relaxed atmosphere, lots of reasonably priced fish and seafood, also cold meats, hot pies and other hot dishes; impressive choice of puddings especially in the good restaurant; good service *(Gp Capt David Hay, D J Bride)*; [Bulbourne – B488 towards Dunstable, next to BWB works; SP9313] *Grand Junction Arms*: Alongside Grand Union Canal, large grounds with free-range chickens and rabbits, tables outside; well kept Benskins, good choice of bar food including vegetarian dishes and childrens helpings, separate restaurant; nr GWG110; children welcome *(Chris and Jacqui Chatfield)*

Turnford [TL3604], *Bulls Head*: Good atmosphere, willing staff, good bar food including excellent steaks, McMullens ales and decent wine; straightforward brocade-furnishing 1930s-style roadhouse *(Ian Phillips)*

Walkern [TL2826], *White Lion*: Welcoming old pub, sensitively restored outside and lots of character inside – cosy alcoves, low beams, nice inglenook with open fire in winter; popular for food in bar and small restaurant, piped music, lots of flowers in garden; in 1711 – when it was called the Rose & Crown – it housed the judges who were the last to sentence a woman to death for witchcraft *(Roger Danes, LYM)*; [B1036] *Yew Tree*: Open fire, wheel-back chairs and lots of brass – clean, welcoming and quite cosy; McMullens real ale, well presented sophisticated rather than typically pubby bar food (but including sandwiches), piped music, restaurant (not Sat lunchtime – maybe two evening sittings); tables on front terrace, McMullens beers *(Lyn and Bill Capper, D L Johnson)*

Watford [Stamford Rd; TQ1196], *Nascot Arms*: Cosy little town pub with dark red flock wallpaper in Edwardian lounge, newly refurbished public bar; Greene King beers, usual pub food *(Stan Edwards)*; [Station Rd] *Pennant*: Clean and spacious Benskins pub with good atmosphere, plenty of seating, well kept ale, polite staff, separate darts alcove; handy for rail and bus stations *(L Baker, L Good)*

Watford Heath [207 Pinner Rd; TQ1196], *Load of Hay*: Good pub food, cheerful staff, pleasant comfortable furnishings *(Gordon Leighton)*; [Watford Green (off Pinner Rd)] *Royal Oak*: Nice furnishings, well kept Watneys-related real ales; nice spot facing green *(S J Edwards)*

Watton-at-Stone [13 High St; A602; TL3019], *Bull*: Picturesque coaching-inn with agreeable and obliging licensee and decent individually cooked food *(D L Johnson)*

Welwyn [TL2316], *White Hart*: Well kept comfortable pub with excellent lunches (booking advised) and first-class ploughman's in bar *(Archie Loveday)*

nr **Wheathampstead** [Gustard Wood; B651 1½ miles N; TL1713], *Cross Keys*: Unspoilt country pub with Benskins real ales and simple but good value bar food; alone in rolling wooded countryside *(LYM)*; [also Gustard Wood] *Tin Pot*: Welcoming, pleasant atmosphere, popular, wide choice of food *(Mr and Mrs F E M Hardy, D L Johnson)*; [Nomansland Common (B651 ½ mile S); TL1712] *Wicked Lady*: Formerly very popular indeed for tremendous range of interesting real ales and other drinks, enterprising bar food, character inside and good garden; but reports since summer 1987 have been generally though not universally uncomplimentary – then in spring 1988 Whitbreads evidently took a hand, with its closure for refurbishment, and we're now keeping our fingers crossed for a revival *(Mrs H A Green, LYM)*

Willian [TL2230], *Three Horseshoes*: Good food and well kept Greene King real ales in warmly welcoming pub very handy for A1(M) – left after Letchworth turn-off *(LYM)*

Wilstone [Tring Rd; SP9013], *Half Moon*: Excellent village pub – a little out of the way but well worth the detour; nr start GWG110 *(Dr and Mrs A K Clarke)*

Humberside

In England it's a general rule that big-city pubs tend to be disappointing: though many of our readers live in cities, it's country pubs that they recommend – and our own inspections confirm that normally the real pub prizes are to be found in the country, or perhaps in small towns. Hull is an important exception to this rule. It has three notable pubs – including the atmospheric Olde White Harte (perhaps the county's most enjoyable pub) and on the waterfront the attractively renovated Minerva, which brews its own beer (a new entry in this edition). Grimsby, too, though so far without a main entry, has several interesting propositions in the Lucky Dip at the end of the chapter (as indeed does Hull). For pub food, it is still the countryside which offers the best hunting ground, with notable places including the welcoming Plough at Allerthorpe, the stylishly simple Queens Head in Kirkburn (with an attractive garden), the Half Moon in Skidby (especially for connoisseurs of the Yorkshire pudding – the pub's got a good deal of character, too, especially in its little front snug), the Pipe & Glass in its attractive surroundings at South Dalton, the warm-hearted Seabirds in Flamborough and (doing well under the licensee who took it over in early 1988) the pleasantly old-fashioned St Vincent Arms in Sutton upon Derwent. The White Horse in Beverley oozes character – decidedly one for lovers of the unspoilt; the unpretentious Triton at Sledmere stands out as an attractive place to stay at. In the Lucky Dip, places to note particularly include the Altisidora at Bishop Burton, both entries under Brandesburton, the Royal Dog & Duck at Flamborough, the Gold Cup at Low Catton, the Gate at Millington (a particular favourite for atmosphere) and the Three Cups at Stamford Bridge.

Boot & Shoe, Ellerton

ALLERTHORPE SE7847 Map 7
Plough ⊗
Off A1079 near Pocklington

Handy for the attractive lily-pond gardens and stuffed sporting trophies of Burnby Hall, this notably welcoming, pretty pub does very good value, home-made bar food: daily specials such as game pie as well as open sandwiches (from 90p), soup or light Yorkshire pudding with onion gravy (£1), spare ribs (£2.50), beef and mushroom pie (£2.75), roast chicken (£2.95), salads such as home-cooked beef or ham (£2.95), steaks (from £5), children's dishes (from £1.10), and very good home-made cheesecake; Sunday roast lunch (best to book). The refurbished two-room carpeted lounge bar has open fires, snug alcoves (including one big bay window), hunting prints and some wartime RAF and RCAF photographs (squadrons of both were stationed here). The games – pool, darts, dominoes, shove-ha'penny, cribbage, fruit machine and space game – have proved so popular that a new extension has been built for them on the public side. Well kept Theakstons Best, XB and Old Peculier on handpump; piped music. There are tables on the gravel outside. *(Recommended by Derek Stephenson, Lee Goulding, Jon Wainwright)*

Free house   Licensee David Banks   Real ale   Meals and snacks   Restaurant tel Pocklington (0759) 302349   Children welcome   Open 12–3, 7–1

BEVERLEY TA0340 Map 8
White Horse ('Nellies')
Hengate, close to the imposing Church of St Mary; runs off North Bar Within

Though John Wesley preached in the back yard in the mid-eighteenth century, the building actually dates from around 1425. The former landlady gave the small rooms the decidedly unspoilt Victorian feel that it still preserves today, with open fires – one with an attractively tiled fireplace – a gas-lit pulley-controlled chandelier, antique cartoons and sentimental engravings, a deeply reverberating chiming clock, and brown leatherette seats (with high-backed settles in one little snug) on bare floorboards. Well kept Sam Smiths on handpump, and remarkably cheap food – roast beef, pork or lamb with carrots, cabbage and potatoes for around £2, say; darts. *(Recommended by T T Kelly, Mark Radford, Lee Goulding, Ian Phillips, J and J W, Jane English)*

Sam Smiths   Real ale   Meals and snacks (lunchtime, not Sun)   Restaurant tel Hull (0482) 861973   Children welcome   Some live music   Open 11.30–2.30, 6–10.30; closes 4 Weds, 5 Sat

ELLERTON SE7039 Map 7
Boot & Shoe [illustrated on page 374]
Village signposted from B1228

Sheltering under a spreading tree, this big, low-tiled sixteenth-century cottage has a comfortable, friendly bar with dove-grey plush wall seats and wheel-back chairs around dimpled copper tables, low black beams, a butter-coloured ceiling, a nice bow window seat, and three open fires. Bar food includes soup (70p), chilli con carne and lasagne (£2.25), chicken and mushroom or steak and kidney pie (£2.95) and sirloin steak (£4.95). Well kept Old Mill and Bulldogs (from Snaith), Tetleys and Youngers Scotch on handpump; darts, dominoes, fruit machine, piped music. Weekend barbecues in the garden at the back. *(Recommended by Jon Wainwright, Graham Howard, Tim Halstead, Phil Asquith, R R Lane)*

Free house   Licensees D Gregg and P McVay   Real ale   Meals and snacks (evenings, not Mon, and Sat and Sun lunchtimes)   Restaurant tel Bubwith (075 785) 346   Open 12–3 (4 Sat), 7.30–11 June–Oct; closed weekday lunchtimes in winter

FLAMBOROUGH TA2270 Map 8
Seabirds
Junction of B1255 and B1229

Close to the open country above the cliffs of Flamborough Head, this pub has an unflurried and nautical atmosphere. The public bar is full of scowling toby jugs and shipping paraphernalia as well as old framed photographs of Flamborough. Leading off this is the lounge, which has a wood-burning stove, pictures and paintings of the local landscape, and a mirror glazed with grape vines. The emphasis here is very much on sea birds: there's a whole case of them (stuffed, of course) along one wall. The hospitality is warm and friendly, and the good value bar food includes sandwiches (from 65p, crab or salmon when available), soup (75p), rollmop herring (£1), ploughman's (£1.50), omelettes (from £2), good fresh local haddock (£1.80) or plaice (priced according to season), scampi (£2), seafood platter (£2.50), a selection of fish salads (again priced according to season) and sirloin steak (£5.50); daily specials such as toad-in-the-hole (£1.90), steak and kidney pie (£2) and smoked salmon mousse (£2.25). Darts, shove-ha'penny, dominoes, cribbage and piped music. *(Recommended by M A and W R Proctor, TR, MA, Dr and Mrs S G Donald; more reports please)*

Free house   Licensees Barrie and Gill Crosby   Meals and snacks (not Sun or Mon evening) Restaurant tel Bridlington (0262) 850242   Children in restaurant   Open 11–3.30, 5.30–11; 11–3, 7–11 in winter

HULL TA0927 Map 8
George
Land of Green Ginger; park just outside town centre and walk in: Land of Green Ginger is a lane at far end of pedestrians-only Whitefriargate, which leads out of centre opposite City Hall

Perhaps best on weekday lunchtimes, this old shuttered coaching-inn has high beams and old latticed windows, squared oak panelling, a Victorian copper and mahogany counter, and high bar stools with sensible little back rests. The long room opens out at the far end of the main bar, with several more tables – come early if you want a place; the dining-room, furnished in traditional plush fashion, is upstairs. Good value food includes light snacks such as pork pies (45p) or home-made Scotch eggs (65p) as well as filled rolls and sandwiches (from 60p), burgers (from 90p), ploughman's or home-made pâté with garlic bread (£1.65), and hot dishes such as lasagne, spaghetti bolognese, chilli con carne (£1.65), with salads such as home-cooked beef or ham (£1.75); well kept Bass and Stones on hand-pump; dominoes, fruit machine and piped music. On your way in, look out for the narrow slit window just to the left of the coach entry; ostlers used to watch for late-night arrivals in case they were highwaymen. The pub is handy for the excellent Docks Museum. *(Recommended by M A and W R Proctor, Lee Goulding; more reports please)*

Bass   Licensee Paolo E Cattaneo   Real ale   Meals (lunchtime, not Sun) and snacks Restaurant tel Hull (0482) 226373   Children in restaurant   No nearby parking Open 11–3, 5.30–10.30

Minerva
From A63 Castle Street/Garrison Road, turn into Queen Street towards piers at central traffic lights; some metered parking here; pub is in pedestrianised Nelson Street, at far end

A great deal of thought and energy has gone into making Hull's old waterfront attractive, with interesting new or converted buildings, a lively marina, and broad prettily paved pedestrian walkways. One of these separates this pub, just around the corner from the Pilot Office, from the Humber. Inside, the floor is raised a few feet above ground level though the windows are down at normal height – so the view out is unusually good. The pub's been thoughtfully refurbished in an old-fashioned style, with several rooms rambling all the way around a central servery, and comfortable seats. Nice touches include interesting photographs and pictures of old Hull (with two attractive wash drawings by Roger Davis), a big chart of the Humber, the tiny snug with room for just three people, and the profusion of varnished woodwork in the back room (which looks out to the marina basin, and has darts). Besides well kept Tetleys Mild and Bitter on handpump, the pub brews its own Pilots Pride (you can see into the microbrewery from the street); evening bar food includes burgers (£1.60), chicken Kiev, plaice or scampi (£2.60), gammon (£3.20) and steaks (from £4), with more snacks at lunchtime. Piped music from the fine reproduction Wurlitzer juke box (the real 'works', with the records, are actually in a completely different place) is loud and clear. Darts, dominoes. *(Recommended by Lee Goulding and others)*

Own brew (Tetleys)   Licensee John Harris McCue   Real ale   Meals (lunchtime) and snacks (not Sun evening)   Children in eating area of bar lunchtime only   Open 11–11 in summer; probably 11–3, 6–10.30 in winter

Olde White Harte ★

Off 25 Silver Street, a continuation of Whitefriargate (see previous entry); pub is up narrow passage beside the jewellers' Barnby and Rust, and should not be confused with the much more modern White Hart nearby

This is a fine place for eating Hull cheese (an eighteenth-century euphemism for enjoying a great deal to drink – the town was known then for its very strong ales). There are attractive stained-glass windows over the bow window seat, polished flooring tiles, carved heavy beams supporting black ceiling-boards, and brocaded Jacobean-style chairs in the inglenook by a fireplace decorated with Delft tiles. The curved copper-topped counter serves well kept Youngers IPA and No 3, and simple, traditional bar food includes sandwiches (60p–80p, hot beef £1.25), ploughman's and steak pie and potatoes (£1.95); Sunday lunch (£4.25); pleasant, efficient service. An excellently preserved handsome old oak staircase takes you up past a grandfather clock to a heavily panelled room where on St George's Day 1642 Sir John Hotham, the town's governor, decided to lock the gate at the far end of Whitefriargate against King Charles, depriving him of the town's arsenal – a fateful start to the Civil War. There are seats in the courtyard outside; dominoes and a fruit machine. *(Recommended by Lee Goulding, David Gittins, M A and W R Proctor; more reports please)*

Youngers   Licensee Mr R Wathey   Real ale   Meals and snacks (not evening, Sun) Lunchtime restaurant tel Hull (0482) 26363   Children in restaurant   No nearby parking Open 11–3, 5.30–10.30

KIRKBURN   SE9855 Map 8

Queens Head ⊗

Village signposted from A163 SW of Great Driffield; pub car park actually on A163

A farmhouse until the previous village pub burnt down in the early nineteenth century, this sensitively refurbished place has an informal, friendly atmosphere and good, efficient service. The small bar has atmospheric black and white photographs of Hull docks and ships, many taken by Mr Mort's father, on the plain walls, and cushioned wheel-back chairs and wall settles on the muted brown-patterned carpet. The home-cooked bar food, praised for its good value and imaginative preparation, includes soup (90p), pâté (£1.55), soused herring (£1.85), ploughman's (£1.90 – lunchtime only), breaded haddock (£2.65), pork casserole in cider or chilli con carne (£2.75), lasagne (£2.80), steak and kidney pie (£2.85), chicken and mushroom pie (£2.95) and goulash (£3.25), with sandwiches at lunchtime and in summer. What used to be a granary is now a reasonably priced galleried restaurant with good crockery and linen, and decorations that include family embroidery and pictures. Darts, dominoes, fruit machine, piped music. The attractive garden, at the back by the car park, has sturdy plain white seats and tables set among fruit trees, shrubs and flower beds. *(Recommended by David Gaunt, Dr and Mrs J Biggs, Roger Bellingham, Pam and Keith Holmes)*

Free house   Licensees Michael and Sophia Mort   Meals and snacks   Restaurant tel Driffield (0377) 89261   Children in small bar and restaurant   Open 12–2.30, 6.30–11 all year

SKIDBY   TA0133 Map 8
Half Moon ⊗
Main Street; off A164

There's a rambling series of little bars and saloons here, with an old-fashioned partly panelled front tap-room, which has a tiled floor, long cushioned wall benches, old elm tables, a little high shelf of foreign beer bottles and miniatures, and a coal fire. The more spacious communicating back rooms have a lighter and airier atmosphere, and there's an unusually big clock back here. The seemingly endless range of enormous (loaf-sized), feather-light Yorkshire puddings are so popular that they're said to get through 60,000 eggs and 7,000 pounds of flour a year; they come in a variety of fillings (from £1.55 for onion and gravy to £3.40 for venison, rabbit and pheasant with red wine sauce); other food, efficiently served, includes soup (85p), four-ounce burgers (from £1.50), ploughman's or chilli con carne (£2), steak and kidney pie (£2.70) and vegetarian dishes; maybe sandwiches. Dominoes, cribbage, fruit machine, piped music; possibly John Smiths on handpump. A landscaped garden area beside the car park has a children's play area, with a newly installed suspended net maze – apparently one of the first in Britain. A black and white windmill is nearby. *(More reports please)*

John Smiths   Licensee Peter Madeley   Meals and snacks   Children welcome   Open all day for a trial period

SLEDMERE   SE9365 Map 8
Triton 🛏
Junction of B1252 and B1253 NW of Great Driffield

Built next to one of the walls that surround Sledmere House, this friendly eighteenth-century posting-inn still bears the notice outside which says 'Licensed to let post horses', and it's easy to imagine windblown rides across this rolling country. Inside, the attractive traditional lounge bar has stately high-backed cushioned settles, and a roaring fire in winter; well kept Youngers Scotch on handpump. Generous bar food includes sandwiches (from 70p), soup (75p), ploughman's or burger (£1.90), chicken breast, scampi or prawn salad (crab when available – all £3.20), steak and kidney pie (£3.50) and steaks (from £5.50); traditional Sunday lunch (£5.25, children £3.30), and enormous breakfasts. The public bar has darts, dominoes, fruit machine, juke box; piped music. *(Recommended by A K Richards, B E Graham, Jon Dewhirst, Alastair Reed, M A and W R Proctor, TR, MA)*

Free house   Licensee John Regan   Real ale   Meals and snacks   Restaurant   Children welcome   Open all day, all year   Bedrooms tel Driffield (0377) 86644; £12 (£17.50B)/ £24 (£34B)

SOUTH DALTON   SE9645 Map 8
Pipe & Glass ⊗
Village signposted off B1248 NW of Beverley

This tiled white pub is charmingly decked with hanging baskets in summer, and there are tables on a quiet lawn by the edge of Dalton Park, with a children's play

area, flower borders, a very fine yew tree, ginger cats and maybe kittens. Inside, both bar rooms have leather seats around their walls and in their bow windows, wheel-back chairs and some rather high-backed settles, plush red carpets, and log fires – a big one in the beamed right-hand room, which has an old map of Yorkshire; the entrance to the main bar is done up as a replica of a stage-coach door. Bar food includes Yorkshire pudding and gravy (95p), nettle and lime soup (£1.10), smoked prawns and lemon mayonnaise (£2.45), chicken piri piri (£2.95) and lasagne verde or duck in orange and kumquat sauce (£3.25), all with carefully cooked vegetables; sandwiches. Besides the restaurant overlooking the lawn, the old separate stableblock has been converted into a weekend winter carvery bar (around £4 – in summer it does weekend barbecues, £2.50–£5). Clarks Bitter, Ruddles County and Websters Choice on handpump; shove-ha'penny, dominoes, fruit machine, piped music. The village itself is best found by aiming for the unusually tall and elegant spire of the church, visible for miles around.
(Recommended by T Nott, Roger Bellingham, Jane and Calum)

Free house Licensee Malcolm Crease Real ale Meals and snacks (not Sun evening) Restaurant tel Dalton Holme (069 64) 246 Children welcome Open 12–3, 7–11 (12–3.30, 6.30–11 Sat); closed evening 25 Dec

SUTTON UPON DERWENT SE7047 Map 7
St Vincent Arms ⊗

B1228 SE of York

Yet again this pub has been lucky in its new landlord: since the change in early 1988, reports are that the good value food is still just that, with sandwiches (from 85p), home-made soup (95p), bacon and prawn pâté (£1.50), ploughman's (from £2.25), salads (from £3.25), steak and kidney pie (£3.75) and fillet steak with oyster sauce (£8.25). The panelled front bar is a cosy, almost parlourish room with a cushioned bow window seat, Windsor chairs, traditional high-backed settles, a coal fire, a massive old wireless set, quite a lot of brass and copper and a shelf of plates just under the high ceiling. Another lounge and separate restaurant opens off here, and a games-room has pool, darts, dominoes, juke box, space game and fruit machine. The well kept ales on handpump change weekly, regularly including Greene King Abbot, Ruddles County and Timothy Taylors. The wide choice of wines by the bottle is unusual for the area; piped music. It's best to book a table if you want a full meal, especially at weekends; the friendly service makes up for the shortage of space. The handsome and large garden has tables and seats.
(Recommended by Graeme Smalley, Ray Wharram, N P Hodgson, Roger Bellingham, Jon Wainwright, Lee Goulding, T Nott, Derek Stephenson)

Free house Licensee Steven Richards Real ale Meals and snacks Restaurant tel Elvington (090 485) 349 Children in restaurant Open 12–2.30, 7–11 all year

Lucky Dip

Besides the fully inspected pubs, you might like to try these Lucky Dips recommended to us and described by readers (if you do, please send us reports):

Aldbrough [1 High St; TA2438], *George & Dragon*: Good evening meals and Sunday lunches from French chef/patron, friendly customers, keen dominoes and darts players, good staff; bedrooms *(Anne Wilks)*
Althorpe [SE8309], *Dolphin*: Friendly, efficient staff and spacious, clean restaurant; landlord is an excellent chef; good wines *(Peter H Clark)*
Arnold [off A165 Hull–Bridlington;

TA1041], *Bay Horse*: One of the very few unspoilt, genuine village locals left in area; one simple decorated room with farming feel; friendly service, real fire in stone fireplace; well kept Camerons Strongarm and occasionally Everards Old Original on handpump; animals tethered outside *(Lee Goulding)*
Beeford [A165 Bridlington–Leven; TA1354], *Black Swan*: Straightforward pub, useful as a

friendly roadside journey-breaker *(Lee Goulding)*

☆**Beverley** *Beverley Arms*: Comfortable and well kept THF hotel with spacious oak-panelled bar, well kept real ales on hand-pump, choice of several places to eat including covered courtyard with interesting inner yard housing impressive bank of former kitchen ranges; good bedrooms, in attractive country town *(Lee Goulding, LYM)*

Beverley [15 Butcher Row (main pedestrian st)], *Angel*: Bustling town-centre pub popular with shoppers – anyone from very old ladies to babes in arms; hot and cold bar food, sheltered back terrace with small fountain *(Neil and Elspeth Fearn)*; [Saturday Mkt] *Kings Head*: Comfortably refurbished, big helpings of good home-cooked food in lounge bar, locally popular public bar, restaurant; bedrooms *(R S Varney)*; [Saturday Mkt] *Push*: Old-fashioned, cosy, warm pub with bare floorboards which livens up in evenings with good music and friendly chatter; well kept Stones and hot and cold bar food *(T T Kelly)*; [North Bar Without] *Rose & Crown*: Good Darleys and Wards ales in relaxing comfortable lounge with good food also games-bar popular with younger people; convenient for racecourse; bedrooms not expensive *(R S Varney, Lee Goulding)*

☆**Bishop Burton** [A1079 Beverley–York; SE9939], *Altisidora*: Good value traditional food in low-beamed modernised lounge with comfortable alcoves, games in saloon bar, seats outside by well kept attractive flower beds, looking over to pretty pond on lovely village green *(Jon Wainwright, M A and W R Proctor, T Nott, LYM)*

☆**Brandesburton** [village signposted from A165 N of Beverley and Hornsea turn-offs; TA1247], *Black Swan*: Spaciously refurbished and attractive pub with good food-ordering system using table numbers, efficient staff – they have to be, as it's popular for lunch; real ales now include Batemans *(W and S McEwan, Nick Dowson, Alison Hayward, T Nott)*

☆**Brandesburton**, *Dacre Arms*: King-size helpings of good value bar food served efficiently in busy and rather vividly modernised but comfortable Georgian posting-inn – snug area on right used to house the local Justices Court; choice of well kept real ales on hand-pump, restaurant; children welcome *(M A and W R Proctor, Lee Goulding, T T Kelly, LYM)*

Brantingham [southern edge; SE9429], *Triton*: Spacious and comfortable modernised pub with well kept Websters Yorkshire, popular buffet in roomy and airy sun lounge, restaurant, games-bar, sheltered garden with children's play area; near wooded dale *(Lee Goulding, BB)*

Bridlington [2 Flamborough Rd; TA1867], *Beaconsfield Arms*: Well laid out Bass pub with comfortable lounge, airy lively public bar, near promenade *(LYM)*; [184 Kingsgate (A165, just outside)] *Broadacres*: Spacious and comfortable Chef & Brewer pub with excellent service, Websters Yorkshire Bitter, good food in snack bar and separate restaurant, pleasant piped music – get there early for a table; children's playground *(Capt Tony Bland, John Gould)*; [Windsor Cres; nr South Beach and harbour] *Windsor*: Very friendly nautical pub, with food and pool; bedrooms *(Lee Goulding)*

Brigg [TA0007], *Angel*: Huge helpings of beautiful fresh plaice with piles of excellent chips, on plates as big as trays; well kept ale, good coffee *(SS)*

Burringham [SE8309], *Ferryboat*: On the east bank of the River Trent – a pleasant spot in summer; good helpings of straightforward food, friendly landlord; swings and climbing-frame in garden *(Alan Bickley)*

Burton Agnes [TA1063], *Blue Bell*: Pleasant service, decent food, real ale *(T Nott, Nick Dowson, Alison Hayward)*

☆**Cottingham** [Parkway; TA0633], *Black Prince*: Pleasant pub notable for its champion sandwiches using home-cooked meats, good self-service salad trolley, fine evening steaks, reasonable wines *(T T Kelly, SY)*

Etton [3½ miles N of Beverley, off B1248; SE9843], *Light Dragoon*: Wide range of bar food including generous sandwiches, also well kept Youngers real ales, in two roomy and recently redecorated comfortable bars with inglenook fireplace; garden with children's play area *(T Nott, LYM)*

☆**Flamborough** [Dog & Duck Sq (junction B1255/B1229); TA2270], *Royal Dog & Duck*: Warm and welcoming, with snug back bar and several other rooms rambling around attractive partly covered back courtyard which has lots of amusements for children – who are treated particularly well here; friendly, efficient and popular restaurant; local fish such as plaice, cod and haddock is a particular strength; bedrooms *(Neil and Elspeth Fearn, Mrs M Warrener, LYM)*

Great Driffield [TA0258], *Bell*: Popular pub with good beer and service, and excellent value bar lunches *(David Gaunt)*

Great Hatfield [TA1843], *Woggarth*: Cosy, friendly free house, well kept Camerons and Tetleys, comfortably furnished lounge, bar food and separate restaurant; children's room *(T T Kelly)*

Grimsby [Brighowgate; TA2609], *County*: Popular bar with interesting food, Youngers Scotch and No 3 on handpump, music loud but bearable; good reasonably priced restaurant; small but well equipped bedrooms *(R Aitken)*; [Riverhead Centre] *Friar Tuck*: Recently refurbished with comfortable seats and first-class restaurant *(Kevin Barwood)*; [Haven Mill, Garth Lane – parking off Baxtergate/ Alexandra Rd with bridge over R Freshney to Haven Mill] *Granary*: Interesting conversion of old canalside granary/ warehouse with enterprising food relying on local supplies – emphasis on fish; local real ale, friendly atmosphere; restaurant is on first floor, closed Sun *(J D K Hyams)*; [Victoria St] *Lloyds Arms*: Former bank converted into smart and busy old-fashioned tavern-style pub *(Kevin Barwood)*

☆ **Hull** [High St; in Old Town to S of centre, quite near Olde White Harte; TA0928], *Olde Black Boy*: Little black-panelled low-ceilinged front smoke room, lofty eighteenth-century back vaults bar with slaving mementoes and fine chandeliers (also TV, fruit machine, juke box strong on golden oldies), well kept Tetleys Mild and Bitter, friendly staff; said to be haunted *(Michael Craig, Lee Goulding, John Gould, BB)*

☆ **Hull** [narrow flagstoned alley off Lowgate; look out for huge blue bell overhanging pavement], *Olde Blue Bell*: Refurbished in traditional style with three snug rooms, well kept Sam Smiths OB, good value simple food, friendly service, bar billiards *(Lee Goulding, Jon Dewhirst, BB)*

Hull [Trinity House Lane], *Bonny Boat*: Small nautical-flavoured pub by market place, collection of model lifeboats, Batemans XB on handpump *(Lee Goulding)*; [Castle St] *Marina Post House*: Comfortable THF hotel overlooking marina with well kept ale and good food, also own leisure club and indoor swimming-pool *(John Gould)*; [Queen St] *Oberon*: Basic pierside pub used mainly by locals and fishermen, lots of local shipping photographs; very friendly, cheapish, good Bass and Stones beers *(Lee Goulding)*; [Jarratt St (opp former North Country Brewery)] *Old English Gentleman*: Relaxed city pub next to renovated New Theatre, autographed actor photographs, Mansfield beers *(Christian Fowler)*; [Princes Dock Rd] *Quayside*: John Smiths Bitter on handpump, lunchtime and evening bar food with three daily specials *(John Gould)*; [Alfred Gelder St (close to Guildhall, city centre – and not the same as our nearby main entry, the Olde White Harte!)] *White Hart*: Quiet city-centre refuge with magnificent green-tiled bar counter and mahogany and glass cabinet surround and backdrop; Mansfield beer *(Lee Goulding)*

Laceby [TA2106], *Saxon Arms*: Good food in bar, carvery and restaurant of country hotel, useful for this area; bedrooms *(J D K Hyams)*

☆ **Low Catton** [between A166 and A1079, near Stamford Bridge; SE7053], *Gold Cup*: Attractive pub/restaurant with well kept Tetleys and excellent food at good prices *(N P Hodgson, Lee Goulding, Ray Wharram)*

☆ **Market Weighton** [SE8742], *Londesborough Arms*: Relatively cheap bar food in elegant high-ceilinged Regency lounge with Cecil Aldin prints, flowers on tables, well kept real ales, friendly service, piped music – useful for area; bedrooms *(LYM)*

☆ **Millington** [Millington Pastures; village signposted from Pocklington; SE8352], *Gate*: Engaging sixteenth-century beamed village pub run and furnished with considerable character, with inglenook seats by the big log fire, food (not Thurs) from sandwiches to steaks and maybe pheasant or wild duck, well kept Bass and Tetleys on handpump, low prices, games room; in good Wolds walking country, near exceptional East Riding views; children welcome; opens noon (not always on winter weekdays) and 7ish; bedrooms *(Jon Wainwright, David Gaunt, Graeme Smalley, LYM)*

New Ellerby [TA1639], *Blue Bell*: Good inn with comfortable lounge, cosy snug, open fire, food, good Bass and Stones beers; very quiet village *(Lee Goulding)*; *Railway*: Beside old Hull & Hornsea railway – full of memorabilia such as station nameplates, signals and lamps; food, friendly atmosphere, quite simple; keg beers *(Lee Goulding)*

North Newbald [SE9136], *Tiger*: John Smiths pub in charming spot by big village green, generous helpings of good food in nicely refurbished downstairs bar, upstairs restaurant *(Mrs P J Pearce, LYM)*

Paull [Main St; TA1626], *Humber Tavern*: Excellent Whitbreads and fine Humber views in riverside local *(Lee Goulding)*

Pocklington [SE8049], *Feathers*: Comfortable and popular open-plan lounge, good solid bar meals, Youngers real ales, friendly staff, children welcome; comfortable motel-style bedrooms *(Calvert C Bristol, LYM)*

Rawcliffe [High St; SE6823], *Neptune*: Nice lounge, good beers, friendly service, good value bar food with wide choice *(J C Clark)*

☆ **Redbourne** [Main St; SK9799], *Red Lion*: Well kept pub with decent food – a real oasis for the area; bedrooms *(Cynthia McDowell, B D Yates)*

Scunthorpe [High St East; SE9011], *Old Mill*: Converted windmill with extensions near old part of Scunthorpe; spacious, well furnished modern interior and limited but good choice of food – excellent steak and kidney pie *(Alan Bickley)*

Sewerby [High St; TA2069], *Ship*: Large, welcoming pub overlooking North Sea, real ale on handpump, good bar food and service, large garden; children's play area and gamesroom *(John Gould)*

Snaithe [SE6422], *Downe Arms*: Excellent summer Sun lunchtime barbecues in attractive courtyard, really good value *(PJP)*

Sproatley [B1238; TA1934], *Blue Bell*: Comfortable and cosy lounge in village local welcoming strangers, John Smiths on handpump, friendly service, food in separate dining-room *(Lee Goulding)*

☆ **Stamford Bridge** [A166 W of town – in fact just over the N Yorks border; SE7155], *Three*

Cups: Spacious and attractive bar with stripped brickwork, beams, panelling and library theme, country furnishings and kitchen range in dining-room, good value food – particularly the generous carvery and family Sun lunches; Bass, Stones and Websters on handpump; children welcome *(M A and W R Proctor, R C Watkins, Ray Wharram, LYM)*

Sutton on Hull [TA1233], *Duke of York*: Very popular Tudor-style old coaching-inn on edge of Hull – outskirts village with attractive church; comfortable lounge, lively bar, Mansfield XXXX *(Lee Goulding)*; *Ship*: Recently discovered well, nicely lit, in family-room; also refurbished lounge, simple bar; well kept Tetleys, children's play area *(Lee Goulding)*

Sutton upon Derwent [SE7047], *Turpins*: Attentive, friendly licensees in well kept pub, generous helpings of good food *(Mr and Mrs R Wharram)*

☆ **Walkington** [B1230; SE9937], *Ferguson Fawsitt Arms*: Attractive mock-Tudor bars in well run pub with buffet counter and wide choice of home-cooked hot dishes in airy flagstone-floored food bar, tables on outside terrace, games-bar with pool-table; unusual puddings *(LYM)*

☆ **Welton** [village signposted from A63 just E of Hull outskirts; SE9627], *Green Dragon*: Spacious and comfortably refurbished, with good range of reasonably priced bar food including children's dishes, evening restaurant; notable as the real-life scene of the arrest of Dick Turpin, though in fact he was a misfit sheepstealer and ruffian rather than the glamorous highwayman of legend *(T Nott, LYM)*

Isle of Wight

As we went to press only one of the pubs listed as main entries here had decided definitely to stay open all day even during the summer under the new Licensing Act, with one or two others considering staying open a little later than previously in the afternoon. This comes as something of a surprise in an area where the tourist trade is so important – we suspect that as time passes afternoon opening may become very much more general here. It is after all true that many of the island's pubs cater notably well for families (all our main entries here make provision for children), and are the sort of places people would drop into for a quiet afternoon snack and a chat maybe – rather than a rowdy booze-up. Our favourite place on the island is the lively Wight Mouse, part of the comfortable Clarendon Hotel at Chale (made more accessible this year by new direct access to the main road – and a special case in point on the family front, with three different rooms for them). The New Inn at Shalfleet continues to notch up the warmest approval for its food – particularly fresh fish. On a summer evening the position of the Fisherman's Cottage right on the beach below Shanklin Chine is hard to beat, though as the sun sinks and the St Catherine's light starts sweeping over the sea the Buddle up on the cliffs at Niton will have its champions – and you couldn't get much more sea-minded than the Folly at East Cowes, so popular with visiting yachtsmen. In the Lucky Dip at the end of the chapter, the three pubs or inns that are under the firmest consideration for promotion to the main entry section are the Crab & Lobster at Bembridge, Chine at Shanklin and George in Yarmouth.

Buddle Inn, Niton

ARRETON   SZ5486 Map 2
White Lion
A3056 Newport–Sandown

The communicating rooms in the spacious and relaxed lounge bar of this attractive old white house have cushioned Windsor chairs on the brown carpet, and beams or partly panelled walls decorated with guns, brass and horse-harness. The smaller, plainer public bar has dominoes, cribbage, fruit machine and, in winter, darts. Good bar food includes sandwiches, ploughman's with Stilton, farmer's platter, generous helpings of crab pâté, and half a chicken (£1.50–£4); Whitbreads Strong Country and Flowers Original tapped from casks behind the bar with an interesting cask-levelling device; pleasant staff, piped music. Outside in the garden (for which they've won brewery competitions) there's a family Cabin Bar – full of old farm tools – and you can also sit out in front by the tubs of flowers. The pub is close to Elizabethan Arreton Manor (which houses the National Wireless Museum) and the twelfth-century village church. (Recommended by Roger Broadie, Nick Dowson, Philip King)

Whitbreads   Licensees David and Maureen James   Real ale   Meals and snacks   Children in eating area of bar   Open 11–3, 6–11

CHALE   SZ4877 Map 2
Clarendon/Wight Mouse ★
In village, on B3399, but now has access road directly off A3055

The perky Wight Mouse bar in this small, well run seventeenth-century hotel (that includes panelling from the Varvassi, an eighteenth-century wreck) has live music on every night of the year – singer/guitarists or jazz. The licensees are keen that the music is soft-pedalled to the extent that it doesn't interfere with talking. Connected by a narrower part along the serving-counter, the two main areas are comfortably but simply furnished. This year, they've added a new family restaurant with white mice depicted in the stained-glass windows, a new porch, and new lavatories. Generous helpings of home-cooked and locally produced food includes sandwiches (from 95p, fresh crab £1.85, toasties 20p extra), home-made soup (£1.05), ploughman's (from £1.60), burgers (from £2.45), ham and eggs (£2.55), salads (from £2.60), home-made pizzas (from £3.10), scampi (£3.25), wiener schnitzel (£3.75), fisherman's platter (£4.60), mixed grill (£5.05) and steaks (from £6.35); puddings such as home-made meringue nests filled with fruit, cream, ice-cream and nuts (£1.20). An excellent collection of around 150 malts (and dozens of other whiskies) is backed up by uncommon brandies, madeiras and country wines, well kept Burts VPA tapped from the cask, and Flowers Original, Fremlins and Whitbreads Strong Country on handpump. Darts at one end, dominoes, fruit machine, piped music; an adjoining games/family-room has pool, shove-ha'penny, space game, juke box, and, outside, pétanque. Picnic-table sets on a side lawn, many more on the big back lawn looking over the fields to the sea, and, for children, swings, slide, seesaw, rabbits and chickens. There's a new car park and a road that now gives access from the main coast road. They run a pick-you-up and drop-you-home mini-bus service for four or more people (£2 per person). (Recommended by Roger Broadie, Nick Dowson, Alison Hayward, Wayne Brindle, Tom Evans)

Free house   Licensees John and Jean Bradshaw   Real ale   Meals and snacks   Restaurant Children in eating areas and three family-rooms   Live music every night   Open 11–3, 6–11 all year, though considering longer afternoon opening on summer weekdays Bedrooms tel Niton (0983) 730431; £17(£19B)/£34(£38B)

The opening hours we quote are for weekdays; in England and Wales, Sunday hours are now always 12–3, 7–10.30.

nr COWES (EAST) SZ5095 Map 2
Folly

Folly Lane – which is signposted off A3021 just S of Whippingham

Big windows in this comfortable pub (first recorded as a proper building in 1792), look out over the boats, as do picnic-table sets on the water's-edge terrace. It's very popular with yachtsmen, and has a VHF radio-telephone, wind speed indicator, barometer and chronometer, mail collection boxes, even showers and a launderette for them. Old wood timbers the walls and ceilings, and there are sturdy old wooden chairs and kitchen tables, shelves of old books and plates, railway bric-à-brac and farm tools, old pictures and brass lights. Sandwiches and popular bar meals; Flowers Original on handpump. There's a good children's playroom. *(Recommended by Alison Hayward, Howard and Sue Gascoyne)*

Whitbreads   Real ale   Meals and snacks   Restaurant tel Isle of Wight (0983) 297171 Children in restaurant and family-room   Rhythm and blues Sun, jazz Tues, easy listening Fri Open 11–3, 6–11 all year

NITON SZ5076 Map 2
Buddle [*illustrated on page 383*]

From A3055 in extreme S of island, take village road towards coast

The comfortable, cosy lounge bar in this busy old smugglers' house has solid furnishings, beams, flagstones, stripped deal panelling, and two log fires in big stone hearths. Bar food includes sandwiches (from 80p), salads (from £1.90), roasts (from £3.10), and home-cooked gammon or scampi (£3.25). Flowers Original, Sam Whitbread, Wethereds, Whitbreads Pompey Royal and Strong Country, and guest beers on handpump or tapped from the cask. The garden has tables spread over the sloping lawn and more on stone terraces which look over the cliffs and St Catherine's lighthouse: at night you can watch its beam sweeping around the sea far below you. Along one side of the lawn, and helping to shelter it, is a Smugglers' Barn cafeteria with darts (not in summer), pool, fruit machine, space game and juke box. *(Recommended by Nick Dowson, Alison Hayward, Howard and Sue Gascoyne)*

Whitbreads   Meals and snacks   Restaurant tel Niton (0983) 730243   Children in eating area, restaurant and Smugglers' Barn (summer)   Occasional jazz, folk, country and western in barn   Open 10.30–3, 6–11 all year

SHALFLEET SZ4189 Map 2
New Inn ★ ⊗

A3054 Newport–Yarmouth

Good food, especially fish and seafood, is the strong point at this cheerful, friendly and popular old pub, though at quiet times the partly panelled public bar is itself a particular attraction: scrubbed deal tables on the flagstones, a cushioned built-in settle and Windsor chairs, a boarded ceiling, and on cold days a roaring log fire in the big stone hearth, which has guns and an ale-yard hanging above it. The landlord was a working fisherman before he took over the pub, and still uses his own small trawler and lobster boat to supply much of his food; depending on what's been caught locally it might include prawns (£1.25 a half-pint), moules marinière (£2), prawn curry (£3.25), poacher's pie (£3.95), Dover sole, cod, plaice, bass and fresh crab and lobster when available; in winter there are live mussels and oysters. The food's not all fish, of course, and as well as a daily changing blackboard menu there's good soup, in winter, sandwiches (from 75p), five different ploughman's (from £1.50), lasagne or chilli con carne (£2.95), a large selection of fresh salads, and steaks (from £4.95). In winter the beamed lounge bar, with its stone walls, Windsor chairs and wall banquettes around small tables, becomes a fish restaurant (bookings essential). Well kept Flowers Original, Fremlins, Whit-breads Strong Country and Pompey Royal, and a guest beer tapped from the cask; efficient staff. There are rustic tables outside by the road, and a garden. *(Recommended by Dr and Mrs R E S Tanner, Keith Houlgate, D Stephenson, Nick Dowson, Alison Hayward, Andy Tye, Sue Hill, Philip King, Maurice Southon, Tom Evans, H G and C J McCafferty, R M Walters)*

Whitbreads Licensee Nigel Simpson Real ale Meals and lunchtime snacks Restaurant tel Calbourne (098 378) 314 Children in eating area and restaurant Open 11–3, 6–11 all year

SHANKLIN SZ5881 Map 2
Crab

High Street, Old Town; A3055 leaving centre for Ventnor

Up some steps in the dimly lit rambling bar of this old thatched pub is an area like part of a sailing-ship, with curved wooden sides and a skylight hold-hatch in its deck-planked ceiling; the rest of the bar has some panelling, low beams, pictures, lots of heraldic shields and an aquarium. Bar food includes sandwiches (from 80p, fresh crab £1.80), quiche Lorraine (£1.05), ploughman's (from £1.45), home-made liver pâté (£1.75), home-made cottage pie (£1.80), home-made fisherman's pie (£1.95), salads (from £2.50, crab £4), and scampi (£2.80). Well kept Flowers Original and Whitbreads Strong Country on handpump. Darts, cribbage, fruit machine, space game, juke box and piped music. There are rustic seats on a sunny paved courtyard surrounded by dwarf conifers, with more seats in a sun porch. *(Recommended by Howard and Sue Gascoyne, Roy McIsaac; more reports please)*

Whitbreads Licensee George William Moore Real ale Lunchtime snacks Children in own room Open all day in summer; 11–3, 6–11 in winter

Fisherman's Cottage

At bottom of Shanklin Chine

Reached by a path zigzagging down the picturesquely steep and sinuous chine (though you can also drive down), this marvellously placed thatched cottage is alone on the beach. There are seats on a terrace which runs straight on to the beach, an outside bar, and evening barbecues in summer. Inside, low-beamed rooms have flagstones, stripped stone walls, and bowls of fresh flowers. Bar food includes sandwiches (from 85p), sausage (£1.60), ploughman's (from £2.30), scampi (£2.45) and seafood platter (£2.60); children's portions (from £1). Coffee is served all day. Darts, fruit machine and piped pop music. *(Recommended by Nick Dowson, Howard and Sue Gascoyne, Maurice Southon)*

Free house Licensee Miss A P P Macpherson Lunchtime meals and snacks Children in eating area Open 11–3 (possibly until 4), 7–11 all year

YARMOUTH SZ3589 Map 2
Bugle 🛏

St James' Square

Abundant woodwork behind the very fine street façade gives this well kept seventeenth-century hotel a nautical feeling that's thoroughly appropriate to this yachting town. The comfortable and relaxed Galleon Bar continues the mood with a serving-counter that looks like the stern of a galleon, and captain's chairs, black plank walls and ceiling with a few burgees hung below it, pictures of ship and marine designs, and a giant photograph of the harbour making up an entire side wall. Good home-made bar food includes filled baked potatoes (from £1), home-made soup (£1.25), open sandwiches (£1.75), ploughman's (from £1.75), grilled sardines (£3.25), salads (£3.50), chilli con carne (£3.75), lasagne (£3.95), and daily specials like steak and kidney pie, pork curry and crab or lobster salad (from £2.95). Flowers Original on handpump; darts, pool, snooker in winter, fruit machine, space game and piped music. The sizeable garden (popular with families) has barbecued Italian-style whole roast pig, rolled in herbs, garlic and wine. The hotel is close to the Tudor castle, the pier, and *Good Walks Guide* Walk 40. *(Recommended by Nick Dowson, Alison Hayward, Howard and Sue Gascoyne, H G and C J McCafferty, JAH)*

Whitbreads   Licensees R Perpetuini and C H R Troup   Real ale   Meals and snacks Restaurant   Children in own room   Singing duo Weds evenings   Open 10.30–3, 6–11 all year   Bedrooms tel Isle of Wight (0983) 760272; £20(£23B)/£35(£42B)

Lucky Dip

Besides the fully inspected pubs, you might like to try these Lucky Dips recommended to us and described by readers (if you do, please send us reports):

Bembridge [Forelands (off Howgate Rd); SZ6487], *Crab & Lobster*: Very good sandwiches (particuarly crab) and local seafood, also other food, well kept Flowers Original and Whitbreads Strong Country on handpump, country wines; good clifftop position near Foreland coastguard lookout, overlooking sea, and path leading down to beach from front terrace; very pleasant atmosphere in both bars and restaurant; bedrooms *(Howard and Sue Gascoyne, Derek Stephenson)*; [Station Rd] *Pilot Boat*: Unusual exterior gives the illusion of a boat in the street; two biggish bars with nautical décor, bar snacks and meals, Flowers on handpump; small simple children's room *(Howard and Sue Gascoyne)*

Bonchurch [Bonchurch Shute (from A3055 E of Ventnor turn down to Old Bonchurch opp Leconfield Hotel); SZ5778], *Bonchurch*: High-ceilinged public bar partly cut into the rocks of the Shute with furnishings that somehow conjure up image of shipwreck salvage, smaller saloon, usual bar food with several Italian dishes too, Whitbreads Strong Country tapped from the cask, games including pool, provision for children, piano Fri–Sat; cafeteria in splendidly arched converted stable across yard; bedrooms *(Michael Thomson, LYM)*

Carisbrooke [B3401 1½ miles W; SZ4888], *Blacksmiths Arms*: Isolated, good views from small garden, cosy front bar with a couple of leatherette sofas and heap of magazines, Flowers on handpump, children's room, pool-table in plain back bar *(Nick Dowson, Alison Hayward)*

Chale Green [SZ4879], *Jolly Brewer*: Good atmosphere, very friendly staff, young people playing pool; name changed from Star after recent facelift by Whitbreads *(Alison Hayward, Nick Dowson)*

Cowes [The Parade; SZ4896], *Globe*: Good views over Solent and harbour entrance, wide choice of reasonably priced hot and cold bar food, Flowers and Wethereds on handpump, friendly efficient service; occasional live jazz in comfortably furnished spacious main bar, darts, pool and juke box in smaller bar, restaurant upstairs; covered terrace popular with yachtsmen and families *(Howard and Sue Gascoyne)*

Downend [B3056, at crossroads; SZ5387], *Hare & Hounds*: Charming thatched Burts pub popular for varied hot and cold food; with skull of someone reputedly hanged nearby in original local bar (gibbet said to form beam over fireplace); more orthodox modern extension behind; parking can be difficult *(Nick Dowson, Alison Hayward, Mark Radford)*

Fishbourne [Fishbourne Rd; from Portsmouth car ferry turn left into no through road; SZ5592], *Fishbourne*: Whitbreads pub with comfortable wall settles and friendly staff; food from ploughman's and home-made pâtés to grills; convenient place to wait for ferry *(Michael Bechley)*

Freshwater [SZ3484], *Red Lion*: Delightful atmosphere, good wholesome food – the wide choice of baked potatoes is specially good *(DRCW)*

Godshill [Newport Rd; SZ5282], *Griffin*: Pleasant seventeenth-century stone-built pub with two comfortable bars and good back family-room leading out to spacious garden with chopped-tree-trunk furniture and caged peacock, surrounded by rolling wooded countryside; good range of bar food, Flowers and Whitbreads Strong Country on handpump *(Howard and Sue Gascoyne)*

Hulverstone [B3399; SZ4083], *Sun*: Pretty pub, decorated outside with lots of flowers; patchwork cushions on the seats, Whitbreads Strong Country tapped from casks behind the bar, friendly attentive service and good food, especially fish *(DRCW, Nick Dowson, Alison Hayward)*

Newchurch [SZ5685], *Pointer*: Pleasant two-bar pub with good local atmosphere, well kept Flowers Original and Whitbreads Strong Country *(Nick Dowson, Alison Hayward)*

Newport [High St; SZ4988], *Castle*: Seventeenth-century beamed and flagstoned pub with panelling, stripped brickwork and huge fireplaces, popular at lunchtime for big good value ploughman's; Sam Whitbread on handpump, piped music *(Nick Dowson, Alison Hayward)*

Niton [SZ5076], *White Lion*: Pleasant, welcoming atmosphere, good reasonably priced hot food, Whitbreads Strong Country on handpump, welcome extended to muddy walkers, dog and children – big recently refurbished family-room *(Dr and Mrs R E S Tanner, Roger Broadie)*

Porchfield [off A3054, 2½ miles from Shalfleet; SZ4491], *Sportsmans Rest*: Cosy pub notable for its Whitbreads Pompey Royal and large children's play area; bright red leatherette seats, reasonable food (recent kitchen refurbishments should eliminate delays), friendly cats *(Nick Dowson, Alison Hayward)*

Rookley [Niton Rd; SZ5084], *Chequers*: Out-of-the-way local with simple easy chairs and settees around open fire, lively flagstoned games-bar, usual pub food at sensible prices, Flowers Original and Whitbreads Strong Country on handpump, restaurant with midnight supper licence, garden with play area for children *(Wayne Brindle, JAH, LYM)*

Ryde [High St; SZ5992], *Castle*: Traditional pub with good, welcoming atmosphere, well kept Gales BBB and HSB and good mix of customers *(J G Wherry)*

Seaview [Esplanade; B3340, just off B3330 Ryde–Brading; SZ6291], *Old Fort*: Good value buffet, fine atmosphere with drinkers and diners mingling in an almost continental way, fresh décor with natural wood furniture; Ind Coope Burton and Gibbs Mew Wiltshire, fine sea views from inside and tables outside *(A J Skull)*; [High St] *Seaview Hotel*: Very pleasant atmosphere in both bars – front one draped with old naval photographs, back one cosy; good range of bar meals, separate restaurant, Burts on handpump, front terrace with Solent views, courtyard back garden; bedrooms *(Howard and Sue Gascoyne)*

Shanklin [Chine Hill; SZ5881], *Chine*: Marvellous wooded setting overlooking chine and beach, with cheap Burts ales in two cosy and homely small bars (one with darts has clinker-built bar counter shaped like a boat), cheap food, and spacious family conservatory attractively draped with flowers and vines *(Nick Dowson, Alison Hayward, Howard and Sue Gascoyne)*

Shorwell [SZ4582], *Crown*: Very pleasant, comfortable and well furnished pub with good food, friendly atmosphere, and attractive garden with trout in stream *(R M Walters, Michael and Harriet Robinson)*

Ventnor [Market St; SZ5677], *Hole in the Wall*: Basic two-bar local with good value simple food and one of the cheapest pints in Britain – Burts VPA, under top pressure; games bar, tables in sheltered yard; children in Barn Bar family-room – kept open all year; on GWG42 *(LYM)*; [Albert St] *Volunteer*: Burts VPA and Mild in unspoilt yellow-walled pub with wooden chairs and benches *(Phil and Sally Gorton, TA)*

Whitwell [SZ5277], *White Horse*: Recently redecorated in country style, good busy atmosphere, friendly efficient staff, well kept Flowers Original and Whitbreads Strong Country, darts; popular in the evening with people from the nearby YHA *(Nick Dowson, Alison Hayward)*

Wootton Bridge [100 yds past Fishbourne Ferry; SZ5492], *Fishbourne*: Well cooked and presented bar food including ploughman's, delicious garlic mussels, grills, fish, salads and puddings; reasonable prices, friendly staff – and after eating, you can watch the ferry traffic *(Roy and Margaret Johnston)*; *Sloop*: Simple main panelled bar with portholes and curved ceiling, games-room with darts and billiards to left, double doors to plainer room with tables for eating overlooking river; Flowers Original on handpump, good lunchtime bar food, riverside garden; children's room and galleon in garden to climb on *(Roger Broadie)*

Wroxall [SZ5579], *Star*: Nice and clean, with reasonably priced Burts VPA, Mild and 4X, some seats outside; nr start GWG42 *(Nick Dowson, Alison Hayward)*

Yarmouth [Quay St; SZ3589], *George*: Well managed old hotel partly built into castle walls, big sofas and easy chairs in panelled smaller bar with oil painting over large fireplace, good choice of real ales including Flowers on handpump, wide range of popular bar food from sandwiches to full meals, nice restaurant, good cheerful service; seats on spacious back lawns overlooking Solent and pier; children in good family-room with sea views; bedrooms *(E G Parish, Howard and Sue Gascoyne)*

Kent

It's very rare for us to find a new entry so good that it comes straight into the Guide *with a star:* this year the George at Newnham does just that – interesting food in delightfully furnished and decorated surroundings, with good drinks too. Other notable new entries, or pubs returning to the main entries after an absence, include the Little Gem at Aylesford (quaint, tiny outside, with a good collection of real ales), the Woolpack at Chilham (a comfortable place to stay in this beautiful village), the Duck at Pett Bottom (food's the draw here), the interesting old Dering Arms in Pluckley, the recently refurbished White Lion down among the orchards at Selling, the secluded yet lively Tiger at Stowting (good value food at both of these, with a popular range of real ales at the Tiger including Everards' eponymous offering), and the Chequer Tree at Weald (having more or less rebuilt the pub themselves, the enthusiastic licensees are now turning their attention to its big garden). Guy Sankey has now successfully transplanted his very popular seafood operation from the Gate in Hildenborough to Tunbridge Wells, under his own name (at first his new Tunbridge Wells place was called the Gate too – he's changing the name to avoid any confusion). Changes at popular entries carried over from previous editions include new licensees for the Dove at Dargate (a wider choice of food and perhaps a quieter atmosphere now), and the fine old Carpenters Arms at Eastling (still good, though food prices are up). The Bull at Wrotham is breaking new ground (or as purists would have it returning to

The Little Gem, Aylesford

traditions of the past) by having customers taken to tables as they come in, where they're served with drinks as well as food; its atmosphere and furnishings are still very much those of a traditional English inn. But many of the old favourites – the Three Chimneys near Biddenden (good food and drink, interesting layout, pretty garden), the lively and unpretentious Gate down by the marshes at Boyden Gate, the smuggly Shipwrights Arms out on the coast near Oare, the splendid old Bell near Smarden – continue very much as ever. There are signs that the Crown at Groombridge is moving towards a star award, and there's been particular warmth in readers' reports on the Black Pig at Staple – we'll be interested to hear what you think over the next few months. Rising stars in the Lucky Dip section at the end of the chapter include the Little Brown Jug at Chiddingstone Causeway, Sun in Faversham, Green Cross outside Goudhurst, Gun & Spitroast at Horsmonden, Brown Trout in Lamberhurst, several pubs in and around Penshurst (or is it just that the surroundings put visitors in an appreciative frame of mind?), Black Horse in Pluckley, Clarendon in Sandgate (if you can track it down), Royal Oak in Sevenoaks and Fox & Hounds on Toys Hill.

ALDINGTON   TR0736 Map 3

Walnut Tree

The charming back Kitchen Bar in this old smugglers' pub, dating back 650 years, has a wood-burning stove and the original side bread oven, a brick floor, and above this what must have been a very cosy cupboard bedroom reached by a ladder. The lively public bar has shove-ha'penny, dominoes, darts and a fruit machine, and there's a comfortable saloon bar; piped music. Bar food includes sandwiches (running up to a steak sandwich, £3.55), smoked mackerel ploughman's (£2.55), mussels (£2.70), home-made pies such as lamb and apricot (£2.75) or steak and kidney (£2.95), vegetarian dishes, fish (£3), home-cured ham (£3.50) and scampi (£3.95); Shepherd Neame on handpump. There are tables in a sheltered garden, with a pool and barbecues in summer. *(Recommended by W E George, John Innes, CMTJ)*

Shepherd Neame   Licensees Mike and Lyn Coggan   Real ale   Meals and snacks   Restaurant   tel Aldington (023 372) 298   Children in eating area and restaurant   Open all day, all year

AYLESFORD   TQ7359 Map 3

Little Gem   [illustrated on page 389]

3 miles from M2 junction 3; A229 towards Maidstone, then first right turn, following signposts to village. Also 1¾ miles from M20 junction 6; A229 towards Maidstone, then follow Aylesford signpost; 19 High Street

Claiming to be Kent's smallest pub, this quaint little place was founded in 1106, and among the interesting oddments is a history of the pub. Heavily timbered, it has a cosy, welcoming atmosphere, a big open fire, and an unusual high-pitched ceiling following the line of the roof; an open staircase leads to a mezzanine floor, a bit like a minstrels' gallery, with a few tables. A fine range of real ales on handpump or tapped from the cask includes Bass, Everards Old Original, Fullers London Pride, Goachers, Greene King Abbot, Marstons Owd Rodger, Ruddles County, Theakstons Old Peculiar, Wadworths 6X, Youngers IPA, Youngs special and one guest each week. Bar food includes various pies, pasties or sausage rolls (£1.60), curry or chilli (£1.75), and plaice or scampi (£2.25). *(Recommended by Peter Griffiths, C Elliott, S J A Velate)*

Free house   Licensee Mrs S Brenchley   Real ale   Meals and snacks (not Sun evening)   Open 11–3, 5–11 all year

BENENDEN   TQ8033 Map 3
King William IV ⊗
B2086

Good, popular bar food in this low-ceilinged village tavern includes toasted sandwiches, soup such as carrot and coriander or leek and watercress (£1), ploughman's (£1.75), garlicky baked potted smoked trout with horseradish or egg and onion mousse on toast (£1.95), French onion tart served with salad and new potatoes (£2.70), stuffed courgettes (£2.75), queen scallops gratiné or beef Stroganoff (£3.50), Arabian-style lamb kebabs (£3.85), red wine casserole (£4.25) or seafood lasagne (£4.35); puddings such as apricot and almond cake with Cointreau (£1). Well kept Shepherd Neame and Mild, as well as some decent French and German wines, and a well made Kir. Carefully unsophisticated furnishings such as half a dozen plain oak and elm tables (one or two behind a standing timber divider) with flowers on them, cushioned shiny pews, kitchen chairs, and an open fire in the carefully restored inglenook fireplace. The public bar has sensibly placed darts, dominoes, video game and juke box. You can sit out on the small but sheltered side lawn. (*Recommended by Theodore and Jean Rowland-Entwistle, E J Cutting, R G and S E Bentley*)

Shepherd Neame   Licensee Nigel Douglas   Real ale   Meals and snacks (not Mon evenings or Sun)   Open 11–2.30, 6–11 all year

nr BIDDENDEN   TQ8538 Map 3
Three Chimneys ★ ★ ⊗
A262, 1 mile W of village

A series of small rooms in this very attractive and well kept country pub is traditionally furnished with old settles, and has low oak beams, some harness and sporting prints on the walls, and good log fires in winter. The food, changing with the season and often using original recipes, includes a choice of at least four starters, four main courses and four puddings. The starters might include good mussel soup (£1.40), spinach and ham mousse (£1.90) and asparagus and cheese pancakes (£2.10); main courses include a choice of quiches such as Brie and broccoli (£3.20), fish lasagne (£4.15), duck and pheasant casserole (£4.50) and chicken and burnt almond salad (£4.75); there are puddings like fruit crumbles (£1.40), lemon and ginger pudding or nutty treacle tart (£1.50), all with Jersey cream. They always have two or three vegetarian dishes, such as aubergine and tomato pie (£3.40). There is a useful overspill Garden Room, popular with families, where you can book tables (Biddenden (0580) 291472); as this part isn't licensed you have to carry your drinks in from the main bar. Besides a range of well kept real ales tapped from the cask, including Adnams Best, Fremlins, Goachers (from Maidstone), Harveys Best, Hook Norton Old Hookey and Marstons Pedigree (and in winter Harveys Old Ale), they keep local cider, and their sensible wine list includes several half-bottles; good service. The simple public bar has darts, shove ha'penny, dominoes and cribbage. The garden is imaginatively planted with flowering shrubs and shrub roses, giving gentle curving borders to the neatly kept lawn. Just down the road from Sissinghurst. (*Recommended by Nigel Paine, Mr and Mrs G D Amos, Greg Parston, Robin and Bev Gammon, J S Evans, AE, GRE, Steve Dark, David Crafts, Mr and Mrs J H Adam, Mrs Shirley Fluck, Martin and Jane Bailey, J E Cross, Margaret Drazin, Tim Halstead, Aubrey Saunders, Mr and Mrs Ken Turner, Dr Venetia Stott, PLC, Dave Butler, Les Storey, Rodney Coe, Gavin May, C M Whitehouse, Wayne Brindle, G Cooper, Stephen Hayes, Brian and Rosemary Wilmot, Anne Morris, Mrs J M Aston, C D T Spooner*)

Free house   Licensees C F W Sayers and G A Sheepwash   Real ale   Meals and snacks Restaurant (see above)   Children in Garden Room   Open 11–2.30, 6–11 all year

BOUGH BEECH   TQ4846   Map 3
Wheatsheaf
B2027, S of reservoir

An attractive sheltered lawn with flower beds, fruit trees, roses, flowering shrubs, and a children's rustic cottage stretches behind this attractive old pub, which is partly tile-hung and partly clad with weatherboarding and roses. Inside, the smart bar has an unusually high ceiling with lofty timbers and a massive stone fireplace. A couple of lower rooms lead off and are divided from the central part by standing timbers. Decorations include cigarette cards, swordfish spears, a stag's head and – over the massive stone fireplace which separates off the public bar – a mysterious 1607 inscription reading *Foxy Galumpy*. Bar food includes freshly cut sandwiches (from 85p, toasties 5p extra), soup (90p), home-made pâté (£1), jumbo sausage (£1.35), ploughman's (from £1.80), omelettes (from £1.90), home-cooked ham with egg (£2.65), salads with home-cooked meats (from £3.25), deep-fried seafood platter (£2.95) and steaks (£6.50); home-made puddings such as apple crumble or walnut, apple and raisin steamed pudding (£1.20). Well kept Fremlins and Flowers on handpump; sensibly placed darts, shove-ha'penny, dominoes, cribbage and fruit machine in the public bar (which has buffalo horns over its fire, and an attractive old settle carved with wheatsheaves); piped music. *(Recommended by KA Read, Alasdair Knowles, Patrick Freeman, J E Cross, S J A Velate, J A Snell, Jon Wainwright)*

Fremlins (Whitbreads)   Real ale   Meals (not Weds evenings or Sun) and snacks (not Weds or Sun evenings)   Children in area set aside for them by public bar   Open 11–2.30, 6–11 all year

BOUGHTON ALUPH   TR0247   Map 3
Flying Horse ⊗ 🛏
Boughton Lees; just off A251 N of Ashford

This fifteenth-century village inn – facing a broad cricket green (with weekly matches in summer) – was probably built for the 'pilgrim traffic'. The friendly and comfortable open-plan bar has lots of standing space by the neat lines of upholstered modern wall benches and tables, and a log fire. Further inside, age shows in the shiny old black panelling and the arched windows (though they are a later Gothic addition). Good food ranges from sandwiches (from 90p, toasties from £1.20), large fresh plaice (£2.95), home-made pies such as steak and kidney or turkey and ham (£2.95), roasts with lamb, beef or pork (£3.30), a cold buffet with home-cooked meats and home-made puddings that might include apple pie, gateaux or flans (from 95p); weekend barbecues are popular with families. Courage Best and Directors on handpump, and good house red wine; fruit machine and piped music. You can sit out in the rose garden. *(Recommended by David Gaunt, S V Bishop, Robin and Bev Gammon, Stanley Matthews)*

Courage   Licensee Leonard Nolan   Real ale   Meals and snacks   Restaurant Sat evenings   Children welcome   Open 11–3, 6–11 all year   Bedrooms tel Ashford (0233) 620914; £15(£20S)/£20(£25–£27S)

BOUGHTON STREET   TR0458   Map 3
White Horse 🛏
¾ mile from M2 junction 7; Boughton signposted off A2; note that this is the village shown on most maps as Boughton Street, though most people actually call it just Boughton – and note that it's a very long way from the Boughton of the previous entry!

The showpiece of its owners, Shepherd Neame, this fifteenth-century inn – very carefully restored after a fire – has a snug dark-beamed bar with a sofa, tapestry-cushioned pews, one table made from a massive highly polished smith's bellows, a little glass-fronted bookcase, a brass-faced longcase clock, some sporting prints, and heavy-horse harness hanging on its stripped brick and timber walls. Beyond the servery another bar has a curved high-backed antique settle by a similar bellows table, and more formal tables and chairs, merging into a communicating restaurant area (with a seafood live tank). Bar food includes sandwiches (from £1.10), home-made soup (£1.20), ploughman's (£1.95), a good choice of omelettes (from £2), burgers (from £2.65), grilled sardines (£2.95), scampi (£3.95) and steaks (from £6.95); well kept Shepherd Neame on handpump. There are tables in the garden behind. *(Recommended by Anthony Lowe, Stuart Taylor; more reports please)*

Shepherd Neame   Real ale   Meals and snacks   Restaurant   Children welcome   Live jazz Sun   Open all day, all year   Bedrooms tel Faversham (0227) 751343; £35B/£45B

BOYDEN GATE   TR2265 Map 3
Gate Inn   ★

Off A299 Herne Bay–Ramsgate – follow Chislet, Upstreet signpost opposite Roman Gallery; Chislet also signposted off A28 Canterbury–Margate at Upstreet – after turning right into Chislet main street keep right on to Boyden

This delightful country pub gives its address as Marshside: though you won't find this on every road map (Boyden Gate itself is much more likely to be marked), it does describe its surroundings well. The bar has hop-bines hanging from the beam, pews with brown velvet cushions around tables of considerable character, bunches of flowers in summer, attractively etched windows, a good log fire in winter (the fireplace serves both quarry-tiled rooms), and a lazy, chatty atmosphere; the walls are covered in photographs, some ancient sepia ones, others new ('MCC' here stands for Marshside Cricket Club – the pub is a focus for many other games, too). Bar food consists of sausages on sticks (28p), sandwiches (from 70p), enterprising toasted sandwiches (65p–£1.10, including appetising bacon ones), prawns (£1.60), a particularly good range of well presented ploughman's (from £1.60), and game or vegetarian pie (£1.95), with some puddings (90p). Well kept Shepherd Neame Bitter, Mild, Best and Old tapped from the cask; sensibly placed darts, shove-ha'penny, dominoes, alley skittles, cribbage and lots of board games. The pub is perhaps at its best on a quiet summer's evening when you can sit at picnic-table sets on the sheltered side lawn, and in front, and the air seems to vibrate with the contented quacking of a million ducks and geese (they sell duck food inside – 5p a bag – and one reader even found a chicken wandering around the bar). *(Recommended by L M Miall, Frank Williams, Rodney Coe, Comus Elliott, Peter Hitchcock)*

Shepherd Neame   Licensee Christopher Smith   Real ale   Snacks   Children welcome (with family-room)   Piano Sun evening, quiz Thurs evening, all sorts of special events   Open all day, all year

CHIDDINGSTONE   TQ4944 Map 3
Castle

Since 1730 this comfortable, busy place – tile-hung from roof to ground – has been an inn, and like the rest of this beautiful village is owned by the National Trust. The neatly modernised bar has an attractive mullioned window seat in one small alcove, well made settles forming booths around the tables on its partly carpeted oak floor, cushioned sturdy wall benches, beams and latticed windows. The food has been sensibly divided between the bar and Reynard's Grill; the bar copes with starters and hot dishes: home-made soup (£1.60), sandwiches (from £1.95), baked potatoes with various fillings (£2.25; there are speciality fillings on certain days), home-made pâté (£2.70), ploughman's (from £2.75), beef and ale pie (£3.15), a very hot chilli con carne or two locally made sausages with a baked potato and cheese (£3.45), salads (from £4.25) and other cold food (self-service) from Reynard's. Well kept King & Barnes and Shepherd Neame on handpump, with quite a number of wines by the bottle; friendly service. The public bar has darts, shove-ha'penny, dominoes and cribbage. The garden behind is pretty, with a small pool and fountain set in a rockery, and tables on a back brick terrace and the neat lawn, surrounded by shrubs. (*Recommended by Nick Dowson, Alison Hayward, Alasdair Knowles, Gethin Lewis, Robin and Bev Gammon, Steve Dark, Jane Palmer, Jon Wainwright*)

Free house　Licensee Nigel Lucas　Real ale　Meals and snacks　Restaurant tel *Penshurst (0892) 870247　Children in garden　Open all day, all year*

CHILHAM　TR0753　Map 3

Woolpack 🛏

Best approached from the signposted village road at junction A28/A252, which leads straight to the inn

Down the lane from the beautiful medieval square which has made the village famous, this has been comfortably renovated by Shepherd Neame, with bedrooms in attractively converted former stable buildings behind. The busy, friendly bar is dominated by the cavernous fireplace with a big log fire and a row of jugs, flagons and kegs above it. There are little brocaded armchairs, a sofa, pews and wall seats, and bar food includes sandwiches (from £1), soup (£1.10), ploughman's (£1.95), four-ounce burger (£2.25), lamb pasties, beef curry (£2.50), smoked salmon (£4.50), steaks (from eight-ounce sirloin £5.50) and Dover sole (£9.50), with an attractive separate carvery. Well kept Shepherd Neame Bitter and Best on hand-pump, cribbage, on our visit unobtrusive piped Stevie Wonder. (*Recommended by Anthony Lowe, David Crafts, Col G D Stafford*)

Shepherd Neame　Licensee John Durcan　Real ale　Meals and snacks　Restaurant Children in eating area and restaurant　Open 10.30–11 all year　Bedrooms tel *Canterbury (0227) 730208; /£35(£45B)*

CHIPSTEAD　TQ4956　Map 3

George & Dragon ⊗

39 High Street

From outside, this well run painted brick house looks handsome on its steep village lane, and there are tables on neatly kept grass, beside roses and tall trees, behind the car park. Inside, upright timbers in the open-plan bar divide it into smaller, cosier areas, two of which have open fires, and the atmosphere is relaxed and friendly; the furnishings, though modern, do tone in with the heavy black beams (some of them nicely carved), oak tables and Windsor chairs on the geometric carpet. Good food includes home-made soup (70p), sandwiches (from 75p, toasties 10p extra), pâté (£1.30), ploughman's (from £1.70), quiche (£1.40), salads (from £2.40), the 'special' (grilled bacon, tomato and cheese on toast, sausage and chips, £2.50), seafood platter (£2.75), ham and egg (£2.80), scampi (£3), gammon steak (£4.20), salads (£4.50) and steaks (from £7.50). Well kept Courage Best and Directors on handpump, and wines on tap; very good service, even when busy. Darts, dominoes, cribbage, piped music. (*Recommended by E G Parish, S J A Velate, R J Foreman, A V Chute, R Houghton, J E Cross*)

Courage　Licensee David Gerring　Real ale　Meals and snacks (not Sun)　Open 10–2.30, 6–10.30 all year

COBHAM　TQ6768　Map 3

Leather Bottle

2½ miles from M2 junction 1; village signposted from A2 (towards London) on B2009

The temptation for a pub with such strong Dickensian connections (it's fondly mentioned in *The Pickwick Papers*) is to make them too obvious, but recently readers have been unanimous in praising the way the large collection of Dickensiana has been used to support a genuinely warm atmosphere here – and the food seems to be on an upswing too. In among all the decorations you'd expect, there are some truly interesting prints of Dickens' characters, including early postcards and teacards. The large, open-plan bar is popular with business people from Rochester as well as tourists, and serves ploughman's (£2.75), cold meat salads (£3.30) and a daily hot dish, as well as Trumans Bitter, Best and Sampson, and Websters Yorkshire. Tables are laid out on the extended back lawn and in the orchard at the bottom there's a large fish pond with a children's play area and, in summer, an outdoors tuck shop. Besides Cobham Park, the village itself is pretty, with medieval almshouses, and outstanding brasses in the church. *(Recommended by Michael and Harriet Robinson, Peter Griffiths, PJP, M J Masters; more reports please)*

Trumans (Watneys) Real ale Snacks (not Sat) Restaurant Children in eating area and restaurant Open 11–2.30, 6–11 all year Bedrooms tel Meopham (0474) 814327; £27.50/ £40(£55B)

CONYER QUAY TQ9665 Map 3
Ship

This cosy, small-roomed pub is on the edge of a creek packed with small boats, which suits its wooden floors, wallboards, a planked ceiling, various nautical knick-knacks and a noticeboard with boating advertisements. Well kept Flowers and Fremlins on handpump; they have a happy hour every night between 6 and 7 (7 to 8 Sundays) when doubles are priced as singles and pints of beer or cider are 10p cheaper. Bar food includes soup (75p), baked potatoes (from £1.65), ploughman's and basket meals such as spicy sausages (£1.65), shepherd's pie (£1.90), vegetable lasagne (£2.75) and curry (£2.95); the restaurant has fresh local oysters and trout. Shove-ha'penny, bar skittles, dominoes, cribbage, Scrabble, dice, backgammon, chess and other board games, and a quiz each Tuesday evening; also a fruit machine, piped music. Used paperbacks are sold and exchanged – proceeds to charity. During opening hours they can supply you with groceries. Tables on a narrow gravel terrace face the waterfront. *(Recommended by Dr and Mrs A K Clarke, Kit Read)*

Fremlins (Whitbreads) Licensee Alec Heard Real ale Meals and snacks Restaurant tel Teynham (0795) 521404 Children in restaurant Open 11–3, 6–11 all year

DARGATE TR0761 Map 3
Dove

Village signposted from A299

New licensees in this popular and attractive, honeysuckle-clad brick house seem to be concentrating more on the food side of things while managing to preserve a friendly, pubby atmosphere. It's a neat, carefully refurbished place with a good log fire in winter and well kept Shepherd Neame Master Brew on handpump; unobtrusive piped music. Home made, the food includes daily specials, sandwiches (from 95p), soup (95p), pâté (£1.75), salads on request (£2.75), main dishes such as baked trout (£5.50), pork chop or swordfish steaks (£5.75), and vegetarian specials like lentil loaf or mushroom and nut fettuccine (£3.50) and lasagne (£3.75). The pub is well known for its very pretty garden with roses, lilacs, paeonies and many other flowers, and picnic-table sets under pear trees; there's also a dovecot – with white doves – and a swing. A bridlepath leads up into Blean Wood. *(Recommended by Dave Butler, Lesley Storey, Rob and Gill Weeks, Lyn and Bill Capper, Denis Mann)*

Shepherd Neame Licensees Peter and Susan Smith Real ale Meals (not Sun evening) and snacks (lunchtimes only) Children in restaurant and eating area Open 11–3, 6–11 all year; closed 25 Dec

Sunday opening is now 12–3 and 7–10.30 throughout England.

EASTLING   TQ9656 Map 3

Carpenters Arms

In the past this old village pub has had not only a food award but also a star; the licensee who made it so popular left at the end of 1987, so these awards have gone into suspension. But early signs are that the character of the place has stayed more or less unchanged, and though food may not be quite so varied as in the past (or so cheap) it's still interesting. The beamed front rooms have easy chairs and pews around simple, candlelit wooden tables of some character decorated with fresh flowers. There are local and sporting prints and some equestrian and other decorative plates on the walls, hop-bines strung along some of the ancient beams, and logs burning in a big brick inglenook fireplace. The two small back rooms have country kitchen chairs, pews and oak tables with candles in bottles, rough-hewn oak beams, and a vast fireplace with well restored bread ovens. Bar food includes sandwiches (£1, toasted £1.50), corn-on-the-cob (£1.50), pizza (£2.50), a large ploughman's (£3.50, with cheese and locally made sausage), scampi or a half-pound burger (£3.50), with daily specials such as beef in ale, game (in season) or shark steak (£4.95); four-course Sunday lunch (£7.50). Well kept Shepherd Neame Bitter and Stock on handpump, decent wines. Shove-ha'penny, dominoes, table skittles, cribbage and a fruit machine; piped music. In summer you can sit, sheltered by the steep-roofed inn's half-timbered brickwork and white clapboarding, by an outbuilding covered with jasmine, clematis and roses. (Recommended by Mrs V Vanderkar, TBB, Dave Braisted, Mrs Penny Mendelsohn, Rodney Coe; more reports on the new regime please)

Shepherd Neame   Licensee Tony O'Regan   Real ale   Meals (not Sun) and snacks (not Sun evening)   Restaurant tel Eastling (079 589) 234   Children in restaurant   Open all day, all year

FORDWICH   TR1759 Map 3

Fordwich Arms ⊗

Village signposted off A28 in Sturry, just on Canterbury side of level-crossing

Though not very old, this tucked-away building repays a close look: the detailed craftsmanship that has gone into it is a pleasure – brick mullions for the handsomely crafted arched windows, oak parquet floor, oak and glass inner porch, and sturdy bar counter. There are comfortable golden-yellow corduroy plush button-back banquettes that sweep in bays around the room, small country prints and a few old local photographs on the dark green hessian walls, plates on a high Delft shelf, and copper pots (some with plants in), antique soda-syphons, pewter jugs and dried flowers. Good value bar food in generous helpings includes sandwiches (from £1.10), soup (£1.10), filled baked potatoes (from £1.35), ploughman's (£2.15), salads (£3.50), and daily specials such as nut roast (£3.45), trout with ginger and spring onions, pork casserole or beef in ale (all £3.75); there's also a special cheese of the week. Well kept Flowers Original and Fremlins on handpump, with a Whitbreads-related guest beer such as Castle Eden changing each quarter; unobtrusive piped music, friendly service. There are white tables, chairs and cocktail parasols on the flagstoned terrace, and a spacious garden by the River Stour – in Roman times sea-going ships came up this far. The lovely little herringbone-brick half-timbered medieval town hall opposite is said to be the smallest and perhaps the oldest in Britain. (Recommended by L M Miall, P Poole, Lyn and Bill Capper, M J Daunton, Kit Read)

Whitbreads   Licensee John Gass   Real ale   Meals and snacks (not Sun)   Children in family-room   Open 11–2.30, 6–11 all year

If we know a pub does summer barbecues, we say so.

GOUDHURST TQ7238 Map 3
Star & Eagle 🏠

Standing close to the thirteenth-century village church, this medieval inn with its wood balconies and timbered gables has a spacious open-plan bar with settles and Jacobean-style seats under its heavy beams; the buttery bar may be used for conferences. At one end of the bar, a special counter now serves the good value food: soup (£1.50, Mediterranean fish soup £2.35), ploughman's (£2.25), lasagne (£3.25), a wide range of salads (from £3.75), home-made steak and kidney pie (£4.35) and beef Stroganoff (£4.65). Well kept Flowers and Fremlins on hand-pump. Three or four white tables out under an old pear tree at the back have a fine view of the hop-fields rolling away to the south; Bedgebury Pinetum, the national collection of conifers, is a couple of miles down the B2079, and the splendid gardens around the moated ruins of Scotney Castle are not much further. *(Recommended by V H Balchin, E G Parish, Wayne Brindle, Gwen and Peter Andrews, Tom Gondris, J H Bell, J S Evans)*

Fremlins (Whitbreads) Licensee Michel Dimet Real ale Meals and snacks Restaurant Children welcome Open 11–2.30, 6–11 all year Bedrooms tel Goudhurst (0580) 211512/211338; £35B(£40B)/£43(£49B)

GROOMBRIDGE TQ5337 Map 3
Crown ⊗

B2110

Though there are two quite separate focuses of attention in the rambling series of small, old-fashioned rooms here, the overall atmosphere is one of busy enjoyment. For drinkers, a central room with a copper-topped serving-bar is filled with masses of old teapots, pewter tankards and so forth, and logs burn in the big brick inglenook. An end room, normally for eaters, has the separate counter where you order the food, fairly close-spaced tables with a variety of good solid chairs, and a log-effect gas fire in a big fireplace. The walls, mostly rough yellowing plaster with some squared panelling and some timbering, are decorated with lots of small topographical, game and sporting prints (often in pretty maple frames), and a circular large-scale map with the pub at its centre; some of the beams have horsebrasses. Quickly served on an entertaining assortment of plates old and new, the food includes good value ploughman's (from £1.80), filled baked potatoes, Greek meatballs with spaghetti (£2.80), salads (from £2.85), steak and mushroom pie (£3), roast duck (£3.20), cold salmon (£3.30), roast sirloin (£3.45) and good puddings. Well kept Adnams Extra, Fremlins and Harveys on handpump, good value house wines; very efficient service. Picnic-table sets on the sunny brick terrace in front of the flower beds by this pretty tile-hung Elizabethan house look down over a steep but beautifully kept village green. Behind is a big tree-sheltered lawn, with a climbing-frame, slide and more picnic-table sets. *(Recommended by Ashley Madden, J A Snell, GSC, Rodney Coe)*

Free house Real ale Meals and snacks (not Sun evening) Children in restaurant Open 11–2.30, 6–11 all year Bedrooms tel Groombridge (089 276) 742; £15/£25

nr HADLOW TQ6349 Map 3
Artichoke

Hamptons; from Hadlow–Plaxtol road turn right (signposted West Peckham – the pub too is discreetly signposted, on an oak tree); OS Sheet 188 reference 623523

The two snug, softly lit rooms in this secluded old cottage – partly tile-hung and shuttered – have beams in the low ceilings, cushioned high-backed wooden settles, wooden farmhouse-kitchen chairs, and upholstered wrought-iron stools matching unusual wrought-iron, glass-topped tables on its Turkey carpet. Decorations include lots of gleaming brass, country pictures (mainly hunting scenes), some antique umbrellas and old storm lamps. One room has an inglenook fireplace and is decked out with jugs, kettles, pots, pans and plates; the other has a wood-burning range. Good bar food includes soup or pâté (£1.25), ploughman's (£2.25), jumbo pork sausage (£2.75), home-made quiche (£3.25), lasagne or chilli con carne (£3.75), home-made steak and kidney pie or mixed grill (£3.95), prawn salads (from £4.75), chicken Kiev (£4.75) and sirloin steak (£7.25). Fullers London Pride, Marstons Pedigree and Youngs Special on handpump, with a good range of spirits; young, friendly service and piped music in the evenings. It's quiet during the day and on many evenings, but fills up quickly on weekend evenings. There are seats on a fairy-lit front terrace with a striped awning, and more built around a tall lime tree across the lane. (Recommended by S J A Velate, Gwen and Peter Andrews, Brandon Broadbent, Simon Small)

Free house   Licensees Barbara and Terry Simmonds   Real ale   Meals (Sun evenings, summer only) and snacks (lunchtimes, not Sat)   Restaurant (Fri and Sat evenings) tel Plaxtol (0732) 810763   Children in eating area   Open 11.30–2.30, 6.30–11 all year; opens 7 in winter

IDE HILL   TQ4851 Map 3
Cock

This comfortably modernised and well kept old village pub has some Windsor chairs and cushioned settles on the polished floorboards and red carpet, lots of polished brass and copper, and a big hearth with an elaborate iron fireback. Good bar food includes attractively presented sandwiches (from £1, toasties from £1.50), home-made soup (£1.20), hot salt beef in a bap (£2), ploughman's (from £2), home-made rough pâté (£2.30), local sausage and egg (£2.50), a range of burgers (from £3), salads (from £3.50), gammon and egg (£3.80), scampi (£4) and tender steak (£7); it may be hard to find a seat at busy times (when parking may be difficult too). Well kept Friary Meux on handpump; service is usually cheerful and very friendly; bar billiards, trivia and piped music. There are seats in front of this pretty, partly tile-hung house. Further down the quiet village road is a patch of National Trust woodland – devastated in the storm in October 1987 – and behind the pub you can get through to a public playing-field with swings, seesaw and slide, overlooking rolling fields and woodland. (Recommended by Jenny and Brian Seller, Lt Col D J Daly, Dave Braisted, AE, GRE, Alison Kerruish, E G Parish, Mrs P J Pearce)

Friary Meux (Ind Coope)   Licensee Robert Arnett   Real ale   Meals (not Sun) and snacks (not Sun evening)   Open 11–2.30, 6–11 all year

LUDDENHAM   TQ9862 Map 3
Mounted Rifleman

3½ miles from M2 junction 6; follow Faversham signpost to A2, turn left on to A2, then follow Oare, Luddenham signpost; take first left turn (signposted Buckland, Luddenham), then turn right just before railway crossing; OS Sheet 178 reference 981627 – hamlet marked as Elverton

Standing alone among quiet orchards, this unspoilt old brick house has a truly old-fashioned standard of welcoming hospitality. The two simply furnished, communicating rooms have bare benches, kitchen chairs and the like on their bare floorboards, and some hunting prints on the ochre walls; behind the bar is the former scullery with stone sink, Aga and kitchen table. The well kept Fremlins is tapped in the cellar and brought up on a tray; sandwiches – with home-pickled onions and eggs – on request (ham 90p); darts, dominoes and cribbage. There are a couple of tables out behind, by the roses on the way to the vegetable patch. (Recommended by Phil Gorton, RH, Mrs Susan Sadler, Dr and Mrs A K Clarke; more reports please)

Whitbreads   Real ale   Snacks (lunchtime, not Sun)   Open 10–3, 6–11

NEWNHAM TQ9557 Map 3

George ★ ⊗

Village signposted from A2 just W of Ospringe, outside Faversham

An attractive sixteenth-century pub of great character, this has a more or less open-plan bar formed from a spreading series of rooms. Everything seems individually chosen and cared for: candlelit tables, prettily upholstered mahogany settles, dining-chairs and leather carving-chairs, rugs on the waxed floorboards, the collection of British butterflies and moths, the early nineteenth-century prints (Dominica negroes, Oxford academics, politicians), the cabinet of fine rummers and other glassware, the table lamps and gas-type ceiling chandeliers, above all perhaps the beautiful and distinctive flower arrangements. Hop-bines hang from the beams, open fires warm each room, there's well kept Shepherd Neame Bitter and Best, and the piped music is unobtrusive, well reproduced and interesting. A wide choice of bar food includes sandwiches (from 80p), soup (£1.20), a good variety of ploughman's (from £2), salads (from £2.20, crab £5), cheese-topped cottage pie (£2.25), interesting vegetarian dishes (£3.25) and steak and kidney pie (£3.50), with, in the evening, grills and a good many specials such as ham and leek quiche (£1.60), chicken and parsley pie (£3.25), smoked sausage, pork and lentil stew (£4.50), venison casserole with chestnut and mushroom dumplings (£6.75), roast guinea-fowl with red wine sauce (£7) and lots of game in season – the winter game pudding (£4.75) is popular. Another favourite is the 'Well' pudding – old-fashioned steamed suet, to a grandmother's recipe. Cribbage, fruit machine. There are picnic-table sets in a spacious sheltered garden with a fine spreading cobnut tree, below the slopes of the sheep pastures. *(Recommended by Ruth Humphrey, M Byrne, G Campion)*

Shepherd Neame   Licensees Simon and Anne Barnes   Real ale   Meals and snacks (not Sun evening, Mon)   Children in eating area   Occasional impromptu pianist   Open 10.30–3, 6–11 all year

OARE TR0062 Map 3

Shipwrights Arms ★

Ham Road, Hollow Shore; from A2 just W of Faversham, follow Oare–Luddenham signpost; fork right at Oare–Harty Ferry signpost, drive straight through Oare (don't turn off to Harty Ferry), then left into Ham Street on the outskirts of Faversham, following pub signpost

The original part of this remote, seventeenth-century pub has three cosy and remarkably dimly lit little bars (there are no mains facilities – lighting is by generator and water is pumped from a well), separated by standing timbers and wood part-partitions or narrow door arches. A medley of seats vary from tapestry-cushioned stools and chairs through some big Windsor armchairs to black wood-panelled built-in settles forming little booths, and there are several brick fireplaces – one with a wood-burning stove. Decorations include copper kettles, boating pictures, flags or boating pennants on the ceilings, and hops and pewter tankards hanging over the bar counter. Bar food, chalked up on a blackboard, has included sandwiches, various ploughman's, seafood pancakes, cottage pie or salads, mild lamb curry, and fresh rainbow trout. Well kept Adnams Best and Extra, Shepherd Neame and Youngers IPA and No 3 tapped from casks behind the counter; farm ciders, including their own called Looney Juice; cribbage and piped music. A larger room with less atmosphere but considerably more light has a food hatch where a loudspeaker tells you your food is ready. The small front and back gardens outside the white weatherboarded and tiled cottage have some picnic-table sets, and lead up a bank to the path above the creek where lots of boats are moored. Unless you land by water (like Kirk Douglas in *The Vikings*), you'll have to drive down a long and extremely bumpy lane across the marshes to reach the pub. Last year eyebrows were raised over the lavatories: we hope they have been taken in hand. *(Recommended by A W Lewis, Quentin Williamson, Paul Wyles, Denis Mann, Stanley Matthews, Colin Humphreys, Patrick Stapley)*

Free house   Real ale   Meals and snacks   Children welcome   Sea shanty trio Mon nights, mid-stream disco Sat nights   Open 10.30–3, 6–11 all year; closed 25 Dec

PETT BOTTOM   TR1552 Map 3

Duck ⊗

From B2068 S of Canterbury take Lower Hardres turn; Pett Bottom signposted from there; OS Sheet 179 reference 161521

It's remarkable that so many people can fit good-naturedly into the two tiny bar-rooms of this remote pub (which has, leading off, a more spacious candlelit restaurant). It's the wide choice of interesting food which is the draw: besides sandwiches (from £1.50), ploughman's (from £2.10) and filled baked potatoes (£2.50), there's vegetable pie or cauliflower cheese (£2.75), lasagne (£3.15), a good few meat pies such as liver and bacon or steak and kidney (£4.20), mussels in wine, cream and garlic (£4.25), one or two changing dishes of the day such as pike quenelles (£4.50) and more expensive specialities such as garlicky chicken en croûte (£7.95), duck done with apple and calvados (£8.95), monkfish with a Dijon mustard and dill sauce (£9.55) and steaks (£9.75); helpings and flavours are robust. Apart from one sofa, a little stripped chest-of-drawers with a mirror on top, and a big fireplace dating from the early seventeenth century, furnishings and décor are very plain. Shepherd Neame and a couple of guest beers such as Greene King IPA, Marstons Pedigree, Palmers or Wadworths 6X tapped from the cask; decent wines by the glass, on our visit rather muffled late-1950s piped pop music. There are some teak tables in front of the tile-hung cottage, by a well and facing usable replica stocks, with more in the sizeable garden; it's a peaceful, pretty valley (and Winston the barky labrador/alsatian you may meet in the car park soon quietens down – especially if you promise him a sip of Pedigree). *(Recommended by PLC, MB, Serena Hanson, Dr and Mrs R O Sadler, Comus Elliott)*

Free house   Licensees Lorraine Brown and Ron Brown   Real ale   Meals and snacks Restaurant tel Canterbury (0227) 830354   Children in left-hand bar and restaurant Open 11–2.30, 6–11 all year

PLUCKLEY   TQ9243 Map 3

Dering Arms 🏩

Near station, which is signposted from B2077 in village

Formerly a part of the Dering estate, this striking old Dutch-gabled place was originally built as a hunting-lodge. Inside, not too much has changed since then: the bars are simply but attractively decorated, with a good variety of solid wooden furniture on the wood and stone floors, log fires, and a relaxed, friendly atmosphere. Good bar food includes sandwiches (from 80p, toasties 10p extra), home-made soup (£1.65), pâté or various ploughman's with home-made chutney (£1.95), chicken (£2.45), home-made pie of the day (£3.65), local trout (£6.25), steak (£6.85), and puddings like fruit crumble (£1.95); daily specials (that always include a vegetarian one) are chalked up on a board, and at weekends they specialise in several fish dishes; they also have gourmet evenings every six weeks. Well kept Adnams Bitter, Goachers Maidstone and a beer they brew for the pub, Shepherd Neame Old and Youngs Special on handpump; darts, bar billiards,

---

The initials GWG – mentioned, for instance, as 'on GWG 22' – stand for our companion Consumers' Association's book *Holiday Which? Good Walks Guide*, and show that the pub is on or near the walk numbered.

dominoes, fruit machine and juke box. *(Recommended by Patrick Stapley, Richard Gibbs, RAB, Ginny Humphreys, RG, B Prosser)*

Free house Licensee James Buss Real ale Meals and snacks Restaurant (closed Sun evening) Children in restaurant and games-room Open 11–2.30, 6–11 all year; closed 25 Dec Bedrooms tel Pluckley (023 384) 371; £20/£32

RINGLESTONE TQ8755 Map 3

Ringlestone ⊗

Ringlestone Road; village signposted from B2163; OS Sheet 178 reference 879558

There are around eight changing well kept real ales in this busy country pub tapped from casks behind the bar and chalked up on a board: Adnams, Batemans, Fremlins, Goose Eye Pommies Revenge, Greene King Abbot, Harveys, Marstons Pedigree, Wiltshire Old Devil, and a beer from the local brewers Goachers, called Ringlestone; they can be quite pricey; country wines are chalked up on a beam over the bar counter. The central room has farmhouse chairs and cushioned wall settles around tables with candle lanterns set into ropework centrepieces, a brick floor, an inglenook fireplace with a wood-burning stove and a small bread oven, and old-fashioned brass and glass lamps on the bare brick walls. An arch from here through a wall – rather like the *outside* of a house, windows and all – opens into a long, quieter room with etchings of country folk on its walls (bare brick too), cushioned wall benches, tiny farmhouse chairs, three old carved settles (one rather fine) and similar tables. Regulars tend to sit at the wood-panelled bar counter, or liven up a little wood-floored side room. Bar food includes a help-yourself hot and cold lunchtime buffet as well as thick vegetable or meat soup with sherry and croûtons (£1.50), filled baked potatoes (£2.25), ploughman's or crab pâté with lemon mayonnaise (£2.75), chilli con carne (£3.65), good home-made pies (chicken and bacon, pork and pear or fisherman's, all £4.50), fresh local trout in oatmeal (£5.50), rump steak (£6.50) and specials such as spiced beef casserole, fish crumble or curry; also, puddings like home-made cheesecake or fruit crumble (£2); cribbage and piped pop music. There are picnic-table sets outside on the large raised lawn with ponds and waterfalls, a rockery above the car park and troughs of pretty flowers along the pub walls. *(Recommended by Robin and Bev Gammon, Mrs W Harrington, Mrs Penny Mendelsohn, Comus Elliott, M J Daunton, S J A Velate, Colin Humphreys, Patrick Stapley, RAB)*

Free house Licensee Michael Buck Real ale Meals and snacks Restaurant tel Maidstone (0622) 859207 Children welcome Open 12–3, 6–11 all year; may stay open longer in afternoon if trade demands Bedrooms with self-catering facilities planned in house next door

ST MARGARET'S AT CLIFFE TR3644 Map 3

Cliffe Tavern Hotel ⊗ ⛏

High Street

In the high part of the little town, back from the National Trust coastal cliffs, this comfortable, friendly inn has tables on its quiet back lawn, sheltered by sycamores and a rose-covered flint wall. Inside, the bar has a striking picture of a Second World War aerial dogfight above the village and there's a larger open-plan lounge. Good, reasonably priced food includes sandwiches (from 90p, fresh crab £1.45), home-made celery and cashewnut soup (£1.80), a range of home-made curries and individual pies such as fish or steak (from £2.50), scampi (£3.10), salads (from £3.30), ten-ounce burger (£3.70), home-made vegetarian dishes like chilli bean and mixed vegetable casserole (£3.60), steaks (from £4.90) and a plate of shellfish (£6.20), with a choice of puddings (from £1.10); there's a dining area next to the back bar. Well kept Fremlins, Ruddles County, Shepherd Neame, Trumans and Websters Yorkshire on handpump; particularly helpful staff. Most of the bedrooms are in two little cottages across the yard from the main building. The inn is near *Good Walks Guide* Walk 43. *(Recommended by Bernard Phillips, M J Daunton, Nigel Williamson, P G Rossington, Allan Kirkwood; more reports please)*

Free house   Licensee Christopher Waring Westby   Real ale   Meals and snacks
Well behaved children in dining area   Open 10.30–2.30, 6–11 all year   Bedrooms tel
Dover (0304) 852749 or 852400; £26.18B/£38.06B

SELLING   TR0456 Map 3
White Lion ⊗

3½ miles from M2 junction 7; village signposted from exit roundabout; village also signposted off A251 S of Faversham

A thriving community of budgerigars, canaries, zebra finches, button quail, golden pheasants, rabbits and guinea-pigs, with their young, enlivens the garden here (and generally seems to drive Timmy and Remi the cats indoors). The bar, refurbished in summer 1988, now has a working spit over the right-hand log fire; it's got a friendly, homely atmosphere, with pews on stripped floorboards and an unusual semi-circular counter serving well kept Shepherd Neame Bitter and Best from handpump, with decent wines by the glass. Generous helpings of bar food include soup (£1.50), pâté and crab pâté (£1.95), a good Stilton ploughman's (£2.10), avocado stuffed with seafood (£2.25), plaice (£3), scampi (£3.50), gammon (£4.95) and steaks (from eight-ounce rump £5.95); darts, fruit machine, maybe piped music – the landlord's a trumpet-player. *(Recommended by John Elias, Ted George, H P Chapman, Comus Elliott)*

Shepherd Neame   Licensees Anthony and Jackie Richards   Real ale   Meals and snacks
Restaurant tel Canterbury (0227) 752211   Children's room   Jazz Sun evening
Open 11–3 (maybe later Sat), 6.30–11 all year; closed 25 Dec

nr SMARDEN   TQ8842 Map 3
Bell ★

From Smarden follow lane between church and The Chequers, then turn left at T-junction; or from A274 take unsignposted turn E a mile N of B2077 to Smarden

Although different in character, the bars here all have a relaxed, friendly atmosphere. The snug little back rooms have low beams, pews and the like around the simple candlelit tables, brick or flagstone floors, bare brick or ochre plastered walls, and an inglenook fireplace. The lively front bar has darts, pool, shove-ha'penny, dominoes, fruit machine, trivia and juke box; part of it is partly set aside for families with children. Good bar food includes home-made soup (£1.10), sandwiches (from £1.10, toasties from £1.20), home-made pâté (£1.80), ploughman's or pizza (from £1.75), home-made shepherd's pie (£2.25), basket meals (from £2.25), salads (from £3), scampi (£2.90), good home-made steak and kidney pie (£3.55), gammon steak with pineapple (£3.95) and steaks (from £6.25) and daily specials; puddings such as home-made chocolate crunch cake (£1.10). There's a fine range of real ales on handpump: Flowers, Fremlins, Fullers London Pride, Goachers, Shepherd Neame and Theakstons Best and Old Peculier; also, six wines by the glass, Biddenden cider, Murphy's Milk Stout, and when the weather calls for it mulled wine. You can sit out at the side, among fruit trees and shrubs, admiring the pub, which is hung with fancy tiles and covered with roses. Every second Sunday in the month at midday, there is a gathering of vintage and classic cars. Basic continental breakfasts only. *(Recommended by Mr and Mrs R Gammon, Greg Parston,*

Stars after the name of a pub show exceptional quality. One star means most people (after reading the report to see just why the star has been won) would think a special trip worth while. Two stars mean that the pub is really outstanding – one of just a handful in its region. The very very few with three stars are the real aristocrats – of their type, they could hardly be improved.

AE, GRE, E G Parish, Rodney Coe, G Cooper, Brian and Rosemary Wilmot, Lance White, C D T Spooner)

Free house   Licensee Ian Turner   Real ale   Meals (not Sun lunch) and snacks   Children in front family area of bar   Open 11.30 (11 Sat)–3 (2.30 weekdays in winter), 6–11 all year; closed 25 Dec   Bedrooms tel Smarden (023 377) 283; £14/£22

SPELDHURST TQ5541 Map 3

George & Dragon ⊗

This big half-timbered house is one of the oldest pubs in the South of England. It's based on a manorial great hall dating from 1212, and there are some of the biggest flagstones you can find anywhere, a massive stone fireplace, heavy beams (installed during 'modernisation' in 1589 – until then the room went up to the roof), snug alcoves, panelling, and antique cushioned settles and Windsor chairs. Good bar food includes sandwiches (from 90p, freshly cut Scotch smoked salmon £1.85), home-made soup (£1.25), ploughman's (£1.75), salads (from £1.85, freshly dressed Cornish crab £4), Speldhurst sausages (£2.50), roast chicken (£3), steak and kidney pie or pudding (£3.25), roast lamb (£3.35), jugged hare (£3.50), cold poached salmon (£4.25), pork chop with baked apple and sirloin steak (£5.50). Well kept Flowers, Fremlins, Harveys and Larkins (from Rusthall, near Tunbridge Wells) on handpump; cribbage and piped music (in the restaurant only). It can get very crowded at weekends, especially in the evenings. The striking first-floor restaurant under the original massive roof timbers serves good but expensive food and is served by a quite splendid wine cellar – a place for special occasions. There are white tables and chairs on the neat little lawn, ringed with flowers, in front of the building. *(Recommended by John Townsend, Alasdair Knowles, M J Masters, Richard Gibbs, Dr and Mrs A K Clarke, F M K Smith, GCS, C D T Spooner)*

Free house   Licensee Mrs Jennifer Sankey   Real ale   Meals and snacks   Restaurant tel Langton (089 286) 3125; closed Sun evening   Children in eating area and restaurant   Open 10–3, 6–11 all year

STAPLE TR2756 Map 3

Black Pig ⊗

Barnsole Road; follow signs to village hall; pub signposted from Wingham–Sandwich back road through Staple, on Sandwich side of village

A nice combination of an old-fashioned country tavern atmosphere with imaginative up-to-the-minute food – and it's not everywhere around here that you can find decent bar food on Sundays, too. The rambling main bar has a heavy beam and plank ceiling, comfortable chairs on the carpet, and an unusual fireplace with a sort of semi-inglenook which may originally have been a smoking cabinet in its massive central chimney. Home-made and freshly prepared bar food includes soup (£1.20), sandwiches (from £1.25, crab £2.20), very good ploughman's with cheeses, home-made pâté, home-cooked ham, beef or turkey, fresh seafood or fresh poached salmon (from £1.75), lasagne (£2.60), chicken curry or scampi (£2.95), salads (from £3.20), steak and kidney pie cooked in Guinness and red wine (£3.25), baked chicken (£3.50) and half a roast duck (£5); daily specials like fresh plaice or skate wings (£3.25), liver and onion casserole (£3.50), fresh poached salmon or guinea-fowl in port (£3.95), and three-course Sunday lunch (£6.50). Well kept Ind Coope Burton and Tetleys on handpump; darts, pool, dominoes, cribbage, trivia, juke box, bat-and-trap in the garden on Wednesday evenings in summer, and piped music. There are seats outside including some under an old yew by the quiet village

---

Pubs shown as closing at 11 do so in the summer, but close earlier – normally 10.30 – in winter unless we specify 'all year'. Often, country pubs don't open as early as we say at quiet times of the year.

lane. *(Recommended by Jack Taylor, Ted George, Mr and Mrs J H Adam, W E George, M J Masters, Rita Davis)*

Free house   Licensees W Culver and J D O Wells   Real ale   Meals and snacks   Restaurant — with dance floor – tel Dover (0304) 812361   Children welcome away from bar servery   Open 10.30–3, 6.30 (6 Sat)–11 all year; closed evenings 25 and 26 Dec

STOWTING   TR1242 Map 3

Tiger ⊗

Village signposted from B2068; coming from N, follow Brabourne, Wye, Ashford signpost to right at fork, then turn left towards Posting and Lyminge at T-junction; coming from S, it's simplest to take the Stowting, Heminge signposted turn, then forking left after nearly a mile to keep along the main road

Simply furnished with plain chairs and dark pews built in against the walls, faded rugs on the dark floorboards, and an abundance of hop-bines draped from the high ceiling, this country pub has a pleasantly open and relaxed atmosphere. There's some floor-to-ceiling plank panelling, shelves of little kegs, stone jugs and copper pots by the brick chimney of the coal-effect gas fire, and candles stuck into bottles. Outside, picnic-table sets and other tables on the front terrace, some under a thinly planted arbour, have a gentle background wash of sheep, farm-animal and other less domesticated noises (on our evening drive here we saw no fewer than six foxes and two badgers); inside, on our visit there was muffled piped pop music – with contented chat the main sound. Bar food, entirely home made, includes sandwiches (£1.25, steak £3.60), soup (£1.70), a half-pint of prawns (£2.60), pork and liver terrine (£2), burger (£2.95), grilled local plaice (£3.75), cod and prawn done with cheese and tomato or steak and kidney pie (£4) and rump steak (£5.95), with local game in season. Well kept Bass, Charrington IPA, Everards Tiger and Ruddles Best on handpump; darts, shove-ha'penny, dominoes and cribbage. *(Recommended by John Bennett, D K and H M Brenchley)*

Free house   Licensees Alan and Linda Harris   Real ale   Meals and snacks   Restaurant tel Lyminge (0303) 862130   Children in eating area (lunchtime)   Jazz Mon   Open 12–2.30 (maybe later Sat), 6–11 all year; closed evening 25 Dec

TUNBRIDGE WELLS   TQ5839 Map 3

Sankeys

39 Mount Ephraim

Having run the Gate in Hildenborough for eight years (and notched up an impressive reputation there), Guy Sankey moved to this Victorian house; at first it too was called the Gate – the name's been changed to make it quite clear that there's no connection with his former pub. There's a little pubby bar that leads into a larger room – used mainly for eating – and decorations include Spy and fish prints, old maps and bottles. Bar food, as before, specialises in fish which is bought direct from source (wherever possible), as well as Billingsgate and Rungis in Paris: potted shrimps (£2.50), fish soup or jellied eels (£2.75), fresh Cornish mussels (£3.50), French rock oysters (£5 for six), Mediterranean prawns (hot or cold £7), paella (£7.50), barracuda baked in an envelope with wine, spring onions and soy or seafood platter (£8.50), Dover sole (£11.75), whole Scottish lobster (from £13.50) and home-made puddings like sherry trifle or lemon and ginger crunch (£2); it's impossible to book at short notice on Saturdays. Well kept Harveys from an antique beer engine salvaged from the late lamented Sussex Arms; the atmosphere is relaxed, the service very friendly. *(Recommended by Isobel May, Patrick Stapley, RAB)*

Free house   Licensee Guy Sankey   Real ale   Meals and snacks (not Sun)   Restaurant (closed Sun) tel Tunbridge Wells (0892) 511422   Children welcome   Open 11–11 weekdays, 11–3, 6–11 Sat; closed bank hols

WEALD   TQ5250 Map 3
Chequer Tree

Village signposted off A21 exit roundabout, at southernmost Sevenoaks exit; in village centre, turn left into Scabharbour Road

In the short time since buying this previously neglected pub from the brewery, the go-ahead licensees have just about trebled its size – doing much of the labour as well as the design themselves. The comfortably modernised open-plan carpeted bar has red plush dining-chairs, captain's chairs and button-back built-in wall banquettes around polished heavy dark wood tables, with a couple of rocking-chairs; there are little country prints on the textured white walls, green velvet curtains for the latticed windows, and gentle piped music. A flagstoned games area has darts, pool, shove-ha'penny, cribbage, a skill game and a fruit machine. Bar food served by neat young waitresses includes sandwiches (from 85p), ploughman's (from £1.60), filled baked potatoes (£1.65), pancake rolls (£1.75), omelettes (from £1.95), cauliflower cheese (£2), lasagne (£2.50), ham and egg (£2.75) and steak and kidney pie (£3.50), served with fresh vegetables; well kept Ruddles Best and County and Websters Yorkshire on handpump. The garden's the chief attraction in summer – masses of space, with fairy-lit terraces, a rambling pond full of plump tadpoles, and young trees and shrubs among the older hawthorns, oaks and ashes; bat-and-trap out here, with weekend barbecues in summer. (Recommended by HMM; more reports please)

Free house   Licensee J L Pocknell   Real ale   Meals and snacks (not Sun or Mon evenings) Restaurant tel Sevenoaks (0732) 463386   Children in eating area and restaurant Open 11–3ish, 6–11 all year; flexible afternoon opening for diners

WHITSTABLE   TR1166 Map 3
Pearsons ⊗

Sea Wall; follow main road into centre as far as you can – then try to park!

This friendly pub is especially popular for its good value, very fresh seafood: cockles (65p), rollmops (£1), delicious crab sandwiches (95p), prawn or smoked salmon ones (£1.15), smoked mackerel (£1.20), peeled prawns (£1.45), king prawns (£3.50) and local oysters in season (three £2.25, six £4.50), with changing fresh fish or shellfish specials; also, other sandwiches (from 75p) and ploughman's (£1.35). The small areas in the downstairs bar are divided by stripped brickwork, and have mate's chairs, sea paintings and old local photographs, a ship's wheel, lobster pots, and rough brown ceiling planking; a lower flagstoned area gets most of its submarine light from a huge lobster tank. Well kept Flowers Original and Fremlins on handpump, decent house wines, piped pop music, fruit machine. Upstairs, in two or three pleasantly close-packed dining-rooms, there's a wider choice (as well as a sea view from some tables – downstairs the sea wall gets in the way); service is kind and very quick. There are some picnic-table sets outside between the pub and the sea. (Recommended by Shirley Pielou, G T Rhys, Ken and Barbara Turner, W E George, John Bell)

Whitbreads   Licensee J S Kray   Real ale   Meals and snacks   Restaurant tel Whitstable (0227) 272005; open all day Sun   Children in restaurant   Open all day

WROTHAM   TQ6159 Map 3
Bull

1¾ miles from M20 junction 2: follow Wrotham and then Bull Hotel signposts

They're initiating an interesting experiment in this small, friendly fourteenth-century coaching-inn, and we're keen to hear what readers think. Instead of heading for the bar when you go in, you are now shown by waitresses to linen-covered tables – which oddly enough used to be the way all inns worked with no bar counter and waitress service: are we heading back that way? All this does seem to carry a price – food now includes a cold buffet and a lunchtime hot daily special (from £4) as well as home-made soup (£1.95), sauté sweetbreads (£3.50), various hors d'oeuvre (£3.75), skewered prawns with sweet peppers (£4.95), whole kidneys rolled in thinly sliced liver with a demi-glace and red wine sauce (£5.95), fresh plaice fillet filled with prawns (£6.95), chicken breast filled with creamcheese and garlic and garnished with avocado (£7.50) and a flambé dish of the day (£9.50); home-made puddings (£1.95) and Sunday roast lunch (main course £4). A changing real ale on handpump such as Greene King IPA; piped music. The two comfortably furnished rooms of the bar still have Battle of Britain pilots' signatures on one part of the ceiling, with a stylised modern relief of pilgrims on another, and upholstered wall benches, one fine long bare wood table among other smaller ones (now clothed), leatherette seats, hunting prints, a big Victorian pilgrimage print, mounted antelope heads, curly brass chandeliers, and a log fire at each end. There are tables on a small sheltered terrace backed by the church. *(Recommended by Mr and Mrs J H Adam, E J Cutting, E G Parish; more reports please)*

Free house   Licensees Michael and Elaine Dunnell   Real ale   Meals   Children welcome Open all day   Bedrooms tel Borough Green (0732) 883092; £26(£35B)/£38(£48B)

WYE   TR0546   Map 3

Tickled Trout

After one of the beautiful walks on the downs on the far side of the village (the pub is near the start of *Good Walks Guide* Walk 46), it's especially nice to sit on the side lawn which runs down under ash trees to the clear, shallow waters of the Great Stour (which have been restocked with carp and bream), with ducks paddling frantically around under the bridge. Inside, it's open-plan, with heavy timbers that have been added to its stripped brickwork, and comfortable wall banquettes around dimpled copper tables; this year there's a new glass-covered restaurant extension. Good bar food includes sandwiches, filled baked potatoes (from 60p), ploughman's (from £1.60), seafood pie (£2.25), salads, trout (£4.95), steaks (from £4.95) and daily specials such as chilli con carne (£2.75). Flowers and Fremlins on handpump. Hard-working, friendly service, maybe piped music. Popular with older people at lunchtime as well as lecturers and students from nearby Wye College. *(Recommended by Paul King, G and S L, Ted George, Robin and Bev Gammon, Anthony Lowe, Sqn Ldr Tony Clarke, Hilary Rubinstein, Geoffrey and Jenepher Newell-Westrow, Mrs S Corrigan, C D T Spooner)*

Fremlins (Whitbreads)   Managers Betty and Jim Grieve   Real ale   Meals and snacks Children in eating area and restaurant   Restaurant tel Wye (0233) 812227   Open 10.30–3, 6–11 all year

Lucky Dip

Besides the fully inspected pubs, you might like to try these Lucky Dips recommended to us and described by readers (if you do, please send us reports):

Acol [TR3067], *Crown & Sceptre*: Small cosy lounge bar with good, reasonably priced bar food in big helpings, good Fremlins *(David Shillitoe)*

Appledore [Stn; TQ9529], *Railway*: Most friendly atmosphere in real family pub with two super log fires, Friary Meux, Harveys, Ind Coope Burton and Tetleys real ales, and extensive choice of good food cooked by licensee's Italian/Swiss wife *(Peter Davies)*;

[The Street] *Red Lion*: Attractive and comfortable Courage pub with wide choice of food, most of it organic – decidedly good if somewhat restaurantish (and not really priced for just a casual meal); exceptionally easy-going and friendly family and staff, a welcome for children (and dogs); freshly squeezed orange juice, real coffee; three bedrooms (one with a four-poster) *(Susan Johnson, Miss P T Metcalfe, Comus Elliott)*

Ash [High St (A257 towards Canterbury); TR2858], *Volunteer*: Friendly, welcoming landlord, very well kept Adnams and Harveys and a varied menu with good home-made food *(Frank Williams, B Prosser)*

Ashford [Park St; TR0042], *Downtown Diner*: Popular American-style bar with very wide choice of food in ample helpings, pleasant staff *(B Prosser)*

Aylesford [High St; TQ7359], *Chequers*: Visually attractive sixteenth-century coaching-inn with friendly staff and riverside terrace looking on to medieval bridge and River Medway; it's been open-planned inside though, and the fruit machines, video games, pop music and indeed many of the customers don't appeal universally *(Peter Griffiths)*

Badlesmere [TR0054], *Red Lion*: Attractive, spacious country pub where time stands still, friendly landlord; draught Fremlins, Wethereds, Flowers Original and Winter Royal; bar food, pleasant garden and paddock for caravans and tents *(Robert Caldwell)*

Bearsted [Weavering Street; TQ7855], *Fox & Goose*: All that a pleasant, friendly local should be *(C Elliott)*

Birchington [Station Rd; TR3069], *Seaview*: Well run, friendly local with well kept Flowers IPA, good bar food; a comfortable place to stay *(P Garrad)*

Bishopsbourne [TR1852], *Mermaid*: Real friendly local in truly small village *(D P Green)*

☆ **Boxley** [TQ7759], *Yew Tree*: Beautifully converted Shepherd Neame pub nestling under the downs (and the M20), with well kept real ale, good sandwiches; very pretty village and church *(Eileen Broadbent, Comus Elliott)*

Brabourne [Canterbury Rd, East Brabourne; TR1041], *Five Bells*: Good comfortable atmosphere, well kept Courage ales and decent food in oak-beamed early sixteenth-century free house with friendly licensees, log fire, garden *(Mr and Mrs L J McKenna, Alison Gurr)*

Brabourne Lees [TR0840], *Plough*: Nice friendly village pub with Shepherd Neame real ales and reasonable food *(C Elliott)*

Bramling [A257 E of Canterbury; TR2256], *Haywain*: First-class Courage Directors in spick-and-span pub, wide choice of good food, tables on lawn, children's playthings *(Ted George)*

☆ **Brasted** [High St; A25 3 miles from M25 junction 5; TQ4654], *Kings Arms*: Inglenook fireplace in the main bar has gleaming brass plates and other knick-knacks and a gas-effect log fire; settles, chairs and stools — upholstered or with cushions — on the parquet floor, a huge carved armchair, and an antique tuba on the wall (it's popular with musicians, and the piano and electric organ do get used); a smaller, plainly furnished bar has bar billiards, shove-ha'penny and darts in separate room; well kept Shepherd Neame ale, lunchtime food and evening snacks, good Sun nibbles, friendly service *(Simon Velate, Michael McEwan)*

☆ **Brasted** [A25], *White Hart*: Friendly and efficient staff and normally quiet relaxed atmosphere in spacious lounge and sun lounge (it can get busy at holiday times or on fine weekends), well kept Bass and Charrington IPA in Battle of Britain bar with signatures and mementoes of Biggin Hill fighter pilots, big neatly kept garden; generous helpings of reasonably priced bar food, restaurant; children welcome; bedrooms *(E G Parish, Margaret Branney, LYM)*

Brasted [High St], *Bull*: Clean comfortable pub with good choice of food, well kept Shepherd Neame ales, decent coffee, garden *(S A Lovett)*; [Church Rd] *Stanhope Arms*: Simple bar food and well kept Friary Meux in cosy and unpretentious village pub near church, with friendly licensee, relaxed atmosphere and traditional games as well as machines; children in eating area; bat-and-trap in pretty garden *(W J Wonham, J E Cross, LYM)*

Brenchley [TQ6741], *Rose & Crown*: Friendly new owners in sturdily timbered old inn with comfortable seats around rustic tables, simple bar food including good home-cured ham, well kept Fremlins, Harveys and Hook Norton real ale; children in eating area, restaurant and family-room, piped music, seats on terrace, garden play area; bedrooms all with private bathroom, though not cheap *(Mr and Mrs G D Amos, LYM)*; [OS Sheet 188 reference 666417] *Walnut Tree*: Well decorated, warm pub with well kept beer, good bar food reasonably priced *(G C Saunders)*

Brookland [just off and signposted from A259 about ½ mile out of village; TQ9825], *Woolpack*: Friendly atmosphere, traditional low beams, good choice at bar, open fire with inglenook seats, adjacent pool-room; built fourteenth century and including ship's timbers that may be twelfth century; garden with stream at bottom *(Matt Buchan)*

Broomfield [TR1966], *Plough*: Whitbreads pub with good, reasonably priced bar food, friendly staff and log fires in winter *(M J Daunton)*

☆ **Burham** [Church St (nr M2 junction 3); TQ7361], *Golden Eagle*: Reasonably priced Malaysian food a speciality in pub with good friendly atmosphere, welcoming landlord, jugs hanging from impressive beams, well stocked bar with well kept Flowers and Fremlins — if they did something about the seating it could be a really fine pub *(B R Wood, Geoff and Teresa Salt)*

Burrs Hill [TQ6840], *Half Way House*: Owners have a trawler, and bring up fish from Rye four times a week — anything from cod through Dover sole to lobster, very good value (even the chips are properly cooked) *(J E Cross)*

☆**Canterbury** [North Lane; TR1557], *Falstaff*: Good ploughman's and other reasonably priced weekday lunchtime bar food and well kept Flowers or Fremlins in clean and friendly pub nicely decorated with stripped woodwork, hop-bines and old coins; cheery barman, waiter in clean butcher's apron; closed Sun lunchtime; note that this is different from the Falstaff Hotel in St Dunstans Street – good, but decidedly not a pub *(Stanley Matthews, A and J Whitley, Gordon Mott)*

Canterbury [Palace St], *Bell & Crown*: Good well kept beer, cheap wholesome food (not Sun) and pleasant service in interesting old pub, though it seems to appeal most to students and youngsters *(Paul Duncan)*; [Rosemary Lane (off Castle St, opp public car park)] *Cardinals Cap*: Robust working man's pub with video disco, settees and good range of food; Fremlins *(Ian Phillips)*; [St Stephens] *Olde Beverlie*: Ancient pub, sympathetically brought up to date and furnished well; good bar food, choice of beers, lots of flower borders and hanging baskets, as well as quaint wooden shelters, around the lawn – centre for the thriving local bat-and-trap team which my great-grandfather captained some 80 years ago *(MB)*; *Phoenix*: Serves good value main-course lunchtime dishes *(R Coe)*; [Watling St] *Three Tuns*: Sixteenth-century building, a well known tavern and coaching-inn by the eighteenth century; beams, sloping floors, comfortable bar areas and conservatory with white metal furniture; Trumans Sampson, various hot dishes, salad bar, piped music; children's room; bedrooms; but they discriminate against the armed forces *(Lyn and Bill Capper)*; [Castle Row; opp tree-shaded square off Castle St] *White Hart*: Friendly, courteous service; popular with businessmen and older people for good variety of well cooked, reasonably priced bar food generously served; Graham Dilley's local – food bar has a mural of Kent CC covering whole wall *(W J Crust, Ian Phillips)*

Challock [Church Lane; TR0050], *Chequers*: Tastefully modernised seventeenth-century country pub with good value bar food (Tues–Sat), well kept Courage ales, friendly atmosphere, terrace *(Anthony Lowe, R Coe)*

☆**Chiddingstone Causeway** [B2027; TQ5146], *Little Brown Jug*: Good welcoming atmosphere in comfortably modernised country pub, pleasant landlord who is a jazz trombonist, at least six well kept real ales, wide choice of good bar food which can also be eaten in restaurant, cheerful if not always speedy service; children allowed in one room; attractive garden with children's play tree and so forth *(J M Price, J G Evans, Mr and Mrs W Harrington, Heather Martin, J A Snell, W J Wonham)*

Chiddingstone Causeway [Charcott, off back rd to Weald; TQ5247], *Greyhound*: Clean and well kept but basic Whitbreads local in quiet village; genuine welcome, good Flowers Original, Sun peanuts and cheese and biscuits on bar and all tables; good value home-made bar food (not Sun – though they may do you a ploughman's then), barbecue out at the front with tables and chairs *(Brian and Jenny Seller, R Coe)*

☆**Chilham** [TR0753], *White Horse*: Beautiful position on prettiest village square in Kent – with couple of tables out on the corner to make the most of it (there are more in a side garden just down the lane); lively lunchtime bustle in summer, good log fire in winter, Fremlins real ale; recent reports on food and service have been mixed *(Wayne Brindle, Robin and Bev Gammon, Ian Phillips, S V Bishop, LYM)*

Cobham [TQ6768], *Ship*: Spacious pub, seven rooms tastefully furnished, long bar, Fremlins and Websters Original Mild *(R A Caldwell)*

☆**Coopers Corner** [TQ4849], *Frog & Bucket*: Friendly new landlord since late 1987, well kept Flowers IPA and good farm cider, good bar food; good views from pleasant garden with seats, tables and barbecue, live jazz Sun lunchtime, other live acts Fri–Sun evenings – very popular with young people, can be too noisy and crowded for older folk *(Jenny and Brian Seller, Alasdair Knowles)*

☆**Cowden** [TQ4640], *Crown*: Friendly attentive licensee and staff in small comfortable bar with homely atmosphere, good wines, good food in bar and small restaurant including steaks grilled over apple-wood; book ahead for restaurant *(Mr and Mrs M J Banbury)*

☆**Cowden** [junction B2026 with Markbeech rd], *Queens Arms*: Clean, friendly and absolutely unpretentious pub with old-fashioned atmosphere, well kept Whitbreads (no lager sold here), incredibly cheap bread, cheese and pickle *(Philip Denison, Phil and Sally Gorton)*

Cranbrook [TQ7735], *Crown*: Friendly basic local with two real ales and exceptional value lunchtime specials such as large wedge of home-made steak and kidney pie with no fewer than six vegetables *(R Coe)*

Crouch [TQ6155], *Olde Chequers*: Very friendly sixteenth-century pub with good choice of bar food (including 'naughty but nice' puddings), real ales and wines; inexpensive restaurant, garden; delightful hamlet nr Great Comp gardens, Old Soare Manor, Ightham Mote; good walks in nearby forest despite hurricane damage *(W J Wonham)*

Darenth [Darenth Rd; TQ5671], *Chequers*: Interesting black and white timbered pub, Courage Best, terrace and garden behind, bar food (Mon–Sat), full Sun lunch *(Anon)*

Dartford [3 Darenth Rd; TQ5373], *Malt Shovel*: Good, quiet old pub, unspoilt public bar and plush lounge with separate eating area; well kept Youngs, good choice of bar food from sandwiches, ploughman's and salads to hot meals and daily specials *(Paul Wyles)*

Deal [Strand; TR3752], *Lifeboat*: Very much connected with the sea; congenial surroundings and good choice of straightforward pub food *(B Prosser)*

☆ **Denton** [Canterbury rd (A260); TR2147], *Jackdaw*: Good food in spotless and welcoming Whitbreads pub with well kept Flowers and Fremlins on handpump; children in eating area at lunchtime *(Comus Elliott, C M Franks, Simon Rees)*

Dover [11 Priory St; TR3141], *Golden Lion*: A most welcoming and friendly pub with very good beer *(J P Swinbourne)*; [opp Martin Mill BR stn] *Ugly Duckling*: Popular real ale pub; welcoming landlord and landlady, good varied menu including seafood *(B Prosser)*

Dunton Green [London Rd; TQ5157], *Dukes Head*: Comfortably modernised pleasant local with friendly licensee, well kept Benskins Best, bar food (not Sun – as one reader with a walking party was upset to discover even though a telephone call had given him to understand differently), garden; maybe Sat pianist *(BB)*

East Peckham [Bush Lane, Peckham Bush; off A26 nr Hadlow; TQ6648], *Bush, Blackbird & Thrush*: Big ploughman's and well kept Fremlins in friendly local *(F M K Smith)*

☆ **Edenbridge** [TQ4446], *Crown*: Cheerful local with Tudor origins and not over-modernised, popular for straightforward bar food, good service from young staff, rack of newspapers for customers' use; one of the last pubs to have kept its 'gallows' inn-sign stretching right across the road *(E G Parish, AE, GRE, LYM)*

Elham [TR1743], *Kings Arms*: Friendly landlord and staff, good beer, pleasant eating room/bar with good fire, good choice of bar food *(L M Miall)*; [B2065] *Palm Tree*: Good but rather pricey range of real ales such as Flowers Original, Fullers ESB, Greene King Abbot, Ringwood Old Thumper, Theakstons Old Peculier and Wadworths 6X, tasteful décor that includes fish tank, olde-worlde atmosphere (but piped music), big garden *(Robert Caldwell)*; *Rose & Crown*: Good beer and superb food in very friendly inn, clean and tidy, with lots of old-world charm and efficient service; tables outside, attractive village; bedrooms *(Ted George)*

☆ **Eynsford** [TQ5365], *Malt Shovel*: Popular Victorian local with interesting décor, history of pub on walls describing appearance of ghost; well kept Courage Best and Directors, good value if not cheap bar food with live lobsters in bar, friendly and prompt service (though Sun lunchtime they tend not to do bar food, as the restaurant's so busy) *(Jenny and Brian Seller, Canon G Hollis)*

Fairseat [Gravesend Rd (A227) – OS Sheet 177 reference 631611; TQ6261], *Vigo*: Really basic traditional country pub – beer-

drinker's delight with friendly young landlord and good beer *(Dr and Mrs A K Clarke)*

☆ **Faversham** [10 West St; TR0161], *Sun*: Fascinating old-world fifteenth-century town pub with interesting rambling bar areas, a good atmosphere, easy-going furniture and unobtrusive Radio 2; individually prepared lunchtime meals that include soup, quiche, several pies, sandwiches, ploughman's with a very comprehensive salad and daily specials that often include fish; well kept Shepherd Neame bitter, friendly staff *(Lyn and Bill Capper, Rodney Coe)*

Faversham [99 Abbey St], *Phoenix*: Amiable and relaxed, with particularly good ploughman's *(Anthony Lowe)*; *Recreation*: This pub recommended in previous editions closed in autumn 1987

Five Wents [A274 Maidstone–Sutton Valence, at B2163 crossroads; TQ8150], *Plough*: Good choice of bar food including nicely presented sandwiches, specials such as chicken and gammon pie, liver and bacon or queen scallops au gratin, and main dishes such as good value gammon and egg or T-bone steak; refrigerated display of desserts, good filter coffee; large bar with restaurant area opening off, piped music, seats in garden, clean lavatories; Courage house, quite handy for Leeds Castle *(TOH)*

Folkestone [TR2336], *Lifeboat*: Friendly staff, very good selection of real ales and tasty bar snacks; beer garden *(T R G Alcock)*

Fordcombe [TQ5240], *Chafford Arms*: Delightful inside and out, nr cricket green *(David Gaunt)*

Fordwich [TR1759], *George & Dragon*: Tables on nice lawn by River Stour, and in covered outdoor area; comfortably cushioned seats inside, bar lunches including ploughman's, baked potatoes, filled rolls, soup, hot dishes, salad bar and puddings, Flowers, Fremlins and Whitbreads, coffee, subdued piped music, fruit machine; afternoon teas, Beefeater restaurant, interesting village *(Lyn and Bill Capper)*

Frinstead [TQ8957], *Kingsdown Arms*: Welcoming atmosphere in free house with lots of swings, slides and so forth in large back garden, bar food even on Sun; out-of-the-way village *(Hazel Morgan)*

Goathurst Common [TQ4952], *Woodman*: Attractively refurbished and extended and tastefully furnished with well spaced tables; good service, young friendly staff, wide choice of good imaginative food in bar and restaurant; in lovely countryside, huge car park – it's very popular *(Margaret Branney, W J Wonham)*

Goodnestone [NB this is in East Kent *not* the other Goodnestone – OS Sheet 179 reference 255546; TR2554], *Fitzwalter Arms*: Typically rural and very friendly place with three bars: big end bar with lovely large cat, middle one for locals, and games-bar; unusual windows like the rest of the village *(W E George)*

☆ **Goudhurst** [A262 W of village; TQ7238], *Green Cross*: Good home-cooked bar food including very nice mushrooms in a cream and port sauce and very good steaks; also freshly smoked salmon, soup, fish, lasagne, lamb chops, salads and puddings; good choice of well kept real ales such as Adnams, Fremlins, Golden Hill Exmoor and Hook Norton; beamed dining-room for residents; bedrooms light and airy, good value (*Sue Hallam, Brian and Rosemary Wilmot*)

Greatstone [Coast Dr; TR0823], *Seahorse*: Very friendly seafront pub with helpful staff, quick service, good choice of cheap bar food including children's meals; big sea-view terrace with play area (*Raymond Palmer*)

☆ **Hadlow** [Tonbridge Rd; TQ6349], *Rose Revived*: Lovely free house with good beers including Harveys and King & Barnes, above-average food including well filled fresh sandwiches; though it had a facelift and name change around 1980, it has a history going back to 1515 (*WHBM, Barry Stevens*)

Ham [Hayhill; TR3254], *Blazing Donkey*: Good menu, good food and beer and friendly staff; children welcome (*B Prosser*)

Harrietsham [TQ8652], *Bell*: Small and spotless, off the beaten track; huge helpings of good food such as home-made turkey and ham pie with four vegetables (*Mrs P Turner*)

☆ **Hawkhurst** [TQ7630], *Oak & Ivy*: Friendly comfortable pub with reasonably priced traditional cooking including Sun roast in bar, roaring log fires, attractive restaurant (*Brian and Rosemary Wilmot, Tim Locke*)

Hawkhurst [Highgate (A268 E); TQ7630], *Royal Oak*: Unspoilt, small hotel with comfortable bar and good value lunchtime food (*R Coe*)

Headcorn [North St; TQ8344], *White Horse*: Comfortable pub with friendly staff; good, wide-ranging choice of bar food reasonably priced, pleasant garden with Wendy house (*Penny Mendelsohn*)

Heaverham [TQ5658], *Chequers*: Big helpings of good varied bar food, friendly licensee, well kept beer; very good jugged hare, venison pie and so forth in attractive restaurant in attached old barn; quiet location in pretty little hamlet (*R J and F J Ambroziak*)

Herne [Herne Common; TR1865], *Fox & Hounds*: Worth including for its good beer and large helpings of enterprising food with decent vegetables at low prices; particularly popular for its restaurant meals (*MB, R Coe*)

Hernhill [TR0660], *Three Horseshoes*: Super little village pub among the apple orchards, strong village identity with own cricket team, simple home-made snacks (*Comus Elliott*)

☆ **Hever** [Luckfield Lane; TQ4744], *Greyhound*: Picturesque white country pub off the beaten track with large L-shaped room, wooden tables and chairs and a relaxed atmosphere, nr GWG50; has been popular for good choice of bar food (fish and puddings particularly recommended), Sun

lunch and good selection of country wines, with Adnams, Flowers and Fremlins on handpump; ramp for wheelchair access; changed hands 1988 (*Heather Sharland, Margaret Branney, E G Parish – reports on new regime please*); *Henry VIII*: Country pub with pondside lawn and Boleyn connections, bought when Lord Astor's estate split up; refurbished and reopened 1987 with purple décor, catering with brisk friendliness for people visiting Hever Castle (*E G Parish, Jon Wainwright, LYM*)

High Halden [TQ8937], *Chequers*: Cosy little pub with real fire, comfortable chairs, good food in separate eating area, Fremlins real ale; bedrooms (*Mark Walpole*)

Hildenborough [Stn; TQ5648], *Gate*: Previously very popular – and very highly rated – for its good seafood; in 1987 the licensee moved his whole operation from here to Tunbridge Wells (see our reports on Sankeys there), but Whitbreads the controlling brewery have kept a seafood operation going here (the starters are said to make good bar snacks); friendly service, well kept Flowers and Fremlins, pubby place with separate restaurant, tables in garden (*Barbara Hatfield, Peter Griffiths, LYM*); *Plough*: Country pub carefully extended, large open log fire; huge choice of real ales including Youngs, Flowers, Fremlins and Fullers ESB; good value bar food and carvery in the Barn (*J A Snell*)

Hollingbourne [A20; TQ8454], *Park Gate*: Several real ales in spacious oak-panelled pub next to Leeds Castle, efficient rather than friendly service, occasional live music, good food including Sun lunch (*Peter Neate*); [B2163, off A20 – OS Sheet 188 reference 833547] *Windmill*: Interesting pub with half a dozen different levels and nooks around the central servery, friendly staff, good food; not too busy even on warm Bank Holiday (*Mr and Mrs R Gammon*)

Horsmonden [TQ7040], *Gun & Spitroast*: Attractive up-market pub overlooking village green with spitroast beef, pork, etc. on alternate days – huge helpings, very good value; other good value food and generous hot or cold sandwiches carved in front of you; well kept Ind Coope Burton, friendly, efficient service from smart staff; restaurant (*Eileen Broadbent, Capt R E G King, Brian and Rosemary Wilmot*)

Ickham [TR2257], *Duke William*: Family-run free house, very friendly, with good value food and Bass, Fullers, Shepherd Neame, Websters, Youngs (*D P Green*)

Ide Hill [TQ4851], *Crown*: Warm welcome, pleasant fire, cheerful service, bar food (*P A Devitt*)

Iden Green [TQ8032], *Royal Oak*: Completely refurbished in 1920s-style with soft, comfortable furnishings, ceiling fans and a warm, welcoming atmosphere; unobtrusive service and good food from a changing menu (*Mr and Mrs P Williamson, J R Leeds*);

Woodcock: Has had remarkably good food provided by friendly girls who've run that side separately under a concession, but we've had no news since the pub came on the market in 1987 *(NM, Miss P T Metcalfe – more reports please)*

Ightham [The Street; TQ5956], *George & Dragon*: Comfortable, well appointed, with very good hot and cold food, pleasantly served *(Margaret Branney)*

Ightham Common [Common Rd; TQ5755], *Harrow*: Small, modest-looking pub with comfortable, friendly bar and restaurant; quite substantial varied fresh food, good value at reasonable prices *(Mr and Mrs P D O Liddell)*

Ivy Hatch [Coach Rd; in village, on bend opposite stores and Post Office; TQ5854], *Plough*: Very friendly free house, attractive and well done-out old brick and timber pub with good log fires, handy for Ightham Mote (open Apr–Oct); has been popular for sandwiches and bar meals with decent coffee; new management autumn 1987, main courses now expensive, but still so popular that you have to get there early for a table; on GWG49 *(Joan Olivier, Margaret Branney – more reports please)*; [Stone Street; TQ5754] *Rose & Crown*: Spacious garden with Fri evening summer barbecues behind straightforward pub in attractive countryside; children's room in barn; food looking up under new licensees, though service may not always be quick; on GWG49 *(LYM)*

Kearsney [B2060; TR2843], *Pickwicks*: Good value food and well kept Fremlins and Wethereds in breweryised pub with tiles and plastic ivy roofing bar, lots of beams and bare brick, Windsor chairs and tapestried settles, high shelf crowded with interesting bottles, flagons and copper jugs, pleasant atmosphere; cheerful friendly service, unobtrusive piped music; tables, swing and slide on big lawn *(Ian Phillips)*

Knockholt [Cudham Lane; TQ4658], *Tally Ho*: Cosy if maybe smoky pub with Ruddles County on handpump and reasonable food servery *(Alison Hayward, Nick Dowson)*

☆ **Lamberhurst** [B2169; TQ6635], *Brown Trout*: Most picturesque, with lovely floral decorations, oast-houses opposite and Scotney Castle entrance almost next door; delightful inside too (and roomier since extension and restaurant added), with very friendly atmosphere and service, well kept beer and good food, especially fish collected specially from Billingsgate thrice weekly – lobster salad is a must; handy for Bewl Bridge Reservoir *(W J Wonham, P H Fearnley, P Gillbe)*

Lamberhurst [School Hill], *Chequers*: Very friendly inn with beamed old bar, very good beer, bar food and hospitality; bedrooms (but on busy noisy road) *(Col G D Stafford)*; *Horse & Groom*: Good food in bar and dining-room; very popular, can be crowded

(Margaret Branney)

Larkfield [London Rd, nr M20 junction 3; TQ7058], *Larkfield*: Relaxing atmosphere in large, open lounge with comfortable furnishings, soft piped music, good lunchtime food; separate Club House restaurant, good service; bedrooms *(Keith Garley)*; [New Hythe Lane] *Monks Head*: Olde-worlde local with low beams and well kept Courage on handpump *(Keith Garley)*

Leeds [TQ8253], *George*: Pleasant if plain village local with compact lounge and public bar, Shepherd Neame on handpump, straightforward bar food; one reader, a long-distance walker, felt he could have been more kindly treated *(S J A Velate)*

☆ **Leigh** [Powder Mills – OS Sheet 188 reference 568469; TQ5446], *Plough*: Amazing variety of seating places including huge old barn, vast log fire, lots of exposed timbers, friendly atmosphere, good food, six real ales on handpump including Adnams, Fremlins, Harveys and King & Barnes, reasonably priced bar food; juke box rivals Concorde in decibel output *(Alison Kerruish, Peter Neate)*

Little Chart [TQ9446], *Swan*: Isolated but comfortable seventeenth-century village inn, keen and obliging landlord, surprisingly good range of food *(Comus Elliott)*

Littlebourne [4 High St; TR2057], *King William IV*: Decorated in tasteful traditionally old English style, with comfortable seating and sensible eating facilities; reasonable choice of good traditional hot or cold food, moderately priced, good service, good range of ales; bedrooms good value *(Mr and Mrs D P Millen, B Prosser)*

Longfield [TQ6068], *Wheatsheaf*: Long low thatched pub dating from fifteenth century, beamed bar with good oak settles, comfortable cask chairs, attractive brick fireplace, collection of cricket blazers and ties, brass milk dippers; simple food including ploughman's, omelettes and ham off the bone; Courage ales, small games-bar *(Ian Phillips)*

Lower Hardres [TR1552], *Three Horseshoes*: Old-fashioned furnishings in country pub with Papas prints of Canterbury, choice of real ales, bar food including wide choice of cheeses for ploughman's *(LYM)*

Luddesdown [TQ6766], *Golden Lion*: Handy for M2 junction 2, yet in peaceful valley for walkers – classified as Area of Outstanding Natural Beauty and Special Landscape Area; simple pub with big wood-burning stove as well as open fire, Trumans and Websters real ales, bar food (not Sun, nor Mon–Thurs evenings) *(LYM)*

☆ **Maidstone** [Penenden Heath Rd; ¼ mile from M20 junction 7, on Maidstone rd; TQ7656], *Chiltern Hundreds*: Well kept and warm, with comfortable furnishings in airy well renovated lounge bar, good value hot dishes and filled crusty rolls, well kept Courage Directors, friendly efficient service, seats on terrace and in conservatory *(Major*

B C Innes, Geoff and Teresa Salt, BB)
Markbeech [TQ4742], *Kentish Horse*: Good home cooking in attractive whitewashed building ablaze with colour in summer; nr GWG50 (*Anon*)
Marsh Green [TQ4345], *Wheatsheaf*: Friendly service from new owners, wide choice of lunchtime and evening bar food including interesting soups and meat dishes (*S J Bentley*)
Martin [TR3346], *Old Lantern*: Ancient house in attractive gardens with good reasonably priced home-made food, attentive service and a happy atmosphere (*Mr and Mrs R Harris, C M Franks*)
Martin Mill [TR3446], *Ugly Duckling*: Good choice of reasonably priced snacks and full meals and good range of beers; friendly welcome, log fires, terrace and garden (*P G Rossington*)
Meopham [Meopham Green; TQ6466], *Cricketers*: Friendly staff, good food (particularly sandwiches) and beer; fine view of cricket on the green (pub's been HQ of cricket team for over 200 years), windmill behind (*David Gaunt, Jeff Cousins*)
Mereworth [Butchers Lane; TQ6553], *Queens Head*: Very good well kept beer, food and restaurant (*Anon*)
☆ **Minster** [2 High St (this is the one nr Ramsgate, at TR3164], *Bell*: Old pub with immense character and comfortable old wooden settles, pleasant atmosphere (in spite of the pipe smoke and customers' big dogs when it gets crowded on Sun lunchtime), well kept Fremlins and Flowers and good bar meals at attractive prices (*Robert Caldwell, D Martin*)
Minster [the same one], *Prospect*: Very popular recently refurbished pub with good choice of food and good beer (*B Prosser*); *Saddlers Arms*: Welcoming if narrow local, Shepherd Neame on handpump, good reasonably priced bar food; could be better ventilated, and beware passing juggernauts (*Robert Caldwell*)
New Romney [North St; TR0624], *Broadacre*: Very reasonably priced pub/hotel with Ind Coope and Tetleys on handpump, good value simple bar snacks, restaurant; bedrooms comfortable, with good breakfasts (*J T Bennett*); *Plough*: A pub since eighteenth century, long bar with log fires, games and pool-room, cosy beamed restaurant, bar food, barbecue and garden (*Rita Bray*)
☆ **Newenden** [A268; TQ8227], *White Hart*: Attractive sixteenth-century pub, very helpful service, low shiny ceilings, beams and timbers in carpeted bar, inglenook fireplace, old-world dining area – good food from snacks to Scotch steaks in bar and restaurant, decent beer (*MA, David Gaunt, A J Woodroffe*)
☆ **Otford** [High St; TQ5359], *Horns*: Well preserved old free house with cheap snacks including well filled sandwiches, good

choice of real ales including Harveys and King & Barnes, winter log fires in big inglenook, attentive service, Nat King Cole-type piped music; busy but quiet and not smoky; nr GWG47 (*GRE, AE, J A Snell*)
Otford, *Bull*: Well kept Courage, first-class food all home cooked, reasonable prices, attractive garden, good family-room (*Barry Stevens*)
Pembury [TQ6240], *Black Horse*: Pub with wine bar next door combining old and new, good food (*Brian Smith*)
Penenden Heath [TQ7656], *Bull*: Well run suburban pub with lots of games including outdoor ones such as boules; bar food, restaurant, barbecues in summer (*BB*)
☆ **Penshurst** [Coldharbour Lane, Smarts Hill; TQ5241], *Bottle House*: Nice cosy family-run pub, a friendly place for a quiet drink and reasonably priced bar snack – varied menu, good cooking, attentive service; comfortable and attractive restaurant, garden (*W J Wonham, Sylvia and Derek Latham*)
☆ **Penshurst** [TQ5243], *Leicester Arms*: Very nicely appointed bar areas in small hotel in village centre, comfortable and full of character, with log fires, lots of atmosphere and good service; comprehensive reasonably priced menu with daily specials; Penshurst Place nearby; on GWG50; bedrooms, some with four-posters (*Lyn and Bill Capper, E G Parish*)
Penshurst [Hoath Corner; TQ4943], *Rock*: Charming ancient pub in beautiful setting, unfussy and unspoilt inside; good real ale, satisfactory ploughman's; on GWG50 (*Tim Locke*); [Smarts Hill, which is signposted off B2188 S of village; TQ5241] *Spotted Dog*: The licensees who made this heavily beamed and timbered pub – licensed since 1520 – so very popular for its atmosphere and its good food in bar and restaurant moved at the end of 1987 to the Woodcock at Felbridge (we'd be very interested to hear about their progress there); first reports on the new regime suggest that something's definitely missing now here, and that prices for a diminished choice of bar food are decidedly on the high side – but the Whitbreads-related real ales are still well kept, the surroundings inside attractive (handsome inglenook fireplace, some antique settles as well as more straightforward bar furnishings, rugs on the tile floor), and of course there's the idyllic summer view over Penshurst Place and the Medway Valley from the split-level terrace outside – though that could be kept cleaner (*M D Hare, J M Caulkin, LYM*)
Petham [B2068 Canterbury–Hythe; TR1251], *Granville*: Almost more restaurant than pub with good lunches at reasonable prices – summer salads, winter hot dishes, gets crowded by 1pm (*I M Phillips*); [Stone Street] *Slippery Sams*: Cosy free house with log fires, where you can dine by candlelight; named after smuggler who lived here; in

beautiful countryside *(John Bell)*

☆ **nr Plaxtol** [Sheet Hill; from Plaxtol, take Tree Lane from war memorial and church, straight through Yopps Green; from A227 nearly a mile S of Ightham, take unmarked turning beside lonely white cottage Bewley Bar, then right at oast-house signposted Plaxtol; TQ6053], *Golding Hop*: Named after one of the finest-flavoured hop varieties, this secluded country pub with its sun-trap streamside lawn has at least in the past had its own farm cider, among others; well priced and well kept real ales such as Everards Tiger and Youngs Special, simple bar food (not Mon evening), straightforward country furniture, maybe rather a take-it-or-leave-it atmosphere; music can be loud *(Alasdair Knowles, Peter Griffiths, LYM)*

☆ **Pluckley** [TQ9245], *Black Horse*: Cosy (reputedly haunted) old local with welcoming staff, low beams, brazier-type fire, dark oak settles and a really huge inglenook; large area given over to restaurant serving tasty business lunches; well kept Fremlins; nice garden for summer evenings, big private car park beside church; always busy *(Eileen Broadbent, Christopher Draper, Anna Jeffery, Richard Gibbs)*

Ramsgate [Ashburnham Rd; TR3865], *Australian Arms*: Good atmosphere, good range of beers and helpful staff *(M J Daunton)*; [Harbour Parade] *Queens Head*: Very friendly and popular fishermen's local, recently refurbished, with pleasant atmosphere, good food and good choice of beer *(B Prosser)*

Ripple [TR3449], *Plough*: Lovely olde-worlde free house specialising in guest real ales; cosy, with flagstone floors, friendly service and adequate choice of food *(Ned Edwards)*

☆ **Rochester** [10 St Margarets St; TQ7467], *Coopers Arms*: Quaint thirteenth-century pub said to be oldest in Kent; two very friendly comfortable bars (not just for locals), attractive garden with summer barbecue, well kept Courage Directors, reasonably priced good food; very close to castle, cathedral and old school *(ND, Dr and Mrs A K Clarke)*

Rochester [16 High St], *Royal Victoria & Bull*: Complex of modernised bars opening off coachyard of substantial hotel, including back Great Expectations bar with Victorian décor – the inn has many Dickens connections; front real ale bar; wide choice of sensibly priced bar food, and restaurant; children welcome; bedrooms (Queen Victoria stayed when storms endangered Medway bridge) *(LYM)*; [Old Watling St] *Three Crutches*: Welcoming old weatherboarded Ind Coope pub, very convenient for A2, with lunchtime bar food *(Brian Green)*

Rolvenden [High St; TQ8431], *Star*: Small homely pub with friendly customers, quite a wide choice of good value food including massive ploughman's (£1.50), real ale, back

garden looking out over countryside; village beautifully kept *(K Kindall)*

Romney Street [TQ5461], *Fox & Hounds*: Quiet pub in lovely countryside with pleasant simple bar, well kept Shepherd Neame Old, good value food, tables and chairs outside in front *(Jenny and Brian Seller)*

St Margarets Bay [on shore below NT cliffs; TR3844], *Coastguard*: Modernised pub included for the marvellous views from its big windows; set by sea below National Trust cliff, loud music, tables outside; on GWG43 *(LYM)*; *Granville*: Lovely clifftop position surrounded by National Trust land (though not actually on it); interesting but limited and rather pricey bar food; on a clear day the Town Hall clock in Calais can be read through the U-boat binoculars on the bar terrace; Shepherd Neame beers; on GWG43; bedrooms *(Lyn and Bill Capper)*

St Mary in the Marsh [TR0628], *Star*: Family-run pub with friendly atmosphere, real ales, good food at reasonable prices; bedrooms attractive with views of Romney Marsh *(G A Trodd)*

St Nicholas at Wade [TR2666], *Bell*: Good fire in saloon bar of true village pub, Flowers and Fremlins kept very well, generous helpings of good plain cheap food; children allowed if well behaved *(Peter Hitchcock)*

☆ **Sandgate** [Brewers Lane; TR2035], *Clarendon*: Classic unchanged pub, popular with mixed bag of very welcoming locals; limited choice of well presented good value food – the landlady's an able cook – and well kept Shepherd Neame; our attempt to make an editorial inspection of this highly recommended pub was foiled by our complete failure to discover it, in spite of directions from several different locals who claimed to know the way and in spite of toiling up and down every street we could find in Sandgate – we gave up at closing time, and if anyone really does know how to describe the way there *exactly* we'd love to hear! *(Tim Locke, Mr and Mrs D I Baddeley, PBK)*

Sandgate, *Ship*: Outstanding fish pie, good service and surroundings; other food also looked home made and of equally good standard *(Carron Greig)*

Sandwich [The Quay; TR3358], *Bell*: Well kept hotel with comfortable carpeted lounge, soft pleasant piped music, usual choice of bar food including sandwiches, ploughman's and main dishes, with extra choice from restaurant menu; bedrooms *(Lyn and Bill Capper)*; [4 High St] *Crispin*: Fifteenth-century inn overlooking river with friendly atmosphere; good lunchtime menu, wide choice of beers and wines *(B Prosser)*; [Strand St (A257)] *Kings Arms*: So basic and unpretentious a local that the striking Elizabethan carving (inside and out) comes as a surprise; simple bar food and bedrooms, well kept Fremlins on handpump, traditional games and pool in public bar, children in restaurant *(LYM)*

Seasalter [Joy Lane; TR0965], *Rose in Bloom*: From the gardens there are the most magnificent views and sunsets *(M J Daunton)*

☆ **Sevenoaks** [Godden Green, just E; TQ5555], *Bucks Head*: Delightful pub in idyllic situation by duck pond on green (handy for walks in Knole Park), good food, prompt cheerful service, well kept Courage ales, very cosy with pleasant atmosphere, copper artefacts on ceiling and several deers' heads on wall; nr GWG49 *(W J Wonham, Jenny and Brian Seller)*

☆ **Sevenoaks** [Bessels Green, just off A21; TQ5055], *Kings Head*: Invariably welcoming, friendly and clean, hot and cold food reliably good, garden a riot of colour in summer; though two of the bar rooms have been converted to restaurant use there is still plenty of room – and they still allow dogs *(WHBM, Margaret Branney)*

☆ **Sevenoaks** [A225 just S (note that this is different from the next-door Royal Oak Hotel); TQ5354], *Royal Oak*: Pleasant bar with lively atmosphere, good range of reasonably priced and imaginative bar food including attractively presented Sun lunch (with special deal for children), friendly waitresses, separate restaurant; almost opposite entry to Knole Park *(Adam Loxley, Debbie Wilkinson, Mrs Elizabeth Loveridge, Mr and Mrs D I Baddeley, PBK)*

Shatterling [TR2658], *Green Man*: Good atmosphere, lively bar, separate restaurant with varied wholesome menu at reasonable prices *(J D Martin)*

Sholden [23 The Street; TR3552], *Sportsman*: Wide choice of good well prepared food (not Sun or Mon) in charming pub with cosy and attractive bars, full of character; get there before 12.30 to find a table; beautiful garden; friendly licensees *(C F Stephens)*

Shoreham [TQ5161], *Kings Arms*: Nice atmosphere in small friendly village pub with good bar food and very good meals in restaurant (not Mon or Tues); live music Tues; nr start GWG47 *(Mrs Penny Mendelsohn)*

Shottenden [TR0454], *Plough*: Pleasant pub, good beer, much cheer *(Anon)*

Smarden [B2077; TQ8842], *Flying Horse*: Lovely small pub on edge of beautiful village; spotless; very obliging landlord; long bar on the left and lounge on the right *(Ted George)*

☆ **Snargate** [Romney Marsh – OS Sheet 189 reference 990285; TQ9828], *Red Lion*: Uneven bare boards, kitchen chairs, very friendly and small – seems it was refurbished last in about 1890; Shepherd Neame real ales, no food, combined with small shop which doubles as games-room; down-to-earth charm of another era *(Phil and Sally Gorton, T George)*

Sole Street [note – this is the Sole Street near Wye; TR0949], *Compasses*: Interesting and largely unspoilt sixteenth-century country pub with big garden, choice of potent local ciders, Shepherd Neame real ales, bar food including decent fish and chips, bar billiards; children welcome *(Keith Brinkman, Richard Coats, LYM)*

Sole Street [the other one, near Cobham; TQ6567], *Railway*: Good food in bar decorated with railway memorabilia; pleasant atmosphere, good friendly service *(G F W Filtness)*

☆ **Southfleet** [Red St; TQ6171], *Black Lion*: Cosy and friendly thatched country pub with massive helpings of interesting food, good beer, log fire; barbecues all summer in well kept gardens *(Elaine Pilkington, Dr and Mrs A K Clarke)*

Southfleet [High Cross Rd], *Wheatsheaf*: Stunning heavily thatched pub dating from 1414, hops, brasses, beams and inglenook inside, friendly atmosphere, morris men *(Mrs Susan Sadler)*

Staple [TR2756], *Three Tuns*: Warm, homely and well kept country pub with very reasonably priced, varied good food in bar and restaurant; bedrooms *(Clem Stephens)*

Stelling Minnis [Stone St (B2068); TR1446], *George*: Good food and service *(Mr and Mrs D B Allan)*

Stone in Oxney [TQ9427], *Ferry*: Wide choice of fish, meat, pasta, curries and good puddings in simple charming cottage with no fuss or frills; board outside still lists the charges for carrying animals and vehicles on the now-defunct Oxney Ferry *(Peter Davies)*

Sundridge [Main Rd (A25); TQ4854], *White Horse*: Smart seventeenth-century low-beamed village pub with comfortable carpeted lounge, more seats and tables behind the open fireplace, and compact public bar with darts; Courage Best and Directors on handpump, piped music, good food including scampi, gammon, good steaks (similar menu in evening restaurant); children's room with snooker-table in outbuilding; small pretty garden with lawn, shrubs and flowers *(SJAV)*

Swanley [TQ5168], *Lamb*: Cosy and friendly Shepherd Neame village local *(Comus Elliott)*

Teynham [Lewson St; TQ9562], *Plough*: Next to Guinness hop farm with very friendly, pleasant atmosphere, well kept Shepherd Neame beer and huge fresh sandwiches *(Keith Widdowson)*

Tilmanstone [A256; TR3051], *Plough & Harrow*: Very pleasant atmosphere in free house with many fine beers and good choice of good food; very popular – get there early *(B Prosser)*

Tonbridge [East St; TQ5946], *Man of Kent*: Small old split-level pub with good lunchtime bar food, well kept Bass *(Dr and Mrs A K Clarke)*

☆ **Toys Hill** [OS Sheet 188 reference 470520; TQ4751], *Fox & Hounds*: Fine old-fashioned pub completely unspoilt and unpretentiously rustic with a hotch-potch of furniture which includes a comfortable old three-piece suite and a motley selection of tables, chairs and stools; open fires, old-world courtesy from refreshingly old-fashioned landlord, magazines dotted around, well kept Ind Coope Burton, lunchtime food limited to generous but basic ploughman's, delicious home-made soup and puddings; very friendly if unhurried service, pleasant garden, occasional live music; in heart of what used to be glorious National Trust woodland – now devastated by October 1987 storm; nr GWG48 (*Comus Elliott, S J A Velate, Alison Kerruish*)

Trottiscliffe [TQ6460], *Vigo*: Unspoilt, basic free house with Dadlums table (*Phil Gorton*)

☆ Tunbridge Wells [Little Mount Sion, off High St; TQ5839], *Compasses*: This promising pub, carefully refurbished in Victorian small-room style, with open fires, imaginative good value home-made bar food and Whitbreads-related real ales, proved so popular that pressure from local residents led to a short licence suspension in early 1988, but it was reopened by the summer – clean, friendly and welcoming (*Adam Loxley, Debbie Wilkinson, T A Woodard, LYM*)

☆ Tunbridge Wells [Spa Hotel, Mt Ephraim], *Equestrian Bar*: Long, light and comfortable room with unusual equestrian floor-tile painting and steeplechasing pictures; wicker and velveteen furnishings, friendly uniformed staff, nicely presented though not cheap lunch snacks, well kept Fremlins and King & Barnes on handpump; bedrooms (*Philip Denison, E G Parish, LYM*)

Tunbridge Wells [Mt Ephraim, behind Royal Wells Hotel], *Beau Nash*: Small, set back from road with ample garden partly under trellis; good choice of real ales, cheap food fair value for area, busy in evenings (*C D T Spooner*); [Mt Ephraim] *Brokers Arms*: Pleasant staff, real ales and wide choice of bar food in attractive black and white pub with bar, small eating area below pavement level, and upstairs restaurant (*E G Parish*); *Sussex Arms*: Previously very popular for great character and interesting bric-à-brac, sadly now closed in redevelopment project (*LYM*)

☆ Ulcombe [Fairbourne Heath, which is sign-posted from A20 (best approach); TQ8548], *Pepperbox*: Just the place for the family in summer – big garden with good facilities for children, extensive range of food from snacks to full meals (fish dishes particularly recommended), good Shepherd Neame ales tapped from the cask, friendly and relaxed comfortable bar with log fires in winter (*Rodney Coe, B R Wood*)

Upstreet [Grove Ferry; off A28 towards Preston; TR2263], *Grove Ferry*: Perfect food, drink and setting – ample helpings of well presented food (*B Prosser*)

Waltham [TR1048], *Lord Nelson*: Good well cooked hot bar meals, plenty of choice, good service, very friendly atmosphere, children's play area in garden behind (*Miss M Brown,*

Miss M Taylor, Victor Spells)

Warren Street [just off A20 at top of North Downs; TQ9253], *Harrow*: Has had good food in bar and restaurant and well kept beers, with restaurant and pleasant reasonably priced bedrooms, but for sale late 1987 and no reports since

☆ West Farleigh [TQ7152], *Chequers*: Locals' pub hugely enlivened by flamboyant decorations and entertaining licensee; well kept Fremlins, straightforward sensible food, piano some evenings, seats in garden; views over upper Medway, with path down to the river and good walks in both directions along it (*S J A Velate, LYM*)

West Kingsdown [TQ1763], *Horse & Groom*: Good value main-course lunchtime dishes (*R Coe*)

West Malling [Swan St; TQ6857], *Swan*: Well kept Bass and Charrington IPA on hand-pump in old inn with suit of armour on the stairs, two friendly cats; good food in bar and restaurant, locally popular; bedrooms – breakfasts very good (*Ken Wright*)

Westerham [TQ4454], *Grasshopper*: Pleasant staff and good atmosphere in originally twelfth-century pub with three connecting bars, lots of old local photographs, model Spitfire and other wartime aeroplanes hanging from ceiling, Churchill memorabilia; wide range of reasonably priced bar food, real ales such as Bass, King & Barnes, Stones and Youngs; nr start GWG48 (*Heather Sharland*); [Market Sq] *Kings Arms*: Elegant, civilised old coaching-inn with comfortable lounge and good bar food, separate restaurant; exceptionally pretty village, interesting houses to visit nearby (*AE, GRE*); [Westerham Hill (A233 to Biggin Hill)] *Spinning Wheel*: Free house – though almost more of a restaurant – with well kept Smiths Yorkshire Bitter, comfortable seating in bar lounge and a rather sedate atmosphere; good bar food from a wide menu and very good service (*E G Parish, WFL*)

Whitstable [Oxford St; TR1166], *Coach & Horses*: Friendly if dimly lit and maybe smoky town local with Shepherd Neame real ales in beautifully polished glasses, good lunchtime bar food (*John Bell (M J Daunton*); [Borstal Hill] *Four Horseshoes*: Friendly licensees, Shepherd Neame in three narrow-seated rooms, jolly atmosphere and well kept Shepherd Neame; can get crowded and smoky (*Robert Caldwell*); [seafront] *Neptune*: Generous helpings of really good value food in basic bars virtually lapped by waves and restaurant with fine sea views (*Canon G Hollis*)

☆ Wickhambreux [TR2158], *Rose*: Delightful quiet and peaceful thirteenth-century pub on pretty village green, very good ploughman's, friendly atmosphere, well kept beer (*Mrs Penny Mendelsohn, Q Williamson*)

☆ Wingham [TR2457], *Red Lion*: Comfortably modernised inn – part of a college founded here 600 years ago by Archbishop of Canterbury; very pleasant, friendly atmosphere, good varied bar food, well kept Fremlins on handpump, restaurant; bedrooms *(Ruth Humphrey, LYM)*

Wingham [High St; TR2457], *Anchor*: Old pub with cosy beamed interior, Fremlins beer, tasty bar food all week, garden *(Q Williamson)*

Wingham Well [TR2356], *Eight Bells*: Comfortably modernised rambling beamed pub near 4000-year-old cave dwelling, ghostly footsteps nearby *(BB)*

Wittersham [B2082; TQ8927], *Ewe & Lamb*: Lots of atmosphere in genuine if basic local with bar food, good range of beers and wines; children welcome, adventure play area *(Leo and Pam Cohen, C H Fewster)*

Worth [The Street; TR3356], *Blue Pigeons*: Recently refurbished welcoming and comfortable Victorian pub close to beach

and golf courses; good, moderately priced decent bar meals and Sun lunch; bedrooms *(B Prosser)*

Wrotham Heath [TQ6458], *Royal Oak*: Service and lunch very good, good choice *(Capt Victor Aubourg)*

Wye [Upper Bridge St; TR0546], *New Flying Horse*: Pleasantly modernised seventeenth-century inn, comprehensive bar menu with daily specials; bedrooms pleasant – especially those in converted outbuildings – with good breakfasts *(Alan Castle)*

Yalding [Yalding Hill; TQ7050], *Walnut Tree*: Cosy, characterful Whitbreads pub with beams and inglenook, very popular for the good food: gorgeous home-made French onion soup, home-cooked ham in sandwiches and huge ploughman's; rather basic cutlery and paper napkins; bedrooms *(Eileen Broadbent)*

Lancashire
(including Greater Manchester and Merseyside)

This is an area where licensees tend to settle into pubs and stay there for a good long time. Indeed, outside Manchester, we didn't hear of changes of management at any of our main entries here during the year leading up to editing this latest edition. The result is that the pubs themselves develop a deeper character than in many other places, where publicans chop and change more often. We believe that this stability is also partly responsible for the area's outstanding record for value for money, with prices of both food and drinks still among the lowest anywhere. Especially when property prices have been inflating so rapidly, incoming tenants and owners – bearing the burden of loan repayments that match the very latest property-price levels – will be more inclined to inflate drinks and food prices, too. So, for low prices, the long-standing owner or tenant is often the best bet. To go

Coal Clough House, Burnley

417

back to character – pubs abounding in this include the busy Black Dog at
Belmont (lots happening there, even a chamber orchestra playing every so often),
the elegant Coal Clough House in its wooded grounds in Burnley (good food),
that moorland pair the old-fashioned Horse & Jockey near Delph (a good range
of real ales) and the Rams Head in Denshaw (part of a farm), the Assheton Arms
in the lovely village of Downham (good food at this new entry, too), Th'owd
Tithebarn by the waterside in Garstang (deliberately quaint and rustic), the
Golden Ball at Heaton with Oxcliffe (sometimes cut off by the tide), the lavishly
turn-of-the-century Philharmonic in Liverpool (fresh from some refurbishments
this year), the ancient Sinclairs Oyster Bar in Manchester, the snug little
Kettledrum at Mereclough above Burnley (good value food at both these), the
Tandle Hill Tavern (part of a farm just outside Middleton), the cottagey Britannia
up above Oswaldtwistle, the Wheatsheaf at Raby, the marvellously idiosyncratic
Stalybridge Station Buffet, the Cross Keys on the moors' edge at Uppermill (the
fact that it doubles as a mountain rescue post shouldn't blind you to its comfort)
and the splendid Inn at Whitewell – good food, a charming place to stay at, and
scoring warmer recommendations from readers than any other pub in the area.
Other pubs where food is a special draw include the comfortable Moorcock up at
Blacko, the White House on Blackstone Edge, Old Rosins up above Darwen
(these three are all moorland pubs – altitude seems to have the mysterious quality
of improving pubs' food), the White Horse at Edgworth, Harpers at Fence (a
warmly enjoyable new entry), the comfortably refurbished Duke of Wellington
near Haslingden, the Mark Addy and Royal Oak in Manchester (both are
outstanding for their tremendous choice of cheeses), the charming Hark to
Bounty at Slaidburn (a civilised place to stay, in fine surroundings), the Red Bull
in Stockport, the Seven Stars at Thornton Hough, and the Old Sparrow Hawk at
Wheatley Lane. A new entrant, the Bushells Arms at Goosnargh, has some of the
most imaginative food of all. The hotel part of another new entry, the Dunk Inn
at Clayton le Moors, is a comfortable place to stay at (very handy for the
motorway), as is the Parkers Arms up at Newton in the Forest of Bowland (yet
another newcomer to these pages). Drinks come first at the Lass o' Gowrie
(which brews its own beers) and Marble Arch (an interesting choice of beers on
draught and from the bottle), both in Manchester. The Lucky Dip section, one of
the fattest in the book, shows how rich the area is in decent pubs – it would take
weeks just to work through the ones suggested for Manchester alone. Elsewhere,
many of the starred Dip entries carry the LYM or BB initials that show they've
been approved by an editorial inspection: of those that don't, we most look
forward to visiting the Lion in Liverpool and Devonshire Arms at Mellor.

nr BALDERSTONE (Lancs)   SD6332 Map 7

Myerscough Hotel

3 miles from M6 junction 31, in Samlesbury; A59 towards Skipton

The softly lit and plushly carpeted bar in this very friendly, homely pub has creaky
eighteenth-century oak beams, well made oak settles around dimpled copper or
heavy cast-iron-framed tables, lots of brass and copper, a Welsh dresser filled with
dainty china, and a high shelf above the oak panelling with more in the way of
ornaments. A fine padded elbow rest cushions the serving-counter, from where you
can order quickly served bar food: home-made soup (£1.10), sandwiches and
toasties (from £1.10), filled baked potatoes (£1.65), ploughman's (£2.35), home-
made steak and kidney pie (£3), salads or a choice of omelettes (from around

£4.15), and sirloin steak (£5.10); well kept Robinsons Best and Mild on hand-pump; some readers aren't keen on the piped music. Just as we went to press in the summer, reports suggested an uncertain beginning for a new regime here: more reports please.

Robinsons   Real ale   Meals and snacks   Children welcome   Open 11.30–3, 6–11 all year

BELMONT (Lancs)   SD6716 Map 7

Black Dog

A675

Outside this friendly old stone house, two long benches on its sheltered sunny side give delightful views of the moors above the nearby trees, and from the village there is a track up Winter Hill and (from the lane to Rivington) on to Anglezarke Moor. There are also paths from the dam of the nearby Belmont Reservoir. Inside, there's a collection of unpretentious small rooms in the original part, tradition showing in cosy coal fires, service bells for the sturdy built-in curved seats, rush-seated mahogany chairs and bygones from railwaymen's lamps to landscape paintings (along with more up-to-date collectables such as the bedpans and chamber-pots); there are various snug alcoves. Wholesome bar food includes sandwiches (from 80p), in winter a home-made broth with suet dumplings (90p), locally made black pudding or steak barm-cake (£1), generous ploughman's (from £1.80), breaded cod (£2), good home-made steak and kidney pie (£2.20), salads with fruit, lamb cutlets (£2.40), curries (from £2.40) and rump steak (£4.25); they do morning coffee. The well kept Holts Bitter and Mild on handpump is among the cheapest you'll find anywhere. An airy extension lounge with a picture window has more modern furnishings; darts, pool, shove-ha'penny, dominoes, fruit machine and piped classical music. Bedrooms are being built in the converted stableblock. *(Recommended by Dr and Mrs A M Evans, Wayne Brindle, Caroline Fisher, Tony Pounder, Yvonne and Don Johnson, AMcK)*

Holts   Licensee James Pilkington   Real ale   Meals and snacks (not Mon or Tues evenings)
Restaurant tel Belmont (0204) 81218; open until 5 Sun   Children welcome until 9
Nine-piece orchestra every two months on a Tues   Open 11–3, 6–11; lounge open until 4.30 Sun

BLACKO (Lancs)   SD8541 Map 7

Moorcock ⊗

A682; N of village towards Gisburn

Surrounded by good walks, this comfortable and spacious pub, high up on the moors, has superb views from its big picture windows. As we went to press they were beginning to redecorate the public areas and adding new lavatories. The clean and straightforward style of the bar won't change much, but new carpets are to be laid, the seating re-upholstered and tables altered. The highly praised, truly home-made food is served willingly until very late in the evening, and there's an unusual range of garlicky Italian and Austrian dishes such as bratwurst (£2.75), authentic goulash (£3.25) and schweinschnitzel (£3.80), as original as anything you're likely to find on the Continent; a wide choice of other food includes soup (£1), sandwiches (from £1, steak £3), pâté (£1.85), chilli con carne (£2.65), lasagne (£2.95), burger or savoury pancakes (£3), steak and kidney pie (£3.25), omelettes (£3.50), and lots of daily specials like Stilton pâté (£1.50), home-made pies and quiches (£2.50) and rump steak with savoury sauce (£4.25); puddings such as home-made cheesecake or fruit tart (£1.25) and excellent fresh Sunday roasts (£3.50); friendly, speedy service (and dogs). Well kept Thwaites Bitter and Best Mild on handpump; juke box. The attractively landscaped back garden is very busy at weekends, though quieter during the week. *(Recommended by Geoff Wilson, Alan and Marlene Radford, Len Beattie, Yvonne and Don Johnson, Gwen and Peter Andrews)*

Thwaites   Licensees Elizabeth and Peter Holt   Meals and snacks   Restaurant   Children welcome   Open 11.30–3, 6.30–12 (supper licence) all year   Bedrooms tel Nelson (0282) 64186; £12.50/£25

BLACKSTONE EDGE (Gtr Manchester)   SD9716   Map 7
White House ⊗

A58 Ripponden–Littleborough, just W of B6138

Past the long enclosed porch where walkers can leave their muddy boots, the main bar area in this isolated, friendly moorland pub has a blazing coal fire in front of a Turkey carpet and under a large-scale map of the area; it opens into the snug Pennine Room, with brightly coloured antimacassars on its small soft settees. Off to the left, a spacious room has comfortable seats around its tables, coloured pins on a map of the world showing where foreign visitors have come from, and a big horseshoe window that looks out over the moors. Good bar food includes home-made vegetable soup (80p), sandwiches (from 80p, steak £1), ploughman's (£1.50), Cumberland sausage with egg (£1.75), quiche Lorraine (£1.85), lasagne or chilli con carne (£2), salads (from £2.50), home-made steak and kidney pie (£2.25) and eight-ounce sirloin steak (£4.25); also daily specials and home-made apple pie (75p). Well kept John Smiths, Marstons Pedigree and Moorhouses Pendle Witches Brew on handpump; fruit machine. *(Recommended by G T Jones, Jon Wainwright, Len Beattie, Caroline Fisher, Tony Pounder, Stephen and Karen Law, Lee Goulding)*

Free house   Licensee Neville Marney   Real ale   Meals and snacks   Restaurant tel Littleborough (0706) 78456   Children welcome until 9   Open 11.30–3, 7–11 all year

nr BROUGHTON (Lancs)   SD5235   Map 7
Plough at Eaves

4½ miles from M6 junction 32: take M55 turn-off, then A6 N, then after about 1 mile N of Broughton traffic lights, first left into Station Lane; after canal bridge bear right at junction, then left at fork; pub on the right; OS Sheet 102 reference 495374

The old-fashioned décor in this spacious, friendly pub includes very low dark beams, little latticed windows, rush-seat chairs around the dark wooden tripod tables, lots of wooden casks, an antique oak linen chest and corner cupboard, a couple of guns over one good copper-hooded open fire and a row of Royal Doulton figurines above another. Generous helpings of bar food include home-made soup (70p), egg mayonnaise (£1.10), triple-decker sandwiches (from £1), baked potatoes (from £1.10), basket meals (from £1.65), ploughman's with three cheeses (£2.45), home-made steak or mince pie (£2.70), home-baked ham (£3) and roast beef (£3.10). Well kept Thwaites Bitter and Mild on handpump; jovial bar staff; darts and dominoes. Metal and wood-slat seats and cast-iron-framed tables run along the front by the quiet lane, and there's a well equipped children's play area behind. *(Recommended by Jon Wainwright, BKA, Sue Cleasby, Mike Ledger, M L Tucker, Lee Goulding, Mr and Mrs M J Leith, Michael Craig, TBB)*

Thwaites   Real ale   Meals and snacks (not Sun–Tues evenings)   Restaurant tel Rochdale (0706) 690233   Children in eating area   Open 12–3, 6.30–11 all year

BURNLEY (Lancs)   SD8332   Map 7
Coal Clough House ★ ⊗   [illustrated on page 417]

Coal Clough Lane; between Burnham Gate (B6239) and A646; OS Sheet 103 reference 830818

Standing in spacious grounds with fine mature trees, this handsome late Victorian house has a seventeenth-century core. It's an elegant and comfortable place, and the spacious oak-panelled lounge has an elaborately moulded high plaster ceiling, antique prints and a lovely carved mantelpiece around the big open fireplace; there's a popular front sun lounge. Good value, quickly served bar food includes home-made soup (70p), sandwiches (from 80p), home-made meat and potato pie (£1.25), ploughman's (£1.75), very good home-made chilli con carne (£2.50), salads (from £2.60), home-made steak and kidney pie or grilled gammon with egg or pineapple (£2.95), daily specials such as stir-fried beef (£2.95) or beef Stroganoff (£3.25), home-made pies or crumbles (95p) and good chips; it's popular with businessmen at lunchtime; fruit machine, maybe piped music. There are tables outside on the terrace by the wistaria, and beside roses on the lawn. *(Recommended by Len Beattie, Alan and Marlene Radford, Wayne Brindle)*

Greenalls   Licensee Stephen Lucie   Meals (lunchtime, not Mon evening) and snacks (not Mon evening)   Restaurant tel Burnley (0282) 28800   Children in restaurant and conservatory   Open 11–3, 6.30–11 all year

CLAYTON LE MOORS (Lancs)   SE7430 Map 7
Dunk Inn 🍺

½ mile from M65 junction 7; A6185 towards Clitheroe, then first left A678 towards Rishton, then first left into Dunkenhalgh Hotel

The hotel itself, standing in extensive mature grounds, is based on a castellated Gothick country house – comfortable and well kept, with many bedrooms in additional matching stone-built wings. The Dunk Inn is tucked away behind, a fairly recent conversion of the former stables. It has a thriving and prosperous feel, and spreads into cosy barrel-vaulted side sections (one with pool and darts). There are lots of heavy brown beams and stonework, with mate's chairs around dark wooden tables on Turkey carpet, but it's lightened by conservatory-style window bays looking out past the sunken entry court to the sloping grass and shrubs beyond. At lunchtime a good help-yourself buffet counter has soup or another starter (80p), salads including juicy rare beef or a few hot dishes (£3.25), and rich gateaux (85p); in the evenings the side areas are served with starters (£1.25) and pasta (£2.75). Though beers are keg, there are decent whiskies, wines and coffee; open fire; dominoes, cribbage, games-table (chess and so forth), fruit machine, piped pop music. *(Recommended by Len Beattie, Wayne Brindle)*

Free house   Licensee Richard Mellor   Meals and evening snacks   Restaurant   Children in eating area   Live music Weds–Sat, disco Sun   Open 11–11 all year   Bedrooms tel Accrington (0254) 398021; £52B/£62B

nr CLITHEROE (Lancs)   SD7441 Map 7
Hodder Bridge Hotel 🍺

At Higher Hodder Bridge, near Chaigley, on the old Clitheroe–Longridge high road that parallels the B6243; OS Sheet 103 reference 699412

Ideally situated for walks along the pretty River Hodder, this country-lane pub has terraces looking down to a salmon pool below, by the bridge, and there are barbecues out here in fine weather; the inn has its own fishing. Inside, the spacious dining-room has picture windows looking out on this same view, and on Sundays serves high teas all day. The L-shaped back lounge has framed old newspapers on the panelling, a coal fire, and is best when it's busy (it can get very quiet on winter weekdays). Bar food includes home-made soup (70p), sandwiches (from 95p), ploughman's (£2.25), plaice or home-made steak and kidney pie (£3), salads (from £3), scampi (£3.25), gammon and eggs, mixed grill or plaice stuffed with cottage cheese, prawns and garlic (£3.50), fresh river trout (£3.50) and sirloin steak (£4.75), with children's dishes (£1) and an eat-as-much-as-you-like Sunday carvery (£6). There's a dinner-dance then disco until 1am on Saturday night (£9). Well kept

Websters and Wilsons on handpump; space game, fruit machine and piped music.
(Recommended by MD, Len Beattie, Dr T P Owen)

*Free house   Licensee Melvyn Clay   Meals and snacks   Restaurant   Children welcome
Open 12–3, 6–11 weekdays; 12–5, 7–11 weekends   Bedrooms tel Stonyhurst (025 486) 216;
£15(£20B)/£25(£30B)*

nr DARWEN (Lancs)   SD6922   Map 7
Old Rosins ⊗

Pickup Bank, Hoddlesden; from B6232 Haslingden–Belthorn, turn off towards Edgeworth
opposite the Grey Mare – pub then signposted off to the right; OS Sheet 103 reference 722227

The big open-plan lounge in this warmly welcoming, homely pub is furnished with
comfortable red plush built-in button-back banquettes, and stools and small
wooden chairs around dark cast-iron-framed tables; there are lots of mugs,
whisky-water jugs and so forth hanging from the high joists, small prints, plates and
old farm tools on the walls, and, in winter, a blazing log fire. The good value food is
virtually all home made and includes soup, sandwiches (from 90p), ploughman's
(£2), meat pie, vegetarian and slimmer's dishes (£2.25), a choice of salads, steak
and kidney pie, beef in Theakstons Old Peculier (£2.95), and daily specials.
Matthew Browns and Theakstons beers are kept under pressure; pool. The moors
and a wooded valley can be seen from the big picture windows, which are heavily
surrounded by trailing plants. There are picnic-table sets on a spacious crazy-paved
terrace, with seesaws, swings and a climber on the lawn; summer barbecues out
here on Friday evenings and Sunday lunchtimes. Watch out for sheep in the cark
park. *(Recommended by Len Beattie, G T Jones, Carol and Richard Glover, Stephen and
Karen Law, Mr and Mrs T F Marshall)*

*Free house   Licensee Bryan Hankinson   Meals and snacks   Restaurant evenings (not Mon)
tel Darwen (0254) 771264   Children welcome   Open 11.30–3, 6–11 all year; open all day
Sun*

nr DELPH (Gtr Manchester)   SD9808   Map 7
Horse & Jockey

Junction of A62 and A670

There's a good range of well kept real ales on handpump in this welcoming
moorland pub that changes fairly frequently: Clarks, Everards, Marstons, Mitchells, Moorhouses Pendle Witches Brew, Oak Best from Cheshire, Timothy Taylors
and Vaux Sunderland. The two dimly lit rooms have bags of character; one is
panelled and served from a high hatch, and both have comfortable settees and easy
chairs as well as Windsor chairs on the carpet, and (except in really warm weather)
log fires. There are lovely views over the high moors, and good local walks,
including one down to the site of a Roman fort by Castleshaw reservoir.
(Recommended by Lee Goulding; more reports please)

*Free house   Licensee David Kershaw   Real ale   No food   Open 7–11 all year; 1–2.30,
7.30–11 Sat*

DENSHAW (Gtr Manchester)   SD9710   Map 7
Rams Head

2 miles from M62 junction 22; A672 towards Oldham – pub N of village

Backing on to the farm of which it is a part, this comfortable moorland pub is
furnished with traditional settles and benches built into the panelling of its
thick-walled small rooms, beam and plank ceilings, and log fires. Well kept
Theakstons on handpump or tapped from the cask; unobtrusive piped music. There
are fine views down the Tame valley and over the moors, and the pub is well placed

for walks – up towards Brushes Clough reservoir, say. It can get crowded on weekend evenings. *(Recommended by Jon Wainwright; more reports please)*

Free house   Real ale   No food   Open 6.30–11 all year; 12–2, 7–10.30 Sun; closed 25 Dec

DOWNHAM (Lancs)   SD7844   Map 7
Assheton Arms ⊗

From A59 NE of Clitheroe turn off into Chatburn (signposted); in Chatburn follow Downham signpost; OS Sheet 103 reference 785443

This charmingly preserved stone-built village, spread out along a pretty winding stream, smiles up at the gaunt dark mass of Pendle Hill; the sixteenth-century pub, opposite the church, looks down on this from the lower slope of the opposite sheep pastures. Its rambling red-carpeted bar is warmly welcoming, with olive plush-cushioned winged settles around attractive grainy oak tables, and a massive stone fireplace helping to divide the separate areas – the two grenadier busts on the mantelpiece gently pun the licensees' name. A wide choice of home-made bar food includes soup (95p), sandwiches (from £1.50 – not Sunday lunchtime), plough-man's, pâté or Stilton pâté (£1.95), hot creamed Morecambe Bay shrimps (£2.75), plaice or steak and kidney pie (£3.50), grilled ham with free-range eggs (£4), game pie (£4.50) and sirloin steak (£5.75), with several children's dishes (£1.50); puddings include special sundaes served with sparklers (£1.95). Well kept Whitbreads Castle Eden and Trophy on handpump; unobtrusive piped music; kind, efficient service. There are picnic-table sets under cocktail parasols outside. *(Recommended by P Booth, Mrs A Booth, G T Jones)*

Whitbreads   Licensees David and Wendy Busby   Real ale   Meals and snacks   Children welcome   Winter dinner-dances Sat   Open 12–3, 7–11 all year   The adjoining cottage is for hire tel Clitheroe (0200) 41227

EDGWORTH (Lancs)   SD7416   Map 7
White Horse ⊗

Bury Street

Very popular at weekends, this friendly village pub has a profusion of highly lacquered dark brown oak panelling, much of it carved. It's comfortably furnished with button-back wall banquettes curved around wooden or dimpled copper tables, a couple of log fires, lots of copper jugs and so forth hanging from the lacquered beams, and a brass ship's clock and barometer. A good range of decent pub food includes home-made half a chicken (£2), plaice or scampi (£2.20), steak pie (£2.40), eight-ounce steak (£4) and home-made pies such as lamb and apricot, pork and apple in cider and fisherman's (£2.75). Well kept Theakstons Old Peculier and XB and Youngers IPA on handpump; darts, pool, dominoes, fruit machine and juke box. *(Recommended by Wayne Brindle, Len Beattie)*

Matthew Browns   Licensee Roy Gorton   Meals and snacks (not Mon lunchtime)   Children welcome   Open 12–3, 7–11

ENTWISTLE (Lancs)   SD7217   Map 7
Strawbury Duck

Village signposted down narrow lane from Blackburn Road N of Edgworth; or take Batridge Road off B6391 N of Chapeltown and take pretty ¾-mile walk from park at Entwistle reservoir; OS Sheet 109 reference 726177

In an area of the moors popular with hikers and ramblers, this remote pub has a fine range of well kept real ales (eight in all): Federation Special, Ind Coope Burton, Ruddles County, Theakstons Old Peculier, Timothy Taylors Dark Mild, Best and Landlord and Walkers Best, all on handpump. The cosy carpeted L-shaped bar has a variety of seats, stools, little settees and pews, Victorian pictures on its partly timbered, partly rough-stone walls, stuffed birds (and in the dining-room a stuffed mongoose struggling with a cobra), a mounted gun, and ceiling-beams – the one over the servery is very low; one of the tables seems to be made from a big cheese press. Bar food includes soup (75p), sandwiches (£1.15), filled baked potato (from £1.25), ploughman's (£1.95), steak and kidney pie or chilli con carne (£2.95), vegetarian dishes (£3.25), and sirloin steak (£5.75); children's menu (from £1.25). Darts, fruit machine, juke box, piped music, and a pool-table in the tap-room. There are tables perched high over the cutting of the little railway line which brings occasional trains (and customers) from Blackburn or Bolton. *(Recommended by Ray and Jenny Colquhoun, Carol and Philip Seddon, Len Beattie, Roger and Kathy, Jon Wainwright, Caroline Fisher, Tony Pounder, Mrs Pamela Roper)*

Free house   Licensees D W and J B Speakman   Real ale   Meals and snacks (not Mon lunchtime)   Restaurant   Children welcome   Open 12–3, 6–11 all year Mon–Thurs; open all day Fri (in summer) and Sat; closed Mon lunchtime Jan–Mar   Bedrooms tel Turton (0204) 852013; £22(£28B)/£29(£37B)

FENCE (Lancs)   SD8237   Map 7

Harpers

2¾ miles from M65 junction 12; follow Nelson, Brierfield sign, then right at T-junction, then at Brierfield's central traffic lights right again to pass station; cross A6068 following Fence, Newchurch signpost into Cuckstool Lane, turn right at T-junction, then first left into Harpers Lane; OS Sheet 103 reference 828376

The imposing portico of this substantial stone-built house takes you into a spaciously modernised and well kept lounge bar. Red plush button-back banquettes curve around dimpled copper tables on the dark red patterned carpet, and pictures on the pale buffy pink flock wallpaper include attractive prints by Vernon Ward (like Russell Flint but demurely dressed for the seaside). The restaurant area is part of the same room, up steps and separated just by a balustrade – which contributes to the thriving warmth of the atmosphere in the evening. Bar food includes soup (90p), sandwiches (from 95p), lasagne (£1.50), chicken and mushroom pancake (£1.75), home-made steak and kidney pie (£2.75), vegetarian dishes (from £2.75), gammon and eggs (£3.75), scampi (£3.95), steaks from eight-ounce sirloin (£5.75), dishes of the day such as mushroom omelette (£3.45) and children's dishes (£1.95); well kept Thwaites Mild and Bitter on handpump; trivia machine, on our visit piped Glen Miller, and good friendly service. *(Recommended by Stephen and Karen Law, Michael Heys, Wayne Brindle, Comus Elliott)*

Free house   Licensee G M Veevers   Real ale   Meals and snacks   Restaurant tel Nelson (0282) 66249   Children welcome   Open 12–3, 7–11 all year

FRECKLETON (Lancs)   SD4228   Map 7

Ship

Off A584; turn off at traffic lights opposite the Plough, towards Naze Lane Industrial Estate, then right into Bunker Street

Looking out over the watermeadows towards the Ribble, this spacious place is the oldest pub on the Fylde. British Aerospace and British Nuclear Fuels are both nearby, and fighters tend to swing down to BAe's Warton aerodrome at alarming speeds and proximity. The roomy main bar has a strong nautical theme to it, with brass marine ordnance shell cases, an engine-room telegraph, a huge ship's wheel, big compass binnacle, ship pictures, varnished wall and ceiling planking, overhead fishing nets and so forth; there are also plenty of cushioned small chairs and settles around tables, and a log-effect gas fire. Bar food includes sandwiches (from 85p), black puddings (£1.30), steak sandwich (£1.90), salads (from £1.95), with a range of daily specials; the airy upstairs pitched-ceiling carvery has an extensive buffet.

Boddingtons Bitter on handpump; darts, dominoes, cribbage, piped pop music; fruit machine and juke box in a smaller bar. There are picnic-table sets out on a lamplit terrace. The pub has a football team. *(Recommended by Jon Wainwright, Brian and Anna Marsden)*

Boddingtons Real ale Meals and snacks (not Mon evening) Carvery Tues – Fri lunchtime, Sat evening tel Preston (0772) 632393 Children in carvery and area partly set aside Open 11.30–3, 6.30–11 all year

GARSTANG (Lancs) SD4845 Map 7
Th' Owd Tithebarn ★ ⊗
Church Street; turn left off one-way system at Farmers Arms

This cleverly converted creeper-covered barn has pews and glossy tables spaced out on the flagstones under the high rafters, masses of antique farm tools, and stuffed animals and birds. One end, with lower beams, is more like a farmhouse kitchen parlour, with an old kitchen range and prints of agricultural equipment on the walls. The atmosphere is jolly and the waitresses wear period costume with mob-caps. Popular food includes soup (90p), home-made pâté (£1.20), good value ploughman's (£1.65), prawns (£1.85), Lancashire hot-pot (£2.45), steak and kidney pie (£2.95), salads (from £3), a choice of roast meats (£3.40) and ham and eggs (£3.85); a huge choice of puddings such as home-made fruit pies (95p), or hazelnut meringue (£1) and a good children's menu (from £1.15); bar billiards. The big stone terrace out by the canal basin has rustic tables overlooking the boats and ducks, and barbecues from Tuesday to Friday (chicken £3.40, steaks £4.95). It can get very busy at weekends. *(Recommended by M A and W R Proctor, Dr J K McCann, Sue Cleasby, Mike Ledger, R H Sawyer, Rob and Gill Weeks, TBB, Michael Cooke, Mike Muston, Wayne Brindle, Lee Goulding, Michael Craig)*

Free house Licensee Kerry Matthews Meals and snacks (not Mon, not Sun evening) Semi-self-service restaurant tel Garstang (099 52) 4486 Children in restaurant Open 11–3, 7(6 Sat)–11 all year; closed Sun evening, all day Mon, and fortnights Apr and Nov

GOOSNARGH (Lancs) SD5537 Map 7
Bushells Arms ⊗
4 miles from M6 junction 32; A6 towards Garstang, turn right at Broughton traffic lights (the first ones you come to), then left at Goosnargh Village signpost (it's pretty insignificant – the turn's more or less opposite Whittingham Post Office)

The inventive food, which has won or scored highly in quite a few trade competitions, is unquestionably the thing here. Some dishes will be familiar to the many readers who praised the licensees' work so highly at their former pub, the White Bull in Ribchester, but the choice is very wide and eclectic, and changes every three months or so. On our visit it included hummus or taramosalata with hot pitta bread (95p), falafel or crispy samosas (£1.60), duck pâté, spicy chicken wings or avocado, one half filled with chervil-flavoured cucumber and yoghurt and the other with prawns (£1.90), ploughman's or an authentic chilli con carne (£2.50), their very popular steak and kidney pie (£3.50), an elaborate fish pie (£4), chicken filled with local goat's cheese and chutney in puff pastry (£4.50), a delicately tangy lamb casserole gently flavoured with lovage and thyme (£5), local sirloin steak (£6.50), several dishes of the day and a good choice of vegetarian dishes (£3.50 – they also have rennet-free cream for the sumptuous puddings). They will do sandwiches if they're not busy, serve some children's things (£1) or child-size helpings, and make the traditional local shortbread flavoured with caraway seeds and known as Goosnargh cakes (the place is pronounced Goozner, incidentally). Vegetables are fresh and crisp, and we were given a choice of rice, chips, diced potatoes baked with cream and peppers, or what turned out to be particularly tasty new potatoes (our only quibble was that butter for them came in a packet). The extensive modernised bar is broken into snug bays each holding not more than two or three tables by walls or part-walls, often faced with big chunks of sandstone (plastic plants and spotlit bare boughs heighten the rockery effect). There are soft red plush button-back banquettes and stools on the green Turkey carpet, with flagstones by the bar. Fruit machine, on our visit piped 1960ish music – and at the moment just keg beers; service is neat and quick (though they warn of possible delays on busy Saturday evenings). *(Recommended by Robert Gartery, John Atherton, W D Horsfield, Ian Clay, AE, GRE)*

Whitbreads   Licensees David and Glynis Best   Meals and snacks   Children in eating area until 8   Open 11–3, 6–11 all year

HASLINGDEN (Lancs)   SD7522 Map 7
Duke of Wellington ⊗

Grane Road; B6232 signposted from Haslingden centre – OS Sheet 103 reference 767228

This well run, pleasant moorland pub is especially popular with families – there's even an indoor play area for children. The softly lit main room has a lot of polished dark woodwork that includes the solid bar counter and the balustered wood and black cast-iron screen dividers which keep the room in separate areas; it's furnished with the odd button-back leather sofa, button-back pink cloth settees and slat-back chairs around its tables, quiet country pictures on the muted pink-papered walls, deco lamps, and bookshelves. The light and airy extension back dining-lounge has big picture windows looking over to the reservoirs nestling below the woods and sheep pastures of Rossendale. Bar food includes soup (70p), sandwiches (from £1.15), Cumberland sausage and egg (£2.40), home-made steak and kidney pie (£2.60), cold platters with salad (from £2.50), ploughman's (£2.65), gammon with egg or pineapple (£3), eight-ounce sirloin steak (£5.25), specials such as mushrooms filled with fresh salmon, prawns and a mayonnaise and tomato sauce (£1.75) or chicken in a white wine, cream and sweetcorn sauce (£3.95), and lots of enterprising ice-cream-based puddings; they also do occasional continental food evenings with Mexican or Greek dishes. Well kept Hartleys XB and Whitbreads Castle Eden on handpump, good coffee; fruit machine, and well reproduced piped music (even in the lavatories). Picnic-table sets on neat grass face the views, and there's a well fenced and well equipped playground. *(Recommended by G T Jones, Carol and Richard Glover, Stephen and Karen Law, Len Beattie)*

Whitbreads   Licensee Adrian Watson   Real ale   Meals and snacks   Children in family-room and in eating area of bar until 8.30   Open 11.30–3, 6 (5.30 Sat)–11 all year; open all day Sun; open noon–9.30 for food; open for lunch 25 Dec, bookings only tel Rossendale (0706) 215610

HEATON WITH OXCLIFFE (Lancs)   SD4460 Map 7
Golden Ball, *known as* Snatchems

Lancaster Road; coming from Lancaster on B5273, turn left by sandy wasteland where sign warns road liable to be under water at high tide (should also be signposted Overton, but sign may be removed by vandals)

Cut off by the tide of the Lune estuary twice a day, this old-fashioned and friendly pub has several cosy little rooms with low beams, cushioned antique settles, old-fashioned upright chairs (one attractively carved, with high arms), and built-in benches around cask tables; also, small flowery-curtained windows, a large collection of sporting rosettes, and good fires in winter. Bar food includes baked potatoes (40p), home-made soup (45p), cheese and onion flan (65p), sandwiches (from 70p), steak or meat and potato pies with mushy peas (95p), steak sandwich (£1.20), sausage and mash (£1.20), curry, bacon ribs or ploughman's (£1.40). Cheap well kept Mitchells Bitter and Mild, on handpump, served from a hatch;

darts and dominoes, and a space game upstairs in the long, neat family-room. Outside, there are old-fashioned teak seats on a raised front. Because of the position, it can get crowded in summer, though it's less isolated now that a large Asda store has been built nearby. (*Recommended by Jeff Cousins, Leith Stuart, Sue Cleasby, Mike Ledger, Dr and Mrs A K Clarke, AE, GRE, John Atherton, C Fisher, Tony Pounder, Jon Wainwright, Wayne Brindle*)

Mitchells   Licensee Fred Jackson   Real ale   Meals and snacks   Children upstairs Open 11–3, 6–11 all year; opens 12 and 6.30 in winter

LIVERPOOL (Merseyside)   SJ4395 Map 7
Philharmonic ★

36 Hope Street; corner of Hardman Street

Careful refurbishments in this opulent gin palace at the end of 1987 included repainting and the addition of period-style wallpapers and some carpets: it's good to know that breweries are still prepared to spend generously looking after such architectural splendour. It's almost worth its star rating for the gents alone – a remarkable period piece, all marble and opulent glinting mosaics (we can't speak for the ladies, but by all accounts they're a less glamourous affair). The mosaic-faced central serving-counter is the hub, and heavily carved and polished mahogany partitions radiate out under the intricate plasterwork high ceiling, dividing off cosy little cubicles from the echoing main hall. This is decorated by a huge mosaic floor, rich panelling, and stained glass including contemporary portraits of Boer War heroes. In a spare moment the licensees should be happy to point out some of the most interesting features. Home-made bar food that includes sandwiches, soup and main dishes such as traditional scouse with red cabbage, quiche, chilli con carne or steak pie, and roast chicken is served in a splendid Grecian room decorated with half-naked art nouveau plaster goddesses reclining high above the squared panelling. Well kept Tetleys on handpump; fruit machine, juke box. There are two plushly comfortable sitting-rooms. (*Recommended by Jon Wainwright, John Roué; more reports please*)

Tetley-Walkers (Ind Coope)   Real ale   Meals (lunchtime, not Sat or Sun) and snacks (not Sat evening, Sun)   Restaurant tel 051-709 1163/708 7469   Children in eating area Jazz Mon–Tues, bands Weds   Metered parking nearby   Open 11.30–3, 5–10.30

LYTHAM (Lancs)   SD3626 Map 7
Captains Cabin

Henry Street; in centre, one street in from West Beach (A584)

This neat and comfortable little pub has been done out in an attractive Victorian style, with a coal-effect gas fire between two built-in bookcases at one end, and well chosen pictures – including local boats – on the muted bird-of-paradise wallpaper. There are dark pink button-back plush seats and captain's chairs in bays around the sides, and quite a bit of stained-glass decoration – in the solid wood screens which divide up the central area, and in the main windows, which have good freestyle stained inserts of fish and gulls. The food is uncomplicated and reasonably priced, including soup, baked potatoes, sandwiches, toasties, pâté, ploughman's and a selection of salads; well kept Hartleys XB, Marstons Pedigree and Whitbreads Castle Eden on handpump; good, friendly staff. Two fruit machines, juke box. (*Recommended by Derrick Turner, Peter Corris, Jon Wainwright, Simon Bates, Mr and Mrs T F Marshall*)

Whitbreads   Real ale   Meals and snacks (lunchtime, not 25 or 26 Dec)   Open 10.30–3, 6–11 all year

There are report forms at the back of the book.

MANCHESTER   SJ8398   Map 7

Lass o' Gowrie

36 Charles Street; off Oxford Street at BBC

The well made malt-extract beers in this popular pub – brewed down in the cellar – are named after their original gravity (strength) – LOG35, which is quite lightly flavoured and slips down very easily, and the meatier LOG42, with well kept Chesters Mild and Bitter on handpump too; in one place seats around a sort of glass cage give a view down into the brewing room. The longish tall room has quite high stools against ledges or unusually high tables, but first-comers get seats around lower tables on a cosier carpeted dais at one end. It's mainly stripped back to varnished bricks, with big windows in its richly tiled arched brown façade, hop-sacks draping the ceiling, and bare unsealed floorboards. Good value home-made food from a separate side servery includes moussaka or shepherd's pie (£1.80), and beef casserole, mince and onion pie, lamb hot-pot or savoury pork (all £1.85). Piped pop music can be very unobtrusive against the buzz of chatter, but it may be louder in term-time when students turn out on a Friday or Saturday evening; fruit machine and trivia. The open gas lighting flares are a nice touch. (*Recommended by Virginia Jones, Peter Race, Dr E Fellow-Smith, M White, Michael Craig, Michael Cooke, Caroline Fisher, Tony Pounder, Lee Goulding, Jon Wainwright, GP*)

Whitbreads/own brew   Real ale   Lunchtime meals (not Sat or Sun) and snacks   Children in small side room and raised area   Open all day weekdays; 11.30–3.30, 6.15–11 Sat; closed 25 Dec

Marble Arch

73 Rochdale Road (A664), Ancoats; corner of Gould Street, just E of Victoria Station

First licensed in 1826 as the Elephants Head, this pub was totally rebuilt in 1888 for the McKennas brewery. There are porphyry entrance pillars, a magnificent glazed brick lightly barrel-vaulted high ceiling, and extensive marble and tiling – particularly the frieze advertising various spirits, and the chimney-breast above the carved wooden mantelpiece. The friendly new licensee has rag-rolled the walls to add to the Victorian feel. The wide range of well kept, regularly changing real ales on handpump make this something of a local CAMRA hangout: Fullers London Pride, Hydes Anvil, Marstons Pedigree, Moorhouses Pendle Witches Brew, Oak Wobbly Bob, Ruddles and Timothy Taylors Landlord; a good choice of bottled beers and a selection of country wines. The bar food includes filled barm-cakes (from 75p), ploughman's (£1.75), and hot dishes such as chilli con carne or beef curry; darts, dominoes, cribbage, chess, fruit machine and juke box. (*Recommended by Brian and Anna Marsden, Lee Goulding, Michael Cooke, Jon Wainwright*)

Free house   Licensee Helene de Bechevel   Real ale   Meals (lunchtime, not Sat or Sun) and snacks (not Sun)   Open all day; closed Sun lunchtime and 25 and 26 Dec

Mark Addy ⊗

Stanley Street, Salford, Manchester 3; look out not for a pub but for what looks like a smoked-glass modernist subway entrance

Elegantly placed on the River Irwell, this very smart place (with evening bouncers) has a stylishly converted series of barrel-vaulted brick bays that were originally waiting rooms for boat passengers, and later the Nemesis boat club; furnishings include russet or dove plush seats and upholstered stalls, wide glassed-in brick arches, cast-iron pillars and a flagstone floor. Photographs around the walls show how it once was in the nineteenth century: a sluggish open sewer from which the eponymous Mark Addy rescued over fifty people from drowning. Bar food includes an extraordinary range of cheeses – up to fifty at a time – from England, Scotland, Wales and several European countries, with granary bread (£1.90) – such is the size of the chunks that doggy-bags are automatically provided; there's also a choice of Belgian pâtés (£1.90), and soup in winter (£1). Well kept Boddingtons on handpump, and quite a few wines; piped music. Service stays efficient even when it gets so busy that there's a queue for food and it's hard to find a table. The canalside courtyard has tubs of flowers around its tables, from which you can watch the ducks. These were actually bred at home by the licensees and brought down here to brighten up what is now a calm stream. *(Recommended by Virginia Jones, R A Hutson, Wayne Brindle, Michael Craig, Lee Goulding, Michael Cook, Caroline Fisher, Tony Pounder, Jon Wainwright)*

Free house Licensee Jim Ramsbottom Real ale Snacks Children welcome Open 11–11

Peveril of the Peak

127 Great Bridgewater Street

There's a surprisingly relaxed family atmosphere in this quaint-shaped green-tiled building once the tide of workers has ebbed away from the surrounding nearby works and high offices. Even at much busier lunchtimes too, the old-fashioned small-roomed layout, with three separate rooms opening off the central servery, has an echo of this. There are various hatches and counters, and a profusion of mahogany and stained glass, and the framed Victorian song-covers and ancient prints of obscure village games such as sack-jumping are worth a look. Furnishings are traditional – red leatherette built-in button-back wall settles, or sturdy red plush ones. Well kept Websters Yorkshire and Choice and Wilsons Original and Mild on handpump; sensibly placed darts, pool, dominoes, fruit machine, juke box and (rarity of rarities now) a bar football table; food consists of sandwiches (from 50p), hot pies such as steak and kidney or cheese and onion (50p), and filled French sticks or gala pie (55p). In summer there are some seats outside on the terrace. The pub had been close to demolition but was saved by local action groups and preservation orders. *(Recommended by Jon Wainwright, Lee Goulding; more reports please)*

Wilsons (Watneys) Licensee Teresa Swanick Real ale Snacks (not Sun) Open 11.30–3, 5–11 all year; closed Sun lunchtime

Royal Oak ⊗

729 Wilmslow Road, Didsbury, Manchester 20

The phenomenal value and the choice of the cheese lunches in this very busy end-of-terrace pub are remarkable. The full range, probably the widest you can find anywhere in the country, and tracked down with great enthusiasm by the landlord over the last thirty-odd years, is spread out over much of the central island serving-counter; there are pâtés too. It remains a mystery how they manage to heap your plate up with so much at the price (£1.90 – there are takeaway bags for what's left over). This year, the pub has been redecorated, though there's still a friendly, local atmosphere, and it's simply furnished with theatrical handbills, porcelain spirit casks, coronation mugs, and old-fashioned brass anti-spill rims around the heavy cast-iron-framed tables; there's a quieter snug bar. Well kept Marstons Burton, Pedigree and Dark Mild on handpump; efficient attractive service. There are some seats outside. *(Recommended by David Wooff, Clarissa Ayman, Simon Barber, Dr and Mrs A K Clarke, Lee Goulding)*

Marstons Licensee Arthur Gosling Real ale Lunchtime snacks (not Sat or Sun) Open all day; closed evening 25 Dec

Sinclairs Oyster Bar ⊗

Shambles Square, Manchester 3; in Arndale Centre between Deansgate and Corporation Street, opposite Exchange Street

It's a surprise to find this traditionally furnished late eighteenth-century pub in the middle of a huge modern shopping complex. The alcovey ground floor has squared oak panelling, a low ochre ceiling, and small-backed stools that run along a tall old-fashioned marble-topped eating-bar. The second servery upstairs, which also serves lunchtime food, is in a quieter, more spacious room with pictures of old Manchester, low old-fashioned wall settles, and a scrolly old leather settee. There's a decent range of bar food, served by neatly uniformed barmaids, such as ploughman's (£1.50), steak pie (£2.50), roast beef, gammon or turkey (£2.75), seafood platter or beef and oyster pie (£3.50) and of course oysters (£4.20 the half-dozen), with sandwiches (hot gammon £1.50), rolls (75p) and side salads upstairs; the menu is limited on Bank Holidays. Sam Smiths OB and Museum on handpump kept under light blanket pressure, chess, fruit machine, and piped music. There are picnic-table sets outside. *(Recommended by Brian and Anna Marsden, Michael Cooke, Jon Wainwright, Wayne Brindle, Lee Goulding)*

Sam Smiths   Real ale   Lunchtime meals and snacks (not Sun)   Nearby parking difficult Open all day; closed 25 and 26 Dec

Tommy Ducks

East Street, Manchester 2

There's a vibrant atmosphere in this pretty black and white pub, and its meticulous Victorian décor makes it unusual for the city centre: heavy swagged velvet curtains, plush button-back banquettes with gold fringes, antique theatrical posters, photographs and music hall cards on the mirrored walls, and in one of its communicating rooms a big old-fashioned black cooking-range. There's even an exuberant collection of knickers, donated by customers, pinned on the red ceiling. Bar food includes sandwiches, steak canadienne, ploughman's, lasagne, chicken pie, chilli con carne or a range of salads, and prawn curry; well kept Greenalls Local and Original on handpump; juke box; very busy on weekday lunchtimes. The building is surrounded by towering new prestige office-blocks and is convenient for the exhibition centre in the former Central Station. *(Recommended by Jon Wainwright, Lee Goulding, Michael Cooke)*

Greenalls   Real ale   Meals (lunchtime, not Sun) and snacks (not Fri–Sun evenings)   Panama Jazz Band Sun evening   Open 11–3, 5.30–11 all year

MERECLOUGH (Lancs)   SD8332 Map 7
Kettledrum ⊗

302 Red Lees Road; from A646 Burnley–Halifax, quickest route is turn off between Walk Mill and Holme Chapel, signposted Over Town, Worsethorne; OS Sheet 103 reference 873305

The most prominent feature of the décor in this warm-hearted pub is sparkling brass – shovels, knockers, measures, corkscrews, keys, scales, weights, spigots, fancy boot-horns, imps, toasting-forks, warming-pans; there are also wooden and copper masks, buffalo horns, gruesome-looking knives by the dozen, and lots more. Furnishings include tapestried wall seats, some sensible angled and padded bottom rests where there isn't room for more formal seats (including one just right for winter, over a radiator), dimpled copper tables, and a solid-fuel stove. A wide choice of food such as home-made soup (90p), sandwiches (from 95p, steak £3.95), ploughman's or omelettes (£2.45), gammon with egg (£3.25), salads (from £3.25), home-made steak and kidney pie (£3.45), home-made lasagne (£3.75), trout (£4.25), a massive mixed grill (£4.95) and sixteen-ounce T-bone steak (£6.25), with good home-made puddings. There's a good value set lunch (£6.25). Well kept Matthew Browns Lion and Mild, Ruddles County, Theakstons Best and XB and Websters Yorkshire and Choice on handpump; darts, dominoes, fruit machine, maybe piped radio. Seats outside look over a low stone wall beyond the quiet road,

Post Office address codings confusingly give the impression that some pubs are in Lancashire when they're really in Yorkshire (which is where we list them).

to Burnley and its surrounding moors. *(Recommended by George Hunt, Len Beattie, Michael Heys)*

Free house   Licensee Roy Ratcliffe   Real ale   Meals and snacks   Restaurant tel Burnley (0282) 24591 (closed Thurs evening)   Children in restaurant   Open 11–3, 5.30–11 all year

MIDDLETON (Gtr Manchester)   SD8606 Map 7
Tandle Hill Tavern

Thornham Lane, Slattocks; this, with Thornham Old Road, is a largely unmade track between A664 and A671 just S of (but not quickly accessible from) M62 junction 20; OS Sheet 109 reference 899090

You'd never guess that this pub – down a rough track which plays havoc with even the sturdiest car's suspension – was within the Manchester built-up area; it's actually part of a farm, surrounded by ducks, ponies and ageing tractors (the landlord, a wrestler, looks big enough to practise his lifts on them). The two snug rooms have spindle-back chairs around dimpled copper tables, and lots of brass candlesticks on the mantelpiece above the coal fire. Cheap sandwiches include prawns and hot beef or steak canadienne; well kept Lees ales on handpump; piped music. There are some benches outside, and paths lead off on all sides. It's handy for the Tandle Hill Country Park. *(Recommended by Jon Wainwright, Yvonne and Don Johnson, Lee Goulding)*

Free house   Real ale   Snacks   Children in tap-room   Open 12–2.30, 7–11

NEWTON (Lancs)   SD6950 Map 7
Parkers Arms 🍺

B6478 7 miles N of Clitheroe

This is a lovely spot – a bowl of tree-sheltered pastures between Waddington Fell and Beatrix Fell, with the River Hodder flowing through, and a cluster of stone cottages angled neatly around steep but trim little lawns. The inn is very much the centre of the picture, and well spaced picnic-table sets on its big lawn make the most of the view. The bar is brightly modernised, with red plush button-back banquettes around dimpled copper tables on a flowery blue carpet, and lots of copper and brass on the neat stone mantelpiece. An arch leads through to a similar area with sensibly placed darts, pool, fruit machine, dominoes and trivia machine; discreet piped music, and an unobtrusive black labrador may wander in. Bar food includes soup (80p), sandwiches (£1.25), burger, steak canadienne or ploughman's (£2), fish or home-made steak and kidney pie (£3), gammon and egg (£3.50) and fresh salmon (£4.95); they do Sunday teas in the big, airy restaurant. *(Recommended by Brian and Elizabeth Carter, Wayne Brindle)*

Whitbreads   Licensee Harry Rhodes   Meals and snacks   Children welcome   Open 10.30–3, 6–11 all year   Bedrooms tel Slaidburn (020 06) 236; £15/£25

nr OSWALDTWISTLE (Lancs)   SD7327 Map 7
Britannia

Haslingden Old Road; junction of A677 with B6231

Several different rooms in this friendly cottagey pub have solid traditional furnishings such as sturdy plush-cushioned settles, wheel-back armchairs, well cushioned pews, cast-iron-framed tables and two fine log-burning black-leaded ranges. There are curly brass lamps, old local photographs and brass platters on the butter-coloured walls, some panelling (particularly the waxed squared panelling screening off the kitchen), boarded ceilings, and rugs on flagstones or stripped floorboards. By the time this book is published, they will have turned the old stable, barn and cartshed into a restaurant and kitchen. Bar food includes soup (70p), sandwiches (from £1), black pudding or pâté (£1.25), slimmers' dishes (from £1.50), ploughman's (from £2.20), a vegetarian dish or steak in ale pie (£2.50), gammon and pineapple (£2.55), and six-ounce sirloin steak (£3.95); children's menu (£1.50). Well kept Thwaites and Mild on handpump; fruit machine, piped pop music and (the only false note) a brash free-standing cigarette machine by the stairs in the central area. There are old-fashioned slat and iron seats and picnic-table sets on a walled sun-trap back terrace, by a play area with a good climber under the nearby trees; at the front, an open-fronted former barn has more seats. *(Recommended by Jon Wainwright, Len Beattie; more reports please)*

Thwaites   Licensee William Stopford   Real ale   Meals and snacks   Restaurant tel Blackburn (0254) 679744   Open 11.30–3, 6–11 all year; open all day Sun

RABY (Merseyside)   SJ3180   Map 7
Wheatsheaf
The Green, Rabymere Road; off A540 S of Heswall

An original seventeenth-century country-hamlet alehouse in a quiet village with a half-timbered exterior, a thatched roof and whitewashed walls. The central room has low beams and red tiles, a nice snug formed by antique settles built in around its fine old fireplace, an old wall clock and homely black kitchen shelves. In a more spacious room there are upholstered wall seats around the tables, small hunting prints on the cream walls and a smaller coal fire. Well kept real ales on handpump include Flowers IPA, Higsons, Ind Coope Burton, Tetleys, Thwaites and Youngers Scotch and No 3, and there's a good choice of malt whiskies. *(Recommended by Mr and Mrs J H Adam, Jon Wainwright)*

Free house   Licensee Mr Cranston   Real ale   Lunchtime meals and snacks (not Sun)   Open 11.30–3, 5.30–10.30

SLAIDBURN (Lancs)   SD7152   Map 7
Hark to Bounty   ★ ⊗ ⌂

In lovely surroundings and off the beaten track, this big stone pub has a cosy, comfortable lounge bar with an antique settee, a Victorian settle, one or two easy chairs, neat armed dining-chairs, and brass and copper over the open fire (there are dried flowers here when it's not lit). Its plain cream walls are decorated with big Victorian engravings, a few Victorian fashion plates, and local photographs. The food is popular with readers, including home-made soup (£1.10), well filled sandwiches (from £1.10), ploughman's with an enormous plate of mixed cheeses, three beautifully grilled, meaty Cumberland sausages (£2.85), salads (from £2.60), home-made steak and kidney pie or scampi (£2.95), fresh haddock with scampi and prawns in a creamy sauce (£4.25), steak (£5.75), daily specials and a carvery in summer. Well kept Youngers Scotch, IPA and No 3 on handpump; friendly, hard-working staff. The oak-panelled Old Courtroom, now used for functions, doubled for local court hearings until 1924. There's lots of room to sit outside – on high days and feast days they may even have a fairground organ. Beyond the gently rolling wooded hills around here there are high fells and fly fishing can be arranged on the nearby Stocks Reservoir. *(Recommended by Derek and Sylvia Stephenson, D Thornton, J E Rycroft, Alan and Marlene Radford, Lee Goulding, Yvonne and Don Johnson, Heather Sharland, ATC, Mrs M Wettern, P H S Wettern, Mr and Mrs T F Marshall, P Howard, E G Parish, Dr R H M Stewart, Hayward Wane, Mike Suddards, Caroline Fisher, Tony Pounder, K McConnochie, David and Ruth Hollands, David Thornton)*

Free house   Licensee Mrs Pat Holt   Real ale   Meals and snacks   Restaurant   Children in eating area and restaurant   Open 11–3, 6–11 all year   Bedrooms tel Slaidburn (020 06) 246; £16B/£32B

Soup prices usually include a roll and butter.

STALYBRIDGE (Gtr Manchester)   SJ9698 Map 7

Stalybridge Station Buffet

Quite unlike any other working station buffet, this privately run place is done out in the Victorian splendour that went with the heyday of the steam train. It's full of railway memorabilia, including barge and railway pictures set into the red bar counter, with more railway pictures and some old station signs on the high walls. The welcome is homely, with very well kept Moorhouses Premier and three guest beers a week from all over the country (including some from home-brew pubs) on handpump, tea (made fresh by the pot) and cheap snacks such as black-eyed peas (30p), chilli beans (40p), sandwiches or hot or cold pies (45p). Proceeds from a paperback library on the piano beside the black coal stove go to a guide dog charity. *(Recommended by Jon Wainwright, M A and W R Proctor, Lee Goulding, Michael Cooke)*

Free house   Licensee Ken Redfern   Real ale   Snacks (not Sun or Tues lunchtime)   Children welcome   Folk singers Sat evening   Open 11.30–3, 5 (7 Sat)–11 all year

STANDISH (Gtr Manchester)   SD5610 Map 7

Crown

4 miles from M6 junction 27; straight through Standish, then at T-junction turn left into Worthington, then left into Platt Lane

Behind an unpromising façade, this friendly pub has a pleasant series of partly panelled knocked-together rooms furnished with Chesterfields and armchairs, bunches of flowers, a coal fire and ship prints. The well kept real ales change regularly, and there are always at least four, typically including Boddingtons, Bass, Cask (Brew X) and Bass Mild, dispensed from handsome brass-mounted hand-pumps on a good solid counter with brass elbow rest and kicking ledge. Attractively presented, good value food includes sandwiches, burgers, plaice, scampi, beef bourguignonne, steak and kidney pie or chilli con carne; piped radio. In summer there may be barbecues out by the pub's own bowling-green, which is up steps from a small back courtyard (but not always open). *(Recommended by J Pearson, Comus Elliott, Jon Wainwright, Roger and Kathy, J H M Broughton, Dr J R Hamilton)*

Free house   Real ale   Meals (lunchtime) and snacks   Children welcome away from bar   Open 11.30–3, 5.30–11 all year

STOCKPORT (Gtr Manchester)   SJ8991 Map 7

Red Bull ⊗

14 Middle Hillgate; turn off A6 beside Town Hall following fingerpost towards Marple and Hyde into Edward Street; turn left at traffic lights – pub almost immediately on your left

This welcoming, old-fashioned pub has open fires, beams, some flagstones, and for decoration lots of brassware, sketches and paintings. The traditionally furnished snug rooms – opening off the efficient central island serving-counter – has substantial settles and seats built into the partly panelled walls. Good value, home-made food includes soup (90p), open sandwiches with home-cooked meats (from £1.45), bacon and egg pie (£2.25), salmon suprême or Moroccan lamb kebabs (£2.35), lamb and almond curry (£2.45) and pork and ham pie (£2.65). Well kept Robinsons Best on handpump; dominoes and cribbage. It can get very crowded and hot in the evenings, but at lunchtime it's very handy for a quiet meal. The outside WC is typical of a Robbies pub. *(Recommended by Jon Wainwright, Lee Goulding; more reports please)*

Robinsons   Licensee Brian Lawrence   Real ale   Meals (lunchtime, not Sun) and snacks (not Sat evening, not Sun)   Children in eating area of bar lunchtime only   Open all day

'Space game' means any electronic game.

THORNTON HOUGH (Merseyside)   SJ3081   Map 7
Seven Stars ⊗
Church Road; B5136 in village centre

Used in the 1840s by travellers to the toll bridge, this relaxing pub has two comfortable rooms linked by arches, with easy chairs and a sofa by the fireplace. Most of the space in the spotless bar is given over to tables with cushioned wheel-back chairs and button-back wall banquettes – note though that you have to be eating to sit here. Served by friendly and neatly uniformed waitresses, the popular food includes soup (40p), sandwiches (from 70p), ploughman's (£1.50), salads (from £1.50), plaice (£2.50), vegetarian dishes (from £3), scampi (£3.50), gammon (£3.70) and steaks (from £4.95); also, lunchtime daily specials – for instance steak and kidney on Wednesday or curry on Friday (from £1.80), and puddings (from 60p). Well kept Whitbreads Castle Eden on handpump; plastic plants hang along the ceiling-trusses, and there's gentle piped music. Seats outside on a terrace and in the small garden have a view of the neighbouring twin churches. It's actually in an estate village built for Lord Leverhulme in the late nineteenth century, and the Leverhulmes still live here. (*Recommended by Alan and Marlene Radford, Jon Wainwright, Mr and Mrs J H Adam, D P Manchett*)

Whitbreads   Licensee C E Nelson   Real ale   Snacks (lunchtime) and meals   Restaurant tel 051-336 4574   Open all day; closed 25 Dec

TOCKHOLES (Lancs)   SD6623   Map 7
Royal Arms
Village signposted from A6062 on S edge of Blackburn; though not signposted, good route on pretty moorland road about 1½ miles N of Belmont, just past AA telephone box (and on opposite side of road) – this is then the first pub you come to

Though the view from this old-fashioned country pub is chiefly of the woods in the country that rolls away below the ridge, if you look hard on a clear day you can make out Blackpool Tower. Inside, the four cosy and friendly little rooms have cushioned wall settles around their tables, rustic decorations, and the panelling-effect walls are dominated by their big log fires in handsome stone fireplaces. Bar food includes sandwiches (80p), ploughman's (£1.65), salads (from £1.65), home-made steak and kidney pie (£1.90), scampi (£2) and maybe steaks done over one of the open fires; well kept Thwaites Bitter and Best Mild on handpump; dominoes, fruit machine, juke box. Outside, there's a sheltered terrace (with a play area in the garden), white doves in a dovecot, geese in the field behind, and a nature trail opposite. (*Recommended by Wayne Brindle, Jon Wainwright, Alan Thorpe, Yvonne and Don Johnson*)

Thwaites   Real ale   Meals and snacks   Children welcome   Open 12–3, 7–11 all year

Victoria
In village

This comfortable and friendly moorland village pub has cushioned banquettes and Windsor chairs around tables in snug alcoves, plates on the partly stripped stone walls, and a nineteenth-century hatter's signboard above a squat wood-burning stove. The good value bar food includes soup (60p), sandwiches (from 70p), burger (85p), ploughman's or home-made pies such as cheese and onion or steak and kidney pie (from £1.50), steak on French bread (£1.65), roast chicken (£1.95), gammon and pineapple (£2.20), daily specials and puddings like home-made apple

---

Stars after the name of a pub show exceptional quality. But they don't mean extra comfort – and though some pubs get stars for special food quality, it isn't necessarily a food thing either. The full report on each pub should make clear what special quality has earned it.

pie (85p); fruit machine and piped music. *(Recommended by Len Beattie; more reports please)*

Free house   Licensee Jack Threlfall   Meals and snacks (not Mon evening)   Restaurant tel Darwen (0254) 71622   Children welcome   Open 11.30–3, 6.30–11 all year; supper licence until 12

nr TOCKHOLES (Lancs)   SD6623   Map 7
Black Bull

Brokenstones Road, Livesey; between Tockholes and Blackburn; OS Sheet 103 reference 666247

From the big windows in this comfortably modernised food pub you can look across the high pastures and down to Blackburn. The carpeted open-plan lounge has wooden pillars that divide it into alcoves, sturdy brown button-back wall banquettes around its tables, and big pictures and horsebrasses on the cream walls. Good straightforward meals include sandwiches (from 80p, toasties from 85p), black pudding (£1.65), plaice or scampi (£2.30), gammon with egg or pineapple (£2.65), pizzas (from £2.75), steaks (from £4.75), and puddings like home-made sherry trifle. Well kept Thwaites Bitter and Mild on handpump; dominoes. There's a fine old slate-bed snooker table in a separate room; some seats outside. From the right-angle bend about three-quarters of a mile east there's a good view towards Darwen. *(Recommended by Len Beattie, Roger Huggins; more reports please)*

Thwaites   Licensee H G Richards   Real ale   Meals and snacks   Children welcome (not evenings)   Open 11.30–3, 7–11 all year; may consider longer afternoon opening Sat

UPPERMILL (Gtr Manchester)   SD9905   Map 7
Cross Keys ★

Runninghill Gate; from A670 in Uppermill turn into New Street, by a zebra crossing close to the chapel; this is the most practical-looking of the lanes towards the high moors and leads directly into Runninghill Gate

Tracks from behind this lively old stone pub – particularly popular with ramblers – lead straight up towards Broadstone Hill and Dick Hill, and it's also the headquarters of the Oldham Mountain Rescue Team and various outdoor sports clubs. Several rambling connecting rooms have low beams, pews, settles, flagstones, and an original cooking range. The decent choice of bar food includes sandwiches, good toasties, soup (65p), and a wide range of dishes such as liver and bacon casserole, Hungarian goulash, chilli con carne, scampi, Chinese spring roll, and salads (all £2.50), with puddings like apricot crumble or apple and blackberry pancake (from 70p). Well kept Lees Bitter and Mild on handpump; darts, dominoes, cribbage and fruit machine. At the back there's a stylish flagstoned terrace, which has bright flowers sheltered by a dry stone wall, and next to it are swings, a slide and a climbing-frame; this year, a new side terrace has been added and the land around the extended car park has been landscaped. The sporting connections are strong: they're annual sponsors of the road running or fell races in the first week in June and on the last Saturday in August (there are lots of colourful photographs of these among the interesting older prints on the walls), and the Saddleworth Clog and Garland Girls practise regularly here. *(Recommended by M A and W R Proctor, Jon Wainwright; more reports please)*

Lees   Licensee Philip Kay   Real ale   Meals (lunchtime) and snacks   Children in eating area of bar   Jazz and clog dancing Mon evenings, folk Weds evenings   Open all day, though may close earlier in winter if weather is bad

---

Remember, this is not just a food guide – pubs earn their place in it for a variety of virtues. If good food is what you want, look for the knife-and-fork symbol or for specific praise of the food.

WHEATLEY LANE (Lancs)   SD8338 Map 7
Old Sparrow Hawk ⊗

Towards E end of village road which runs N of and parallel to A6068; one way of reaching it is to follow Fence, Newchurch 1¾ signpost, then turn off at Barrowford ¾ signpost

Furnishings in the big semi-circular bar of this busy pub include three stuffed sparrowhawks and an owl above the gleaming copper hoods of the log-effect gas fires, studded leather seats and long button-back banquettes, dark oak panelling, stripped stonework, and an unusual stained-glass ceiling-dome. Even when it's busy you can find a snug quiet corner in the communicating room areas. Reliable food served from an efficient food servery includes a good range of sandwiches (from 70p, double-deckers £4.25, toasties from 95p, steak £2.45), home-made soup (95p), ploughman's (£1.95), and lots of attractively presented salads or cold plates including smoked or roast ham, Grosvenor pie, roast meats and smoked salmon (from £2.25), and a range of at least five hot daily specials such as lasagne, steak and kidney pie or beef carbonnade. A mock-Tudor carvery serves good roasts (lunch, not Saturday, £7.95; dinner £8.95 – including starter, second helpings and pudding). Well kept Bass on handpump, with Cask Bitter (Brew X) on electric pump; good coffee (65p). Tables on a good-sized terrace give a view over to the moors behind Nelson and Colne, and Pendle Hill rises behind the pub. *(Recommended by L F Beattie, R Aitken, Simon Bates)*

Bass   Licensee Don Butterworth   Real ale   Meals and snacks   Restaurant tel Burnley (0282) 64126   Children welcome   Open 11–11 all year

WHITEWELL (Lancs)   SD6546 Map 7
Inn at Whitewell ★ ★ ⊗ ⊨

Easily reached by B6246 from Whalley; road through Dunsop Bridge from B6478 is also good

One reader cycles twenty miles to this long, low stone house, alone by a church and surrounded by well wooded rolling hills set off against higher moors, with lawns running down to the River Hodder. Inside, the atmosphere is sometimes more that of an old-fashioned country house than a pub, with sonorous clocks, heavy curtains on sturdy wooden rails, antique settles, oak gate-leg tables, old cricketing and sporting prints, and log fires (the lounge has a particularly attractive stone fireplace); one area has a selection of newspapers, local maps and guidebooks. Lunchtime bar food includes soup (£1), fish pâté (£2.45), ploughman's (£3.10), spiced sausages in red wine, Cumberland sausage, very good steak, kidney and mushroom or fish pie (all £3.50), and salads (from £3.50); in the evenings there are spinach, bacon and avocado salad (£3), delicious seafood pancakes (£3.25), Bradenham smoked ham and egg (£3.50) and gravadlax with dill mayonnaise (£5.50); also freshly made puddings such as strawberry Pavlova or blueberry pie (£1.50). They serve coffee and cream teas all day. Well kept Moorhouses Premier and Pendle Witches Brew on handpump; civilised, friendly service. The public bar has darts, pool, shove-ha'penny, dominoes, fruit machine, space game and juke box, with a 1920s game-of-skill slot machine; there's a piano for anyone who wants to play. Seats outside in front catch the afternoon sun. The inn has six miles of trout, salmon and sea-trout fishing on the Hodder, and can also (with notice) arrange shooting. It also houses a wine merchant (hence the unusually wide range of wines available here), an art gallery, and a shop selling cashmere and so forth. *(Recommended by Derek and Sylvia Stephenson, Lynn Stevens, Gill Quarton, Philip and Carol Seddon, E Lee, C Gray, Heather Sharland, Lee Goulding, W D Horsfield, George Hunt, Charles McFeeters, David and Ruth Hollands, Dr and Mrs R Hodgkinson, Jon Wainwright, Simon Bates, Brian and Anna Marsden, Denis Mann, N K Crace, G L Archer)*

Free house   Licensee Richard Bowman   Real ale   Meals and snacks (not Sat evening if a big function is on)   Restaurant   Children welcome   Pianist Fri evenings   Open 11–3, 6–11 all year   Bedrooms tel Dunsop Bridge (020 08) 222; £32(£32B)/£39(£43B)

Lucky Dip

Besides the fully inspected pubs, you might like to try these Lucky Dips recommended to us and described by readers (if you do, please send us reports):

Accrington [Manchester Rd; SD7528], *Hargreaves Arms*: Decent town-centre pub with plush banquettes and velveteen drapes, frosted glass shutters over the bar, stuffed birds and a fox behind, well kept Matthew Browns Bitter *(Anon)*

Affetside [Watling St; SD7513], *Pack Horse*: Nice, warm, friendly atmosphere, good views down from moors, reasonable food *(Caroline Fisher, Tony Pounder, M Thomas, A Matheson)*

Altham [Whalley Rd; SD7632], *Greyhound*: Good local, welcoming fire in winter, good Sam Smiths and pleasant sandwiches and ploughman's *(Len Beattie)*; [A678 Padiham–Clayton-le-Moors] *Martholme Grange*: Interesting creeper-clad former manor house with attractive panelled lounge bar which often has live entertainment – very popular with older customers; good Tetleys ales, carvery *(Wayne Brindle)*

Altrincham [42 Victoria St; SJ7788], *Old Roebuck*: Usually quiet and cosy beamed Tudor-style pub with well kept Wilsons ales served from original timber counter, appealing choice of hot dishes *(Lee Goulding, R G Ollier)*

Ashton Under Lyne [52 Old St; SJ9399], *Gamecock*: Friendly pub, entirely beer-orientated with a dozen or more real ales and décor recalling spit-and-sawdust days *(Lee Goulding)*

Audenshaw [Audenshaw Rd (B6390); SJ8896], *Boundary*: Good varied choice of well cooked food at prices to suit all pockets, in clean friendly pub with well equipped bar and friendly staff; horse-drawn boat trips on adjacent Peak Forest Canal *(N Hesketh)*

Aughton Park [B5197; SD4006], *Derby Arms*: Excellent food, good value *(A A Worthington)*

Bamber Bridge [main rd (former A6), nr M6 junction 29; SD5625], *Olde Hob*: A real rarity – a thatched pub in industrial Lancs; pleasant food, small interconnecting rooms running the length of the pub *(Wayne Brindle)*

Bamford [off Ashworth Rd – NB this is the Bamford in Manchester; SD8612], *Egerton Arms*: Surrounded by fields, this popular, smart and plush place is cosy in winter *(David and Valerie Hooley)*

Barley [SD8240], *Pendle*: Pleasant pub in quiet village below Pendle Hill with friendly licensees, Bass and good ploughman's *(Len Beattie)*

☆ **Barnston** [Barnston Rd (A551); SJ2883], *Fox & Hounds*: Attractively refurbished eighteenth-century country pub with good food weekday lunchtimes, lovely character and atmosphere, well kept Websters and Wilsons real ales; pianist Sun lunchtime

(Mr and Mrs J H Adam, Guy Chessall)

Barrowford [Gisburn Rd (A682); SD8539], *White Bear*: One of the county's oldest pubs – looks great outside at night with all its lights on *(Wayne Brindle)*

Barton [A6 N of Preston, 200 yds from Barton Grange Garden Centre; SD5137], *Boars Head*: Nicely decorated pub with friendly staff and good value separate food bar *(I Wilson)*

Bashall Eaves [SD6943], *Red Pump*: Character pub in beautiful Forest of Bowland countryside, overlooking Longridge Fell and filled with antique furniture; decent food, log fires, stoves, quite busy even on winter weekdays *(David Thornton, Wayne Brindle)*

Belthorn [Elton Rd (B6232 S); SD7224], *Grey Mare*: Well run clean and tidy pub on moorland road with breathtaking views from its hilltop site; fairly wide choice of reasonably priced food lunchtime and evening, well kept Thwaites on handpump *(P Corris)*; *Pack Horse*: The feel of an Italian restaurant with a pub bar attached; Matthew Browns and Theakstons Old Peculier *(Anon)*

Bispham [Chorley Rd (B5246 2 miles N of Parbold); SD3139], *Farmers Arms*: Isolated pub overlooking Parbold Hill, large and friendly with cosy red seats in several warm rooms *(Wayne Brindle)*

Blackburn [Exchange St; SD6828], *Borough Arms*: Cheerful, friendly, comfortable and almost always busy; cheap lunchtime food, good Bass, perhaps the best atmosphere of any town pub here *(Wayne Brindle)*; [Penny St] *Daniels*: Rather self-consciously smart, by Thwaites main brewery and museum – named after Daniel Thwaites; as you'd expect, excellent Thwaites Bitter *(Anon)*; [Royal Oak Rd/Revidge Rd, nr A6119 ring rd – OS Sheet 103 reference 681302] *Royal Oak*: Cosy and well decorated eighteenth-century local with well kept Matthew Browns, good lunchtime sandwiches and other snacks – remarkably peaceful surroundings considering its closeness to the ring road and town centre *(Len Beattie, Wayne Brindle)*

☆ **Blackpool** [35 Clifton St (just behind Town Hall); SD3035], *St Martins Tavern*: Stylish Whitbreads cafe-bar with marble, columns, statues, lofty coffered ceiling, solid ash bar counter in central sunken area, home-made food, keg beers, espresso machine; used to be a bank and when first opened was called the Mint *(R H Sawyer, LYM)*; *Saddle*: Straight out of 1920s, original glasswork, tiles, snugs and pictures; good atmosphere, Bass Mild and Special *(Graham Bush)*

☆ **Blacksnape** [Grimehills; SD7121], *Crown & Thistle*: Isolated and excellent little pub, on the Roman road over the moors – on such a steep hill that its several rooms are on different levels *(Wayne Brindle, Peter Corris)*

Bolton [Pool St; SD7108], *Howcroft*: Hidden gem – traditional local with great beer and a welcome for strangers *(Denis Mann)*; [262 Bridgeman St (off A579)] *Lodge Bank*: Good Lees beer, friendly welcome, nourishing food *(J R Fen)*

Bolton by Bowland [SD7849], *Coach & Horses*: Friendly and comfortably refurbished pub in picturesque village near lovely stretch of river; newish young licensees concentrating on food in bar and restaurant – get there early at weekends for a table; well kept Chesters *(E G Parish)*

Bowdon [The Firs (by church); SJ7686], *Stamford Arms*: Smart, lively, friendly pub, public bar with games and sedate lounge, first-class Boddingtons, useful restaurant *(Lee Goulding)*

☆ **Bramhall** [Redford Dr (towards Hazel Grove, via Grange Rd from Bramhall Lane); SJ8985], *Shady Oak*: Unusual design of modern pub in recent housing development, bare bricks, open fire, usually five changing and well kept real ales, welcoming staff, good atmosphere, food, tables outside, special-interest evenings eg Tues quiz night *(Lee Goulding, Paul Corbett, Mike Suddards)*

Bretherton [Croston Rd (B5247); SD4720], *Blue Anchor*: Small cosy pub, very well refurbished by Whitbreads – impressive bar counter with stained-glass blue anchors, lots of stuffed animals; lively but friendly atmosphere, well kept Chesters, Hartleys XB, Whitbreads Castle Eden; bar food *(Lee Goulding)*

Brierfield [Higher Reedly Rd; SD8436], *Lane Ends*: Good value home-cooked food, pleasant friendly atmosphere, well kept beer; oak beams and brasses in large single bar *(J H Cleave)*

☆ **Brindle** [B5256, off A6 from M6 junction 29; SD6024], *Cavendish Arms*: Attractive, whitewashed village local by church; interesting inside, with several small rooms including tiny bar with TV, plush lounge; open fires, stained-glass windows, well kept Burtonwood, darts, friendly licensees and locals *(Jon Wainwright, Wayne Brindle, J T C Heslop)*

Bromley Cross [Chapeltown Rd; SD7213], *Railway*: Full of interesting mementoes for railway enthusiasts *(Wayne Brindle)*

Brookhouse [3 miles from M6 junction 34 – village signposted off A683 towards Settle; SD5464], *Black Bull*: Simple bar meals and well kept Thwaites real ales in comfortably modernised stone pub just below moors *(LYM)*

nr Burnley [High Halstead; from central traffic lights in Briercliffe turn off A56 into Halifax Rd and keep on, turning right at T-junction towards Worsthorne – OS Sheet 103 reference 884337; SD8833], *Roggerham*

Gate: Alone on moors road near Swinden reservoirs, spacious, simple and airy inside, with good value plain food, well kept Youngers Scotch and IPA, friendly welcome and bedrooms; close to nice walks *(P Wayne Brindle, Len Beattie, BB)*; [Cliviger; A646, just into W Yorks; SD8631] *Staff of Life*: Old and eccentric pub full of bits and bobs, superb cider *(Wayne Brindle)*

Burscough [Martin Lane; SD4310], *Martin*: Good friendly service, John Smiths real ale, imaginative good value food from bar and restaurant, friendly licensees; handy for Peter Scott Nature Reserve *(Mr and Mrs Peter Sephton and friends)*; [Lathom, just off A5209; SD4610] *Ring o' Bells*: Very pleasantly placed by canal, picture windows in well furnished lounge with massive oak beams; Higsons real ales *(Wayne Brindle)*

Bury [Clifton St; SD8010], *St Martins*: Décor particularly attractive – especially the pillars and high swivel chairs; not sure about the plastic plants or loud juke box and piped music *(Anon)*

Caton [SD5364], *Ship*: Good plain food in fine refuge from Lancaster, no loud music *(MGBD)*

Chatburn [SD7644], *Brown Cow*: Recently refurbished – included for its dining-room food (not midweek evenings) and well kept Whitbreads Castle Eden *(Wayne Brindle)*

Cheadle [Wilmslow Rd; SJ8688], *Station*: Nicely renovated old station house with pleasant atmosphere – but can get very crowded; food (not Sun), well kept Banks's Mild and Bitter on electric pump *(Brian and Anna Marsden)*

Chipping [Windy St; SD6243], *Sun*: Popular stone village local in shadow of Longridge Fell, well kept Boddingtons (stream through cellar keeps it cool), open fire, friendly service, good value food; said to be haunted *(Lee Goulding)*

☆ **nr Chipping** [Hesketh Lane Village; crossroads of Longridge rd with Inglewhite–Clitheroe one – OS Sheet 103 reference 619413], *Dog & Partridge*: Comfortable little bar lounge with easy chairs around low tables and log fire, generous home-made bar food except Sat evening and Sun lunchtime, Tetleys on electric pump, restaurant; attractive country setting *(Wayne Brindle, LYM)*

Chorley [Bolton Rd – A6 S; SD5817], *Yarrow Bridge*: Comfortably modernised, with open fire and Chesterfields in big baronial hall of a room, also large bar; Greenalls, good value food *(Paul Finan)*

☆ **nr Chorley** [White Coppice, 2 miles from M61 junction 8; signposted from A674 towards Blackburn; SD6118], *Railway*: Simple comfort by the North-West Pennine Recreational Park, well kept Matthew Browns Bitter and Mild, decent bar food with half-price children's helpings; weekend cricket on the green, clay pigeon shoots winter Suns, fine cigarette card collection,

Sat evening live entertainment in winter, monthly in summer *(Brian Green, LYM)*

nr **Chorley** [A674; SD5818], *Red Cat*: Very friendly, clearly popular with Italian-style restaurant; decent coffee *(Sue Cleasby, Mike Ledger)*

Churchtown [off A565 from Preston, taking B5244 at Southport; SD3618], *Bold Arms*: Large, simple pub with well kept Ind Coope Burton *(Jon Wainwright)*; *Hesketh Arms*: Attractive, thatched pub sheltered by trees; spacious inside, with well kept Tetleys on handpump from central servery; handy for botanic gardens *(Jon Wainwright)*

Churchtown [note that this is the different one, off A586 Garstang–St Michaels-on-Wyre, at SD4843], *Horns*: Friendly, with good value food in very big helpings – very good choice of puddings *(M A and W R Proctor)*; *Punchbowl*: Lovely, peaceful village pub nr church with attractive mock-Tudor interior, good fires, well kept Tetleys, superb bar food *(Wayne Brindle, Miss E Thickett)*

Clayton Green [just off B5256, not far from M1 junction 29; SD5723], *Lord Nelson*: Large secluded pub, locally popular for food; nice inside, with plenty of exposed stone and pictures, Matthew Browns beers *(Wayne Brindle)*

Clayton le Moors [Burnley Rd; SE7430], *Martholme Grange*: Atmosphere quite good, with very good value carvery upstairs; pub is a feeder for the popular cabaret lounge behind *(Anon)*

Cowpe [Cowpe Lane; SD8320], *Buck*: Warm, welcoming pub in terrace of houses with good choice of Timothy Taylors beers; strongly local but friendly atmosphere, pool-table and juke box *(Jon Wainwright)*

Croston [Out Lane (A581); SD4818], *Lord Nelson*: Fine unspoilt village pub with lively, friendly bar, cosy adjoining snug, quieter lounge and tiny games-room with table skittles; well kept Boddingtons and Higsons ales *(Lee Goulding)*

Dalton [look out for Ashursts Beacon – pub next to cricket pitch; SD5007], *Prince William*: Comfortably furnished with good food and beer, and superb views – from the car park you can see nine counties on a clear day; quaint cricket field next door *(Wayne Brindle)*

Denton [Stockport Rd; SJ9295], *Fletchers Arms*: Spacious bar with well kept Robinsons, decent wine and good plentiful food, large library, pond in garden with lots of space for children to play *(John Gould)*

Diggle [Sam Rd, Saddleworth; SE0008], *Diggle*: Very welcoming pub with old stone fireplace in one of its three cosy rooms, superbly kept Timothy Taylors Landlord; lovely position, with fine Tame valley views from beside the entrance to Standedge railway tunnel; food popular *(Lee Goulding)*

Dobcross [SD9906], *Swan*: Lively and wel-coming villagey atmosphere, good ale and nice food at reasonable prices; Sun folk night *(Dominic Cullearn)*

Dunham Woodhouses [B5160 – OS Sheet 109 reference 724880; SJ7288], *Vine*: Busy local with well kept Sam Smiths on electric pump, pleasant atmosphere, straightforward cheap food; landlord may play the electric organ *(Jon Wainwright, Brian and Anna Marsden)*

Eccles [Church St (A57 – very close to M602 junction 2); SJ7798], *Duke of York*: Recent change of landlord at this recently renovated Victorian pub, formerly popular for its no-smoking room and interesting choice of well kept real ales *(Up-to-date reports please)*; [off A57] *Hare & Hounds*: Remarkably low-priced good food in pub in pedestrianised central area, plenty of free parking nearby *(A A Worthington)*; [33 Regent St (A57)] *Lamb*: Large, friendly, four-roomed pub with good etched windows, bell tower and separate billiards-room; good value Holts beers *(Richard Sanders)*; [133 Liverpool Rd, Patricroft, a mile from M63 junction 2; SJ7698] *White Lion*: Busy, popular three-roomed corner local with etched windows and passageway servery; well kept Holts *(Richard Sanders)*

Edenfield [Bury Rd; SD7919], *Duckworth Arms*: Lively and popular Whitbreads pub, recently refurbished without losing its character, in broadly similar style to Duke of Wellington near Haslingden (see main entries); good food and service *(Miss C Haworth)*

Edgworth [N of village; SD7416], *Toby*: Friendly, isolated moorland pub with pleasant views of surrounding countryside, modern-style renovations, well kept Tetleys ales, good adjoining Italian restaurant *(Wayne Brindle)*

☆ **Fence** [300 Wheatley Lane Rd], *White Swan*: The fine collection of about a dozen well kept real ales is the main attraction at this lively local with simple comfortable furnishings and roaring fires in all three separate communicating areas; landlord could be more obliging to strangers, and pub may not open before 1pm on weekdays *(Simon Bates, Len Beattie, LYM)*

Fence [Wheatley Lane Rd; SD8237], *Bay Horse*: Good all round, with well kept Matthew Browns, decent food, garden, attractive surroundings *(Comus Elliott)*; [just off A6068] *Fence Gate*: Biggish Georgian hotel with attractive open-plan yet cosy bar, friendly service, good atmosphere, Thwaites and Youngers beers *(Len Beattie)*

Forton [A6, handy for M6 junction 33 – OS Sheet 102 reference 492505; SD4851], *New Holly Hotel*: Warmly welcoming, with good value bedrooms and fine breakfasts; new owners have settled in well *(E Lee)*

Frankby [SJ2487], *Farmers Arms*: Recently extended, busy pub *(E G Parish)*

Freckleton [SD4228], *Coach & Horses*: Old-fashioned, fairly plain but clean Boddingtons house with three small rooms – one carpeted and pleasantly furnished, with glass partitions and so forth; a fine old friendly pub *(Comus Elliott)*

Galgate [A6 towards Lancaster; SD4755], *Boot & Shoe*: Attractive, with friendly service and good food *(Tony Pounder, Caroline Fisher)*

☆ **Garstang** [northbound section of one-way system; SD4845], *Wheatsheaf*: Small and cosy, with gleaming copper and brass, glossy brown low beams with creaky ceiling-planks, little plush-cushioned black settles and dining-chairs, good service, warm atmosphere; food notable for good specials such as mussels in garlic butter, barbecued pork kebab and grilled halibut with prawn sauce *(M A and W R Proctor, Michael Williamson, Wayne Brindle, BB)*

Garstang [Church St] *Farmers Arms*: Friendly and popular, pleasant interior *(M A and W R Proctor)*

Gisburn [SD8248], *White Bull*: Excellent atmosphere, good food quickly served *(A A Worthington)*

☆ **Goosnargh** [pub signposted from village; SD5537], *Horns*: Old black and white Tetleys country pub, interesting and attractive inside with period furnishings, good if not cheap bar food (not Mon) including well filled beautifully presented sandwiches, hot dishes using local produce; coal fire, nice restaurant *(Wayne Brindle, Miss E Thickett)*

☆ **Greasby** [Greasby Rd (off B5139 in centre); SJ2587], *Greave Dunning*: Spacious revamp of eighteenth-century farm, lofty manorial-hall-like main lounge with upstairs food gallery, cushioned pews in flagstoned locals' bar with cosy snugs leading off, well kept Boddingtons, Tetleys and Websters Yorkshire, games-room *(E G Parish, Jon Wainwright, Mr and Mrs J H Adam, LYM)*

Greasby [Frankby Rd], *Red Cat*: Attractively refurbished Whitbreads local with decent choice of beers and wines, bar food, tables on raised terrace, small garden *(E G Parish)*; *Twelfth Man*: Extensively renovated, good food *(E G Parish)*

Great Eccleston [Market Pl (just off A586); OS Sheet 102 reference 428402; SD4240], *White Bull*: Friendly, quiet village local with pleasant décor, two open fires, old black range and comfortable seats; Bass on handpump, Chinese chef cooking Chinese food Weds, Fri, Sat, Sun; Weds is market day so gets busy *(John Atherton)*

Great Harwood [Harwood New Rd; SD7332], *Park*: Well kept and tastefully decorated, with good Matthew Browns beer and substantial food bar *(Anon)*

Great Mitton [B6246 – OS Sheet 103 reference 716377; SD7139], *Aspinall Arms*: In pleasant surroundings on banks of River Ribble, plush seats in comfortable warm bars with soft piped music; Hartleys and Whitbreads Castle Eden on handpump, wide choice of bar food from sandwiches to sirloin steak *(Mike Tucker)*

Grindleton [SD7545], *Duke of York*: Pleasant and friendly biggish village-centre pub, good bar food includes splendid properly made steak and kidney pie *(Oliver Howes)*

Hambleton [off A588 next to toll bridge; SD3742], *Shard Bridge*: Included for its lovely position overlooking the River Wyre *(Wayne Brindle)*

Hapton [2 Accrington Rd; SD7932], *Hapton*: Friendly atmosphere, pleasant staff, consistently good home-cooked food, excellent real ale *(K A Skilling)*

Haskayne [Rosemary Lane – turn right at Kings Arms heading towards Southport on A5147; SD3507], *Ship*: Character canalside pub with rich nautical flavour, cheap good food, attentive service, well kept Tetleys, lots of bric-à-brac; in a lovely spot *(Wayne Brindle)*

☆ **Hawk Green** [SU9687], *Crown*: Sprawling and popular black and white food pub with big helpings of pizza, salad, steaks and other grills, good (if pricey) restaurant, lively atmosphere – recent alterations give two distinct halves separated by screen, with more room for drinkers (well kept Robinsons on handpump) *(David Waterhouse, John Gould, Lee Goulding)*

Helmshore [Holcombe Rd; B6235; SD7821], *Robin Hood*: Small local near Higher Mill working cotton museum, with views of viaduct and tumbling river from back windows; table football, juke box and reasonably priced Wilsons *(Jon Wainwright)*

Heswall [Pensby Rd; SJ2782], *Harvest Mouse*: Relatively new Greenalls pub built as a windmill, complete with sails; galleried interior, reasonably priced food *(Peter Corris)*

Heywood [Pilsworth Rd; SD8612], *Three Arrows*: Lively atmosphere, friendly bar staff, open-plan but with separate areas decorated with plates, bottles and so forth – one part has black-leaded kitchen range with side oven *(Len Beattie)*

High Lane [A6 Stockport–Disley; SJ9585], *Red Lion*: A shame about the 'improved' open-plan layout with extension in non-matching brick, but very comfortable, with waiter-served well presented good food *(Mr and Mrs John Watson)*

Higham [Main St; SD8036], *Four Alls*: Pleasantly done-up Whitbreads pub, good beer, cheap bar food, friendly welcome *(Wayne Brindle)*

Holme Chapel [A646 Burnley–Todmorden; SD8829], *Ram*: Dark beams, white walls, brasswork and restrained lighting in roadside pub with spacious back dining area – wide choice of reasonable food and children welcome here; juke box (not too loud), fruit machine, well kept Bass, good cider *(George Hunt, Wayne Brindle)*

Horton [A59 Skipton–Gisburn; SD8550], *Coronation Arms*: Delicious sandwiches and chips, though style rather that of a hotel bar *(Wayne Brindle)*

Hurst Green [B6243 Longridge–Clitheroe; SD6838], *Eagle & Child*: Decidedly a local (a bit the sort where everyone goes quiet when strangers come in), but worth noting for its well kept Matthew Browns ales and views of the Ribble valley from the lovely garden with lovingly tended flower beds *(Wayne Brindle)*

Hutton [A59 on roundabout by Longton turnoff, just S of Hutton; SD4826], *Anchor*: Busy roadside inn with comfortable traditional décor, games-room, good Matthew Browns and Theakstons beers; in bustling commuter village *(Lee Goulding)*

nr **Hyde** [Werneth Low – OS Sheet 109 reference 958926; SJ9592], *Hare & Hounds*: Isolated but spacious hilltop pub with superb views – on a clear day you can see Liverpool Cathedral 35 miles away, and the Welsh mountains; stripped stonework, bar food, well kept Boddingtons, seats outside, good walks all around; children allowed for meals – also play area; in Werneth Low Country Park *(Lee Goulding)*

☆ **Lancaster** [Canal Side (parking in Aldcliffe Rd behind Royal Lancaster Infirmary, off A6); SD4862], *Water Witch*: Pitch-pine panelling, flagstones, bare masonry and rafters in simply furnished canalside pub with hearty bar food, waterside summer barbecues, and hot beverages as well as cheap wines and Tetleys, Thwaites and McEwans 70/-; games-room, juke box; run as a Yates Wine Lodge; children allowed in eating areas; service could be better, and it's really the location which earns its star *(Lee Goulding, Brian and Pauline Fullam, Caroline Fisher, Tony Pounder, Wayne Brindle, HRH, LYM)*

Lancaster [Green Lane (heading N on A6, last turn on right leaving speed restriction)] *Howe Ghyll*: Neat and spacious conversion of former mansion in most attractive grounds on edge of town, well kept Mitchells real ales, efficient quick-service lunchtime food counter, games in public bar; children in family-room – but it's the garden that has most attraction for them *(R P Taylor, J F Atherton, LYM)*; [Lower Church St] *Stonewell Tavern*: Comfortably modern atmosphere in genuinely old pub, airy and high-ceilinged at the front but snugger behind, with steps up to a dining area serving good value straightforward lunchtime food (not Sun); well kept Thwaites Bitter and Mild, good evening pop music; children in eating area *(Chris Fluck, LYM)*

Laneshaw Bridge [SD9240], *Emmott Arms*: Very friendly welcome, freshly cooked and nicely presented food from a varied menu *(Miss S Wild)*

Lea Town [SD4731], *Saddle*: One of the most popular pubs on the Fylde – deservedly *(Wayne Brindle)*

Littleborough [Halifax Rd (A58), just through rly arches; SD9316], *Red Lion*: Friendly, comfortable multi-roomed traditional pub with real fires, extensive range of ciders and well kept Wilsons and Websters, seats outside *(Dr Michael Clarke)*

☆ **Liverpool** [4 Hackins Hey (off Dale St); SJ4395], *Hole in Ye Wall*: Smallish Walkers pub, well restored, with several different areas in the pleasant panelled bar; friendly staff, beer unusually fed by gravity via pillars from upstairs cellar; side food servery popular at lunchtime with local businessmen; uncertain evening opening hours – may be closed by 7ish, always by 9 *(Jon Wainwright, Richard Sanders, John Roué)*

☆ **Liverpool** [67 Moorfields], *Lion*: Splendidly preserved Walkers pub with etched glass and serving-hatches in central bar, curious wallpaper, large mirrors, panelling and tilework in two of the rooms, fine domed structure behind, well kept beer, cheap value lunchtime bar food, well kept Bitter and Mild *(Jon Wainwright, Richard Sanders, Brian Greenwood)*

☆ **Liverpool** [Albert Dock Complex], *Pump House*: Despite preponderance of lagers and keg beers, notable for its ideal position by the water; stylish and interestingly laid out two-level conversion of listed dock building, good value food *(J A Jones, Jon Wainwright, Wayne Brindle)*

Liverpool [Regent Rd, Sandhills], *Atlantic*: Dock road pub, plain and clean décor, live folk music or jazz most nights; Boddingtons and Higsons on handpump *(Peter Corris)*; [Ranelagh St (opp Central Stn)] *Central Commercial*: Mahogany woodwork, sumptuous engraved glass, marble pillars, an elaborately moulded domed ceiling in Victorian pub with reasonably priced hot and cold buffet, well kept Ind Coope real ales, loud but good juke box *(Richard Sanders, LYM)*; [13 Rice St] *Cracke*: Entertaining students and eccentrics crowd several small uncarpeted rooms; well kept Boddingtons and Marstons, including Merrie Monk *(Jon Wainwright and others)*; [25 Matthew St – closed Sun] *Grapes*: Friendly central pub with well kept Higsons and Boddingtons on handpump, cheap lunchtime bar food, attractive unaltered décor *(Peter Corris)*; [Dale St] *Rigbys*: Nelson theme – he used this when it was a coaching-inn *(John Roué)*; [Wood St] *Swan*: A fine beer-drinker's pub *(Jon Wainwright)*

Longridge [Longridge Fell, off B6243 Longridge–Clitheroe above Ribchester – OS Sheet 103 reference 644391; SD6439], *New Drop*: Good bar meals and restaurant in welcoming pub with real fires *(J H M Broughton)*; [junction of B6243 to Preston leaving town – OS Sheet 103 reference 605365] *Old Oak*: Matthew Browns/Theakstons pub with good atmosphere, always friendly even when busy, open fires, well kept; good food including excellent chip butties and sandwiches *(J T C Heslop)*

Lydiate [Southport Rd; SD3604], *Scotch Piper*: Thatched pub with real fire, real ale, donkey and hens; claims to be oldest in Lancs *(A V Fontes)*

Lytham [SD3627], *County*: Marvellous cheap food in restaurant *(Ian Robinson)*; [Forest Dr] *Hole-in-One*: Comfortable Thwaites house close to golf course with golfing memorabilia, paintings and photographs; well kept Bitter on handpump *(Peter Corris)*

☆ **Manchester** [50 Great Bridgewater St (corner Lower Mosley St); SJ7796], *Britons Protection*: Fine tilework and solid woodwork in smallish rather plush front bar, attractive softly lit inner lounge with coal-effect gas fire, battle murals in passage leading to it; well kept Ind Coope Burton, Jennings and Tetleys, popular at lunchtime for its simple well prepared food, quiet evenings; handy for GMEX centre *(Caroline Fisher, Tony Pounder, Jon Wainwright, C J Dyall, Lee Goulding, Michael Cooke, BB)*

☆ **Manchester** [Shambles Sq (behind Arndale Centre, off Market St)], *Old Wellington*: Flagstones and gnarled oak timbers, well kept Bass and Stones on handpump, oak-panelled bar and small second-floor restaurant (useful in having sandwiches in the evening too); often packed lunchtime *(Wayne Brindle, Brian and Anna Marsden, Lee Goulding, Jon Wainwright, BB)*

Manchester [Albert Rd (off Wilmslow Rd, Didsbury)], *Albert*: Irish pub with clean traditional layout – bar, two cosy snugs; very friendly service, well kept Hydes beers, simple food including very hot hot-pot, collections of film-star photographs and caricatures, cigarette cards *(Lee Goulding, Michael Cooke)*; [Gt Ducie St] *Brewers Arms*: Boddingtons show pub, next to the brewery – naturally the beer's good, but so is the interesting bar food, in enormous helpings; very clean *(J A H Townsend)*; [Oldham St (about 200 yards from Piccadilly)] *Castle*: Very friendly traditional city-centre pub, lively at weekends *(Lee Goulding)*; [Cateaton St (nr cathedral and Arndale Centre)] *Chesters Pie & Ale House*: Recent Whitbreads recreation of Victorian alehouse, bare boards, stripped walls, beams with anti-spitting notices, Victoriana such as clay pipes, games, plumbing taps – good period feel in spite of piped pop music; seems run as a free house, with other beers like Marstons Pedigree and Thwaites as well as Whitbreads' own; pies and other food, reasonable prices, service unusually friendly for city centre, often fairly quiet *(Lee Goulding)*; [86 Portland St; SJ8398] *Circus*: Tiny character pub with two cosy panelled rooms, wall seating, minuscule bar counter with well kept cheapish Tetleys Bitter; so popular that they may shut the door when full; opens 8.30pm Sat and Sun *(Lee Goulding)*; [Kennedy St] *City Arms*: Very popular with business people at lunchtime for good food in lounge, quieter in evening; well kept Ind Coope Burton, Jennings and Tetleys *(Lee Goulding)*; [St Annes Sq] *Corbieres Wine Cavern*: Cellar bar popular with young people for its imaginative choice of music on juke box; well kept Marstons Pedigree on handpump, foreign bottled beers, decent wines *(Lee Goulding, Michael Cooke)*; [Windsor Crescent (A6), opp Salford Univ] *Crescent*: Basic décor of panelling and plaster in four-room pub with three serving-bars, old mangle piled high with old magazines, good pubby atmosphere (not studenty despite position); character landlord extending range of real ales, and runs mini beer festivals; piped laidback 1970s rock music *(Lee Goulding)*; [41 Hilton St (off Newton St, nr Piccadilly)] *Crown & Anchor*: Smartly renovated pub with comfortable red plush wall seats; well kept Chesters Best Mild, Timothy Taylors Landlord and Ram Tam and Whitbreads Castle Eden on handpump, popular lunchtime food *(Graham Gibson, Michael Cooke)*; [Oldham Rd] *Crown & Kettle*: Ornate if rather brightly refurbished high-ceilinged Victorian pub; panelling from R100 airship in smaller room, breakfast served from 10am, well kept Wilsons real ale, weekday lunchtime bar food *(LYM)*; [95 Cheetham Hill Rd (A665)] *Derby Brewery Arms*: Large two-roomed Holts brewery tap, reasonable bar food; children allowed lunchtime *(Richard Sanders)*; [Dutton St, Strangeways] *Dutton Arms*: Not exactly smart but interesting and friendly, ancient fireplace with brass blowlamps above it, stained-glass windows, particularly cheap Hydes beers *(Lee Goulding)*; [Collier St (off Greengate, Salford)] *Eagle*: Seems to have been untouched since the 1950s – absolutely no frills, with notably cheap well kept Holts *(Lee Goulding, Richard Sanders)*; [Scholes Lane, Prestwich] *Friendship*: Large, friendly Holts local, low prices, customers all ages, good Fri night organist *(Yvonne and Don Johnson)*; [Grafton St] *Grafton*: Good modern pub with friendly local atmosphere in both bars – escape from students in nearby pubs; exceptionally cheap Holts beer, pool *(Lee Goulding)*; [Portland St (nr Piccadilly)] *Grey Horse*: Very small pub popular for lunchtime food; well kept Hydes ales, some unusual malt whiskies, old Manchester photographs *(Lee Goulding)*; [47 Ducie St] *Jolly Angler*: Very small and friendly, tucked away behind works; warm coal fire, well kept Hydes ale, comfortable enough *(Michael Cooke, Richard Sanders, BB)*; [Bootle St (off Deansgate)] *Lord Abercrombie*: Recently refurbished central pub with good choice of well prepared bar food – very popular for office-worker lunches; Australian landlord *(Yvonne and Don Johnson)*; [set back off Hyde Rd, Gorton, nr Tan Yard Brown] *Lord Nelson*: Cottagey pub with cosy, dimly lit lounge and plainer back overspill; friendly welcome, Wilsons real ales and bar food *(Lee Goulding)*; [5 Royce Rd] *Mancunian*: Popular pub with quick service, wide variety of lunchtime bar food, loyal regulars *(Stephen Napper, John Povall)*; [Wilmslow Rd, Didsbury] *Manor House*: Amazingly friendly for a town pub; good lunchtime food *(SY)*; [Cross St] *Mr Thomas Chop House*: Refurbished under new management; well kept Thwaites Mild and Bitter, cheap bar food, good staff; can be crowded lunchtime and early evening *(Mike Suddards, John Gould)*; [Bottomley Side, Blackley – best reached on foot from Delauneys Rd entrance of ICI Organics] *Old House At Home*: Surprisingly cottagey pub sandwiched between North Manchester Hospital and ICI; friendly, with superbly kept Wilsons ale *(Lee Goulding, Michael Craig)*; [Bloom St (by Charlton St National Express Coach Stn)] *Paddys Goose*: Smart city pub with superb tilework and ornate glass in façade, comfortable inside with one or two cosy alcoves; lunchtime food, well kept ales including Websters Choice and Wilsons *(Lee Goulding)*; [Wilmslow Rd, Withington] *Red Lion*: Busy Marstons pub with bowling-green – landlord is a bowls champion; cosy front bar popular with locals and students *(Lee Goulding)*; [Sackville St] *Rembrandt*: Entertaining and friendly, helpful management, good value food, Lees real ale; worth knowing for its comfortably refurbished but attractively priced bedrooms – and the breakfasts are good *(A J Ritson)*; [Lloyd St (off N side of Albert Sq by Square Albert pub)] *Sir Ralph Abercrombie*: Pleasant Whitbreads pub with good lunchtime food, Chesters Mild and Best on handpump, conscientious staff; popular with men from the next-door police station *(Brian and Anna Marsden, Lee Goulding)*; [35 Swan St; SJ8284] *Smithfield Tavern*: Terrific atmosphere on live music evenings – pub well laid out for these and gets packed at weekends when the music is among the best in town; at other times a quiet local, though distinguished by well kept Boddingtons and charming young landlady; good juke box, pool on separate little railed-off dais *(Michael Cooke, Lee Goulding, R A Hutson, BB)*; [Back Hope St, Higher Broughton; just off Bury New Rd (A56)] *Star*: Cosy character local in timeless cobbled-street location; tiny bar with TV and good Robinsons including Old Tom, bigger lounge with brass horns, sword, piano, games-room with pool, good value bar snacks; regular folk music, otherwise usually very quiet – a place like this could only be in Salford *(Lee Goulding)*; [682 Wilmslow Rd] *Station*: Small basic pub with excellent welcome and beer *(Dr and Mrs A K Clarke)*; [Errwood Rd, Burnage] *Sun in September*: Useful for the area *(Lee Goulding)*; [525 Ashton Old Rd] *Travellers Call*: Unusually good for the area – friendly and comfortable with well kept Boddingtons, Marstons Pedigree and Tetleys, popular food *(Lee Goulding)*; [Kirk St, Gorton] *Vale Cottage*: Three cosy rooms in an almost countrified pub, full of interesting bits and pieces such as a seat made from a barrel and an antique wall telephone; genuine, friendly welcome, well kept Wilsons and big helpings of reasonably priced bar meals; nice tree-lined terrace *(Lee Goulding)*; [Kennedy St] *Vine*: Young person's pub with bright but interesting décor and features, John Smiths real ale, good-looking cellar food bar *(Lee Goulding)*

☆ **Marple** [Ridge End (off A626 via Church Lane, following The Ridge signposts – OS Sheet 109 reference 965867); SJ9588], *Romper*: Comfortably furnished food pub with softly lit knocked-through oak-beamed rooms, well kept Ruddles County and Timothy Taylors Landlord, helpful staff, wide choice of food; superb setting alone on the steep side of the Goyt Valley; can get packed at weekends – get there early for a table; children welcome *(David Waterhouse, John Gould, Lee Goulding, LYM)*

Marple [130 Church Lane (by canal, Bridge 2 – OS Sheet 109 reference 960884)], *Ring o' Bells*: Big friendly pub with excellent value food, very efficiently served, and well kept Robinsons; tables in small garden with summer barbecues overlooking water – but piped music even out here; children welcome; boat trips can be arranged here (it takes 16 locks to raise the Macclesfield Canal 210ft through Marple) *(Dr and Mrs C D E Morris, John Gould)*

Marple Bridge [Ley Lane; SJ9689], *Hare & Hounds*: Good country-pub atmosphere with open fire, shining brasses and beautiful setting; welcoming owner, super varied bar snacks *(Mrs M Cox)*; [48 Town St] *Royal Scot*: Pleasantly unsmoky pub with attentive staff, piped music in lounge though not in other two bars, well kept real ale and good toasted sandwiches *(Lorraine Shaugnessy)*

Mawdesley [Croston–Eccleston rd, N of village; SD4915], *Robin Hood*: Two-room pub with friendly atmosphere, well kept Whitbreads Castle Eden and a guest beer such as Hartleys XB on handpump, good value food in bar and upstairs restaurant, where the steaks are popular; children allowed until 8.30 *(P Corris)*

Melling [Prescot Rd; note that this is the one in Merseyside, nr Kirkby, at SD3800], *Hen & Chickens*: Friendly pub with good choice of food including vegetarian dishes, well kept Tetleys ales *(J A Harrison)*

Melling [this is the other one – in Lancs, on A683 Lancaster–Kirkby Lonsdale at

SD6071], *Melling Hall*: Comfortable saloon bar, cosy but not precious, with well kept real ales such as Boddingtons, Hartleys and Moorhouses; good home-cooked bar food including exceptional pizzas, obliging service, restaurant worth knowing, attractive situation; bedrooms good too *(Derek and Sylvia Stephenson, R A Harkness)*

Melling Mount [SD4001], *Pear Tree*: Friendly pub refurbished tastefully with Victorian pictures, etc.; good bar snacks, Greenalls on handpump *(T L Mathias)*

☆ **Mellor** [Longhurst Lane; this is the Mellor near Marple, S of Manchester at SJ9888], *Devonshire Arms*: Small, light and comfortable bar with old photographs of pub and lots of antiques, nice little second room, fires in both; friendly and efficient service, well kept Robinsons, and interesting attractively priced food; charming village *(John Derbyshire, Geoff Wilson, J Walsh)*

Mellor [Shiloh Rd – same village], *Moorfield Arms*: Freshly sandblasted former chapel, with beams, stonework and original panelling; good hill views, well kept Boddingtons, decent wine, friendly staff, coal fire, filling food – decorations could be more tasteful, and piped music less penetrating *(John Gould)*

Mellor [this is the other one, up near Blackburn; SD6530], *Millstone*: Plush hotel with recently refurbished bars, in nice village *(Wayne Brindle)*

Middleton [Long St; SD8606], *Old Boars Head*: Partly twelfth-century black and white timbered building of enormous potential, though not seen by editorial team since a couple of years ago, when it had cheap well kept Lees ales but was only partly in use, with basic furnishings *(Progress reports please)*

Milnrow [Newhey Rd (¼ mile from M62 junction 21); SD9212], *Slip*: Cosy three-roomed pub with friendly welcome; well kept Sam Smiths, good bar food *(Dr Michael Clarke)*

Moreton [Frankby Rd, Newton (A553 Birkenhead–West Kirby); SJ2589], *Ridger*: Opened a few years ago – good value for lunch, excellent décor, nice atmosphere *(Peter Corris)*

Mossley [Manchester Rd (A635 N); SD9802], *Roaches Lock*: Very well kept pub by Huddersfield Canal, interesting inside with bare stone walls, fan, hunting-horns and tropical fish; four real ales, food including good value three-course Sun lunch, swift service, good views of canal from garden *(Lee Goulding)*

Much Hoole [Liverpool Rd (A59); SD4723], *Black Bull*: Well kept Greenalls on handpump in spacious three-room pub with reasonably priced varied food including children's helpings; horsy feel, with lots of prints and brasses *(Lee Goulding)*

Nether Burrow [SD6275], *Highwayman*: Comfortably plush and spacious bar with well kept Tetleys, Theakstons and Youngers

Scotch, usual range of bar food in generous helpings, restaurant, welcoming service, French windows to terrace with swing and climbing-frame beyond; children in eating area and restaurant *(Lee Goulding, LYM)*

Newton [the one on A583 Kirkham–Preston in Lancs, at SD4431], *Highgate*: Several spacious and well furnished rooms in recently refurbished roadside pub; well kept Tetleys *(Wayne Brindle)*

Norden [SD8514], *Edgerton Arms*: Cosy, quiet pub with separate restaurant, said to be haunted *(Ian Briggs)*

Oldham [Dunham St, Waterhead (off A62); SD9305], *Gardeners Arms*: Remarkable location by stream with ducks, surrounded by hulking mill buildings; friendly public bar full of brass platters and so forth and trophies won by pool teams; well kept Robinsons real ales including Old Tom at times *(Lee Goulding)*

☆ **nr Oldham** [Grains Bar, junction A672/ B6197; SD9608], *Bulls Head*: Gleaming brass and copper in snug two-room moorland pub with cheap bar food, well kept Bass and Cask Bitter and Mild on handpump, and nostalgic singalongs to theatre organ played with gusto by Mr Wilson the landlord on Weds, Fri, Sat and Sun evenings; good views, particularly from war memorial a few yards away *(Lee Goulding, LYM)*

☆ **Osbaldeston** [Whalley Rd; SD6431], *Bay Horse*: Unpretentious but cosy and spruce, well kept Thwaites, notably good home-made food including first-class soup, huge attractively filled baps and lots of daily specials; friendly and efficient service *(K A Skilling, Eileen Broadbent)*

Oswaldtwistle [Haslingden Rd, well outside; SD7327], *Coach & Horses*: High on the moors, very welcoming on a cold night, with a good atmosphere and well kept Tetleys *(Wayne Brindle)*; [Union Rd] *Golden Cross*: Good lively atmosphere, with well kept Boddingtons; former almshouses, became an inn in 1814; children's play area behind *(Len Beattie)*

Parbold [Alder Lane; SD4911], *Stocks*: Clean and attractive, with good food, efficient service, well kept ales *(Philip and Carol Seddon, John Roué)*; [A5209] *Wiggin Tree*: Now a Whitbreads 'Brewers Fayre' pub with decent beers and service, good value (rather than cheap) food and the advantage of a magnificent view *(Comus Elliott, Wayne Brindle)*

Pendleton [SD7539], *Swan With Two Necks*: Friendly welcome in spotless village pub prettily placed below Pendle Hill, good value homely food, well kept ale *(LYM)*

Pleasington [Victoria Rd – OS Sheet 103 reference 642266; SD6426], *Butlers Arms*: Comfortably modernised village pub with its own bowling-green, in lovely quiet village; well kept Matthew Browns, tasty snacks (though not always available); particularly nice in summer *(Wayne Brindle)*

Port Sunlight [SJ3485], *Olde Bridge*: Interesting combination of mock-Tudor exterior, quasi-Victorian inside, and mainly American memorabilia including prints of US sailing ships – even some American food *(John Roué)*

Preesall [Park Lane; SD3647], *Saracens Head*: Friendly, cheery pub with good Thwaites Bitter, straightforward food; bedrooms *(John Atherton, Dave Bentley, Robin Parker)*

Preston [Friargate (by Ringway); SD5530], *Old Black Bull*: Busy mock-Tudor town pub with small vault and big L-shaped lounge with bulls' horns hanging from ceiling; well kept cheapish Boddingtons *(Lee Goulding)*; [London Rd] *Shaws Arms*: Excellent fairly plush games-room with big picture windows overlooking bridge over River Ribble *(Wayne Brindle)*; [Garden St] *Winckley*: Newish pub with wide range of food, gets crowded at lunchtime as this town isn't overstocked with good pubs *(R H Sawyer)*

Rawtenstall [Church St, Newchurch; SD8222], *Boars Head*: Friendly hilltop local with fine Pennine views, full of darts trophies, Bass Special *(Jon Wainwright)*; [371 Bury Old Rd (A56 towards Edenfield – OS Sheet 103 reference 803217)] *Whitchaff*: Well renovated, with attractive exposed eighteenth-century stonework in warm and comfortable open-plan bar; friendly welcome, tasty bar food, well kept Tetleys and Websters, flame-effect gas fire *(Wayne Brindle, Len Beattie)*

Ribchester [Main St (B6245); SD6435], *Black Bull*: Good atmosphere, well kept Thwaites ales, good cider *(Wayne Brindle)*; [outside village] *Halls Arms*: Welcoming, cottage-like atmosphere, well kept Whitbreads, good bar food *(Wayne Brindle)*; [Dinckley (off B6245 before Ribble bridge); SD6835] *Tanners*: Pleasant country pub in isolated spot outside village – path beside pub takes you to a lovely reach of the River Ribble; well kept Matthew Browns ales *(Wayne Brindle)*; [Church St (sharp turn off B6245 at Black Bull)] *White Bull*: Worth noting for its unique 1900-year-old Tuscan door pillars – the second-oldest component of any British pub we know *(LYM)*

Riley Green [A675; SD6225], *Royal Oak*: Good atmosphere, well kept Thwaites ales, good cider; warm and cosy, with several open fires; fifteenth-century, some associations with James I *(Wayne Brindle)*

Roby Mill [not far from M6 junction 26 – off A577 at Up Holland; SD5107], *Fox*: Nicely placed traditional pub, wide range of good food in bar and adjacent Hungry Fox restaurant *(G T Kendal)*

Rochdale [470 Bury Rd (A6222); SD8913], *Cemetery*: Excellent traditional four-room pub with over half a dozen real ales and interesting bottled beers from many countries; good bare-boarded parlour, two comfortable lounges, remarkable tree mural decorating stairs from back car park *(Lee Goulding)*

☆ nr **Rochdale** [3 miles from M62 junction 20 – on A671 Oldham Rd, just S of where it underpasses M62; SD8809], *Yew Tree*: Stripped stone walls give the cosy feel of a moorland pub, without having to clamber up some mountainside to get there; well kept Sam Smiths, relaxed country atmosphere, good value food, Pullman railway carriage dining-room *(Wayne Brindle, Lee Goulding, LYM)*

nr **Rochdale** [Cheesden, Ashworth Moor; A680 – OS Sheet 109 reference 831161], *Owd Betts*: Warm and cosy low-beamed moorland pub, open fires, brass and other objects on stripped stone walls, reasonably priced home-cooked food; tends to get snowed in in winter *(Carol and Richard Glover, Wayne Brindle)*

Romiley [Stockport Rd; SJ9390], *Duke of York*: Cheap John Smiths on handpump in older building with lots of woodwork, some brasses, creaky boards; welcoming landlord, a few character regulars, big helpings of good food in upstairs restaurant *(Simon Turner, Caroline Bailey)*

☆ **Simonstone** [Trapp Lane, off School Lane towards Sabden – OS Sheet 103 reference 776356; SD7734], *Higher Trapp*: Lovely views from bar overlooking terrace and lawns beyond, quiet and refined, bamboo chairs and ceiling-fans, well kept Thwaites Bitter; bar food evenings only ; bedrooms *(Len Beattie)*

Slaidburn [Woodhouse Lane; SD7152], *Parrock Head Farm*: Not a pub, but worth knowing as an attractively furnished farmhouse alternative in 200 acres, relaxing atmosphere, friendly staff, excellent food from interesting menu including fine English cheese choice, lovely seafood au gratin and good selection of wines ; comfortable bedrooms *(RCR)*

Slyne [SD4866], *Slyne Lodge*: Nice pub atmosphere, good range of well kept beer; bedrooms marvellous value, with small kitchen attached *(Mrs Graham)*

Stalybridge [Mottram Rd; SJ9698], *Hare & Hounds*: Tastefully redeveloped Bass house, well kept beer, good atmosphere *(Jon Wainwright)*

☆ **Stockport** [Market Pl; SJ8991], *Bakers Vaults*: Cosy old-fashioned pub with good welcome and excellent food using fresh produce, including open sandwiches, salads and monthly four-course banquet; well kept Robinsons Mild and Bitter, pleasant service, live music three nights a week *(Brian and Anna Marsden, Roy Fidler)*

☆ **Stockport** [533 Didsbury Rd, Heaton Mersey – off A5145], *Griffin*: Four simply furnished and unimproved Victorian rooms open off central servery with largely original curved-glass gantry, cheap well kept Holts real ales, thriving local atmosphere – decidedly a drinker's (and talker's) pub; seats outside

(C F Walling, Richard Sanders, Brian and Anna Marsden, Lee Goulding, John Gould, BB)

Stockport [Millgate], *Arden Arms*: Quaint, amazingly clean and tidy little pub; quiet, with very polite licensee and well kept beer *(Dr and Mrs A K Clarke)*; [Heaton Moor Rd] *Elizabethan*: Former gentlemen's club, now a spacious pub with good well priced home-made food and well run bar, improved with out losing its atmosphere; large garden *(John Gould)*; [Wellington St, off Wellington Rd S (A6)] *Little Jack Horners*: Excellently priced bar meals in small pub on several levels, nice friendly service, Wilsons real ale; restaurant *(Paul Corbett, Patrick Godfrey)*; [82 Heaton Moor Rd, Heaton Moor] *Plough*: Good plentiful home-cooked food and fine well kept ale on handpump, good village-local atmosphere *(John C Gould)*; [Wellington Rd, Heaton Chapel] *Rudyard*: Hotel rebuilt from ground upwards, two spacious drinking areas, good choice of plentiful food at reasonable prices, keg beer; great for children; bedrooms good value *(J C Gould)*; [Hillgate] *Star & Garter*: Good weekday lunchtime bar food, well kept Robinsons ales, games room *(David Waterhouse)*; [Shaw Heath] *Swan*: Friendly and clean, with freshly made home-cooked food, good service, beer, wines and coffee *(H R Edwards)*; [Underbank] *White Lion*: Good clean pub with good food and service – opens early for coffee, hot tea-cakes and so forth, tends to fill quickly at lunchtime *(H R Edwards)*

Thornton [Victoria Rd; SD3342], *Bay Horse*: Friendly pub with tasty well prepared and reasonably priced food served with a smile; well kept Tetleys *(Dave Bentley, Robin Parker)*

Thornton Hough [SJ3081], *Cheshire Cat*: Modern pub in grounds of country-house hotel, comfortable seating, discreet piped music, sedate atmosphere; smartly dressed and helpful staff, tempting bar food well presented *(E G Parish)*

Timperley [SJ7988], *Hare & Hounds*: Quite atmospheric for a suburban pub, with Marstons ales and frequent live music; vigorously promotes its restaurant *(G T Jones)*

Tockholes [SD6623], *Rock*: Comfortable atmosphere and plush furnishings with plenty of brass, friendly licensee, substantial bar food, well kept Thwaites Bitter *(Len Beattie)*

Treales [SD4333], *Derby Arms*: Pleasant and comfortable Brewers Fayre pub *(Simon Bates)*

Tyldesley [Elliott St; SD6802], *Mort Arms*: Real 'Rovers Return'-style pub popular with older locals, especially in lounge; rich in accents and character with crowds huddled around TV for Sat horseraces; friendly landlord, good value Holts beer *(Jon Wainwright)*

☆ **Uppermill** [Runninghill Gate, nr Dick Hill; SD9905], *Church*: Well kept real ales and bar food in partly stripped-stone old pub on steep moorland slope by isolated church,

annual gurning championship, piped classical music *(Jon Wainwright, LYM)*

Waddington [SD7243], *Higher Buck*: Well appointed and welcoming, with good snacks, great cider, nice location in beautiful village *(Wayne Brindle)*; *Lower Buck*: Well kept cheap Thwaites Bitter and cider in small, basic village pub with interesting old-fashioned layout *(Wayne Brindle, BB)*

nr **Waddington** [OS Sheet 103 reference 719467], *Moorcock*: Large hotel/pub with magnificent views and moorland surroundings; quiet restaurant, well kept beer; bedrooms *(Wayne Brindle; more reports on decorative order please)*

Walshaw [Hall St; SD7711], *White Horse*: Pleasant, tidy Thwaites pub in quiet village with friendly customers *(Jon Wainwright)*

Waterloo [Bath Rd; SJ3298], *Victoria*: Popular but relaxing Walkers local, good value lunchtime food *(Peter Corris, Jon Wainwright)*

Weeton [B5260; SD3834], *Eagle & Child*: Spacious well kept village local *(Simon Bates, Jon Wainwright)*

Weir [178 Burnley Rd (A671 Bacup–Burnley); SD8625], *Weir*: Well kept Thwaites Bitter and especially Mild on handpump, large lounge and tap-room with darts, TV and trivia machine, limited choice of reasonably priced food, roadside tables; friendly licensee *(C Dempsey)*

West Bradford [SD7444], *Three Millstones*: Small cosy cottagey pub with well kept Matthew Browns, particularly good value food, friendly licensee *(Wayne Brindle)*

☆ **Westhoughton** [590–592 Chorley Rd – nr M61 junction 6; SD6505], *Brinsop Arms*: Smartly decorated and considerably extended pub – one room with sofas and newspapers, another simpler decorated with old documents, a more spacious room with occasional bands; wide choice of bar food, lots of real ales *(Jon Wainwright, Lee Goulding)*

☆ **Wharles** [Church Rd – OS Sheet 102 reference 448356; SD4435], *Eagle & Child*: Clean and homely thatched pub in quiet spot (though surrounded by forest of radio masts), notable for its well kept Boddingtons and usually three guest beers such as Goose Eye, Moorhouses, Sam Smiths, Timothy Taylors or Theakstons; friendly landlord, two nice coal fires, no food; surprisingly spacious inside, window seats and carved settle *(John Atherton, Jon Wainwright, Simon Bates)*

Wheelton [SD6021], *Top Lock*: Very friendly, renovated old pub on canal bank, decorated with narrowboat theme; rather limited though generously served bar food; popular with locals in evening *(Col G D Stafford)*

Whiston [Mill Lane; SJ4792], *Manor*: Tastefully restored manor farm with varied and well prepared lunches and well kept Burtonwood beers; good restaurant *(Herbert J Sullivan)*

unpretentious Beehive there, with its remarkable living inn-sign (the 'newcomer' is in fact Mr Bull's son – he's retired now, but his son is keeping up the tradition for doing the ploughman's which Mr Bull virtually invented); the comfortable Marquess of Exeter at Lyddington also has new licensees (a suggestion that it's getting more foody), as does the Bull & Swan at Stamford (though their Portuguese predecessors are a hard act to follow, the new people have already been earning praise from readers) and the Mill on the Soar at Sutton in the Elms (no major changes at this popular and successful conversion). The landlord who took over the friendly old Kings Arms at Wing brings it back into these pages after an absence. Completely new entries this year include the friendly King William in the old estate village of Scaftworth (a big garden and good food, particularly pies and game), the Cross Keys at Upton (the young licensee, born and brought up at the oldest coaching-inn in Newark, practised as a chartered surveyor before taking over this engagingly rambling pub a few years ago – a good range of beers and interesting food), the Black Horse just off the motorway at Walcote (a good range of beers here too, but the real surprise is the good food – all Thai) and the comfortable and very popular Wheatsheaf at Woodhouse Eaves. Among older favourites, we've granted a star to the highly traditional Cap & Stocking at Kegworth, where the cautious changes made by the newish licensees have thoroughly proved their worth now. The best pub in the region still remains the Crown at Old Dalby, though the grand old George of Stamford is hard to beat for interest, or on a summer's day when they're barbecuing in its attractive courtyard, and a great many other pubs in these three counties have particular individual merits worth travelling quite a long way to uncover. If one had to characterise the differences between the three counties' pubs in broad terms, one would probably conclude that Nottinghamshire scored for uncompromisingly good value (with some startlingly low prices to be found here and there), while Leicestershire and Lincolnshire go for civilised comfort and good food – but of course, as always, it's the exceptions that prove the rule! In the Lucky Dip section at the end of the chapter, pubs to focus on particularly include the Tally Ho at Aswarby, Leagate at Coningsby, reopened Cotes Mill at Cotes, Fox & Hounds at Exton, Woodlark at Lambley, Neville Arms at Medbourne, Nickerson Arms at Rothwell, Black Horse at Sheepy Magna, Saracens Head in Southwell, Three Horseshoes at Stoke Golding, Hercules at Sutton Cheney, White Hart at Tetford and Finches Arms at Upper Hambleton.

BICKER (Lincs)   TF2237 Map 8

Red Lion

A52 NE of Donington

The comfortably modernised, clean red-carpeted lounge of this seventeenth-century pub has masses of china hanging from its bowed black beams, guns, Youngers advertising mirrors and a sporran on stripped stone or rough-cast cream walls, and a very realistic log-effect gas fire in its huge fireplace. They serve good value food, and well kept Ind Coope and Burton on handpump; fruit machine and maybe piped radio. There are white tables on a terrace and small tree-shaded lawn; it's very flat roundabout, and nearby you can in some places still find the remains of the Roman dykes that circled nearly ten square miles of a former sea inlet here. A real refuge for the area. *(Recommended by A V Lewis; more reports please)*

Free house   Real ale   Meals and snacks   Open 11–3, 6–11 all year

Prices of main dishes usually include vegetables or a side salad.

BRAUNSTON (Leics)   SK8306 Map 4
Old Plough ⊗

Village signposted off A606 in Oakham

The good variety of wholesome bar food in this slate-roofed stone-built village house includes filled rolls (from £1.25), ploughman's (£2.75), a large steak sandwich (£3.95), daily specials like chicken Kiev (£6.95), and Scotch salmon or fresh crab salad in season, and twenty-ounce T-bone steak (£8.95). There's quite a contrast between the sturdily traditional black-beamed lounge bar, with its leatherette seats around heavy cast-iron-framed tables and brass ornaments on the mantelpiece, and the modern conservatory dining-room at the back. This has dainty cane furniture, cream-painted brickwork and frilled pastel curtains swagged back. Well kept John Smiths on handpump; cheerful service. The carpeted public bar has a fruit machine and winter darts; maybe piped pop music. There are picnic-table sets among fruit trees on a small sheltered back lawn; they play boules in summer. The inn-sign is of a ploughman on night shift. *(Recommended by Peter L Astbury; more reports please)*

John Smiths (Courage)   Licensees John and Lindsey Berry   Real ale   Meals and snacks Restaurant tel Oakham (0572) 2714   Children in restaurant   Open 11–2.30, 6–11 all year; closed evenings of 25 Dec, 26 Dec, 1 Jan

BURROUGH ON THE HILL (Leics)   SK7510 Map 7
Stag & Hounds

Village signposted from B6047 in Twyford, 6 miles S of Melton Mowbray

In the last edition we described this village pub as own brew; to all intents and purposes it still is – though there are new licensees, Barry Parish, the former owner, still owns the brewery (probably Britain's smallest) across the road, and supplies its extraordinary range of own-brew beers: Parish Bitter, Mild, the stronger Poachers Ale, and Baz's Bonce Blower, which is the strongest real ale kept on handpump anywhere in the country; in addition there's a weekly guest beer, such as Sam Smiths OB and Vaux Samson or Lorimers Scotch. The new licensee is a chef, so, as you'd expect, the range of bar food has been extended, now including sandwiches (from 65p), soup (85p), smoked mackerel in a Stilton sauce (£1.15), ploughman's (£1.95), beef in one of the Parish ales (£3.25), local Rutland trout (£5.49), and the landlord's special dish, duck in port and redcurrant sauce (£5.95); the three-course Sunday lunch is excellent value at £3.50. They still have the inclusive three-course dinner or cold buffet in the restaurant for groups; this includes a brewery tour and as much beer as you want all evening – £11.50, Monday–Thursday, minimum ten people with a week's notice. As we were going to press extensive refurbishment and redecoration was under way in the bar, the car park was being enlarged and a children's play area was being installed in the garden. Close to *Good Walks Guide* Walk 112. *(Recommended by Rob and Gill Weeks, David Fisher, Tim and Lynne Crawford, Stewart Argyle, Michael Bolsover, Richard Sanders)*

Free house   Licensees Peter and Sue Bishop   Real ale   Meals and snacks (evenings) Restaurant tel Somerby (066 477) 375   Well behaved children welcome until 8.30 Open 7pm–11, and 12–3 Fri, all day Sat

DRAKEHOLES (Notts)   SK7090 Map 7
Griff Inn

Village signposted from A631 in Everton, between Bawtry and Gainsborough

Under new licensees, bar food in this civilised and well kept pub includes soup (75p), sandwiches (from £1.25), ploughman's (£1.95), lasagne (£2), roast beef or steak and kidney pie (£2.90, lunchtime only), scampi (£3.75), steak (£4.10), seafood platter (£4.25), as well as a lunchtime carvery on weekdays and Sundays; puddings (£1.25). The well kept lounge bar has small grey or dusky pink plush seats around its neat tables, and little landscape prints on the silky-papered walls; Tetleys and Whitbreads on handpump. Besides the main restaurant, a continental-style summer restaurant communicates through an arch with a functions room, and there's a cosy cocktail bar. Bedrooms, planned under the former licensees the Griffiths, have recently become available. The neatly landscaped gardens have tables which look out over the flat valley of the River Idle and a basin of the old Chesterfield Canal. (*Recommended by Norman G W Edwardes, Frank Williams, ILP; more reports on the new regime please*)

Free house   Licensee Michael Edmanson   Meals and snacks   Restaurant (not Sun evening) tel Retford (0777) 817206   Children welcome   Open 12–2, 7–11 all year; closed Mon Bedrooms (prices unavailable at time of going to press)

DYKE (Lincs)   TF1022   Map 8
Wishing Well ⊗

21 Main Street; village signposted off A15 N of Bourne

Home-cooked bar food in this friendly village inn includes toasted sandwiches (£1.25), ploughman's with Cheddar or Stilton (£1.50), fish (£2.15), cottage pie (£1.95), seafood platter, scampi, home-made lasagne or steak and kidney pie (£2.75), and a reasonably priced three-course Sunday lunch (£4.99). There are green plush button-back low settles and wheel-back chairs around nice wooden tables, with dark stone walls, heavy dark beams, sparkling horsebrasses and twinkling candles; well kept Adnams, Greene King IPA and Abbot and Marstons Pedigree on handpump. The quite separate public bar, smaller and plainer, has sensibly placed darts, pool, dominoes, fruit machine, space game and juke box. The eponymous wishing well shares the dining end of the long, rambling room with a massive open fireplace. (*Recommended by Dr A V Lewis, S A and P J Barrett, D Stephenson, Nick Dowson, Alison Hayward*)

Free house   Licensee G R Jones   Real ale   Meals and snacks (not Sun) Restaurant   Children welcome   Open 10.30–2, 6.30–11 all year; closed 25 Dec Bedrooms tel Bourne (0778) 422970; £15B/£19.50B

EAST LANGTON (Leics)   SP7292   Map 4
Bell ⊗

The Langtons signposted from A6 N of Market Harborough; East Langton signposted from B6047

More of a bistro than a pub, this stylish and civilised place is kept in our pages by readers' consistent praise for its food; the style is British New Cooking, with starters like whitebait (£1.50) or moules marinière (£2.25), and main dishes such as swordfish steak (£4.95) and plaice (£5); they also do a ploughman's (£1.75) and the best value is Sunday lunch (£8.50); tables can be booked. The most pubby part, still popular with diners, has stripped oak tables and brown banquettes against bare stone walls, below pink beams in a white ceiling; on a weekday it's a quiet and peaceful place for a drink and a chat. Manns and Websters Yorkshire on handpump, kept under light blanket pressure, maybe unobtrusive piped jazz or classical music. The attractive village is set in peaceful countryside. (*Recommended by R J Haerdi, Mel Bodfish, Patrick Freeman, R P Hastings*)

Manns (Watneys)   Licensee Pascal Trystram   Meals (not Sun evening or Mon) and snacks (not Mon)   Restaurant tel East Langton (085 884) 567   Children welcome   Open 12–3, 6.30–11 all year; closed Sun evening and Mon

---

Places with gardens or terraces usually let children sit there – we note in the text the very very few exceptions that don't.

EMPINGHAM (Leics)   SK9408   Map 4

White Horse ⊗ 🛏

Main Street; A606 Stamford–Oakham

On the edge of Rutland Water (Europe's largest man-made lake, with good water-sports facilities), this is a simple but stylishly comfortable inn. The modernised open-plan lounge bar has russet plush wall seats, stools and armchairs with little silver scatter-cushions around its dark tables, and a big log fire below an unusual free-standing chimney-funnel. The cream walls are decorated with reproduction sporting prints and prints of local scenery or of farm tools, and old Rutland maps. Home-made bar food includes soup (95p), pâtés (£1.75), ploughman's with a good choice of cheese including local Stilton (£2.75), vegetarian burgers or vegetarian chilli con carne (£3.95), kedgeree or Grimsby cod (£4.20), stir-fried chicken or their award-winning steak and kidney pie (£4.45), salads (from £4.50), and pork kebabs or lamb chops (£4.75); puddings such as gooseberry and marshmallow pie or a genuine trifle (£1.35); some of the ingredients come from the family farm. They serve coffee and croissants from 8am (£1.25) and cream teas (£1.50). Friendly, efficient service; well kept John Smiths on handpump; fruit machine and piped music. There are rustic seats and tables in front, among urns filled with marigolds; the best bedrooms are those in the attractively converted stableblock behind – away from any noise from the main road. (*Recommended by Stanley and Eileen Johnson, KC, D McD Wilson, M J Steward, Gordon Theaker, Mrs Graham, Wilf Plater-Shellard*)

John Smiths (Courage)   Licensees Robert and Andrew Reid   Real ale   Meals and snacks Restaurant   Children welcome   Open 11–2.30, 6–11 all year   Bedrooms tel Empingham (078 086) 221/251; £19.50(£26.50B)/£29.50(£37.50B); closed exc for residents evening 25 Dec and 26 Dec

GLOOSTON (Leics)   SP7595   Map 4

Old Barn ★ ⊗ 🛏

From B6047 in Tur Langton follow Hallaton signpost, then fork left following Glooston signpost

Since becoming a main entry last year, this attractively restored sixteenth-century pub has found an enthusiastic following, with the bedrooms (new last year) coming in for particular praise. The ever-increasing range of well kept real ales on handpump is another plus-point this year; they now serve Adnams Extra and Broadside, Badger Best and Tanglefoot, Batemans, Flowers Original, Hook Norton Old Hookey, Marstons Pedigree, Theakstons Best and Old Peculier, and Wadworths 6X and Old Timer. There's an abrupt change of levels between the stylishly simple front dining-room, with its attendant bar, and the much lower back bar; the servery is between, and it's fairly nerve-racking watching the charming bar staff negotiating the steep steps involved, a hair's breadth below a hostile beam. This back cellar bar has stripped kitchen tables and country chairs on its green Turkey carpet, an open fire, pewter plates on a beam, Players cricketer cigarette cards, and four curved steps up to a little platform alcove with easy chairs and attractive country prints. The lighting is excellent – soft, yet perfectly clear – and the atmosphere relaxed and civilised. Bar food, all freshly made from fresh ingredients, includes sandwiches (90p), ploughman's (£1.85), beef, tomato and prawn pie (£3.25), chilli con carne, pasta provençale or cream and garlic mushroom pie (£3.95), gammon, pizza or ham hock with onion salad and parsley sauce (£4.25)

Post Office address codings confusingly give the impression that some pubs are in the Midlands when they're really in the Derbyshire, Leicestershire or Shropshire areas that we list them under.

and steak (£5.50); piped music. There are a few old-fashioned teak seats in front, with picnic-table sets by roses under the trees behind. *(Recommended by Roger Broadie, Dr John Innes, Mr and Mrs Jocelyn Hill, Dr A V Lewis, Rob and Gill Weeks, David Surridge, Douglas Jarvis, Ted George, Miss E K Cloud)*

Free house   Licensees C D and S J Edmondson-Jones and S P Sturge   Real ale   Meals and snacks (not Sun evening)   Restaurant (not Sun evening)   Well behaved children welcome   Open 12–2.30, 7–11 all year; closed Sun evening (exc for residents)   Bedrooms tel East Langton (085 884) 215; £29.50B/£39.50B

GRANTHAM (Lincs)   SK9135 Map 8

Angel & Royal ⊗ ⇔

High Street

The carving on the stone façade (still just visible despite the effects of pollution) includes the heads of King Edward III and his queen, to honour their visit over six hundred years ago, when this was a Commandery and Hospice of the Knights Templar; and it had already been welcoming visitors for well over a century before that. On the left of the coach entry, the plush hotel bar has an elegantly restored and historically atmospheric oriel window jutting out over the road. Opposite is the popular main bar, high-beamed, with tapestry hangings and a massive inglenook fireplace where whole pigs, venison or barons of beef are spit-roasted once a month or so in winter – details of timings from the inn. Bar food under the new licensees includes sandwiches, mushroom and Stilton fritters (£1.50), Lincolnshire chine or chicken in a lightly curried mayonnaise with banana and pineapple (£2.50), plaice (£2.75), home-made steak and kidney pie (£3.25), salad (£4.35), smoked Scotch salmon (£5.25) and aubergine and mushroom lasagne (£5.95); well kept Adnams, Bass and Greene King Abbot on handpump in the right-hand bar; they mix non-alcoholic and children's cocktails, and serve morning coffee and afternoon teas. *(Recommended by Rob and Gill Weeks, E J and J W Cutting, Ian Phillips; more reports on the new regime please)*

Free house (THF)   Licensee David Dain   Real ale   Meals and snacks   Restaurant   Children welcome   Open 11–3, 6–11 all year; may open longer, afternoons   Bedrooms tel Grantham (0476) 65816; £55.95B/£68.90B

Beehive

Castlegate; from main street turn down Finkin Street opposite the George Hotel

Mr Bull practically invented the ploughman's lunch some twenty-five years ago; his son is now continuing the tradition, serving a properly basic one with cheese or ham (£1.20 – or a small version from just 70p); other attractively priced bar food includes a wide choice of freshly cut sandwiches (from 55p), soup (55p), filled baked potatoes (from 70p), salads (from £1.30) and home-cooked ham and eggs (£1.30). But the really remarkable thing here is the unique inn-sign, a beehive mounted up in a lime tree. It's been the sign certainly since 1830, and probably since the century before, and must be one of the oldest populations of bees in the world – so well established here that when they swarm they invariably come to rest in the same place. The comfortable bar has a fruit machine, space game and good juke box. They now serve Ruddles County on handpump, under air pressure. *(Recommended by Ian Phillips; more reports please)*

Free house   Real ale   Licensee John Bull   Meals and snacks (lunchtime, not Sun)   Open 11–4 (3 Sat), 7–11 all year

---

Meal times tend to vary from day to day and with the season, depending on how busy the pub hopes to be. We don't specify them as our experience shows you can't rely on them. Avoid the disappointment of arriving just after the kitchen's closed by sticking to normal eating times for whatever area the pub is in.

HALLATON (Leics)   SP7896   Map 4

Bewicke Arms ★ ⊗

On good fast back road across open rolling countryside between Uppingham and Kibworth; village signposted from B6047 in Tur Langton and from B664 SW of Uppingham

This thatched village pub is a cheerful and unpretentious place; the beamed main bar has two small oddly shaped, cosy rooms with old-fashioned furniture, and four gleaming copper kettles over the log fire in its stone hearth. Bar food includes soup (£1.20), ploughman's (from £2.10), half a roast chicken (£3.80), daily fish specials like baked trout with apples, cider and cream or grilled swordfish steaks with herbs and garlic butter (£4.60), two changing chicken dishes (from around £5.20) and eight-ounce sirloin steak (£6.35); bar meals can be booked on Saturday evening. Well kept Marstons Pedigree, Ruddles Best and County and Websters Yorkshire on handpump; darts, and a fruit machine in the side corridor. Picnic-table sets on a crazy-paved back terrace look over the ex-stableyard car park to the hills behind. The attractive village has a traditional Easter Monday 'bottle-kicking' race (actually miniature barrels). Though the Old English sheepdog died at Christmas, they've now got a very large Bernesel Mountain puppy, who shares his predecessor's interest in bitter drinkers. (Recommended by Rob and Gill Weeks, Michael Bolsover, Capt F A Bland, Rita Horridge, Dave Braisted, Michael Craig; more reports please)

Free house   Licensee Neil Spiers   Real ale   Meals and snacks   Restaurant (Tues–Fri evenings, bookings only) tel Hallaton (085 889) 217   Well behaved children welcome   Open 12–3, 7–11 all year; may open longer afternoons

HORBLING (Lincs)   TF1135   Map 8

Plough

4 Spring Lane; off B1177

This inn is almost unique in being owned by the parish council (the Royal Oak in Meavy – see Devon Lucky Dip – is the only other we know of). It's preserved a friendly village atmosphere in the lounge bar, and at the price the bar food represents fine value: toasted sandwiches (95p), home-made burger or soup (from 95p), varying home-made pies (from £2.50), four-ounce rump steak (£3.15) and a good mixed grill (£4.75). Well kept Greene King IPA and Abbot and guest beers on handpump; sensibly placed darts, pool, dominoes, fruit machine and juke box in the lively public bar. (Recommended by Dave Braisted, Rita Horridge; more up-to-date reports please)

Free house   Licensees David Kawalec and Wendy Hambelton   Real ale   Meals and snacks   Children in eating area   Open 11–2, 7–11 (11–11 Sat) all year   Bedrooms tel Sleaford (0529) 240263; £10/£18

HOSE (Leics)   SK7329   Map 7

Rose & Crown ⊗

Bolton Lane

The range of ales in this comfortably modernised village pub is interesting; they usually have half a dozen on handpump. A typical set might be Arkells Kingsdown, Batemans XB, Big Lamp, Cotleigh Old Buzzard, Glenny and Wards Sheffield Best. They change frequently, and as you can see are drawn from an unusually wide range of sources, often rare for the area, with the occasional strong ale such as Hoskins & Oldfields Old Navigation tapped from the cask. The neat beamed lounge bar is warmly atmospheric, and its green plush seats around dimpled copper tables are separated into two areas by three broad carpeted steps. Bar food consists of filled baps (from 80p), ploughman's (from £2, local Stilton £2.30), and vegetarian pie (£2.50), as well as dishes from the larger main restaurant menu such as home-made soup (90p), scampi (£2.95), a very good range of salads (from £4.75), and steaks (from six-ounce rump, £4.30). The simpler public bar has pool, a fruit machine, space game and juke box. There are tables on a fairy-lit sheltered terrace behind the building. *(Recommended by Derek and Sylvia Stephenson, D Frankland, Dr and Mrs M Rayner, Dave and Angie Parkes, Dave Butler, Lesley Storey)*

Free house   Licensee Carl Routh   Meals and snacks   Restaurant tel Bingham (0949) 60424 Children in restaurant (lunchtimes) and eating area   Open 11.30–2.30, 7–11 all year

HOUGHTON ON THE HILL (Leics) SK6703 Map 4
Rose & Crown

69 Uppingham Road; A47 Leicester–Uppingham

Italian-run, this comfortably modernised pub serves home-made pasta such as spaghetti (from £3), lasagne (£3.50) and cannelloni (£3.80), with soup (80p), lunchtime sandwiches (£1.20), ploughman's (from £2.40), help-yourself salads (from £3.50), with a wider choice in the evening. The lounge bar is relaxing, with purple plush bucket armchairs, button-back wall banquettes and gilt-trimmed panelling; Bass on electric pump, piped music. There are good summer weekend barbecues, and monthly 'theme' evenings. *(Recommended by RJH, D R Linnell; more reports please)*

M&B (Bass)   Licensees Tino and Elaine Vandelli   Real ale   Meals (not Sun or Mon evenings) and snacks (not Mon evening)   Well behaved children welcome   Live music with theme evenings   Open 10.30–2.30, 6–11 all year

ILLSTON ON THE HILL (Leics) SP7099 Map 4
Fox & Goose

Village signposted off B6047 Market Harborough–Melton Mowbray, 3 miles S of A47

You name it, they've probably got it – especially if it's to do with hunting, though we hope the human skull doesn't fall into quite the same category as the foxes' masks and brushes, gamecocks, badger head, squirrel and other trophies that share the crowded walls with gin-traps, grass hooks, sheep-shears, ancient bottles, gas masks, helmets, Jubilee celebration photographs, Fernie hunt pictures and commemorative plates, and lots of McLachlan original cartoons. As all this might suggest, this entertaining tiled-floor village pub is most idiosyncratic; but there's nothing quirky about the well kept Adnams Bitter and Everards Tiger on handpump, the warm winter coal fire, and the sandwiches and Cornish pasties (65p). Darts, dominoes, piped classical music, and a tankful of goldfish. A cosy sitting-roomish front lounge is opened when there are enough customers to justify it. It's said that a poltergeist gets to work when it decides things are a bit too quiet. *(More reports please)*

Everards   Licensee Jack Scott   Real ale   Snacks   Open 11–2 (2.30 Sat), 7–11 all year

KEGWORTH (Leics) SK4826 Map 7
Cap & Stocking ★

Under a mile from M1 junction 24: follow A6 towards Loughborough; in village, turn left at chemist's down one-way Dragwall opposite High Street, then left and left again, into Borough Street

Such is readers' enthusiasm for the friendly local atmosphere and the warmth of the welcome here that we've decided to give it a star this year. A particularly charming feature is the way the reasonably priced Bass and M&B Mild are still brought in a jug from the cellar, though they are now poured at a small L-shaped bar counter

---

If we know a pub has a no-smoking area, we say so.

instead of the original hatch – and the jug is stainless steel. The licensee has earned a lot of praise for his warm friendliness, and on a rare quiet moment (it's usually pretty busy, particularly in the evenings) may find the time to show you round the cellar. The two original rooms of the front bar have a very traditional feel, and in the tap-room there are fabric-covered wall benches and heavy cast-iron-framed tables, lots of etched glass, and walls decorated with stuffed birds and locally caught stuffed fish, with a coal fire in its cast-iron range. The smoke-room has another coal fire, and a vintage juke box caught somewhere in the 1960s or early 1970s. Bar food consists of filled rolls (from 50p), ploughman's (from £1.20p), and a range of hot lunchtime dishes such as chilli con carne (£1.95), Lancashire hot-pot, vegetarian spaghetti or beef carbonnade (£2.25); dominoes, shove-ha'penny, cribbage, fruit machine. The back bar has French windows leading out to the garden. *(Recommended by Roger Bellingham, TRA, MA, S R Holman, Dave Butler, Lesley Storey, Stewart Argyle, Rob and Gill Weeks, Richard Sanders, Wilf Plater-Shellard, Mr and Mrs P A Jones, S R Holman, Frank Cummins, Ian Phillips, Mrs Jenny Seller, Michael Bolsover, Virginia Jones)*

Bass   Licensees Bil and Linda Poynton   Real ale   Meals (not evenings) and snacks   Open 12–3, 6–11 all year; may open longer, afternoons

LEICESTER (Leics)   SK5804   Map 4

Tom Hoskins

131 Beaumanor Rd; from A6 at Red Hill Circle (huge roundabout N of centre) follow Motorway, Burton, Coventry signpost into Abbey Lane (A5131), take second left into Wade Street – pub on left at next crossroads

Although this backstreet pub is part of the small Hoskins brewery, it's run as a free house, keeping a changing selection of real ales from other breweries as well as its own Bitter, Mild, Penns, and in summer Premium, all on handpump. In contrast with the tapestried seats, elegantly etched windows, panelling and old brewing equipment of the Grist Room (actually the brewery's old malt loft), the smoky wood-floored tap-room is very basic – lots of chaps chatting or at dominoes, darts or cribbage, varnished pews around cast-iron-framed tables, and flagstones by the servery; for one reader the atmosphere here makes it quite the best tap-room he knows. Bar food consists chiefly of a limited supply of filled rolls, with hot dishes in winter; beer prices are low. The adjoining brewhouse can be visited day or night by previous arrangement (*tel* Leicester (0533) 661122). *(Recommended by Graham Bush, Richard Sanders, Alastair Lang, Lee Goulding, Mr and Mrs P A Jones, Michael Cooke)*

Hoskins   Real ale   Snacks (weekday lunchtimes)   Open 11.30–2.30, 5.30–11 all year

LINCOLN (Lincs)   SK9872   Map 8

Wig & Mitre   ★   ⊗   [illustrated on page 448]

29 Steep Hill; just below cathedral towards centre

This attractive fourteenth-century building, on a steep and picturesque alley not far below the cathedral, can get crowded on summer weekends – not least because it serves food right through from 8am to midnight (last orders around 11pm), even on Sundays. It's on two floors, with pews and other seats around the tables on the tiled floor of its cheerful downstairs bar, and a more relaxed oak-raftered upstairs dining-room. This, with ancient and modern pictures elaborating the theme of the pub's name, has an almost clubby atmosphere, with newspapers set out to read, shelves of old books, settees, elegant small settles, Victorian armchairs and an open fire. Throughout, restoration of the medieval building has been most careful, showing the original timbers and other materials without making heavy weather of it. Food varies twice daily and covers a remarkable range. Besides sandwiches (from 95p), ploughman's (£2.75) and all-day breakfast dishes (full fried breakfast £3.25), there are usually two or three soups (£1.25), a choice of pâtés (£2.65), two or three enterprising vegetarian or vegan dishes such as avocado and orange salad (£2.75), half a dozen other main dishes like pork and mustard casserole (£3.45), gammon (£4.25), and good puddings (£1.65). You can also choose from the less quickly changing restaurant menu, which includes more expensive dishes such as steaks (from £6.95) and chicken breast with Parma ham (£7.65). A very wide though not cheap choice of wines by the glass, many more by the bottle, Sam Smiths OB and Museum on handpump, and freshly squeezed orange juice. There are seats on a small sheltered back terrace, with a small pool and fountain. (*Recommended by Guy Sowerby, ILP, Tim Halstead, Mike and Kay Wilson, Geoff Wilson, G N G Tingey, R F Neil, Rob and Gill Weeks, Nick Dowson, Alison Hayward, Lee Goulding, Richard Trigwell, J and J W*)

Sam Smiths   Licensees Michael and Valerie Hope   Real ale   Meals and snacks   Restaurant tel Lincoln (0522) 35190   Children in eating area and restaurant   Open 8am–midnight (with supper licence), including Sun; closed 25 Dec

LYDDINGTON (Leics)   SP8797   Map 4

Marquess of Exeter ⊗ ⇌

Village signposted off A6003 N of Corby

Early indications are that the new licensees are maintaining the civilised and welcoming atmosphere in this attractive stone-built inn, with perhaps more emphasis on the hotel and food side than before. The comfortable rambling beamed lounge has red plush seats including one or two wing armchairs, and a good log fire in its handsome stone fireplace; it's mainly carpeted, with flagstones by the serving-counter. On a busy lunchtime, room is made in the hotel dining-room. Neatly uniformed waiters and waitresses serve a good range of bar food, including sandwiches (from 95p, crab when available £1.95, steak £3.50), soup (£1.10), ploughman's (from £2.30), lasagne, moussaka or curry (£2.50), home-made specials like braised oxtail or pie (£3.45) and beef bourguignonne (£3.95) and sirloin steak (£4.45); puddings (£1.45); well kept Batemans and Ruddles Best on handpump; piped music. The charming village has long been owned by the Burghley family. (*Recommended by Derek Stephenson, Dr A V Lewis; more reports on the new regime please*)

Free house   Licensee N L Martin   Real ale   Meals and snacks   Evening restaurant Children welcome   Open 11–11 (12 Sat) all year   Bedrooms tel Uppingham (0572) 822477; £39.50B/£48B

MARKET BOSWORTH (Leics)   SK4003   Map 4

Olde Red Lion

1 Park Street; from centre, follow Leicester and Hinckley signpost

The L-shaped main bar in this carefully restored pub (one of the first to be acquired by the Hoskins brewery in Leicester) has an intimate atmosphere, with stripped original beams, and traditional settles set back-to-back around cast-iron tables. A cosy little Victorian snug has benches built into its walls, and a cream-painted wooden plank ceiling, and there's a well equipped central children's room: bar billiards, fruit machine. Bar food includes filled cobs (70p), soup (£1), ploughman's (£1.95), omelettes (from £2.50), scampi or whitebait (£2.45) and steaks (from six-ounce rump, £2.55); excellent value three-course lunch (£3.75, not Sunday). There's a decent range of real ales on handpump: Holdens Mild, Hoskins Bitter, Mild, Penns, Premium in summer and Old Nigel in winter, Ma Pardoes and regular guest beers; piped music. There are tables in the sheltered courtyard behind, which

---

If you're interested in real ale, the CAMRA Good Beer Guide – no relation to us – lists thousands of pubs where you can get it.

has swings, slides and a seesaw; in front, hanging baskets and window boxes have been based on pictures of the pub in the 1920s. *(Recommended by Ian Blackwell, W S Wright, T Nott, Derek Stephenson, Michael Craig, Lee Goulding; more reports please)*

Hoskins   Licensees John and Shirley Kesler   Real ale   Meals and snacks (not Sun evening)   Children welcome   Easy-listening jazz Sun, trad jazz Thurs, pianist Sat   Open 11–11 all year   Bedrooms tel Market Bosworth (0455) 291713; £17.50(£19.50B)/£34(£38B)

MARKET DEEPING (Lincs)   TF1310 Map 8
Bull

Market Place

This engaging early Georgian market-town pub is pleasantly atmospheric, and serves decent bar food, including sandwiches, soup (£1), ploughman's (£2), curry (£2.90), lunchtime salads or daily specials (around £3), steak and kidney pie (£3.20), swordfish steaks (£4.90) and beef steaks (from sirloin, £5.20). Little corridors and low-ceilinged alcoves give a pleasantly old-fashioned feel, at its strongest in the comfortable Dugout Bar, a long, cellar-like narrow room down a few steps, with heavy black beams and roughly plastered walls made from enormous blocks of ancient stone. Though there are handpumps up in the main bar down here they tap the well kept Adnams, Everards Tiger and Old Original and a guest beer direct from a row of casks. Bar billiards, fruit machine, space game, piped music; you can sit out in the pretty back coachyard. *(Recommended by Derek Stephenson, Nick Dowson, Alison Hayward; more reports please)*

Everards   Licensees David and Shirley Dye   Real ale   Meals and snacks (not Mon or Sun evening)   Restaurant   Children in eating area, restaurant and upstairs room   Nearby daytime parking may be difficult   Open 11–3, 5.30–11 all year   Bedrooms tel Market Deeping (0778) 343320; £16/£28

NEWARK (Notts)   SK8054 Map 7
Old Kings Arms ⊗

19 Kirkgate; follow To The Market Place signpost opposite Maltby agricultural engineers on A46

As you'd expect with a licensee who is a former chairman of the Campaign for Real Ale, the beers here – Marstons Burton, Merrie Monk, Pedigree and Owd Rodger – are notably well kept on handpump. Though the no-nonsense cushioned wall benches and other traditional seats around plain stripped deal tables in the vaulted bar suggest a certain ascetic character, there's no mistaking the warmth of the welcome and the wholesomeness of the food; this includes sandwiches (from £1, steak £2.50), ploughman's (from £1.20), chilli con carne or lasagne (£1.50 or £2.25, depending on size of helping), tuna and peanut risotto (£1.80 or £2.70), salads (from £2.40), and a range of several other hot dishes such as steak and kidney pie, beef in Guinness, spicy pork in tomatoes, chicken or vegetable curry and carbonnade of beef (around £2.75–£3). Prices are rather higher in the evening, when the choice is a bit different and the food is served upstairs; there's always something for vegetarians. Shove-ha'penny, dominoes, cribbage, a fruit machine, juke box. The coat of arms outside is unusually handsome, and the castle ruins are just a stroll away. *(Recommended by Richard Sanders, Graham Bush, Scott W Stucky, Mrs L Moore)*

Marstons   Licensee Christopher Holmes   Real ale   Meals (not Sun or Mon evenings) and snacks   Upstairs restaurant Tues–Sat evenings tel Newark (0636) 703416   Children upstairs   Trad jazz Mon, general music night Sun   Restricted nearby parking   Open 11–11 all year

---

If a pub is on or near one of the walks described in *Holiday Which? Good Walks Guide*, also published by Consumers' Association, we mention this – giving the walk's number.

NEWTON (Lincs)   TF0436 Map 8
Red Lion ⊗

Village signposted from A52; at village road turn right towards Haceby and Braceby

Once again readers have been unanimous in their praise for the impressive consistency of the food in this quietly civilised village – especially the excellent and attractively displayed cold carvery. You choose as much as you like of the salads, with four different types of fish such as fresh salmon, cold meats and pies, and the friendly and attentive landlord serves you. Prices depend on how much you want: a small helping is £4.50, normal £5 and large £6.50; children's helpings are £1; the soups are also very good. The partly rendered stone walls of the communicating rooms are covered with farm tools, maltsters' wooden shovels, stuffed birds and animals, pictures made from pressed flowers, a dresser full of china, old advertisements, hunting and coaching prints, even a penny-farthing cycle. Besides cushioned wall benches, there are old-fashioned oak and elm seats and a Gothick carved settle. Very well kept Batemans XB on handpump, decent wine; fruit machine, and during the day and at weekends two squash courts run by the pub can be used by non-members. The neat, well sheltered back garden has tables under cocktail parasols on the grass and on a terrace, and a swing. (*Recommended by Jane Palmer, Frank Williams, Guy Sowerby, Amanda Rusholme, Brian and Anna Marsden, David and Ruth Hollands, Jilly Mills, E J Cutting, Michael Bolsover, Derek and Sylvia Stephenson, Dave Butler, Lesley Storey*)

Free house   Licensee John William Power   Real ale   Meals and snacks (not Sun evening or Mon, exc bank hols)   Children welcome   Open 11–2.30 (3 Sat), 6–11 all year; closed Mon lunch exc bank hols

NOTTINGHAM (Notts)   SK5640 Map 7
Bell

18 Angel Row; off Old Market Square

Very popular, this quaint little yellow building (dwarfed by the neighbouring eleven-storey office block) has enough rooms to allow for a bit of peace somewhere, however busy it gets. Upstairs – the Belfry – is usually quieter in the evenings, and at the back you can see the rafters of the fifteenth-century crown post roof; at lunchtime it functions as a family restaurant. There are lower beams at the front, with heavy panelling by the windows looking down on the street. Downstairs, the nicest bar is the Elizabethan – cosy, with lots of black beams, and thickly cushioned banquettes forming booths around the tables. The good range of real ales on handpump – Bass, Greene King Abbot, Marstons Pedigree, Ruddles County, Theakstons Best and Old Peculier and a weekly guest beer (from a choice of twenty-seven from twelve different breweries) – are kept well in a marvellous sandstone cellar thirty feet below ground (groups may be able to arrange cellar tours); good value wines; a fairly priced hot and cold buffet at lunchtime, with filled rolls and other food from the back snack bar; piped music. They arrange various festivities, such as the malt whisky festival built around Burns Night in January, and a Beaujolais nouveau event with Burgundian food on the third Thursday in November. The pub's been in the same family since the end of the last century, and from 1820–36 its landlord was William Clarke, the captain of the first All England cricket XI, and founder of the Trent Bridge ground. In summer there's waiter service to the tables on the pavement outside. (*Recommended by Graham Bush, BKA, T Mansell, Derek Stephenson, Revd B K Andrews*)

Free house   Licensees David and Paul Jackson, Manager Richard Jackson   Real ale   Meals (lunchtime, not Sun) and snacks (lunchtime)   Restaurant (closed Sun)   Children in restaurant lunchtimes   Trad jazz Sun lunchtime and evening, Mon and Tues evenings   Open 10.30–11 all year

New Market Hotel

Lower Parliament Street, at junction with Broad Street; inner ring road passes the pub

Although the owners of this home-brew pub, Scottish & Newcastle (McEwans/
Youngers), are again putting financial pressure on the licensee, the price of both
beer – well kept Mild and Bitter on handpump – and spirits remains outstandingly
low. Its exterior is nondescript, but inside there's no mistaking its pubby character.
The high-ceilinged front bar is unashamedly practical, but the back lounge is
comfortably furnished with curvy button-back banquettes and pretty wallpaper.
Reasonably priced bar food includes filled cobs (from 45p), baked potato with
cheese (85p), quiche with coleslaw (£1.15), ploughman's (£1.25) and dishes of the
day such as steak and kidney pie, lasagne or coq au vin (£1.95). Darts, shove-
ha'penny, table skittles, dominoes, cribbage, backgammon, chess, draughts, juke
box and fruit machine in the front bar; seats on a back terrace. Dogs allowed (rare
for the area). Dodger, the licensee, is a chatty ex-policeman. *(Recommended by Guy
Sowerby, Stewart Argyle, Graham Bush, Richard Sanders, Ian Phillips)*

*Home   Licensee Tony (Dodger) Bill Green   Real ale   Meals and snacks   Children in back
lounge   Open 11–3, 5.30–11 all year*

Olde Trip to Jerusalem ★

Brewhouse Yard; from inner ring road follow The North, A6005 Long Eaton signpost until you
are in Castle Boulevard then almost at once turn right into Castle Road; pub is up on the left

This highly unusual pub is mainly seventeenth-century, though its caverns may have
served as cellarage for an early medieval castle brewhouse which stood here (hence
the pub's claims to great antiquity). The upstairs bar (not always open) is unique:
cut into the sandstone rock below the castle, its panelled walls soar narrowly into
the dark cavernous heights above. The friendly downstairs bar is also mainly carved
from the rock, with leatherette cushioned settles built into the dark panelling, barrel
tables on the tiles or flagstones, and more low-ceilinged alcoves; there's a great deal
of atmosphere; friendly, helpful staff. A good range of real ales on handpump
includes Bass (alternating weekly with Wards), Marstons Pedigree, Ruddles Best,
Sam Smiths OB and a weekly guest beer; fruit machine, ring the bull; seats outside.
They serve filled baps at lunchtime. *(Recommended by Richard Sanders, Graham Bush,
Stewart Argyle, Barry and Anne, Ian Phillips, Phil and Sally Gorton, MM, T Mansell, Jon
Wainwright, Colin Gooch, C D T Spooner)*

*Free house   Licensee Janet Marshall   Real ale   Snacks (lunchtime)   Open 11–2.30,
5.30–11 all year; may open longer weekends*

OLD DALBY (Leics)   SK6723   Map 7

Crown ★ ★ ⊗

By school in village centre turn into Longcliff Hill then left into Debdale Hill

There's a fine range of real ales, all tapped straight from the cask, in this
hidden-away pub: Adnams, Baileys Best, Batemans XXXB, Greene King Abbot and
IPA, Hardys & Hansons, Hoskins and Oldfield HOB, Mansfield Riding, Marstons
Pedigree, Owd Rodger and Merrie Monk, Ruddles County, Theakstons XB and
Old Peculier, and Wadworths 6X. Its many little rooms are furnished almost like
the farmhouse that it once was, with one or two antique oak settles and Windsor
armchairs, easy chairs, Cecil Aldin and Victor Venner hunting prints on the white
walls, and snug open fires (one fireplace is covered in summer by an embroidered
bird-of-paradise firescreen); friendly, unspoilt atmosphere. The attractive garden
has plenty of tables on a terrace – idyllic in summer, by the big, sheltered lawn
sloping down among roses and fruit trees. The food is well above the standard of
the area; it includes sandwiches (from £1.25), soup (£1.25), Welsh rarebit (£2.25),
a bumper ploughman's (£3.95), melted Stilton dip with crudités (£2.75) and main

dishes like stuffed whole peppers (£3.95), skate wings in a light beer batter with mint and watercress sauce, tagliatelle or carbonnade of beef (£4.50) and sirloin steak (£6.95). What was once the old kitchen and utility-room is now a second small, cottagey restaurant area, matching the charm of the first one. One room has darts, dominoes, cribbage and table skittles. (*Recommended by Stewart Argyle, Dr Paul Kitchener, Clifford Spooner, Dave Butler, Lesley Storey, Guy Sowerby, Syd and Wyn Donald, Michael Cooke, PLC, Michael Bolsover, Dave and Angie Parkes, J E Bland, Ken and Barbara Turner, Gill and Rob Weeks, Ted George, Virginia Jones*)

Free house   Licensees Lynne Bryan and Salvatore Inguanta   Meals and snacks (not Sun evenings)   Restaurant tel Melton Mowbray (0664) 823134   Children in eating area and restaurant   Open 12–3, 6–11 all year; may open longer afternoons

SCAFTWORTH (Notts)   SK6692   Map 7

King William ⊗

Village signposted (not prominently) off A631 Bawtry–Everton

The big garden's a special plus in summer at this friendly pub: well sheltered, it has white tables spaced out generously among shrubs and lots of young trees, with swings, slides and climber for children, chickens poking around, and occasional barbecues (with a covered area for these). Cows graze in the meadows on the far side of the River Idle. Inside, three connecting rooms are pleasantly furnished with a variety of seats from ordinary spindle-back chairs through high-backed settles to a Liberty-print sofa. There are bunches of flowers on French-style waterproof floral tablecloths, Delft shelves of knick-knacks, hunting and other prints, lots of brasses, and an unusually big mirror; the ginger cat's a friendly creature, and the open fires are welcoming in winter. One simply furnished room's no-smoking, and there's a good, recently decorated family-room with milk churns as seats. Bar food includes soup (95p), salads or ploughman's (£2.75), Basque ratatouille, chilli con carne or curry (£3.30), a good many interestingly flavoured pies such as Stilton and celery or steak and kidney (£3.50), and a mixed grill (£4.20), with a lunchtime fry-up (£2.20); usefully they still do things like burgers late in the evening, and have a good deal of local game in season. Well kept Camerons Strongarm, Everards Old Original and Whitbreads Castle Eden and Trophy on handpump, with a very good range of malt whiskies, decent wines and an espresso coffee machine; dominoes, cribbage, fruit machine, space game, maybe unobtrusive piped music. (*Recommended by Derek and Sylvia Stephenson, Alastair Lang, RAB, William and Patrick Stapley*)

Free house   Licensee Michael Wright   Real ale   Meals and snacks (not Mon, not Tues or Weds lunchtime)   New restaurant tel Doncaster (0302) 710292   Children in eating area, restaurant and family-room   Midsummer festival weekend with morris men, clog dancers, mummers, Punch & Judy   Open 12–2.30 (3 Sat), 7–11 all year; closed lunchtime Mon–Weds, 25 Dec

SIBSON (Leics)   SK3500   Map 4

Cock ⊗

A444 N of Nuneaton

Dating back in part to 1250, this charming thatched and timbered black and white pub has a quaint atmosphere and look: heavy black beams and timbers, latticed windows, strikingly low doorways, and in the room on the right what was once an immense fireplace, its chimney big enough to hold a party in, now turned into an alcove with built-in seats. There are other comfortable seats around cast-iron-framed tables in here, and the room on the left has country kitchen chairs around wooden tables. The good value bar food includes sandwiches (75p), home-made soup (90p), ploughman's (from £1.75), omelettes (£2.25), salads (from £2.25), home-made steak and kidney pie (£2.95), lasagne (£3) and steaks (from eight-ounce rump or sirloin £5.25), with children's dishes (£1.25) and cold puddings (90p).

Well kept Bass and M&B Brew XI and Mild; friendly service; piped music. There's popular restaurant (in a former stableblock), and in summer you can sit out on the back lawn, which had a cockpit until 1870. (*Recommended by Ian Blackwell, W S Wright, Jon Wainwright, Ken and Barbara Turner, C D T Spooner*)

M&B (Bass) Licensee J R McCallion Real ale Meals (not Sat evening or Sun) and snacks (not Sat or Sun evenings) Restaurant (not Sun evening) tel Tamworth (0827) 880357 Children in eating area and restaurant Open 11.30–2.30, 7–11 all year

SOUTH LUFFENHAM (Leics) SK9402 Map 4
Boot & Shoe ⊗ 🛏

10 The Street; turn off A6121 at the Halfway House, then first right

Very much a community pub, this notably welcoming pub has a snug and comfortably carpeted lounge bar. It rambles through several areas where stripped stone walls have been knocked through, with red plush easy chairs by the log fire, lots of brass and copper, and varnished beams. The lively public bar has darts, pool, shove-ha'penny, dominoes, cribbage, fruit machine, trivia game and juke box. Bar food is cooked by the landlord, and is interesting and wide-ranging, including home-made soup (£1), sandwiches, several starters or light snacks, two filled baked potatoes (£1.75), ploughman's (£2.50), a good choice of vegetarian dishes such as mushroom and nut fettuccine (£2.95), chilli con carne or beef and ginger curry (£3.25), steaks (from six-ounce sirloin £4.75), locally caught trout (£5.25) and a massive seafood platter (£6.95 – free half-bottle of wine for anyone who can finish the whole thing on their own; it makes more sense to share it between two); good puddings (£1.20). Well kept Camerons on handpump, piped music. There are old-fashioned seats on the quiet lawn of the neatly kept small garden, and more on a sunny back terrace by the car park. (*Recommended by EC, Gwen and Peter Andrews; more reports please*)

Melbourns (Camerons) Licensees Alan and Angela Wright Real ale Meals and snacks (not Mon) Restaurant Children welcome Open 12–2.30 (3.30 Sat), 7–11 all year; closed Mon lunchtime exc bank hols Bedrooms tel Stamford (0780) 720177; £12.50/£25

STAMFORD (Lincs) TF0207 Map 8
Bull & Swan ⊗

High Street, St Martins; B1081 leaving town southwards

New licensees in this old stone inn are intent on maintaining the good atmosphere in its cosy and comfortably modernised low-ceilinged bar; on three levels (with shallow steps leading up and down), it has heavy beams hung with lots of highly polished copper kettles and brass, sturdy red plush seats, a wood-burning stove set into one stripped stone wall, and an open log fire in another part of the open-plan room. The bar food is all home made, and includes sandwiches (from 90p, steak £2.75), soup (£1), a choice of ploughman's (£2), chicken (£2.60), dishes of the day such as chilli con carne or curries (around £3), seafood platter (£3.70), gammon (£4.20) and mixed grill (£5.60); well kept Camerons on handpump; fruit machine, space game and piped music. An arched passageway leads back to the old coachyard, where there are tables in summer. (*Recommended by T Mansell, JFH, John Roué, Mr and Mrs R Williamson, Mrs R Horridge; more reports on the new regime please*)

Melbourns (Camerons) Licensee M Desadeleer Real ale Meals and snacks Restaurant Children in separate room Open 11–2.30, 6–11 all year Bedrooms tel Stamford (0780) 63558; £28B/£35B

Please keep sending us reports. We rely on readers for news of new discoveries, and particularly for news of changes – however slight – at the fully described pubs. No stamp needed: The Good Pub Guide, FREEPOST, London SW10 0BR.

George ★ ⊗ 🛏

71 St Martins

Though a comfortable and sizeable hotel, its interesting rambling bars are decidedly pubby, with a particularly congenial atmosphere. It's a very handsome building, full of heavy beams, sturdy timbers and broad flagstoned corridors; it's mainly Elizabethan, though the magnificent and cunningly lit arched stone fireplace amid lots of exposed stonework in the comfortable and spacious central lounge looks older. A Norman pilgrims' hospice stood here previously, and the crypt under the present cocktail bar may pre-date even that. A pair of front rooms are still named after the destinations of the coaches – twenty a day each way to London and York – which changed horses here in the eighteenth and nineteenth centuries. The quietly ornate London Room has plush chairs around neat mahogany tables, carved panelling where some claim to be able to see a ghostly face, and tall shuttered windows; the York Room opposite by the bar servery, also panelled, has sturdier furniture. The most pleasant place for lunch is the imaginative Garden Lounge, with its central tropical grove of flowers, ferns, banana trees, rubber plants and creepers surrounded by well spaced white cast-iron furniture on herringbone glazed bricks. Food, served here or in the bars, is by no means cheap, but it is of a very high standard, including soup (£2.45), generous Danish open sandwiches (from £3.90), stir-fried vegetables in black-bean sauce (£4.85), delicious grilled lamb-burger with a yoghurt and mint dressing or lasagne verde (£4.90), fritto misto (£6.35), grilled lemon sole with anchovy butter (£7.95) and a large seafood platter (£11.95); good puddings. The best drinks are the Italian wines, many of which are good value (they don't sell real ales); efficient friendly service. The charming cobbled courtyard at the back is attractively planted with tubs of plants, weeping shrubs and birches, and bright hanging flower baskets. It's a delightful place for a summer drink or bar lunch, its comfortable chairs and tables covered with William Morris fabric. Besides the regular bar food, there are frequent barbecues out here. It leads on round to a well kept walled garden, with a sunken lawn where croquet and outdoor chess are often played. This is the headquarters of Ivo Vannocci's small but illustrious empire of Poste Hotels. (*Recommended by Syd and Wyn Donald, AE, RMS, RLG, John Townsend, John Roué, G L Archer, T Mansell, Dave Butler, Lesley Storey, Sir Charles Innes Bt*)

Free house   Licensees Ivo Vannocci and Philip Newman-Hall   Meals and snacks Restaurant   Children welcome   Open 11–11 all year   Bedrooms tel Stamford (0780) 55171; £55B/£80B

STRETTON (Leics)   SK9416   Map 7

Jackson Stops ★ ⊗

From A1 follow village signposts

This idiosyncratic place has the difficult task of balancing its considerable popularity against the friendly informality that's been its hallmark. It's decidedly a food place, and diners have first call on the tables in the lounge; people who want a drink then have to find space in the small public bar (at busy times the snug seems to be pretty firmly a locals' preserve). But the compensation is the high quality and value of the food, including soup (90p), lunchtime sandwiches (from £1) or ploughman's (£1.60), Somerby sausages (£1.90), salads (from £2), home-made pie (£2.90), lamb cutlets or trout (£4), gammon and egg (£4.50), mixed grill (£4.95) and sirloin steak (£6.95), with various puddings (90p). The bar has old-fashioned high-backed settles, country tables and chairs, armchairs, open fires, rugs and so forth, with yokes, antlers and stuffed animal heads on the walls. Darts, dominoes, nurdles; well kept Ruddles Best and County and Sam Smiths OB on handpump. The pub, as you might guess from the picture on its inn-sign, used to be called the White Horse, but got its present name from the estate agent's sign that it carried a good many years ago, when it was up for sale for quite a time. It's handy for the A1. *(Recommended by Roger Bellingham, Dr A V Lewis, Mrs Jenny Seller, C J Dowling, G W Judson, Michael Cooke)*

Free house   Licensees Frank and Sue Piguillem   Real ale   Meals and snacks   Restaurant tel *Stamford (0780) 81237   Children in eating area   Open 11–2.30, 6–11 all year; closed 25 Dec*

SUTTON IN THE ELMS (Leics)   SP5194 Map 4
Mill on the Soar ⊗

3¼ miles from M69 junction 2, but can leave motorway only southbound, rejoin only northbound – alternative access via junction 1, or via M1 junction 21; Coventry Road – junction B4114/B581

New licensees here have kept things much as they found it – namely a well run place with a buoyant atmosphere. One thing that probably will change is the range of food, which at the moment includes sandwiches (from 75p), ploughman's (£1.85), main dishes like chicken and leek pie or bacon and eggs (around £2.30–£3.25), and children's dishes (from £1.35). The building itself is a fine conversion of a substantial brick mill building. The main bar spreads very extensively below brown beams and sturdy joists, hung with whisky-water jugs and some huge aluminium pans; it's flagstoned, with some rugs and carpet, and masses of tables. At each end the bare brick walls are painted with big cartouches of mill and barge scenes, and there's a high Delft shelf with toby jugs and similarly decorative pottery figures. Up at the serving end you can see the restored millwheel turning outside; a spacious conservatory with a curved roof, and white cast-iron furniture, has an armoured glass floor panel showing the millstream below. Fruit machine, space game, maybe piped music. The pub stands in a spread of low meadows around the stream. There's a good play area out here; occasional barbecues. It can get very busy in the evenings and at weekends. *(Recommended by Roger Broadie, Robert Aitken; more reports on the new regime please)*

Free house   Licensee Mr Cook   Meals and snacks (not Sun lunchtime)   Evening restaurant (not Sun)   Children in eating area and restaurant   Open 11–2.30, 5.30–11 all year   Fishing tel *Sutton Elms (0455) 282223   Bedrooms* tel *Sutton Elms (0455) 282419; £34.50B/£44B*

SWITHLAND (Leics)   SK5413 Map 7
Griffin

Village signposted from A6

The three communicating beamed rooms of this comfortably modernised and warmly welcoming country pub have brocaded wall seats around dimpled copper tables, hunting prints on the partly panelled walls, and easy chairs by the fire in the end room – where it's usually quietest. Besides well kept Adnams Bitter and Everards Bitter, Mild, Tiger and Old Original on handpump, they usually have a changing guest beer; good fresh bar snacks; darts, dominoes, cribbage, fruit machine and juke box, and a skittle alley in the quite separate back Stable Bar. A small stream runs along the grass behind the big car park. *(Recommended by Richard Sanders, Dave Butler, Lesley Storey; more reports please)*

Everards   Licensees Norman and Brenda Jefferson   Real ale   Meals (not Sun) and snacks (only sandwiches Sun)   Children welcome   Open 11–2.30, 6–11 (11–11 weekends) all year

TUR LANGTON (Leics)   SP7194 Map 4
Crown

Off B6047; follow Kibworth signpost from village centre

The two rooms of this beamed village pub have a more individual flavour than many around here. The Turkey-carpeted room on the right has little high-backed settles and red leather dining-chairs around the tables, an antique curved settle built in opposite the serving-counter, and a raised central coal fire. The lounge on the left, with another coal fire, has chintz easy chairs on its pastel flowery carpet, a dresser of blue and white china, a Delft shelf with more plates, and copper pans and jugs hanging from the beams; well kept Bass, Marstons Pedigree and Shipstones on handpump. There are tables in a sheltered back courtyard with hanging baskets, and on attractive grassy terraces with fat conifers. Note that they're not open at lunchtimes, and may keep irregular hours. *(Recommended by T Nott, Michael Cooke, Louise Collins; more reports please)*

Free house   Real ale   Restaurant tel East Langton (085 884) 264   Open 6–11 (and 12–3 Sat) all year

UPTON (Notts)   SK7354   Map 7

Cross Keys ⊗

Main Street (A612 towards Southwell)

The bar of this friendly seventeenth-century pub (a listed building) is given a good deal of character by its rambling layout, its heavy beams, the unusual carved bar counter, and pews and more interesting chairs among the more orthodox seats; pictures are uncommon, too, including a Cardiff Arms Park print by Alan Fearnley signed by all the Welsh team to commemorate the 1981 centenary Wales/England match. This vein of individuality runs through the food, which besides sandwiches changes day by day and might include potted shrimps or Stilton and walnut pâté (£1.95), cheese and courgettes baked in layers (£2.75), pork casseroled with lemon and lime, lamb soubise or beef and ginger (£3.45) and beef done with orange and walnuts (£3.65); they don't do chips. Well kept Batemans XXB, Flowers IPA and Marstons Pedigree on handpump, with guest beers such as Yates; piped pop music unobtrusive (as is the dog), darts, dominoes, with logs burning in the two-way fireplace in winter. A few tables shelter in the bays of the neatly plant-lined fence behind. As this edition of the *Guide* is published, a new restaurant should be under construction in the former dovecot, for opening Thursday to Saturday evenings, with Sunday lunches until four o'clock. *(Recommended by Mr and Mrs David Hollands, Angie and Dave Parkes, M L Tucker, Douglas Bail, Derek Stephenson, Peter Burton)*

Free house   Licensee Michael Kirrage   Real ale   Snacks (lunchtime) and meals   Restaurant planned (see above) tel Southwell (0636) 813269   Children in restaurant, lunchtimes too Folk music winter Sun evening   Open 11.30–2.30, 6–11 all year; closed evening 25 Dec

French Horn ⊗

A612

This busy, friendly pub serves a wide range of reliably good home-made food in generous helpings, including filled rolls (from 65p), home-made soup (85p, Stilton and leek 95p), chicken liver and brandy pâté (£1.95), ploughman's (from £1.95), chilli con carne with tortilla chips (£2.75), beef and Guinness casserole or steak and kidney pie (£2.95), salads (from £2.95), chicken Kiev (£4.95) and sirloin steak (£6.20), with vegetarian dishes (£2.75) and lots of puddings (from 85p). The comfortable open-plan bar is neatly kept, with cushioned captain's chairs and wall banquettes around glossy tables, and frequent shows of local artists' work on its partly panelled walls; pleasant service. Well kept John Smiths on handpump and a good range of decent wines. Outside, there are picnic-table sets on a big sloping back paddock, which looks out on farmland. *(Recommended by Derek Stephenson, PLC, RJH, George and Jill Hadfield; more reports please)*

John Smiths (Courage)   Licensees Graham and Linda Mills   Real ale   Meals and snacks Restaurant tel Southwell (0636) 812394   Children welcome   Open 11–2.30, 6.30–11 all year

WALCOTE (Leics)   SP5683   Map 4
Black Horse ⊗

1½ miles from M1 junction 20; A427 towards Lutterworth

At first sight this is a straightforwardly decent and welcoming English pub – russet plush button-back built-in wall banquettes around cast-iron and other heavy tables, more booth-like seating at the side, pale mate's chairs in an airier section up steps, with a quietly chatty local atmosphere and an open fire in the stripped stone fireplace. The first suggestion that it's out of the ordinary comes with the enterprising choice of well kept beers on handpump: Flowers IPA, Hook Norton Best and Hoskins & Oldfields HOB with a couple of guests such as Brakspears SB and Hook Norton Old Hookey. The real surprise is the landlady's home cooking – wholly Thai. About eight dishes, half spicy and half savoury, include nasi goreng (fried rice with meat and egg, £2.50), a Thai mixed grill, strips of beef in oyster sauce or khau mu daeng (marinated pork – all £3) and various curries such as gaeng pak (vegetables) or gaen pla (fresh fish – £3–£3.50). The eclectic range of bottled beers includes Singha from the Boon Rawd Brewery in Thailand; country wines; seats in the back garden. (Recommended by Dave Butler, Lesley Storey, Cdr Patrick Tailyour, Alan and Jenny Ling, J C and D Aitkenhead, W Rich)

Free house   Licensee Michael Tinker   Real ale   Meals   Restaurant by arrangement only tel Lutterworth (045 55) 2684   Children in eating area   Open 12–3, 5 (6 Sat)–11 all year

WALTHAM ON THE WOLDS (Leics)   SK8024   Map 7
Royal Horseshoes 🛏

A607

Facing the thirteenth-century village church, this is an attractive Tudor pub; apparently it was just the Horseshoes until Queen Victoria, staying at Belvoir Castle, enjoyed refreshments here while a horse being ridden by one of her party was reshod nearby. There's a hot and cold help-yourself buffet (£4.25) in the lounge, as well as soup (95p), ploughman's (£2.30), a hot dish of the day such as steak braised in red wine (£3.25) and sirloin steak (£5.95), with a four-course Sunday roast lunch (£5.95) and home-made puddings such as apple pie with cream. The bar has sturdy cushioned wall seats and plush stools around copper-topped tables, a glass window behind the servery, a large old hunting painting over one of the three open fires, and piped music. The smaller public bar has darts, dominoes and a fruit machine; John Smiths on handpump, decent wines. There's a bench on a verandah, and a few other seats by the back car park. As the village name implies, this is fine rolling Wolds country. (Recommended by Mel Bodfish, John Oddey, Derek and Sylvia Stephenson, RMS, RLG)

John Smiths (Courage)   Licensee Maurice Wigglesworth   Meals and snacks (not Sun evening)   Children welcome   Open 10.30–2.30, 6–11 all year; closed 25–26 Dec Bedrooms tel Waltham on the Wolds (066 478) 289; £21.50B/£37B

WEST LEAKE (Notts)   SK5226   Map 7
Star

Village signposted from A6006

Rooted in the past, this secluded old village pub has a simple but wholesome selection of food, including soup (60p), salads (from £2.75), a daily hot dish (around £2.75) and puddings (65p). The beamed public bar has a strong hunting and sporting theme, with plain oak tables and heavy settles on its tiled floor; the till consists of just a wooden tray. The dimly lit carpeted lounge is a bit more up to date: partly panelled, with comfortable armed chairs, more familiar copper and brass decorations, and a good log fire; well kept Bass and M&B Springfield on handpump; pleasant service. There are picnic-table sets in front of the old house, which stands on a quiet village lane. The atmosphere can feel rather feline – they have six cats. *(Recommended by Roger Broadie, Stewart Argyle, Richard Sanders, Jill and George Hadfield, Frank Cummins, Michael Bolsover, Rob and Gill Weeks, M P Le Geyt, Tim Crawford)*

Bass   Licensee F Whatnall   Real ale   Meals and snacks (lunchtime, not Sat or Sun) Children in eating area   Open 10.30–2.30, 6–10.30

WHITWELL (Leics)   SK9208 Map 8
Noel Arms ⊗

Although much of the space in this thatched Rutland pub is to be found in the attractive spreading back extension, plushly comfortable and partly curtained off as an eating area, the real heart of the place remains the small-roomed original part. This has simple wheel-back chairs and pews, local illustrated maps on the walls, an older chair by the coal fire, pot plants in the local type of vertical spit-roasting cage, a box for fishermen's catch returns, and a decidedly local atmosphere. Good waitress-served bar food includes sandwiches (from 85p), home-made soup (from £1.20), ploughman's or sausage and bread (£2.20), daily specials such as home-made pie or a fish dish (£3.95) and fillets of pork (£4.95), and in the evening mixed grill and steaks (from £5.95); afternoon teas (not Monday), and interesting puddings like green figs in port (£1.75). Well kept Ruddles Best and County and Tetleys on handpump, and an extensive wine list; fruit machine, maybe piped music. The sun-trap back terrace which slopes up behind is sometimes used for summer barbecues. Beware that the narrow entrance to the car park can be rather trying, though things have improved with the new tarmac; close to Rutland Water. *(Recommended by Mrs J Stocks, Jamie and Sarah Allan, Stewart Argyle, Malcolm Steward, Rob and Gill Weeks, Jon Wainwright, Tom Evans)*

Free house   Licensee Sam Healey   Real ale   Meals and snacks   Restaurant   Children in eating area   Open 11–2.30, 6–11 all year   Bedrooms tel Empingham (078 086) 334; £20/£29(£39B)

WILSON (Leics)   SK4024 Map 7
Bulls Head ⊗

Village signposted from A453 Ashby de la Zouch–Castle Donington

The comfortably modernised beamed bar in this friendly pub opens into an attractive variety of quiet little alcoves, with maroon plush seats around black tables on its Turkey carpet; there are striking modern prints of immensely magnified insects, and well kept Ind Coope Burton on handpump. It serves generous helpings of good value, popular food, with pride of place going to the buffet counter – a very wide range of attractively presented salads using good fresh ingredients (from £3), including dressed crab, cold fresh salmon or freshly cut smoked salmon when available. There are also sandwiches (from 95p), soup (65p), ploughman's (from £1.75), a daily special (£3.25) and hot roast beef (£4.25). It's not far from the Donington race track – hence the old sepia racing-car photographs on the wall. *(Recommended by David Gaunt, M A and W R Proctor, Michael and Alison Sandy, Dr and Mrs A K Clarke, Dr Keith Bloomfield)*

Ind Coope   Licensee Michael Johnson   Real ale   Meals and snacks (not Sun or Mon evenings)   Children in eating area lunchtimes   Open 11–2.30, 6–11 all year

---

Real ale to us means beer which has matured naturally in its cask – not pressurised or filtered. We name all real ales stocked. We usually name ales preserved under a light blanket of carbon dioxide too, though purists – pointing out that this stops the natural yeasts developing – would disagree (most people, including us, can't tell the difference!).

WING (Leics)   SK8903 Map 4
Kings Arms
Top Street

This simple and friendly early seventeenth-century stone inn serves good value home-cooked bar food that includes sandwiches (from £1), soup (95p), sausage and beans (£1.95), ploughman's (£2.25), daily specials, omelettes (from £3.25), mixed grill (£5.95) and steak or jumbo prawns (£6.95); well kept Batemans, Greene King IPA and Ruddles Best and County on handpump. The lounge has an attractive window seat, an antique settle and an unusual central open fireplace under a gleaming copper chimney-funnel, as well as some conventional wheel-back chairs. In the recently refurbished back bar (formerly a family-room) there are beams and a stone fireplace. The sunny yard has wooden benches; a medieval turf maze some seventeen yards across is just up the road. *(Recommended by Derek Stephenson, Dr A V Lewis, Peter Hall)*

Free house   Licensee M Moreno   Real ale   Meals and snacks   Restaurant   Children welcome   Open 10.30–2.30, 6–11 all year   Two-bedroom flat tel Manton (057 285) 315; £70 a week

WOODHOUSE EAVES (Leics)   SK5214 Map 4
Wheatsheaf
Brand Hill; follow Main Street straight through town off B591 S of Loughborough

Foxes' masks and lots of sporting prints, especially of the Quorn hunt, set the mood in this low-ceilinged and gently lit pub. It's open-plan but well done and civilised, with a log fire and brown plush built-in wall banquettes around dimpled copper tables in two front parlour areas, and a further comfortable area behind – a far cry from its humble nineteenth-century origins as the Slate Splitters Arms, a tavern for the men working the quarry-pits behind and in the Swithland woods (it had its six-day alehouse licence right up to 1964). Bar food includes soup (£1.20), mushrooms and bacon in garlic butter (£2.30), four-ounce burger or lasagne (£2.30), scampi (£3.30) and good charcoal-grilled steaks (from eight-ounce sirloin £5.95); well kept Bass, Marstons Pedigree and Ruddles County on handpump. It can get packed in the evenings and at weekends, but service is always quick and friendly. There are picnic-table sets under cocktail parasols beyond the coach entry, on the way to the car park, with summer barbecues. No motor-cycles or leathers. *(Recommended by Tim and Lynne Crawford, A J Hill)*

Free house   Licensees Mr and Mrs Tony Marshall   Real ale   Meals and snacks (not Sun evening)   Restaurant tel Woodhouse Eaves (0509) 890320   Children in restaurant   Open 11–2.30, 5.30 (6 Sat)–11 all year

---

Lucky Dip

Besides the fully inspected pubs, you might like to try these Lucky Dips recommended to us and described by readers (if you do, please send us reports):

Anstey, Leics [Bradgate Rd; SK5408], *Hare & Hounds*: Recently renovated local, with several tastefully refurbished rooms, wide range of home-made food (especially chilli con carne), well kept Marstons Pedigree and friendly atmosphere; car park small, with narrow entry *(Mr and Mrs P A Jones)*
Ashby de la Zouch, Leics [The Mews; SK3516], *Mews*: A wine bar rather than a pub, but worth knowing for its food *(Jill Hadfield)*
Ashby Folville, Leics [SK7011], *Carrington*

Arms: Good game pie and home-made steak and kidney, real ales including Adnams *(Nicholas Kingsley)*
Ashby Parva, Leics [turn off N in Bitteswell just through Lutterworth; nr M1 junction 20; SP5288], *Holly Bush*: Comfortable and well furnished bar lounge, knocked through to games area; well kept real ales such as Hook Norton Old Hookey, Marstons Pedigree and Ruddles County, seats outside, summer barbecues *(Gill and Ted George)*
☆ **Aswarby**, Lincs [A15 Folkingham–Sleaford;

TF0639], *Tally Ho*: Lovely seventeenth-century hunting inn with open fires, well kept Adnams and Batemans XB on hand-pump, good value straightforward bar food, adaptable and helpful staff, well maintained gardens; delightful comfortable bedrooms in former stableblock across courtyard *(Jane Kingsbury, A K Grice, Angie and Dave Parkes, Derek and Sylvia Stephenson)*

Aubourn, Lincs [SK9262], *Royal Oak*: Large helpings of good food in pretty, very friendly country pub with garden *(Mr and Mrs Mark Smith)*

Awsworth, Notts [quite handy for M1 junction 26, via A610/A6096; SK4844], *Hog Head*: Huge helpings of good fresh traditional food and excellent beers in friendly family-run pub, very modern and clean *(John Balfour)*

Barholm, Lincs [TF0810], *Five Horseshoes*: Well kept Adnams, Batemans and guest beers in homely easy-going village local with horsy connections and paddocks behind the garden tables *(Steve Coley, LYM)*

Barkby, Leics [off A607 6 miles NE of Leicester; SK6309], *Brookside*: At the end of a no-through road in pretty village with a brook running past the front door; inside, lots of toby jugs, brass and copper; Ind Coope Burton and Mild on handpump; also Ansells; try the beef puff *(A C Lang)*

☆ **Bassingham**, Lincs [High St; SK9160], *Five Bells*: Eighteenth-century village inn using only fresh ingredients for imaginative home-cooked food from sandwiches to steaks, in big helpings, served in separate eating area raised above main bar; well kept Ind Coope and Tetleys, good choice of wine, liqueur coffees *(Carolyn Jell, Frank Williams)*

Baston, Lincs [Church St; TF1113], *Spinning Wheel*: Good choice of beers including Bass, fine food in bar and restaurant – affordable prices, outstanding value *(C E Tyers)*

Beckingham, Lincs [off A17 E of Newark; SK8753], *Black Swan*: Colourfully presented good food and good service in restaurant *(H C Jackson)*

Belmesthorpe, Leics [Shepherds Walk; TF0410], *Bluebell*: Olde-worlde pub with lively atmosphere and entertaining landlord; well kept Marstons Pedigree and Ruddles County, value-for-money lunchtime pub food (not Sun) *(C E Tyers)*

Billesdon, Leics [Church St; SK7202], *Queens Head*: Cheerful service, good atmosphere and good restaurant food *(Cdr Patrick Tailyour)*

Blackfordby, Leics [SK3217], *Bluebell*: Good home cooking including Sun lunch, well kept Marstons Pedigree *(B Hazzard)*

Blidworth, Notts [SK5956], *Bird in Hand*: Cosy old-fashioned local with superb view over Sherwood Forest, Mansfield Riding on handpump, good choice of food, lots of cups, tankards, plates and so forth on the walls, friendly staff, good food lunchtime and evening all week; swings and other playthings in garden; children welcome *(Dominic Dixon, Stewart Argyle)*

Blyth, Notts [SK6287], *Angel*: Cheerful pub, formerly an early eighteenth-century coaching-inn but much modernised, with a comfortable and quite lively lounge, well kept Hardys & Hansons real ales, public bar and pool-room, seats in garden; bar food basic, but includes good ham off the bone, and is usefully served on Sun too (rare around here), so handy for A1; children welcome; bedrooms very simple, though OK for a stopover *(Tony Gayfer, Jim Wiltshire, LYM)*

Boston, Lincs [Witham St; TF3244], *Carpenters Arms*: Enterprising young landlord has kept traditional atmosphere in backstreet inn – very friendly, vibrant with locals and young people, well kept Batemans Mild and XB, good lunchtime food all home cooked; bedrooms reasonably priced *(R H D Rowling)*; [Spilsby Road (A16) – OS Sheet 131 reference 338453] *Mill*: Good helpings of simple food lunchtime and some evenings, Batemans ales *(G N G Tingey, R F Neil)*

Brandy Wharf, Lincs [TF0197], *Hankerin*: Own moorings on River Ancholme, unusual lounge bar with very wide choice of ciders, friendly landlord, basket meals, seats outside; attached Olde Jam and Sydre Shoppe open summer afternoons (not Mon or Tues) *(Mrs A C Fallon)*

Branston, Leics [Main St; SK8129], *Wheel*: Friendly 300-year-old two-roomed pub with skittle area and boules piste in summer; Batemans XB on handpump; good bar food, some showing German influence *(Richard Sanders)*

Breedon on the Hill, Leics [SK4022], *Holly Bush*: Friendly old building – beware low seventeenth-century beams; pretty outside, decked with flower baskets; Ansells and Ind Coope on handpump *(Dave Braisted)*; [A453] *Three Horse Shoes*: Well kept Marstons beer and good buffet *(Dave Braisted)*

Burbage, Leics [SP4294], *Cross Keys*: Charming building with nice snugs and good atmosphere, well kept Marstons real ale; can watch cricket from end of garden *(Graham Bush)*

Burton on the Wolds, Leics [Melton Rd (B676); SK5921], *Greyhound*: Though the redevelopment of this eighteenth-century pub doesn't appeal to all readers, it is at least praised for warm comfort, with good value food and friendly service *(Alan Ward, R C Clark)*

☆ **Castle Donington**, Leics [90 Bondgate; B6504; SK4427], *Cross Keys*: Well kept Vaux Samson and Wards Best, attractive atmosphere, with good fire and good mix of customers *(Dave Butler, Lesley Storey, Richard Sanders)*

☆ **Castle Donington** [Kings Mills], *Priest House*: Unusual drinks and hearty snacks and grills in rambling beamed bars of inn with medieval tower in attractive spot by River Trent, popular with young people; children's play area; decent bedrooms *(Michael Bolsover, G Bloxsom, LYM)*

Clipstone, Notts [Old Clipstone; B6030 Mansfield – Ollerton – OS Sheet 120 reference 606647; SK6064], *Dog & Duck*: Comfortably modernised pub with three rooms and a friendly welcome; good home-made hot meals at decent prices, well kept Home ales; not far from Center Parc at Rufford; children's room *(Alan and Marlene Radford)*

Coleby, Lincs [Far Lane; SK9760], *Bell*: Reliably good value carvery, cold table with wide range of salads, and hot food, friendly atmosphere, efficient service, open fires *(R Trigwell, Russell Wakefield)*

Colston Bassett, Notts [SK7033], *Martins Arms*: Charming setting, interesting fireplace, unusual scales, plenty of brasses, Bass and Ruddles County – almost part of the front room of the house *(Tim Crawford)*

☆ **Coningsby**, Lincs [Boston Rd (B1192); TF2258], *Leagate*: Seventeenth-century coaching-inn full of character, original beams and antique furniture, priest's hole above fire, good range of real ales, wide choice of good reasonably priced bar food, big restaurant, spacious garden with Koi carp in pond and children's play area *(R H D Rowling, Kevin and Mary Shakespeare, Neil and Elspeth Fearn, Mike and Kay Wilson)*

Cossington, Leics [SK6013], *Cossington Mill*: Friendly and efficient service and very good Sun lunch with an unusually good soup; pleasant surroundings; coffee in separate room makes for 'unhurried' feel about the place *(Dr A J Gillham)*

☆ **Cotes**, Leics [Nottingham Rd (A60); SK5520], *Cotes Mill*: Large and attractively placed converted watermill reopened after careful 1987 refurbishments; view of waterwheel from foyer, pleasant whitewashed lounge with view of cows grazing, friendly atmosphere, bar food including good cold pies, Bass, Vaux, Wards Best and maybe Lorimers Scotch on handpump; separate upstairs restaurant, garden next to mill pond; children's area *(Barry and Anne, Richard Sanders, LYM – more reports please)*

☆ **Cottesmore**, Leics [Main St; SK9013], *Sun*: Limited range of top-quality home-made food, beautifully presented and most reasonably priced, in charming seventeenth-century stone pub with friendly reception and real ales; very popular with the locals *(John Oddey)*

Cropston, Leics [Station Rd (B5328); SK5510], *Bradgate Arms*: Good value old-fashioned formerly simple village pub refurbished 1988 by Hoskins, its new owners; well kept real ales, family area and biggish garden; has had rather clubby atmosphere *(LYM)*

Dadlington, Leics [SP4097], *Dog &*

Hedgehog: Food pub with friendly atmosphere, real ale, generous helpings; in pretty village – pub rather hidden behind village green *(F N Clay)*

East Kirkby, Lincs [OS Sheet 122 reference 334623; TF3362], *Red Lion*: Good, clean, cosy Batemans pub full of clocks that chime and ring for ten minutes around each hour; friendly and welcoming landlord *(Phil and Sally Gorton)*

Eastwood, Notts [Giltbrook; B6010, off A610 – near M1 junction 26; SK4646], *New White Bull*: Reasonable food in friendly local with traditional working men's bar in front, nice back lounge, friendly service, unpretentious atmosphere, well kept Hardys & Hansons ales, garden behind *(Michael Bolsover)*

☆ **Edenham**, Lincs [A151; TF0621], *Five Bells*: Friendly waitresses, wide choice of bar food, well kept Camerons ales and log fire in spacious modernised lounge with neatly ranged tables; piped music, soft lighting, good play area in garden; children welcome *(LYM)*

Edwinstowe, Notts [Mansfield Rd; SK6266], *Manvers Arms*: Good reasonably priced food, good friendly and quick service *(Mrs M A Bradley)*

Elkesley, Notts [SK6975], *Robin Hood*: Very cosy and cheerful village pub with open fires and comfortable atmosphere, big helpings of good wholesome food all cooked by landlady – no convenience foods *(Mr and Mrs Sherlock)*

Epperstone, Notts [SK6548], *Cross Keys*: Very warm welcome, happy atmosphere, good choice of food, and good range of well served beers *(Geoff Moore, Stewart Argyle)*

Everton, Notts [SK6991], *Blacksmiths Arms*: Well kept popular pub with comfortable furnishings and nice atmosphere *(ILP)*

☆ **Ewerby**, Lincs [TF1247], *Finch Hatton Arms*: Well kept Wards Sheffield Best, good value food in very pleasant new restaurant – well prepared, ample helpings, quick service; lovely old building *(Richard Cole, R D Murray)*

☆ **Exton**, Leics [The Green; SK9211], *Fox & Hounds*: Elegant high-ceilinged lounge in comfortable and attractive village inn, in pretty surroundings; good value bar meals, well kept Sam Smiths real ales, quite separate lively public bar, restaurant; children in eating areas; bedrooms *(Ann Parker, T Nott, LYM)*

Farndon, Notts [SK7651], *Rose & Crown*: Well kept pub with good atmosphere and carefully prepared food *(B M A Hopkins)*

Frisby on the Wreake, Leics [Main St; SK6917], *Bell*: Well kept pub with good food including home-made soups and fruit pies, obliging staff, tables in yard overlooking village crossroads, fair range of wines, piped music *(RJH)*

Gainsborough, Lincs [Morton Terrace; SK8189], *Elm Cottage*: An oasis in this part of the world – nice local atmosphere, comfortable cottagey interior, friendly staff, well kept Bass on handpump, good traditional pub food at anachronistic prices *(David and Ruth Hollands)*

Gedney, Lincs [Chapelgate; TF4024], *Old Black Lion*: Much praised by loyal regulars for its food, homely atmosphere and real ale *(Anon)*

Glaston, Leics [SK8900], *Monkton Arms*: Good food in pub with lively atmosphere and unusual bar layout adding to ambience; often crowded at night *(David Surridge)*

Grantham, Lincs [Vine St; SK9135], *Blue Pig*: Ancient, attractive half-timbered pub decorated with hanging baskets in summer, connecting rooms; friendly staff, bar food served quickly and in generous helpings *(David and Ruth Hollands)*

Great Casterton, Lincs [TF0009], *Crown*: Good simple food, beer well kept, friendly atmosphere; pretty village *(N and J D Bailey, A V Lewis)*

Greetham, Leics [B668 Stretton–Cottesmore; SK9214], *Wheatsheaf*: Friendly staff and service, good atmosphere and attractive bar and restaurant area; extensive, sensibly priced choice of well cooked, generously served food on hot plates; good Marstons Pedigree, Sam Smiths and others *(M and J Back)*

Grimsthorpe, Lincs [A151; TF0422], *Black Horse*: Stripped stone, beams and blazing log fire in restaurant with good food; bedrooms *(Anon)*

☆ **Grimston**, Leics [SK6821], *Black Horse*: Cosy, well run pub full of cricket memorabilia: bats, plates, letters and items of clothing from famous cricketers; fresh home-cooked bar food includes delicious chicken soup, good gammon and superb choice of puddings – fine value *(Norman Edwardes)*

Halam, Notts [SK6754], *Wagon & Horses*: Immaculate village pub with open fire, well kept Marstons Pedigree on handpump, and wide range of good food served in separate dining area *(P Manning)*

Haltham, Lincs [Main Rd; TF2463], *Marmion Arms*: Small, comfortable two-bar pub in tiny hamlet, locally popular for food *(Mike and Kay Wilson)*

Hinckley, Leics [Upper Brook St; nr Police Stn; SP4294], *Black Horse*: Small and cosy true local where the Marstons always seems really well kept despite management changes; good food and nice atmosphere – particularly in winter *(Graham Bush)*; [New Buildings] *Greyhound*: Young, lively atmosphere, occasional jazz and well kept Marstons *(Graham Bush)*; [Watling St (A5)] *Lime Kilns*: Cosy atmosphere, well kept Marstons Pedigree in recently refurbished pub *(Clifford Spooner, Graham Bush)*; [The Borough] *Union*: Hotel which has been popular for its charming lounge and main entrance and good lunchtime bar food, undergoing building work summer 1988; bedrooms *(Graham*

Bush); [Coventry Rd, not far from M69 junction 1] *Wharf*: Old unspoilt many-roomed pub with collection of toby jugs in pleasant lounge, basic bar area, old-world snug with beams and brasses; good Marstons Burton and Pedigree *(G P Dyall)*

Horncastle, Lincs [Bull Ring; TF2669], *Bull*: Good reasonably priced food and good beer in pleasant pub; bedrooms *(A J Woodroffe)*; *Durham Ox*: Unspoilt pub with dark bar full of old cardboard drink advertisements, copper ornaments and stuffed animals *(Phil Gorton)*

Hose, Leics [Bolton Lane; SK7329], *Black Horse*: Clean, three-roomed classic village local with quarry-tiled floor in bar, settles in lounge, open fires, well kept Home Bitter and Mild, bar food, skittle alley, garden *(Richard Sanders)*

Hoton, Leics [A60; SK5722], *Packe Arms*: Spacious and comfortable Bird Bar and refurbished original older front part in welcoming pub with decent food, efficient service *(BB)*

Huthwaite, Notts [Blackwell Rd; off M1 junction 28; SK4759], *Miners Arms*: Has been a fine example of how locals used to be, seeming unchanged in character since built, with good Home ales on handpump, pub games, no food and local characters; but friendly landlady, in her 80s, retiring summer 1988 (as is Bruce the labrador who disposed of any unwanted nuts and crisps) – will Scottish & Newcastle change it all? *(Angie and Dave Parkes)*

Jacksdale, Notts [Stoneyford; SK4551], *Boat*: Beams, brasses, antlers, stripped walls and settles in comfortable bar with food from sandwiches to hot dishes including very good steak and kidney pie; carvery lunches (not Sat) and Weds–Sat evenings; bedrooms *(Cdr Patrick Tailyour)*

☆ **Kibworth Harcourt**, Leics [Main St (just off A6); SP6894], *Three Horseshoes*: Splendid well kept pub in delightful surroundings, reasonably priced good food including Sun lunch served in separate section, Marstons Pedigree on handpump *(C M Holt, Christopher Baker)*

Kirby Bellars, Leics [A607 towards Rearsby; SK7117], *Flying Childers*: Very friendly staff, good value food and Ind Coope Burton *(Dave Braisted)*

Kirby Muxloe, Leics [Main St; SK5104], *Royal Oak*: Reasonably priced food well above average in bar or restaurant of well refurbished village pub *(J P Sumner)*

☆ **Lambley**, Notts [Church St; SK6245], *Woodlark*: Well preserved and interestingly laid out mining-village pub with relaxing, quiet and timeless atmosphere, navy memorabilia on walls, a cheerful welcome for strangers and outstanding value cheap snacks; well kept Home ales, wide range of pub games including pool-room, table skittles and skittle alley; children in annexe

(Pete Storey, LYM – more reports please)

☆ **Langham**, Leics [Bridge St; SK8411], *Noel Arms*: Rather mixed reports on this neighbour to Ruddles Brewery since it came up for sale in late 1987; interesting furnishings in comfortable low-ceilinged lounge divided by big log fire in central chimney, smart covered terrace, and still has its extensive spread of help-yourself salads on a long refectory table *(Rob and Gill Weeks, LYM)*

Leadenham, Lincs [High St; A17; SK9552], *George*: Main attraction at this friendly stone-built pub is its large variety of good wine, beer (including Ruddles County and Theakstons Old Peculier) and Scotch whiskies; quickly served bar food available almost whenever inn is open, though service may not be speedy at busiest times; restaurant; children in games-room; bedrooms *(Rob and Gill Weeks)*

☆ **Leicester** [Silver St, nr covered market; SK5804], *Globe*: Period features including gas lighting and original woodwork, though its recent comfortable refurbishment could have been more sympathetic; reasonably priced lunchtime food upstairs, well kept Everards real ale with a guest beer such as Adnams *(Mr and Mrs P A Jones, Richard Sanders, Graham Bush, LYM)*

☆ **Leicester** [Charles St], *Rainbow & Dove*: Converted Post Office social club with full range of Hoskins beers and a guest such as Holdens Mild all kept well, good value lunchtime bar food, friendly landlord, attractive atmosphere (can't say the same for the bright décor – or indeed for all the customers), interesting collection of commemorative beer-bottles, large relief map of Britain with breweries marked, and jazz Sun evening *(Pete Storey, Graham Bush, Richard Sanders, Dave Butler, Lesley Storey)*

Leicester [Welford Rd], *Bricklayers Arms*: Recently extended lively pub, very busy for food and well kept Shipstones *(Graham Bush)*; [London Rd] *Marquis Wellington*: Adnams, Everards and Sam Smiths in pub which has been renovated without losing its old décor; popular at lunchtime for wide range of snacks and meals *(Alastair Lang)*; [King St] *Vin Quatre*: Enjoyable wine bar/pub with well kept Marstons Pedigree, attracting young trendy (not to say alternative) customers *(Michael Cooke)*

Linby, Notts [Main St; SK5351], *Horse & Groom*: Spacious pub with old-fashioned furniture, lots of plants, and wide choice of reasonably priced food and drink; children welcome *(Dominic Dixon)*

☆ **Lincoln** [Waterside North; SK9872], *Green Dragon*: Noble waterside Tudor building – carved sixteenth-century façade gave its homelier name 'The Cat Garret'; attractively timbered and beamed bar comfortably modernised with good use of interior wall partition, John Smiths beers, friendly staff (but somewhat regimented tables and chairs,

intrusive fruit machines); downstairs restaurant *(Nick Dowson, Alison Hayward, LYM)*

Lincoln [Steep Hill; SK9872], *Browns Pie Shop*: Competition for the neighbouring Wig & Mitre (see main entries); good cheap food, staff working really hard to please, well kept and reasonably priced Everards Tiger *(Heather Sharland)*; [Alfred St, off High St] *City Vaults*: Hatch service of well kept Wards ales, including Mild, in simple friendly town pub *(BB)*; [44 Bailgate] *Duke William*: Oak-beamed inn with stone walls, good lunchtime food in spacious pleasant bars, well kept Darleys, Wards and Youngers Scotch; bedrooms clean and cheerful *(Mary Henderson)*; [21 High St] *Golden Eagle*: Good Batemans beers and food, warm welcome *(J R Fen)*; [Greetwell Gate] *Morning Star*: Well kept Wilsons in very friendly pub close to cathedral and castle *(Dominic Williams)*; [Moor St/Newland St West] *Queen in the West*: Delightful family-run town pub well maintained, well kept Wards and Youngers No 3, home-cooked bar food, reasonably priced simple cooking *(David and Ruth Hollands)*; [310 High St] *Roebuck*: Well kept Shipstones ale in cosy and unpretentious town pub with low-key lighting and relaxed atmosphere *(Dominic Williams)*; [83 Westgate] *Strugglers*: Very good cheap Bass and Bass Mild on handpump in classic small two-room pub; very busy, near the castle *(Richard Sanders)*; [Union Rd] *Victoria*: Very busy two-room free house behind the castle, with well kept Timothy Taylors Landlord and other real ales such as Batemans XB, Everards Old Original and Old Mill; good lunchtime bar food, children's room *(Richard Sanders)*; [Waterside North] *Witch & Wardrobe*: Quite simple, with good value food including superb chips *(Revd Richard Hanson)*

Little Steeping, Lincs [TF4362], *Eaves*: Well kept beer, nice premises, very good value straightforward food *(Kevin and Mary Shakespeare)*

Long Sutton, Lincs [TF4222], *Bull*: Unspoilt, old-fashioned hotel, unchanged since 1920s judging by décor; bar counter off main passage, divided from it by Victorian sash window screen, and serving Bass on handpump; bedrooms *(Phil Gorton)*

Long Whatton, Leics [SK4723], *Falcon*: Good service and bar food, including marvellous well filled cobs and superb steaks *(Jill Hadfield, Tony Gallagher)*

Loughborough, Leics [canal bank, about ¼ mile from Loughborough Wharf; SK5319], *Albion*: Busy, welcoming, canalside local with friendly licensees, two rooms and central bar, whitewashed walls, brasses and mirrors; well kept Banks's Mild and Bitter, Hoskins & Oldfields HOB and Old Navigation, John Thompsons Lloyds Best and Shipstone Mild and Bitter; good value bar food including steak and kidney pie, lovely home-cooked beef rolls and occasional barbecues;

wonderful budgerigar aviary *(Pete Storey)*; [Meadow Lane] *Gate*: Friendly, small three-roomed pub with open fires, popular darts and dominoes, well kept Marstons Pedigree and Border Mild, reasonable lunchtime food, pleasant back garden with summer Sat barbecues *(Richard Sanders)*; [The Rushes (A6)] *Swan in the Rushes*: Well kept Batemans XXXB, Marstons Pedigree and weekend guest beers in rather austerely decorated two-room pub which is part-owned by owner of the Old Kings Arms in Newark (see main entries) and has good range of rather similar food, reasonably priced; juke box, fruit machine, live blues music Weds *(Richard Sanders)*

Louth, Lincs [Upgate; TF3387], *Greyhound*: Very warm welcome in friendly local inn with good open fire and nice collection of old artefacts; pleasant good value bar food such as lasagne, fish or steak and kidney pie, variety of traditional pub games, Sun evening quiz (with sandwiches on the house); bedrooms *(Francis Josephs)*; *Masons Arms*: Worth knowing for its good imaginative bar food, good chips too *(Nicholas Kingsley)*; [Pawn Shop Pass, Kidgate] *Scarfes*: Interesting choice of food, wine and local beers, friendly easy atmosphere *(J D K Hyams)*

Mansfield, Notts [Nottingham Rd; (a mile from centre); SK5561], *Talbot*: Friendly little two-roomed local refurbished 1988 by new licensee, good value food (evenings and Sun lunch too now), well kept Shipstones on handpump, open fires, pleasant atmosphere *(Angie and Dave Parkes, Derek and Sylvia Stephenson)*

Maplebeck, Notts [signposted from A616/A617; SK7160], *Beehive*: Deep in the country, snug little beamed bar with plain traditional furnishings, tables on small terrace with grassy bank running down to small stream, open fire, Mansfield or Websters Yorkshire real ale; an idyllic spot *(Rob and Gill Weeks, LYM – is the welcome for strangers still as warm?)*

Mapperley, Notts [187 Plains Rd; SK6043], *Tree Tops*: Completely refurbished, comfortable place with friendly service and very popular home-made lunches *(TWG)*

Marston, Lincs [2 miles E of A1 just N of Grantham; SK8943], *Thorold Arms*: Pleasant, peaceful atmosphere and efficient, cheerful service; plentiful hot food from a limited but reasonable menu *(Mr and Mrs G H Rosenthal)*

Medbourne, Leics [SP7993], *Neville Arms*: Lovely appearance and setting, with river and wooden bridge in front; very attractive front bar with well kept Hook Norton and Marstons Pedigree, good generously served reasonably priced food; very practical large family-room/dining-hall; pub often very busy *(Dave Butler, Lesley Storey, Dr A V Lewis)*

Minting, Lincs [The Green; off A158 Lincoln–Horncastle; TF1873], *Sebastopol*: Cosy, low-beamed old pub of character, under new

management (no more Batemans beer) with a fish tank set into wall; good hot food (not Sun) *(Frank Williams, Mike and Kay Wilson)*

Morton, Notts [SK7251], *Full Moon*: Pleasant atmosphere, relaxing décor, music in poolroom; Marstons Pedigree on handpump and good house wines, interesting and reasonably priced bar food, good service *(Derek and Sylvia Stephenson, F N Clay)*

Navenby, Lincs [SK9858], *Butchers Arms*: Ploughman's and big helpings of steak and kidney pie, casseroles, cod in cider and other food served quickly in friendly, very cosy (but spacious) and nicely kept pub with garden, popular with locals; clean and tidy; the potatoes sauté in garlic butter are particularly good *(Mrs P J Turner)*; [car park behind is off East Rd] *Kings Head*: Extensive range of good bar snacks and home-cooked specials in cosy bar/lounge, also evening restaurant and Sun lunch; well kept Sam Smiths beer *(Mr and Mrs HS)*

Nettleham, Lincs [The Green; TF0075], *Plough*: Friendly village pub in picturesque village centre and overlooking village green; well kept Batemans; RAF prints on walls *(Frank Williams)*

☆ **Newark**, Notts [Riverside; SK8054], *Navigation Co Brasserie*: Delightful warehouse conversion with genuine brasserie atmosphere and Everards Tiger *(Geoff Wilson)*

Newark [Market Pl], *Clinton Arms*: Spacious and smoothly if plainly modernised lounge bar, with Home real ales and restaurant; in the past this was a base of highwayman John 'Swift Nicks' Nevison; bedrooms *(LYM)*

Newington, Notts [Newington Rd; off A614 at Misson signpost; SK6794], *Ship*: Unpretentious and friendly roadside pub with well kept Home ales and lively public bar *(LYM)*

North Kilworth, Leics [4½ miles from M1 junction 20; A427 towards Market Harborough; SP6081], *White Lion*: Well kept Marstons Pedigree, good food in quality and quantity, restaurant *(Christopher Baker)*

☆ **North Muskham**, Notts [Ferry Lane; SK7958], *Muskham Ferry*: Lovely position by River Trent, friendly efficient staff, good bar food, cold buffet and restaurant; garden with children's slide, own moorings, slipway, private fishing *(E G and M L Peters, AE, GRE)*

Norton Disney, Lincs [SK8859], *St Vincent Arms*: Pleasant pub with photographs of Lincoln around the turn of the century on the lounge walls; Adnams, Batemans XXXB, Everards and Marstons; good range of vegetarian dishes, very good vegetable soup and enormous mixed grills; large well equipped play area for children *(Derek Stephenson)*

☆ **Nottingham** [Canalside; SK5640], *Morton Clayton & Fellows*: Newness has worn off this interesting canalside conversion with its own brewery attached, with lots of nooks and crannies, old dining-tables and so forth, very good collection of whisky-water jugs, extensive range of wines, rather loud 1960s pop music, bar food including magnificent hot beef sandwiches *(Ian Phillips, Dave Butler, Lesley Storey, T Mansell)*

☆ **Nottingham** [Canning Circus, Derby rd], *Sir John Borlace Warren*: Lots of comfortable small rooms, clay pipes and other old knick-knacks in cases, comfortable Chesterfields and small cast-iron-framed tables, big bay windows; nice location opposite Georgian almshouses in rather stately part of old Nottingham, at its highest point; well kept cheap Shipstones; well run, usually busy *(Ian Phillips, Stewart Argyle)*

Nottingham [Parliament St], *Blue Bell*: Well run city-centre pub with well kept Home ales, food reasonably priced and pleasant staff *(Stewart Argyle, D Simmonite)*; [Gt Northern Cl, off Canal St] *Grand Central*: Recently opened free house, converted railway buildings and viaduct arches; spacious bar, cosy seats in mock-up of Orient Express at top of iron stairs, furnishings and décor in keeping with theme; Tetleys and other real ales on handpump; good bar food and separate Victorian dining area *(David and Ruth Hollands)*; [Clumber St] *Lion*: Built in 1684, thoroughly modernised, one-roomed city-centre pub, Home Bitter, good cheap lunchtime meals *(Angie and Dave Parkes)*; [Canal St] *Narrow Boat*: Large Shipstone pub, good beer, hot lunchtime bar food *(Richard Sanders)*; [Wilford St; end of A453 into city, at canal bridge] *Navigation*: Refurbished in canal style with brightly coloured painted panels; waterside seats and tables, canal trips pick up here; Banks's Bitter and Mild on electric pump, lunchtime food *(Michael Bolsover)*; [Stony St] *Old Angel*: Well kept Home ales and lunchtime snacks in old two-room pub in the Lace Market area; upstairs room was used for forming many trade unions and is still used as a union chapel *(Richard Sanders)*; [Castle Rd, on corner opp castle grounds entrance] *Old Castle*: Traditionally decorated upstairs lounge with brass ornaments, stained-glass windows, reasonable lunchtime bar food, well kept Ansells, Ind Coope and occasional guest beers; downstairs bar, more studenty, has piano played some lunchtimes; some refurbishment due *(Michael Bolsover)*; [Lower Parliament St] *Old Dog & Partridge*: Good generously served ploughman's in variety and well kept Shipstones on handpump *(Angie and Dave Parkes)*; [Mansfield Rd] *Peacock*: Small, attractive two-roomed city-centre pub, lounge bar with bells for waiter service, no piped music, Home ales *(Stewart Argyle)*; [Market St] *Robin Hood*: This entertaining place done out as a medieval street, with a good range of reasonably priced food and less reasonably priced real ales, was closed in 1988 to make way for shopping centre; [Maid Marion Way] *Salutation*: The

ancient back part is attractive (the front part is plush modern), and new landlord has made a feature of the old cellars which can be visited at quiet times by arrangement; Whitbreads-related real ales, reasonably priced bar food – including snacks even late in the evening *(Ian Phillips, Graham Bush, BKA, BB)*; [Market Pl] *Talbot*: Very large, popular Yates wine lodge recently restored, with first-floor conservatory overlooking market place and basic, simple ground-floor bar; good lunchtime food; live music evenings *(Graham Bush)*; [402 Derby Rd] *Three Wheatsheaves*: Rambling old pub with flagstones, traditional furnishings, somewhat basic feel but good atmosphere; bar food, well kept Shipstones, summer lunchtime barbecues in big garden *(LYM)*; [Waverley Rd] *Vernon Arms*: Good value bar food in comfortable Italian-run suburban pub with tables on terrace and smart restaurant *(LYM)*

Oadby, Leics [Harborough Rd; A6 just SE of Leicester; SK6200], *Oadby Owl*: Attractive ex-coaching-inn with many rooms, good range of bar snacks and lunches, Marstons on handpump, darts and fruit machine, garden behind *(C Baker)*; [Harborough Rd, next to Wilkinsons] *Swinging Sporran*: Comfortably refurbished, attractively priced lunches, separate pool area (away from bar, so good for younger players); a Scottish & Newcastle pub *(C Baker)*

☆ **Oakham**, Leics [Market Pl; SK8508], *George*: Friendly old stone coaching-inn with oak-beamed and panelled lounge opening into cosy eating area, well kept Ruddles Best and County on handpump, children allowed in eating area, restaurant; bedrooms *(LYM)*

Oakham [Mill St], *Rutland Angler*: Good meals in well kept dining-room, Marstons Pedigree and Sam Smiths, pleasant licensee *(A E Alcock)*

Old Somerby, Lincs [SK9633], *Fox & Hounds*: Notable for good range of food including some spectacular sandwiches; good number of rooms with copper-topped tables and hunting-print wall benches and stools, good choice of real ales – Banks & Taylors SPA, Marstons Pedigree, Ruddles County and Theakstons Old Peculier *(Rob and Gill Weeks)*

Peatling Magna, Leics [SP5992], *Cock*: Very small, with uncrowded village atmosphere, reasonably priced wholesome food, nice character and very picturesque location in hamlet; hunt sometimes meets here *(J T C Heslop)*

Plumtree, Notts [just off A606 S of Nottingham; SK6132], *Griffin*: Popular for lunch, well kept Hardys & Hansons beer, good parking; interesting village church *(E Osborne)*; *Perkins*: Good food with extensive use of fresh products and all imaginatively prepared, good range of wines in cross between pub and restaurant – on balance more pub though not open Sun or Mon, and no real ale *(H J Stirling)*

Potterhanworth, Lincs [Cross St; TF0565], *Chequers*: Village free house, piano in lounge bar, cheerful landlady and landlord, creamy Mansfield 4X, wide range of bar food including superb gammon *(Frank Williams)*

Preston, Leics [Uppingham Rd; SK8602], *Kingfisher*: Though this warm and friendly pub has recently been reported by some readers as serving nicely cooked fresh food, others say there's none *(Mr and Mrs R G Ing – confirmation please)*

Quorndon, Leics [Meeting St; SK5616], *Blacksmiths Arms*: Popular and atmospheric two-roomed old pub, low ceilings, well kept Marstons Pedigree, lunchtime bar food, friendly staff *(Richard Sanders)*; [corner Meeting St and A6] *Royal Oak*: Popular pub with small snug at front, good Bass and M&B Mild, bar food *(Richard Sanders)*

Ratby, Leics [Boroughs Rd; SK5105], *Plough*: Cheerful unpretentious village local with lively Fri night singalongs, well kept Marstons real ales, simple cheap lunchtime food and good play area in big back garden; the snag is that you do feel a stranger *(LYM)*

Ravenshead, Notts [Main Rd (B6020); SK5956], *Little John*: Well organised modern pub with comfortable airy lounge, good value bar food, games in public bar, restaurant popular for lunch *(LYM)*

Rippingale, Lincs [High St; just off A15 Bourne–Sleaford; TF0927], *Bull*: Lovely warm convivial atmosphere, friendly personal service by happy staff, well kept Camerons, changing unusual food at low prices, wide choice of restaurant dishes, very big children's play area *(R D Murray, Mrs M G Longman)*

Rothwell, Lincs [Caistor Rd (A46); TF1599], *Nickerson Arms*: Friendly and relaxed atmosphere in attractive stone pub with well kept Batemans, Timothy Taylors and Tetleys on handpump, several guest beers, lunchtime meals Mon – Fri including very good home-made steak and kidney pie with fresh vegetables, seats outside; children's room *(Mrs A C Fallon, Mrs M E Lawrence)*

Salmonby, Lincs [TF3273], *Cross Keys*: Roomy and comfortable Wolds pub with friendly staff, well kept Websters and guest beers, above-average very reasonably priced food; bedrooms clean and comfortable, large breakfast *(Kevin and Mary Shakespeare)*

Sandilands, Lincs [TF5280], *Grange & Links*: Really good welcoming atmosphere, log fires, wide choice of beer, good choice of well prepared food in bar and dining-room; comfortable bedrooms *(C J Dowling)*

Scamblesby, Lincs [Old Main Rd; TF2879], *Green Man*: Virtually unspoilt basic pub with several rooms, only one being used regularly, with open fire and piano; known as Wyn's Place after long-serving landlady *(Phil Gorton, Dr and Mrs A K Clarke)*

☆ **Scotter**, Lincs [High St; SE8801], *Gamekeeper*: An oasis in this part of the world – old, with five rooms on different levels leading into each other; beams, panelling, Delft shelves and abundant china, stuffed birds and animals, varied seating; well kept Darleys, Wards and Youngers on handpump, wide choice of food *(David and Ruth Hollands)*

Scrooby, Notts [SK6591], *Pilgrim Fathers*: Nice cosy pub with recent conservatory extension filled with plants (not to mention a huge green plastic frog lurking in the undergrowth), snug even in winter; small choice of good food *(Sue Cleasby, Mike Ledger)*

Seacroft, Lincs [Vine Rd; off Drummond Rd; TF5660], *Vine*: Big surprise to find a seventeenth-century pub – where Lord Tennyson stayed – around Skegness; well run hotel, good bar snacks, Batemans real ale, pictures of variety artistes who have played at Skeg and stayed here; bedrooms *(John Honnor)*

☆ **Sharnford**, Leics [B4114; SP4791], *Falconer*: Falcons mewed at the back distinguish this well kept local, which also has an eagle owl and pets such as rabbits, ducks and kids; inside has stuffed ferrets, foxes, hawks and other birds, collection of jesses, hoods and so forth behind the bar; well kept Ansells Mild and Bitter and Tetleys on handpump, wide choice of good value food, quieter tables in wine-bar area behind bar, well reproduced pop music *(Ted George, BB)*

☆ **Sheepy Magna**, Leics [Main St (B4116); SK3201], *Black Horse*: Decently kept village pub with generous helpings of good value bar food including a very wide choice of cheeses for the ploughman's and particularly good steaks; well kept Marstons Pedigree and maybe Border ales, games in lively public bar, family area *(M J Williamson, Jon Wainwright, M and J Back, Geoff Lee, Cliff Spooner, LYM)*

☆ **Sileby**, Leics [Swan St; SK6015], *White Swan*: Comfortable and welcoming book-lined dining-lounge with good often interesting food – even the rolls are home-made, and the puddings are wonderful (no food Sun or Mon); friendly service *(P T Sharpe, Rodney R Elsley)*

☆ **Skendleby**, Lincs [Spilsby Rd; off A158 about 10 miles NW of Skegness – OS Sheet 122 reference 433697; TF4369], *Blacksmiths Arms*: Tiny village pub with a black-leaded fireplace in one of its two low-ceilinged rooms, open fire, no juke box or fruit machine, and Batemans XB particularly well kept – the largest cask size they use is six gallons, so they can always serve it at its peak; talk of possible sale – news please *(Richard Sanders, Phil and Sally Gorton)*

Somerby, Leics [Main St; SK7710], *Stilton Cheese*: New owners keeping up previous high standards – good choice of real ales on handpump, wide choice of imaginative food in ample helpings *(G I Carver)*

South Rauceby, Lincs [Main St; TF0245], *Bustard*: Friendly atmosphere, good well kept beers including a guest beer tapped from the cask, good value bar food *(Derek and Sylvia Stephenson, Bob Sutherland)*

South Thoresby, Lincs [about 1 mile off A16; TF4077], *Vine*: Very friendly little inn with fair choice of beers and bar food; bedrooms *(Chris Fluck)*

☆ **Southwell**, Notts [SK6953], *Saracens Head*: Interesting old THF hotel with well kept John Smiths on handpump, good value bar lunches in main beamed Smoke Room bar which has a good deal of character, pleasant helpful staff; they've recently uncovered an old wall painting in room where Charles I spent his last free night; children in eating area or restaurant; bedrooms comfortable and well kept, though some are small *(Mr and Mrs Bill Muirhead, E J and J W Cutting, David and Ruth Hollands, Rob and Gill Weeks, M D Hampson, A V Lewis, LYM)*

Southwell, Notts [Church St (A612); SK6953], *Bramley Apple*: Named after the apple that originated here, this pub boasts an unusual 3-D sign, one comfortably furnished room split into two by corridor, Batemans XXXB on handpump, good food *(Angie and Dave Parkes)*

Spilsby, Lincs [TF4066], *White Hart*: Well kept Bass on handpump, generous helpings of speciality home-cooked ham salads, friendly service *(Mr and Mrs David Hollands)*

☆ **Stamford**, Lincs [Broad St; TF0207], *Lord Burghley*: Splendidly renovated and popular town-centre pub with a fine range of well kept real ales such as Adnams, Greene King IPA and Abbot and Marstons Pedigree; nice atmosphere and good choice of bar lunches served by friendly staff; garden *(T Mansell, Dr A V Lewis, Steve Coley)*

Stamford [High St, St Martins], *Anchor*: Large and friendly old stone-built pub with good bar food, spacious open-plan modern bar, very pleasant service, popular with younger people at night; bedrooms *(John Roué, T Mansell)*; [All Saints Pl] *Crown*: Good bar with pleasant atmosphere, well kept Bass and Ruddles County, good range of bar food, separate dining-room; bedrooms *(T Mansell)*; [East St] *Dolphin*: Friendly staff, well kept Charles Wells ales and good value bar food in small back-street pub with good atmosphere *(T Mansell)*; [Casterton Rd] *Green Man*: Recently comfortably refurbished free house with well kept real ales and friendly landlord; can get rather noisy and smoky *(Steve Coley, A V Lewis)*; *Hole in the Wall*: Good choice of beers and wine, good food, lively atmosphere; full of character, with oak beams *(Martin Ball)*; [Maiden Lane] *Kings Head*: Small two-roomed pub with interesting coin collection, notably welcoming staff serving well kept Ind Coope ales, decent bar food, separate restaurant

(T Mansell, Steve Coley); [St Marys St] *St Marys Vaults*: Low-beamed local with log fire in front room, hunting prints on the walls and friendly service; well kept beer and good food; popular with younger people in the evening *(T Mansell)*; [Scotgate] *White Swan*: Nice quiet Manns pub *(C E Tyers)*

Stanton under Bardon, Leics [Main St; 1½ miles from M1 junction 22, off A50 towards Coalville; SK4610], *Old Thatched Inn*: Large, friendly, one-roomed thatched pub divided into four drinking areas, one with open fire; Marstons Pedigree and maybe Border Mild on handpump; lunchtime and evening bar food including good grills (Mon to Sat, Sun lunch by prior booking) *(Richard Sanders)*

Staunton in the Vale, Notts [SK8043], *Staunton Arms*: Warmly welcoming village pub with first-class reasonably priced food; closed summer 1988 for renovations *(B M A Hopkins)*

Stickford, Lincs [A16; TF3560], *Red Lion*: Small homely inn with good value bar food, limited choice of good beers; bedrooms *(Chris Fluck)*

Stoke Bardolph, Notts [Riverbank Rd; SK6441], *Ferryboat*: Imaginative well presented food, tasteful mix of modern and old-style decoration with nautical flavour, friendly efficient service, nice spot by River Trent with tables outside and play area, Shipstones beer; can be very popular weekends and evenings *(Michael Bolsover)*

☆ **Stoke Golding**, Leics [High St; SP3997], *Three Horseshoes*: Good choice of food from hot and cold buffet, and traditional Sun lunch, in nicely decorated village pub with good service in roomy canalside bar with friendly staff and well kept real ales such as Marstons and Ruddles; also cocktail bar and big restaurant; children welcome *(Mrs M Lavender, C D T Spooner, Mandy and Mike Challis, F N Clay)*

Stoney Stanton, Leics [Long St; SP4894], *Blue Bell*: Popular local with well kept Everards Bitter, Tiger and Old Original on handpump, good value straightforward food; busy at weekends *(Mike Tucker)*

Stow, Lincs [SK8882], *Cross Keys*: Carefully modernised to give space without losing homely style, inviting food, good atmosphere; in shadow of massive cathedral-like village church *(Richard Trigwell)*

Stretton, Leics [Great North Rd (A1); SK9416], *Ram Jam*: Much refurbished old inn with very good Ruddles and outstanding house wine in large, comfortable bar; varied imaginative and sensibly priced food in bar and restaurant; breakfasts and simpler dishes served 7–11am, main menu 11–11; good service, tables outside; bedrooms most attractively decorated and thoughtfully equipped, *(Joy Heatherley)*

☆ **Surfleet**, Lincs [A16 nearby; TF2528], *Mermaid*: Family-run riverside free house with good bar and restaurant food, well kept beer, pleasant staff, garden *(Oliver Tame, D A Green)*

☆ **Sutton Bonington**, Leics [3 miles from M1 junction 24; SK5025], *Old Plough*: Good value bar food and well kept Shipstones real ales in roomy well run modern pub with good local atmosphere and roaming cats *(Peter Storey, Lesley Storey, LYM)*

☆ **Sutton Cheney**, Leics [Main St; off A447 3 miles S of Market Bosworth; SK4100], *Hercules*: Always a pub to please some but not others, this is most notable for its extensive range of well kept real ales, changing frequently and including rarities as well as one or two brewed for the pub; the previously very old-fashioned bar has recently been modernised (the old high settles have gone, and carpet has encroached on the flagstones), and the lounge is now more of a restaurant; piped pop music may be loud, the licensees are very friendly *(Lee Goulding, Michael Cooke, Jon Wainwright, C D T Spooner, T Nott, Gill Austin, Rob Weeks, Gwen and Peter Andrews, Ian Blackwell, W S Wright)*

Sutton in Ashfield, Notts [Alfreton Rd; off M1 junction 28; SK5059], *Duke of Sussex*: Consistently good value bar food (not Mon), especially steak sandwich, in friendly pub with quiet lounge and lively tap-room; Hardys & Hansons on electric pump *(Angie and Dave Parkes)*

☆ **Tattershall Thorpe**, Lincs [TF2259], *Blue Bell*: Very friendly landlord, good reasonably priced food, real ale, cosy and comfortable pub very attractive outside and in; loud juke box in pool-room *(Kevin and Mary Shakespeare, Mike and Kay Wilson)*

Tetford, Lincs [OS Sheet 122 reference 333748; TF3374], *White Hart*: Small and friendly sixteenth-century inn with stone floor, settles and open fire in very pleasant back bar, small snug bar too; well kept Batemans, nice choice of very reasonably priced good food; nr GWG114, in lovely Wolds countryside; bedrooms *(Kevin and Mary Shakespeare, Phil and Sally Gorton)*

Thrussington, Leics [SK6415], *Star*: Friendly village pub in fox-hunting country, good sandwiches, remarkably good Ind Coope Bitter and Burton, knowledgeable and efficient bar staff *(Dave Butler, Lesley Storey)*

☆ **Tugby**, Leics [Main St; village signposted off A47 E of Leicester, bear right in village; SK7600], *Black Horse*: Good value home-made evening meals in cosy and attractively traditional small rooms of picturesque black and white thatched village pub, Ansells on handpump, friendly service, log fire; children welcome; closed lunchtime *(Michael Craig, LYM)*

☆ **Upper Hambleton**, Leics [village signposted from A606 on E edge of Oakham; SK9007], *Finches Arms*: Well kept Marstons and

Ruddles County in country pub on the high ground that's now largely surrounded by Rutland Water – the Upper part of the village's name is really redundant now, as what was Lower Hambleton is under water; unpretentious, though there's now a large restaurant extension at the back *(Rob and Gill Weeks, Michael Bolsover, Mel Bodfish, LYM)*

Uppingham, Leics [High St West; SP8699], *White Hart*: Friendly pub, John Smiths on handpump, piped music, wide range of good fresh food, comfortable dining area *(Dr M S Saxby)*

☆ **Wainfleet**, Lincs [High St; TF5058], *Angel*: Very friendly and obliging young licensees, good home-made food, well kept real ales on cask with unusual guest beers; restaurant; children very welcome *(Mrs Karen Mitchell, C M Clements)*

Walkeringham, Notts [off B1403; SK7792], *Brickmakers Arms*: Well kept beer, friendly atmosphere, good bar food *(G A Hannam)*

Walton on the Wolds, Leics [Loughborough Rd; SK5919], *Anchor*: Good food, especially sausages and puddings, good sparkling wine; well kept real ale at weekends *(Dave Butler, Lesley Storey)*

Washingborough, Lincs [TF0270], *Ferry Boat*: Friendly village pub with reconstructed millwheel; Ruddles County and Wilsons on handpump; separate eating area with own bar and salad bar *(Frank Williams)*

West Bridgford, Notts [SK5837], *Trent Bridge*: Old pub with associations with neighbouring Test cricket ground; good beer, good hot and cold bar food *(David Gaunt)*

Wilford, Notts [Main Rd; SK5637], *Ferry*: Large Shipstones pub on banks of River Trent near riverside church, plush lounge, pleasant main bar, large varied clientele *(J L Thompson)*

Wilsford, Lincs [TF0042], *Plough*: Good choice of beers including changing guest beers from all over the country, good value food *(C J Dowling)*

Woodhall Spa, Lincs [Tattershall Rd; TF1963], *Abbey Lodge*: Pleasant surroundings, welcoming fire, above-average food though there may be quite a wait for it, well kept John Smiths real ale *(Peter Burton, J A Stuart)*; [Broadway] *Golf*: Big black and white hotel just outside village, good cheap bar food popular with locals and visitors, good service *(Mike and Kay Wilson)*

Woodhouse Eaves, Leics [SK5214], *Bulls Head*: Bright and cheerful, with quickly served good food *(Jill Hadfield)*

Wymeswold, Leics [SK6023], *Hammer & Pincers*: Well kept Bass and occasional guest beers, small choice of reasonably priced food; nice atmosphere – never too busy *(Michael Bolsover)*

Lincolnshire *see* Leicestershire

Midlands (Northamptonshire, Warwickshire and West Midlands)

Changes in this big area include new licensees at the interestingly laid out Royal Oak in Eydon (much redecoration), the Fox & Hounds at Great Wolford (flagstones uncovered, tap-room reopened, bedrooms redone, a new terrace outside), the very lively Little Dry Dock in Netherton, the Wharf at Old Hill (lots of real ales, changing every few days), the atmospheric Old Mint at Southam, and the Three Conies at Thorpe Mandeville (friendly and relaxed, doing all their own food – nothing bought in). The latest development in the saga of that famous own-brew pub, the Old Swan in Netherton, is that Hoskins have taken it over; still well worth visiting, and still brewing just as before. The Butchers Arms at Farnborough which has been very popular for food seems well back on form now – as its reinstated food award shows. Food's a particularly strong point too at several of the entirely new entries: the friendly Chequers at Ettington, the spacious and well run White Hart at Newbold on Stour, the White Bear at Shipston on Stour (particularly imaginative; this well decorated place is under the same ownership as our popular Gloucestershire entry the Fossebridge Inn at Fossebridge), the Slug & Lettuce in Stratford (imaginative dishes here too) and

The Boat, Stoke Bruerne

the Plough in the pretty village of Warmington (we had a delicious simple bar lunch from the very new licensees here). Another new entry also has very new licensees quickly making a name for themselves – the civilised Rose & Crown at Charlton, with a fine range of real ales and other drinks. Besides the many main entries to follow up (this area's strong in combining real individuality and character in a pub with the more sybaritic virtues of good beer and food – even at the simplest level of that excellent local delicacy the hot pork or beef sandwich), lots of the Lucky Dip entries at the end of the chapter look specially promising. We'd mention particularly the Kings Head at Aston Cantlow, the Cottage of Content at Barton, both the Old Windmill and the Town Wall in Coventry, the Bottle & Glass in Dudley (a living museum piece – but it keeps museum hours), the Case is Altered at Five Ways, the Little White Lion in Halesowen and the Pie Factory in Tipton (two of Mr O'Rourke's entertaining and slowly growing small chain of 'Little' pubs), the Howard Arms at Ilmington, the Saltwells at Quarry Bank and the Rose & Crown at Ratley.

ALDERMINSTER (War) SP2348 Map 4
Bell ⊗

A34 Oxford–Stratford

There's a firm emphasis on the high quality, home-made food in this attractively refurbished pub: sandwiches, soup such as bortsch (£1.50), various pâtés (£2.25), ploughman's (£2.45), seafood and mushroom scallop (£2.50), salads (from £3.75), and lots of changing specials such as red-hot pork spare ribs or braised sausage in red wine (£4), crispy topped lamb in cider, chicken in tarragon or steak, kidney and oyster pie (all £5), and seafood platter (£7.95), with puddings such as chocolate mousse or raspberry parfait. Flowers IPA and Original on handpump, and a good range of wines (from Berry Bros & Rudd); friendly service; darts, dominoes, piped music. The spacious rambling bar has several different communicating areas that manage to keep an old-fashioned feeling of cosiness. There are plenty of stripped slat-back chairs around wooden tables (each with a plant on it), a panelled oak settle, little vases of flowers, small landscape prints and swan's-neck brass-and-globe lamps on the cream walls, a solid-fuel stove in a stripped brick inglenook, and bare boards and flagstones at one end, with a russet carpet at the other. There are white tables under cocktail parasols on the sheltered grass of what must once have been a coachyard. (*Recommended by Simon Turner, T Nott, Ian Phillips, M A and C R Starling, S J A Velate, H G Bown*)

Free house   Licensee Keith Brewer   Real ale   Meals and snacks (not Mon evening) Restaurant tel *Alderminster (078 987) 414   Children welcome   Pianist Fri, Sat, Weds in summer, Sat in winter   Open 12–2.30, 7–11 all year; closed Mon evenings and 25 Dec*

ASHBY ST LEDGERS (Northants) SP5768 Map 4
Old Coach House ★ ⊗

4 miles from M1 junction 18; A5 S to Kilsby, then A361 S towards Daventry; village signposted left

The lounge bar in this friendly dark stone house is made up of several snug little rooms with high-backed winged settles on the polished black and red tiles, old kitchen tables with candles and flowers, harness on a few standing timbers, hunting pictures (often of the Pytchley, which sometimes meets outside), Thelwell prints, and a big log fire in winter. Even readers who feel there's still scope for some smartening up (and the pub does now seem to be largely on top of its earlier housekeeping problems) still like the feel of the place with its relaxed atmosphere and lived-in feel. A front room has darts, and there are pool, and piped music

Please use this card to tell us which pubs *you* think should or should not be included in the next edition of *The Good Pub Guide*. Just fill it in and return it to us – no stamp or envelope needed. And don't forget you can also use the report forms at the end of the *Guide*.

ALISDAIR AIRD

Your name and address (block capitals please)

☐ *Please tick this box if you would like extra report forms*

REPORT on   *(pub's name)*

Pub's address:

☐ YES MAIN ENTRY   ☐ YES *Lucky Dip*   ☐ NO don't include
Please tick one of these boxes to show your verdict, and give reasons and descriptive comments, prices etc:

☐ Deserves FOOD award   ☐ Deserves PLACE-TO-STAY award

REPORT on   *(pub's name)*

Pub's address:

☐ YES MAIN ENTRY   ☐ YES *Lucky Dip*   ☐ NO don't include
Please tick one of these boxes to show your verdict, and give reasons and descriptive comments, prices etc:

☐ Deserves FOOD award   ☐ Deserves PLACE-TO-STAY award

The Good
Pub Guide

The Good Pub Guide
Freepost
London SW10 0BR

(anything from Brahms to Tina Turner). Bar food includes giant prawns or slices of local pork pie, Danish herrings (£1.50), ploughman's, pâté (£2.25), a good helping of mixed meats (£3.75), turkey and game casserole, a wide and very popular range of good salads, herrings in madeira sauce, duckling (£6.25), and steak in pepper sauce (£6.50); also, vegetarian dishes, puddings (£1), children's reductions, and enormous breakfasts. Besides well kept Everards, Flowers and Sam Smiths on handpump, there are guest beers. They stock quite a grand collection of wines by the bottle, and do hot toddy in winter. In summer, barbecues are held outside or in the conservatory/vinery, and there are seats among fruit trees and under a fairy-lit arbour, with a climbing-frame, slide and swings. The attractive village has thatched stone houses, with wide grass verges running down to the lane. (*Recommended by Clare Greenham, Bernard Phillips, BKA, M R Watkins, Jeremy and Margaret Wallington, Nick Dowson, Alison Hayward, R P Hastings, Cynthia McDowell, Ken and Rob and Gill Weeks, Rachel Waterhouse, Barbara Turner, GAC, MJC, A J Davenport, Michael O'Driscoll, Jane and Calum, Mr and Mrs J H Adam, Yvonne Healey, Mr and Mrs G D Amos*)

Free house Licensees Douglas and Frederika Jarvis Real ale Meals (not Sun or Mon) and snacks (not Sun evening) Children in family areas exc after 8 Landlady sometimes sings with guitar Open 12–2.30 (3 Sat), 6–11 all year; opens 7 in winter; closed evening 25 Dec Bedrooms (four-posters in all rooms) tel Rugby (0788) 890349; £27.50B/£35B

BERKSWELL (W Midlands) SP2479 Map 4
Bear

Spencer Lane; village signposted from A452

The cannon in front of this picturesque timbered building is a veteran of the Crimean War and blasted nearby buildings when it was fired with blank ammunition during local festivities some years ago. The pub is popular and unassuming, with good bar food that includes rolls and five changing main dishes such as braised liver and onions or chilli con carne (£3.10), steak and kidney pie, sweet-and-sour pork or fish pie (£3.20), and roast loin of pork (£3.25); on weekday lunchtimes they have a cold table with quiches, cold meats and cheese and help-yourself salads (£3). Ruddles County and Wilsons Bitter on handpump; friendly service, piped music. There are tables and chairs out on the tree-sheltered back lawn. In the village, the church, in a very pretty setting, is well worth a visit. (*Recommended by J S Evans, J Harvey Hallam, Charles Gurney, Rob and Gill Weeks, Tim Heslop, G Cooper, Lyn and Bill Capper, Gill Rigg, Neil Patrick*)

Manns (Watneys) Real ale Meals and snacks Restaurant tel Berkswell (0676) 33202 Children welcome if eating Open 11–2.30, 6–10.30

BIRMINGHAM (W Midlands) SP0786 Map 4
Bartons Arms ★ ★

Birmingham 6; 2 miles from M6 junction 6; leave junction on A38(M) towards city centre but take first exit, going right at exit roundabout into Victoria Road, and left at next big roundabout into Aston High Street – A34 towards city centre; pub on the next corner at Park Lane (B4144); car park just past pub on opposite side of road; pub also an unmissable landmark on A34 going N from town centre

Some pubs that are architecturally splendid can be lifeless museum pieces. This one, though, manages to combine magnificent Edwardian opulence with a bustling atmosphere. There's a variety of rooms from palatial salons to cosy snugs with lots of highly polished mahogany and rosewood, elaborate richly coloured and painted tilework (perhaps its most striking feature), sparkling cut-glass mirrors and stained glass, rich curtains, plush seating, heavy brass hanging lamps, and a full set of painted cut-glass snob screens – little swivelling panels that you open when you want a drink, and shut when you want privacy – around its central bar counter. Bar food includes sandwiches (from 60p), ploughman's (£1.50), scampi (£1.95), daily specials like beef and Guinness pie, lasagne or chilli con carne (£2.30), and a cold table. Well kept M&B Mild and Brew XI on handpump; fruit machine, space game and juke box. *(Recommended by Jon Wainwright, Rob and Gill Weeks, H G and C J McCafferty, Brian Jones, Dave Butler, Les Storey, E J Alcock, GB, David Mabey)*

Mitchells & Butlers (Bass) Licensee Stephen Lefevre Real ale Lunchtime meals and snacks (not Sat or Sun) Restaurant tel 021-359 0853 Jazz club Fri, free and easy Sun, nostalgia first Sun lunchtime in month, big band first Mon in month, Hatbox orchestra first Sat evening in month, blues last Thurs in month Open 11–2.30, 5.30–10.30

CHARLTON (Northants) SP5236 Map 4
Rose & Crown

Village signposted from A41 at W edge of Aynho, and from Kings Sutton

The friendly new licensees (and their quiet collie Boltby) had been at this neat thatched stone house for only a few weeks when we inspected – yet the atmosphere already had that civilised and solid feel that usually comes only with long tenure. The fine choice of real ales on handpump, Arkells, Everards Tiger, Marstons Burton and Pedigree, Tetleys, Wadworths 6X and a guest beer, were well kept, too, and there were some *recherché* malt whiskies among the better known ones. The beamed bar has a sofa and winged armchairs as well as seats that match its sturdy country-kitchen tables, and there are shelves of books by the big open fireplace. Walls are mainly stripped to the carefully coursed masonry, with two or three good prints. Bar food includes sandwiches (from 70p), ploughman's (£1.75), spaghetti bolognese or steak and kidney pie (£2.50), salads (from £2.50), Barnsley chop (£3.75) and steaks (from £5.50); there are a couple of picnic-table sets on a small front terrace by the village lane, with a few more on gravel behind. They hope to have bedrooms ready by the 1989 Grand Prix. *(Recommended by James Ogier, John Croft, Michael O'Driscoll, P G M Connolly, Dr and Mrs A K Clarke)*

Free house Licensee Peter Reeves Real ale Meals and snacks Restaurant tel Banbury (0295) 811317 open until 4 Sun Children's room Open 11–2.30ish, 5.30–11 all year Bedrooms planned

EASTCOTE (Northants) SP6753 Map 4
Eastcote Arms

Gayton Road; village signposted from A5 3 miles N of Towcester

This stone-built village pub has a profusion of pictures above the dark brown wooden dado that reflects an individual taste (running to cricket, fishing and other sports, and to militaria) much more than in most pubs, and include many linked to the pub and its history; there are fresh flowers on tables, two log fires in winter, and simple traditional seats have cushions matching the flowery curtains. The well kept real ales include a fine fragrant beer brewed for them by Banks & Taylors especially for them (though now sold elsewhere too) as well as Adnams Extra, Marstons Pedigree, Sam Smiths OB and a guest beer changing monthly such as Brakspears SB. Food includes rolls (65p), soup (85p), sandwiches (from 85p), good big home-made pasty with gravy (£1.55), ploughman's (£1.85), and daily specials like lasagne or goulash (£2.45) or steak and kidney pie (£2.55); dominoes, cribbage and unobtrusive piped music – conversation clearly takes precedence here. There are picnic-table sets and other tables in an attractive back garden, with roses, geraniums and other flowers around the neat lawn. *(Recommended by Dr and Mrs A K Clarke, Nick Dowson, Alison Hayward)*

Free house Licensees Mike and Sheila Manning Real ale Lunchtime snacks (not Sun or Mon) Open 12–2.30, 6–10.30; closed Mon lunchtime, exc bank hols

Food details, prices, timing, etc. refer to bar food – not to a separate restaurant if there is one.

ETTINGTON (War)   SP2749 Map 4
Chequers
A422 Banbury–Stratford

Decidedly one for the inner soul, this outwardly straightforward pub serves
enterprising and carefully cooked food such as a good vegetarian bake (£3.35),
cockaleekie pie (£3.45), tripe and onions (£3.50), smoked haddock pasta (£3.85)
and pigeon breast marinated in red wine and juniper berries and served with bacon
and mushrooms (£4.25), besides more usual pub food such as sandwiches (from
90p), ploughman's with a good choice of cheeses (£2.60), steaks (from eight-ounce
sirloin £7.30) and children's dishes (£1.40); they price the additional help-yourself
summer buffet according to how much you take (£2.95–£5.95). The main bar's at
the back: brown leatherette wall seats and modern chairs, attractive Ros Goody
Barbour-jacket-era sporting prints, a shih-tzu called Nemesis and a Hungarian
vizsla called Alex (a father for the first time this year – with no fewer than a dozen
pups, he seems well on the way to making this breed a lot less rare). Well kept
Adnams, M&B Brew XI and Marstons Pedigree on handpump, thoughtful and
friendly service; sensibly placed darts, dominoes, trivia machine and juke box in the
simple front bar, pool-room, and on our visit unobtrusive piped country music.
There are tables out on the neat back lawn and on an awninged terrace, with lots of
hanging baskets. *(Recommended by Frank Cummins, S V Bishop, T Nott)*

*Free house   Licensees Jan and Fred Williams   Real ale   Meals and snacks   Well behaved
children allowed   Open 11–2.30, 6–11 all year; closed evening 25 Dec*

EYDON (Northants)   SP5450 Map 4
Royal Oak
Lime Avenue; village signposted from A361 Daventry–Banbury in Byfield, and from B4525

The several small idiosyncratic and recently decorated rooms in this stone village
pub are linked by a central corridor room, with its own serving-hatch. The other
place to get bar service is the room on the right as you go in – flagstones, cushioned
wooden wall benches built into alcoves, seats in a bow window, low beams, some
cottagey pictures, and an open fire. Well kept Banks's Bitter, Hook Norton, and
Ringwood Fortyniner on handpump, with guest beers like Batemans or Hansons
Black Country; friendly informal service. As we went to press, they only had
sandwiches (60p) and basket meals (from £1.20), but were in the process of
working out a proper bar menu and opening a restaurant. Darts, dominoes,
cribbage, fruit machine and piped music, with table skittles in a separate room.
There should be a club room for under-18s by the time this book is published.
(Previously recommended by John Thompson, John and Joan Wyatt)

*Free house   Licensee A Macari   Real ale   Meals and snacks   Restaurant tel Daventry
(0327) 60470   Children in lounge and own club room   Open 11–2.30, 6.30–11*

FARNBOROUGH (War)   SP4349 Map 4
Butchers Arms ⊗
This is now decidedly a dining pub, very much enjoyed by readers for superior
home-made food – meals rather than snacks, at prices to match. Recent redecoration symbolises the freshened-up feel of the place, which this year seems firmly back
on form. The farmhouse-style main lounge bar is furnished with simple, well made
stripped deal pews and stout deal tables on the carpet; this opens into a barn-like
extension with a flagstone floor, huge timbers, furniture made from old pine
including a very long table, pretty fabrics and lots of plants, and the walls are
decorated with brass, copper and bric-à-brac; at one end French windows overlook
a colourful rockery. There is a carpeted front public bar. Though the bar meals can

be delicious and interesting, and there's a range of attractive salads (from £3.50), a typical price is now £4.95 for home-made pies, casseroles, vegetarian dishes and so forth, with quite a bit of concentration on more elaborate restaurantish food (around £6–£11 for main dishes); very good Sunday lunch (£5.95). If you are depending on a meal, it might be wise to ring first. Well kept Flowers IPA and Original and a guest beer that changes every couple of months, such as Everards, Hook Norton or Whitbreads Pompey Royal on handpump, and cocktails; dominoes and piped music. The pub, with its matching stableblock opposite, is set well back from the village road, and the safely fenced-in front lawn is equipped with playthings such as climb-in toadstools, a sandpit, a sputnik with slide and so forth. There are tables and swings by a yew tree on another flower-edged lawn which slopes up behind. (*Recommended by S V Bishop, Jon Wainwright, J C Proud, Mr and Mrs R Tod, Virginia Jones, Tom Evans, Rob and Gill Weeks*)

Free house   Real ale   Meals and snacks   Restaurant   Children welcome (not in public bar) Restaurant tel Farnborough (029 589) 615   Open 11–2.30, 6–11 all year; may consider opening longer in afternoon if trade demands; closed 25 Dec except 1 hour lunchtime

FOTHERINGHAY (Northants)   TL0593   Map 5
Falcon ⊗

Village signposted off A605 on Peterborough side of Oundle

Though there is a simpler public bar which the landlord prefers to keep for the locals, the comfortable lounge in this pretty stone pub has antique engravings on its cream walls, cushioned slat-back armchairs and bucket chairs, winter log fires in stone fireplaces at each end, and a hum of quiet conversation. Good bar food includes home-made soups (£1.20), home-made chicken pâté (£1.40), ploughman's (£1.50), sweet spiced herring salad (£1.70), moussaka (£3), steak and kidney pie (£3), rabbit in cider with apples and walnuts (£4.20), gammon (£4.40), fresh Grimsby cod (£5), steaks (from £6), and puddings like fresh fruit salad or rhubarb and ginger crumble (£1.40); prices are slightly cheaper at lunchtime. On weekend lunchtimes they only do a cold buffet. Well kept Adnams, Elgoods Greyhound, and Greene King IPA and Abbot on handpump; darts, shove-ha'penny, dominoes, cribbage. Quietly welcoming service; magazines to read. There are seats in the neat side garden. The pub carries the sign of the Yorkist falcon – which, gilded, also tops the striking lantern tower of the vast church (well worth a visit) just behind it. (*Recommended by T Nott, G N G Tingey, R F Neil, Dr A V Lewis, Dave Butler, Lesley Storey, Amanda Flint*)

Free house   Licensee Alan Stewart   Real ale   Meals (not Mon or weekend lunchtimes) and snacks (not Mon evening)   Children in eating area   Open 10–2.30, 6–11 all year; closed Mon evening in winter

GREAT WOLFORD (War)   SP2434   Map 4
Fox & Hounds 🛏

New licensees have taken over this sixteenth-century Cotswold-stone inn and have made some alterations – the flagstone floors have been uncovered, a small tap-room re-opened, the bedrooms re-done, and there's a new terrace with a well. The beamed open-plan bar has a pair of high-backed old settles and other comfortable armchairish seats around a nice collection of old tables, well cushioned wall benches and window seat, and a large stone fireplace with a good winter log fire by the marvellous old bread oven. There are old hunting prints on the walls, which are partly stripped back to the bare stone. Food includes watercress soup (£1.05), pâté (£1.75), ploughman's (£1.90), lasagne (£2.95), salads (£3.45), steak and kidney pie (£3.95), Turkish-style lamb or sweet-and-sour pork (£4.25), sirloin steak in red wine sauce (£6), and puddings like spotted dick with custard or chocolate mousse (£1.45). Well kept Flowers IPA and Original, Whitbreads Pompey Royal and a guest beer on handpump or tapped from the cask; darts, shove-ha'penny, dominoes, chess, draughts, cards, spoof, fruit machine, and occasional piped music. *(Recommended by Paul S McPherson, GDH, Dave Braisted, J S Evans; more reports on the new regime please)*

Free house   Licensees David and Joan Hawker   Meals and snacks   Weekend restaurant   Children in eating area of bar   Open 11–2.30, 6.30 (6 Sat)–11 all year; opens 7 in winter   Bedrooms tel Barton-on-the-Heath (060 874) 220; £15B/£30B

HIMLEY (W Midlands – though see below)   SO8889   Map 4
Crooked House   ★

Pub signposted from B4176 Gornalwood–Himley, OS Sheet 139 reference 896908; readers have got so used to thinking of the pub as being near Kingswinford in the Midlands (though Himley is actually in Staffs) that we still include it in this chapter – the pub itself is virtually smack on the county boundary

This pub – formerly known as the Glynne Arms – is literally staggering: as a result of mining it has subsided wildly, with very steeply sloping walls and floors – even getting the doors open is an uphill struggle, and on one sloping table a bottle on its side actually rolls 'upwards' against the apparent direction of the slope. A large new (straight) back extension with local antiques has been built, though it's not visible from the front, and on the whole readers don't feel it's spoilt the character too much. Bar food includes sandwiches, plaice or home-made faggots (£1.95), home-made steak and kidney pie (£2.65) and sirloin steak (£4.45). Well kept cheap Banks's Bitter or Mild (on electric pump); dominoes, fruit machine and piped music. Tables out on an extensive terrace in surprisingly remote-seeming countryside. *(Recommended by Pamela and Merlyn Horswell, E J Alcock, Rob and Gill Weeks, C Elliott)*

Banks's   Licensee Gary Ensor   Real ale   Lunchtime meals and snacks (not Sun)   Children in eating area   Open 11.30–11 in summer for trial period; 11.30–3, 6–11 in winter

KENILWORTH (War)   SP2871   Map 4
Virgins & Castle

High Street; opposite A429 Coventry Road at junction with A452

The entrance corridor in this recently redecorated, old-fashioned town pub is flanked by a couple of simply furnished small snugs, one with rugs on its bare boards and the other with flagstones. A larger room down a couple of steps has a big rug on ancient red tiles, heavy beams, and matching seat and stool covers. The carpeted lounge, with more beams and some little booths, has hatch service, a good warm coal fire and a fruit machine (there's another in a lobby). Popular bar food includes rolls and sandwiches, ploughman's, salads, and daily specials; well kept Davenports and Wem Special on handpump, and farm cider from the inner flagstones-and-beams servery. Seats outside in a sheltered garden. *(Recommended by S J Curtis, M S Hancock, Rob Weeks, Gill Austin)*

Davenports   Real ale   Meals and snacks   Live music Tues   Open 11-2.30, 6–11 all year

LANGLEY (W Midlands)   SO9788   Map 4
Brewery   ★   ⊗

1½ miles from M5 junction 2; from A4034 to W Bromwich and Oldbury take first right turn signposted Junction 2 Ind Estate then bear left past Albright & Wilson into Station Road

The refurbishment here has been done exceedingly well – it seems like a genuine Victorian pub, though the décor is no older than 1984. The cosy Parlour, on the left, has flowery wallpaper matching a soft-toned carpet, lacy net curtains, plates and old engravings on the walls, brass swan's-neck wall lamps, a corner china cabinet, nice dining-chairs or sturdy built-in settles around four good solid tables, and a coal fire blazing in a tiled Victorian fireplace with china on the overmantel. Shelves of Staffordshire pottery and old books divide this off from the similarly furnished red-tiled Kitchen which has lots of copper pans around its big black range. The Tap Bar is more simply furnished, but on much the same general lines, and in a back corridor tractor seats give a view into the brewhouse (a charmingly think-small subsidiary of Allied Breweries, the Ind Coope empire) through a big picture window. They specialise in exceptional-value sandwiches, double-deckers, and hot beef or lamb, dripping with gravy in thick doorsteps of bread (60p–75p), and there's also soup and a hunk of bread (45p); the beer to drink is the Entire brewed here, full-flavoured and quite strong, well kept on handpump – also Bitter and Mild, both brewed up in Warrington; friendly staff. Darts, dominoes and piped music. *(Recommended by Roger Broadie, Frank Cummins, R M Sparkes, Mark and Caron Bernhoft, Rob and Gill Weeks, R P Taylor)*

Holt, Plant & Deakin (Ind Coope)　*Licensee Vic Norton*　*Real ale*　*Lunchtime snacks*
Open 11–2.30, 5.30–10.30

MARSTON ST LAWRENCE (Northants)　SP5342　Map 4
Marston Inn

A fine example of a quite unspoilt village pub. The well kept Hook Norton Best, splendidly cheap, is drawn from a cask in the back room (there's no bar counter), and you can drink it either in a purple carpeted sitting-room (TV – and antique hunting prints) or in the plain room by the serving-hatch (darts here, and a fire in winter). The back garden is a peaceful place to sit in summer, with interesting foreign birds in its aviary, vegetables grown in front of the pub, and there are ducks and geese in the car park. Nicely placed near Sulgrave Manor with its George Washington connections; rolling countryside surrounds the village. *(Recommended by Jill and Ted George; more reports please)*

Hook Norton　*Real ale*　*Open 11–2.30, 7–11 all year*

NASSINGTON (Northants)　TL0696　Map 5
Black Horse ⊗

When this seventeenth-century pub was completely modernised a few years ago, a splendid big stone fireplace in the lounge bar was uncovered; it was probably brought from Fotheringhay Castle (which had been destroyed some time earlier) when the pub was built. There are easy chairs and small settees, a beamed ceiling, and a pleasant, relaxed atmosphere. The bar servery, with panelling from Rufford Abbey, links the two comfortable rooms of the restaurant. Here, good, interesting – though not cheap – food includes soup (£1.85), pâté (£2.65), devilled crab (£2.95), alligator (£3.50), toasted steak sandwich (£3.75), pasta and vegetable au gratin or basil and tomato meatballs with fusilli (£4.35), scampi (£5.25), chicken breast with asparagus spears in a wine, cream and mushroom sauce or Brazilian duckling with peaches, banana and brazilnuts (£7.25), and steak (from £7.75); there's a daily choice of fresh fish (from £4.95), home-made puddings (from £1.85) and Sunday lunch (£9.25). They will normally do sandwiches, ploughman's or omelettes on request. Well kept Adnams, Greene King IPA and Wadworths 6X on handpump. You can sit out on the neatly kept and attractive sheltered lawn. *(Recommended by T Nott, PLC, Derek Stephenson, Mrs R Horridge, Virginia Jones)*

Free house　*Licensee Tom Guy*　*Real ale*　*Meals and snacks*　*Restaurant tel Stamford (0780) 782324　Children in eating area of bar　Open 10.30–3, 6.30–11 all year; closed evening 25 and 26 Dec*

If you know a pub's ever open all day now that the licensing laws have changed, please tell us.

NETHERTON (W Midlands) SO9387 Map 4
Little Dry Dock

Windmill End, Bumble Hole; you really need an A–Z street map to find it – or OS Sheet 139 reference 953881

Everything in this red, white and blue painted pub is cheerfully over the top; winches and barge rudders flank the door, and somehow they've squeezed a whole beached narrowboat into the bar on the right (its engine is in the room on the left) to use as the servery. There are lots of brightly coloured bargees' water-pots, lanterns, jugs and lifebuoys, a curving green-planked ceiling with pierced ribs, marine windows, a huge model boat in one front transom-style window, and vivid paintwork throughout. High point of the menu is the Desperate Dan Pie, complete with horns (and a badge if you finish it – £3.25), with other generous food served from the end galley such as soup (95p), sandwiches on request, pâté (£1.45), filled baked potatoes (from £1.95), omelettes (from £2.20), salads (from £2.50), vegetarian dishes (£2.60), trout (£3.30) and sirloin steak (from £4.70), with good value daily specials such as lamb curry, goulash or pizza. In common with the other pubs in the chain, they have their own Little Lumphammer ale as well as Ansells Mild and Ind Coope Burton; catchy Irish piped music. Others in Mr O'Rourke's small young chain of Black Country pubs include one in Halesowen in the Lucky Dip section, and main entries in Bewdley and Kidderminster (Hereford & Worcester). The Dudley Canal embankment is behind the pub. *(Recommended by Rob and Gill Weeks, Dr Iain McColl, Dave Braisted, P and K McAteer, E J Alcock)*

Free house   Licensee Robin Newman   Real ale   Meals and snacks   Children welcome Irish folk music Mon   Open 11–2.30, 6ish–10.30

Old Swan ★

Halesowen Road; A459 towards Halesowen just S of Netherton centre

One of the rooms in this extended pub (taken over by Hoskins in October 1987) is called 'Ma Pardoe's Bar' in memory of the late Doris Pardoe who ran the pub for twenty-five years and who gave tremendous impetus to the movement towards pubs brewing their own real ale. This room has been recently decorated with 1920s bric-à-brac, though is fitted out very much in keeping with the rest of the building, using recycled bricks and woodwork, and even matching etched window panels. The original bar is unchanged, keeping its lovely patterned ceiling with the big swan centrepiece, the swan design engraved in the mirrors behind the bar, old-fashioned cylinder stove with its chimney angling away to the wall, good solid new but traditional furniture, and its easy-going, unspoilt atmosphere. The home-brewed beer is fresh, fragrant and very good value, and there are pre-arranged brewery trips with the brewer (who was here for many years under Doris Pardoe herself, and whose father was brewmaster here, too). Bar food includes sandwiches, black pudding and cheese (£1.50), and home-made pies, chilli con carne, curry or pork in cider (all £2); darts, fruit machine and piped music. A sizeable car park has been opened at the back of the pub. *(Recommended by PLC, Graham Gibson, Rachel Waterhouse, Rob and Gill Weeks, C Elliott, P and K McAteer, Brian Jones)*

Own brew (Hoskins)   Licensee Valerie Harris   Real ale   Meals (not Sun evening)   Children in smoke-room   Will probably open 11–11

NEWBOLD ON STOUR (War) SP2446 Map 4
White Hart ⊗

A34 S of Stratford

Quarry-tiling throughout makes for a clean simplicity in this well run pub, which has reddish russet cord plush cushions for the modern high-backed winged settles in its spacious beamed main bar, seats set into big bay windows (there's some traffic noise), a gun hanging over the log fire in one big stone fireplace, brass twinkling here and there, and gleaming copper-topped tables. Stub walls and the main chimney slightly divide up the room without spoiling its fresh and open feel. Reliable bar food includes ploughman's (£1.75), taramosalata or hot prawns in a tarragon and wine sauce (£1.95), and changing hot dishes such as lasagne (£3.25), home-cooked ham stuffed with spinach and topped with Stilton sauce or kidneys with a garlic, sherry and cream sauce (£3.50). The roomy back public bar has darts, pool, dominoes, fruit machine and juke box; well kept Bass on handpump; there seems to be no objection to well behaved dogs. The friendly and helpful licensee used to work at the Kings Head in Wellesbourne in what local people now tend to think of as its golden days. There are some picnic-table sets under cocktail parasols in front of the pub, which has well tended hanging baskets in summer. *(Recommended by S V Bishop, Frank Cummins, M E France, S J A Velate)*

M&B (Bass)   Licensees Mr and Mrs Jim Cruttwell   Real ale   Meals and snacks (not Sun evenings in winter)   Restaurant tel Stratford-upon-Avon (0789) 87205 Fri and Sat evenings, Sun lunch   Children welcome   Open 11–2.30 (3 Sat), 6–11 all year; closed evening 25 Dec

nr NORTHAMPTON   SP7560   Map 4
Britannia

3¾ miles from M1 junction 15; A508 towards Northampton, following ring road, then take A428 towards Bedford; shortly, pub is to the left on Bedford Road

The rambling open-plan bar in this popular beamed and flagstoned pub has several roomy alcoves with Victorian prints and enamelled advertising placards on its stripped vertical plank panelling, stripped pine kitchen tables and pews, matching cupboards and shelves holding plates and books, and dim coloured lanterns. A side room is a converted eighteenth-century kitchen, and its cast-iron cooking-range and washing-copper are still intact. Generous helpings of bar food such as ploughman's (£1.95), lasagne, steak and kidney pie and so forth can be eaten in a conservatory facing the River Nene. Well kept Ruddles Best and County on handpump; fruit machine, space game, juke box and piped music. *(Recommended by Nick Dowson, Rob and Gill Weeks)*

Manns (Watneys)   Licensee John Clark   Real ale   Lunchtime meals and snacks   Children in eating area of bar   Disco Tues, Thurs, Sun   Open 10.30–2.30, 5.30–11 all year

OLD HILL (W Midlands)   SO9685   Map 4
Wharf

Station Road, which is off Halesowen Road (A459) in Cradley Heath; this entrance involves a hideously steep wooden canal bridge – the back way into the car park, from Grange Road off Waterfall Lane, is much easier

The neat bar in this pretty cottagey pub, by the largely disused Dudley Canal, has a quarry-tiled front room with red leatherette settles, cribbage and a fruit machine, and a carpeted back room with tapestry-cushioned mate's chairs around black tables, a plum-coloured fabric ceiling and well reproduced pop music. Stripped brick arches open between the two, as does a gas-effect coal fire, and little touches like the curly brass and etched-glass wall lamps give a pleasantly old-fashioned feel. The new licensee has kept the enormous range of well kept real ales; changing every four days, they might include Belhaven, Big Lamp, Brains, Burton Bridge, Cotleigh, Flowers, Gales, Hook Norton, Knightley and Black Knight Stout (completely new to us), Marstons Burton, Pedigree Merrie Monk and Owd Rodger, Moorhouses, Pitfield, Ringwood, Thwaites, Wadworths, and Whitbreads Pompey Royal; farm cider on handpump. Bar food at lunchtime includes curry or spaghetti bolognese (£1.75), faggots (£1.95), steak and kidney pie (£2.50) and steaks (from £4.50); also, sandwiches, black pudding and onion roll (70p), burger (£1.30), cod (£1.50) and fish pie (£2.50); a chatty atmosphere, and piped music. There are picnic-table sets in a sheltered side garden which has a good children's play area with a fort and drawbridge. (*Recommended by SP, E J Alcock, Dave Braisted, R P Taylor*)

Free house (owned by but not tied to Premier Midland Ales)   Licensee Mandy Collins   Real ale   Meals and snacks (not Sun evening)   Restaurant tel 021-559 2323   Children in restaurant   Live music Mon evenings   Open 11.30–3, 5–11; open all day Sat

PRESTON BAGOT (War)   SP1765 Map 4
Olde Crab Mill
B4095 Henley-in-Arden–Warwick

An attractive and comfortable series of communicating rooms here have lots of cosy nooks and crannies, black beams in the low ochre ceilings, old-fashioned small-paned windows, and four log fires; furnishings include cushioned antique carved settles, chintz-cushioned wicker easy chairs and other seats (similarly upholstered), and antique prints. Bar food includes soup, filled baked potatoes, ploughman's, vegetarian quiche, basket meals, home-made Mexican tacos, lasagne or steak and kidney pie, and evening grills. Well kept Flowers Original, Marstons Pedigree, Sam Whitbread and Wadworths 6X on handpump, with monthly guest beers. Some seats shelter outside in an angle of the roadside house and there's a children's tree-giant. (*Recommended by Roger Taylor, Wayne Brindle, HDC, J and M Walsh, Chris Cooke, J A Velate, John Tyzack, C D T Spooner, J T C Heslop, GB, Rob and Gill Weeks, Tom Evans*)

Whitbreads   Real ale   Meals and snacks (not Sun evening)   Children in eating area and area next to kitchen   Open 10.30–2.30, 6–11 all year; closed 25 Dec

PRIORS MARSTON (War)   SP4857 Map 4
Holly Bush ⊗
From village centre follow Shuckburgh signpost, but still in village take first right turn by telephone box, not signposted

Partly candlelit at night, the rambling small rooms in this quaint, family-run thirteenth-century building have beams, some stripped stone walls, old-fashioned pub seats, leather upholstered stools and chairs, and two log fires. Bar food includes home-made soup (£1.35), sandwiches (from 95p, toasties from £1.35), burgers (from £1.35), home-made pâté (£2.35), ploughman's or home-made fresh pies like steak and kidney or haddock and spinach (£2.85), and fresh mango and curried egg (£3.85); fresh vegetables are extra; Sunday roast lunch. Well kept Everards Tiger, Hook Norton, Marstons Pedigree, Theakstons Old Peculier and Wadworths 6X are served from handpumps on the copper-topped bar counter, with a monthly guest beer such as Hicks; friendly staff. Darts, dominoes, pool (round table) and video game. The peaceful lawn beside this golden stone house has hitching posts for customers on horseback and there's an adventure playground. The village has some most attractive stone houses. (*Recommended by David Crafts, Paul McPherson, Charles Gurney, S V Bishop, Derek Stephenson, John Atherton, Mrs Pamela Roper, Rob and Gill Weeks*)

Free house   Licensee K J Robinson   Real ale   Meals and snacks   Restaurant tel Byfield (0327) 60934   Children welcome   Live music on special occasions   Open 11–3 (4 Sat), 6.30–11 all year

Though English and Welsh pubs have to stop serving bar drinks between 3 and 7 on Sundays, they are allowed to serve drinks with meals in a separate dining-room all afternoon.

All main entries have been inspected anonymously by the Editor or Assistant Editor. We accept no payment for inclusion, no advertising, and no sponsorship from the drinks industry – or from anyone else.

ROWINGTON (War)   SP2069   Map 4
Tom o' the Wood
Finwood Road; from B4439 at the N end of Rowington follow Lowsonford signpost

Close to the Grand Union Canal, this comfortably modernised pub has several communicating rooms with Windsor chairs and cushioned rustic seats set around dark varnished tables, and log-effect gas fires. Good bar food includes sandwiches (from 85p), home-made chilli (£2.55), home-made lasagne (£2.75), scampi (£3.90), gammon and egg or pineapple (£4.05) and very good steaks (from £6.55), with lunchtime additions such as sausage or bacon with egg and chips (£1.90). Well kept Flowers IPA and Original and Sam Whitbread on handpump; fruit machine, maybe piped music. There are picnic-table sets on a neat side lawn, with more on a terrace by the big car park. (*Recommended by Mr and Mrs W H Crowther, Brian Jones, J T C Heslop, Mandy and Michael Challis, Lyn and Bill Capper*)

*Flowers (Whitbreads)   Real ale   Meals and snacks   Restaurant tel Lapworth (056 43) 2252
Children in restaurant and large lounge   Open 11.30–2.30, 6.30–11 all year*

SAMBOURNE (War)   SP0561   Map 4
Green Dragon ⊗
This friendly pub faces the village green and looks very pretty with roses climbing against its shuttered and timbered façade. Inside, the comfortably modernised, communicating rooms have beams, little armed seats and more upright ones, some small settles, and open fires. Good bar food, served by helpful and cheery staff, includes sandwiches (from 70p), soup (95p), pâté (£1.80), ploughman's (from £1.95), sausage and egg (£2.50), omelettes (from £2.80), home-made steak, mushroom and onion pie or breakfast which is served all day (£2.95), gammon (£3), curries (£3.15), a fish dish of the day (£3.50), salads (from £3.50, fresh crab £4.50), steaks (£6.50), and daily specials (from £2.85); well kept Bass, M&B Brew XI and Springfield on handpump. There are picnic-table sets and teak seats among flowering cherries on a side courtyard, by the car park. (*Recommended by Roger Broadie, S V Bishop, Richard Maries, Mr and Mrs P M Dowd, Mrs Iris Smith*)

Bass   Licensee Philip Burke   Real ale   Meals and snacks (not Sun)   Restaurant tel Astwood Bank (052 789) 2465   Children welcome   Open 11–3, 6–11 all year

SHIPSTON ON STOUR (War)   SP2540   Map 4
Bell 🛏
Sheep Street

What used to be the coach entry is now a narrow lounge running right through to the little back courtyard. A chatty, relaxed place, it has brocaded wall seats around white cast-iron-framed tables in one place, sofas in another, and even an old barred jail door on one side; they still keep the ball and chain, though usually the two cats (black and white Susan and three-legged Tuppence) keep the customers in order without resort to that. On the left a nice little bar is screened off by a partly glazed partition: brocaded settles in booths around tables, a log-effect gas fire, shooting prints on the stripped-stone walls, whisky-water jugs and decorative mugs hanging thickly from the two beams. Bar food includes soup (80p), sandwiches (from £1), coarse pâté (£1.75), ploughman's (£2.25), salads (from £2.45), plaice (£2.95) and steak and kidney or steak, mushroom and Guinness pie (£3.25); Flowers IPA and Original on handpump, faint piped music. A front games-room has a well lit pool-table, fruit machine and juke box. (*Recommended by Rob and Gill Weeks, G T Rhys*)

*Flowers (Whitbreads)   Licensees George and Frances Rooney   Real ale   Meals and snacks
Restaurant   Children in eating area and games-room   Open 10–2.30, 7–11 all year
Bedrooms tel Shipston on Stour (0608) 61443; £22.50(£34.50)/£28(£34.50)*

White Bear ⊗ 🛏

High Street

The pictures in the bar on the left are worth a close look: charming pen and wash drawing of Paris cafe society, and sporting and other cartoons from Alken through Lawson Wood to bright modern ones by Tibb; the spacious back lounge, with rather plain but comfortable modern furniture, has bigger Toulouse-Lautrec and other prints of French music-hall life. The left front bar, quite narrow, has massive stripped settles, attractive lamps on the rag-rolled walls, and newspapers out for customers; on the right a subsidiary bar has a wood-burning stove in a big painted stone fireplace, with a fruit machine round at the back. Enterprising bar food, frequently changing, might include onion soup (£1), mushroom gratiné or kidneys in tomato sauce (£1.95), chicken livers done with onion and bacon (£2.25), lasagne (£2.95), scallops with bacon (£3.25), steak and kidney pie (£3.95) and lemon sole served with pink peppercorn sauce or seven-ounce rump steak (£5.95). Well kept Bass and M&B Brew XI and Springfield on handpump, with decent wines; darts, shove-ha'penny, dominoes. It can get very busy, but service is efficient; there may be dogs. There are some white cast-iron tables in a small back yard, and benches face the street. (*Recommended by Brian Green, BKA, S V Bishop, Lyn and Bill Capper*)

M&B (Bass) Licensees Hugh and Suzanne Roberts, Managers Lynn and Geoff Chapman Real ale Meals and snacks (not 25–26 Dec, nor bank hols) Restaurant Children in eating area and restaurant Open 11–2.30, 6–11 all year; open 11–11 Sat Bedrooms tel Shipston on Stour (0608) 61558; £27B/£38B

SHUSTOKE (War) SP2290 Map 4
Griffin

5 miles from M6 junction 4; A446 towards Tamworth, then right on to B4114 and go straight through Coleshill; pub is at Church End, past Shustoke centre

The L-shaped bar in this quaint little brick house has an old-fashioned settle and cushioned cafe seats (some quite closely packed) around sturdily elm-topped sewing trestles, lots of old jugs hanging from the low beams, log fires in both stone fireplaces (one's a big inglenook), and a relaxed, friendly atmosphere. Good value bar food includes appetising sandwiches (from 75p), home-made steak and kidney pie (£2.30), salads (£2.50) and good local gammon and egg (£3.25 – they may have local fresh eggs for sale too); very well kept Everards Old Original, M&B Mild, Marstons Pedigree, Theakstons Old Peculier and Wadworths 6X on handpump, and about three other changing beers, say Arkells Kingsdown, Everards Old Bill and Gibbs Mew Bishops Tipple from a bar under one of the lowest, thickest beams anywhere; there are plans for a family-room. Outside, there's a terrace, and old-fashioned seats and tables built on to the back grass by the edge of the playing-field. (*Recommended by Rob and Gill Weeks, John Baker, Ted George, Frank Cummins, C D T Spooner*)

Free house Licensee Michael Pugh Real ale Meals (lunchtime, not Sun) and snacks Open 12–2.30, 7–11 all year

SOUTHAM (War) SP4161 Map 4
Old Mint ⊗

Coventry Street; A423, towards Coventry

Named after the fact that in the Civil Wars it was used to melt down commandeered silver for coin to pay King Charles' troops before the Battle of Edge Hill, this medieval stone building has an interesting shaped bar with two snug, heavy-beamed rooms. Furnishings include sturdy old seats and settles, masses of toby jugs behind the serving-counter, two cosy little alcoves, walls peppered with antique guns, powder flasks, rapiers, sabres, cutlasses and pikes, and an open fire. Bar food includes sandwiches, soup (90p), filled baked potato (from 95p), cheese and bacon flan or ploughman's (£1.80), cottage pie (£1.90), deep-fried mushrooms alsacienne (£2.50), steak and kidney pie (£3), grilled gammon and pineapple (£3.30), scampi special (£4.50), and steaks (from £6). Well kept Adnams, Marstons Pedigree, Sam Smiths OB, Theakstons XB and Old Peculier, Wadworths 6X and changing guest beers on handpump; fruit machine, piped music. Through the medieval arch of the back door there are tables and chairs in the sheltered, extended garden, with more on the cobbles and laid bricks of a sheltered yard, which has clematis on a side wall and is fairy-lit at night. *(Recommended by David and Ruth Hollands, Roger Broadie, Geoff Wilson, Dr J R Hamilton, Mrs P Fretter, John Parsons, Rob and Gill Weeks, Charles Gurney)*

Free house   Licensees Harry and Pauline Poole   Real ale   Meals and snacks   Restaurant tel Southam (092 681) 2339   Children welcome   Open 11–3, 6–11 all year

STOKE BRUERNE (Northants)   SP7450 Map 4

Boat   [illustrated on page 479]

3½ miles from M1 junction 15: A508 towards Stony Stratford, then Stoke Bruerne signposted on the right

The old-fashioned, low-ceilinged bar and tap-room in this thatched pub – owned and run by the same family for over a century – look out on to the neatly painted double locks of the Grand Union Canal, the colourful narrowboats, and on the other side a handsome row of eighteenth-century warehouses and houses (where there's an interesting canal museum). These rooms have simple, brightly coloured vignettes of barges and barge life painted on the walls, built-in wall benches, worn tiled floors, and a separate alley for the vigorous local game of hood skittles. Behind the pub (and away from the canal) is a lounge bar extension, with stripped stone walls and a stylish high timber ceiling. Sandwiches (from 95p), burgers (from £1.25), basket meals (from £1.30), ploughman's (from £1.40), home-made lasagne (£2.75), salads (from £2.95), mini-grill (£3.50) and steak (£5.50). Everards Old Original, Marstons Pedigree and Merrie Monk, Ruddles County and Sam Smiths OB on handpump; dominoes, cribbage, a fruit machine, trivia, and piped music; canalside tea-rooms serve the bar food all day from March to October. There are tables on the canal bank. It can get very crowded at peak times. A narrowboat is available for party or individual hire, and there's a new cocktail bar for restaurant customers. *(Recommended by Michael and Alison Sandy, Rob and Gill Weeks, Mrs G K Herbert)*

Free house   Licensee John Woodward   Real ale   Meals and snacks   Restaurant tel Roade (0604) 862428   Children in lounge bar, restaurant and tea-room   Live entertainment Nov and Dec, and by arrangement at other times   Parking may be difficult at peak holiday times   Open 11–2.30, 6–11 all year; may open longer in afternoon if trade demands

STRATFORD-UPON-AVON (War)   SP2055 Map 4

Garrick

High Street; close to Town Hall

Run by the same family since 1933, this striking, elaborately timbered building has small and often irregularly shaped rooms: long upholstered settles and stools, heavy wall timbers, high ceiling-beams, some walls stripped back to bare stone, with others heavily plastered with posters, sawdust on the wood floor, and a talking mynah bird (Tuesday to Friday); the back bar has an open fire in the middle of the room with a conical brass hood. Bar food includes filled rolls, ploughman's (£1.85), steak and kidney pie (£1.90), game pie (£2.60) and cottage pie or lasagne (£3.10). Well kept Flowers IPA and Original on handpump, kept under light blanket pressure; a fruit machine and thoughtfully chosen piped music. The adjoining house was the family home of Katherine Harvard whose son founded America's best-known university. *(Recommended by S V Bishop, S J A Velate)*

Flowers (Whitbreads)   Licensee E N Eborall   Real ale   Lunchtime meals (not Sun or Mon) and snacks   Children in dining-room Tues–Sat lunchtimes only   Nearby daytime parking difficult   Open 11–4 (3 Mon), 6–11

Slug & Lettuce ⊗

38 Guild Street, corner of Union Street

Done up well in the currently popular 'old' style, this has pine kitchen tables and chairs on rugs and flagstones, a few period prints on stripped squared panelling, sprays of flowers on the tables, and a rack of newspapers for customers. At the back a small flagstoned terrace, with lanterns and floodlighting at night, has lots of flower boxes and sturdy teak tables under cocktail parasols, with more up steps. Enterprising bar food changes frequently and might include tomato and orange soup (£1.50), black pudding with bacon and cheese or garlic mushrooms with bacon (£2.75), fried Brie (£2.95), tagliatelle (£3.25), marinated pork kebab or lamb chops with fresh mint sauce (£5.50) and roast duck with plum and brandy sauce or roast guinea-fowl done with pork and bacon strips (£6.50). You can watch some food being prepared at one end of the long L-shaped bar counter. The staff are friendly; if you tell them you're going to an RSC matinee they'll serve you quickly. They have decent wines and do a good Pimms, as well as well kept ABC Best, Ansells, Ind Coope Burton and another Ind Coope-related beer named for the pub on handpump. *(Recommended by S J A Velate, Dr J R Hamilton, Maggie Jo St John, Tony Dudley Evans, Dr and Mrs A M Evans, Charles Gurney, V N Hill)*

Ansells (Ind Coope)   Licensees Mr and Mrs A Harris   Real ale   Meals and snacks   Children in eating area   Open 11–11 all year; closed 25–26 Dec, 1 Jan

White Swan

Rother Street; leads into A34

This was the Kings Head in Shakespeare's day, and a popular enough inn then for him to have almost certainly drunk here. The old-fashioned bar is a long, quiet room where, during renovations in 1927, a 1560 wall painting of Tobias and the Angel with the miraculous fish was discovered, hidden until then by the highly polished Jacobean oak panelling which covers much of the rest of the room. There are heavy beams, cushioned leather armchairs, carved ancient oak settles, plush smaller seats and a nice window seat; one fireplace has a handsomely carved chimney-piece, another smaller one an attractive marquetry surround. A staffed food counter outside serves filled rolls, ploughman's (£2.25), a daily hot dish (£3.25) and there are salads from a self-service bar with quiche (£2.50) and ham off the bone (£3.25). Well kept Courage Best, Flowers Original, Marstons Pedigree and Wadworths 6X on handpump. *(Recommended by Wayne Brindle, S J A Velate, I R Hewitt, Rob and Gill Weeks, C A Gurney)*

Free house (THF)   Licensee David Warnes   Real ale   Lunchtime snacks   Restaurant; open 12.30–6 Sun   Children in eating area of bar   Open 11–11 all year   Bedrooms tel Stratford-upon-Avon (0789) 297022; £58.95B/£79.90B

THORPE MANDEVILLE (Northants)   SP5344 Map 4
Three Conies ⊗

In village, just off B4525 Banbury–Northampton

Over the last year this pleasantly isolated early seventeenth-century pub has become less restaurantish – more of a place where anyone dropping in will feel at home. The cosy low-beamed and carpeted lounge bar has tapestried built-in settles and spindle-back chairs around its tables (which may have fresh flowers), and little hunting prints and polished brass on the walls, which are partly stripped back to golden stone. Beyond the servery, the public bar has bigger pictures on its stripped stone walls, and bar billiards, cribbage and fruit machine. Home-made bar food (nothing is brought in) includes sandwiches (from 95p), soup (£1), salmon pâté (£1.95), ploughman's (from £1.95), mushrooms in a garlic and cream sauce (£2.25), salads (from £3.25), steaks (from £5.95), and daily specials like cottage pie, chilli con carne, steak and kidney pie (from £2.95); puddings such as home-made ice-creams, sherry trifle or chocolate eclairs (from £1.50), and Sunday roast lunch (£3.95). Well kept Hook Norton Best on handpump and a good selection of wines and spirits. There are old-fashioned teak and curly iron seats on a lawn that merges into an orchard outside the pub, which is handily placed for Sulgrave Manor (George Washington's ancestral home) and Canons Ashby House (the Dryden family home). *(Recommended by G T Rhys, Joan Olivier, Tom Evans)*

Hook Norton   Licensees John and Maureen Day   Real ale   Meals and snacks   Restaurant
tel Banbury (0295) 711025   Children in eating area   Open 11–2.30, 6–11 all year; may open
longer in afternoon if trade demands

TITCHMARSH (Northants)   TL0279   Map 4
Wheatsheaf
Village signposted from A604 and A605

This extended village pub has comfortable little plush bucket seats and a sweep of button-back banquettes around tables in one spacious area, as well as Windsor rocking-chairs in the smaller original beamed lounge. Good bar food includes home-made soup (80p), pâté (£1.55), home-made dishes such as steak and mushroom pie, lasagne or chilli con carne, or fresh cod (£3.55), scampi, pork kebab or gammon and pineapple (£3.85) and steaks (from £4.65). Ind Coope Bitter and Tetleys on handpump; friendly service. There is a pool-table in a separate room, darts, fruit machine and piped music. Out on the grass, among flowers by the car park, are some picnic-table sets. *(Recommended by N A Wood; more reports please)*

Free house   Licensee James Wells   Meals and snacks (not Mon, or Tues–Fri lunchtimes)
Restaurant tel Thrapston (080 12) 2203   Children in eating area and restaurant
Open only Tues–Fri evenings 7–11 all year, and Sat and Sun 12–2.30, 7–11

TWYWELL (Northants)   SP9478   Map 4
Old Friar
Village signposted from A604 about 2 miles W of Thrapston

The beams in this refurbished old pub – like the brick fireplaces – are decorated with wooden carvings of friars, and furnishings include comfortable tub chairs, settles and good plain wooden tables – most of which are set out for eating (the dining area is no-smoking). Bar food includes sandwiches, soup (95p), oriental parcels (£2.25), daily specials (£3.45), meat pies (£3.95), lamb moussaka (£4.75), vegetarian meals (£4.55), gammon (£5.95), steaks (from £5.95), a hot and cold carvery (£4.55; vegetarian £2.95, children's helping £2.25), and puddings such as spotted dick and treacle pudding. Well kept Ruddles Best and County and Websters Yorkshire on handpump served from the brick bar counter; dominoes, fruit machine and piped music. No dogs. *(Recommended by Frank Cummins, Comus Elliott, G W Judson)*

Manns (Watneys)   Licensee David Crisp   Real ale   Meals and snacks   Restaurant tel
Thrapston (080 12) 2625   Children welcome   Open 11–3, 6–11 all year; open all day Sat

---

Post Office address codings confusingly give the impression that some pubs are in the Midlands when they're really in the Derbyshire, Leicestershire or Shropshire areas that we list them under.

WARMINGTON (War) SP4147 Map 4
Plough ⊗

Village just off A41 N of Banbury

A few yards up the quiet village lane from a broad sloping green, this golden ironstone pub is very pretty – especially in autumn, when the creeper over it turns crimson. The black-beamed and softly lit bar is largely stripped back to the stonework, and cosy seating includes a small settee, an old high-backed winged settle, leatherette-cushioned wall seats and lots of comfortable Deco small armed chairs and library chairs. There are good log fires in winter. Quickly served simple but good lunchtime bar food includes sandwiches (from 95p, crab £1.15), pâté (£1.50), a good choice of ploughman's (£2.50), cheese and onion puffs (£2.75), scampi (£3.25) and flavoursome home-baked ham and eggs (£3.50); well kept Hook Norton Best, Marstons Pedigree and Wadworths 6X on handpump; on our visit, faint piped pop music. (*Recommended by Mrs J Budfield, N F Doherty, Gordon and Daphne, Gill and Rob Weeks*)

Free house   Licensees E J and D L Wilson   Real ale   Meals and snacks (lunchtime, not Sun) Occasional live music   Open 11.30–2.30, 6–11 all year; closed evening 25 Dec

WARWICK (War) SP2865 Map 4
Saxon Mill

Guy's Cliffe; A429 N of town

Restyled last year as a Harvester (a chain of family restaurants run by a subsidiary of THF, with historical links to Courage), this is done well to recreate an almost cottagey atmosphere in the pub part – with brasses, bookshelves, beams, pine cladding, open fireplaces and so forth. The centrepiece is the great wheel turning slowly behind glass, and the mill race rushing under a glass floor panel – though it hasn't worked as a watermill since 1938. The rooms ramble around with beams and flagstones in places, and there are fine views of the Avon weir. Bar food includes winter soup (70p), filled baps (£1), sausage in French bread (£1.50), various ploughman's (£2.50), salads (£2.95), and three or four daily specials like moussaka, curries, pies or casseroles (£3.50); children's helpings. Well kept Courage Best and Directors on handpump; gentle piped music. There are picnic-table sets on a terrace below and out under the surrounding trees, a fishing club (anyone can join), weekend barbecues – weather permitting – and a children's play area with slides, swings and so forth. (*Recommended by Mr and Mrs Markham, Rob and Gill Weeks, TBB*)

Free house (THF)   Manager John Cumming   Real ale   Lunchtime meals and snacks Restaurant tel Warwick (0926) 492255; open all day Sun   Children welcome   Rock music Tues, jazz Thurs, country and western Sun   Open 11–11 Mon–Sat, 12–3, 7–10.30 Sun

WEEDON (Northants) SP6259 Map 4
Crossroads ★ 🛏

3 miles from M1 junction 16; A45 towards Daventry – hotel at junction with A5 (look out for its striking clock tower)

The serving-counters in the exuberantly decorated and friendly main bar here are made from the elaborate mahogany fittings of an antique apothecary's shop; there are also shelves of plates, sets of copper jugs, antique clocks, various cosy alcoves, softly cushioned old settles and bucket seats on the pastel-toned carpet. A cosy parlourish room leading off has soft easy chairs. Smartly served bar food includes home-made soup (£1.25), ploughman's with a selection of cheeses or smoked mackerel, prawns, home-cooked ham and pâté and salads (from £2.85), scampi or a hot dish of the day such as steak and kidney pie (£3.95), and puddings such as excellent lemon sorbet. Well kept Bass, Ruddles County and Wilsons on hand-pump, freshly squeezed orange juice, and regular, organised wine tastings; shove-ha'penny, piped music. The light and airy coffee parlour, open all day, makes this spreading modern main-road hotel a useful motorway break. (*Recommended by J C and D Aitkenhead, Rob and Gill Weeks, Alison Hayward, Nick Dowson, Robert and Vicky Tod, Mr and Mrs J H Adam, A Duff, RW*)

Free house   Licensee Richard Amos   Real ale   Meals and snacks – also see above   Children in lounge and snug   Restaurant   Open 10.30–2.30, 5.30–11 all year; closed 25 and 26 Dec Bedrooms tel Weedon (0327) 40354; £46B/£56B

WELFORD-ON-AVON (War)   SP1452 Map 4
Bell

High Street; village signposted from A439

A thorough-going overhaul has left the character of this seventeenth-century pub more or less unchanged. The low-ceilinged lounge bar is comfortable with sober seats and tables that suit its dark timbering, beams and open fireplaces (which have an open fire in one and an electric fire in the other). The flagstoned public bar has a juke box and fruit machine, and there's a refurbished family-room. Flowers Original and IPA on handpump; efficient staff; darts, pool, dominoes, cribbage, fruit machine, trivia, juke box and piped music. A varied bar menu includes sandwiches, cottage pie (£2.25), salads (from £2.90), home-made steak and kidney pie (£3), fresh plaice (£3.05), crispy prawns (£3.10), gammon and eggs (£3.30), and escalope of turkey (£3.35). You can sit in the pretty garden area and back courtyard. The lane leading to the village church has pretty thatched black and white cottages. (*Recommended by S V Bishop, S J A Velate, Rob and Gill Weeks, I R Hewitt*)

Whitbreads   Licensee Mike Eynon   Real ale   Meals and snacks   Restaurant tel Stratford-upon-Avon (0789) 750353   Children in restaurant   Open 11–2.30, 6–11 all year; midnight supper licence

WEST BROMWICH (W Midlands)   SP0091 Map 4
Manor House

2 miles from M6 junction 9; from A461 towards Wednesbury take first left into Woden Road East; at T-junction, left into Crankhall Lane; at eventual roundabout, right into Hall Green Road

This remarkable moated and timbered building is listed in the Domesday Book as being held by William Fitz Ansculph, Baron of Dudley. The main bar is a great hall, with twin blue carpets on its flagstones, and plenty of tables. Tremendous oak trusses support the soaring pitched roof (the central one, eliminating any need for supporting pillars, is probably unique), and a fine old sliding door opens on to stairs leading up to a series of smaller and cosier timbered upper rooms, including a medieval Solar, which again have lovely oak trusses supporting their pitched ceiling-beams. Up here, there are comfortably cushioned seats and stools around small tables, with the occasional settle; a snug Parlour Bar is tucked in beneath the Solar. Bar food served from the efficient side food bar includes beef in ale, chicken chasseur, steak and kidney pie, sweet-and-sour pork and chicken curry. Well kept Banks's Bitter and Mild on electric pump; friendly service, everything very neatly kept, piped music and fruit machines. The car park is kept well out of sight behind some modern ancillary buildings, giving a very picturesque entrance through the ancient gatehouse. A broad sweep of grass stretches away beyond the moat towards the modern houses of this quiet suburb. (*Recommended by John and Pat Smyth, AE, Rob and Gill Weeks*)

Banks's   Real ale   Meals and snacks   Open 11–2.30, 6–10.30

It's very helpful if you let us know up-to-date food prices when you report on pubs.

WHATCOTE (War)   SP2944 Map 4
Royal Oak

Village signposted from A34 N of Shipston on Stour; and from A422 Banbury–Stratford, via Oxhill

Some of the heavy beams in this very pretty stone-built pub are so low that it's not so much your head that's in danger as your shoulders. The small rooms of the original bar have a miscellany of stools, cushioned pews and other seats around their tables, with old local photographs, brasses, a sword, and a stuffed peewit on the walls, and coins, bookmatches and foreign banknotes behind the beams behind the high copper bar counter. The huge inglenook fireplace has rungs leading up to a chamber on the right – perhaps a priest's hiding-hole, or more prosaically a smoking-chamber for hams. There's a more spacious (and more straightforward) bar on the left. A wide choice of home-made bar food includes sandwiches (if they're not busy), soup (80p), ploughman's (£2), cold ham (£2.80), trout (£3), seafood platter (£3.10), chicken Kiev (£4.20), sirloin steak (£6) and specials such as vegetarian lasagne (£2.80), steak and kidney pie (£3.30), lamb Shrewsbury or beef bourguignonne (£4), with puddings like treacle tart (£1). Well kept Hook Norton Best, with guest beers tapped from the cask, during the cooler months, and a good range of wines. Darts (winter), dominoes, fruit machine and piped music; Shadow the German shepherd is very welcoming – even to other dogs. There are strong traditions associating the pub with Cromwell and his skinheads, and when the Sealed Knots re-enact the Battle of Edgehill around 20–30 October they come here in period costume for lunch. The front terrace has some picnic-table sets, and there are more on grass at the side. *(Recommended by J S Evans, S V Bishop, A J Hill, Gill and Rob Weeks)*

Free house   Licensee Mrs Catherine Matthews   Real ale (maybe not in summer)   Meals and snacks   Children in eating area of bar   Occasional live music   Open 10.30–2.30, 6–11 all year; afternoon meals by arrangement

WITHYBROOK (War)   SP4384 Map 4
Pheasant ⊗

4 miles from M6 junction 2; follow Ansty, Shilton signpost; bear right in Shilton towards Wolvey then take first right signposted Withybrook – or, longer but wider, second right into B4112 to Withybrook

This well kept food pub is so popular that they now take your name when you arrive, and sit you down in order (a good idea), giving you time to relax with a drink early beforehand. Served by neat and cheerful waitresses, the wide menu includes sandwiches (from 85p), soup (90p), several pâtés (£1.65), ploughman's (£1.95), home-made lasagne (£2.15), omelettes (from £3), home-made steak and kidney pie or fresh quiches (£3.15), salads (from £2.95, assorted salami £3.75, fresh crab in season £4.25), scampi (£3.25), sweetbreads (£3.50), braised guinea-fowl royale (£4.95), mixed grill (£5.75) and steaks (from £6.30); a vegetarian menu has dishes like ploughman's with vegetarian Cheddar (80p), ratatouille crumble (£2.50) or spinach and mushroom lasagne (£3.25); good Sunday lunch (£6.25; they don't do other food then). The extended lounge has a few farm tools on its cream walls, lots of plush-cushioned wheel-back chairs and dark tables on the patterned carpet, and good fires in winter. The serving-counter, flanked by well polished rocky flagstones, has well kept Courage Best and Directors and Hook Norton Bitter on handpump. A fruit machine in the lobby, and piped music. There are tables under

---

We say if we know a pub has piped music.

Ring the bull is an ancient pub game – you try to lob a ring on a piece of string over a hook (occasionally a bull's horn) on the wall or ceiling.

fairy lights on a brookside terrace, and the bank opposite is prettily planted with flowers and shrubs. *(Recommended by Michael and Alison Sandy, Dr and Mrs B D Smith, Roy Bromwell, D P Cartwright, Mandy and Mike Challis, PLC, Rob and Gill Weeks, R A Slater, D P Manchett, Alan Worthington, Lyn Malkin, Edward Clarkson)*

Free house   Licensee Derek Guy   Real ale   Meals and snacks (not 25 and 26 Dec; see text for Sun)   Restaurant tel Hinckley (0455) 220480   Children welcome   Open 11–3, 6.30–11 all year; closed evenings 25 and 26 Dec

---

Lucky Dip

Besides the fully inspected pubs, you might like to try these Lucky Dips recommended to us and described by readers (if you do, please send us reports):

Alcester, War [Stratford Rd; SP0857], *Cross Keys*: Small, well established inn with pleasant atmosphere, Ansells real ale and generous helpings of good bar food *(A J Woodhouse)*

Ansty, War [Ansty–Shilton rd, E of Coventry; between M6 junction 2 and B4029; SP3983], *Crown*: Unspoilt old pub popular with canal users, well kept M&B Mild and Bitter, good open fires in both low-beamed bars, interesting food, friendly service *(Lyn Malkin, Edward Clarkson)*

Armscote, War [SP2444], *Wagon Wheel*: Good interesting food and Bass real ale; recently completely – and tastefully – refurbished; menu, all home made, changes daily, no food Sun *(B S Bourne)*

☆ **Aston Cantlow**, War [SP1359], *Kings Head*: Attractive black and white timbered pub in centre of village and close to church where Shakespeare's parents are supposed to have married; a few tables and chairs in compact, carpeted low-beamed main bar area on left, with more in the flagstoned 'snug'; inglenook, cheery log fire and settles; dining-room seems to be used as overflow area, lounge bar now set out with tables as in a restaurant; well kept Flowers IPA and Original; bar food includes good thick vegetable soup *(S J A Velate, Rob and Gill Weeks, Oliver Howes, J Walsh, J S Evans, T George, Chris Cooke, LYM)*

Austrey, War [Church Lane; SK2906], *Bird in Hand*: Attractive thatched and black-beamed pub, immaculately kept with friendly atmosphere and well kept Marstons Pedigree, welcoming coal fire, benches around walls; near Twycross Zoo *(H S Harries, C D T Spooner)*

☆ **Aynho**, Northants [SP5133], *Cartwright Arms*: Promising new regime in sixteenth-century inn, with well kept Bass and M&B Springfield in neatly modernised lounge and bar which may develop some character as the changes wear in, attentive service by polite staff, good bar food, interesting restaurant with fresh fish flown in daily from Jersey, a few tables in pretty corner of yard; bedrooms being comfortably refurbished; one to watch *(Gordon Theaker, BB)*

☆ **Badby**, Northants [village signposted off A361; SP5559], *Windmill*: As we went to press this stone village inn was really too much in a state of flux to include as the main entry it had been in previous editions – with only the front bar more or less open and a Portaloo on site, most of the pub was being fundamentally rejigged, with bedrooms being added – though they still had a good choice of real ales such as Adnams, Bass, Bodicote Porter, Hook Norton Best, Marstons Pedigree; we have hopes that the outcome will be good, and await reports *(A E Alcock, Michael O'Driscoll, LYM)*

Baginton, War [SP3474], *Old Mill*: Converted watermill with gardens leading down to the R Sower; the oldest and most interesting part, with the river views and great millwheel, is given over to the restaurant and its cocktail bar (popular with businessmen), which seems the central feature here; the spacious beamed and panelled side bar has Watneys-related and maybe guest real ales, with old settles as well as its mainly modern seats *(LYM)*

☆ **Barton**, War [a mile E of Bidford; SP1051], *Cottage of Content*: Cosy and very small old stone pub with friendly atmosphere and enormous helpings of reasonably priced bar food with home-baked bread – the Weds night winter specials are recommended; real ales – and tea, coffee or hot chocolate; very rural setting on R Avon *(Andrew Ludlow, Elsie and Les Tanner, HDC)*

Bidford-on-Avon, War [High St; SP1051], *White Lion*: Attractive riverside location, Everards Old Original on handpump, tasty well presented food with plenty of variety, very cheerful competent staff; bedrooms *(C H Lamb, F M Bunbury)*

Billesley, W Mid [SP0980], *Stags Head*: Interesting timbered old building with real ale and good value bar food *(Grahame Archer)*

Bilston, W Mid [High St; SO9495], *Greyhound & Punchbowl*: Ornate plaster ceilings and big fireplaces in fifteenth-century building, a real surprise for the area; extremely friendly licensees, highly recommended mixed grill, small back garden *(E J Alcock)*

Birmingham [Ravenhurst St, Camp Hill;

SP0786], *Brewer & Baker*: Well kept real ales in plain but atmospheric inner-city pub, walls covered with plates; limited range of bar snacks and rolls, darts, juke box, fruit machine *(C P Gooch)*; [Church St (nr Eye Hospital)] *Cathedral*: Gorgeous painted ceilings and lots of wooden fittings in city-centre pub with friendly staff and very reasonably priced food; busy at lunchtime *(Roy Bromell, C P Gooch)*; [Church Lane, Perry Barr] *Church*: Large recently refurbished pub decorated with old-fashioned bric-à-brac, small panelled side room with open fire and serving-hatch, friendly bar, secluded and sheltered garden; outstanding chip butty, weekend barbecues *(E J Alcock)*; [Cambrian Wharf, Kingston Row, off Broad St] *Longboat*: Friendly and welcoming modern city-centre pub overlooking the recently renovated canal, quick service even during busy lunchtime periods, typical but tasty pub food, fruit machines, space game, juke box; terrace and balcony over the water *(Colin Gooch)*; [176 Edmund St] *Old Contemptibles*: Spacious Edwardian pub crowded with business people there for good value lunchtime cold table in high-ceilinged main bar, well kept Bass, good happy hour; popular with younger people in evening for good loud pop music (quiet side and upstairs bars then) *(C M Whitehouse, LYM)*; [Woodbridge Rd, Moseley] *Trafalgar*: Friendly local, some old-world old-world charm despite renovation, well kept Ansells and Ind Coope Burton on handpump, good folk evening Weds *(N F Doherty)*; [Temple St] *Trocadero*: Small, friendly city-centre pub with two bars, reasonably priced food, well kept M&B beers, fruit machine, 'quiet' juke box and restaurant; busy at lunchtime *(Colin Gooch)*; [Stephenson St, off New St] *Victoria & Albert Bar*: Formerly the Midland Hotel's Peel restaurant, revamped in Victorian style with cane chairs, larger tables (and quieter music) in one area, wide choice of food lunchtime and early evening such as quiche, cold meats, roasts, salads – no sandwiches; popular meeting-place, real ales; bedrooms *(C M Whitehouse)*

Blakesley, Northants [High St (Woodend rd); SP6250], *Bartholomew Arms*: Two cosy beamed bars cluttered with knick-knacks, Marstons Pedigree on handpump, well filled rolls and decent ploughman's ready-made; very popular Fri evening, calmer Sat lunchtime; back garden with summerhouse *(Nick Dowson)*

Bloxwich, W Mid [Park Side; SK0002], *Chimneys*: Good choice of real ale and good food in busy town-centre pub with very friendly management *(Tim Wootton)*

Bodymoor Heath, War [Dog Lane; SP2096], *Dog & Doublet*: At least three log fires, lots of beams, and lots of bargees' painted ware – in keeping with setting by Birmingham and Fazeley Canal; reasonably priced bar snacks,

meals in separate dining-room, pleasant garden with dovecot; close to Kingsbury Water Park; can be packed Sun lunchtime *(Mike and Sue Wheeler, Gill and Rob Weeks)*

Brackley, Northants [SP5837], *Bell*: Very good daily special such as home-made steak and kidney pie, plenty of tasty cheese and fresh salad with ploughman's, good beer, pleasant atmosphere *(Mrs M E Lawrence)*; [20 Market Sq] *Crown*: Classically refurbished, good value bar food and good restaurant; bedrooms extremely comfortable with all facilities *(Lorna Hawkins)*

Braunston, Northants [SP5466], *Admiral Nelson*: Lovely canalside position, about a mile along the towpath from the village; Manns and Wilsons real ales, open fire, darts, table skittles *(Jane and Calum)*

☆ **Brierley Hill**, W Mid [Delph Rd; B4172 between A461 and A4100, nr A4100], *Vine*: No-nonsense Black Country tap for neighbouring Bathams brewery, with cheap and well kept Bitter, Mild (unusually full-flavoured) and winter Delph Strong, old-fashioned sturdy ham cobs, fresh seafood; the three rooms can get crowded in the evenings and some lunchtimes (esp Fri); jazz Mon evening; known as the Bull & Bladder *(LYM)*

Brierley Hill, W Mid [Delph Rd; SO9187], *Bell*: Cosy Holts pub with roaring coal fires, lots of old knick-knacks, good value lunchtime bar food *(E J Alcock)*

Brigstock, Northants [SP9485], *Olde Three Cocks*: Clean, well run pub with well above average bar food; also restaurant *(Cdr Patrick Tailyour)*

Brinklow, War [Fosse Way; A427, fairly handy for M6 junction 2; SP4379], *Raven*: Good beer, friendly staff and customers, good value and generously served bar food *(Geoff Lee, Comus Elliott)*

Broom, War [SP0853], *Broom Hall*: Very comfortable lounge bar with good choice of reasonably priced food and choice of beers; bedrooms comfortable *(A Royle)*

Buckby Wharf, Northants [A5 N of Weedon – OS Sheet 152 reference 607654; SP6065], *New Inn*: Simple food and Marstons real ale in several rooms radiating from central servery, hood skittles and other games, canalside terrace *(LYM)*

Churchover, War [SP5180], *Haywaggon*: Carefully modernised old pub on edge of village which on weekday lunchtimes has been functioning solely as a restaurant (the reason it isn't a main entry) serving good food, also dinners Thurs to Sat evenings; well kept Hook Norton Best and Ruddles County, friendly pubby atmosphere *(BB)*

Claverdon, War [SP1964], *Red Lion*: Major attraction is the wide range of reasonably priced bar food, quickly served and well presented, though it can get full; pleasant main bar has red plush seats, lots of beams, a real fire and bookable tables in a side room

(it does get booked up on Sat evening);
Flowers Original and a Whitbreads-related
guest beer *(Rob and Gill Weeks, Dave Braisted)*
Coleshill, War [High St; not far from M6
junction 4; SP1989], *George & Dragon*:
Clean and well decorated bar and lounge,
well kept M&B Brew XI, good food at very
low prices, especially grills and daily specials
(T R G and A E Alcock)
Collyweston, Northants [Main St; on A43
4 miles SW of Stamford; SK9902], *Cavalier*:
Good range of real ales including Ruddles
County, pleasant atmosphere, good value
food in bar and restaurant; open fire, glass
floor between bar and lounge showing stone
cellar stairs below; bedrooms *(Michael
Bolsover, C E Tyers)*
Corley Moor, War [SP2884], *Bull & Butcher*:
Off the beaten track, small lounge and two
larger bars all with real fireplaces, good
choice of M&B ales, good bar food *(Clive
Davies)*
Cosgrove, Northants [Thrupp Wharf;
SP7942], *Navigation*: Good range of real ales,
very nice family-room, large canalside
garden, usual bar food *(Liz and Tony Hall)*
Cottingham, Northants [Blind Lane; SP8490],
Royal George: Wide range of traditional
dishes and half a dozen stupendous curries in
a choice of three different degrees of curry
taste; very old pub with bags of character
(Cdr Patrick Tailyour); [1 High St] *Spread
Eagle*: Modern pub with good value food
well above average in its dining lounge –
service well above average, though it gets
very busy *(Cdr Patrick Tailyour)*
☆ **Coventry**, W Mid [Spon St; called Ma
Browns; SP3379], *Old Windmill*: Interesting
and unspoilt timber-framed sixteenth-
century pub in otherwise reconstructed
ancient street, fine ancient fireplace, good
atmosphere in lots of small rooms one of
which has carved oak seats on flagstones;
lunchtime food, well kept Watneys-related
real ales, gets very busy Fri and Sat evening
*(Lyn Malkin, Edward Clarkson, Dr Graham
Bush, Rob and Gill Weeks)*
☆ **Coventry** [Bond St, behind Coventry
Theatre], *Town Wall*: Lovely compact Victorian pub with small lounge and bar and even
smaller donkey-box (which has room for six
friendly people), open fire, well kept Bass,
quite remarkably cheap bar food, flower-
filled back yard; still has Atkinsons engraved
windows and much as was in 1940s; can get
very busy *(Lyn Malkin, Edward Clarkson, Rob
and Gill Weeks, Dr Graham Bush)*
Coventry [Sutton Stop – close to M6 junction 3, via Black Horse Rd, off B4113
Coventry Rd], *Greyhound*: Welcoming pub
by Coventry Canal, beautiful food at reasonable prices *(Mr and Mrs R Holroyd)*; [Barnett
Green] *Peeping Tom*: Free house with good
choice of beers on handpump, including
good Marstons Pedigree; changing choice of
good food *(Mr and Mrs M D Jones)*; [Foleshill

Rd] *Saracens Head*: Pleasant pub with
beams, feature fireplace and little private
alcoves; well kept cellar and good value
food; pool-table, loud juke box *(Mr and
Mrs N Beckett)*
Cranford St John, Northants [SP9277], *Red
Lion*: Family-run pub in a delightful village
with thick stone walls, beautifully polished
tables and wooden settles; Watneys-related
real ales, bar food (not Mon) *(Gwen and Peter
Andrews)*
Crick, Northants [a mile from M1 junction
18; A428; SP5872], *Red Lion*: Lovely old
stone inn, licensed since 1766; large L-
shaped room with big log fire and second fire
in small inglenook by bar, very good food,
darts in small room by entrance; can get
crowded in evening *(Ted George)*
Denton, Northants [SP8358], *Red Lion*:
Small unpretentious local in sleepy hollow of
thatched stone houses, family atmosphere,
spotless lavatories, locals playing skittles, bar
food; canaries in outside aviary *(BB)*
Duddington, Northants [SK9800], *Royal
Oak*: Outstandingly good food *(Mr and Mrs
G Olive)*
☆ **Dudley**, W Mid [Black Country Museum;
SO9390], *Bottle & Glass*: Dismantled brick-
by-brick and rebuilt within the museum – all
fittings, decoration and even heating system
original, and the friendly old-fashioned
atmosphere seems just right (the only thing
that's not authentic is the price of the well
kept Hansons on handpump); only open
during the day while the museum is open,
but well worth a visit; good sandwiches
*(E J Alcock, David Fisher, Patrick and Mary
McDermott)*
☆ **Dunchurch**, War [SP4871], *Dun Cow*: Classic
coaching-inn layout with big central courtyard, pubby front bars (linked by hallway
with settles and antiques) have heavy beams,
brasses, warm fires in inglenooks, old-
fashioned furnishings, panelling; good
atmosphere, particularly in evenings;
bedrooms *(Lyn and Bill Capper, LYM)*
Edge Hill, War [SP3747], *Castle*: Terrific garden as perched over steep slope of Edge Hill,
with lovely views through the trees; unfortunately the atmospheric octagon room of this
intriguing battlemented folly, previously the
lounge bar, has been turned into a restaurant
and the duller previous public bar has
become the lounge, so it's less interesting
inside; well kept Hook Norton real ales, bar
food *(Gordon and Daphne, Gill and Ted
George, SP, Rob and Gill Weeks, LYM)*
Ettington, War [Banbury Rd (A422);
SP2749], *Houndshill*: Traditional country
pub with friendly service and a large choice
of good value bar meals *(R C Coates)*; *White
Lion*: Inviting atmosphere, friendly staff,
good lunchtime bar food, open fire, clean
lavatories *(F M Bunbury)*
Exhall, War [Coventry Rd, nr M6
junction 3; SP3385], *Black Bank*: Popular

pub with well kept Bass, comfortable lounge, lunchtime bar food *(Clive Davies)*

Fenny Compton, War [SP4152], *George & Dragon*: Canalside pub with good reasonably priced food in small restaurant *(Mr and Mrs K R Watkins)*

☆ **Five Ways**, War [follow Rowington signpost off A41 at A4177 roundabout, then right a few yards after roundabout – OS Sheet 151 reference 225701; SP2270], *Case is Altered*: Quite unspoilt old pub with cosy and homely sitting-room (open only Fri and Sat evening) and rather basic whitewashed public bar with tiled floor and posters from long-defunct local breweries; Ansells Bitter and Mild and Flowers Original dispensed from unique 1930s cask pumps behind interesting bar counter carved specially for pub; sandwiches at lunchtime, bar billiards machine which still takes sixpences *(Gill and Rob Weeks, SP)*

Frankton, War [about 1¼ miles S of B4453 Leamington Spa–Rugby; SP4270], *Friendly*: Friendly old low-ceilinged village pub with wooden settles, very good value lunchtime bar food, coal fire *(Gill and Ted George, J C Proud)*

Gaydon, War [B4451, just off A41 Banbury –Warwick; SP3654], *Malt Shovel*: Modernised pub with pleasant atmosphere, good service, Flowers Original and IPA, good, cheap bar food *(Mark Evans)*

Gayton, Northants [High St; SP7054], *Eykyn Arms*: Games are a particular attraction in this pub with old cockfighting connections; good Charles Wells *(Dr and Mrs A K Clarke)*; *Queen Victoria*: Wide choice of real ales in refurbished village pub which has comfortable back lounge with hunting prints and lively front public bar with darts and hood skittles (also pool-room); often popular for bar food from modern servery area *(Dr J R Hamilton, LYM)*

Grafton Regis, Northants [A508; SP7546], *White Hart*: Pleasant pub with hood skittles, well kept beer and big garden *(Dr and Mrs A K Clarke)*

Great Houghton, Northants [up No Through Road just before the White Hart; SP7958], *Old Cherry Tree*: Very cosy low-beamed pub with single servery for two alcovey areas, Charles Wells Eagle and Bombardier on handpump, cheap well filled cheese sticks; slightly up-market – no bikers, but not snobby *(Nick Dowson)*

☆ **Halesowen**, W Mid [Cowley Gate St; just off A458 to Stourbridge, at Cradley Heath – OS Sheet 139 reference 941847; SO9683], *Little White Lion*: One of the engagingly light-hearted 'Little' chain – bright red and blue paintwork here, with white lions all over the place, cask tables, six-foot papier-mâché bear, windows painted as if stained glass; good value freshly made bar food in massive helpings, and besides Ind Coope Burton has the group's Little Lumphammer real ale; live music Tues, otherwise quiet piped nostalgic pop music *(Rob and Gill Weeks, Dave Braisted)*

Halesowen [next to Halesowen FC], *King Edward*: Popular at lunchtimes for the good value food and Ansells ales *(Roger Huggins)*

Halford, War [SP2545], *Halford Bridge*: Large, modernised old hotel, Ruddles County on handpump, good though not cheap bar food, restaurant; bedrooms *(Mr and Mrs J H Wyatt)*

Hampton in Arden, W Mid [High St; SP2081], *White Lion*: Attractive stuccoed old village local with well kept Bass and M&B; fast and friendly service, lots of atmosphere and regulars of all ages (can sometimes seem clubby); children in special room *(R Houghton, N F Doherty)*

Hampton Lucy, War [SP2557], *Boars Head*: Friendly and cosy atmosphere in Flowers pub with garden behind; in nice village, handy for visitors to Charlecote Park; usual food *(W J Wonham)*

☆ **Harborne**, W Mid [not far from M5 junction 3; SP0284], *Bell*: Lovely little pub in Botanic Gardens area; bar at foot of stairs and queue formed along passageway for drinks, or if in snug served through hole in the wall; large, comfortable lounge, much of snug actually within chimneybreast of former vast open fireplace, with old leather settles and lots of bowls trophies won by local bowls club – a balcony overlooks the green; M&B Mild, full range of reasonably priced lunchtime bar food *(Ian and James Phillips)*; [High St] *Harborne*: Bar snacks and well kept cellar in small family pub which does a lot for local old people – even keeps a holiday caravan for OAPs *(Michael Chapman)*; [High St] *Junction*: Good reasonably priced food, friendly staff *(Michael Chapman)*; [Metchley Lane] *Lazy Fox*: Though ordinary externally, is well furnished and decorated inside, with very reasonably priced good food *(J R Green)*

Harbury, War [Crown St; SP3759], *Crown*: Pleasant stone pub with real fire in lounge, usual range of bar food in separate eating area, Flowers real ales *(Lyn and Bill Capper)*; [Chapel St] *Gamecock*: Popular for enormous choice of very good value bar food, staff extremely pleasant *(Lyn and Bill Capper, Elisabeth Kemp)*; *Shakespeare*: Popular and welcoming village pub with beams, horse-brasses on bare stone walls, two inglenook fireplaces in lounge, big helpings of food, well kept beer *(Gill and Rob Weeks)*

Harlestone, Northants [A428; SP7064], *Fox & Hounds*: Listed sixteenth-century building, very well furnished inside, mixture of old and new; quite spacious through lounge, raised snug opposite servery, separate bar; wide choice of good lunchtime food, Watneys-related real ales, decent choice of wines, garden *(Ted George)*

Harpole, Northants [High St; nr M1 junction 16; SP6860], *Bull*: Pleasant atmosphere in clean pub with good food – nothing too much for the licensees *(S Clarke)*

Hartshill, War [SP3393], *Stag & Pheasant*: Big Whitbreads pub with overwhelmingly friendly welcome, Flowers Original, assorted replica guns, horns, swords, plates and prints on flock wallpaper, inglenook fireplace; maybe live music; can get smoky *(Cliff Spooner)*

Henley in Arden, War [High St; SP1466], *Blue Bell*: Small, clean, well run and cosy country pub with friendly efficient service, well kept Flowers, good plain food at attractive prices; modern furnishings under the beams – it's one of many impressive timber-framed buildings here *(J Keppy, Mr and Mrs P M Dowd)*

Hinton in the Hedges, Northants [SP5536], *Crewe Arms*: Relaxing atmosphere in simply furnished bar and comfortable lounge, choice of beers including Marstons Pedigree, reasonably priced bar food, separate dining area for Sun roasts, etc., summer barbecues *(Michael O'Driscoll)*

Hockley Heath, W Mid [Stratford Rd; A34 Birmingham–Henley-in-Arden; SP1573], *Barn*: Children genuinely welcomed in restaurant and lounge, running about enjoying themselves; décor includes little houses built into the rooms, well kept Whibreads beers on handpump, decent food *(M T Casey)*; [Stratford Rd;] *Wharf*: Fairly typical big Chef & Brewer pub; reasonably priced bar food, if not very imaginative, piped pop music, fruit machines *(Grahame Archer)*

☆ **Ilmington**, War [SP2143], *Howard Arms*: Attractive Cotswold-stone pub on village green, open fires and well polished flagstones in beamed lounge, doing very well under new tenants; first-class unpretentious décor and furnishings, and above all big helpings of interesting food which changes from day to day – husband cooks, wife serves as well; darts in smaller room, Whitbreads-related beers, evening dining-room *(S V Bishop, P J Hanson)*

Iron Cross, War [A435 Evesham–Alcester; SP0552], *Queens Head*: Nicely decorated and very friendly old pub with good choice of food, well kept Flowers; children welcome *(Patrick Godfrey)*

Islip, Northants [SP9879], *Woolpack*: Renovated with prints and brass rubbings on bare stone walls, good furniture and carpet, weekday bar food, Sun lunch in restaurant; Charles Wells beers *(Tom Evans)*

☆ **Kenilworth**, War [High St; SP2871], *Clarendon House*: Based on old timber-framed 1430 Castle Tavern, oldest domestic building here and an inn even then; painstakingly restored with original beams and lots of panelling, antique prints, metalware and porcelain, relaxing cherry-red armchairs, reasonably priced lunchtime bar food, well kept Flowers IPA and Original, Hook Norton Best and a guest beer, good choice of liqueurs, malt whiskies and vintage port;

good restaurant, and recently discovered well in inner dining area of bar; bedrooms *(Rob and Gill Weeks, Sue White, Tim Kinning)*

Kenilworth, War [Chesford Bridge; SP2871], *Chesford Grange*: Large and largely modern hotel, but very good bar food and good service from pleasant staff; bedrooms good *(B Hazzard)*

Kettering, Northants [Victoria St; SP8778], *Alexandra Arms*: Superb value home-made lunchtime food and good choice of real ales including Ruddles County; interesting and extensive collection of ashtrays on wall in front lounge *(Tony Smith)*

Knowle, W Mid [about 1½ miles S off A41; SP1876], *Black Boy*: Small canalside pub with large garden and field – a popular stop for boats; M&B beers and food (not tried); though enlarged, is still atmospheric *(Dave Braisted)*

Ladbroke, War [A423 S of Southam; SP4158], *Bell*: Pleasant surroundings, well kept Davenports Bitter, well served and good value bar food, garden *(Charles Gurney)*

Lapworth, War [Old Warwick Rd (B4439); SP1670], *Boot*: Interesting old pub backing on to Grand Union Canal, coal fires in lounge and bar with darts area; lunchtime food (not Sun) includes sandwiches, ploughman's, main courses, cold buffet, starters and puddings; Flowers and Whitbreads beers, no piped music; extensive wine list, locally popular; nr GWG105 *(Lyn and Bill Capper)*; *Navigation*: Well kept Bass and M&B Mild on handpump and good value lunchtime food including good salads in canalside bar; waterside garden, children in room beyond bar, at least at lunchtime *(Brian Jones, G N G Tingey, R F Neil)*

Leamington Spa, War [Lansdowne St; SP3165], *Greyhound*: Very pleasant atmosphere in central side-street pub with well kept Flowers IPA and Original on handpump *(Charles Gurney)*; *Sommerville Arms*: Though nothing special architecturally, it is a useful local with good Ansells Bitter and Mild, Ind Coope Burton and Tetleys *(Graham Bush)*; [Clarendon Ave] *White Horse*: Recently restored, with small snug screened off from bar, separate lounge and cocktail bar, well kept Bass and M&B on handpump *(Geoff Wilson)*

☆ **Lilbourne**, Northants [Rugby Rd; 4 miles from M1 junction 18; A5 N, then first right; SP5677], *Bell*: Spaciously comfortable modern lounge bar with low-priced quickly served good value simple bar food, warm welcome for all (including children), seats outside, also a climbing-frame – well worth knowing as a relaxing motorway break *(Jill Hadfield, Tony Gallagher, LYM)*

Litchborough, Northants [B4525 Banbury –Northampton; SP6353], *Red Lion*: Pleasant and friendly, with slightly tarted-up inglenook, very good reasonably priced home-cooked ham, well kept Wilsons

Original, cheerful company *(Tom Evans)*

Little Addington, Northants [SP9573], *Bell*: Popular village pub with beams and exposed stone giving its long lounge bar an olde-worlde atmosphere; Adnams, Ansells, Ind Coope Burton and Tetleys real ales, good food in bar and restaurant, summer barbecues in pleasant garden *(Keith Garley, Barry Stevens)*

Little Brington, Northants [also signposted from A428; 4½ miles from M1 junction 16; first right off A45 to Daventry; SP6663], *Saracens Head*: Old-fashioned village pub, harking back to an idealised memory of the 1950s – spick-and-span brass and copper, cosy seats by the lounge fireplace, games in big L-shaped public bar, tables in neat back garden overlooking quiet fields; piano singalong Sat evening, real ale *(LYM)*

☆ **Little Compton**, War [off A34; SP2630], *Red Lion*: Simple but civilised Cotswold-stone inn with generously served good value bar food, open fire, well kept Donnington ales, friendly welcome from attentive landlord, traditional games in public bar, safe play area in garden; bedrooms comfortable and good value *(Dr Fuller, Barry and Anne, LYM)*

Long Buckby, Northants [A428; SP6267], *Buckby Lion*: Friendly and plushly refurbished country pub with picture windows overlooking rolling wooded countryside, real ales, lunchtime bar food, restaurant *(LYM)*

Long Compton, War [A34; SP2832], *Red Lion*: Stripped stone and bare beams in bottom bar with old-fashioned built-in settles and flagstones, well kept Bass, M&B Brew XI and Worthington on handpump, log fire, bar food and restaurant; very mixed reports on the new regime, though; bedrooms *(Paul McPherson, RF, LYM)*

☆ **Long Itchington**, War [off A423; SP4165], *Two Boats*: Friendly canalside pub with good mooring on Grand Union Canal, small and can be busy; well kept Flowers Original, good value food (trout, mixed grill and puddings all recommended); friendly youngish licensees, good lavatories; children welcome *(Mike and Sue Wheeler, Dr R Hodkinson)*

Long Itchington, War, *Buck & Bell*: Fine old-fashioned pub, down-to-earth charm of another era; locals sit or stand in passage, served through small hatch, with long benches and positively gleaming tables in another room which you may well have to unlock yourself *(T George)*; [Church Rd] *Harvester*: Good selection of beers, good value for money bar snacks and small restaurant *(T R G Alcock)*

Lower Boddington, Northants [off A361 Banbury–Daventry – OS Sheet 151 reference 481521; SP4852], *Carpenters Arms*: Popular local run by cricketing Yorkshireman and wife, well kept beer and wide range of snacks including super fry-ups *(David Gittins)*

Lowick, Northants [off A6116; SP9780], *Snooty Fox*: Recently renovated fourteenth-century inn with original oak beams, large, warm and comfortable; smartly dressed barmaids, well kept Adnams, Ruddles Best and County, Paines EG, good though rather pricey lunchtime and evening bar food, separate restaurant, garden with picnic tables *(Michael and Alison Sandy, N A Wood)*

Lowsonford, War [OS Sheet 151 reference 188679; SP1868], *Fleur de Lys*: Canalside pub with lots of beams and open fires in attractive bars, good waterside summer garden; popular for food, dogs allowed *(Rob and Gill Weeks, Robert and Vicky Tod)*

☆ **Lye**, W Mid [Pedmore Rd; SO9284], *Shovel Inn*: Refurbished pub with pleasant lounge and homely and unpretentious bar, serving generous helpings of good value for money steaks and other bar food; constantly changing guest beers such as Bathams and Hook Norton Old Hookey, friendly cheerful staff; can get very crowded, and parking isn't easy *(SP, E J Alcock, Dr Iain McColl)*

Marton, War [signposted off A423 Coventry–Banbury; SP4069], *Hare & Hounds*: Very clean village pub, partly sixteenth century, unobtrusively extended, with low beams, copper-topped tables, wood-burning stoves; cheap food, Ansells real ales, usually fairly quiet – piped music not irritating *(Gill and Rob Weeks)*

Meer End, W Mid [SP2474], *Tipperary*: Friendly comfortable pub with bar snacks, Davenports real ale, enormous goldfish in piano-aquarium, guinea-fowl pen in garden *(LYM)*

Middleton, War [OS Sheet 139 reference 175984; SP1798], *Green Man*: Very attractive garden – imaginative, even; popular for food (meals rather than snacks, though they do have filled cobs); bedlam in nice sort of way Sun lunchtime *(Dr and Mrs C D E Morris)*

Monks Kirby, War [Bell Lane; just off A427 W of Pailton; SP4683], *Bell*: Nicely decorated, with slabbed and cobbled floor, lots of brown beams, wood-burning stove; open-plan, but split into several areas and the extensions fit in well; friendly people and good, plentiful food both in bar and restaurant closed all day Mon, Tues–Fri lunchtimes; no food Sat evening, Sun lunchtime; children in restaurant only *(Mandy and Michael Challis)*; *Denbigh Arms*: Village pub tastefully decorated, well kept M&B beers on handpump, darts and pool-room, wide variety of good bar food up to 2½ lb steaks, separate restaurant busy at weekends *(A E Alcock)*

Napton, War [SP4661], *Crown*: Village local with plain but comfortable lounge, Manns real ale, games-bar *(C D T Spooner)*; [A425] *Napton Bridge*: Quite reasonably priced bar food in open-plan lounge well split up by remaining parts of walls – comfortable, with beams and open fire; Davenports ales, skittle alley in converted stable (used to be canalbarge horse-changing station) *(Rob and Gill Weeks)*

Nassington, Northants [Station Rd; TL0696], *Queens Head*: Lovely food including good range of good value pies, very friendly service, Greene King ales *(Virginia Jones)*

Nether Whitacre, War [Whitacre Heath; Station Rd – OS Sheet 139 reference 220928; SP2292], *Swan*: Quite attractive, pleasant service, decent food at tables set out for meals between bar and kitchen *(431)*

Newbold on Avon, War [B4112; canalside; SP4777], *Boat*: Lovely old canalside pub with pleasantly extended lounge/eating area; good Davenports real ales, very good value food well cooked and served; can get packed on sunny days even in winter *(Ted George, J C Proud)*

Northampton, Northants [11 Fish St; SP7560], *Fish*: Town-centre pub with good value food in bar and small, delightful restaurant; bedrooms comfortable *(Lorna Hawkins)*

Nuneaton, War [Bull St, Attleborough; SE of centre; SP3592], *Bull*: One of Ansells Heritage Inns refurbishments, with real ales on handpump, freshly made food, coal fire, darts, dominoes and cribbage opened late eighteenth century, run early this century by Jack Dickens, father of present Jack (Jnr) *(I Blackwell)*; [Eastborough Way] *Crows Nest*: New one-room single-storey Banks's pub furnished with a large collection of old farm tools; very good filled rolls and lively lunchtime trade *(I Blackwell)*

Offchurch, War [off A425 at Radford Semele; SP3565], *Stags Head*: Four-hundred-year-old thatched pub, good food from German cook, Ansells and Tetleys ales, though concentration on the food has turned former lounge area into restaurant – drinkers rather cramped into side bar; village name derived from Offa's Church – which is reputed to house his coffin *(A J Hill)*

☆ **Oxhill**, War [just S of A422; SP3145], *Peacock*: Lovely old stone country inn with open fire in big inglenook, tidy cosy bar tastefully furnished in keeping, some emphasis on good lunchtime food at affordable prices, Bass, M&B and guest real ales; seats on big lawn, nice village *(Ted George, Nick Dowson, S V Bishop)*

Pailton, War [SP4781], *Fox*: Clean pub, well kept M&B Brew XI, reasonably priced good bar food; bedrooms *(T R G Alcock)*

Pelsall, W Mid [Walsall Rd; SK0203], *Old House*: Pleasant, comfortable surroundings, well kept Banks's Mild and Bitter and limited but good value lunchtime bar snacks *(Paul Noble)*

Pensnett, W Mid [A4101 Dudley–Kingswinford; SO9188], *Fox & Grapes*: Holts pub with odd mixture of ancient and modern décor; landlord's attractive theory is that you pay for the food, if you like it *(Dave Braisted)*

Polebrook, Northants [TL0687], *Kings Arms*: Very friendly thatched pub with good local beers and very good value food; good location in lovely village *(Mark Bowman)*

Potterspury, Northants [A5; SP7543], *Old Talbot*: Watneys-related real ales in brightly decorated bar with friendly staff, food in bar and small restaurant, simple public bar with darts and other games; bedrooms *(LYM)*

Preston on Stour, War [SP2049], *Radbrook Manor*: Newly opened renovated country house with poolside bar (and bar food) as well as restaurant, panelled coffee-room, lots of leisure facilities, bedrooms; have to pay entrance or membership fee and hardly a suitable case for these pages, but included as interesting new venture by owner of the popular Holly Bush at Seighford – see Derbys/Staffs main entries; bedrooms *(Anon)*

Princethorpe, War [junction A423/B4453; SP4070], *Three Horseshoes*: Popular roadside inn with well kept Flowers and open fires, and lounge more or less given over to the reasonably priced food which comes in big helpings; nice garden with lots of children's playthings *(J C Proud, Rob and Gill Weeks)*

Priors Hardwick, War [SP4756], *Butchers Arms*: What was the lounge of this medieval stone inn is now attached to the restaurant (with lots of beams, oak panelling, antique furniture) doing food such as caviare and roast quail, with fine wine list; public bar something of a sideline, with big inglenook, beams, sloping floor; keg beers, attractive gardens *(C Fisher Price)*; *Falcon*: Sixteenth-century stone-built pub which has been popular for well kept Flowers, Everards, Hook Norton Best and Old Hookey and Sam Smiths real ales, with log fire, bar food and restaurant; but being sold early 1988 – more news please *(Gill and Rob Weeks)*

☆ **Pytchley**, Northants [SP8574], *Overstone Arms*: Delightful bustling Manns pub with nice garden, friendly professional service, superb food, good Pimms *(D M C Creighton Griffiths, Dr Paul Kitchener)*

☆ **Quarry Bank**, W Mid [Saltwells Lane; Quarry Bank signposted off Coppice Lane, off A4036 nr Merry Hill Centre – OS Sheet 139 map reference 934868; SO9386], *Saltwells*: Surprisingly modern hotel at end of rough lane – books on shelves in nice main lounge carefully refurbished by the new owners, cheap straightfoward bar food, Banks's and Hansons ales, play equipment in garden and family-room; it's a veritable haven in these industrial parts, in a nature reserve by Mushroom Green – perfect for walking off your lunch, with woods, quarry, reservoir and canals; bedrooms *(Dave Braisted, E J Alcock, Dr and Mrs C D E Morris)*

Radford Semele, War [A425 2 miles E of Leamington Spa – OS Sheet 151 reference 343645; SP3464], *White Lion*: Plain old pub with wide choice of good value cheap, cheerful and generously served lunchtime food –

they specialise in ploughman's; Davenports ales, garden (*G N G Tingey, R F Neil*)

☆ **Ratley**, War [OS Sheet 151 reference 384473; SP3847], *Rose & Crown*: New licensees have comfortably refurbished this golden stone building; previously a flagstones-wood-and-candlelight pub, it's now carpeted, with lots of interesting brasses, smarter tables, more emphasis on food, with wide choice and new restaurant separated off by two big fireplaces; Donnington SBA, Hook Norton Best and Wadworths 6X, attentive service; seats on small back terrace, lovely church next door – it's a picturesque village (*Pete Storey, Rob and Gill Weeks, Gordon and Daphne*)

☆ **Rockingham**, Northants [SP8691], *Sondes Arms*: Civilised and attractive old pub, cosy and warm, with friendly service, well kept Charles Wells Bombardier and Eagle and good range of food – good helpings, nicely cooked and very reasonably priced (*Joy Heatherley, AE, Derek Stephenson*)

Rowington, War [SP2069], *Cockhorse*: Open all day from 10am for reasonably priced food; low beams, big inglenook with log fire, Flowers real ales, subdued lighting (*Rob and Gill Weeks*)

Rugby, War [Lawford Rd; SP5075], *Half Moon*: Very cosy – probably the town's smallest pub; extremely friendly licensees, good atmosphere, well kept beer; only filled rolls at lunchtime (*Ted George*); [nr M6 junction 1: A426 towards Rugby centre] *Old Crown*: Very good and most reasonably priced food in clean bar, snug and spacious lounge; popular at lunchtime with young local businessmen; an M&B pub (*John Roué*)

Sedgley, W Mid [Bilston St (A463); SO9193], *Beacon*: Recently refurbished Victorian home-brew pub brewing potent Dark Ruby Mild; good atmosphere, original furniture and fittings in hatch-served passageway bar, four other rooms and family-room; also stocks guest beers such as Bathams, Burton Bridge and Holdens; seats on terrace (*David Fisher, R A Sanders, E J Alcock*)

Shipston on Stour, War [Station Rd (off A34); SP2540], *Black Horse*: Ancient thatched stone-built inn now rather improbably surrounded by housing estate; log fire in big inglenook, lots of beams, cheap drinks including Wadworths real ales, cheap food (*Rob and Gill Weeks*)

Shrewley, War [off B4439 Hockley Heath –Warwick; SP2167], *Durham Ox*: This otherwise straightforward pub gains its place for its spacious garden, with beer-barrel dovecots on telegraph poles housing a flight of white doves – the new M40 being built beyond it completes the transport scene, with railway and canal already cutting past; cheap very basic snacks (not Sun lunchtime), M&B beers (*S R Holman, LYM*)

Shustoke, War [SP2290], *Plough*: Several small bars without connecting doors in old low-beamed pub with very friendly atmosphere, well kept Bass, friendly considerate licensees and simple good value food (*Mrs Pamela Roper, Colin Grout*)

Sibbertoft, Northants [SP6782], *Red Lion*: Simple village pub with well kept Flowers, upholstered bench seats, brightly patterned carpet, open fires in bar and restaurant, good service from young licensees, usual bar food, piano, darts and skittles (*Cdr Patrick Tailyour*)

Smethwick, W Mid [SP0288], *New Chapel*: Welcoming landlord who talks to children, well kept beer, good hot roast pork sandwiches (*Roger Taylor*); [Uplands/Meadow Rd] *Old Chapel*: Delightful little pub tucked away in residential area with black and white half-timbered extension and timber-effect lounge; M&B Brew XI and Springfield on electric pump, well kept Mild on handpump, really welcoming landlord, all fresh food including fine hot roast pork sandwiches with or without apple sauce (*R P Taylor*); [Waterloo Rd – junction A457/A4136/ A4092] *Waterloo*: Decidedly unpretentious atmosphere in splendidly tiled Victorian public bar with cheap M&B and Springfield ales, more orthodox comfortable lounge, grandly decorated basement grill room (*LYM*)

Stonnall, W Mid [Main St, off A452; SK0503], *Old Swan*: Good choice of good reasonably priced hot and cold food lunchtime and early evening, warm hospitality, good service, Bass and M&B ales, reasonable choice of wines (*C N Blakemore*)

Stourbridge, W Mid [Amblecote Rd (A491); SO8984], *Moorings*: Large, busy pub by canal spur; reasonably priced bar food, pleasant terrace at back (*E J Alcock*); [Church St] *Old Crispin*: Refurbished pub, now extended into a sun-lounge covered terrace; superb food that includes vegetarian dishes, good Hook Norton Old Hookey and Marstons; popular with students from art college opposite (*SP*)

☆ **Stratford-upon-Avon**, War [Riverside; SP2055], *Black Swan*: Charmingly placed sixteenth-century pub with attractive terrace looking over the riverside public gardens, handy for the Memorial Theatre (and popular with RSC players), well kept Flowers IPA and Original, children allowed in restaurant (*C D T Spooner, S V Bishop, Wayne Brindle, I J McDowall, LYM; more reports please*)

☆ **Stratford-upon-Avon** [Chapel St], *Shakespeare*: Smart THF hotel based on handsome lavishly modernised Tudor merchants' houses, stylish public rooms and accommodation, also comfortable Froth & Elbow bar with good choice of well kept real ales and bar food; tables in back courtyard (*S V Bishop, LYM*)

Stratford-upon-Avon [Clopton Bridge], *Alveston Manor*: THF hotel with good public bar and good lunchtime snacks, handy for shops on that side of Clopton Bridge and for pre-theatre drinks *(S V Bishop)*; [opp United Reform Church, handy for Friday Market] *Lamplighters*: Attractive low-ceilinged lounge and flagstoned public bar with real ales such as Ansells, Courage Best and Directors and Tetleys, reasonably priced food *(S V Bishop)*; [Rother St/Greenhill St] *Old Thatch*: Small thatched Whitbreads pub, pleasant and warm inside, with well kept beer, reasonable bar food (their idea of a sandwich is thick Vienna loaf that you need two hands for) and quick service *(S V Bishop)*; [Bridgefoot;], *Swans Nest*: Same advantages as Alveston Manor *(S V Bishop)*; [Church St] *Windmill*: Attractive Whitbreads pub, though a bit dark inside; food good value *(S V Bishop)*

☆ **Studley**, War [Icknield St Dr; left turn off A435, going N from B4093 roundabout; SP0763] *Old Washford Mill*: The pretty waterside gardens are in summer perhaps the best part of this extensive and popular watermill conversion (and have a good play area); inside, there's old mill machinery, lots of different levels with various quiet alcoves (though at night the music gets rather loud, giving a sort of night-clubbish atmosphere), and a variety of catering; real ales; provision for children *(Gill and Ted George, PLC, LYM)*

Tanworth in Arden, War [SP1170], *Bell*: Roomy lounge which has been popular particularly with older people for its low lunchtime food prices, well kept Flowers IPA and Original on handpump from the bar at one end, outlook on peaceful village green and lovely fourteenth-century church; children in eating area and restaurant *(LYM – reports on current regime have been very mixed)*

Temple Grafton, War [1 mile E, towards Binton; SP1255], *Blue Boar*: Popular for good bar food – same menu as in restaurant – with well kept Flowers ale; tastefully extended building with spacious dining-room, stripped stonework, recently exposed fireplace in bar, new flagstoned darts area *(HDC, S V Bishop)*

☆ **Thornby**, Northants [Welford Rd (A50); SP6775], *Red Lion*: New licensees rejuvenating this pub making it cheerful and interesting; interior is pleasantly crowded with pictures and plates, open log fire, comfortable settees and highly polished benches; Marstons and Everards, above-average food in bar and small separate no-smoking restaurant (Fri-Sat evening, Sun lunch) *(Roy Herbert, Cdr Patrick Tailyour)*

Thrapston, Northants [A604 to Kettering, just W of main bridge; SP9978], *Woolpack*: Solid traditional inn with good home-cooked bar food, two or three communicating bar rooms with stone-clad walls and wood-burning stove, pleasant service; bedrooms *(C J Cowlin)*

Tipton, W Mid [Hurst Lane, Dudley Rd; towards Wednesbury, junction A457/A4037 – look for the Irish flag; SO9592], *M A D*

O'Rourkes Pie Factory: New addition to Mr O'Rourke's chain of 'Little' pubs, set in former butcher's shop with interesting original décor (all sorts of ancient meat-processing equipment) and the usual larger-than-life atmosphere; good value food including not only gargantuan Desperate Dan cow pie with horns but also gerbil giblets (don't worry, it's just a nickname) and black pudding thermidor; traditional puddings, well kept real ales, jazz Mon; children welcome *(Elaine Kellet, James Billingham, Colin Dowse, PLC, E J Alcock)*

Towcester, Northants [104 Watling St – village signposted from A5; SP6948], *Brave Old Oak*: Cheerful and comfortable, well kept Ruddles Best and County; pleasant dining-room with good food and reasonable prices; can get packed some evenings with motor-cyclists and other youngsters; small basic bedrooms *(Douglas Bail)*; [Watling St] *Saracens Head*: Attractive building with strong *Pickwick Papers* connections, cavernous fireplace with cooking-range in the bar, friendly owners; bedrooms *(LYM)*

Tredington, War [SP2543], *White Lion*: Very hospitable welcome on very busy Sun with a good atmosphere and food (fairly short menu) appetising and well served; large garden *(Ian Meredith)*

Ufton, War [White Hart Lane; just off A425 Daventry–Leamington, towards Bascote; SP3761], *White Hart*: Pleasant location near top of hill overlooking Avon Vale; Davenports ales *(Dave Braisted)*

Upper Benefield, Northants [SP9889], *Wheatsheaf*: Welcoming hospitality with personal attention to detail, good beer and wines, good value food in bar and restaurant, log fires, seats in garden *(Martin Ball)*

☆ **Upper Brailes**, War [SP3039], *Gate*: Old-world atmosphere, log fires, low ceilings, beams, genial host, good service, bar food including lots of sandwiches, extensive gardens – good value all round *(D H Carr, Derrick Turner)*

Warley, W Mid [Freeth St, Oldbury; SO9987], *Waggon & Horses*: Old Holts pub with superb Edwardian tiled bar, good variety of food (curries and steaks) and varied real ales *(SP)*

Warmington, War [A41 towards Shotteswell; SP4147], *Wobbly Wheel*: Warm welcome, nice situation, attractive bar and lounge, choice of real ales and very original and enjoyable food (some dishes rather pricey); restaurant *(M S Hancock, Michael O'Driscoll)*

☆ **Warwick** [St Nicholas Church St; SP2865], *Barn*: Long popular as a restaurant, especially for fish, but now open as a pub as well, doing lunchtime bar food in converted barn – a surprising survivor almost in Warwick's centre; very well done conversion with natural colour beams, exposed brickwork and flagstones, and pub/bistro feel from sewing-machine trestle tables with candles and fresh flowers, stripped wood chairs, tractor-seat bar stools, old farm tools, open fire; tables in enclosed courtyard with well *(Rob and Gill Weeks)*

Warwick [Smith St], *Roebuck*: Particularly good sandwiches *(Roy and Pamela Wade)*; [West St, between Lord Leycester Hospital and racecourse, towards Stratford] *Wheatsheaf*: Welcoming town pub with Ansells, Ind Coope and Tetleys; attractive bar food *(Dave Braisted)*; [11 Church St] *Zetland Arms*: Good value simple food and well kept Davenports beer in lively pub with charmingly well kept sheltered back garden *(LYM)*

Weedon, Northants [Stowe Hill (A5, S); SP6259], *Narrow Boat*: Spacious terrace and big garden with pheasants and peacocks sweeping down to Grand Union Canal (though that makes it sound smarter than it is), good canal photographs in main bar, high-raftered ex-kitchen family-room, quickly served bar food, summer barbecues, restaurant; well kept Charles Wells real ale; very busy in summer *(Neil and Angela Huxter, BG, Derek Stephenson, LYM)*

Weedon [Daventry Rd], *Heart of England*: Friendly manageress, good service and good food; bedrooms superbly decorated, one with four-poster *(Lorna Smith)*; [High St] *Wheatsheaf*: Friendly, welcoming and pleasantly fussy little pub jam-packed with brasses, substantial lunchtime baps *(Dr and Mrs A K Clarke)*

Welford, Northants [SP6480], *Shoulder of Mutton*: Agreeable pub with good simple food, well kept beer and big garden behind *(Yvonne Healey)*

Welford on Avon, War [Maypole; SP1452], *Shakespeare*: Whitbreads pub very popular for food, tastefully presented and reasonably priced – get there early for a table; concentration on food has restricted space for quiet drinking at bar, though; welcoming owners (especially if you're a golfer), helpful staff, prettily planted garden and hanging baskets *(S V Bishop, Michael Craig, R W and E J Richardson, J M Reading)*

Wellesbourne, War [SP2755], *Kings Head*: Old-fashioned high-ceilinged bar of inn handy for Stratford (but cheaper), M&B Brew XI on electric pump, separate public bar with lots of games, seats in garden facing church; new tenants 1987, with talk of a possible expensive refurbishment; bedrooms *(LYM – news please)*

West Bromwich, W Mid [High St; SP0091], *Old Hop Pole*: Cosy Holts pub with lots of old knick-knacks, roaring fire in black-leaded grate, well kept real ale, superb doorstep sandwiches – especially the local speciality, hot pork *(E J Alcock, AJH)*; [High St, opp bus stn] *Sandwell*: Edwardian hotel beside shopping precinct with extensive room surrounding the bar on three sides – one side is for food – and non-smoking area between bar and food counter; deep pink furnishings, cheerful and efficient service, Springfield Bitter on handpump and good value food – all dishes £1.75; bedrooms *(Frank Cummins)*; [High St] *Wheatsheaf*: Cheerful lively licensee, well kept Holdens and good food – lunchtime hot pork sandwiches a real treat *(AJH)*

West Haddon, Northants [about 3 miles from M1 junction 18; A428 towards Northampton; SP6272], *Wheatsheaf*: Very comfortable pub with pool-table in small cosy downstairs bar, snug and tastefully furnished upstairs lounge, good bar meals and wide choice of courteously presented good food in big candlelit dining-room *(Ted George)*

Weston, Northants [SP5846], *Crown*: Good food and range of ale, really warm welcome, in old pub with highwayman connections; handy for NT Canons Ashby *(David Gittins)*

Wicken, Northants [Deanshanger Rd; SP7439], *White Lion*: Lovely unspoilt old pub with good beer *(Dr and Mrs A K Clarke)*

Wilmcote, War [Aston Cantlow Rd; SP1657], *Masons Arms*: Friendly, snug and tidy pub with well kept Flowers IPA and Original, wide choice of good value bar food *(Andrew Ludlow, T George)*

Wixford, War [B4085 Alcester–Bidford – OS Sheet 150 map reference 085546; SP0954], *Fish*: There has been an inn here for centuries and this one is tastefully refurbished with a roomy L-shaped bar and snug, beams, polished wood wall panels, carpets over the flagstones and upholstered wall settles, Windsor chairs and stools; well kept Bass on handpump, reasonably priced bar food and pleasant, efficient service *(Frank Cummins)*

Wollaston, W Mid [from Stourbridge on A458, 400 yds past shops, on left at hill brow; SO8984], *Forresters Arms*: Good food in friendly pub with well kept real ale *(Mr and Mrs W H Crowther)*

Wolston, War [Main Rd; SP4175], *Half Moon*: Friendly, olde-worlde pub, deep leather sofas by open fire, good range of beers, good though loud juke box, reasonably priced bar food, restaurant *(Mr and Mrs N Beckett)*

Wolverhampton, W Mid [Park Lane, Park Village; SO9198], *Paget Arms*: Medieval-style lounge with heavy oak refectory tables, wide choice of beers including Premier from Stourbridge, good value food *(Miss G L Paget – no relation)*; [51 Compton Rd] *Quarter House*: Homely, lively and friendly, with exceptional personal attention from licensee *(J R Green)*

Wolvey, War [near M65 junction 1; SP4287], *Blue Pig*: Friendly olde-worlde pub with nice atmosphere and super char-grilled mixed grill at very reasonable prices; does get busy at weekends *(Mandy and Mike Challis)*

Wolvey Heath, War [OS Sheet 140 reference 436890; SP4390], *Axe & Compass*: Rightly popular for wide choice of bar food (including lots of daily specials), crowded with diners by 7pm; Bass, M&B Brew XI, silent fruit machine, quiet piped music *(R Aitken)*

☆ **Woodford Halse**, Northants [SP5452], *Fleur de Lys*: Taken over 1988 by Derek Hettenbach, formerly of Royal Oak, Eydon: his record there – it was highly rated in the *Guide* – suggests that this will be well worth watching *(JT)*

Wootton Wawen, War [N side of village; SP1563], *Bulls Head*: L-shaped lounge in sixteenth-century black and white pub is low-ceilinged and heavily beamed, and there are some massive upright timbers as well; keg beers and no evidence of bar snacks, but restaurant very popular *(S J A Velate)*

Yardley Gobion, Northants [30 High St; SP7644], *Coffee Pot*: Comfortable, friendly atmosphere with good value food counter *(H Rust)*

Yardley Hastings, Northants [SP8656], *Rose & Crown*: Wide choice of reasonably priced bar food, including carvery, in recently redecorated village-centre pub *(Mr and Mrs Ray)*

Norfolk

Quite a few changes in this county over the last year include new licensees at the cheerful Bluebell in Hunworth, the Capt Sir William Hoste in Burnham Market (they've been upgrading it, and rather directing attention to its restaurant – the bar food's good value, too), and the grand old Scole Inn at Scole (still very much as before: there's been little change to the popular food, and housekeeping standards are as high as ever). The Ship at Brandon Creek, in its lovely isolated waterside position, has rejigged its food service, combining the restaurant and the bar together – so that there's now the same choice of food, wherever you want to sit. And the marked upswing in the standard of cooking in Norfolk pubs that's been noticed by many readers has resulted in new food awards for that friendly country-house pub the King's Head at Letheringsett, the little Adam & Eve in Norwich (besides being probably the city's most attractive pub, it's certainly its oldest) and the cosy and atmospheric Lifeboat at Thornham, with its five log fires keeping out the chill of the winter salt marshes. The new place-to-stay award for the Fishermans Return at Winterton-on-Sea is recognition of the friendly good value offered by this snugly traditional seaside-village inn. Besides the Scole Inn already mentioned, another comfortable inn here is the attractively placed old Buckinghamshire Arms at Blickling. That too has particularly good food, as does the Jolly Sailors busily living up to its name at Brancaster Staithe, the Ostrich in the attractive village of Castle Acre, and the Rose & Crown at Snettisham, with its rambling series of charmingly furnished small rooms. A couple of delightfully placed waterside pubs are the Ferry House at Surlingham and the Sutton Staithe Inn at Sutton Staithe – while the Kings Arms in Blakeney's just a stroll from the sea. The idiosyncratic Admiral Nelson in Burnham Thorpe earns special praise

The Fishermans Return, Winterton-on-Sea

from many readers for its relative freedom from cigarette smoke, though its primary virtues are its unspoilt period flavour and its fine collection of Nelson material. Several of the Lucky Dip entries at the end of the chapter are beginning to suggest themselves as potential main entries, and we'd be particularly interested in readers' views on these, as we'd like to devote quite a bit of effort to inspection in the county over the coming year. Those which spring most obviously to attention are the Ferry at Reedham, the Gintrap at Ringstead and the Manor at Titchwell, and there's also growing support for the Hare & Hounds at Baconsthorpe (make sure you head for the right one, up near Holt — we spent a wasted morning trying to find the pub in the other Baconsthorpe, down near Attleborough!), the Spread Eagle at Erpingham (particularly among beer enthusiasts), the Windmill at Great Cressingham and the Crown at Mundford.

BLAKENEY   TG0243 Map 8
Kings Arms
West Gate Street

The date 1760 is picked out in black tiles on the red roof of this pretty white cottage. Inside, the three knocked-together, simply furnished rooms are relaxed and friendly; there's a banquette facing the bar counter, slat-backed seats around traditional cast-iron tables, and framed reprints of old Schweppes advertisements and photographs of the *Black and White Minstrels* (the licensees are both ex-theatricals) on the walls. Regulars tend to favour the red-tiled end room, where the flint walls have been exposed above low panelling. Good bar food includes sandwiches (from 80p, local crab in season £1.20), a wide choice of ploughman's, including locally smoked ham, home-cooked silverside and rollmops (£2.30 to £4.35), hot snacks (£2.75) and a daily special (£3.25), with evening dishes such as fresh cod (£3.60), gammon or trout (£4.70) and steak (£6.95); also, puddings like fruit crumble or bread pudding. Ruddles County and Websters Yorkshire on handpump; darts, dominoes and fruit machine. There are picnic-table sets on the grass and gravel outside. As the pub is near the harbour, it tends to get packed at busy times. (*Recommended by Guy Sowerby, David and Ruth Hollands, Jill Hadfield, Ian Phillips*)

Manns (Watneys)   Licensee Howard Davies   Meals and snacks   Restaurant tel Cley (0263) 740341; open all day from noon on Sun   Children welcome   Open all day

BLICKLING   TG1728 Map 8
Buckinghamshire Arms ⊗ 🛏

Outside this civilised Jacobean inn, picnic-table sets shelter under cocktail parasols on the lawn (they serve food from an outbuilding here in summer), and there's a wide stretch of neatly raked gravel between the inn and a splendid Dutch-gabled stableblock; climbing-frame, slide and swing. Inside, the simply furnished little snug front bar has fabric cushioned banquettes, some brass tack above the open fire and an antique seed-sowing machine in an alcove. It sometimes gets so busy that you can scarcely get through the door, though you can then use the bigger lounge, which has neatly built-in pews and stripped deal tables, and landscapes and cockfighting prints. The home-made country food is not cheap, but well served in generous helpings, and includes sandwiches (from £1.30, in French, brown or white bread), soup (£1.65, home-made stockpot soup with croûtons (£1.65), ploughman's (£2.60), salads (from £2.65, fresh Cromer crab in season £4.50), and home-made pâté or vegetarian hors d'oeuvre (£3). Well kept Adnams, Flowers, and Greene King IPA and Abbot on handpump; good service. Neighbouring National Trust Blickling Hall is open from April to mid-October only, and closed Mondays and

Thursdays, though you can walk through the park at any time. *(Recommended by G and M Brooke-Williams, T Nott, Paul and Margaret Baker, Barbara Hatfield, Guy Sowerby, S V Bishop, Susan Masquire, Mrs A Roberts)*

Free house   Licensee Nigel Elliott   Real ale   Meals and snacks   Restaurant   Children in restaurant   Open 10.30–2.30, 6–11 all year; closed 25 Dec   Three double bedrooms tel Aylsham (0263) 732133; £36/£46

BRANCASTER STAITHE   TF7743 Map 8

Jolly Sailors ★ ⊗

Licensed by 1789, this informal country pub has a happy atmosphere and a warm welcome from the staff. The three bar rooms have antique high-backed settles as well as more modern seats on the broad old flooring-tiles, shorebird pictures on the white-painted rough stone or bare brick walls, and three stuffed albino birds. The log fire has one of those old-fashioned sturdy guards to sit on. The winter mussels, baked with garlic butter or white wine and cream, have the distinction of coming from the only natural harbour – just across the road – in England and Wales passed as pollution-free by a recent EEC survey. Other home-made bar food includes soup (from 80p), sandwiches (crab £1.40), ploughman's (from £1.90), macaroni in a cream sauce with ham (£2.80), chicken pâté (£3.20), curry (£3.40), chicken quarter in barbecue sauce (£4), lasagne (£4.20), seafood pancake (contains no mussels, £4.30) and steak and kidney pie (£6.40); puddings (from £1) and children's dishes (£1.20). Well kept Greene King Abbot and IPA on handpump; sensibly placed darts in one room; also shove-ha'penny, dominoes, table skittles, and warri. There are seats by flowering shrubs on a sheltered lawn, or on a canopied side terrace, a hard tennis court (which can be booked up to seven days in advance), and a children's play house. The pub is on the edge of thousands of acres of National Trust dunes, salt flats and Scolt Head Island nature reserve. *(Recommended by Michele and Andrew Wells, Guy Sowerby, S V Bishop)*

Free house   Licensee Alister Borthwick   Real ale   Meals and snacks   Restaurant tel Brancaster (0485) 210314   Children in eating areas and darts room   Open 11–11 July and Aug; 11–3, 6–11 rest of year; closed evening 25 Dec (no food that lunchtime)   Local bed and breakfast can be arranged

BRANDON CREEK   TL6091 Map 5

Ship

A10 Ely–Downham Market

Steps by the wood-burning stove in the bar of this out-of-the-way pink-washed pub drop down into a sunken area that was a working forge until not long ago – as the massive stone masonry and photographs on the walls show. The rest of the bar is spaciously comfortable, with soft lighting, slat-back chairs and one or two upholstered settles, and an open fire at one end; the very long bar counter is decorated above with shepherds' crooks made from intricately plaited corn stalks. As we went to press, the licensees were revising their food operation, and introducing one menu that would serve both the bar and restaurant, and could be eaten in either area (this means that it won't be just restaurant diners who can enjoy the river view); tables can be reserved in advance. At lunchtime food includes sandwiches (from £1), soup (£1.20), seafood pancake (£1.40), filled baked potatoes (from £1.50), ploughman's (from £2), poacher's pie or vegetable crumble (£3), home-cooked ham and egg (£3.25), salads (from £3.75) and a roast of the day (£4); in the evening there are extras such as spare ribs (£1.75), pasta or cheese fondue (£3), lamb kebabs (£3.50), mixed grill (£4.25), and whole lemon sole (£6); also, Sunday roast lunch. Well kept Ruddles Best and County, and Websters Yorkshire on handpump. Besides shove-ha'penny, they have books on general knowledge, quizzes, short stories and so forth, and their quiz league is on Tuesday and

Wednesday evenings from September to May; piped music. Outside, there are tables by the pub's own moorings at the junction of the creek with the high-banked Great Ouse. *(Recommended by B R Shiner, R P Hastings, P Gillbe, G N G Tingey, R F Neil)*

Manns (Watneys)   Licensees Geoff and Jean Preston   Real ale   Meals and lunchtime snacks Restaurant tel Brandon Creek (035 376) 228   Children in eating area of bar until 8.30 Occasional Sun evening entertainment in summer   Open 10.30–4, 5–11 all year; closes 2.30 Sun in winter

BURNHAM MARKET   TF8342   Map 8
Capt Sir William Hoste ⊗
The Green; B1155

A good bow-window seat in the lounge of this friendly pub – named after one of Nelson's officers born nearby – looks out past pots of geraniums to the Georgian-fronted houses surrounding the green. The age of the pub itself can be seen in the curved door in from the little entrance hall, the hatches hinged up over the bar servery, and the old brick tiles alongside it. There are captain's chairs and wheel-back chairs around oak tables, bar seats with comfortable back rests and arms, and Turkey carpets; the big brick fireplace here has a fine log fire, as does the one in the black-panelled Nelson Room (which is decorated with naval paintings); friendly dog. The new licensee has changed the style of bar food which now includes soup, mussels, seafood quiche (£2.95), steak and mushroom pie or chicken Kiev (£3.25), baked avocado with lobster and cheese sauce (£3.50), potted brown shrimps (£3.75), special steaks in good sauces, a help-yourself salad bar and amazing Pavlovas. The attractive restaurant has a naval theme. Well kept Ruddles County and Websters Yorkshire on handpump; attentive service; Kenco coffee. In summer there are seats outside in front, and in a back courtyard looking past a honeysuckle-covered pergola to a paddock. *(Recommended by R C Vincent, Patti McNaught, David and Ruth Hollands, Guy Sowerby, Linda and Alex Christison, S V Bishop, R C Vincent, Ian Phillips, P Gillbe, Andy Blackburn)*

Manns (Watneys)   Licensee Nick Turner   Real ale   Meals and snacks   Restaurant Children in family-room   Open 11.30–3, 6.30–11 all year   Bedrooms planned tel Burnham Market (0328) 38257

BURNHAM THORPE   TF8541   Map 8
Admiral Nelson
Village signposted from B1155 and B1355, near Burnham Market

In the village where Nelson was born, this unpretentious little pub has a cosy family atmosphere and sixty pictures on show connected with Nelson – though this is just part of the licensee's fine collection of over two hundred items; he's very knowledgeable on the subject, and should be keen to tell the odd historical anecdote. Some come as a delightful surprise, such as the photograph of Indian huts lining the now-forgotten little upstream island of San Juan which was briefly a focus of international naval strategy when Nelson stormed it. These line the entrance corridor as well as the bar itself – a small room with a sheathed cutlass on one beam, a cabinet of miniature bottles, well waxed antique settles, and worn red flooring-tiles. Well kept Greene King IPA and Abbot are tapped from the cask in a back still-room; the glasses are simply stacked by the spotless sink, separated off from the rest of the room by two high settle-backs, below a window overlooking a lawn swarming with cats. It's well positioned by the village green. You are asked not to smoke. *(Recommended by Roger Huggins, C Elliott, Jonathan Williams, K R Harris, Tom McLean)*

Greene King   Licensee Les Winter   Real ale   No food   Open 11.30–3, 7–11 all year

CASTLE ACRE   TF8115 Map 8
Ostrich ⊗

Stocks Green; village signposted from A1065 N of Swaffham; OS Sheet 144 reference 815153

This largely eighteenth-century ex-coaching-inn (built on the site of a sixteenth-century building) is the only inn on the ancient Peddar's Way. The end wall in the back room has exposed sixteenth-century masonry, a very high pitched ceiling with exposed oak beams and trusses, and a strong local atmosphere. Good value, tasty bar food includes sandwiches (from 60p, a lovely crab and smoked salmon double-decker £1.90), pizzas (from £1.20), a wide range of ploughman's (from £1.50), various basket meals (from £1.15), omelettes (from £2), salads (from £2.50), rainbow trout (£3.50), daily specials such as braised duck in paprika and pineapple or squid and prawn salad (£3.50), and several good vegetarian dishes such as peanut loaf in tomato sauce (from £2.20). In winter there are good log fires both in here and in the simply furnished lower-ceilinged L-shaped front bar's huge old fireplace, which has a swinging potyard below its low mantelbeam – used in winter for cooking soups and hams. Through here there are big photographs of the local sites on hessian walls. Well kept Greene King IPA, Abbot and XX Mild on handpump; fruit machine, piped music, and picnic-table sets in the sheltered garden, where you can play boules. The public bar has dominoes, cribbage and rota-snooker. The pub is on the tree-lined green near the ruins of a Norman castle, and there's a Cluniac monastery in the village. *(Recommended by Mark Sheard, R P Hastings, Guy Sowerby, David and Ruth Hollands, G N G Tingey, R F Neil, P Gillbe, Mrs A Roberts)*

Greene King   Licensee Ray Wakelen   Real ale   Meals and snacks   Children in decent adjacent family-room   Jazz second Tues in month, folk/blues last Weds in month   Open 11–2.30, 6–11 all year; may stay open longer in afternoons during school and bank hols; closed evening 25 Dec   Bedrooms (single only) tel Castle Acre (076 05) 398; £10

HUNWORTH   TG0635 Map 8
Bluebell

Village signposted off B roads S of Holt

The warm L-shaped bar here serves generous helpings of fresh bar food that includes sandwiches (90p, open sandwiches £1.70), ploughman's (£1.70), plaice (£2.90), steak and kidney or chicken and mushroom pies, ham salad or scampi (all £3), gammon and pineapple (£4), sirloin steak (£5.90), and daily specials such as lamb provençale, quiche or chilli con carne (£2.50). There are comfortable settees – some of them grouped around the log fire – as well as Windsor chairs around dark wooden tables, and Norfolk watercolours and pictures for sale hanging above the panelling dado. A good choice of well kept real ales includes Adnams, Greene King Abbot, Woodfordes Wherry, and weekly changing guest beers such as Adnams Broadside; darts, dominoes, cribbage, piped music, and a children's room. In good weather there's bar service to the tables under cocktail parasols on the back lawn, where there are fruit trees – heavily laden in summer. *(Recommended by R P Hastings, Brian and Anna Marsden, Mrs A Roberts)*

Free house   Licensee T P King   Real ale   Meals and snacks   Children welcome   Open 11–2.30, 6–11 all year

LETHERINGSETT   TG0538 Map 8
King's Head ⊗

A148 just W of Holt

This is an exceptionally friendly place, with something of a family atmosphere. The main bar is décorated with picturesque advertisements, a signed John Betjeman poem, lots of Battle of Britain pictures especially involving East Anglia, a panoramic view of Edward VII's first opening of Parliament, and jokey French pictures of naughty dogs. There's also a small plush lounge, and a separate games-room has darts, pool, dominoes, cribbage, fruit machines and a space game. Good value bar food includes sandwiches (from 85p, crab £1.30, evening toasties £1.25), soup (90p), home-made pasty (£1.20), four-ounce burgers (£2), basket meals (from £2.80), home-cooked ham or steak and kidney pie (£2.95), salads (from £2.50, local crab £3.25 when available), steaks (from £6.25, evenings only), and daily specials; also cheaper children's helpings. Well kept Adnams, Bass and Greene King IPA and Abbot on handpump; darts, pool, dominoes, cribbage, pinball, fruit machine, space game, and piped music. It's surrounded by a spacious lawn with lots of picnic-table sets; park and paddock slope up beyond a post-and-rails fence, and the church over the road has an unusual round tower. No dogs. *(Recommended by R C Vincent, Charles Turner, Guy Sowerby, R P Hastings, S V Bishop, Mrs A Roberts, Tom McLean, Ian Phillips)*

Free house Licensee Thomas King Real ale Meals and snacks Restaurant tel Holt (0263) 712691 Children in eating area of bar Country and western Mon Open 11–3, 6–11 all year

NORWICH   TG2308   Map 5

Adam & Eve ⊗

Bishopgate; follow Palace Street from Tombland N of Cathedral

This welcoming and very pretty Dutch-gabled brick and flint house is Norwich's oldest pub, parts of it dating from 1249; the ghost of Lord Sheffield who was killed during Kett's Rebellion in 1549 is said to wander around. It's traditionally furnished, with cosy bars upstairs and downstairs: old-fashioned high-backed settles, one handsomely carved, cushioned benches built into partly panelled walls, and tiled or parquet floors. Good, imaginative home-made bar food includes sandwiches (from 95p, excellent prawn £1.60), filled French bread (from £1), ploughman's (from £1.65), shepherd's pie (£2.10), vegetable bake (£2.20), salads (from £2.20), chicken curry (£2.45), casserole of pork in cider and rosemary (£2.55), very filling fish pie or ham and egg (£2.65), chicken breasts with orange and brandy sauce (£2.90), and daily specials such as scallops, steak and kidney pie or cod Wellington (£2.65); Sunday roast lunch (£2.85) and puddings (from 95p). Ruddles Best and County, and Websters Yorkshire on handpump from a serving-counter with a fine range of pewter tankards, and around thirty-four different wines (from 95p a glass); efficient, friendly service. There are seats on the pretty quiet terrace, hung with clematis and baskets of flowers. *(Recommended by Tim Baxter, Gwen and Peter Andrews, G C Hixon, Ian Phillips, Colonel and Mrs L N Smyth, G and M Brooke-Williams, David and Ruth Hollands, Quentin Williamson, BKA)*

Manns (Watneys) Licensees Colin and Phyl Burgess Real ale Lunchtime meals and snacks Children in eating area off bar Open 11–11

SCOLE   TM1576   Map 5

Scole Inn ★ ⊗ ⊨

Built for a rich Norwich merchant in the seventeenth century, this Dutch-gabled brick mansion used to be famous for its enormous round bed that could sleep thirty people at a time (feet to the middle) and for its elaborately carved and sculptured giant 'gallows' sign spanning the road; it's one of the few pubs to be covered by a Grade 1 preservation listing. The high-beamed lounge bar has antique settles, leather-cushioned seats and benches around oak refectory tables on its Turkey carpets, a big fireplace with a coat of arms iron fireback, a handsomely carved oak mantelbeam, and a seventeenth-century iron-studded oak door. In the bare-boarded public bar there's another good open fire, and stripped high-backed settles and kitchen chairs around oak tables. Waitress-served, freshly made bar food includes home-made soup (£1), sandwiches (from £1.10, crab £1.80), good ploughman's (from £1.60), home-made pâtés – smoked mackerel or Stilton, celery and port (£1.90), chicken livers in herb butter (£2.20) – salads (from £2.20, crab £4.40), and charcoal-grilled steaks (from £6.50), with hot daily specials such as cheese and tomato flan or plaice (£2.50), steak and kidney pie, burger, roast chicken or Elizabethan pork chop (all £3.20), and home-made puddings (£1). Well kept Adnams Bitter and Broadside, and Greene King Abbot on handpump; unobtrusive piped music, darts, dominoes, and a fruit machine. (*Recommended by Michele and Andrew Wells, Barbara Hatfield, Brian and Anna Marsden, Gavin May, Mrs D A Biggs, Michael Craig*)

Free house   Licensee Steve Condrad   Real ale   Meals and snacks   Restaurant   Children welcome   Open 10.30–2.30, 6–11 all year   Bedrooms tel Diss (0379) 740481; £38B/£53B

SNETTISHAM   TF6834 Map 8

Rose & Crown ⊗

Old Church Road; just off A149 in centre

At the front of this busy pub there's an old-fashioned beamed bar with cushioned black settles on the red tiled floor, lots of carpentry and farm tools, and a great pile of logs by the fire in the vast fireplace (which has a gleaming black japanned side oven). Beside it, an airy carpeted room has green plush seats around tables with lacy tablecloths, and pictures for sale on the wall. The back locals' bar has perhaps the nicest atmosphere – a cosy place with a big log fire and tapestried seats around cast-iron-framed tables. Right at the back, an extensive modern summer bar with bentwood chairs and tractor seats has a clean Scandinavian look, with its tiled floor, bare brick walls and narrow-planked ceilings. Quickly served bar food includes soup (£1), ploughman's (£1.95), open baps with home-cooked honey-roast ham (£2.50) or rare topside of beef (£2.75), gammon with pineapple or eggs or pork chop (£4.95), salads (from £5.25), three lamb chops (£5.75), scampi (£5.95), steaks (from £5.95), and cold seafood (£6.50); there's a daily special, puddings like home-made apple pie (£1.40), children's dishes (£1.40) and a barbecue menu (from £3.75, children from 95p). Bass (called Rose & Crown here), Adnams Bitter, Greene King IPA and Abbot and Woodfordes Best on handpump; an old-fashioned penny slot game. There are picnic-table sets on a neat sheltered lawn and terrace. (*Recommended by Angie and Dave Parkes, R P Hastings, Dr R C Roxburgh*)

Free house   Licensee Margaret Trafford   Real ale   Meals (not Sun evening, exc barbecue) and snacks   Restaurant tel Dersingham (0485) 41382; not Sun   Children in restaurant and own room   Open 11–11 in summer, probably 11.30–2.30, 6–11 in winter

SURLINGHAM   TG3206 Map 5

Ferry House

From village head N; pub is along a track (beware of potholes) which both back village roads fork into

When the lane was the main road between Beccles and Wroxham, this friendly pub was built for the old chain ferry on the River Yare, and there's still a rowing-boat to take you across; you can use their moorings free for up to twenty-four hours. The big, softly lit modernised bar is comfortably furnished with banquettes and tables which line the walls and give a good view of this stretch of the river. Bar food includes large granary rolls, plaice (£2.85), scampi (£3.50), four vegetarian dishes (£3.75), beef in stout (£3.95), steaks (from £5.75), and a children's menu (from £1.55); a loudspeaker announces your food order; given advance notice, they'll cook you almost anything you want. Ruddles County and Websters Yorkshire on handpump; darts, dominoes, cribbage, table skittles, Connect-4, shut-the-box, fruit machine, piped music. A gas barbecue can be hired if you feel inclined to cook your own. (*Recommended by Ian Phillips; more reports please*)

Manns (Watneys)   Licensee Mike Morley-Clarke   Real ale   Meals and snacks   Restaurant tel *Surlingham (050 88) 227   Children welcome   Occasional live entertainment   Open* 11–2.30, 6–11 *all year; opens 8 in winter*

SUTTON STAITHE   TG3823 Map 8
Sutton Staithe
Signposted as Sutton Staithe from A149

Its surroundings in a particularly unspoilt part of the Broads is one of the main reasons for visiting this rustic inn – once a notorious haunt of poachers and smugglers. The open bars have little alcoves, built-in seats, a cushioned antique settle and Windsor chairs; one bar opens on to a front terrace where there are three or four tables among roses and small trees. Well kept Adnams Best and Old and occasional guest beers tapped from the cask; bar food includes soup (95p), sandwiches (from 85p, double-deckers £1.95), quiche or sausage and mash (£1.95), salads (from £2.25), scampi (£2.95), and sirloin steak (£6.75); also, a daily special (£2.25), and children's menu (from £1.25). Fruit machine, space game and piped music. Good nearby moorings. (*Recommended by Brian and Anna Marsden, M Quine, BKA*)

Free house   Licensee Norman Ashton   Real ale   Meals and snacks   Restaurant   Children in eating area of bar and restaurant   Open 11–11 *in summer; closed* 2.30–7 *in winter Bedrooms* tel *Stalham (0692) 80244; £17.50(£22.50S)/£25(£32.50S)*

THORNHAM   TF7343 Map 8
Lifeboat ★ ⊗
Turn off A149 by Kings Head, then take first left turn

The series of small cosy rooms in this atmospheric inn are furnished with low settles, window seats, pews, carved oak tables, panelling, shelves of china, rugs on the tiled floor, and are decorated with masses of guns, black metal mattocks, reed-slashers and other antique farm tools. It's perhaps at its best in winter – though it can get very busy even out of season – when curtains are drawn across the heavy wooden rails to keep out the chill of these remote coastal salt flats, the romantic antique lamps hanging from the great oak beams are lit, and no fewer than five open fires blaze away. Home-made, popular bar food includes soup (£1.50), sandwiches (from £1.15) various ploughman's (£2.50), deep-fried chicken wings with garlic mayonnaise (£1.95), salads (from £2.95, Cromer crab £4.25, cold poached salmon £5.35), cheese and tomato quiche or deep-fried fresh cod with home-made tartare sauce (£3.50), burger (£3.75), curried beef with apple, coconut, a plate of crudités and date chutney, ragout of chicken (£3.95), sirloin steak (£7.25), and home-made puddings like ginger sponge (£1.35); children's dishes (from £1.45) and a barbecue menu (from £4.95). The quaint and pretty little restaurant does a good value set menu with some choice (£11.95 including a glass of wine); booking recommended. Well kept Adnams, Greene King IPA and Abbot, and Rayments BBA on handpump, and changing guest beers; shove-ha'penny, dominoes, and an antique penny-in-the-hole bench. At the back there's a courtyard eating area which opens out beyond a glazed protected terrace with a flourishing vine; there are old-fashioned seats among small trees, a summer barbecue, a rustic climbing-frame, toys under shelter, and a donkey; the pub is near *Good Walks*

Post Office address codings confusingly give the impression that some pubs are in Norfolk when they're really in Suffolk (which is where we list them).

Guide Walk 116. *(Recommended by Angie and Dave Parkes, Michele and Andrew Wells, A T Langton, Frank Cummins, Deirdre Woodcock, R P Hastings, S V Bishop, Mrs A Roberts, D Stephenson)*

Free house   Licensees Nicholas and Lynn Handley   Real ale   Meals and snacks Restaurant; not Sun lunch   Children welcome   Occasional folk singer   Open 11–11 in summer; maybe 11–3, 5.30–11 in winter   Bedrooms tel Thornham (048 526) 236; £17.50/£29

WINTERTON-ON-SEA   TG4919   Map 8

Fishermans Return 🍺 *[illustrated on page 509]*

From B1159 turn into village at church on bend, then turn right into The Lane

Not far from a sandy beach, this pretty brick inn is much older than the rest of the village, which has expanded around it so extensively for holiday-makers. The white-painted panelled lounge bar has neat brass-studded red leatherette seats, a good log fire in winter, and a cosy, relaxed atmosphere; the low-ceilinged public bar, also panelled, has a glossily varnished nautical air. There's a separate serving-counter in the back bar, which opens on to a terrace and good-sized sheltered garden, and more seats face the quiet village lane. Bar food includes toasted sandwiches (from 90p), taramosalata with pitta bread or ploughman's (£2), burgers (from £2), chilli con carne or fish pie (£2.50), salads (from £3), scampi or omelette (£3.50) and Dover sole (£7.50) and steaks (from £7), with children's dishes (£1.50) and home-made cheesecake (£1). Well kept Ruddles Best and County, and Websters Yorkshire on handpump; friendly service; pool, darts, shove-ha'penny, dominoes, cribbage, with a fruit machine and juke box in the public bar. *(Recommended by Simon Tubbs, Michael Lawrence, David and Ruth Hollands, R P Hastings)*

Manns (Watneys)   Licensee John Findlay   Real ale   Meals and snacks   Children welcome Probably open 11–11 in summer; 10.30–2.30, 6–11 in winter   Bedrooms tel Winterton-on-Sea (049 376) 305; £18/£30

nr WROXHAM   TG2917   Map 8

Green Man

Rackheath; A1151 towards Norwich

The terrace behind this roadside pub borders a beautifully kept bowling-green. Inside, the open-plan, beamed and timbered bar has wheel-back chairs, green plush button-back banquettes, and easy chairs on its Turkey carpet, log fires, and, on a higher level, a quieter dark green area. The bar food is popular and includes French bread sandwiches, home-made soup served with croûtons or choice of ploughman's (£1.30), good steak and kidney pie (£2.50) and roast beef (£3.45); in the evenings they serve only fish. Steward & Patteson, Ruddles County and Websters Yorkshire on handpump; fruit machine and piped music. A functions room at the back caters for large parties. *(Recommended by R P Hastings, Mr and Mrs HS, Mr and Mrs A R Ward)*

Manns (Watneys)   Real ale   Meals (not evenings) and snacks   Children in eating area Open 11–2.30, 6–11 all year

Lucky Dip

Besides the fully inspected pubs, you might like to try these Lucky Dips recommended to us and described by readers (if you do, please send us reports):

Aylmerton [A148; TG1840], *Roman Camp*: Worth knowing about for cheap good food such as home-made steak and kidney pie and sirloin steak; keg beers *(Anon)*

Baconsthorpe [Hempstead Rd; TG1237], *Hare & Hounds*: Landlord has demod- ernised it by revealing flagstone floors and inglenook fireplace, and fitting stripped pine furniture; own well kept Hobsons Choice Bitter brewed by Woodfordes, good inventive bar food including three dishes of the day and interesting vegetarian dishes;

friendly atmosphere, big garden, play area
(David and Ruth Hollands, Stuart Smith)
Banham [The Street; TM0687], *Red Lion*:
Friendly atmosphere, good reasonably priced
food and juke box *(Miss J M Smith)*
Bawburgh [TG1508], *Kings Head*: Smart,
rather expensive place *(Ian Phillips)*
Binham [TF9839], *Chequers*: Small, unspoilt
village pub close to Binham Priory; with
friendly atmosphere, Batemans, Mitchells
and Woodfordes on handpump, small but
enterprising bar menu *(R P Hastings)*
Blakeney [The Quay; TG0243], *Blakeney
Hotel*: Elegant economical variety of lunchtime bar food served in restaurant – good
food, first-class service, delightful views over
the quay; bedrooms *(Kenneth Finch)*; *White
Horse*: Attractive modernisation, lounge bar
decorated with old ads such as Andrews
Liver Salts, ships' crests and prints, friendly
staff *(S V Bishop)*
Bodham Street [TG1240], *Red Hart*: Real
village pub with two small bars, Ruddles on
handpump, interesting bar food
(R P Hastings)
Bressingham [Thetford Rd; TM0781],
Garden House: Popular family pub, friendly
and efficient, with well kept beer and ample,
varied good food; juke box *(Anon)*
Brisley [TF9521], *Bell*: Just like someone's
front room with no bar, large central table,
armchairs, open fire and beer brought from
the back; no food *(Stephanie Pattenden, MM)*
Burnham Market [TF8342], *Lord Nelson*:
Very homely atmosphere, with excellent
varied home cooking, no-smoking area,
interesting pictures; barbecue on terrace
(Mrs V Lovegrove)
Castle Acre [A1065 nearby; TF8115], *George
& Dragon*: Pleasant surroundings and
atmosphere, well kept Ruddles, wide range
of reasonably priced hot and cold bar food
(Richard Fawcett)
☆ **Castle Rising** [TF6624], *Black Horse*: Small
and comfortably furnished country pub with
wide range of good bar food from sandwiches to trout or salmon, including tip-top
ploughman's and children's dishes, also carvery and restaurant; cheerful smiling service,
well kept Adnams and Charringtons IPA on
handpump, unobtrusive pop music; children
welcome *(Frank Cummins, Kenneth Finch)*
Caston [TL9597], *Red Lion*: Most friendly
welcome, food which is both tasty and
eminently reasonably priced *(J D Cranston)*
Cawston [TG1323], *Ratcatchers*: Friendly
and comfortable village pub with well kept
Adnams – nothing too fancy *(Martin Dooner)*
Cley-next-the-Sea [TG0443], *Three Swallows*:
Attractive old-world pub, not too
modernised, next to church and overlooking
village green; unusual elaborately carved
wooden bar, well kept Ruddles County, well
presented good food including various children's dishes, very friendly *(R P Hastings)*
☆ **Cockley Cley** [TF7904], *Twenty Church-*

wardens: Small pub in lovely setting, delightfully friendly and cosy, good value food,
good choice of well kept beers including
Adnams; handy for Oxburgh Hall (NT)
(K R Harris, Patrick Godfrey, Derek Pascall)
Colkirk [TF9126], *Crown*: Greene King house
in pleasant village, well furnished, bar food,
own bowling-green behind *(R G Tennant)*
☆ **Coltishall** [Church St (B1354); TG2719], *Red
Lion*: Attractive sixteenth-century pub with
very good value bar food showing real care
in the cooking, and including a rather special
fresh fruit trifle; efficiently run, with
Wethereds real ale, Rombouts coffee, excellent friendly service, cool quiet atmosphere,
tables under cocktail parasols outside; bedrooms *(J D Cranston)*;
Coltishall, *Rising Sun*: Superb spot on pretty
bend of River Bure; rather expensive but well
presented food, courteous staff, choice of
Watneys-related real ales, waterside and
other outside tables, family-room *(Col and
Mrs L N Smyth, LYM)*
Cromer [Front; TG2142], *Bath House*: Welcoming landlord, excellent sandwiches
(Margaret and Roy Randle); *Red Lion*: Most
interesting bar, good real ale and food that's
good value for the area *(R P Hastings)*
☆ **Dersingham** [Manor Rd (B1440 towards
Sandringham); TF6830], *Feathers*: Solidly
handsome dark sandstone seventeenth-
century inn with relaxed and comfortably
modernised dark-panelled bars opening on
to neatly landscaped garden with play area;
well kept Charrington and maybe Adnams
on handpump, reasonably priced bar food,
restaurant (not Sun evening); children welcome; bedrooms *(Quentin Williamson, LYM)*
Dilham [TG3325], *Cross Keys*: Olde-worlde
pub with friendly atmosphere, pleasant licensees; well kept Websters Yorkshire, good
cheap bar food, lovely bowling-green and
garden behind *(Mr and Mrs G Hawksworth)*
Diss [9 St Nicholas St (town centre, off
B1077); TM1179], *Greyhound*: Some handsome Tudor features such as the high
moulded beams in otherside comfortably
refurbished carpeted lounge, with big brick
fireplace, well kept Watneys-related real ales,
reasonably priced popular bar food, games in
public bar; children in eating area *(Louise
Findlay, LYM)*
East Barsham [B1105 3 miles N of
Fakenham on Wells road; TF9133], *White
Horse*: Attractive food, well kept
Woodfordes, good retreat from Walsingham
(Mark Sheard)
East Runton [A149; TG1942], *Fishing Boat*:
Interesting interior, good real ale, limited
choice of well cooked food not too expensive
(RPH)
☆ **Edgefield** [TG0934], *Three Pigs*: Well kept
Adnams and Bass, home-cooked food at
reasonable prices, friendly licensees, nicely
furnished with settles and cane-back chairs;
seats on terrace *(Charlie Salt, R P Hastings)*

Elsing [TG0516], *Mermaid*: Good value well presented steaks, well kept Adnams and Woodfordes, comfortable recent refurbishment *(Mark Sheard)*

Erpingham [OS Sheet 133 reference 191319; TG1931], *Spread Eagle*: Included particularly for the fine Woodfordes beers which they brew here, and enthusiasts will find it well worth the pilgrimage (though otherwise it's not so special); children allowed in games-room *(Mr and Mrs A R Ward, Reg and Marjorie Williamson)*

Fakenham [Market Pl; TF9229], *Crown*: Friendly unpretentious front bar in Elizabethan inn with dimly lit front snug, nice carved oak furniture, interesting former gallery staircase now glassed in; bedrooms *(S V Bishop, AE, LYM)*; [Greenway Lane] *Henry iv*: Good food including fantastic value six-course steak meals in well kept inn; bedrooms *(M D Hampson)*

Framingham Earl [B1332; TG2702], *Railway*: Well kept open-plan modern pub with character and relaxing atmosphere; several well kept beers such as Websters Yorkshire, reasonably priced well served food (advisable to book at weekends) *(T Nott, D E and A H Clarke, Dr R Fuller)*

Garboldisham [TM0081], *Fox*: Willing service in well run pub, conveniently placed on main crossroads in sparsely populated area *(Mr and Mrs HS)*

Gayton [TF7219], *Crown*: Elegant old Greene King pub with unusual features, friendly and well kept, with good beer and food; children's facilities *(Mrs A Roberts, LYM)*

Geldeston [TM3991], *Locks*: Several real ales, home-made wine, usually bar food, summer evening barbecues in remote old pub (with big extension for summer crowds) by River Waveney; closed weekdays in winter *(LYM)*

Great Cressingham [OS Sheet 144 reference 849016; TF8501], *Windmill*: Friendly and spacious yet cosy, with several rooms opening off either side of main bar area, collection of farm tools; good reasonably priced bar food, quick service, Adnams, Ruddles and Sam Smiths; conservatory for families, well kept big garden *(Mark Sheard, R G Tennant)*

Great Yarmouth [Berney Arms Stn – OS Sheet 134 reference 464049; TG4604], *Berney Arms*: Unspoilt and remote, by River Yare at head of Breydon Water – access only by water, rail, or a walk of several miles; but we never hear again from the readers who tell us they're going to visit it – they're either still there, or they fall in on the way back *(Editor)*; [St Olaves – A143 towards Beccles, where it crosses R Waveney; TM4599] *Bell*: Attractive Tudor herringbone brickwork and heavy oak timbering underline its claim to be the oldest Broads pub; comfortably modernised inside, with bar food, Wethereds on handpump, games in public bar; barbecues and good children's play area in riverside garden; children in restaurant *(LYM)*

Happisburgh [by village church; TG3830], *Hill House*: Very friendly and pleasant under new owner, with good value, tasty food; bedrooms *(Maj B G Britton)*

Hempstead [TG1037], *Hare & Hounds*: Stripped beams, inglenook, friendly atmosphere, good beer (including guests) and home-cooked food at reasonable prices *(R P Hastings, N A Bentley)*

Hethersett [TG1505], *Kings Head*: Homely and cheerful pub with lunchtime bar food, comfortable carpeted lounge, traditional games in cosy public bar, attractive and spacious back lawn; well kept Watneys-related real ales *(LYM)*

☆ Heydon [village signposted from B1149; TG1127], *Earle Arms*: Where else can you find stabling still in use behind a pub that overlooks such a decidedly unpretentious village green? Flagstones, bare boards, well kept Adnams tapped from the cask and served through a hatch – and absolutely no pretensions or concessions to current fashions in pub design; readers who like it say proudly that 'basic' is an understatement; bedrooms (cheap and simple) *(Rena Myskowski, LYM)*

Hillborough [TF8100], *Swan*: Pleasant bar snacks and good range of beers including Adnams and Greene King on handpump in eighteenth-century pub with good mix of locals and passers-by; real fire, restaurant, garden *(Brian and Pam Cowling)*

☆ Holkham [A149 near Holkham Hall; TF8943], *Victoria*: Several simply furnished but comfortable hotel-ish bar rooms in pleasantly informal coastal inn by entry to Holkham Hall, with bar food from generous sandwiches to sirloin steak, Tolly real ale; tables in former stableyard and on front terrace; handy for Holkham Hall, beaches and nature reserves a half-mile away – nr start GWG118; children welcome; bedrooms *(Derek Pascall, Kenneth Finch, LYM)*

Horning [Lower St; TG3417], *Swan*: Handsomely modernised, pleasant service and nice restaurant; bedrooms spacious and well equipped – good value *(Anon)*

Horsey [just visible down lane 'To The Sea' from B1159 in S bends; TG4522], *Nelsons Head*: Isolated basic Whitbreads pub, near coast and actually below sea level (Horsey Gap down the lane a weak part of sea defences); small and quaint, limited bar snacks; reported now to have well kept Adnams *(RPH, BB)*

Kings Lynn [London Rd; TF6220], *London Porterhouse*: Small, friendly, lively pub with a good mix of customers and well kept Greene King IPA and Abbot tapped from the cask *(Nigel Paine)*; [St Nicholas St] *Tudor Rose*: Large choice of beers, wines and whiskies, attractive bar food and efficient, friendly service *(Neil Colombe)*

Langham [TG0041], *Blue Peter*: Satisfactory food and beer in pub with upstairs shoe museum, recent old-world external restoration *(Paul McPherson)*

Larling [A11; TL9889], *Angel*: Long red ochre building, nice inside with friendly service, good reasonably priced food, Watneys-related beers on handpump *(T A V Meikle)*

Lessingham [outside village; TG3928], *Victoria*: Well kept Adnams and Greene King ales, very friendly atmosphere, good food *(N F Doherty)*

Mundford [Crown St; TL8093], *Crown*: Ancient posting-inn, rebuilt in eighteenth century, in charming village, excellent food at good prices, very welcoming staff, happy atmosphere; bedrooms superb value *(Dr S G Donald, J A Flack, AAW)*

Narborough [TF7412], *Ship*: Pleasant for lunch – good food *(Peter Burton)*

Neatishead [TG3420], *White Horse*: Very good reasonably priced home-cooked food in homely and friendly pub only a few minutes' walk from the staithe *(Mrs M G Longman)*

New Buckenham [TM0890], *George*: Pleasant inn on corner of village green, delicious beautifully presented food in dining-room *(J Ferreira)*

Newton [TF8315], *George & Dragon*: Friendly licensees, excellent bar food, well kept Ruddles Best and County on handpump; children in small restaurant area and games bar; some space for touring caravans *(Richard Palmer)*

North Walsham [B1150 a mile NW – OS Sheet 133 reference 292311; TG2730], *Blue Bell*: Modern but pleasant, well kept Watneys-related real ales, eating area with very good range of excellent value food in huge helpings; play area in garden *(R P Hastings, Mr and Mrs A R Ward)*

☆ **Norwich** [King St; TG2308], *Ferryboat*: Traditional beamed old-fashioned front part, refurbished restaurant, spacious raftered and flagstoned back area where you may find pianist in action, well kept and attractively priced Greene King IPA and Abbot; slide and climbing-frame in riverside garden with barbecue *(Rena Myskowski, Brian and Anna Marsden, LYM)*

Norwich [Timber Hill], *Bell*: Former coaching-inn now a thriving multi-bar pub in useful spot near castle; good quiche, home-made shepherd's pie and other food, brisk service *(Ian Phillips)*; *Gardiners Arms*: Characterful free house with exposed beams and wall timbers, and many levels with small intimate areas as well as a separate functions area; half a dozen well kept real ales such as Adnams, Bass and Woodfordes *(Mark Walpole)*; [St George St] *Wild Man*: Not large, so gets busy as it's known for its good value lunchtime bar food *(K R Harris)*

☆ **Ormesby St Michael** [TG4614], *Eels Foot*: Superb setting with spacious waterside lawn, courteous professional bar staff, pleasant atmosphere, good food *(G D Crouch, LYM)*

Overstrand [High St; TG2440], *White Horse*: Good honest local with well kept Watneys-related real ales, limited choice of well cooked and inexpensive meals, very friendly *(RPH)*

Ranworth [village signposted from B1140 Norwich–Acle; TG3514], *Maltsters*: Included for its fine position across quiet lane from Ranworth Broad; rather nautical décor, Watneys-related real ales *(A T Langton, LYM)*

☆ **Reedham** [Ferry Rd (B1140); TG4101], *Ferry*: Well run pub, secluded and relaxing, overlooking old chain-driven car ferry, good choice of well kept beers including Adnams and Woodfordes, cheerful welcome, interesting bar, log fire, comfortable seats, good service, excellent hot and cold bar food; provision for children, waterside tables, good moorings *(Mr and Mrs J D Cranston, Brian and Anna Marsden, J E Rycroft, Q Williamson, G A Farmer, CDC)*

Reepham [Market Sq; TG0922], *Old Brewery House*: Friendly and helpful, cosy atmosphere, good choice of well kept beers, reasonably priced straightforward food; bedrooms *(Guy Sowerby, N Kirkby)*

☆ **Ringstead** [OS Sheet 132 reference 707403; TF7040], *Gintrap*: Pleasant well kept bar with hanging gin-traps, some converted to electric candle-effect wall lights, cheerful log fire in stone fireplace; friendly new landlord serving even bigger helpings than before of good home-cooked bar food, and upping the strength of his Gintrap Bitter (brewed by Woodfordes – they also keep Adnams); helpful advice to walkers (pub is few minutes' walk from Peddar's Way, part of Norfolk Long Distance Path); children welcome in dining-room; no food Sun or Mon evenings; tables in walled garden behind *(Frank Cummins, David and Ruth Hollands, Derek Stephenson)*

Roydon [Thetford Rd (A1066); TM0980], *White Hart*: Partly fifteenth-century pub with nicely refurbished bar and pleasant dining-room, formerly Benskins but being sold freehold 1988 *(Up-to-date news please)*

Salhouse [Bell Lane; TG3014], *Bell*: Pleasant and friendly, with good real ales and limited choice of inexpensive food *(R P Hastings)*; [Vicarage Rd (off A1151)] *Lodge*: Pleasant rural pub, nicely set in its own grounds and popular with older people, with good range of well kept beers such as Greene King IPA and Abbot, Marstons Pedigree and Woodfordes Wherry and Phoenix; good range of food served efficiently; children tolerated in eating area; garden with play area and barbecue *(Brian and Anna Marsden)*

Sheringham [TG1543], *Crown*: Overlooks sea, with nice terrace, good bar food; nr start GWG117 *(N Kirkby)*; *Lobster*: Log fire in attractive lounge with charts on ceiling, fishing-nets and lobster-pots on walls – also show-business pictures (licensees were Black & White Minstrels); very friendly, good food, family-room *(Charlie Salt)*; *Two Life-boats*: Locals' pub right on sea (children can play on beach if tide is out); bedrooms very comfortable, breakfast very good *(Charlie Salt)*

South Wootton [Knights Hill Village; TF6422], *Farmers Arms*: Farming hamlet attractively converted into pub, restaurant and hotel; the pub part is a huge old barn with lots of farm tools on the walls, church pews on the uneven stone floor *(Mr and Mrs T Scheybeler)*

Stalham [High St; TG3725], *Kingfisher*: Modern bar (part of restaurant/motel complex) with well kept Adnams, cheap well cooked bar food served efficiently; bedrooms not noted for their outlook, but comfortable *(R P Hastings, PR)*; [Wayford Bridge; TG3424] *Woodfarm*: Friendly entertaining pub, lots of real ales and good food *(Dr P R Simpson, W A Lawrence)*

Stoke Ferry [TL7099], *Blue Bell*: Good beef sandwiches *(Mr and Mrs H T Colmer)*

Stokesby [TG4310], *Ferry House*: Traditional atmosphere in Broads pub with own moorings, choice of real ales, good food; children welcome *(CDC)*

☆ **Stow Bardolph** [TF6205], *Hare Arms*: Friendly and pleasant country pub opposite Stow Hall, recently refurbished; cheerful licensees, well kept Greene King Abbot, good value bar food (including rare roast beef sandwiches), elegant restaurant open in evenings, greenhouse for children *(R G Tennant, P Gillbe)*

Stradsett [A134/A1122; TF6604], *Folgate*: Good food and beer in old low-beamed but modernised pub with plenty of character *(Mark Walpole)*

☆ **Surlingham** [TG3206], *Coldham Hall*: Beautiful waterside setting on edge of Broads with attractive, well kept gardens; good bar food (tasty venison sausages), well kept beer, pleasant service; family-room *(Sue Cleasby, Mike Ledger, P Gillbe)*

Swanton Morley [B1147, E end of village; TG0216], *Darbys*: Rural, beamed pub, tractor seats and potato sacks as cushions at bar, real ales, excellent bar food, separate restaurant; children's room *(Mr and Mrs J D Cranston)*

☆ **Thetford** [King St; TL8783], *Bell*: Clean, tidy and pleasant bar area in attractively beamed and timbered Tudor part of otherwise modern THF hotel; reasonably priced bar snacks, Adnams and Greene King real ales *(Kenneth Finch, Quentin Williamson, BB)*

☆ **Thetford** [White Hart St], *Thomas Paine*: Good Adnams and Tolly Original in friendly, spacious and comfortable hotel lounge bar, good value bar food – especially triple-decker sandwich, but wide range of other sandwiches, omelettes and hot dishes; excellent service, small fire in big fireplace; children welcome *(Ian Phillips, J Ferreira, LYM)*

Thompson [Chequers Rd – OS Sheet 144 reference 923969; TL9196], *Chequers*: Charming fifteenth-century thatched house, long and low, with series of quaint rooms – was highly rated main entry, but closed spring 1987 and reopened only in spring 1988; first reports suggest pleasantly refurbished with good new lavatories and well kept Adnams, Bass and Charrington IPA on handpump, but possibly intrusive piped pop music, and some way to go yet on the food side *(RGT, LYM – more news please)*

Thornham [TF7343], *Chequers*: Attractive pub in picturesque village with good beer, nicely presented good value food and friendly atmosphere *(Linda and Alex Christison, J F Stock)*; [Church St] *Kings Head*: Good bar food – especially the well presented ploughman's, big enough for two; nr GWG116; bedrooms *(A T Langton)*

☆ **Titchwell** [TF7543], *Manor*: Attractive two-storey inn, warm and welcoming, with consistently high standards and friendly service from the family who took it over in 1986; catering for birdwatchers and the like, helpful to disabled people, good food in bar and restaurant, reasonable prices, lovely gardens, Greene King IPA and Abbot on handpump; comfortable bedrooms *(Dr and Mrs M Rayner, A T Langton, T A V Meikle)*

Titchwell [A149], *Three Horseshoes*: Has had friendly atmosphere and good help-yourself carvery, but up for sale summer 1988 *(Anon)*

☆ **Tivetshall St Mary** [Ram Lane; TM1686], *Old Ram*: Popular, comfortable and well run, with well kept beer, good bar food (book Sun lunch ahead) and friendly service; children welcome *(Dr R Fuller, KB, Paul Cort-Wright)*

Toft Monks [TM4294], *Toft Lion*: Above-average village pub, clean and friendly, with good simple bar food and well kept Adnams *(A V Chute)*

☆ **Upper Sheringham** [TG1441], *Red Lion*: Real village pub with no frills – lots of stripped pine and stone floors, well kept Adnams, Greene King IPA and Marstons, masses of malt whiskies, good home cooking (no chips), friendly welcome to counterbalance the rather austere décor; bedrooms *(N A Bentley, R P Hastings)*

Walpole Cross Keys [A17 8 miles W of Kings Lynn; TF5119], *Woolpack*: Old low-beamed pub with adjoining tiled stables, tables under cocktails parasols on side lawn; has had well kept Adnams and good food, but no news since it came on the market in late 1987 *(Mark Walpole)*

Walsingham [Shire Hall Plain; TF9236], *Bull*: Enjoyed good beer in good company of five priests, several pilgrims (it's a short walk from the shrine), a tramp on the scrounge and cheery locals; no food at all in evening – very pleasant drinking man's pub *(S V Bishop)*

Weasenham St Peter [A1065 Fakenham–

Swaffham; TF8522], *Fox & Hounds*: Good value food, fresh ingredients only, no salt added, such as huge plaice, steak and kidney pie or Stilton and port soup; good service in friendly, clean and roomy pub *(H S King)*

☆ **Wells-next-the-Sea** [The Buttlands; TF9143], *Crown*: Pleasantly friendly, well kept Adnams and Marstons, good food in bar and restaurant including freshly caught fish; comfortably refurbished bedrooms *(Dr R Fuller, John Townsend, A K Grice)*

West Beckham [Bodham Rd; TG1339], *Wheatsheaf*: Pleasant and friendly in quiet backwater, with cottage doors, beamed ceiling, cosy wood fires, comfortable chairs and banquettes; reasonably priced drinks, good bar food including three daily specials, children's room, garden; bedrooms *(J D Cranston, Tim Halstead)*

West Runton [TG1842], *Village Inn*: Large pub with olde-worlde interior, good and often unusual bar food, large garden (with space for campers) *(K R Harris)*

☆ **West Somerton** [B1159/B1152; TG4619], *Lion*: It's the genuinely warm and friendly welcome which lifts this airy and comfortable roadside pub out of the average; good value efficiently served bar food, well kept Greene King and guest real ales, handy for Martham Broad; children in family-room *(LYM)*

Wighton [TF9340], *Sandpiper*: Small modest inn in attractive village, with dogs, cats, pony, donkey and goats on green opposite; friendly licensees; good value bedrooms *(NBM)*

Worstead [TG3025], *Rising Sun*: Well worth knowing *(Mark Sheard)*

☆ **Wymondham** [2 Bridewell St; TG1101], *Queens Head*: New licensees previously made the Swan at Hoxne popular with many readers for its food; they're now doing excellent things here in bar and restaurant, perfectly presented, a good varied choice very reasonably priced *(Sharon Hall)*

Wymondham [Market Pl], *Cross Keys*: Friendly, with good value food, good service, well kept real ale; partly Tudor timbered, partly Georgian, old-fashioned inside *(Mark Sheard, Quentin Williamson)*

Oxfordshire

Quite a few changes in the county this last year include new licensees for the picturesque Barley Mow at Clifton Hampden, the Red Lion opposite the churchyard at Cropredy, the Bear & Ragged Staff in Cumnor, the stately Old Swan at Minster Lovell, the rambling White Hart in Nettlebed, the cosy Beehive tucked away at Russell's Water (unusual in being a father-and-daughter team), the stylish Mason Arms at South Leigh, and the White Hart at Wytham (here, they're keeping the famous cold table instituted by long-serving Mr Godden, who's left to open a craft shop in a converted barn). In all of these, early visits by readers who report to us regularly show firm grounds for optimism, though at the Bear & Ragged Staff we can't yet be sure that the food, satisfactory enough, will be up to the very high standard set by the previous landlord. The Wheatsheaf in East Hendred has also changed hands, but so recently (just as we finally went to press) that our preliminary approval has to be based chiefly on the cheery character of the pub itself – which is what readers have always liked most. The Clanfield Tavern in Clanfield has been on and off the market, with some consequent fluctuation in its standards; the most recent series of readers' reports has been favourable. Pubs which in the last year have done particularly well include the old-world Lamb in Burford (a fine place to stay at), the idiosyncratic Woodman at Fernham (though the licensee to whom it owes so much of its character was toying with the idea of moving on, we're glad to say that he's decided to stay in place), the charmingly old-fashioned Falkland Arms in the pretty village of Great Tew, the King William IV up on the Chilterns at Hailey (full of farm antiques – you can even get there on a horse-drawn waggon), the homely Plough at Noke (cheap simple food) and the Oxford Brewhouse in Oxford (it bakes its own bread as well as brewing its own beer – a splendidly lively place). Another lively pub, the Perch & Pike at South Stoke, is on a decided upswing under the licensees who took over a couple of years ago – definitely one to note. The White Hart at Adderbury has also been consolidating a growing reputation for good food – it gains a food award this year. Newcomers include the Bull at Burford (successfully rebuilt as an almost exact replica of how it was before a bad fire), the Star at Stanton St John (doing remarkably well under the licensees who took over a couple of years ago – and charmingly refurbished), and the riverside Trout at Tadpole Bridge (another careful renovation – it had been standing derelict). There are so many pubs in this area where food stands out as being of special merit that it would be pointless to list them all; pressed to narrow the choice, we'd probably pick the Bottle & Glass at Binfield Heath, the Sir Charles Napier above Chinnor (very stylish – and pricey, particularly in the restaurant which is the real focus of attention here), the Five Horseshoes at Maidensgrove, the Bell at Shenington, the Lamb at Shipton-under-Wychwood and the Harcourt Arms at Stanton Harcourt (some people think it's getting too much like a restaurant, but the food is good – and it's a comfortable place to stay at). The Lucky Dip section at the end of the chapter, fatter than ever this year, has a good many particularly promising pubs: among them, outstanding prospects include the Abingdon Arms at Beckley, the Hunters Lodge at Fifield, the Gate Hangs High near Hook Norton, the Victoria Arms in Marston, the Nut Tree at Murcott and the White Horse at Woolstone.

ADDERBURY   SP4635 Map 4
White Hart ⊗

Tanners Lane: off Hornhill Road (signposted to Bloxham) towards W end of village

There's a warm and friendly welcome in the heavily beamed bar of this cosy little pub. Attractive furnishings include eighteenth-century seats and other old-fashioned settles and armchairs, paintings and antique prints. At lunchtime the good home-made food consists of a hot and cold buffet – three courses and coffee (around £6). This may include soup, fish pâté, spicy meatballs, sweet-and-sour pork, chicken and mushrooms in a port and cream sauce, vegetarian quiche, salads, pasta, and puddings such as cheesecake, apple and passion-fruit pie or chocolate ganache. In the evening there are three starters such as pâté-stuffed mushrooms (£2), six main courses like chicken with lychees with Chinese boiled noodles or rognons Turbigo (kidneys and chipolata sausages in a sherry and wine sauce, both £3.50), and prawns in a mild creamy curry sauce or a really authentic mutton curry made with around twenty ingredients and several side dishes (£4), and a larger choice of puddings. They don't take bookings. Well kept Hook Norton on handpump; they have a Happy Hour between 6.30 and 7.30; piped music. *(Recommended by Andy Tye, Sue Hill, F M Steiner, R Simmonds, Hazel Church, Richard Balkwill)*

Free house   Licensee Andrina Coroon   Real ale   Meals and snacks (not Sun or Mon)   Open 12–2.30, 6.30–11 all year; closed evening 25 Dec

BINFIELD HEATH   SU7478 Map 2
Bottle & Glass ⊗

Village signposted off A4155 at Shiplake; from village centre turn into Kiln Lane – pub at end, on Harpsden Road (Henley–Reading back road)

The low-beamed bar in this thatched, fifteenth-century black-and-white timbered pub has a bench built into black squared panelling, spindle-back chairs, ancient tables (so scrubbed that one or two are almost like silvery-grey driftwood), fine old flagstones and tiles, and huge logs in the big fireplace. The side room is furnished along similar lines, and one window has diamond-scratched family records of earlier landlords. Bar food, often imaginative, includes sandwiches (from £1.25), home-made pâté (£1.95), fresh grilled sardines or ratatouille (£2.50), cottage pie (£2.65), cauliflower with prawn sauce, chicken livers with bacon or courgettes with prawns in a cheese sauce (all £2.95), seafood with mushrooms, fresh smoked trout or rich wine casserole (£3.50), and twelve-ounce rump steak (£6.95); well kept Brakspears Bitter, SB and Old on handpump; friendly service. In the garden there are old-fashioned wooden seats and tables under little thatched roofs, and an open-sided shed like a rustic pavilion. *(Recommended by Nick Dowson, Jamie and Sarah Allan, Mrs H Church)*

Brakspears   Licensee T C Allen   Real ale   Meals and snacks (not Sun)   Open 11–2.30, 6–10.30

BLOXHAM   SP4235 Map 4
Elephant & Castle

Humber Street; off A361

As this friendly old stone inn is built on the side of a steep hill, the airy public bar is perched high above the street. It's attractively simple, with an elegant seventeenth-century stone fireplace and a strip-wood floor. The comfortable lounge has a good winter log fire in the massive fireplace in the very thick wall which divides it into two rooms. The food prices here really are remarkably low: good sandwiches (from 50p, with crusty bread from 65p), ploughman's (from 90p), sausage or ham with eggs (£1.35), chicken or haddock (£1.95), seafood pie (£2), salads (from £2), steak and kidney pie (£2.10), steak (£4.50), and daily specials (from around £2); the well kept Hook Norton Best and Old Hookey on handpump are attractively priced, too. Sensibly placed darts, dominoes, cribbage, a fruit machine, and shove-ha'penny – the board is over a century old, and there's an Aunt Sally pitch up in the flower-filled yard (summer only). *(Recommended by Tom Evans, Sheila Keene, Ted George)*

Hook Norton   Licensee Chas Finch   Real ale   Lunchtime meals and snacks (not Sun) Restaurant (closed Sun) tel Banbury (0295) 720383   Children welcome   Open 11–2.30 (3 Sat), 6–11 all year; may open longer Sat afternoon

BRIGHTWELL BALDWIN   SU6595 Map 4

Lord Nelson ⊗

Brightwell signposted off B480 at Oxford end of Cuxham

A listed seventeenth-century building, this comfortably modernised pub was originally called the Admiral Nelson until the man himself got his peerage in 1797. The plain white walls in the bar are decorated with pictures and prints of the sea and ships – often associated with Nelson – with some ship design plans; a naval sword hangs over the big brick fireplace in the wall which divides off a further room. The very good lunchtime food in the bar is the same as that served in the restaurant, so most things are more than just a snack (though if that's all you want you can choose from the starter menu): soup (£1.30), pâté or mushrooms in garlic (£1.85), Welsh rarebit with crispy bacon (£3.25), home-made chilli con carne topped with crispy bacon (£4.95), salads (from £4.95), seafood pancakes au gratin (£5.25), lemon sole or large scampi (£5.75) and fillet of pork (£5.95), with evening dishes (you can also have the restaurant menu) such as home-made steak and kidney pie (£4.95) and prawn risotto or minute steak (£5.95); vegetarian meals are available if ordered in advance; Sunday lunch (from £8.50). There are wheel-back chairs (some armed), country kitchen chairs and dining-chairs around the tables on its Turkey carpet, candles in coloured glasses, orange lanterns on the walls, and pretty fresh flowers; tables are not bookable (except in the restaurant), so it's best to get here early at weekends. Brakspears PA on handpump, and a very decent wine list, including a good range of cheaper French wines; faint piped music, neat and friendly waitress service (and two friendly St Bernards). There's a verandah at the front, and tables on a back terrace by the attractive garden or under its big weeping willow, beside the colourful herbaceous border. *(Recommended by D L Johnson, Bob Rendle, PLC, NW)*

Free house   Licensees Barry Allen and David and Muriel Gomm   Real ale   Meals and snacks (not Mon)   Restaurant (closed Sun evening) tel Watlington (049 161) 2497   Children over seven in restaurant only   Open 11.30–2.30, 6.30–11 all year; closed Mon, exc bank hols

BURFORD   SP2512 Map 4

Bull

High Street

Founded in 1475 and one of the most popular stops on the western coach routes in the late seventeenth century, this old inn has been attractively rebuilt on traditional lines following a fire; some readers who knew it well before could scarcely tell the difference. The main beamed and panelled bar is divided by a central stone fireplace, and there's another adjacent room, as well as a dining-room. It's comfortably furnished with cushioned settees, Windsor chairs and other wooden seats, and there are log fires. Imaginative food includes sandwiches (95p, not Sunday), home-made soup (£1.10), good crudités with four dips (£2.10), ploughman's or home-made chicken liver pâté (£2.25), deep-fried stuffed mushrooms (£2.75), vegetable pot or vegetable burger (£3.95), fisherman's pie or home-made lasagne (£4.95), good steak and kidney pie (£5.50), Mediterranean prawns (£5.95), and children's dishes (£2.50). Well kept Wadworths IPA and 6X on handpump, and efficient, friendly service; darts, dominoes, cribbage and piped music. (*Recommended by BKA, Jason Caulkin, G H Theaker, Frank Cummins*)

Free house   Licensee M Cathcart   Real ale   Meals and snacks   Restaurant (closed Sun evening)   Children welcome   Open 11–11 in summer; 11–3, 6–11 in winter   Bedrooms tel Burford (099 382) 2220; £24(£28B)/£42.50(£48.50B)

Lamb ★ ★ 🏠

Sheep Street

The bars in this fifteenth-century old Cotswold inn are delightfully old-fashioned, and an antique handpump beer engine serves the well kept Wadworths IPA from a glassed-in cubicle. The big, beamed main lounge has bunches of flowers on polished oak and elm tables, distinguished old seats including a chintzily upholstered high winged settle, ancient cushioned wooden armchairs, easy chairs and seats built into its stone-mullioned windows. There are shelves of plates and other antique decorations, a grandfather clock, a writing-desk, attractive pictures, oriental rugs on the wide flagstones and polished oak floorboards, and a good log fire in winter under its elegant mantelpiece. Furnishings in the public bar are traditional, with more high-backed settles and old chairs on flagstones in front of its fire. The rest of the building is decorated in similar style, with simple, old-fashioned, chintzy bedrooms. Bar lunches rotate on a daily basis, and should typically include soup (£1.10), ploughman's or devilled whitebait (£2.25), steak sandwich (£2.95), guinea-fowl casserole, fish dishes like grilled sardines, good liver with orange sauce, or steak, mushroom and oyster pie (£3.50) and smoked salmon salad (£4.95); free dips at Sunday lunchtime. Wadworths IPA and 6X on handpump, with, in winter, Old Timer tapped from the cask down in the cellar. There's a real sun trap of a garden, totally enclosed by the warm stone of the surrounding buildings, with a pretty terrace leading down to small neatly kept lawns surrounded by flowers, flowering shrubs and small trees. Dogs welcome. (*Recommended by Ewan McCall, Roger Huggins, Tom McLean, K A Read, Jason Caulkin, Neville Burke, BKA, M C Howells, Simon Velate, Dave Loukidelis, Jon Wainwright, S C Collett-Jones, T O Haunch, Wilfred Plater-Shellard, Wayne Brindle, Leith Stuart, Tom Evans, B Walton, Gill and Rob Weeks, Sally Watson, Paul McPherson*)

Free house   Licensees R M de Wolf and K R Scott-Lee   Real ale   Meals and snacks (lunchtime, not Sun)   Restaurant   Children welcome   Open 11–2.30, 6–11 all year   Bedrooms tel Burford (099 382) 3155; £23.50/£45(£52B)

nr CHINNOR SP7500 Map 4

Sir Charles Napier ⊗

Spriggs Alley; from B4009 follow Bledlow Ridge sign from Chinnor; then, up beech wood hill, fork right (signposted Radnage and Spriggs Alley); OS Sheet 165 reference 763983

The reader who told us that the stylishly relaxed atmosphere here tends to turn his quick visits into whole evenings speaks for many. The emphasis in this remote and idiosyncratic little Chilterns pub is strongly on the food, and almost everyone in the bar is on their way through to the smart restaurant, though at lunchtime during the week, when there's a quieter pubby feel, it's possible to eat lunch at one of the highly polished tables in the bar. The brief bar menu includes soup (£1.75), oeufs Benedict (£2.50), smoked ham with melon (£2.75), prawn salad (£3), warm chicken salad with avocado and orange or pasta carbonara (£4.50), and poached cod with fennel sauce or liver and bacon (£6.50). There are bare oak boards in the low ceiling, a plain wood-block or tiled floor, narrow spartan benches by the wall of the small bar, and a good log fire in winter (with gleaming copper pipes running from the back boiler behind it); good music is excellently reproduced by the huge loudspeakers. Champagne is served on draught at £2 a glass, they have well chosen wines by the bottle, well kept Wadworths IPA tapped from the cask, and freshly squeezed orange juice; friendly, unhurried staff. The decorations in the restaurant include works by two local artists – sketches of Francis Bacon by Claire Shenstone, commissioned by him to do his portrait, and sculpture by Michael Cooper; Sunday luncheon is possibly the most fashionable meal of the week, though it tends to work out at around £25 a head. In summer they serve lunch in a charming crazy-paved back courtyard with rustic tables by an arbour of vines, honeysuckle and wistaria (lit at night by candles in terracotta lamps), and there are peaceful views over the croquet lawn and the paddocks by the beech woods which drop steeply away down this edge of the Chilterns. (*Recommended by David and Flo Wallington, Dr J R Hamilton, Peter Hitchcock, John Tyzack, JMC, M A and C R Starling, Mr and Mrs T F Marshall, Dick and Penny Vardy*)

Free house   Licensee Mrs Julie Griffiths   Real ale   Lunchtime bar meals (not Sun or Mon)   Restaurant (open 12–5 Sun) tel Radnage (024 026) 3011   Children welcome lunchtimes, in evenings if over eight   Open 11.45–5, 6.30–12.30 weekdays; 11.45–4.30, 6.30–1am Sat (the late extensions are for diners); closed Sun evening and Mon

CHIPPING NORTON   SP3127   Map 4
Crown & Cushion   🛏

High Street

Windows in this comfortable three-hundred-year-old coaching-inn look out on the narrow brick-paved creeper-hung coach entry, which leads back to tables out on a sun-trap terrace. Inside, an attractively old-fashioned bar counter, which has warm-coloured ancient flagstones alongside it, serves well kept Donnington, Wadworths IPA and 6X, and changing guest beers on handpump. Some of the walls in the cosy, beamed and carpeted bar are partly knocked through or stripped to bare stone; there are old-fashioned cloth-upholstered seats around the wooden tables, some of them in a snug low-ceilinged side alcove, and a log fire in winter; the atmosphere is relaxed and the locals cheery. The bar food is freshly prepared and includes double-decker sandwiches (£1.20), home-made pâté (£1.75), omelettes (from £2.20), ploughman's (£2.85), grilled rainbow trout or steak and mushroom pie (£2.95), sirloin steak (£4.75), and maybe a daily special (£2.95); piped music. They are planning a back garden. (*Recommended by S V Bishop, Tom Evans, Margaret and Trevor Errington*)

Free house   Licensee Jim Fraser   Real ale   Meals (not Fri or Sat evenings) and snacks (not Sun lunchtime, not Fri or Sat evenings)   Restaurant (closed Sun lunchtime)   Children in eating area of bar and in restaurant; no children under three   Open 10.30–2.30, 6–11 all year   Bedrooms tel Chipping Norton (0608) 2533; £33B/£54B

CHRISTMAS COMMON   SU7193   Map 4
Fox & Hounds

Hill Road from B4009 in Watlington; or village signposted from B480 at junction with B481

This simple and unspoilt tiny cottage has a beamed bar on the left with two sturdy logs to sit on in the big inglenook – which has a fire burning even in summer – three tables and wooden wall benches or bow-window seats, a little carpet on the red and black flooring-tiles, and a framed Ordnance Survey walker's map on one cream wall. A small room on the right is similar. Well kept Brakspears PA, SPA and Mild are tapped from casks in a back still-room ; dominoes, cribbage. Lunchtime food includes soup (75p), sandwiches (from 85p), ham and eggs (£1.95) and scampi (£3.30); note that they do only soup and sandwiches on Sundays and Mondays.

Outside there's a rampant Albéric Barbier rose climbing the walls, old-fashioned garden seats and sitting-logs by the roses and buddleja on the front grass beyond a small gravel drive, and picnic-table sets under a sumac beside the house. There are fine Chilterns walks all around. (*Recommended by Phil Gorton, Gordon and Daphne; more reports please*)

Brakspears   Real ale   Snacks (lunchtime)   Children in games-room off one bar   Open 11–2.30, 6–11 all year

CLANFIELD   SP2801   Map 4
Clanfield Tavern   (⊗)
A4095

Although the Nadins had been planning to move out during 1988, a sale they arranged fell through and as we went to press they had still not decided whether the pub would be put back on the market. Around the time the pub was originally on the market, although the majority of readers' reports continued to be favourable about the pub itself and the food, there were one or two important exceptions – including people who had been previous reporters. We hope the period of uncertainty is now over – during the summer the quality seemed to even out again, with a stream of favourable reports. The carpeted main bar has heavy stripped beams, various chairs, seats cut from casks and settles around the tables, brass platters and hunting prints on the old stone walls, vases of flowers or bowls of spring bulbs, and a handsome open stone fireplace with a big log fire, and a seventeenth-century plasterwork panel above it; several small rooms with flagstones open off here. Good bar food includes minestrone soup, sandwiches, generous ploughman's, ham off the bone with salad, local trout, vegetarian sesame stir-fry tossed in peanut oil and served with a hunk of garlic bread (£3.50), creamy chicken with avocado (£4.20), Asian marinated rack of lamb (£4.50), sirloin steak cooked with honey, orange juice and almonds (£6.50), and puddings like banoffi pie or treacle tart. The Arkells BBB, Hook Norton Best and Morlands are well kept on handpump; darts, dominoes, shove-ha'penny, cribbage, fruit machine and space game, and there is a proper skittle alley. Tables and chairs on a small lawn with a flower border and roses look across to the village green and pond. (*Recommended by Andy Blackburn, Heather Sharland, M E Lawrence, G B Pugh, Patrick Freeman, DMJ, John Bell*)

Free house   Licensees Keith and Sue Nadin   Real ale   Meals and snacks   Cottagey restaurant   Children welcome (but not near bar servery)   Open 11.30–2.30, 6–11 all year Bedrooms tel Clanfield (036 781) 223; £12.50/£25

CLIFTON HAMPDEN   SU5495   Map 4
Barley Mow
Back road S of A415 towards Long Wittenham

Reckoned as the quaintest and most old-world inn on the Thames by Jerome K Jerome, this popular seven-hundred-year-old building – with a new licensee – has a very low-beamed lounge with old-fashioned furnishings (including antique oak high-backed settles), and old engravings on the walls. The black-flagstoned public bar is broadly similar, and there's a side family-room with handsome squared oak panelling. Bar food includes ploughman's (from £1.90), a good value selection of meats, pies and salads from a buffet table (£2.95), home-made daily specials such as lamb and orange or steak and kidney pie, lasagne or chilli con carne (£3), a roast of the day (£4), and puddings like apple or fruit pies (£1.25). Ruddles County, Ushers Best and Websters Yorkshire on handpump; dominoes, cribbage, fruit machine, maybe piped music; efficient if rather impersonal service. There are rustic seats among the flowers on a well kept sheltered lawn, and the Thames bridge is a short stroll away. Beware the public car park some way down the road – there may be thefts. *(Recommended by Nancy Witts, Joan Olivier, GRE and AE, Dr J R Hamilton, Michael and Alison Sandy, Gwen and Peter Andrews, John Bell, Mike and Kay Wilson)*

Ushers (Watneys)   Licensee Mrs Welsh   Real ale   Meals and snacks   Restaurant (closed Sun evening)   Children in oak room   Open 11–2.30, 6–11 all year   Bedrooms tel Clifton Hampden (086 730) 7847; £27/£43

CROPREDY   SP4646   Map 4

Red Lion

Off A423 4 miles N of Banbury

In an attractive village setting, this old brown-stone thatched pub is cosy and welcoming. It's simply furnished in a traditional style, with high-backed settles under its beams and brasses on the walls, a fish tank, and a fine open fire in winter. Home-made bar food includes sandwiches, home-made soups (£1.25), home-made pâtés and terrines (£1.95), burgers or traditional ploughman's (from £1.95), quiches (£2.35), vegetarian curry and lasagne (£2.95), plaice (£3.65), home-made steak and kidney or game pies (from £3.95), gammon steak (£4.15), rump steak (£5.95), and home-made puddings; Sunday roast lunch (it's best to book – £4.95). Well kept Ruddles Best and County and Websters Yorkshire on handpump; darts, shove-ha'penny, dominoes, cribbage, pool, fruit machine, trivia and juke box. There are seats in the back garden, a raised churchyard opposite, and the Oxford Canal a hundred yards away. Although it is generally very quiet, parking could be problematic at summer weekends. *(Recommended by Jon Wainwright, Andrew Stephenson, Mr and Mrs K J Baxter, Derek Stephenson, Tom Evans, Gill and Rob Weeks)*

Manns (Watneys)   Licensee J J Hunt   Real ale   Meals and snacks   Children welcome Open 11–3.30 (10–4 Sat), 5.30–11 all year

CUMNOR   SP4603   Map 4

Bear & Ragged Staff

Village signposted from A420: follow one-way system into village, bear left into High Street then left again into Appleton Road – signposted Eaton, Appleton

Now part of a smallish chain called 'Buccaneer Inns', this twin-gabled sixteenth-century farmhouse has several knocked-together room areas: easy chairs and sofas as well as more orthodox cushioned seats and wall banquettes, soft lighting, polished black sixteenth-century flagstones in one part and Turkey carpet elsewhere, and a large open fire with log basket. The new licensees have put in a food bar serving quite a wide choice including baked herrings in oatmeal (£3.45), curry or goujons of plaice (£3.95), home-made beef pie, chicken in a cream and tarragon sauce or spare ribs (£4.25), and a cold buffet with meats and salads (from £3); on the whole, readers' reports are favourable. Well kept Morrells and Varsity on handpump; friendly service. There's a children's play area, with a swing and climbing-frame at the back by the car park. The pub can get crowded at weekends. *(Recommended by Mr and Mrs D A P Grattan, TBB, William Rodgers, Dr and Mrs S Pollock-Hill, John Tyzack, Frank Cummins, BKA, Stanley Matthews, Dr and Mrs A K Clarke)*

Morrells   Licensee Michael Kerridge   Real ale   Meals and snacks   Restaurant (closed Sun evening) tel Oxford (0865) 862329   Children in eating area of bar   Open 12–2.30, 6–11 all year

DORCHESTER SU5794 Map 4
George ⊗ 🛏

Village signposted from A423

Five hundred years ago, this timber and tile inn was built as a brewhouse for the Norman abbey which still stands opposite. There are some beams, comfortable old-fashioned furniture including cushioned settles and leather chairs, a big fireplace, and carpet on the wood-block floor of the bar. At lunchtime food includes home-made soup, sandwiches (from £2, steak and bacon sandwich £3.80), filled baked potatoes (from £3.20), home-made pasties (from £3.50), steak and kidney pie (£4), and scampi (£4.50). Brakspears and Morlands on handpump, good wine by the glass; immaculate service. The pub is near *Good Walks Guide* Walk 96. *(Recommended by JMC, Dr Keith Bloomfield, Margaret and Roy Randle, G H Theaker)*

Free house Licensees Brian Griffin and M Thompson Real ale Lunchtime meals and snacks (not Sun) Restaurant Children in eating area of bar Open 11–2.30, 6–11; closed Christmas week Bedrooms tel Oxford (0865) 340404; £43B/£54B

EAST HENDRED SU4588 Map 2
Wheatsheaf ⊗

Chapel Square; village signposted from A417

There are seats outside this black and white timbered pub on the back grass among roses and other flowers, conifers and silver birches, and a budgerigar aviary. The attractive village itself is just below the downs, and its church has an unusual Tudor clock with elaborate chimes but no hands. Inside (the new licensees aren't planning any changes), the main area has high-backed settles and stools around tables on quarry tiles by an open fire, cork wall-tiles and some vertical panelling, a minute parquet-floored triangular platform by the bar, and a friendly local atmosphere. Low stripped deal settles form booths around tables in a carpeted area up some broad steps. The food, generously served, is simple and home made, including sandwiches (from 90p, big baps from £1.50), three-cheese ploughman's (£1.90), vegetable lasagne (£1.95), filled baked potatoes (from £2.25), spare ribs or chops (£3.75), orange and honey-glazed chicken (£3.95), marinated pork kebabs (£4.75), and T-bone steak (£7.95). Well kept Morlands Mild, Bitter and Best on handpump; darts, Aunt Sally, and piped music. *(Recommended by Mrs Margaret Dyke, R C Watkins, Mr and Mrs D Towe, A T Langton)*

Morlands Licensees Liz and Neil Kennedy Real ale Meals and snacks Children in separate room Open 11–2.30, 6–11 all year

FARINGDON SU2895 Map 4
Bell ⊗ 🛏

Market Place

The old-fashioned bar in this comfortable, well run coaching-inn still has the ancient glazed screen through which customers would watch the coaches trundling through the alley to the back coachyard – now the hallway; it's attractively furnished with red leather settles, and has a seventeenth-century carved oak chimney-piece over its splendid inglenook fireplace, some unusual fragments of ancient wall painting, Cecil Aldin hunting prints, and maybe Bess the charming labrador. A side room has an attractive modern panoramic mural by Anthony Baynes. As we went to press there were rumblings of future structural changes, though it was too early in the proceedings to get any specific information – we'd be grateful for reports from readers on this. The bar food is consistently good, with sandwiches (£1, sizeable open French bread sandwiches £2), soup (£1.75), lasagne, chicken and ham pie or mushrooms in a garlic mayonnaise (from £3), daily specials such as cottage pie, chilli con carne or steak and kidney pie (all £2.75), and puddings like home-made apple pie, trifle or cheesecake (£1.20). Well kept Wadworths 6X on handpump, with Old Timer in winter; good coffee; dominoes, shut-the-box. The cobbled and paved yard, sheltered by the back wings of the inn, has wooden seats and tables among tubs of flowers. *(Recommended by Joy Heatherley, Ewan McCall, Roger Huggins, Tom McLean, Frank Cummins, Patrick Freeman, Gordon and Daphne, Sian Rees)*

Wadworths   Licensee William Dreyer   Real ale   Meals and snacks   Restaurant   Open 10.30–2.30, 5.30–11 all year, though may open longer in afternoons Apr–Oct   Bedrooms tel Faringdon (0367) 20534; £21.50(£29.75B)/£27.75(£33.75B)

FERNHAM   SU2992   Map 4
Woodman ★

The heavily beamed rooms in this seventeenth-century village pub are decorated with boomerangs, milkmaids' yokes, leather tack, coach horns, an old screw press, and good black and white photographs of horses. The candle-lit tables are made simply from old casks, there are pews and Windsor chairs, and cushioned benches are built into the rough plaster walls. Some unusual touches include a big central log fire that sometimes has a hot-pot simmering over it in winter, hot saki, clay pipes ready filled for smoking, and a collection of hats above the bar. A games-room in the barn has darts, dominoes, pool, fruit machine, space game and piped music. The reasonably priced bar food, served at your table, includes chicken soup (£1.25), baked potato (£1.50), mushroom quiche (£1.75), ploughman's (£2), ham salad (£2.40), hot-pot, steak and kidney pie or lasagne (£2.50), moussaka (£2.75), and steak sandwich (£2.95). Well kept Morlands PA and BB, Theakstons Old Peculier and Hook Norton Old Hookey or Gibbs Mew Bishops Tipple tapped from casks behind the bar; regular OAPS have been paying 30p a pint; friendly dog.
(Recommended by Ewan McCall, Roger Huggins, Tom McLean, Frank Cummins, John Bell)

Free house   Licensee John Lane   Real ale   Meals and snacks (not Mon evening)   Children welcome   Live music Fri or Sat every three weeks and every Sun   Open 11–2.30, 6–11 all year, though may open longer in afternoons if trade demands

FYFIELD   SU4298   Map 4
White Hart

In village, off A420 8 miles SW of Oxford

This marvellously preserved pub was built for Sir John Golafre in about 1450 to house priests who would pray for his soul for ever. They were thrown out after the Reformation and the building was bought by St John's College, Oxford, who have now run it as a pub for four hundred years. The main room is a hall with soaring eaves, huge stone-flanked window embrasures, and an attractive carpeted upper gallery looking down into it. A low-ceilinged side bar has an inglenook fireplace with a huge black urn hanging over the grate. The priests' room is now a dining area, as is the barrel-vaulted cellar. The impressive range of well kept real ales, which changes from time to time, typically consists of Boddingtons Bitter, Gibbs Mew Bishops Tipple, Morlands Bitter, Ruddles County, Theakstons Old Peculier, Uley Pigs Ear, Wadworths 6X and Farmers Glory, and guest beers. Good bar food includes sandwiches on request (as they make their own bread daily, it might be too fresh to cut), soup (£1.15), pâté (from £1.95), pan-fried sardines (£2.15), chilli con carne or vegetarian curry (£2.95), good moussaka (£3.15), local trout (£3.75), a range of home-made pies (all £3.95) and steaks (from £6.25); daily specials are usually available; good if sometimes casual service. Dominoes, cribbage, fruit machine, and quiet piped music. There's a fine rambling and sheltered back lawn (with quite a few cats), and the pub is not far from the delightful gardens of Pusey House. *(Recommended by Lyn and Bill Capper, Mr and Mrs G D Amos, H G Allen, Neville Burke, Anne Morris, David Loukidelis, Dick Brown, Mike Tucker)*

Free house Licensees Edward Howard and John Howard Real ale Meals and snacks Restaurant (closed Sun) tel Oxford (0865) 390585 Children in three or four rooms for families and in eating area of bar Open 10.30–2.30, 6.30–11 all year; they may stay open longer on Sat afternoon if trade demands; closed 25 and 26 Dec

nr GORING   SU5080 Map 2

Olde Leatherne Bottle

Cleeve; off B4009, about a mile towards Wallingford

Unusual for its unspoilt setting and friendly, unpretentious atmosphere, this Thames-side pub has lots of window seats in the three connecting rooms of the bar and dining-room looking out to the quiet stretch of river, over a terrace with a black gondola. There is some very old stone masonry, and an assortment of interesting décorations from stuffed fish to drinking-horns and wooden caryatids. Bar food includes filled rolls (from 60p), home-made soup (£1.10), ploughman's or filled baked potato (£2), quiche salad (£2.75), home-made lasagne or chilli con carne (£2.95), vegetarian crumble (£3.10), and hunter's pie (£3.50); roast Sunday lunch in winter (£4), and barbecues in summer – weather permitting. Well kept Brakspears PA and SB on handpump, XXXX Old tapped from the cask, coffee or hot chocolate; shove-ha'penny, dominoes, cribbage and fruit machine. Watch out for the life-size statue of the drunken seaman outside. *(Recommended by Charles Gurney, Ian Phillips, BRD, M S Hancock, Gary Wilkes)*

Brakspears Licensee Colin Tebbit Real ale Meals and snacks Children in two rooms off bar area Open 11–2.30, 6–11 all year

GREAT TEW   SP3929 Map 4

Falkland Arms ★ ★ 🛏

Off B4022 about 5 miles E of Chipping Norton

Apart from more space – it can get packed – the only change readers look forward to in this idyllically old-fashioned pub is refurbished lavatories (they are a couple of doors down the lane). Otherwise, try to go at a quiet time and keep your fingers crossed that everyone else doesn't have the same idea. Most readers love the partly panelled bar, with its dim converted oil-lamps and one, two and three handled mugs hanging from the beam and board ceiling, high-backed settles around plain stripped tables on flagstones and bare boards, a wonderful inglenook fireplace, and shutters for the stone-mullioned latticed windows. The bar counter, decorated with antique Doulton jugs, mugs and tobacco jars, always serves several reasonably priced and well kept guest beers – more in summer, when the surge of customers means less risk of casks lingering on beyond their peak – as well as the regular Donnington and Hook Norton Best. They also keep country wines and draught and farm ciders, do mulled wine in winter, and even have clay pipes filled ready to smoke, and some fifty different snuffs. Lunchtime bar food is mostly home made and includes sandwiches, country cider and beef hot-pot, lamb and leek or pork and Stilton pie, fishcakes or tuna and pasta bake (all £3.50); friendly and cheerful service; darts, shove-ha'penny, dominoes, cribbage and table skittles. On a summer weekday, sitting on the wooden seats among the roses on the front terrace, with doves cooing among the lumpy cushions of moss on the heavy stone roof-slabs, can feel quite special. This is because the village around you is extremely pretty – an outstanding conservation area, full of golden-stone thatched cottages and secluded wooded slopes. The pub is part of the manor of Great Tew which belonged to the Falkland family until the end of the seventeenth century; the fifth Viscount Falkland who was treasurer of the navy in 1690 also gave his name to the Falkland Islands. *(Recommended by Alan Glen, I R Hewitt, H G Bown, T George, Rob and Gill Weeks, A J Hughes, Richard Gibbs, Jason Caulkin, S V Bishop, PADEMLUC, Nick Dowson, Neil Barker, M E Dormer, Lady Quinny, Neville Burke, ACP, Lindsey Shaw Radley, J E Rycroft, Brian and Rosemary Wilmot, Julie Vincent, A and K D Stansfield, A J Hughes, Michael O'Driscoll, Sian Rees, Tom Evans, Phil and Sally Gorton, Ken Howard, Lyn and Bill Capper, A E Loukidelis, David Loukidelis, Grahame and Brenda Blair, Michael Bolsover, J Walsh, Stanley Matthews, R H Inns, E J Alcock, David and Ann Stranack, Gill and Rob Weeks, C Elliott, Jon Wainwright)*

Free house Licensee John Milligan Real ale Lunchtime meals (not Mon) and snacks (not Sun or Mon) Children in eating area of bar Folk music Sun evening Open 11–2.30, 6–11 all year; opens 11.30 in winter; closed Mon lunchtime Three bedrooms tel Great Tew (060 883) 653; £17/£25(£28S) (double rooms only)

HAILEY SU6485 Map 2
King William IV ★

Signposted with Ipsden from A4074 S of Wallingford; can also be reached from A423; OS Sheet 175 reference 641859

A friend of the landlord's operates horse and wagon rides from Nettlebed to this country pub, where you have a ploughman's or supper and then gently return through the woods and via Stoke Row back to Nettlebed (from £6 a head; phone Ian Smith on Nettlebed (0491) 641364). A museum of well restored farm tools hang from the beams in the glossy ruby-smoked ceiling and timbered bare brick walls: forks, ratchets, shovels, crooks, grabbers, man-traps, wicker sieves and so forth. On the tiled floor in front of the big winter log fire, there's good sturdy furniture, and two broadly similar carpeted areas open off. In winter the atmosphere is quiet and cosy, and in summer it's busy and friendly. Well kept and reasonably priced Brakspears PA, SB, XXXX Old and Mild tapped from casks behind the bar, and good filled rolls such as ham, cheese and pickle, corned beef (from 45p – the only evening food), and pies, pasties or Stilton ploughman's with home-made soup (£2.20 – the soup alone, a winter thing, is £1). There are seats out among smartly painted veteran farm equipment, such as cake-breakers and chaff cutters, on the lawn behind, looking down over a fine rolling stretch of wood-fringed Chilterns pasture. *(Recommended by Dr J R Hamilton, Maureen Hobbs, Sharon Taylor, Tim Irish, Mrs M J Dyke, Jane and Calum, Gordon and Daphne)*

Brakspears Licensee Brian Penney Real ale Snacks Children in eating area Open 11–2.30, 6–11 all year

HENLEY-ON-THAMES SU7882 Map 2
Three Tuns ⊗

5 Market Place

This unspoilt and cosy pub has an unusual pricing system that shows a complete disregard for the decimal system: soup with a sort of Vienna stick (56p), sandwiches (from 63p, two-rasher bacon, lettuce and tomato £1.40, hot salt-beef £2.03), Cornish pasty (96p), home-made chicken liver pâté (£1.39), filled baked potatoes (from £1.55), ploughman's (called boatman's here, from £1.74), vegetarian lasagne (£2.27), egg, bacon, sausage and tomato (£2.37), home-made lasagne (£2.60), a pie of the day (£3.03), gammon with egg or pineapple (£3.93), mixed seafood (£4.17), and six-ounce sirloin steak (£6.19). Besides chips, they also do croquettes. Food is served throughout the afternoon in the buttery, as well as during normal hours. Two small rooms open off a long tiled and panelled corridor (which leads to a small back terrace). The panelled front public bar has shove-ha'penny, dominoes, cribbage and fruit machine; then, beyond the old-fashioned central servery, is a snug and unpretentious heavily beamed buttery, with a central chimney and log-effect gas fire dividing off its back part. Well kept Brakspears PA and SB on handpump, with Mild and XXXX Old tapped from the cask; in winter, hot cider punch and hot chocolate as well as coffee or tea; quick, polite service; piped music. The pub is near *Good Walks Guide* Walk 68. (*Recommended by Mrs Margaret Dyke, Quentin Williamson, Sheila Keene, D Stephenson, David Regan, TBB*)

Brakspears   Licensees Jack and Gillian Knowles   Real ale   Meals and snacks all day Children in eating area of bar   Open 10–11 all year; noon to 10.30 Sun; closed evening 25 Dec

LITTLE MILTON   SP6100 Map 4

Lamb ⊗

3 miles from M40 junction 7; A329 towards Wallingford

This honey-coloured stone pub concentrates on a wide choice of pleasantly served, home-made food: sandwiches (not weekends), ploughman's with warmed bread, good fresh salads, and main dishes such as lamb and courgette casserole (£3.95), grilled Portuguese sardines or venison in red wine (£4.25) and steaks (from £6.25); there are good simple puddings such as lemon charlotte. The softly lit carpeted bar has lots of tables with wheel-back chairs, a few beams in its low cream ceiling, and cottagey windows in its stripped stone walls that are so low you have to stoop to look out. Well kept Ind Coope Burton and Tetleys on handpump, good coffee; fruit machine, piped music. This thatched seventeenth-century building is one of the reasons why the rolling farmland area is now a conservation area. It's decorated in summer with hanging baskets and tubs of flowers, and you can sit in the quiet garden, with swings, roses, a herbaceous border and fruit trees. (*Recommended by SC, George and Jill Hadfield; more reports please*)

Halls (Ind Coope)   Licensee David Bowell   Real ale   Meals and snacks   Bookings tel Great Milton (084 46) 527   Open 11–2.30, 6.30–11 all year

MAIDENSGROVE   SU7288 Map 2

Five Horseshoes ⊗

W of village, which is signposted from B480 and B481; OS Sheet 175 reference 711890

Secluded and tranquil, this well run and friendly little seventeenth-century brick house serves stylishly prepared food such as home-made soup (from £1.50), ploughman's (from £2.20), filled baked potatoes (from £2.75), home-made pâtés like smoked trout or avocado and walnut (mostly £3), chilli con carne (£3.50), steak and kidney pie (£3.95), a casserole of the day, seafood lasagne (£5.25), stir-fried beef (£5.95), Scotch salmon (£6.50) and Scotch steak (from £7.50); specials include vegetable lasagne or breaded butterfly prawns (£5.50), and there are puddings such as good treacle tart with walnuts. Though furnishings in the main bar are mainly modern – wheel-back chairs around shiny dark wooden tables – there are some attractive older seats and a big baluster-leg table as well as a good log fire in winter; darts. Well kept Brakspears PA and SB on handpump; efficient helpful service. Get there early to be sure of a table – it does get very busy indeed, with people waiting for seats at weekends. It's popular with walkers on the lovely common, high on the Chiltern beech woods, and there's even a separate bar in which boots are welcome. There are picnic-table sets on the sheltered lawn and under a fairy-lit Perspex arbour. (*Recommended by Stephen King, J Roots, Alison Hayward, Nick Dowson, Don Mather, F M Bunbury, Gordon and Daphne, Doug Kennedy, Jane and Calum, Dave Loukidelis*)

Brakspears   Licensees Graham and Mary Cromack   Real ale   Meals and snacks (not Sun evening)   Open 11–2.30 (3 Sat), 6–11 all year

Pubs brewing their own beers are listed at the back of the book.

MINSTER LOVELL SP3111 Map 4
Old Swan ★ 🏠

Just N of B4047; follow Old Minster signs

Three or four quiet and attractive low-beamed rooms in this beautifully placed and smartly modernised old stone inn open off the small central bar. There are Turkey carpets on the polished flagstones, Liberty-print easy chairs, good china in corner cupboards, an antique box settle, and big log fires in huge fireplaces. Lunchtime bar food includes soup (£1.25), sandwiches (from £1.25), home-made pâtés (from £2.25), ploughman's (£2.50), a slimmers' salad (£3), and prawns in a spicy dip (£3.50); well kept Tetleys on handpump pulled by a neatly dressed barman. The restaurant is housed in what used to be the brewhouse. On the way out to the garden there's a medieval well, and then a neatly kept lawn with seats, a lily pond, flowers and shrubs, and some shade from chestnut and sycamore trees. The nearby bridge over the pretty River Windrush is remarkably narrow – to help the toll collector count the sheep being herded from Wales to market in London. *(Recommended by Brian and Rosemary Wilmot, Chris Cooke, Nancy Witts, R P Taylor, HKR, J R Smylie, William Meadon, Richard Steel, Jon Wainwright, Frank Cummins, Wayne Brindle)*

Halls (Ind Coope) Licensee A R Taylor Real ale Lunchtime meals and snacks (not Sun) Restaurant Children welcome Open 11–11 all year Bedrooms tel Witney (0993) 75614; £35B/£49B

MOULSFORD SU5983 Map 2
Beetle & Wedge 🏠

Ferry Lane; off A329, 1½ miles N of Streatley

Big windows in the airy main lounge bar (and in the restaurant) look out over the hotel's own moorings to the river, with reeds, willows and open pastures beyond; the waterside lawn, flanked by roses, has white cast-iron tables and friendly ducks and geese. The lounge has comfortable seats with copper-topped tables around the walls, and a big opened-up fireplace. Bar food includes soup (£1.20), various ploughman's or filled baked potato (£2.20), spaghetti bolognese (£3), curries (£3.30), chilli con carne (£3.50) and steak, kidney and mushroom pie, haddock in cheese sauce or salads (£3.90); well kept Courage Best and Directors on handpump; fruit machine, trivia and piped music. The hotel is near the start of *Good Walks Guide* Walk 97. *(Recommended by Lyn and Bill Capper, A T Langton, Paul McPherson, Wayne Brindle)*

Free house Licensees Mr and Mrs D Tiller Real ale Meals and snacks Restaurant Children welcome until 9 Open 11–2.30, 6–11 all year Bedrooms tel Cholsey (0491) 651381; £42B/£55B

NETTLEBED SU6986 Map 2
Carpenters Arms

Crocker End; hamlet signposted from A423 on W edge of Nettlebed

This friendly and well kept little brick cottage, on a very quiet side turning into woods, has flowery-cushioned dark small pews, wheel-back chairs, and country pictures on the cream walls of the carpeted main room. The partly panelled side saloon bar has a small settee, comfortable seats cushioned in plush deep red, and old prints on its walls; there are three log fires in winter. Bar food includes sandwiches (from £1), ploughman's (from £1.90), home-made cottage pie (£3.20), beef curry, steak and kidney pie or lasagne (£3.95), with evening extras such as gammon (£5) or steak (£5.95). Well kept Brakspears PA, SB and Mild on handpump; darts, shove-ha'penny, dominoes, cribbage and piped music. On the sunny front terrace white tables and seats stand by the climbing roses and shrubs. *(Recommended by Don Mather, G and S L, Joan Olivier, David Carter, Mr and Mrs T G Morris)*

Brakspears   Licensee David Bicknell   Real ale   Meals and snacks (not Sun, Mon or Tues evenings)   Children in saloon until 8.30   Open 11–2.30, 6–11 all year

White Hart

A423, in centre

The civilised, beamed lounge bar in this relaxing ex-coaching inn (which has friendly new licensees) has been knocked through into an extensive series of sitting areas, with shallow steps between: there's a highly polished grand piano in one snug side area, another has a good log fire in winter, and there's a big Act of Parliament wall clock. Furnishings include cosy leather easy chairs, and other old-fashioned seats and settles. Bar food includes sandwiches, grilled avocado and cheese or mushrooms in a Stilton sauce (£2.75), home-made charcoal-grilled burgers (£2.95), pies (£3.50) and nut cutlets or vegetarian salads (£3.95); children's helpings available. Brakspears PA and SB on handpump; shove-ha'penny, backgammon and chess. There are tables and benches outside. *(Recommended by Mike Tucker, Don Mather, Joan Olivier, Colin and Caroline, Robert Timmis)*

Brakspears   Licensee Gregory Leith   Real ale   Meals and snacks   Restaurant   Children welcome   Open 11–2.30, 6–11 all year   Bedrooms tel Nettlebed (0491) 641245; £18/£30

NEWBRIDGE   SP4101 Map 4
Rose Revived

A415 7 miles S of Witney

It's the lovely garden outside this spacious old stone inn that is the main attraction; it stretches along a quiet reach of the upper Thames, with a long lawn, crazy-paved paths, weeping willows, spring bulbs or a colourful summer herbaceous border, and is prettily lit at night by superannuated street-lamps. Bar food includes sandwiches, ploughman's (£1.95), mixed meat salad (£2.50) and home-made lasagne or steak and kidney pie (£2.95); well kept Morlands PA and Old Masters on handpump; fruit machine and piped music. There are cushioned antique settles on polished flagstones, deep ochre ceilings, attractive curtains, lots of pictures, and a log fire. In the inner bistro, with its candles in bottles, pianist, handsome sixteenth-century stone fireplace with an oak mantelbeam, and polished tile floor, they do three-course evening meals. *(Recommended by GS, Gwynne Harper, Nicholas Walter, T A V Meikle)*

Morlands   Licensees Mr Jefferson and Mr Losey   Real ale   Meals and snacks   Restaurant Children welcome   Jazz Sun evening   Open 11–11 in summer; probably afternoon closing in winter   Bedrooms tel Standlake (086 731) 221; £25B/£38B

NOKE   SP5413 Map 4
Plough ★ ⊗

Village signposted from B4027 NE of Oxford

The main bar in this very friendly, homely and bustling pub consists of three knocked-together rooms which have settles and other closely spaced seats on the dark brown carpet, dark beams covered in brightly pictorial plates, and several dogs and cats. Generous helpings of cheap, fresh and simple food, ordered through a hatch to the kitchen, includes sandwiches if they're not too busy (from 65p, toasties 5p extra), home-made French onion soup (95p), ploughman's (from £1.20), sausages and egg (£1.75), good value fry-up (£2.50), home-made steak and kidney or chicken and mushroom pie (£2.75), lamb chops (£3), scampi (£3.50), steak braised in Guinness gravy (£3.75), and roast duckling (£6.25), with puddings such as good home-made fruit pie (75p); best to get there early on Sunday lunchtimes in summer. Well kept Courage Best and Directors on handpump; well chosen piped music. In summer there are plenty of seats out in the pretty garden, which backs on to farmland, and walks in the nearby Otmoor wilderness. *(Recommended by M A and C R Starling, PAB, Roger Barnes, Helen Stanton, W J Wonham)*

Courage   Licensee Peter Broadbent   Real ale   Meals and snacks (not Weds evening) Children at kitchen end of bar   Country music Tues, trad jazz first Sun of month Open 12–2.30 (3 Sat), 7–11 all year

OXFORD   SP5106   Map 4

Bear

Alfred Street

Parts of the surviving structure of this ex-coaching-inn date back seven hundred years, and even the handpumps – serving well kept Halls Harvest and Ind Coope Burton – are over a century old. The four low-ceilinged and partly panelled rooms have traditional built-in benches and plain tables, a collection of seven thousand or so club ties, all neatly arranged behind glass (there are still regular additions), and an old-fashioned and cosy atmosphere; they can't always cope with the people who flock here – particularly in term-time with students from Oriel and Christ Church Colleges – and often you'll find as many people drinking out on the street, by the tables on the side terrace. Home-made bar food includes sandwiches or filled rolls, omelette or Cornish pasty (£1.80), ploughman's, quiche or lasagne (£1.85), chicken, pies or plaice (£2.10), and steak sandwich or ham and egg (£2.75), all served generously with chips and beans. *(Recommended by Jon Wainwright, Graham Bush, C D T Spooner, Alison Hayward, HKR)*

Halls (Ind Coope)   Real ale   Meals and snacks   Children welcome   Nearby parking very limited   Open 11–2.30, 5.30–11 all year

Oxford Brewhouse ★

14 Gloucester Street; by central car park and Gloucester Green bus station

Quiet and cosy at lunchtimes and very lively and popular in the evenings, this well run place, largely done out in wood and stripped brick, has steps leading up to three linked mezzanines which look out into the main area and down into a two-level pit. There are lots of basic junk-shop-style chairs, rocking-chairs, pews and tables, with some benches let into the walls of the main area, and a big wood-burning stove. Decorations include big dark tuns perched on brick pillars, brass cask spigots, and an airborne brewers' dray loaded with casks labelled for the pub's own beers. You can see these brewing through a window at the back: Tapper, Best, Oxbow and Porter, all on handpump (served most efficiently, and sold more cheaply for take-away, with twenty-four hours' notice); interesting, if a little pricey. A couple of guest beers change weekly. Enterprising food comes from the attached bakery (open from 8.30am), changing day by day, with a wide choice including soup, exotic salads such as beans, egg and chorizo (£2.35), caraway-seed bread 'trenchers' (big sandwiches – hot salt-beef £2.70), evening pizzas, and quiche (£3). Well reproduced piped jazz, and very good live jazz; good service. There are picnic-table sets in a small, neat back courtyard under a tall ash tree. *(Recommended by John and Joan Wyatt, Jon Wainwright, Brian Marsden, Graham Bush, Stanley Matthews, B Prosser)*

Own brew   Real ale   Meals and snacks (not Sat or Sun evenings)   Children in upper levels Jazz Weds evening (not Aug) and Sun lunchtime   Open 10.30–2.30, 5.30–11 all year

---

Please tell us if the décor, atmosphere, food or drink at a pub is different from our description. We rely on readers' reports to keep us up to date. No stamp needed: *The Good Pub Guide*, FREEPOST, London SW10 0BR.

Perch

Binsey; leaving Oxford on A420, keep your eyes skinned for narrow Binsey Lane on the right – it's just before Bishops' furniture depository

Surrounded by lovely riverside meadows, this spacious thatched pub has something of a secluded country atmosphere, despite being within walking distance of the busy town centre. Inside, the rambling rooms have wooden dividers between stone pillars, some flagstoned areas, high-backed built-in settles, cushioned wheel-backs, and a couple of log fires in winter. The bare stone walls have several pictures of perches, including the us submarine *Perch*, sunk in 1942, and high shelves of plates; incidentally, if you see a figure dressed in old-style naval uniform, he's a ghost. Bar food includes curried beef (£3.30), Somerset pork or Kentish beef (£3.45), harvest pie (£3.55) and a help-yourself salad bar; they also do weekend afternoon teas in summer. Arkells, Halls Harvest and Ind Coope Burton on handpump. The one-and-a-half acres of beautifully kept gardens have picnic-table sets, a children's play area with slides and castles, and a weeping willow on the edge of the meadows. There's a large landing stage for boats. *(Recommended by Jon Wainwright, Paul McPherson, Tim Brierly; more reports please)*

Halls (Ind Coope)   *Real ale   Meals (not Sun evening, or winter Mon)   Children in eating area   Live entertainment Sun – from morris dancers to electric guitarist   Open 11–2, 5.30–11 all year*

Turf Tavern

Bath Place; via St Helen's Passage, between Holywell Street and New College Lane

Though Whitbreads have taken over this ancient pub, buried in its hidden courtyard, their agreement with Merton College (the owners) means that a decent range of real ales from other brewers has been kept on – Archers Headbanger, Brakspears, Theakstons Old Peculier, and Uley Old Spot, as well as Whitbreads ales such as Flowers Original. But the chief reason for including the pub remains its character: dark beams and low ceilings, flagstoned or gravel courtyards, and its seclusion from the modern bustle of the city by the high stone walls of some of its oldest buildings, including part of the ancient city wall. Bar food includes soup (£1), Stilton ploughman's (£2.95), steak and kidney pie or lasagne (£3.25), and puddings like apple and cranberry pie (£1.45); service can be slow on a busy weekend; trivia machine. The pub is popular with foreign visitors. *(Recommended by Geoff Wilson, Charles Gurney, Joan Olivier, GS)*

Whitbreads   *Licensee Stephen Shelley   Real ale   Meals and snacks   Children welcome No nearby parking   Open 11–11 all year*

PISHILL   SU7389   Map 2
Crown ⊗

B480 N of Henley

The warmly welcoming and friendly latticed-window bar in this ancient pub has old photographs on the partly panelled walls in the front area, a central black-beamed and red and gold carpeted part with little blocky country chairs and stools around wooden tables, and an elegant corner cabinet of decorated plates. The rear section is knocked-through, with standing oak timbers. Good, home-made bar food includes sandwiches, deep-fried mushrooms with a garlic dip or deep-fried Brie with a celery and apple dip (£2.25), vegetarian curry or casserole (£2.95), home-made meat or vegetable lasagne (£3.75), steak, kidney and mushroom pie (£3.95), and a wide range of daily specials. Well kept Arkells BBB and Kingsdown, Huntsman Dorchester and Palmers Bridport on handpump; piped music. An

---

It is illegal for bar staff to smoke while handling your drink.

attractive side lawn outside the wistaria-covered pub has picnic-table sets, and the surrounding valley is quiet and pretty. *(Recommended by Stephen King, Gary Wilkes, Alison Hayward, I Meredith, Michael and Alison Sandy, Doug Kennedy)*

Free house   Licensee Jeremy Capon   Real ale   Meals and snacks (not Sun or Mon evenings) Restaurant tel Turville Heath (049 163) 364   Children in restaurant   Jazz Sun evening Open 11–2.30 (3 Sat), 6–11 all year

RUSSELL'S WATER   SU7089   Map 2
Beehive ⊗

Up short rough track past duck pond from centre of village, which is signposted from B481 S of junction with B480

In an isolated Chilterns hamlet, this olde-worlde pub has a friendly, relaxed atmosphere in its main bar, as well as some old-fashioned settles (including one elaborately carved in Jacobean style), armed Windsor chairs, high wrought-iron bar stools with slung leather seats, and a copper-bound bar counter; wooden ceiling-supports sprout from barrels, there's a big wood-burning stove and subdued red lighting. Good food from a menu that changes daily includes two soups such as tomato and basil or Mediterranean fish soup (from £1.50), various ploughman's (£2), interesting salads like vegetarian mange-tout and almond (£3) or warm duck breast with garlic and parsley (£4), steak and kidney pie (£3.50), lasagne (£4), home-made pasta dishes like tagliatelle with salmon, cream, fennel and tomatoes (£5), sauté monkfish with mustard and chives (£7.50), steaks (from £8), and home-made puddings like chocolate truffle cake or raspberry and vanilla charlotte (£2). Well kept Brakspears, Wadworths 6X and Farmers Glory on handpump; darts, cribbage and piped music. There are tables outside in front, on a rose-fringed terrace or under a fairy-lit arbour. *(Recommended by M J Dyke, Dick Brown, Ian Howard, A T Langton)*

Free house   Licensees John and Lydia Jenkins   Real ale   Meals and snacks (not Mon) Restaurant (Fri evening–Sun lunch) tel Henley (0491) 641306   Children in family-room Trad jazz Tues or Weds evening   Open 11–2.30, 6–11; closed evening 25 Dec

SHENINGTON   SP3742   Map 4
Bell ⊗

Village signposted from A422 W of Banbury

This neatly kept seventeenth-century pub is part of a row of little golden Hornton-stone cottages. The civilised yet friendly, mainly carpeted lounge has heavy oak beams, brown cloth-cushioned wall seats and window seats, tables with vases of flowers, old maps and documents on the cream wall, and flagstones on the left – where the wall is stripped to stone and decorated with heavy-horse harness. On the right, it opens into a neat little pine-panelled room, with decorated plates on its walls. Popular home-made bar food includes sandwiches or soup such as parsnip and orange (£1.25), and a good choice of other dishes, changing daily, such as curried prawns or mushrooms on toast (£2.50), ham and noodles tetrazini (£3.50), ham and asparagus quiche (£4.25), marmalade-glazed ham or sausage-meat hot-pot (£4.25), crispy-topped lamb in cider (£4.50), curries for which they grind and mix their own spices (£4.75), beef casserole (£4.75), game pie or halibut in crab sauce (£5), and puddings such as treacle tart (£1.85). Main dishes are served with four or five fresh vegetables. Well kept Flowers IPA on handpump, and a good choice of wines from Berry Bros; darts, shove-ha'penny and dominoes. The tortoiseshell cats are called Myrtle and Mittens and are very calm about dogs – which are welcome (the pub's own labrador/border collie cross is called Sophie).

You are now allowed twenty minutes after 'time, please' to finish your drink – half an hour if you bought it in conjunction with a meal.

There are two or three tables out in front. At the last minute we heard that the pub was up for sale – more news, please. (*Recommended by Bernard Phillips, I R Hewitt, Mr and Mrs M Pearlman, S V Bishop, Gill and Rob Weeks, H G Bown, Michael O'Driscoll*)

Free house   Real ale   Meals and snacks (not Sun evening)   Restaurant   Children welcome in pine-panelled room on right in the evening   Open 12–2.30, 7–11 all year; closed Sun evening Bedrooms tel Edge Hill (029 587) 274; £12(£15B)/£24(£30B)

SHIPTON-UNDER-WYCHWOOD   SP2717   Map 4

Lamb ⊗ 🛏

Just off A361 to Burford

Smart and well kept, this friendly stone village inn is especially nice in summer when you can sit at tables among the roses at the back and enjoy the excellent cold buffet. The comfortable, pretty bar has beams, a fine oak-panelled settle and long pews on the good wood-block floor, a solid-oak bar counter, flowery curtains in the small windows of the old partly bared stone walls, and a stylishly relaxed atmosphere; well kept Hook Norton Best and Wadworths 6X on handpump. Good value, popular bar food includes home-made soup, duck and orange pâté (£2), Scandinavian hash (£3.50), Cotswold pie (£4), seafood tart or duck in cherry sauce (£5.50), poached salmon and shrimp sauce (£6.50), and puddings such as treacle tart or strawberry Pavlova (£1.50); efficient, helpful service. (*Recommended by Gordon Mott, Barbara Hatfield, Patrick Freeman, Gordon Theaker, S V Bishop, Nancy Witts, Liz and Tony Hall, Stanley Matthews, R C Lang, Gwen and Peter Andrews, Dr J F Loutit, Lyn and Bill Capper, JH*)

Free house   Licensees Hugh and Lynne Wainwright   Real ale   Meals and snacks Restaurant   Children in restaurant   Open 11.30–2.30, 6–11; closed last week Feb and first week Mar   Bedrooms tel Shipton-under-Wychwood (0993) 830465; £25B/£40B (double rooms only)

Shaven Crown ⊗ 🛏

Originally a hospice for the monastery of Bruern in the fourteenth century, this substantial inn was then used as a hunting-lodge by Elizabeth I. The magnificent double-collar braced hall roof and front lounge, with its lofty beams and sweeping double stairway down the stone wall, are original Tudor. Bar food is served in the fine beamed bar at the back of the courtyard which has a relief of the 1146 Battle of Evesham, as well as seats forming little stalls around the tables and upholstered benches built into the walls. It includes sandwiches, soup (95p), ploughman's (£1.85), garlic mushrooms (£1.90), home-made chicken liver pâté or Canadian-style potato skins (£2.05), omelettes (from £2.20), home-baked ham with salad or plaice (£2.75), mushroom and walnut pancake (£2.95), scampi (£3.25), steak sandwich (£3.75), spinach and bacon lasagne or coronation chicken (£3.85), steak, kidney and mushroom pie (£3.95), lightly curried prawns with saffron rice (£4.85) and sirloin steak (£5.45), with a choice of puddings like home-made ice-creams and sorbets (95p) and treacle tart or chocolate and apple cake (£1.10); Flowers Original and Hook Norton Best on handpump; cheerful, friendly service. The medieval courtyard garden makes a pleasant place to sit in summer, surrounded as it is by the heavily stone-roofed buildings, with a lily pool, roses, and old-fashioned seats set out on the stone cobbles and crazy-paving. It has its own bowling-green. (*Recommended by Simon Velate, Dr J F Loutit, Frank Cummins, Lyn and Bill Capper, Bronia Suszczenia*)

Free house   Licensee Trevor Brookes   Real ale   Meals and snacks   Restaurant   Children welcome   Open 11–2.30, 6–11 all year   Bedrooms tel Shipton-under-Wychwood (0993) 830330; £24/£56B

Please tell us if any Lucky Dips deserve to be upgraded to a main entry – and why. No stamp needed: *The Good Pub Guide*, FREEPOST, London SW10 0BR.

SOUTH LEIGH   SP3908   Map 2
Mason Arms
Village signposted from A40 Witney–Eynsham

There's been another change of licensees at this thatched fifteenth-century Cotswold-stone pub, though early reports from readers are of a warm welcome and very good home-made food: soup (£1.50), sandwiches (from £1.80), ploughman's (£2.50), seafood pancake (£3.25), vegetarian or meat lasagne, steak, kidney and Guinness pie, salt-beef salad, marinated spare ribs and spicy sauce, trout or lamb kebabs (all £3.90), smoked salmon roulades (£6.50), and puddings such as trifles or profiteroles (£1.75). Well kept Adnams and Glenny Witney (from nearby Witney) on handpump. The cosy lounge, separated into two halves by a wrought-iron divider, has a flagstone floor, built-in cushioned settles curving around the corners, an open fire with a stone hearth at one end, and a log-effect gas fire at the other. There should be peacocks and a couple of chickens in the big, pretty garden, where a small grove of what look like Balearic box trees shelter picnic-table sets. *(Recommended by Roger Taylor, Mrs M Lawrence, Edward Hibbert, D Stephenson, Aubrey Saunders, Trevor Boswell, Joan Olivier)*

Free house   Licensees Geoff and Josie Waters   Real ale   Meals and snacks (not Mon) Restaurant (closed Sun evening) tel Witney (0993) 702485   Children in restaurant Open 11–2.30, 6.30–11 all year; closed Mon

SOUTH STOKE   SU5983   Map 2
Perch & Pike ⊗
Off B4009 2 miles N of Goring

Just a field away from the Thames, this lively and unspoilt flint pub has benches by tubs of flowers and honeysuckle, and a spacious flower-edged lawn (past a black wooden barn) with a slide, seesaw and swings; there are barbecues in summer. Inside, the public bar has low beams, a brick floor, stuffed perch and pike on its shiny orange walls, and a collection of plates painted with fish. A good choice of bar food from a changing menu includes French bread rolls (from £1.25), various ploughman's (from £2.20), soup such as Stilton and watercress or smoked salmon pâté (£2.40), cannelloni or lasagne (£3.25), smoked salmon and lumpfish roe (£4.95), chicken in tarragon and white wine or giant Mediterranean prawns and hot garlic dip (£5.50), beef in Guinness and orange pie (£5.95), steaks (from £6.25), and curries, stews, pheasant and fresh salmon. Brakspears PA, SB and Old on handpump; darts, bar billiards, shove-ha'penny, dominoes, cribbage, fruit machine, boules, Aunt Sally and piped music. *(Recommended by Jane and Calum, Joan Olivier, Dennis and Janet Johnson, I Meredith, Col A H N Reade)*

Brakspears   Licensees Susie and Roy Mason-Apps   Real ale   Meals and snacks (limited Sun and Mon evenings in summer; no food then in winter)   Restaurant tel Goring (0491) 872415 Children in restaurant   Assorted guest musicians Thurs evening, singing guitarist landlord (ex-pro) Sat evening   Open 10.30–3 (5 Sat in summer), 6–11 all year; they may open longer on weekday afternoons if trade demands

STANTON HARCOURT   SP4105   Map 4
Harcourt Arms ⊗ 🛏
B4449 S of Eynsham

The emphasis in this busy, picturesque inn is very much on food, and in the evenings, at least, every table is taken up by people eating meals. These aren't cheap, but they are all home made and very generously served: soup (£1.75), chicken satay or stuffed and boned leg of chicken with a spicy apricot sauce (£2.95), grilled king prawns or mussels in white wine and cream (from £3.25), steak and kidney pie (£5.90), smoked haddock crumble (£6.75), liver and bacon (£7.95), fillet steak (£10), and home-made puddings (£1.75). The steaks are often done on a grid-iron over the log fire in one of the room's massive stone fireplaces. Well kept Wadworths 6X on handpump; pleasant, cheerful service; piped music. The attractively decorated three dining areas are simply furnished with spindle-back chairs around wooden tables. In the annexe room there are Windsor-back chairs and framed Ape and Spy caricatures from *Vanity Fair*; tables on a neat side lawn. *(Recommended by Frank Cummins, D M Anderson, Stephen and June Clark, Nancy Witts, Col G D Stafford, Grahame and Brenda Blair, Mr and Mrs T A Towers)*

Morrells   Licensee G A Dailey   Real ale   Meals and snacks   Restaurant tel Oxford (0865) 882192   Children welcome   Open 11–3, 6–11 all year; closed 25 Dec   Bedrooms tel Oxford (0865) 882192; £35B/£49.50B

STANTON ST JOHN   SP5709   Map 4

Star ⊗

Pub signposted off B4027; village signposted off A40 heading E of Oxford (heading W, the road's signposted Forest Hill, Islip instead)

Though the original part of the pub is nice enough – a couple of cheery little low-beamed rooms, one with ancient brick flooring-tiles and the other with carpet and quite close-set tables – it's the recently refurbished extension up a flight of stairs (but on a level with the car park) which has real character. There are rugs on flagstones, an interesting mix of dark oak and elm tables with old-fashioned dining-chairs around them, shelves of good pewter, terracotta-coloured walls left fairly free of decoration (just one portrait in oils, a stuffed ermine, and pairs of bookshelves on each side of an attractive new inglenook fireplace). Lighting's thoughtful – like the crystal chandelier above a little group of tables on a small railed-in platform. The atmosphere's chatty and relaxed; the licensees took over in 1987 (he's fresh from fifteen years in the Royal Fleet Auxiliary), and Mick Robertson, Mrs Tucker's father, is much in evidence, too. Mrs Tucker's a careful cook, and dishes which have been praised recently include spring vegetables in a white sauce, pork oriental (£2.95), bulghur wheat and walnut casserole (£3), corned-beef hash (£3.05) and plaice stuffed with prawns (£3.95), besides a wide range of other things from toasted sandwiches (£1.10) or Stilton ploughman's (£1.80) to sirloin steak (£5.80), and puddings from banana splits to interesting fruit-filled pancakes. The pub's run spotlessly. Well kept Wadworths IPA, Farmers Glory and 6X on handpump, with Devizes (in summer) or Old Timer (in winter) tapped from the cask, and a guest beer such as Badger Tanglefoot; shove-ha'penny, dominoes, cribbage, piped music. The pretty walled garden has picnic-table sets and swings among shrubs. *(Recommended by Joan Olivier, P J Wheeler, Graham Richardson, Edward Hibbert, Dr D A Sykes, V T Morgan, Jane and Niall)*

Wadworths   Licensees Nigel and Suzanne Tucker   Real ale   Meals and snacks   Children in lower room   Open 10.30–2.30, 6.30–11 all year; closed 25 Dec

STEEPLE ASTON   SP4725   Map 4

Red Lion ⊗

Off A423 12 miles N of Oxford

This welcoming and civilised little village pub has a beamed bar with an antique settle among other good furniture, a collection of rather crossword-orientated books, and dark hessian above its panelling. Very good lunchtime bar food includes stock-pot soup (75p), sandwiches such as thickly cut rare beef (£1.20), Cheddar ploughman's with local crusty bread (£1.65), home-made pâté or taramosalata (£1.85), and in winter varying hot-pots such as bouillabaisse, mussels in white wine or game (from £2.20), with salads in summer instead (from £3.30, fresh crab or salmon from £3.40). On Tuesday to Saturday evenings there are full meals in the small dining-room (£13.40), with main courses such as sweetbreads. Well kept Badger Tanglefoot, Hook Norton Best and Wadworths 6X on handpump, a choice of sixty or so malt whiskies, and around 120 good wines in the restaurant (they ship their own wines from France). The terrace outside the stone house is a real sun trap. *(Recommended by I R Hewitt, C Elliott, Peter Storey, Dr J R Hamilton, Dr and Mrs James Stewart, Rob and Gill Weeks, M Mullett, R H Inns, Dr R Fuller, A S Bridgwater)*

Free house   Licensee Colin Mead   Real ale   Snacks (lunchtime, not Sun)   Restaurant tel Steeple Aston (0869) 40225   *Open 11–2.30, 6–11 all year; closed 25 Dec*

STEVENTON   SU4691 Map 2
North Star

The Causeway; central westward turn off main road through village, which is signposted from A34

Through a low-ceilinged tiled entrance passage in this unspoilt village pub is the main bar, with its traditional snug formed by high cream-painted settles around a couple of elm tables by an electric bar fire. It's decorated with veteran steam engine pictures – reflecting the fact that it's named after an 1837 steam engine – and there are interesting local horsebrasses. The side tap-room (which has no bar counter) serves Morlands Mild, Bitter and Best tapped from the cask, and there are colourful stacks of crisps, bottles, barrels and so forth. The small parlourish lounge has an open fire, and there's a very simply furnished dining-room; cribbage. Cheap bar food includes a celebrated so-called mini ploughman's – two rolls, a thick slice of wholemeal bread, chunks of Cheddar, blue cheese and a soft plain cheese, a big slice of pressed beef, fresh tomato, cucumber, onion, spring onion, lettuce and chutney. A few large old-fashioned benches stand out on the side grass, by roses and cabbages. The wooden gateway to the pub used to be cut through a living tree. *(Recommended by Gordon Smith, Gordon and Daphne, Phil and Sally Gorton)*

Morlands   Real ale   Meals and snacks (weekday lunchtimes only)   Open 10.30–2.30, 6.45–11 all year

STOKE ROW   SU6784 Map 2
Crooked Billet

Newlands Lane

Readers feel this little country pub (under a new licensee since it was last in the *Guide*) is as good as ever: that's to say, to everyone's surprise it's kept the simple and distinctively old-fashioned charm which marked it in Nobby's time. One or two small changes – an open fire with an attractive rug in front of it in the little parlour that's the real heart of the place, a renovated lounge opened up beyond it – are changes for the better. Mostly, though, it's business as usual. Well kept Brakspears PA, SP, Mild and XXXX Old, tapped from casks in a back room, and brought into the parlour, where everyone sits around a big table under the single lamp hanging from the single bowed beam; good, reasonably priced ploughman's, home-made pies and Arbroath smokies. The public bar hasn't changed much, either – a couple of scrubbed deal tables in front of a vast open hearth; shove-ha'penny, cribbage, trivia and candle snuffing. There's a three-acre garden/paddock for organised games or camping. From the pub, where there are benches in front by the very quiet lane (the only noise is from the geese and bantams in the back yard), you can walk straight into Chilterns beech woods. *(Recommended by Gordon and Daphne, Dick Brown, Jane and Calum, Phil and Sally Gorton)*

Brakspears   Licensee Ben Salter   Real ale   Meals and snacks   Children in club room Gypsy jazz Fri evening   Open 12–3, 6–11 all year

SWINBROOK   SP2712 Map 4
Swan

Back road 1 mile N of A40, 2 miles E of Burford

A warm welcome and idyllic surroundings are the makings of this unpretentious pub. It's close to the River Windrush and there are old-fashioned benches, a fuchsia hedge, and a smothering of wistaria on the seventeenth-century walls. Inside, there are country benches, a wood burning stove on a simple flagstone floor, and good value lunchtime bar food that includes various snacks like salmon and prawn sandwiches (£1.80) and hot dishes, with evening food such as duck pâté (£1.80), prawns with garlic mayonnaise (£2.25), beef in ale (£4.25), venison in lager (£4.75), pheasant (£5.70), duckling with cherry sauce (£5.80), and puddings like meringue nest filled with chestnut purée, whisky and cream (from £1.60). Well kept Morlands Bitter and Wadworths 6X on handpump; darts, shove-ha'penny, dominoes, cribbage, trivia and occasional piped music. *(Recommended by Graham Tayar, Mrs E M Lloyd, Paul S McPherson, Nancy Witts, William Meadon, Richard Steel, Bronia Suszczenia)*

Free house   Licensee H J Collins   Real ale   Meals (not Tues evening) and lunchtime snacks Small restaurant (closed Sun lunch)   Open 11.30–2.30, 6–11 all year   Two bedrooms tel Burford (099 382) 2165; £18/£30

TADPOLE BRIDGE   SP3203 Map 4
Trout

Back road from Bampton–Buckland, 4 miles NE of Faringdon

The reason why even fairly local people may not have heard of this eighteenth-century pub is that is was closed for nearly two years. After standing empty for a while, it was completely refurbished by its new owners, and is now one of the nicer upper Thames-side pubs. There are picnic-table sets among small fruit trees on an attractive side lawn, pretty hanging baskets and flower troughs, moorings for customers and a 1¾-mile stretch of river where you can fish (the pub sells day tickets). Inside, the flagstoned L-shaped bar has reasonably priced food such as sandwiches, steak and kidney pie (£1.50), ploughman's (from £1.60), pâté (£1.75), home-cooked ham and egg (£2.60), lasagne, scampi (£3.75), gammon with egg or pineapple (£4.50), rump steak (£5.95) and daily specials; well kept Archers Village and Wadworths 6X on handpump; darts, dominoes, piped music and Aunt Sally; pleasant staff. There's a caravan and camping site for five. *(Recommended by Joan Olivier, Frank Cummins)*

Free house   Licensee K C King   Real ale   Meals and snacks   Children in dining-room at lunchtime   Open 11–2.30, 6–11; closed all day Weds Nov–Mar

WATLINGTON   SU6894 Map 4
Chequers ⊗

2¼ miles from M40 junction 6; Love Lane – B4009 towards Watlington, first right turn in village

A particularly relaxing and quiet atmosphere warms the rambling bar in this red-tiled old white pub. There are character chairs such as a big spiral-legged carving-chair and a low panelled oak settle around a few good antique oak tables, low oak beams in a ceiling darkened to a deep ochre by the candles which they still use, and rugs, red carpet and (in one corner) red and black shiny tiles on the floor; a pale grey cat dozes in front of one of the two open fires. Interesting, carefully served bar food includes ploughman's (£2.50), smoked salmon roulade (£3.40), dressed crab (£3.85), cauliflower and crispy bacon gratin (£3.95), home-made lasagne (£4.20), salads such as home-cooked ham (£4.60), very good steak and kidney pie, prawn curry (£4.80) and steaks from rump (£6.60) to 1½-pound T-bone (£13.20), with some snacks such as chilli con carne with granary bread. Good home-made puddings include crème brûlée, apple and raspberry pie, or treacle tart (£1.75). Brakspears on electric pump. On the right there are steps down to an area with more tables. The pretty back garden has picnic-table sets under apple and pear trees, and sweet-peas as well as roses, geraniums, begonias and so forth; there are rabbits too. It's cosily tucked away in a back alley. *(Recommended by TBB, HKR, SC, BKA, Mrs Jane Reason, Stanley Matthews)*

Brakspears   Licensee John Valentine   Real ale   Meals and snacks   Open 11.30–2.30, 6–11 all year

WROXTON   SP4142 Map 4
North Arms ⊗
Church Street; off A422 at hotel

The modernised lounge in this friendly thatched stone pub has a big stone fireplace taking up one wall, and several beige plush high-backed settles, tapestried seats, wheel-back chairs and an armchair on its swirly carpet. It's a popular and very peaceful lunchtime retreat for businessmen from Banbury. Bar food includes sandwiches (from 80p, good crusty ones from £1.20), home-made soup (£1.10), ploughman's (from £1.75), pâté (£2.75), cold beef or ham (£3.25), plaice or scampi (£3.50), trout or gammon (£4.50) and steaks (from £5.75); well kept Banks's Bitter on handpump. The building looks down its well tended garden to the tall trees around Wroxton Abbey (which is now an outpost of Farleigh Dickinson University). The well spaced picnic-table sets out here are idyllic in summer, with just the birds singing and woodpigeons drowsily burbling. As we went to press we heard that the brewers are to install a juke box and bar billiards, and that the licensee may leave after twenty years here. *(Recommended by I R Hewitt, S V Bishop, Michael O'Driscoll, Rob and Gill Weeks)*

Banks's   Licensee Robin Russell   Real ale   Meals (not Sun) and snacks (not Sun evening) Restaurant tel Wroxton St Mary (029 573) 318   Children in restaurant   Open 12–3, 7–11 all year

WYTHAM   SP4708 Map 4
White Hart ⊗
Village signposted from A34 ring road W of Oxford

Creepers swathe this tall seventeenth-century stone pub, and the flagstoned bar has wheel-back chairs and high-backed black settles built almost the whole way around its cream walls, with a shelf of blue and white plates above them, and a fine relief of a heart on the iron fireback; the atmosphere is cosy and relaxed. The new licensees have kept on the excellent self-service cold table (between £2.35 and £3 for as much as you want) with some fourteen salads and a good choice of cold meats and home-made pies. At lunchtime in winter there is home-made soup (£1) and one hot dish such as a casserole or hot pie (around £3.50). In the evenings there are hot dishes too throughout the year, from gammon (£3.30) through chicken Kiev (£3.70), to steaks (from £3.75); get there early if you want a table, especially on Sundays. Well kept Ind Coope Burton and Tetley Walkers on handpump, and a good choice of malt whiskies. The concrete back yard has a Perspex roof over its picnic-table sets, and even a heater in cold weather, and there are more seats outside in the garden. *(Recommended by Nancy Witts, F N Clay, Tim Brierly)*

Ind Coope   Licensees Rob Jones and Carole Gibbs   Real ale   Meals and snacks   Children in eating area and conservatory   Open 11–2.30, 6–11 all year

Lucky Dip

Besides the fully inspected pubs, you might like to try these Lucky Dips recommended to us and described by readers (if you do, please send us reports):

Abingdon [Bridge; SU4997], *Nags Head*: Friendly new licensees, Ruddles County on handpump, good bar food; comfortable bedrooms with good breakfasts (ST); [St Helens Wharf] *Old Anchor*: Characterful Morlands pub in tucked-away riverside location; recently repainted and refurbished and now serves food; good mix of customers, flagstoned back bar with little shoulder-height serving-hatch, little front bar looking across Thames, bigger lounge (Graham Bush, Gordon and Daphne); [15 Oxford Rd] *Ox*: Consistently good, clean and well run pub serving hot and cold bar food at reasonable prices (V T Morgan)

Appleton [SP4401], *Three Horseshoes*: Good range of bar food in good local (D R Reeve)

Ascott under Wychwood [SP3018], *Wychwood Arms*: Good friendly country inn with terrace and walled garden, sandwiches, salads and other bar food, log fires; bedrooms comfortable, all with private bath (E G and M L Peters)

Ashbury [SU2685], *Rose & Crown*: Friendly atmosphere and emphasis on good food in bar and restaurant, but real ales too; very busy at weekends, quiet during the week; log fire, games-room; nr Ridgeway and Wayland's Smithy – good for walkers; bedrooms comfortable (F A Rabagliati, E Turner-Nedelev)

Asthall [just off A40 3 miles on Oxford side of Burford; SP2811], *Maytime*: Popular up-market food pub in old Cotswold-stone building; wide choice of dishes, reasonably priced Sun lunch, Morrells Varsity and Wadworths 6X, prompt service; in tiny hamlet – stunning views of Asthall Manor and watermeadows from car park (R W B Burton, John Bell, Nancy Witts, David Surridge, BB)

Bampton [Bridge St; SP3103], *Romany*: Friendly atmosphere, good home-cooked food in bar and restaurant; good value bedrooms (Mrs D Farmer)

Banbury [Parsons St, off Market Pl; SP4540], *Reindeer*: Good value bar food in refurbished Hook Norton pub with long history; its 'gallows' inn-sign, spanning street, is one of only half a dozen left (LYM); [George St] *Wheatsheaf*: Small, lively pub with friendly landlord and bar staff; the young/fun atmosphere they generate attracts all ages; Bass (Graham Bush)

Barford St Michael [SP4332], *George*: Rambling thatched pub, modernised and open-plan inside, very pretty outside; well kept real ales, pleasant garden (LYM)

Beckley [High St; SP5611], *Abingdon Arms*: Delightful little stone-built pub in lovely village on ridge overlooking Otmoor wilderness; very comfortable lounge with excellent food – especially Sun lunch; good courteous service, tables and good summerhouse in orchard, attractive walks round about (Annie Taylor, Tim Brierly, Sir Nigel Foulkes)

Begbroke [A34 Oxford–Woodstock; SP4613], *Royal Sun*: Clean and attractively decorated open-plan pub with good choice of quickly served food, friendly quick service, small garden; pleasant surroundings though on trunk road (M V Fereday, Joan Olivier)

Bessels Leigh [A420; SP4501], *Greyhound*: Two big well furnished bars with excellent well priced lunchtime food, good courteous service and well kept Morlands Best (Ken Howard)

Bix [A423; SU7285], *Fox*: Good well kept pub (HKR)

☆ **Blewbury** [Chapel Lane, off Nottingham Fee – narrow turning N from A417; SU5385], *Red Lion*: Well kept Brakspears real ales and bar food from sandwiches and ploughman's to salads and changing hot dishes in well run downland village pub with beams, quarry tiles and big log fire; tables on back lawn; children in small restaurant, no piped music, pleasant licensees (K G Latham, Joan Olivier, LYM)

Broadwell [SP2503], *Five Bells*: Small village pub with big garden, welcoming children; has been noted for friendliness and good value bar food, but changed hands early 1988 – no news since (F M Bunbury, M J Dyke)

Burcot [SU5695], *Chequers*: Lovely thatched pub, comfortably furnished (a bit Laura Ashley-esque in the 'Gallery'); well kept Ushers ales on handpump, good landlord, pleasant atmosphere (Mr and Mrs P Burton-Johnson)

☆ **Burford** [High St], *Mermaid*: Pleasant and friendly, well kept Courage Best and Directors, wide choice of really good if rather pricey food in bar and restaurant (they've been finalists in the trade magazine Pub Caterer of the Year competition two years running), very attentive service (E J Knight, Andrew Hudson, CAJS, Jason Caulkin)

Burford [Sheep St], *Bay Tree*: Really a small hotel: go past the restaurant to find the bar with its high-backed wooden armchairs and several longcase clocks on wooden and flagstone floors; rooms vary from very low ceiling to areas with soaring eaves; nicely laid out gardens; good restaurant (Gill Austin, Rob Weeks); [High St] *Dragon*: Seventeenth-century Cotswold pub with bare beams, stripped stone walls, wheel-back chairs – but Chinese food in bar as well as restaurant (Anon); [A433 W of village] *Portman Arms*:

Clean, comfortable village pub with friendly staff and customers; good range of food in generous helpings (K R Harris)

Cassington [SP4510], *Chequers*: Friendly atmosphere in recently refurbished pub with choice of good bar food, carvery, attentive staff, Morrells ales, tables in garden; shy but friendly mongrel Trixie – no other dogs allowed; children welcome (Joan Olivier)

Caulcott [SP5024], *Horse & Groom*: Basic but pleasant food and atmosphere; quiet and characterful, with good service (Anon)

Chalgrove [SU6396], *Red Lion*: Free house with pleasant staff, good range of beers and food that's available all through opening hours; children; big garden (Richard Hallwood)

☆ Charlbury [SP3519], *Bell*: Small seventeenth-century hotel, comfortable bedrooms often used by people at nearby conference centres, warm welcome in quiet and civilised flag-stoned bar with stripped stone walls and enormous open fire, good value bar lunches, Wadworths real ales; children in eating area (E G Parish, L Diaz, Ian Patterson, LYM)

Charlbury, *Bull*: Lots of character, friendly service, open fires, Charrington IPA on handpump; two rooms with good simple food in separate eating area (Ned Edwards); [Market St] *White Hart*: Excellent friendly local with good reasonably priced food lunchtime and evening, Hook Norton and Marstons on handpump, extremely wide range of good, often obscure, malt whiskies, good restaurant, garden; jazz most Thurs (Peter Wright)

Chazey Heath [Woodcote Rd (A4074 Wallingford–Reading); SU6977], *Pack Horse*: Well kept, friendly and attractive old pub with big log fire in simply furnished lounge bar, well kept Gales ales and country wines, good value home-cooked bar food, sizeable back garden with play area and fairy-lit barbecue terrace, family-room, Shetland ponies and boxers (Sharon Taylor, Tim Irish, BB); [same rd, a bit further along] *Pack Saddle*: Engagingly 1950s-ish pub with alligator skins, African spears and masks, old rifles, Spanish bullfighting pictures, tartan-blanket carpet, nostalgic pop music, cheery atmosphere, well kept Gales ales, country wines, basic food; pool in lounge bar (BB)

☆ Checkendon [OS Sheet 175 reference 666841; SU6683], *Black Horse*: Small and cottagey three-room pub, one with bar, others with easy chairs and sofas as in 1950s front room; nostalgic old-fashioned smell of camphor and cabbage; spick and span, nice open fire, well kept beer brought through from the back by the two friendly elderly sisters who run it; lunchtime opening can be erratic (Geoffrey Griggs, Phil and Sally Gorton); [map reference 663829] *Four Horseshoes*: Old, thatched and beamed, with spacious lounge and bar, very welcoming

atmosphere, friendly landlord, well kept Brakspears, huge helpings of very good cheap food; summer barbecues (Bill Ibbetson-Price)

Chinnor [SP7500], *Red Lion*: Friendly pub with a quick hot meal service, good beer, comfortable chairs, big old fireplace (Mr Savage)

☆ Chipping Norton [SP3127], *Blue Boar*: Excellent choice of reasonably priced food in comfortable free house with good range of beers and decent cider; under same ownership as Black Horse, Woburn (see Cambs main entries) and Crown of Crucis, Ampney Crucis (see Gloucs) (D W Davison, Wayne Brindle); *Fox*: Ancient stone pub – rambling lounge comfortably furnished with antique oak settles, open fire, food in bar and restaurant, Hook Norton real ales (LYM)

Chislehampton [B480 Oxford–Watlington, opp B4015 to Abingdon; SU5998], *Coach & Horses*: Sixteenth-century inn with plush seats in heavily beamed red-carpeted bar, friendly and relaxed; well kept Morlands real ale, fine old stove in lovely fireplace; food only in good restaurant, popular on weekday lunchtimes with local businessmen; bedrooms (nine) around courtyard (Gwen and Peter Andrews, Joan Olivier)

Churchill [3 miles from Chipping Norton on Bledington rd; SP2824], *Chequers*: Cosy, friendly village pub with attractive and comfortable furnishings, a variety of interesting foods that are well prepared and presented, well kept beer and good value house wines (Susan Hardy, W G Roebuck)

Clanfield [SP2801], *Plough*: Substantial old stone inn with lovely Elizabethan façade, attractive gardens and civilised atmosphere; comfortable lounge bar, good restaurant food at a price; bedrooms (HS, LYM)

Clifton [B4031 Deddington–Aynho; SP4831], *Duke of Cumberlands Head*: Superb country pub with quite outstanding and original food, cordial welcome (I Meredith)

Clifton Hampden [SU5495], *Plough*: Ancient low-ceilinged pub said to be haunted by a presence felt rather than seen or heard; friendly licensee, Ushers ales, variety of bar food, childrens' play area (Joan Olivier)

Cookley Green, *Jolly Ploughman*: Sadly this little pub, mentioned in previous editions, has now been closed by Brakspears

Crawley [SP3412], *Lamb*: Splendid eighteenth-century pub under new Australian management; stone walls, heavy oak timbers and inglenook fireplace; Witney Glenny and Hook Norton, also Australian wines; new dining-room (where the piped music may be rather loud) has some Malaysian dishes as well as more usual pub food from ploughman's to steaks; darts, maybe even teatime bridge (Joan Olivier)

Cropredy [OS Sheet 151 reference 466465; SP4646], *Brasenose*: Useful pub about ten minutes' stroll from canal, with lots of cricketing pictures, friendly atmosphere and real ale; bar food lunchtime, evening meals *(Mr and Mrs K R Watkins, Jon Wainwright, Mr and Mrs J T Fallon)*

Crowell [2 miles from M40 junction 6; SU7499], *Catherine Wheel*: Oldish brick and flint ABC pub with church pews and other oldish furniture (including a grandfather clock), reasonably priced bar food (not Sun evening, nor all day Mon) *(Joan Olivier)*

Culham [A415 Abingdon–Dorchester; SU5095], *Waggon & Horses*: Old coaching-inn, log fires, play area and barbecue park in garden; can get very crowded in the evening – especially winter *(A T Langton, Joan Olivier)*

Cumnor [Abingdon Rd; SP4603], *Vine*: Delightful pretty pub with pleasant atmosphere, delicious salads, amiable service and pretty garden *(Joan Bowen)*

Cuxham [SU6695], *Half Moon*: Idiosyncratic and attractive old-fashioned pub in pretty streamside village, parking difficult, filled rolls and range of well kept Brakspears real ales, spotless and friendly, seats outside, children welcome – all too like several other village pubs which Brakspears have recently closed *(LYM)*

Deddington [SP4361], *Kings Arms*: Pleasant black-beamed L-shaped bar, with several malt whiskies and other liquors as well as Halls Harvest and Marstons Pedigree; very wide choice of bar snacks, wine list includes a whole page of English and another of country wines *(Gwen and Peter Andrews)*

Dorchester [now bypassed by A423; SU5794], *White Hart*: Ancient coaching-inn, well modernised and friendly, with good food and good choice of wines in oak-beamed restaurant – romantic for weekends away, in unspoilt historic village; nr GWG96; comfortable bedrooms *(HMT, John Bell)*

Drayton St Leonard [SU5996], *Three Pigeons*: Friendly village local with good reasonably priced bar food *(Margaret and Roy Randle)*

East End [SP4014], *Leather Bottle*: Four-hundred-year-old pub with solid beams, thick stone walls, Courage Best and Directors on handpump, wide choice of food including several vegetarian dishes; neat garden transformed by current licensees *(Joan Olivier)*

East Hendred [Orchard Lane; SU4588], *Plough*: Good village pub with beams, farm tools and so forth, Morlands ales, occasional live music, food often using vegetables from own garden, friendly licensees, nice garden with good play equipment *(Mr and Mrs D Towe, BB)*

☆ **Enslow** [Enslow Bridge – off A4095 about 1½ miles SW of Kirtlington; SP4818], *Rock of Gibraltar*: Large rambling eighteenth-century stone-walled canalside pub with cosy nooks, beams and open fires – one with

interesting dog-driven spit; bar billiards in games area downstairs overlooking large garden with barbecue; friendly landlord and staff, Watneys-related real ales, good choice of bar food; children's adventure playground, live music Sun *(E J Alcock, Mr and Mrs J T Fallon)*

Enstone [A34 Chipping Norton–Woodstock; SP3724], *Harrow*: Pleasant and friendly main-road pub with Morrells Varsity, delicious filled rolls, attractive buffet, good value steaks in recently refurbished lounge bar *(Neil and Angela Huxter and others)*

☆ **Exlade Street** [SU6582], *Highwayman*: Rambling beamed pub dating from fourteenth century, formerly the Greyhound, with unusual layout including sunken seats in central inglenook, good collection of ancient-looking paintings; friendly staff, good food, real ales such as Palmers Tally Ho, Theakstons Old Peculier and XB, Ushers and Wadworths 6X on handpump; children's bar, no bikers, overlooks fields – gets busy *(Gary Wilkes, Gordon and Daphne)*

Eynsham [Newlands St; SP4309], *Newland Arms*: Small country pub peaceful, comfortable and quiet, with limited but good food in bar and dining-room, Halls ales, log fire, friendly and attentive but not over-assertive service *(MO, Michael Quine)*; [B4044 towards Swinford Bridge] *Talbot*: Very hospitable pub about half-mile from river, good service by kind staff, good choice of well presented food; popular at weekends with Oxford students *(B Prosser)*

Faringdon [Market Pl; SU2895], *Crown*: Well kept real ales such as Hook Norton, Glenny Wychwood, Morlands and Theakstons, friendly staff, flagstones, panelling, varnished wooden tables, roaring log fires in winter and lovely courtyard for summer; after some initial doubts, recent reports suggest that quality of both bar food and bedrooms is evening out at a good level as the newish licensees settle in; children welcome *(Mike Muston, Frank Cummins, David Brown, D Stephenson, Pamela and Merlyn Horswell, LYM)*; *Faringdon*: Pleasant comfortable bar *(Pamela and Merlyn Horswell)*; [Coxwell (outside town); SU2894], *Plough*: Good range of beers such as Arkells, Halls Harvest, Wadworths 6X and superb choice of pub food; restaurant behind; children in room off main bar *(Stan Edwards)*

☆ **Fifield** [A424; SP2318], *Hunters Lodge*: Isolated but warm and friendly stone inn partly dating from the thirteenth century, reopened 1987 under this name (previously the Merrymouth) after extensive tasteful refurbishments; warm welcome – especially from the dog; big helpings of bar food (though service may be on the slow side), well kept Donnington beers *(Tom Atkins, Helen Wright, Joan Olivier, A T Langton, LYM)*

Filkins [village signposted off A361 Lechlade –Burford; SP2304], *Five Alls*: Free house with friendly new licensees, lounge (summer lunchtimes), bar and restaurant (evenings, Sun lunchtime); Courage Best on handpump, good range of bar food, garden; nearby working wool-weaving mill in splendid eighteenth-century barn *(Joan Olivier)*; *Lamb*: Friendly free house, Morlands on handpump, wine by the glass, good choice of hot and cold bar food at reasonable prices, garden with children's play area; bedrooms should be available by the time this edition is published *(Joan Olivier)*

☆ **Forest Hill** [SP5807], *White Horse*: Cosy stone-walled bar with wide range of good well presented food including splendid ploughman's, well kept Morrells ales on handpump, welcoming licensees; tables in dining-room; children welcome *(Michael Dunne, Robert Gomme)*

☆ **Godstow** [SP4708], *Trout*: It's the marvellous position that makes this creeper-covered medieval pub special, with a lovely terrace by a stream clear enough to see the fat trout lazily holding position in it, and more extensive grounds where peacocks wander – one of the nicest summer spots in England; apart from that it's pretty commercialised, though the bar snacks in a modern extension are satisfactory, and they have Bass and Charrington IPA *(Lyn and Bill Capper, Graham Bush, Margaret and Roy Randle, Mr and Mrs J T Fallon, Joan Olivier, LYM)*

Goosey [SU3591], *Pound*: Nice little Morlands pub, recently improved, with lovely old brickwork opened up in bar; wide choice of nice food in massive helpings, humorous Welsh landlord, well kept real ale *(Gordon and Daphne, John Bell)*

Goring [Manor Rd; SU6080], *John Barleycorn*: Nice little Brakspears country pub with good bar food *(Gordon and Daphne)*

☆ **Great Bourton** [just off A423, 3 miles N of Banbury; opp church; SP4545], *Swan*: Nice atmosphere in popular thatched village pub, with good range of well kept Wadworths beers and enjoyably promising food under new landlord, including many vegetarian dishes, though in early 1988 décor could have done with some attention; bedrooms *(Jon Wainwright, S V Bishop, Grahame Archer, LYM – more reports please)*

Great Bourton [SP4545], *Bell*: Friendly local with juke box, darts, lots of trophies and well kept Hook Norton ales *(Jon Wainwright)*

Great Milton [SP6202], *Bull*: Excellent food and service in sixteenth-century pub *(Margaret and Trevor Errington)*

Hanwell [SP4343], *Moon & Sixpence*: Recently refurbished former Red Lion, good bar food, pleasant and efficient service – unusual in having a Sicilian licensee *(T Nott)*

Harwell [A417; SU4988], *Kingswell Farm*: Good choice of home-cooked meals and snacks (even Sun and bank hols), quick efficient service, children welcome in family bar-restaurant, also play area *(C H Fewster)*

☆ **Headington** [London Rd; SP5407], *White Horse*: Large bars extensively and comfortably refurbished with exposed brickwork and beamery, mahogany and stained-glass screens separating areas, well kept Morrells beers; useful for its reasonably priced bar food served all day (separate children's menus – one for under-sevens, the other for under-twelves); prompt service; busy lunchtimes, piped music, fruit machines *(Joan Olivier, Mrs Margaret Dyke)*

Headington [Wharton Rd], *Quarry Gate*: Varied choice of decent food from sandwiches to meals, reasonable prices, Ushers ales, tables in garden, fruit machine but no piped music; popular *(Joan Olivier)*

☆ **Henley** [Market Pl; SU7882], *Argyll*: Well run pub with long tartan-carpeted lounge, Highland pictures; popular lunchtime food is good value, well kept Morlands ales, seats on back terrace, handy parking behind; nr GWG68 *(LYM)*

Henley, *Old White Hart*: Friendly and comfortable, with good plain food and nice location by Thames; popular with regulars, but still quiet, and welcoming to visitors *(Lindsey Shaw Radley)*; [Wargrave Rd] *Two Brewers*: Comfortable, rambling rooms with wooden beams around central bar, oldest part dating back 600 years; open log fire, darts, fruit machine, friendly service; good range of reasonably priced bar food; back children's room *(Lyn and Bill Capper)*

☆ **Henton** [a mile off B4009 Chinnor–Princes Risborough; SP7602], *Peacock*: Courteously run and smoothly modernised well kept inn below the Chilterns, peacocks wandering all around outside (and over the thatch); well kept Brakspears and Hook Norton ales on handpump, mulled wine in winter, popular if somewhat pricey food with duck and steak specialities, good log fires; bedrooms in back block *(B R Shiner, HKR, Lindsey Shaw Radley, BB)*

Highmoor [SU6984], *Dog & Duck*: Cosy two-bar Brakspears pub, cottagey-looking outside, with small comfortable bars, open fires, and good choice of food for dining area towards the back *(Gordon and Daphne)*

☆ **Hook Norton** [a mile N towards Sibford, at Banbury–Rollright crossroads; SP3533], *Gate Hangs High*: Snug and spotless pub with friendly landlord, attractive inglenook, home-grown ingredients in good value home-cooked meals and salads served generously, well kept Hook Norton real ales, country garden; isolated, quite near Rollright Stones *(Brian and Rosemary Wilmot and others, LYM)*

Hook Norton, *Bear*: Theakstons and Davenports real ales, good choice of bar food, pleasant garden *(Dr A Y Drummond)*; *Pear Tree*: Readers who've been going for 20 years find little change – friendly landlord, well kept Hook Norton beers from the nearby brewery, open fire, two bars, sandwiches (not always available when it's busy, as it is on summer weekends – though there's plenty of room in garden) *(Robert Gomme, Brian Jones)*

☆ **Islip** [B4027; SP5214], *Red Lion*: Very wide choice of well presented food including attractive buffet, Halls ales, nice bar with fantastic collection of drinking-vessels; a group of former agricultural buildings behind now converted into Old Barns with its own bar, skittle alley and dining area; lavatories for the disabled; garden *(Joan Olivier, G N G Tingey, R F Neil, I Meredith)*
Islip, *Swan*: Pretty country village pub, attractively refurbished *(BB)*

Kennington [off A4142 (Oxford eastern bypass); SP5202], *Tandem*: Popular pub with two bars and garden; Morlands ales, friendly service and good food; no dogs except for guide dogs; family-room *(Joan Olivier)*

Leafield [Lone End; SP3115], *Spindleberry*: Comfortable bar, Wadworths 6X, good if pricey bar food, up-market restaurant *(Dr A Y Drummond)*

☆ **Letcombe Regis** [follow Village Only sign as far as possible; SU3784], *Sparrow*: Relaxed and unpretentious village-edge pub below prehistoric Segsbury hill-fort, well kept Morlands Bitter and Mild, simple lunchtime food from soup and toasted sandwiches to fry-ups (the home-cooked ham and eggs is a favourite), friendly landlord; tables, swings and climbing-frame in safely fenced garden *(Dave Braisted, Derek and Sylvia Stephenson, LYM)*

Long Hanborough [A4095 Bladon–Witney; SP4214], *Bell*: Small and friendly, with open fires and good pub food *(MO)*; *George & Dragon*: Friendly old stone village pub, low beams, Halls ales and bar food from sandwiches (not weekends) or big filled baps to steaks; restaurant, garden with children's play area and car park *(Joan Olivier)*; *Shepherds Hall*: Good choice of home-cooked food in clean and very friendly pub; good service, wide choice of drinks *(Stanley Matthews)*

Long Wittenham [SU5493], *Machine Man*: Family-run free house, the father shoots game and this is reflected in the mother's cooking; the son is a real ale fanatic; Ringwood Old Thumper, Ind Coope Burton and Wadworths 6X, home-made cider too; lounge, public bar (with darts) and dining-room *(Chris and Sue Hubbard)*; *Plough*: Big riverside garden with pitch-and-putt course, rustic furniture in small low-beamed lounge, lots of horsebrasses around the inglenook fireplace; bar food, Watneys-related real ales, games in public bar, children allowed in separate pool-room; bedrooms *(Joan Olivier)*; *Vine*: Morlands house with two bars separated by fireplace, variety of hot and cold bar food from sandwiches to enormous steaks, garden with play area *(Joan Olivier)*

Longworth [A420 Faringdon–Kingston Bagpuize; SU3899], *Lamb & Flag*: Good value Buccaneer Inn welcoming children, with large car park and park for Caravan Club members; serves breakfast 9.30–11 *(Joan Olivier)*

☆ **Lower Assendon** [SU7484], *Golden Ball*: Superb home-made pies in earthenware dishes, well kept Brakspears ales *(Ian Robinson, A T Langton)*

☆ **Marston** [Mill Lane, Old Marston – OS Sheet 164 reference 520090; SP5208], *Victoria Arms*: Spacious and comfortably refurbished pub in attractive setting by the River Cherwell, well kept Wadworths including Old Timer, friendly staff, open-plan bar with flagstone floor, open fires, old prints, no juke box, lively atmosphere; very wide choice of reasonably priced straightforward bar food from sandwiches to steaks; lavatories OK for the disabled, children welcome; big garden with play area *(Joan Olivier, Tim Brierly, J Treadgold, GCS, Edward Hibbert)*

☆ **Middle Assendon** [SU7385], *Rainbow*: Friendly local with wide choice of consistently very good plain food using fresh vegetables, well served in pleasant setting; well furnished with small tables, limited number of chairs as opposed to stools; full range of Brakspears ales; nice garden *(V P Prentice, Mr and Mrs H J F Marriott, CGB)*

Middle Barton [SP4325], *Carpenters Arms*: Friendly stone-built beamed village inn, generous helpings of reasonably priced food in bar or alcove eating area, Halls beers, coal-effect gas fire, garden; bedrooms *(Rob and Gill Weeks, Byrne Sherwood)*

Middleton Stoney [SP5323], *Jersey Arms*: Very good food in friendly beamed and panelled bar and restaurant of old inn with log fires in big fireplaces; bedrooms large and well furnished, one with four-poster *(Alan Bickley)*

Milton [SU4892], *Admiral Benbow*: Small friendly pub with Morrells ales, reasonably priced simple bar food such as piping hot home-made steak and kidney pie, quiet atmosphere; garden; by entrance to seventeenth-century Manor (open Sun afternoons Easter–Oct) *(Joan Olivier)*

☆ **Murcott** [SP5815], *Nut Tree*: Immaculate white thatched pub with duck pond and interesting garden (it's obvious that they look after their animals well); particularly good range of drinks from changing real ales such as Burton Bridge, Glenny, Halls Harvest and Wadworths 6X kept under light carbon dioxide blanket to worthwhile whiskies and wines; very much concentrates on food, with almost all tables laid for this, giving rather a restaurant atmosphere; the food, though somewhat pricey, is normally good – particularly Scotch steaks *(Peter and Barbara Atkins, I Meredith, Dr Paul Kitchener, Charles Gurney, LYM – more up-to-date reports please)*

Nettlebed [SU6986], *Sun*: Small friendly pub with collection of taps, 'time flies' clock, well kept Brakspears, good ploughman's, freshly made sandwiches, vegetarian and other food *(Dr J R Hamilton)*

Newbridge [A415 7 miles S of Witney; SP4101], *Maybush*: Low-beamed bar in unassuming Thames-side pub with waterside terrace, popular under previous tenants for good value food, low prices compared with the obvious competitor, and welcoming atmosphere – now under management for Morlands (same man runs the Rose Revived) *(Joan Olivier, A T Langton, LYM – more reports on the new regime please)*

North Leigh [Park Rd; SP3812], *Masons Arms*: Carefully refurbished former work-house with two small and friendly low-beamed inglenook bars, open fires, bar billiards room, bar food from sandwiches upwards (perhaps even occasional dishes cooked by the New Zealander owners in the traditional Maori hangi – a sort of under-ground oven); restaurant, off licence and garden *(Joan Olivier)*

Northmoor [off A415; SP4202], *Dun Cow*: Morlands real ale in simple pub with no bar counter, domino-worn Formica-topped traditional tables on lino floor *(Phil and Sally Gorton)*

Osney [SP5005], *Watermans Arms*: Under new ownership and undergoing some rede-coration, on island by attractive stretch of canal; Morlands ales and wide variety of reasonably priced and generously served bar food *(Nick Long)*

Oxford [off Cornmarket St (in alley near McDonalds, more or less opposite Boots); SP5106], *Crypt*: Cellar-type wine bar with sawdust on floor and terrific atmosphere; smart service, good food with excellent pies and nibbles on bar; numerous wines, ports, fresh orange juice and bottled beers *(Stanley Matthews)*; [Little Clarendon St (just off St Giles)] *Duke of Cambridge*: Well kept smart and popular pub with flamboyant, efficient barmen; bottled beers from all over the world, a wide range of spirits, good cocktails and freshly squeezed juices; bar food includes scrambled eggs with smoked salmon and bangers and mash *(Stanley Matthews)*; [St Giles] *Eagle & Child*: Friendly, old-fashioned pub refurbished a year or two ago to regain the old-fashioned feel of its several panelled rooms; simple good value bar food, Halls Harvest and Ind Coope Burton on handpump, classical piped music in back conservatory, little sun-trap terrace; young licensees *(GL, SL, Michael and Alison Sandy)*; [Merton St] *Eastgate Hotel*: Tastefully redone, with some sections of bar panelled off for intimacy; quiet and up-market rather than pubby, but with friendly efficient staff, good helpings of traditional pub snacks and well kept Courage ales; bedrooms *(Alison Hayward, Martin Hamilton)*; [39 Plantation Rd – 1st left after Horse & Jockey going N up Woodstock Rd] *Gardeners Arms*: Recently given open-plan revamp with walls knocked down, mock beams, old local photographs, antique plates and brasses, college shields; but still has Morrells Bitter and in winter College, and readers not too attached to its previous small-roomed sim-plicity still find the atmosphere enjoyable; home-made bar food, garden-room *(Jon Wainwright, LYM)*; [Paradise St] *Jolly Farmers*: Busy traditional free house with fine reasonably priced real ale, pool-table in basement bar, good lunchtime food (esp Sun), back garden, car park nearby; close to BR stn *(Barry Shapley)*; [Holywell St] *Kings Arms*: Very big roomy pub with Wadworths 6X among good range of well kept beers, smaller more comfortable and rather more select back rooms opening off the main area which throngs with students in term-time; popular bar food, especially wide choice of filled baked potatoes *(GL, SL, BKA, C D T Spooner)*; [Temple Rd, Cowley] *Marsh Har-rier*: Halls and Ind Coope Burton, very good value food in nicely decorated pub, very warm and friendly; darts, bar billiards, juke box and fruit machine *(GCS)*; [Hythe Bridge St] *Nags Head*: Sandwiches generously filled real bread, friendly staff, Halls Harvest beer; decent fire and games such as Trivial Pursuit in lounge; handy for bus and train stations *(Alison Hayward)*; [Cranham St, Jericho] *Radcliffe Arms*: Excellent value salads and pizzas, well kept Ushers, friendly atmos-phere; live music *(J Treadgold)*; [Market St] *Roebuck*: Very good value and well kept beer *(B Prosser)*; [North Parade] *Rose & Crown*: Welcoming landlord, who remem-bers you even if you've only been once before – his care for customers shows up in their attitudes to him; Halls Harvest *(M Quine)*; [Woodstock Rd] *Royal Oak*: Friendly unassuming local with fine Burton ale – open the front door and you're right at the bar *(John Branford)*

Pyrton [SU6896], *Plough*: Friendly service in very civilised pub, nicely presented food (not Sun evening) from sandwiches to full meals, with baked potatoes a speciality; good beers such as Adnams and Theakstons XB, open fire one end of lounge, no piped music or machines; restaurant (bookings only) *(HKR, Lyn and Bill Capper)*

☆ **Radcot** [Radcot Bridge; A4095 2½ miles N of Faringdon; SU2899], *Swan*: Unpretentious inn, delightful in summer for its riverside lawn, with Thames boat trips from pub's camping-ground opposite; well kept Morlands Bitter, Best and Mild, pub games; children in eating area; bedrooms clean and good value, with hearty traditional breakfast *(Andy Blackburn, Joan Olivier, HKR, LYM)*

Roke [SU6293], *Home Sweet Home*: Well refurbished seventeenth-century oak-beamed pub which has had good unusual food in bar and attractive restaurant, Flowers and Wethereds real ales, and big pretty garden; under new management from summer 1988 *(S Clark – news please)*

Sandford on Thames [SP5301], *Catherine Wheel*: Fifteenth-century pub, supposedly haunted by former landlord who keeps an approving eye on how each successive set of licensees looks after his pub – it's currently run by a friendly young couple; garden with play area *(Joan Olivier)*; [Church Rd – OS Sheet 164 reference 531013] *Kings Arms*: Big helpings of very good vegetarian food, wide range of cocktails, fairly quiet at lunchtime; exposed brickwork, tiled floor; next to Sandford Lock, with moorings *(Mr and Mrs J T Fallon)*

Satwell [just off B481; 2 miles S of Nettlebed, take Shepherds Green turning; SU7083], *Lamb*: Unspoilt in spite of being freshened up by new licensees (there's even an indoor gents now), this Chilterns cottage by a farmyard has low black beams, tiled floors, well kept Brakspears, huge logs smouldering, simple cheap bar food, traditional games – no frills *(Gordon and Daphne, LYM)*

Shillingford Bridge [SU5992], *Shillingford Bridge*: Food excellent in very friendly well furnished hotel bar and restaurant, idyllic spot with peaceful Thames-side lawn and outdoor swimming-pool; bedrooms comfortable, good value for area *(BB)*

Shiplake [A4155 towards Reading – OS Sheet 175 reference 746768; SU7476], *Flowing Spring*: Well kept Fullers ales in three cosy rooms of friendly and interesting countrified pub with open fires and floor-to-ceiling windows overlooking the water-meadows; big attractive garden *(TBB, G V Price, LYM)*

Shiplake [by stn; SU7578], *Baskerville Arms*: Friendly landlord and customers; well kept beers and good choice of food, jazz Thurs; bedrooms clean and good value *(Ken Sharp)*; *Plowden Arms*: Good food and beer and very friendly bar staff in cosy small beamed bar with newsletters from 1800 on wall; peaceful location with fine surrounding countryside *(Gary Wilkes)*

Shiplake Row [SU7578], *White Hart*: Location, welcome and food all good (worth booking for meals) *(Ian Meredith)*

Sibford Gower [SP3537], *Wykham Arms*: Impressive food has pleased several readers in this welcoming pub *(John and Joan Wyatt, Roy Davies)*

Sonning Common [SU7080], *Butchers Arms*: Taken over by Leon Banks who made the Old Crown at Skirmett in Bucks so popular for its old-fashioned atmosphere and ambitious food *(Anon)*

Souldern [SP5131], *Bear*: Delightful Cotswold-stone pub with Flowers, Hook Norton and Sam Smiths real ales, bar food, very friendly landlady *(John Bell)*

Stadhampton [signposted in village on A329; SU6098], *Bear & Ragged Staff*: Characterful free house, darkly crowded with atmosphere and people; strong real ales on handpump, good interesting bar food (the glutton burger has been such a favourite with regulars that when the pub was for sale in late 1987 they formed a consortium to buy it and keep it as they like it); music popular with young people *(Colin and Caroline, Mr and Mrs P Burton-Johnson)*

Steventon [SU4691], *Cherry Tree*: Popular for its wide choice of over half a dozen well kept real ales including Hook Norton; good range of snacks such as soup, ploughman's, pizza *(Dick Brown)*

☆ **Stoke Row** [Kingwood Common; 1 mile S of Stoke Row, signposted Peppard and Reading – OS Sheet 175 reference 692825; SU6784], *Grouse & Claret*: Cosy and attractive rebuilt pub, isolated in woodland setting; popular though expensive, with good food and helpful staff; restaurant *(Gordon and Daphne, Ian Meredith)*

Stonor [SU7388], *Stonor Arms*: Amiable staff, well kept Brakspears and maybe a guest beer, decent food; bedrooms good value *(Ian Robinson)*

Sutton Courtenay [B4016; SU5093], *Fish*: Tastefully modernised, with very good food in bar and restaurant, Morlands real ales *(A T Langton)*

Swalcliffe [Bakers Lane, just off B4035; SP3737], *Stags Head*: Thatched stone pub which is one of the few to house the village post office; friendly new licensees, hot and cold bar food, morning coffee, garden behind, little front terrace too; the village is pronounced Swaycliff *(Joan Olivier)*

Tackley [SP4720], *Gardiners Arms*: Friendly chatty and polite landlord and staff, tolerant of canal-holidaying youngsters and dogs (ours was given a bone); well presented, tasty and good value food from a varied menu; prompt service too *(Graham Darke)*

Tetsworth [A40, not far from M40 junction 7 – OS Sheet 164 reference 685020; SP6801], *Swan*: Old inn which has been popular with readers for good food in bar and restaurant, but damaged by fire and closed 1988 for refurbishment and possible extension (application by new owners for 40-room extension) *(Anon)*

Thame [High St; SP7005], *Abingdon Arms*: Nothing seems too much for the polite and friendly young staff in this low-beamed old pub with tasty food and real ale including guests such as Jennings *(E G Parish)*; *Bird Cage*: Short, reasonably priced bar lunch menu and Courage Best and Directors in quaint black and white beamed and timbered pub, once a medieval jail (and top room said to have ghost of a leper boy who died there); sandwiches, ploughman's and home-made soup good *(Frank Cummins, LYM)*; *Black Horse*: Old-fashioned calm in panelled and chintzy back lounge, little sheltered courtyard, bar meals and restaurant; bed-rooms *(LYM)*

Tiddington [SP6504], *Fox*: Very clean, warm and welcoming pub with comfortable seats, good food including fresh salads, Flowers, Halls Harvest, Ind Coope and Tetleys beers *(Brian Green)*

Toot Baldon [village signposted from A423 at Nuneham Courtenay, and B480; SP5600], *Crown*: Friendly village pub, popular at lunchtime for good food; benches and tables on terrace *(Joan Olivier)*

Towersey [Chinnor Rd; SP7304], *Three Horseshoes*: Flagstones, old-fashioned fur-nishings and good log fire make for a warm country atmosphere; well kept ABC real ale, bar food (rather pricey), piped pop music, biggish garden with playthings among fruit trees; children allowed at lunchtime *(Mike Tucker, Nancy Witts, TBB, LYM)*

Uffington [SU3089], *Fox & Hounds*: Very friendly pub with good food *(Michael Thomson)*

Wallingford [SU6089], *George*: Much done-up series of bars and places to eat in hotel with spacious and attractive sycamore-shaded courtyard; bedrooms *(LYM)*

☆ **Wantage** [Mill St, past square and Bell; down hill then bend to left; SU4087], *Lamb*: Snugly comfortable low-beamed pub with choice of attractively furnished seating areas, well kept Morlands, popular nicely presented bar food, good play area *(LYM)*; *Shoulder of Mutton*: Draught Morlands in bar with ochre floor-to-ceiling tongue-and-groove woodwork — Wantage's dominoes centre *(Phil and Sally Gorton)*

☆ **Warborough** [The Green South (just E of A329, 4 miles N of Wallingford); SU5993], *Six Bells*: Low-ceilinged thatched pub with country furnishings, big fireplace, antique photographs and pictures, fairly priced good bar food; tables in back orchard, cricket green in front, boules in summer; children in eating area *(I Meredith, Joan Olivier, Gordon and Daphne, LYM)*

Wardington [A361 Banbury–Daventry; SP4845], *Hare & Hounds*: Good value food and well kept Hook Norton beers in well run pub *(David Gittins)*

Watlington [Town Sq; SU6894], *Hare & Hound*: Recently refurbished, with panel-ling, prints, bookcases, stuffed animals, inglenook, new open fires; Bass, Ind Coope Burton, Marstons Pedigree and Morrells, friendly, obliging service and ample, reasonably priced bar snacks *(Joan Olivier, A T Langton)*

West Hendred [off A417 – OS Sheet 174 reference 447891; SU4488], *Hare*: Young couple doing good food; well kept Morlands *(A T Langton)*

Weston on the Green [SP5318], *Ben Jonson*: Friendly, welcoming and very attentive landlord in attractive stone pub with lovely window boxes; good bar food including

several vegetarian dishes *(Mrs Dorothy Pickering)*

Whitchurch [SU6377], *Greyhound*: Pretty old cottagey pub in riverside village with toll bridge; low beams, open fires, relaxing atmosphere, wonderful collection of miniature bottles in glass cases *(Gordon and Daphne)*

Witney [17 High St; SP3510], *Royal Oak*: Cosy and welcoming with log fire and good lunchtime bar snacks; attractive courtyard *(Mrs F Abbot)*

Woodstock [A34 leading out; SP4416], *Black Prince*: Interesting fairly authentic Mexican food as well as more conventional dishes, good choice of mind-crippling strong ales *(PLC, B Prosser)*; *Crown*: First-class real ale and popular food *(B Prosser)*; [A34 2 miles N] *Duke of Marlborough*: Clean and friendly, excellent food and service *(Frank Letch)*; [Market St] *Feathers*: Traditional hotel with sedate older-fashioned garden bar, good light lunches including excellent baked ham and other salads; bedrooms *(G Heap)*; [Park Lane] *Kings Head*: Pleasant atmos-phere, quick and friendly service, good bar food including enormous filled baked pota-toes *(Mrs Margaret Dyke)*; [Oxford St] *Marlborough Arms*: Courteous welcome in attractive lounge bar of Best Western hotel with cheerful fire, well kept beer, good reasonably priced food; bedrooms warm and cosy, not cheap and not spacious but good value *(E G Parish, B Prosser)*; *Punch Bowl*: Good beer and food in enjoyable surround-ings *(B Prosser)*; [59 Oxford St] *Queens Own*: Warm, one-bar pub with friendly licensees, lovely, reasonably priced food and well kept Hook Norton ales; unobtrusive juke box, darts, dominoes *(Barry Shapley)*; [22 Market St] *Star*: Good home-made food with plenty of vegetables, friendly cat, busy, good fire *(Stanley Matthews)*; *Woodstock Arms*: Tasty food (not cheap but good value) and great atmosphere in quaint old inn; bedrooms *(Wayne Brindle, B Prosser)*

☆ **Woolstone** [SU2987], *White Horse*: Attractive partly thatched sixteenth-century pub in ideal setting, very good reasonably priced food, very friendly new landlady, two big open fires in beamed and partly panelled bar, careful recent refurbishments; picturesque location perfect for walkers; Flowers and Wethereds real ales, children allowed in side eating area *(Lady Quinny, Dr A Y Drummond, Jenny Cantle)*

Wroxton [A422 2 miles W; SP4142], *New*: Attractively refurbished Hornton stone food pub, with central log fire and stripped walls at either end; has had friendly licensees and Bass-related real ales, but up for sale early summer 1988 *(Anon)*; [A422] *White Horse*: Good helpings of cheap food such as gammon, home-made steak and kidney pie, salads, served in bars and separate dining area; keg beers *(Michael O'Driscoll)*

Shropshire

It's becoming clear that Shropshire has quite a treasure-trove of splendid 'undiscovered' pubs and inns. More than half the main entries here are new to the Guide in just the last two or three years. Three years ago, the Lucky Dip section for this county had fewer than twenty entries; in this latest edition it has more than sixty. This year's newcomers to the main section include the Green Dragon at Little Stretton (currently, readers' first choice in this charming village below the Long Mynd), the rambling White Horse at Pulverbatch (its food lures a stream of people down the lanes from Shrewsbury each mealtime), the Wenlock Edge Inn delightfully placed on Wenlock Edge itself (this old place gives one of the warmest welcomes you can find in the area), the pretty little Willey Moor Lock by the canal just north of Whitchurch, and the Plough at Wistanstow (though its food is good value, its main lure is the fine range of Woods beers brewed here). An important change to note in the county is Greenalls' closure of the Wem brewery in early 1988 – the Wem real ales that you'll still find in the area are now brewed not in Shropshire but in Birmingham, so pubs used to being supplied locally now find themselves at the far end of a relatively much longer supply-line. The Blacksmiths Arms at Loppington (a good place for food, incidentally) is one pub previously tied to Wem which has now become a free house, and we suspect that others may follow suit. On a much more local scale, we should also note new licensees for the Red Lion by the Teme at Llanfair Waterdine (though many people will miss the Rhodes now they've retired, others will be glad of the real ales introduced by their successors). Many readers will miss from the main entries the Crown at Hopton Wafers – in the past it's been much the highest-rated pub in the area. A change of ownership is the cause of its demotion to the Lucky Dip, but in the late spring of 1988 it changed hands yet again. The latest owners formerly ran an Oxfordshire pub that's done well in this Guide, and during the

The Horseshoe, Llanyblodwel

summer (though too late for the reinspection that might have restored it to the main entries) we've had promising reports that things are decidedly looking up again at the Crown. Many of the area's nicest pubs happily go on without any marked change – for food, we'd pick out both contrasting entries in Much Wenlock, and the interestingly laid out Hundred House at Norton (a comfortable place to stay at, too). And for character, ones to note are the Three Tuns at Bishop's Castle (still brewing its own beers in its unique Victorian tower brewery), the welcoming Royal Oak in Cardington, the massively timbered Crown at Claverley, the Pheasant at Linley with its cheerful poaching mural, and the warren-like though admittedly pretty basic medieval Horseshoe at Llanyblodwel. Lucky Dip entries that have been attracting particular interest recently include the Railwaymans Arms in Bridgnorth, Old Jack at Calverhall, Bradford Arms at Llanymynech, Feathers and Wheatsheaf in Ludlow, and Stiperstones Inn at Stiperstones.

BISHOP'S CASTLE   SO3289   Map 6
Three Tuns
Salop Street

Across the yard from this unspoilt and family-run pub is the many-storeyed towering Victorian brick brewhouse – virtually unique and a Grade I listed building, with various stages of the brewing process descending floor by floor; the beers from it are XXX Bitter, Mild and an old-fashioned, dark, somewhat stoutish ale called Steamer; brewery tours can be arranged. Home-made bar food such as baps, hot beef and ham in French bread (£1.75), ratatouille and cheese or cottage pie (£2.25), ploughman's (from £2.25), chilli con carne and pitta bread (£2.50), salads (from £3), lasagne (£3.25), and steaks (from £6.50); also vegetarian dishes. Darts, dominoes and cribbage in the public bar. *(Recommended by Derek and Sylvia Stephenson, T Nott, Nicholas Walter)*

Own brew   Licensee Jack Wood   Real ale   Meals and snacks   Children welcome   Open 11.30–2.30, 6.30–11 all year

CARDINGTON   SO5095   Map 4
Royal Oak
Village signposted off B4371 Church Stretton–Much Wenlock; pub behind church; also reached via narrow lanes from A49

Tables beside roses in the front court of this remote old village pub look over to hilly fields, and a mile or so away, from the track past Willstone (ask for directions at the pub), you can walk up Caer Caradoc Hill which has magnificent views. Inside, a carefully furnished room has old standing timbers of a knocked-through wall, low beams, gold plush, red leatherette and tapestry seats solidly capped in elm, and a vast inglenook fireplace with its roaring log fire in winter, a cauldron, black kettle and pewter jugs. Good value lunchtime bar food includes sandwiches (£1, toasties £1.60), ploughman's (£2) and at least seven dishes – served without vegetables – such as macaroni cheese (£1.60), cauliflower cheese (£1.80), chicken cobbler, lasagne or cottage pie (£2), and steak and kidney or fidget pie or quiche (£2.20). The choice in the evening (no orders after 8.30) is generally similar, and always includes plaice or chicken curry (£2.80), gammon and egg (£4.25), rump steak (£5.25) and occasional evening specials. Well kept Ruddles County and Wadworths 6X on handpump, with Bass and Springfield, also on handpump, kept under light blanket pressure. Besides darts, dominoes and cribbage in the main bar,

---

a brightly lit upstairs room has pool, a fruit machine, space game and juke box. *(Recommended by T Nott, A Royle, A B Garside, E Mitchelmore, Dr Venetia Stent, Claire Davies)*

Free house Licensee John Seymour Real ale Meals and snacks (not Sun evening) Children welcome lunchtime, must eat in evening Open 12–2.30, 7–11; closed Mon lunchtime Nov–Mar exc school hols One self-contained double bedroom tel Longville (069 43) 266; £19.50S/£29S

CLAVERLEY   SO7993   Map 4

Crown

High Street

This four-hundred-year-old timbered pub, in one of Shropshire's prettiest villages, is close to a fine red sandstone church notable for its set of Norman paintings of armed knights on horseback representing the Battle of the Virtues and the Vices. Though it's been refurbished this year, the pub hasn't changed much, and the comfortable and neatly kept upper lounge has heavy beams, cushioned seats around the wooden tables on its patterned carpet and an open fire. The friendly and cosy lower bar has cushioned wall seats, an old-fashioned settle, a coal fire in winter and is served from a hatch. Another hatch serves a little lobby by the garden entrance. Good, home-made lunchtime bar food includes sandwiches (90p), ploughman's (£1.95), good steak and kidney or cottage pie or salads (£2.50), gammon and pineapple, goujons of fresh plaice or scampi (£2.95) and eight-ounce sirloin steaks (£3.95); evening dishes are similar but more expensive. Well kept Banks's Bitter on electric pump; pleasant, efficient service; dominoes, cribbage and unobtrusive piped music. The fairy-lit back terrace has tubs of flowers, roses and clematis and some tables by a waterpump, and beyond an arch through the old stableblock is an extensive lawn sheltered by trees and shrubs, with more tables and a children's play area. Back here, a children's shop sells sweets, ices and so forth on fine weekends and evenings (when there are barbecues too). Dogs are allowed. *(Recommended by Alan and Audrey Chatting, I Meredith, Robert and Vicky Tod)*

Hansons Licensee Leslie Stewart Real ale Meals and snacks (not Sun–Weds evenings) Children in eating area of bar Open 12–3 (4 Sat), 7–11 all year; they may open longer in afternoon if trade demands

CLUN   SO3081   Map 6

Sun 🏨

High Street; B4368 towards Clunton

In a village surrounded by wooded hills, this small Tudor inn has a beamed lounge bar with a quietly relaxed atmosphere, one or two high-backed winged settles, built-in cushioned wall benches, a carved antique oak armchair, some attractive old tables and sturdy wall timbers; it opens on to a sheltered back terrace with tables among pots of geraniums and other flowers. The L-shaped public bar has traditional settles on its flagstones, an enormous open fire, and dominoes, cribbage, chess, backgammon and tippet; there's a friendly Scotty dog. Bar food includes sandwiches, home-made soup (£1.20), garlic mushrooms (£2), scampi (£4), gammon and egg (£4.95), chicken breast in a wine and cream sauce (£5.95), steaks (from £6.25), vegetarian dishes, a daily special and puddings like home-made fruit pie (£1.50). Well kept Banks's on handpump. *(Recommended by Paul McPherson, William Rodgers, Pete Storey, Hazel Ricketts, PLC, E Kinnersly, John Atherton, John Innes, Mrs M E Collins)*

Free house Licensee Keith Small Real ale Meals and snacks Restaurant Children in eating area and restaurant Open 11–3, 6–11 all year; open 11–11 Sat Bedrooms tel Clun (058 84) 559 or 277; £16/£32(£35B)

LINLEY   SO6998   Map 4
Pheasant
Pub signposted off B4373

Much of this friendly, traditional pub is several hundred years old, though the feel is more up to date – as is the entertaining and colourful poaching mural covering one wall of an airy green-carpeted side room. The main bar has a mixture of seats including a flowery-cushioned pew and big-backed country kitchen armchairs, rugs on red quarry tiles, low black beams, a stuffed pheasant with a collection of pheasant-decorated plates, and log fires at each end. Simple food includes rolls (40p), sandwiches (from 60p, toasties 90p), good ploughman's with three cheeses (£1.75), sausage and egg (£2.30), home-made lasagne (£2.60), cod or haddock (£2.80), scampi (£2.95), gammon with their own free-range eggs (£3.85) and rump steak (£4.70). Well kept Banks's Mild, Marstons Burton and Holdens Special on handpump; dominoes; fruit machine and juke box in a separate room. There are some picnic-table sets under damson trees on the side grass, by a pretty flower border. They can tell you a good circuit walk from here. Strictly no children. *(Recommended by Jon Wainwright, A D Goff, Brian and Anna Marsden)*

Free house   Licensee R S A Reed   Real ale   Meals (not Sun) and snacks   Open 11.30–2.30, 6.30 (6 Sat)–11 all year; opens 7 in winter

LITTLE STRETTON   SO4392   Map 6
Green Dragon ⊗
Ludlow Road; village well signposted from A49

Clean and welcoming, this busy pub has a warm and friendly yet relaxing atmosphere, with green plush banquettes and stools around the well spaced polished dark tables of its neatly carpeted lounge bar. Good value well presented bar food, served efficiently, includes soup (85p), filled rolls (90p – or sandwiches on request), plaice or vegetarian lasagne (£3.20), scampi (£3.25), steak and kidney pie (£3.50), halibut (£4.75) and steaks (from sirloin £5.95). Well kept Manns, Ruddles County and Woods on handpump; maybe unobtrusive piped music. There are picnic-table sets under cocktail parasols on the lawn of a prettily planted garden beside the creeper-covered white house. *(Recommended by R M Walters, T Nott, A A Worthington)*

Free house   Licensee R B Jones   Real ale   Meals and snacks (not Sun evenings in summer) Restaurant tel Church Stretton (0649) 722925   Children in restaurant   Open 11.30–2.30, 6–11 all year; closed 25 Dec

LLANFAIR WATERDINE   SO2476   Map 6
Red Lion 🛏
Village signposted from B4355; turn left after crossing bridge

One of the joys of Shropshire is that when other attractive parts of the country are overrun with summer visitors, here you can still find peace and quiet even in a fine old riverside pub like this. The rambling lounge bar has cosy alcoves, easy chairs, some long, low settles and little polished wooden seats on its Turkey carpet, an unusual grandfather clock, earthenware jugs hanging from the beams, and a big open fire. The small black-beamed tap-room has plain wooden chairs on its polished brick floor, a wood-burning stove, and table skittles, dominoes, and sensibly placed darts. The new licensees have introduced home-made bar food and real ale: soup (85p), ploughman's (from £1.65), flans (£1.95), vegetable moussaka or meat lasagne (£2.50), jugged prawns, steaks (£5.50) and puddings like delicious toffee and banana (from 85p); John Smiths and Marstons Pedigree on handpump. There are seats on flagstones among roses by the quiet lane in front of the pub, with more on the grass at the back looking down over the River Teme (the licensees have given over part of their own garden); there's a track, before you get to the main road, that leads to a good stretch of Offa's Dyke and the long-distance walkway there. *(Recommended by T Nott, Mike Tucker, Ned Edwards)*

Free house   Licensee David Thomson   Real ale   Meals and snacks   Restaurant (if booked a day ahead)   Children in eating area of bar lunchtime and early evening   Open 12–2.30, 6.30–11 all year   Bedrooms tel Knighton (0547) 528214; £18/£30(£36B)

LLANYBLODWEL   SJ2423   Map 6

Horseshoe   [illustrated on page 555]

Village and pub signposted from B4396

Dating from the early fifteenth century, this black and white timbered inn has several rambling low-beamed rooms; the style is decidedly basic. The simple front inglenook bar has traditional black built-in settles alongside more modern chairs around oak tables, a collection of china and bottles on a high beam, brass buttons and other brass, and a collection of over two hundred key fobs. Bar food includes sandwiches, chilli con carne (£1.30), ploughman's (£1.40), pâté (£1.50), roast chicken (£2.25), chicken chasseur (£2.60), sirloin steak (£4.60) and various weekly specials such as stuffed plaice (£2.80). In the various rooms leading off you will find darts, pool, shove-ha'penny, dominoes, cribbage, a space game and piped music. There are tables in front of the building by the River Tanat which rushes around the boulders under a little red stone bridge, and a mile of fly-fishing for trout or grayling – free for residents; day tickets otherwise. *(Recommended by Rob Weeks, Gill Austin, Mr and Mrs Ray; more reports please)*

Marstons   Licensee Philip Hindley   Meals and snacks   Children in eating area until 9   Open 11–3, 6–11 all year; opens 7 in winter   Bedrooms tel Llansantffraid (069 181) 227; £10/£18

LOPPINGTON   SJ4729   Map 6

Blacksmiths Arms ⊗

Village signposted from B4397 W of Wem

In February this year, the Wem brewery (just three miles away) which supplied this pub's well kept Bitter and Best was shut down by its owners, Davenports of Birmingham, who have taken over production of the beers. This year the licensees have upgraded the kitchens, are improving the lavatories and have bought new picnic-table sets and other garden seats for the terrace. The central bar has spindle-back chairs on its red tiled floor, two seats by the inglenook fireplace, and a collection of farm and thatching tools. Off to the left there are dark plush built-in button-back banquettes around neat tables (with a vase of flowers), and country prints on the timbered walls. On the right a smallish room has more neat seats and tables and shooting prints. Good value home-made bar food includes sandwiches or toasties and filled baked potatoes (from £1), Cumbrian hot-pot (£2), vegetable pancake (£2.50), very good steak and oyster pie (£3), duck and oyster pie (£3.50), chicken Kiev (£4) and steaks (from £5.25); Bass and Davenports Bitter; shove-ha'penny and dominoes. There's a play area in the attractive garden. *(Recommended by William Rodgers, G E Rodger, R G Ollier)*

Free house   Licensees Wilf and Dorothy Jackson   Real ale   Meals and snacks (not Tues)   Restaurant tel Wem (0939) 33762   Children in restaurant (not Sat evening)   Open 12–2.30 (3 Sat), 7–11 all year; closed Tues lunchtime

Ideas for a country day out? We list pubs in really attractive scenery at the back of the book – and there are separate lists for waterside pubs, ones with a really good garden, and ones with lovely views.

MUCH WENLOCK   SJ6200   Map 4

George & Dragon ⊗

High Street

Deliberately unrefined, this busy, town pub has a front bar, popular with locals, with a few antique settles as well as wheel-back chairs packed in around the wooden tables, and a couple of attractive Victorian fireplaces (with coal-effect gas fires); there's a collection of about six hundred water jugs hanging from the beams (the biggest pub collection in England), some George and the Dragon pictures, old brewery and cigarette advertisements, and lots of bottle labels and beer trays; it can get smoky. At the back, the quieter snug old-fashioned rooms have black beams and timbering, little decorative plaster panels, tiled floors, a big George and the Dragon mural as well as lots of smaller pictures (painted by local artists), a stained-glass smoke-room sign, and a little stove in a fat fireplace. Very good food at lunchtime includes sandwiches, home-made soup (£1.50), ploughman's with home-made chutney (from £2.25), home-made pâté (£2.75), lentils and vegetable gratin (£3), fisherman's pie or chicken in a lemon and tarragon sauce (£3.25), fresh trout stuffed with prawns, mushroom and ginger or lamb curry (£3.50), and puddings like home-made sherry trifle (£1.50); evening meals are served in Eve's Kitchen, with starters such as Stilton and pear pâté (£2.25), and main courses such as lamb's liver (£6.25) or the house speciality, duck (£8.50). Well kept Hook Norton Best, Marstons Pedigree and guest beers on handpump; friendly service; music from a vintage wireless. (*Recommended by Colin Dowse, Lynne Sheridan, Bob West, Maggie Jo St John, Dudley Evans, Derek and Sylvia Stephenson, M A and W R Proctor, Robert and Vicky Tod, N J Neil-Smith, Robert Alton, A Royle, Robert Timmis, Prof A P M Coxon, Jon Wainwright, A Pinder*)

Free house   Licensees Eve and Brian Nolan   Real ale   Lunchtime meals and snacks Evening restaurant tel Much Wenlock (0952) 727312; closed Sun and Mon evenings Older children in restaurant if well behaved   Open 10.30–2.30, 6–11 all year; opens 7 in winter

Talbot ⊗

High Street

Quite different in character from our other main entry here, this very neatly kept and comfortable old pub has several opened-together carpeted areas with green plush button-back wall banquettes around cast-iron-framed tables, walls decorated with prints of fish, and with shives, tuts, spices and other barrel-stoppers, low ceilings, lovely flowers, and two big log fires (one in an inglenook decorated with a hop-bine). Good home-made bar food includes soup (£1); home-made pâté (£1.95), Danish-style open sandwiches (from £2.35), filled baked potatoes (£1.95), ploughman's (from £2.65), quiche (£2.95), spicy pancake (£3), omelettes (from £2.95), steak and kidney pie with first-class pastry (£3.25), locally produced sirloin steak (£5.25) and daily specials such as lamb and apricot or oxtail casserole, shepherd's pie or leek and ham pie (under £3); in the evening there's more concentration on main dishes such as grilled trout (£4.75), lamb chops (£5.25) or scampi provençale (£6.25). Home-made puddings include fruit crumble and daily specials (£1.25), and they do a roast Sunday lunch (best to book). Ruddles Best and Websters Yorkshire on handpump; piped music; very friendly service. Through the coach entry, there are white seats and tables in an attractive sheltered yard. (*Recommended by Alison Graham, T Nott, Kit Read, Abbie Bryce, Robert Alton, Emily Gill, M A and W R Proctor, Jon Wainwright*)

Free house   Licensee Timothy Lathe   Real ale   Meals and lunchtime snacks   Restaurant (to stay open until 4 Sun)   Well behaved children welcome (no prams)   Open 10–2.30, 6–11 all year   Bedrooms tel Much Wenlock (0952) 727077; £25B/£40B

NORTON   SJ7200 Map 4

Hundred House ★ ⊗ 🛏

A442 Telford–Bridgnorth

Three or four more or less separate areas in this carefully and interestingly refurbished old place have a warm and chatty atmosphere, attractive lamps, old quarry tiles at either end and modern hexagonal ones in the main central part, which has high beams strung with hop-bunches and cooking-pots. Steps lead up past a little balustrade to a partly panelled eating area, where stripped brickwork looks older than that elsewhere. Handsome fireplaces – one a great Jacobean arch with fine old black cooking-pots – have log fires or working Coalbrookdale ranges, and around the sewing-machine tables are a variety of interesting chairs and settles, some with long colourful patchwork leather cushions. Good, though not cheap, home-made bar food includes duck liver pâté (£2), ploughman's (lunchtime, from £2), prawns (half-pint £2), a cold buffet of cheeses, lean beef and salads (from £3.75), a changing vegetarian dish (£4), lasagne or steak and kidney pie (£4.95), steaks (from £7.25), daily specials such as local pigeon (£4.95), lemon sole poached in white wine (£5.75), local pheasant, hare or rabbit, or charcoal-grilled lamb cutlets done as pink as you like (£5.95), and salmon cooked with dill and Pernod (£6.95); herbs come from their own garden. In the evening prices are about fifteen per cent higher. Well kept Chesters Mild, Flowers Original and a guest beer such as Wadworths 6X or Whitbreads Durham Mild, with Heritage (light and refreshing, not too bitter) and the stronger Ailrics Old Ale at the moment brewed for them by a small brewery. Darts, shove-ha'penny, dominoes, cribbage, table skittles, fruit machine, and unobtrusive piped music; no dogs; seats out in a neatly kept and prettily arranged garden. The village bowling-green is next to the inn. *(Recommended by Laurence Manning, Derek Stephenson, Dave Butler, Lesley Storey, M A and W R Proctor, Eileen and Michael Brecker, Tony Heath, T E Heywood, Lynne Sheridan, Bob West)*

Free house   Licensees Henry, Sylvia, David and Stuart Phillips   Real ale   Meals and lunchtime snacks   Restaurant, open Sun afternoons   Children welcome   Open 11–11 all year   Bedrooms tel Norton (095 271) 353; £45B/£54B

PULVERBATCH   SJ4202 Map 6

White Horse ⊗

From A49 at N end of Dorrington follow Pulverbatch/Church Pulverbatch signposts, and turn left at eventual T-junction (which is sometimes signposted Church Pulverbatch); OS Sheet 126 reference 424023

The decided Scots influence here extends to tasty cullen skink as a soup (90p), well hung proper steak in sandwiches (£2.25 – outstanding value) or on its own (from £4.25), and a good choice of malt whiskies as well as the well kept Wethereds SPA and Flowers Original or maybe Whitbreads Pompey Royal on handpump (and several decent wines by the glass); there's even a good Thorburn print of a grouse among the other country pictures. It's a homely, rambling pub, with unusual fabric-covered high-backed settles as well as the brocaded banquettes on its Turkey carpet, sturdy elm or cast-iron-framed tables in its several interconnected snug areas, black beams and heavy timbering, an open coal-burning range with gleaming copper kettles, a collection of antique insurance plaques, big brass sets of scales, willow-pattern plates, pewter mugs hanging over the serving-counter – in short, plenty to look at. The wide choice of other bar food includes sandwiches (from 75p), burgers (from £1.50), ploughman's (from £1.75), omelettes (from £1.80), fresh fish of the day (£2.25), salads (from £2.35), gammon (£3.25), home-made curries (from £3.25), a popular fry-up (£3.85), trout (£3.95) and children's dishes

---

Please let us know of any pubs where the wine is particularly good.

(from 75p); darts, juke box, friendly efficient service. The quarry-tiled front loggia with its sturdy old green leatherette seat is a nice touch. *(Recommended by PLC, W D Hammond, Dr Keith Bloomfield)*

Whitbreads   Licensee James MacGregor   Real ale   Meals and snacks   Children welcome Open 11.30–3, 7–12 all year

SHREWSBURY   SJ4912 Map 6
Boat House

New Street; leaving city centre via Welsh Bridge, follow Bishop's Castle A488 signpost into Port Hill Road

The long, quiet lounge bar in this comfortably modernised pub has good views down over the River Severn to the park – which, as you can see from a 1732 engraving that shares the panelling with rowing photographs and a collection of oars, hasn't changed much over the centuries. Well presented bar food includes filled rolls, ploughman's (from £1.60), chicken and herb pâté (£1.75), pork and apple or chicken and mushroom pie or vegetarian or meat quiches (£2.45), chilli con carne or chicken curry (£2.50), and moussaka (£2.65); summer barbecues. Well kept Flowers Original and IPA on handpump; fruit machine, space game, trivia and piped music. There's a summer bar on a sheltered and attractive terrace, a lawn with roses, and a footbridge that leads across to the park (where there are quite a few events). *(Recommended by C P Scott-Malden, Quentin Williamson, W D Hammond)*

Whitbreads   Licensee Brian Branagh   Real ale   Lunchtime meals and snacks   Children in eating area   Live guitarist duo last Weds evening of month   Open 11–3 (2.30 in winter), 6–11 all year

WENLOCK EDGE   SO5796 Map 4
Wenlock Edge Inn ⊗ ⇌

Hilltop; B4371 Much Wenlock–Church Stretton; OS Sheet 137 reference 570962

An exceptionally friendly warmth marks this carefully restored inn, in its fine position just by the Ippikins Rock viewpoint and lots of walks through the National Trust land that runs along the Edge. It's a family – father, mother, son and daughter – escaped here from Nottingham, who've so rejuvenated it; both father and daughter were lawyers there. Built originally around 1795 as a pair of quarrymen's cottages, it then became the Plough, and now (reopened after a period of disuse) has two cosy bar rooms with a fine bar counter made – like the small booths in the left room – from local oak. The one on the right, with a big wood-burning stove in its big inglenook, leads into a little dining-room. Home-cooked bar food, using fresh ingredients and worth waiting for, includes soup (£1.20), pâté (£1.60), scampi (£2.95), steak and mushroom pie (£3) and dishes of the day such as vegetarian ratatouille flan (£3) or Elizabethan pork (£4.20), with evening steaks (eight-ounce, £5.95) and attractive puddings. Well kept Wem Best and Special, interesting whiskies, decent wines by both glass and bottle, and no music – unless you count the deep-throated chimes of Big Bertha the fusee clock. There are some tables on a front terrace and the side grass – giving a ringside view of the twenty-two housemartins we found nesting under the eaves. *(Recommended by Ian Howard, Lynne Sheridan, Bob West, Colin Dowse)*

Free house   Licensees Harry, Joan, Stephen and Diane Waring   Real ale   Meals and snacks (not Mon)   Restaurant   Children in restaurant (not under 10 after 8 Sat)   Open 11–2.30 (3 Sat), 6–11 all year; Sat lunchtime 12–2.30 in winter; closed Mon lunchtime exc bank hols Twin bedroom tel Much Wenlock (074 636) 403; £17S/£29S

If you report on a pub that's not a main entry, please tell us any lunchtimes or evenings when it doesn't serve bar food.

WHITCHURCH SJ4947 Map 7
Willey Moor Lock
Pub signposted off A49 just under 2 miles N of Whitchurch

Park down a short bumpy track, use the footbridge to cross the Llangollen Canal and the rushing sidestream by the lock, and go into the low fairy-lit pub that looks out over the colourful narrowboats. The several low-ceilinged carpeted rooms are neatly decorated – crisp black and white paintwork, red velvet curtains for the little windows, brick-based brocaded wall seats, stools and small chairs around dimpled copper and other tables, a decorative longcase clock and a shelf of toby jugs. Bar food includes good freshly cut sandwiches, steak and kidney pie (£2.50), scampi (£3), salads (from £3), gammon (£4.25) and rump steak (£5.25), with children's dishes (£1.50); well kept McEwans 70/- on handpump; fruit machine, trivia machine, piped background music. White tables under cocktail parasols on the terrace outside the building, which used to be the lockkeeper's cottage, let you watch the boats go by. *(Recommended by Graham Gibson, E Mitchelmore)*

Free house   Licensee Mrs E Gilkes   Real ale   Meals and snacks   Children in eating area   Open 11–2.30, 6–11 all year; closed lunchtime Mon–Sat Nov–Feb

WISTANSTOW SO4385 Map 6
Plough ⊗
Village signposted off A49 and A489 N of Craven Arms

Most pubs which brew their own beer have a markedly back-to-basics décor and atmosphere – but not this one. Its lounge bar is high-raftered and airy, with big windows and orange or dark blue leatherette chairs around the many tables spread over its swirly patterned carpet. It recalls a smartish working-men's club or NAAFI of a decade or two ago (or, more exactly for those who know it, Jersey Airport's Horizon Bar). Good value home-cooked food includes ploughman's with three English cheeses (£2), cottage pie (£2), lasagne (£2.50), gammon and egg (£2.75), steak and kidney pie (£2.95), salads or scampi (£3), chicken breasts in vermouth and cream (£4.20), halibut Mornay (£4.50), and maybe fresh salmon (£5), with an attractive show of home-made puddings. The brewery is actually separate, an older building right by the pub, and the beers are among the best from any brewery – Woods Parish, Special, the strong Wonderfull and the seasonal Christmas Cracker. They also keep two farm ciders, and there's a fine display cabinet of bottled beers. The games area has darts, pool, dominoes, cribbage, fruit machine, space game and juke box; there may be piped music. There are some tables under cocktail parasols outside. *(Recommended by Lynne Sheridan, Bob West, Derek and Sylvia Stephenson, SP, Paul and Joanna Pearson, T Nott)*

Own brew   Licensee R G West   Real ale   Snacks (lunchtime, not Sun) and meals (not Mon evening)   Children in eating area   Open 11–2.30, 7–11 all year

Lucky Dip

Besides the fully inspected pubs, you might like to try these Lucky Dips recommended to us and described by readers (if you do, please send us reports):

All Stretton [SO4695], *Yew Tree*: Friendly and obliging landlord and bar staff, good value bar food *(Gary Merrell – and Harrow & Wembley YHA Group)*

Alveley [Birds Green; SO7684], *Mill*: Excellent layout either for eating or for drinking, good food and reasonably priced drinks, delightful terrace and garden *(D I Baddeley)*

Aston Munslow [OS Sheet 137 reference 512866; SO5187], *Swan*: Old pub with several bars, log fires, pool-room, real ales, good bar food, garden *(Lynne Sheridan, Bob West)*

☆**Bridgnorth** [Hollybush Rd; SO7293], *Hollyhead*: Varied choice of excellent food, reasonable prices; inn run by two charmingly friendly and attentive couples, obviously out to please; bedrooms – and excellent breakfasts (*G M K Donkin, G B Pugh*)

☆ **Bridgnorth** [Stn – A458 towards Stourbridge, opp the Hollyhead], *Railwaymans Arms*: A real curiosity, recreating the atmosphere of bustling station bars in the 1940s, and forming part of the Severn Valley steam railway terminus (the station car-parking fee is refundable against either your train ticket or what you spend in the pub); very basic amenities, basic snacks, a fine range of well kept real ales including Bathams, Timothy Taylors Landlord, Woods and good Milds; children welcome (*Dave Braisted, Jon Wainwright, LYM*)

Bridgnorth [B4364 to Ludlow], *Punch Bowl*: Homely old-fashioned quiet country pub with good food and beer, armchairs and an open fire in winter (*Elaine Kellet*); [High St] *Swan*: Attractive old half-timbered pub, comfortable, with well kept beer and good food (*Quentin Williamson*)

☆ **Brockton** [SO5894], *Feathers*: Bar food and well kept real ales in comfortable country pub with large collection of little china houses and pretty little covered back terrace (*Mr and Mrs D Nicklin, LYM*)

☆ **Calverhall** [New St Lane; SJ6037], *Old Jack*: Elegantly furnished and attractively decorated bar with Windsor chairs, oak tables, lovely flower arrangements; wide choice of good reasonably priced bar food including steaks cooked to perfection, well kept beer, good service, restaurant; bedrooms (*J Taylor, L S Manning*)

Chorley [SO6983], *Duck*: Village pub with excellent food – duck is the speciality – and M&B ales; friendly owners (*Clifford Blakemore*)

Church Aston [A518 Newport–Wellington, outside village; SJ7418], *Red House*: Pleasant atmosphere, reasonable blend of modern decoration and old relics, Ansells real ale, good food (*Dave Braisted*)

Claverley [SO7993], *Plough*: Rambling old but modernised pub, extensive back garden with sales shed for customer sales and children's play equipment; extensive range of home-cooked food including good Sun lunch – restaurant a pleasantly converted barn (*Mr and Mrs J Halsey, SP*)

Cleobury Mortimer [SO6775], *Old Lion*: Friendly old pub with oak beams, antique settles, longcase clock, Banks's Bitter and Mild on electric pump, particularly good value food including excellent Sun lunch (*EJ*); *Talbot*: Good food in bar and restaurant; bedrooms of a high standard (*N A Hawkins*)

Clun [SO3081], *Buffalo*: Happy, friendly bar staff, vivacious gang of customers (*Paul McPherson*); *Old Post Office*: Restaurant with bedrooms rather than a pub, but comfortable, good food, really cordial landlord – and it does have a lounge/bar area (*Paul McPherson*)

☆ **Coalport** [SJ6903], *Woodbridge*: Pretty and well kept old inn with terraced Severnside garden overlooking the world's second iron bridge (1799); good food including excellent steaks, well kept beers, small nooks and crannies, hops hanging from ceiling, attentive staff (*Elaine Kellet, G M K Donkin*)

Coalport [Salthouse Rd – over footbridge by chinaworks museum; OS Sheet 127 reference 693025], *Boat*: Handy for the museums, with tables on grass by River Severn – idyllic in summer sunshine; well kept Banks's on electric pump, outdoor barbecue (*Dr and Mrs C D E Morris*)

☆ **Corfton** [SO4985], *Sun*: Friendly and welcoming licensees, well cooked and presented bar food at reasonable prices, pleasant surroundings, big garden with children's play area (*S Pearce, Mr and Mrs R A Gethen*)

Coton [B5476 Wem–Whitchurch – OS Sheet 126 reference 528343; SJ5335], *Bull & Dog*: Old coaching-inn with excellent food and well kept Wem ales; named after early nineteenth-century Sun bull-baiting here (*A J Hill*)

Cross Houses [SJ5406], *Fox*: Clean refuge from busy road, good varied food including vegetarian at reasonable prices, efficient landlord (*G C Hixon*)

Ellesmere [Scotland St; SJ4035], *Black Lion*: Friendly sixteenth-century pub with good reasonably priced food, Border and Marstons beers; convenient for the mosses and meres of Shropshire's lake district (*A J Hill*)

Grinshill [off A49; SJ5323], *Elephant & Castle*: Early Georgian pub with fine food and Ansells ales; the hill is an excellent viewpoint over Shropshire to the distant Welsh hills; nr GWG99 (*A J Hill*)

Harmerhill [SJ4922], *Bridgewater Arms*: Large bar with central serving area, pleasant staff, good straightforward pub food, real ales; seats at front and in small garden (*Mike and Kay Wilson*)

Hodnet [SJ6128], *Bear*: Relaxing warm atmosphere in well refurbished old inn with interesting underfloor garden in what was the old bearpit, in the cocktail bar; opposite Hodnet Hall gardens; four comfortable bedrooms (*T E Heywood*)

Hookagate [SJ4609], *Cygnet*: Well kept Flowers and maybe even Pompey Royal, good atmosphere, good value food includes pleasantly served fresh pizzas (*W D Hammond*)

☆ **Hopton Wafers** [A4117; SO6476], *Crown*: Very highly rated in previous editions for its combination of an interestingly individual layout and furnishings with a particularly wide choice of unusual bar food; in late 1987 and early 1988, under different management, the food became more orthodox and restricted and the atmosphere suffered, but from May 1988 – under new owners Howard and Polly Hill-Lines – warmth has returned to readers' reports on food, atmosphere and the well kept Wadworths; children welcome; more reports please *(F A Noble, Robert and Vicky Tod, Mr and Mrs D A P Grattan, LYM)*

Ironbridge [Wharfage; SJ6704], *Malt House*: Large, long room popular with tourists, bar at one end with well kept Davenports and Wem Special, useful if not cheap food served from other end; across road is Severn *(Jon Wainwright, A Royle)*; [11 High St at Blists Hill Open Air Museum; SJ6903] *New*: Well worth the museum entrance fee to sample what a pub of the 1880s could offer; it's very much a 'spit and sawdust' pub with the bar staff dressed in the style of the working class of the industrial towns of this part of the world; real ales, good ploughman's (an excusable anachronism – that pub staple wasn't really invented until the 1950s) and no juke box, fruit machines, cigarette machines or fancy drinks; open lunchtime – can be hired during the evening *(Colin Gooch)*; *Olde Robin Hood*: Good home-made food in carpeted lounge with comfortable pink plush seats, handsome collection of clocks and beautifully burnished brasses *(Mr and Mrs Ken Turner)*; *Swan*: Cosy pub with good sheep, simple food *(A Royle)*

Kemberton [SJ7304], *Masons Arms*: Cheerful welcome and good value food in country pub handy for business visitors to Halesfield industrial estate in Telford *(T E Heywood)*

Ketley [Holyhead Rd – nr M54 junction 6; SJ6810], *Unicorn*: Brews a wide range of beers including an old ale named Old Horny; has had good food *(David Fisher)*

☆ **Leebotwood** [A49 Church Stretton–Shrewsbury; SO4898], *Pound*: Above-average food and reasonably priced drinks including well kept beer in pleasantly appointed main-road pub with helpful licensee and good atmosphere; can be very busy on Ludlow race days *(G B Pugh, F A Noble, T Nott)*

Little Stretton [Ludlow Rd – village well signposted off A49; SO4392], *Ragleth*: Attractive sixteenth-century pub with open fires, comfortable bay-windowed lounge, huge inglenook in public bar, real ales, tables on lawn by tulip tree; popular, particularly for food in bar and restaurant, under previous American landlord, but taken over by two new couples in early 1988 and first reports very mixed – so more news please; children have been allowed in eating area and restaurant; beware of the car park – one reader who'd lunched at the pub then gone for a walk (it's nr GWG102) came back to find his car locked in, and couldn't get it out without paying a penalty; bedrooms *(T Nott, LYM)*

☆ **Llanymynech** [A483 – OS Sheet 126 reference 267207; SJ2721], *Bradford Arms*: Elegant lounge, well kept Marstons Burton and Pedigree, good choice of attractive and interesting bar food including lots of puddings, separate restaurant, small garden *(Lynne Sheridan, Bob West, D A Lloyd)*

☆ **Ludlow** [Bull Ring; SO5175], *Feathers*: Famous for exquisitely proportioned and intricately carved timbered frontage, and a fine hotel inside – Jacobean panelling and carving, period furnishings; for snacks or a casual drink (they have Whitbreads-related real ales) you may well now be diverted to a plainer more modern side bar; bedrooms comfortable, if not cheap *(T Nott, LYM)*

☆ **Ludlow** [Lower Bridge St], *Wheatsheaf*: Pleasant little pub spectacularly built into ancient town gate, good atmosphere, well kept Bass on handpump, friendly welcome, good interesting food *(Chris Cooke, Wayne Brindle, T Nott)*

Ludlow [Broad St], *Angel*: Attractive front in lovely architectural street; entrance via alley to distinctive long lounge with comfortable sofas; well kept Flowers IPA and Original, good value baked potatoes at lunchtime, friendly; bedrooms *(A Cook)*; [Church St] *Church*: Food a bit pricey but decent – and good, pleasant atmosphere *(Anon)*; [Bull Ring] *Old Bulls Head*: Solid old-fashioned town pub with good beer and nice choice of bar food (also restaurant); busy at lunchtime *(A Royle)*

Madeley [Coalport Rd; SJ6904], *All Nations*: Friendly pub brewing its own beer – as it has done for decades; no food nor any other concession to modernity, being run wholly for its local custom *(Lynne Sheridan, Bob West)*

Market Drayton [High St; SJ6734], *Corbet Arms*: Pleasant pub/hotel with wide choice of beers and excellent buffet lunch at very reasonable cost – a former coaching-inn; plenty of seating *(E G Parish)*

Marton [B4386 Chirbury–Westbury; SJ2902], *Lowfield*: Attractive fairly remote country pub, immaculate inside and out; restrained décor, with generous log fire in lounge, friendly and helpful landlord, M&B and Worthington beers, above-average bar food *(G W Tanner)*

Munslow [SO5287], *Crown*: Attractive old building in pleasant countryside with flagstones, bare stone walls, original cupboards and doors; generous food, good cheap beer *(Quentin Williamson)*

Myddle [A528 7 miles N of Shrewsbury – OS Sheet 126 reference 468239; SJ4724], *Red Lion*: Clean and comfortable free house with pleasant spacious lounge, exposed beams and log fire, good value bar food, well kept Woods real ale *(F and E Rossiter, BNR)*

Newcastle [B4368 Clun–Newtown; SO2582], *Crown*: Friendly, well kept and well furnished pub with attentive service from hard-working young owners, nicely presented good food including some interesting dishes as well as the more usual ones, wide choice of well kept beer; beer garden, lovely countryside *(G Holliday, Mrs P J Hughes)*

Nordley [B4373 N of Bridgnorth; TQ4952], *Swan*: Friendly small country pub, warm welcome for strangers, good home-cooked food even on a Sun evening, Wem real ale *(Simon Barber)*

Priorslee [SJ7109], *Lion*: Cosy, well run pub serving well kept Wem Mild and Bitter, good value weekday lunchtime food with interesting puddings *(Roger and Judy Tame)*

Shifnal [SJ7508], *White Hart*: Tastefully restored, comfortable, cosy village pub, good range of beers, bar food with excellent specials *(Bob Alton)*

☆ **Shrewsbury** [Wyle Cop – follow City Centre signposts across the English Bridge; SJ4912], *Lion*: Grand old inn with distinguished history, cosy oak-panelled bar and sedate series of high-ceilinged rooms opening off, comfortably refurbished by THF; obliging staff, Bass under light blanket pressure, bar food – which may be served in the restaurant if it's not busy; children welcome; bedrooms comfortable *(Paul and Margaret Baker, KC, Wayne Brindle, LYM)*

Shrewsbury [Swan Hill/Cross Hill; SO3983], *Coach & Horses*: Licensed as alehouse for nearly 300 years, carefully exposed old brickwork, ships' timbers stripped back to original worn split grain, generous helpings of food, well kept Bass on handpump, unobtrusive piped music, cosy atmosphere *(John Green)*; [Longden Rd, Coleham] *Crown*: Excellent range of well kept beers including ones that are decidedly uncommon around here, good atmosphere, pleasant river view, summer boat hire *(W D Hammond)*; [42 Wenlock Rd] *Peacock*: Charming atmosphere and staff, good snacks and coffee, pleasant white wine; in summer the hanging baskets are most attractive *(Cynthia McDowell)*; [The Square] *Plough*: Decent town pub, busy at lunchtime, with good choice of reasonably priced food, satisfactory beer *(A Royle)*

Stiperstones [OS Sheet 126 reference 364005; SO3697], *Stiperstones Inn*: Old pub nestling below Stiperstones Ridge (remote, good walks – the pub's on GWG100), simple but good cheap bar food including homemade pies, vegetarian or vegan meals, maybe local whimberry pie; well kept Whitbreads and Woods real ales, cheap for area; oak beams, brasswork, local paintings, pine tables and chairs, fresh flowers, and tables outside in attractive setting; village shop seems to be part of pub *(Mrs M E Collins, J Phillips)*

Stottesdon [SO6783], *Fighting Cocks*: Delightful old half-timbered pub in unspoilt countryside, low ceiling, open fire, equestrian pictures, good substantial simple food *(Anon)*

Telford [Foregate; SJ6710], *Telford Moat House*: Pleasant bar in modern hotel serving good and reasonably priced bar food *(Mrs H March)*

☆ **Tong** [A41 towards Newport, just beyond village; SJ7907], *Bell*: Friendly service, well kept Banks's beer, good hot dishes and cold table, also good value Sun lunch; big family-room, small dining-room, no dogs, busy at lunchtime; nr Weston Park in attractive area *(Mr and Mrs R Tod, B H Pinsent, AE)*

Upton Magna [SJ5512], *Corbet Arms*: Very friendly spacious pub with good range of interesting food *(Gordon Theaker)*

Wellington [Church St; SJ6611], *Charlton Arms*: Nice furnishings including antique carved grandfather clock, friendly atmosphere; courteous, helpful staff, excellent food, reasonable prices; bedrooms comfortable *(Dennys Wheatley)*

Wem [High St; SJ5128], *Castle*: Good old smart pub with pleasant atmosphere and popular bar meals; Wem ales on electric pump *(Dr and Mrs C D E Morris)*

Wentnor [SO3893], *Crown*: Friendly and welcoming atmosphere, good food in bar and restaurant including good choice for vegetarians, excellent value wines and good coffee, cosy and pleasant dining-room; bedrooms cheap and comfortable, caravan and camping facilities *(Jackie Wynn)*; *Green*: Newish pub in East Onny Valley, comfortable lounge, very good food (not cheap), satisfactory beer; restaurant *(A Royle)*

Whittington [A5; SJ3331], *Olde Boot*: Welcoming pub attractively placed by thirteenth-century castle, good range of bar snacks, Robinsons beer; restaurant; children welcome; bedrooms *(G H Theaker)*

Woore [Nantwich Rd; SJ7342], *Coopers Arms*: Pleasant, comfortable pub decorated with coopers' tools and beer engines; well kept Bass, good bar food and pleasant service *(K G S Adams)*

Somerset and Avon

Several pubs where we welcomed new licensees in the last edition have been going from strength to strength since – the King William in Catcott, the interesting Cat Head at Chiselborough (gaining a place-to-stay award this year, to go with its food award – and the tie has changed from Ushers to Gibbs Mew), the bustling Poachers Pocket in Doulting (good food here too), and the unspoilt Ring o' Bells in Hinton Blewett. Licensees have changed yet again at the Ashcott Inn (food's been its main attraction – it's still too early to say whether it's heading back into the top rank, though early indications are promising), and there are new people this year at the Globe in Appley (making cautious changes – determined not to spoil its old-fashioned appeal), the Half Moon at Horsington (mixed reports to start with – but the old team was a very hard act to follow), and the Kings Arms in Montacute (both the civilised atmosphere and the popular cold table are still widely praised by readers). The Boars Head at Aust and Royal Oak at Withypool (which is a nice place to stay at) both gain food awards this year, and the neatly kept Hood Arms at Kilve (good value food) gets a place-to-stay award. Among new entrants, or pubs returning to the main entries after a gap, the Black Horse in Clapton in Gordano impressed us so much with its simple, unforced traditionalism that we were tempted to award it a star right away; the New Inn at Dowlish

The Ship, Porlock

Wake scores highly for food, drink and atmosphere; the Royal Oak at Over Stratton, a very popular food pub, has a stylishly low-key old-fashioned décor; the promise of the magnificent stone frontage doesn't mislead you when you go into the George & Pilgrims in Glastonbury; and the prettily placed Royal Oak at Winsford is good both for food and to stay at. Other pubs to note for food include the Square & Compass at Ashill, the Ralegh's Cross up on the Brendon Hills, the Wheatsheaf at Combe Hay, the Bull Terrier at Croscombe (a nice place to stay in, too – and notable for its wines), the Three Horseshoes at Langley Marsh, the Windbound alone by the Severn at Shepperdine, the Crossways at West Huntspill and the Red Lion at Woolverton. Pick of the area's pubs, with inventive food and a fine atmosphere, is now the Notley Arms in Monksilver, which seems surprisingly unspoiled by its growing fame. In general, it's strong character that tends to mark out most of the county's better pubs, and this is especially so with the Coronation Tap (a Bristol cider house), the rustic King William at Catcott, the Crown at Churchill (a notable collection of real ales), the stylish old Luttrell Arms in Dunster (a fine place to stay at), the Tucker's Grave at Faulkland (its main bar is quite minute), the defiantly basic Rose & Crown at Huish Episcopi, the ancient George at Norton St Philip (more of a sense of age here than at any other pub in the county), the cheerful Ship at the foot of Exmoor in Porlock (good value as a place to stay), the Pack Horse in South Stoke (celebrating its half-millennium this year), and the Greyhound at Staple Fitzpaine. The Lucky Dip pubs at the end of the chapter are particularly well endowed with the stars that show readers' reports suggest special merit. Among them, the most promising seem to be the Princes Motto at Barrow Gurney, White Horse at Exford, Crown at Kelston, Olde Kings Arms at Litton, Hope & Anchor at Midford, George in Nunney, Carpenters Arms at Stanton Wick, White Hart at Trudoxhill and Red Lion at West Pennard; and if you get them on the right day, the Stag at Hinton Charterhouse and Ship at Porlock Weir can be hard to beat. Incidentally, that nice pub the Hop Pole at Limpley Stoke which has featured in previous editions hasn't been dropped; though its postal address does indeed put it in this area, readers' letters have prompted us to look more closely at the map – it's really in Wiltshire, and included now in that chapter.

ALMONDSBURY (Avon)   ST6084 Map 2

Bowl

1¼ miles from M5 junction 16 (and therefore quite handy for M4 junction 20); from A38 towards Thornbury, turn first left signposted Lower Almondsbury, then first right down Sundays Hill, then at bottom right again into Church Road

By the church (in what is now mainly rather a modern village), this tiled white house has a friendly, welcoming atmosphere. The long, neatly kept bar has low beams, most walls stripped to bare stone, traditional black-lacquered built-in seats, mate's chairs, one or two Windsor armchairs, and elm tables; in winter there's a big log fire at one end and a wood-burning stove at the other. Good home-made bar food includes sandwiches (85p), soup (£1), a choice of ploughman's (£1.59), four-ounce burger (£1.65), good mushrooms in garlic sauce, macaroni and leek gratin (£1.70), omelettes (from £2.60), quiche (£3), chilli beef tacos or chicken and ham pie (£3.55), salads (from £3.55) and scampi (£3.75); well kept Courage Bitter, Best and Directors and John Smiths on handpump, some enterprising bottled beers, good value wines, tea or coffee; cribbage (the pub has a hot winter team), fruit machine, maybe piped country and western music. The hanging baskets are very pretty in summer; there are picnic-table sets in front, and a children's play area in the garden behind – though this is not open at quiet times. *(Recommended by J L Cox, A D Jenkins, W A Harbottle, Gwen and Peter Andrews, Tom Evans)*

Courage   Real ale   Meals and snacks (not Sun evening)   Restaurant tel Almondsbury (0454) 612757 (closed Sun and Mon evenings)   Children may be allowed   Open 10.30–2.30, 6–11; closed evening 25 Dec

APPLEY (Somerset)   ST0621   Map 1
Globe

Hamlet signposted from network of back roads between A361 and A38, W of B3187 and W of Milverton and Wellington; OS Sheet 181 reference 072215

An entry corridor in this five-hundred-year-old country pub – largely untouched by the passing of time – leads to a serving-hatch where Ind Coope Burton and Cotleigh Tawny (a local brew) are on handpump. A simple front room has benches and a built-in settle, bare wood tables, beams and a brick floor; the back room has a pool-table (and a big Victorian chromolithograph of 'The Meet of the Four-in-Hand Club' on its white-panelled wall); yet another room has easy chairs and superannuated office chairs. Bar snacks include filled rolls, sandwiches and ploughman's; darts, pool, dominoes, alley skittles and fruit machine. The hilly pastures which surround this maze of twisting lanes are very pretty, and there are seats outside in the garden; the path opposite leads eventually to the River Tone. *(Recommended by Phil and Sally Gorton; more reports please)*

Free house   Licensees A W and E J Burt, R and J Morris   Real ale   Meals (not Mon) and snacks (not Mon lunchtime)   Restaurant tel Greenham (0823) 672327   Children in eating area and restaurant   Open 11–2.30, 6.30–11 all year; closed Mon lunchtime, exc bank hols

ASHCOTT (Somerset)   ST4337   Map 1
Ashcott Inn

A39

This attractive food pub (now part of the small chain of Buccaneer Inns and under a new licensee) is more laid out for eating than for drinking, and has good oak and elm tables, some interesting old-fashioned seats among more conventional ones, beams, stripped stone walls and a gas-effect log fire in its sturdy chimney. Generously served, the food includes soup (£1.25; in winter they do soup and baked potato £2.95), ploughman's (£2.35), macaroni cheese (£2.95), a cold table (from £3.50), steak and kidney pie (£3.95), fresh sardines or parsnips and tomato au gratin (£4.50), seafood pie (£4.75) and whole grilled plaice (£5.35); children's menu (from 75p). Well kept Butcombe Bitter, Flowers Original and monthly guest beers on handpump; shove-ha'penny, a fruit machine, alley skittles and piped music. There are seats on the newly built terrace and in the pretty garden. *(Recommended by Dave Butler, Lesley Storey, K R Harris, John and Pat Smyth, Alan Carr, Margaret and Douglas Tucker, Tom Evans, Paul McPherson, G J Brook)*

Free house   Licensee Thom Carroll   Real ale   Meals and snacks   Restaurant tel Ashcott (0458) 210282   Children in eating area   Open 11–2.30, 5–11 all year

nr ASHILL (Somerset)   ST3217   Map 1
Square & Compass ⊗

Windmill Hill; turn off A358 at Stewley Cross Garage

As we went to press, this comfortable and friendly country pub was up for sale. Upholstered window seats overlook the rolling pastures around Neroche Forest, and it's furnished with brown leatherette armchairs on the brown carpet, there's an open fire in winter, and an extra room for eating. The wide range of home-made, freshly prepared food includes sandwiches, soup (95p), tuna-stuffed peaches

(£1.10), lasagne or savoury pancake (£2.75), salads (from £3.10), local farm trout (from £3.25), fondues (from £3.45 for cheese, £6.25 for steak), pie of the day (£3.50), beef bourguignonne (£4.45), and steaks (from £5.95); also, three vegetarian dishes, daily specials, children's dishes (£1.10), and puddings like home-made cheesecakes or sweet stuffed pancakes (£1.15). Well kept Butcombe on handpump; helpful service. Darts, dominoes, cribbage and piped music. Outside on the grass there are picnic-table sets, a swing, climbing-frame and bright blue hay wagon, and a cook-it-yourself barbecue. There's also a touring caravan site. *(Recommended by the Barrett family, Mrs Crease, PLC, S J Edwards, J E F Rawlins)*

Free house   Real ale   Meals and snacks (not Tues) Children in restaurant and garden Occasional guitar and music nights   Restaurant tel Hatch Beauchamp (0823) 480467 Open 11.30–2.30, 7–11 all year; closed Tues

AUST (Avon)   ST5789 Map 2
Boars Head ⊗

½ mile from M4 junction 21; village signposted from A403

Near the village church – which is unique for being nameless – this friendly, small-roomed village pub has well polished country kitchen tables and others made from old casks, old-fashioned high-backed winged settles in stripped pine, some walls stripped back to the dark stone, big rugs on dark lino, and decorative plates hanging from one stout black beam; the log fire in the main fireplace may, in summer, have a bunch of dried flowers in the opening for its former side bread oven. In another room with a wood-burning stove there's a little parakeet and a pair of gerbils, and a third room has dining-tables. Bar food, all cooked by the landlady, includes soup (£1.25), open sandwiches (from £1.65), toasties from £1.45), ploughman's (from £1.85), pâté (£2.30), a wide choice of filled baked potatoes (from £1.70), lots of omelettes (from £4.25), a tremendous spread of up to thirty help-yourself salads (from £4.25, seafood platter £10.95), and daily specials. The puddings include filled crêpes (from 90p), and children's helpings are available on request. Well kept Courage Best and Directors on handpump. There's a medieval stone well in the pretty and sheltered garden, and a touring caravan site. *(Recommended by D Godden, T H G Lewis, S J Edwards)*

Courage   Licensee Charles Broome   Real ale   Meals and snacks (not Sun)   Children in own room until 9.30   Open 11–3.30, 6–11; closes 10.30 Mon–Thurs

BATH (Avon)   ST7565 Map 2
Bladud Arms

Gloucester Road, Lower Swainswick (A46)

There's a good mix of customers in this friendly and simple pub who enjoy the well kept real ales, cheap and cheerful food, and lively games-room. The reasonably priced beers include Bass, Butcombe, Marstons Pedigree, Wadworths 6X and Whitbreads West Country on handpump. Good value lunchtime food consists of sandwiches (from 70p), giant hot dog (85p), ploughman's (£1.65), ham and egg, curry, chilli con carne or goulash (all £2), salads (from £2), and chicken, scampi or mixed grill (around £2.30). Upstairs or downstairs you can play darts, pool, cribbage, fruit machine, space game, trivia, juke box, piped music, and outside there's a full-scale skittle alley. Furnishings and décor are sensibly simple, including a couple of nice old high-backed settles. You can sit outside in summer. *(Recommended by H P S Forster, Frank W Gadbois, Dr and Mrs A K Clarke)*

Free house   Licensee Meylan Donald   Real ale   Lunchtime snacks (not Sun)   Open 11–3, 6–11 all year

---

Real ale to us means beer which has matured naturally in its cask – not pressurised or filtered.

BRADLEY GREEN (Somerset)   ST2538 Map 1
Malt Shovel 🍺

Pub signposted from A39 W of Bridgwater, near Cannington

Even though this little country pub is popular with locals, there's a warm welcome for visitors too. The main bar has cushioned window seats, sturdy modern winged high-backed settles around wooden tables, some nice modern elm country chairs and little cushioned cask window seats; a black kettle stands on a giant fossil by the wood-burning stove, and there's a tiny red-hessian-walled snug. Good value food includes sandwiches (from 50p, crusty French rolls from 60p), ploughman's (from £1.50), smoked haddock cheesy bake (£1.75), filled baked potatoes (mostly £1.75), salads (from £2.50), home-made pies such as steak and kidney (£2.75), fisherman's (£3.10) or excellent duck (£3.25), scampi (£3), chicken Kiev (£4.25) and steaks (from £5.20); also, starters and puddings chalked up on a blackboard, and children's meals on request. Well kept Butcombe, Wadworths 6X and one guest ale on handpump; faint piped music, and a separate skittle alley. On the grass behind the pub there are picnic-table sets (an adjoining field may be used by touring caravans). West of the pub, Blackmore Farm is a striking medieval building. *(Recommended by Simon Barber, G Jones, Mr and Mrs P A Jones, Tom Evans, Sue Cleasby, Mike Ledger)*

Free house   Licensees Robert and Frances Beverley   Real ale   Meals and lunchtime snacks   Restaurant   Children in eating area of bar   Open 11.30–3, 6.30–11; 11.30–2.30, 7–11 in winter; may open longer in afternoons if trade demands   Bedrooms tel Combwich (0278) 653432 (previously Spaxton (027 867) 332); £14/£22; family-room £32

BRENDON HILLS (Somerset)   ST0434 Map 1
Ralegh's Cross ✕

Junction of B3190 Watchet–Bampton with the unclassified but good E–W summit road from Elworthy to Winsford

Close to the old mineral railway (they have a good collection of photographs of it, running between here and Watchet), this isolated roadside inn is nearly 1200 feet high on the Brendon Hills. From the spacious lawns there are lots of walks, and they hold whippet racing on Sundays in summer. Inside, the spacious bar has little red leatherette armchairs around the tables, button-back banquettes along its strip-panelled walls, and in cool weather a couple of open fires. Good bar food brought to your table includes sandwiches (from 90p), soup (£1.10), pear and walnut starter or pâté (£1.50), omelettes (from £2.30), sausage, egg and bacon (£2.35), ploughman's (£2.50), salads (from £2.50), liver and bacon (£2.55), plaice (£2.80), gammon and pineapple (£3.90), local trout (£3.95), scampi (£4.10), mixed grill or steak (£6.75), with puddings (from £1.05); children's menu (£1.50). Well kept Flowers Original and Golden Hill Exmoor and Exmoor Dark on handpump; gentle piped music. *(Recommended by Richard Gibbs, Brian and Anna Marsden, Gwen and Peter Andrews)*

Free house   Licensees Peter and Elizabeth Nash   Real ale   Meals and snacks   Restaurant; closed Sun   Children in restaurant and family-room   Open 11–11 July–Sept; 10.30–2.30, 6–11 rest of the year; closed Feb   Bedrooms tel Washford (0984) 40343; £15B/£30B

BRISTOL (Avon)   ST5673 Map 2
Coronation Tap

Between Sion Place and Portland Street, Clifton

A stroll away from Clifton Suspension Bridge and at the end of a quiet cul-de-sac, this lively and friendly low-ceilinged little pub sells only ciders and beers, including well kept Courage Best and Directors on handpump; rows of big cider-barrels dominate its otherwise warmly red décor. Bar food includes sandwiches or ploughman's; dominoes and cribbage. *(Recommended by Alan Merricks; more reports please)*

Courage *Real ale* *Meals (lunchtime, not Sun) and snacks (lunchtimes and Mon–Fri evenings)* *Open 11–2.30, 5.30–10.30 (7–11 Fri and Sat evenings)*

CATCOTT (Somerset)   ST3939   Map 1
King William
Village signposted off A39 Street–Bridgwater

This traditional cottagey pub has stone floors with a rug or two, window seats, kitchen and other assorted chairs, and brown-painted built-in and other settles; there are log fires in big stone fireplaces (one with its side bread oven turned into a stone grotto with kitsch figurines), and Victorian fashion plates and other old prints. A large extension at the back includes a new skittle alley and a recently discovered well. Good bar food includes sandwiches (from 70p), home-made soup (£1), filled baked potatoes (£1.30), ploughman's (from £1.75), salads (from £2.50), home-made meat or vegetable lasagne (£2.75), cheese and bacon flan (£2.85), beef curry (£2.95), scampi or home-made seafood pie (£3.20), pork in cider (£5.75), veal paprika (£6.25), duck in orange sauce (£7.85), and puddings (from £1.10). Well kept Bass, Huntsman Dorchester and Royal Oak and Palmers IPA on handpump and good Wilkins farm cider; darts, dominoes, fruit machine and piped music. *(Recommended by Keith Walton, Mr and Mrs John Smyth, Jon Wainwright, S J Edwards, Hilary Roberts)*

Free house *Licensee Michael O'Riordan* *Real ale* *Meals and snacks* *Children welcome* *Open 11.30–3, 6–11 all year*

CHISELBOROUGH (Somerset)   ST4614   Map 1
Cat Head ⊗ 🛏
Village signposted off B3165 between A3088 and A30 W of Yeovil

This striking old place has an old-fashioned atmosphere in the main bar, chairs and settles in Italian tapestry coloured to blend with the honey-coloured velvet curtains, a flagstone floor, and a big solid-fuel stove. This year they've decorated the lavatories. Good, popular bar food, mostly home made and using home-grown vegetables where possible, includes sandwiches (from £1), soup (£1.10), pâté (£1.15), Imam Bayildi (a Turkish dish with aubergine and a spicy filling £1.95), ploughman's (from £1.80), home-made vegetable pie or butter-bean stew (£2.50), home-made fish pie or lasagne (£2.95), moussaka with Greek spices and herbs or ham salad (£3.50), chicken Kiev (£4.95), steaks (from £6.25), and puddings (from £1.10). Sunday roast lunch (main course £3.95). At busy times there may be quite a wait – check if you're at all short of time. Good Gibbs Mew Wiltshire, Salisbury and Bishops Tipple on handpump; rosehip tea is also available; friendly service. Sensibly placed darts, dominoes, cribbage, fruit machine and juke box, and piped music. There is a separate skittle alley, and you can sit outside in an attractive garden with its new borders and plants, looking up to the small surrounding hills. *(Recommended by John Nash, Mrs Mary Hallem, Nigel Paine, Rod and Christine Ward, Margaret Drazin, Phil and Sally Gorton, David and Ann Stranack, Alan and Audrey Chatting)*

Gibbs Mew *Licensees David and Rosemary Bowden* *Real ale* *Meals and snacks (not Mon lunchtime or Sun evening)* *Children in restaurant* *Live music Sat evening every six weeks* *Restaurant; closed Sun evening* *Open 12–2.30, 7–11; closed Mon lunchtimes* *Bedroom tel Chiselborough (093 588) 231; £13.50/£20*

If a pub is on or near one of the walks described in *Holiday Which? Good Walks Guide*, also published by Consumers' Association, we mention this – giving the walk's number.

CHURCHILL (Avon)   ST4560   Map 1
Crown

Skinners Lane; in village, turn off A368 at Nelson Arms

A good range of well kept real ales is stocked in this rather stylish rambling old cottage: a nice light but well hopped bitter brewed for the pub by Cotleigh, plus Cotleigh Tawny, Felinfoel Double Dragon, Fullers London Pride, Marstons Pedigree, Oakhill Farmers, Stout (under some top pressure), and Titanic – four on handpump, with others tapped from casks at the back. There's a lively local atmosphere, well crafted seats (some built in), stone or slate floors, neat steps between the small rooms, and a log fire in one big stone fireplace. Lunchtime bar food includes a home-made soup, ploughman's, baked potatoes and steak and kidney pudding; there are picnic-table sets on a smallish back lawn, and the pub is near the start of *Good Walks Guide* Walk 1. *(Recommended by Anne Morris, Frank Cummins; more reports please)*

Free house   Real ale   Meals and snacks   Open 11–2.30, 6–11 all year

CLAPTON IN GORDANO (Avon)   ST4773   Map 1
Black Horse

4 miles from M5 junction 19; A368 towards Portishead, then B3124 towards Clevedon; village signposted in North Weston, then in village turn right at Clevedon, Clapton Wick signpost

Unchanging and unspoilt, this friendly tucked-away pub dates from the fourteenth century – though it's the early years of this century that it recalls inside. The main room, partly flagstoned and partly red tiled, has winged settles around narrow tables, no fewer than three competing wall clocks, a big log fire, and lots of cigarette cards. An inner snug has high-backed settles – one a marvellous carved and canopied creature, another with an art nouveau copper insert reading *East, West, Hame's Best* – lots of mugs hanging from its black beams, lots of little prints and photographs, and a window still barred from the days when this room was the petty-sessions jail. The separate games-room has darts, pool, dominoes and cribbage, and there are old rustic tables out on the flagstones in front of the very prettily flower-decked white house, with more behind. The garden has swings and a climber. Bar food includes soup (£1) and a few hot dishes such as quiche or steak and kidney pie (£2.25); well kept Courage Bitter and Best, tapped from the cask. Paths from here lead up Naish Hill or along to Cadbury Camp. *(Recommended by Steve and Carolyn Harvey, Tom Evans, William Meadon, Richard Steel)*

Courage   Licensee R A Womersley   Real ale   Meals (lunchtime, not Sun) and snacks   Children welcome   Open 11–2.30 (3 Fri and Sat in summer), 6–11 all year

COMBE HAY (Avon)   ST7354   Map 2
Wheatsheaf ⊗

Village signposted from A367 or B3110 S of Bath

Set into the wall of the front bar is a worn stone coat of arms, probably of the Hungerford family, found when the fireplace was opened up some ten years ago. The low-ceilinged, attractive rooms have a welcoming atmosphere, brown-painted settles, pews and rustic tables, a very high-backed winged settle facing one big log fire, old sporting and other prints, and earthenware jugs on the shelf of the little shuttered windows. A wide choice of very good food includes such dishes as home-made tomato and herb soup (£1.25), garlic mushrooms (£1.95), ploughman's (£1.50), quiche and salad (£1.95), vegetable chilli or hot-pot (£2), chilli con carne (£2.50), squid and prawn vinaigrette (£3.25), braised lamb chop or chicken chasseur (£3.50), whole pigeon in red wine sauce or pork chop in orange sauce

(£3.75), vast gammon steak with pineapple, and a selection of fish specials like lovely Cheddar-baked lemon sole or scallops in white wine (£3.50) and whole fresh crab (£5.50). Well kept Courage Best and Directors tapped from the cask; courteous, friendly staff; shove-ha'penny. There's a couple of friendly dogs. Tables outside on the spacious sloping lawn, perched on the side of a steep wooded valley, look down past the enterprising plunging garden to the church and ancient manor stables. (*Recommended by S J A Velate, Steve and Carolyn Harvey, M A and W R Proctor, Donald Godden, R Baskerville, Miss J Vincent, Wilfred Plater-Shellard*)

Courage   Licensee M G Taylor   Real ale   Meals and snacks   Restaurant tel Bath (0225) 833504   Children welcome   Open 11–11 all year

CROSCOMBE (Somerset)   ST5844 Map 2
Bull Terrier ⊗ ⇐

A371 Wells –Shepton Mallet

By a medieval cross, this welcoming and neatly kept old village pub has a good range of well kept beers such as Butcombe, Greene King Abbot, Palmers IPA and Bull Terrier Best Bitter (a strongish beer brewed for the pub) on handpump, as well as several wines both by the glass and by the bottle. Very good bar food includes sandwiches (from 75p, steak bap £2.95), soup (£1.05), basket meals (from £1.45, scampi £3.15), salads (from £2.25, home-cooked roast beef £4.25), spaghetti bolognese (£2.75), vegetarian lasagne (£2.90), Brazilnut loaf (£3.15), home-made oriental chicken (£3.25), home-made steak and kidney pie (£3.30, one reader thought it was the best he'd ever eaten), home-made red-hot beef (£3.50), Barnsley chop (£3.95), trout and almonds (£4.25), and steaks; lovely puddings. Dominoes, chess, cribbage and piped music. The lounge has cushioned wooden wall seats and wheel-back chairs around neat glossy tables, a red carpet on its flagstone floor, pictures on its white walls, attractively moulded beams, and a log-effect gas fire in a big stone fireplace with a fine iron fireback. A communicating room has more tables with another gas-effect log fire, and there's a third in the parquet-floored 'Common Bar', by the local noticeboard. (*Recommended by Dr F Peters, Brian and Jenny Seller, Donald Godden, Mrs V Thomas, Major and Mrs D R C Woods, Margaret and Douglas Tucker, Virginia Maner, N A Wood*)

Free house   Licensees Mr and Mrs S A Lea   Real ale   Meals and snacks (not Sun evenings or Mon, winter)   Children in family-room   Open 12–2.30, 7–11; closed Mon 1 Nov–31 Mar Bedrooms tel Wells (0749) 3658; £11/£28B

DOULTING (Somerset)   ST6443 Map 2
Poachers Pocket ⊗

Follow Chelynch signpost off A361 in village, E of Shepton Mallet

One leading light in the catering trade felt his quick lunchtime stop at this little pub had in itself made buying the *Guide* worthwhile. There's an especially warm and friendly atmosphere, as well as flagstones by the bar counter (though it's mainly carpeted), a few black beams, stools, small wheel-back or captain's chairs, and one or two settles around the tables, gundog pictures on the white walls, and a log fire in the end stripped-stone wall; as we went to press an extension was being added to the bar. Very good, popular food (in generous helpings) includes sandwiches (from 95p), pâté or egg mayonnaise (£1.05), ploughman's (from £1.70), home-made quiche Lorraine (£2.35), cauliflower cheese (£2.65), delicious home-made steak and kidney pie with good chips or home-cooked ham (£2.65), scampi (£3.05), and pan-fried steak (£4.45); an evening charcoal grill serves a selection of pork chops and lamb cutlets (£4), gammon steak and pineapple (£4.30) and steaks (from £6); puddings range from sherry trifle or cheesecake (£1.05) to meringue surprise (£1.45). Well kept Butcombe Bitter and Wadworths 6X and Farmers Glory on handpump. *(Recommended by Ted George, Barry and Anne, D J Wallington, Pamela and Merlyn Horswell)*

Free house   Licensees Derrick and Margaret Taylor   Real ale   Meals and snacks (not Mon lunchtime)   Children welcome   Open 11.30–2.30, 6.15–11; closed Mon lunchtime

DOWLISH WAKE (Somerset)   ST3713 Map 1
New Inn ⊗

Village signposted from Kingstone – which is signposted from A303 on W side of Ilminster, and from A3037 just S of Ilminster; keep on past church – pub at far end of village

With most of the pubs we visit, however good they are, it's clear to us that they'll appeal much more to some readers than to others. It's rare to find a pub – particularly a smallish one – that seems bound to please everyone. This is one that really should do just that, with good food, good drink, distinctive old-fashioned décor, spotless cleanliness and an interested, hospitable landlord. The Swiss landlady does the cooking: besides bar food that includes sandwiches (from 85p), soup (£1.15), ploughman's (from £1.75), ham and egg (£2.15), omelettes (from £2.25) and sirloin steak (£5.75), she's praised for dishes such as squid or grilled sardines (£2), raclette (£4.50), duck and pigeon breast (£6.50) and crab thermidor (£6.75). There are attractive sturdy tables with a mixture of chairs and high-backed settles under the dark beams, which are strung liberally with hop-bines; the stone inglenook fireplace has a wood-burning stove. Besides well kept Butcombe, Theakstons Old Peculier and Wadworths 6X on handpump (a well matched trio), and a decent choice of whiskies, there's a selection of Perry's ciders. These come from just down the road, and the thatched sixteenth-century stone cider mill is well worth a visit for its collection of wooden bygones and its liberal free tastings (you can buy the half-dozen different ciders in old-fashioned earthenware flagons as well as more modern containers; it's closed on Sunday afternoons). There may be piped music, and in a separate area they have darts, shove-ha'penny, dominoes, table skittles as well as alley skittles and a fruit machine. There's a rustic bench in front of the stone pub, which is decorated with tubs of flowers and a sprawl of clematis. *(Recommended by Richard Dolphin, Brian and Pam Cowling, Jonathan and Helen Palmer, Mr and Mrs J Holden)*

Free house   Licensees Therese Boosey and David Smith   Real ale   Meals and snacks (table bookings tel Ilminster (0460) 52413)   Children in new garden-room   Open 11–2.30, 6–11 all year; 11–11 July–Sept, at least on Sat

DUNSTER (Somerset)   SS9943 Map 1
Luttrell Arms ⊨

A396

Firmly based on a great hall built for the Abbot of Cleeve five hundred years ago, this imposing building (now a comfortably modernised THF hotel) was altered during Tudor times and again around 1600. It's kept a lot of character, especially in the the back bar where there are old settles as well as more modern furniture, bottles, clogs and horseshoes hanging from the high beams, and a stag's head and rifles on the walls. Ancient black timber uprights glazed with fine hand-floated glass, full of ripples and irregularities, separate the room from a small galleried and flagstoned courtyard. Good bar snacks include an attractive cold buffet, plaice and a speciality mixed grill, as well as unusual evening meals; well kept Bass and Golden Hill Exmoor on handpump. The town, on the edge of Exmoor National Park, is pretty. *(Recommended by Mr and Mrs W A Rinaldi-Butcher, Wayne Brindle, Michael and Alison Sandy)*

Free house (THF)   Managers Mr and Mrs R A Mann   Real ale   Meals and snacks Restaurant   Open 11–2.30, 6–11 all year   Bedrooms tel Dunster (0643) 821555; £50B/£70

EAST LYNG (Somerset)   ST3328   Map 1
Rose & Crown
A361 about 4 miles W of Othery

A friendly and relaxing retreat from the trunk road, this charming pub has good, freshly prepared food such as sandwiches (from 85p; steak £2.40), soup (£1.10), pâté (£1.45), ploughman's (from £1.95), home-cooked ham and egg (£2.30), excellent liver and bacon (£2.45), omelettes (£2.50), salads (£3.10), scampi or trout (£3.95), steaks (from £5.75), mixed grill (£6.25), and puddings like delicious apple crumble (from £1.10). Well kept Butcombe, Devenish Royal Wessex, Palmers IPA and Huntsman Royal Oak on handpump. Beamed and open-plan, the big lounge bar has traditional furnishings such as a corner cabinet of glass, china and silver, a court cabinet, a winter log fire in a modernised fine old stone fireplace, and stacks of old copies of *Country Life* on a bow window seat by an oak drop-leaf table; piped music. The prettily planted back garden (largely hedged off from the car park) has picnic-table sets, and there's also a full skittle alley. They're pleased with the way their new, intimate little restaurant has turned out. *(Recommended by Alan Carr, J Harvey Hallam, D Goodger)*

Free house   Licensee P J Thyer   Real ale   Meals and snacks   Restaurant tel Taunton (0823) 69235; not Sun lunchtime   Children in eating area of bar and restaurant   Open 10.30–2.30, 6.30–11 all year

FAULKLAND (Somerset)   ST7354   Map 2
Tucker's Grave
A366 E of village

The flagstoned entry into this roadside farm cottage – the smallest pub in the *Guide* – opens into a tiny room with casks of well kept Bass and Butcombe Bitter on tap and Cheddar Valley cider in an alcove on the left. Two old cream-painted high-backed settles face each other across a single table on the right, and a side room has shove-ha'penny. There's a skittle alley, and seats outside. *(Recommended by Roger Huggins, Ewan McCall, Tom McLean, Phil and Sally Gorton)*

Free house   Licensees Ivan and Glenda Swift   Real ale   Open 11–2.30, 6–11 all year

GLASTONBURY (Somerset)   ST5039   Map 2
George & Pilgrims
High Street

Built in the 1470s by the Abbot of Glastonbury, chiefly for pilgrims, this inn has a remarkable carved stone façade very handsomely restored by the brewery. The comfortably modernised lounge bar has some traditional oak seats, sporting prints and a log-effect gas fire, though probably the nicest place to sit is in the great fifteenth-century traceried bay window. Good bar food includes soup (from 95p), excellent sandwiches (from 95p), quiche Lorraine (£1.10), ploughman's (from £1.50), salads (from £2.80), scampi (£3.10), puddings (around £1.25), and daily specials such as Cumbrian stew (£2.75) and trout (£3.20). Well kept Bass on handpump. One cornice shield has the intertwined initials I S (no 'J' in Latin) for John of Selwood, the abbot. *(Recommended by Mea Horler, Joy Heatherley, S V Bishop)*

Bass (part tie only)   Licensee Jack Richardson   Real ale   Meals and snacks   Children in restaurant and abbot's parlour   Restaurants   Open 10–2.30, 6–11 all year; probably open all day Sat   Bedrooms tel Glastonbury (0458) 31146; £36B/£48B

Please keep sending us reports. We rely on readers for news of new discoveries, and particularly for news of changes – however slight – at the fully described pubs. No stamp needed: The Good Pub Guide, FREEPOST, London SW10 0BR.

HINTON BLEWETT (Avon)   ST5957   Map 2
Ring o' Bells

Village signposted from A37 in Clutton

Tables and chairs in the sheltered front yard outside this stone-built village pub, with pretty hanging baskets and window boxes in summer, look over the quiet road to rolling fields and hedgerows. Inside, the simply but comfortably furnished bar has red plush button-back wall banquettes, round stools, shiny brasses on the low black beams that support its white ceiling-planks, and perhaps Smokie the collie. Reasonably priced and well kept Wadworths Devizes and 6X on handpump, and good ploughman's (£1.95), steak and kidney pie (£3.45) or gammon steak (£4.45). The dining area doubles as a family-room; shove-ha'penny, dominoes, cribbage and piped music. *(Recommended by T H G Lewis; more reports please)*

Wadworths   Licensee Christopher Greaves   Real ale   Meals and snacks (not Sun evening) Restaurant tel Temple Cloud (0761) 52239; closed Sun evening   Children welcome Open 11–2.30, 6–11 all year

HORSINGTON (Somerset)   ST7023   Map 2
Half Moon

Village signposted off A357 S of Wincanton

This listed building (under new owners) has been licensed since 1725, and before that was a slaughterhouse – as you go in look out for traces of what used to be the chimney of the smoking chamber used then. The knocked-through beamed bars have wheel-back chairs, one or two pews and cushioned window seats around neat tables, good log fires in big stone fireplaces at either end, and maybe Robby the young black labrador or Khan the large white cat; decorations include blown-up old photographs of New South Wales forestry, Victorian chromolithographs, gin-traps, and thatching or forestry tools on the stripped stone walls. Bar food includes sandwiches, garlic mushrooms, steak and kidney pie, turkey or vegetable curry (£3.75), Spanish pork, beef Stroganoff or plaice in mushroom sauce (£3.95), prawn curry (£4.25), a weekend carvery, and a cold display in summer. Well kept Butcombe, Golden Hill Exmoor and Wadworths 6X on handpump; fruit machine and piped pop music. There are picnic-table sets on the raised front lawn, with more tables in a bigger garden behind, which has barbecues in summer and a children's play area with a large wooden fort, swing and slide. Four of the seven bedrooms are in a recently converted ancient stableblock behind. *(Recommended by Nigel Paine, MM; more reports on the new regime please)*

Free house   Licensees Philip and Valerie Bobby   Real ale   Meals and snacks   Restaurant Children welcome   Live music planned   Bedrooms tel Templecombe (0963) 70140; £17(£22B)/£28(£32B)   Open 11–11 July–Sept; 11–2.30, 6–11 in winter

HUISH EPISCOPI (Somerset)   ST4326   Map 1
Rose & Crown

A372 E of Langport

Readers who love this pub as a last bastion against the incursions of spray-on cleanliness, plush banquettes and plastic plants by the yard will have shivered when they heard of plans for refurbishment. Rest assured: it's just a matter of painting (first outside, then here and there inside). Otherwise, this continues proudly as before, with its engaging rough-and-ready attitude to creature comforts. The pub has been in the family of the present licensee for 120 years or more, and, as you can see from the Sturgeon print in one front room, the pub hasn't changed externally much over the years, either. To get a drink, you just walk into the central flagstoned still-room and choose from the casks of well kept Bass and Butcombe or the wide choice of Somerset farm ciders and country wines which stand on ranks of shelves around it; prices are very low. This servery is the only thoroughfare between the casual little front parlours, with their unusual pointed-arch windows, old rugs on stone floors, and seats which are inching into decrepitude. Food is simple and cheap: assorted rolls (weekends only, 40p), sandwiches (from 60p, toasties from 70p), beans on toast (70p), soup (75p), ploughman's (£1.20), and home-made Scotch eggs using their own free-range eggs. There's a fruit machine in one of the front rooms, and shove-ha'penny, dominoes and cribbage are available. A much more orthodox big back extension family-room has darts, pool, fruit machine and juke box; there's a skittle alley. Outside, there's now a lawn and new tables. *(Recommended by the Barrett family, Mrs Crease, Gordon and Daphne, Phil and Sally Gorton, Professor A N Black, Roger Huggins)*

Free house   Licensee Mrs Eileen Pittard   Real ale   Snacks   Children welcome   Impromptu live music   Open 11–2.30, 5.30–11 all year

KILVE (Somerset)   ST1442   Map 1
Hood Arms ⊗ ⇦

A39 E of Williton

Very good and generously served home-made food, comfortable bedrooms and a tremendously friendly atmosphere continue to draw readers to this well run village inn. Food at lunchtime includes sandwiches (from 75p), good soup (£1), pâté (£1.10), good ploughman's (from £1.85), enormous salads (from £1.95), hot daily specials such as country-style chicken, steak and kidney pie, smoked salmon quiche or cauliflower, celery and Stilton bake (all £2.95), grilled local trout (£3.25), and puddings (from £1.10); in the evenings the main bar takes on much more the style of a restaurant, with full meals. Well kept Flowers IPA and Original on handpump; dominoes, cribbage, pool, alley skittles and gentle piped music. The carpeted main bar is straightforwardly comfortable and there's a wood-burning stove in the stone fireplace (decorated with shining horsebrasses on their original leathers). It leads through to a little cosy lounge with red plush button-back seats. A sheltered back terrace, by a garden with a prettily planted old wall behind, has white metal and plastic seats and tables. *(Recommended by Mrs J M Gillman, David and Ruth Hollands, Derek and Jennifer Taylor, W G Davis, SC, T H G Lewis, R M Pearson, Ian Blackwell, A B and K H Cutting, Anne Morris, Michael Thomson)*

Free house   Licensees Robbie Rutt and Neville White   Real ale   Meals and snacks Restaurant; closed Sun   Children in restaurant   Open 10.30–2.30, 6–11 all year Bedrooms tel Holford (027 874) 210; £24B/£40B

LANGLEY MARSH (Somerset)   ST0729   Map 1
Three Horseshoes ★ ⊗

Village signposted off A361 from Wiveliscombe

The two rooms of this friendly, well run pub with its imaginative home cooking and good range of well kept real ales, give a choice between comfort in the back bar (low modern settles, polished wooden tables with plants, dark red wallpaper, a piano, a local stone fireplace, banknotes papering the wall behind the bar and planes hanging from the ceiling), and the lively front room with sensibly placed darts, shove-ha'penny, table skittles, dominoes, cribbage, fruit machine and piped music. Good value and entirely fresh food from a constantly changing and imaginative menu includes baps (from 90p), home-made soup (£1.25), ploughman's (from £1.65), butter-bean bourguignonne (£2.45), salads (from £2.65), lovely courgette and mushroom bake or Mexican taco shells (£2.95), fish pie with

---

Pubs with outstanding views are listed at the back of the book.

perfect pastry (£3.25), and beef Stroganoff (£3.45); no chips or fried food; puddings include good mincemeat, apple and brandy pancakes or excellent cheesecake with cherry topping. Well kept Adnams, Badger Tanglefoot, Bass, Cotleigh Tawny, brewed down the road in Wiveliscombe, Fullers London Pride, and Palmers IPA on handpump or tapped from the cask; the guest ales change continually. Quick, attentive service. This year they've added a skittle alley and functions room. You can sit on rustic seats on the verandah or in the sloping back garden, with a climbing-frame, swing and slide, maybe the pub Alsatian (Guinness), and a view of farmland. (*Recommended by Heather Sharland, J L Simpson, S Matthews, D Stephenson, Mr and Mrs D A P Grattan, M C Howells, David and Ruth Hollands, Frank Cummins*)

Free house   Licensee J Hopkins   Real ale   Meals and snacks   Children in dining-room and area set aside for them   Singalongs Sat evenings and occasional spontaneous 'fiddle/squeeze-box' sessions with local morris dancing musicians   Open 11–11 in summer for trial period; probably 12–2.30, 6–11 in winter

MONKSILVER (Somerset)   ST0737   Map 1
Notley Arms ★ ⊗
B3188

One reader feels this pub has got better and better in the seven years he's been coming here – as he says, a very rare occurrence these days. 'Refreshingly different' and 'original' is how several people describe the very good food that changes frequently; regular dishes include soup (£1), sandwiches (from 80p), filled baked potatoes (from £1.65), ploughman's (from £1.85), shepherd's purse (wholemeal pitta bread generously filled with garlicky lamb and salad, £1.75), home-made pasta or vegetarian curry (£2.75), lovely salads (local cured ham £3.50), superb Chinese-style pork with stir-fry vegetables (£4.25), and correctly cooked vegetables; puddings like stunning nectarine cheesecake (£1.20), and evening extras such as fresh local trout (£3.75) and sirloin steak (£6). Well kept Ushers Best and Ruddles County on handpump, and country wines such as rhubarb or raspberry; hard-working, efficient and cheerful staff. The L-shaped beamed bar has a relaxing, friendly atmosphere, and small settles and kitchen chairs around the plain country wooden and candle-lit tables, Old Master and other prints on the black-timbered white walls, and a couple of wood-burning stoves; dominoes and alley skittles, well reproduced classical music, and a bright little family-room; dogs welcome. The charming cottage garden behind this quiet village inn runs down to a swift clear stream. (*Recommended by PLC, Margaret Mawson, David and Ruth Hollands, Wayne Brindle, D H, M C Watkinson, Heather Sharland, Richard Dolphin, M W Barratt, Mr and Mrs R Gammon, M E Dormer, Mr and Mrs W A Rinaldi-Butcher, Joy Heatherley, SC, Mrs J Richards, P and H B, Frank Cummins, Mr and Mrs R Tod, Sally Watson*)

Ushers   Licensee Alistair Cade   Real ale   Meals and snacks   Children in own room   Open 11–2.30, 6–11 all year; closed 25 Dec

MONTACUTE (Somerset)   ST4951   Map 2
Kings Arms ⊗

It's rewarding to find a place that appeals to the most civilised tastes, and yet which still manages to preserve a genuinely friendly atmosphere. The new licensees have not changed the bar food much; it still includes soup with home-made bread (95p), a very good value, popular buffet, and daily specials such as steak and kidney pie, chicken chasseur or ham and asparagus bake (£3.45 or £3.95); best to book for Sunday lunch (when people tend to dress smartly). The comfortable lounge bar has grey-gold plush seats, soft armchairs, chintz sofas, a high curved settle, and towards the front – where parts of the walls are stripped back to the handsome masonry – plush seats around tables; Bass and Gibbs Mew Salisbury tapped from the cask.

The village includes the stately Elizabethan mansion of the same name, and behind the hotel the wooded St Michael's Hill is owned by the National Trust. (*Recommended by D K and H M Brenchley, G and S L, the Barrett family and Mrs Crease, C H Beaumont, Gwen and Peter Andrews, Margaret Drazin, Cecil Eimerl, J E F Rawlins, Mrs Anne Fowler*)

Free house   Licensee S D Price   Real ale   Meals and snacks   Children in eating area of bar Restaurant   Open 11–2.30, 6–11 all year; closed 25 Dec and evening of 26 Dec   Bedrooms tel Martock (0935) 822513; £38B/50B

NORTON ST PHILIP (Somerset)   ST7755   Map 2

George

A366

It's the building itself which makes this pub worth visiting: high mullioned windows, massive stone walls, wide bare floorboards, lofty beams hung with harness and copper preserving pans, and the charming half-timbered and galleried back courtyard – which has an external Norman stone stair-turret (and maybe a young tame jackdaw). Furnishings are simple, with plain old tables, leather seats, square-panelled wooden settles, and a long, stout table that serves well kept Bass, and Wadworths Devizes and 6X from handpump. Bar food includes sandwiches, ploughman's, and a couple of daily specials. A panelled lounge is furnished with antique settles and tables. Off the courtyard is the cellar Dungeon Bar (opened only at busy times), named to recall the men imprisoned there after the rebel Duke of Monmouth had been defeated. A stroll over the meadow behind the pub leads to an attractive churchyard around the medieval church whose bells struck Pepys (here on 12 June 1668) as 'mighty tuneable'. (*Recommended by Roger Huggins, Ewan McCall, Tom McLean, Gary, C Elliott; more reports please*)

Wadworths   Licensee M F Moore   Real ale   Snacks   Children in eating area of bar and in two family-rooms   Restaurant tel Faulkland (037 387) 224; closed Sun evening Open 11–2.30 (4 Sat), 6–11 all year

OLDBURY-UPON-SEVERN (Avon)   ST6292   Map 2

Anchor ⊗

Village signposted from B4061

This neat and attractively modernised village pub has a good selection of well kept beers such as Bass, Butcombe, Marstons Pedigree and Theakstons Best on handpump, or tapped straight from the cask. Popular food includes soup (95p), quiche Lorraine (£2.30), very good steak and kidney pie or mushroom and nut fettuccine (£2.75), locally made pork and garlic sausages or vegetable curry (£2.95), chicken marengo (£3.05), prawn and apricot curry or lamb kebab (£3.25), gammon with pineapple (£4.50), sirloin steak (£5.45), and puddings (from £1.05). The beamed lounge is comfortably furnished with cushioned window seats, a curved high-backed settle facing an attractive oval oak gate-leg table, winged seats against the wall, easy chairs, and a big log fire in winter. Darts, shove-ha'penny, dominoes and cribbage. You can sit outside in the garden in summer. St Arilda's church nearby is interesting, on its odd little knoll with wild flowers among the gravestones, and there are lots of paths over the meadows to the sea dyke or warth which overlooks the tidal flats. (*Recommended by PLC, W D Horsfield, Pamela and Merlyn Horswell, John and Joan Wyatt, Tom Evans, Adrian Kelly, W A Harbottle; more reports please*)

Free house   Licensee Peter Riley   Real ale   Meals and snacks   Children in dining-room Open 11.30–2.30 (3 Sat), 6.30–11 all year

Pubs with particularly interesting histories, or in unusually interesting buildings, are listed at the back of the book.

OVER STRATTON (Somerset)   ST4315 Map 1

Royal Oak ⊗

Village signposted off A303 Yeovil–Ilminster

The spacious series of dark-flagstoned rooms in this popular sixteenth-century thatched food pub has been simply but carefully decorated and furnished to give a relaxed, old-fashioned feel. The beams have been prettily stencilled with an oakleaf and acorn pattern, and where walls aren't stripped to bare stonework they've been attractively ragrolled red. Most of the tables are scrubbed deal farmhouse kitchen ones, with a mixture of similar or dining-chairs, pews and settles. There are candles in bottles, plants in the windows, log fires (even in summer), some hop-bines, a stuffed pheasant, and maybe unobtrusive piped music. Bar food includes soup (£1.35), salads (from £2.75), squid (£2.95), chicken, Brie and ham pasty (£3.25), smoked goose (£3.45), filled pancakes (from £3.45), home-made burgers (£3.95), steak and kidney pie (£4.75), lamb kebabs (£5.45), scampi-stuffed chicken (£6.25) and steaks (from ten-ounce rump £6.95), with children's dishes (from £1.50). Well kept Boddingtons, Butcombe and a guest beer such as Wadworths 6X on handpump, and an extensive wine list. There are lots of picnic-table sets on a floodlit reconstituted-stone terrace sheltered by the back wings of the building, with more on a further sheltered gravel terrace with a barbecue; the play area is large and well equipped – there's even a big trampoline. *(Recommended by Alison Grenville, Sue Hallam, Dr and Mrs A K Clarke, Richard Dolphin, the Barrett family, Mrs Crease, C R and M Southcombe)*

Free house   Licensees Derek and Claire Blezard   Real ale   Meals and snacks   Restaurant tel Ilminster (0460) 40906   Children in restaurant   Open 12–3, 6.30–11 all year

PORLOCK (Somerset)   SS8846 Map 1

Ship ★ ⇐ *[illustrated on page 567]*

A39

Smart and comfortable as a place to stay, this also scores as an unpretentious pub, popular with locals. It's a partly thirteenth-century thatched village cottage set at the foot of Porlock Hill – which from here climbs over six-hundred feet to the Exmoor plateau in little more than half a mile. The low-beamed front bar has an inglenook fireplace at each end, traditional old benches on the tiled and flagstoned floor, and hunting prints on the walls. Good generous bar food includes home-made soup (80p), sandwiches (from 90p, including fresh prawn), generous plough-man's or ham and egg (£1.75), plaice (£2.50) and a range of daily specials like pheasant or venison casserole or dressed crab and king prawns (£3.50); the dining-room has a spit roast and grill; good breakfasts. Well kept Bass, Cotleigh Old Buzzard, and Courage Best on handpump; good local cider. The carpeted back lounge room has plush red banquettes, a Gothic settle and a chimney seat; shove-ha'penny, dominoes, cribbage, bar billiards, and fruit machine, a separate pool-room (which has sensibly placed darts too in winter), and a full skittle alley. You can sit in the extended back garden, which is almost higher than the roof, with lovely views of the sea and moor; there's a children's play area. *(Recommended by Alan and Ruth Woodhouse, Wayne Brindle, Brian and Anna Marsden, Anthony Sargent, Sally Watson, Mark Walpole, Melanie Byrne, WHBM, BJN, W A Rinaldi-Butcher, Paul McPherson, Neil and Debbie Hayter, Stanley Faulkner, David and Ruth Hollands, Mrs Jenny Seller, Michael and Alison Sandy)*

Free house   Licensee C M Robinson   Real ale   Meals and snacks   Children welcome Restaurant   Open 10.30–2.45, 5.30–11 all year   Bedrooms tel Porlock (0643) 862507; £14.50(£18.50B)/£29(£33B)

Real ale to us means beer which has matured naturally in its cask – not pressurised or filtered.

SHEPPERDINE (Avon)   ST6295 Map 4

Windbound

From B4061 just N of Thornbury turn off at Oldbury signpost, then right at Shepperdine signpost, then next left into Shepperdine Lane; some maps and signposts spell it Sheperdine

On the sheltered fairy-lit lawn outside this extended pub there are picnic-table sets among brightly coloured summer flowers, swings and slides, and more seats up on the dyke; you can walk along the banks of the Severn Estuary to Sharpness. It's the spacious and recently refurbished upper dining-lounge, laid out rather as a restaurant, which has extensive views over the water to the hills beyond; the downstairs bar is below the level of the sea dyke; this lower bar (which is to be refurbished later this year) has dining-chairs and straight-backed small settles forming booths around the tables, one or two local watercolours and prints with the wicker fish-traps on its walls, cheerful service, a good fire in winter, and maybe piped airport-ish music. Bar food includes sandwiches (from 80p), home-made soup (85p), ploughman's (from £1.75), cold home-cooked ham (£2.75), omelettes or salads (from £2.75), a home-made vegetarian dish (£3.50), grilled lamb kebabs (£4.25), duck with orange sauce (£5.75), steaks (from £5.95), and puddings (from £1.50); also daily specials, a children's menu (£1.50), Sunday lunch (£3.75), afternoon teas from June to September, and barbecues in fine weather. Darts, dominoes, cribbage and a separate skittle alley. Ind Coope Burton, Smiles, Tetleys, Wadworths 6X and guest beers on handpump. It's popular with older people on weekday lunchtimes, though there's a much wider range of customers at weekends. *(Recommended by Gwen and Peter Andrews, Julian Jewitt, John Bell, Tom Evans)*

Halls (Ind Coope)   Licensee Neil France   Real ale   Meals and snacks   Restaurant tel Thornbury (0454) 414343; open noon–9pm Sun   Children in area partly set aside for them Live music Sat evening   Open 11–11 weekdays (until 1am Sat – supper licence); 11–3, 7–11 in winter

SOUTH STOKE (Avon)   ST7461 Map 2

Pack Horse

Village signposted opposite the Cross Keys off B3110, leaving Bath southwards – just before end of speed limit

In 1989 this unspoilt, three-gabled old stone house will be celebrating its five-hundredth year with lots of events – as we went to press we had no further details, but anyone interested can write to them for dates. The main room, popular with locals, has rough black shutters for the stone-mullioned windows, a heavy black beam and plank ceiling, antique oak settles (two well carved), leatherette dining-chairs and cushioned captain's chairs on the quarry-tiled floor, a cheery log fire in the handsome stone inglenook, some Royalty pictures and a chiming wall-clock; shove-ha'penny boards are set into two of the tables, and there are darts, dominoes and cribbage. There's another room down to the left. An entrance corridor – actually a public right of way to the church – takes you to a central space by the serving-bar, with well kept Courage Best on handpump and a choice of ciders. Very good value bar food includes home-baked cider ham in rolls (from 60p), home-made pasties (£1), sausage plait (£1.65), ploughman's, home-made lasagne or curries (£1.85), and fresh Cornish mussels (Thursday and Friday £2); friendly staff. The spacious back garden looks out over the stolid old church and the wooded valley. *(Recommended by Nick Dowson, Alison Hayward, Roger Huggins, Ewan McCall, Tom McLean)*

Courage   Licensee Tim Brewer   Real ale   Meals (lunchtime) and snacks   Children in eating area of bar lunchtimes only   Open 10.30–3, 5.30–11 all year

---

Pubs close to motorway junctions are listed at the back of the book.

STAPLE FITZPAINE (Somerset)   ST2618   Map 1
Greyhound

Village signposted from A358 Taunton–Ilminster at Hatch Beauchamp; or (better road) from Shoreditch on B3170, just after crossing M5 S of Taunton

This popular creeper-covered Georgian house has flagstone floors, antique furnishings and log fires. Reasonably priced food includes home-made soup (£1.15), pâté or ploughman's (£1.95), salads (from £2.95), lasagne or vegetable biriani (£3.95), grilled fillet of bream with savoury butter (£4.95), and evening charcoal grills like gigot of lamb (£4.75), kebabs (£4.95) and steaks (from £7.45), with home-made puddings such as treacle tart or profiteroles (from £1.75), Friday summer evening specials like fish or Mexican dishes, and Sunday lunch (£4.95). Well kept Flowers IPA, Golden Hill Exmoor, Huntsman Royal Oak and Whitbreads Strong Country on handpump, with frequent guest beers such as Badger Tanglefoot or Youngs Special, and lots of country wines and a fair number of whiskies. Service is friendly but can be rather slow; piped classical music. There are some seats ouside in front of the pub among troughs of flowers, with more in the gravelled stableyard behind; also, a children's play area with a Wendy house and slide, and a barbecue. Just to the south you can walk in the hillside woods of Neroche Forest, which has a signposted nature trail. *(Recommended by John Tyzack, CED, Patrick Young, H W Clayton, Richard Dolphin, Julie Vincent, PLC, Jane English, Margaret and Douglas Tucker, Della Thompson, Alan and Audrey Chatting, D C Jacobs)*

Free house   Licensees Paul Aiston and David Townsend   Real ale   Meals and snacks   Jazz or occasional rhythm and blues Thurs evenings   Children in garden and eating area Restaurant tel Hatch Beauchamp (0823) 480227   Open 10.30–2.30, 5.30–11 all year; may open longer on weekend afternoons

STOGUMBER (Somerset)   ST0937   Map 1
White Horse

Three generations of one family were made very welcome at this little inn, having travelled on the West Somerset Railway from Minehead to the station a mile or so away. The comfortably furnished long bar has settles and cushioned captain's chairs around the heavy rustic tables on its patterned carpet, a coal fire in cool weather, and a red-tiled floor at one end with old-fashioned built-in settles. Well kept Cotleigh Tawny and Golden Hill Exmoor on handpump and local farm cider. Good food includes sandwiches (from 60p), home-made soup (90p), filled baked potatoes (from £1.10), ploughman's (£1.65), salads (from £1.70), vegetable lasagne (£1.80), liver and bacon (£2.50), steak and kidney pudding (£2.80), chicken with peaches (£3.10), trout (£4.20) and steaks (from £5.75); puddings such as walnut tart or apple crumble (from 85p) and Sunday lunch (£5.70). A side room has sensibly placed darts and a fruit machine; shove-ha'penny, dominoes, cribbage, space game and soothing piped piano and strings music; also, a separate skittle alley. The garden behind is quiet except for rooks and lambs in the surrounding low hills. *(Recommended by K R Harris, Wayne Brindle, Mrs J M Gillman, D Stephenson, M C Howells, Alan Carr, Mr and Mrs P A Jones, David Gaunt, Alan and Audrey Chatting)*

Free house   Licensee Peter Williamson   Real ale   Meals and snacks   Restaurant   Open 11–2.30 (3 Sun), 6–11 all year   Bedrooms tel Stogumber (0984) 56277; £28B

TINTINHULL (Somerset)   ST4919   Map 2
Crown & Victoria

Farm Street; from village, which is signposted off A303, follow signs to Tintinhull House

This comfortable old place has a friendly welcome, low modern settles, Windsor chairs or more old-fashioned higher-backed chairs on the carpet, and a couple of easy chairs by the big winter log fire in one bared stone wall. Food includes sandwiches, lasagne (£2), scampi (£3.25), gammon (£3.75), steaks (from £5.50), and daily specials such as chicken in cream and cider (from £2.75). Well kept Bass, Flowers IPA, Wadworths 6X, Youngs Special on handpump; bar billiards, table skittles, alley skittles, dominoes, cribbage, fruit machine, trivia and piped music. In summer, the big lawn behind the pub is attractive and peaceful with cocktail parasols, white chairs, swings and a goldfish pool set in a rockery; there's a children's play area. Tintinhull House with its beautiful gardens is close by. *(Recommended by the Barrett family, Mrs Crease, E A George, J S Evans, Bernard Phillips, A J Triggle, John Milroy)*

Free house   Licensees Richard and Sherry Knight   Meals and snacks (not Sun)   Children in eating area of bar (ask first)   Open 10.30–2.30, 6–11 all year

TOLLDOWN (Avon)   ST7576 Map 2
Crown

Under 1 mile from M4 junction 18; A46 towards Bath; village not marked on many maps

The two comfortable little bars in this well run Cotswold-stone pub have some heavy beams, a mixture of seats including long cushioned settles and an antique carved armchair, open fires, a dresser with plates in one room, and dominoes, cribbage, darts and a fruit machine. Efficiently served in generous helpings, the lunchtime bar food includes soup (£1.20), ploughman's (£2.50), chicken or cold smoked chicken (£2.60), vegetarian quiche (£2.80), chilli con carne (£3.30) or home-made pies; evening extras include omelettes (£2.80), chicken Kiev (£5), mixed grill (£6) and steaks (£8.30). Well kept Wadworths IPA and 6X on handpump. The fenced-in garden has an equipped play area for children. The National Trust's Dyrham House, with its large deer herd, is situated nearby. *(Recommended by Adrian Kelly, Mrs Margaret Dyke, M G Hart, G S Crockett)*

Wadworths   Licensees John and Pat Collins   Real ale   Meals and snacks   Children in eating area of bar   Open 11–11 in summer; 11–2.30, 6–11 end Oct–Easter   Bedrooms tel Bath (0225) 891231; £14/£28

TORMARTON (Avon)   ST7678 Map 2
Compass

Under 1 mile from M4 junction 18; A46 towards Stroud, then first right turn

The nicest of the various rooms in this well run, busy roadhouse is the light and spacious conservatory with flowers and a few orange and fig trees dotted around the tables; it's attractively lit at night. Home-made bar food includes home-made soup (£1.15), sandwiches (from £1.20), ratatouille au gratin (£2.25), ploughman's (from £2.25), pâté (£2.45), home-made cheese flan (£3.15), home-cooked meats (from £3.45), filled baked potatoes (from £3.85), fresh poached salmon or dressed crab (£4.95), and good puddings (£1.25). Archers Village, Bass and Wadworths 6X on handpump, with maybe mulled wine in winter; darts, dominoes, cribbage, fruit machine and piped music. Outside, the crazy-paved terrace has bright flowers and some stone tables. Badminton and Dodington are close by. *(Recommended by Aubrey and Margaret Saunders, Jenny and Brian Seller, Pamela and Merlyn Horswell, Sue Cleasby, Mike Ledger, Tom Evans, David Regan, Heather Sharland, Wilfred Plater-Shellard, Richard Dolphin)*

Free house   Licensee P Monyard   Real ale   Meals and snacks; limited menu from 2.45–5 Restaurant; closed Sun lunchtime   Children in eating area of bar   Open 11–11 all year Bedrooms tel Badminton (045 421) 242/577; £27.50(£34.95B)/£39.95(£49.95B)

We accept no free drinks or payment for inclusion. We take no advertising, and are not sponsored by the brewing industry – or by anyone else. So all reports are independent.

WELLOW (Avon)   ST7458 Map 2

Fox & Badger

In an attractive village, this fine old stone-built tavern has a lounge bar decorated with curtains to match the cushions of the small winged settles and the seats built into snug alcoves; there's a flagstone floor, a handsome fireplace, flowers on the tables, and a pleasantly chiming clock. Bar food includes sandwiches (from 85p), ploughman's with three cheeses (£2.15), honey-roast ham off the bone and salad (£2.65), steak and kidney pie (£3.15), mixed grill (£4.40), and home-made apple pie (£1.20); there are evening specials (fish on Thursday and steak or kebabs on Saturday), Sunday lunch (£3.15), afternoon teas on Saturday and Sunday in summer, and they'll even make up picnic boxes (£2.50). Well kept Ruddles Best and Ushers Best on handpump. The cosy carpeted public bar has shove-ha'penny, dominoes, a juke box and fruit machine, and there's also a skittle alley. The inn-sign is rather striking, showing the two animals in Regency dress. (*Recommended by S J A Velate, M A and W R Proctor, Roger Huggins*)

Ushers (Watneys)   Licensee Wendy Dymond   Real ale   Snacks (not Sun lunchtime) and meals   Restaurant tel Bath (0225) 832293; closed Sun evening   Well behaved children welcome   Open 11–3, 6–11 weekdays; 11–11 Sat; 11–2.30, 6.30–11 in winter

WEST HUNTSPILL (Somerset)   ST3044 Map 1

Crossways ⊗

2¾ miles from M5 junction 23 (A38 towards Highbridge); 4 miles from M5 junction 22 (A38 beyond Highbridge)

The main area of the rambling bar in this spacious and popular food pub has a mixture of settles, dining-room chairs and seats built into one converted brick fireplace, and good log fires in winter. At one end there's more of a dining-room, with neat red seats, prettily decorated with old farm machinery engravings, Albert and Chic cartoons (chiefly about restaurants), 1920-ish hunting prints, and a brass colonial fan in its dark ceiling (Friday and Saturday bistro menu here). The other end has an area with big winged settles making booths, and there's a family-room with bamboo-back seats around neat tables (and a space game). A wide choice of good food includes various home-made soups (90p), sandwiches (from 90p), pâté (£1.80), ploughman's (from £1.80), prawns by the half-pint (£2.30), salads (from £2.20, cider-baked ham £3.80), quiche Lorraine (£2.50), broccoli, chicken and ham Mornay (£2.80), steak and kidney pie or lasagne (£2.90), deep-fried seafood (£3.20), gammon with egg or pineapple (£3.80), grilled fresh trout (when available, £4), steak (from £5), and daily specials such as ham and mushroom tagliatelle (£2.50) or garlic sausage and smoked bacon kebab (£3). The home-made puddings are good and served with double cream – treacle tart, bitter-sweet chocolate pudding or lemon cheesecake (£1.10). Well kept Butcombe Bitter, Flowers IPA and Original, and Huntsman Royal Oak on handpump, with a changing guest beer such as Hook Norton Old Hookey; friendly, prompt service; fruit machine and skittle alley. There are picnic-table sets among fruit trees in quite a big garden. (*Recommended by Patrick Young, Tom Evans, C F Stephens, W F Coghill, A V Chute, Antonia Cutbill, Verney and Denis Baddeley*)

Free house   Licensee Michael Ronca   Real ale   Meals and snacks   Children in family-room Open 11–2.30, 5.30–11 all year; closed 25 Dec   Bedrooms tel Burnham-on-Sea (0278) 783756; £10/£20

Stars after the name of a pub show exceptional quality. One star means most people (after reading the report to see just why the star has been won) would think a special trip worth while. Two stars mean that the pub is really outstanding – one of just a handful in its region. The very very few with three stars are the real aristocrats – of their type, they could hardly be improved.

WHEDDON CROSS (Somerset)   SS9238 Map 1
Rest & Be Thankful
Junction of A396 and B3224, S of Minehead

Under Dunkery Beacon, this carefully extended and refurbished seventeenth-century pub has a comfortable lounge bar divided into two communicating rooms by its central chimney (with log fires in cool weather); it's decorated with plush burgundy built-in banquettes and chairs around modern wood tables, a graceful goldfish in a big aquarium, and a white plank ceiling. Good bar food includes sandwiches (from 80p – not Sunday lunchtime), home-made soup or pâté (£1.05), three sausages (£1.90), ploughman's (from £1.90), macaroni cheese (£2.10), salads (from £2.35), pork cooked with Stilton (£5.33), and steaks (from £6.05). Well kept Ruddles County, Ushers Best and Websters Yorkshire on handpump; gentle piped music. A communicating games area has pool, darts, fruit machine, space game and juke box; there is a skittle alley and a buffet bar. *(Recommended by C F Stephens, PHF, Colin Donald, Michael and Alison Sandy, Mrs H Church, Mrs Jenny Seller, Michael Cooke)*

Free house   Real ale   Meals and snacks   Restaurant tel Timberscombe (064 384) 222 Children in restaurant, eating area and family-room   Open 10.30–2.30, 6–11 all year; opens 7 in winter

WINSFORD (Somerset)   SS9034 Map 1
Royal Oak ⊗ 🛏
Village signposted from A396 about 10 miles S of Dunster

In the seventeenth century, customers to this thatched Exmoor inn were regularly plundered by the Exmoor highwayman Tom Faggus on his strawberry roan, in exploits which R D Blackmore, a frequent visitor, worked into *Lorna Doone*. The partly panelled and cosy lounge bar has a relaxed, friendly atmosphere, Windsor armed chairs and cushioned seats on the red carpet, horsebrasses and pewter tankards hanging from the beam above the attractively panelled bar counter, and a splendid iron fireback in the big stone hearth (with a log fire in winter); another similarly old-fashioned bar has good brass, copper, wall prints and darts. Good home-made bar food includes soup (£1.20), sandwiches (£1.25), traditional ploughman's or chicken liver and bacon pâté (£2.50), home-cooked ham (£2.55), very good home-made chicken, leek and mushroom or excellent game pies (£3.95), and home-made puddings (£1.50). Well kept Flowers IPA and Original on handpump; friendly staff. Plenty of nearby walks, for example up Winsford Hill for magnificent views, or over to Exford. *(Recommended by Heather Sharland, D Stephenson, Don Mather, Brian and Anna Marsden, Mr and Mrs W A Rinaldi-Butcher, Julie Vincent, Mrs Jenny Seller, JKW)*

Free house   Licensee C R Steven   Real ale   Meals and snacks   Restaurant   Children in eating area of bar   Open 11–11 all year   Bedrooms tel Winsford (064 385) 232; £52.50B/ £62.50B

WITHYPOOL (Somerset)   SS8435 Map 1
Royal Oak ⊗ 🛏
Village signposted off B4233

This pleasantly situated country inn has a cosy beamed lounge bar with a log fire in a raised stone fireplace, comfortable button-back brown seats and slat-backed chairs, and a stag's head and several foxes' masks on its walls; another quite spacious bar is similarly decorated. A wide range of good bar snacks includes sandwiches (from 90p, giant filled rolls from £1.40, open sandwiches from £2.80), home-made soup (£1), home-made pâté (£2.25), ploughman's (from £2.40), home-cooked ham (£2.80), two large sausages (a choice of pork and garlic, pork and herb, venison and bacon or spicy tomato £3.50), smoked turkey breast salad (£3.80), steaks (from £4.50) and large Mediterranean prawns with garlic mayonnaise (£6). Well kept Ruddles County and Ushers Best on handpump; good, friendly service; shove-ha'penny, dominoes and cribbage. Outside, there are white metal and plastic chairs and tables under cocktail parasols on the front terrace. The village is tucked down below some of the most attractive parts of Exmoor – there are grand views from Winsford Hill just up the road, tracks lead up among the ponies into the heather past Withypool Hill, and the River Barle runs through the village itself, with pretty bridleways following it through a wooded combe further upstream. For guests, they can arrange for salmon and trout fishing, riding (stabling also), clay pigeon shooting, rough shooting, hunting, sea fishing from a boat and trips to see wild red deer. *(Recommended by Don Mather, Wayne Brindle, Dr and Mrs A R H Worssam, David and Ruth Hollands, B S Bourne, J C Smith, Dave Braisted, J Pearson, Colin Donald, Anthony Sargent, Simon Levene, Mrs Jenny Seller, JDL)*

Free house   Licensee Michael Bradley   Real ale   Meals and snacks   Restaurant; closed Sun lunchtime   Open 11–2.30, 6–11 all year; closed 25 and 26 Dec   Bedrooms tel Exford (064 383) 506/7; £22(£35B)/£36(£48B)

WOOLVERTON (Somerset)   ST7954 Map 2
Red Lion ⊗

A36, at N end of village on E side of road

Originally called the Woolpack, this old ex-farm building has cushioned farmhouse chairs, a winged high-backed settle by the big stone hearth with a log-effect gas fire, beams, flagstones and old panelling. The main area has an expanse of parquet flooring with oriental-style rugs, and lots of comfortably cushioned seats around decent elm tables. The atmosphere is friendly and relaxed, even when it's busy. Huge helpings of popular food include sandwiches (from £1), ploughman's (from £1.75), lots of interesting filled baked potatoes (from £2, prawn, ham and asparagus £3.10), delicious salad bowls such as garlic croûtons, walnuts, ham and cheese (£2.60), egg, tomato, smoked sausage, mushrooms and garlic croûtons (£3.15), or tuna, prawns, avocado, pineapple, sweetcorn and orange dressing (£3.75), chicken Korma (£4.95), seafood platter (£5.15), and daily specials. Well kept Wadworths IPA and 6X on handpump. You can eat outside, under the trees. *(Recommended by Dr Stewart Rae, Steve Dark, Roger Huggins, Mrs H Astley, John Baker, Mike Tucker, D Stephenson, Frank Cummins, Alan and Audrey Chatting, Len Beattie, D Godden)*

Wadworths   Licensee Barry Lander   Real ale   Meals and snacks   Children welcome Open 11–11 in summer; possibly 11–2.30, 6–11 in winter; closed 25 Dec

Lucky Dip

Besides the fully inspected pubs, you might like to try these Lucky Dips recommended to us and described by readers (if you do, please send us reports); in Bath and Bristol we give OS references for places out of the centre.

Ansford, Somerset [ST6333], *Wagon & Horses*: Excellent value food, particularly pastry, vegetables and Sun roast; drink good too, in this very clean pub *(Charles Hudson)*
Axbridge, Somerset [The Square; handy for M5; ST4255], *Lamb*: Tucked away in the corner of the village square in a beautiful part of the country with first-class good value food and well kept beer; nice lounge and bar *(Ted George, Tom Evans)*
Barrow Gurney, Avon [Barrow St (link rd,

just off A370/A38); ST5268], *Princes Motto*: A favourite, for outstanding quality of a wide choice of real ales such as Bass, Butcombe, Boddingtons, Courage, Smiles and Wadworths 6X, attractively priced – also decent coffee; unpretentious and old-fashioned but friendly, with log fire, generous snacks including delicious crusty sandwiches and coffee; pleasant garden with rural views; parking may not be easy *(Hugh Minett, Dr and Mrs A K Clarke, Tom Evans, Michael and*

Harriet Robinson, S J A Velate)

☆Bath, Avon [2 Bathford Hill; ST7965], *Crown*: Just taken over by the Worralls, who made the Crown at Kingsclere very popular with readers, and highly rated by us both for food and for atmosphere, during their time there a few years ago *(Anon)*

☆Bath, [Mill Lane, Bathampton (canalside); ST7766], *George*: Attractive canalside pub, busy but pleasant, with wide choice of well cooked and nicely served food including vegetarian dishes; dining-room leads directly off the canal towpath; outside seats, garden bar; can be approached by peaceful 3-mile walk from centre *(George Little, G G Calderwood, Wayne Stockton, T C and A R Newell)*

Bath, [Abbey Green; ST7565], *Crystal Palace*: Big sheltered courtyard is chief attraction of modernised Georgian pub with Huntsman ales under light top pressure, bar food (service could perhaps be quicker), family area in pleasant heated conservatory *(Roger Huggins, Pamela and Merlyn Horswell, Michael and Alison Sandy, Dr J D Bassett, LYM)*; *Grapes*: Busy city-centre pub with friendly efficient service, lively but not overcrowded, good value bar meals – especially fish and seafood *(J Mitchell)*; [Lansdown Hill] *Hare & Hounds*: Comfortable raj-style atmosphere (rather than that of a pub), with lots of cane chairs, elephant pictures and plastic palms; friendly staff, lovely views, reasonably priced food, well kept Courage Best and Directors, good-sized neat garden with swings, slides and so forth, conservatory, family-room *(Wilfred Plater-Shellard, Mrs E Pollard, Mrs Gill Avis)*; [North Parade] *Huntsman*: Good choice of excellent well cooked and tasty food (chips and vegetables charged extra), real ales *(Alastair Campbell)*; [12 Green St] *Old Green Tree*: Unspoilt, small, friendly pub with panelled walls, well kept Ushers ales, friendly service, good choice of cold food (the crab rolls are hotly tipped); separate smoking-room *(M A and W R Proctor, L Diaz, Ian Patterson)*; [central pedestrian area] *Roundhouse*: Interestingly shaped bar with Watneys-related real ales, wide choice of bar food, upstairs restaurant *(Alastair Campbell)*; [Saracen St/Broad St] *Saracens Head*: Spacious and interesting beamed bars with Courage real ales and good value cold buffet lunches *(O Richardson)*; [ST7565] *Theatre Royal Brasserie*: Very good well prepared food, choice of decent wines by the (smallish) glass *(T H G Lewis)*

Bayford, Somerset [ST7229], *Unicorn*: Former coaching-inn, well kept and spacious yet still intimate, one area with traditional settle and dark wood, fine choice of beers and wines, wide range of hot and cold food, small cheerful restaurant *(Major J A Gardner)*

Bishops Hull, Somerset [A38 W of Taunton; ST2124], *Stonegallows*: Very enjoyable set-price carvery dinner, Ushers ales, pleasant log fire *(Hugh Butterworth)*

Bishops Lydeard, Somerset [A358 towards Taunton; ST1828], *Kingfishers Catch*: Previously the Rose Cottage – a main entry with very well cooked food in pretty and truly cottagey cosy little rooms, especially good puddings; though keeping Huntsman ales and its pub licence, it's now really a restaurant – small and attractive, with good food, friendly service and in summer morning coffee and afternoon teas *(Shirley Pielou, David and Ruth Hollands, Heather Sharland, LYM)*; [ST1629] *Lethbridge*: Cosy, good atmosphere, good value innovative food, notable collection of Graham Clark prints, Whitbreads beers; live music weekends; bedrooms *(W B and S Dent, Elizabeth Lloyd)*

Blackford, Somerset [ST4147], *Sexeys Arms*: Well prepared and reasonably priced bar snacks such as delicious individual cottage pie, excellent dinner menu in small restaurant *(T H G Lewis)*

Blagdon, Avon [A368; ST5059], *Live & Let Live*: Cosy partly panelled back bar with log fire and sporting prints, generous bar food, well kept Courage Bitter and Best, sensibly placed darts, pool and other pub games; handy for fishing on Blagdon Lake; bedrooms *(Dr N M Hall, LYM)*; *New*: Very friendly atmosphere, spacious with three bar areas - open fires in two; good value well prepared food, well kept beer; the setting's an asset too, overlooking Blagdon Lake *(P D Weight-Vowden, Tom Evans, Pamela and Merlyn Horswell)*

Brent Knoll, Somerset [ST3350], *Red Cow*: Extensive menu served in lounge and (through separate hatch) delightful sheltered garden, with fields sloping beyond to Brent Knoll – lovely setting for this Whitbreads pub *(S J Edwards)*

Bridge Yate, Avon [junction A420/A4175; ST6873], *Griffin*: Good range of well kept beers and generous helpings of fine value food *(Margaret and Douglas Tucker)*

Bristol, Avon [off Boyce's Ave, Clifton; ST5673], *Albion*: Friendly and unpretentiously old-fashioned pub with unusual flag-stoned courtyard off cobbled alley, well kept Courage real ales *(LYM)*; [Alma Vale Rd, Clifton] *Alma Vale*: Well kept Courage and Wadworths 6X, good value bar snacks, small pleasant garden *(Paul Dennis)*; [Bell Hill, Stapleton; ST6176] *Bell*: Warm and friendly local on edge of city, good early evening atmosphere, lunchtime bar food *(B V Cawthorne, A Moggridge)*; [Prince St] *Bristol Clipper*: Convenient for Arnolfini Gallery, harbour, lifeboat museum; good bar food, real ale – but can get too busy *(KC)*; [Quayside Leisure Centre] *Bristol Lochiel*: Former Scottish islands steamer adapted by Courage, plenty of room and very cheerful atmosphere – window seats away from quay let you imagine you're floating off down the Avon; children's play area *(GA, PA)*; [Montpelier; ST5974] *Cadbury House*: Fascinating collec-

in sheltered courtyard and peaceful garden with unusual playthings, popular bar food; children welcome (except in bars); bedrooms more than adequate for the price *(Diane Duane, Mrs Pamela Roper, LYM)*

Minehead, Somerset [Harbour; SS9746], *Old Ship Aground*: Friendly Victorian pub with Ushers real ale, bar food and terrace, just by lifeboat station, and handy for Bristol Channel cruises on *Balmoral* or paddle steamer *Waverley* (both belong to a preservation society); parking might be difficult *(Joan Olivier)*

Monkton Combe, Avon [ST7762], *Wheelwrights Arms*: Attractively laid out bar with some interesting features, Flowers Original, IPA and Wadworths, extensive choice of food including first-class rare beef sandwiches (some of the more elaborate dishes evening only); very firm about ending food service at a set time; comfortable well furnished bedrooms; more reports on the current regime, please *(S J A Velate, LYM)*

☆ **Nether Stowey**, Somerset [Keenthorne – A39 E of village; not to be confused with Apple Tree Cottage; ST1939], *Cottage*: Big helpings of good value simple bar food and well kept Youngers Scotch on handpump (not that common around here), friendly service, comfortable red plush seats in lounge with wood-burning stove, aquarium and interesting pictures in eating area, games-room including two pool-tables (children allowed here), skittle alley *(The Barrett family, Mrs Crease, Roy McIsaac, LYM)*

North Cadbury, Somerset [ST6327], *Catash*: Warm and welcoming, real fires, hot fresh food which changes daily, Huntsman Royal Oak; two bedrooms *(P H S Wettern)*

North Curry, Somerset [Queens Sq; ST3225], *Bird in Hand*: Pleasant, friendly place with excellent salads and other bar snacks, good evening meals, Courage Directors, tables outside *(Derrick Turner)*

North Petherton, Somerset [High St (nr M5 junction 24); ST2932], *Walnut Tree*: Welcoming and attentive staff, good value food, well kept Wadworths and comfortable bedrooms with walnut furniture – but this is a hotel rather than a pub *(G Turner)*

☆ **Nunney**, Somerset [11 Church St; ST7345], *George*: Well kept Butcombe and Oakhill Farmers and hugely generous portions of good food in rambling pub opposite the castle, with several interconnecting rooms all comfortably furnished; helpful and friendly service; bedrooms quiet, clean and well equipped *(John Baker, Joy Heatherley)*

Old Sodbury, Avon [junction of A46 with A432, 1½ miles from M4 junction 18; ST7581], *Cross Hands*: Comfortably done-up spacious inn where the Queen took refuge from 1981 blizzard; real ales, two restaurants, comfortable bedrooms *(LYM)*

Oldland, Avon [North St; ST6771], *Crown & Horseshoe*: Lovely stone pub a little off the beaten track; rather surprising to find an original like this in rather drab surroundings *(Dr and Mrs A K Clarke)*

Othery, Somerset [ST3831], *London*: Unspoilt traditional pub *(Anon)*

Paulton, Avon [Bath Rd; ST6556], *Somerset*: Attractive Courage house with wonderful view over Cam Valley, well kept beer, good bar food, pleasant garden *(Mike Walters)*

Pennsylvania, Avon [A46, quite handy for M4; ST7373], *Swan*: Popular little pub on busy main road, good quick food, folk music each Tues; new management spring 1988 *(Peter and Rose Flower)*

Pensford, Avon [ST6263], *Rising Sun*: Good choice of named wines by the glass, and good variety of hot and cold food *(T H G Lewis)*

Porlock, Somerset [SS8846], *Castle*: Friendly and welcoming low-beamed pub with good atmosphere, well kept real ales such as Golden Hill Exmoor, good and well served food in eating area off spacious open-plan bar with pool and games *(Don Mather, Mark Walpole, Melanie Byrne)*

☆ **Porlock Weir**, Somerset [separate from but run in tandem with neighbouring Anchor Hotel; SS8547], *Ship*: Little thatched inn near peaceful harbour on lovely unspoilt coast below Exmoor; atmospheric original Ship Bar behind, with stone floor, well kept real ales including Golden Hill Exmoor; this bit's sadly often closed, when you must make do with the more modern front Mariners Bar; bar food, restaurant, children's room; bedrooms creaky and comfortably characterful in Ship itself – a nice place to stay *(Mrs Anne Fowler, Wayne Brindle, Stanley Faulkner, D H and M C Watkinson, LYM)*

Portbury, Avon [½ mile from A369 (off M5 junction 19); ST5075], *Priory*: Comfortably modernised ancient building with good food, excellent Bass *(Tom Evans)*

Portishead, Somerset [ST4777], *Portishead Bay*: Exceptional value food such as really tasty steak and kidney pie *(Tom Evans)*

Priddy, Somerset [off B3135; ST5251], *New*: Excellent no-fuss food at basic prices in fifteenth-century former farmhouse which keeps its character in the bars, with lovely fireplace, low beams, horsebrasses and so forth; well kept Huntsman Royal Oak and Wadworths 6X, good local cider, friendly service, good position on quiet village green; bedrooms very comfortable and homely *(Mr and Mrs H Gaydon, Sue Cleasby, Mike Ledger)*; *Queen Victoria*: Good, cosy family pub with large garden and family-room *(Dr and Mrs A K Clarke)*

☆ **nr Priddy** [from Wells on A39 pass hill with TV mast on left, then next left – OS Sheet 183 reference 549502], *Hunters Lodge*: Very unassuming basic walkers' and potholers' inn with good range of interesting real ales including well kept Badgers and Oakhill Farmers tapped from casks behind the bar, log fire, flagstones, friendly licensees; simple bar food, tables in garden; bedrooms clean and adequate given the price *(Mr and Mrs J M Elden, Dr and Mrs A K Clarke, Phil and Sally Gorton, Sue Cleasby, Mike Ledger, LYM)*

Queen Camel, Somerset [ST5924], *Mildmay Arms*: Consistently good pub, piped music in public bar *(Jack Taylor)*

Redhill, Avon [ST4963], *Arlington*: Very good food at very reasonable prices in family-run pub *(P D Weight-Vowden)*

Rode, Somerset [ST8153], *Red Lion*: A cluster of unspoilt little rooms and a main bar with interesting old paintings on the walls, large fireplace, wooden floor and traditional cider; very friendly landlord and landlady *(Andy Mason)*

Ruishton, Somerset [A358, just off M5 junction 25; ST2624], *Blackbrook*: Rangy pub of character with unusual furniture, well kept Ushers ale, good food; usually busy in summer *(Tom Evans)*

☆ **Seavington St Michael**, Somerset [A303 – getting in and out of the car park not exactly soothing; ST4015], *Volunteer*: Dates from 1500s, but much modernised and comfortable; well kept Badger Best, excellent Perry's cider from Dowlish Wake, wide choice of good value straightforward food using local ingredients *(C P Scott-Malden, AE, WAG, the Barrett family, Mrs Crease, RD, B H Pinsent, BB)*

Seven Ash, Somerset [A358 Taunton–Watchet; ST1433], *Stags Head*: Very reasonably priced home-cooked food from a wide menu with especially delicious puddings *(Miss C Scott)*

Shepton Montague, Somerset [off A359; ST6731], *Montague*: Pleasant and friendly new owners – jovial New Zealander landlord, wife does attractive home cooking *(W M Elliott)*

☆ **Simonsbath**, Somerset [SS7739], *Exmoor Forest*: Attractively placed Exmoor inn with several bar rooms including games-room, straightforward furnishings, log fires, lots of whiskies, well kept Whitbreads PA and a beer brewed for the pub, popular for family meals; decent bedrooms (but inn scored a black mark for its treatment of one reader who had to cancel a booking); nine miles of good trout fishing for residents, and nr start GWG30 *(Wayne Brindle, Hans Swift, BJN, LYM)*

Somerton, Somerset [ST4828], *Globe*: Friendly, comfortable atmosphere, reasonably priced bar food, large garden with terrace *(The Barrett family, Mrs Crease)*; *White Hart*: Pleasant old Courage pub built on site of Somerton Castle, Courage Best and Directors, excellent value bar food including children's helpings in two small eating rooms, airy, spacious and well furnished family room *(Ted George, Roger Huggins)*

Sparkford, Somerset [A303; ST6026], *Sparkford Inn*: Pleasant service, reasonable food and beer; busy in summer *(G C C Bartlett)*

Stanton Drew, Avon [off B3130; ST5963], *Druids Arms*: Nice pub where they sell real pickled eggs, friendly local voices, tables under bright awning look out over green fields *(Paul McPherson)*

☆ **Stanton Wick**, Avon [ST6162], *Carpenters Arms*: Many small rooms with bars and dining-rooms, in attractive building originally converted from row of thirteenth-century cottages; good service and reasonably priced cold buffet, hot fish and puddings; fine choice of well kept real ales such as Bass, Butcombe, Flowers Original and Wadworths 6X, extensive wine list; children welcome; same owners as our main entry Ashcott Inn at Ashcott *(Mr and Mrs F H Stokes, Mr and Mrs D S, John Bell, Aubrey and Margaret Saunders, Steve Dark)*

Staplegrove, Somerset [ST2126], *Staplegrove*: Good roadside pub, recently renovated, with good beer and bar food *(David Gaunt)*

Stathe, Somerset [ST3729], *Black Smock*: Lively local, especially on Sat night, well kept Butcombe *(Mark Spurlock)*

Stoke St Mary, Somerset [W of A358 Chard–Taunton; ST2622], *Half Moon*: Really good reasonably priced food, good choice of wines; children allowed in attractive dining area *(Guy Harris, Rear-Admiral E N Poland)*

Stratton on the Fosse, Somerset [A367 towards Radstock, at junction with B3139; ST6550], *White Post*: Very clean, comfortable and well furnished country pub with good home-cooked food and Ushers ales *(K R Harris)*

Tatworth, Somerset [ST3206], *Old Station*: Decent pub with comfortable bar and large, life-like coal-effect gas fire; real ale, good choice of reasonably priced food *(Alastair Campbell)*; *Olde Poppe*: Interesting old thatched pub, two bars, one long with antiques, saddle-back chairs and plenty of tables for eating; wide choice of beers and bar food at reasonable prices, garden with barbecue *(The Barrett family, Mrs Crease)*

Taunton, Somerset [ST2224], *County*: Reliably very good food in lounge bar of big bustling THF hotel, likeable staff, excellent Golden Hill Exmoor *(Anon)*; [Magdalene St] *Masons Arms*: Nice choice of well kept beers, very popular at lunchtime for good value food, bedrooms very clean and reasonably priced *(A A Bonella, NE)*

Thurloxton, Somerset [ST2730], *Maypole*: Well kept Whitbreads-related real ales and wide choice of bar food in spacious bar, separate skittles room *(Ian Blackwell)*

Tickenham, Avon [B3130 Clevedon–Nailsea; ST4571], *Star*: Light and airy lounge with modern pine furniture, delicate green and cream décor; wide choice of bar food, piped music – which can be loud *(Tom Evans)*

Timbercombe, Somerset [SS9542], *Lion*: Very reasonably priced evening bar food, good farm cider *(Michael Thomson)*

Timsbury, Avon [North Rd (B3115; ST6658],

Seven Stars: Cheerful and brightly lit village local with big wood-burning stove, cheap well kept Courage Best and Directors, well reproduced juke box, pub games *(LYM)*

Tintinhull, Somerset [ST4919], *Lamb*: Very clean and well run M&B pub, with friendly helpful licensee; normal range of food in comfortable bar and lounge, big garden *(K R Harris)*

Tockington, Avon [ST6186], *Swan*: Reasonable food and atmosphere, good facilities and plenty of room *(Anon)*

Triscombe, Somerset [signposted off A358 Crowcombe–Bagborough; ST1535], *Blue Ball*: Old thatched cottagey pub on slopes of Quantocks, old open fire and settles in single spruced-up bar with timbered ceiling, peaceful relaxed atmosphere (though there's piped music and it may be busy at weekends), well kept real ales, local cider, friendly licensee, simple but extensive and unusual menu of good value food from sandwiches to steak (there may be a wait); hens, chickens or goslings may hope to share your food out on the lawn *(Muriel Pope, SC, Mrs Shirley Pielou, T H G Lewis)*; [OS Sheet 181 reference 156355] *Bull*: Traditional Quantocks pub, unspoilt in spite of space game *(KG)*

☆ **Trudoxhill**, Somerset [ST7443], *White Hart*: Very friendly landlord and staff in pub with excellent, generously served food in bar and interesting restaurant, farm cider and well kept beer; it claims to be the only pub outside Scotland serving Caledonian 80/-; wide, unusual range of fruit and flower wines, and landlord liked Bishops Best so much that when brewing in Wellington ceased he bought the brewery to keep it in production *(Andy Mason, Dr and Mrs A K Clarke)*

Uphill, Avon [ST3158], *Dolphin*: Bar serving three areas with tables and cushioned settles; fair range of reasonably priced hot and cold food, Courage ales, cheerful service and piped music *(Lyn and Bill Capper)*

Upton, Somerset [OS Sheet 181 reference 006293; SS9928], *Lowtrow Cross*: Warm welcome in lonely country inn with well kept Cotleigh Tawny, nice low-beamed bar with enormous inglenook, simple attractively priced bar food, skittle alley, provision for children *(CS, LYM)*

Upton Noble, Somerset [ST7139], *Lamb*: Excellent food including Sun roasts in restaurant, with extensive views beyond large garden; closed Mon *(W M Pinder)*

Wadeford, Somerset [ST3010], *Haymaker*: Pleasant friendly bar, cheerful staff, good local beer, bar food at reasonable prices, separate pool and billiards room; a firm rein on bad language here *(John Tyzack, Derrick Turner)*

Watchet, Somerset [Market St; ST0743], *Bell*: Early sixteenth-century beamed pub with warm welcome, Ushers ales, good range of bar snacks; by harbour and quite convenient for Minehead–Bishops Lydeard

steam railway *(Stanley Faulkner)*

Waterrow, Somerset [A361 Wiveliscombe–Bampton; ST0425], *Rock*: Friendly pub in small village with log fire, wide choice of bar food, restaurant *(Jonathan and Helen Palmer)*

Wedmore, Somerset [ST4347], *George*: Traditional furnishings in stripped-stone bar of rambling coaching-inn with real ale, bar food, lively locals' bar, sheltered lawn; bedrooms *(Tom Evans, LYM)*; [outside village] *Trotters*: Full of armchairs and boxer dogs (which may adopt you); has had the horse-brass treatment but recovered; well kept Butcombe real ale *(Phil and Sally Gorton, MM)*

Wells, Somerset [Market Pl; ST5545], *Crown*: Good atmosphere in pleasant old coaching-inn close to cathedral, magnificent fireplace behind bar; well kept Courage Directors and John Smiths, good variety of decent if somewhat pricey bar food; William Penn arrested in 1685 for speaking to 3000 outside here *(John Roué, Ted George, S V Bishop)*; [St Thomas St] *Fountain*: Friendly and pleasant with good well served food, particularly in Boxers restaurant where it can be really interesting and not too expensive; very busy for Sun lunch *(G G Calderwood, E F P Metters, Margaret Drazin)*; [High St] *Kings Head*: Friendly fourteenth-century inn with pleasant, friendly atmosphere and generously served, reasonably priced good food in ample helpings; Courage Best and Directors and John Smiths on handpump; free newspapers for customers, live music some evenings *(Alastair Campbell, P Bromley)*; [High St] *Star*: Busy pub, bar snacks in Chimney Room – friendly service and good attractive food; seats outside this fine former coaching-inn *(S V Bishop, K Baxter, Dr and Mrs A K Clarke)*

West Buckland, Somerset [very near M5 junction 26; ST1720], *Blackbird*: Sixteenth-century pub with very pleasant beer garden and unusual statue, good food (especially Sun lunch) and real ale *(Richard Meredith)*; *Crown*: Excellent value simple bar food – good choice, very generous helpings; very friendly, Ushers Best on handpump, garden; children welcome *(P and K McAteer)*

☆ **West Harptree**, Avon [B3114 half mile NW of village; ST5657], *Blue Bowl*: Friendly, smart but cosy pub with good Courage Best and Directors, excellent value simple food, cheerful atmosphere, peaceful and pleasant garden; bedrooms nice, with excellent breakfasts *(G J Brown, J P Alderson, Mrs Wadham)*

West Huntspill, Somerset [ST3044], *Orchard*: Comfortable bars with a good range of beers, bar snacks and excellent carvery *(R F Davidson)*

West Monkton, Somerset [ST2728], *Monkton Inn*: Recently rebuilt Ushers pub with popular new young licensees, excellent food (especially mixed grills), well kept real ale, reasonable prices *(Richard Dolphin)*

☆ **West Pennard**, Somerset [A361 Glastonbury–Shepton Mallet; ST5438], *Red Lion*:

Spacious, welcoming and comfortable bar with flagstoned floor, beams and stonework in carefully restored seventeenth-century inn, charming atmosphere unchanged since one reader's previous visit in 1951; well kept real ales and remarkably wide and interesting choice of meals and snacks – snug for eating, small restaurant; bedrooms well equipped and comfortable, in recently converted barn – a good touring centre; no pets *(ACMM, Ted George, Dr and Mrs A K Clarke, Mr and Mrs J L Burns)*

West Pennard, [A361], *Apple Tree*: Very clean, spacious pub with wide selection of lunchtime snacks, good furnishings, well kept Watneys-related real ales, two restaurants *(John and Pat Smyth, Ted George)*

Westerleigh, Avon [ST7079], *Olde*: Exceptional value food, especially baked potatoes and salad; cosy lounge and bar, good beers *(Ceri Jarr)*

Weston in Gordano, Avon [B3124 Portishead–Clevedon; ST4474], *White Hart*: Attractive cream-washed village pub with good furniture (some very fine small settles); cheerful, cosy and in 'pubby' good taste, no-smoking restaurant area, family-room and garden with children's play area – flower-bedecked walls; has had well kept Courage ales and good food, but in 1988 licensees who'd made it so popular moved to Swan at Tickenham *(Tom Evans; reports on the new regime please)*

Weston-super-Mare, Avon [ST3261], *Claremont Vaults*: Good service, excellent views, friendly atmosphere *(M W Barratt)*

Whatley, Somerset [ST7347], *Sun*: Good beer and really delicious filled baked potatoes – the pub's speciality; try the huge chicken curry *(Andy Mason)*

Wick, Avon [ST7072], *Rose & Crown*: Good value food, olde-worlde charm, attractive location *(Gill Avis)*

Widcombe, Somerset [OS Sheet 193 reference 222160; ST2216], *Holman Clavel*: Ancient but comfortably modernised Whitbreads pub named after its massive holly chimney-beam; full of locals and country folk, good value bar food, well kept beers, helpful landlord, restaurant; handy for Blackdown Hills and Widcombe Bird Garden; said to be rumbles of ghostly skittle balls at nights, in the skittle alley – one tale is that the haunter is a monk who stayed on too long here when it was a hospice for Glastonbury Abbey pilgrims *(John Tyzack, BB)*

Williton, Somerset [A39; ST0740], *Foresters Arms*: Comfortable, clean interior, good mix of customers, well kept beer, good value bar food, pleasant garden *(Wayne Brindle)*; [outskirts of village, on B3191 for Watchet] *Masons Arms*: Thatched village pub with cheerful atmosphere, good value bar food, quick and friendly service, separate restaurant *(Wayne Brindle)*

Winterbourne, Avon [41 High St; ST6580],

Wheatsheaf: Worth a visit for the interesting windows – but also very welcoming, with well kept real ale *(Dr and Mrs A K Clarke)*

Witham Friary, Somerset [OS Sheet 183 reference 745409; ST7441], *Seymour Arms*: Excellent very friendly traditional pub, bar counter in entrance lobby with Victorian-style sash-windowed screen, two very high-ceilinged rooms – one with open fire, basic benches and tables, the second with bar billiards; Ushers real ale *(Phil and Sally Gorton)*

☆ Wookey, Somerset [B3139; ST5245], *Burcott Inn*: Friendly, popular country local with good service, well kept Butcombe, Cotleigh and maybe the even rarer Miners Arms on handpump; good choice of wine and food in bar and restaurant, walled garden *(Phil and Sally Gorton, A J Ritson)*

Wookey, [ST5145], *Ring o' Bells*: Small, pleasant country pub with beamed ceiling, wooden tables, open fireplace, friendly landlord, well kept Bass and hot and cold bar food *(W A Harbottle)*

Wookey Hole, Somerset [ST5347], *Wookey Hole*: Friendly inn with good value bar food; children welcome in separate dining-room and amusement machines room; bedrooms *(Keith Walton)*

Wootton Courtney, Somerset [SS9343], *Dunkery*: Though at first sight this looks like a residential hotel (it does have bedrooms) the main bar is very friendly, with superb views to the Beacon; well kept Flowers tapped from the cask, efficiently served snacks and light meals including good value ploughman's; tables outside *(Mrs Jenny Seller, Anthony Sargent)*

Wrantage, Somerset [near M5 junction 25 – 3 miles E on A378; ST3022], *Wheelwrights Arms*: Consistently good welcome, very good individual steak and kidney pie and cottage pie, well filled tasty sandwiches *(T H G Lewis)*

Wrington, Avon [High St; 2½ miles off A370 Bristol–Weston, from bottom of Rhodiate Hill; ST4662], *Plough*: Friendly, rural atmosphere, wide choice of home-made food, good service *(H S Harries)*

Yate, Avon [North Rd; ST7283], *Cross Keys*: Pleasant and friendly old ivy-covered pub with excellent beer *(Mr and Mrs A K Clarke)*; [Church Rd] *Lawns*: Old pub well refurbished, lunchtime food popular with local businessmen, good beer *(Dr and Mrs A K Clarke)*; [Shopping Precinct] *Swan*: Good food in busy, lively surroundings *(Anon)*

Yatton, Avon [High St; ST4365], *Butchers Arms*: Unspoilt, fairly basic pub with well kept Courage Best and a welcoming atmosphere *(Dr and Mrs A K Clarke)*

Yeovil, Somerset [Wine St; ST5516], *Wine Vaults*: Neat and popular town pub with well kept Bass, friendly atmosphere, rather winebar-like décor *(LYM)*

Staffordshire *see* Derbyshire

Suffolk

New entries for this well-endowed county include the Bull at Barton Mills (a well run coaching-inn), the Dobermann at Framsden (interestingly refurbished by its enthusiastic licensees), the Crown in Long Melford (an unusually comfortable lounge bar, matching the dignity of this lovely village), the Plough at Rede (exceptional cooking unexpectedly found in a little rustic hamlet), the Black Horse at Thorndon (attractively priced food in a nicely laid out sixteenth-century pub) and the Four Horseshoes at Thornham Magna (very popular for its food, and a comfortable place to stay at). We've this year awarded a star to the Pickerel at Ixworth – charming refurbishment, and good food including outstanding seafood. So it joins in the top rank of the county's pubs the elegantly restored Peacock in Chelsworth (an attractive place to stay at, with good food – sometimes including spit roasts in the bar), the Victoria at Earl Soham (its chief merit is the range of good beers brewed on the premises, but its attractively simple old-fashioned layout and food are worth mention, too), the civilised White Horse in Easton (for its outstanding nouvelle cuisine), the odd Kings Head at Laxfield (old-fangled all round – even to table drinks service and its own bowling-green), the small-roomed Jolly Sailor near the water at Orford, and the Golden Key at Snape (good food and friendly service in attractive surroundings). Many people would add to these the Crown at Southwold (another nouvelle cuisine pub, with outstanding wines by the glass, and comfortably refurbished bedrooms), and three pubs which seem to be moving towards a star rating at the moment are the Crown at Westleton (good food, good value to stay at), the cosy Beehive at Horringer (another with good food) and the beautifully restored Elizabethan Swan at Hoxne. Particular changes to note include new licensees at two very popular pubs, the cheerful Queen's Head at Blyford and the carefully refurbished Crown in Great Glemham (a comfortable place to stay at). Early reports suggest that they are doing well – both places have a food award. Another change is that

The Butt & Oyster, nr Chelmondiston

the Ship at Blaxhall (as joyfully traditional as you'd expect from a pub in George Ewart Evans' village), formerly tied to Tolly, has thrown off its tie and is now a free house. Besides the other main entries here, the Lucky Dip includes many fine prospects; among them, we'd note as specially promising the Dukes Head at Coddenham, White Horse at Kersey, Swan in Lavenham, Bull in Long Melford and Angel at Stoke by Nayland.

ALDEBURGH   TM4656 Map 5
Cross Keys
Crabbe Street

Even when the town fills with visitors in summer, this sixteenth-century pub manages to keep a lively and friendly local atmosphere. The two communicating rooms are divided by a sturdy central chimney with wood-burning stoves on either side, and good bar food includes sandwiches, haddock smokie (£1.85), plough-man's (from £1.90), salmon and prawn pot (£1.95), home-made pâté (£2.35), home-made lasagne or steak and kidney pie (from £3.25) and crab salad (£4). Well kept Adnams Bitter, Extra, Broadside and winter Old on handpump; shove-ha'penny, dominoes, cribbage and fruit machine. Outside, the back gravel court-yard has wooden seats and tables, and opens directly on to the promenade and shingle beach. *(Recommended by Heather Sharland, Alan and Ruth Woodhouse; more reports please)*

Adnams   Licensees Peter and Jenny Cresdee   Real ale   Meals and snacks   Children in eating area of bar only when wet   Open 11–3, 6–11 all year

BARTON MILLS   TL7173 Map 5
Bull ⊗ ⇐
Just off A11 Newmarket–Thetford

Opposite the main hotel entrance, beyond the old coach entry, is a friendly rambling bar, partly candlelit in the evening. It's comfortably modernised, with gold plush button-back built-in wall banquettes, matching stools and studded seats, old and more recent panelling, beams and joists showing through the plasterwork, big fireplaces, and various cosy alcoves – one with attractive antique sporting prints on a Delft shelf. Well kept Adnams and Greene King IPA on handpump, with a good selection of decent wines – particularly whites; on Sundays they may set out cheese cubes, nuts and crisps. The good range of bar food includes French bread rolls heaped with beef or ham (from £1.10), ploughman's (£2.25) and salads, and the restaurant does fine seafood (it was these licensees who originally gave the Bell at Kennett in Cambridgeshire its reputation for that – they moved here a couple of years ago). Piped pop music, fruit machine. The pretty seventeenth-century coachyard has a pigeon loft above its neatly converted high-doored stables. *(Recommended by Ian Phillips, Lesley Donner)*

Free house   Licensees Ian and Annie Cooper   Real ale   Meals and snacks   Grill-room and restaurant   Open 11.30–2.30, 6–11 all year   Bedrooms tel Mildenhall (0638) 713230; £30B/£45B

BLAXHALL   TM3657 Map 5
Ship
This is George Ewart Evans' village, and the public bar of this early eighteenth-century house – originally the Sheep – is all you'd hope from that: low beams, antique high-backed settles on the red tiles, a log fire, local notices on the cream walls and plenty of local regulars; the cosy wallpapered lounge has spindle-back

chairs around the neat tables on its carpet. There's now a walkway between these two rooms to allow easy access to the new lavatories. Generously served bar food includes sandwiches (from 55p, toasties 10p extra), soup (60p), burgers (£1.20), sausage and egg (£1.65), ploughman's (£1.80), salads (from £2), cod (£2.25), chicken (£2.50), scampi (£2.85) and steaks (from £5.50). Well kept Tolly Bitter and Mild, and Marstons Pedigree on handpump; darts, pool, shove-ha'penny, dominoes, cribbage, fruit machine and piped music. On the front terrace are some seats, and a caravan is used as a children's playroom in the back garden. (*Recommended by Peter Bush; more reports please*)

Free house Licensees Jim and Sue Grubbs Real ale Meals and snacks (not Mon, except bank hols) Children in eating area of bar Folk music bank hol lunchtimes Open 11–3, 7–11 all year; closed Mon morning, exc bank hols Two bedrooms tel Snape (072 888) 316; £12.50/£25; also tent and caravan site

BLYFORD TM4277 Map 5
Queen's Head ⊗
B1123

Even though this thatched fifteenth-century village pub is a popular place to enjoy good home-made food, the atmosphere remains very much that of a friendly pub, with a good mix of locals and visitors. It's attractively furnished, with low oak beams, some antique settles, pine and oak benches built into its cream walls, heavy wooden tables and stools, and a huge fireplace with good brickwork. The new licensees have introduced home-made bar food from a menu that changes daily and includes soup (£1.40), pâté (from £1.95), hummus (£1.45), fresh skate in orange and cider or cod in soya and ginger (£3.75), asparagus or warm onion tart (£2.95), steak and kidney pie (£3.25); interesting salads, home-made puddings (from £1.20) and Sunday roast lunch (£3.45). A full range of well kept Adnams on handpump; dominoes and piped music. There are seats on the grass outside, and a small village church opposite. (*Recommended by Alison Hayward, Nick Dowson, Derek and Sylvia Stephenson, Heather Sharland, Doreen and Toby Carrington, Anna Jeffery, Chris Draper*)

Adnams Licensee P J Honeker Real ale Meals and snacks Children welcome Open 10.30–2.30, 6–11 all year

BLYTHBURGH TM4575 Map 5
White Hart
A12

In a lovely spot above the marshes, this old building – an inn since 1548 – has a spacious lawn, a pétanque pitch, canaries and oriental pheasants in an aviary, free-running ducks and fowls, and a dovecot. Inside, it's open-plan, with a busy food operation, including soup (75p), sandwiches (from £1), salad or fresh local fish (£2.75), with daily specials (£2.75) and a selection of roast meats (£5.45). There are log fires at each end, and between the bar and dining-room they've opened up the large circular open fire; if you look around you can find some lovely curved oak beams, a fine Stuart staircase and Elizabethan woodwork. Well kept Adnams on handpump; table skittles, dominoes, cribbage and piped music. If you want a table in summer, turn up early. The marshy flats beyond the pub stretch along the River Blyth, and there's a right of way from the pub along the drily earthed-up river bank. The church down the lane on the other side of the main road is one of East Anglia's grandest. (*Recommended by A W Lewis, Derek Stephenson, David and Jocelyn Smith, John Townsend, Mrs D A Biggs, Heather Sharland*)

Adnams Real ale Meals and snacks Restaurant tel Blythburgh (050 270) 217; open all afternoon, and from 8.30am Children in garden, eating area and restaurant Open 10.30–2.30, 6–11 all year

BRANDESTON   TM2460 Map 5

Queens Head

Towards Earl Soham

On Thursday nights this well run, friendly country pub reverts to Tilley-lamp lighting and there may be free baked potatoes. The big open-plan bar is divided into separate bays by the stubs of surviving walls; brown leather banquettes and old pews are built around them, and there's some panelling. Bar food is home made and good value: sandwiches (from 70p), ploughman's (from £1.75), steak and kidney pie (£2.10), lamb and courgette bake (£2.30), quiche (£2.75) and fisherman's pie (£2.95). Well kept Adnams on handpump; helpful staff; cribbage, fruit machine, faint piped music, and (in a separate family-room) pool and table skittles. There's a big garden with tables on neatly kept grass among large flower beds and a play tree, climbing-frame and slide. The inn has a caravan and camping club site at the back. You can visit a nearby vineyard or the new cider farm. *(Recommended by Paul and Rhian Hacker, Doreen and Toby Carrington)*

Adnams   Licensee Ray Bumstead   Real ale   Meals and snacks   Children in family-room Open 11–2.30, 5.30 (6 Sat)–11 all year   Bedrooms tel Earl Soham (072 882) 307; £12/£22

nr CHELMONDISTON   TM2037 Map 5

Butt & Oyster   [illustrated on page 598]

This unspoilt old bargeman's pub has a fine view of the big ships coming down the river from Ipswich from the big bay window of the main bar (and in the separate dining-room), and it's interesting to see the long lines of black sailing-barges moored outside. One of the best times to visit the pub would be on the first Saturday in July for the annual Thames Barge race. The small, half-panelled smoke-room is decorated with model sailing-ships, and has high-backed and other old-fashioned settles on the tiled floor; spare a glance for the most unusual carving of a man with a woman over the mantelpiece. Bar food is good and generously served, and includes sandwiches (not on Saturday or Sunday lunchtimes), ploughman's with a choice of granary or crusty white bread, a choice of salads, home-made pies and quiches, changing home-made hot dishes such as casseroles or steak and kidney pie, giant prawns in garlic butter, chicken fillets, plaice, seafood platter and so forth; Tolly Bitter, Original and Mild on handpump with Old Strong in winter tapped from the cask; darts, shove-ha'penny, table skittles, dominoes and cribbage. *(Recommended by P J and S E Robbins, Margaret and Trevor Errington, Rob Weeks, Gill Austin, Heather Sharland)*

Tolly Cobbold   Real ale   Meals and snacks   Children in two separate rooms   Open 11–2.30, 5–11 all year; opens 6.30 in winter; closed evenings 25 and 26 Dec

CHELSWORTH   TL9848 Map 5

Peacock ★ ⊗ 🛏

The Street; B1115

This elegantly restored fourteenth-century inn has a relaxed, friendly atmosphere in its large beamed bar, which has a splendid stone inglenook fireplace and is divided into several areas by a partly open timbered partition. The cosy inner lounge has some exposed Tudor brickwork and the walls are decorated with local paintings for sale (there is a craft shop behind the garden). Home-made bar food includes sandwiches (from 90p), soup, burger (£1.30), ploughman's (£2), salads (from £3.80), a good cold buffet in summer with quiche, home-cooked beef and so forth (from £3.75) as well as daily specials such as home-made beef and game pie (£4.50), vegetable lasagne (£4.20) and fish dishes such as salmon cutlet (£5.50); they also do afternoon teas. Well kept Adnams, Greene King IPA and Abbot and Mauldons on handpump, and sometimes there are nibbles such as stuffed olives or nuts on the tables. Helpful, courteous staff; darts and piped music, and maybe a friendly Jack Russell. The rich parkland of Chelsworth Hall is just over the bridge. *(Recommended by Gwen and Peter Andrews, I S Wilson, D J Amery, J S Evans, Miss E T A Bennett, MBW, JHW, Alison Hayward, Nick Dowson, Brenda Gentry, Margaret and Roy Randle, Rob Weeks, Gill Austin, Heather Sharland, Jenny Cantle, Mrs H M T Carpenter)*

Free house   Licensees Mrs L R Bulgin and A F Marsh   Real ale   Meals and snacks   Children in eating area   Jazz Fri evenings   Open 11–2.30, 6–11 all year   Bedrooms tel Bildeston (0449) 740758; £16/£32

CLARE   TL7645 Map 5
Bell

This small hotel in the market place is an attractive building, and the lounge bar – rambling around under splendidly carved black beams – has panelling and woodwork around the open fire, armchairs on the green carpet and local notices on the hessian walls. Another room leads off, and to eat you go through to the wine bar with masses of prints mainly to do with canals on its walls: food here includes soup (90p), ploughman's (from £1.80), home-made lasagne (£3.25) and steaks (from £5.95); toasted sandwiches in the comfortable lounge bar. Well kept Nethergate and Ruddles on handpump; quick service. There are some tables on a back terrace by the small, sheltered lawn. Several other striking buildings in the village include the remains of the priory and the castle (which stands on prehistoric earthworks). *(Recommended by Mrs R Wilmot, Rob and Gill Weeks, W T Aird, John Brandford, R L and A V Roberts, S White, T Kinning, Melvin D Buckner)*

Free house   Licensees Brian and Gloria Miles   Real ale   Meals and snacks   Children in reception lounge   Open 11–2.30, 5–11 all year   Bedrooms tel Clare (0787) 277741; £25(£30B)/£35(£40B)

DUNWICH   TM4770 Map 5
Ship

The main bar in this pretty, old-fashioned inn has a dusky ochre ceiling, tiled floor, cushioned wall benches, pews, captain's chairs, a wood-burning stove (cheerfully left open in cold weather), and a friendly, relaxed atmosphere (perhaps a bit too easy-going for some readers). Bar food, all home-made, includes soup (65p), cottage pie (£2), lasagne (£2.50), vegetarian dishes or fresh local fish (£3), with evening dishes such as garlic mushrooms (£1.75), scampi (£5.25), steaks (£6.25), fresh prawn or crab salads (£6.50), and puddings like home-made ice-cream. Well kept Adnams Bitter and Greene King Abbot on handpump, and James White farm cider (very strong) at the handsomely panelled bar counter. The public bar area has darts, dominoes, cribbage, fruit machine, space game and piped music. There's a conservatory with a vine and jasmine, a sunny back terrace, and a well kept garden with an enormous fig tree. *(Recommended by Peter Bush, K Howard, Andy Tye, Sue Hill, Alison Hayward, Nick Dowson, David and Jocelyn Smith, Mr and Mrs O'Gorman, Gwen and Peter Andrews, Mrs D A Biggs, J P Selby, John Tyzack, Heather Sharland, Doreen and Toby Carrington, Mrs J M Gillman, Jill Hadfield)*

Free house   Licensees Stephen and Ann Marshlain   Real ale   Snacks (lunchtime) and meals   Restaurant   Children welcome (not in Ship bar)   Open 11–2.30, 6–11 all year; opens 7 in winter; closed evening 25 Dec   Bedrooms tel Westleton (072 873) 219; £15/£30; not Christmas/New Year

The initials GWG – mentioned, for instance, as 'on GWG 22' – stand for our companion Consumers' Association's book *Holiday Which? Good Walks Guide*, and show that the pub is on or near the walk numbered.

EARL SOHAM SM2363 Map 5
Victoria ★ ⊗

A1120 Stowmarket–Yoxford

The furnishings in this friendly little country pub are nicely chosen – kitchen chairs and pews, plank-topped trestle sewing-machine tables and other simple country tables with candles, tiled or board floors, open fires, stripped panelling, a piano and an interesting range of pictures of Queen Victoria and her reign. Reasonably priced bar food includes sandwiches (from 70p), home-made soup (£1), ploughman's (from £1.75), kipper (£1.75), chilli con carne (£2), corned beef hash (£2.25), vegetarian lasagne (£2.50) and steak, kidney and mushroom casserole (£2.75). Very good home-brewed beer (they do a takeaway service too) includes a Bitter, a mild called Gannet, another called Victoria and a stronger ale called Albert (you can visit the brewery). Darts, shove-ha'penny, dominoes and cribbage; there are seats out in front and on a raised back lawn. The pub is close to a wild fritillary meadow at Framlingham and a working windmill at Saxtead. (*Recommended by Mr and Mrs J H Wyatt, N A Wood, A V Chute, E J and S H J Colgate, Jenny Cantle, Nick Dowson, Rob and Gill Weeks*)

Own brew Licensees Clare and John Bjornson Real ale Meals and snacks Frequent and impromptu folk music Open 11.30–2.30, 5.30–11 all year; may try longer hours at weekends

EASTON TM2858 Map 5
White Horse ★ ⊗

N of Wickham Market, on back road to Earl Soham and Framlingham

In what is after all such a relatively small village pub, it's a surprise as well as an enormous pleasure to find such imaginative food, presented so attractively: various ploughman's with cheeses, Scotch egg, pork pie and so forth, as well as a hot and cold buffet with spicy and meaty sausage casserole with lentils, Cromer crabs, fresh fish and Gressingham duck; well kept Tolly Bitter on handpump. The two enlarged rooms of the bar have country kitchen chairs, good small settles, cushioned stripped pews and stools, and open fires; the attractive duck and goose decoys looking down on the very large fluffy cat are carved by the owner/chef (who has been joined by a chef who has won a regional award). The lavatories are now inside. The terrace has barbecue facilities and the garden has a well equipped children's play area. Easton Farm Park is worth visiting. (*Recommended by Alan and Ruth Woodhouse, A V Chute, Dr and Mrs R M Belbin*)

Tolly Cobbold Licensees David and Sally Grimwood Real ale Meals and lunchtime snacks Restaurant, closed Sun, tel Wickham Market (0728) 746456 Open 11–11 in summer; 11–2.30, 6–11 in winter; closed evenings 25 and 26 Dec

FRAMLINGHAM TM2863 Map 5
Crown 🛏

Market Hill

This small and friendly black and white Tudor inn once had coaches clattering through what is now a prettily planted flagstoned courtyard (with a cheerful winter-flowering cherry). The cosy bar has high heavy beams, one or two settles (including an antique carved one), dark green plush armed seats, a log fire, and a window overlooking the unusual sloping triangular market place (market day is Saturday, when nearby parking may be difficult); off this is a comfortable lounge, with wing easy chairs beside the fire, and there are more seats in the hall. Bar food includes home-made soup (£1), sandwiches, home-made quiche (£2.20), plough-man's (£2.20), pâté (£2.35), shepherd's pie (£2.60) and cold meat salads or a daily special (£3.60). Adnams and Ruddles on handpump; pleasant, efficient staff, piped music. *(Recommended by A G Tucker, Heather Sharland, Alison Hayward, Nick Dowson, Wayne Brindle, Rob and Gill Weeks, Anna Jeffery, Chris Draper)*

Free house (THF)   Licensee P Senior   Meals and snacks   Restaurant   Children in restaurant   Open 11–4, 6–11 all year   Bedrooms tel Framlingham (0728) 723521; £44B/£59B, excl breakfast

FRAMSDEN   TM1959 Map 5
Dobermann

The Street; pub signposted off B1077 just S of its junction with A1120 Stowmarket–Earl Soham

Engagingly restored and shiningly well kept, this friendly thatched pub is divided by a central fireplace, its log fire open to both sides. On one there's a big sofa (a favourite with the tabby cat), a couple of chintz wing armchairs, and by the big window a refectory table. The other side has a mix of chairs, plush-seated stools and winged settles around scrubbed rustic tables. The white walls are decorated with photographs of and show rosettes won by the owners' dogs; the pale stripped beams are very low. Bar food includes sandwiches (maybe hot beef, £1.75), basket meals such as scampi (£2.90), Stilton ploughman's (£3.10), gammon and egg (£3.95), trout and home-made chicken and mushroom or steak and kidney pie (£4.50), and a special such as lasagne (£3.50). Well kept Adnams Bitter and Broadside, Greene King IPA, a beer brewed for the pub by Tolly, and a guest beer such as Everards Tiger, all on handpump, with a decent choice of spirits; shove-ha'penny, dominoes, cribbage, fruit machine, and on our visit piped Radio 1. They play boules outside, where there are picnic-table sets by trees and a fairy-lit trellis, with summer barbecues. *(Recommended by Nick Dowson, Alison Hayward, Donald Rice)*

Free house   Licensees Susan and Richard Frankland   Real ale   Meals and snacks   Open 11.30–2.30, 7–11 all year   Bedroom tel Helmingham (047 339) 461;/£30

GREAT GLEMHAM   TM3361 Map 5
Crown ⊗ 🛏

There's a cosy, relaxed atmosphere in this old brick house, helped by an enormous double fireplace in the middle of the open-plan lounge, with a black wood-burning stove on one side and logs blazing on the other; it's well kept, and furnished with red cord button-back wall banquettes and captain's chairs around stripped and waxed kitchen tables, one or two big casks, beams, and local paintings and drawings on the white walls. A side eating room has flowers and pot plants. Good, reasonably priced bar food includes sandwiches or soup (75p), French bread sandwiches (£1.15), pâté (£1.30), ploughman's (£1.40), smoked mackerel (£1.50), omelettes (from £1.50), chilli con carne (£2), curry (£2.50), salads (from £1.90), scampi (£2.35), fisherman's platter (£2.50) and steak (from £5.50); good breakfasts. Well kept Adnams, Flowers, Greene King IPA and Abbot, and Mauldons on handpump; warmly welcoming new licensees; darts, dominoes, cribbage, fruit machine and piped music. There's a neat, flower-fringed lawn, raised above the corner of the quiet village lane by a retaining wall; seats out here. *(Recommended by Chris Fluck, Jenny and Brian Seller, C Williams, Peter Griffiths, W J Wonham, A V Chute)*

Free house   Licensees Roy and Eve Wood   Real ale   Meals and snacks   Evening restaurant, not Mon   Children in eating area   Open 11–2.30, 6.30–11 all year   Bedrooms tel Rendham (072 878) 693; £15/£28.50B

The letters and figures after the name of each town are its Ordnance Survey map reference. *How to use the Guide* at the beginning of the book explains how it helps you find a pub, in road atlases or large-scale maps as well as in our own maps.

HORRINGER   TL8261 Map 5
Beehive ⊗
A143

Cottagey rooms in this buoyantly friendly pub radiate from a central servery, with a shiny ragged ochre ceiling, some very low beams in some of the furthest and snuggest alcoves, stripped panelling or brickwork, picture-lights over lots of nineteenth-century prints, deep brown velvet curtains on brass rails, and a couple of quiet dogs including an aloof borzoi. There are carefully chosen dining-chairs and country kitchen chairs, one or two wall settles around solid tables, and a wood-burning stove. Very good food from an unusual menu includes sandwiches (from £1), home-made parsley soup (£1.10), ploughman's or home-made taramo-salata (£2.25), Mexican omelette (£2.50), baked avocado Bloody Mary (£3), oyster Mornay (£3.50), lovely gravadlax (£3.75), scrambled eggs with smoked salmon (£3.95), and specials such as a salmon and seafood mayonnaise (£4.75), garlic roasted baby chicken (£5.95), steak au poivre (£7.50) and grilled fresh lobster (£10.95); good puddings. Well kept Greene King IPA and Abbot on handpump, decent house wines; young, cheerful service; fruit machine. A most attractively planted back terrace has picnic-table sets, with more seats on a raised lawn. *(Recommended by Frank Gadbois, W T Aird, Derek and Sylvia Stephenson, John Baker, John Hurworth)*

Greene King   Licensee Gary Kingshott   Real ale   Meals and snacks (not Sun evening) Table bookings tel Horringer (028 488) 260   Children in eating area   Open 11.30–2.30, 7–11.30

HOXNE   TM1777 Map 5
Swan

A great deal of work has gone into restoring this herringbone brick and timbered pub to its former Elizabethan glory: heavy oak floors have been installed, the ancient timber and mortar of the walls are now visible, and the ceilings on the ground floor have been stripped to reveal gigantic grooved and fluted oak beams (some of them reputedly installed during Henry VIII's reign). In the front bar there are two brand new solid oak bar counters, and a deep-set inglenook fireplace (the dining-room now has an original wooden fireplace too); in the back bar a fire divides the bar area and snug. Bar food includes sandwiches (£1.30), ploughman's (£1.55), rump steak (£4.95) and daily specials such as garlic mushrooms (£1.55), grilled sardines (£1.95), pancake filled with mushrooms and cheese (£2.50) and seafood gratin or lamb kebab (£3.95); puddings range from Cotswold apple-cake to coffee and walnut cheesecake (from £1.35). Well kept Adnams tapped from the cask and Ruddles County on handpump; darts, shove-ha'penny and dominoes, and there is also a separate pool-room with a high fluted beamed ceiling, an open fire and a juke box. The extensive lawn behind the inn used to be a bowling-green – a nice place to sit in summer on the hand-made elm furniture, sheltered by a willow and other trees and its shrub-covered wall; it's close to the site of King Edmund's martyrdom on 20 November 870. *(Recommended by Nick Dowson, Gavin May, Robert and Vicky Tod, Mrs C O'Callaghan, A V Chute, Mr and Mrs E K Smith)*

Free house   Licensees Tony and Frances Thornton-Jones   Real ale   Meals (not Mon, not Sun evening) and snacks (not Mon or Sun)   Restaurant tel Hoxne (037 975) 275/652   Children in garden and eating area   Open 12–2.30, 7–11 all year; considering earlier opening in summer

---

If you have to cancel a reservation for a bedroom or restaurant, please telephone or write to warn them. A small place – and its customers – will suffer if you don't. And recently people who failed to cancel have been taken to court for breach of contract.

HUNDON   TL7348 Map 5
Plough ⊗

Brockley Green; on Kedington road, up hill from village

On one of the few hills around, this well kept and warmly welcoming country pub
has big windows that look out past a pretty post and rails paddock to quiet East
Anglian countryside. Inside, there's a double row of worn old oak timbers to mark
what must have been the corridor between the two rooms of the carpeted bar.
There are low side settles with Liberty-print cushions, spindle-back chairs and
sturdy low tables, and most walls are stripped back to bare brick, and decorated
with striking gladiatorial designs for Covent Garden by Leslie Hurry, who lived
nearby. As we went to press, they had just obtained planning permission to add on
an extension which would be used for eating – they also hope to put in bedrooms
here. Good bar food includes sandwiches (90p), home-made soup (£1.10), ploughman's (from £1.40), devilled whitebait in paprika or pâté (£1.95), omelettes (from
£2.55), seafood platter (£3.25), trout with almonds (£3.45), steak and kidney pie
(£3.85), rump steak (£4.95) and daily specials; puddings (from £1.25) and
children's dishes (£1.75). Well kept Greene King IPA, Nethergate and a house beer
brewed by Mauldons ('Furrowed Brew') on handpump; shove-ha'penny, dominoes,
trivia and cheerful piped music. Besides rustic wood tables and chairs on a side
lawn, there's a summer marquee and barbecue. It's also a certified location for the
Caravan Club, with a sheltered site to the rear for tourers. *(Recommended by Frank
Gadbois, Melvin D Buckner, Kevin Blick)*

*Free house   Licensee David Rowlinson   Real ale   Meals and snacks   Restaurant tel Hundon
(044 086) 248   Children welcome   Open 12–2.30, 5 (7 Sat)–11*

IXWORTH   TL9370 Map 5
Pickerel ★ ⊗

Village signposted just off A143 Bury St Edmunds–Diss

Exceptional value, very good food, a friendly welcome and charming furnishings
earn this carefully restored old inn a star this year. Several small rooms lead off
from the central servery, and have panelling that varies from ancient to eighteenth-
century, attractive brickwork, moulded Elizabethan oak beams, big fireplaces, and
a relaxed atmosphere. The chairs and pews are cushioned to match the curtains,
there are flowers (and heaps of magazines) on the tables, and lots of engravings on
dark squared panelling. Kerstin Burge, who does the cooking, may ask you to
choose from the fresh fish in her kitchen when she takes your order (on a sensible
combination menu and order form, with tick boxes). The wide choice includes half
a pint of cockles (95p), lots of excellent open sandwiches (from £1.25), ploughman's (£1.95), a pint of whole prawns (£3.45), dressed crab (£3.25), seafood
platter (£4.95), fresh fish such as sardines (£3.25), Scotch salmon (£5.85), fried
Dover sole (£6.25) and lobster (from £7.95) and steaks (from £5.95). The
two-roomed dining-room shares the same menu; its two pretty rooms have
stripped-pine tables and dressers, stripped pine dado, blue patterned wallpaper and
a high shelf of plates. Well kept Greene King Abbot and IPA on handpump, freshly
squeezed orange juice, and very reasonable house wines; the public side has
shove-ha'penny, table skittles, dominoes, cribbage and fruit machine. A small back
sun lounge faces a sway-backed Elizabethan timbered barn across the old
coachyard. There are picnic-table sets on a goodish stretch of grass, under a giant
sycamore. *(Recommended by Simon Tubbs, B H Pinsent, A V Chute, Alan and Ruth*

Most of the big breweries now work through regional operating companies, with different
names. If a pub is tied to one of these regional companies, we put the parent company's name in
brackets – in the details at the end of each main entry.

Woodhouse, K N Symons, Stephen and June Clark, John Baker, Alison Hayward, Nick
Dowson, K Howard, Mel Buckner, Heather Sharland, W T Aird)

*Greene King   Licensees Nigel and Kerstin Burge   Real ale   Meals and snacks   Children
welcome   Restaurant tel Pakenham (0359) 30398; to stay open until 4 weekends   Open
11–2.30, 5.30–11; 11–11 Sat and bank hols; all year; considering longer opening in lounge
bar in summer*

KERSEY   TL9944   Map 5
Bell

Village signposted off A1141 N of Hadleigh

Just up the village street from a ford with ducks and geese, this old building has a
jettied upper floor and attractively carved black timbers. Inside there are latticed
windows and fine old timberwork, and doors off a worn brick-tiled corridor open
into a bar and lounge divided by a brick and timber screen decorated with copper
and brassware. The low-beamed public side has simple seating on its tiled floor and
a log fire; the lounge side has comfortable red plush button-back banquettes and a
swirly red carpet. Bar food includes soup (£1.15), sandwiches, ploughman's
(£2.25), plaice (£3.90), salads (from £4.35), steak and kidney pie (around £7, with
a smaller lunchtime helping around £4), eight-ounce rump steak (£7.20) and game
pie (£7.48). Well kept Adnams, Flowers Original, Wethereds and guest beers on
handpump; white cast-iron tables and chairs out on the sheltered back terrace,
some under a fairy-lit side canopy; steel quoits available. *(Recommended by Mrs R
Wilmot, J S Evans, Paul and Margaret Baker, Gordon Theaker, Heather Sharland, Rob and
Gill Weeks)*

*Free house   Real ale   Meals and snacks   Restaurant tel Ipswich (0473) 823229   Children
welcome   Open 11–2.30, 6–11 all year*

LAXFIELD   TM2972   Map 5
Kings Head ★

Behind church, off road toward Banyards Green

An old-fashioned atmosphere and traditions have been preserved at this unspoilt,
friendly Tudor pub with the barman serving you at your table. The tiled-floor front
room has an open fire cosily surrounded by a high-backed built-in settle, and a
couple of other rooms have pews, old seats, scrubbed deal tables, and a quietly
ticking clock. Well kept Adnams Bitter and Broadside, Mauldons and James
White's farmhouse cider – mulled, if you want – are tapped from casks in a back
room; darts, dominoes, cribbage and trivia. Bar food includes sandwiches, lovely
home-made soup (£1), oak-smoked kippers or ploughman's (£1.60), vegetarian
chilli (£2.70), Lancashire hot-pot or steak and kidney pie (£2.75), rainbow trout or
pigeon casserole (£2.95), Suffolk gammon (£3.50) and rump steak (£4.50); full
evening meals if booked two days in advance. Going out past the casks in the back
serving-room, you find benches and a trestle table in a small yard. From the yard, a
honeysuckle arch leads into a sheltered little garden, where there's a pets corner,
with vegetables at the far end, and to the pub's own well kept and secluded
bowling- and croquet-green. *(Recommended by Pete Storey, Gavin May, Gwen and Peter
Andrews, Nick Dowson, Alison Hayward, David Mabey)*

*Free house   Licensee Mrs Janet Parsons   Real ale   Meals and snacks (not Mon exc bank hols)
Restaurant tel Ubbeston (098 683) 395   Children in eating area until 9   Occasional folk
music   Open 10.30–3 (4 Sat), 6–11 all year; maybe longer afternoon opening if trade
demands*

MARTLESHAM   TM2547 Map 5
Black Tiles

A12; W side of village, on N side of road

Quickly served, fairly priced food is the main draw to this well kept, spacious roadhouse: lots of sandwiches (from 80p), home-made soup (90p), burger (from £1.30), a choice of ploughman's (from £1.75), tacos or chilli con carne (£2.50), salads (from £3.20), home-made steak and kidney pie (£3.50), scampi (£4.40) and steaks (from £5.50); Sunday lunch (£3.50). Well kept Adnams Bitter and Broadside on handpump; fruit machine and piped music. The grass outside, floodlit at night, has picnic-table sets, and a fish pond and fountain in front, and is quieter now the village has been bypassed. *(Recommended by Wayne Brindle, A V Chute; more reports please)*

Adnams   Licensee Don Williamson   Real ale   Meals and snacks   Restaurant   Children in restaurant   Open 11–11 all year; closed evening 25 Dec and 1 Jan, all day 26 Dec

LONG MELFORD   TL8645 Map 5
Crown

Friendly new owners and staff look after you well in this comfortable two-roomed lounge bar – quietly sedate on a weekday lunchtime, but busy at weekends and in high season. It's gently decorated in pale buff, soft pink and cream, with big easy chairs and sofas and fringed table lamps in one part, smaller chairs and cushioned pews in another. Besides some rugwork 'pictures' of birds and flowers, there's a stained-glass panel picture of *A Midsummer Night's Dream*. Bar food includes big filled rolls and sandwiches (from £1), soup (£1.25), ploughman's (from £1.65), gammon or lasagne (£2.95) and scampi or chicken (£3.50); well kept Adnams, Greene King IPA, Mauldons and Nethergate or Tetleys on handpump, good Sunday nibbles on the bar (when the three-course lunch is good value at £4.95); soft piped music, newspapers for customers. They also do morning coffee and afternoon teas. There are picnic-table sets on the lawn of the walled garden, which has a play area. *(Recommended by Gwen and Peter Andrews, Gordon Theaker, Heather Sharland)*

Free house   Licensees B W and K H Heavens   Real ale   Meals and snacks   Restaurant (open all day Sun)   Children welcome   Open 11–11 all year   Bedrooms tel Sudbury (0787) 77666; £22.50(£27.50B)/£35(£37.50B)

ORFORD   TM4250 Map 5
Jolly Sailor ★

This waterside smugglers' inn stands by a busy little quay on the River Ore, opposite Orford Ness and close to marshy Havergate Island, where avocets breed. The pub is built mainly from the timbers of ships wrecked nearby when the sea ran closer in the seventeenth century, and the floor of one room is made of flagstones that in the days before tarmac were part of the street. Several cheerful rooms are served from counters and hatches in an old-fashioned central cubicle, which has well kept Adnams Bitter on handpump; friendly staff (and dogs). In the corner of one main room, warmed in winter by a good solid-fuel stove, there's an uncommon spiral staircase. Often, seats are pews: one little room is popular with the dominoes, darts, cribbage and shove-ha'penny players, another has pool and a fruit machine; piped music. There are some curious stuffed 'Chinese muff dogs', about half the size of a chihuahua – said to be Tudor, though no one's sure. Bar food includes sandwiches, scampi (£2.50), ploughman's or smoked mackerel (£2.70), seafood (£3), steaks (£5.50) and a daily special such as beef and vegetable or cottage pie (£2.50). Orford has always specialised in the odd: in the twelfth century fishermen netted the Wild Man of Orford – a strange half-human bald-headed hairy thing that later escaped back to the sea. (*Recommended by Dave Butler, Lesley Storey, Angus Lindsay, Pete Storey, Heather Sharland, A V Chute, R Aitken, Marcus and Marcella Leith*)

Adnams Licensee Patrick Buckner Real ale Meals and snacks Children in own room Live music most Sat evenings Open 11–2, 6–11 all year Bedrooms tel Orford (0394) 430243; £14.50/£24

Kings Head ⊗

Front Street

Parts of this predominantly Tudor inn date back seven hundred years, and there are carved black oak beams in the main bar, as well as one or two fine old wooden chairs, comfortable blue leatherette seats and cushioned wall benches grouped around the low tables on its carpet, and an open fire. Very good fresh fish at lunchtime in the bar includes home-cooked fresh plaice (£2.50), white fish soufflé (£3), home-made fish pie (£4.25), monkfish and lobster with shellfish sauce (£4.75), scallops in sherry and cheese sauce with mushrooms (£4.95), king prawns in garlic butter (£6.50); also, home-made soup (£1.50), ploughman's (from £1.85), home-made pâté (£2.25), and home-made puddings such as tropical fruit sorbet or brown bread and honey ice-cream (from £1.25); good breakfasts often include grilled sole or poached whiting. Note though that they don't do sandwiches. Well kept Adnams on handpump; fruit machine. There are views from the well restored keep of the nearby twelfth-century castle. (*Recommended by Angus Lindsay, Andrew and Alison Beardwood, M C Howells, Geo Rumsey, Heather Sharland, D Stephenson, Gwen and Peter Andrews, Heather Sharland, R Aitken*)

Adnams Licensee Phyllis Shaw Real ale Snacks (not Mon or Sun evenings) and lunchtime meals Restaurant Children in restaurant Open 11–2.30 (2 in winter), 6–11 all year; 11–11 Sat in summer Bedrooms tel Orford (0394) 450271; £17/£29

RAMSHOLT TM3141 Map 5

Ramsholt Arms

Village signposted from B1083; then take turning after the one to Ramsholt Church

It's the setting that distinguishes this from other pubs in the area. The isolated guardian of an old barge quay on the River Deben which winds past to the sea, it's surrounded by quiet pine woods, and silent but for the distant noise of gulls, curlews and other waders. Simple furnishings include red leatherette or green upholstered seats, red tiles or parquet flooring, some neatly nautical woodwork, tide tables and charts, and a big picture window. Well kept Adnams, Flowers Original and Tolly on handpump; home-baked rolls, a choice of ploughman's, hot smoked mackerel and smooth duck pâté, good seafood platter, steak and kidney or chicken and ham pies, with evening hot meals including steaks; sensibly placed darts, shove-ha'penny, dominoes, fruit machine. There are tables outside, on crazy paving, and a lot of boating activity on summer weekends. (*Recommended by P A Bush, MBW, JHW, Gwen and Peter Andrews*)

Free house Real ale Meals and snacks Children in dining-room Steep longish walk down from car park Open 11.30–2.30, 6.30–11 all year; opens 7 in winter

REDE TL8055 Map 5

Plough ⊗

Village signposted off A143 Bury St Edmunds–Haverhill

It's really the dishes of the day which earn our food award for what would otherwise be an unassuming local. On a typical day, they might be spicy beef (£3.95), steak and kidney pie (£4.25), lamb hot-pot (£4.50) and poached salmon or stuffed quail with black cherry sauce (£6.25), with scrumptious puddings. They do a lot of game in season, such as rabbit cooked in cider, roast partridge or pheasant casserole. There is a wide choice of other hot bar dishes and salads, too (most around £3; ploughman's in variety from £1.90), and the little evening restaurant does things like moules au gratin, lemon sole stuffed with prawns and mushrooms, and steaks. The snug bar is simple and traditional, with copper measures and pewter tankards hanging from low black beams, decorative plates on a low Delft shelf and surrounding the solid-fuel stove in its brick fireplace, and red plush button-back built-in wall banquettes. The atmosphere's truly warm and pubby, with the well lit pool-table by no means relegated to some back area; also trivia machine, fruit machine, unobtrusive piped radio; keg Greene King beers. There are picnic-table sets in front of the pretty pink-washed partly thatched pub, with more in a sheltered cottage garden behind; it's a lovely quiet spot, with not much sound beyond the birds in the aviary (and the surrounding trees) or the burbling white doves in the dovecot. *(Recommended by Mr and Mrs D E Milner, W T Aird)*

Greene King   Licensees Brian and Joyce Desborough   Meals and snacks (not Sun or Mon evenings)   Restaurant (bookings preferred tel Hawkedon (028 489) 208), evenings, Sun lunch   Children in eating area and restaurant   Open 11–3, 6.30–11 all year

SAXTEAD GREEN   TM2665   Map 5
Volunteer

B1119

This friendly, tiled pink-washed house has a light and airy lounge bar with an open fire in winter, little pictures on the cream walls, and comfortable dark russet plush furniture on its green carpet. Reasonably priced, well presented bar food includes home-made pasties, plain or toasted sandwiches, ploughman's, ham and crusty bread, plaice, a choice of salads, and a dish of the day. Well kept Tolly and Original are drawn from handpumps on a remarkably solid bar counter. The public bar has shove-ha'penny, dominoes, cribbage, a fruit machine and juke box. A pretty little back terrace has a small rockery pool. *(Recommended by Chris and Sandra Taylor, Mrs D A Biggs, Alison Hayward, Nick Dowson, Eric Walmsley)*

Tolly Cobbold   Real ale   Meals and snacks   Children in corner bar   Open 10.30–2.30, 6–11 all year

SIBTON   TM3669   Map 5
White Horse

Halesworth Road; village – and in Peasenhall even pub – signposted from A1120

Attractively furnished in an old-fashioned style, this sixteenth-century inn has little red plush armchairs by a wood-burning stove, cushioned settles, lots of tack, horsebrasses and plates on the yellowing walls, and a big rug on the black and red tiled floor. Five steps take you up past an ancient partly knocked-through timbered wall into a carpeted gallery with comfortable armed seats around rustic tables. Good bar food includes sandwiches, soup (55p), ploughman's (£1.80), lasagne, chilli con carne or trout (£2.75), rump steak (£4.60), duck à l'orange or coq au vin (£5.40) and a selection of home-made vegetarian dishes. Well kept Adnams Bitter on handpump; darts, shove-ha'penny, dominoes, cribbage and piped music. There are tables under parasols on the gravel and pretty cobblestone courtyard, and more in the big garden where there's a children's play area and space for caravans. *(Recommended by Nick Dowson, Mr and Mrs J Wilmore, Peter Bush, Jeff Cousins, Mr and Mrs G P Bishop, Mr and Mrs M Johnson, Jenny Cantle, Doreen and Toby Carrington)*

Free house   Licensees Tony and Fay Waddingham   Real ale   Lunchtime snacks and meals (not Sun evening)   Children in eating area and restaurant until 9   Open 11.30–3, 6–11 all year; opens 7 in winter; closed Mon lunchtime Sept–Mar   Bedrooms tel Peasenhall (072 879) 337; £12B/£24B

SNAPE TM3959 Map 5
Golden Key ★ ⊗

Priory Lane

The stylish low-beamed lounge bar in this civilised place has a solid-fuel stove in its big fireplace, stripped modern settles around heavy Habitat-style wooden tables on a Turkey carpet, and nice pictures on the cream walls – pencil sketches of customers, a Henry Wilkinson spaniel and so forth. The serving end has an open log fire in winter, an old-fashioned settle curving around a couple of venerable stripped tables and a tiled floor; a brick-floored side room has sofas and more tables. Very good, home-made food includes soup (£1.25), ploughman's with Cheddar, Stilton, Brie or ham (from £2.45; pity about the little pats of butter), pâté with salad and French bread (£2.75), spinach and mushroom or smoked haddock quiche or sausage, egg and onion pie (£3.50), locally caught crab (£3.75), steak (£7.45), lobster and daily specials such as rare roast beef, cottage pie or steak and kidney pie (around £4); a choice of puddings such as fruit pies or lemon cake (£1–£1.20). Well kept Adnams Bitter and Broadside on handpump, with Old ale and Tally Ho in winter, and James White's cider; friendly staff. There are tables on the gravel in the small, sheltered front garden – a lovely mass of flowers in summer. *(Recommended by Peter Griffiths, Jenny and Brian Seller, Patrick Young, BKA, Heather Sharland)*

Adnams Licensee Max Kissick-Jones Real ale Meals and snacks Open 10.30–2.30, 5.30–11 all year, with afternoon and evening extensions during Aldeburgh Festival

SOUTHWOLD TM5076 Map 5
Crown ⊗ 🛏

High Street

Adnams Bitter and Extra on handpump in this rather smart, comfortable place are in superb condition – it's the nearby Adnams brewery's flagship. But to start by describing the beers really gives the wrong impression. The place's character is better defined by the eighteen wines or so, kept perfectly on a Cruover machine, chosen monthly by Simon Loftus (so always interesting). The fine modern cooking, from an unusual bar menu which changes each day, includes soups (£1.20–£1.40), four or so starters (around £3.15) such as pleasant duck rillettes – these could also be considered as light but elaborate snacks – and up to four main dishes at around £4, such as Cromer crab, steamed cod with soya and ginger, tasty seafood casserole, or salmon and plaice roulade. Cheeses are carefully chosen, puddings delicious (£1.30–£1.75). Helpings are of a size to suit the older customers, and vegetables are cooked very lightly indeed – too lightly for some tastes; good breakfasts; very good service. The main carpeted bar has plain wooden tables with chairs and long settles that give a slightly churchy feel – first-comers sit by the wall, then later people stand up to let them out – green-grained panelling, and Georgian-style brass lamps. A smaller back oak-panelled bar, which can get very full (and possibly smoky), has brassy navigation lamps and a brass binnacle to give a nautical impression, and there are some tables in a sunny sheltered corner outside. In winter they arrange wine tastings and other events such as classical music evenings. *(Recommended by Stephen and June Clark, M C Howells, Geo Rumsey, Derek and Sylvia Stephenson, Patrick Young, Rob and Gill Weeks, Gwen and Peter Andrews, Anna Jeffery, Chris Draper, Dave Butler, Les Storey, A V Chute, Chris Wauton, Alex Mark, Hope Chenhalls, J P Selby)*

Adnams Real ale Meals and snacks Restaurant Children in eating area and restaurant Open 10.30–3, 6–11 all year Bedrooms tel Southwold (0502) 722275; £22B/£35B

Most pubs in this book sell wine by the glass. We mention wines only if they are a cut above the – generally low – average. Please let us know of any good pubs for wine.

Harbour

Blackshore Quay; entering Southwold on A1095, turn right at Kings Head and go past golf course and water tower

This friendly old waterside pub – standing among the small black huts (where you can buy fresh fish) – is a sort of unofficial clubhouse for fishermen and has a ship-to-shore radio as well as a wind speed indicator in the bar. The back bar has cushioned built-in wooden wall benches, rustic stools, stripped panelling, brass shellcases on the mantelpiece over a stove, model ships, a number of local ship and boat photographs, smoked dried fish hanging from a line on a beam and a lifeboat line launcher. The low-beamed front bar, with antique settles, is tiled and panelled, and is served from a hatch high in the wall. It specialises in good fish and chips, served in newspaper (£1.65 – an extra 3p if you want a fork), and also serves sausages (£1.10), burgers (£1.30), chicken (£1.80) and scampi (£2.20); only cold food on Sundays, with ploughman's and crab or mackerel salads. Well kept Adnams Bitter and Broadside on handpump, attractively priced; darts and juke box. There is often locally smoked eel for sale, for your freezer. A couple of picnic-table sets behind (where there are animals in pens and a children's play area) with more in front facing the jumbly waterfront bustle. *(Recommended by Gavin May, Mr and Mrs J H Wyatt, Nick Dowson, N A Wood, A V Chute, Jeremy Kemp, Heather Sharland)*

Adnams   Licensee Ron Westwood   Real ale   Meals (not Tues or Thurs evening)   Open 10.30–2.30, 6–11 all year; 7 – evenings in winter

SUTTON   TM3046   Map 5

Plough ⊗

B1083

There are picnic-table sets in front and more by the fruit trees behind this tiled white house which is surrounded by Sutton Common. Inside, the cosy front room has button-back wall banquettes, and there's a more spacious room round the side. Good value bar food includes sandwiches (from 75p, home-baked gammon 90p, toasties 5p extra), home-made soup (£1.10), ploughman's (from £1.65), burgers (from £1.65), salads (from £2.75), plaice or chicken (£2.75), scampi (£3.95) and steaks (from £6.40). In the evening a rather grander choice concentrates more on fish, with starters like mixed seafood (£3.20) or scampi (£3.35) and main courses such as grilled halibut steak with prawns or garlic butter (£5.85) or Dover sole (£10.50), and also steaks (from £6.40); daily specials include steak and Guinness or ratatouille pie and there are house specialities (twenty-four hours' notice) such as roast local pheasant in red wine sauce (£6.95) or chateaubriand (£8.95). Steward & Patteson Best and Ruddles Best on handpump; jugs of Pimms or sangria (£2.35); good service; shove-ha'penny, dominoes, cribbage, fruit machine and piped music. *(Recommended by Dr F O Wells, H Dawson; more reports please)*

Watneys   Licensees Michael and Anne Lomas   Real ale   Meals (not Sun evening or Mon) and snacks (not Sun or Mon evenings)   Restaurant tel Shottisham (0394) 411785   Children in eating area and restaurant   Open 11–2.30 (3 Sat), 6.30–11 all year

THORNDON   TM1469   Map 5

Black Horse ⊗

Village signposted off A140 and off B1077, S of Eye

Well laid out, this quietly friendly pub has scrubbed ancient red flooring-tiles and a glass-doored solid-fuel stove in the big fireplace of its central core. On one side of this is a games-room with sensibly placed darts, well lit pool and juke box. On the other, a carpeted area has small tapestried settles and country dining-chairs around stripped country tables or glossy darker ones; above a second huge fireplace a wall clock ticks ponderously between stuffed animal heads. There are dark low beams, some standing timbers, and quite a bit of stripped brick and studwork. A wide choice of attractively priced bar food includes soup (85p), sandwiches (from 90p, steak £1.95), filled baked potatoes (from 90p), filled croissants (from £1.25), burgers (from £1.30), omelettes (£1.95), several vegetarian dishes (from £2), salads (from £2.65), steak and kidney pie (£2.95) and charcoal-grilled steaks (from six-ounce rump £3.25). The restaurant (converted stables, with the original stalls) has a Friday seafood night, and good value three-course Sunday lunch (£4.95, children £3). Adnams Extra, Courage Best and Greene King Abbot on handpump are kept well under light blanket pressure, and the young licensees take their wines seriously; well reproduced and interesting late 1950s and 1960s pop music on our visit; there are white metal and plastic tables on the lawn that spreads round to the back. *(Recommended by H D Boyden, E G N Alcock, Miss J M Smith)*

Free house   Licensees Paul and Katrina Stephen   Real ale   Meals and snacks   Restaurant tel Occold (037 971) 523   Children in eating area and restaurant   Monthly folk nights, morris dancing   Open 11.30–2.30, 7 (6.30 Sat)–11 all year

THORNHAM MAGNA   TM1070   Map 5
Four Horseshoes ⊗ 🏠

Off A140 S of Diss; follow Finningham 3¼ signpost, by White Horse pub

This thatched inn is said to date back in part to the twelfth century, and the extensive bar has low and heavy black beams throughout. It's well divided into alcoves and distinct areas, and there are some character seats such as tall Windsor chairs as well as the golden plush banquettes and stools on its spread of fitted Turkey carpet. The black-timbered white walls are decorated with country pictures and farm tools, and logs burn in big fireplaces. But it's food that everyone's here for – generous helpings, quickly served by uniformed waitresses. The wide choice includes sandwiches (from 70p), soup (95p), ploughman's (from £1.60), savoury rolls (£2.20), salads (from £2.40), scallops or lasagne (£3.50), steak and kidney pie (£3.60), tagliatelle or a mild chicken curry (£3.80) and well hung steaks (£5.90); meat comes from the owners' own butcher's shop, most vegetables from their own market garden. Well kept Greene King IPA and Abbot and Websters Yorkshire on handpump; the juke box is rarely used; fruit machine. Picnic-table sets stand by flower beds on a sheltered lawn and on an even more sheltered back terrace. *(Recommended by Mrs S Mackay, Miss M A Bunting, M Quine)*

Free house   Managers Malcolm Moore and Caroline Ruth   Real ale   Meals and snacks Restaurant   Children welcome   Open 12–3, 7–11 all year   Bedrooms tel Occold (037 971) 777; £29B/£39.50B

TOSTOCK   TL9563   Map 5
Gardeners Arms

Village signposted from A45 and A1088

In summer, the sheltered lawn beside this pretty sand-coloured house is a lovely place to sit at the picnic-table sets among roses and other flowers and watch the local team playing steel quoits on the pitch here. Inside, there are low heavy black beams in the friendly lounge bar, and lots of what used to be called carving-chairs (dining-chairs with arms) around the black tables. Good bar food includes sandwiches (from 75p), home-made soup (£1), ploughman's with home-made granary rolls (£1.80), home-made vegetarian pizza (£2.60), steak sandwich (£3.25), cold salt beef (£3.25) and prawns (£3.75), with supper dishes (bookings only) like ratatouille with peanuts and cheese topping (£1.50), poached salmon steak (£6.10) and sirloin steak (£6.50). Well kept Greene King IPA and Abbot on handpump;

friendly, efficient staff. The lively tiled-floor public bar has darts, pool, shove-ha'penny, dominoes, cribbage, juke box, fruit machine and a quiz league. *(Recommended by Andrew and Alison Beardwood, Nick Dowson, E J and J W Cutting, Richard Fawcett)*

Greene King   Licensee R E Ransome   Meals and snacks (not Mon or Tues evenings or Sun lunchtime)   Restaurant tel Beyton (0359) 70460: Sun opening 8–10pm   Children in restaurant   Open 11–2.30, 7–11 all year

WALBERSWICK   TM4974 Map 5
Bell

Just off B1387

Sheltered by a hedge from the worst of the sea winds, the sizeable lawn here is a quiet place to sit at the seats and tables among roses and other flowers. Inside, the oak-beamed bar has an easy-going atmosphere, and rambles attractively around with curved high-backed settles on well worn flagstones, tiles and flooring-bricks that were here when this sleepy village was a flourishing port six hundred years ago. There is a wood-burning stove in the big fireplace, and tankards hang from oars above the bar counter, which serves well kept Adnams and Mild from handpump; to one side there is a smarter and more conventionally comfortable area, decorated with local photographs. Bar food includes sandwiches (85p, toasted 95p), plough-man's (£2, ham £2.30), freshly caught plaice (£2.75), with a good choice of summer salads from smoked mackerel or home-made quiche (£3), scampi (£3.30) and prawns or crab (£3.85); in winter there are more hot dishes; one reader was surprised to find plastic knives and forks in what is otherwise a traditional place. Shove-ha'penny, cribbage, fruit machine, space game. The bedrooms all look over the sea or the river. *(Recommended by Mr and Mrs O'Gorman, John Townsend, Gavin May, Anna Jeffery, Chris Draper, Margaret and Roy Randle; more reports please)*

Adnams   Real ale   Meals and snacks (lunchtime)   Restaurant   Children in small room off bar   Open 11–2.30, 6.30–11 all year; closed 25 Dec   Bedrooms tel Southwold (0502) 723109; /£36(£40B)

WESTLETON   TM4469 Map 5
Crown ⊗ 🛏

The comfortably furnished bar in this well kept and friendly village inn has a growing collection of old photographs and postcards of Westleton, pews, stools and settles, and a good open fire in winter. Bar food includes sandwiches (from 80p), home-made soup (£1.45), pâté (£2.15), ploughman's (from £2.15), salads (from £2.90, quiche £3.25), good freshly caught local fish such as cod and sole (from £3.50), steak and kidney pie (£3.75) and sirloin steak (£5.75); lovely puddings (£1.45); helpful service. Well kept Adnams Bitter and Broadside, Greene King IPA and Abbot, Mauldons and Rayments on handpump; dominoes, shove-ha'penny and cribbage. There are seats out in the garden (which they hope to have landscaped by Easter; they hope to have built a conservatory by then too). The Minsmere bird reserve is a couple of miles away, and in that direction there are good walks (the 'Westleton Walks') – perhaps over to our Lucky Dip entry at Eastbridge. *(Recommended by Jenny and Brian Seller, Shirley Pielou, Richard Fawcett, Robert and Vicky Tod, Derek and Sylvia Stephenson, Amanda Rusholme, Heather Sharland, NJB)*

Free house   Licensees Richard and Rosemary Price   Real ale   Meals and snacks (lunchtime)   Evening restaurant (that doubles as an art gallery)   Children in restaurant Open 11–2.30, 6–11 all year; closed 25 and 26 Dec   Bedrooms tel Westleton (072 873) 273; £27.50B/£40.50B

Tipping is not normal for bar meals, and not usually expected.

Lucky Dip

Besides the fully inspected pubs, you might like to try these Lucky Dips recommended to us and described by readers (if you do, please send us reports):

Aldeburgh [The Parade; TM4656], *Brudenell*: Smart, comfortable THF hotel with large cocktail bar open to non-residents; very good bar meals, rather expensive drinks including Adnams on handpump and (if you're lucky) a table with spectacular sea views; pleasant, helpful staff; children welcome; nr start GWG120 *(Heather Sharland, Anna Jeffery, Chris Draper)*

Aldringham [TM4461], *Parrot & Punchbowl*: Good food in cosy and unpretentious pub with uncommonly wide choice of wines by the glass, but could be more flexible with bar food service, and only dining-room meals Fri/weekend – when booking essential *(K R Harris)*

Badingham [TM3068], *White Horse*: Attractive and old-fashioned pub included particularly for its own neat bowling-green; well kept Adnams, wide choice of cheapish bar food including summer lunchtime cold buffet, vegetarian and children's dishes as well as usual pub food; more expensive busy restaurant, nice rambling garden *(Jenny Cantle, LYM)*

Blundeston [from B1074 follow Church Lane, right into Short Lane, then left; TM5197], *Plough*: Handy for Jacobean Somerleyton Hall – smartly modernised Watneys pub which was the home of Barkis the carrier in *David Copperfield (LYM)*

Boxford [Broad St; TL9640], *Fleece*: Well kept Tolly and enterprising food in partly fifteenth-century pink-washed pub, recently under new management, with former back restaurant area opened up and made lighter, medieval fireplace revealed and brought into use in lounge bar, panelled side bar, some distinctive old furniture, new restaurant opening upstairs; English home cooking *(Gwen and Peter Andrews, LYM)*

Bramfield [A144; TM4073], *Queens Head*: Obviously a lot of thought, time and money have gone into redecoration of beautiful carefully refurbished hall-type building with wonderful high beams, panel of original wattle and daub by lavatories, clean and pleasant; Adnams Bitter and Old on handpump, bar food, big log fire *(Nick Dowson)*

Brandon [by level crossing, A1065 N; TL7886], *Great Eastern*: Smart pub, well kept Adnams, bar food *(John Baker)*

Brantham [junction A137/B1080; TM1033], *Bull*: Wide choice of home-cooked bar food, reasonable prices, friendly staff, big log fire; small zoo behind with peacocks and so forth; good restaurant; children welcome, with children's helpings *(C H Fenster, Miss M A Bunting)*

Bromeswell [TM3050], *Cherry Tree*: Generous helpings of good bar food in straightforward local; comfortably modernised beamed lounge with open fire and velvet curtains; seats outside, charming inn-sign *(BB)*

Bury St Edmunds [Angel Hill; TL8564], *Angel*: Bustling town-centre hotel with comfortable lounge; cheerful, friendly service, Adnams real ale, excellent food; good bedrooms *(AE)*; [Eastgate St] *Fox*: Well kept and clean, with excellent service from Yorkshire landlord and wife, good value food, cooked and served extremely well; close to centre, with adequate parking *(Capt J Hurworth)*; [Whiting St] *Mason Arms*: Excellent choice of reasonably priced food, very friendly landlord makes all welcome, good beer and freshly squeezed orange juice, lovely surroundings, handy for town centre *(Mr and Mrs J M Glynn)*; [Traverse, Abbeygate St] *Nutshell*: Very pretty little one-roomed Greene King pub with old handpumps recessed into part of bar, curios and pictures on wall, rooms upstairs; said to have smallest interior of any pub; closed Sun and Holy Days *(Heather Sharland, Peter Hitchcock)*

Buxhall [TM0057], *Crown*: Charming sixteenth-century pub behind its plain Victorian façade, oak beams and cosy log fire, friendly landlord, well kept Greene King IPA and Abbot, good reasonably priced food including unusual cheeses with French bread; reputedly haunted *(Kevin and Mary Shakespeare)*

Cavendish [TL8046], *George*: Smallish, intimate and well decorated, good beer, very good food cooked to order and moderately priced; lovely surroundings, pleasant helpful staff; children and dogs welcome in bar *(KH)*

Charsfield [off B1078; TM2556], *Three Horseshoes*: Friendly pub with reasonably priced and slightly different home-cooked food (not Sun), well kept Tolly ales, friendly and efficient owners; nearby Akenfield Garden is worth a summer visit *(Geo Rumsey, RAS)*

☆ **Clare** [Callis St; TL7645], *Cock*: Fine pub with well kept Adnams, quick service, warm atmosphere and enthusiastic local following; good value food (especially evening meals in restaurant) *(Melvin D Buckner, Alison Krohn, Tim Bell)*

Clare [Nethergate St], *Seafarer*: Smartened-up L-shaped bar with style almost of a city pub but relaxing atmosphere, friendly young licensees (not to mention Maxwell the borzoi who's rehearsing the part of a lapdog), Nethergate, Greene King and Websters Yorkshire real ales and good small wine list, seats in garden; bedrooms *(Gwen and Peter Andrews, John Branford, LYM)*

☆ **Coddenham** [1¼ miles E of junction A45/ A140; TM1354], *Dukes Head*: Well kept

Tolly ales, choice of wines, and good help-ings of interesting food using fresh local produce cooked by imaginative landlord who took over 1987; stripped pine and simple atmosphere, welcoming landlady, pin-table in public bar, seats in steep garden behind; promising; three bedrooms *(Col and Mrs L N Smyth, Wayne Brindle, LYM)*

Cretingham [TM2260], *New Bell*: Simply furnished modernised pub, converted from fifteenth-century cottages 20 years ago; timbered walls and standing timbers, exposed beams, spacious old fireplace; tradi-tional games in quarry-tiled public bar, seats outside in rose garden and on front grass, children in eating area and restaurant; new licensees do well kept real ales, reasonably priced bar food, and jazz *(Gill and Rob Weeks, LYM)*

☆ **Dalham** [TL7261], *Affleck Arms*: Good atmosphere in thatched village pub by stream, log fire in cosy low-beamed locals' bar, good value food in more comfortable and intimate rambling dining-bar on right; some tables outside *(Frank W Gadbois, LYM)*

☆ **Darsham** [Darsham Stn; TM4069], *Strad-broke Arms*: Cheery high-ceilinged pub with good value well presented food in bar and restaurant, Adnams real ale, high-backed settles, darts and bar billiards, pretty garden with primroses and bluebells under ash trees *(Peter Bush, BB)*

Debenham [High St; TM1763], *Red Lion*: A happy place with likeable landlord, good bar menu, Tolly ales and pleasant atmosphere; fine sixteenth-century plaster ceiling in nicely furnished lounge *(E G N Alcock, BB)*

☆ **Dennington** [TM2867], *Queens Head*: Good food at average prices in attractive Tudor pub with charming stylishly simplified beamed open-plan main bar, more spartan public bar, good range of real ales, garden; attractive spot next to church *(Kevin and Mary Shakespeare, Alison Hayward, Nick Dowson, LYM)*

Earl Soham [SM2363], *Falcon*: Well kept split-level bar with mainly local customers in sixteenth-century beamed pub opposite bowling-green, open fire, popular bar food, Adnams and maybe Whitbreads Strong Country on handpump, restaurant; three comfortable double bedrooms *(Mrs S Mackay)*

☆ **East Bergholt** [Burnt Oak – on road to Flatford Mill; TM0734], *Kings Head*: Attrac-tively decorated lounge with fine corner cup-board, comfortable seats, coal fire, reason-ably priced home-cooked food including excellent salads, attentive and friendly licen-see, well kept Tolly Bitter, Original and XXXX on handpump, juke box in uncar-peted public bar; fresh filter coffee; pleasant garden with flower-decked hay wain *(Gwen and Peter Andrews, Mr and Mrs P W Dryland)*

Eastbridge [TM4566], *Eels Foot*: Simple country local well placed for Minsmere bird

reserve, Sizewell pebble beach (a good place to hunt semi-precious stones) and heathland walks (it's at the start of GWG122); crisp varnish, red leatherette, bright carpet or linoleum, well kept Adnams, basic bar food (no winter evening meals); tables on small front terrace, children in eating area *(Peter Griffiths, LYM)*

Erwarton [village signposted off B1456 Ipswich–Shotley Gate; TM2134], *Queens Head*: Good home-smoked Suffolk ham and other home-cooked food in unassuming six-teenth-century pub with old-fashioned fur-nishings; well kept Tolly (including Mild), picture window with fine view over fields to Stour estuary; seats in orchard behind *(Rob and Gill Weeks, LYM)*

Eye [Castle St; TM1473], *Horseshoes*: Idiosyncratic décor with Christmas decora-tions all year round, huge log fire and viva-cious bar staff; Adnams, Flowers, Whit-breads and Wethereds and good bar food; bedrooms exellent, with TV and video *(Andrew Dawson)*; *White Lion*: This formerly unpretentious inn interesting for its Eliza-bethan oak-beamed bar, panelled lounge and Georgian ballroom has sadly been closed down for redevelopment *(LYM)*

☆ **Felixstowe Ferry** [TM3337], *Ferry Boat*: Well kept Tolly real ales and simple bar food in neatly kept seventeenth-century pub close to sand dunes, Martello tower and harbour *(LYM)*

Framlingham [OS Sheet 156 reference 286637; TM2863], *Framlingham Castle*: Small pub right by the castle, one open-plan bar made from many small rooms, Watneys-related real ales, good value food, family eating area *(R Aitken)*

Harkstead [TM1834], *Bakers Arms*: Attrac-tive, with pleasant atmosphere and garden; food includes delicious roast beef melt – beef on melted cheese and bread with fried onion rings and salad *(S Boswell)*

Hartest [B1066 S of Bury; TL8352], *Crown*: A real village pub with two bars and pleasant licensee; simple lunchtime food, good beer and fine log fire *(W T Aird)*

Haughley [TM0262], *Kings Head*: New licen-see serving wide range of very good reason-ably priced straightforward food, well kept Greene King Abbot; charming well furnished lounge, attractive village; particularly good for lunch *(Kevin and Mary Shakespeare)*; [by level crossing towards Old Newton] *Railway*: Popular free house with well kept Mauldons Bitter, traditional bar food at low prices *(John Baker)*

Hawkedon [between A143 and B1066; TL7952], *Queens Head*: Beautifully simply furnished true village pub with big open fireplace and charming landlady; good value food includes prawn and courgette bake, spicy pancakes and good fresh chilli con carne, with real old-fashioned snacks such as sardines, eggs on toast and rarebit; though it doesn't seem large from the outside, there's room for quite a crowd; children welcome *(W T Aird)*

Huntingfield [TM3374], *Huntingfield Arms*: Friendly pub on small green close to Heveningham Hall; new licensees renovating imaginatively, well prepared ploughman's *(MT)*

Icklingham [TL7772], *Red Lion*: Locally popular thatched pub with inglenook fireplace in comfortable lounge, restaurant section beyond wrought-iron divider, good value bar food, games in big public bar, seats outside; handy for West Stow Country Park and Anglo-Saxon village *(Martin, Jane, Simon and Laura Bailey, LYM)*

Ipswich [St Peters Dock; TM1744], *Malt Kiln*: Dockside malt kiln converted into free house but keeping many of its original features, popular bar food, three floors, so surprisingly spacious; waterside tables – a good place to view the Thames barges gathered here for the annual races *(Rob and Gill Weeks)*; [St Margarets Green, corner of St Margarets St] *Mulberry Tree*: Good food and well kept Tolly Original in up-market town-centre pub; carvery, grill some evenings *(Mark Walpole)*; [1 Fore St] *Spread Eagle*: Busy local with regulars' noticeboard and trophy cabinet, neat rooms, polite staff, well kept Tolly Bitter, Mild, XXXX on handpump *(Roger Broadie)*; [King St] *Swan*: Old low-beamed pub with well kept Tolly Bitter, Original and XXXX *(Mark Walpole)*

Ixworth Thorpe [TL9173], *Oak*: Cheerful simply furnished country pub with popular food, sensibly placed darts and pool-table, quite near Bardwell working windmill *(BB)*

Kersey [The Street; TL9944], *White Horse*: Pretty pink-washed village pub with delightful very friendly atmosphere, real fire in the public bar's range Victorian range, beams and timbering, wooden furniture, well kept real ales such as Adnams Extra and Old, Nethergate and perhaps a guest beer, good choice of well presented home-cooked food including fine ploughman's and Suffolk ham, good service; children allowed in lounge bar – there's also a play area behind car park *(Rob and Gill Weeks, Peter King, C H Fewster, Mr and Mrs P W Dryland)*

Lavenham [TL9149], *Swan*: Handsome and comfortable Elizabethan hotel, with in its heart a pubby little bar with leather seats on its tiled floor and well kept Adnams and Greene King; spacious overflow into numerous communicating but cosy seating areas with beams, timbers, armchairs and settees; bar food, lavishly timbered restaurant, pleasant garden; a magnet for American and other tourists, and has recently been through a phase in which it seemed perhaps too much of a hotel and too pricey for our pages – but it seems now to be recovering its appeal *(Barbara Hatfield, AE, Mrs R Wilmot, Gwen and Peter Andrews, J S Evans, Heather Sharland, G H Theaker, J M M Hill, LYM)*

Lavenham, *Angel*: Simple well prepared reasonably priced food with children's special; well kept Ruddles *(Richard Fawcett)*; *Greyhound*: Friendly and simple pub in picturesque (if expensive) village, excellent food *(Tom, Lorna, Audrey and Alan Chatting)*

Laxfield [TM2972], *Royal Oak*: Lovely fire in beautiful fireplace, Adnams, reasonable food *(Nick Dowson, Alison Hayward)*

Layham [Upper Layham; TM0340], *Marquis of Cornwallis*: Good variety of simple pub food, well presented and fresh, in generous helpings *(Tom Gondris)*

Leiston [Station Rd; TM4462], *White Horse*: More hotel than pub, but lively atmosphere, charming staff; good range of pub-priced hot dishes and salads in restaurant – serving late for this area, with generous helpings; brilliant adventure playground with inflatable, giant boot and so forth; bedrooms very comfortable – only snag is traffic noise, this being a busy crossroads *(K R Harris, Anna Jeffery, Chris Draper)*

☆ **Levington** [Gun Hill; village signposted from A45, then follow Stratton Hall signpost; TM2339], *Ship*: Engaging three-roomed traditional pub with ship pictures, chatty Amazon parrot, well kept Tolly ales, thoughtful bar lunches including plump kippers and home-smoked ham ploughman's; seats in front with distant sea view; might well be a main entry still if licensee deigned ever to return our fact-checking questionnaires *(John Baker, K R Harris, LYM)*

Lidgate [TL7257], *Star*: Attractive old building, partly an old cottage, friendly and welcoming landlord, large open fire with Sun spit roasts, good bar food *(Mr and Mrs P W Dryland)*

☆ **Lindsey Tye** [TL9843], *Red Rose*: Clean and attractive pink-washed beamed pub with open fires, fresh flowers on tables, lively Amazon parrot, well kept Adnams, Greene King and a beer brewed for them by Mauldons, big helpings of reasonably priced and well cooked hot food in bar or restaurant; standing timbers from knocked-through walls save it from feeling too open-plan, unobtrusive piped music *(Rob and Gill Weeks, M J Clarke)*

☆ **Long Melford** [TL8645], *Bull*: Fine black and white timbered building, originally a medieval manorial hall and an inn since 1580, in beautiful village; interesting rooms, with woodwose – Suffolk wild man – carved on high beam in lounge, log fire in big fireplace, charming antique furnishings; currently on an upswing, with good value (though not cheap) bar food in spacious and attractive back dining-lounge (not Sun – the restaurant lunch is good then), well kept Adnams and Greene King IPA on handpump, civilised and efficient service, newspapers and magazines set out for customers; tables out in central courtyard; bedrooms either entertainingly ancient or very comfortably modern *(Heather Sharland, Dave Butler, Les Storey, Gwen and Peter Andrews, Ian Phillips, J S Evans, LYM)*

Long Melford, *Black Lion*: It's closed its public bar and is no longer a pub, but this small seventeenth-century hotel is worth knowing for imaginative well presented food in lounge bar, well kept Nethergate on handpump, and comfortable bedrooms with lovely views; the classical piped music may be a bit intrusive; seats out on green *(Heather Sharland, C M and D D Lloyd)*

Mendham [TM2782], *Sir Alfred Munnings*: Cheery atmosphere in big open-plan bar of inn with well kept Adnams and Courage Directors, bar food, restaurant; children welcome, bedrooms, swimming-pool for residents *(LYM)*

Mill Green [nr Edwardstone; TL9542], *White Horse*: Simple remote pub with traditional atmosphere, many locals, quiet welcome *(Dr Paul Kitchener)*

Newmarket [High St; TL6463], *Rutland Arms*: Well kept and comfortable Georgian hotel with good value food; when George Osbaldeston set his 1831 record for riding 200 miles, his time of under 8¾ hours included his single stop, here, for cold partridge and brandy *(W T Aird)*; [High St] *White Hart*: Comfortable central hotel with racing pictures and open fire in spacious lounge, solid back cocktail bar, and pleasant lobby between; bar food, well kept Tolly, restaurant *(Rob and Gill Weeks, Howard and Sue Gascoyne, LYM)*

North Cove [TM4789], *Three Horseshoes*: Pleasant pub with cosy atmosphere, bricks and rustic timberwork, open fire, tapestried seat coverings, piped music, horsebrasses and fruit machine; well kept Ruddles County on handpump, bar food and separate restaurant *(Nick Dowson, Jon Reed)*

Oulton Broad [Commodore Rd; TM5292], *Commodore*: Well done modernised pub with friendly and helpful staff, wide choice of good value food and attractive terrace looking over the Broad *(Jon Reed)*

Pakefield [TM5390], *Jolly Sailors*: Excellent value carvery in comfortable well kept pub *(Anon)*

Rattlesden [TL9758], *Brewers Arms*: Friendly and unpretentious village pub with lively public bar (pool, darts and so forth) *(LYM)*

Rickinghall [A143 Diss—Bury St Edmunds; TM0475], *Hamblyn House*: Sixteenth-century building, large lounge with copper and brassware and good atmosphere; Adnams, Greene King IPA and Abbot, good range of bar food; bedrooms with exposed timbers *(Roger Huggins)*

Risby [TL7966], *Crown & Castle*: Friendly licensees in nicely refurbished timbered pub with winter log fire, Greene King real ale, and wide choice of home-made food including charcoal grills *(Michael Wigg)*;

White Horse: Comfortable pub, spacious and uncrowded, with well kept Greene King beers, bar food *(LYM)*

St James South Elmham [OS Sheet 156 reference 320812; TM3181], *White Horse*: Two quaint bars – one with a painted highbacked settle around fireplace; cosy lounge bar and friendly service, Adnams on handpump, fruit machines *(Alison Hayward, Nick Dowson)*

Saxmundham [High St; TM3863], *Queens Head*: Reasonably priced good bar meals, friendly surroundings, Whitbreads real ale; children's room, aviary by car park *(Peter Bush)*

☆ **Snape** [TM3959], [The Maltings], *Plough & Sail*: Tastefully modernised narrow L-shaped bar with alcoves and small restaurant leading off, carpets on the tiled floor, Liberty-print curtains, well kept Adnams, welcoming staff, good range of bar food; can get very full when there are concerts *(Gwen and Peter Andrews, Mr and Mrs J H Wyatt, Heather Sharland)*; [B1069] *Crown*: Front room supposed to be the model for the Boar in Britten's *Peter Grimes*, in much done-up pub which very much caters for visitors to the Maltings; chatty landlord, tremendously wide choice of food served with lots of vegetables, Adnams real ales, barn-like children's room, interesting ducks and geese on pond; well equipped bedrooms *(Dr and Mrs R M Belbin, BKA, LYM)*

Southolt [TM1968], *Plough*: Heavily beamed sixteenth-century pub by church on village green, good food in bar and small bookable restaurant *(Mrs Mackay, Mr Margarson)*

☆ **Southwold** [South Green; TM5076], *Red Lion*: Well kept Adnams ales, good lunchtime snacks and salads in brown-panelled bar with big windows on to green, nice atmosphere, ship pictures, brassware and copper, elm-slab barrel tables; also welcoming family-room and summer buffet room *(Derek and Sylvia Stephenson, BB)*

Southwold, *Kings Head*: Cheerful proper pub, friendly, with pleasant red wine *(A V Chute)*; [42 East St] *Lord Nelson*: Well kept Adnams, close to town centre and beach; bedrooms excellent value, one overlooking sea *(Mr and Mrs P A Jones)*; [7 East Green] *Sole Bay*: Good value simple lunchtime trade (not Sun) and well kept Adnams – this very friendly Victorian local is just across the road from the brewery, and only a stroll from the sea *(Derek and Sylvia Stephenson, Jeremy Kemp, LYM)*; [Market Pl] *Swan*: Good prints and pictures in Georgian hotel's attractive lounge bar, Adnams ales – including full range of the interesting bottled ones; bar food *(LYM)*

Spexhall [Stone St (A144); TM3780], *Huntsman & Hounds*: Excellent food in nicely decorated fourteenth-century pub with log fire and prompt service by pleasant staff; some tables bookable *(Mrs Mackay, Mr Margarson)*

Stoke by Nayland [TL9836], *Angel*: Pleasant pub, originally a set of old cottages, most attractively refurbished by young licensees; spacious, with beams, timbers, exposed brickwork and log fires; well kept Adnams, Greene King IPA and Abbot, Mauldons and Nethergate, wide range of fine bar meals from fresh asparagus or Greek salad through interesting omelettes or aubergine fritters to trout or grilled grey mullet (only problem is that you may have to wait quite a while for a table and even up to an hour for food if they're very busy); relaxed atmosphere, pleasant service, piped music, enterprising restaurant (Tues evening to Sun lunch – must book), seats on terrace, beautiful village; bedrooms open off gallery *(Gwen and Peter Andrews, John Brooks, B J E Phillips, D J Milner, Mr and Mrs Bill Muirhead)*; *Crown*: Spacious series of comfortably modernised rooms in lounge bar with reliable food including excellent home-made pies, Tolly on handpump, restaurant; bedrooms *(Margaret and Roy Randle, LYM)*

Stradbroke [TM2374], *White Hart*: Good food in pleasant pub with nice fire and brasses *(Nick Dowson)*

Stradishall [A143; TL7452], *Cherry Tree*: Included for its most attractive back garden with lots of space and small lake; amiable landlord, Greene King beers, sandwiches, ploughman's and some hot dishes *(W T Aird)*

Stutton [Manningtree Rd; TM1534], *Kings Head*: Spotless sixteenth-century pub in pretty village, amazing value bar food, well kept Tolly ales, very hospitable staff *(Chris Fluck)*

Thorington Street [TM0035], *Rose*: Deservedly very popular for decent choice of reasonably priced good hot food *(M J Clarke)*

Thurston [Barrells Rd]; village signposted from A1108 N of Norton, then turn left on S-bend by Bayer Experimental Farm, then first right – OS Sheet 155 reference 939651; TL9365], *Black Fox*: Thanks to many readers for putting us right about the location of this unusual traditional pub, wrongly listed under Thurston End in the 1988 edition; an old drovers' tap-room almost like a private house, with a good choice of real ales including Adnams and Greene King tapped from barrels in a back room, good atmosphere, open fire, frequent singsongs *(Rob and Gill Weeks, John Baker)*

Tunstall [TM3555], *Green Man*: Good value food including terrific burgers, and well kept Tolly, in comfortable and airily modern village pub with comfortable lounge and small games-bar; bedrooms *(Chris Fluck, BB)*

Wangford [A12 to Wrentham; TM4679], *Plough*: Good, clean pub where decent dress is expected, well kept Adnams, pleasant landlord and staff, simple well cooked food –

smoked and fresh salmon a speciality *(GMG, AVC)*

Washbrook [TM1042], *Brook*: Warm, cosy pub with very friendly service and excellent steak *(Andrew Pye)*

Wenhaston [TM4276], *Star*: Simple friendly local with sun-trap small lounge, well kept Adnams ales, games in public bar, bar food, spacious lawn; simple bedrooms *(LYM)*

West Creeting Green [TM0758], *Red Lion*: Unusual and welcoming landlord – he feeds parrots by letting them take tidbits from between his lips; well kept Greene King beer *(D S Fowles)*

West Row [TL6775], *Judes Ferry*: Riverside free house with tables and chairs along bank; open fire, friendly landlord, good range of well kept ales on handpump change weekly, large choice of freshly prepared bar food, fruit machines *(Frank Gadbois)*

☆ **Westleton** [TM4469], *White Horse*: Good welcome, friendly atmosphere, well presented good value food including fine Stilton ploughman's served on a breadboard; nice position by village pond, and handy for Minsmere RSPB reserve; bedrooms comfortable *(A T Langton, Geo Rumsey, J B Robinson, Ian and Gillian Edgar)*

Wetherden [TM0062], *Maypole*: Friendly village pub with strikingly beamed and timbered open-plan bar, bar food, well kept Adnams, live music Fri and Sat, disco Weds and Sun *(LYM)*

☆ **Wetheringsett** [TM1266], *Cat & Mouse*: Fifteenth-century free house with friendly licensees, several bars, no fewer than 15 well kept real ales on handpump, bar food, barbecues by stream, separate dining-room, outside tables *(Frank Gadbois)*

Wickhambrook [TL7554], *Cloak*: Excellent friendly service, good beer and food; children welcome *(Steve Monk)*

Woodbridge [The Thoroughfare; TM2749], *Crown*: Reasonable priced bar meals including good daily specials, fresh fish and steaks; bedrooms *(Geo Rumsey)*; [Market Sq] *Kings Head*: Friendly pub with scrubbed kitchen tables around spacious bar and inglenook fireplace; well kept Tolly and good bar food *(Angus Lindsay)*; [Pytches Rd] *Melton Grange*: Wide choice of good reasonably priced bar meals in pleasant bar, Flowers and Stones beers; bedrooms *(Geo Rumsey)*; [off Market Sq] *Olde Bell & Steelyard*: Fascinating old local, derricks from steelyard still in place over street, fires, well kept Greene King IPA and Abbot on handpump *(Angus Lindsay)*

☆ **Woolpit** [TL9762], *Swan*: Neatly kept partly panelled and beamed sixteenth-century bar with open fires, low settles, seats in bay windows, good value bar food (not Thurs –Sat evenings), well kept Watneys-related real ales; clean, bright and airy bedrooms *(LYM)*

Surrey

As elsewhere in the South-East, there have been more changes of licensees in the last year here than we'd normally expect: at the heavily beamed Whyte Harte in Bletchingley, the Crown at Chiddingfold (one of Britain's oldest licensed inns, and certainly the oldest in the county), the attractively laid out Cricketers in Dorking (the previous licensee's departure unfortunately comes too late for us to predict how the new regime will turn out; fingers crossed, therefore), the traditional Queen's Head at East Clandon, the Windmill in its marvellous position on the steep wooded hills above Ewhurst (perhaps the nicest surroundings of any pub in the county), the interesting old White Horse in the picture-book village of Shere, and the Wotton Hatch at Wotton. Several of the newcomers to the Guide have been steered into these pages by new or relatively new licensees, too: the cosy and traditional Plough at Coldharbour (the highest pub in South-East England, in a most attractive spot; popular with dogs too – they get a free biscuit), the calm and relaxing Black Horse at Gomshall, and the rambling and lively Dog & Duck out in the country near Outwood (unusual for the area in being tied to Badger; its young licensees, brother and sister, are doing food all day). Other newcomers are the White Bear at Fickleshole (a remarkable find for the area, with its rambling rooms and its big garden full of animals and birds), the Bell in Godstone (beside a fine traditional bar it's gone out of its way to cater separately and very successfully for children), the bustling spick-and-span Plough overlooking the village green in Leigh (particularly good food), and its fairly near neighbour the pretty Seven Stars. We've noticed a trend here for pubs to split their menus – relatively simple good value traditional bar food at

The Punch Bowl, nr Ockley

lunchtime, and more expensive dishes in the evening, when the atmosphere may become more dining-outish. It will be interesting to see whether this spreads, over the next few months. We'll also be interested to watch the progress of several pubs that are currently looking particularly prominent among the Lucky Dip entries at the end of the chapter – the Abinger Hatch on Abinger Common, Dog & Pheasant at Brook, Woolpack at Elstead, Thames Court by the river in Shepperton, Volunteer at Sutton and Three Horseshoes at Thursley.

BATTS CORNER SU8240 Map 2
Blue Bell

Take road signposted Rowledge, Dockenfield, Frensham off A325 S of Farnham, by Halfway House pub at Bucks Horn Oak; after ¾ mile turn left into village lane; OS Sheet 186 reference 820410

Right on the edge of Alice Holt Forest and overlooking rolling countryside, this very civilised country pub – run with a good deal of character – has a spacious garden with seats built around fairy-lit apple trees, tables on a terrace, tubs of flowers, and a tree-house and swings for children and toddlers. Inside, the snug and low-ceilinged original room has bulgy white-painted stone walls, a big fireplace, and leatherette seats around low tables on the carpet. Other rooms open off: one, through an arch, has wheel-backs and settles on a tiled floor; another is higher-ceilinged, a long room with wheel-back chairs around its tables. It in turn opens into an airy big-windowed extension with button-back leatherette banquettes. Simple bar food such as home-made sandwiches (from 95p), soup (£1.05) and ploughman's (from £1.40). Well kept Ballards Best and Wassail, Brakspears SB, Courage Best and Fullers ESB tapped from the cask; darts, shove-ha'penny, dominoes and cribbage. Large car park. *(Recommended by G B Longden, Lyn and Bill Capper; more reports please)*

Free house Licensee Moira Yells Real ale Lunchtime meals (not Sat or Sun) and snacks Open 11–2.30, 6–11 all year

BETCHWORTH TQ2049 Map 3
Dolphin
The Street

Though surrounded by decidedly G and T country, this flagstoned and gaslit pub firmly defends older traditions. At the back, the black-panelled and carpeted saloon bar has robust old-fashioned elm or oak tables, and a sonorous longcase clock; the front bar has kitchen chairs, plain tables and big open fireplaces. Well kept Youngs Bitter and Special on handpump; a good choice of well made sandwiches, Cheddar or Stilton ploughman's, good home-made shepherd's pie and other hot dishes. There are some seats in the small laurel-shaded front courtyard, and more beyond the car park, opposite the church. No leather jackets allowed. *(Recommended by Phil and Sally Gorton, Dave Butler, Jenny Seller, John Branford)*

Youngs Real ale Meals (not Sun or Mon evenings) and snacks (not Sun evening) Open 10.30–2.30, 5.30–11

BLACKBROOK TQ1846 Map 3
Plough ⊗

On byroad E of A24, parallel to it, between Dorking and Newdigate, just N of the turn E to Leigh

The light and airy saloon bar (there is a no-smoking area) has copper-topped trestle tables from which to enjoy the good, interesting food: specials might include spinach and mushroom soup (£1.25), deep-fried prawns with satay sauce (£2.95), West Indian lamb pepperpot, beef pasandahr or paella (£4.75), baked tuna with ginger sauce (£5.25); other food includes good ploughman's (£2.25), basket meals (from £2.25, scampi £3.95), salads (from £2.65, fresh prawn £4.75), plaice (£3.45), ham steak with pineapple (£3.75), lasagne, ratatouille niçoise, chilli con carne or moussaka (all £3.95), prawn curry (£4.45) and steaks (from £6.25). Well kept King & Barnes Sussex, Festive, Mild (in summer) and Old Ale (in winter) on handpump; the pub regularly wins its brewery's annual best-kept cellar competition. There are fourteen wines by the glass; friendly service. Down some steps, the public bar has quite a formidable collection of ties as well as old saws on the ceiling, and shove-ha'penny, dominoes, cribbage and piped music. You can sit outside at the front under the fourteen hanging baskets, or more quietly on the grass or a small terrace at the back, which in summer is full of tubs of flowers. At Christmas time they hold annual carol concerts and there are free mince pies and punch. Just south is a good stretch of attractive oak wood with plenty of paths – and a big pond. *(Recommended by Norman Foot, Mike Muston, S A Lovett, Jason Caulkin, WFL, Mr and Mrs W Harrington, Capt F A Bland, John Branford)*

King & Barnes   Licensee Robin Squire   Real ale   Meals and snacks (not Mon evening) Open 11–2.30, 6–11; closed 25, 26 Dec and 1 Jan

BLETCHINGLEY   TQ3250 Map 3

Whyte Harte

2½ miles from M25 junction 6; A22 towards East Grinstead then A25 towards Redhill

For nearly three centuries this well run, busy pub has been in business, though it probably wasn't licensed as an inn until the coaching era. As we went to press new licensees were just moving in and have plans to extend their food operation: home-made bar food includes sandwiches (from £1.80, smoked salmon £3), ploughman's (£2.50), hot dishes such as cottage pie, lasagne, moussaka and chilli con carne (from £3.20), mixed grill (£6.50) and sirloin steak (£7); three-course Sunday lunch (£7.50). Well kept Friary Meux, Ind Coope Burton and Tetley Bitter on handpump; also a fair range of wines. The big, mostly open-plan bars have comfortable old plush-covered settles and stools, rugs on the neat wood-block floor, dark low ceiling-beams, old-fashioned prints on the walls and an inglenook fireplace with a heavily sagging chimney-beam; they are considering having bar skittles and shove-ha'penny. There are tables on a strip of lawn behind, sheltered by an old stone wall and the backs of two of the Tudor cottages that are a feature of this pretty village; you can also sit out in front, sharing the cobbles with tubs of flowers, looking across the wide, sloping village street to the church. *(Recommended by E G Parish, Simon Small, Paul and Margaret Baker, Mrs R F Warner, John Branford)*

Friary Meux   Licensees Helen and David Cooper   Real ale   Meals and snacks   Children in eating area   Open 11–2.30, 6–11 all year; considering longer afternoon opening on Sat Bedrooms tel Godstone (0883) 843231; £23(£25B)/£34(£38B)

CHIDDINGFOLD   SU9635 Map 2

Crown ⊗ ⊨

One of the oldest licensed inns in England, this lovely timbered building has oak beams over two feet thick, fine oak panelling, a magnificently carved inglenook fireplace, massive chimneys, and a cabinet of coins going back some four hundred years found here during renovations. The recently refurbished lower back area has a wood cooking fire with a central chimney dividing it into two separate rooms. Bar food includes sandwiches, smoked mackerel and apple pâté or spinach and cream cheese roulade (£2.20), beef and Guinness pie or chicken in tarragon and lemon sauce (£3.50), and fresh puddings such as strawberry vacherin (£1.50). Well kept

Adnams Bitter on handpump. The restaurant is panelled and tapestry-hung. There are seats outside looking across the village green to the church, which is much the same age, and other tables in a sheltered central courtyard. In early summer the inn is a marvellous sight, with wood mullions, laburnum, lilac and wistaria. On 5 November there is a fireworks party on the village green. The village has copses of sweet chestnut and ash specially grown for umbrella handles and walking-sticks. *(Recommended by Charles and Mary Winpenny, Gwen and Peter Andrews, Lyn and Bill Capper, Mike and Kay Wilson, Doug Kennedy, Peter Griffiths, Hope Chenhalls)*

Free house   Licensee Andrew Kitson   Real ale   Meals and snacks   Restaurant   Children in eating area   Open 11–11 all year   Bedrooms tel Wormley (042 879) 2255; £38B/£71B

Swan ⊗

Petworth Road (A283 S)

On the walls of the comfortable and spacious bar in this well run tile-hung pub there are a good many hunting, shooting and fishing pictures and objects. This enthusiasm of the licensee is also reflected in the food, with game and game fish probably bagged by him or his family. Other dishes (maybe using produce from the family farm) include sandwiches (from 95p), home-made soup (£1.10), filled baked potatoes (from £1.30), cottage pie (£1.75), ploughman's (from £1.95), squid with home-made garlic mayonnaise (£2.50), herby grilled sardines (£2.65), home-made steak and kidney pie (£3.40) and eight-ounce sirloin steak (£7.25); there is a special curry night (from £2.75) and evening seasonal specials such as fillet of carp in coriander and cream (£7.10) or goose in fresh sage, apple and cream (£9.25). The restaurant is strong on fish, local game and venison. Well kepts Benskins, Friary Meux and Gales HSB on handpump, and decent wines. There are good log fires in winter, a friendly pub atmosphere and a back den; fruit machine and trivia. Some seats outside. *(Recommended by James Cane, Lyn and Bill Capper, Capt and Mrs L R Sowka)*

Friary Meux (Ind Coope)   Licensee Neil Bradford   Real ale   Meals and snacks   Restaurant tel Wormley (042 879) 2073; may stay open late at lunchtime   Children in eating area and restaurant   Open 11–3, 6–11 all year; maybe longer afternoon opening if trade demands

CHIPSTEAD   TQ2757 Map 3
Well House

3 miles from M25 junction 8; A217 towards Banstead, turn right at second roundabout following Mugswell, Chipstead signpost; can also be reached from A23 just W of Coulsdon

Quite alone in a country valley, this pretty pub has a pleasantly rustic character, big low fourteenth-century beams and inglenook fireplaces. The central room, mainly used for standing, has a few tables and wheel-back chairs around the edge, and red Turkey carpeting sweeps through from here into a quieter room with many more tables and comfortable tapestried seats. A side room has darts. Home-made bar food includes sandwiches, filled baked potatoes (from £1.10), chicken curry, cheese and onion pie or chilli con carne (£2.35), spinach and mushroom quiche with baked potato and coleslaw (£2.60), steak pie (£2.70) and puddings like apple, raspberry, apricot or blackcurrant pies with cream (£1). Well kept Bass and Charrington IPA on handpump. The garden is particularly attractive in summer with hanging baskets, neat small flower beds, an old yew coppice then taller trees behind and masses of birdsong. There is a well – a Wishing Well (proceeds to charity) – on the sheltered back terrace. *(Recommended by GRE, AE, Mike Muston, Dave Butler, Les Storey, R P Taylor, Lance White)*

Charringtons   Licensee W G Hummerston   Real ale   Meals and snacks (lunchtime, not Sun)   Children in eating area   Open 11–2.30, 5.30 (6 Sat)–11 all year

It's against the law for bar staff to smoke while handling food or drink.

COBHAM   TQ1060 Map 3
Cricketers

Downside Common; from A245 on Byfleet side of Cobham follow Downside signpost into
Downside Bridge Road, follow road into its right fork – away from Cobham Park – at second
turn after bridge, then take next left turn into the pub's own lane

Overlooking the broad green, this rambling country pub has a neat and charming
garden with standard roses, dahlias and other bedding plants, urns and hanging
baskets. Inside, there are some time-bowed standing timbers, beams so low they
have crash-pads on them, and places where you can see the wide oak ceiling-boards
and ancient plastering laths; bar furnishings are simple and traditional, there are
horsebrasses and big brass platters on the walls, and a good log fire in winter; piped
music. Good bar food includes sandwiches (from £1.25), ploughman's (from
£1.50), salads (from £2.50), and hot dishes such as lasagne (£2.95), vegetarian
pasta, liver and bacon or pork chops in orange sauce (£3.25). Well kept Ruddles
Best and County, and Websters Yorkshire on handpump; helpful service. *(Recommended by Norman Foot, Alasdair Knowles, K and D E Worrall, Derek Pascall, WFL, Doug
Kennedy, John Branford, Michael and Harriet Robinson)*

*Watneys   Licensee B J W Luxford   Real ale   Meals and snacks   Restaurant tel Cobham
(0932) 62105   Children in restaurant and stable bar   Open 11–2.30, 6–11 all year*

COLDHARBOUR   TQ1543 Map 3
Plough

Village signposted in the network of small roads around Abinger and Leith Hill, off
A24 and A29

At eight hundred feet, this is the highest pub in South-East England – a pretty
black-shuttered white house in a quiet hamlet by Buryhill Woods, with attractive
views from its peaceful garden, which has a fish pond with waterlilies and is fairy-lit
at night. Inside there are two bars, with stripped light beams, timbering in the
warm-coloured dark ochre walls, quite unusual little chairs around the tables in the
snug red-carpeted room on the left, little decorative plates on the walls and a big
open fire in the one on the right – which leads through to the restaurant. The
enthusiastic new licensees who took over in early 1988 (he was a Fleet Street
journalist before) are to some extent still feeling their way – there may be some
renovations. But they've already won firm approval for their food: perhaps a
simpler choice than before, but all home cooked using good ingredients. It includes
vegetable soup (£1.25), sandwiches (from £1.30), filled baked potatoes (from
£1.50), vegetarian lasagne (£2.50), very popular ham and egg (£3) and a good few
pies such as pork and apple in cider, lamb with apricot and steak and kidney pie
(£3.25). And the range of well kept real ales is wider than ever, with Badger Best,
Buckleys, Ringwood Old Thumper and Theakstons Old Peculier on handpump,
and guests such as King & Barnes Festive or Pilgrims Progress changing every three
weeks; there may be piped music. Besides the garden, there are picnic-table sets in
front, with one or two tubs of flowers. The games-bar on the left has darts and
pool; dogs and walkers are welcome (the dogs get a free biscuit). *(Recommended by
Ray Challoner, R P Taylor, D J Penny, Gary Wilkes, Mrs Jenny Seller, TOH, John Branford)*

*Free house   Licensees Mr and Mrs Norman Luck   Real ale   Meals and snacks   Restaurant
tel Dorking (0306) 711793   Children welcome (not in main area at weekends)   Open
11.30–2.30, 6.30–11 all year; considering longer opening Sat*

There are report forms at the back of the book.

The details at the end of each main entry start by saying whether the pub is a free house or if it's
tied to a brewery (which we name).

COMPTON SU9546 Map 2
Harrow ⊗
B3000

Fairly close to the North Downs Way, this friendly country pub is mainly popular for its unusual range of attractively presented food: sandwiches such as smoked turkey and avocado (from £1.50), and hot dishes that change every two weeks such as pizzas (from £3.25), fish, vegetarian or Indian dishes (from £3.50) and seafood platter (£11.50). Well kept Friary Meux Bitter, Ind Coope Burton and Tetleys Bitter on handpump; cordial service. The main bar has an attractively relaxed atmosphere, some interesting racing pictures below the ancient ceiling, mostly portraits of horses such as Nijinsky, jockey caricatures and signed race-finish photographs; other beamed rooms with latched rustic doors open off it. Piped music, two trivia machines. You can sit outside this friendly country pub in summer, round by the car park but looking out to gentle slopes of pasture. In the pretty village the art-nouveau Watts Chapel and Gallery are interesting, and the church itself is attractive; Loseley House is nearby too. *(Recommended by TOH, Charles and Mary Winpenny, Ian and Liz Phillips, Jenny Seller, Mrs A Mager, John Estdale, KC, Dr I J Thompson)*

Friary Meux   Licensee Roger Seaman   Real ale   Meals and snacks   Children in eating area   Open 11–2.30, 5.30–11 all year

DORKING TQ1649 Map 3
Cricketers ⊗
81 South Street; from centre follow signs to Horsham (A2003)

As Dorking is one of relatively few towns (as opposed to villages) in the Home Counties to have a really fine pub, we're surprised we don't get more reports on this one. The comfortably modernised, attractive bar has a notably friendly atmosphere, and library chairs around cast-iron-framed tables, well cushioned sturdy modern settles, and a central servery with a big modern etched-glass cricketers mirror. The stripped-and-sealed brick walls are decorated with Spy cricketer caricatures and other cricketing pictures, and there's a log-effect gas fire. Popular lunchtime bar food includes very fresh rolls, ploughman's (£1.20), liver and mushroom pâté (£1.75), smoked mackerel (£1.80), chilli with noodles (£1.90), fish and chips (£1.95) and scampi (£2.20), with daily specials such as moussaka or chicken and prawn risotto (£1.90), stuffed marrow, cottage pie, curry or lasagne (£1.95), bacon and mushroom quiche or steak and kidney pie (£2) and lamb kebabs with saté sauce or beef goulash (£2.05). Really well kept Fullers Chiswick, ESB and London Pride on handpump; darts, chess, cards and piped music. Up steps at the back there's a very pretty little sheltered terrace, interestingly planted with roses, a good red honeysuckle, uncommon shrubs and herbaceous plants, and gently floodlit at night. The landlord left just before this book was to be published: though there's no denying the companionable atmosphere has owed a lot to him, he leaves behind a very well laid out pub, with a good many points of merit – it shouldn't be too difficult for his successor to keep up the pub's fine reputation. *(Recommended by Keith Garley, D J Penny; more reports please)*

Fullers   Real ale   Meals (lunchtime, not Sat or Sun) and snacks (not Sun)   Nearby daytime parking difficult   Children (excl babies) welcome   Open 11–2.30, 5.30–11

EAST CLANDON TQ0651 Map 3
Queen's Head
In a quiet cluster of cottages, this civilised and traditionally furnished half-timbered pub has comfortable upholstered chairs, little beer-keg seats, a fine elm bar counter,

a faded but interesting Victorian foxhunting embroidery, brasses and copper, and a big inglenook fireplace. As we went to press the licensee told us he was leaving in a few weeks, so the choice of unusual food may change; it has included Mrs Beeton's good family soup (£1.10), sandwiches, fresh prawns from Selsey (£2.65), a range of pies (£4.40) and steaks (£6.30). Our only advice to the new licensee is to invest in a more efficient extractor fan. Friary Meux and Ind Coope Burton on handpump. It can get crowded in the evenings. You can sit on roadside benches in front, or by the flowers round a tree-sheltered side lawn. The car park backs on to an orchard behind the pub, where children can run wild. Off the road south to Shere, you can walk through splendid beech woods. *(Recommended by J S Evans, Dave Braisted, Nick Dowson, Alison Hayward, S V Bishop, A Bloxsome, A T Langton, I S Wilson)*

Friary Meux   Real ale   Snacks (lunchtime) and meals   Open 11.30–2.30, 6.30–11; closes 10.30 in winter

nr EWHURST   TQ0940 Map 3
Windmill ★ ⊗

Ewhurst–Shere back road; follow Shere signposts from E end of Ewhurst main street, or ask for Pitch Hill

This pub's position is one of the finest in the South, and makes it well worth a visit – particularly in summer when you can sit at sheltered tables among flowers and shrubs and look out over the beautifully kept terraced lawns that drop steeply away below. On a clear day you can see right across to the South Coast – useful in the days when this pub was a smugglers' lookout, and the woods are marvellous for walking (the pub is on *Good Walks Guide* Walk 55). There may well be changes to the menu as the new licensee settles in: soup (95p), sandwiches (from £1.45), sausages and mash (£1.90), salads (from £2.95), curry (from £3) and chicken casseroled in red wine (£4.40). Well kept King & Barnes Sussex and Youngs Special on handpump. The main bar has easy chairs and a patterned carpet, and a sparser back bar, without the view, has darts, dominoes, shove-ha'penny, fruit machine, space game. *(Recommended by Charles and Mary Winpenny, TOH, Ian and Liz Phillips, Nick Dowson, Alison Hayward, Ninka Sharland, Richard Balkwill, Mr and Mrs W Harrington, Gwen and Peter Andrews, Christopher Fluck, T O Haunch, Jenny Seller)*

Free house   Real ale   Meals and snacks   Children in back bar or two furnished porches Possible parking difficulties on sunny summer weekends   Open 10.30–2.30, 6–11; closed 25 Dec

FICKLESHOLE   TQ3860 Map 3
White Bear

Off A2022 Purley Road just S of its junction with A212 roundabout; at The Willows follow Addington Court Golf Club signpost into Featherbed Lane and keep on

Remarkable for the outer fringes of London, this friendly country pub has a rambling series of dimly lit rooms dating in parts to the fifteenth century. Some are quite spacious and some very snug indeed, with polished flagstones, quarry tiles and oak parquet, bay windows inset with stained-glass panels, an attractive variety of seating including some antique settles, low and heavy black beams, and decorations ranging from china on Delft shelves through halberds and pikes to a handsome Act of Parliament clock. There are open fires and solid-fuel stoves. Outside (where there are plenty of tables) the country mood deepens – besides a big play area, there is a walk-through paddock with hens, ducks, geese and white doves, pheasants and rabbits in big pens, and a Nubian goat; other paddocks have a donkey, ponies and sheep. A lunchtime bar food servery does soup (65p), quiches (from £1.25), ploughman's in variety (from £2), salads (from £2.75) and a few hot dishes such as liver and onions or fish pie (£3.60). There's a three-course Sunday lunch (£7.50), and evening food includes basket meals (from £2) and more expensive dishes such as gammon (£4.95) and steaks (from £6.50); well kept Felinfoel Double Dragon and Fullers London Pride and ESB on handpump; darts (winter), three fruit machines, inoffensive piped music. (*Recommended by Ray Challoner, W J Wonham, Alasdair Knowles, AE, GRE, E G Parish, Janet Homewood*)

Free house   Licensee Mrs C Waice   Real ale   Meals and snacks   Children in eating areas Open 11–2.30, 6–11 all year; may open all day Sat

FOREST GREEN   TQ1240 Map 3
Parrot
Near B2126/B2127 junction

This quaint old pub, which overlooks the village cricket field, has rambling bars full of parrot designs, ingeniously worked into some of the most unlikely materials. A comfortable carpeted area by the old central fireplace has massive beams (and blazing logs in winter), and a plainer section, with walls partly bare stonework and partly cream-painted brick, has a brick floor that has been worn to a fine lustre by generations of drinkers. The changing range of beers might typically consist of Courage Best and Directors on handpump, and one brewed for the pub called Parrot. Good, interesting food includes salads, moules marinière, mixed grills and daily specials; cream teas in summer. Darts, shove-ha'penny, dominoes and fruit machine. On Sunday evenings the live entertainment goes on until 11.30 and free snacks are handed round at 10.30. Outside there is plenty of room; on one side there's a good-sized terrace by a lawn with apple trees and rose beds, and on another a bigger stretch of grass has some swings and fallabout bouncy castle. The pub is handy for the good woodland walks in the hills around Abinger.
(*Recommended by N D Foot, Christopher Fluck, T O Haunch, R P Taylor, Mr and Mrs W Harrington, E G Parish, I S Wilson*)

Free house   Licensee M S Babister   Real ale   Meals and snacks   Restaurant open until midnight (1am Thurs–Sat)   Children welcome   Open 11–11 all year

GODSTONE   TQ3551 Map 3
Bell
Under a mile from M25 junction 6; village signposted down B2236 from exit roundabout – 128 High Street

There's still something of the atmosphere of its former coaching days here – especially in the spacious beamed and partly panelled main bar, even if its beams are now festooned with copper petrol cans, buckets and churns and glass, brass or pottery mugs. It has big open fires at each end, comfortable seats on its blue Turkey carpet, well kept Benskins Best, Ind Coope Bitter and Burton, Friary Meux Best and Tetleys on handpump, and a cheerful atmosphere. A smaller Carriage Bar with timbering as well as more beams has some nice prints, and is set out more for eating. It's where you order bar food such as sandwiches (from 80p, crab £1.80), home-made soup (£1), filled baked potatoes (£1.50), toasted Stilton (£1.60), a wide choice of ploughman's (from £1.80), omelettes (from £2.50), steak and kidney pie (£3.50) and sirloin steak (£6.20), with children's dishes (£1.50); the evening choice leans more to main dishes and grills. Unusually, a lot of effort's gone into the big and nicely furnished children's room, where they bounce around to a juke box and have a fruit machine, space game and pin-table; cribbage and a trivia machine are in the main bar. Out in the big garden too there's a family atmosphere in summer, with rockers, a shoe-house and a tree-house, and three sets of swings; there's a quieter sheltered terrace with a vine pergola, and they have summer barbecues. The

---

Children welcome means the pub says it lets children inside without any special restriction; readers have found that some may impose an evening time-limit – please tell us if you find this.

gents' lavatory at least is quite a picture-gallery. *(Recommended by E G Parish, W J Wonham, Linda Egan, John Branford, Alan Merricks)*

Ind Coope   Licensees John and Cindy Courtney   Real ale   Meals and snacks   Restaurant (evenings, not Tues)   Children in restaurant and children's room   Occasional live music Open 10.30–2.30, 5.30–11 all year; may be all day Sat   Bedrooms tel Godstone (0883) 843133; £25(£35B)/£32(£42B)

GOMSHALL   TQ0847 Map 3
Black Horse
A25 Dorking–Guildford

Since the M25 opened and much of the traffic's left this road, the Black Horse has recovered a calm, relaxing and decidedly conversational atmosphere that suits its spacious saloon bar, with its dark squared panelling, gothick dining-chairs and sideboard, open fire with copper hods for logs and coal, and old-fashioned leaded-light bar counter. Food's included sandwiches (from 90p), soup (£1), burgers (from £1.50), ploughman's (from £1.95), filled baked potatoes (from £2.25), steak and kidney pie (£3.95) and more expensive evening dishes such as local trout (£4.75) and eight-ounce rump steak (£7.45); well kept Youngs Bitter and Special on handpump. The public bar on the other side has darts, shove-ha'penny, dominoes, cribbage, fruit machine and space game. There are tables under cocktail parasols on a back terrace and up on a spacious sloping lawn with fruit trees – and good swings including a gondola one. The licensees changed just as we went to press, with suggestions of a new approach to food – news please. *(Recommended by John Branford, Don Mather, BMS, TOH, I S Wilson)*

Youngs   Real ale   Meals and snacks   Restaurant (to be open all day)   Children in restaurant   Open 11–11 all year; closed evening 25 Dec   Bedrooms tel Shere (048 641) 2242; £16.10/£32.20

HASCOMBE   TQ0039 Map 3
White Horse

You can eat in the light and airy extension of this friendly rose-draped country pub, or in an inner beamed area with quiet small-windowed alcoves. If you want a table, it's best to get there early as people flock here from Godalming for business lunches; the ham sandwiches are especially good, with thick slices of meat, and there is a variety of hot dishes, such as home-made soups and burgers, chicken in cream and tarragon sauce, and swordfish or plaice. Well kept Friary Meux Bitter, Ind Coope Burton and Gales HSB on handpump. The main lounge is cosy and attractive with flock wallpaper and piped classical music; darts, shove-ha'penny, dominoes and fruit machine in the plainer bar. There are some tables in several places outside – on a little patio by the front porch, in a bower and under a walnut tree; children might enjoy the swings and haywain on the lawn. Nearby, Winkworth Arboretum (B2130 towards Godalming) has walks among beautiful trees and shrubs. *(Recommended by R P Taylor, Denis Weiner, Dr I J Thompson)*

Friary Meux   Licensee Mrs S Barnett   Real ale   Meals and snacks (not Sun evening) Restaurant tel Hascombe (048 632) 258   Children in eating area   Open 11–2.30, 5.30–11 (11–11 Sat) all year

HASLEMERE   SU9032 Map 2
Crowns ⊗
Weyhill; B2131 towards Liphook, close to railway bridge

Formerly known as the Crown & Cushion, this friendly, busy pub has a pleasantly light and airy bar with comfortable chairs, shelves of books, interesting lamps, wall prints, flowers on the tables and piped music. Good value food includes deep-fried Camembert with gooseberry sauce (£2.55), mussels with garlic stuffing (£2.85), baked avocado with crab (£3.50), pasta with salmon and dill (£3.85), swordfish steak in garlic sauce (£4.50), prawn and haddock pie (£4.95), rabbit in mustard and marjoram (£5.25) and peppered chicken in a cream and Dijon sauce (£5.45). Well kept Friary Meux, Ind Coope Burton and Tetleys on handpump, and a sensible choice of wines. There are tables outside, front and back; the pub is on *Good Walks Guide* Walk 53. (*Recommended by Maggie and Derek Washington, Doug Kennedy, Mrs Jo Corbett*)

Friary Meux (Ine Coope)   Licensee B Heath   Real ale   Meals and snacks   Restaurant tel Haslemere (0428) 3112   Children welcome, daytime   Open 10.30–2.30, 6–11; closed 25 and 26 Dec

HORLEY   TQ2842   Map 3

Olde Six Bells

3 miles from M23 junction 9: from Gatwick turnoff follow A23 towards Reigate and London, then Horley signpost at roundabout; after 600 yards pub signposted by sharp left turn into Church Road, which is first real left turn

Parts of this interesting old building are said to date back to 830 and the carpeted saloon area is thought to have been a chapel – the inn was a hospice for the Dorking monastery in the fourteenth century; you can still see memorial niches in the wall on the right. The busy open-plan bar has heavy beams, butter-coloured plaster walls and ceiling, a tiled floor and some copper measuring dippers for decoration. Upstairs is quieter, carpeted, with high rafters and heavy wall timbering: you can book tables up here for the popular home-made food, such as rolls (from £1.20), ploughman's (from £1.85), vegetable lasagne, turkey and ham pie, or chilli con carne (all £2.80) and salads (from £2.95), with evening meals such as lamb marengo, pork normandie or veal korma (all £4.75). Well kept Bass and Charrington IPA on handpump; shove-ha'penny, dominoes, darts, fruit machine and piped music. Beyond a sheltered back flagstone terrace with jasmine on the wall is a sizeable garden beside the little River Mole. (*Recommended by Comus Elliott, E G Parish, Jenny Seller*)

Charringtons   Licensee David Beaumont   Real ale   Meals and snacks   Restaurant tel Horley (0293) 782209   Children in restaurant   Open 11–11 all year

LALEHAM   TQ0568   Map 3

Three Horseshoes ⊗

B377

This thirteenth-century inn was one of Edward VII's bolt-holes when he was Prince of Wales. It's a busy, friendly place, and the comfortably modernised open-plan bar has lots of big copper pots and pans hanging from beams, interesting cock-fighting prints on the red walls, padded leather-look seats on the red carpet, and blacksmith's tools hanging over the main fireplace (the pub is named after the old village forge next door); one small alcove has high-backed settles. Good, reasonably priced bar food specialises in huge filled baked potatoes (from £2.50, prawns £3.75) as well as an excellent choice of sandwiches (from £1, crab £1.80), ploughman's (£2.25), salads (from £3.75), and a selection of daily specials such as lasagne (£2.85), steak and ale pie or lamb biriani (£2.95) and home-made chicken Kiev (£3.25). Well kept Ruddles Best and County, Trumans Best Bitter and Websters Yorkshire on handpump; decent wines; they have a happy hour. The inn's façade is almost hidden by wistaria, hanging baskets and cartwheels, and the garden has some statues and plenty of tables – some under a cleverly rainproofed 'arbour' of creepers. The lane opposite leads down to a stretch of the Thames that is popular for picnics and sunbathing. *(Recommended by Ian Phillips, Miss L Masolle, S Matthews, Simon Collett-Jones, Neil and Elspeth Fearn, R A Corbett, E Kinnersly, Grahme and Brenda Blair, Mr and Mrs G Holliday)*

Watneys   Licensee Philip Jones   Real ale   Meals and snacks (not Sun evening)   Restaurant tel Staines (0784) 52617   Open 11–3, 5–11; 11–11 Sat; all year

LEIGH   TQ2246 Map 3
Plough ⊗

3 miles S of A25 Dorking–Reigate, signposted from Betchworth (which itself is signposted off the main road); also signposted from South Park area of Reigate; on village green

Spick and span, this pretty tiled and white-boarded cottage is bright with geraniums in summer, and has picnic-table sets under cocktail parasols in an attractive side garden bordered by a neat white picket fence. The lounge on the right is so low-beamed that it really does need its crash-pads; it has flowers on its tables, with a good many Cecil Aldin prints on its timbered white walls. There are more of these on the yellowing walls of the more local bar on the left, which has a good bow-window seat (and darts, shove-ha'penny, dominoes, table skittles, cribbage, fruit machine and piped radio). Lunchtime bar food, all made from fresh ingredients, includes sandwiches (from 85p), ploughman's (from £1.75), salads (from £2.70), very popular ham and eggs (£3.10) and dishes of the day such as fresh sardines portugaise or salmon; they also do children's helpings. In the evenings (except at weekends) the food takes a turn towards dishes such as duck or lemon sole poached in wine with prawns (£5.30) and steaks (from £6.95). Well kept King & Barnes Sussex, Festive, Mild and in winter Old on handpump; Gales country wines, more sensible soft-drinks pricing than usual, and a much wider choice of crispy nibbles than in most other pubs that give as much attention as this one to main dishes. Limited nearby parking. *(Recommended by Lyn and Bill Capper, Mrs Pamela Roper, TOH)*

King & Barnes   Licensees Mr and Mrs Graham Walker   Real ale   Meals and snacks Restaurant tel Dawes Green (030 678) 348   Children in eating area and restaurant Morris dancers about once a month, mainly summer   Open 10.30–2.30, 6–11 all year; may open longer, especially Sat

Seven Stars

In the comfortable saloon bar of this pretty country pub there's a 1633 inglenook fireback with the royal coat of arms in the smoke-blackened brick inglenook fireplace, and an early eighteenth-century sign painted on the wall, reading '...you are Wellcome to sit down for your ease pay what you call for and drink what you please'; also, lots of racing pictures and horsebrasses. The plainer public bar has an alley set aside for darts. Good bar food, Sunday barbecues in summer; well kept Ind Coope Burton and Friary Meux real ale. Outside in the flower-filled garden you are quite likely to see people ambling by on horseback. *(Recommended by R P Taylor, W A Lund, Jason Caulkin, J Knighton)*

Ind Coope   Real ale   Meals and snacks   Children welcome   Open 10.30–2.30, 6.30–11

NEWDIGATE   TQ2042 Map 3
Surrey Oaks

Parkgate Road

The main lounge of this friendly, family-run country pub has tapestried seats in little partly curtained booths, and rustic tables lit by lanterns hanging low from fairy-lit lowered beams. A much older part on the right has a little snug beamed room by a coal-effect gas fire, then a standing area with extraordinarily large flagstones and an open fire. Good bar food includes vegetarian dishes such as bulghur wheat and walnut casserole (£3) and non-vegetarian food – all with help-yourself salad – such as sandwiches (from £1.40), ploughman's (£2), moussaka, cannelloni, lasagne or chilli con carne (£2.75), mixed grills and steaks; on Sunday lunchtimes they do a carvery (£8.25) and on Sunday evenings (weather permitting) there's a barbecue in the garden, with beefburgers, kebabs, chicken and steaks (£1.65–£4.95). Well kept Friary Meux, Ind Coope Burton and Taylor-Walker on handpump. A separate games-room has a well lit pool-table, darts, shove-ha'penny, dominoes, cribbage, a fruit machine, space game, juke box and piped music. The spacious garden is most attractive, with a large patio, a rockery with illuminated pools, fountains and waterfall, and a flock of pure-white doves; they also have sheep, a calf, and an aviary of budgerigars, and all sorts of fowls. You can buy their free-range duck, hen and goose eggs from the bar. A little way down the lane there is a bridlepath through Reffolds Copse, the oak wood behind the pub. *(Recommended by Mrs I Sears, E G Parish, W J Wonham, T O Haunch)*

Friary Meux   Licensee Colin Haydon   Real ale   Meals and snacks (not Sun evening) Restaurant tel Newdigate (030 677) 200   Children in eating area and restaurant Middle-of-the-road live music Sun evening   Open 11–3, 6–11 all year

nr OCKLEY   TQ1439 Map 3
Punch Bowl   ★   [illustrated on page 620]

Oakwoodhill (some maps and signposts spell it Okewoodhill); village signposted off A29 S of Ockley

Pleasantly traditional, this fine old house has polished, big dark flagstones, many beams and some timbering, an antique settle among simpler country seats and scrubbed deal tables, an inglenook fireplace with huge logs smouldering gently on the vast round hearth, and a relaxed, friendly atmosphere. Good, popular food includes a regularly changing range of home-cooked specials such as chicken curry, sweet-and-sour crispy duck or ham and eggs (£3.25), scampi (£3.75), steak and kidney pie (£4) and rump steak (£6.95) as well as sandwiches and ploughman's (£1.75). Well kept Badger Best and Tanglefoot, King & Barnes Sussex, Youngs Special and a guest ale on handpump; a good choice of whiskies. Another plainer bar has sensibly placed darts, a juke box and fruit machine. You can sit outside this partly tile-hung building with a heavy slab roof at tables on several different birdsong-serenaded terraces, and fields with oak trees and woods stretching away on all sides. *(Recommended by T O Haunch, Tim Halstead; more reports please)*

Free house   Licensee Robert Chambers   Real ale   Meals and snacks (not Sun and Mon evenings)   Restaurant tel Oakwood Hill (030 679) 249; to stay open all afternoon, weekends Children in upstairs room   Open 10.30–2.30, 5.30–11; 11–11 Sat

OUTWOOD   TQ3245 Map 3
Bell   ★   ⊗

In summer, the well managed garden outside this traditional country pub is a peaceful place to sit among flowers and shrubs on the sheltered lawn and look past its bordering pine trees to the fine view over rolling fields, dotted with oak trees and woods. Inside, the long carpeted front bar has low beams, elm and oak tables and chairs, some in Jacobean style, and a vast stone inglenook fireplace; there's another lounge bar at the back. Efficiently served bar food includes main dishes such as steak and kidney pie (£4.60), fresh whole plaice (£5.75), English rack of lamb (£5.95), char-grilled sirloin or rump steak (£6.25), chicken breast stuffed with Stilton and mushrooms (£6.95) and fillet steak topped with duck pâté (£8.80). They do sandwiches (from £1.10), ploughmans (£2.25), filled baked potatoes (£2.75) and salads (£3.95) at lunchtime; also, morning coffee and an all-year barbecue (Sunday to Tuesday evenings) outdoors in summer. Several readers have been disappointed by the fact that you have to book several days in advance to get a table. Well kept Batemans XXXB, Charrington IPA, Fremlins, King & Barnes Sussex and Festive and Pilgrim Progress on handpump. *(Recommended by Mike Muston, Chris Fluck, GRE, AE, Alasdair Knowles, Andy Tye, Sue Hill, J H Bell, M E A Horler, T O Haunch, Jenny Seller, Gwen and Peter Andrews, Ian Howard, Dave Butler, Les Storey)*

Free house   Licensee Harry Pam   Real ale   Meals and lunchtime snacks   Children over seven if booked in advance   Open 11–2.30, 6–11 all year

Dog & Duck ⊗

From A23 in Salfords S of Redhill take Station turning – eventually, after you cross M23, pub's on your left at T-junction; coming from village centre, head towards Coopers Hill and Prince of Wales Road

This isolated partly tile-hung country cottage has the happy knack of somehow making space for far more people than you'd ever imagine possible, when you compare the number of cars parked outside with its small size. It rambles about more than you'd expect, with comfortable settles and oak armchairs as well as more ordinary seats, rugs on the quarry tiles, a good log fire, ochre walls and stripped dark beams; the atmosphere's cheerful and lively. Enterprisingly, the bar food's now served all day (until 5pm on Sundays, too); it includes ploughman's in variety (£2), kebab in pitta or a half-pint of prawns (£2.95), cannelloni (£3.45) and ham and egg (£3.50), with daily summer barbecues if it's fine. In the evening the choice is more on the lines of soup (£1.50), avocado with crab (£3), trout or halibut (£6) and steaks (from sirloin £6.95). Well kept Badger Best and Tanglefoot on handpump, with a couple of guest beers such as Everards Tiger and Shepherd Neame Best; decent wines; newspapers out for customers; also shove-ha'penny, dominoes, ring the bull, cribbage, backgammon, Scrabble, Trivial Pursuit; there may be unobtrusive piped music. The restaurant area, with another huge fireplace, really only functions separately in the evening – during the day it's more part of the bar that it communicates with. Picnic-table sets under cocktail parasols on the grass outside look over a safely fenced-off duck pond to the meadows. There's a pleasant walk to the old windmill in the village – the round trip's about about an hour. *(Recommended by Alasdair Knowles, Mr and Mrs M J Banbury, Mrs J Pescod, John Kimber, Dominic Williams, S A Lovett)*

Badger   Licensees Amanda and Timothy Buchanan-Munro   Real ale   Meals and snacks served all day   Restaurant tel Smallfield (034 284) 2964   Children in restaurant   Open 11–11 all year; closed evening 25 Dec

PIRBRIGHT   SU9455   Map 2
Royal Oak ⊗

Aldershot Road; A324S of village

This friendly, tile-hung extended Tudor cottage has heavy beams and timbers, ancient stripped brickwork, gleaming brasses set around the big low-beamed fireplace, and a rambling series of side alcoves; it's furnished with wheel-back chairs, tapestried wall seats and little dark church-like pews set around neat tables. Bar food consists of sandwiches (from £1), ploughman's (from £1.75), pâté (£2.75), salads using produce from their own garden (from £3.50), gammon, lamb chops, or pork cutlets (£3.75) and rump steak (£4.60); particularly well kept Badger Best, Huntsman Royal Oak, King & Barnes and another real ale (likely to be Flowers, Marstons Pedigree or Wadworths) on handpump. As this is run rather proudly as a genuinely old-fashioned pub, the licensee doesn't believe in serving coffee. A pleasant absence of games, machines and music. In summer the beautifully kept gardens (for which they have won a local award) are a mass of colour, and even in

---

Cribbage is a card game using a block of wood with holes for matchsticks or special pins to score with; regulars in cribbage pubs are usually happy to teach strangers how to play.

winter the many dwarf conifers keep them cheerful before the first spring bulbs show. *(Recommended by K Chenneour, Lyn and Bill Capper, J P Berryman, J T Alford, KC)*

Free house   Licensee Geoffry Walkling   Real ale   Lunchtime meals and snacks (not Sun) Evening restaurant   Open 11–2.30, 6–10.30 (11 Sat); closed evenings 24 and 26 Dec

PUTTENHAM   SU9347 Map 2

Jolly Farmer

Village signposted just off A31 Farnham–Guildford

Several communicating room areas in this big tile-hung house have an air of quiet prosperity: brown beams and joists, a stripped pine dado topped by a frieze of blue and white tiles, lots of Victorian and later prints, paintings, drawings and sporting prints on the attractively papered walls, glass-fronted bookcases, and mounted topi and sable antelope heads; comfortable seats range from cushioned wheel-back chairs around traditional cast-iron-framed tables to sofas and easy chairs, and there are rugs on bare polished boards or good brown carpet. Last year the restaurant was extended into a Harvester family steak and salad place. Bar food consists of a good choice of ploughman's (around £1.90), hot dishes such as steak and kidney pie, lasagne, or chilli con carne (£3.25) and salads (around £3). Well kept Courage Best and Directors on handpump; good coffee; good service; fruit machine, trivia machine, maybe unobtrusive piped music. There are picnic-table sets under cocktail parasols on the terrace in front of the pub. *(Recommended by F J Walters, R B Crail, Tony Bland; more reports please)*

Part Courage tie (THF)   Licensee Rob White   Real ale   Meals and snacks   Restaurant tel Guildford (0483) 810374   Children welcome   Open 11–2.30, 6–11; closed evening 25 Dec

PYRFORD LOCK   TQ0458 Map 3

Anchor

Lock Lane; service road off A3 signposted to RHS Wisley Gardens – continue past them towards Pyrford

Alone in the country, this spacious pub is included for its lovely position by a busy canal lock and for its masses of picnic tables on a big pink and white terrace. Inside, it's well kept, and the comfortably modern open-plan bar has big picture windows where you get a fine view of the narrowboats leaving the dock and edging under the steeply hump-backed road bridge. Courage Best and Directors on handpump, and standard bar food. The Royal Horticultural Society's nearby gardens are open every day (members only on Sunday mornings). *(Recommended by Peter Griffiths, Ian Phillips, Michael and Alison Sandy)*

Courage   Real ale   Meals and snacks (lunchtime, not Mon)   Open 11–2.30, 6–11

REIGATE HEATH   TQ2349 Map 3

Skimmington Castle ★

3 miles from M25 junction 8: A25 through Reigate, then on W edge of Reigate District turn S into hamlet of Reigate Heath; after about ½ mile turn left into Bonny's Road (unmade, very bumpy track); after crossing golf course fork right up hill

The bright main front bar in this popular, old-fashioned, cottagey pub has shiny brown vertical panelling decorated with earthenware bottles, decorative plates, brass and pewter, a brown plank ceiling, a miscellany of chairs and tables and the uncommon traditional game of ring the bull. It leads off a small but efficiently run central serving-counter, framed in dark simple panelling, with a collection of oddly shaped pipes (and a skull among them) dangling over it. The back rooms are partly panelled too – cosy, with old-fashioned settles and Windsor chairs, and perhaps Basher the black and white cat; one has a big brick fireplace with its bread oven still beside it. Bar snacks include local sausages (30p), soup (75p), sandwiches (from 60p, creamcheese and prawn with walnuts £1.25, steak rolls from £1.50), basket meals (from £1.20, scampi £3), ploughman's (from £1.40), cod (£2), salads (from £2.80, crab £3.50), gammon steak with egg (£3.80), steaks (from £5.80) and daily specials. Friary Meux Best, Ind Coope Bitter and Burton, and Tetleys on hand-pump; the stuffed fox leering out of the crisp packets is commonly known as Derek. A small room down steps at the back has space games, and there are darts, shove-ha'penny and dominoes. You can sit outside on the crazy-paved front terrace or on the grass by lilac bushes, and paths from here wind into the surrounding wooded countryside. *(Recommended by Mike Muston, John Day, John Branford, Derek Pascall, Mrs Pamela Roper, T O Haunch)*

Friary Meux Licensee Andrew Fisher Real ale Meals (lunchtime, not Sun) and snacks Children in special small room at all times Open 11–3, 5.30–11 all year

RUNFOLD SU8747 Map 2
Jolly Farmer
A31 just E of Farnham

At one end of this friendly roadside pub, big windows look out on the back garden and terrace, where there are plenty of tables among some flowers and shrubs, and a good adventure playground. Comfortable furnishings include some massive rough-cut elm tables and chairs as well as more conventionally comfortable seats, and there's an unusual painted vineleaf dado around its cornices. Popular with businessmen at lunchtime, the bar food includes ploughman's (from £2.40), pie or plaice (£3.30), quiche (£3.60), meats (£5.45), puddings (£1.75) and a daily special; evening dishes tend to be considerably more ambitious. Well kept Courage Best and Directors on handpump; also children's cocktails (and adult ones); darts, shove-ha'penny, dominoes, cribbage, fruit machine and unobtrusive piped music. *(Recommended by John Innes, Lyn and Bill Capper; more reports please)*

Courage Real ale Meals and snacks Restaurant tel Runfold (025 18) 2074 Children in restaurant Open 10.30–2.30, 5.30–11 all year

SHEPPERTON TQ0867 Map 3
Kings Head
Church Square; E side of B375

This busy, cheerful pub – parts of which date from the fourteenth century – has lost some of the garden to make more room inside. The several small rooms have oak parquet flooring, an inglenook fireplace and generous helpings of good, imaginative food: Welsh rarebit to a secret recipe (£1.95), Maria's pie (£2.25), chilli con carne (£2.50) and a dish of the day such as cauliflower au gratin (£2.65). Well kept Courage Best and Directors on handpump and a good range of wines; fruit machine and juke box in the public bar. Outside, there are window boxes and black shutters and a view across the attractive village square to the brick and flint church. *(Recommended by Simon Collett-Jones, Ian Phillips, GB, CH, S E and C L Manning, John Branford)*

Courage Licensee David Longhurst Real ale Meals and snacks (not Sun) Restaurant (closed Sun) tel Walton-on-Thames (0932) 221910 Children in eating area lunchtimes only Open 11–3 (12–4 Sat), 5.30–11 all year

SHERE TQ0747 Map 3
White Horse
The floors in this interesting old half-timbered pub are uneven – no foundations, just salvaged ships' timbers plunged into the ground some six hundred years ago.

The open-plan main lounge bar has massive beams, a huge inglenook fireplace, antique oak wall seats, old manuscripts on the walls, and elegant Tudor stonework in a second inglenook fireplace through in the Pilgrim's Bar. Since the new licensee took over, the tenor of readers' reports has been such that we are not yet sure the pub still deserves the star award it has had in the past. Bar food includes a wide range of sandwiches (from £1.40), ploughman's (from £1.95), steak, kidney and Guinness pie or scampi (£3.95) and sirloin steak (£6.75). Well kept Websters Yorkshire on handpump. There are seats outside on a sunny cobbled courtyard among carefully planted troughs of flowers and bright hanging baskets; good walking in the beech woods on the road north towards East Clandon. Because the village is so pretty, the pub does get very busy. *(Recommended by Gary Wilkes, Alasdair Knowles, J and M Walsh, Doug Kennedy, B A Websdale, E G Parish, Wilfred Plater-Shellard, John Branford)*

Watneys Licensee M Wicks Real ale Meals and snacks (not Sun evening) Children in eating area Open 11–2.30, 6–10.30 (11 Sat) all year; closed 25 Dec

STAINES TQ0471 Map 3
Swan

The Hythe; south bank of Thames, over Staines Bridge

The two main bars of this carefully restored old inn have good river views, and for summer there's a charming sycamore-shaded terrace by the towpath with some tables protected by an overhanging upper balcony. In the two well run bars there are upholstered settles, seats and armchairs, and carefully exposed original fireplaces. Bar food includes sandwiches (from 85p, toasted 15p extra), home-made soup (£1.15), jumbo sausage and chips or filled baked potatoes (from £1.75), ploughman's (from £1.95), lasagne or chilli con carne (£2.70), basket meals such as scampi (£3), and salads (from £3.20, beef £3.80). Fullers London Pride and ESB on electric pump; fruit machine, piped music. *(Recommended by Dr J D Bassett, Ian Phillips, Mrs G K Herbert, Quentin Williamson, A J Leach)*

Fullers Real ale Meals and snacks Restaurant tel Staines (1784) 52494 Children in eating area and restaurant Occasional live music Open 11–11; 11–2.30, 5.30–11 in winter Bedrooms tel Staines (1784) 52494; £22/£32

WARLINGHAM TQ3658 Map 3
White Lion

B269

This is probably the closest you can get to a really interesting and unspoilt pub in what virtually amounts to a suburb of London. It's based on two fifteenth-century cottages with tales of a secret passage from behind the fine inglenook fireplace to nearby almshouses. A warren of dimly lit black-panelled rooms have extremely low beams, deeply aged plasterwork, lots of nooks and crannies, wood-block floors, and high-backed settles by the fireside. Bar food includes sandwiches, pâté, salads and hot dishes such as steak and kidney pie; well kept Bass and Charrington IPA on handpump (from the central bar, by the door as you come in). A side room with some amusing early nineteenth-century cartoons has darts, fruit machine and space game. There are good sturdy wooden seats on the immaculate back lawn, surrounded by a herbaceous border, with a goldfish pond. *(Recommended by Alasdair Knowles, Philip Denison, Mr and Mrs R Bray, E G Parish)*

Charringtons Real ale Meals and snacks (lunchtime, not Sun) Restaurant tel Warlingham (088 32) 4106 Children in middle room Open 10.30–2.30, 5.30–11; closes 10.30 in winter

---

Children – if the details at the end of an entry don't mention them, you should assume that the pub does not allow them inside.

WOTTON   TQ1247 Map 3

Wotton Hatch

A25 Dorking–Guildford; coming from Dorking, start slowing as soon as you see the Wotton village sign – the pub's around the first bend

Most of the space in the low-ceilinged front bar of this well kept seventeenth-century pub is standing-room only, though there are some cushioned wheel-back chairs around copper-topped tables on its patterned carpet. To one side a handsome cocktail bar has gentle piped music and medieval-style seats ranked around its panelled walls under a high frieze of plates and Victorian pilgrim's-progress wallpaper; on the other side a tiled-floor public bar has darts, shove-ha'penny, dominoes, cribbage and a fruit machine. Bar food changes daily and might typically include sandwiches, soup (£1.10), ploughman's (£1.95) and pork chop or beef Stroganoff (£2.90). Well kept Fullers Chiswick, London Pride and ESB on handpump. Outside on a neat lawn there's a white pergola, and beyond a screen of roses and sweet peas, on a second lawn, there are picnic-tables sets by a pavilion and a new children's play area. *(Recommended by Mr and Mrs R Gammon, Doug Kennedy, R P Taylor)*

Fullers   Licensee Winston Legg   *Real ale   Meals and snacks   Restaurant* tel *Dorking (0306) 885665; open until 4 Sun   Children in restaurant   Open 11–2.30, 5.30–11 all year; closed evening 25 Dec*

Lucky Dip

Besides the fully inspected pubs, you might like to try these Lucky Dips recommended to us and described by readers (if you do, please send us reports):

Abinger Common [Abinger signposted off A25 W of Dorking – then r to Abinger Hammer; TQ1145], *Abinger Hatch*: A great favourite for its position near the church in a clearing of the rolling woods; a good deal of character inside, with big log fires, heavy beams, flagstones – and an interesting range of well kept real ales such as Badger Tanglefoot, Gibbs Mew Bishops Tipple and Wadworths 6X; bar food, restaurant, children allowed in area partly set aside for them, tables outside; can get very busy indeed at weekends; lease sold early 1987, and first reports on the new regime are very promising – more news please *(R B Crail, Doug Kennedy, LYM)*

Addlestone [Hamm Moor Lane; corner A318/B385; TQ0464], *Pelican*: Entertaining canalside pub with good beer and lively clientele *(Dr and Mrs A K Clarke)*; [New Haw Rd; opposite corner A318/B385] *White Hart*: Cheerful local with attractive waterside garden, good value simple food, Courage real ales, darts, bar billiards, juke box; pianist Sat *(LYM)*

Albury [TQ0547], *Drummond Arms*: Good food with wide choice, pretty garden backing on to small river; pleasant quick service *(Peter Nash)*

Albury Heath [Little London; OS Sheet 187 reference 065468; TQ0646], *William IV*: Pleasant building and atmosphere in main bar with flagstones, open fire and benches and tables; similarly furnished darts room, another room up some steps with tables for eating, and an upstairs restaurant; reasonably priced snacks, well kept Courage beer and maybe live piano and saxophone; can get crowded and smoky Sun lunchtime *(Phil and Sally Gorton)*

Alfold [B2133; TQ0334], *Crown*: Cheerful pub with home-made bar food; several rooms, well kept garden, in quiet village *(LYM)*; [Dunsfold Rd] *Three Compasses*: Remote country inn on quiet back lane with inglenook public bar and airy saloon *(LYM)*

Ashford [Woodthorpe Rd; TQ0671], *District Arms*: Small one-bar pub close to Heathrow with well kept Courage beer and good lunchtime food; pleasant efficient service even though it gets crowded *(RH)*

Bagshot [High St; SU9163], *Three Mariners*: Very old pub with curvy walls, low ceilings and beams from an old ship; pleasant, friendly atmosphere though a bit smoky in the two bars (one with pool); doesn't allow crash helmets or leathers; can get packed *(Gary Wilkes)*

Beare Green [TQ1842], *Dukes Head*: Atmospheric public bar in pretty roadside Ind Coope pub with well kept real ales and pleasant garden *(LYM)*

Betchworth [TQ2049], *Red Lion*: Very pleasant bar, well kept Bass, pretty garden for sitting out, friendly staff, good choice of reasonably priced food well presented and quickly served *(Mrs Jenny Seller, TOH)*

Bishopsgate [OS Sheet 175 reference

979721; SU9871], *Fox & Hounds*: Now two-thirds restaurant, with most people in the bar on their way to a meal – the food's good though pricey by pub standards, but they do have sandwiches too, well kept if pricey Courage Best, a cheerful atmosphere, log fires and a good location, with a pleasant front garden; parking difficult at times *(SCCJ, Ian Phillips)*

Bisley [OS Sheet 175 reference 949595; SU9559], *Hen & Chickens*: Perhaps 600 years old (though only the beams show its great age), notable for pleasant efficient management, good lunchtime food; Courage *(WHBM)*

☆ **Bletchingley** [Little Common Lane; 3 miles from M25 junction 6; off A25 on Redhill side of village; TQ3250], *William IV*: Good choice of bar food in country local, prettily tile-hung and weatherboarded, with well kept Bass and Charrington IPA, darts, dominoes, cribbage and fruit machine in back bar, seats in nice garden with summer barbecues on Sat evening and Sun lunchtime, food lunchtime (not Sun) *(John Kimber, E G Parish, TBB, LYM)*

Bletchingley [2 High St; A25, on E side of village], *Plough*: Newish tenants doing wide range of hot and cold lunchtime bar food, real ale, imaginative menu for full evening meals *(Gordon Smith)*; *Prince Albert*: Relaxed pub with very friendly Dutch owner; superb food – huge steaks and tasty fish – from a regularly changing menu; no booking so arrive early *(G Turner)*; [A25, Redhill side] *Red Lion*: Pleasant staff and well kept Friary Meux in traditional and cosy old pub with friendly atmosphere and reasonably priced, though rather limited , bar food *(Dominic Williams, W J Wonham)*

☆ **Blindley Heath** [Tandridge Lane; TQ3645], *Red Barn*: Friendly, attractive country pub with jolly atmosphere, lovely inglenook fireplace, nicely furnished library bar, period atmosphere, discreet piped music, excellent service, imaginatively presented bar food including big tasty home-baked crusty rolls; good choice of beers *(E G Parish, Jenny and Brian Seller)*

Bramley [High St; TQ0044], *Jolly Farmer*: Pleasant atmosphere in cheerful Watneys pub with two log fires, beer-mats on ceiling, tremendous choice of bar food brought to table, well served and presented, large restaurant; handy for Winkworth Arboretum (NT) and Loseley House; bedrooms *(W J Wonham)*

Brockham [Brockham Green; TQ1949], *Dukes Head*: Friendly place with good food, well kept Friary Meux, unusual set of badger pictures and open fires – real logs one end, coal-effect gas the other *(Mrs P J Pearce, R J Groves)*; *Royal Oak*: Idyllic village green pub used in Fosters lager advertisement with Paul Hogan; pretty in summer, with enjoyable food *(Peter Corris, TOH)*

☆ **Brook** [A286 – OS Sheet 186 reference 930380; SU9337], *Dog & Pheasant*: Pleasant atmosphere in busy and friendly pub, full of character; low-beamed ceiling decorated with polished walking-sticks, no piped music, fruit machine; well kept Benskins, Friary Meux, Ind Coope Burton and Tetleys, home-cooked food, and restaurant where manager Bazz Norton plays the piano Weds–Sun evenings; seats in garden, lovely setting opposite cricket green *(Lyn and Bill Capper, Gordon Hewitt, David Gaunt)*

Caterham [235 Stanstead Rd; Whitehill, Caterham on the Hill; TQ3354], *Harrow*: Busy pub with log fires, good choice of simple bar food, popular with young people; garden nice in the summer *(Gordon Smith)*

☆ **Charlton** [TQ0869], *Harrow*: Snug little pub, said to be the oldest inhabited building in what used to be Middlesex – low and thatched, with skull-cracking beams in tiny rooms, scrubbed deal tables, brick fireplace; Watneys-related real ales, food during week, tables in little front yard with pump and stone trough; farmyard beyond lilac- and lavender-bordered garden *(Ian Phillips, John Branford)*

Charlwood [Church Rd; TQ2441], *Half Moon*: Plainly modernised old Friary Meux pub with good local atmosphere, freshly made sandwiches, bar billiards, shove-ha'penny, space game, darts and fruit machine *(BB)*

☆ **Chertsey** [Ruxbury Rd, St Anns Hill (nr Lyne); TQ0466], *Golden Grove*: Attractive brick pub with low tongue-and-groove ceilings and walls, boarded floors; Friary Meux Bitter with guests such as Gales HSB, good value lunchtime bar food with separate pine table eating area; wooded pond and large, pleasant garden; children welcome *(Ian Phillips, Rodney Coe, Gary Wilkes)*

Chertsey [High St (A317)], *George*: Friendly old local with reasonably priced food; mentioned in H G Wells' *War of the Worlds*, said to be haunted *(LYM)*; [Windsor St, on left heading towards Windsor] *Swan*: Warm and friendly old pub, comfortable seats, good choice of good bar food, Wethereds Bitter and SPA on handpump, evening restaurant *(F J Walters, R B Crail)*

Chilworth [Dorking Rd; TQ0247], *Percy Arms*: Well kept Friary Meux in popular pub below North Downs, upholstered settles and stools in carpeted lounge, soft piped music, wide choice of bar food including sandwiches, baked potatoes, ploughman's, salads and hot dishes (may not be cold snacks Sun), restaurant, conservatory and garden; nr start GWG54 *(Lyn and Bill Capper)*

Chobham [just N of village – OS Sheet 176 reference 970633; SU9761], *Four Horseshoes*: Useful Courage pub with surprisingly good smoked salmon sandwiches *(WHBM)*; [High St – 4 miles from M3 junction 3] *Sun*: Low-beamed lounge bar in quiet timbered Courage pub with good food, friendly atmosphere, prompt service *(W J Wonham, LYM)*

Cobham [Pains Hill; TQ0960], *Little White Lion*: Well kept pub with Ruddles on hand-pump and good choice of hot and cold food *(Dr R B Crail)*; [Plough Lane] *Plough*: Courage pub with comfortably modernised low-beamed lounge bar, cheerful lively atmosphere (piped music may be a bit on the loud side in the evening, when customers seem rather wine-barish – and it can get smoky); straightforward popular food, well kept real ale, traditional games in public bar, seats outside the pretty black-shuttered brick house *(Michael and Harriet Robinson, LYM)*

☆ **Compton** [Withies Lane; SU9546], *The Withies*: Smart dining-pub with immaculate garden, tiny beamed bar with settles and inglenook, some lunchtime snacks, pricey Friary Meux; children in restaurant *(Ian Phillips, LYM)*

Cranleigh [The Common; TQ0638], *Cranley*: Newly decorated pub under new management with good, reasonably priced food *(Anon)*; [Bookhurst Rd; Parkmead estate – towards Shere] *Little Park Hatch*: Well kept real ales, seats outside, ample parking *(Anon)*

Crondall [SU7948], *Plume of Feathers*: Generous helpings of well prepared food at moderate prices, fresh atmosphere in pleasantly furnished bar decorated with interesting historical and other items, friendly courteous service, more austere public bar, some tables outside *(A C Godfrey)*

Dorking [170 High St; TQ1649], *Murrays*: Good choice of beer including King & Barnes on handpump, as well as food and wine; friendly, reasonable prices, piped music *(WFL)*

☆ **Dunsfold** [TQ0036], *Sun*: Elegantly symmetrical eighteenth-century pub overlooking green, Ind Coope real ales with a guest such as Gales HSB, exposed beams, comfortable seats and courteous service; recent reports of good value food – though prices are not low; lively smartly casual young crowd – not to mention Tabitha the well behaved collie and Parsnip the perky Jack Russell; separate cottage dining-room *(Dr John Innes, Prof and Mrs Keith Patchett, LYM)*

East Horsley [Epsom Rd; TQ0952], *Thatchers*: Spacious, relaxing lounge with efficient waiter service, drinks come with coasters, daily papers, good food and separate restaurant pâté with Cumberland sauce, super hot food; bedrooms *(Stanley Matthews)*

East Molesey [TQ1267], *Paddock*: One large, attractive and comfortable bar with good carvery (not Sun evening) and Ruddles County, Trumans Bitter and Best Bitter and Websters Yorkshire *(Clem Stephens)*

☆ **Effingham** [Orestan Lane; TQ1253], *Plough*: Welcoming landlord and staff, well kept Courage Best and Directors – outselling lager by seven to one here; nice range of food beyond ordinary range of bar snacks, attractive atmosphere, pleasant tables outside *(J S Evans, Mrs I Sears, TOH)*

Effingham Junction [TQ1055], *Lord Howard*: Large pub with good bar food, well kept Friary Meux and Ind Coope Burton, friendly bar staff; children well provided for, with family-room and special menu *(Simon Pink)*

☆ **Elstead** [SU9143], *Woolpack*: Good traditional English and colonial food from snacks to main dishes, changing daily, in picturesque old-world pub with numerous relics of wool industry in tastefully renovated oak-beamed lounge; well kept real ale tapped from the cask, pleasant licensees, friendly welcome (from large dog too if he's awake) *(W M Elliott, Mrs J P Crawford, Michael and Harriet Robinson, Mr and Mrs J C Dwane, WAG)*

Englefield Green [34 Middle Hill; SU9970], *Beehive*: Friendly, courteous, helpful service, Gales ales (it's no longer a free house) and country wines, attractive bar food, nice atmosphere, early-evening happy hour *(Simon Collett-Jones, Gary Wilkes)*

Epsom [East St; TQ2160], *Common Room*: Far from traditional – school theme; well kept Ruddles County and other beers, good weekday pub food, Fri and Sat evening trendy pub for young people keen on up-to-date music and videos *(H E Swift)*; [East St] *Kings Arms*: Cheerful and friendly at lunchtime, with attractive (if softly lit) bar, handpump beer, simple honest food at moderate prices, willing polite service, picnic-table sets in small garden *(E G Parish)*; [West St (junction with High St)] *Marquis of Granby*: Comfortable town pub with attractive wooden ceiling in bar, fresh flowers on lounge tables; popular at lunchtime for its good value bar food – the sandwiches are delicious, including formidable hot salt beef ones known as Tram-stoppers; good service *(E G Parish)*

Esher [82 High St; TQ1464], *Albert Arms*: Good range of real ales and sensibly priced French regional wines in lively Victorian pub/bistro with good value bar food including interesting pâtés and well kept cheeses *(Richard Balkwill, LYM)*; [A307 at Weston Green between Esher and Kingston] *Cricketers*: Good value sandwiches, courteous service, well kept Courage ales *(Nigel Williamson)*; *Moor Place*: Berni Inn, limited but good range of bar food at very fair prices, including really fresh salad with the cheese or meat plates; lovely sweeping lawns with wide views *(Ian Phillips)*; [West End; off A244 towards Hersham, by Princess Alice Hospice] *Prince of Wales*: Well run and attractive, with Watneys-related real ales on handpump, good variety of hot and cold bar food (also restaurant), pleasant conservatory, well laid out garden *(Robert Crail)*; [on green]

Wheatsheaf: Cosy, spacious bar facing village green, with Watneys-related real ales on handpump and well arranged food counter with tasty daily specials and home-made puddings; no music or fruit machines *(G T Rhys)*

Ewell [45 Cheam Rd; TQ2262], *Glyn Arms*: Previously a main entry for its rambling series of rooms connected by lobbies and passages, its cheerful Antipodean staff, and its cheap food, but readers have been less enthusiastic since the licensees left to go to the Fox & Hounds, Walton on the Hill – more reports please *(LYM)*; [Broadway, Stoneleigh] *Stoneleigh*: Spacious and very lively, with good food, friendly staff and good parking *(David Clare)*

Ewhurst [The Street; TQ0940], *Bulls Head*: Newly decorated pub under new management with skittle alley, beer garden and promising food; start GWG55 *(Anon)*

Farley Green [Farley Heath; TQ0645], *William IV*: Very nice pub with lots of character, good wine *(C Gray)*

☆ Farncombe [SU9844], *Ram*: Known locally as the Cider Hole as it has no beer, only draught cider; a rural retreat in suburbia with discreet, simple rooms and a shaded garden; tends to get very busy with Guildford students at weekends *(Jon Dewhirst)*

Farnham [Castle St; SU8446], *Nelsons Arms*: Good value triple-decker sandwiches in long low-beamed pub with polished tables and settles, Courage ales, wide choice of food and some naval mementoes; next to almshouses in fine Georgian street leading up to the castle *(Liz Phillips)*; [Bridge Sq] *William Cobbett*: Cobbett's picturesque birthplace, now a lively young people's pub with good value cheap food, well kept Courage Directors and lots of amusements *(Gary Wilkes, LYM)*

Felbridge [TQ3639], *Woodcock*: A promising future, as it's been taken over by the Joneses who made the Spotted Dog near Penshurst (in Kent) particularly popular with readers for good food and drink in a civilised yet pleasantly pubby atmosphere *(Anon; reports please)*

Friday Street [TQ1245], *Stephan Langton*: Welcoming, friendly pub in walking area with well kept real ale, unusual bar snacks; on GWG52 *(Jenny Seller)*

Godalming [Ockford Rd; SU9743], *Anchor*: Comfortable, tastefully old-fashioned pub, friendly staff and locals; Fullers London Pride, Huntsman Royal Oak and bottled Gales Prize Old Ale, bar food, pleasant garden and terrace *(P M Brooker)*; *Inn on the Lake*: Especially good for families, with good food and service, well kept Flowers and Wethereds, log fire, lakeside garden, summer barbecue *(Dr I J Thompson)*; [High St (A3100)] *Kings Arms & Royal*: Really cheap good value lunches in busy but friendly warren of little partitioned rooms and rather

splendid Tsar's Lounge – substantial eighteenth-century coaching-inn; bedrooms *(BB)*

Godstone [Bletchingley Rd; TQ3551], *Hare & Hounds*: Friary Meux house opposite village green, attractive exterior, welcoming atmosphere, mock oak beams and cosy nooks, good bar food and service *(E G Parish)*

Grafham [Smithbrook (A281 Horsham Rd); TQ0241], *Leathern Bottle*: Well kept King & Barnes ales, wide choice of food, roaring log fire; by no means plush – pleasantly pubby; has recently changed management, and the licensees who made it particularly popular with readers have moved to the Crabtree at Lower Beeding *(C Elliott, Lyn and Bill Capper)*

Guildford [123 High St; SU9949], *Bulls Head*: This massively beamed and timbered pub, popular with many readers and the brave survivor of one attempt to devour it in a property-development scheme, closed in summer 1988 after being sold to another property developer – we fear the worst *(LYM)*; [Quarry St] *Kings Head*: Lots of beams and stripped brickwork in large corner pub converted from former cottages, lovely big inglenook, spacious banquettes, lots of intimate nooks and crannies, subdued piped music, well kept Courage Best, full range of good value pub food, coffee *(Ian Phillips)*; [Sydenham Rd] *Rats Castle*: Owned by same people as Crowns, Haslemere, and food has been as good – a haven in a surprising backwater for pubs, though décor has little atmosphere *(Dr I J Thompson)*; [Trinity Churchyard] *Royal Oak*: Very friendly Courage pub with super big log fires in winter, lots of stools around small tables, good value simple bar food *(Liz and Ian Phillips)*; [Chertsey St] *Spread Eagle*: Recently refurbished Whitbreads house – surely the fad for stripping pub walls has gone too far when it reveals perfectly plain brickwork; friendly welcome, large range of bar food at reasonable prices *(Ian Phillips)*; [Blackheath] *Villagers*: Delightful atmosphere in genuinely old-world pub, very good bar food, outside service for garden in summer, good range of drinks *(J Nichols)*

Headley [TQ2054], *Cock*: Good pub with lots of room *(TOH)*

Hindhead [SU8736], *Punch Bowl*: Welcoming place with a pleasant atmosphere and quickly served food *(J A Uthwatt)*

☆ Holmbury St Mary [TQ1144], *Kings Head*: Very friendly new landlord in quiet country pub with plenty of tables, log fires, six changing real ales on handpump such as Badger Tanglewood, Batemans XXB, Flowers Original, King & Barnes, Ringwood Old Thumper and Tetleys on handpump, big helpings of food such as basic ploughman's, children accepted; rarely too busy, yet surrounded by good walking country *(R P Taylor, John Booth, M D Hare)*

Holmbury St Mary [TQ1144], *Royal Oak*:

Civil and comfortable cottagey pub in fold of the hills with view over green and ample tables in front; very neat and tidy, with Friary Meux beer and good bar food; no hikers, no dogs *(TOH)*

Horley [TQ2842], *Coppingham Arms*: Very good real ale and reasonably priced good straightforward food *(A R Hardy)*; [Victoria Rd] *Foresters Arms*: A surprising find in this modern town centre – genuinely old and unspoilt pub with high bar hatch for tiny back rooms *(LYM)*

Horsell Common [A320 Woking–Ottershaw; SU9959], *Bleak House*: Warm, friendly, Friary Meux pub belying its name (though it's isolated, surrounded by heath), real ale on handpump and decent hot and cold bar food; décor could be improved *(R B Crail)*

Irons Bottom [Irons Bottom Rd; off A217; TQ2546], *Three Horseshoes*: Friendly free house with real ales such as Arkells, Brakspears, Everards and Fullers, good food *(C Elliott)*

Kenley [Old Lodge Lane; left (coming from London) off A23 by Reedham Stn, then keep on; NB is actually in Gtr London; TQ3259], *Wattenden Arms*: One of very few real country pubs on the outskirts of London (and actually within London's boundary, though by long tradition we list it here under Surrey); cosy and friendly, with dark panelling, traditional furnishings, firmly patriotic décor, well kept Bass and Charrington IPA on handpump, bar food (not Sun lunch), seats on small side lawn *(G Shannon, E G Parish, LYM)*

Kingswood [Waterhouse Lane; TQ2455], *Kingswood Arms*: Particularly enjoyed for quality and variety of bar food (though sandwiches may be too doorstep-like for some); spacious attractive building *(TOH)*

Leatherhead [Chessington Rd; A243 nr M25 junction 9 – OS Sheet 187 reference 167600; TQ1656], *Star*: Big pub which gets packed with people – it's popular for lunches and for evening charcoal-grilled steaks, with real ales such as Ruddles County and Whitbreads Strong Country; congenial, good service *(Keith Douglas, Dorothy Waldeck)*

Limpsfield Chart [TQ4251], *Carpenters Arms*: Pretty, recently decorated pub on delightful green, clean, well run and pleasantly laid out; Friary Meux, Benskins Best; good bar food including vegetarian dishes *(Jenny and Brian Seller)*

Little Bookham [TQ1254], *Windsor Castle*: Old building, repeatedly but carefully extended and on the up and up; friendly, with Watneys-related real ales on handpump, wide choice of good reasonably priced food (almost a restaurant, though they also do ploughman's and so forth), huge garden with children's play things *(WFL, Roger Taylor)*

☆ **Mickleham** [Byttom Hill – OS Sheet 187 reference 173538; TQ1753], *King William IV*: Delightfully cosy rambling free house approached by steep roads and paths with lovely views (you may see badgers on a warm evening); well kept Badgers, Flowers, King & Barnes Mild and Bitter, home-made good value bar food, pretty garden on four layers with terraces and an abundance of seats and tables *(Christopher Allen, R P Taylor)*

Mickleham [London Rd], *Running Horses*: Straightforwardly decorated pub with good atmosphere, reasonably priced bar food with some concentration on restaurant, friendly staff, well kept Friary Meux and Ind Coope Burton, nice enclosed courtyard with folding roof for weather protection; conveniently placed for walkers *(Ian Phillips, Mrs Jenny Seller, TOH)*

Mogador [from M25 going up A217, it's signposted off after the second roundabout, on the edge of Banstead Heath; TQ2452], *Sportsman*: All on its own down a country lane, yet near London and easily accessible: lots of character, good beer, darts and bar billiards *(Mike Muston)*

Norwood Hill [TQ2343], *Fox Revived*: Good lunch, pleasant friendly atmosphere *(J H Bell)*

Oatlands [Anderson Rd; TQ0965], *Prince of Wales*: Very comfortable and remarkably spacious for what from outside looks a typical little corner pub; good range of food – sandwiches, generous ploughman's and casseroles all recommended; nice staff, separate dining-room, small garden; parking may be difficult *(Ian Phillips, Minda and Stanley Alexander)*

Ockham [Cobham Lane, on Effingham Junction crossroads; TQ0756], *Black Swan*: Old free house recommended for its range of very well kept beers; fairly well extended, garden, reasonable food *(WFL)*; [Ockham Lane – towards Cobham] *Hautboy*: This spectacular red stone Gothick building goes through phases when it's a restaurant/brasserie rather than a pub, but at least in summer 1988 the unusual darkly panelled high-raftered upstairs bar with its minstrels' gallery was doing real ales, ploughman's and other bar food (at a price); there are lots of seats outside *(John Branford, Simon Pink, LYM)*

☆ **Ockley** [Stane St (A29); TQ1439], *Cricketers Arms*: Roses around the door, inglenook, flagstones, low oak beams and shinily varnished rustic furniture in fifteenth-century stone village pub with simple bar food, well kept real ales such as Badgers, Fullers, King & Barnes and Pilgrim Progress (brewed in Surrey), country wines, friendly staff, log fires, piped music, small attractive dining-room decorated with cricketing memorabilia; seats outside *(M Webb, Chris Fluck, LYM)*

☆ **Ockley**, *Red Lion*: Decent choice of real ales in seventeenth-century former coaching-inn, refurbished with stable/loose-box theme under its genuine old beams – giving a cosy feel, though it's actually pleasantly spacious;

good value food, pleasant efficient service; children welcome *(Esme Hilliard, Mr and Mrs R Harrington, TOH, BB)*
Outwood [Miller Lane; TQ3245], *Castle*: Good atmosphere, unpretentious décor; welcoming, friendly landlord; Websters, King & Barnes; good value bar food *(Jenny and Brian Seller)*
Oxted [High St, Old Oxted; TQ3951], *Old Crown*: Well kept Adnams, Fremlins and Wethereds on handpump in small cosy downstairs bar with good helpings of food such as good vegetarian tagliatelle full of fresh vegetables; recently renovated pine wine bar and restaurant upstairs; barbecues in raised back garden; parking can be difficult; good Pimms *(Jason Caulkin)*
Pirbright [The Green; SU9455], *White Hart*: Popular cheap bar food, separate restaurant upstairs, good service, beautifully kept garden *(Shirley MacKenzie)*
Ranmore Common [towards Effingham Forest, past Dogkennel Green – OS Sheet 187 reference 112501; TQ1451], *Ranmore Arms*: Deep in the country, wide range of beers including Badger, food, open fire, lots of horseracing photographs, log fire; play area in big garden (which perhaps understandably is not at its tidiest in winter); children welcome *(R P Taylor)*
Redhill [A25 towards Reigate; TQ2650], *Red Lion*: Popular at lunchtime for reasonably priced straightforward food *(BB)*
Ripley [High St; TQ0556], *Anchor*: Low-beamed Tudor inn with lunchtime bar food, darts and video games in public bar, Ind Coope real ales, tables in coachyard *(Mike Muston, LYM)*; [Newark Lane] *Seven Stars*: Very near River Wey, very attentive staff, interesting choice of reasonably priced food, very big helpings – on the up and up *(Brian Frith)*; [High St] *Talbot*: Straightforward bar food in olde-worlde former coaching-inn with lounge comfortably rebuilt after 1987 fire; bedrooms *(J S Evans)*
Row Town [off Addlestone–Ottershaw rd, sharp left past church up Ongar Hill; TQ0363], *Cricketers*: Pleasant, well run pub with Watneys-related real ales on handpump, good choice of reasonably priced food; very clean and friendly *(Robert Crail)*
Rowledge [Cherry Tree Rd; SU8243], *Cherry Tree*: Pleasant out-of-the-way pub with good lunchtime food, big garden; can be very busy *(John Innes)*; [OS Sheet 186 reference 822434] *Hare & Hounds*: Courage beer, reasonably priced bar food, lovely garden *(Dr John Innes)*
Send [TQ0155], *New*: Attractively placed right on Wey Navigation canal, with big garden; wide choice of reasonably priced very well cooked and presented food, cheerful staff; can seem a bit bleak inside – big games machine, loud juke box with video screens *(Brian Frith, Jane Palmer)*
Shackleford [SU9345], *Cyder House*: New

licensees have made considerable improvements; despite name there's a better selection of beers (and food) than of cider; nice setting *(Dr I J Thompson)*
Shalford [The Street; TQ0047], *Sea Horse*: Large roadside pub with very nice garden and good car park, opposite the ancient Shalford Mill; Gales Butser and HSB, friendly landlord, bar snacks *(JS)*
Shamley Green [B2128 S of Guildford; TQ0343], *Red Lion*: Has had attractive range of enterprising food (which should be back to normal after some problems in the past year) in surroundings of some character – handsome settles and country furniture, antique clocks, old photographs; well kept Ind Coope Bitter, Best and Burton tapped from casks behind the bar *(Christopher Hill, P S Luckin, LYM)*
☆ **Shepperton** [Shepperton Lock, Ferry Lane; off B375 towards Chertsey, 100 yds from Sq; TQ0867], *Thames Court*: Delightful riverside spot, large rambling 1930s pub full of character, opened out inside with gallery up spiral stairs giving lovely view of the Thames and mooring boats, lots of dimly lit intimate nooks and crannies with oak-panelled walls and Windsor chairs; relaxed atmosphere even when busy, Bass and Charrington IPA, good value home-cooked food from separate bar, pleasant efficient service, large garden with weeping willows; very popular on a summer Sun *(Simon Collett-Jones, Ian and Liz Phillips, Gary Wilkes, Minda and Stanley Alexander)*
Smallfield [Plough Rd; TQ3143], *Plough*: Friendly place with very good, generously served fish Fri, hard-working staff, large attractive garden with lots of flowers *(Derek and Maggie Washington)*
South Godstone [Tilburstow Hill Rd; TQ3648], *Fox & Hounds*: Very old half-tiled black and white building, said to be haunted by highwayman – low-beamed bars, high settles, old prints, big helpings of food such as turkey and ham pie, very simple pleasant garden *(Mrs Pamela Roper)*; [Eastbourne Rd] *Wonham House*: Attractive nineteenth-century hotel with bow-windowed lounge overlooking fields, warm welcome, friendly service, real ales on handpump including Greene King, tasty bar meals; bedrooms *(E G Parish)*
Staines [124 Church St; TQ0471], *Bells*: Good bar food in pleasantly decorated pub *(Mrs G K Herbert)*
Stoke d'Abernon [Station Rd, off A245; TQ1259], *Plough*: Comfortably modernised pub with coal fire in small, cosy and homely old part, and airy conservatory eating area; well kept Watneys real ales and reasonably priced sensible bar food; big window seats, sizeable garden *(H E Swift, BB)*
Sunbury [French St; TQ1068], *Jockey*: Unpretentious side-street Charringtons local, very homely and comfortable, distinguished by its

extensive collection of chamber-pots hanging from bar ceiling; cat in front of gas fire, dogs in bar, leatherette seats, lots of old family photographs *(Ian Phillips)*; [Thames St] *Phoenix*: Thames pub with riverside terrace and landing-stage, occasional summer barbecues; good reasonably priced food, two lounges and back games-room; attractive view, opposite Sunbury lock *(Ian Phillips)*

☆ **Sutton** [B2126 – this is the Sutton near Abinger; TQ1046], *Volunteer*: Charming intimacy in traditional atmospheric interior without the bustle of busier pubs (and food service doesn't seem geared to any substantial number of customers); food's good value, with sandwiches, ploughman's and changing hot dishes; well kept Friary Meux and Ind Coope Burton; beware the low-flying beams; nicely set garden *(TOH, Liz and Ian Phillips, Doug Kennedy)*

Tandridge [off A25 W of Oxted; TQ3750], *Barley Mow*: Well kept ales including Courage Directors in lively village pub with large bright functional bar area; food in restaurant section *(Dominic Williams)*

☆ **Tandridge** [Tandridge Lane; TQ3750], *Brickmakers Arms*: Warm, friendly atmosphere and exemplary amiable service in pleasant country pub, revitalised by its new German landlord, with impressive choice of well kept real ales and imaginative and extensive range of bar food; seats in garden *(E G Parish, Tim Powell)*

Thames Ditton [Queens Rd; TQ1567], *Albany*: Overlooking Hampton Court grounds and the Thames, pleasant atmosphere, three real fires, Bass on handpump, ample helpings of averagely priced well presented home-cooked bar food *(Ian Phillips)*; [Summer Rd] *Olde Swan*: Civilised black-panelled upper bar overlooking quiet Thames backwater, bar food and restaurant *(LYM)*

☆ **Thursley** [SU9039], *Three Horseshoes*: Dark and cosy, with lovingly polished furniture, well kept Gales HSB and a good range of other drinks, well made sandwiches and imaginative hot dishes changing each day (not Sun lunchtime or Mon–Thurs evenings – at lunchtime they don't serve food until 12.30); very highly rated by many readers – and by ourselves – for its atmosphere, which depends on the character (not to say whim) of the landlord; though not all readers have felt so happily treated here, if you find you like it you'll love it *(Ray Challoner, C Gray, Ian Phillips, Lyn and Bill Capper, LYM)*

Tilford Common [SU8742], *Duke of Cambridge*: Very rural, with climbing-frames and so forth in long garden, tables on high grassy terrace at one end – so you can keep an eye on the children *(Neil and Elspeth Fearn)*

☆ **Walliswood** [Walliswood Green Rd; TQ1138], *Scarlett Arms*: The new licensee is preserving the old-fashioned atmosphere here – deeply polished flagstones, heavy oak

beams, simple furnishings, well kept King & Barnes Festive and maybe Old ale (on hand-pump now, rather than tapped from the cask), big log fire, two friendly cats, flowers from the well kept garden; limited food *(D J Penny, Phil and Sally Gorton, LYM)*

Walton on Thames [Station Approach; TQ1066], *Ashley Park*: Refurbished in Edwardian style, Benskins, Friary Meux and Ind Coope Burton on handpump, fair choice of reasonably priced bar food, attractively priced meals in restaurant; bedrooms good value *(F J Walters, R B Crail)*

Walton on the Hill [Chequers Lane; TQ2255], *Chequers*: Well laid out series of rooms rambling around central servery, good value food bar, popular restaurant, well kept Youngs real ale, quick friendly service even when it's crowded, terrace and neat garden with summer barbecues; traditional jazz Thurs; children in restaurant *(Patrick Young, R C Vincent, LYM)*; [Walton St] *Fox & Hounds*: Attractive cottage-style pub in centre of village; cosy with open fire, well kept Bass and Charrington IPA and good, well presented food and snacks; the new licensees previously notched up a good record in this *Guide* at the Glyn Arms, Ewell *(R H Reeves)*

☆ **West Clandon** [TQ0452], *Onslow Arms*: Well laid out beamed country pub with soft lighting, comfortable seats, lots of nooks and crannies and a touch of class (prices to match); meals (rather than snacks) in bar and restaurant, open fire, well kept real ales such as Brakspears, Youngs and Courage Directors, friendly service, great well lit garden; convenient for nearby NT properties; children welcome *(Roger Taylor, A R Lord, Lyn and Bill Capper, LYM)*

West Horsley [TQ0753], *Barley Mow*: Friendly, welcoming atmosphere; beamed bars, traditional oak furniture; courteous service; good, home-made food served in separate dining-room *(Denis Waters)*

☆ **West Humble** [just off A24 below Box Hill – OS Sheet 187 reference 170517; TQ1651], *Stepping Stones*: Wide choice of food, especially pizzas in a variety of fillings and sizes, and good choice of help-yourself salads in big popular pub with circular bar counter, real ale, pool-table; terrace and garden with barbecue and children's play area *(TOH, Roger Taylor)*

Westcott [Guildford Rd; TQ1448], *Cricketers*: Friendly recently refurbished pub with good local atmosphere, half a dozen real ales, food, pool-table in sunken area *(Ray Challoner)*

☆ **Weybridge** [Thames St; TQ0764], *Lincoln Arms*: Behind its own green on the Weybridge side of Shepperton Lock, very near the Thames; divided inside by snob-screen-style partitions, with sash bar shutters, country kitchen chairs and tables, the odd stuffed bird, prints and paintings, log-effect gas fires; light and airy, with four big bay windows facing green, pleasant staff; formerly a free house, it's now tied to Ind Coope-related beers with a guest such as Gales HSB; well presented good food *(Ian Phillips, R Houghton, Robert Crail)*

☆ **Weybridge** [Bridge Rd], *Queens Head*: Reopened 1987 after extensive renovations, good friendly atmosphere in intimate beamed bar with open fire, lots of stripped brick and rugby souvenirs, big helpings of good bar food, Watneys-related real ales; spacious restaurant with its own separate bar; benches outside; can get very busy *(Ian Phillips, Gary Wilkes, David Clare)*

Weybridge [Thames St], *Old Crown*: Extended old weatherboarded pub near (though not on) river with intimate sun-trap back yard, good atmosphere, good sand-wiches and more elaborate lunchtime food; Courage ale and other drinks – including wine at what seem like off-licence prices – all well served *(Ian Phillips)*

☆ **Windlesham** [Church Rd; SU9264], *Half Moon*: Busy and very friendly pub run by mother and son, recently carefully refur-bished, with fifteen real ales such as Badger, Fullers ESB and London Pride, Greene King Abbot, Marstons Pedigree, Ringwood Old Thumper, Ruddles County, Timothy Taylors Landlord, Theakstons Old Peculier, Wilt-shire Old Devil and Weedkiller, Youngers No 3; lovely garden overlooking nearby church and field with horses, good straight-forward food (not Sun), barn restaurant *(Gary Wilkes)*

☆ **Witley** [Petworth Rd (A283); SU9439], *White Hart*: Easy-going atmosphere in largely Tudor pub with good oak furniture, pewter tankards hanging from beams, inglenook fireplace where George Eliot drank; Watneys-related real ales, traditional games, unobtrusive piped music, straightforward bar food, friendly labrador; children in restaurant and eating area, seats outside, playground; nearby partly Saxon village church with interesting early twelfth-century frescoes *(Lyn and Bill Capper, E G Parish, W A Lund, LYM)*

Woking [Arthurs Bridge; TQ0159], *Bridge Barn*: Good atmosphere with lots of alcoves to hide away in, well kept Brakspears beer; a Beefeater *(Kit Read)*; [Chertsey Rd, nr stn] *Old Stillage*: Good range of real ales such as Hook Norton Best, Marstons Pedigree and Wadworths 6X in pleasant town-centre pub done up with beamery and so forth to give wine-bar atmosphere; good food, particu-larly pizzas, in restaurant area with pine tables, piped music *(Kit Read)*; [West End; TQ0058] *Wheatsheaf*: Genial, friendly licensee, good value bar food, pleasant garden with apple trees, ducks and chickens *(S L Hughes)*

Wonersh [The St; TQ0245], *Grantley Arms*: Popular half-timbered sixteenth-century local, busy on Sun, friendly service, real ale, imaginative bar food; arms commemorate Fletcher Norton who prosecuted Wilkes for his essay *On Women* and initiated recall of the punitive American expedition *(J S Evans)*

☆ **Wood Street** [SU9550], *White Hart*: Comfort-ably furnished, with straightforward bar food (not sandwiches), well kept changing real ales such as Gales HSB, Brakspears and Flowers on handpump, piped music, res-taurant; in cul-de-sac off attractive village green, tables outside *(Lyn and Bill Capper, F J Walters, R B Crail)*

☆ **Woodmansterne** [High St; TQ2760], *Wood-man*: Splendid garden with plenty of room for kids to play; often packed inside, with good Bass and Charrington IPA, character, homely atmosphere, comfortable settees and armchairs (if you can get one), decent food, pleasant staff *(Mike Muston, E G Parish)*

Worplesdon [take Worplesdon Stn rd from Guildford–Woking rd; SU9753], *Jolly Far-mer*: Fine range of well kept real ales – at a price – in simply furnished L-shaped bar, bar food, piped music, pleasant staff, big shel-tered garden; children in restaurant *(Lyn and Bill Capper, LYM)*

Sussex

Some notable changes at popular pubs here include new licensees at the Three Horseshoes at Elsted (still a fine pub, with excellent food), the cosy Black Horse in Nuthurst (popular for food, too), and the pretty Gribble down at Oving (brewing its own beer now). Several of the entirely new entries are particularly interesting – the Fox Goes Free at Charlton, cunningly redone by its new graphics-designer owner to capture an old-fashioned atmosphere (the pub itself is nearly five hundred years old), the grand old Spread Eagle in Midhurst (no need for special effort here to call up the mood of the past), the Crab & Lobster tucked away from the tourist crowds just outside Sidlesham (old-fashioned simplicity, a lovely little garden looking out to Pagham harbour), and the rambling New Inn at Winchelsea (good food in interesting, convivial surroundings); the neatly kept Olde White Horse at Easebourne does good food, too. Overall, the proportion of pubs combining good food with real character is remarkably high here – as can be seen from the unusual number that we've granted food awards to. Indeed, as the large number of Lucky Dip entries at the end of the chapter shows, this is an area where it's quite difficult to go anywhere without finding at least a reasonably good pub; we'd rate Sussex as among the very best-pubbed areas of Britain. The

The Cat, West Hoathly

stars against many of these Lucky Dip entries show that readers' reports or our own knowledge give really solid grounds for valuing their merit. Ones that are particularly worth noting are, in East Sussex, the Bell at Burwash, Juggs at Kingston Near Lewes, Sloop at Scaynes Hill and Golden Galleon near Seaford, and, in West Sussex, the Oak at Ardingly, Rainbow at Cooksbridge, George & Dragon at Coolham, Sussex Brewery at Hermitage, Lickfold Inn at Lickfold, White Hart at Stopham and Keepers Arms at Trotton.

ALCISTON TQ5103 Map 3
Rose Cottage ⊗
Village signposted off A27 Polegate–Lewes

The snugness is part of the charm in the bar of this well run little cottage (where there's a talking parrot in the mornings), and even when it gets a bit full the atmosphere stays relaxed and friendly. There are perhaps half a dozen tables, with wheel-back chairs and red leatherette seats built in around them; the black joists are hung with harness, traps, a thatcher's blade and lots of other black ironware, and a model sailing-ship, a stuffed kingfisher and other birds sit on shelves above its dark panelled dado, or in the etched-glass windows. A small low-beamed and parquet-floored area by the bar counter has a wall bench and little side bench. Good simple lunchtime bar food includes soup (£1), home-made pâté (£1.50), ploughman's (from £1.55), big salads (from £2, prawn £3.50), quiche (£2.15), ham and egg (£2.25), first-class home-made steak and kidney pie (£2.75), scampi (£3.50) and steaks such as ten-ounce porterhouse (£6.95), with evening extras like smoked salmon cornet (£2.75) or roast duck (£5.95). Well kept Harveys (sold as Beards here) tapped from the cask under light blanket pressure, King & Barnes on handpump, and a good Kir or buck's fizz; maybe cheap free-range eggs and local game; quietly friendly staff. There are some seats outside, by the tangle of wistaria over this tiled white cottage, and a small paddock beside the car park with a goat and chickens, and ducks on a pond. *(Recommended by Theodore and Jean Rowland-Entwistle, J Caulkin, Heather Sharland, PAB, Patrick Young, Peter Corris)*

Free house Licensee Ian Lewis Real ale Meals and snacks Small restaurant (evenings, not Sun) tel Alfriston (0323) 870377 Children in eating area and restaurant Open 11–2.30, 6.30 (7 Sat)–11 all year

ALFRISTON TQ5103 Map 3
Market Cross ('The Smugglers Inn')
In the early nineteenth century this medieval pub was the home of Stanton Collins, a particularly bloodthirsty gangster who used to smuggle brandy at nearby Cuckmere Haven, and was eventually transported to Australia for stealing sheep; he once hid eight of his gang up the chimney here. As a reminder of its smuggling history, a couple of cutlasses hang over the big inglenook fireplace in the low-beamed L-shaped bar; it's comfortably modernised with Liberty-print cushions on the window seats, Windsor chairs, and some brass on the walls (which have quite a lot of nautical-looking white-painted panelling). A snugger little room leads off. Bar food includes freshly cut sandwiches (from 75p), vegetarian flan (£2.40), basket meals such as cod (£2.40) or scampi (£2.95), gammon or trout (£4.35) and steaks (from good nine-ounce rump, £5.50), and at lunchtime good value plough-man's (from £1.35); last orders 1.45pm and 8.45pm. Well kept Courage Best and Directors on handpump. There's a beer garden behind. The cliff walks south of here are superb, though, if you're feeling lazier, Old Clergy, a house in the village, is

---

Pubs shown as closing at 11 do so in the summer, but close earlier – normally 10.30 – in winter unless we specify 'all year'.

worth visiting for its fine Elizabethan furniture. *(Recommended by Nick Dowson, Alison Hayward, Peter Corris, Wayne Brindle, Heather Sharland, B A Websdale)*

Courage   Real ale   Meals (not Sun lunchtime) and snacks   Public car park only fairly close Open 10–2.30, 6–11 all year

Star 🛏

Fine brightly painted medieval carvings decorate the front of this ancient inn, originally built by the monks of Battle Abbey as a hostel for pilgrims going to the shrine of St Richard in Chichester. The striking red lion is known by local people as Old Bill – probably a figurehead salvaged from a seventeenth-century Dutch shipwreck, like the one decorating the Red Lion in Martlesham (see Suffolk's Lucky Dip section). Inside, the elegant bar has a Tudor fireplace, massive beams supporting the white-painted oak ceiling-boards (and the lanterns used for lighting), and handsome furnishings that include a heavy oak Stuart refectory table with a big bowl of flowers and antique Windsor armchairs worn to a fine polish. Lunchtime food includes home-made soup (95p), sandwiches (£1.25), ploughman's (from £2.10), a mixed meat salad (£3.25) and home-made dishes of the day such as chicken casserole or good steak and kidney pie (£3.25); puddings (from 95p). Bass, John Smiths and Websters Yorkshire on handpump (drinks prices are very reasonable here, considering the style of the place). Friendly service and a relaxed atmosphere. *(Recommended by Nick Dowson, Alison Hayward, WHBM, Kenneth Finch, Jenny Seller, Simon Collett-Jones, Tom Evans, Heather Sharland, Dave Butler, Lesley Storey)*

Free house (THF)   Manager Michael Grange   Real ale   Lunchtime snacks and meals (not Sun)   Restaurant   Children welcome   Open 11–11 all year   Bedrooms tel Alfriston (0323) 870495; £52.25B/£77.50B

ARUNDEL   TQ0107   Map 3
Swan ⊗ 🛏

High Street

There's a good choice of well kept real ales in this cosy, friendly inn that includes Badger Best and Tanglefoot, Courage Directors, Harveys, King & Barnes, Youngs Special and a guest bitter all on handpump. Reasonably priced bar food, using fresh local produce, includes home-made soup (£1), sandwiches (from 95p, home-cooked beef with horseradish £1.20, toasties 20p extra), ploughman's (£1.50), garlic mushrooms (£1.50), basket meals (from £1.90, scampi or seafood £3.90), bacon, sausages and eggs or chilli con carne (£2.50), salads (from £2.50, home-cooked chicken £3, smoked salmon £6.50), gammon with pineapple (£4.95), steaks (from £8.50); puddings such as home-made fruit pie with cream or cheesecake (95p). The spacious L-shaped Turkey-carpeted bar has red plush button-back banquettes, red velvet curtains, and a casual local atmosphere; fruit machine, trivia machine and piped music. *(Recommended by A V Chute, Mrs R F Warner, Michael and Alison Sandy)*

Free house   Licensees Diana and Ken Rowsell   Real ale   Meals and snacks   Restaurant Children in eating area   Jazz first Sun night of month, 1950s and 1960s live music on other Sun nights   Open 11–11 all year   Bedrooms tel Arundel (0903) 882314; £33B/£40B

ASHURST   TQ1716   Map 3
Fountain ⊗

B2135 N of Steyning

On the right as you go into this friendly pub is a charmingly unspoilt sixteenth-century room with scrubbed flagstones, a couple of high-backed wooden cottage armchairs by the brick inglenook fireplace, a cushioned pew built right around two sides, two antique polished trestle tables, brasses on the black mantelbeam, and a friendly pub dog. Good home-made bar food includes soup and sandwiches (£1), ploughman's (from £1.50) and various daily specials such as moussaka or cheese and broccoli (£2.75) and tasty steak and kidney pie; candlelit suppers on Thursday and Friday evenings (booking advisable). Well kept Flowers Original, Fremlins, Whitbreads Strong Country, Pompey Royal and a guest beer such as Wethereds SPA or Winter Royal on handpump or tapped straight from the cask; cheerful service. A bigger carpeted room (no dogs in this one) has spindle-back chairs around its circular tables, a wood-burning stove, and darts, shove-ha'penny, dominoes, cribbage and fruit machine. There are two garden areas, one with fruit trees, roses, swings, a seesaw and a tiled-roof weekend barbecue counter, the other with picnic-table sets on gravel by an attractive duck pond. *(Recommended by Gordon Smith, Mr and Mrs R Gammon, Roger Danes, Dave Butler, Lesley Storey)*

Whitbreads   Licensee Maurice Christopher Caine   Real ale   Meals (lunchtime, not Sun) and snacks (not Sun)   Children in eating area lunchtime only   Open 11–2.30, 6–11 (11–11 Fri and Sat) all year; closed evenings 25 and 26 Dec

nr BILLINGSHURST   TQ0925 Map 3

Blue Ship

The Haven; hamlet signposted off A29 just N of junction with A264, then follow signpost left towards Garlands and Okehurst

On summer evenings you can sit outside this remote and friendly country pub at the tree-shaded side tables or out on benches in front by the tangle of honeysuckle around the door. Inside, the unspoilt front bar is served from a hatch, there's a snug bar down a corridor at the back and another room furnished with kitchen chairs and post-war Utility tables. Good home-made bar food includes sandwiches made with wholemeal bread (from 95p), ploughman's (from £2), with evening dishes like grilled gammon or stuffed plaice (£4.30) and T-bone steak (£8.25). Well kept King & Barnes Bitter tapped from the cask, and Old in winter. A games-room has shove-ha'penny, cribbage and a fruit machine. It can get crowded with young people at weekends. The pub has its own shoot. *(Recommended by N D Foot, Phil and Sally Gorton, MM, KG, Gary Wilkes, Philip King, RJF)*

King & Barnes   Real ale   Meals and snacks   Children in side back room   Occasional morris dancing   Open 10.30–2.30, 6–11 all year

BLACKBOYS   TQ5220 Map 3

Blackboys ★ ⊗

B2192, S edge of village

It's well worth wandering through the lovely series of old-fashioned small rooms in this fourteenth-century building to find interesting odds and ends such as Spy cricketer caricatures and other more antique prints, a key collection hanging from beams, a stuffed red squirrel, a collection of ancient bottles on a high shelf, a snug armchair by the inglenook fireplace, and so forth. Good waitress-served home-made food includes soup (£1.20, fish soup £1.90), sandwiches (from £1.20, prawn £1.90), ploughman's (£2.40), steak sandwich (£2.50), mussels in garlic butter (£2.75), seafood pancakes (£3.95), salads (from £3.50, local crab and prawns £5.25), rib-eye steak (£5.75), lots of puddings (from 80p), and children's portions (from £1.20). Well kept Harveys PA, BB and in winter Old on handpump; darts, shove-ha'penny, dominoes, table skittles, cribbage, fruit machine, space game and juke box. Seats among flowers and shrubs in front of the pub overlook a pretty pond where ducklings bob about among yellow flag irises. Altogether, there are about sixteen acres; the orchard behind, with rustic tables among apple trees and a children's play area with two wooden castles linked by a rope bridge, has goats, friendly rare pigs, ponies, guinea-fowl, rabbits and even peacocks, and there is a big

There are report forms at the back of the book.

well equipped playroom in the barn. (*Recommended by Comus Elliott, Revd Brian Andrews, G and S L, Dave Butler, Lesley Storey, Nick Dowson, Michael Bolsover, E G Parish*)

Harveys   Licensee Patrick Russell   Real ale   Meals and snacks (not Sun evening) Restaurant tel Framfield (082 582) 283   Children in areas set aside for them, restaurant and eating area   Open 11–11 initially

BYWORTH   SU9820 Map 3
Black Horse
Signposted from A283

The garden of this pub – a friary in the fifteenth century – is particularly attractive, dropping steeply down through a series of grassy terraces, each screened by banks of flowering shrubs (but still with a view across the valley to swelling woodland); a bigger lawn at the bottom is set beside a small stream and a line of old willows. Inside, it's simply, even austerely furnished, with stripped pews and scrubbed tables on bare floorboards, candles in bottles, decoration confined to a collection of old sepia photographs in the back part, and has a friendly atmosphere. In contrast with the simplicity of the décor, there's an elaborate choice of bar food: over twenty starters such as French onion soup (£1.30), ploughman's (from £1.60), pâté (£1.70), salads (from £1.85), and well over two dozen main dishes from shepherd's pie (£1.90) to jumbo prawns in garlic (£6.60). Well kept Ballards and Youngs Bitter and Special on handpump. (*Recommended by Mr and Mrs J H Adam, M E A Horler, S J A Velate, Lyn and Bill Capper, S A Lovett, B V Harmes, Dr I J Thompson*)

Free house   Real ale   Meals and snacks   Restaurant tel Petworth (0798) 42424   Children in restaurant   Open 11–2.30, 6–11; closed 25 Dec

CHALVINGTON   TQ5109 Map 3
Yew Tree
Village signposted from A27 and A22; pub on road to Golden Cross; OS Sheet 199 reference 525099

Outside this isolated country pub, beyond a little walled terrace garden with a sundial, unusually extensive grounds include the pub's own cricket pitch (they also play stool ball), rustic seats and tables (some of them chunks of tree-trunk) among plump conifers and hawthorns, an unusually high swing, and a big wooden climbing-frame. They have summer barbecues out here. Inside, it's kept deliberately simple and has lots of small oak pews around stripped kitchen tables on the brick or flagstone floor, good new elm seats built into its plain walls (some are bare brick, others cream plaster or plank-panelling), low beams, and there's an inglenook log fireplace in the back bar. Straightforward but carefully done bar food includes sandwiches, ploughman's (£1.85), and three main dishes such as steak and kidney pie or shepherd's pie (£3.10); well kept Harveys (sold here as Beards) and Fremlins on handpump; darts, dominoes and cribbage. The pub can get very busy with young people on Friday and Saturday evenings. (*Recommended by Robert Buckle; more reports please*)

Free house   Licensee Rhett Coomber   Real ale   Lunchtime meals and snacks   Open 11–2.30, 6–11 all year

CHARLTON   SU8812 Map 2
Fox Goes Free ⊗
Village signposted off A286 Chichester–Midhurst just N of West Dean; also from Chichester–Petworth via East Dean

Attractively reworked since being taken over from its former owners (Phoenix/ Watneys) three years ago, this friendly and well run sixteenth-century pub serves good bar food such as sandwiches (from £1), soup (£1.40), ploughman's (£2), filled baked potatoes (from £2.35), lasagne (£3.25), steak and kidney pie (£3.45), salads (from £3.65), seafood in hot garlic butter (£5.25) and sirloin steak (£6.25), with dishes of the day such as lamb and apricot pie (£3.45) or game pie (£5.50). The partly carpeted brick-floored main bar has elm benches built against its yellowing walls, a big brick fireplace, and blond wood tables and mate's chairs, with a small but entertaining hat collection; a nice little low-beamed snug has a sturdy elm settle and a big inglenook fireplace. A new extension in rustic style gives extra eating space for bar lunches, and becomes an evening restaurant (with the same menu as the bar). Well kept if pricey Ballards Wassail, Flowers Original, Fremlins, Gales HSB, King & Barnes Festive and a guest beer on handpump, decent house wines and country wines, piped music, fruit machine; they also have darts, shove-ha'penny, dominoes, table skittles, cribbage and some old-fashioned Victorian games. Tables among fruit trees in the back garden looking up to the downs have a summer soft-drinks servery and children's play area. (*Recommended by Gwen and Peter Andrews, Mrs C Jensen*)

Free house   Licensee Roger Waller   Real ale   Meals and snacks   Restaurant tel Singleton (024 363) 461   Children in eating area and restaurant   Live music Sun evening   Open 10.30–2.30ish, 6–11 all year

CHIDDINGLY   TQ5414 Map 3

Six Bells ★ ⊗

Under the low beams in this old-fashioned, warmly welcoming pub there are simple but attractive furnishings that include tall Windsor armchairs, pews, scrubbed or polished tables, an antique box settle, some panelling and old engravings, and a good fire in winter. In the back bar there's a pianola with many rolls which can be played with the landlord's permission. Consistently good home-made food includes sandwiches, French onion soup (50p), filled French bread (70p), cheesy garlic bread (95p), landlord's special (£1.20), steak and kidney, beef and vegetable or shepherd's pies (£1.40), vegetarian or meaty lasagne (£1.60), chilli con carne (£2.20), spicy prawns or spare ribs in barbecue sauce (£2.20), with generous banana splits, treacle pie and other puddings (£1.20). The elaborately carved bar counter – part of which did service as a makeshift bridge over a stream for some years, after it was removed from a nearby pub that closed down – serves well kept Courage Best and Directors and Harveys on handpump or tapped from the cask. Darts, dominoes, cribbage. There's a fine collection of enamelled advertising signs in the gents. Outside at the back, there are some tables beyond a goldfish pond. (*Recommended by C R and M A Starling, Theo and Jean Rowland-Entwistle, Nick Dowson, Dave Butler, Lesley Storey; more reports please*)

Free house   Licensee Paul Newman   Real ale   Meals and snacks (not Mon)   Small children's room and more room in music bar   Live bands Fri, Sat and Sun evenings, jazz Sun lunchtime   Open 10–2.30, 6–11 all year; closed Mon exc bank hols

COWBEECH   TQ6114 Map 3

Merrie Harriers

Village signposted from A271

There's still something of the atmosphere of an old-fashioned farm parlour in the friendly panelled public bar of this white clapboarded ex-farmhouse: beams, pewter tankards hanging by the bar counter, a curved high-backed settle by the brick inglenook fireplace (with a log-effect gas fire now), pot-plants in the window, and two friendly cats. The communicating lounge has spindle-back chairs around the tables on its flowery carpet. Good value, popular food includes filled cottage rolls, sandwiches and ploughman's at lunchtime, with soup, pâté, egg and prawn mayonnaise, salads from mixed cheese to mixed meats or smoked salmon and prawn cornets, hot dishes such as gammon and pineapple, steak and kidney pie or lasagne, lemon sole and puddings like home-made fruit pie with cream. Charringtons IPA, Flowers Original and well kept Beards (Harveys) on handpump under light top pressure; also country wines and biscuits to nibble on the counter. Darts, dominoes, cribbage. Outside the pub is a flower garden and a lawn with a swing and rustic seats. *(Recommended by AE, D J Penny, Prof A N Black, Gwen and Peter Andrews)*

Free house   Meals and snacks (limited Sun)   Open 11–2.30, 6.30–11; opens 7 in winter Two-bedroom letting cottage in grounds tel Hailsham (0323) 833108

nr DALLINGTON   TQ6619 Map 3

Swan ⊗ 🛏

Wood's Corner; B2096, E of Dallington

As nothing is nearly as high between here and Beachy Head, the views behind this welcoming fourteenth-century tile-hung inn are marvellous – either from the picnic-table sets in the neatly kept back flower garden or from the big picture windows in the simply furnished back bar. The main bar has sturdy wooden tables with little bunches of flowers, tapestry-cushioned stools and built-in wooden benches, well polished horsebrasses on the few beams and timbers in the cream walls, windows with more flowers and hanging copper saucepans, and a log fire. The menu changes day by day, serving mostly home-made dishes – they clearly mark those that are, such as sandwiches, cottage pie, cod and mushroom bake, lasagne or prawn au gratin (all £2.85), pies such as steak and kidney or chicken, ham and mushroom (£3.80), and puddings like apple pie, bread pudding or sherry trifle (£1); vegetarian flans. On Sundays little dishes of nuts, crisps and Cheddar cheese are put out on the bar counter. Well kept Harveys, King & Barnes Festive and Marstons Pedigree on handpump; decent house wines; attentive service. Bar billiards, shove-ha'penny, dominoes, chess, a trivia machine and unobtrusive piped music. From the bedrooms, the night view of the tiny distant lights of Eastbourne is stunning. Good woodland walks nearby, especially in Dallington Forest. *(Recommended by B R Shiner, J A H Townsend, V H Balchin, E G Parish, Dr Paul Kitchener, Philip King, Chris Fluck, K Soutter, K Smurthwaite, G F Scott, WHBM)*

Beards (who no longer brew)   Licensees John and Marie Blake   Real ale   Meals and snacks   Restaurant   Children in restaurant and area set aside for them   Occasional folk nights   Open 11–3, 6–11 all year   Two bedrooms tel Brightling (042 482) 242; £15/£25

EASEBOURNE   SU8922 Map 2

Olde White Horse ⊗

A286 just N of Midhurst

Reliable for good value simple food, this neat and well kept stone pub has a snug little modernised lounge with Leech and other sporting prints on its white-painted partly panelled walls, and a small log fire. The bigger public bar, with wall settles on its woodstrip floor, has darts, dominoes, cribbage, a fruit machine and juke box. One seat is the preserve of Guy the cat, even on those busy days when a shooting or polo party's in. The food includes sandwiches (from 70p), burgers (£1.75), haddock (£1.95), shellfish platter (£2.75) and gammon (£2.85), with quite a few dishes of the day such as cochin beef or grilled trout (£2.95), lemon sole (£3.25) and six-ounce sirloin steak (£3.95). On Tuesday to Saturday evenings a much wider choice includes a variety of popular soufflé omelettes (£5.50), steaks and more elaborate dishes. Well kept Friary Meux and Ind Coope Burton and Mild on handpump. There are tables out in a small courtyard, with more on the sheltered and well tended back lawn. *(Recommended by Steve and Carolyn Harvey, Mrs W S McCaw, C Harwood, Sylvia Matthews)*

Friary Meux (Ind Coope)   Licensees Alan and Christine Hollidge   Real ale   Meals and snacks   Evening restaurant (may be used as weekend lunchtime overflow) tel Midhurst (073 081) 3521   Children in restaurant   Open 11–2.30ish, 6–11 all year; closed evening 25 Dec

EAST DEAN   SU9013 Map 2
Star & Garter

Village signposted from A286 and A285 N of Chichester

Tucked away in a little village below the South Downs, and looking down to the big, peaceful green, this well kept and happy pub has three rooms comfortably knocked together, with captain's chairs, leatherette armchairs, some corn dollies, and local oil paintings above the lower panelling. Lunchtime bar food includes home-made soup (80p), sandwiches (from 80p, toasties from 90p), bacon and egg (£1.20), ploughman's (from £1.65), jumbo sausage (£1.45), three-egg omelettes (£2.10), gammon and pineapple (£3.50), scampi (£3.80) and sirloin steak (£5.60), with evening extras such as ambitious salads (from £3), trout (£4.25) and giant mixed grill (£6.60). On Goodwood race-days and Bank Holidays they do a lunchtime salad bar and barbecue instead – occasionally with country and western singers and/or a brass band – in a marquee in their pretty flower garden, which has rustic seats and a swing by a long herbaceous border, a giant of an apple tree, and a flower-ringed little pool. As the garden is completely walled in, it's good for families. Well kept Friary Meux and Ind Coope Burton on handpump; sensibly placed darts, shove-ha'penny, dominoes, cribbage and fruit machine. Close to the South Downs Way, the pub welcomes walkers. *(Recommended by G B Longden, R P Taylor, A V Chute)*

Friary Meux (Ind Coope)   Real ale   Meals and snacks   Children in eating area   Occasional jazz or country and western bank hols only   Open 10.30–2.30, 6–11

EASTDEAN   TV5597 Map 3
Tiger

Pub (with village centre) signposted – not vividly – from A259 Eastbourne–Seaford

Perhaps the main attraction to this long, low, tiled white cottage is the very pretty setting; it faces a quiet cottage-lined green, and has a big bright painting of a tiger on a branch, lots of window boxes, clematis and roses, and some rustic seats and tables on the brick front terrace. The lane (very bumpy around the green) leads down to the coast at Birling Gap, then on to Beachy Head – much of the land between here and the sea is National Trust. The pub is on *Good Walks Guide* Walk 60. Inside, two low-beamed ochre-walled rooms are decorated with old photographs of the pub (often with a hunt meeting on the green), Victorian engravings, horsebrasses, pewter measures and china mugs hanging from beams, a big kitchen clock facing the bar, some handbells over the counter, and a stuffed tiger's head. There are low rustic tables and padded seats and (in the inner room) antique oak settles, one with a big bowed back and another attractively carved, housekeeper's chairs and old-fashioned tables; a relaxed and cheerful atmosphere. Bar food includes toasted sandwiches in winter, pâté (£1.75), ploughman's (from £1.80), a wide choice of salads (from £3), chicken or scampi (£3.25), fresh sole or curry (£3.50), gammon (£4.50) and eight-ounce sirloin steak (£5.50). Well kept Courage Best and Directors on handpump; good choice of wines by the glass and hot toddies; fruit machine and piped music. *(Recommended by Peter Corris, Jenny and Brian Seller, Gwen and Peter Andrews)*

Courage   Licensee James Conroy   Real ale   Meals and snacks (limited Sun lunchtime, not Sun evening)   Open 11–11; 11–2.30, 6–10.30 in winter

ELSTED   SU8119 Map 2
Three Horseshoes ★
Village signposted from B2141 Chichester–Petersfield

At the end of summer 1987, new owners took over this pub and since then the
majority of reports have been warmly favourable, though there have been a few
grumbles – mainly about food prices. The four cosy connecting rooms have low
beams, rugs on sixteenth-century bricks, on tiles or on bare boards, antique
high-backed settles, studded leather seats, oak benches, and good tables (candlelit
at night), attractive engravings and old photographs on the deep ochre walls, log
fires, and simple latch and plank doors; there are newspapers on racks. Changing
food might include soup in winter (£1.50), ploughman's with a good choice of
cheeses (from £2.50), garlic-stuffed mussels (£3.25), baked potatoes with interesting fillings (£3.50), chilli con carne (£3.75), scampi (£3.95), steak and kidney in
Guinness pie (£4.50), wing of skate in black butter (£6.25), good grilled prawns in
garlic butter (£6.50), steaks (from £6.95), and puddings such as tasty cinnamon and
nutmeg pie or treacle tart (£1.50). The pretty little rustic dining-room with candles
in brass holders on its plain wooden tables now serves the same food as the bar.
Well kept changing ales tapped from the cask might include Badger Best, Ballards
Best and Wassail, Fullers London Pride, Harveys BB and Gales HSB, and they keep
Churchward's farm cider and Gales country wines; dominoes, cribbage and
shut-the-box; rather rushed young staff, though perfectly pleasant. They sell local
eggs. The pretty tiled house is set at the end of the hamlet, below the sweep of the
South Downs; it has picnic-table sets out in a biggish garden with a good
herbaceous border, new rose beds and a pets corner with a lamb, goat, pigs and
ornamental fowl; extended car park. (*Recommended by Shirley Fluck, Dr John Innes, Dr
I J Thompson, HEG, Peter Hitchcock, Drs S P K and C M Linter, Gwen and Peter Andrews,
M C Howells, Ian Phillips, Harvey Hallam, Wendy Arnold, YMH, Gary Wilkes, J Walsh, A J
Kentish, R Hutchings*)

Free house   Licensees Ann and Tony Burdfield   Real ale   Meals and snacks   Restaurant tel
*Harting (073 085) 746; open until 4.30 Sun   Children in eating area and restaurant   Open
10–11 all year; closed evening 25 Dec*

FITTLEWORTH   TQ0118 Map 3
Swan ⊗
Lower Street; B2138

This pretty tile-hung fifteenth-century inn is now part of the Chef & Brewer chain;
the main bar has wooden truncheons over the big inglenook fireplace (which has
good log fires in winter), a big collection of bottle openers behind the bar, and is
comfortably furnished with Windsor armchairs on the patterned carpet. Good
home-made bar food includes sandwiches (from 95p), and open sandwiches on
French bread (from £1.25), soup (£1.10), baked potatoes (from £1.20), ploughman's (from £2.40), lasagne (£2.50), vegetarian dishes and curries (£3), steak and
kidney (£3.60), salads (from £3.50), and puddings such as trifle or summer pudding
(from 90p); children's meals (£1.80), Sunday lunch with a choice of four starters
and four main courses (£7.95); good coffee. The attractive panelled room is
decorated with landscapes by Constable's brother George. Well kept Ruddles Best
and County, and Websters Yorkshire on handpump; perhaps soft classical piped
music, and the smaller public bar has darts and a fruit machine. There are good
nearby walks in beech woods. In summer perhaps the nicest place to sit is at one of
the white tables spaced well apart on the big back lawn, sheltered by flowering
shrubs and a hedge sprawling with honeysuckle, and there are benches by the

---

village lane in front of the building. *(Recommended by Charles and Mary Winpenny, Lyn and Bill Capper, Mr and Mrs W Harrington, WHBM, Mr and Mrs J Halsey)*

Phoenix (Watneys)   Licensees Chris and Nikki Hunt   Real ale   Meals and snacks   Restaurant   Children welcome   Open 10.30–2.30, 6–11 all year; closed evening 25 Dec   Bedrooms tel Fittleworth (079 882) 429; £27.50(£31.50B)/£38(£44B)

FULKING   TQ2411   Map 3

Shepherd & Dog   ★

From A281 Brighton–Henfield on N slope of downs turn off at Poynings signpost and continue past Poynings

Even on a grim winter weekend, the very warm low-ceilinged bar in this charming little slate-hung cottage can get packed; it's best visited during the week, out of season. The partly panelled walls are decorated with shepherds' crooks, harness, stuffed squirrels, mounted butterflies and blue and white plates. There's a big log fireplace in one stripped wall hung with copper and brass, an antique cushioned oak settle, stout pegged rustic seats around little gate-leg oak tables, and attractive bow-window seats. There may be a long queue at the food servery: sandwiches (not Sunday, from £1, locally smoked Scotch salmon £2), various ploughman's (from £2.15), salads (from £4.55), and in the evening dishes such as home-made soup, home-made liver or smoked salmon pâté (£2.55), beef and Guinness pie or duck and apple pancakes (£4.95) and porterhouse steak (£6.95); puddings such as lemon crunch or chocolate and rum mousse. King & Barnes Festive, Ruddles Best and County, and Websters Yorkshire on handpump; darts, shove-ha'penny, dominoes and cribbage. The garden – nestling below the seven-hundred-feet slope of the steep downs – has a series of prettily planted grassy terraces, some fairy-lit, with an upper tree-sheltered play lawn with veteran farm machinery, swings, seesaw and an old-lady-who-lived-in-a-shoe playhouse. The stream running through washes into a big stone trough where the shepherds bringing their flocks to sell at Findon sheep fair used to clean up their merchandise – while having a nip of the illicit liquor sold by one of the twin cottages which later became this pub. *(Recommended by J Caulkin, Jon Wainwright, Hugh Morgan, Mrs J M Aston, IAA, G Kahan, W J Wonham)*

Phoenix (Watneys)   Licensees C M E Bradley-Hole and S A Ball   Meals and snacks (not Sun evening exc summer barbecues)   Open 10.30–2.30, 6–11 all year; maybe longer afternoon opening on Sat if trade demands; closed evenings 25 and 26 Dec

GUN HILL   TQ5614   Map 3

Gun   ⊗

From A22 NW of Hailsham (after junction with A269) turn N at Happy Eater

Two good reasons for visiting this neatly kept family-run pub are the friendly welcome and good choice of quickly served food: ploughman's (from £1.80), cauliflower cheese (£3.20), home-made steak and kidney pie or a cold buffet (from £3.50), vegetarian or meaty lasagne (£3.60), scampi (£4.50), steak Wellington (£5.70) and steaks (not lunchtime, from £6); puddings such as crisp apple and raisin pancake (£1.50). The mainly carpeted rambling rooms have some fifteenth-century flooring-bricks and tiles, beams hung with pewter measures and brasses, small pictures on the cream walls, latticed windows with flowery curtains, and several fires in winter (one in an inglenook decorated with brass and copper). Red curtains mark the openings between different room areas – one, furnished more as a dining-room, has attractive panelling. Well kept Bass and Charrington IPA on handpump, good choice of wines by the glass, and country wines; friendly service, with a good mix of age-groups among the customers. Outside the pretty tiled and timbered house – covered with clematis, honeysuckle, hanging baskets and heavy flower tubs – there are tables in the spacious garden, which has swings, fairy-lit trees and flower borders. *(Recommended by Neil Barker, Brian Smith, D L Johnson, Gwen and Peter Andrews, Richard Davis)*

Free house   Licensee R J Brockway   Real ale   Meals and snacks   Children in eating area   Open 11–11; 11–3, 6–10.30 in winter; closed 25 and 26 Dec   Bedrooms tel Chiddingly (0825) 872361; £20B/£25(£30B)

HALNAKER   SU9008   Map 2
Anglesey Arms ⊗
A285 Chichester–Petworth

There's a lively local atmosphere in the right-hand bar of this well run roadside pub as well as stripped deal settles and wall seats around candlelit stripped deal tables on the flagstones, and modern paintings on the cream walls; at the back there's a rather more dining-roomish carpeted area. Generously served home-made food includes sandwiches (from £1, not Sunday lunchtimes in winter), toasties (from £1.20), soups such as cream of watercress (£1.20), spinach or courgette quiche (£1.55), omelettes (from £1.75), ploughman's (£1.95), crab pâté (£1.95), fry-ups (£2.65), good dressed Selsey crab (£3.75), giant prawns (£5.65), sirloin steak (£4.95) and fillet steak (£5.95); Sunday roast lunch in winter. Well kept Friary Meux and Ind Coope Burton on handpump. Dominoes, cribbage, fruit machine, yatzee, draughts and shut-the-box. There are picnic-table sets on the side grass, and white metal and plastic seats and tables in a sheltered back beer garden by a fig tree. *(Recommended by J M M Hill, Prof A N Black)*

Friary Meux (Ind Coope)   Licensees C J and T M Horseman   Real ale   Meals and snacks (exc Sun lunchtime in winter)   Restaurant (open until 4 Sun) tel Chichester (0243) 773474   Children in eating area and restaurant   Open 10.30–2.30, 6–11; closed 24, 25, 26 and 31 Dec and 1 Jan

HARTFIELD   TQ4735   Map 3
Anchor ⊗
Church Street

Diners in this very friendly food pub aren't segregated from drinkers so the atmosphere is still very much that of a village pub. Very good – and generously served – it includes soup (£1.20), sandwiches (from £1.50, steak £3.95), ploughman's (from £2), salads (from £2.50), kebabs (from £5.50), steak (£6.50) and daily specials such as steak and kidney pie (£2.35), but the emphasis is on seafood – crab or prawn sandwiches (£2), fresh plaice (£2.75), scampi (£3.75), hot garlic prawns (£4), grilled lemon sole or skate (£5) and a giant seafood salad (£28 for two). The evening restaurant is used as a lunchtime overflow if the bar is full. Very well kept Adnams, Fremlins, Flowers Original, King & Barnes Bitter and Festive and a guest beer such as Whitbreads Pompey Royal on handpump. Service is notably courteous and efficient. The heavy beamed and carpeted bar rambles around the servery, with cushioned spindle-back chairs and wall seats, old advertisements and little country pictures on the ochre walls, a brown panelled dado, and houseplants in the small-paned windows. Darts in a separate lower room; shove-ha'penny, dominoes, cribbage and unobtrusive piped music. A front verandah gets packed on warm summer evenings, and there are some seats outside behind. This pub is near the start of *Good Walks Guide* Walk 62. *(Recommended by N D Foot, E G Parish, Jenny and Brian Seller, I D Shaw, Mr and Mrs M J Banbury, Ron Williams, Moira and Hugh Latimer)*

Free house   Licensee Ken Thompson   Real ale   Meals and snacks   Restaurant tel Hartfield (089 277) 424   Children in restaurant and games-room   Open 11–3, 6–11; closed evening 25 Dec

If you're interested in real ale, the CAMRA *Good Beer Guide* – no relation to us – lists thousands of pubs where you can get it.

sensibly placed darts and bar billiards, plus shove-ha'penny and cribbage. You can sit outside at rustic wooden tables on the lawn beside this pretty weatherboarded house, which used to be a village brewhouse. *(Recommended by V H Balchin, Mr and Mrs R J Welch, Mr and Mrs W Harrington, Donald Clay, Gavin May, Patrick Stapley, RAB)*

Free house   Licensee Richard Leet   Real ale   Meals and snacks   Restaurant   Children in restaurant   Open 11–2.15 (2.45 Sat), 5.45 (6 Sat)–11 all year; closed 25 Dec   Bedrooms tel Mayfield (0435) 872200; £28B/£40B

MIDHURST   SU8821 Map 2
Spread Eagle 🛏
South Street

Hilaire Belloc, who lived just around the corner from our editorial office, called this place 'the oldest and most revered of all the prime inns of this world'. Its spacious lounge bar certainly has bags of character – oriental rugs on broad boards, old leather wing armchairs, Chesterfields, wicker settees, original Victorian caricatures, timbered ochre walls, massive beams, big leaded windows, a huge fireplace with a 1608 fireback (there's said to be a secret room up one chimney, about six feet up). Badger Best and Ballards on handpump (not cheap), decent wines by the glass, courteous service, shove-ha'penny, dominoes and cribbage. A neat and cheerful barrel-vaulted cellar bar with crisp white paintwork, tiled floor and big oak cask seats or brocaded settles serves good value filled French bread or baked potatoes (£1.50), ploughman's (from £1.85) and salads (£2.95); darts in one bay, well reproduced piped music. *(Recommended by J S Evans, Keith Houlgate, E G Parish, Guy Harris)*

Free house   Licensee George Mudford   Real ale   Bar meals and snacks (lunchtime) Restaurant   Children welcome in cellar food bar (lunchtime)   Open 11–2.30, 6–11; closed evening 25 Dec   Bedrooms tel Midhurst (073 081) 6911; £52B/£60B

NUTHURST   TQ1926 Map 3
Black Horse
Village signposted from A281 SE of Horsham

In spite of a couple of changes in management over the last few years, this cosy pub has kept its friendly and welcoming atmosphere and its cheerful service; Badger, Harveys and King & Barnes Sussex are as well kept as ever. The black-beamed bar has a couple of armed Windsor chairs and a built-in settle on the big Horsham flagstones in front of its inglenook fireplace; it opens out into other carpeted areas with more seats and tables. Bar food includes ploughman's (from £1.75), ham and egg (£2.25), beef or lamb curry (£3.25), vegetarian dishes (from £3.25), steak and kidney pie (£3.75) and grilled gammon (£3.95); children's meals (£1.50); Sunday evening barbecues (weather permitting). You can sit outside in front or in the attractive back garden by a little stream. There are good woodland walks nearby. *(Recommended by G T Rhys, Peter Hall, Aubrey and Margaret Saunders, Stuart Barker, Dave Butler, Lesley Storey, Harvey Hallam)*

Free house   Licensees K W Beadle and A Latham   Real ale   Meals and snacks   Restaurant tel Lower Beeding (040 376) 272   Children in eating area   Live music Tues evenings   Open 11–2.30, 6–11 all year

---

We checked prices with the pubs as we went to press in summer 1988. They should hold until around spring 1989 – when our experience suggests that you can expect an increase of around 10p in the £.

People named as recommenders after the main entries have told us that the pub should be included. But they have not written the report – we have, after anonymous on-the-spot inspection.

OVING   SU9005   Map 2
Gribble ⊗

Between A27 and A259 just E of Chichester, then signposted just off village road; OS Sheet 197 reference 900050

This English country cottage is named after Rosa Gribble, who lived here for over ninety years. The lively bar has old heavy beams, timbered bare bricks, wheel-back chairs and cushioned pews around the old wooden country tables on its carpet, and a big log fire. On the left, a family-room, with more pews and rugs on its oak parquet floor, has bar billiards and darts; also shove-ha'penny, dominoes, cribbage and fruit machine. Besides Gribble Ale there are well kept Badger Best and Tanglefoot and Ringwood Old Thumper on handpump. Well presented bar food includes sandwiches (from 80p, fresh Selsey crab £1.85, toasties from £1.75), soup (95p), home-made burgers including a vegetarian one (£1.50), ploughman's (from £1.95), home-made cottage pie (£2.25), pâté of the day (£2.45), delicious home-baked ham and eggs (£3.15), home-made turkey and ham or steak and mushroom pie (£3.25), salads (from £3.25, Selsey crab £4.50), scampi (£3.50) and sirloin steak (£5.95); there are a few smaller (and cheaper) portions for those with not much appetite. A small open-sided barn opens on to the garden where there are rustic seats under the apple trees. *(Recommended by YMH, J P Berryman)*

Own brew   Licensees Connie and James Wells   Real ale   Snacks (not Sun and Mon evenings) and meals (not Sun, or Mon evening)   Children in family-room   Open 11–2.30, 6–11 all year

nr PUNNETTS TOWN   TQ6220   Map 3
Three Cups

B2096 towards Battle

The low-beamed bar in this cottagey pub has a welcoming atmosphere, dark brown panelling, dark old plush chairs on its oak parquet floor (there are tiles by the door), fishing-rods and mugs hanging from the low and heavy beams, lots of pewter tankards over the serving-counter, and a large stone inglenook fireplace with a log fire in winter. Comfortable plush cushioned seats in the bow window look out over a spreading front green where bantams stroll between the picnic-table sets. Reasonably priced bar food includes sandwiches, home-made cottage pie, local prize-winning giant sausages, ploughman's (the only food sold on Sundays), lasagne or butter-bean and mixed vegetable gratin, salads (including home-cooked ham), and evening dishes like pâté, breaded chicken and sirloin steak; there are daily specials and summer cook-your-own barbecues. Well kept Courage Best and Directors on handpump, and a good range of fortified wines in cut-glass decanters. The family-room has pool, shove-ha'penny, dominoes, cribbage and a sitting space game. There is a small covered back terrace, seats in the garden beyond, and a safe play area for children; a games hut has a pool-table and space games. There are clay-pigeon shoots every alternate Sunday (by prior appointment), and three pétanque pitches; they have space for five touring caravans. *(Recommended by J A H Townsend, Mr and Mrs W Harrington; more reports please)*

Courage   Licensee R Davis   Real ale   Meals (not Sun) and snacks (not Sun evening) Children in eating area and family-room   Open 11–3, 6–11 all year

nr RINGMER   TQ4412   Map 3
Cock

A26, N of Ringmer turn-off

Refurbishments and rebuilding here include a new restaurant and two new no-smoking lounges. The pub is cosy and friendly, with small Windsor chairs, heavy beams, soft lighting, winter log fires in an inglenook fireplace, and a young black labrador. Waitress-served bar food (if they could get the staff they'd like to offer table service for drinks too) includes open sandwiches (from £1.50), pâté (£1.95) and quite a few main dishes such as ham and egg (£3.25), moules marinière (£3.50), fresh dressed crab (£3.75), good fresh salmon salad (£5.50) and tandoori chicken kebab (£5.75); as the food is freshly prepared, there may be delays at peak times. Ruddles Best and County and Websters Yorkshire on handpump, and a good selection of wines; eclectic and enjoyable piped music. The sizeable fairy-lit lawn outside this white weatherboarded house is attractively planted with fruit trees, shrubs, honeysuckle and clumps of old-fashioned flowers, and there are seats on a good terrace. *(Recommended by Charles and Mary Winpenny, Emilia Marty, D L Johnson, Dave Butler, Les Storey, G Cooper)*

Phoenix (Watneys)   Licensee Brian Cole   Real ale   Meals (not Sun lunchtime) and snacks Restaurant tel Ringmer (0273) 812040   Well behaved children in restaurant and two no-smoking rooms   Open 11–11; 10–2.30, 6–11 in winter; closed 25 Dec

ROWHOOK   TQ1234 Map 3
Chequers
Village signposted from A29 NW of Horsham

The snug front bar in this sheltered country pub has black beams in its white ceiling, upholstered benches and stools around the tables on its flagstone floor and an inglenook fireplace; up a step or two, there's a carpeted lounge with a very low ceiling. Home-cooked lunchtime food includes home-made soups and pâtés (from £1.25), chicken and onion tagliatelle (£2.75), mushroom and bacon au gratin (£2.95) and home-cooked ham (£3.25); in the evening there are chicken satay (£4.25), king prawns with garlic butter (£4.50), chicken breast baked with avocado and garlic (£5.50) and steaks (from £6); home-made puddings like cheesecake and chocolate fudge (from £1.25); best to book at weekends. They do traditional roasts on Sunday lunchtimes and barbecues on Sunday evenings. Well kept Flowers Original, Fremlins and Whitbreads Strong Country on handpump, served from the elaborately carved bar counter; darts, shove-ha'penny, dominoes, cribbage and piped music; friendly service. Outside, sunny benches overlook the quiet country lane, and there are picnic-table sets in the big, peaceful side garden among roses and flowering shrubs, and under cocktail parasols on a crazy-paved terrace. *(Recommended by Jim Matthews, Mr and Mrs C H Kinnersly, Nick Dowson, Alison Hayward, Tim Halstead, Capt Tony Bland, Mrs Shirley Fluck)*

Whitbreads   Licensee G M Culver   Real ale   Meals and snacks   Restaurant tel Horsham (0403) 790480   Children in restaurant   Open 11–11 all year

RUSPER   TQ2037 Map 3
Plough
Village signposted from A24 and A264 N and NE of Horsham

Originally a blacksmith's and wheelwright's, this seventeenth-century village pub has a wide collection of real ales on handpump or tapped from the cask: Badger Best, Boddingtons, Courage Directors, Everards Old Original, Fullers London Pride and ESB, Gibbs Mew Bishops Tipple, Harveys BB, King & Barnes Sussex (and Old ale in winter), Marstons Owd Rodger, and guest beers such as Marstons Pedigree and Theakstons Old Peculier. The comfortably modernised, partly panelled bar has very low beams, a big inglenook fireplace with a good log fire, and a medley of brass and copper implements. Bar food includes a fine collection of cheeses, fresh salmon and meats with help-yourself salads, as well as home-made fisherman's pie or steak and kidney pie, lasagne and barbecued chicken. A small end room has a couple of space games and a fruit machine, and there may be piped music; upstairs, a room with exposed rafters has more seats, darts and bar billiards. In the back garden there is a pond, fountain and old well; the pretty front terrace has hanging baskets. *(Recommended by Don Mather, Mike Muston; more reports please)*

Free house   Real ale   Meals and snacks (lunchtime)   Children welcome   Open 11–2.30, 6–11

RYE   TQ9220 Map 3
Mermaid

The back bar of this classic black and white timbered Tudor inn, on its steep and much photographed cobbled lane, has hardly changed over the last sixty-five years – as a picture there shows. Though it's unassuming and unpretentious, it has interesting antique seats (one of them carved in the form of a goat) around its timbered walls, a huge fireplace with a halberd and pike mounted over it, some eighteenth-century carving, and a longcase clock. Other rooms have panelling, heavy timbering and wall frescoes. Bar food includes sandwiches, home-made soup, ploughman's and a salad buffet, but in 1988 was not served before March; Bass, Fremlins and Wethereds on handpump. There are seats on a small back terrace. *(Recommended by Alison Hayward, Nick Dowson, Peter Corris, Richard Gibbs, Wayne Brindle, J R Leeds, Tom Evans)*

Free house   Real ale   Meals and snacks (lunchtime)   Restaurant   Open 11–2.30, 6–11 all year; but may be closed, particularly at lunchtime, mid-week out of season   Bedrooms tel Rye (0797) 223065; £30(£37B)/£44(£56B)

SELSFIELD   TQ3434 Map 3
White Hart ⊗

Ardingly Road; B2028 N of Haywards Heath, just S of junction with B2110 at Hartfield; close to West Hoathly (which is its postal address)

This friendly old timbered and tiled building stands alone on a pretty tree-lined road, just above a wooded combe which drops steeply away below the picnic-table sets on the lawn at the side. Inside, there are some old black wooden-plank tables, black oak beams in the dark ochre ceiling, and a couple of very thick elm tables by the big log fire which serves to divide the bar into two areas. Good bar food includes home-made soup (£1.50), ploughman's (from £1.55), a choice of omelettes (from £1.60), hot daily specials such as home-made steak and kidney pie or lasagne (£2.95), beef Stroganoff (£3), curries (£3.50), plaice (£3.75) and scampi (£4.25); three-course Sunday lunch. Well kept Adnams, Benskins, Fullers London Pride, Hook Norton Old Hookey, King & Barnes Festive, Ruddles and Tetleys on handpump; piped music. A sixteenth-century barn from Wivelsfield has been moved here and sensitively reconstructed as a restaurant. The pub is handy for Wakehurst Place and Ingwersen's alpine plants nursery; it is also on *Good Walks Guide* Walk 64. *(Recommended by Norman Foot, Derrick Turner, Chris Fluck, Dominic Williams)*

Free house   Licensee Keith Noquet   Real ale   Meals and snacks (lunchtime)   Restaurant tel East Grinstead (0342) 715217   Children welcome   Open 11–3, 6–11 all year

SIDLESHAM   SZ8598 Map 2
Crab & Lobster

Off B2145 S of Chichester, either Rookery Lane N of village (on left as you approach) or Mill Lane from village centre

Picnic-table sets in the little back garden, filled prettily with sweet peas, gladioli, foxgloves, snapdragons, roses and so forth, look out across a meadow to the coastal flats; the pub stands in a small group of houses right by silted Pagham harbour, and is comfortably well away from the main tourist places. The bar is a welcome relief from most around here – quite unimproved, with wildfowl prints on the ochre walls, elderly dark green leatherette wall benches and a good log fire; there's also a plusher side lounge. The simple food's good value: filled baked potatoes (from £1.50), toasties such as egg and bacon (£1.60), crab or prawn sandwiches (£1.90), chicken satay (£2.60) and Selsey crab (£3.50). Well kept Friary Meux and Ind Coope Burton on handpump, and a decent choice of other drinks. Sadly, the magnificent mulberry opposite was a victim of the October 1987 storm. *(Recommended by Hope Chenhalls, Peter Griffiths, Mr Adams)*

Friary Meux (Ind Coope) *Licensee Brian Cross* *Real ale* *Meals and snacks* *Open 10.30–2.30, 6–11 all year; closed evenings 25–26 Dec*

nr TICEHURST TQ6830 Map 3

Bull ✪

Three Legged Cross; coming into Ticehurst from N on B2099, just before Ticehurst sign, turn left beside corner house called Tollgate (Maynards Pick Your Own may be signposted here)

Delightfully tucked away, this fourteenth-century pub has several low-beamed rooms (including a very popular restaurant extension) with flagstone, brick or oak parquet floors, heavy oak joined tables, kitchen seats, flowery cushions on benches and settles, and a big central fireplace (which the soft grey tabby heads for). Good lunchtime bar food includes home-made soup (90p), sandwiches (from 70p, hot gammon £1, steak £2), ploughman's (from £1.50), smoked mackerel pâté (£2), smoked haddock (£2.75), steak and kidney pie or winter oxtail stew (£3.50), ten-ounce rib-eye steak (£4) and home-made puddings (from £1.25). In the evenings (when they prefer bookings) they do more elaborate meals. Well kept Harveys BB, Ruddles County and Best, and Shepherd Neame Master Brew on handpump; darts, dominoes and cribbage. The sheltered garden has old-fashioned seats with fruit trees, climbing roses and clematis, and a pool by a young weeping willow – all very pretty, and quiet but for birdsong. *(Recommended by Heather Sharland, Mrs Jane Reid, Tim Halstead, Margaret Drazin, M Reese, G L Tong)*

Free house *Licensee Mrs Evelyn Moir* *Real ale* *Meals and snacks* *Restaurant tel Ticehurst (0580) 200586* *Well behaved children in eating area* *Occasional live music Open 10.30–3, 6–11 (11–11 Sat and bank hols); considering longer afternoon opening in summer*

WEST ASHLING SU8107 Map 2

Richmond Arms ✪

Mill Lane; from B2146 in village follow Hambrook signpost

In just seven years, the enthusiastic licensees of this simple, out-of-the-way and very friendly village pub will have served over four hundred different real ales from their fourteen handpumps. Besides the three quickly changing guest beers, they keep a fairly permanent range of Adnams Broadside, Boddingtons Bitter, Harveys XX, King & Barnes Festive and Sussex Bitter and Theakstons Old Peculier on handpump. They also have Wilkin's Farmhouse cider tapped from the cask, Newquay Steam stout, most bottle-conditioned English beers, and one of the best ranges of good foreign bottled beers in the South, including all five Trappist beers, raspberry, wild cherry beers and brown ale from Belgium, and some of the rarer German ales. The real food fits in well: besides sandwiches (from £1.50, croque-monsieur £2.25), ploughman's (from £1.85), and steak sandwich (£3.25), there are filled baked potatoes (from £1.95), home-made chilli con carne, curry, lasagne or cottage pie (£2.50), vegetarian dishes such as quiches and lasagne (£2.95), with winter specials such as beef in beer or steak and kidney pie; summer salads and local seafood (in season). There are long wall benches, library chairs and black tables around the central servery, a fire in winter and numbered decoy ducks hanging on the wall; bar billiards, shove-ha'penny, dominoes, cribbage, and trivia and fruit machines. The old skittle alley has been renovated and doubles as a functions and family-room; if booked, food can be served. There's a pergola, and some picnic-table sets by the car park. (*Recommended by Nigel Paine, David and Sarah Gilmore, Ian Phillips, Richard Houghton, Mrs R Sims, HEG, F N Clay, R Hutchings*)

Free house   Licensees Roger and Julie Jackson   Real ale   Meals and snacks (lunchtime, not Sun)   Children in skittle alley/functions room   Folk music Thurs, pianist Sun Oct–Easter Open 10.30–2.30 (3 Sat), 5.30–11 all year

WEST FIRLE   TQ4607 Map 3
Ram

Signposted off A27 Lewes–Polegate

Though they've not been here long, the Leisters have given this three-hundred-year-old village inn a marvellous feel, combining a really welcoming atmosphere with the lively warmth of a pub that has preserved very vigorous local connections. The brightly lit main bar has a few oak chairs and three or four sturdy tables spaced well apart, and the lounge bar is similar, though with more chairs and is more comfortable. Good value bar food includes home-made soup, a notable ploughman's with cheese and home-pickled onions or sweet pickle (Cheddar 90p, Brie, sausage or pâté £1), and home-made spinach pie or broccoli and cheese flan (£2); breakfasts are huge. Well kept Charringtons IPA and Youngs Special on handpump; darts, shove-ha'penny, dominoes, cribbage and toad-in-the-hole. There are seats in the large walled garden behind. Nearby Firle Place is worth visiting for its collections and furnishings. The pub is just below a particularly fine stretch of the South Downs and close to Glyndebourne. (*Recommended by Jenny and Brian Seller, H and P B, Patrick Young, Kenneth Finch*)

Free house   Licensees Mr and Mrs C Leister   Real ale   Lunchtime meals and snacks Traditional folk music every second Mon   Open 11–3, 6.30–11 all year   Three good value bedrooms tel Glynde (079 159) 222; £11/£22

WEST HOATHLY   TQ3632 Map 3
Cat   [illustrated on page 644]

Village signposted between A22 and B2028 S of East Grinstead

You can sit among roses on the small sun-trap terrace outside this old smugglers' pub and look across to the church nestling among its big yew trees (if you walk through the churchyard to the far side there's an even better view). The pub is near the start of *Good Walks Guide* Walk 64. Inside, the open-plan, partly panelled bar has a friendly, old-fashioned atmosphere and comfortable, traditional furnishings; note the interesting ancient carving around the massive central chimney. Good bar food includes a delicious ploughman's as well as some very tasty Italian dishes. Well kept Harveys BB, XX Mild and Old ale (sold as Beards here) and King & Barnes on handpump. (*Recommended by James Cane, M C Howells, Jenny Cantle, B V Harmes, S A Loveat*)

Beards (who no longer brew)   Real ale   Meals (not Sun) and snacks (not Sun evening) Children in dining-room and entrance lobby only   Open 11–2.30, 6–10.30

WINCHELSEA   TQ9017 Map 3
New Inn ⊗ 🏠

Just off A259

Though it rambles through three quite spacious rooms (one's no-smoking), the pleasantly old-fashioned lounge bar does fill up on weekend lunchtimes, as word about the good value food's got around. It includes soup (£1.25), sandwiches (not

Sunday lunchtimes or Bank Holidays), garlic mushrooms (£1.95), ploughman's (£1.95, not Friday or Saturday evening), a vegetarian dish (£3.50), curry (£3.95), gammon and mushroom or steak and kidney pie (£4.25), locally caught fish such as a whole plaice (£4.95), pork kebabs (£5.50) and steaks (from eight-ounce sirloin £6.95), with children's dishes (95p, not after 7.30) and Sunday lunches. There are wall banquettes, settles, sturdy wooden tables, good log fires, masses of hop-bines hanging from the beams, with walls painted a deep terracotta, and decorations including old farm tools, china, pewter and copper on Delft shelves, old local photographs and so forth, with a pleasant buzz of conversation and efficient waitress service. Well kept Courage Best and Directors on handpump, decent wines by the glass. The wholly separate public bar has darts, well lit pool, cribbage, fruit machine, and there may be unobtrusive piped music. There are picnic-table sets and swings in a neat and good-sized orchard garden, and some of the pretty bedrooms look out on a charming medieval scene, with a lime tree and swathes of bluebells around the church opposite. *(Recommended by Heather Sharland, Mrs D Lambourne, Aubrey Saunders, E G Parish, Theo and Jean Rowland-Entwistle, Cdr G R Roantree)*

Courage   Licensee Richard Joyce   Real ale   Meals and snacks   Children allowed away from bar   Open 11–2.30, 6–11 all year   Bedrooms tel Rye (0797) 226252; £15/£25

WINEHAM   TQ2320 Map 3
Royal Oak
Village signposted from A272 and B2116

Above the serving-counter in this handsome black and white timbered pub, the very low beams are decorated with ancient corkscrews, horseshoes, racing plates, tools and a coach horn, and the furniture throughout is fittingly simple and old-fashioned. The enormous inglenook fireplace carries the smoke stains of centuries, and the brick floor in front of it is well worn. Well kept Whitbread Pompey Royal is tapped from casks in a still-room on the way back through to the small snug; darts, shove-ha'penny, dominoes, cribbage; toasted sandwiches (75p). There are rustic wooden tables on the grass by a well in front, and on a clear day you can just see Chanctonbury Ring from the window in the gents, far beyond the nearby meadows and oak trees. *(Recommended by IAA; more reports please)*

Whitbreads   Real ale   Snacks (not Sat evening or Sun)   Open 10.30–2.30, 6–10.30; closed 25 Dec and evening 26 Dec

---

Lucky Dip

Besides the fully inspected pubs, you might like to try these Lucky Dips recommended to us and described by readers. If you do, please send us reports. We'd also like your guidance on an experiment we've tried – splitting the entries into East Sussex and West Sussex. If you find this either more or less help than in the other chapters that combine more than one county – where we've listed the pubs in alphabetical order but named the counties – please let us know.

EAST SUSSEX

☆Alfriston [TQ5103], *Deans Place*: Comfortable hotel with armchairs in roomy bar, good bar food such as steak and kidney pie or cold roast meats with help-yourself salads, surprisingly reasonable prices, lots of room in beautiful garden with croquet lawn; children welcome; changed hands late 1987 with talk of a leisure complex, but during 1988 at least

continuing very much as before *(D L Johnson, Heather Sharland)*
Alfriston [High St], *George*: One of England's oldest inns, first licensed 1397; well decorated long heavily beamed bar, pleasant staff, good bar snacks, ambitious dining-room menu; very well kept; bedrooms well regarded *(Heather Sharland)*
Arlington [TQ5407], *Yew Tree*: Neatly kept and comfortably modernised village pub

with big garden, local atmosphere, usual range of bar food from sandwiches and filled baked potatoes through steak and kidney pie to steak; Courage Directors and Harveys on handpump *(BB)*

☆ Barcombe [TQ4114], *Anchor*: Charming gardens and boating on very peaceful river outside remote inn with small bar (sandwiches) and restaurant; comfortable bedrooms *(D Pearman, LYM)*

Battle [High St; TQ7416], *George*: Old pub in attractive High Street, well kept Harveys Bitter and good bar food with cold table in restaurant; comfortable bedrooms *(John Townsend)*; [Mount St] *Olde Kings Head*: Fine town-centre pub with good value bar snacks – especially the French bread rolls – and Courage Best and Directors on handpump *(Peter Corris)*

Beckley [TQ8523], *Rose & Crown*: Old coaching-inn; pub has been on site since Edward III's day; plenty of character, friendly welcome from licensees, good food and service, piped music *(Theodore and Jean Rowland-Entwistle)*

☆ Berwick [by stn; TQ5105], *Berwick*: Excellent children's playground behind well run family pub with attractive Perspex-roofed garden bar, good choice of food and real ales *(Comus Elliott, Tom Evans, LYM)*

☆ Berwick [Milton Street, which is signposted off A27 ¼ mile E of Alfriston roundabout; TQ5304], *Sussex Ox*: Marvellous play area and big lawn outside country pub just below downs; can get very busy (though nice winter atmosphere – simple country furniture, brick floor, wood-burning stove); good home cooking, family-room *(R and S Bentley, LYM)*

Bexhill [Egerton Park Rd; TQ7407], *Traffers*: Good food (upstairs restaurant has been extended by new owners), real ales including Harveys, King & Barnes Festive and Tetleys, very friendly barmaids *(Nigel Paine)*

Blackham [TQ4838], *Sussex Oak*: Unspoilt traditional atmosphere in spite of flock wallpaper; no tables in main bar *(MM, KJM)*

☆ Bodiam [TQ7825], *Curlew*: Refurbished 1987 by very friendly and efficient licensee, well kept Adnams and King & Barnes, sensibly priced wines; popular food including outstanding home-made pies *(Richard Davis, John Townsend, John Knighton)*

☆ Bodle Street Green [off A271 at Windmill Hill; has been shut Mon Oct–Easter, opens 7pm; TQ6514], *White Horse*: Wide choice of excellent food (usually have to book now) shows considerable flair at times, well kept Harveys and King & Barnes ales, very friendly welcome in clean pub with pleasant atmosphere and quick service *(John Townsend, J H Bell)*

☆ Brighton [Castle Sq; TQ3105], *Royal Pavilion*: Efficient service from central food counter – good choice, good value; well laid out series of rooms attractively done up for old-fashioned look, including intimate candlelit winebar area (good big glasses), lots of panelling, successful pastiche full of character; choice of real ales *(Mr and Mrs J H Adam, D L Johnson, LYM)*

Brighton [The Lanes], *Bath Arms*: Pretty, heavy stone exterior in delightful Lanes area; basic décor in single bar with rugged wooden furniture, fireplace, mirror and bookshelves; friendly bar staff, variety of customers including some characters; Watneys-related real ales and own-brewed Bathwater with malty taste *(Peter Griffiths)*; [Kings Rd Arches; on beach below prom, between the piers] *Belvedere*: Lively and youthful real-ale pub squashed into long arch below the road, right on the beach; with its similar next-door sister-pub the Fortune of War (which is lined with marine planking and may be a bit quieter) it has a good two-drinks-for-the-price-of-one happy hour, 7–8pm; live music *(BB)*; [8 Sydney St] *Green Dragon*: In the North Lanes area with a young and lively local clientele, well kept Courage beers and a good range of bottled lagers, good value sandwiches and rolls, and lots of chamberpots hanging from the ceiling *(Dave Butler, Les Storey)*; [St James St, Kemp Town] *Hand in Hand*: Small lively pub with good range of well kept beers such as Adnams, Badger Best and Tanglefoot, Gales HSB, Harveys and King & Barnes Festive, walls covered with newspapers and old Brighton photographs *(Mark Walpole)*; [13 Marlborough Pl] *King & Queen*: Medieval-style main hall, straightforward food, good jazz most evenings, aviary in flagstoned courtyard *(LYM)*; [Trafalgar St] *Lord Nelson*: Early Victorian town-centre pub with tasty good value unpretentious home cooking, well kept Harveys, farm cider; good mix of customers, with far fewer poseurs than at other similar pubs here; Sun quiz evenings; handy for stn *(Brian and Pam Cowling)*; [Old North Rd] *Princess Victoria*: Busy, friendly pub with extensive choice of reasonably priced food including daily specials; good range of beers *(JH)*; [Queens Rd (nr stn)] *Queens Head*: Friendly staff, unobtrusive music, good value and imaginative bar food, handy for stn *(Mrs Margaret Dyke)*; [Southover St] *Sir Charles Napier*: Small, friendly town local with excellent beer, good pub food, no-smoking room; lively in evenings; children welcome *(A Hunt)*; [Manchester St] *Star*: Immaculately kept pub with lounge bar filled with clown collection, real ales, very clean cellar bar serving good food, smashing atmosphere, pianist twice a week *(Mrs M Openshaw)*

☆ Burwash [TQ6724], *Bell*: Delightful bar, wonderful hot mulled wine, well prepared and presented bar food, well kept Fremlins, Harveys and King & Barnes, comfortable dark green plush furnishings, newspapers on sticks, traditional games; opposite church in prettily conserved village; nr start GWG67; children in dining-room; nearby parking can

be difficult; bedrooms quiet, clean and pleasant *(H B Smith, Peter Corris, Mr and Mrs A F Walker, G and M Brooke-Williams, LYM)*
Burwash, *Rose & Crown*: Tucked away down side street in quaintly restored village, all timbers and beams, with wide choice of real ale such as Bass, Charrington IPA and Shepherd Neame, decent wines, helpful cheerful licensee, quite enterprising bar food, restaurant; tables on quiet lawn; nr start GWG67 *(Tim Halstead, BB)*
Burwash Common [Stonegate Rd; TQ6322], *Kicking Donkey*: Rustic old pub getting plenty of attention from current licensees, good cheap bar food, play area; alone down a country lane, by a cricket field *(Brian Smith)*
Burwash Weald [A265 two miles W of Burwash; TQ6624], *Wheel*: Friendly and well kept open-plan local with big log fire, well kept real ales and generous helpings of good value straightforward food; some seats on small front terrace *(David and Marguerite Warner, John Chapman, BB)*
Buxted [High St; TQ4923], *Buxted*: Excellent food, wonderful main course and vegetables *(Mrs V A Bingham)*
Catsfield [The Green; TQ7213], *White Hart*: Excellent cheap ploughman's in family-run pub popular with locals and visitors, log fire one end of bar, other end opens into hall used for children as well as for functions *(Nigel Paine)*
Colemans Hatch [signposted off B2026; or off B2110 opp church; TQ4533], *Hatch*: Simple and delightfully traditional Ashdown Forest pub with lunchtime snacks, pub games including elderly one-arm bandit, well kept Adnams and Harveys BB on handpump, tables on bluff of grass by quiet lane *(Phil and Sally Gorton, Chris Fluck, Roger and Kathy, Ian Howard, LYM)*
Cousleywood [TQ6533], *Old Vine*: Busy little pub with a bistro-type atmosphere in attractive lounge bar, wide choice of good food, pleasant and efficient service, live entertainment; can get very busy lunchtime *(Wayne Brindle, G L Tong, Kit Read)*
Cripps Corner [TQ7721], *White Hart*: Good reliable pub, reasonably priced food, well kept Courage Best; somewhat dimly lit *(John Townsend)*
Dale Hill [by Dale Hill golf club; junction A268 and B2099; TQ6930], *Cherry Tree*: Nice building with good friendly atmosphere, excellent Youngs real ales, wide choice of tasty well cooked food served in generous helpings, pleasant service *(Kit Read, Richard Trigwell, D A Benson)*
Danehill [School Lane, off A275 opp The Crocodile; TQ4027], *Coach & Horses*: Run by young couple who have brought it up to date rather than modernising it, and have converted the small stableblock into a space for eaters (not a restaurant which they don't want at any cost) with simple, really good value home-cooked food; well kept Harveys,

with a guest beer each week and excellent house wine *(E Boisseau, B V Harmes)*
☆ **Ditchling** [2 High St (B2112); TQ3215], *Bull*: Warm welcome in spacious and beautifully kept pub with interesting old furniture in its two comfortable bars, well kept Whitbreads Flowers and Pompey Royal, straightforward bar food, friendly attentive service, terrace and garden; bedrooms *(Jenny Cantle, AE, Mr and Mrs G Holliday, Charles and Mary Winpenny)*
East Hoathly [TQ5216], *Kings Head*: Welcoming staff in comfortable pub in pretty countryside; period atmosphere, horse-brasses, plush-upholstered settles, real ales, good value straightforward food; fairy-lights around bar *(E G Parish, Nick Dowson)*
Eastbourne [Beachy Head; TV6199], *Beachy Head*: Excellent position, nice bars, good beer and bar food, very friendly atmosphere, very good restaurant which has restarted its outstanding lunchtime carvery *(J H Bell)*; *Terminus*: Very busy town-centre pub with popular lunchtime food and well kept Harveys; tables and chairs outside in the precinct *(Peter Corris)*
Ewhurst Green [TQ7925], *White Dog*: Reopened 1987 after extended closure; fine position above Bodiam Castle, imaginative food, friendly and enthusiastic service; bedrooms comfortable and well equipped *(Catherine Budgett-Meakin, LYM)*
Fletching [signposted off A272 W of Uckfield; TQ4223], *Griffin*: Delightfully peaceful village; very good bar food that includes excellent seafood pancakes (salmon, cod, prawns) and strawberries; Thursday is 'fish' evening; friendly service; restaurant *(Derek and Maggie Washington)*
Hartfield [Gallipot St; TQ4735], *Gallipot*: Welcoming and well cared-for old inn, well kept Charrington and Flowers real ales, wide range of bar snacks, good log fire, no music or machines; handy for Ashdown Forest walks, and on GWG62 *(John Kimber)*
Hartfield [A264; TQ4735], *Haywaggon*: Good food in bar and restaurant, very clean; nr start GWG62 *(Roy and Shirley Bentley)*
Hastings [TQ8109], *Old Pump House*: Friendly wood-floored pub with beams, lots of character and well kept ales; well laid out; nr start GWG63 *(Gary Wilkes)*; [The Ridge] *Robert de Mortain*: Welcoming bar carefully restored after chimney crashing through in October 1987 storms, handsome wallpaper, comfortable carpet and furnishings; well presented varying bar food, basement restaurant doing well under new owners *(Theo and Jean Rowland-Entwistle)*
Hollingbury [Carden Ave; TQ3108], *Long Man of Wilmington*: Beautifully furnished spotless pub, well kept real ales and good food; collection of lions; pool and darts *(Mrs M Openshaw)*
Horsted Keynes [TQ3828], *Green Man*:

Good pub atmosphere and well kept beer (*M C Howells*)

☆ **Icklesham** [TQ8816], *Queens Head*: Interesting old pub with splendid view over Brede to Rye, friendly, bustling and comfortable, with good choice of well presented home-cooked food, children welcome with special menu, good choice of beers, collection of old farm tools, cosy in winter; on the edge of fields, with footpath running down the Brede Valley (*C H Fewster, Theo and Jean Rowland-Entwistle, Dr Paul Kitchener*)

Isfield [TQ4417], *Laughing Fish*: Well kept Beards ales and lively local atmosphere in simple modernised pub; robust food (*BB*)

☆ **Kingston Near Lewes** [TQ3908], *Juggs*: Good atmosphere in pretty fifteenth-century free house with beams, big log fire with copper hood, prints of local scenes, wooden settles and furniture, lath-and-plaster bar with rows of gleaming glass tankards above it, horse tackle on walls; Harveys BB and King & Barns on handpump, soft-drinks counter, no music, interesting bare garden/family-room; good hot and cold bar food with children's helpings; seating outside with neat, newly planted flower beds, wooden climbing-frame and play area (*Heather Sharland, David Crafts, Theo and Jean Rowland-Entwistle, M Rising, Keith Walton*)

☆ **Lewes** [Castle Ditch Lane, Mount P1; TQ4110], *Lewes Arms*: Friendly local with satisfactory food at lunchtime, wider choice at weekends, well kept Harveys ales (*G N G Tingey, R F Neil, Neil Barker*); [High St, St Anne's] *Pelham Arms*: Well kept town pub, locally popular for good value food, with friendly service; nr GWG61 (*Dr M D Wood, BB*)

Maresfield [TQ4624], *Chequers*: Good range of well prepared bar food from very good value ploughman's or home-made soup to hot dishes and daily specials – nothing prepacked in sight; real ales such as Badger Best, Fullers ESB, Harveys and Tanglefoot on handpump (*Robert Gomme*)

Netherfield [Netherfield Hill; TQ7118], *Netherfield Arms*: Attentive, friendly licensees, quiet piped music; reasonably priced bar food including good choice of vegetarian dishes (*Theo and Jean Rowland-Entwistle*)

☆ **Newhaven** [West Quay – OS Sheet 198 reference 450002; TQ4502], *Hope*: Nautical theme in eighteenth-century inn facing harbour entrance – downstairs has polished planks, seafaring bric-à-brac and pictures, upstairs is the 'bridge' with good view of Newhaven harbour and Seaford Bay; good food, especially locally caught fish, well kept Whitbreads Pompey Royal on handpump; children in conservatory area (*Chris Fluck, Mr and Mrs N E Friend*)

Northiam [The Green; TQ8224], *Hayes Arms*: Very peaceful old bar part at back of hotel which stands back from village green; bedrooms (*Heather Sharland*); *Six Bells*: Has

been good atmosphere in very friendly old-fashioned local with three rooms radiating from central servery; solid old furniture, good log fire, lots of beams; has been popular for good food, but no news since new owners took over 1988; bedrooms (*Heather Sharland, H Fewster*)

Nutley (A22; TQ4427], *William IV*: Friendly staff and locals, quickly served bar meals and good sandwiches, well kept King & Barnes and Ushers, garden (*Alan Bickley, Joan Olivier*)

☆ **Oxleys Green** (just outside Brightling; TQ6921], *Fullers Arms*: Friendly stone-built and beamed pub with log fires, good reasonably priced no-nonsense food including unusual dishes, well kept Harveys real ales with wines including English ones; nice position, convenient for Bateman's; on GWG67 (*Paul and Margaret Baker, Bruce Wass, V F Ammoun*)

Peasmarsh [TQ8822], *Horse & Cart*: Free house with very well kept Adnams, Websters Yorkshire, extensive but simple choice of very good food – almost all home made, ample helpings, sensible prices (*E J Cutting*)

Pett [TQ8714], *Two Sawyers*: Very friendly village pub with charming waitresses, great dane, well kept beer and variety of reasonably priced food (*Mr and Mrs E Hardwick, Byrne Sherwood*)

Pevensey [High St; TQ6304], *Priory Court*: Hotel in shadow of Pevensey Castle with newly refurbished bar, welcoming log fire, Harvey and Flowers beer on handpump, various bar food, extensive garden with pond; bedrooms (*David Crafts*)

Playden [TQ9121], *Peace & Plenty*: Good atmosphere, very wide choice of slightly unusual dishes in generous helpings – good value (*Karen Gardner*)

Ringles Cross [A22; TQ4721], *Ringles Cross*: Useful well kept roadside pub with reliable food including good steaks, well kept real ale (*BB*)

Ringmer [B2192; TQ4412], *Anchor*: Comfortable banquettes in bays of main bar, more tables in adjoining room; good choice of bar food, Watneys-related real ales with a guest such as King & Barnes; spacious pretty garden, children's play area (*TOH*)

Rotherfield [TQ5529], *Kings Arms*: Present owner has considerably improved this very old attractive pub which was once owned by Maurice Tate the former cricketer (*P H Fearnley*)

☆ **Rushlake Green** [signposted off B2096; TQ6218], *Horse & Groom*: Old country pub overlooking quiet village green, rustic bar with big log fire on the right, cosier carpeted rooms on the left, traditional games, bar food, restaurant, garden with weekend barbecues, well kept Sussex ales; children in eating area (*Chris Fluck, LYM*)

Rye [High St; TQ9220], *George*: On Sat night bar lively with locals, lounge more sedate with sofas and log fire; Fremlins Bitter on handpump, good staff; THF hotel, comfortable bedrooms *(Alison Hayward, Nick Dowson, Pamela and Merlyn Horswell)*; [The Mint] *Standard*: Busy, lively pub, juke box, King & Barnes Festive on handpump, reasonably priced bar food; popular with young people *(Alison Hayward, Nick Dowson)*; [East St] *Union*: Clean and tidy split-level town pub with warm atmosphere, piped music, well kept real ales such as Flowers Original, Fremlins, King & Barnes Festive and Ruddles Best, bar food good but rather pricey *(Alison Hayward, Nick Dowson, Mr and Mrs G D Amos)*; [Gun Gdn, off A259] *Ypres Castle*: Unrefined cosy local with Whitbreads real ales including Flowers Original, Fremlims and Pompey Royal; fresh French bread and good Stilton, approach by steep flight of stone steps *(WHBM, Alison Hayward, Nick Dowson)*

Rye Harbour [TQ9220], *William the Conqueror*: Functional pub with cheap food, well sited on undeveloped harbour edge *(Dr Paul Kitchener, BB)*

Scaynes Hill [Freshfield Lock; off A272, via Church Lane signposted; TQ3623], *Sloop*: Birdsong in neat garden by derelict Ouse Canel, comfortable sofas and armchairs in long saloon, traditional games-room off public bar, bar food including popular baked potatoes, well kept Harveys and King & Barnes; handy for Bluebell steam railway, not far from Sheffield Park; children in eating area and small games-room *(M J Masters, T Nott, LYM)*

Scaynes Hill, *Farmers*: Superb situation by lake, several delightful bars including a conservatory with masses of fuchsias and geraniums, friendly service, handy for Sheffield Park and the Bluebell Line *(W J Wonham)*

Seaford [near Cuckmere Valley; A259; TV4899], *Golden Galleon*: Very good food including remarkable fish and chips, quick service, wide choice of beers and decent wine, reasonable prices, friendly and wonderfully relaxed atmosphere; a treasure in summer, with lots of tables outside, on a gentle slope with lovely views of the river and sea cliffs, ten minutes' easy walk to unspoilt uncrowded beach *(Sqn Ldr Tony Clarke, Debby Jellett, Jenny and Brian Seller, Rosemary Dudley Lynch, Tom Evans)*

Sedlescombe [TQ7718], *Queens Head*: Beautifully kept pub on village green with well maintained old farm machines in front, seats, trees and forge behind; toby jugs on beams of main panelled and carpeted bar with plenty of good tables and chairs and good settles – copper, brass and horse yoke show links with working forge; also pewter, glass mugs, some good hunting prints, framed collection of bottled beer labels, big inglenook log fire; Flowers real ale, bar food, restaurant; space games in separate bar *(Heather Sharland)*

Sharpthorne [Station Rd; TQ3732], *Bluebell*: Friendly landlord, cheap food in unpretentious pub on edge of village, close to Sussex Border Path *(TAB)*

☆ **Shortbridge** [Piltdown – OS Sheet 198 reference 450215; TQ4521], *Peacock*: Attractive fourteenth-century country pub which has had good range of real ales including Harveys, King & Barnes and Youngs, lovely inglenook fire in old-world bar with rustic furniture, good food in bar and restaurant; beautiful gardens front and back with barbecue and children's area – very popular in summer *(S F James, P Ashley, C Pollard, TOH; more reports please)*

Uckfield [Eastbourne Rd (A22); 2 miles S, nr Framfield, on left going S; TQ4721], *Barley Mow*: Good food, fast friendly service; run by son of former owner of the Star at Old Heathfield (see Heathfield main entry) *(Brian Smith)*; [in town] *Brickmakers Arms*: Tiny bar in small old pub with unusual beers and wide choice of good cheap bar food *(Brian Smith)*; [Eastbourne Rd (A22)] *Highlands*: Food very promising under new landlord *(Brian Smith)*

Udimore [TQ8619], *Kings Head*: Small village pub with much character, open fire in winter and low ceilings, attentive landlord, well kept Fremlins, bar food *(Michele and Andrew Wells)*

Upper Dicker [TQ5510], *Plough*: Fine country pub with three separate rooms, restaurant; a Watneys pub but has King & Barnes on handpump; good atmosphere, busy in the evening *(Peter Corris)*

Waldron [Blackboys–Horam side road; TQ5419], *Star*: Wide choice of good plentiful food, from sandwiches upwards; Charrington IPA and maybe M&B Mild, very friendly atmosphere, popular with locals and regular visitors; large garden, children's playground *(G and J U Jones)*

☆ **Warbleton** [TQ6018], *Warbil in Tun*: Isolated, in a lovely setting; kind and friendly licensees – he's a master butcher, so good meats are a speciality; brasses and cuirass in spacious beamed L-shaped bar with plum-coloured chairs, stools and carpet, big log fireplace; Flowers IPA and Harveys on handpump *(Gwen and Peter Andrews, Tony Reid)*

Westfield [TQ8115], *Plough*: Popular, well run with good atmosphere, friendly landlord; community spirit with pub supporting darts and football teams and local charities; bar food and separate restaurant; small garden with bench tables *(Theodore and Jean Rowland-Entwistle)*

Wilmington [TQ5404], *Wilmington Arms*: Conversion of private house and a comfortable, civilised place for eating but little pub atmosphere *(WHBM)*

☆ **Withyham** [TQ4935], *Dorset Arms*: Unspoilt feel in unusual raised bar with massive Tudor fireplace, beams and oak floorboards, well kept Harveys real ales, good home-made bar food – chosen in 1987 as one of *Newsweek*'s World's Best Bars; nr GWG62 *(Richard Gibbs, Leo and Pam Cohen, LYM)*

WEST SUSSEX

Adversane [TQ0723], *Blacksmiths Arms*: Historic old pub, spacious and roomy yet cosy with pleasant atmosphere, good value and varied if not cheap menu, friendly service *(Anon)*

Albourne [London Rd (A23); TQ2616], *Kings Head*: Unusual pub, interesting décor in Munster bar, 1940s-style juke box, Watneys-related real ales with a guest such as King & Barnes Festive, good choice of bar food *(John Hayward)*

☆ **Amberley** [off B2139; TQ0212], *Black Horse*: Unspoilt, attractive village pub, up a flight of steps, its beams festooned with sheep and cow bells and other downland farm equipment; flagstones, well kept Friary Meux and Ind Coope Burton, good bar food including local shellfish, garden; children in eating area and restaurant; occasional folk music *(David Shillitoe, LYM)*

Amberley [Houghton Bridge], *Bridge*: Free house close to Chalk Pit Museum, open-plan lounge neatly decorated with local prints, well kept Harveys and Flowers real ales, daily specials such as fresh dressed crab as well as usual pub food; children in lounge; bedrooms *(Michael Bechley)*

Angmering [The Square; TQ0704], *Lamb*: Good choice of beers, good value food very popular at lunchtime, well placed in quiet Sussex village *(J Russell)*; *Spotted Cow*: Good snacks even on Sun – when there are free cheese cubes and biscuits; ample staff, jovial landlord, nice welcome; plenty of room outside with good children's play area separate from main garden; dogs welcome; at start of lovely walk to Highdown hill fort *(Ian Phillips)*

Ansty [2 miles from Ansty on A272 at junction with B2036; TQ2923], *Ansty Cross*: Popular local, modern bar, log fire, horse-brasses, darts and fruit machine, good straightforward hot dishes and more original salads, large garden *(C R and M A Starling)*

Apuldram [Birdham Rd; SU8403], *Black Horse*: Comfortable, well run pub, well kept Friary Meux and Ind Coope Burton, good food at reasonable prices *(Peter Ames)*

☆ **Ardingly** [Street Lane; TQ3429], *Oak*: Wide choice of good bar food, Watneys-related and Gales real ales on handpump in fourteenth-century building with beams, antique furnishings and lovely log fire in magnificent old fireplace; new licensee *(Gwen and Peter Andrews, Jenny and Brian Seller, Norman Foot)*

☆ **Arundel** [Mill Rd – keep on and don't give up!; TQ0107], *Black Rabbit*: Lovely peaceful spot, with riverside tables looking across to bird-reserve watermeadows and castle; long

bar with big windows and log fires, lots of spirits as well as well kept Youngers Scotch and IPA, pub games, good choice of bar food (not Sun evening), airy side restaurant; children in eating and family areas; bedrooms comfortable for the relatively low price, with good breakfast *(Capt Tony Bland, Cyril Higgs, Mrs Val Rixon, Roger Taylor, WFL, LYM)*

Arundel [Chichester Rd (A27)], *White Swan*: Pub with motel outside the town – very attractive, spacious and well kept; good choice of food, friendly efficient service; bedrooms *(JH)*

Balls Cross [signposted off A283 N of Petworth; SU9826], *Stag*: Unspoilt pub with two rooms, one with flagstones and an inglenook fireplace, the other with a carpet; well kept King & Barnes real ales *(Phil Gorton)*

☆ **Billingshurst** [High St (A29); TQ0925], *Olde Six Bells*: Partly fourteenth-century flag-stoned and timbered pub with well kept King & Barnes real ales, food, inglenook fireplace, pretty roadside garden *(LYM)*

Binstead [Binstead Lane; about 2 miles W of Arundel, turn S off A27 towards Binstead – OS Sheet 197 reference 980064; SU9806], *Black Horse*: Unusual menu including first-class omelettes such as kidney and bacon cooked in Gales HSB, in very friendly, clean and well polished little village local on quiet country lane, secluded back garden with good view over meadows towards coast; Gales HSB, BBB and XXXL, good draught cider, sensibly placed darts; no food Sun evening; bedrooms *(S A Lovett, Keith Houlgate)*

Birdham [B2179 1 mile S of village; SU8200], *Lamb*: Attractive and comfortable pub, well kept Ballards, good bar food at reasonable prices, pleasant garden ideal for children *(S Breame)*

Bosham [High St; SU8003], *Anchor Bleu*: Lovely sea views and waterside position are what recommend this pub with low ceilings and open fires, Watneys-related real ales, and straightforward food; readers report most enthusiastically out of season *(HS, Charles Turner, LYM)*

Bucks Green [TQ0732], *Queens Head*: Personal attention from friendly owners, good food, wide choice of beers, very pleasing décor and atmosphere *(Anthony Barreau)*

Burgess Hill [TQ3118], *Top House*: Consistently good and reasonably priced food *(Clifford Sharp)*

Burpham [take Warningcamp turn off A27 outside Arundel: follow road up and up; TQ0308], *George & Dragon*: Food now the centre of interest at this much renovated pub, also well kept Harveys and King & Barnes, airy uncluttered feel inside, pleasant tables and masses of windows boxes; close to Norman church in quiet village with good walks and fine views over Arundel Castle *(Ian Phillips, BB)*

Bury [A29 Pulborough–Arundel; TQ0113], *Black Dog & Duck*: Good bar food such as potato and leek soup and game pie, welcoming, courteous and efficient landlord, Gales ales on handpump *(R A Anderson)*

Chichester [St Martins St; SU8605], *Hole in the Wall*: Large and popular (the Rotary meet here), with old beams, good open fire, reddish upholstery; food in one bar, and grills and so forth in restaurant *(Heather Sharland)*; [St Pauls St] *Rainbow*: Friendly, welcoming bar staff, good food and plenty of tit-bits at bar; small garden with aviary *(Mrs F Abbot)*

☆ **Chidham** [Cot Lane; off A27 at Barleycorn pub; SU7903], *Old House At Home*: Pretty old pub in remote, unspoilt farm-hamlet location, notable for enterprising range of real ales usually including Badger and Ringwood (they no longer brew their own); welcoming atmosphere, open fire in winter, seats outside in summer; bar food including vegetarian dishes *(RJF, HEG, J Williams, Ian Phillips, LYM)*

☆ **Chilgrove** [actually at Hooksway, which is signposted off B2141, down steep hill – OS Sheet 197 reference 814163; SU8214], *Royal Oak*: Unspoilt pub in remote country setting with low ceilings, open fires in winter, piped classical music; well kept real ales such as Gales HSB, Gibbs Mew Bishops Tipple, Ringwood Old Thumper and Ruddles Best and County, country wines, good and reasonably priced bar food, separate restaurant *(Neil Lusby, Prof A N Black, LYM)*

Chilgrove, *White Horse*: Lovely long low white building, very well maintained – it's the good, expensive restaurant (closed Sun and Mon) which people talk of most, and though the ochre-walled beamed bar divided by timbers, with pictures on the walls, is not too tarted up it's not exactly pubby; there is bar food, good but not cheap *(HS)*

Coldwaltham [pub signposted down lane about 2 miles S of Pulborough – OS Sheet 197 reference 027167; TQ0216], *Labouring Man*: Clean and comfortable pub with friendly atmosphere, cheerful new licensees (who are also tenants of the White Hart at Stopham), well kept real ales such as Batemans XXXB, Courage Directors, Flowers, King & Barnes Festive and Whitbreads Castle Eden, home-made food *(S A Lovett)*

Compton [SU7714], *Coach & Horses*: Simply decorated pub in small Sussex village, with remarkably good food in attached restaurant *(Rod Stoneman)*

☆ **Cooksbridge** [junction A275 with Cooksbridge and Newick rd; TQ3913], *Rainbow*: Absolutely massive menu, particularly good food, attractive building, reasonable prices, very pleasant staff *(G B Pugh, B V Harmes, Philip Haggar)*

☆ **Coolham** [Dragons Green; TQ1423], *George & Dragon*: Lovely old pub in huge garden;

big inglenook, unusually low beams, well kept King & Barnes ales, pub games; previously popular for home-made food, and first indications are that the friendly new licensees are keeping up the reputation for good value, with big helpings, though perhaps the choice is not yet what it was, and at least in their first few months the licensees had not yet curbed the regulars' enthusiasm for piped music – definitely one to watch *(W H B M, Heather Sharland, T Nott, S J A Velate, Dr and Mrs J Levi, N D Foot, Theo and Jean Rowland-Entwistle, LYM)*

Copthorne [A264 just E of village; TQ3139], *Abergavenney Arms*: Modernised, but with conservative furnishings, relaxed atmosphere, well kept real ale, popular lunchtime food; paddock behind garden *(BB)*

☆ **Cuckfield** [South St; TQ3025], *Kings Head*: Robustly subtle modern cooking with an almost French concern for fresh ingredients in the two restaurant areas of this otherwise straightforward pub; the food side has been separately franchised to an inventive chef; bedrooms *(P S Simpson and others)*

Cuckfield [A272], *White Harte*: Popular medieval pub close to church, comfortably modernised, keen darts teams, well kept Watneys real ales *(LYM)*

☆ **Dell Quay** [SU8302], *Crown & Anchor*: Modernised fifteenth-century pub on site of Roman quay, yacht-harbour views from bow window and garden, good generous food with local fish dishes, evening restaurant food mostly grills; log fire, plenty of tables outside overlooking water, Watneys-related real ales *(Heather Sharland, BB)*

Devils Dyke [TQ2511], *Devils Dyke*: Staggering views night and day from busy touristy pub perched on downs above Brighton *(LYM)*

Dial Post [A24/B2244; TQ1519], *Crown*: Well kept friendly pub with good food in bar and reasonably priced restaurant; Badger beer *(Brenda Gentry)*

Eartham [SU9409], *George*: Good buffet, service and beer *(Mr and Mrs W Harrington)*

East Grinstead [TQ3938], *Dunnings Mill*: Gas lighting and back-to-basics furnishings in low-ceilinged three-roomed sixteenth-century mill cottage built right over stream (pretty garden); bar food, range of real ales, children welcome; handy for Standen (NT) *(Neil Barker, LYM)*

East Lavant [SU8608], *Earl of March*: Good food including recommended mussels in garlic, pancakes and rabbit pie, good for supper before Chichester Theatre (food served in good time), well kept beer, big comfortable gimmick-free bar; children welcome *(Prof A N Black)*

Elsted [Elsted Marsh; nearer to Midhurst than the Three Horseshoes, same road; SU8119], *Ballards*: Simple roadside country pub popular for the good Ballards beers brewed here (they also stock other real ales such as King & Barnes and Marstons Pedigree); has been up for sale *(WFL, Mrs Kate Ford)*

Fairwarp [TQ4626], *Foresters*: Well sited by village green in Ashdown Forest; pleasant inside with welcoming and obliging landlord; well kept King & Barnes Festive, good value ploughman's, garden with tables and chairs *(Brian and Jenny Seller)*

Fernhurst [SU9028], *Red Lion*: Good old pub overlooking village green, lots of atmosphere, winter log fires, really welcoming licensees, good value first-rate food *(Andrew Johnson)*

Findon [TQ1208], *Gun*: Large helpings of good standard food, well presented, friendly service, and Flowers and Whitbreads Strong Country on handpump in comfortably modernised pub with attractive sheltered lawn, in quiet village below Cissbury Ring *(Michael Bechley, LYM)*

Fishbourne [A27 Chichester–Emsworth; SZ8404], *Sussex Barn*: Large bar with rustic décor and atmosphere, friendly service; Ruddles Best and County, Gales HSB, Websters Yorkshire and King & Barnes on handpump; good bar food and separate restaurant *(A R Lord)*

Gatwick [Airport; TQ2941], *Country Pub*: Worth knowing – reasonably comfortable considering all the air-traveller customers, and decent simple food *(J S Rutter)*

Hadlow Down [OS Sheet 199 reference 532241; TQ5323], *New*: Difficult to believe that a pub like this exists in SE England – management extremely friendly but, like the pub and its immediate surroundings, unlikely to win awards for style *(Phil and Sally Gorton)*

Handcross [TQ2529], *Red Lion*: Welcoming, friendly atmosphere; remarkable value in Barnabys Carvery, good coffee, good value wines *(Dr Richard Neville)*; [Horsham Rd] *Royal Oak*: Huge helpings of good lunchtime food, with wide choice, prompt courteous service; handy for Nymans Gardens (NT) *(Mark Radford)*

Henfield [TQ2116], *George*: Olde-worlde pub in pretty village with pleasant atmosphere, good helpings of good value bar food and well kept Gales HSB and Ushers; separate restaurant *(Chris Fluck)*

Henley [SU8925], *Duke of Cumberland*: Small wistaria-covered pub with good food – including trout fresh from their own stewponds outside *(C Gray)*

☆ **Hermitage** [36 Main Rd (A27); SU7505], *Sussex Brewery*: Four good own-brewed beers and well kept guest bitters, good home-cooked food and carefully traditional atmosphere (sawdust on the flagstones, stripped brickwork, simple furnishings); wide choice of food including occasional shellfish fresh from local fishermen, efficient friendly service even when busy *(Nigel Lander, P M Brooker, Richard Houghton)*

Heyshott [SU8918], *Unicorn*: Nice local

atmosphere in L-shaped bar with tables around walls, good range of well presented bar food, friendly staff, restaurant, barbecue in garden; in attractive country at the foot of the downs *(J S Evans, Mr and Mrs I McCaw)*

Horsham [North Parade; TQ1730], *Dog & Bacon*: Pleasant local on the outskirts; well kept King & Barnes beer *(Dr and Mrs A K Clarke)*

Hurstpierpoint [High St; TQ2716], *New*: Old-fashioned local with charming traditional back room, bar billiards in panelled snug, simpler public bar, well kept Bass and Charrington IPA *(LYM)*

Kirdford [TQ0126], *Foresters*: Well run pub with brilliant cooking by licensee's wife *(Jim Gavin)*; [opp church] *Half Moon*: Good original food, garden *(AB)*

☆ **Lambs Green** [TQ2136], *Lamb*: Recently extended but still cosy plush bar with beams and open fire in friendly pub with wide choice of quickly and generously served food and normally well kept real ales such as Badger Best, Gales HSB, King & Barnes and Ruddles County on handpump; big glass-walled garden-room *(Mike Muston, David and Sarah Gilmore, Dr A V Lewis, BB)*

☆ **Lickfold** [SU9225], *Lickfold Inn*: Tudor pub with a good deal of character and attractively landscaped garden, big log fires, heavy beams, Georgian settles, herringbone brickwork, praiseworthy range of interesting well kept real ales, summer barbecues, children allowed in eating area; has had its ups and downs but latest reports suggest it's been decidedly on an up recently, with friendly service and good though not cheap bar food from sandwiches to steaks; has been closed Mon evening *(Mary Billam, Gary Wilkes, Neil Lusby, Mr and Mrs J C Dwane, Mr and Mrs R Harrington, LYM)*

Littlehampton [westwards towards Chichester, opp railway stn; TQ0202], *Arun View*: Built out on to the harbour edge, with extensive views of the river – busy here with seagoing vessels; comfortable banquettes, accurate drawings of barges and ships worked into counter-top, Wethereds and Sam Whitbread on handpump, wide choice of bar food and restaurant, flower-filled terrace; summer barbecues evenings and weekends *(Ian Phillips)*

☆ **Lower Beeding** [TQ2227], *Crabtree*: Large pub with public bar, snug and back bar with inglenook fireplace; good welcome, well kept King & Barnes, good bar food and dining-room; recently taken over by licensees who earned many plaudits from readers at the Leathern Bottle near Graffham in Surrey *(Phil and Sally Gorton)*

Lower Beeding [Plummers Plain; TQ2128], *Wheatsheaf*: Popular; walls and ceiling decorated with military memorabilia; good food, well kept King & Barnes on handpump *(David Fisher)*

☆ **Lurgashall** [signposted off A283 N of

Petworth – OS Sheet 186 reference 936272; SU9327], *Noah's Ark*: Interesting old pub on edge of quiet village green, simple attractive furnishings, open fires including big ingle-nook in lounge, straightforward bar food, well kept Friary Meux and Ind Coope real ale, traditional games and bar billiards, children allowed in dining-room *(E G Parish, Mr and Mrs J C Dwane, LYM)*

Lyminster [TQ0204], *Six Bells*: Good food, friendly atmosphere, well kept real ale *(Mike and Shirley Hyde)*

Midhurst [North St; SU8821], *Angel*: Old coaching-house with beams, dark wood-work, crimson plush seats and fresh flowers in its two main bars, polite and helpful long-serving staff, well kept Gales, bar food, separate restaurant, large garden; bedrooms *(Doug Kennedy)*; [Petersfield Rd (A272 just W)] *Half Moon*: Good reasonably priced food and good service and friendly and comfortable well run pub *(AB)*; [A286 towards Chichester] *Royal Oak*: Good range of real ales and bottled beers, and barbecues in the fine extensive garden which surrounds this country pub with its little rambling rooms – it was originally a fifteenth-century farm-house *(Steve and Carolyn Harvey, LYM)*; [South St/Market Sq] *Swan*: Split-level Harveys pub with very attentive licensees, evidently trying very hard; interesting choice of freshly cooked and attractively served food – one to watch *(Aubrey and Margaret Saunders)*; [Wool Lane] *Wheatsheaf*: Tastefully decorated, with good food and King & Barnes beer *(Anon)*

Milland [A3; SU8328], *Fox*: Well kept beer, good cheap bar food, huge garden with animals and swings *(Ray Challoner)*

Nep Town [TQ2015], *Gardeners Arms*: Good choice of real ales, good food in restaurant, comfortable lounge bar with good mix of ages among customers *(Dr David Stanley)*

Northchapel [SU9529], *Half Moon*: Friendly village pub with rustic atmosphere, farm tools, subdued lighting, open fire, pool-room, honest value food – especially Sun lunch *(Michael and Harriet Robinson, Charles and Mary Winpenny)*

Pease Pottage [by M23 junction 11; TQ2533], *James King*: Comfortable bar, well kept King & Barnes, extensive bar food and cold buffet, separate restaurant *(Norman Foot)*

Petworth [Angel St; SU9721], *Angel*: Pleasant spacious pub with relaxed atmosphere and surroundings and friendly staff, straightfor-ward decent bar food, Watneys-related real ales with a guest beer such as Gales, huge winter log fire; bedrooms *(D J Penny, Norman Foot, NHB)*; [A285 1½ miles towards Chichester] *Badger & Honeyjar*: Though it looks ordinary there's a warm and friendly welcome from the landlord and an extensive and interesting range of bar food; Whit-breads-related real ales *(TOH)*; *Red Lion*:

Old and interesting if hardly smart, very friendly landlord, attractive food; upstairs part is a wine bar, and the good wine is served downstairs too *(Dave Butler, Les Storey)*; [A283 towards Pulborough] *Well-diggers*: Low-ceilinged food pub very popular for its good value restaurant-style meals – hardly a place for just a drink now – and attractive lawns and terraces *(LYM)*

Pulborough [99 Lower St; TQ0418], *Oddfellows Arms*: Notable for its marvellous ploughman's – well kept and comfortable *(Guy Harris)*

Rake [A3 S of Liphook; SU8027], *Flying Bull*: Well kept Huntsman ales, very good staff; county border runs through pub *(M C Wheeler)*

☆ **Rogate** [A272; SU8023], *White Horse*: Old seventeenth-century coaching-inn with wide range of beers, pleasant comfortable atmos-phere, good red plush seats under low beams, very good food nicely served (even with tablecloths), several real ales, notably clean lavatories *(Dr and Mrs A K Clarke, Prof A N Black)*

Rudgwick [Church St; TQ0833], *Kings Head*: Friendly and efficient service, three-course Sun lunch a real bargain; backs on to lovely old church in attractive small village *(L V Nutton)*

Rusper [Friday Street (a mile or two from village); TQ2037], *Royal Oak*: Very well run by particularly welcoming and wholly genuine licensees, good honest-to-goodness pub food, pleasant surroundings in quiet lane *(Brian Fender, N D Foot)*

Selsey [Albion Rd; SZ8593], *Lifeboat*: Good lunches in beautiful garden, very clean; friendly staff *(Stella Crist)*; *Seal*: Homely inn, in residential road back from seafront; very wide choice of beers and other drinks, busy at lunchtime – but very quiet dining area with good choice of very reasonably priced good food; good value bedrooms *(Mrs Shirley Fluck)*

☆ **Sharpthorne** [Horstead Lane; TQ3732], *Ravenswood*: Magnificent spacious period bar with handsome panelling in converted Victorian house, Badger Best and Tanglefoot on handpump, restaurant; extensive grounds with lake, summerhouse, tables behind house *(D J Penny)*

Singleton [SU8713], *Horse & Groom*: Comfortable, relaxing pub with real fires and large helpings of good food – Suns also; within walking distance of Weald and Downland Open Air Museum *(NHB)*

Sompting [TQ1605], *Smugglers*: Though really a restaurant, it has a beamed bar with an inglenook fireplace; also a terrace in the walled garden; restaurant closed Sun evening, Mon *(Unity and George Denton)*

☆ **South Harting** [B2146; SU7819], *White Hart*: Lovely old attractive place with two log fires and welcoming and attentive licensees and staff; good to find a pub with a real public bar for locals and young instead of usual open-plan gentrification; good fresh food, well served *(Jack Hanson, MCG)*

☆ **Stedham** [School Lane; SU8622], *Hamilton Arms*: Good English food in well kept clean pub with friendly owners and staff; nr GWG57 *(Mr and Mrs I McCaw)*

☆ **Stopham** [off A283 towards Pulborough, TQ0218], *White Hart*: Friendly old beamed pub with big lawn, play area, and grass walks by pretty junction of Arun and Rother rivers; open fire in one of the snug rooms, good freshly made bar food (not Sun evening), restaurant specialising in unusual fresh fish, well kept Flowers Original and Whitbreads Strong Country, unobtrusive piped music; quiet now the new bridge diverts the traffic; children welcome, also play area; the tenants have now bought the Labouring Man at Coldwaltham – see above – and are running that in tandem *(Lyn and Bill Capper, B V Harmes, LYM)*

Stoughton [signposted off B2146 Petersfield –Emsworth; SU8011], *Hare & Hounds*: Much modernised seventeenth-century brick and flint downs village pub, pine cladding, red leatherette, big open fires in dividing chimney, an airy feel; cheerful bar food, well kept Gales ales, friendly young staff, winter restaurant, back darts room, pretty terrace; children in eating area and restaurant; nr start GWG56 *(LYM)*

Sutton [nr Bignor Roman Villa; SU9715], *White Horse*: Good choice of bottled beers as well as real ales such as Badger Tanglefoot, Ballards, Gales HSB and King & Barnes on handpump (and a Pils from a vast porcelain machine); pleasant unpretentious small two-bar pub with cream wood banquettes, brass lamps, wood floor, open fires; busy with locals, friendly to strangers; newspapers on poles, even Metaxas brandy; good food, separate restaurant *(Patrick Young)*

☆ **Tillington** [SU9621], *Horseguards*: Perched above village lane, with lovely view from bow window; well kept King & Barnes beers at low prices, good value food including several vegetarian dishes, traditional and other games, tables on terrace and in garden *(Steve and Carolyn Harvey, Norman Foot, S J A Velate, Chris Fluck, R and S Bentley, LYM)*

Tismans Common [TQ0732], *Mucky Duck*: Oak beams, timbers and flagstones in cheery well run country pub with simple homecooked food, good choice of well kept real ales, lively evening atmosphere, play area and garden seats *(LYM)*

☆ **Trotton** [OS Sheet 197 reference 837222; SU8323], *Keepers Arms*: Straightforwardly furnished L-shaped bar angling around to restaurant area in beamed and timbered tile-hung pub, standing on a little rise – country views from its latticed windows and from teak tables on a narrow terrace; Badger Best and Tanglefoot and Ruddles County on handpump, decent spirits, lots of non-alcoholic drinks, quietly chatty atmosphere, decent straightforward food cooked nicely *(WHBM, J H Bell, J S Evans, Mrs Beryl Rosenbaum, BB)*

☆ **Turners Hill** [East St; TQ3435], *Crown*: Homely and friendly olde-worlde sixteenth-century pub, prompt friendly service, good choice of wines and reasonably priced food; secluded well kept lawn behind; handy for Wakehurst Place aad Standen; very popular; two bedrooms *(W J Wonham, C F Stephens, Ruth Moynard)*

Washington [just off A24 Horsham–Worthing; TQ1212], *Frankland Arms*: Roomy pub with wide range of food, good selection of beers and prompt service by pleasant staff; garden with play area *(M Sayer, Mr and Mrs R A Kingsnorth)*

West Hoathly [TQ3633], *Vinols Cross*: Good bar food and well kept Badger and Fullers beers; start GWG64 *(Donald Owen)*

West Marden [B2146 2 miles S of Uppark; SU7713], *Victoria*: Pleasant surroundings, well kept Gales ales, decent house wines, good home-made food including generous ploughman's; quick courteous service *(Col and Mrs L N Smyth, R Sims)*

Westergate [SU9305], *Wilkes Head*: Small, very friendly pub with flagstones and open fire; well kept Burton and Friary Meux, good food and pleasant landlord *(C R T Low)*

☆ **Wisborough Green** [TQ0526], *Three Crowns*: Comfortable and careful refurbishment in late 1987 – oak beams, brick walls, parquet and carpeted floors; well kept Friary Meux, wide choice of good bar food, good service *(Norman Foot, A Banister)*

Worthing [High St; Tarring; TQ1303], *George & Dragon*: Cheerful family atmosphere in clean pub with light and airy lounge and good range of attractive food, with Watneys-related real ales; attractive sheltered terrace and garden *(Capt Tony Bland)*; [Old Brighton Rd; TQ1402] *Royal Oak*: Large pub strategically placed next to Beach Hill Park, the mecca for bowls; very friendly atmosphere, reasonably priced food, efficient service, Watneys-related real ales, draught milk and Bovril *(D L Johnson, M O'Mara)*

Yapton [North End Rd; SU9703], *Black Dog*: Good reasonably priced food and good variety of beers such as Whitbreads Pompey Royal; particularly nice terrace and covered seating areas; large park, children's play area *(Anon)*

Warwickshire *see* Midlands
West Midlands *see* Midlands

Wiltshire

Several popular main entries here have had new licensees this year. These include the Weight for Age at Alvediston (though to readers' relief the French chef has stayed on), the rustic Compasses at Chicksgrove (lots of copper and brass on the walls now), the friendly White Hart at Ford (recent reports warmly praise the food), and the civilised Bell at Ramsbury. Two engaging country pubs that are quite new to the Guide are the Harrow in the attractive village of Little Bedwyn (new young licensees are doing good food here) and the Vine Tree at Norton (interestingly done up rather like a wine bar, but concentrating firmly on thoroughly pubby virtues – including good beer, good food and a fine garden for children). Though we haven't included the Hop Pole at Limpley Stoke in the Wiltshire chapter before, it's not exactly a newcomer; in previous editions we've had it in the Somerset and Avon chapter (the county boundary bisects the village), and are responding to having our geographical knuckles rapped by repositioning it here. Pubs which stand out for good food include the welcoming Maypole (beside the country's tallest) at Ansty, the Waggon and Horses at Beckhampton (with its droll menus), the picturesque old Chequers in Box, the cottagey Dove at Corton, the Bear in Devizes (with a rambling old-fashioned lounge – it's useful for serving bar food until very late – and is a comfortable place to stay at), the Crown at Giddeahall (with its strongly charactered collection of rambling rooms), the Royal Oak at Great Wishford (good for families), the civilised Lamb at Hindon (the curries are popular), the Silver Plough at Pitton (particularly for its fresh fish – worth the wait), the newly rethatched George & Dragon in Potterne (with good value bedrooms and a remarkable antique indoor shooting-gallery), the cosy Benett Arms at Semley (comfortable bedrooms, too), and the increasingly popular thatched Royal Oak at Wootton Rivers. The sparkling little Horseshoe at Ebbesbourne Wake is now run by the son of the previous licensees – which gives good hope of preserving its charming atmosphere; the Haunch of

Weight for Age, Alvediston

Venison in Salisbury is another pub which stands out through sheer force of character. Pubs in particularly attractive surroundings include the unspoilt old Rising Sun just outside Lacock (with the best views of any pub in the county from its garden – and good real ales), and the Spread Eagle at Stourton (it's part of this lovely National Trust property, and is a comfortable place to stay at). Among the pubs in the Lucky Dip section at the end of the chapter, some particularly notable possibilities include the Fox & Hounds at Farleigh Wick, Cross Keys at Fovant, Up The Garden Path at Manton and Avon Brewery in Salisbury; the M4's junction 15 seems to be particularly well served with handy pubs, around Wanborough.

ALVEDISTON ST9723 Map 2

Weight for Age ⊗ 🛏 [illustrated on page 674]

The two open-plan beamed rooms in this friendly thatched pub are comfortably furnished with deeply upholstered seats on the red patterned carpet, subdued lighting and a fire at one end. Home-made bar food includes sandwiches (from 65p, including open sandwiches), soup (95p), baked potato with various fillings (from £1.20), ploughman's (from £1.60), fresh whitebait or home-made pâté (£1.90), breaded plaice (£2.90), giant sausage (£2.95), moules marinière (£3.25), steak and kidney pie (£3.60) and chicken Kiev (£4.70); a children's menu (£1.45) and Sunday lunch (£5). Service is efficient and readers note French staff. Well kept Huntsman Dorset and Wadworths 6X on handpump; darts, shove-ha'penny, a trivia machine and piped music. If you stay, readers tip the National Room. Facing a farmyard with ponies and other animals, the attractive garden, on different levels around a thatched white well, is nicely broken up with shrubs and rockeries among the neatly kept lawns; there is also a new children's play area. *(Recommended by Norman Rose, WHBM, Nigel Paine, Gwen and Peter Andrews, S N Hancock, Roy McIsaac, Dr R Conrad)*

Free house Licensee W D Johnson Real ale Meals and snacks Restaurant Children in family-room Open 11–11; 11–3, 6–11 in winter; all year One bedroom tel Salisbury (0722) 780335; /£25

ANSTY ST9526 Map 2

Maypole ⊗

Village signposted from A30 Shaftesbury–Salisbury

Originally the ale or beer house for the workers on the estate during most of the last century, this white-shuttered brick and flint pub was sold into private hands in 1881. The present landlord is courteous and welcoming, and his popular bar food includes sandwiches (from 95p, home-cooked ham £1.25), soup (£1.10), filled baked potatoes (from £1.45), good ploughman's (from £1.95), basket meals such as curry pancake rolls, chicken or scampi (from £2.50), lasagne (£2.95), salads (from £3.25, home-topside of beef £4.25), seafood platter (£4.75), breaded chicken with creamcheese and pineapple filling (£4.50), gammon steak with egg or pineapple (£4.95), fresh trout with almonds (£6.25) and steaks (from £6.95). Well kept Hook Norton Best, Marstons Pedigree and Wadworths 6X on handpump; piped music. The dark green hessian walls are hung with old local photographs and drawings and hunting prints, and around the tables on the Turkey carpet there are spindle-back chairs, cushioned wall seats and winged settles. There are seats in front and in the back garden. Maypoles have been here since the fifteenth century, and the present one is England's tallest – ninety-six feet; there are jolly celebrations

---

Most pubs kindly let us have up-to-date food prices as we went to press in summer 1988; with those that didn't – normally recognised by the absence of a licensee's name – we've assumed a 10 per cent increase.

on May Day. The pub is near *Good Walks Guide* Walk 34. *(Recommended by Nigel Paine, V Thomas, Bob Smith, Guy Harris, Mr and Mrs B E Witcher)*

Free house   Licensees Brian and Pat Hamshere   Real ale   Meals and snacks (not Sun evening or Mon)   Restaurant   Children over five in eating area   Open 11–3, 6.30–11; closed Mon, exc bank hols (they then close the next day)   Bedrooms tel Tisbury (0747) 870607; £15B/ £30B

BECKHAMPTON   SU0868   Map 2

Waggon and Horses ⊗

A4 Marlborough–Calne; OS Sheet 173 reference 090689

This lovely family-run old thatched coaching-inn has a wide choice of bar food that usually includes home-made soup (£1), lots of sandwiches and filled rolls (£1, double-deckers £1.75, specials like toasted French stick with garlic butter, ham and cheese £1.25), Stilton and mushroom pâté (£1.50), ploughman's (£1.50), home-made steak and kidney pie (£2.60), or an unspecified hot special which you have to order as a pig in a poke (£2.75), a big choice of salads (£3.25), grills like chicken (£4.60), gammon with pineapple (£4.95) or sirloin steak (£5.60), daily specials, vegetarian dishes and home-made puddings such as strawberry cheesecake or pot-luck pudding (£1.25); they carefully follow food fashion – polyunsaturate fats, wholemeal flour, and no salt in cooking. Well kept Wadworths IPA, 6X, Farmers Glory and in winter Old Timer on handpump. The open-plan bar has beams in the shiny ceiling where walls have been knocked through, a large, old-fashioned high-backed settle on one side of the room, with a smaller one opposite, as well as red cushioned Windsor chairs, leatherette stools, comfortably cushioned wall benches, and a warm, solid-fuel fire in winter; the lounge is more cosy, but similarly furnished; piped music. Shove-ha'penny, dominoes and fruit machine. In summer you can sit at picnic-table sets on the big front cobbles, among troughs of flowers, by the massive stone walls of the inn – a welcome sight to coachmen coming in from what was notorious as the coldest stretch of the old Bath road. Silbury Hill – a prehistoric mound – is just towards Marlborough, and Avebury stone circle and the West Kennet long barrow are very close too. *(Recommended by Frank Cummins, D H Voller, TBB, M C Howells, Oliver Howes, C Elliott)*

Wadworths   Licensees Jon and Lesley Scholes   Real ale   Meals and snacks (not Mon evening)   Children in side room if eating   Open 11.30–2.30, 6–11; closed Mon evening and evening 25 Dec

BOX   ST8268   Map 2

Chequers ⊗

Pub signposted from A4 E of junction with A365 – keep eyes skinned for the sign, and the turning is sharp and narrow

With its little stone-mullioned windows, this old stone building gives a greater feeling of age than almost all Wiltshire pubs – certainly the uncommonly steep and twisting narrow lanes around it were designed more for packhorses than for carts (let alone cars!). Inside, there are cushioned wall seats (some in a bow window), wheel-back chairs and green plush round stools on the partly carpeted old oak parquet floor, a little bureau is built into one stripped stone wall, and the handsome old stone fireplace has a warm log fire in winter. The end dining-room has flowers and candles on its tables, and a fine big yachting print. A wide choice of home-made bar food, changing with the seasons, might include filled ploughman's (£1.95), hot chilli con carne or cauliflower bake (£1.95), a wide range of vegetarian dishes (from £1.95, vegetable curry £2.95), steak, kidney and Guinness pie (£2.95), chicken curry (£5.95) and steaks (from £6.20). Ushers Best and Websters Yorkshire on handpump, from a servery decorated with hop-bines; friendly and efficient service;

darts, shove-ha'penny, table skittles, dominoes, cribbage, quiet fruit machine, sitting space game and piped music. *(Recommended by Jane and Calum, Steve and Carolyn Harvey, GRE and AE, CED)*

Ushers Licensee Kenneth Martin Real ale Meals and snacks Restaurant Children in eating area Open 11–2.30 (3 Sat), 6–11 all year Bedroom tel Box (0225) 742383; /£30B

nr BRADFORD-ON-AVON ST8060 Map 2
Cross Guns

Avoncliff; pub is across footbridge from Avoncliff Station (first through road left, heading N from river on A363 in Bradford centre, and keep bearing left), and can also be reached down very steep and eventually unmade road signposted Avoncliff – keep straight on rather than turning left into village centre – from Westwood (which is signposted from B3109 and from A366, W of Trowbridge); OS Sheet 173 reference 805600

Though this old-fashioned pub has been changing hands so often that it's been hard for us to keep up with it, readers took us to task when we demoted it to the Lucky Dip. It's included for its beautiful position with floodlit and terraced gardens overlooking the wide river Avon and a maze of bridges, aqueducts (the Kennet and Avon Canal) and tracks winding through this quite narrow gorge. Inside, there are low seventeenth-century beams, stone walls, rush-seated chairs around plain sturdy oak tables, and a large ancient fireplace with a smoking-chamber behind it. Bar food includes sandwiches, home-made steak and kidney pie or cottage pie, scampi, plaice and steak; well kept Badger Best and Tanglefoot, Butcombe, Smiles and Wadworths 6X, and a beer brewed for the pub on handpump; efficient, cheerful service. Darts, dominoes, cribbage, fruit machine and piped music. *(Recommended by Philip King, Juliet Streatfield, Neil Evans, James and Susan Trapp, Nick Dowson, Alison Hayward, WHBM, Roger Huggins)*

Free house Real ale Meals (not Mon or Tues lunchtime or Sun evening) and snacks (not Sun evening) Open 11–2.30, 6–11 all year; opens 7 in winter Bedrooms tel Bradford-on-Avon (022 16) 2335; /£30B

CASTLE COMBE ST8477 Map 2
White Hart

Village centre; signposted off B4039 Chippenham–Chipping Sodbury

The lovely stone village attracts enough visitors to make this cheerful old stone pub – one of the most attractive buildings here – rather crowded at times, overflowing from the beamed and flagstoned main bar into a family-room and a small central covered courtyard. The old-fashioned furnishings include an antique elm table as well as Windsor chairs, a traditional black wall bench built into the stone mullioned window, and a big winter log fire in the elegant stone fireplace. Things haven't changed under the new regime, with home-made bar food that includes hot specials such as good prawns in bacon, vegetarian dishes and a help-yourself salad bar in summer. Well kept Badger Best and Wadworths Farmers Glory on handpump, and a good range of country wines; darts, shove-ha'penny, dominoes and cribbage. As well as the courtyard, you can also sit in the garden. *(Recommended by Ted George, G Bloxsom, Rob and Gill Weeks, Roger Baskerville, Patrick Young, S V Bishop, W A Harbottle)*

Free house Real ale Meals (winter, not Sat or Sun) and snacks Children in family-room Parking nearby may be difficult; village car park is up steep hill Open 10.30–2.30, 6–10.30

Though lunchtime closing time is now 3 on Sundays in England and Wales (with 20 minutes' drinking-up time), some pubs hope to close a bit earlier – please let us know if you find this happening.

CHARLTON ST9588 Map 2
Horse & Groom ⊗
B4040 towards Cricklade

The lounge, on the left in this tiled stone pub, has an atmosphere of relaxed well-being; also, kitchen armchairs and attractive pine built-in stall seats around scrubbed deal kitchen tables, a Turkey carpet, red velvet curtains, dark red Anaglypta walls (stripped to stone in some places), a pine-panelled bar counter and log fires in winter. A more spacious parquet-floored bar on the right has darts, dominoes and shove-ha'penny; friendly, chatty landlord. Bar food ranges from filled rolls (from 80p) or ploughman's (from £1.85) to vegetarian platter (£5.50), trout (£5.95), chicken in cranberry and wine sauce (£6.75) and steak (£8.65), with a wide and interesting choice of specials such as cream of celery soup (£1.30), mushroom and walnut pâté (£1.75), smoked salmon pâté (£2), cottage pie (£3.50), steak and kidney pie (£4.50) and pork in cream and mushroom sauce (£5.50); there are country puddings such as apple crumble or orange cheesecake (£1.40). The lounge has a £5.50 minimum food charge on Friday and Saturday evenings. Well kept Archers Village, Moles and Wadworths 6X on handpump, good quality wines on the recently extended list. Tables with cocktail parasols are set out on the grass in front of the pub – the road doesn't carry much traffic. *(Recommended by Godfrey Smith; more reports please)*

Free house   Licensee Richard Hay   Real ale   Meals and snacks (not Sun evening or Mon) Restaurant tel Malmesbury (0666) 823904   Children welcome (not in lounge bar); over-eights in restaurant in evenings   Open 12–2.30, 7–11; closes 10.30 in winter; closed Sun evening, all day Mon

CHICKSGROVE ST9629 Map 2
Compasses ⊗
From A30 5½ miles W of B3089 junction, take lane on N side signposted Sutton Mandeville, Sutton Row, then first left fork (small signs point the way to the pub, but at the pub itself, in Lower Chicksgrove, there may be no inn sign – look out for the car park); OS Sheet 184 reference 974294

Old bottles and jugs hang from the beams above the roughly timbered bar counter, there are farm tools and brasses on the partly stripped stone walls, and high-backed wooden settles form snug booths around the tables on the mainly flagstone floor. A wide choice of reasonably priced, home-cooked bar food includes sandwiches (from 80p), ploughman's (from £1.95), chilli con carne or lasagne (£2.95), home-made steak and kidney pie (£3.45), trout (from £3.50), scampi (£3.75), gammon (from £4.50) and steaks (from £6.25). Well-kept Wadworths 6X, IPA and Farmers Glory on handpump; darts, shove-ha'penny, table skittles, dominoes and cribbage; prompt and friendly service. The lane past here carries very little traffic, and it's peaceful sitting out in the big garden or on the flagstoned farm courtyard. *(Recommended by Mr and Mrs R Marleyn, Nigel Paine, R H Inns, Paul McPherson, Gordon and Daphne)*

Free house   Licensee P J Killick   Real ale   Meals and snacks   Restaurant   Children in eating area   Open 11–3, 7 (6 Sat)–11 all year   Bedrooms tel Fovant (072 270) 318; £15/£30B

CHILMARK ST9632 Map 2
Black Dog
B3089

It's not unusual to find a group of Americans in this comfortably modernised fifteenth-century pub, as early settlers from this area nostalgically opened their own Black Dog Tavern in Massachusetts and visitors are clearly quite moved to see the original tavern. The carpeted lounge bar has a friendly local atmosphere, armchairs, horsebrasses on the beams, equestrian plates on the walls and a big fireplace with logs burning in winter and a big display of brasswork in summer. The Quarry Bar has had the plaster stripped back so that you can see fossil ammonites in the stone (from Chilmark quarry – the same stone as Salisbury Cathedral), and a third bar, the Brew House, is favoured by people from the huge nearby RAF base. Good bar food includes sandwiches, cod (£2.20), plaice (£2.60), ham or chicken salad (£2.90), scampi (£3.10) and beef salad (£3.15); Sunday roast lunch (£6); prompt service. Well-kept Courage Best and Directors on handpump; darts, shove-ha'penny, dominoes, cribbage and fruit machine. There are white tables and chairs on the pretty daisy-covered lawn, well screened by the tiled house from any road noise. The village, off the main road, is most attractive. *(Recommended by Harry Jackson, Lyn and Bill Capper, Roy McIsaac, C P Scott-Malden)*

Courage   Licensee Geoffrey Price-Harris   Real ale   Meals and snacks   Restaurant tel Teffont (072 276) 344   Children welcome   Open 11–3, 6–11 all year

CORTON   ST9340   Map 2
Dove ★ ⊗

Village signposted from A36 at Upton Lovell, SE of Warminster; this back road on the right bank of the River Wylye is a quiet alternative to the busy A36 Warminster–Wilton

There's considerable emphasis on the excellent home-made food in this beautifully kept and welcoming cottagey pub: home-made soup (£1.20), pâté (£1.75), variations on ploughman's with cheese, smoked loin of pork, home-cooked gammon, fish, quiche or pie (from £2.50), changing specials like pork casseroled in cider, vegetable and egg curry or shepherd's pie (£3.30), salad platters (£4.50), several vegetarian dishes and good puddings (£1.50). It's elegantly and individually furnished with a cane settle with colourful cushions by a pretty little chest-of-drawers in an alcove under the stairs, red bentwood cane chairs on the brick-tiled floor, cushioned brick side benches, and a rug in front of the small log fire; some of the attractive pictures are for sale. Well kept kept Ushers Best on handpump, good wines and properly made cocktails; impeccable service. There are rustic seats on the grass behind the stone building, which has dovecots by the climbing roses on its walls, and white doves on its tiled roof. Full marks for the charming ladies' lavatory here. *(Recommended by Dave Butler, Lesley Storey, Peter and Rose Flower, Norman Rose, DP, Mark Spurlock, K N Symons, Mrs A Cotterill-Davies)*

Ushers   Licensee Michael Rowse   Real ale   Meals and snacks (not Sun evening or Mon) Restaurant   Children in restaurant   Open 11–2.30, 6–11; closed Sun evening, Mon (exc bank hols), two weeks mid-Jan and first week Oct

DEVIZES   SU0061   Map 2
Bear ⊗ 🛏

Market Place

In the 1770s, this imposing stone inn was run by the father of Thomas Lawrence, the portrait painter who was later knighted; when he was six, Thomas was shown off to customers and became famous even among people like Sheridan and Dr Johnson for reciting vast chunks of Milton. A simply furnished grill- and snack-room is named after him, and is specially useful for serving food until the bar closes. At lunchtime this has buffet service (you can take food through into the bar), with salads such as turkey and ham pie with cranberry topping (from £2.80) and daily hot dishes such as sausage plait with tomato, cheese and herbs or spicy meatloaf with tomato sauce (£2.80). In the evening it reverts to a waitress-served charcoal grill-room, with most of the lunchtime food as well as decent grills such as mustard and honey chops (£3.10), a generous mixed grill (£4.25) and steaks (from £6.50);

tempting puddings. There is a special children's menu (not after 8pm). Quick snacks such as a good range of sandwiches (from 85p, toasties from 85p, roast sirloin of beef with horseradish £1.50, vegetarian wholewheat crispbread sandwich £1.10, bacon and tomato £1.48, smoked salmon with capers £2.95), jumbo sausage and egg (£1.20) and ploughman's (from £1.40) are served from the bar, with a wider choice ordered from the Lawrence Room waitress in the evening. Sunday roast lunches, good breakfasts and afternoon teas. The friendly and spacious beamed main bar rambles through the main hall, and has groups of seats including one or two easy chairs as well as the black winged wall settles around oak tripod tables, fresh flowers here and there, old prints on the walls, big logs on the fire in winter, and an old-fashioned bar counter with shiny black woodwork and small panes of glass. Well kept Wadworths IPA and 6X on handpump; it's brewed in the town, and from the brewery you can get it in splendid old-fashioned half-gallon earthenware jars; freshly ground coffee; cheerful, helpful service. This used to be one of England's great coaching-inns. *(Recommended by Roger Broadie, Mr and Mrs G J Packer, Neal Clark, Kathleen and David Caig, Aubrey and Margaret Saunders, Brig A F Freeman, Jamie and Sarah Allan)*

Wadworths   Licensees W K and J A Dickenson   Real ale   Meals and snacks   Restaurant Children in eating area   Frequent bar piano music   Open 11–11; closed 25 and 26 Dec Bedrooms tel Devizes (0380) 2444; £28(£33B)/£38(£45.50B)

EBBESBOURNE WAKE   ST9824 Map 2
Horseshoe

This delightfully simple and old-fashioned village local has been taken over by the landlord's son, which should mean that the charming character preserved so carefully, and for so long, by Mr and Mrs Tom Bath will survive their retirement. The beautifully kept and carpeted public bar is a friendly parlour, its beams crowded with lanterns, farm tools and other bric-à-brac, and there's an antique kitchen range in the big chimney embrasure. The tables are usually decorated with fresh flowers from the most attractive little garden, where seats look out over the small, steep sleepy valley of the River Ebble. Simple bar food consists of sandwiches and ploughman's (£1.90), with other hot dishes such as home-made steak and kidney pie (£2.50), lemon sole with crabmeat (£3.95) and chicken Kiev (£4.50) served in the restaurant. Well kept Wadworths 6X and Farmers Glory drawn straight from the row of casks behind the bar; darts and piped music. *(Recommended by Byrne Sherwood, WFL, Nigel Paine, J Roots, Dr and Mrs A K Clarke)*

Free house   Licensees A C T Bath and P I Bath   Real ale   Meals and lunchtime snacks Restaurant; open until 4 Sun   Open 12 (11 Sat)–4, 6–11; 12–3, 6.30–11 in winter Bedrooms tel Salisbury (0722) 780474; £10(£12B)

EVERLEIGH   SU2054 Map 2
Crown

Outside this striking seventeenth-century building with twin eighteenth-century wings, the spacious walled garden (safe for children) has animals as well as fowls, and the inn's extensive stables are now used by the trainer Richard Hannon (customers may tie their horses up outside). Dry-fly fishing for residents. Inside, the well kept, airy bar has a restful, friendly atmosphere, lots of polished copper, fresh flowers, sporting prints on the walls, and a mixture of upright rush-seated chairs, big Windsor armchairs and little easy chairs, as well as log fires in winter. Hearty home-made bar food relies heavily on fresh vegetables and local meat and includes sandwiches, soup (£1.30), potted Stilton with port (£1.75), home-cooked ham and egg (£3.50), and venison with port sauce (£7.40); the eggs used in the cooking come from the ducks, chickens and geese that wander in the garden; Sunday roast lunch. The downstairs public bar (the one for muddy boots) has darts, pool, shove-ha'penny, dominoes, cribbage, fruit machine, juke box and background music – none of this audible in the lounge – and a family-room has a piano and games. Well kept Wadworths IPA and 6X on electric pump; playful cat. *(Recommended by Stan Edwards, J B Whitley; more reports please)*

Free house   Real ale   Meals and snacks   Restaurant   Children in restaurant and family-room   Open 10.30–2.30, 6–11; closed 25 Dec   Bedrooms tel Collingbourne Ducis (026 485) 223; £16/£25(£29B)

FORD   ST8374 Map 2
White Hart ⊗ 🍴

A420 Chippenham–Bristol; follow Colerne sign at E side of village to find pub

In summer you can drink outside at the front of this little stone building, and there is another terrace behind, by a stone bridge over the By Brook, and for residents a secluded swimming-pool. Inside, the L-shaped cosy bar has polished wooden tables, tub armchairs, heavy black beams supporting the white-painted boards of the ceiling, and a relaxed atmosphere; there are small pictures and a few advertising mirrors on the walls, gentle lighting and in winter the warmth of a big log-burning stove in the old fireplace that's inscribed 1553. Good bar food includes sandwiches, home-made pâté (£1.95), chilli con carne (£2.60), Burgundy beef casserole (£2.95), mixed meat salad or steak and kidney pie (£3.20) and scampi (£3.45); very good breakfasts. Well kept Badger Best and Tanglefoot, Fullers ESB and London Pride, Greene King Abbot, Marstons Pedigree, Smiles Exhibition and Wadworths 6X on handpump; quick, friendly service even when busy. Dominoes, cribbage and piped music. *(Recommended by Alison Hayward, Nick Dowson, KC, Dr and Mrs B D Smith, Mr and Mrs J M Elden, Dennis Heatley, D S Rusholme, Frank Cummins, Neil and Elspeth Fearn, Pamela and Merlyn Horswell, Tom Evans)*

Free house   Licensee Bill Futcher   Real ale   Meals and snacks   Restaurant   Children in eating area and restaurant   Open 11–3, 6–11 Mon–Thurs; 11–11 Fri and Sat all year Bedrooms tel Castle Combe (0249) 782213; £32B/£45B

GIDDEAHALL   ST8574 Map 2
Crown ⊗

A420 W of Chippenham

Some four hundred years old, the rambling rooms in this listed building have been put together by incorporating the old private parlour and a neighbouring cottage. The main area has red plush window seats and wall seats, two wicker armchairs by the big fireplace where there are log-burning stoves, a brass iron-holder and frying-pan, a crook and so forth over its mantelpiece, a dark red ceiling, and a fluted stone plinth made from the base of an old column. Through behind the bar, there are red plush wall seats (some in curtain-draped alcoves), and in the end room dark red plush button-back wall banquettes with little pillars holding a velvet-fringed canopy over them, Victorian ointment posters, two cases of small stuffed birds and a stuffed rough-legged buzzard. Good value, imaginative home-made food cooked to order includes sandwiches (from 75p), platters of cheeses, mixed meats or fish (from £1.60), three-egg omelettes (from £1.65), salads (from £2.15) and steaks (from £6.55); puddings such as steamed golden roll (85p) or Southern walnut pie (£1.10); Sunday lunch (£3.55) with children's helpings (£2.20). Well kept Marstons Pedigree, Moles, Smiles Exhibition, Wadworths 6X and Youngers Scotch and IPA on handpump; dominoes, cribbage and fruit machine. *(Recommended by Aubrey and Margaret Saunders, Mr and Mrs G J Packer, Steven Farmer, Gordon Hewitt, Mr and Mrs D A P Grattan, Tom Evans)*

Free house   Licensees David and Theo Ross   Real ale   Meals and snacks   Restaurant; closed Sun and Mon until extension work completed   Children welcome   Open 11–11 all year   Bedrooms tel Castle Combe (0249) 782229; £25B/£40B

GREAT WISHFORD   SU0735 Map 2
Royal Oak ⊗

In village, which is signposted from A36

The unusually large menu in this busy flint village pub includes home-made soup (£1.15), sandwiches (from 95p), nine varieties of ploughman's with Wiltshire ham or superb Stilton and home-baked bread (from £2.35), a range of filled jacket potatoes and pizzas (from £2), three-egg omelettes (from £2.75), salads (from £3), burgers (from £3.25), Wiltshire ham and eggs (£3.85), lasagne or Mexican beef chilindron (£4.25), pies such as pork and cider, veal and cream or steak and oyster (from £5), vegetarian dishes such as vegetarian niçoise or crumbly nut and mushroom roast (£4) and steaks (from £7.99); fresh seasonal fish is delivered three times a week, with starters (from £2.75) and main courses (from £4.25) such as plaice, grilled salmon cutlet or scallops in cream; puddings include raspberry and peach crumble, treacle roly-poly, bread-and-butter pudding, chocolate fudge bake and lots of ice-creams and sorbets, all home made (£1.95). Children's menus (from £1.50); breakfasts and cream teas (summer only); efficient, cheerful service. Besides a good choice of some twenty reasonably priced wines by the glass and others by the bottle, there are well kept Ruddles County and Ushers Best on handpump, and they do a number of cocktails. The friendly and relaxed main bar has beams, cushioned pews, small seats and some easy chairs on its brown carpet, and in winter a log fire at each end; a cheery family area, just behind, has sturdy bleached wood tables. Darts, shove-ha'penny, dominoes, cribbage and piped music. The garden behind the pub has swings; and you can go home with a jar or two of Mrs Fisher's home-made jam, marmalade or chutney, or some home-made meringues. *(Recommended by Keith Walton, Mr and Mrs D I Baddeley, Gwen and Peter Andrews, Roger Mallard, Dave Butler, Les Storey, Peter Hall, JAH, Roy McIsaac, JMW)*

Ushers (Watneys)   Licensee Colin Fisher   Real ale   Meals and snacks   Restaurant tel Salisbury (0722) 790229   Children in eating area and restaurant   Open 11–11; 11–3, 7–11 in winter; closed 25 Dec

HINDON   ST9132 Map 2
Lamb ⊗

B3089 Wilton–Mere

The long bar in this solidly built and well cared for inn – popular with locals and visitors – is divided into three sections: we like best the two lower ones. One end has a window seat with a big waxed circular table, spindle-back chairs with tapestried cushions, a high-backed settle, brass jugs on the mantelpiece above the small fireplace, and a big kitchen clock; the middle – and main – area has a long polished table with wall benches and chairs, and a big inglenook fireplace. Up some steps, a third, bigger area has lots of tables and chairs. The varied choice of good bar food includes a very popular curry which comes with six side dishes (£3.95), soup (£1), sandwiches (from 75p), toasties (from 90p), home-made liver pâté (£1.65), ploughman's with granary bread (£1.90), home-made steak and kidney pie (£2.95) and salads (from £3.75) with home-cooked ham or fresh salmon (£5.95); Sunday lunch (£7.95). Well kept Wadworths IPA and 6X on handpump kept under light top pressure, and good wine from a local vineyard (off-sales as well). Friendly service; shove-ha'penny; no dogs. There are picnic-table sets across the road (which is a good alternative to the main routes west). *(Recommended by J S Evans, Roger Broadie, John Townsend, Major and Mrs D R C Woods, A R Tingley, Mr and Mrs R Gammon, Mr and Mrs D I Baddeley, S V Bishop, J S Evans, Major R A Colvile, Patrick Young, J and M Walsh, C P Scott-Malden, W A Gardiner, Nigel Paine, K R Harris)*

Free house   Licensee A J Morrison   Real ale   Meals and snacks   Restaurant   Children in eating area, restaurant and residents' lounge   Open 11–11 all year   Bedrooms tel Hindon (074 789) 225; £25(£35B)/£30(£40B)

KILMINGTON ST7736 Map 2
Red Lion
Pub on B3092 Mere–Frome, 2½ miles S of Maiden Bradley

There's a strong local atmosphere in this fifteenth-century country pub, underlined by the lively photographs on the beams, and racing gossip or games of shove-ha'penny in front of the deep fireplace with its fine old iron fireback. The atmosphere is relaxed, and there are flagstones, a curved high-backed black settle blocking off draughts from the door, red leatherette wall and window seats and maybe Lady, the black labrador. As we went to press we learnt of plans to extend the bar to provide additional seating (due to be completed by autumn 1988). Home-made bar food – no chips or fried food – includes soup (65p), baked potatoes (from 65p), toasties (from 95p), open sandwiches (from £1.45), pâté (£1.50), ploughman's (from £1.50), a hot daily dish (£2.50) and salads (£2.50); well kept Butcombe Bitter and Charringtons IPA on handpump, with quickly changing guest beers such as Batemans, Marstons Pedigree, Moles Bitter, Smiles or Theakstons; sensibly placed darts, dominoes, spoofing and cribbage; friendly service. Picnic-table sets in the large garden overlook White Sheet Hill (riding, hang-gliding and radio-controlled gliders), which can be reached by a road at the side of the pub; the National Trust Stourhead Gardens are a mile away, and Longleat Safari Park is fairly handy too. *(Recommended by Lyn and Bill Capper, S V Bishop, Dr K Bloomfield)*

Free house   Licensee Christopher Gibbs   Real ale   Meals and snacks (lunchtime)   Children welcome   Occasional live music   Open 11–3, 6.30–11; maybe longer afternoon opening if trade demands; closed 25 Dec   Bedrooms tel Maiden Bradley (098 53) 263; £10/£20

LACOCK ST9168 Map 2
Carpenters Arms
Village signposted off A350 S of Chippenham

Several cottagey areas open off each other in this big, attractively refurbished pub: one room, on the way to the candlelit raftered restaurant, has a plush porter's chair and a deep country-house sofa; another has polished boards instead of the carpet elsewhere, and a dresser filled with plates, and there are country wooden chairs unpainted or stripped to match the tables, as well as some older ones. It's decorated with old documents, bugles, trumpets, antlers, brass implements, old and modern prints, and lots of houseplants. Bar food includes soup (£1.10), ploughman's, steak and oyster pie (£3.85), steaks (from £6.75), daily specials, and puddings (£1.50); they have a bakery producing their own bread, rolls, pastries and scones. Well kept Ushers PA, Best and Founders on handpump; shove-ha'penny, dominoes, table skittles, cribbage and piped music (sometimes rather obtrusive). The bedrooms are by no means grand. *(Recommended by S V Bishop, G D Stafford, Laurie Nutton, Mrs C Jennings, Norman Rose, Philip King, John Knighton, Roger Huggins)*

Ushers   Real ale   Meals and snacks   Restaurant   Tea-room open outside licensed hours Children in eating area   Jazz Mon and Weds evenings, folk some Sun evenings   Open 10.30–2.30, 6–10.30   Bedrooms tel Lacock (024 973) 203; £30S/£40S (small shared lavatory)

George
One of the oldest buildings in the village and dating from 1361, this very friendly inn has a low beamed ceiling, upright timbers in the place of knocked-through walls making cosy corners, armchairs and Windsor chairs, seats in the stone-mullioned windows and flagstones just by the bar. A three-foot treadwheel set into the outer breast of the big central fireplace was originally for a dog to drive the turnspit. Bar food includes sandwiches and home-made dishes such as delicious stew and

dumplings and evening grills such as fresh trout (£4.95) or twelve-ounce rump steak (the licensee is shy of giving us prices for these – up-to-date reports welcomed). Well kept Wadworths IPA, 6X and in winter Old Timer on handpump; good coffee; darts and cribbage. There are seats in the back garden, and a bench in front that looks over the main street. (*Recommended by Alan Castle, Joan Olivier, Frank Cummins, David R Crafts, Leith Stuart, Mr and Mrs J H Adam, Roger Huggins, RAB, Patrick Stapley, Richard Gibbs, Penny Markham*)

Wadworths   Licensee John Glass   Real ale   Meals and snacks   Restaurant tel Lacock (024 973) 263   Children welcome   Open 11–11; 11–2.30, 6–10.30 in winter

Red Lion

High Street

Divided into separate areas by cart shafts, yokes and other old farm implements, the bar in this tall red brick Georgian inn has old-fashioned furniture, Turkey rugs on the partly flagstoned floor and a big log fire at one end. It's decorated with branding-irons hanging from the high ceiling, and plates, oil-paintings and Morland prints, more tools, and stuffed birds and animals on the partly panelled walls. Good home-made bar food includes soups (£1.30), ploughman's (£2.15), filled baked potatoes (from £2.20), duck liver terrine and pickled damsons or smoked trout and garlic mayonnaise with home-baked bread (£2.25), giant local sausages or home-made rissoles (£3.50), tasty beef pie (£3.95), chicken in cream and tomato sauce (£4.95) and puddings such as apple and almond crumble (£1.50). Wadworths IPA, 6X and in winter Old Timer on handpump; darts; warm and friendly service. They serve morning coffee from 10am. A stableblock is now used for teas, with fresh home-made scones and friendly waitresses. The pub is very popular in the latter half of the evening, particularly with younger people. Lacock Abbey and the Fox Talbot Museum are close by. (*Recommended by Mr and Mrs Maitland, Barbara Hatfield, L Walker, Nigel Williamson, Philip King, Joan Olivier, Jonathan Williams, James Bedell, Roger Huggins, RAB, Patrick Stapley, Richard Gibbs, Penny Markham*)

Wadworths   Licensee John Levis   Real ale   Meals and snacks   Children in eating area Open 11–2.30, 6–11 all year; closed 25 Dec   Bedrooms tel Lacock (024 973) 456; £25(£34B)/£40B

nr LACOCK   ST9168 Map 2

Rising Sun ★

Bowden Hill, Bewley Common; on back road Lacock–Sandy Lane

This isolated little country pub is a warmly welcoming, refreshingly simple place, with an L-shaped series of three rooms: one – mainly standing room – has the bar counter, a coal-effect gas fire and sensible darts area; another has flowery cushioned wall benches, a mix of old chairs and a couple of basic kitchen tables on the stone floor, antlers on the wall, and dried flowers and plants in the windows; the third has a big case of stuffed birds, stuffed badger, grandfather clock, some old woodworking planes, a shotgun on the wall and a few country pictures. Good bar food includes generous sandwiches, toasties, ploughman's and daily specials such as home-made leek and potato soup with Wiltshire bacon scone (£1.45), home-made lasagne (£2.75), moussaka (£3.10), lamb and apricot casserole (£3.50) and home-made puddings such as apple strudel (£1.10). Well kept Moles Bitter, 97 and Blind Dog (brewed by Moles to the landlord's recipe, with part of the price going to guide dogs for the blind) and Wadworths 6X on handpump, with several uncommon guest beers such as Bunces Best and Gibbs Mew Salisbury. Dominoes, cribbage and other card games; there is a young Gordon Setter and a friendly white and marmalade cat. You can sit outside at the picnic-table sets on the two-level terrace with tubs of flowers and enjoy the magnificent view (especially at sunset)

Pubs with attractive or unusually big gardens are listed at the back of the book.

looking out over the Avon valley, some twenty-five miles or so. *(Recommended by Peter and Rose Flower, Joan Olivier, Frank Cummins, Phil and Sally Gorton, RAB, Patrick Stapley, Richard Gibbs)*

Free house   Licensees R S and L Catte   Real ale   Lunchtime snacks (not Tues or Sun) Children welcome   Folk and country singer/guitarist Weds evenings   Open 12–2.30 (11–3 Sat), 7–11; closed Tues lunchtime

LIMPLEY STOKE   ST7760   Map 2

Hop Pole

Coming S from Bath on A36, 1300 yds after traffic-light junction with B3108 get ready for sharp left turn down Woods Hill as houses start – pub at bottom; if you miss the turn, take next left signposted Limpley Stoke then follow Lower Stoke signs; OS Sheet 172 reference 781610

This friendly pub has lots of dark wood panelling on the walls and ceilings of its two cosy bars. On the left, the spacious Avon Bar, with an arch to a cream-walled inner room, is pleasantly furnished and has a log-effect gas fire; the room on the right has lantern lighting, a log fire, red velvet cushions for the settles in its alcoves, some slat-back and captain's chairs on its Turkey carpet, and the slow tick of a big kitchen clock. Good value bar food includes burgers (from £1.20), Gloucester sausage and egg, ratatouille with garlic bread or cauliflower cheese with mushrooms (all £1.95), ploughman's or filled baked potatoes (£2.25), omelette (£2.45), salads (from £3.25), rump steak (five-ounce £3.25, eight-ounce £6.65), scampi or home-made fish pie (£3.25) and pork with Jamaican sweet-and-sour sauce or poached trout with prawn sauce (£3.95). Well kept Courage Bitter, Best and Directors on handpump; darts, dominoes, cribbage and piped music.
(Recommended by Nick Dowson, Alison Hayward, S J A Velate, M A and W R Proctor)

Courage   Licensee Graham Claude Titcombe   Real ale   Meals and snacks   Children in own room   Open 11–11 all year

LITTLE BEDWYN   SU2966   Map 2

Harrow ⊗

Village signposted off A4 W of Hungerford

New owners are serving interesting but unpretentious food, all home made from good ingredients, in this small but refreshingly light and airy village pub. On our summer visit it included onion soup (£1.75), chicken liver pâté (£1.95), ploughman's with a choice of cheeses (£2.50), macaroni cheese done with bacon and mushrooms (£2.95), a spicy chickpea casserole (£3.25), pork loin with fresh apple sauce (£3.95), ham baked with honey and orange (£4.25 – very tasty), fresh salmon (£5.95) and eight-ounce fillet steak with a nutty sherry sauce (£9.95). Their puddings (£1.75) are good – especially the chocolate roulade. With so much temptation, it's no surprise that Peter the alsatian is decidedly food-minded. Of the three rooms, the front one is the best for eating in, with a mixture of country chairs and simple wooden tables on its well waxed boards (one table in the bow window), flowery curtains, pale walls with large-scale local Ordnance Survey maps and a big wood-burning stove. The two inner rooms are chattier; decorations include a fine silvery model of a bull, and locally done watercolours and photographs for sale. Four changing well kept real ales (on our visit Archers Best, Golden Hill Exmoor, Hook Norton Best and Marstons Pedigree) on handpump, with decent wines by the glass and a sensible small selection of malt whiskies. Service is quietly friendly and helpful, the atmosphere relaxed. On your way to the lavatories you'll go through what's recently become the village post office, with the original Victorian sit-up-and-beg counter. Though they don't exactly take bookings, they do suggest telephoning to let them know you're coming, especially on Wednesday to Saturday evenings and for Sunday lunch; dominoes, cribbage, unobtrusive piped music.

There are seats out in the garden, and the pub's a couple of hundred yards from the Kennet and Avon Canal. *(Recommended by Frank Cummins, C H Pipe-Wolferstan, D Stephenson)*

Free house   Licensees Jacki and Richard Denning   Real ale   Meals and snacks   Restaurant tel Marlborough (0672) 870871   Children over ten allowed   Open 12–3, 5.30–11 all year; opens 7 in winter; closed Mon lunchtime exc bank hols

LOWER CHUTE   SU3153   Map 2
Hatchet ⊗

The Chutes well signposted via Appleshaw off A342, 2½ miles W of Andover

Inside this neatly kept Downland pub there are very low beams, a big winter log fire in front of a splendid seventeenth-century fireback in the huge fireplace, and a mix of captain's chairs and cushioned wheel-backs set neatly around oak tables. The new licensees are friendly, though some readers have felt that there's now less of a country-pub atmosphere. Good bar food includes home-made soup (from £1.50), ploughman's (from £1.70), pâté (£1.75), cheese herbies (£2.25), snails with hot garlic bread or grilled fresh sardines (£2.50), home-cooked ham salad, grilled trout with almonds or roast beef and Yorkshire pudding (£4.50), Mexican beef casserole or braised steak in red wine (£4.75), fillet steak au poivre (£8.50), and puddings like apricot crumble, strawberry cheesecake or chocolate brandy mousse (£1.50). Well kept Adnams, Ballards, Bass, Courage Directors and Wadworths 6X on handpump. Darts, shove-ha'penny, dominoes and piped music. There are seats out on a crazy-paved terrace by the front car park, and on the side grass. *(Recommended by Guy Harris, R H Inns, D P Maguire, Dr and Mrs A K Clarke, Michael Andrews)*

Free house   Licensee Jackie Chapman   Real ale   Meals and snacks   Restaurant tel Chute Standen (026 470) 229   Children in restaurant   Open 11–2.30, 6–11; all day Tues, Thurs and probably Sat

MALMESBURY   ST9287   Map 2
Suffolk Arms

Tetbury Hill; B4014 towards Tetbury, on edge of town

This Virginia creeper-covered stone house has an imaginatively knocked-through bar that uses a stone pillar to support the beams, leaving a big square room around the stairs which climb up apparently unsupported. The comfortable seats include a chintz-cushioned antique settle, sofa and easy chairs as well as captain's chairs and low Windsor armchairs, and there are soft lights among the copper saucepans and warming-pans on the stripped stone walls. What was the restaurant has now been changed into a lounge. Home-made bar food includes sandwiches (from 80p), filled baked potatoes or ploughman's (from £1.50), smoked mackerel pâté (£1.70), sausage and baked potatoes (£1.95), salads (from £2.40), steak and kidney pie (£3.35), chicken Marsala and swordfish steaks. Wadworths IPA and 6X on handpump; attentive service. There are seats on the neat lawns outside. *(Recommended by Alison Hayward, Nick Dowson, Mr and Mrs R Marleyn, P H Fearnley)*

Wadworths   Licensee John Evans   Real ale   Meals and snacks   Children over ten in eating area   Open 10.30–2.30, 6–11 (10.30 in winter)

MARKET LAVINGTON   SU0154   Map 2
Green Dragon ⊗

High Street; B3098 towards Upavon

When several of the Bloomsbury set were staying here in 1908, the mood predictably sank into depths of chilly introspection until Rupert Brooke – always a man to liven up a pub – was brought in as an emergency pick-me-up. Run by an individualist, this pub shows a lot of character in its rambling bar; there are old kitchen chairs, smart dining-room chairs or massive boxy settles, fancy Victorian wallpaper or stripped deal panelling, a Spy cartoon of Sir Henry Irving, photographs of the town in the old days, and Highland views and corn dollies. Good home-made bar food includes soup (95p), sandwiches (from 90p), filled French rolls (from £1.40), ploughman's (£1.75), salads (from £2.45), chilli bean pot (£2.65), liver and bacon or scampi (£3.25), lamb kebab or smoked haddock pie (£3.75), steak and mushroom pie (£3.95), sirloin steak (£5.45) and puddings such as lemon cheesecake or English trifle (from 95p); they use home-cooked and locally bought meat and vegetables (when the latter are not grown in their garden); prices of some dishes may be slightly more in the evenings. Well kept Wadworths IPA and 6X on handpump and wide range of wines. Darts and bar billiards in a raised, communicating section; also shove-ha'penny, dominoes and cribbage; classical piped music. There's a garden fenced off behind the car park. *(Recommended by S Leggate, Ron Walker; more reports please)*

Wadworths   Licensee Gordon Godbolt   Real ale   Meals and snacks (not Sun)   Restaurant (closed Sun) tel Lavington (038 081) 3235   Children (if booked) in restaurant until 8.30 Open 11–2.30, 6–11, though may open longer in afternoons if trade demands; closed evening 25 Dec

NORTON   ST8884 Map 2

Vine Tree ⊗

4 miles from M4 junction 17; A429 towards Malmesbury, then left at Hullavington, Sherston signpost, then follow Norton signposts; in village turn right at Foxley signpost, which takes you into Honey Lane

It's a surprise in this quietly placed country pub to find a décor almost like that of a successful London wine bar – yet it works well, with the atmosphere welcoming and warmly pubby, and clearly appealing to a very broad cross-section of the local community. The three bars which open together have ochre or dark green walls, lots of stripped pine with candles in bottles on the tables (the lighting's very gentle), some old settles, and lively decoration that includes plates and small sporting prints, a cuckoo clock giving cheek to a sonorous grandfather clock, carvings, hop-bines, a mock-up mounted pig's mask and even a working model of a lager-drinking Aussie. Besides well kept Archers Best, Fullers London Pride, Wadworths 6X, a guest beer such as Devenish or Everards Tiger and a beer brewed for them by a Mr Kemp (a light well balanced taste reminiscent of Courage Bitter – good value), they have decent wines. Bar food includes ploughman's (from £1.85), open prawn sandwiches or deep-fried courgettes (£2.50), burgers and nutburgers (£3.25), beef kebabs (£4.25), chicken done in white wine or gammon (£5.95) and steaks (from ten-ounce rump £6.95 to thirty-ounce whoppers £15.95), with game in season; puddings are all home made. There are picnic-table sets under cocktail parasols in a vine-trellised back garden with young trees and tubs of flowers, and a well fenced separate play area with a fine thatched fortress and other goodies – they have stables at the back. *(Recommended by Julie Trott, Drew Smith, Miles Elwell, Ken Wright)*

Free house   Licensees Brian and Tina Mussell   Real ale   Meals and snacks   Restaurant tel Tetbury (0666) 837654   Children in eating area   Open 12–3, 6.30–11; 12–2.30, 7–11 in winter; closed Tues

PITTON   SU2131 Map 2

Silver Plough ★ ⊗

Village signposted from A30 E of Salisbury

The comfortable and spacious Turkey-carpeted front bar in this well run hillside pub is full of interest. The timbered white walls have pictures that include Thorburn and other gamebird prints, original Craven Hill sporting cartoons, and a big naval battle glass-painting; its black beams are strung with hundreds of antique boot-warmers, and there are stretchers, pewter and china tankards, copper kettles, brass and copper jugs, toby jugs, earthenware and glass rolling-pins, painted clogs, glass net-floats, coach-horns and so forth. The comfortable seats include half a dozen red-velvet-cushioned antique oak settles, one elaborately carved beside a very fine reproduction of an Elizabethan oak table. The back bar is broadly similar, though more restrained, with a big winged high-backed settle, cased antique guns, substantial pictures, and – like the front room – flowers on its tables. Food is notable. Though they don't aim to serve many snacks, they do filled freshly baked rolls, fresh vegetable soup (£1.50), home-made pâté (£2.15), a good ploughman's with a handsome choice of cheeses (£2.45) and in the evening chilli con carne or lasagne (£3). Their more substantial bar meals, though, make this a place to eat out in style. With frequent variations, these might include green New Zealand mussels (£3.50), various pasta dishes such as curried crunchy vegetable pasta (£3.75) or smoked chicken and wild mushroom pasta (£4.50), smoked salmon and spinach tartlet with dill and yoghurt sauce (£4.50), skate with black butter (£5.50), lemon sole with sorrel butter or saddle of rabbit (£6.50), calf's liver or salmon with basil sauce (£8.25), loin of veal (£8.75) and lobster with wild mushroom sauce (£10.95); their particular strengths are fresh fish and seafood, and game in season, and choice is best from Wednesdays onwards. Well kept Courage Best and Directors, Wadworths 6X and John Smiths on handpump, decent wines, good country wines, and a worthy range of spirits (Macallan on optic, for instance – always the sign of a licensee who knows his whiskies). The separate skittle alley has a fruit machine, and there may be unobtrusive piped music. There are picnic-table sets and other tables under cocktail parasols on a quiet lawn, with an old pear tree. *(Recommended by J M Watkinson, Ian Scrivens, Dr S P K and C M Linter, J B Whitley, Wayne Brindle, Dr and Mrs A K Clarke, Roy McIsaac)*

Free house   Licensee Michael Beckett   Real ale   Meals and snacks   Restaurant tel Farley (072 272) 266   Children in restaurant and skittle alley   Occasional guitarist   Open 11–2.30, 6–10; opens 7 in winter; may be longer afternoon opening if trade demands; closed 25 Dec

POTTERNE   ST9958   Map 2

George & Dragon ⊗ 🏠

A360 beside Worton turn-off

Through a hatch beyond the pool-room in this extensively restored and recently re-thatched Tudor village inn, there's a unique indoor .22 shooting-gallery. It opens on a twenty-five-yard shoulder-high tube, broad enough at its mouth to rest your elbows in, but narrowing to not much more than the width of the target. The small bull is an electric bell-push, which rings when hit. After your nine shots (two for practice), you pull a rope which lifts a brush from a whitewash bucket to whiten the target for the next marksman. Other features include the exposed old beamed ceiling and fireplace of the original hall, and old bench seating and country-style tables. Bar food includes sandwiches (from 70p), home-made soup (95p), ploughman's (£1.35), filled baked potatoes (from £1.85), salads (from £2.30), home-made steak and kidney or chicken, ham and cheese pie (£2.40), lasagne (£2.40), beef curry or mini-grills (from £2.50), scampi (£4), venison, rabbit and bacon in rich sauce (£5.10), sirloin steak (£5.75) and various puddings such as peach or apple crumble (£1.35); Sunday roasts; good breakfasts. Well kept Wadworths IPA and 6X on handpump; helpful, enthusiastic landlord. A separate room has pool and fruit machine; also, darts, shove-ha'penny, dominoes and cribbage, and there's a full skittle alley in the old stables. A museum of hand-held agricultural implements

---

Please tell us if any Lucky Dips deserve to be upgraded to a main entry – and why. No stamp needed: *The Good Pub Guide*, FREEPOST, London SW10 0BR.

has recently been opened at the pub. There's a pleasant garden and a sun-trap yard with a grapevine. The simple bedrooms are good value. *(Recommended by B K Plumb, Philip King, Roy McIsaac, Peter Ogilvie, Peter Hitchcock, John Parsons, Brian Barefoot)*

Wadworths   Licensee Roger Smith   Real ale   Meals and snacks (not Mon)   Children in pool-room   Open 11.30–2.30, 6.30–11 all year   Bedrooms tel Devizes (0380) 2139; £11.50/£21.50

RAMSBURY   SU2771   Map 2

Bell ⊗

Village signposted off B4192 (still shown as A419 on many maps) NW of Hungerford, or from A4 W of Hungerford

The atmosphere in this very well kept and civilised pub is rather elegant, and the barman wears a dark suit and tie. Two bar areas, separated by a chimney-breast with a wood-burning stove, have polished tables, fresh flowers, and window settles in two sunny bay windows (one with Victorian stained-glass panels); no noisy machines or piped music. Bar food includes soup (£1.35), salads (from £2.80), spaghetti bolognese, toad-in-the-hole or ratatouille (£2.80) and speciality pies (£3.25). Well kept Wadworths IPA and 6X on handpump; friendly, attentive service. There are picnic tables on the raised lawn. Roads lead from this quiet village into the downland on all sides. *(Recommended by Lyn and Bill Capper, Frank Cummins, GB, CH, Peter Hitchcock, Mrs H Church, Mr and Mrs W Smurthwaite, Christine Herxheimer)*

Free house   Licensee Guy Marshall   Real ale   Meals and snacks (not Sat evening) Restaurant (to stay open until 4, 3.30 Sun) tel Marlborough (0672) 20230   Children in room between bar and restaurant and in restaurant   Open 10–2.30, 6–11

SALISBURY   SU1429   Map 2

The pubs mentioned here are all within a short stroll of one another. The Old George, which used to be one of the finest old inns – Shakespeare probably performed in its yard – has now been rebuilt as a shopping arcade, but it's still very well worth visiting for its façade, and the upstairs coffee shop which gives some idea of what it was like inside

Haunch of Venison ★

1 Minster Street, opposite Market Cross

This is the city's most ancient pub and its chief attraction is that it manages to combine great character with an utterly genuine atmosphere of cheerful friendliness. There are beams in the ochre ceiling of the cosy main bar, a black and white tiled floor, stout red cushioned oak benches built into its timbered walls, genuinely old pictures, and an old-fashioned – and as far as we know unique – pewter bar counter with a rare set of antique taps for gravity-fed spirits and liqueurs. Well kept Courage Best and Directors on handpump. An upper panelled room has a splendid fireplace that dates back some six-hundred years, to when this was the church house for St Thomas's, just behind, as well as antique settles and a carved seat around several small tables. In 1903 workmen found a smoke-preserved mummified hand holding some eighteenth-century playing-cards in here; it's now behind glass in a small wall slit. Lunchtime bar food – served in the lower half of the restaurant – includes sandwiches (from 75p, toasties 15p extra), home-made soup (95p), baked potatoes (from £1), ploughman's (from £1.60), home-made pies such as tasty game, ham and mushroom or splendid steak and kidney (£1.50), savoury pancakes (from £2.50) and good puddings; attentive and friendly service.

If you stay overnight in an inn or hotel, they are allowed to serve you an alcoholic drink at any hour of the day or night.

(Recommended by Gordon and Daphne, S J A Velate, Chris Fluck, J P Berryman, B S Bourne, Neville Burke, Dr A V Lewis, Nigel Paine, Dr John Innes, Roy McIsaac, Gwen and Peter Andrews, R J Bryan, William Fairclough, Heather Sharland)

Courage   Licensees Antony and Victoria Leroy   Real ale   Snacks (not Sun evening) and lunchtime meals   Restaurant tel Salisbury (0722) 22024; closed Sun evenings Oct–June Children in eating area and restaurant   Nearby parking may be difficult   Open 11–11 all year

King's Arms 🏨

St John Street; the main one-way street entering city centre from S

This creaky old inn, with Tudor timbering, has fireplaces of the same Chilmark stone as the cathedral, so may be just as old. The dark-panelled bars have red leatherette benches built around their walls: one has attractive Windsor armchairs under its heavy beams, with carving around its fireplace and door; the other, more local, has darts, a trivia machine and maybe piped music. The panelling in the pleasantly old-fashioned residents' lounge upstairs and in the heavily beamed restaurant, which has snug high-backed settles, is considerably older. Well kept Ushers Best and Ruddles County on handpump; sandwiches (evenings only), pâté, basket meals, hot daily specials and salads from a buffet counter. Car parking (welcome in this city) free by arrangement with the neighbouring White Hart. *(Recommended by Dr John Innes, Margaret Drazin, Heather Sharland)*

Host (Watneys)   Licensee P R Craven   Real ale   Meals and snacks   Restaurant   Children in eating area   Open 11–2.30, 6–11   Bedrooms tel Salisbury (0722) 27629; £32B/£48B

Red Lion 🏨

Milford Street

The stylishly medieval restaurant in this extensively renovated grand coaching-inn is as old as it looks – there's a tradition that this part of the hotel housed the draughtsmen who worked on the cathedral. The knocked-through rooms of the bar have some antique settles and leather chairs as well as more modern, comfortable button-back banquettes, coaching prints on the timbered walls and piped music. An overflow into the spacious and sedately attractive hall, with old-fashioned furniture, has some curiosities such as the elaborate gothick longcase clock with little skeletons ringing bells to mark the hours. Lunchtime bar food includes sandwiches (from 90p), ploughman's (£1.75), pâté (£1.65), sausages (£1.70), and gammon salad or Spanish chicken (£2.50). Well kept Bass, Courage Best, Ruddles Best, Ushers Best and Wadworths 6X on handpump; a beer festival is held here in July. The sheltered and creeper-hung courtyard (dotted with quite a pride of cheery red lions) has a nicely old-fashioned glass loggia sheltering a row of cushioned Windsor armchairs. *(Recommended by R H Inns; more reports please)*

Free house   Licensee Michael Maidment   Real ale   Meals and snacks (lunchtime) Restaurant   Children in eating area   Nearby daytime parking may be difficult   Open 11–2.30, 6–11   Bedrooms tel Salisbury (0722) 23334; £45B/£65B

SANDY LANE   ST9668 Map 2

George

A342 Chippenham–Devizes

This fine Georgian building, overlooking a small green just off the main road, looks more like a small manor house than a pub. The well kept main bar is carpeted, with comfortable cushioned wall benches, decorative wall beams, horsebrasses, old pistols and photographs and a log fire; an arch leads through to the attractive back lounge. Good value home-made food includes soup (£1), burgers (£1.60), ploughman's (£1.80), very good moussaka, fisherman's pie (£2.95), plaice (£3.20), steak and kidney pie, steak (£5.80), duck (£5.90) and cold puddings. Well kept Wadworths 6X and IPA; pleasant, friendly service. There are wooden benches and tables in front of the pub, with picnic-table sets on the neat side lawn. *(Recommended by Frank Cummins, S G Game, David R Crafts, Tom Evans)*

Wadworths   Licensee T J M Allington   Real ale   Meals and snacks   Children in eating area (lunchtime)   Open 11–2.30, 6–10.30 (11 Sat) all year

SEMLEY   ST8926   Map 2

Benett Arms   ★ ⊗ ⇔

Turn off A350 N of Shaftesbury at Semley Ind Estate signpost, then turn right at Semley signpost

Across the green from the church, this very welcoming small village inn has good bar food served by a neat waitress: home-made soup (£1), very good ploughman's (from £2), omelette (£2.35), chilli con carne (£2.75), local ham and egg (£2.95), salads (from £3.15), steak and kidney pie (£3.15), home-made venison pie (£3.55), fresh trout (£3.65), gammon with pineapple (£3.95), scampi (£4.45), steak (£6.30), and home-made puddings such as apple pie (£1.25); children's menu. Well kept Gibbs Mew Salisbury and Godsons Black Horse on handpump; good house wines and a wide range of spirits. Dominoes, cribbage and piped music. The two cosy rooms of the bar, separated by a flight of five carpeted steps, have deep leather sofas and armchairs, one or two settles and pews, ornaments on the mantelpiece over the log fire, a pendulum wall clock, carriage lamps for lighting, and hunting prints. Down by the thatched-roof bar servery, the walls are stripped stone; upstairs, there is hessian over a dark panelling dado. There are seats outside. If you stay, they do good breakfasts. Well behaved dogs welcome. *(Recommended by John Nash, Philip King, Colin and Caroline, Nigel Paine, Tom Evans)*

Gibbs Mew   Licensees Annie and Joseph Duthie   Real ale   Meals and snacks   Restaurant Children in eating area, restaurant and upper bar   Open 10.30–2.30, 6–11; closed 25 Dec Bedrooms tel East Knoyle (074 783) 221; £19.50B/£32B

STOURTON   ST7734   Map 2

Spread Eagle   ⇔

Church Lawn; follow Stourhead signpost off B3092, N of junction with A303 just W of Mere

It's the lovely setting, among the other elegant National Trust stone buildings at the head of Stourhead Lake, that attracts so many leisurely parties of mostly older customers. There are very well spaced solid tables, antique panel-back settles, studded leather chairs, library chairs, a green sofa, and handsome fireplaces with good log fires in winter; decorations include smoky old sporting prints, coaching prints, ones of Stourhead, and standard lamps or swan's-neck brass wall lamps; one room by the entrance has armchairs, a longcase clock and a corner china cupboard. Lunchtime bar food includes sandwiches (from 95p), hot dishes (from £1.20) and salads (from £4.20); in the evening there's also fried mushrooms stuffed with Dorset pâté (£1.90), toasted sandwiches (£2), scampi (£4.10), chicken Kiev (£5.05), gammon with pineapple (£5.60) and sirloin steak (£6.90). Well kept Bass and Charringtons IPA on handpump kept under light top pressure; friendly staff; darts, shove-ha'penny and cribbage. There are benches in the courtyard behind. *(Recommended by Pamela and Merlyn Horswell, Gwen and Peter Andrews, S V Bishop, Lyn and Bill Capper)*

Bass   Licensee R M M Wills   Real ale   Meals and snacks   Restaurant   Children in restaurant and bars at lunchtime   Open 11–2.30, 7–11; closed 25 Dec   Bedrooms tel Bourton (0747) 840587; £25B/£35B

Please let us know what you think of a pub's bedrooms. No stamp needed: *The Good Pub Guide*, FREEPOST, London SW10 0BR.

WEST DEAN   SU2527   Map 2
Red Lion
Village signposted from A27 in Whiteparish

Set among lime and chestnut trees in a peaceful downland village, this little tiled brick inn looks down over a small green to a pond with ducks, geese and flag irises – clean and fresh, as a small stream flows through it. The simple lounge (which on the left spreads into a dining area) has flowery-covered easy chairs around rustic tables, sailing-ship plates, gundog pictures and miniature cricket bats signed by Test teams on its cream walls, with an open fire in winter and maybe unobtrusive piped music; the small plain back public bar has darts, pool, dominoes, cribbage, fruit machine, space game and juke box. A wide choice of bar food in generous helpings, and using fresh produce, includes burgers or hot dogs (from 85p), sandwiches (from 95p), basket meals (from £1.75), cold platters (from £1.95), vegetarian dishes (£2.50), home-made curries (from £2.50), home-made steak and kidney pie or pork chop (£2.95), and Sunday roasts (£3.25); well kept Flowers Original, Fremlins and Whitbreads Pompey Royal and Strong Country on handpump. There are picnic-table sets on the front terrace. (*Recommended by J Walsh, G S Burrows*)

Whitbreads   Licensee John-Paul Sharp   Real ale   Meals and snacks   Children welcome Open 10–2.30, 6–11   Bedrooms tel Lockerley (0794) 40469; £15/£27

WOOTTON RIVERS   SU1963   Map 2
Royal Oak ⊗
Village signposted from A346 Marlborough–Salisbury and B3087 E of Pewsey

In an attractive tucked-away Pewsey Vale village by the Kennet and Avon Canal, this pretty sixteenth-century thatched pub is very popular for its wide choice of good value food. Lots of specials might include crispy vegetables with savoury dip (£2.25), stuffed vine-leaves (£2.75), vegetable bake (£3.50), home-made steak and kidney pie (£5), roast rack of lamb (£8.50) or grilled Dover sole (£11.50). Regular dishes run from soup or sandwiches (from £1) through ploughman's (£1.60), basket meals (from £1.60) and lots of salads to chicken Kiev (£6.50) and steaks (from £7). The L-shaped dining-lounge (where they take table bookings – people do dress up to come and dine here) has a friendly atmosphere, a low ceiling with partly stripped beams, partly glossy white planks, slat-back chairs, armchairs and some rustic settles around good tripod tables and a wood-burning stove; it's decorated with discreetly colourful plates and small mainly local prints, drawings, water-colours and photographs. Well kept Wadworths 6X tapped from the cask, and decent wines (running up to some distinguished ones); friendly service. The timbered bar on the right is comfortably and more or less similarly furnished, though with fewer tables – so seems more spacious; it has pool, dominoes, cribbage, fruit machine, shut-the-box and juke box. There are tables under cocktail parasols in the back gravelled yard by the car park. (*Recommended by Stan Edwards, Jim Gavin, Anna Jeffery, Jack Charles, Lady Quinny, Dr and Mrs A K Clarke, T E Cheshire*)

Free house   Licensees John and Rosa Jones   Real ale   Meals and snacks (not Sun evenings Oct–June, nor 26 Dec)   Restaurant   Children in restaurant and area partly set aside   Open 11–11; 11–3, 6.30–11 in winter; midnight supper licence; closed 25 Dec   Bedrooms (in adjoining house) tel Marlborough (0672) 810322; £13.50 (£15S)/£25S

Lucky Dip

Besides the fully inspected pubs, you might like to try these Lucky Dips recommended to us and described by readers (if you do, please send us reports):

Aldbourne [SU2675], *Blue Boar*: Quiet fifteenth-century true village pub set by the green; stuffed boar's head over attractive inglenook fireplace of its single bar, well kept Wadworths 6X on handpump and good but very limited bar snacks *(Ian Howard, Neville Burke)*; *Crown*: Busy, comfortable and very welcoming Ushers pub with good bar food and real ale; the village is pretty *(Ian Howard)*

Alderbury [SU1827], *Green Dragon*: Much-modernised fifteenth-century village pub with Courage real ales – Dickens, using it as the Blue Dragon in *Martin Chuzzlewit*, cheekily named its landlady Mrs Pugin after the wife of his friend the neighbouring grandee (who designed the Houses of Parliament) *(LYM)*

☆ **Amesbury** [High St; SU1541], *George*: Gibbs Mew real ales, bar food, restaurant and daytime coffee-lounge in rambling coaching-inn with unusually extensive surviving coachyard; has gradually been undergoing thorough refurbishment; pool and other games in cheerful public bar; bedrooms *(Roger Broadie, Michael Samuel, Margo and Peter Thomas, LYM)*

Amesbury [Church St], *Antrobus Arms*: Coaching-inn with décor reflecting its history, bar food and drinks unexpectedly at normal prices despite plush surroundings; bedrooms *(R H Inns)*; [Earls Court Rd] *Greyhound*: Smart pub with a somewhat up-nice market lounge, nice atmosphere and good beer *(Dr and Mrs A K Clarke)*

Atworth [ST8666], *White Hart*: Friendly pub in nice Cotswold village with superb value three-course Sun roast, very popular with locals *(Brian and Rosemary Wilmot)*

Avebury [A361; SU0969], *Red Lion*: Right in the heart of the stone circles – much-modernised comfortable thatched pub with Whitbreads and other real ales such as Wadworths, friendly staff, simple but good food including steaks in interesting dining-room *(GB, CH, Graham Richardson, LYM)*

Axford [SU2370], *Red Lion*: Roadside village pub with friendly informal bar service, wood floor and beams and local clientele; real ales such as Wadworths 6X, Archers Village, Whitbreads Strong Country straight from the cask, bar food which may include local fish *(Anne Morris)*

☆ **Barford St Martin** [junction A30/B3098 W of Salisbury; SU0531], *Green Dragon*: Old-fashioned panelled front bar with big log fire and larger games-bar in pub with decent bar food, well kept Badger real ales, tables in little courtyard, children's playthings; bedrooms simple, clean and cosy *(PJP, R H Inns, S G Game, Colonel and Mrs L N Smyth, LYM)*

Beckington [Bath Rd/Warminster Rd; ST8051], *Woolpack*: Used to be a stop-off for condemned men on the way to the gibbet for a last drink; they say one unfortunate individual refused this option, was taken up the hill and hanged just five minutes before his reprieve arrived from London; good range of food *(Mark Spurlock)*

Berwick St John [ST9323], *Talbot*: Unspoilt heavy-beamed bar in friendly Ebble Valley pub, huge inglenook fireplace, well kept Badger real ales, sandwiches and ploughman's (summer), tables on back lawn with swings for children; start GWG35 *(LYM)*

Biddestone [ST8773], *Biddestone Arms*: Well kept village pub with simple but comfortable and friendly lounge, games in public bar, well kept Ushers Best and Wadworths 6X, good value bar food, swings in fairy-lit garden *(Mrs Carol Mason, Mr and Mrs John Smyth, BB)*; *White Horse*: Beautifully placed, very welcoming, super home-made casseroles *(John Broughton)*

Boscombe [Tidworth Rd; SU2038], *Plough*: Very enthusiastic new licensee who is progressively upgrading and updating (tastefully), with plans for widening range of beers, adding range of food and enlarging garden *(Mark Spurlock)*

Box [A4, Bath side; ST8268], *Northey Arms*: Homely décor, coal fire, potted plants, friendly landlord, piped music, Wadworths ale, appetising choice of bar food at reasonable prices *(Mr and Mrs E J Smith)*

Bradford-on-Avon [35 Market St; ST8261], *Ancient Fowl*: Included as a fine place to eat at – a restaurant really, with bar attached *(Graeme Barnes)*; [Silver St] *Bunch of Grapes*: A converted shop that's now a really delightful and spotlessly clean pub with a charming landlord; friendly, warm atmosphere and cheap good food in big helpings *(Derrick Turner, Graeme Barnes)*; [top of Masons Lane] *Castle*: Good mix of people, mainly local but very friendly, and an interesting matchbox collection in the main bar; Ushers *(Andy Mason)*; [1 Church St; car park off A363 Trowbridge rd, beside bridge over Avon, in centre] *Swan*: Good bar food and three ales in recently enlarged and improved bar of old coaching-inn; bedrooms *(Ian Blackwell, GDPT, LYM)*; [55 Frome Rd; on bottom rd out, by big car park by stn] *Three Horseshoes*: Cosy, comfortable one-roomed pub close to canal bridge, Watneys-related real ales, restaurant *(Roger Huggins)*

Bremhill [ST9773], *Dumbpost*: Extremely good beer and food at low prices; long view from the bar, garden *(R Inns)*

Broad Chalke [SU0325], *Queens Head*: Modest frontage, real ales, good choice of bar food, efficient service, garden; bedrooms *(Canon and Mrs G Hollis)*

Broad Hinton [A361 Swindon–Devizes; SU1076], *Bell*: Old country pub, beautifully kept and furnished, good bar food *(F E M Hardy)*; [in village, signposted off A361] *Crown*: Big open-plan bar with good home-cooked bar meals, help-yourself salad bar and restaurant section, cheerful piped music, unusual gilded inn-sign; bedrooms *(LYM)*

☆ **Bromham** [ST9665], *Greyhound*: Two bars – back one has jade and mug collection, seashells and a beautifully lit well; front bar has pool and darts; very friendly landlord, good food and a good choice of real ales, skittle alley, big garden, small intimate restaurant *(P B Webb, Lady Quinny)*

Broughton Gifford [ST8763], *Fox & Hounds*: Welcoming, friendly pub with well kept beer *(Dave Marks, Tiff Wilson)*

Burbage [A338 Marlborough–Andover; SU2361], *Bullfinch*: Friendly, short basic menu of well cooked and presented food, hot food on Sun too; children welcome *(Dave Braisted)*

Burcombe [SU0730], *Ship*: Well kept Gibbs Mew and cheerfully served palatable food in village local *(Roy McIsaac)*

Burton [ST8179], *Old House at Home*: Good choice of Wadworths real ales, varied menu with generous helpings of beautifully cooked food, log fire *(J R Jewitt)*; *Plume of Feathers*: Comfortable, friendly and simply furnished village inn, with log fire and well behaved alsatian; good Ushers and acceptable house wine; staggering range of good bar food including Sinhalese dishes and an award-wining pasty-shaped steak and kidney pie among many other dishes; bedrooms *(Joy Heatherley)*

Castle Combe [ST8477], *Castle*: Jocular licensee creates good atmosphere in old-world country pub, good service and choice of ales in nicely furnished bars, quite good bar food; bedrooms *(E G Parish)*; [The Gibb – OS Sheet 173 reference 838791] *Salutation*: Lovely old pub hung with colourful flower baskets in tiny hamlet (pronounced The Jib), very good Whitbreads, vast menu including lots of interesting specials, new restaurant in converted barn adjoining *(Peter and Rose Flower)*

Castle Eaton [High St; SU1495], *Red Lion*: Particularly nice in summer, with pleasant garden *(Ewan McCall, Roger Huggins, Tom McLean)*

Chapmanslade [ST8247], *Three Horse Shoes*: Popular homely local, plenty of atmosphere, quick pleasant service, well kept Ushers, good food reasonably priced, separate restaurant, small garden *(Charlie Salt, E A Turner)*

Chilton Foliat [SU3270], *Wheatsheaf*: Friendly pub, good service, small choice of decent bar food *(John Hill)*

Chippenham [Market Pl; ST9173], *Rose & Crown*: Tudor pub whose licensees, taking over in 1985, won their brewery's Innkeeper of the Year competition in 1987; lunchtime bar food, children allowed at lunchtime, barbecues on terrace *(Anon)*

nr **Chippenham** [Pewsham; A4 towards Calne – OS Sheet 173 reference 948712], *Lysley Arms*: Eighteenth-century free house under new management, completely refurbished with olde-worlde bar and open fire, good choice of food including menu for vegetarians and children; play area on pleasant side lawn with picnic tables *(Mr and Mrs D A P Grattan)*

Chiseldon [6 New Rd; SU1879], *Patriots Arms*: Very friendly staff and good beer in theme pub with much military memorabilia including facsimile D-Day tapestry *(Dr and Mrs A K Clarke)*

Coombe Bissett [Blandford Rd (A354); SU1026], *Fox & Goose*: Friendly local with recently refurbished open-plan bars and wide choice of quickly served bar food including takeaway service; real ales; children's section *(Canon G Hollis)*

Corsley [A362 Warminster–Frome; ST8246], *White Hart*: Pleasantly furnished, well kept Bass, good lunchtime and (pricier) evening bar food, close to Longleat Safari Park *(Don Mather)*

Cricklade [SU0993], *Kings Head*: Good beer and sherry, popular food, very friendly staff and landlady *(JMW)*

Dauntsey [Dauntsey Lock; A420 – handy for M4 junctions 16 and 17; ST9782], *Peterborough Arms*: Particularly friendly welcome from landlord and his wife, good selection of food, good choice of real ales including monthly guest, pool-table, lovely location, children's playground *(Pat and Lee Crosby, P and K Davies)*

Derry Hill [ST9570], *Lansdowne Arms*: Good value home cooking in bar and restaurant, lunchtime and evening *(Mr and Mrs D A P Grattan)*

Devizes [Long St; SU0061], *Elm Tree*: Very friendly atmosphere, well kept ale; bedrooms *(Jamie and Sarah Allan, Mr and Mrs F E M Hardy)*; [Maryport St] *Three Crowns*: Friendly town pub with well kept local Wadworths real ales, George I backsword blade (recently found hidden in inn's ex-stables) decorating one hessian wall, seats in small sheltered yard *(BB)*

Dinton [SU0131], *Penruddocke Arms*: Spacious and comfortable country pub, good real ales, country wines, popular bar food, good pub games in public bar *(Dr and Mrs A K Clarke, LYM)*

Downton [A338 Salisbury–Fordingbridge; SU1721], *Bull*: Very long bar in enlarged ex-fishing inn with food including generous sandwiches, cold table and daily hot special, tables in many alcoves, brasses and ancient pistols on walls, dining area at one end; bedrooms *(LYM)*; [High St (A3080)] *Kings Arms*: Goods Gibs Mew Salisbury and

Wiltshire on handpump, very cheap fresh food cooked to order *(Mark Kibble)*; *White Horse*: Fairly big place with Flowers IPA and good bar food including outstanding value Sun lunches; seats outside, children welcome *(Simon Turner, Caroline Bailey)*

East Chisenbury [SU1452], *Red Lion*: Unspoilt and basic country village pub where locals in the old-fashioned snug around the big winter fire function as a sort of garden-ers' brains trust – a pub for devotees of times past, though the beer's keg; very friendly licensee, play area on lawn *(Phil and Sally Gorton, LYM)*

East Knoyle [ST8830], *Fox & Hounds*: Though enlarged still has nice friendly country atmosphere; good bar food including home-made pasties and puddings, superb view over Vale of Blackmoor, seats in garden and on village green *(Anne and Alan Oakley)*

Easton Royal [SU2060], *Bruce Arms*: One very basic room with bare floor, benches and tables, another with old easy chairs, Whitbreads real ale tapped from the cask *(Phil Gorton)*

Farleigh Wick [A363 Bath–Bradford; ST8064], *Fox & Hounds*: Good welcome in the several cleanly kept rooms of quiet, relaxing and attractively furnished old-world seventeenth-century Bath-stone pub; well kept Ushers ales, good imaginative food such as big local mushrooms with salad and garlic oil, splendid service, log fire, no music; packed at weekends, lovely garden *(J L and E B Burns, B R Woolmington, E G Parsons)*

Farley [SU2229], *Hook & Glove*: Well kept warm and friendly pub in scenic area, good choice of good reasonably priced food *(Mark Spurlock)*

Fovant [A30 Salisbury–Shaftesbury; SU0128], *Cross Keys*: Fifteenth-century pub with attractive rooms, first-class and well priced bar food (the choice of cheeses for ploughman's is particularly good), separate restaurant, good service, very friendly landlady, nice fire in quiet main bar – no juke box or fruit machine; bedrooms old and attractive *(Philip King, Chris and Val McPhee, Jack and Claudia Russell, Canon G Hollis)*

Ham [SU3362], *Crown & Anchor*: Free house with good choice of beers and draught cider; welcoming, cheerful landlord; well furnished, neat lounge bar; good variety of hot food at reasonable prices *(F A Rabagliati)*

Heddington [ST9966], *Ivy*: Simple thatched village pub with big log fire in good ingle-nook fireplace, low beams, timbered walls, well kept Wadworths real ales tapped from the cask, very limited bar food, children's room; seats outside the picturesque house *(Maureen Hobbs, Tom Evans, LYM)*

Heytesbury [Main St; ST9242], *Red Lion*: Nice comfortable pub, good Watneys-related real ales, pleasant licensees *(Mr and Mrs D R Thornley)*

Highworth [Market Pl; SU2092], *Saracens*

Head: Good popular inn with good food; bedrooms good *(Jenny Cantle)*

Hilperton [ST8659], *Lion & Fiddle*: Cheerful atmosphere, wide choice of good bar snacks and home-cooked meals at very reasonable prices, with fresh vegetables and salads; log fire, well kept Ushers Best, delightful garden, restaurant; ample parking *(Mr and Mrs R A Diaper)*

Hindon [ST9132], *Grosvenor*: Good food and drink, friendly landlord and locals, very good atmosphere *(J M Watkinson)*

☆ **Horningsham** [ST8141], *Bath Arms*: Comfortable pub in pretty village and at gates of Longleat, good food with plenty of variety including superb smoked trout, good service; bedrooms *(Mr and Mrs Maitland, Kathleen and David Caig, Don Mather)*

Landford [off B3079; SU2519], *Cuckoo*: Rustic pub with bantams and penned peacocks and rabbits out by spacious play area; inside best described as simple, with ploughman's and well kept Badger and Wadworths real ales; occasional folk music; children in small room off bar *(Mark Kibble, Phil and Sally Gorton, LYM)*

☆ **Liddington** [just off A419; SU2081], *Village Inn*: Comfortable, clean, welcoming village inn, good value bar food, quiet, pleasant, good range of real ales such as Flowers IPA and Original, Wadworths 6X and a guest beer; bedrooms *(K R Harris, Dr and Mrs A K Clarke, Philip King)*

Limpley Stoke [Lower Limpley Stoke; ST7760], *Limpley Stoke Hotel*: Food well presented, generous, good value, very friendly service, good views, good location for touring; bedrooms comfortable, breakfast very 'full' *(Cecil Eimerl)*

Littleton Drew [B4039 Chippenham–Chipping Sodbury; ST8380], *Plough*: Tiny thatched pub in sleepy little village, amazingly clean and comfortable – nice to find a pub that doesn't do food but just serves good beer *(Peter and Rose Flower)*; *Salutation*: Very friendly place with recently converted and newly furnished barn that provides a new bar and a very good range of bar food *(Mr and Mrs D A P Grattan)*

Lockeridge [signposted off A4 Marlborough –Calne just W of Fyfield – OS Sheet 173 reference 148679; SU1467], *Who'd A Thought It*: Three carpeted areas around small bar, with plush-cushioned Windsor and other chairs, wood-effect tables, fireplace with polished copper hood, welcoming pleasant service, well kept Wadworths IPA and 6X on handpump, big helpings of well presented bar food – simple but good value; tables on back lawn, family-room *(Frank Cummins)*

Longbridge Deverill [ST8740], *George*: Good choice of food and snacks in three cosy bars *(E A Turner)*

Lower Woodford [SU1235], *Wheatsheaf*: Good food, beer in very good condition; very

pleasant atmosphere, though very busy
(*JMW*)

Lydiard Millicent [SU0985], *Sun*: Neat little
pub with friendly service and well kept beer
(*Dr and Mrs A K Clarke*)

☆ **Malmesbury** [Abbey Row; ST9287], *Old Bell*:
Sensitively redecorated old hotel looking
across churchyard to Norman abbey, traditionally furnished, with Edwardian pictures
and recently uncovered early thirteenth-
century hooded stone fireplace, attractively
old-fashioned garden, Ushers Best and
Wadworths 6X on handpump; mixed views
on food value for money, and bar can get
smoky, but has a distinctive traditional
appeal; bedrooms rather expensive (*Pamela
and Merlyn Horswell, David Gittins, Rob and
Gill Weeks, LYM*)

Malmesbury [29 High St], *Kings Arms*:
Historic old coaching-inn with modest bars,
lounge and restaurant; full of character with
extensive and interesting range of home-
cooked food (without chips; Wiltshire ham a
speciality); cosy restaurant off lounge; real
ales; bedrooms unpretentious (*SP*)

☆ **Manton** [SU1668], *Up The Garden Path*:
Small unspoilt village pub, well kept inside
and out, central bar, some tables in room on
left, darts in small snug on right, padded wall
settles, stools and chairs, locomotive pictures, hanging plants, house plants on tables;
well kept real ales such as Archers BB,
Flowers Original and Hook Norton Best,
three farm ciders, decent traditional food,
picnic-table sets on neat lawn by flower bed,
pleasant friendly service, discreet piped
music (*Frank Cummins, Neville Burke, T E
Cheshire*)

☆ **Marlborough** [High St; SU1869], *Sun*: Good
atmosphere in bar on right with black panelling, heavy sloping beams, big fireplace,
plainer lounge on the left, well kept Ushers
ales, bar food, seats in small sheltered back
courtyard; bedrooms rather basic, a do-it-
yourself element in the breakfasts (*Neville
Burke, T E Cheshire, Mr and Mrs A W Medus,
Miss A M Burton, David Gittins, LYM*)

☆ **Marlborough** [High St], *Wellington Arms*:
Friendly atmosphere in cosy well run pub
with lots of commemorative and decorative
mugs hanging from ceiling, newspapers on
canes, steps down to eating area with wide
range of good bar food including soup,
ploughman's, salads, omelettes, steaks and
dishes such as ham or stuffed peppers; well
kept Flowers on handpump, tables in courtyard; bedrooms (*P J and S E Robbins, BB*)

Marlborough [High St], *Castle & Ball*: Well
kept and comfortable small bar with well
kept Wadworths 6X (*Dr and Mrs A K Clarke*);
[High St] *Green Dragon*: Good choice of
well prepared food, good value; bedrooms
(*F E M Hardy*); [The Parade] *Lamb*: Very
good cheap food, friendly atmosphere, real
ale served from barrel behind bar (*T E
Cheshire*); [London Rd] *Roebuck*: Very wel-

coming new licensee doing extremely well for
this old coaching-inn, a Grand Met hotel – so
tied to Ushers (*F E M Hardy*)

Marston Meysey [SU1297], *Spotted Cow*:
Raised open fireplace, civilised atmosphere;
friendly, knowledgeable staff, well kept
Ruddles County (*Ewan McCall, Roger
Huggins, Tom McLean*)

Melksham [Market Pl; ST9063], *Kings Arms*:
Restored sixteenth-century coaching-inn in
town centre, well kept Wadworths beer, bar
food, tables in cobbled courtyard,
restaurant; bedrooms well furnished
(*Alan Bickley*)

☆ **Mere** [Castle St; ST8132], *Old Ship*: Interesting sixteenth-century building with open fire
in cosy hotel bar, lots of games in spacious
and wholly separate public bar; bar food,
Badger Best under light blanket pressure;
children allowed in eating area; bedrooms
(*E G Parish, Mr and Mrs P W Dryland, KC,
Hans Swift, John Innes, PJP, P J and S E
Robbins, LYM*)

Middle Woodford [SU1136], *Wheatsheaf*:
Old and interesting family pub in the lovely
Woodford valley; warm, welcoming and
comfortable with friendly service and a very
good range of reasonably priced and generously served food, nice restaurant; no juke
box, big garden (*J and M Walsh, Mark
Spurlock*)

Milton Lilbourne [SU1860], *Three
Horseshoes*: Pleasant country free house
with well kept real ales amd good value food
(*DBB*)

Minety [SU0290], *White Horse*: Pleasant and
friendly atmosphere, good home-cooked bar
food including fresh fish (*Mrs C Tuohy*)

Monkton Farleigh [ST8065], *Kings Arms*:
Fine local with super atmosphere and
splendid landlord (*Dr and Mrs A K Clarke*)

Netherhampton [SU1029], *Victoria & Albert*:
Cosy, friendly and interesting thatched pub
with reliably good beer and nice crab pâté
(*R H Inns, Dr and Mrs A K Clarke*)

Newton Toney [off A338 Swindon–
Salisbury; SU2140], *Malet Arms*: Well kept
Ushers and Wadworths 6X, good food,
reasonable prices (*S White, T Kinning*)

Nunton [SU1526], *Radnor Arms*: Friendly
atmosphere in spacious lounge bar with good
food seven days a week, big garden (*William
Dickson*)

Pewsey [A345 Marlborough rd; SU1560],
French Horn: Lovely furniture made from
local elm in central carpeted lounge, cosy
atmosphere, warm welcome, open fires, well
kept Wadworths IPA, 6X and Old Timer,
limited choice of good value food; darts,
pool and so forth in public bar, piped music
or juke box, Guinness cartoons in eating area
(*Ned Edwards*)

Porton [just off Winterslow Rd; SU1936],
Porton: Good range of Gibbs Mew beers and
good value food, cosy in winter; satellite
television in public bar; bedrooms

reasonably priced *(Mark Spurlock)*
Poulshot [ST9559], *Raven*: Popular pub, small, intimate lounge and bar, well kept Wadworths real ales, friendly efficient barmaid, nice garden; the brewery dray horses stop here for a pint on their way to their fortnight's summer holiday *(Roger Huggins, A J Triggle)*
Purton [B4041 Wootton Bassett–Cricklade; SU0887], *Ghost Train*: Friendly old stone pub, good helpings of good food, Courage Directors on handpump, darts and two pooltables in games-room, skittle alley, children's playground *(Pat and Lee Crosby)*
Salisbury [Castle St; SU1429], *Avon Brewery*: Good service, exceptional value for money, with the busy atmosphere of a thriving London pub at lunchtime; superb sandwiches include unparalleled bacon ones with several crispy rashers, and other food is good value too; clean bar nicely decorated with old prints, comfortable chairs, notably good landlord, well kept Huntsman Royal Oak; back garden, parking nearby, occasional folk music; children welcome *(William Fairclough, Col E Richardson, R H Inns, Byrne Sherwood)*
Salisbury [Harnham Rd – at southernmost ring rd roundabout (towards A354 and A338) an unclassified rd not signposted City Centre leads to pub], *Rose & Crown*: Worth a visit for the view – almost identical to that in the most famous Constable painting of Salisbury Cathedral; elegantly restored inn with friendly beamed and timbered bar, popular simple bar food, Bass real ale, charming garden running down to River Avon, picture-window bedrooms in smart modern extension as well as the more traditional ones in the original building *(LYM)*
Salisbury [The Maltings], *Bishops Mill*: Tastefully decorated and very spacious new split-level place with pricey restaurant on the upper level, wide range of drinks in big bar, views of River Avon *(Mark Spurlock)*; [Market Sq] *City*: Fine central pub with very pleasant décor, well kept real ale; fairly quiet even on Sat night *(J Mitchell)*; [New St] *New Inn*: Creaky-beamed ancient timbered local with good choice of simple food, friendly atmosphere, Badger beers *(Gordon and Daphne, BB)*; [St John St] *White Hart*: Former coaching-inn, rebuilt late eighteenth century, now a THF hotel – good buffet with help-yourself salads *(DP)*; *Wyndham Arms*: Home-brew pub opened 1987, brewing Gilberts First Brew (GFB) and HBS *(David Fisher)*
Seend [ST9461], *Bell*: Traditional and very friendly country local with well kept beer and good food including home-made soup and sandwiches prepared by the landlord's daughter; well kept Wadworths IPA and 6X, beautiful garden; children allowed in dining-room; quarter-mile from canal *(T C and A R Newell, BCL, T P Heavisides)*
Seend, *Barge*: This former canalside pub

has closed down
Semington [A350 2 miles S of Melksham – OS Sheet 173 reference 898608; ST8960], *Somerset Arms*: Long room with drinks bar at one end and food-order bar at the other, leading into another room where you can reserve tables, with yet another room at the back; beams, carpets, chintz-upholstered wall settles and stools, cushions on tub chairs; quite attractive artificial flower displays, brassware, watercolours for sale, piped pop music; wide choice of good value cheerfully served bar food, well kept Watneys-related real ales, garden *(Frank Cummins, B R Woolmington)*
Shalbourne [SU3163], *Plough*: Popular village pub with friendly welcome and well kept beer *(Dr and Mrs A K Clarke)*
Sherston [ST8585], *Carpenters Arms*: Lovely comfortable country Whitbreads pub with scrubbed wooden floors and tables, good open fire; the dining extension hasn't spoilt the attractive garden; charming helpful landlady, good beer and great food *(Roger Huggins)*; [B4040 Malmesbury–Chipping Sodbury – OS Sheet 173 reference 854859] *Rattlebone*: Seventeenth-century free house with two well furnished beamed and stone-walled bars; public bar with fruit machine, hexagonal pool-table and table skittles, small central room; big dining-room with window settles, Windsor-back chairs, polished tables, big stone fireplace; well kept Archers Village and Wadworths 6X on handpump, good choice of lunchtime and evening bar food, pebbled terrace, attractive walled back garden *(Frank Cummins)*
Stapleford [Warminster Rd; SU0637], *Pelican*: Immaculately kept by new licensees from Yorkshire, long rectangular room now largely (though not too largely) a restaurant, with very promising food – soup served in tureens with melba toast, curry with proper side dishes *(WHBM)*
Stibb Green [SU2363], *Three Horseshoes*: Olde-worlde beams and inglenooks, well kept Wadworths, real cider, friendly landlord and locals and very good food *(L M Alen)*
Stockton [just off A36 Salisbury–Warminster, near A303; ST9738], *Carriers*: Recently upgraded and enlarged with bar food and good selection of beer *(Mark Spurlock)*
Sutton Mandeville [ST9828], *Lancers*: Good food and very pleasant service *(Heather Hodd)*
Swindon [Prospect Hill; SU1485], *Beehive*: Very interesting pub oozing with character, very friendly, good Morrells beer *(Lady Quinny)*; [Cold Harbour Lane, Blunsdon, off A361; SU1389] *Cold Harbour*: Spacious, well decorated and very comfortable Chef & Brewer pub; good food from a wide fixed menu that includes daily specials, huge piping hot helpings – reasonably priced and

efficiently served; separate restaurant, Watneys-related real ales, pretty garden *(M E A Horler, Jenny Cantle)*; [Newport St] *Wheatsheaf*: Recently extended, without losing simple local appeal; public bar can get rather crowded but exudes cheery atmosphere; well kept Wadworths beer *(Neville Burke, Lady Quinny)*

☆ **Teffont Magna** [ST9832], *Black Horse*: New licensees doing good food with frequently changing specials in pretty pub with comfortable and welcoming lounge; well kept real ales, limited but reasonably priced range of wines, more basic public bar; in attractive village *(H J Stirling, Dr and Mrs A K Clarke, LYM)*

Trowbridge [7/8 Castle St; ST8557], *Peewees*: Live (mainly rock) bands most weekends and the people who go with it – landlord is the singer of the local band; good range of beer and traditional cider *(Andy Mason)*; [Chilmark Rd; left off A363 Bath rd opp Citroen garage, then right, then left again] *Wiltshire Yeoman*: Fine old stone farmhouse with big helpings of good, value-for-money bar food and Ushers beer; almost entirely surrounded by a fairly modern housing estate but you look out on open country from the bar windows; garden *(GDPT)*

nr **Trowbridge** [Strand, Seend; A361 near Keevil – OS Sheet 173 reference 918597], *Lamb*: Popular eating pub, several rooms knocked together though still some attractive furnishings, good value food, children welcome *(LYM)*

Upavon [SU1355], *Antelope*: Well kept Wadworths real ales and good choice of bar food (big helpings) in spotless and friendly seventeenth-century village local; also restaurant (no food Mon evening); three good value bedrooms *(A J Triggle)*

Upper Minety [SU0191], *Old*: Lovely old Cotswold pub with Wadworths real ales *(Dr and Mrs A K Clarke)*

☆ **Wanborough** [2 miles from M4 junction 15; B4507 towards Bishopstone; SU2083], *Black Horse*: Friendly landlord and staff in unpretentious country pub with swings, climbing-frame and assorted livestock in garden – maybe even a lamb; generous helpings of well priced food weekday lunchtimes including fine ploughman's and good home-made faggots (only snacks Sun), well kept Arkells Bitter, separate homely dining-room with own bar serving-hatch; fine views *(Mr and Mrs B E Witcher, R G Ollier)*

☆ **Wanborough**, *Harrow*: Beautiful thatched and whitewashed pub, flowers outside, very welcoming and busy in, big fireplaces in each of the two oak-beamed bars, raised floor level at the back, well kept Flowers IPA and Original and maybe Whitbreads Pompey Royal, prompt service, decent food, enjoyable atmosphere *(Jenny Cantle, Tony Bland, Dr and Mrs A K Clarke)*

Wanborough [Upper Wanborough; from

A419 coming through Wanborough, right at crossing, 1½ miles on left], *Olde Shepherds Rest*: Relaxed, friendly and comfortable, very nice food lunchtime and evening *(Neil Barker)*

Westbrook [A3102 about 4 miles E of Melksham; ST9565], *Westbrook Inn*: Big helpings of good value food including mild curries and vegetarian dishes are the main interest in this small and cleanly renovated pub, with farm tools and prints of seventeenth-century German towns on the walls; Watneys-related real ales on handpump, piped music; may be crowded *(Frank Cummins, Aubrey and Margaret Saunders, LYM)*

Westbury [Market Pl; ST8751], *Lopes Arms*: Friendly atmosphere, nice furnishings and decorations, good food, very pleasant landlord; bedrooms *(Mr and Mrs D R Thornley)*

Westwood [main rd; ST8059], *New Inn*: Cheerful pub with oak beams, friendly atmosphere and lovely open fires; well kept beer and good bar food *(Andy Mason)*

Whiteparish [Main St; SU2423], *Village Lantern*: Friendly, lively pub with generous menu; some smartish young customers *(Mark Spurlock)*

☆ **Wilcot** [SU1360], *Golden Swan*: Ancient steeply thatched village inn, very picturesque, with rustic tables on pretty front lawn; well kept Wadworths IPA and 6X in two small rooms of comfortable bar decorated with lots of china jugs and mugs hanging from beams; bar food, friendly old retriever, simple bedrooms, dining-room *(Dr and Mrs A K Clarke, BB)*

Wilton [North St; SU0931], *Six Bells*: One of Ushers' most successful refurbishments in this smart little town with historic house and carpet factory *(Dr and Mrs A K Clarke)*

Wingfield [ST8256], *Poplars*: Friendly pub with well kept Wadworths ales and own cricket pitch *(LYM)*

Winterslow [A30, W of junction with A343; SU2332], *Pheasant*: Big welcoming roadside inn; bedrooms *(Dr and Mrs A K Clarke)*

Woodborough [Bottlesford – OS Sheet 173 reference 112592; SU1059], *Seven Stars*: Although difficult to find, this rather smart pub is worth the detour; an interesting-looking menu, little rooms, magazines and so forth *(Dr and Mrs A K Clarke)*

Wootton Bassett [High St; SU0682], *Angel*: Pleasant sixteenth-century coaching-inn, well kept Flowers, friendly atmosphere; lounge area leads back to bistro with wide choice of reasonably priced food; bedrooms *(Keith Garley)*

Wroughton [SU1480], *White Hart*: Bar food and Wadworths real ales in spacious lounge with old stone fireplace, lively public bar and skittle alley; handy for M4 junction 16 *(LYM)*

☆ **Wylye** [just off A303; SU0037], *Bell*: Beautiful old pub, comfortable, friendly and spotlessly kept; tables set out rather formally in restaurant style, but food above average, well cooked and well presented; pleasant service, reasonable wine list *(Stella Crist, Roy McIsaac, B H Pinsent, Mr and Mrs P W Dryland)*

Zeals [A303; ST7832], *Hunters Lodge*: Good food and service, helpings almost too generous – speciality steak and kidney pie made with Guinness *(Mr Edwicker)*

Yorkshire

Yet again this has been an area of tremendous change, at least from the point of view of this Guide. There are new licensees at several old favourites: the Game Cock at Austwick, the Buck at Buckden, the Garden Gate in Leeds, the Fountaine at Linton in Craven (they previously notched up a good record at the Craven Arms in Appletreewick), the Kings Head in Masham, the White Horse above Rosedale Abbey and the Fox & Hounds at Starbotton (advances in kitchen and bedrooms). Besides several pubs making their way back into these pages after an absence (including the interesting Old Hall at Heckmondwike, doing well under its new Sam Smiths colours), completely new entries include the Kings Arms in the lovely village of Askrigg (on balance perhaps our favourite of all these new entries), the friendly Crown charmingly tucked away at Bolton Percy, the Abbey Inn opposite Byland Abbey (better known as Mrs Bush's in its former days, a humble place with just two owners from the start of this century until it was auctioned a couple of years ago – it's been wholly reworked inside, to great advantage), the neatly kept Devonshire Arms at Cracoe (Maurice Jaques' new place – he formerly made a great success of the Bull at Broughton), the homely Red Lion up in the Dales at Langthwaite, the idiosyncratic Sair in Linthwaite (run with great verve by that compulsive brewer Ron Crabtree), the well kept Half Moon up above Pateley Bridge, the tie-filled Nags Head at Pickhill (distinguished food), the civilised Sawley Arms at Sawley (its soups and puddings are specially prized), the Fat Cat in Sheffield (lots of good beers, interesting food, a no-smoking room) and the lively Frog & Parrot there (it brews the strongest draught beer in the world), the Boat by the River Don at Sprotborough (very popular since its conversion to a pub a year or two ago), the quietly convivial Royal Oak at Staveley, the enthusiastically run Buck at Thornton Watlass (if you're reading this before Christmas 1988 you'll get a chance to see what its bar looks like in the sixth episode of the latest All Creatures Great and Small series then) and the Old Hall at Threshfield (done out very successfully over the last couple of years). Among older favourites, the Malt Shovel at Oswaldkirk still holds the palm. Looking to the end of the chapter, among the Lucky Dip entries there ones to note particularly at the moment are the Birch Hall at Beck Hole, Strines at Bradfield, Golden Cock at Farnley Tyas, Cow & Calf at Grenoside, Shears in Halifax, the entries we list for Helmsley (for its size far too well supplied with good pubs), the Blacksmiths Arms at Lastingham, the Tan Hill Inn, and the Wensleydale Heifer at West Witton.

ALDBOROUGH (N Yorks)   SE4166 Map 7

Ship ⊗ ⇌

Village signposted from B6265 just S of Boroughbridge, close to A1

Since taking over a couple of years ago, the licensees of this attractive fourteenth-century pub have quickly established a firm claim to readers' affections. They do good value home-made food such as soup (95p), excellent sandwiches (from 90p, cheesburger £1.05), ploughman's, home-made pâté or sausage and egg (£1.50), haddock or plaice (£2.75), scampi (£2.80), local gammon and egg (£3.50 – their most popular dish), good chicken Kiev or Cordon Bleu (£3.85), exceptional mixed grill (£4.20) and steaks (from £4.55); puddings such as home-made apple pie (95p), and a big bowl of first-class chips (50p). On Sundays there's an eat-as-much-as-you-can buffet, with hot and cold dishes (£3.75). There's a warm, friendly atmosphere in the heavily beamed main bar, and old-fashioned seats around heavy cast-iron tables, sentimental engravings on the walls, a coal fire in the stone inglenook fireplace and seats looking through latticed windows to the ancient village church across the lane. A quieter back room (decorated with ship pictures) has a buffet bar, waitress service and lots more tables. Well kept Tetleys on handpump; darts, shove-ha'penny, dominoes, fruit machine and piped music; summer seats on the spacious grass behind. The Roman town for which the village is famous is mainly up beyond the church. *(Recommended by Dr J R Hamilton, Wayne Brindle, John Knighton, KC, A W Wallens, Alan and Ruth Woodhouse, Jon Wainwright, M Thomas, A Matheson, W A Rinaldi-Butcher, P G Race, GB)*

Free house   Licensees David and Liz Vose   Real ale   Meals and snacks   Well behaved children in eating area of bar   Open 11–11 all year   Bedrooms tel Boroughbridge (090 12) 2749; £20B/£32B

ARNCLIFFE (N Yorks)   SD9473   Map 7
Falcon
Off B6160

This quite unspoilt moorland inn stands right by a bridleway leading up to Malham Tarn and beyond (and is on *Good Walks Guide* Walk 151), and run by a family which has been here for four generations, with a fifth growing up. Youngers ales are tapped from casks in a small servery at the back, with hatch service to a couple of functional little rooms with heavy settles and cast-iron tables, a fire (if you're lucky enough to get near it) and some old humorous sporting prints; there's also an airy conservatory-room behind, and a homely front lounge. Simple bar food includes baked potato with cheese (70p), soup (75p), sandwiches (from 80p, toasties 95p), cheese and onion pie (95p) and ploughman's (£2.20); dominoes. *(Recommended by Tim Halstead, Phil Asquith, Mr and Mrs C France)*

Free house   Licensee D M Miller   Real ale   Lunchtime snacks   Children in conservatory (lunchtime only)   Open 12–3, 6.30–11 in summer; 12–2, 7–11 in winter   Bedrooms tel Arncliffe (075 677) 205; £15.50/£31 (may not be available in winter)

ASKRIGG (N Yorks)   SD9591   Map 10
Kings Arms ⊗ 🛏
Village signposted from A684 Leyburn–Sedbergh in Bainbridge

This beautiful Dales village is protected against too heavy an influx of visitors by being a bit off the beaten track, though many people are drawn here just to see the vet's Skeldale House of the TV version of James Herriot's *All Creatures Great and Small*, across the road from the inn (in real life he practises in Thirsk). The inn itself, which in the series is the Wagoners Arms, is a similarly attractive former Georgian manor house, with bags of character. Its very high-ceilinged central room has a real coaching flavour still, with its saddle-hooks still in place, the kitchen hatch in the panelling, the curving wall with the high window that shows people bustling up and down the stairs, the huge stone fireplace, the hunting prints, nineteenth-century fashion plates and stag's head, and the attractive medley of furnishings including a fine sturdy old oak settle. A small low-beamed front bar has more oak panelling, with brocaded wall settles in its side snugs and a fire in a lovely green marble fireplace. There's yet another fire in a simply furnished flagstoned back bar, which has a fruit machine, trivia machine and juke box; also darts, shove-ha'penny, dominoes and cribbage. There are seats in the inner courtyard beyond. Bar food includes sandwiches (from 75p), soup (85p), filled baked potatoes (from 95p), burgers (£1.50), ploughman's (from £1.75), salads (from £2.25), steak and kidney pie (£2.95), gammon and egg (£3.25) and steak (£5); well kept McEwans 80/- and Youngers Scotch and No 3 on handpump, good coffee (served before the bar opens, too). The atmosphere's very friendly; breakfasts are good. *(Recommended by Betsy and David White, Ken and Dorothy Worrall, John H Jackson, Nick Long)*

Free house   Licensees Ray and Liz Hopwood   Real ale   Meals and snacks   Restaurant Children in eating area   Open 11–11 all year; closes afternoons weekdays in winter Bedrooms tel Wensleydale (0969) 50258; £17B/£34B

AUSTWICK (N Yorks)   SD7668 Map 7
Game Cock ⊗

Popular with climbers and walkers, this welcoming inn has a simply furnished but cosy back bar with beams, well made built-in wall benches and plain wooden tables, a few cockfighting prints on the butter-coloured walls, and a good fire in winter; there is a more comfortable lounge. Well presented bar food includes sandwiches (ham £1, open prawn £2.25), crispy crab and vegetable parcels (£2.45), roast chicken (£2.75), steak and mushroom pie (£2.95), scampi (£3.25) and puddings such as apple and blackberry pie or chocolate and pear pudding (£1.20); substantial three-course breakfasts. Well kept Thwaites on handpump; darts and dominoes. There are some seats in a glass-enclosed sun loggia, and outside. Above the green pastures around this quiet village of rose-covered stone houses rise the crags and screes of the Dales National Park and the Three Peaks. *(Recommended by J A Jack, Hilarie Miles-Sharp, A W Wallens, Caroline Fisher, Tony Pounder, Patrick Stapley, Gwen and Peter Andrews, David Barrett, Simon Bates)*

Thwaites   Licensee Alan Marshall   Real ale   Meals and snacks   Open 11–3, 6–11 Bedrooms tel Clapham (046 85) 226; £12.50/£25

BAINBRIDGE (N Yorks)   SD9390 Map 10
Rose & Crown ⊗ 🛏
A684

A cluster of solid old stone houses, grouped loosely around a broad green, includes this ancient, friendly inn. The beamed and panelled front bar has antique settles and other old furniture, a butterfly collection, flowers and a cheerful fire; the spacious main bar (which they are hoping to extend in 1989) has big windows overlooking the green. They are also hoping to built a conservatory. Good bar food includes excellent home-made soup (£1), an impressive choice of sandwiches (from 95p, open sandwiches £3), ploughman's (from £2), home-made sausages (£2.30), chilli bean pot (£2.75), tuna-fish casserole (£2.95), salads with home-cooked meats or lasagne (£3.25), home-made pie of the day (£3.50), sirloin steak (£5.50), daily specials, home-made puddings (£1) and children's menu (£2). John Smiths, Theakstons and Youngers Scotch on handpump; extensive wine list; darts, pool, dominoes, fruit machine and juke box. Each winter night the buffalo horn is taken out to the village green and blown sonorously three times – a seven-hundred-year-old tradition, originally to guide herdsmen down from the misty moors. *(Recommended by Dr and Mrs R J Ashleigh, Mr and Mrs J H Adam, Helen and John Thompson, G Jones, Dr and Mrs A K Clarke, Brian and Elizabeth Carter, Lynda Brown, Rob and Gill Weeks, Michael Bolsover)*

Free house   Licensee Penny Thorpe   Real ale   Meals and snacks   Evening restaurant Children welcome (not after 9)   Open 11–3, 6–11 weekdays, 11–11 Sat   Bedrooms tel Wensleydale (0969) 50225; £18.50(£22B)/£37(£44B)

Bedroom prices normally include full English breakfast, VAT and any inclusive service charge that we know of. Prices before the '/' are for single rooms, after for two people in double or twin (B includes a private bath, S a private shower). If there is no '/', the prices are only for twin or double rooms (as far as we know there are no singles).

BLAKEY RIDGE (N Yorks)   SE6799   Map 10

Lion ⊗ 🛏

From A171 Guisborough–Whitby follow Castleton, Hutton le Hole signposts; from A170 Kirkby Moorside–Pickering follow Keldholm, Hutton le Hole, Castleton signposts; OS Sheet 100 reference 679996

Mainly sixteenth-century (though parts are older), this friendly, rambling inn is the fourth highest in England, at 1325 feet above sea level, and has spectacular moorland views in virtually every direction. Inside, there are low beams, stripped stone walls, dim lamps, photographs of the pub under snow (it can easily get cut off in winter – but there are good fires) and some old engravings. Besides lots of small dining-chairs on the Turkey carpet, it has a few big high-backed rustic settles around cast-iron-framed tables and a nice leather settee. Very large helpings of good bar food include soup (80p), sandwiches (85p) or ploughman's (£2.45 – both these lunchtime only), steak sandwich (£1.95), home-made steak and kidney pie, curry, home-cooked ham and egg, fruit and nut pilaff or salads (all £3.45), steaks (from £4.95), puddings (£1.35), children's menu (£1.95) and good Sunday roasts (£5.45, children £2.95). Well kept Tetleys and Theakstons Best and Old Peculier on handpump; dominoes, fruit machine and piped music. Get there early for lunch at weekends or in summer. The two-room restaurant is smarter than you'd expect for this isolated spot. *(Recommended by Lynn Stevens, Gill Quarton, Linda and Alex Christison, Bob Gardiner, Steve Dykes, G T Jones, Rob and Gill Weeks, F E M Hardy, Comus Elliott, T George, R A Hall, J M Steward)*

Free house   Licensee Barry Crossland   Real ale   Meals and snacks   Restaurant; open all day Sun   Children welcome   Occasional live music Weds evenings   Open 11–11 all year Bedrooms tel Lastingham (075 15) 320; £15/£30

BOLTON PERCY (N Yorks)   SE5341   Map 7

Crown

Signposted with Oxton from Tadcaster – first real right turn after crossing bridge, heading out from centre on York road

With the brewery just over three miles away, it's not surprising to find the Sam Smiths OB on electric pump in tip-top condition – and it's cheap here, too. But the real attraction is the pub itself: unpretentious and homely, tucked away by a striking medieval gatehouse behind the village church. Its two rooms are simply furnished, and decorated with brass ornaments, a stuffed falcon, a Delft shelf of fox-hunting plates and a big print of shire horses – very peaceful indeed on a weekday lunchtime, probably with just Teal the spaniel and Coot and Gipsy the labradors for company. There are plenty of real birds outside: ornamental pheasants in a row of pens beside the biggish terrace, which has picnic-table sets among fruit trees, and a very long wooden cat-walk footbridge that snakes out over a slow dark stream and its bordering nettle flats. They have summer barbecues on Saturday evenings, and do sandwiches, bar snacks and good steaks at other times. Darts. *(Recommended by Syd and Wyn Donald, Tim Halstead, T Nott, JAH, HCH, Jon Wainwright)*

Sam Smiths   Licensees Geoff and Angela Pears   Real ale   Meals and snacks   Open 11.30–2.30, 6.30–11 all year

BUCKDEN (N Yorks)   SD9278   Map 7

Buck ⊗

B6160

Of the many fine pubs in and around Wharfedale, this is perhaps the most usefully placed for the hill walks – indeed, you can aim from here for our other main entries at Arncliffe, Cray, Starbotton, Litton or Hubberholme. The modernised and extended open-plan bar has upholstered built-in wall banquettes and square stools around shiny dark brown tables on its carpet – though there are still flagstones in the snug original bit by the serving-counter, decorated with hunting prints and willow-pattern plates. The wall by the big log fire (where the cats like to sit) is stripped to bare stone, with others left buttery cream and decorated with local pictures, the mounted head of a roebuck and fresh flowers. Good value bar food includes home-made soup (75p), sandwiches (from £1), toasties (£1.25), Yorkshire pudding with onion gravy (lunchtime only) or sausage, egg and bacon (£2), a generous ploughman's or a choice of omelettes (£2.50), mixed meat salad (£3), home-made steak, kidney and mushroom pie (£3.50), gammon with eggs or pineapple (£3.75), baked local trout (£4), mixed grill (£5) and sirloin steak (£6.50). Well kept Theakstons Best, XB and Old Peculier and Youngers No 3 on handpump; darts, pool, dominoes and piped music. Seats on the terrace and beyond the sloping car park in the shelter of a great sycamore have good views of the surrounding moors. *(Recommended by J E Rycroft, Dr and Mrs T E Waine, Tim Baxter, Professor S Barnett, Len Beattie, Lyn Stevens, Gill Quarton, Jon Wainwright, Colin and Caroline, Mrs M E Collins, D W Stokes, Mrs D M Everard, Mr and Mrs Jon Payne, Michael Bolsover, W B Knox)*

Free house   Licensee Trevor Illingworth   Real ale   Meals and snacks   Restaurant; not Sun lunchtime   Children welcome   Open 11–3, 6–11 all year   Bedrooms tel Kettlewell (075 676) 227; £17(£19.50B)/£34(£39B)

BURNSALL (N Yorks)   SE0361   Map 7
Red Lion

B6160 S of Grassington, on Ilkley road; OS Sheet 98 reference 033613

White tables on the cobbles in front of this family-owned, pretty stone-built pub look over the quiet road to the village green (which has a tall maypole) running along the banks of the River Wharfe. The busy, friendly main bar has flowery-cushioned sturdy seats built into the attractively panelled walls (decorated with pictures of the local fell races), Windsor armchairs, rugs on the floor, and steps up past a solid-fuel stove to a back area with sensibly placed darts (dominoes players are active up here, too). The carpeted front lounge bar, which is served from the same copper-topped counter through an old-fashioned small-paned glass partition, has a coal fire. Well kept Tetleys and Theakstons on handpump, and good lunchtime bar food such as sandwiches (from 80p), home-made soup (90p), ploughman's (from £2.20), home-made steak and potato pie, Yorkshire sausages or salad (all £2.60) and scampi (£3); evening dishes include home-made pâté (£1.80), local trout (£4) and steaks (from £5). *(Recommended by J E Rycroft, Mike Suddards, Len Beattie, J R Leeds, Eileen Broadbent)*

Free house   Licensee Patricia Warnett   Real ale   Snacks   Restaurant   Children welcome Open 11–3, 6–11 all year   Bedrooms tel Burnsall (075 672) 204; £24.75(£33B)/ £33(£44B)

BYLAND ABBEY (N Yorks)   SE5579   Map 7
Abbey Inn ⊗

The Abbey has a brown tourist-attraction signpost off the A170 Thirsk–Helmsley

Alone in a spectacular setting opposite the abbey ruins, this pub – formerly very simple indeed – was completely refurbished in 1987 by its new owners. They've done it with great verve, preserving the old-fangled character by leaving the rambling series of separate rooms more or less intact, by gently highlighting some of its original features (polished boards and flagstones, big fireplaces, discreet stripping back of some plaster to show the ex-abbey masonry), and by furnishing it very much in character. There are carved oak seats, oak and stripped deal tables, settees, Jacobean-style dining-chairs, china cabinets, and for decoration bunches of flowers among the candles, various stuffed birds, cooking implements, little etchings, willow-pattern plates and so forth. In a big back room this country theme rather runs riot – as well as lots of rustic bygones an uptilted cart shelters a pair of gnomelike waxwork yokels. Though it's quiet in the early evening it quickly fills up with people after the food, which might include crab pâté (£2), sweet-cure herring (£2.25), vegetarian dishes, moussaka or steak pie (£3.75), fresh cod or pork cooked with lime and lemon sauce (£4), sirloin steak (£6.75) and lots of puddings; it's also popular for Sunday lunch. Well kept Theakstons Best on handpump, interesting wines, efficient food service by neat waitresses, inoffensive piped music. No dogs. There's lots of room outside, though the garden's in its earliest days yet. *(Recommended by Mr and Mrs C France, Peter Race, Roger Barnes, Helen Stanton)*

Free house   Licensees Peter and Gerd Handley   Real ale   Meals and snacks (not Sun evening, not Mon)   Children welcome before 8.30   Open 10–2.30, 6.30–11 all year; closed Mon lunchtime

CADEBY (S Yorks)   SE5100   Map 7

Cadeby Inn ★ ⊗

3 miles from A1(M) at junction with A630; going towards Conisbrough take first right turn signposted Sprotborough, then follow Cadeby signposts

The cheerful friendliness of this well kept, busy sixteenth-century pub quickly makes you feel at home. The serving-bar is in the main lounge at the back: comfortable seats around wooden tables, a high-backed settle made in the traditional style to fit around one stone-walled alcove, an open fire in the big stone fireplace, lots of houseplants, some silver tankards and a stuffed fox and pheasant. There's a quieter front sitting-room, and, decently out of the way, a fruit machine (they also have darts, shove-ha'penny, dominoes, cribbage, trivia and piped music); there are plans afoot for a new extension. Good bar food includes a lunchtime salad bar (£3) and carvery (£3.30), as well as soup (60p), sandwiches (from 85p), ploughman's (from £1.75), home-made steak and kidney pie (£2.10), seafood platter (£2.95), gammon with pineapple and egg or scampi (£3.25) and good value steaks (from £4.50); their traditional Sunday lunches (£3.30) are very popular. Well kept Sam Smiths OB and Museum, Tetleys, Timothy Taylors and a regular guest beer on handpump, attractively priced, and over 140 whiskies. There are seats in the front beer garden, and in summer they have barbecues out here. *(Recommended by Michael and Alison Sandy, M A and W R Proctor, T Nott, ILP, Alastair Lang, Ned Edwards, Wayne Brindle, Rob and Gill Weeks, Jon Wainwright)*

Free house   Licensee Walter William Ward   Real ale   Meals and snacks   Children in eating area of bar   Open 11–11 all year

COXWOLD (N Yorks)   SE5377   Map 7

Fauconberg Arms ★ ⊗ 🛏

The two cosy knocked-together rooms of the well kept lounge bar in this civilised and spotlessly kept inn are comfortably furnished with cushioned antique oak settles – including one that's handsomely carved and another curved to fit the attractive bay window – an oak porter's chair and Windsor armchairs; there are gleaming brasses on one beam, matting on the flagstones, and a good log fire in the unusual arched stone fireplace. Lunchtime bar snacks include soup (£1) and attractively served first-rate sandwiches such as salami and beetroot, roast ham or beef and cheese and tomato (£1.30) or specials like fresh crab (£1.75) and hot dishes such as stew and dumplings (around £2.95); good breakfasts. Well kept Tetleys, Theakstons and Youngers Scotch on handpump. The locals' spacious back public bar has a fruit machine and piped music. The pub is close to Shandy Hall, the home of Laurence Stern the novelist. The broad, quiet village street is pretty, with tubs of flowers on its grass or cobbled verges. *(Recommended by Laurence Manning, Barbara Hatfield, Mrs Shirley Pielou, Syd and Wyn Donald, Wayne Brindle, John Adams, Hon G Vane, W J and R Webster, E J and J W Cutting, Rob and Gill Weeks, Jon Dewhirst, Jon Wainwright)*

Free house   Licensee Richard Goodall   Lunchtime snacks (not Sun or Mon)   Restaurant Open 10.30–2.30, 6–11; restaurant closed 2 weeks each Feb and Oct   Bedrooms tel Coxwold (034 76) 214; £22(£24S)/£38(£40S)

CRACOE (N Yorks)   SD9760   Map 7
Devonshire Arms ⊗

B6265 Skipton–Grassington

Polished flooring-tiles with rugs here and there, sturdy rustic or oak tripod tables, green plush cushioned dark pews and built-in wall settles give a comforting feel of neat solidity here. Copper pans around the stone fireplace glint with the firelight, white planks creak above the low shiny black beams, and above the dark panelled dado are old prints, engravings and photographs, with a big circular large-scale Ordnance Survey map showing the inn as its centre. Readers particularly enjoy uncommon soups such as cream of turnip or orange and coriander (£1.10), scrambled egg done with smoked salmon (£2.95) and steaks; a wide range of other bar food includes sandwiches (from £1), ploughman's (£2.85), salmon pâté (£3.15), fresh haddock (£3.95), steak and kidney pie (£4.20) and salads (£4.25); well kept Youngers Scotch and No 3 on handpump, decent coffee, friendly and attentive service. A fruit machine is tucked discreetly away by the entrance; there's a gentle old labrador; darts, maybe unobtrusive piped music. A terrace flanked by well kept herbaceous borders has picnic-table sets. *(Recommended by Joan Webon, G Milligan, David Burrows, Dr and Mrs A K Clarke, Wayne Brindle)*

Youngers   Licensees M Jaques and Miss C Kurz   Real ale   Meals and snacks   Restaurant Tues–Sat evenings   Children welcome until 9   Open 11–3, 6.30–11 all year   Bedrooms tel Cracoe (075 673) 237; £18/£30

CRAY (N Yorks)   SD9379   Map 7
White Lion ★

This unspoilt and friendly little stone-built country pub is the highest in Wharfedale, 1100 feet up by Buckden Pike, and the surrounding countryside is superb. Inside, the bar (where walkers are welcome) has seats around tables on the flagstone floor, a high dark beam and plank ceiling, shelves of china, iron tools and so forth, a lovely open fire (even in summer) and a traditional atmosphere. Well kept Youngers Scotch and Goose Eye on handpump. Bar food – snacks at lunchtime only – includes good sandwiches, pork pie and mushy peas, hot crusty ham roll, generous ploughman's, beef curry, beef casserole, and ham and eggs; dominoes, ring the bull. There are picnic-table sets in a pretty little garden above the very quiet, steep lane, and great flat limestone slabs (pleasant to sit on) in the shallow stream which tumbles down opposite. *(Recommended by Lynn Stevens, Gill Quarton, Mark Sheard, Brian and Anna Marsden, Len Beattie, Alan and Ruth Woodhouse)*

Free house   Real ale   Snacks (lunchtime, limited Sun) and meals (not Sun)   Limited parking   Open 11–3, 5.30ish–11; closed Mon in winter

CRAYKE (N Yorks)   SE5670   Map 7
Durham Ox

This distinctive old inn has a pleasantly relaxed atmosphere – except at the busiest times. At one end of the old-fashioned lounge bar there's an enormous inglenook fireplace, and antique seats and settles around venerable tables on the partly carpeted flagstone and tiling floor, pictures and old local photographs on its dark green walls, and a high shelf of plates and interestingly satirical carvings in its panelling (birds hanging a fox, say). Some of the panelling here divides off a bustling public area with a good lively atmosphere and more old-fashioned furnishings; darts. Bar food includes soup (£1), open sandwiches or omelettes (£2.25), Yorkshire pudding with a choice of fillings (£2.75), and salads (from £2.75); good Sunday lunch. Well kept Theakstons Best and XB on handpump. The tale is that this is the hill which the Grand Old Duke of York marched his men up. *(Recommended by David and Ruth Hollands, Jeremy and Margaret Wallington, Jon Wainwright, Syd and Wyn Donald, PLC, John Dewhirst, Lee Goulding, Flt Lt A Darroch Harkness)*

Free house Real ale Meals and snacks Restaurant Children in restaurant Open 11–3, 5.30–11 Bedrooms tel Easingwold (0347) 21506; £20/£30

CRIDLING STUBBS (N Yorks)   SE5221 Map 7

Ancient Shepherd

4 miles from M62 junction 33: S of A1, first left signposted Cridling Stubbs; 3½ miles from M62 junction 34: S on A19, first right; pub signposted from village

A welcome respite from the motorway, this carefully decorated, friendly pub has a décor of soft browns, comfortable seats and sentimental engravings on the walls. Bar food includes home-made soup (£1.10), sausages (£1.90), vegetable curry (£2.80), gammon with fresh pineapple (£2.95), seafood vol-au-vent (£3), chicken in white wine (£3.35) and home-made puddings (£1.50). The serving-bar is in an attractive flagstoned hall, with soft lighting and stone pillars: well kept Ruddles, Tetleys and Timothy Taylors on handpump; friendly service. The public bar has darts and dominoes. *(Recommended by Tony Gayfer, Mr and Mrs T A Towers)*

Free house Licensees David and Carole Craven Real ale Meals and snacks (not Sat lunchtime, not Sun or Mon) Restaurant (not Sat lunchtime, Sun or Mon) tel Knottingley (0977) 83316 Children in eating area of bar Open 12–3, 7–11 all year; closed lunchtime Sat, all day Mon

EAST LAYTON (N Yorks)   NZ1609 Map 10

Fox Hall Inn ⊗ ⇔

A66

The panelled bar in this tall roadside inn has settles built in to make cosy booths around the tables, and the back part is more open, with a big south-facing window (where Sam, the friendly boxer, likes to sit). It's decorated with prints covering a wide range of sporting pursuits and a high shelf of plates. Good bar food includes home-made soup (£1.10), home-made pâté (£1.75), salads (from £2.25), ploughman's (£2.95), steak and kidney pie or gammon with egg or pineapple (£3.50), steaks (from £5.75, the T-bone is very popular at £5.95), and daily specials like fillet of pork in Dijon mustard sauce (£3.75), swordfish steaks in garlic butter (£3.95), and, in winter, game pie or rabbit casserole; helpful, enthusiastic service. Dominoes, cribbage, sensibly placed darts. Trivial Pursuit, mah-jong, backgammon and piped music. There's a new back terrace with tables and chairs. Down the nearby lane to Ravensworth (which climbs to fine views of the rolling countryside) is a ruined medieval castle. Be careful entering or leaving the pub's car park, as some of the traffic on this road is dangerously fast. Well behaved dogs welcome. *(Recommended by Ian Gordon, Michael and Alison Sandy, Hon G Vane)*

Free house Licensee Jeremy Atkinson Meals and snacks Evening restaurant (not Mon or Tues) Children welcome Open 10.30–3, 6–11 Bedrooms tel Darlington (0325) 718262; £15(£20B)/£25(£30B)

EAST WITTON (N Yorks)   SE1586 Map 10
Blue Lion
A6108 Leyburn–Masham

Coming into this old stone house (marked just by a faded heraldic lion, no pub or brewery name) is like stepping back at least fifty years. The friendly licensee – who took over from her mother over half a century ago – pulls well kept and very cheap Theakstons Mild from an antique brass handpump in a back room, brings it through on a tray, then chats to you in a simple and truly old-fashioned room: high-backed winged settles, glossy brown woodwork, ham-hooks in the high ceiling, an open fire (lit if there's a local shoot on or something, though not perhaps for a lone casual visitor), a table full of houseplants and a window seat looking out over the cobbled courtyard to the long village green lined neatly with stone cottages. The lively Jack Russell is called Susie. *(Recommended by Mrs V Carroll, Phil and Sally Gorton)*

Free house   Licensee Bessie Fletcher   Real ale   Open 11–3, 6–11; closed Sun

EGTON BRIDGE (N Yorks)   NZ8105 Map 10
Horse Shoe
Village signposted from A171 W of Whitby; via Grosmont from A169 S of Whitby

Outside this attractive stone house, by a little stream with ducks and geese, there are comfortable seats and tables on a quiet terrace and lawn; a footbridge leads to the tree-sheltered residents' lawn which runs down to the River Esk. The moors rise steeply from this sheltered valley. Inside, there are wall seats and spindle-back chairs around the modern oak tables, high-backed built-in winged settles, and a log fire; the walls are decorated with a big stuffed trout (caught near here in 1913), a fine old print of a storm off Ramsgate and other pictures. Well kept John Smiths, Tetleys and Theakstons on handpump. The young couple who took it over nearly two years ago are working hard to make a success of the place. Their bar food includes sandwiches (£1), cod (£2.50), gammon (£3.75) and steaks (£6). *(Recommended by G T Jones, Nick Dowson, Alison Hayward, M A and W R Proctor, Mr and Mrs Tim Crawford, Eileen Broadbent, Tony Bland, Jon Dewhirst)*

Free house   Licensee Brian Walker   Real ale   Meals and snacks   Restaurant (not Sun lunch)   Children welcome   Open 11–3, 6.30–11; closes 2.30 lunchtime in winter Bedrooms tel Whitby (0947) 85245; £15/£25

Postgate ⊗ 🛏
Though she's been here only since May 1987, the landlady has firmly consolidated the pub's position in the local community – dominoes every Monday evening raises money in aid of two local churches and the village hall, and there are three men's and one ladies' darts teams. She's also won a number of friends among our readers for the friendly welcome and good home-made food: sandwiches (from £1.10), ploughman's (£2.50), vegetable curry (£2.75), seafood pie (£3.25), good steak and kidney pie, chicken fricassé or sweet-and-sour pork (all £3.50), salmon steaks (£4.50), steak (£6.50) and fruity puddings; Sunday lunch (main course £3, three courses £6 – best to book) or large Yorkshire pudding with beef and gravy (£1.95), and fresh crabs and prawns when available. Camerons Lion and Strongarm on handpump. The well kept and carpeted lounge bar has upholstered modern settles and seats in a sunny window, with a high shelf of cups and bottles, and Windsor chairs; the public bar has darts, dominoes, trivia and piped music, and there are open fires. This year the dining-room, bedrooms and lavatories have been refurbished. Seats outside on a sunny flagstoned terrace look down the hill. This is one of the prettiest parts of the moors, down the steep twisty valley of the lovely River Esk – used by the British Rail Est Valley line, which links at nearby Grosmont

with the magnificent private North Yorkshire Moors line. *(Recommended by Lynn Stevens, Gill Quarton, R D Jolliff, Robert Gartery, A W Wallens, Eileen Broadbent, Mr and Mrs G Olive, Sheila M Rochester, Nick Dowson, Alison Hayward, M A and W R Proctor, PLC)*

Camerons   Licensee Penny Zweep   Real ale   Meals and snacks (not Sun evening) Restaurant (not Sun evening)   Children welcome   Open 11.30–4, 6.30–11 all year; 12–2, 7–11 weekdays in winter   Bedrooms tel Whitby (0947) 85241; £15/£30

ELSLACK (N Yorks)   SD9249 Map 7

Tempest Arms ⊗

Just off A56 Earby–Skipton; visible from main road, and warning signs ¼ mile before

This very welcoming French-run eighteenth-century pub is especially popular for the carefully cooked and well presented food: sandwiches (from £1.40, steak £3.50), three soups – including an exceptional French onion soup (from £1) – fish pie (£2.60), liver and onion (£2.75), Cumberland sausage (£3), steak and kidney pie, gammon and egg (£3.50), fresh salmon (£4.50) and daily specials that concentrate on fresh fish and shellfish (from £3.25); their low-calorie platter (£3.25) makes dieting seem no hardship, though the puddings (£1.25) are tempting enough to be a slimmer's subsequent undoing. The many tables are spread carefully through a softly lit series of quietly decorated areas, with quite a bit of stripped stonework, and a log fire in the dividing fireplace; there are chintzy cushions on the comfortable built-in wall seats, and small chintz armchairs. Tables outside are largely screened from the road by a raised bank. Well kept Tetleys Mild and Bitter and Thwaites Bitter on handpump; darts, dominoes and piped music. *(Recommended by J Whitehead, Dr S G Donald, Prof S Barnett, J G Bridger, Wayne Brindle)*

Free house   Licensee Francis Boulongne   Real ale   Meals and snacks   Restaurant tel Earby (0282) 842450   Children welcome until 8   Open 11.30–3, 6.30–11 all year; may open longer Sat afternoons; opens 7 Sat in winter; closed evening 25 Dec

GOOSE EYE (W Yorks)   SE0340 Map 7

Turkey

On high back road between Haworth and Sutton-in-Craven, and signposted from back roads W of Keighley; OS Sheet 104 reference 028406

In an ex-milling village at the bottom of a steep valley with high-walled lanes, this warm and cosy pub serves home-brewed beers – Goose Eye Bitter and Pommies Revenge; they also keep Tetleys Bitter, Mild and Landlord on handpump. It's simply refurbished and has comfortable button-back banquettes built into its various snug alcoves, barrel tops set into the concrete floor, and a good old-fashioned copper-topped bar counter. Good value food includes home-made soup (75p), pie and peas (£1), sandwiches (from £1.10), giant Yorkshire pudding (£1.30), hot dog or burger (£1.35), ploughman's or home-made pâté (£1.85), chilli con carne (£2.10), haddock (£2.55) and daily specials which might include chicken Madras curry (£2.30), steak and onion pie or prawn and mushroom crêpe (£2.45), scampi (£3) and steaks (from £4.35), with a range of puddings such as passion cake or blueberry pie (£1.05); there's a barbecue on Saturdays. A separate games area has darts, dominoes, various space games, juke box and fruit machine. *(Recommended by Jon Wainwright, R Mitchell)*

Own brew   Real ale   Meals and snacks   Children welcome   Live evening entertainment Open 11.30–3, 6–midnight; 12–3, 7–11 Sun

Stars after the name of a pub show exceptional quality. But they don't mean extra comfort – and though some pubs get stars for special food quality, it isn't necessarily a food thing either. The full report on each pub should make clear what special quality has earned it.

GREAT AYTON (N Yorks)   NZ5611   Map 10
Royal Oak ⊗
High Green; off A173 – follow village signs

Bow windows in the dark-panelled main bar of this busy, friendly inn look out on the square of elegant houses around the village green – some Georgian, some older, either bare stone or rendered in grey or (like the inn) white. There are sturdy settles – some of them antique – and wheel-back chairs around its traditional cast-iron-framed tables, an inglenook fireplace (big enough to hold two of the tables), thick butter-coloured plaster on the humpy stone walls, and beams supporting wide white ceiling-planks. An adjoining longer room is set with more tables for the bar food, which at lunchtime includes hot beef baps (80p), fine soup or quiche Lorraine (95p), pâté (£1.25), smoked haddock in creamy cheese sauce (£1.65), mushrooms in garlic mayonnaise (£1.95), delicious salads (from £2.20), braised lamb cutlets (£2.45), ploughman's or lasagne (£2.50), steak and kidney pie (£2.95), baked cod in cheese sauce (£3.25) and steaks (from £5.20); Sunday roast lunch (£2.95). Well kept Youngers No 3 on handpump. The public bar has darts, dominoes, a fruit machine and piped music. *(Recommended by Laurence Manning, RB, Ian Gordon)*

Scottish & Newcastle   Licensee Derek Monaghan   Meals and snacks   Singer Weds evening   Restaurant   Children in eating areas   Open 11–11 all year   Bedrooms tel Great Ayton (0642) 722361; £20(£30B)/£28(£40B)

HARDEN (W Yorks)   SE0838   Map 7
Malt Shovel
Follow Wilsden signpost from B6429

In a lovely spot by a bridge over Harden Beck, this handsome dark stone, low building has a bustling, old-fashioned atmosphere. The bar has three rooms (some of them panelled) with red plush seats built into the walls, kettles, brass funnels and the like hanging from the black beams, horsebrasses on leather harness and stone-mullioned windows. Simple but good bar food includes sandwiches, ploughman's, steak and kidney pie and salads; well kept Tetleys Bitter and Mild on handpump; dominoes. From the other side of the bridge you can walk upstream beside the river. *(Recommended by Dr A V Lewis, Wayne Brindle, Syd and Wyn Donald, Mike Tucker, P Howard)*

Tetleys   Real ale   Meals and snacks (not Sun evening)   Open 11.30–3, 5.30–11

HAROME (N Yorks)   SE6582   Map 10
Star ★ ⊗
2 miles south of A170, near Helmsley

In this part of Yorkshire there are several decidedly civilised pubs, and this is one of the more rarefied: heavy, deeply polished dark rustic tables with bunches of fresh flowers, cushioned old settles on the Turkey carpet, a dark bowed beam and plank ceiling hung with ancient bottles (some pointed) and glass net-floats, and unobtrusive classical music. A very clean glass cabinet holds kepis, fine china and Japanese dolls, there's a copper kettle on the well polished tiled kitchen range (with a ship in a bottle on its mantelpiece), and other decorations include a fox's mask with little spectacles and a lacy ruff. Bar food includes tasty home-made soup (90p), some twenty good, generous sandwiches that include chicken or prawn curry, good roast beef, ham, egg and cress, tuna, smoked salmon and so forth (£1.40–£2.80), a daily hot dish and various salads; there's a coffee loft up in the thatch. Well kept Camerons Lion and Theakstons Best and Old Peculier on handpump; piped music. In summer there are seats and tables outside this thatched building on a sheltered front flagstoned terrace, with more in the garden behind which has an old-fashioned swing seat, fruit trees and a big ash. No animals. *(Recommended by M A and W R Proctor, Laurence Manning, E Lee, Wayne Brindle, Rob and Gill Weeks, G Bloxsom, J C Proud, Sue Cleasby, Mike Ledger, H Edwin Scott, John Wainwright)*

Free house   Licensee Peter Gascoigne-Mullett   Real ale   Snacks (lunchtime)   Children in dining-room lunchtime only if weather bad   Open 11.30–2.30, 6–11; closes 10.30 in winter; closed 25 Dec

nr HARROGATE (N Yorks)   SE3155 Map 7
Squinting Cat ⊗

Whinney Lane, Pannal Ash (singposted off B6162 W of Harrogate); OS Sheet 104 reference 296517

After many delays, this friendly, rambling eighteenth-century country pub was hoping to begin major structural work as we went to press; they will be doubling the size of the pub to give more room for diners, and adding a new car park. While the floor and cellar work is being carried out, the pub will close for two or three weeks. Though they will be adding lots of new dishes, bar food includes sandwiches (90p), six home-made pâtés (from £1.95), chilli con carne (£2.45), home-made lasagne (£2.75), steak and kidney pie or scallops of turkey in garlic (£2.95) and a cold buffet (from £3.50). Well kept Tetleys Imperial, Mild and Bitter on hand-pump; dominoes and fruit machine. The garden is pretty, with tables on the terrace and on one of several small lawns divided by roses, lilacs, flower borders, a silver birch and so forth; daily barbecues in summer. The North of England Horticultural Society's fine gardens on the curlew moors at Harlow Car are just over the B6162. *(Recommended by Sally Watson, A J Leach, Neil Patrick, Gill Rigg, Prof S Barnett; more news please about the changes)*

Tetleys   Licensee Ken Attewell   Real ale   Meals and snacks   Children welcome   Open 11.45–2.30, 6–11 all year

HATFIELD WOODHOUSE (S Yorks)   SE6808 Map 7
Green Tree ⊗

1 mile from M18 junction 5: on A18/A614 towards Bawtry

The spacious series of connecting open-plan rooms and alcoves in this big but comfortably modernised and well run pub always has plenty of room, even when it's busy. There's an expanse of Turkey carpet, brown leatherette seats and Windsor chairs around the tables, fresh flowers and a warm atmosphere. Good bar food includes soup (85p), sandwiches (from 75p), ploughman's (£1.90), a pint of fresh prawns, fresh haddock or plaice from Grimsby (£2.50), home-made steak and kidney pie (£2.65), salads (from £2.75), grilled gammon (£2.95), mixed grill (£3.95), steaks (from £3.95) and puddings such as cherry and apple pie (85p). They do a seafood buffet on Friday and Saturday evenings, serving cockles, mussels, whelks and prawns. Well kept Darleys and Wards on handpump; friendly staff; fruit machine and piped music. *(Recommended by M A and W R Proctor, John Baker, ILP, Sue Cleasby, Mike Ledger, Jon Woodhouse)*

Wards (Vaux)   Licensee Trevor Hagan   Real ale   Meals and snacks   Restaurant (not Sun evening) tel Doncaster (0302) 840305   Children in eating area of bar   Open 11–3, 6–11 all year

HEATH (W Yorks)   SE3519 Map 7
King's Arms

Village signposted from A655 Wakefield–Normanton – or, more directly, turn off opposite Horse & Groom

The gas-lit dark-panelled original bar in this extraordinarily old-fashioned pub has plain elm stools and oak settles built into the walls, some heavy cast-iron-framed tables on the flagstones, a fire burning in the old black range (with a long row of smoothing-irons on the mantelpiece) and a built-in cupboard of cut glass. A more comfortable extension (with a fitted red carpet, even) has carefully preserved the original style, down to good wood-pegged oak panelling, a high shelf of plates, and more of the swan's-neck gas lamps; a new beamed and panelled restaurant fits in well too. Quiet on weekday lunchtimes, it's more popular for an evening outing. The range of bar food changes daily, but typically should include soup (70p), Yorkshire pudding and gravy (75p), hot beef sandwich (£1), savoury mince pancake or chicken liver pâté (£2), savoury quiche (£2.20), rabbit pie (£2.50) and minted lamb chops, gammon steak or roast pork lunch (£2.75). Well kept Theakstons Bitter, XB and Old Peculier from antique hand-tap beer engines (or a tighter creamier head from the more orthodox handpumps in the new bar); dominoes. *(Recommended by Roger Huggins, Comus Elliott, Lee Goulding)*

Free house   Licensee David Kerr   Real ale   Meals and snacks (not Sun evening)   Restaurant (not Sun evening) tel Wakefield (0924) 377527   Children in eating area of bar   Open 11.30–3, 6.30–11

HECKMONDWIKE (W Yorks)   SE2223   Map 7
Old Hall

New North Road; B6117 between A62 and A638; OS Sheet 104 reference 214244

A sensitively restored, fine old manor house – dating from 1470 – that was the home of the Nonconformist scientist Joseph Priestley. It's partly knocked through inside, showing lots of oak beams and timbers, stripped old stone or brick walls (with pictures of Richard iii, Henry vii, Katherine Parr and Priestley), and latticed mullioned windows with worn stone surrounds. The central part has a high ornate plaster ceiling, and snug low-ceilinged alcoves lead off this – with an upper gallery room, under the pitched roof, looking down on the main area through timbering 'windows'. Comfortable furnishings include cushioned oak pews and red plush seats, some with oak backs, on a sweep of Turkey carpet (there are flagstones by the serving-counter). Bar food brought to your table by efficient staff includes home-made soup (70p), sandwiches (from 85p), pâté (£1.20), chilli con carne (£2.45), ploughman's (£2.50), scampi (£2.60), salads (from £2.75), steak (£5.75) and daily specials (£2.50). Well kept Sam Smiths OB on handpump; fruit machine, light piped music and darts in a wall cupboard. *(Recommended by M A and W R Proctor, PLC)*

Sam Smiths   Licensee Julie Cliff   Real ale   Meals   Children in eating area of bar lunchtime only   Open 11–3, 6–11 all year

HELMSLEY (N Yorks)   SE6184   Map 10
Feathers

Market Square

Though the main inn is a handsomely solid three-storey stone block with a comfortable lounge bar, the adjoining pub part is low and cosy, with heavy medieval beams, dark panelling, a venerable wall carving of a dragonfaced bird in a grape-vine, a big log fire in the stone inglenook fireplace, and unusual cast-iron-framed tables topped by weighty slabs of oak and walnut; a relaxed atmosphere and efficient service. Popular, good value bar food includes lots of changing specials as well as sandwiches, soup, ploughman's, good garlic mushrooms, fresh Scarborough haddock, scampi and steaks. Well kept Theakstons XB and Youngers No 3 on handpump; darts, dominoes, fruit machine and juke box. There's an attractive back garden. This is a pleasant and relaxing town, close to Rievaulx Abbey (well worth

---

Looking for a pub with a really special garden, or in lovely countryside, or with an outstanding view, or right by the water? Such pubs are listed separately at the back of the book.

an hour's visit). *(Recommended by G Owens, Jill Hadfield, Tony Gallagher, Tony Pounder, E Lee, M A and W R Proctor, Jon Wainwright, Jane Palmer, Jon Dewhirst, Roger Bellingham, Rob and Gill Weeks, B J and A C Normand)*

Free house   Licensee J Feather   Real ale   Meals and snacks   Restaurant   Children welcome   Open 10.30–2.30, 6–11   Bedrooms tel Helmsley (0439) 70275; £17(£21B)/ £34(£42B)

HETTON (N Yorks)   SD9558 Map 7

Angel ★ ⊗

This attractively decorated Dales pub has a welcoming, homely atmosphere in the four rooms of the rambling bars, though the main draw is the very wide choice of imaginatively presented food. This includes cream soups with fried croûtons or clear soups with cheese croûtes and a touch of wine or cognac (£1.10), provençale fish soup with garlic croûtons £1.60), sandwiches (from £1.45, open smoked salmon salad £3.30), home-made terrine (£2.75), a plate of home-smoked and cured fish (£3.30), home-made steak and kidney pie or grilled gammon with egg or pineapple (£3.85), lamb cutlets with tarragon butter (£4.35), char-grilled calf's liver with sweet home-cured bacon (£4.75), eight-ounce sirloin steak (£5.75) and cold Scotch salmon (£5.95, when available); also, daily specials, home-made puddings (£1.50) and a Friday fish menu (fillet of baby cod £3.65, crab salad £4.25 and fresh halibut steak £5.25). It gets packed with families and walkers by 1pm (seats may be hard to find a quarter of an hour before that) when there can be quite a long wait for food, and they may want to move you on when you've finished to make space for someone else. There are lots of cosy alcoves with some beams, standing timbers and panelling, Ronald Searle wine snob cartoons and older engravings and photographs, and comfortable country-kitchen chairs or button-back green plush seats; they've just installed a lovely Victorian farmhouse range in the big stone fireplace of the main bar (there are other log fires and a solid-fuel stove). Well kept Theakstons Bitter, XB and Old Peculier, Timothy Taylors Landlord and Youngers Scotch on handpump, a decent choice of wines by the glass or bottle (chalked up on a blackboard, and often bin-ends), and quite a few malt whiskies; darts and dominoes. Sturdy wooden benches and tables are built on to the cobbles outside this pretty house, in the little village which is very much quieter than nearby Grassington. *(Recommended by Alan and Marlene Radford, E Lee, J E Rycroft, Robert Gartery, Alan Bickley, Tim Halstead, Phil Asquith, Len Beattie, Dr S G Donald, Stephen Sarraff, Margaret and Roy Randle, Michael Bolsover)*

Free house   Licensee Denis Watkins   Real ale   Meals and snacks   Restaurant (not Sun evening) tel Cracoe (075 673) 263   Children in eating area of bar and restaurant   Open 11.30–2.30, 6–11; closed 25 Dec

HUBBERHOLME (N Yorks)   SD9178 Map 10

George ★

Village signposted from Buckden; about 1 mile NW

This attractive and unspoilt eighteenth-century building was J B Priestley's favourite pub and is in Yorkshire's smallest conservation area – just the inn, bridge and church. It looks out on a lovely swirly stretch of the River Wharfe, where they have fishing rights, and they still let riverside land, in aid of a church charity, on the first Monday of the New Year (with a licensing extension to nearly midnight then); seats and tables look up to the moors which rise all around. Inside, the two small and well kept flagstoned bar-rooms have dark ceiling-boards supported by heavy beams, walls are stripped back to bare stone, there are simple seats around shiny copper-topped tables, and an open stove in the big fireplace throws out plenty of heat. At lunchtime, cheerful walkers crowd in for food, mainly fresh from the Aga, that includes home-made soup, hefty warm rolls filled with big slices of juicy fresh ham, cheese or bacon (around £1.25), pâté (£1.90), steak and kidney or chicken and ham pie with the lightest of crusts (£3.20), and good apple pie; very well kept Youngers Scotch and No 3 on handpump, and a good choice of malt whiskies; darts, dominoes and cribbage. *(Recommended by Lynn Stevens, Gill Quarton, David Forsyth, Jacqueline Howard, Jon Wainwright, Alan and Ruth Woodhouse, Rob and Gill Weeks, J E Rycroft, M F S Hoggett, Malcolm Steward, Mrs D M Everard, Robert Gartery, Len Beattie, M S Hancock)*

Free house   Licensee John Fredrick   Real ale   Meals and snacks   Evening restaurant Children welcome   Open 11.30–3, 6.30–11 all year; opens 7 in winter; closed evening 25 Dec   Bedrooms tel Kettlewell (075 676) 223; £28 (twin only)

KILBURN (N Yorks)   SE5179   Map 7

Forresters Arms 🛏

Signposted from A170 E of Thirsk

The Thompson furniture workshop next door has supplied most of the furniture here, sturdy yet elegant, usually oak, always with the trademark of a little carved mouse sitting, standing or running in some discreet corner of the piece. That's also the source of the fine bar counter and the great slab shelf along the wall of the inner room – lights beneath it throw the stripped stonework into striking relief (parts of the inn are said to date back to the twelfth century). This inner room has tables for people eating; the smaller outer bar's chairs are much more for sitting and chatting by the log fire in its unusual rounded stone chimney-breast. Well kept Tetleys on handpump, a good choice of popular bar food from sandwiches to steaks, a friendly welcome from the licensees who've been here for a bit over two years now, unobtrusive and pleasantly chosen piped music, fruit machine kept discreetly out of the way. There are white tables out on the front terrace, looking across to pretty village gardens interspersed with planked oak trunks weathering for the workshop. Dogs welcome. *(Recommended by T George, Steve Breame and others)*

Free house   Licensees Brian and Kristine Livingstone   Real ale   Meals and snacks Restaurant   Children welcome   Open 11–3, 5.30–11 all year; all day Sat in summer Bedrooms tel Coxwold (034 76) 386; /£35B

KIRBY HILL (N Yorks)   NZ1406   Map 10

Shoulder of Mutton 🛏

Signposted from Ravensworth road about 3½ miles N of Richmond; or from A66 Scotch Corner–Brough turn off into Ravensworth, bear left through village, and take signposted right turn nearly a mile further on

This is a very quiet spot, looking out from a bluff over the ruin of Ravensworth Castle, with just the breeze sighing through the limes and chestnuts in the churchyard opposite, and the unusually tuneful bell of the church clock. It's neat and shipshape inside; the licensee came to the pub after thirty years in the Navy, and his wife's father and grandfather were in the service too. The bar, on the left of a communicating entry hallway with a pretty 1880s watercolour of boats in a misty estuary, is comfortably modernised, with muted blues and reds for the carpet and the plush wall settles around simple dark tables; it's got a good welcoming atmosphere, and an open fire. Decent bar food includes ploughman's (£2.25), lasagne, chicken and bacon or steak and kidney pie (£2.50), a large plateful of haddock and chips (£3.75) and scampi (£3.95), and the stripped stone restaurant is noted for its generous helpings. Well kept Theakstons XB, Websters Choice and Youngers No 3 on handpump; darts, dominoes, cribbage, with pool and juke box in a side room and a fruit machine around the back. The yard behind has picnic-table sets. Bedrooms are comfortably modern (though the inn was originally converted from a farm some time in the 1830s), with first-class breakfasts. *(Recommended by John Roué, Hon G Vane and others)*

Free house   Licensees Hylton and Shirley Pyner   Real ale   Meals and snacks (not Mon lunchtime)   Restaurant   Children welcome   Open 12–3, 7–11 all year   Bedrooms tel Richmond (0748) 2772; £12.90 (£15.50B)/£25.80 (£31B)

LANGDALE END (N Yorks)   SE9491 Map 10
Moorcock

Best reached from A170 at East Ayton (signposted Forge Valley, just E of bridge), or A171 via Hackness; OS Sheet 101 reference 938913

This quite unspoilt village pub, in a beautiful valley, has its bar in a neat little parlour in a whitewashed stone terraced cottage, with simple old settles around a scrubbed table, clean red quarry tiles and one or two calendars on the wall. The beer is poured in a back room and brought out on a tray, and the sandwiches with ham, cheese and tomato (70p) are freshly cut. You can expect a cheery welcome with a warm fire (over which there's a brass plaque to six victims of the 1914–18 War, including Chris Martindale), and there's even tea or coffee and biscuits if you wish. *(Recommended by SG, T George)*

Free house   Licensee Maud Martindale   Evening snacks (not Sun)   Open 10.30–3, 6–11 all year; closed Sun

LANGTHWAITE (N Yorks)   NZ0003 Map 10
Red Lion

Just off Arkengarthdale road from Reeth to Brough

Footpaths from this charming cluster of houses thread their way along the Arkle beck and up the moors on either side; it's a delightful spot, and this unpretentiously cottagey little pub fits in perfectly. It's kept spick and span, with comfortably cushioned wall seats, flowery curtains, a fox's mask, a few decorative plates on a Delft shelf and a beam and plank ceiling; if you think that one's low, try the burrow-like side snug. A sensibly short choice of simple good value bar food includes toasted sandwiches (from 80p), pizza (£1.20), ploughman's (£1.65), vegetarian goulash (£1.75) and curries or Old Peculier casserole (£2.25); the Theakstons ales are kept under pressure; service is very friendly. They have carved horn beakers, signed copies of books by Herriot and Wainwright, and Ordnance Survey maps, and very helpfully open at 10.30 for coffee on Sundays in summer, keeping open for meals then until 3. There are some picnic-table sets out in the tiny village square. *(Recommended by R A Hall, TOH, G T Jones)*

Free house   Licensee Mrs Rowena Hutchinson   Meals and snacks   Children in eating area until 8   Open 10.30–3, 6–11 all year

LEDSHAM (W Yorks)   SE4529 Map 7
Chequers ⊗

The small, individually decorated rooms in this friendly, pleasant pub open off an old-fashioned little central panelled-in servery, and there are lots of cosy alcoves, low beams, and log fires. Good bar food includes soup (80p), sandwiches (from £1.10), ploughman's (£1.95), scrambled eggs and smoked salmon (£2.25), lasagne or steak pie (£2.75), salads (£3), and good ham and eggs (£3.65). Well kept Theakstons and Youngers Scotch on handpump; good service. A sheltered two-level terrace behind the creeper-covered stone village house has tables among roses.

Most pubs in the *Guide* sell draught cider. We mention it specifically only if they have unusual farm-produced 'scrumpy' or specialise in it. Do please let us know about any uncommon draught cider you find in a pub.

(Recommended by J C Proud, J H Tate, Brian Green, A V Lewis, John Oddey, M A and W R Proctor, PLC, Dr S G Donald)

*Free house   Licensee George Wraith   Real ale   Meals and snacks (lunchtime, not Sun)
Children in own room   Open 11–11 Thurs, Fri, Sat; may close earlier afternoons on other days; closed Sun*

LEEDS (W Yorks)   SE3033   Map 7
Garden Gate ★

37 Waterloo Road, Hunslet; leaving Leeds centre on A61, turn right at traffic lights signposted Hunslet Centre P, Belle Isle 1½, Middleton 3, park in public car park on your right, and walk through – the pub is obvious

Because it's surrounded by a modern development, the marvellously preserved Victorian layout and décor of this lively pub seem especially striking. Four old-fashioned rooms open off a tiled corridor panelled in mahogany and deep-cut glass; the finest, on the left as you enter, has a mosaic floor and a lovely free-flowing design of tiles coloured in subtle tones of buff, cream and icy green: the bar counter itself, its front made from elaborately shaped and bowed tiles, is the masterpiece (with hatch service to the corridor too). It's very much a working men's pub (we saw no women here), in a depressed part of the town. We found the best kept Tetleys Bitter and Mild we've come across here, on handpump – the brewery is just up the Hunslet Road. Ham or cheese salad sandwiches; darts, dominoes (very popular here), cribbage and fruit machine. *(Recommended by J C Proud; more reports please)*

Tetleys (Ind Coope)   Licensee Dennis Ashman   Real ale   Snacks (not Sat or Sun)   Open 11–3, 5.30–11 Mon–Thurs; 11–11 Fri and Sat

Whitelocks ★ ⊗

Turks Head Yard; gunnel (or alley) off Briggate, opposite Debenhams and Littlewoods; park in shoppers' car park and walk

This splendidly preserved, very popular and lively city-centre tavern has hardly changed since 1886. The long old-fashioned narrow room has red button-back plush banquettes and heavy copper-topped cast-iron tables squeezed down the side and facing the fine bar counter decorated with polychrome tiles, and there are grand advertising mirrors and stained-glass windows. Good, reasonably priced lunchtime bar food includes bubble and squeak (35p), home-made Scotch eggs (60p), soup (65p), Yorkshire puddings (65p with onion gravy, £1.20 with fillings), sandwiches (from 80p, with good big meat ones cut straight from home-cooked joints, in white or granary bread from £1.50), sausage and mash (£1.50) and meat and potato pie (£1.60), fresh salads (from £1.75), and jam roly-poly or fruit pie (65p); when it gets busy you may have to wait for your order. Well kept McEwans 80/- and Youngers IPA, Scotch and No 3 on handpump. At the end of the long narrow yard another bar has been done up in Dickensian style. *(Recommended by Wayne Brindle, Jon Wainwright, Professor S Barnett, T Nott, Geoff Wilson, John Thorndike, J C Proud)*

Youngers   Licensee Mark Clarke   Real ale   Meals and snacks   Restaurant tel Leeds (0532) 453950   Children in restaurant   Open 11–11 all year

LEVISHAM (N Yorks)   SE8391   Map 10
Horseshoe

Pub and village signposted from A169 N of Pickering

This friendly and well kept pub looks down the broad grass-edged village road to the moors beyond. The extended bar has been refurbished this year and has plush seats and new tables, a log fire in a stone fireplace, and bar billiards, dominoes and piped music; the restaurant has spread into what was the sun lounge. Well presented bar food includes soup (80p), sandwiches (from £1.15), ploughman's (£1.85), home-made goulash (£2.65), salads (from £2.95), good steak and kidney pie (£3.15), good prawn thermidor (£3.50), fresh fisherman's platter (£3.95) and steak (£4.95); home-made apple pie (£1.10). Well kept Tetleys Bitter and Theakstons Best on handpump. Twice a day each way in spring and autumn, and four times in summer, steam trains of the North Yorkshire Moors Railway stop at this village. *(Recommended by F Haworth, R D Jolliff, M A and W R Proctor)*

Free house   Licensee Roy Hayton   Real ale   Meals and snacks   Restaurant   Children in eating area of bar and restaurant   Open 11–11 in summer; 11–3, 7–11 in winter   Bedrooms tel Pickering (0751) 60240; £15/£30

LINTHWAITE (W Yorks)   SE1014 Map 7
Sair

Hoyle Ing, off A62; as you leave Huddersfield this is one of the only left turns in Linthwaite, and the street name is marked, but keep your eyes skinned for it – it burrows very steeply up between works buildings; OS Sheet 110 reference 101143

The reason for unearthing this hidden-away pub is the remarkable range of ales brewed by Mr Crabtree, who was previously one of the founders of the West Riding Brewery; he describes his microbrewery here as 'very Heath-Robinson', but still manages to turn out an astonishing range, from the pleasant and well balanced Linfit and Linfit Mild through Old Eli, Leadboiler and a Christmas Ale that has a habit of turning up at the most unseasonable times to the redoubtable Enochs Hammer (named for its impact, which makes a Luddite hammer look pretty small beer). He even does stout (English Guineas) and a pasteurised Hoyleingerbrau lager, and in all turns out nine different brews – not to mention his Hoyle Ing Sider. The place was an own-brew pub back in the last century, and they say that the name Sair ('sour') dates back to a time around the turn of the century when the beer was off; folk don't forgive easily around here. But it's evident that there are no complaints now – most evenings the quaint cluster of rooms is crowded with people chatting happily as they down their pints. There are big stone fireplaces (in winter almost as many fires as beers), pews, more comfortable leatherette banquettes or smaller chairs, rough flagstones in some parts and carpet in others, bottle collections, beer-mats tacked to beams; usually it's kept tidy, but on a busy weekend evening it's not exactly neat, and as so often in Yorkshire the air-cleaner then fights rather a losing battle. The room on the right has darts, shove-ha'penny, dominoes and a juke box (mainly golden oldies – and not noticed in the other rooms). The view down the Colne Valley is very striking. *(Recommended by Lee Goulding, N F Dohert, Jon Wainwright, Mr and Mrs P A Jones, Ben Wimpenny, Rob and Gill Weeks)*

Own brew   Licensee Ron Crabtree   Real ale   Well behaved children welcome in two of the rooms   Open 7–11 on weekdays, 12–4 too Sat and bank hols, all year; otherwise closed weekday lunchtimes

LINTON IN CRAVEN (N Yorks)   SD9962 Map 7
Fountaine

New licensees have taken over this traditional pub, and have introduced a more home-made menu: home-roasted local beef or pork, sausages made specially for them with spices, herbs and walnuts, a daily vegetarian dish such as broccoli and Stilton quiche (£2.95), and daily specials like smoked quails' eggs, liver and onions, nine-inch-thick Yorkshire puddings with various toppings, or tandoori sausage. They also have soup (£1.10), open sandwiches (from £1.30), black pudding with mild mustard sauce (£1.75), ploughman's (from £2.65), scampi (£3.45), salads (from £3.50), gammon with eggs or pineapple (£4.25), mixed grill (£6.95), and salmon or Dover sole when available. High-backed settles and copper-topped tables form a square snug around the big open fireplace, with a series of little rooms opening off here. Well kept Theakstons Best and Old Peculier and Youngers Scotch on handpump; darts, dominoes, ring the bull and fruit machine. *(Recommended by Mark Sheard, Dr and Mrs A K Clarke, Mr and Mrs M Tarlton, Len Beattie, Wayne Brindle)*

Free house   Licensees Gordon and Linda Elsworth   Real ale   Meals and snacks   Children in own room   Open 11.30–3, 6.30–11; 11–11 bank hols

LITTON (N Yorks)   SD9074   Map 7
Queens Arms 🛏

Attractively refurbished, this friendly seventeenth-century inn is in a lovely spot – a sheltered valley with moors rising all around. The main bar, on the right, has a seat built into the stone-mullioned window, stools around cast-iron-framed tables on its stone and concrete floor, stripped rough stone walls, a brown beam and plank ceiling, and a good coal fire. On the left, the red-carpeted room has more of a family atmosphere, with varnished pine for its built-in wall seats, and for the ceiling and walls themselves, and there's another coal fire. Food at lunchtime includes home-made soup (90p), good sandwiches (90p, steak canadienne £1), hot pork pie with mushy peas (£1), ploughman's (£1.90) and salads (£2.95); more substantial evening meals include pork sausage with apple sauce and sage and onion stuffing (£2.20), ham with eggs or pineapple (£3.20) and rump steak (£5.95); excellent generous breakfasts. Well kept Youngers Scotch on handpump; darts, dominoes, cribbage and piped music. A track behind the pub leads over Ackerley Moor to Buckden, and the quiet lane through the valley leads on to Pen-y-ghent. *(Recommended by Hilaire Miles-Sharp, Mrs D M Everard, Andy Tyne, Sue Hill, D A Adams, Neil and Angela Huxter, Colin and Caroline, Tim Halstead, Phil Asquith, Dr D K M Thomas, J T Smith, K McConnochie, Mike Suddards)*

Free house   Licensee Freda Brook   Real ale   Meals (evening) and snacks   Children welcome   Open 11–3, 6–11; opens 7 weekdays in winter   Bedrooms tel Arncliffe (075 677) 208; £12.50/£25

MASHAM (N Yorks)   SE2381   Map 7
Kings Head 🛏
Market Square

Facing the broad partly tree-shaded market square, this tall handsome stone inn has a spacious and neatly kept lounge bar – two rooms opened together – with green plush seats around heavy cast-iron-framed tables on its patterned carpet, a dark green ceiling, and a high shelf of Staffordshire and other figurines. There's a big War Department issue clock over the imposing slate and marble fireplace, which is decorated with four tall brass coffee-pots (usefully, they serve coffee before the bar opens), and lots of houseplants including a big rubber plant. Bar food includes soup (95p), sandwiches (from 95p), Yorkshire pudding (£1.10), omelettes (£1.75), ploughman's (from £2.75), steak and kidney (£2.95), chicken Kiev (£3.25) and a daily special; well kept Theakstons Best, XB and Old Peculier on handpump; fruit machine, space game, dominoes, unobtrusive low-key piped pop music. The pub is attractively decorated with hanging baskets, and there are picnic-table sets under cocktail parasols in a partly fairy-lit coachyard. *(Recommended by TRA, MA, Alan Bickley, Barry Stevens, PJA, Nicolas Walter, Neil Patrick, Gill Rigg, David Barrett)*

Theakstons   Licensee Michael Beckett   Real ale   Meals (not Sat evening or Sun lunchtime) and snacks (not Sat evening)   Restaurant, open noon–10 Sun   Children welcome   Open 11–11 all year   Bedrooms tel Ripon (0765) 89295; £25.50B/£37.50B

All *Guide* inspections are anonymous. Anyone claiming to be a *Good Pub Guide* inspector is a fraud, and should be reported to us with a name and description.

soup (£1.25), granary bread open sandwiches (from £1.80), hot poached pear with blue cheese dressing or port and brandy flamed kidneys (£2.70), ham and leek pancake (£3.45), curried chicken and Indian pickles in a cottage loaf (£3.65), chicken suprême in tangy orange sauce (£4.35), lamb's liver in red wine and onions (£4.50), home-made casserole or suprême of chicken with basil and tomato (£4.70), sea-trout with cream and watercress sauce (£6.30), steaks (from £7.95) and puddings (from £1.80); vegetables are good and fresh. Very well kept Sam Smiths OB and Museum on handpump, traditional cocktails, a dozen or so interesting wines by the glass (including mature vintage port); darts, shove-ha'penny, dominoes and piped classical music. The licensee's own character is very much in evidence, and for most customers this is decidedly part of the pleasure – though one or two would have preferred something lower-key. Outside, subtly floodlit at night, there are plenty of snug corners to sit in. *(Recommended by Gill and Neil Patrick, Peter Burton, G Owens, Lynn Stevens, Gill Quarton, Laurence Manning, M A and W R Proctor, Guy Sowerby, E Lee, JAH, HCH, Wayne Brindle, J C Proud, Mrs M Wettern, B J and A C Normand, PLC, Sue Cleasby, Mike Ledger, Derek Stephenson, Peter and Fern Horsburgh, Jon Wainwright, Warwick Peirson, Rob and Gill Weeks, R R Lane, Carol Boothby, Prof S Barnett, Dave Webster, Sue Holland)*

Sam Smiths   Licensee Ian Pickering   Real ale   Meals and snacks (limited Mon evening, not Tues evening)   Restaurant (not Sun lunchtime)   Children in eating area and restaurant Open 11–2.30, 6.30–11   Three bedrooms tel Ampleforth (043 93) 461; £16/£28

nr OTLEY (W Yorks)   SE2045 Map 7
Spite ⊗

Newall-with-Clifton, off B6451; towards Blubberhouses about a mile from Otley, and in fact just inside N Yorks

Until a century ago, this hillside country pub was the Roebuck, but one regular got into such a row with the landladies of this and a long-closed nearby pub called the Travellers for splitting his loyalties between the two that his heartfelt complaint ('There's nowt but spite and malice up here') won new names for them both. It's now a comfortable, welcoming place with good food (especially the award-winning ploughman's) and beautifully kept real ale – Websters Yorkshire, Choice and Green Label on handpump. There are wheel-back chairs and plush or leatherette stools around the orderly tables, Turkey carpet as you go in and a blue and brown patterned one over by the bar, some wildfowl prints and a collection of walking-sticks on the plain white walls, and a good log fire as well as central heating; unobtrusive piped music. The generous range of home-made food includes soup (£1.25), two-tone sandwich (£2.50), the magnificent award-winning ploughman's (a range of cheeses, quiche, pâté, potato, roll and butter on one plate, £3.50), salads with home-made roasts (£4), hot specials such as the substantial steak pie (£4), fresh halibut, salmon or fillet steak (all £7.95) and home-made puddings (£1.50). There are white tables and chairs in a neat little garden. *(Recommended by Tim and Lynne Crawford, Ned Edwards, William Halstead)*

Websters (Watneys)   Licensees Eric and Irene Law   Real ale   Meals (not Mon, not Sun evening) and snacks (not Mon lunchtime)   Restaurant (closed Sun evenings) tel Otley (0943) 463063   Open 11–3, 7–11 all year

nr PATELEY BRIDGE (N Yorks)   SE1966 Map 7
Half Moon ⊗

Fellbeck; B6265 3 miles E

The open-plan bar has a spread of russet plush button-back built-in wall banquettes and light-wood country kitchen chairs around decent wooden tables, with a big

---

We say if we know a pub has piped music.

sofa and easy chairs by the entrance, near a fat free-standing wood-burning stove. The cream walls with a Delft shelf, and the spaciousness, make a refreshing change from what can become a surfeit of olde-worlde stonework and close-packed beamery in this area. Well kept Timothy Taylors Landlord, Theakstons BB and Youngers Scotch on handpump; big helpings of simple but properly home-cooked bar food such as sandwiches (from 85p), soup (90p), ploughman's (£2.25), omelettes (from £2.25), fresh haddock (£2.75), steak and kidney pie (£2.90), gammon (£3.85) and sirloin steak (£5.25) – you may see the friendly landlord coming in from the garden with freshly picked herbs. A back area has darts, pool, dominoes and a juke box; there's a caravan park behind the pub. *(Recommended by Prof S Barnett, Chris Fluck)*

Free house   Licensees David and Sheila Crosby   Real ale   Meals and snacks   Children welcome until 9.30   Open 11–3, 6.30–11 all year; all day Sat   Bedrooms tel Harrogate (0423) 711560; £18B/£26B

PICKHILL (N Yorks)   SE3584 Map 10
Nags Head ⊗

Village signposted off A1 N of Ripon, and off B6267 in Ainderby Quernhow

The convivial tap-room on the left is the bar most readers head for: masses of ties hang as a frieze from a rail around the red ceiling, with jugs, coach horns, ale-yards and so forth hanging from the beams. One table's inset with a chessboard, and they also have darts, shove-ha'penny, dominoes, table skittles, cribbage, a silenced fruit machine and faint piped music in here, with pool in a separate room. There's a warm and thriving atmosphere, and it's comfortable too, with muted pastel red plush button-back built-in wall banquettes around dark tables. A smarter bar with deep green plush banquettes and a carpet to match has pictures for sale on its neat cream walls. But it's the food that people get enthusiastic about. They buy the ingredients carefully, and have a changing choice of about fifteen dishes depending wholly on what looked good – maybe only a couple of helpings of some things (but their definition of a helping is pretty massive). On our visit the choice included asparagus and chicken soup (£1.25), smoked oysters with bacon (£3.25), fresh cod (£4.50), braised rabbit with orange sauce (£5.25), grilled halibut (£6.90) and rod-caught sea-trout (£7.50); they will do sandwiches. Well kept Tetleys, Theakstons Best and XB and Youngers Scotch on handpump, decent wines by the glass. Creaky-boarded bedrooms, huge breakfasts. *(Recommended by Neil and Gill Patrick, Brian Lawrence, Tim Halstead, Robert Gomme, Alan Bickley, Kevin Blick)*

Free house   Licensees Raymond and Edward Boynton   Real ale   Meals and snacks Restaurant tel Thirsk (0845) 567391   Children allowed in eating area until 8   Open 11–3, 5–11 all year   Bedrooms tel Thirsk (0845) 567570; £23B/£34B

RAMSGILL (N Yorks)   SE1271 Map 7
Yorke Arms ⇌

This fine inn was the shooting-lodge of the Yorke family's Gouthwaite Hall, which now lies drowned under the nearby reservoir named after it. Behind its warm stone façade are comfortable sofas and easy chairs, as well as some fine older oak furniture including two or three heavy carved Jacobean oak chairs and a big oak dresser laden with polished pewter. With the sun streaming in through the stately stone-mullioned windows, this is a fine place to sit with a pot of coffee before setting off up the magnificent if strenuous moorland road to Masham, or perhaps on the right-of-way track that leads along the hill behind the reservoir, also a bird sanctuary. Bar food includes sandwiches (from 80p), soup (85p), smoked haddock quiche or chilli con carne (£2.40), cottage pie (£2.45) and game pie (£3.30). The inn's public rooms are open throughout the day for tea and coffee, and shorts are served in cut glass. Dominoes and cribbage. *(Recommended by Wayne Brindle, A J Leach, Tim Halstead, Phil Asquith, Ian Phillips)*

Free house   Licensee J S Ralston   Meals and snacks   Restaurant   Children welcome   Open 11–11 all year   Bedrooms tel Harrogate (0423) 75243; £16(£26B)/£32(£52B)

REDMIRE (N Yorks)   SE0591   Map 10
Kings Arms ⊗

Wensley–Askrigg back road: a good alternative to the A684 through Wensleydale

This friendly and unpretentious thick-walled old pub, popular with horse-trainers and jockeys, has small windows looking south to the fells. One end of the long room is set out with tables for diners and the other has simple furnishings that include a long soft leatherette wall seat and other upholstered wall settles, red leatherette cafe chairs, round cast-iron tables and a fine oak armchair (its back carved like a mop of hair); there are lots of interesting photographs – of old local scenes (including folk-singers recording here in three-piece suits), of local filming for *All Things Great and Small*, of the licensee's RAF squadron, and of his steeplechasing friends such as John Oaksey. Home-made bar food includes sandwiches, soup (95p), pâté (£1.90), meat or walnut and spinach lasagne (£3.25), steak and kidney pie, omelettes or grilled local trout (£3.85), lamb (£4.75), venison (£5.15) and steaks (from £5.95); Sunday roast lunch (from £3.25; best to book); well kept John Smiths on electric pump; very obliging service. Darts (under fluorescent light at one end), dominoes; seats in the small garden. *(Recommended by Dr and Mrs B D Smith, Mr and Mrs M Tarlton, SS, Mr and Mrs D H Riley, Patrick Young)*

Free house   Licensee Roger Stevens   Meals and snacks   Restaurant (closed Sun evening)   Children welcome   Open 11–11 all year   Bedrooms tel Wensleydale (0969) 50258; £12/£19

REETH (N Yorks)   SE0399   Map 10
Black Bull ⇌

B6270

From this big white coaching-inn you can look across the wide sloping village green to the great swell of Marrick Moor. Inside, the cosy beamed L-shaped bar, with its high-backed wall benches and cheery fires, has a relaxed, friendly atmosphere; more seats can be found in the lounge bar and outside. Good value bar food includes soup (70p), sandwiches (from 70p), home-made pâté (£1.25), ploughman's with three cheeses (£1.40), home-made cottage pie (£1.95), vegetarian dishes such as nut and fruit pilaff (£2.20), home-made pies like steak and kidney or pork and apple (£2.40) and home-roasted ham salad (£2.75). Well kept John Smiths on electric pump, with Theakstons XB and Old Peculier tapped from the cask; darts, pool, dominoes, cribbage, fruit machine, trivia and juke box. The hotel has its own fishing on the Swale. *(Recommended by Helen and John Thompson, Dr and Mrs B D Smith, G T Jones, Richard Dolphin, J C Braidwood, Mike Lawson, Cynthia McDowell)*

Free house   Licensee R E Sykes   Real ale   Meals and snacks   Restaurant   Children welcome (not after 8.30)   Open 11–11 all year   Bedrooms tel Richmond (0748) 84213; £13.95/£27.90

RIPPONDEN (W Yorks)   SE0419   Map 7
Old Bridge ⊗

Priest Lane; from A58, best approach is Elland Road (opposite Golden Lion), park opposite the church in pub's car park and walk back over ancient hump-backed bridge

The fine structure of this well kept and welcoming medieval house (which has been in the same hands for over twenty-five years) has been carefully restored:

plasterwork is stripped away just here and there to show the handsome masonry, and ceilings have been removed to show the pitched timbered roof. The three communicating rooms, each on a slightly different level, are comfortably furnished with rush-seated chairs, oak settles built into the window recesses of the thick stone walls, antique oak tables, a few well chosen pictures and a big wood-burning stove. On weekday lunchtimes a popular cold meat buffet always has a joint of rare beef as well as spiced ham, quiche, Scotch eggs and so on (£5.25, with salads). In the evenings, and at lunchtime on Saturdays (when you may have to wait some time for your food), good filling snacks include home-made soup (£1), breadcrumbed mushrooms with garlic mayonnaise (£1.85), potted smoked trout with lime butter (£2), chicken, ham and broccoli pancake (£2.50), tagliatelle verde (£3), pepper pot beef casserole (£4) and weekend specials such as cheese and onion pie (£2). They will cut fresh sandwiches. Service can get a bit pushed when it's busy. Well kept Marstons, Timothy Taylors and Youngers on handpump. The pub has a good restaurant, across the very pretty medieval bridge over the little river Ryburn. *(Recommended by Brian and Anna Marsden, Jon Wainwright, Ian Clay, Lee Goulding)*

Free house Licensee Ian Beaumont Real ale Meals (evening, not Sun) and snacks (not Sat lunchtime or Sun) Restaurant tel Halifax (0422) 822595; closed Sun Children tolerated in eating area, lunchtime Open 11.30–3.30 (3 Sat), 5.30–11 all year

ROBIN HOOD'S BAY (N Yorks) NZ9505 Map 10

Laurel

This cosy white pub is right at the heart of one of the prettiest and most unspoilt fishing villages on the North-East coast, and is near *Good Walks Guide* Walk 160. The snug and friendly beamed main bar has a good local atmosphere and is decorated with old local photographs, Victorian prints and brasses. Well kept – they've won a local award for this – Camerons Bitter, Strongarm and Tetleys Bitter on handpump; darts, dominoes, cribbage, maybe piped music. In summer, the hanging baskets and window boxes are lovely. The self-catering flat above the bar is enticing; *tel* Whitby (0947) 880400. Please note: they no longer do food. *(Recommended by Sally Durnford, Graeme Smalley, G T Jones, Eileen Broadbent, M A and W R Proctor, Nick Dowson, Alison Hayward, Mr and Mrs Tim Crawford)*

Free house Licensee Mrs J D Tucker Real ale Children in snug bar Open 11.30–3, 7–11 all year

ROSEDALE ABBEY (N Yorks) SE7395 Map 10

Milburn Arms ★ ⊗ ⇦

Easiest road to village is through Cropton from Wrelton, off A170 W of Pickering

Surrounded by splendid steep moorland, this civilised and friendly eighteenth-century stone inn is popular for the imaginative home-made food served in the big, well run bar. At lunchtime this includes wholemeal buns (from 90p), soup (95p), chicken liver pâté or mariner's hot-pot (£1.95), ploughman's (£2.50), calf's liver, onion and bacon (£3.25), local rainbow trout or chicken curry (£3.75), home-made game pie with green ginger wine (£4.95), sirloin steak (£5.95) and puddings like treacle tart (£1.45), with evening extras such as cottage pie (£3.90), home-made steak and kidney pie or chicken in wine sauce (£4.75) and lamb cutlets with rosemary (£5.75). On Sunday there's also a range of cold meats, fish, quiche and cheese with salads, and roast lunch (£2.25). As we went to press they told us that in November the bar is going to be repositioned, a new snug created, the banquettes re-covered and new curtains hung. There are sentimental engravings (The Poor Poet, The Pensionist) by Karl Spitzweg, sporting prints with an emphasis on rugby and cricket, and black beams in the bowed cream ceiling by the log fire; wine box ends are a sign of the licensee's previous days in the wine trade. Well kept Camerons

Lion and Theakstons XB on handpump, and Stowford Press cider; lots of malt whiskies and freshly ground coffee. Unobtrusive piped classical music at lunchtime; sensibly placed darts, with pool-table, shove-ha'penny, dominoes, cribbage, space game, backgammon, board games and fruit machine in a separate balconied area with more tables up a few steps; seats outside. They have a keen cricket team, and would welcome enquiries from other teams (they provide free beer and a proper cream tea). *(Recommended by A C Lang, Jane Palmer, G Bloxsom, R G and A Barnes, F A Noble, G L Archer, Dr R Hodkinson)*

Free house   Licensees Stephen and Frances Colling   Real ale   Meals and snacks Restaurant   Children in eating area, restaurant and large family-room   Occasional jazz, blues and country   Open 11–3, 6–11; 11.30–2.30, 6.30–10.30 in winter   Bedrooms tel Lastingham (075 15) 312; £27.50B/£43B

White Horse ⊗ 🛏

Above village, 300 yards up Rosedale Chimney Bank – the exhilarating 1-in-3 moorland road over Spaunton Moor to Hutton-le-Hole

Views of the high surrounding countryside (the inn itself has eleven acres with a pedigree flock of Jacob sheep) from the picnic-table sets on the stone front terrace are marvellous. They are almost as good from the windows of the beamed bar, which has red plush cushioned pews salvaged from a church in Wakefield, captain's chairs and wooden tables, a welcoming log fire and several foxes' masks, a stuffed heron and peregrine falcon, various antlers, horns and a reindeer skin on the stone walls. (The fine collection of china pub tankards left with the old licensees.) Generously served bar food includes soup (90p), sandwiches (from £1.10), home-made pâté (£1.95), ploughman's (from £2.20), mussels in white wine (£2.25), salads (from £3.50), grilled plaice or local trout (£3.70), home-made pies (£3.90) and eight-ounce sirloin steak (£5.60), with children's dishes such as fishfingers (from £2), puddings like home-made brandy-snaps and cream (from £1.20) and Sunday roast lunch (£4.30). Well kept John Smiths and Tetleys on handpump, and a good choice of malt whiskies; dominoes and piped background music. *(Recommended by Jytte Cumberland, G L Archer, Simon Holmes, Dave Braisted)*

Free house   Licensees Howard and Clare Proctor   Real ale   Meals and snacks Restaurant   Children in bar if eating until 8.30, and in restaurant   Monthly folk night and varied live entertainment all year   Open 12–2.30, 6.30–11; may open longer in afternoons if trade demands; closed 25 Dec   Bedrooms tel Lastingham (075 15) 239; £27B/£42B

SAWLEY (N Yorks)   SE2568   Map 7
Sawley Arms ⊗

Village signposted off B6265 W of Ripon

Handy for Fountains Abbey (the most extensive of the great monastic remains – floodlit on late summer Friday and Saturday evenings, with a live choir on the Saturday), this decidedly civilised place has a series of small and cosy Turkey-carpeted rooms. Comfortable furnishings range from greeny-gold wall banquettes and small softly cushioned armed dining-chairs to the wing armchairs down a couple of steps in a side snug. While we were waiting for our meal, the courteous black-bow-tied barman (the landlady's son) brought us the *Yorkshire Post* to read. (We're indebted to an article in that edition for the answer to a question which had always bemused us – how to pronounce the brewer Vaux; it rhymes, as the paper's city correspondent put it, with walks, talks, or more appropriately corks.) The food is certainly worth the short wait: interesting soups such as celery and apricot or mushroom with cumin, all made with proper stock (£1.20), good sandwiches (from £1.20), ham, spinach and almond pancake or ravioli done in red wine (£2.40), salmon mousse (£2.50), a Stilton, port and celery pâté (£2.60), egg, bacon and

---

Food details, prices, timing, etc. refer to bar food – not to a separate restaurant if there is one.

mushroom cocotte (£2.80), freshly smoked trout (£3.10), steak and mushroom pie with a fine buttercrust pastry (£3.90), salads (from £3.90) and sirloin steak (£7), with puddings such as apple and blueberry pie or a meringue glacé in the shape of a swan (£1.60). Decent house wines (the beers are keg), log fires, unobtrusive piped piano music, passe-temps; there's a silkily engaging half-Siamese grey cat. An attractive and well kept small garden has two or three old-fashioned teak tables. *(Recommended by A L Leach, E R Thompson, Mrs J H Vallance)*

Free house   Licensee Mrs June Hawes   Real ale   Meals and snacks   Restaurant Children old enough to behave as adults (at least nine) allowed in restaurant   Open 11–3, 6.30–11 all year

SHEFFIELD (S Yorks)   SK3687 Map 7

Fat Cat

23 Alma Street

It's the wide range of well kept real ales and foreign bottled beers (particularly Belgian ones) which draws most people to this relaxed pub; on our visit they had Brakspears SB, Huntsman Royal Oak, Ma Pardoes (from the Old Swan at Netherton, included in the Midlands chapter), Marstons Pedigree, Merrie Monk and Owd Rodger, Old Mill, Timothy Taylors Landlord and Woods Wonderful (from the Plough at Wistanstow, Shropshire) on handpump. There were also country wines, several organically grown wines and farm cider. Cheap bar food includes big sandwiches (70p), soup (80p), quiche or chilli (£1.20), hot dishes and ploughman's (£1.65) – they do a number of vegetarian dishes such as carrot and parsnip bake, tagliatelle with courgette and mushroom sauce or mushroom and pepper pizza, beside things like beef and pepper casserole and Sunday roasts (£1.80). The two small downstairs rooms have simple wooden tables and grey cloth seats around the walls, with a few advertising mirrors and an enamelled placard for Richdales Sheffield Kings Ale; the one on the left is no-smoking and both have coal fires. Steep steps take you up to another similarly simple room (which may be booked for functions), with some attractive prints of old Sheffield; there are picnic-table sets in a fairy-lit back courtyard. The atmosphere's friendly and chatty, service efficient; cribbage. Kelham Island Industrial Museum is close. *(Recommended by Mrs M Lawrence, Michael O'Driscoll, G N G Tingey, R F Neil, John and Helen Thompson, W P P Clarke, Lynn Stevens, Gill Quarton)*

Free house   Licensee Stephen Fearn   Real ale   Meals and snacks (lunchtime)   Children allowed upstairs. if not booked, until 8   Open 11–3, 5.30–11 all year

Frog & Parrot

Division Street, corner of Westfield Terrace

A lofty brown ceiling, huge windows, bare boards and high stools at elbow-height tables are the rule at this popular place, though one side (with an old neatly blacked kitchen range in a brick chimney-breast) is carpeted, and an area up a few steps has blue plush button-back built-in wall banquettes. Up here, you can see down into the basement brewhouse where they produce the pub's speciality – Roger and Out, a hefty 1125 OG ale (at nearly 17 per cent alcohol about five times the strength of an ordinary bitter), which they sell in third-pint glasses (£1), restricting customers to one pint a session. The other beers here are Old Croak (by contrast very light and easy to drink), Reckless and Conqueror, with a winter Porter and occasional commemorative strong ales. The pub has a good conversational atmosphere, and is well laid out to take a lot of people; besides the blue and yellow macaw in a splendidly spacious cage, they're reputed to keep a tank of frogs somewhere, but we didn't see this (the place was so busy on our visit that we'd have been hard put even to find a tank of giant Sumatran toads); fruit machine, trivia machine, piped music. Cheap bar food includes soup (75p), Yorkshire puddings with onion gravy (95p), eight-ounce burgers or omelettes made with three free-range eggs (£1.75), sweet-and-sour pork (£2.45) and roast beef (£2.95); fruit machine, with a very wide range of fish from haddock, ling, herring, cod and plaice to halibut, salmon and red mullet, served in a variety of ways (mostly £2.25–£3.45). *(Recommended by J L Thompson, T T Kelly)*

Own brew (Whitbreads)   Licensee Roger Nowill   Real ale   Meals and snacks (lunchtime, not Sun)   Restaurant tel Sheffield (0742) 721280   Children in restaurant   Folk night Mon Open 11–11 all year; closed Sun lunchtime

SOWERBY BRIDGE (W Yorks)   SE0623 Map 7
Moorings ⊗
Off Bolton Brow (A58) opposite Ash Tree

Overlooking the basin where the Calder and Hebble Canal joins the Rochdale Canal (part of which has been partially reopened, and there's now a circular walk), this attractively converted ex-canal warehouse has tables out on a terrace with grass and small trees; other old canal buildings here are now crafts workshops and shops. Inside, the very high ceiling and big windows contribute to a relaxed and airy atmosphere, and it's pleasantly furnished with fabric-covered seats built against the stripped stone walls (which are decorated with old waterways maps and modern canal pictures), rush-seated stools and tile-top tables. Big openings lead to a family-room alongside, similarly furnished and with the same charming view. Reasonably priced, good bar food includes sandwiches (from 95p), home-made soup (85p), home-made chicken liver pâté (£1.50), a lunchtime help-yourself buffet (from £2), ploughman's or spinach and mushroom lasagne (£2.50), steak, kidney and mushroom pie or fusilli oriental (£3), home-made puddings (95p) and children's dishes (from £1); friendly service. Besides well kept Moorhouses Bitter, McEwans 80/-, Youngers Scotch and No 3 and a regularly changing guest beer on handpump, there is a range of sixty foreign bottled and canned beers (many Belgian bottle-conditioned real ales – also Dutch Lineboom which they import themselves), over eighty whiskies (including seven Irish), reasonably priced house wines, and cocktails – including children's specials. Dominoes and piped music. *(Recommended by Derek and Sylvia Stephenson, Wayne Brindle, G Bloxsom, Brian and Anna Marsden, Rob and Gill Weeks)*

Free house   Licensees Ian Clay and Andrew Armstrong   Real ale   Meals and snacks Restaurant tel Halifax (0422) 833940   Children in family-room until 8.30   Open 11.30–3, 5.30–11 all year

SPROTBROUGH (S Yorks)   SE5302 Map 7
Boat ⊗
2¾ miles from M18 junction 2; A1(M) northwards, then A630 towards Rotherham, then first right, signposted Sprotbrough, by Texaco garage; immediate left after crossing river

In a peaceful spot by the River Don, this was a pub called the Ferry Boat from when it was built in 1652 until about 1850 (Scott's reputed to have used it while he was writing *Ivanhoe*). It then became a farm, and stayed that way until a local solicitor reopened it as a pub in early 1987. It's since been bought by John Smiths, though they've made few changes. The conversion's a successful one – three spacious areas running together, with dark brown beams, latticed windows, prints of bygone scenes, a rack of guns, big cases of stuffed birds, a couple of longcase clocks, the odd bronze, open fires in rather portentous stone fireplaces, and a pleasant mixture of comfort and character in the seating. Bar food includes rabbit casserole or steak and kidney pie (£2.75), salads (from £2.75), haddock (£3), a roast (£3.25) and several dishes of the day such as half a roast chicken (£3.50), grilled trout (£4.50) or Dublin Bay prawns (£6.50); well kept John Smiths on handpump; unobtrusive piped music, friendly service. A big enclosed brick-paved courtyard has picnic-table sets, and you can wander round to watch the barges and water-bus on the river (as the embankment's quite high you don't see much from the bar). *(Recommended by ILP, John Wainwright, Alastair Lang)*

John Smiths (Courage)   Licensee Peter Wolthuis   Real ale   Meals (not Sat evening, not Sun)   Restaurant (Tues–Sat evening, Sun lunch) tel Doncaster (0302) 857188   Children in restaurant   Open 11–11 all year

STANSFIELD MOOR (W Yorks)   SD9227   Map 7
Sportsmans Arms

Hawks Stones, Kebcote; on old packhorse road between Burnley and Hebden Bridge, high above Todmorden; OS Sheet 103 reference 928273

There's an unpretentious but comfortable mix of old and new furnishings in this remote and very welcoming moorland pub: big heavy russet plush settles face the open fire in the back area, mustard-coloured leatherette seats elsewhere, and stone-mullioned windows. Also, some dark squared panelling, beams hung with mugs and horsebrasses, a few toby jugs and other decorative china on a high shelf, swords, knives, assegais, and heavy-horse harness; the colour photographs of show horses and of a pony and trap are a clear clue to the licensee's interests. Good quality bar food includes sandwiches (from £1.10), sausage and egg (£2.25), chilli con carne (£2.50), steak pie (£2.75), gammon (£3.25), trout (£4.45) and steaks (from £5.30); Sunday roast lunch (£3.35). Well kept Ruddles County, Websters Yorkshire and Choice on handpump, with quite a few decent malt whiskies. A separate room has pool, fruit machine, space game and juke box. *(Recommended by Len Beattie, John Gumbley)*

Free house   Licensee Jean Greenwood   Real ale   Meals and snacks (not Mon lunchtime)   Evening restaurant tel Todmorden (0706) 813449   Children welcome   Open 12–3, 7–11 all year; midnight supper licence; closed Mon lunchtime

STARBOTTON (N Yorks)   SE9574   Map 7
Fox & Hounds

OS Sheet 98 reference 953749

As we went to press, new licensees had just moved into this beautifully placed Dales pub and were adding bathrooms to the bedrooms and re-fitting the kitchen (during this time there are only sandwiches or ploughman's). The decent pubby atmosphere remains, as does the good mix of customers – locals, walkers and motorists. There's an antique settle and other solid old-fashioned furniture on the flagstones, high beams supporting ceiling-boards, a big stone fireplace (and enormous fire in winter). Well kept Theakstons Best and Old Peculier and Youngers Scotch on handpump; darts and dominoes. There are sturdy tables and benches in a sheltered corner outside the pretty stone-slab-roofed inn; here you can look out to the hills all around this little hamlet – there's a bracing walk up over Buckden Pike to the White Lion at Cray. *(Recommended by Peter Race, Len Beattie, Mr and Mrs M Tarlton, Tim Halstead, Robert Gartery, K McConnochie, Dr J C Barnes; we'd be grateful for reports on the changes)*

Free house   Licensee Pam Casey   Real ale   Meals and snacks   Open 11.30–3, 6.30–11 Bedrooms tel Kettlewell (075 676) 269; no prices available as we went to press

---

Children welcome means the pub says it lets children inside without any special restriction. If it allows them in, but to restricted areas such as an eating area or family-room, we specify this. Places with separate restaurants usually let children use them; hotels usually let them into public areas such as lounges. Some pubs impose an evening time-limit – let us know if you find this.

STAVELEY (N Yorks)   SE3662 Map 7
Royal Oak ⊗

Village signposted from A6055 Knaresborough–Boroughbridge

Dark settles and a big check-clothed Victorian table in the broad bow window underline the genuine country atmosphere in this small tiled-floor pub – as do the picnic-table sets under cocktail parasols on the neatly flower-bordered front lawn, dominated as they are by the great lime tree standing over them, beside the village church. A dark-beamed and carpeted inner room has small topographical prints on the walls, but is otherwise similar. Popular lunchtime bar food includes soup (£1.50), sandwiches (from £1.75), ploughman's (£2.95), salads (£3.75), steak and kidney pie (£3.85) and game pie (£4.05; they sell this to take away, too); in the evening the pub turns into a restaurant, with main dishes such as poached salmon with prawn and cucumber sauce (£7.90). Well kept Theakstons Best on handpump; darts, dominoes; the *Independent* or *Telegraph* for the rare customers who don't find themselves joining in the general conversation. *(Recommended by Stephanie Sowerby, Dr S G Donald, Prof S Barnett)*

Free house   Licensees Peter and Elizabeth Gallagher   Real ale   Snacks (lunchtime) and meals   Restaurant tel Harrogate (0423) 340267   Children welcome   Open 12–3, 7–11 all year; closed 25 Dec

SUTTON (S Yorks)   SE5512 Map 7
Anne Arms   ★

From A1 just S of Barnsdale Bar service area follow Askern, Campsall signpost; Sutton signposted right from Campsall

A cosy and friendly creeper-covered stone house, starred by us for its profusion of ornaments: a throng of toby jugs collected over many years; lots of colourful five-litre and smaller Bavarian drinking-steins; latticed glass cases thronged with china shepherdesses and the like; oak dressers filled with brightly coloured plates; fruit plates embossed with lifesize red apples; wooden figures popping out of a Swiss clock when it chimes the quarter-hours. A separate room is filled with brass and copper, and there's a new Victorian-style conservatory. Good value food includes a choice of six main dishes, a help-yourself salad buffet, and puddings such as trifles or meringues. *(Recommended by T Nott, D P Cartwright, Malcolm Steward, Sue Cleasby, Mike Ledger, Patrick Young, Richard Cole)*

John Smiths (Courage)   Meals and snacks   Children in buffet room/snug   Open 10.30–3, 6–10.30

SUTTON HOWGRAVE (N Yorks)   SE3279 Map 7
White Dog ⊗

Village signposted from B6267 about 1 mile W of junction with A1

The two main rooms in this pretty village cottage have flowers on the polished tables and are furnished with comfortably cushioned Windsor chairs. On one side of the black-beamed bar there's an open kitchen range with a welcoming fire in cool weather; friendly cat. Good, popular bar lunches include sandwiches (from £1), French onion soup (£1.25), mariner's hot-pot (£2.50), salads (from £2.50), omelettes (from £2.75), fish pie (£2.85), steak and kidney pie (£3.25), chicken and mushroom casserole (£3.25), sirloin steak (£5.95) and puddings (£1.50). The pub stands at the end of a little farming hamlet by a peaceful green with field maples and sycamores. Its upper windows are almost hidden in summer by the flowers in the window boxes and two clematis, and there are picnic-table sets among flower beds on the grass beside the pub. *(Recommended by Wayne Brindle, Mr and Mrs M Fox, J E Rycroft, KC, H E Scott)*

Free house   Licensee Basil Bagnall   Lunchtime meals and snacks (not Mon, not Sun evening)   Restaurant (not Sun evening) tel Melmerby (076 584) 404   Open 12–2.30, 7–11 all year; closed Sun evening, all day Mon, 25 Dec and 1 Jan

THORNTON WATLASS (N Yorks)   SE2486 Map 10
Buck ⊗ 🛏

Village signposted off B6268 Bedale–Masham

Part of a row of low stone cottages, this peaceful country pub looks past a grand row of sycamores to the village cricket green (the pub itself forms part of the boundary). The bar on the right is pleasantly traditional, with handsome old-fashioned wall settles, cast-iron-framed tables, a high shelf packed with ancient bottles, and several mounted foxes' masks and brushes (the Bedale hunt meets in the village). Bar food includes soup (£1.20), bacon and tomato in French bread (£1.70), a vegetarian dish such as broccoli and courgette au gratin (£2.50), omelettes (£2.70), steak and kidney pie (£3.20), sugar-baked ham (£3.70), fresh Whitby cod (from £3.70 – picked out by several readers) and tandoori chicken (£5.50), with smaller helpings for OAPs; well kept Tetleys and Theakstons Best and XB on handpump. A bigger plainer bar has darts, dominoes, pool and trivia machine, and the garden has two quoits pitches, with league matches on Wednesday evenings in summer, and practice on Sunday morning and Tuesday evening. The inn has trout fishing on the Ure. *(Recommended by E R Thompson, Frank Cummins, Mr and Mrs K Hicks, William Langley, David Gaunt, A Sharp, JF)*

Free house   Licensees Michael and Margaret Fox   Real ale   Meals and snacks Restaurant   Children in functions room at lunchtime and in bar until 8.30   Organ singalong and dancing Sat and Sun evening   Open 11–2.30, 6–11 all year, all day for cricket matches and so forth   Bedrooms tel Bedale (0677) 22461; £11.50/£22

THRESHFIELD (N Yorks)   SD9763 Map 7
Old Hall ⊗

B6265, just on Skipton side of its junction with B6160 near Grassington

Completely reworked by its new owners in 1987, this friendly inn has three communicating rooms, with a high beam and plank ceiling hung with pots, a tall well blacked kitchen range, cushioned pews built into the white walls, and simple crisp decorations, nothing fussy – old Cadburys advertisements, decorative plates on a high Delft shelf. Food too is imaginative without being pretentious or over-ambitious: a pair of Yorkshire puddings with onion gravy (95p), celery and Stilton soup (£1.10), sweet-and-sour herrings or ratatouille (£1.75), ploughman's (£2.50), lamb and spinach curry or pork goulash (£3.50), steak pie or chicken with sweet mustard and almond sauce (£3.75), twelve-ounce gammon (£3.95), a huge mixed salad (£4.50) and fish Mornay (£4.95). Well kept Timothy Taylors Best and Youngers Scotch on handpump, darts, dominoes and on our visit piped pop music, fruit machine. There are tables in a neat side garden, partly gravelled, with young shrubs, a big sycamore, and an aviary with cockatiels and zebra finches; they should have a conservatory open here by the time we publish. It's the back part – dating from Tudor times, and the oldest inhabited building in Wharfedale – that gives the inn its name; this ancient part is being turned into additional bedrooms. This is of course a fine base for Dales walking, and the inn is on *Good Walks*

Meal times are generally the normal times at which people eat in the region. But they tend to vary from day to day and with the season, depending on how busy the pub hopes to be. We don't specify them as our experience shows you can't rely on them.

Guide Walk 150. *(Recommended by G N G Tingey, R F Neil, J Whitehead, Prof S Barnett, Wayne Brindle, P Howard)*

Free house Licensees Ian and Amanda Taylor Real ale Meals and snacks Restaurant Children in eating area and conservatory Open 11–3, 5.30–11 all year Bedrooms tel Grassington (0756) 752441; £15/£30

THRUSCROSS (N Yorks) SE1558 Map 7
Stone House Inn ⊗

Village signposted from A59 Harrogate–Skipton at Blubberhouses, or off B6265 Grassington–Pateley Bridge at Greenhow Hill; OS Sheet 104 reference 159587

This enthusiastically friendly moorland pub has a black beam and board ceiling, a very powerful wood-burning stove in the elaborately carved wooden fireplace below a collection of brass blow-torches, sturdy cushioned seats built in around oak tables in the carpeted part by the left, and some dark squared panelling, stripped stone and flagstones round towards the right where there's another open fire; here, two cats (Grace and Flower) doze on a chintz armchair, and there's a very friendly dog. Generous helpings of good value bar food include sandwiches (from 85p), late breakfast (£2.95), seafood platter or gammon (£3.15), special salad (£5.75), steak (£7.95), mixed grill (£9.45) and puddings (£1.10). Well kept Theakstons Best, XB and Old Peculier on handpump; darts, shove-ha'penny, dominoes, cribbage, fruit machine and unobtrusive piped music. Tables outside in front are sheltered by attractive stone bays planted with geraniums and other flowers. *(Recommended by Mark Sheard, Chris Fluck, Len Beattie, Jenny Seller, Prof S Barnett, Ann McClurkin)*

Free house Licensee B W Nicholson Real ale Meals and snacks Restaurant (closed Sun evening) tel Blubberhouses (094 388) 226 Children welcome Open 11–11 all year

WATH-IN-NIDDERDALE (N Yorks) SE1558 Map 7
Sportsmans Arms ⊗ 🛏

You should really stay overnight in this friendly country inn and enjoy a good leisurely dinner to get the best of the young chef's excellent cooking. There's a very sensible and extensive wine list, and service is attentive. Bar lunches, much simpler, are good too: home-made soup (£1.25), chicken liver pâté (£2.50), locally made Coverdale and double Gloucester ploughman's (£2.50), pasta with garlic mushrooms (£2.85), locally made black pudding (£2.95), rarebit with grilled bacon (£3.50), chicken sauté chasseur (£3.95), late breakfast (£4), and fresh Nidderdale trout and puddings (£1.60); three-course restaurant Sunday lunch (£8.50), and fresh fish daily from Whitby. The comfortable blond-panelled bar has big gamebird prints on Madras cotton wallhanging, dominoes and piped music. The valley setting is charming. *(Recommended by Lynn Stevens, Gill Quarton, Geoff Wilson, Andy Tye, Sue Hill, K A Chappell, Len Beattie, David and Flo Wallington, W F Coghill, Mrs C Forster)*

Free house Licensee J R Carter Lunchtime meals and snacks (not Sun) Evening restaurant (not Sun evening) Children welcome Open 12–3, 7–11 all year; closed evenings 24 and 31 Dec, all day 25 and 26 Dec and 1 Jan Bedrooms tel Harrogate (0423) 711306; £25(£27S)/ £35(£40B)

WELBURN (N Yorks) SE7268 Map 7
Crown & Cushion

Village signposted from A64 York–Malton

The two connecting rooms of the carpeted lounge in this pleasant old stone inn have a relaxing atmosphere, a collection of over 265 water jugs, high shelves of plates, little pictures between strips of black wood on the cream walls, wheel-back chairs and small cushioned settles around wooden tables, and open fires in winter. Bar food includes soup (95p), sandwiches (from £1), pâté (£1.80), ploughman's (£2.50), salads (from £3), lasagne (£3.10), steak and kidney pie (£3.45), scampi or gammon with pineapple (£4.35) and steaks (from £5.95). Well kept Camerons Lion and Strongarm on handpump; brisk service. Darts, dominoes, fruit machine and juke box in the public bar; piped music. The pub is close to Castle Howard. Please note that they no longer do bedrooms. (*Recommended by Mr and Mrs F W Sturch, Bernard Phillips, John Roue', John and Alison Logan, Scott W Stucky, R A Gomme*)

Camerons   Licensee David Abbey   Real ale   Meals and snacks (not Mon)   Restaurant tel Whitwell on the Hill (065 381) 304   Children in eating area of bar and restaurant   Open 11–2.30, 6.30–11; opens 7 in winter

WENTWORTH (S Yorks)   SK3898   Map 7
George & Dragon ⊗

3 miles from M1 junction 36: village signposted from A6135; can also be reached from junction 35 via Thorpe; pub is on B6090

You'll find the warmest of welcomes in the pleasantly rambling bar as well as an assortment of old-fashioned seats and tables, blue plates on the walls, steps splitting the front area into separate parts, and a lounge (back by the little games-room) with an ornate stove. Good food includes a wide choice of salads with interesting ingredients from a help-yourself counter, and sandwiches, ploughman's, savoury hash and nut rice; they also sell home-made jams, marmalade and cake. A wide range of well kept ales includes Oak Double Dagger, Timothy Taylors Bitter, Landlord and, in winter, Porter, and Tetleys and Theakstons Old Peculier on handpump; also scrumpy cider. There are benches in the front courtyard, where there's a barn and shop. (*Recommended by M A and W R Proctor, Dr R V Watson, Brian Green; more comments please – up-to-date food prices would be very helpful!*)

Free house   Licensee Margaret Dickinson   Real ale   Lunchtime meals and snacks   Children in dining area   Open 12–3, 7–11 all year

WEST TANFIELD (N Yorks)   SE2678   Map 7
Bruce Arms

A6108 (a quiet road) N of Ripon

The snug little front bar in this unspoilt and attractive old village inn has red plush cushioned Jacobean-style seats, a cushioned curved-back antique settle, carved oak armchair, spindle-back chairs around rustic tables, and an unusual open stone bread oven beside its log fire; the back bar is more or less similar. Cheap bar food includes pasties or burgers (65p), sandwiches (from 70p), home-made soup (90p), good ploughman's (£1.30), with main meals such as shepherd's pie (£1.10), scampi or haddock (£2.20), chicken and mushroom or steak and onion pie (£2.40), grilled ham and eggs (£4.10) and steaks (from £5.50); well kept John Smiths and Theakstons Best and XB on handpump; darts, dominoes, cribbage, juke box and space game, and – sharing a lobby with an attractive pew, with fine carved finials – a fruit machine. Tables on a flagstoned side terrace are sheltered by roses and flowering shrubs, with a fine pear tree trained against the inn's wall. The back stables are still in use. (*Recommended by Rob and Gill Weeks, Mr and Mrs M Tarlton, Wayne Brindle*)

Free house   Real ale   Meals and snacks (not Mon)   Restaurant tel Bedale (0677) 70325   Children welcome lunchtimes   Open 10.30–2.30, 5.30–11; closed Mon lunchtime exc bank hols

WIDDOP (W Yorks)   SD9333 Map 7
Pack Horse ⊗

The Ridge; from A646 on W side of Hebden Bridge, turn off at Heptonstall signpost (as it's a sharp turn, coming out of Hebden Bridge road signs direct you around a turning circle), then follow Slack and Widdop signposts; can also be reached from Nelson and Colne, on high, pretty road; OS Sheet 103 reference 952317

Popular with walkers (the Pennine Way passes quite close by), this isolated moorland pub has an unpretentious welcome. There are sturdy furnishings, window seats cut into the partly panelled stripped stone walls which look out over the moors, and warm fires in winter. Good, straightforward bar food includes sandwiches (from 80p, home-cooked ham or roast beef 90p, double-deckers from £1.50, open sandwiches on French bread from £1.75), burger (£1.75), cottage hot-pot (£2.20), ploughman's (£2.30), salads (from £3), gammon with two eggs or home-made steak and kidney pie (£3.50) and steaks (from £5.25); be prepared for a wait on summer weekends, when it's crowded. Well kept Thwaites, Youngers IPA and guests on handpump, and decent malt whiskies. There are seats outside. *(Recommended by Wayne Brindle, Len Beattie, Simon Bates)*

Free house   Licensee Peter Jackson   Real ale   Meals and snacks (not Mon evenings in winter) Children welcome until 9   Open 12–2.30 (3 Sat), 7–11 all year; closed weekday lunchtimes Oct–Apr, exc Christmas and Easter week

WIGHILL (N Yorks)   SE4746 Map 7
White Swan ★

Village signposted from Tadcaster; also easily reached from A1 Wetherby bypass – take Thorpe Arch Trading Estate turn-off, then follow Wighill signposts; OS Sheet 105 reference 476468

While a huge lovingly restored tractor engine idled outside next to two horses, the riders and boiler-suited drivers nipped into this friendly, unaffected and remarkably relaxing pub to enjoy the well kept Stones and Theakstons Best, XB and Old Peculier on handpump. The central bar serves a small lobby as well as several separate rooms, each attractively furnished by this family over the half-century that they've kept the pub. At the back, for instance, there are leather bucket seats and a curly-armed mahogany settle, a very deep square-sided Second Empire cane sofa (in need of recaning), small sporting prints and a dark oil painting, a longcase clock and – as in all the other rooms – a coal fire. The bar snacks are good value: well filled sandwiches (from 80p), ploughman's with a choice of cheeses (£2.14), giant crusty-bread sandwiches (from £1.80), and salads (up to £3.60), with soup on cold winter days; the dignified but friendly dog (mainly golden labrador) is called Wooster. French windows from an extension lead on to a patio area overlooking the garden. *(Recommended by AE, Graeme Smalley, T Nott, Jon Wainwright)*

Free house   Licensee Peter Swale   Real ale   Lunchtime snacks   Children in three rooms Open 12–3, 6–11 all year

WORMALD GREEN (N Yorks)   SE3065 Map 7
Cragg Lodge ⊗

A61 Ripon–Harrogate, about half way

The collection of malt whiskies at this comfortably modernised roadhouse is probably now the widest in Britain – maybe the world. There are well over five hundred, including for example a dozen Macallans going back to 1937 (£2.30 – a remarkable bargain, smooth as silk yet glowing with deep character). They have sixteen price bands, between 80p and £7, depending on rarity – with a seventeenth 'by negotiation' for their unique 1919 Campbelltown; and happy-hour price cuts betwen 6 and 7. Not being too single-minded, they also have well kept John Smiths,

Tetleys Bitter and Mild and Theakstons Best, XB and Old Peculier on handpump, several distinguished brandies, and mature vintage port by the glass; friendly service; dominoes, cribbage, fruit machine and piped music. The extensive open-plan bar has a dark joist and plank ceiling, little red plush chairs around dark rustic tables, and a coal fire; bar food includes home-made soup (80p), sandwiches (from 80p), game and liver pâté (£1.40), ploughman's (£2), nut cutlets (£2.50), salads (from £2.50), home-made steak and kidney pie or curry (£2.90), gammon with egg or pineapple (£3.95), steaks (from £5.50) and a daily roast; also, puddings such as home-made cheesecake (£1.15), children's meals (from £1), and they do morning coffee and snacks from 10am. There are picnic-table sets under cocktail parasols on the side terrace. (*Recommended by Mandy and Mike Challis, Barbara Hatfield, Audrey and Alan Chatting, Wayne Brindle*)

Free house   Licensee Garfield Parvin   Real ale   Meals and snacks   Restaurant   Children in eating area of bar   Open 11–2.30, 6–11   Bedrooms tel Ripon (0765) 87214; £15(£24B)/£20(£32B)

YORK (N Yorks)   SE5951   Map 7

Black Swan

Peaseholme Green; inner ring road, E side of centre; the inn has a good car park

Built over five hundred years ago, this very interesting building was quite plain and plastered until complete restoration before the Second World War revealed its splendid timbered, jettied and gabled façade and original lead-latticed windows in the twin gables. Inside, there's a great deal of evocative character: the back bar has very heavy beams and a big log fire in a vast brick inglenook, while the panelled front bar, with its little serving-hatch, is more restful. The crooked-floored hall between the two has a fine period staircase (leading up to a room fully panelled in oak, with an antique tiled fireplace). Bar food includes sandwiches including delicious prawn (from 80p), home-made soup (90p), ploughman's (£2.30), excellent Yorkshire puddings filled with beef stew (£2.50), and home-made fruit pie (80p). Dominoes, cribbage, fruit machine and piped music. (*Recommended by Dr C D E Morris, Audrey and Alan Chatting, Graeme Smalley, J C Proud, Jon Wainwright, Chris Cooke, Nick Dowson, Alison Hayward*)

Bass   Licensee Robert Atkinson   Meals and snacks (lunchtime, though they will do evening food for party bookings)   Children welcome   Folk night Thurs and jazz Sun lunchtime Open 11–11 all year   Bedrooms tel York (0904) 25236; /£30B

Kings Arms

King's Staithe; left bank of Ouse just below Ouse Bridge; in the evening you should be able to get a parking space right outside, turning down off Clifford Street; otherwise there's a quarter-mile walk

Flooding happens so often in this lively and very busy old pub that its 'cellar' is above ground in an adjacent building, and there's a level meter on one of the walls recording some of the more severe deluges. The pub has bowed black beams, a flagstoned floor, bare brick and stone walls, and good thick cushions on stone window seats that look out over the river. Bar food includes burgers (£1), ploughman's (£1.80), prawn platter (£2), steak and kidney pie or home-made curry (£2.40), and scampi or plaice (£3); fruit machine, juke box. Outside, on a cobbled riverside terrace in a fine spot by the river, are some picnic-table sets. (*Recommended by Graeme Smalley, Jon Wainwright, Andy Tye, Sue Hill, Quentin Williamson, Nick Dowson, Alison Hayward, Rob and Gill Weeks*)

Sam Smiths   Licensee I C Webb   Meals and snacks (not Sat evening)   Open 11–11 all year

---

Though English and Welsh pubs have to stop serving bar drinks between 3 and 7 on Sundays, they are allowed to serve drinks with meals in a separate dining-room all afternoon.

Olde Starre ⊗

Stonegate; pedestrians-only street in centre, far from car parks

The beamed rooms in this very busy pub ramble happily around with some little oak Victorian settles, heavy cast-iron tables and a stained-glass hatch servery with a copper-topped bar counter; the snug has been turned into a wine bar. A good choice of self-service bar food includes sandwiches (from £1), burgers (from £2.20), ploughman's (£2.30), fresh cod (£2.60), steak and kidney pie (£2.85), scampi (£2.90) and chilli con carne or lasagne (£3). Well kept Camerons Lion and Strongarm and Everards Old Original on handpump. A games-room has darts, dominoes, cribbage, fruit machine and piped music. The courtyard tables have a view up above the chimneys and tiled roofs of York's medieval Shambles to the minster's towers. The pub can get extremely crowded at weekends. *(Recommended by Dr Stephen Hiew, Jon Wainwright, Mr and Mrs J H Adam, F A Noble, Scott W Stucky, Ian Phillips, M A and W R Proctor)*

Camerons   Licensee Gaynor Hartley   Real ale   Meals and snacks (not Fri or Sat evenings) Children in parlour bar and games-room   Open 11–11 all year

---

Lucky Dip

Besides the fully inspected pubs, you might like to try these Lucky Dips recommended to us and described by readers (if you do, please send us reports):

Aberford, W Yorks [SE4337], *Arabian Horse*: Well kept Tetleys and Youngers No 3 in beamed pub with blazing winter log fires, lunchtime sandwiches, pleasant landlord, friendly service; in heart of pretty village *(Mr and Mrs J A Smith)*

Ainderby Quernhow, N Yorks [SE3581], *Black Horse*: Out-of-the-way, but worth finding for its good food, and such nice people *(Mr Edwicker)*

Ainderby Steeple, N Yorks [SE3392], *Wellington Heifer*: Long low-ceilinged bar and lounge on two levels, with brown woodwork making no pretence at age; good choice of generously served bar food and beers, quick friendly service *(Anon)*

Ainthorpe, N Yorks [NZ7008], *Fox & Hounds*: Sixteenth-century country pub with oak beams, horsebrasses, real fires and homely atmosphere; Theakstons, reasonably priced bar food, outside tables for summer; cheap bedrooms *(E R Thompson)*

Aislaby, N Yorks [A170 W of Pickering; SE7886], *Blacksmiths Arms*: Friendly welcome in bar with original smithy fire and bellows, though this is really for people going on to eat in the good restaurant *(J F Derbyshire)*

☆ **Almondbury**, W Yorks [bear left up Lumb Lane; village signposted off A629/A642 E of Huddersfield – OS Sheet 110 reference 153141; SE1615], *Castle Hill*: Perched high above Huddersfield on site of prehistoric hill fort, with terrific views of the moors dwarfing the mill towns; lots of coal fires in the rambling partly panelled bar, sturdy traditional furnishings, well kept Timothy Taylors Best and Landlord and Tetleys,

simple bar food (not Sun–Tues evenings), popular Sun lunch *(Rob and Gill Weeks, LYM)*

Appleton Roebuck, N Yorks [SE5542], *Shoulder of Mutton*: Good bar food, separate restaurant *(R C Watkins)*

☆ **Appletreewick**, N Yorks [SE0560], *Craven Arms*: Fine country pub in beautiful surroundings, with roaring fires in both bars, main one in old iron range; good lighting, and good view across River Wharfe – convenient for Dales walkers; it's also been much praised by readers for its well kept Tetleys and Theakstons XB and Old Peculier on handpump, good bar food at reasonable prices and friendly welcome, but the licensees concerned moved in 1988 to the Fountaine at Linton in Craven (see main entries) – just too early for us to hear how their successors have been faring *(Tim Baxter, Nick Long, P Howard, Geoff Wilson and others – reports on the new regime, please)*

Appletreewick, *New Inn*: Good welcome from enthusiastic licensees, good wholesome home cooking prepared and served with care – great ploughman's with three different kinds of cheese; massive choice of beers and lagers *(the Shand family)*

Asenby, N Yorks [just off A168, handy for A1; SE3975], *Shoulder of Mutton*: Thatched stone pub with shutters, old bread oven in lounge, Bass, Shipstone Mild, Stones Best, Theakstons Best, XB and Old Peculier; cheap food, often unusual – rabbit pie, jugged hare, poacher's pie *(Rob and Gill Weeks)*

Askrigg, N Yorks [SD9591], *Crown*: Good home-cooked ham sandwiches and home-made burgers in pleasant pub, not large, in the village where James Herriot's 'Skeldale

House' was filmed for the BBC TV series *All Creatures Great and Small (N Burrell)*

Austerfield, S Yorks [A614 N of Bawtry; SK6694], *Austerfield Manor*: Opened only in 1983, with a spacious, spotless and comfortable L-shaped bar, picnic-table sets on terrace, quickly served bar food, Youngers No 3 on handpump; children welcome, restaurant; very useful for the area *(A G Rose, ILP, LYM)*

Aysgarth, N Yorks [SE0088], *Palmer Flatt*: Moorland hotel near broad waterfalls and carriage museum, medley of largely modernised bars but some interesting ancient masonry at the back recalling its days as a pilgrims' inn, restaurant, seats outside, fishing rights; sold spring 1988 – reports on the new regime, please *(LYM)*

Barden Bridge, N Yorks [SE0557], *Barden Tower*: Steeped in history, very unusual, though not exactly a pub – part of the ancient monument itself and at least in summer has been serving food all day; in a lovely part of Wharfedale *(Wayne Brindle)*

Bardsey, W Yorks [A58; SE3643], *Bingley Arms*: Ancient pub and decorated to look it, popular if pricey picturesque restaurant, charming terrace *(George Little)*

Barkisland, W Yorks [SE0520], *Fleece*: Good choice of well kept real ales in comfortable pub on moors edge, with food including Tues spit-roasts, trad jazz Sun afternoons, and disco-bar – open until small hours *(Wayne Brindle, BB)*; [Stainland Rd] *Griffin*: Previously popular (and highly rated in this *Guide*) for timeless old-fashioned appeal of its small rooms – particularly the cosy little oak-beamed parlour – with good value simple bar food, well kept Burtonwood on unusual Nole pumps, and games in the lively tap-room; when passing in 1988 we've found it closed, but peering through the windows everything still seemed in order *(LYM – news please)*

Barwick in Elmet, W Yorks [Main St; SE4037], *Gascoigne Arms*: Cosy country pub with 200-foot maypole outside, its history and that of other old village traditions detailed in pictures inside; well kept hand-pumped Tetleys and good food (lunchtime, not Sun and Weds–Fri evenings) *(T T Kelly)*

☆ **Beck Hole**, N Yorks [OS Sheet 94 reference 823022; NZ8202], *Birch Hall*: Unusual and interesting pub by bridge over river in beautiful village; comprised of three rooms – public bar, village shop and coffee lounge; home-made butties, hot pies and drinks (no real ale – though in such a lovely spot the chilled Youngers Tartan tastes as nice as it's ever likely to) are served from a hole in the wall from the shop side, to a room with kitchen chairs, plain benches and tables and coal fire; tables outside, garden reached by set of steep steps, and it's close to Thomason Fosse, a waterfall, with lots of attractive walks in the area – it's on GWG159 *(Martin Parker, Dr R Hodkinson, Mr and Mrs Tim Crawford)*

Beckwithshaw, N Yorks [SE2753], *Smiths Arms*: Bright, friendly pub with good bar food and carvery *(Peter Race)*

Bedale, N Yorks [Market Pl; SE2688], *Green Dragon*: Good reasonably priced food and good Theakstons beer *(A J Woodroffe)*

Bingley, W Yorks [Ireland Bridge; B6429 just W of junction with A650 – OS Sheet 104 reference 105395; SE1039], *Brown Cow*: Small snug areas divide spacious open-plan bar of comfortable pub just below pretty bridge over River Aire; bar food (not Sun or Mon evenings) fairly robust – especially their Yorkshire pudding; good range of Timothy Taylors beers normally well kept, summer barbecues, children in eating area and small snug; has been found still closed 7.30 Sun evening; bedrooms in shared adjoining cottages *(Michael Bolsover, Mike Tucker, LYM)*; [Otley Rd, High Eldwick; SE1240] *Dick Hudsons*: Pleasant and very busy pub with fine views over Dales to Bradford, friendly staff, paintings of local scenes for sale, good food – remarkable value Sun lunch; well kept Tetleys *(J P Day, Mike Tucker)*; [Gilshead Lane] *Glen*: Very welcoming atmosphere, railway memorabilia, good sandwiches with lavish salad and other cheap food, Tetleys Mild and Bitter on handpump, play area; pleasant rural setting *(D Stokes)*

Birstwith, N Yorks [SE2459], *Station*: Interesting collection of porcelain and china and friendly staff in pleasant village pub; good real ale on handpump *(Chris Fluck)*

Booth Wood, W Yorks [3 miles from M62 junction 22, towards Halifax; opp reservoir – OS Sheet 110 reference 021162; SE0216], *Turnpike*: Very isolated moorland pub on very quiet Pennine road; three rooms, some panelling and flagstones, food, first-class Youngers real ales, extremely welcoming; good views to Deanhead, with the M62 at its highest point a distant ribbon *(Lee Goulding)*

☆ **Bradfield**, S Yorks [Strines Reservoir; signposted from A57 Sheffield–Ladybower – OS Sheet 110 reference 222906; SK2692], *Strines*: Ancient thirteenth-century manor with sixteenth-century Worrall coat of arms carved in stone over porch; wonderful views over reservoir and Dark Peak, home-made broths and soups, filled rolls and bar meals (open all day for food); also evening carvery Weds–Sat and Sun buffet lunch – first-floor restaurant with open fires, oak panelling in two rooms; particularly good coffee *(Jane English, Rob and Gill Weeks)*

☆ **Bradford**, W Yorks [Barkerend Rd; up Church Bank from centre, on left few hundred yds past cathedral; SE1633], *Cock & Bottle*: Notable Victorian décor in well preserved small rooms, good value cheap lunchtime snacks, unusually well kept Tetleys real ales, live music Fri and Sat evenings; down-to-earth atmosphere, no frills *(LYM)*

Bradford [74 Frizing Hall Rd], *Black Swan*:

Better known as the Mucky Duck – popular with younger people, busy most evenings *(Anon)*; [7 Stone St, off Manor Row] *Le Nouveau*: Downstairs wine bar with daily board menu, very homely service and well kept Websters; very pleasant glass-enclosed upstairs restaurant; parking impossible *(Ronald Monjack, J E Rycroft)*; [731 Gt Horton Rd], *White Horse*: Very fine Castle Eden and other Whitbreads ales in very spacious friendly pub *(Ian Robinson)*

Brodsworth, S Yorks [Pickburn; SE5107], *Pickburn Arms*: Spacious recently built pub, efficiently run and spotlessly clean, with pleasant atmosphere with sun streaming in through windows and French doors at lunchtime; straightforward bar food, Barnabys carvery; lawns, outside tables, summer barbecues – a cheerful haven for travellers in an area with few good pubs *(ILP)*

Brompton on Swale, N Yorks [SE2299], *Crown*: Well kept real ale, good bar food, friendly staff *(P Gillbe)*

Broughton, N Yorks [SD9351], *Bull*: Well kept Youngers in cosy pub, comfortable and smartly modernised, with pleasant atmosphere and friendly service; food in bar and restaurant *(Mike Suddards, LYM)*

Burniston, N Yorks [TA0193], *Oak Wheel*: Good wholesome food, pleasant service *(Stanley Robinson)*

Burnlee, W Yorks [Liphill Bank Rd; just off A635 Holmfirth–Manchester; SE1307], *Farmers Arms*: Small, unspoilt pub in remote hamlet with new regime now providing cheap lunchtime and evening bar food; well kept Greenalls and Timothy Taylors; children welcome *(Robert Gartery)*

Calder Grove, W Yorks [Broadley Cut Rd; just off M1 junction 39; A636 signposted Denby Dale, then first right; SE3116], *Navigation*: Well kept Tetleys and simple food in profusely decorated canalside pub with tables outside – very handy for the motorway, though piped music can be loud *(Keith Noble, LYM)*

Campsall, S Yorks [SE5413], *Old Bells*: Good choice of bar snacks and restaurant meals, good service, good value for money *(Pat Smith)*

Carleton, N Yorks [SD9749], *Swan*: Roaring fire in unpretentious bar with comfortable chairs, very good value food (same in bar and restaurant) including many good vegetarian dishes; very friendly staff, well kept Websters *(PJA)*

Carlton, N Yorks [OS Sheet 93 reference 509044; NZ5104], *Blackwell Ox*: Atmosphere relaxed and friendly in low-beamed lounge overlooking quiet village street from elevated position among lovely village buildings, though food value doesn't seem quite what it used to be under former owners *(Anon)*

Carlton Husthwaite, N Yorks [SE5077], *Carlton*: Good cheerful efficient service, very

well kept Youngers on handpump, good food in bar and dining-room – especially large succulent fillet steaks, salmon with mushroom and prawn cream sauce, well cooked interesting vegetables such as potatoes in herb sauce and sliced cauliflower in batter *(W A Rinaldi-Butcher)*

Carlton Miniott, N Yorks [Thirsk Rd (A61 Thirsk–Ripon); SE3981], *Old Red House*: Close to BR station – good value bedrooms and real ale *(Alan Gough)*

Carperby, N Yorks [SE0189], *Wheatsheaf*: Good range of beers and other drinks, pleasant friendly atmosphere *(Anon)*

Carthorpe, N Yorks [off A1 N of Ripon, via Burneston and B6285; SE3184], *Fox & Hounds*: Busy food pub with unpretentious exterior and cosy interior; friendly service, Camerons on handpump and good range of bar meals *(Tim Halstead)*

Castleton, N Yorks [NZ6908], *Moorlands*: Hotel with pleasant split-level bar, good bar food at reasonable prices; bedrooms *(Mr and Mrs F W Sturch)*

Chapel le Dale, N Yorks [SD7477], *Old Hill*: Basic moorland pub with well kept Theakstons real ales, popular with walkers and climbers for its unfussy welcome – except at the quietest times there's normally a big open fire in the cosy back parlour; live music in barn most summer Sats; children welcome; bedrooms simple *(LYM)*

Clifton, W Yorks [Westgate; off Brighouse rd from M62 junction 25; SE1623], *Black Horse*: Attractive and substantial old inn with low ceilings, long corridors and exposed beams; well kept Whitbreads Castle Eden on handpump, very friendly service, cheerful landlord, wide choice of bar food including good Yorkshire pudding butties at lunchtime, traditional Sun lunches; good garden with barbecue area; bedrooms beamed and comfortable *(Mr and Mrs J A Smith, Stephen Sarraff)*

Cloughton Newlands, N Yorks [TA0196], *Bryherstones*: Good food, pleasant surroundings, facilities for children *(Stanley Robinson)*

Collingham, W Yorks [off A58; SE3946], *Barley Corn*: Spacious pub serving good value bar food and Sun lunches *(C Edwards)*

Collingham, W Yorks [SE3946], *Star*: Good pub with separate restaurant, bar can be crowded *(T Nott)*

☆ **Constable Burton**, N Yorks [SE1791], *Wyvill Arms*: Comfortably converted farmhouse with elaborate stone fireplace and fine plaster ceiling in inner room; under new management, with fresh décor, well kept Theakstons, good value bar food attractively presented including ploughman's with three local cheeses, piped music – kindly turned down on request *(Dr and Mrs B D Smith, LYM)*

Cropton, N Yorks [SE7689], *New Inn*: Very good beer brewed on the premises, nice atmosphere and good – but a bit pricey – food *(J H Tate)*

Cullingworth, W Yorks [Manywell Heights; B6429/A629 Halifax–Keighley; SE0636], *Five Flags*: Impressive hotel complex with comfortable and cosy lounge bar among striking theme bars, popular restaurant *(Wayne Brindle)*

Darley Head, N Yorks [B6451; SE1959], *Wellington*: Small pub with warm, cosy atmosphere and log fires; well kept Tetleys on handpump and limited bar food; new restaurant extension *(Chris Fluck)*

Denby Dale, W Yorks [Wakefield Rd; SK2208], *Travellers Rest*: Good value hot or cold bar food in comfortable surroundings, Tetleys and Theakstons; open fires in winter *(A D and S A Gamble)*

Dishforth, N Yorks [nr junction A1/A168; SE3873], *Black Swan*: Good welcome, roaring fire, well kept John Smiths on handpump, home-cooked daily specials including vegetarian dishes *(Gill and Neil Patrick)*

Doncaster, S Yorks [Cleveland St; SE5703], *Corner Pin*: Friendly atmosphere in central pub with well kept John Smiths, bar snacks and charity-conscious licensees *(Alastair Lang)*; [Frenchgate; on edge of central pedestrian precinct] *White Swan*: Front room so far below counter level that you need a high reach for your well kept Wards Sheffield Best; snacks *(BB)*

Easingwold, N Yorks [Market Pl; SE5270], *George*: Terraced village inn with food in cosy lounge bar, well kept Youngers IPA and Scotch, quiet and relaxing at lunchtime; in picturesque village; bedrooms *(Lee Goulding)*

☆ **East Marton**, N Yorks [SD9051], *Cross Keys*: Interesting old-fashioned furnishings, well kept Theakstons, bar food and friendly service in pub quite close to Leeds and Liverpool Canal; separate children's room *(LYM)*

East Morton, W Yorks [SE1042], *Busfeild Arms*: Friendly well kept pub with well kept Bass and Stones; good bar meals and snacks Mon to Sat lunchtime *(Mr and Mrs J E Rycroft)*

East Witton, N Yorks [over ½ mile on road to Middleham; SE1586], *Coverbridge*: Very old, unspoilt place with good bar food and characterful bar food *(David Gaunt)*

Ebberston, N Yorks [SE8983], *Grapes*: Good well cooked food – get there early for lunch *(Stanley Robinson)*

Egton, N Yorks [NZ8106], *Wheatsheaf*: Popular and welcoming village local with well kept McEwans 80/-, wide choice of bar food, smallish simple bar, very plush lounge, attractive separate restaurant; attractive outside – especially lit up in the dark *(Mr and Mrs Tim Crawford, Nick Dowson, Alison Hayward, Eileen Broadbent, M A and W R Proctor)*

Embsay, N Yorks [Elm Tree Sq; SE0053], *Elm Tree*: Recently refurbished village-centre pub with open-plan bar and beams, brass plates, old-fashioned prints and gas-effect log fire; one end has a pool-table, darts, fruit machine, dominoes and TV which is popular with locals, and the other is quieter, though there is a juke box; Whitbreads ales and bar food; well run by pleasant new landlord *(George Hunt)*

Emley, W Yorks [SE2413], *White Horse*: Village free house with well kept Tetleys Yorkshire No 1 *(Jon Wainwright)*

Escrick, N Yorks [SE6343], *Black Bull*: Very pleasant setting and atmosphere, comfortable if not unusual inside, reasonably priced straightforward bar food, decent house wines; can get very busy *(Roger Bellingham, Tim Halstead, T Nott)*

☆ **Esholt**, W Yorks [Main St, just off A6038 Shipley–Otley; SE1840], *Commercial*: Very clean and attractive inside and out, bright and spick and span with lots of shining brass, well kept Whitbreads Castle Eden, friendly atmosphere, good bar food, in pleasant village – which doubles as Beckindale in *Emmerdale Farm* TV series, with pub as Woolpack (quite often see filming outside pub) *(Mrs Jenny Seller, Andrew Rice)*

☆ **Fadmoor**, N Yorks [SE6789], *Plough*: Friendly landlord in traditionally furnished pub overlooking quiet village green, lunchtime bar food has included big filled Yorkshire puddings in winter but may be confined to soup and sandwiches, restaurant meals including Sun lunch; Websters and Wilsons real ale; comfortable bedrooms *(Peter Race, Bob Gardiner, T George, Jon Dewhirst, LYM)*

Fairburn, N Yorks [just off A1; SE4727], *Bay Horse*: Very good value three-course dinner; quite full even on a Mon evening *(M D Hampson)*

☆ **Farnley Tyas**, W Yorks [SE1612], *Golden Cock*: Set out more like a bistro than a pub with a warmly welcoming small cosy bar with coal fire and well kept Bass on handpump, very good new upstairs charcuterie restaurant which specializes in carvery and casseroles; fresh flowers on tables, pleasant panelling, discreetly attentive service, thoughtful wine list, unobtrusive piped music *(K A Chappell, David and Gerda Scott, John Keighley)*

Felixkirk, N Yorks [SE4785], *Carpenters Arms*: Old-world food pub with well kept John Smiths and Younger Scotch on handpump, friendly attentive licensees and good bar meals in cosy, comfortable bar and attractive character dining-room; good coffee; high chair available for children *(T W Simpson, Mrs Irene Smith, SS)*

Filey, N Yorks [The Crescent; TA1281], *Victoria Court*: Pleasant bar with reliably good food, service always congenial *(Dr R J Kerry)*

Follifoot, N Yorks [SE3452], *Radcliffe Arms*: Short choice of good generous one-price main dishes such as roast beef, huge

Aberdeen haddock, steak and kidney pie, very good puddings; always busy, especially on weekend evenings, with a nice party atmosphere – not rowdy *(Dr S G Donald)*

Galphay, N Yorks [SE2573], *Galphay*: Lovely atmosphere in friendly and very popular food pub – there's often a queue for a table when it opens at 7; open fire, very good choice of enterprising and generously served main dishes, good value if not cheap *(C Hackett, P G Race, Audrey and Alan Chatting)*

Gargrave, N Yorks [A65 W of village; SD9354], *Anchor*: Popular and very big family pub with wide range of real ales (their Timothy Taylors Landlord is particularly praised) and simple reasonably priced food, including children's dishes; efficient service, lots of amusements, piped music; canalside tables and play area; restaurant *(Stephen and Karen Law, Mrs M Warrener, R H Sawyer, Prof S Barnett, Len Beattie, LYM)*

Gargrave, *Masons Arms*: Typical Yorkshire Dales village pub – a cosier and much more traditional contrast to our other entry here – with dominoes in one lounge, bowling-green at back and popular bar food *(Wayne Brindle)*

Garsdale Head, N Yorks [junction A684/B6259; near Garsdale stn on Settle–Carlisle line; SD7992], *Moorcock*: Isolated in good walking country; good food, well and quickly produced, pleasant staff *(D T Taylor)*

Gayles, N Yorks [NZ1207], *Bay Horse*: Much done-up open-plan bar in friendly farm pub with small open fires, well kept McEwans 80/-, Newcastle Exhibition and Youngers Scotch on handpump, darts, straightforward food including good home-cooked ham; closed Weds *(Hon G Vane, BB)*

Goathland, N Yorks [opp church; NZ8301], *Mallyan Spout*: Good beer from Malton Brewery, very comfortable bar with good food such as braised oxtail, huge Yorkshire puddings with venison or steak and kidney, proper puddings; also popular restaurant; nr GWG159; bedrooms *(Anon)*

Goldsborough, N Yorks [two miles from A1; SE3856], *Bay Horse*: Traditional stone-built Yorkshire pub with fine restaurant food and bar food now served evenings as well as lunchtime; beamed front lounge bar has coal-effect gas fire, is decorated with weaponry, and has massive cast-iron chandelier over the copper-topped tables; off the beaten track, so good for a quiet drink; well kept Whitbreads Castle Eden and Trophy; bedrooms *(Rob and Gill Weeks)*

Grange Moor, W Yorks [A6142 Huddersfield–Wakefield; SE2216], *Kaye Arms*: A collection of whiskies decorates the walls and there's a large range of bar snacks with specials chalked up on a blackboard; good rare beef sandwiches, very good thick fillet steak, ploughman's with good home-made chutney and interesting soups such as carrot and orange or cream of celery *(K A Chappell)*

Grassington, N Yorks [Garrs Lane; SE0064],

Black Horse: Good Theakstons ales, very good food, comfortable and friendly; nr start GWG150; bedrooms good value *(Alan Brooke)*; [The Square] *Devonshire*: Pleasant and popular inn with interesting pictures and good window seats overlooking the attractive sloping village square; Youngers Scotch Ale and No 3 on handpump, good range of bar food; nr start GWG150; bedrooms reasonable, good breakfasts *(Jon Wainwright, C M T Johnson)*

Great Barugh, N Yorks [off A169 Malton –Pickering – OS Sheet 100 reference 749790; SE7579], *Golden Lion*: Interesting country pub with lots of horse tackle, helpful landlord, light classical piped music; Tetleys on handpump; good, reasonably priced food and friendly staff; separate dining-room with Sun lunch; seats outside; children welcome *(Mrs B E Asher, AE)*

☆ **Great Broughton**, N Yorks [High St; NZ5405], *Wainstones*: Under efficient new ownership with good bar food including lovely Yorkshire puddings for the Sun bar lunches, Bass and Stones on handpump, good restaurant; bedrooms *(E J and J W Cutting, Lyn Marsay)*

Great Ouseburn, N Yorks [SE4562], *Three Horseshoes*: Good atmosphere and character, exceptionally friendly and attentive staff, superb freshly cooked food at attractive prices *(Capt and Mrs F Allen)*

☆ **Grenoside**, S Yorks [Skew Hill Lane; 3 miles from M1 junction 35 – OS Sheet 110 reference 328935; SK3394], *Cow & Calf*: Good high settles in the several rooms of this neatly converted farmhouse in its walled yard; well kept Sam Smiths, weekday food, splendid views of Sheffield, welcoming atmosphere; animal noises off; children in good family area, with children's shop in farmyard *(W P P Clarke, Greg Parston, J C and D Aitkenhead, James Walker, Jon Wainwright, LYM)*

Grenoside, [Main St], *Old Red Lion*: Recently refurbished Whitbreads town pub with pleasant atmosphere, friendly service, very good value bar lunches, real ales; piped music and TV, but unobtrusive *(Gordon Theaker)*

Grewelthorpe, N Yorks [SE2376], *Crown*: Friendly village pub with generous helpings of good bar food including Grewelthorpe giant sausages, much attention to detail; very pleasant surroundings *(Mr and Mrs John Watson, Audrey and Alan Chatting)*

Gristhorpe, N Yorks [off A165 Filey–Scarborough; TA0982], *Bull*: Spacious open-plan low-beamed bar with cushioned banquettes, lots of sporting pictures and village scenes; good value bar food including lunchtime cold buffet; games area; well kept Youngers Scotch and No 3 *(Margaret and Roy Randle, LYM)*

Gunnerside, N Yorks [SD9598], *Kings Head*: Good, classic Dales pub with nice beer and food *(Jon Dewhirst)*

Halifax, W Yorks [Paris Gates, Boys Lane – OS Sheet 104 reference 097241; SE0924], *Shears*: Superbly tucked away down narrow cobbled alleys, shut in by towering mills and the bubbling Hebble Brook; very dark but always tidy inside, with décor reflecting sporting links with local teams; also collection of pump clips and foreign bottles; particularly well kept Taylors, Youngers and unusual guest beers, well priced lunchtime food *(Jon Wainwright, I Clay)*

Hambleton, N Yorks [A170; SE5530], *Hambleton*: Conveniently near Cleveland Way and Sutton Bank, well kept Theakstons, wide choice of food *(Tony Pounder)*

Hampsthwaite, N Yorks [about 5 miles W of Harrogate; SE2659], *Joiners Arms*: Clean, warm, well decorated and comfortable with a good choice of well presented reasonably priced bar food; gets full quickly at lunchtime, children and dogs seem welcome; in pleasant village *(Denis Waters, H Edwin Scott)*

Hardrow, N Yorks [SD8791], *Green Dragon*: The reason for visiting this pub has been its exclusive garden access to Britain's highest single-drop waterfall; the pub, which has bedrooms and lots of ground, changed hands in summer 1988, and we'd like news of the new regime; on GWG147 *(LYM)*

Harmby, N Yorks [A684 about 1½m E of Leyburn; SE1389], *Pheasant*: Two-roomed, comfortably furnished, friendly pub with good Tetleys on handpump and a genuine landlord keen on traditional values *(Jon Dewhirst)*

Harrogate, N Yorks [1 Crescent Rd; SE3155], *Hales*: Simple but good lunchtime food *(J Sheldrick)*; [A59/B6161] *Travellers Rest*: No-nonsense pub that lives up to its name with Yorkshire welcome, good beer, unpretentious but comfortable décor, open fires and good plain cheap and quickly served food – especially the poor man's mixed grill *(Dr R Hodkinson, Neil and Gill Patrick)*; [6 Cold Bath Rd, across green from main part of town] *William & Mary*: Wine bar down stone steps in large Victorian house with interesting seating areas; very friendly, prompt service and popular with locals at lunchtime; upstairs restaurant *(B Pain)*

☆ **Hartoft End**, N Yorks [SE7593], *Blacksmiths Arms*: At the foot of Rosedale, extended and modernised sixteenth-century farmhouse with two large bars, open wood fires, attractive dining-room; well kept Tetleys on handpump and good wines by the glass; good home-made food, friendly service; pool-table and fruit machine, tables in garden; bedrooms *(SS)*

Hawes, N Yorks [SD8789], *Crown*: Pleasant atmosphere, good choice of bar food *(Helen Thompson)*; *White Hart*: Tidy lounge bar with open fire, well kept John Smiths, friendly licensees, good food in bar and dining-room *(Peter Bedford)*

Haworth, W Yorks [Main St; SE0337], *Black Bull*: Splendid old Yorkshire pub in pretty village, gorgeous big Yorkshire puddings; this used to be Branwell Brontë's main drinking place, and the Museum Bookshop opposite was the druggist where he got his opium; bedrooms *(AE)*; [Main St] *Fleece*: Good, friendly pub with flagstones, very well kept Timothy Taylors and wholesome, good value food; morris dancers on bank hols, gets crowded in summer *(A and K D Stansfield)*

Hebden, N Yorks [SE0263], *Clarendon*: Well kept Timothy Taylors and Tetleys Mild and Bitter, good food – especially big steaks; friendly service, laconic in typically Yorkshire way; bedrooms clean and comfortable *(Mark Sheard, J Corcoran)*

Hebden Bridge, W Yorks [Thistle Bottom; SD9927], *Stubbings Wharf*: Good friendly atmosphere in clean, bright pub with helpful, cheerful landlord, good choice of well kept beers and good cheap food *(R A Hall)*

☆ **Helmsley**, N Yorks [Market Pl; SE6184], *Black Swan*: Striking Georgian house and adjoining Tudor rectory included primarily as a place to stay, with particularly well equipped and comfortable bedrooms and a charming sheltered garden; though the small saloon bar on the corner is quite ordinary, the beamed and panelled hotel bar (sharing the same servery, and the well kept real ale) has attractive carved oak settles and Windsor armchairs, and opens into cosy and comfortable lounges with good open fires and a good deal of character – one of THF's nicest inns *(Laurence Manning, BB)*

☆ **Helmsley**, [Market Sq], *Crown*: Good friendly atmosphere in simply but pleasantly furnished beamed front bar and bigger central dining bar with good value lunchtime snacks and home-made scones and biscuits for afternoon teas; friendly and efficient service, roaring fires, tables in sheltered garden behind with covered conservatory area; nice bedrooms *(Peter Race, Ninka Sharland, Wayne Brindle, M A and W R Proctor, Rob and Gill Weeks)*

Heptonstall, W Yorks [SD9827], *Cross*: Welcoming pub in friendly steep Pennine moorside village, good Timothy Taylors ales, adequate bar snacks *(G T Jones)*; *White Lion*: Local atmosphere and well kept Castle Eden ale in quiet friendly pub, delightful Pennine village; bedrooms simple *(LYM)*

Higham, S Yorks [Higham Common Rd (off A628); SE3107], *Engineers*: Good Pennine views, well furnished dark wood lounge with juke box; good Sam Smiths OB and well cooked bar food in generous helpings; children's outside play area *(Roger Ollier)*

Honley, W Yorks [SE1312], *Coach & Horses*: Good well kept pub, hard-working licensee; can be smoky *(Ninka Sharland)*

Horton in Ribblesdale, N Yorks [SD8172], *Crown*: Well kept beer in well run pub with good value bedrooms – a nice place to stay at

(Chris Brasher)
Hovingham, N Yorks [SE6775], *Worsley Arms*: Good value bar food and Tetleys and Theakstons on handpump in neat, plain locals' back bar with lots of Yorkshire cricketer photographs, especially of 1930s and 1940s; comfortable hotel with pleasant bedrooms, swifts and house-martins nesting under the eaves – a nice place to stay at *(BB)*

Huddersfield, W Yorks [New St; SE1416], *Jug & Bottle*: Interesting and attractive stone-built pub on city-centre pedestrian way, beautifully kept Sam Smiths OB and Museum on handpump, good choice of food from separate counter, popular with wide range of ages *(Geoff Wilson, R G Ollier)*

Huddersfield [Chapel Hill], *Rat & Ratchet*: Good range of real ales and guest beers in interesting pub, formerly the Grey Horse, handy for town centre and very busy at weekends; good cheap food *(Ben Wimpenny)*; [Lockwood (A616ish)] *Shoulder of Mutton*: Warm and friendly atmosphere and good range of well kept beers such as Everards, Marstons, Tetleys and Theakstons *(N F Doherty)*; [Bradford Rd] *Slubbers Arms*: Locals' free house built in tight V-shape, good real ales including Barnsley Bitter, Marstons Pedigree, Timothy Taylors and guests, country wines, good value cheeseburger with generous side salad, friendly regulars and landlord, real coal range; wonderful Dickensian journey to the lavatories *(Mr and Mrs P A Jones)*

Hunton, N Yorks [SE1992], *New Inn*: Most friendly welcome, typical local atmosphere but bar meals exceptional for originality and variety *(J H M Broughton)*

Hutton le Hole, N Yorks [SE7090], *Crown*: Country village pub in pleasant dales and moors surroundings, well kept Camerons ales and good bar food; handy for Rye Dale Museum *(E R Thompson, A J Woodroffe)*

Hutton Rudby, N Yorks [NZ4706], *Bay Horse*: Pleasant and roomy interior belies exterior, choice of real ales, varied menu in generous portions, garden *(Mrs Shirley Pielou)*

Hutton Sessay, N Yorks [off A19 S of Thirsk; SE4876], *Horsebreakers Arms*: Quite a bit of character, good atmosphere, good Theakstons *(Wayne Brindle)*

Ilkley, W Yorks [Stockel Rd; off Leeds–Skipton rd; SE1147], *Ilkley Moor*: Pleasantly decorated and refurbished Victorian Tetleys pub known locally as the Taps or the Vaults, a good early-doors pub with well kept Taylors and Tetleys, giant lunchtime Yorkshire puddings, real fires, separate games-room and family-room *(Sally Watson)*; [Skipton Rd] *Listers Arms*: Well kept beers and friendly service in solid inn with basement nightclub; bedrooms *(LYM)*; [Ben Rhydding, SE1347] *Wheatley*: Large, warm and friendly pub, big helpings of good bar food and Sun lunches *(C Edwards)*

Ingbirchworth, S Yorks [Welthorne Lane, off A629; SE2205], *Fountain*: Pleasant lounge in Tetleys Wayfarer Inn with good value food, well kept Tetleys Bitter and Mild on handpump, friendly staff, lovely open views over Pennine countryside; children in nice family-room separate from main lounge, with special food helpings – also playground outside *(Alan and Yvonne Hall, W P P Clarke, Roger Huggins)*

Ingleton, N Yorks [SD6973], *Wheatsheaf*: Pleasant, relaxing décor with photographs of old Ingleton, friendly staff, Theakstons and good vegetarian and other bar food *(Anna Jeffery)*

☆ **Keighley**, W Yorks [not a pub, but the buffet car on Keighley–Oxenhope steam trains; SE0641], *Worth Valley Railway*: Ex-BR buffet-car painted in old Midland Rly colours, marvellous views of Brontë and *Railway Children* country; friendly weekend volunteers serve Clarkes, Timothy Taylors and Youngers from handpump, and best sandwiches, as well as full range of other drinks; occasional White Rose Pullman wine-and-dine trains too; can simply change platforms from BR at Keighley – best way to reach Haworth; tel Haworth (0535) 43629 for talking timetable of the five-mile steam service serving Ingrow, Damems, Oakworth (the prettiest station), Haworth and Oxenhope *(Mr and Mrs P A Jones, Charles Hall)*

☆ **Kettlesing**, N Yorks [signposted 6 miles W of Harrogate on A59; SE2256], *Queens Head*: Very good local in pleasant surroundings with wide range of good, popular bar food including good steaks, well kept John Smiths and Theakstons ales, good wine list; friendly service, nicely maintained *(J E Rycroft, G Milligan, David and Ruth Hollands)*

Kettlesing, *Bull*: Very friendly, with well kept John Smiths – and golf balls practically dropping into your hand! *(Wayne Brindle)*

Kettlewell, N Yorks [SD9772], *Bluebell*: Nice atmosphere in knocked-through bar of simple Wharfedale village inn with well kept real ales, bar food and restaurant; nr start GWG151; bedrooms *(Len Beattie, LYM)*; *Kings Head*: Lively and cheerful, Youngers real ales, pool-room; bedrooms *(BB)*; *Racehorses*: Quiet and sedate open-plan hotel bar, comfortable and well furnished with a good atmosphere, well kept real ales such as Goose Eye, Tetleys, Websters and Youngers; nr start GWG151; bedrooms *(Len Beattie, BB)*

☆ **Kilnsey**, N Yorks [Kilnsey Crag; SD9767], *Tennant Arms*: Friendly, lively Dales country pub with beams and flagstone floors, well kept Tetleys and Theakstons Old Peculier, good value bar food including local farm trout, venison pie and children's dishes, open fires (one in an ornate carved fireplace), series of interconnecting rooms each with its own character; views over spectacular Kilnsey Crag from restaurant; on

GWG150; comfortable bedrooms all with private bathrooms *(Rob and Gill Weeks, Len Beattie, Peter Race)*

Kirk Smeaton, N Yorks [SE5216], *Shoulder of Mutton*: Friendly old village pub with lots of character – and characters; Whitbreads Trophy *(Alastair Lang)*

Kirkby Malham, N Yorks [SD8961], *Queen Victoria*: Village pub with good bar snacks, small terrace garden, well kept Tetleys and Theakstons, dog called Albert; bedrooms *(J A Snell)*

Kirkbymoorside, N Yorks [Market Pl; SE6987], *Black Swan*: Picturesque and lively, wide choice of bar snacks, Camerons real ales; bedrooms simple *(LYM)*; *George & Dragon*: Cosy atmosphere, especially in winter with open fire, well kept Theakstons on handpump, good bar food *(R W K Gardiner)*

☆ **Lastingham**, N Yorks [SE7391], *Blacksmiths Arms*: Very attractive village setting for neat stone inn with comfortable and traditional bar – oak beams, built-in wall seats, potyards swinging over cooking-range; well kept Matthew Browns John Peel and Theakstons Best, XB and Old Peculier, piped music, simple bar food and Sun roasts; closed weekday lunchtimes Nov–Feb; children in eating area; lovely surrounding countryside, good for easy walking; simple bedrooms *(Kelvin Lawton, T George, G Bloxsom, LYM)*

Ledston, W Yorks [SE4328], *White Horse*: Friendly pub, good for lunchtime food – set in attractive village *(M A and W R Proctor)*

☆ **Leeds** [9 Burley Rd; junction with Rutland St – OS Sheet 104 reference 293336; SE3033], *Fox & Newt*: Done up in cheerful Victorian style – bright paintwork, dark panelling, bare floorboards, What The Butler Saw machine (not working), well reproduced but not obtrusive piped music or juke box; reasonably priced bar food, but main draw has probably been the range of beers brewed on the premises *(Graeme Smalley, Jon Wainwright, LYM)*

Leeds, [Arkwright St, off new Armley Rd], *Albion*: Splendid refurbishment of Victorian city pub *(Comus Elliott)*; [North St] *Eagle*: Pubgoers' pub which was popular for its wide range of real ales, then taken over by Sam Smiths, now let to Timothy Taylors – with their real ales kept well *(LYM)*; [Gt George St] *George*: Cheerful central pub with good Tetleys on handpump, good varied bar food with daily specials; increasingly popular with people using the nearby Crown Court *(JRP)*; [18 Kirkstall Lane] *Kirkstall Lites*: New pub with comfortable, pleasant atmosphere, well kept Courage Directors, John Smiths and Tetleys and generous helpings of well presented, reasonably priced food; special OAPs budget meals on Tues and Thurs *(A J Woodhouse)*; [Roundhay Pk] *Mansion*: Cosy, warm atmosphere and wide choice of decent food

at quite low price; well placed *(Christopher Edwards)*; [Gt George St, just behind Town Hall] *Victoria*: Large, opulent-looking high-ceilinged pub with dim lighting, mirrors, ample plush alcoved seating, well kept Tetleys ale, efficient service, bar food *(Graeme Smalley, Jon Wainwright)*; [55 Wetherby Rd] *White House*: Good food at reasonable price, friendly atmosphere; spacious, with tables in pleasant garden *(Christopher Edwards)*

Lepton, W Yorks [Paul Lane, Flockton Moor; SE2015], *Dartmouth Arms*: Good food, especially steak and onion pie with large chunks of tender meat with a thick shortcrust top, cut from a real large pie, proper chips; brisk waitress service *(K A Chappell)*

☆ **Leyburn**, N Yorks [Market Pl; SE1191], *Golden Lion*: Homely, with comfortable seats around big pine tables, good value food such as ploughman's, home-made steak and kidney pie, fine crisp Yorkshire puddings, haddock fresh from Whitby that day, chocolate fudgecake served efficiently from food counter; good unusually flavoured Oliver Johns beer brewed here, decent house wines and malt whiskies, friendly atmosphere; bedrooms good value – especially the bargain breaks *(Mrs V Carroll, Mr and Mrs Tarlton)*

Leyburn [just off Market Pl], *Sandpiper*: Good choice of moderately priced bar food from freshly cut sandwiches to big helpings of hot food often served with good Yorkshire pudding, cheerful and pleasant staff, well kept Theakstons *(SS, W M Sharpe)*

Linthwaite, W Yorks [Blackmoorfoot Rd; SE1014], *Bulls Head*: Superb Bass and Boddingtons on handpump in moorland pub above the town, food particularly good and all prepared at the pub, with a choice of about ten main lunch dishes – seems to be getting better all the time under the licensees who've made such an improvement here since they took over fairly recently; friendly service, good atmosphere *(Robert Gartery)*

☆ **Linton**, W Yorks [SE3947], *Windmill*: Polished charm in carefully preserved small rooms with antique settles, oak beams, longcase clock, well kept Youngers Scotch and No 3, decent spirits and wines *(J E Rycroft, T Nott, LYM)*

Lockton, N Yorks [A169 N of Pickering; SE8490], *Fox & Rabbit*: Bustling family pub on moors, well kept real ales, good value simple food, seats outside and in sun lounge; children's room *(LYM)*

Luddenden, W Yorks [SE0426], *Lord Nelson*: Cheerful modernised eighteenth-century local with interesting features, where Branwell Brontë borrowed books; attractive very steep streamside village *(LYM)*

Lumbutts, W Yorks [Mankinholes Rd; SD9523], *Shepherds Rest*: Good spacious and welcoming family country pub with superb moor views, good choice of drinks, endly service, superb cheap meals (lunches eekends only, supper all week), open fires *'vonne and Don Johnson, Wayne Brindle)*

alham, N Yorks [SD8963], *Buck*: Well kept heakstons in comfortable panelled bar, also kers' bar; straightforward food including cent ploughman's; nr start GWG152 *Margaret and Roy Randle)*

alton, N Yorks [Commercial St; SE7972], *ornucopia*: More restaurant than pub: ood meals, well set out; good service *(R S arney)*; [Wheelgate] *Crown*: Unspoilt place, same family for generations, brewing its vn beers — Double Chance and Auld Bob; ood value bedrooms *(Simon Feisenberger)*

ankinholes, W Yorks [SD9523], *Top Brink*: arge moorland pub packed with rsebrasses and so forth, licence extension midnight *(Wayne Brindle)*

arsden, W Yorks [Manchester Rd (A62); 0412], *Olive Branch*: Log fire in winter, utch landlord/chef, good, unusual bar food reasonable prices — especially the bargain nners on Weds evening *(Mr and Mrs G awksworth)*

arton-cum-Grafton, N Yorks [village sign-osted off A1 3 miles N of A59; SE4263], *lde Punch Bowl*: Easy-going service with avy beams, open fires and plenty of tables expansive open-plan bar; Tetleys and oungers Scotch and No 3, generous lunch-ne bar food, restaurant; games and juke x in public bar, pretty garden, space for ravans; children welcome *(Sue Cleasby, ike Ledger, Rob and Gill Weeks, P T Young, ayne Brindle, J R Leeds, EC, Jon Wainwright, YM)*

exborough, S Yorks [S of A6023: follow aterbus' signs; SE4800], *Ferry Boat*: Old-shioned with some traditional furnishings, vely friendly atmosphere, good welcome; ite near canal *(LYM)*

iddleham, N Yorks [SE1288], *Black Swan*: ice and comfortable, with dark wood bles, friendly licensees and attractive back rrace; big helpings of bar food really over-ad the plates, restaurant *(Mrs V Carroll)*; *Market Pl] White Swan*: Very friendly mosphere, good plain cooking; bedrooms otless and good value, with big breakfasts *r and Mrs M Tarlton)*

iddleton Tyas, N Yorks [NZ2306], *Shoul-er of Mutton*: A labyrinth of small lounges, ir rafters, dark wood and a wealth of iual ornaments in small stone village pub ith good beer, quick cheerful service, con-ntional pub food including good pâté; ood value three-cup pot of coffee *(Anon)*

idhopestones, S Yorks [just off A616 W of ocksbridge — OS Sheet 110 reference 38995; SK2399], *Club*: Little old country ib close to reservoir and Peak Park bound-y, totally unspoilt, cosy, welcoming, full of aaracter; Wards Sheffield Best on hand-imp, bar food *(W P P Clarke)*

inskip, N Yorks [SE3965], *White Swan*:

Varied, reasonably priced good bar meals including sirloin steak done to perfection; a John Smiths pub *(N Burrell)*

Mirfield, W Yorks [just off A644 towards Dewsbury; SE2019], *Ship*: Spacious pub, good food, big restaurant *(Ian Robinson)*

☆ **Newton on Ouse**, N Yorks [SE5160], *Daw-nay Arms*: Very picturesque, right by River Ouse with lovely garden running down to moorings; comfortable and spacious inside, good beer, tasty food at reasonable prices *(Wayne Brindle, Mrs Shirley Pielou)*

Norland, W Yorks [Hob Lane; SE0723], *Hobbit*: Pleasant atmosphere, friendly staff, good bar snacks and full meals, wide choice of beers, reasonable prices; bedrooms com-fortable and well equipped *(SM)*

North Stainley, N Yorks [SE2977], *Lightwater Valley*: Pleasant surroundings, food from own farm — good solid fare, eat as much as you want *(P G Race)*

Nun Monkton, N Yorks [off A59 York —Harrogate; SE5058], *Alice Hawthorn*: Modernised beamed bar with dark red plush settles back to back around dimpled copper tables, open fire in big brick fireplace, keen darts players; on broad village green with pond, near River Nidd *(H C Hutchinson, BB)*

Ogden, W Yorks [A629 Denholme–Halifax: SE0631], *Causeway Foot*: Large spacious pub with several local beers and food that's served until late evening *(Ian Robinson)*; *Moorland*: Free house smartened up well with lots of beams, dark woodwork, brasses, log-effect gas fire and subdued lighting; Rud-dles County on handpump, juke box, pool-table; lunchtime bar food, separate small restaurant; antique farm machinery outside; children at lunchtimes *(George Hunt)*

☆ **Oldstead**, N Yorks [SE5380], *Black Swan*: Friendly inn in beautiful surroundings with pretty valley views from two big bay win-dows and picnic-table sets outside; engaging licensees (he's an American — and the dog's called Duke), decent bar food including lots of grills, well kept Tetleys and Youngers No 3 on handpump, rather fuzzy piped music, evening restaurant; children welcome; bedrooms in comfortable modern back extension *(Greg Parston and Ann Casebeer, Michael Swallow, BB)*

☆ **Osmotherley**, N Yorks [Staddlebridge; A172 towards Middlesbrough, just off its junction with A19 — OS Sheet 99 reference 444994; SE4499], *Cleveland Tontine*: Good log fire in huge stone fireplace of prosperous and attractive cellar bar, lovely busy atmosphere, huge vine worked into unusual old ceiling plasterwork; good soups and generous help-ings of interesting hot dishes and salads, cheerful service; at peak times it becomes a virtual restaurant, with most tables reserved for diners *(Mr and Mrs M Masterman)*

Osmotherley, N Yorks [The Green; SE4597], *Golden Lion*: Candlelit tables in small pub with very good value meals and John

Smiths beers *(Dave Braisted)*

Ossett, W Yorks [20 Horbury Rd (B6128); SE2820], *Crown*: Comfortably old-fashioned stone-built pub with attractive doll collection, pictures on wood-effect panelling, lots of brass and copper, toby jugs, keys, swords, washstand sets; good well cooked food, especially the light and tasty Yorkshire puddings *(Mrs K Chappell)*; [Dale St] *Royal*: Modernised town-centre Victorian pub with remarkable value lunchtime food (not Sun) such as mouth-watering beef topside (though called brisket) with true fresh Yorkshire pudding; Tetleys on handpump *(Geoff Wilson)*

Otley, W Yorks [Otley Chevin; SE2045], *Chevin*: Smallish pub, like going into someone's front room – every wall decorated with brass, plates and knick-knacks *(Ian Robinson)*; [Westgate] *Crosspipes*: Friendly pub recently redecorated by new landlord, John Smiths on handpump, good home-made food; good value bedrooms *(Tim Baxter)*; [Yorkgate, 300 yds from surprise view on Otley Chevin] *Royalty*: Good pub with several rooms including family-room, good value food; tables outside, garden *(Tim Baxter)*

Oxenhope, W Yorks [off B6141 towards Denholme; SE0335], *Dog & Gun*: Busy pub with plenty of character and atmosphere, separate bistro-style restaurant; well kept Taylors and Tetleys on handpump; good, reasonably priced bar food *(J E Rycroft, Wayne Brindle)*; *Lamb*: Friendly landlord and family, real fires, Websters and Wilsons, good reasonably priced bar food *(Charles Hall)*; [A6033 Keighley–Hebden Bridge] *Waggon & Horses*: Free house up on the moorside outside town with good views, comfortable surroundings, fleeces on stripped stone walls, good beer and food *(A J Woodroffe, LYM)*

Pateley Bridge, N Yorks [SE1666], *Crown*: Formal stone frontage on narrow steep main street, cosy lounge with railed-off dining area alongside; stone walls, not too many horse-brasses; good choice of food including good sandwiches, decent beer *(Anon)*

Patrick Brompton, N Yorks [SE2291], *Green Tree*: Nicely refurbished pub with new owners, well kept Theakstons, good cider and very good fresh well cooked bar food varying from day to day *(Mr and Mrs W A Rinaldi-Butcher)*

Penistone, S Yorks [Mortimer Rd; outskirts, towards Stocksbridge – OS Sheet 110 reference 248021; SE2403], *Cubley Hall*: Large stone-built country house recently converted into stylish attractive pub, set in own grounds with seating areas and gardens; several good ales on handpump including Tetleys and Wards; good food at reasonable prices (lunchtime and evening), noted for its chip butties, Yorkshire-style; children in conservatory and certain internal rooms *(W P P Clarke)*

☆ **Pickering**, N Yorks [Market Pl; SE7984], *White Swan*: Most inviting small bar run by friendly and enthusiastic hotel staff, good friendly locals, good food including chicken and mushroom pie with for once no chips served; bedrooms *(Jon Wainwright)*

Pickering [Market Pl], *Bay Horse*: Roaring fire, old-fashioned unpretentious décor and furnishings, warm welcome from young licensees who've brought in Camerons real ale; imaginative well served bar food including ploughman's with four types of cheese; very reasonable prices; can be smoky *(Dr R Hodkinson, R D Jolliff)*; [18 Birdgate] *Black Swan*: Big old pub, fairly well modernised with John Smiths on handpump and limited range of food – with generous helpings of vegetables; no dogs; bedrooms *(Dr John Innes)*; [Westgate; SE8083] *Sun*: Small friendly local with seats around wall of central bar, Tetleys on handpump *(Dr John Innes)*

Potto, N Yorks [NZ4704], *Potto Hall*: Country-house hotel and attractive restaurant, courteous and attentive staff; bedrooms *(J E M Ruffer)*

Rainton, N Yorks [under a mile from A1 Boroughbridge–Leeming Bar; SE3775], *Bay Horse*: Friendly village atmosphere with collections of blow-lamps, bank notes and cigarette cards; superb, inexpensive and very generous menu, very popular locally *(Gill and Neil Patrick)*

Reeth, N Yorks [SE0499], *Buck*: Attractive, welcoming and enjoyable country inn with log fire in pleasant bar, good choice of beers and cider, good bar food including sandwiches and hot meals; bedrooms *(BB Porter)*

Richmond, N Yorks [Finkle St; NZ1801], *Black Lion*: Ground floor all bars, including cosy panelled back snug with good fire in winter; pleasant spot for a drink after shopping, substantial bar meals; flamboyant and instructive sign over door of this small hotel; bedrooms *(Anon)*; [Market Pl] *Castle Tavern*: Small and friendly pub – one of eight in market square; photographs of the Green Howards there *(John Roué)*

Ripon, N Yorks [SE3171], *Golden Lion*: Free house with pool-table, darts, friendly licensees, well kept Matthew Browns, Theakstons Best and XB, generously served bar food, small restaurant *(Geoff Hall)*; [nr cathedral] *Old Deanery*: Enterprising food and drink in ancient surroundings, Swiss landlord, plenty of imaginative dishes *(P G Race)*

Robin Hood's Bay, N Yorks [The Dock, Bay Town; NZ9505], *Bay*: Wonderful sea views from welcoming and busy public bar (which doubles as breakfast-room – breakfasts are huge) and waterside terrace, well kept real ale, hounds basking in front of winter fire; friendly if basic place to stay *(Dave Webster, Sue Holland, Roger Bellingham)*; *Olde Dolphin*: Good olde-worlde pub with wide choice of food including lots of seafood, well kept Camerons Bitter and Strongarm on handpump *(Simon Holmes, Tony Pounder)*

Roecliffe, N Yorks [SE3766], *Crown*: Very small Tudor-style country inn with rather olde-worlde décor, friendly atmosphere, big helpings of good home-cooked food, attentive family service – good value sandwiches too *(Mrs R Mason, H E Scott)*

Rotherham, S Yorks [Moorgate Rd; SK4393], *Belvedere*: Tastefully decorated pub with horseshoe-shaped bar which has one end sectioned off for food; Whitbreads beers and good selection of wines *(David Tonkin)*

☆ **Runswick Bay**, N Yorks [NZ8217], *Royal*: Cheerful and lively atmosphere, well kept John Smiths, nautical back bar and lovely views down over fishing village and bay from big-windowed front bar and terrace; good choice of bar food, comfortable bedrooms, big breakfasts *(M A and W R Proctor, LYM)*

Sandal, W Yorks [48 Stanbridge Lane; SE3418], *Star*: Friendly and comfortable, with good choice of food including Yorkshire puddings and good garlic mushrooms (you can imagine still tasting them a week later); spacious and interesting garden *(Stephen Sarraff)*

☆ **Sandsend**, N Yorks [NZ8613], *Hart*: Quaint and cosy pub with log fires in winter, near the water in notably attractive seaside village; current licensees serving a variety of good home-cooked food and notably well kept Camerons Strongarm; super service; sea views and good garden *(Peter Kitson, Bridgett Sarsby, Eileen Broadbent)*

☆ **Saxton**, N Yorks [by church in village, 2½ miles from A1 via B1217, or near A162; SE4736], *Greyhound*: Whitewashed stone pub next to the church, smothered in climbing roses, and quite unspoilt and undiscovered three small beamed and flag-stoned rooms all with open fires, narrow passage to bar where Sam Smiths OB is still aged behind the counter, small snug with attractive engraved window looking into bar and some old brewery mirrors, separate games area with darts and table skittles *(Rob and Gill Weeks)*

Scarborough, N Yorks [Cambridge Terrace; TA0489], *Cask*: Decent choice of real ales in lively conversion of big Victorian house, buzzing with young people *(Margaret and Roy Randle, LYM)*; [Vernon Rd] *Hole in the Wall*: Welcoming atmosphere in comfortable lively bar – three narrow connecting rooms descending hill; well kept Theakstons and enterprising guest beers, above-average low-priced food, walls worth reading; very varied clientele *(Sue Holland, Dave Webster)*; [St Marys St] *Leeds Arms*: Well kept beers and pleasant relaxed atmosphere, pronounced nautical feel; interesting location in the old part of town *(R A Hutson)*

☆ **Scawton**, N Yorks [SE5584], *Hare*: Low and pretty pub, said to date back in part to twelfth century and fairly handy for Rievaulx Abbey; apart from a dark beam and plank ceiling in the innermost bar it's much modernised inside, with simple wall settles, stools, little wheel-back armchairs and wood-effect or trestle tables, and inoffensive piped music; cheerful welcome, well kept John Smiths on handpump, decent straightforward food from sandwiches through home-made steak and kidney pie to big steaks; steps up to pool-table area, seats outside, nice inn-signs *(GG, N P Hodgson, BB)*

Scorton, N Yorks [B1263 Richmond–Yarm; NZ2500], *Royal*: Dark and cosy bar with bow window overlooking green; good well garnished sandwiches at quiet times, bigger menu when busier; cheerful service, big fire, pool-table, darts; formal frontage *(Anon)*

Scotton, N Yorks [Main St; SE3359], *Guy Faukes*: Warm and homely atmosphere in modernised sixteenth-century building with very well kept John Smiths, Old Mill and Tetleys; good food in bar and restaurant including good soups *(T Houghton)*

Settle, N Yorks [SD8264], *Golden Lion*: Easy chairs, sofas and big Windsor armchairs in high-beamed lounge bar, well kept Thwaites ales, good open fire, particularly friendly service, games in lively public bar, horses still stabled in coachyard; bedrooms *(Tony Pounder, LYM)*; *Royal Oak*: Good range of fantastic value food in spacious dark-panelled hotel lounge (with rather restauranty atmosphere) – the Yorkshire fat rascals are puff pastry and raisins concoctions served hot with cream, and the turkey sandwiches are particularly good; good choice of beers; a surprise to find those naughty doggy cartoons in full open view rather than in the gents *(Margaret and Roy Randle and others)*

Sheffield, S Yorks [Handsworth Rd], *Cross Keys*: Ancient friendly pub inside churchyard; well kept real ales, open fires, local atmosphere *(W P P Clarke, LYM)*; [Manchester Rd] *Crosspool*: Well run plush stone-built suburban pub with good value carvery, popular with businessmen at lunchtime, service friendly and efficient, keg beers *(P G Race, K and D E Worrall)*; [Baslow Rd (A621), opp Totley police stn – OS Sheet 119 reference 305798] *Fleur de Lys*: Good lunchtime food including superb chips, Stones ales, garden *(G N G Tingey, R F Neil)*; [18 Pitt St] *Red Deer*: Good all round – nearly always full *(WPPC)*; [Charles St – handy for railway stn] *Red Lion*: Friendly and very comfortable, with pleasant atmosphere, good Wards beer, limited choice of reasonably good food *(Brian and Pam Cowling, W P P Clarke)*; [Redmires Rd, Lodge Moor; SK3687] *Shiny Sheff*: Large 1960s estate-type pub on theme of HMS *Sheffield*, useful locally for fair choice of reasonably priced food, well cooked and served; small but attractive conservatory-style restaurant (Dorothy and Ken Worrall); [Church St] Stone House: Plush well kept pub with clever pastiche of Dickensian cobbled shopping-square in central courtyard – cobbled streets, olde-worlde shopfronts; can be very crowded, beer is keg (T T Kelly, LYM)

Shelley, W Yorks [Royd House; SE2011], Three Acres: Rather smart food which they call bistro meals (with prices to match) including very good steak and kidney pie, good range of real ales, pleasantly comfortable (K A Chappell, Geoff Wilson)

Shepley, W Yorks [Penistone Rd; SE1909], Sovereign: Food's definitely the main thing in this friendly, clean and welcoming refurbished pub – big helpings, good value; Stones ale; very busy at weekends (A J and R A Buchan, Geoff Wilson, Gillian Hamilton, K A Chappell)

Shipley, W Yorks [SE1537], Ring of Bells: Popular with lovers of good beer for its well kept Tetleys on handpump (Anon)

☆ Sicklinghall, N Yorks [OS Sheet 104 reference 363485; SE3648], Scotts Arms: Consistently good value home-cooked food in lively and friendly stone village pub with big inglenook fireplace, cosy nooks; well kept Youngers Scotch and No 3, pool-room, tables outside; children in restaurant and two family-rooms (Syd and Wyn Donald, T Nott, LYM)

☆ Skipton, N Yorks [Canal St; from Water St (A65) turn into Coach St, then left after canal bridge; SD9852], Royal Shepherd: Local near canal with Chesters, Hartleys, Whitbreads Castle Eden and Trophy and a changing guest beer – always well kept; large bar with games, juke box, snug and dining-room with open fires and pictures of town and canal in bygone days; unusual whiskies, simple, generously served lunchtime food (inc Sun), good mix lunchtime customers, students in evening; friendly atmosphere (though Petrol the dog isn't exactly chummy); seats outside; children allowed in dining-room lunchtime (George Hunt, Lynn Stevens, Gill Quarton, Alan Wilford)

Skipton, N Yorks [Market Sq], Red Lion: Cheerful and bustling (next to the market), well furnished, with pleasant food and Whitbreads ales (Wayne Brindle)

Slingsby, N Yorks [High St; SE7075], Grapes: Straightforward but popular food including good steaks and sausages in stone-built village local with cast-iron-framed tables on patterned carpet, children in room off bar (Eileen Broadbent, BB)

Snape, N Yorks [SE2784], Castle Arms: Welcoming fairly new landlord, very good food and beer; Catherine Parr came from the eponymous castle (Simon Feisenberger)

South Anston, S Yorks [3 miles from M1 junction 31; SK5183], Loyal Trooper: Cheerful village local, handy for M1 junction 31, with well kept Tetleys and tables in lounge

set at lunchtime for good value straightforward bar food; lively public bar (Brian Green, LYM)

South Stainley, N Yorks [SE3163], Red Lion: Good value food and relaxed atmosphere, very friendly (P G Race, B J E Phillips)

☆ Sowerby Bridge, W Yorks [Wharf St; main rd, opp entrance to canal basin; SE0623], Ashtree: Smart exterior and entrance, unpretentiously comfortable inside, warmly welcoming bar; bar food notable for delicious Indonesian dishes; separate restaurant, efficient but unobtrusive service, decent beers (Dr and Mrs A K Clarke, Anthony Pounder, Dr Stephen Hiew)

Sprotbrough, S Yorks [Melton Rd; SE5302], Ivanhoe: Good service and first-class food, all home made and reasonably priced; modernised pub with good view of cricket ground (Pat Smith)

☆ Staithes, N Yorks [NZ7818], Cod & Lobster: Included for superb waterside setting in unspoilt fishing village under sandstone cliff; well kept Camerons, friendly local atmosphere (M A and W R Proctor, Tony Pounder, LYM)

Stanbury, W Yorks [SE0037], Old Silent: Popular moorland village inn near Haworth, small rooms packed with bric-à-brac, real ale, bar meals; bedrooms (LYM); [OS Sheet 104 reference 008371] Wuthering Heights: Comfortable atmosphere in clean and friendly moorland village pub with good simple bar meals and well kept Websters Yorkshire (Len Beattie)

☆ Stapleton, N Yorks [NZ2612], Bridge: Food quite exceptional, using top-quality fresh ingredients, in cosy Victorian pub with heavy brown Anaglypta walls and log-effect gas fire; pleasant helpful and efficient service; children allowed, with special helpings and prices, if they eat early; restaurant (Mrs P Sachs, J F Pearce, Dr R C Keith)

Steeton, W Yorks [Station Rd; SE0344], Steeton Hall: Good welcome, friendly atmosphere, good food; bedrooms comfortable – so much so that you may end staying longer than planned (J B Robinson, Mr and Mrs Norman Morris)

Stutton, N Yorks [SE4841], Hare & Hounds: Popular old stone-built pub with nice atmosphere, very good bar food from wide menu and well kept Sam Smiths on handpump; restaurant (H B Smith, M D Hampson, Warwick Peirson)

Summer Bridge, N Yorks [junction B6451/ B6165; SE2062], Flying Dutchman: Village inn in beautiful Nidderdale setting, quiet relaxed atmosphere, well kept Sam Smiths; bedrooms good, with huge breakfast (Chris Fluck)

Sutton under Whitestonecliffe, N Yorks [A170 E of Thirsk; SE4983], Whitestonecliffe: Busy pub, extensive choice of good lunchtime and evening bar food at reasonable prices, restaurant used as extension to bar

(Mr and Mrs F W Sturch)
Swainby, N Yorks [NZ4802], *Black Horse*: Good food, good service and garden with aviary and tree house; separate dining-room with Sun lunch; children welcome *(Mrs B E Asher)*

☆ **Tadcaster**, N Yorks [Bridge St; SE4843], *Angel & White Horse*: The pub's coachyard has the stables for the Sam Smiths team of dappled grey shire horses – as you can see from the handsomely fitted oak-panelled bar; cheap well kept Sam Smiths ales, good value weekday bar food, restaurant; brewery tours can be arranged – tel Tadcaster (0937) 832225 *(H B Smith, Michael O'Driscoll, Jon Wainwright, LYM)*

☆ **Tan Hill**, N Yorks [Arkengarthdale rd from Reeth to Brough, at junction with Keld and W Stonesdale rd; NY8906], *Tan Hill*: At 1732 feet Britain's highest pub – some five miles from nearest neighbours, often snowed in, needing its two big fires even in summer; a haven for walkers on the Pennine Way, with well kept Theakstons Best, XB and Old Peculier, cheery food, decidedly simple furnishings, flagstone floors and very few frills (apart from the juke box); occasional accordion and singsong sessions; children welcome; bedrooms basic *(Steve Dykes, Yvonne and Don Johnson, C P Fenton, Rob and Gill Weeks, Gwen and Peter Andrews, TOH, Dave Braisted, Wayne Brindle, G J Proudlock, C Elliott, Mike Lawson, LYM)*

Thirsk, N Yorks [Market Pl; SE4382], *Black Bull*: Friendly welcome, good Camerons Mild and Bitter and good value Sun roast lunch; a comfortable place to stay at *(Alan Gough)*; [Market Pl] *Golden Fleece*: Comfortable THF hotel with good beer and food; no music; bedrooms *(Prof S Barnett)*

Thorganby, N Yorks [SE6942], *Jefferson Arms*: Lovely pub with superb food – everything a pub should be; bedrooms *(Michael Swallow)*

Thurlstone, S Yorks [A628 – OS Sheet 110 reference 230034; SE2303], *Huntsman*: Old stone-built well run free house, friendly landlord with taste for jazz records, good staff, wide range of well kept real ales including Marstons Pedigree, Ruddles County, Stones and several guest beers like Rockside Thurlstone; lunchtime bar food; landlord occasionally runs trips to Marstons brewery for selected regulars *(W P P Clarke)*

Todmorden, W Yorks [550 Burnley Rd, Knotts; OS Sheet 103 reference 916257; SD9324], *Staff of Life*: A pub of real character in the narrowest part of the Cliviger Gorge; interconnecting rooms with stripped stone walls, beams, interesting collection of bedpans, bar food, and real ales such as Timothy Taylors, Theakstons and Moorhouses beers including good Pendle Witches Brew; the owner's been setting up his own microbrewery nearby, to brew two or three real ales for the pub *(Len Beattie)*

Tosside, N Yorks [SD7755], *Dog & Partridge*: Old-fashioned, cosy village free house with big log fire in lounge, good, reasonably priced food; Thwaites *(Yvonne and Don Johnson)*

Ulley, S Yorks [Turnshaw Rd; nr M1 junction 31 – off B6067 in Aston; SK4687], *Royal Oak*: Popular country pub on site of old blacksmith's, wood beams decorated with farm tools and horse tackle, wooden chairs and tables; Sam Smiths on handpump, good wine list; lunchtime and evening bar food including children's portions; family-room, garden with play area *(W A Harbottle)*

Wakefield, W Yorks [SE3321], *Harewood Arms*: Pleasantly refurbished with cheap, good beer and nice atmosphere for a city-centre pub *(Comus Elliott)*

☆ **Warthill**, N Yorks [SE6755], *Agar Arms*: Quite small (so can get packed), well refurbished and pleasant single partly split-level room, accent on promptly served food with steaks highly recommended, good Sam Smiths; tables outside overlook village pond *(JAH, HCH, J C Proud)*

Weaverthorpe, N Yorks [SE9771], *Star*: Good Theakstons, especially XB, first-class food at very reasonable prices in bar and restaurant, very friendly licensees; bedrooms a little sparse but good value at their low price *(DW)*

Wentworth, S Yorks [3 miles from M1 junction 36; SK3898], *Rockingham Arms*: Pleasant village pub with comfortable bar, popular food, Youngers real ales, bowling-green in attractive garden *(M A and W R Proctor, John E Robinson, LYM)*

West Burton, N Yorks [SE0287], *Fox & Hounds*: Unspoilt, basic pub on village green in idyllic Dales spot; one small bar with friendly staff, John Smiths Bitter on handpump, simple bar food *(C W T Johnson)*

☆ **West Witton**, N Yorks [SE0688], *Wensleydale Heifer*: Pretty whitewashed stone inn with comfortable rooms, good log fire in inglenook, pleasant décor, interesting prints, chintz-upholstered furniture; well kept John Smiths, but emphasis is firmly on well cooked and imaginative bar food (not cheap) served in large helpings; stall seating in separate bistro; bedrooms *(Dr and Mrs B D Smith, Rob and Gill Weeks, C J Cuss)*

Wetherby, W Yorks [A1; SE4048], *Alpine*: Quick, well mannered service and an especially good fish pie *(Jill Hadfield)*

Whitby, N Yorks [Flowergate; NZ9011], *Little Angel*: Clean and cosy pub with very friendly licensees, good Tetleys, good value food, friendly regulars; children if well behaved *(John and Sally Emmerson)*

Whixley, N Yorks [SE4458], *Anchor*: Building looks nothing special from outside, but, inside, brickwork has been used very effectively to give unstable-looking walls, and each room has its own character; one has lots of old tins over fireplace with hot open fire; John Smiths and Theakstons, and very good value bar food, which is also served in adjacent dining area; they've obviously had fun doing the pub up over the last few years (Rob and Gill Weeks)

Wigglesworth, N Yorks [SD8157], Plough: Imaginative well presented food, especially savoury pancakes – not the cheapest place, but very good value; civilised atmosphere, always a friendly welcome, lovely restaurant in converted barn, quick and efficient service even on a bank hol Mon; bedrooms (Dr R Hodkinson, Prof S Barnett)

Winksley, N Yorks [SE2571], Countryman: Pleasant pub, good bar food, separate dining-room; children welcome (Audrey and Alan Chatting)

Worsall, N Yorks [NZ3909], Ship: Very much enlarged, with good choice of well presented food including good puddings (RAMS)

Yeadon, W Yorks [Nunroyd House; SE2141], Inn on the Park: Newly decorated pub in the centre of a park with value-for-money good food (Tim Baxter)

Yedingham, N Yorks [SE8979], Providence: Good country pub with wide choice of beautifully cooked food, good helpings (Stanley Robinson)

☆ York [Merchantgate – between Fossgate and Piccadilly; SE5951], Red Lion: Low-beamed rambling rooms with some stripped Tudor brickwork, relaxed old-fashioned furnishings, well kept John Smiths real ale, bar snacks and summer meals, tables outside, good juke box or piped music (Nick Dowson, Alison Hayward, Jon Wainwright, LYM)

☆ York [26 High Petergate], York Arms: Cosy and quiet, with compact and attractive front bar and more spacious comfortable rooms behind giving distinctive character; very well kept Sam Smiths OB and Museum real ales, cheeerful staff, friendly grey cat; good lunchtime and early evening bar food, partly no-smoking; a couple of strides from awe-inspiring view of minster (Jon Dewhirst, Dr Stephen Hiew, Nick Dowson, Alison Hayward)

York [Goodramgate], Anglers Arms: Small friendly pub, ful of atmosphere, with unusual shape and décor; supposedly

haunted by several ghosts including one who turns off the pumps (Paul Corbett); [Blossom St] Bay Horse: Lots of nooks and alcoves in rambling rooms of Victorian pub, can be smoky (LYM); [17/19 Bootham] Exhibition: Genuine marble fireplace, good atmosphere in spacious open-plan bar; John Smiths real ale (Ian Phillips); [23 Market St] Hansom Cab: Pleasant, comfortable pub with uphol-stered leather furnishings, wood-panelled walls and old-fashioned carved tables; mod-ern lighting and good music (louder as even-ing wears on); good handpumped Sam Smiths (T T Kelly); [High Petergate] Hole in the Wall: Small and cosy, feels old (John Roué); [Lendal] Lendal Cellars: Broad-vaulted medieval cellars carefully spotlit to show up the stripped masonry; hand-crafted furniture and cask seats on stone floor, series of interconnected rooms and alcoves, can be packed in the evening with younger people, quieter at lunchtime (Nick Dowson, Alison Hayward, LYM); [Kings Staithe; on Ouse bank not 50 yds from Kings Arms – see main entries] Lowther: Large open-plan bar crowded with young and middle-aged cus-tomers – good atmosphere (John Roué); [7 Stonegate] Punchbowl: Decibels ring out to Scotland and beyond, jiving to juke box in front bar, singing Ye Bonnie Banks and Braes to two guitars in back room; fun, everyone welcome to join in (Ian Phillips); Red House: Small hotel, courteous and help-ful service, good value wine; bedrooms (Jill Hadfield, Ann Roberts); [Ouse Bridge] River-side: On banks of the River Ouse, in heart of city; reasonable carvery food (John Roué); [Walmgate] Spread Eagle: Tremendous range of beers, with admirable display of OG and price both inside and outside the pub; none of its unique atmosphere lost in spite of careful improvements to pleasantly spartan décor and good new lavatories; reasonably priced food (Jon Wainwright, Graeme Smal-ley); [Micklegate] Walkers: Good friendly pub, well kept Theakstons real ales, unusual atmosphere and furnishings including chan-delier, peculiar artefacts, mynahs (Scott W Stucky, Jon Wainwright)

London

London

Under the new licensing laws which allow all-day opening, London's pubs stand out as far more likely to stay open than those in any other area of England and Wales. In all, about two-thirds of the main entries here are now open all day, on at least one day of the week, though there are interesting variations, like the Black Friar in Central London (a marvellous architectural flight of fancy inside) which is opening from 11.30 through until 9, then closing – and closing altogether at weekends. It's quite notable though that mostly pubs here are either staying open throughout the day or sticking with the old hours. Only a handful of pubs have made minor adjustments to the tradiitonal hours, like the ever-individualistic Cross Keys (also Central), staying open until 4 and then closing until 5.30, or the Old Wine Shades (Central) opening a little earlier at 5 in the evening. Changes unconnected with the hours here include new licensees at the Grenadier, Olde Cheshire Cheese and Olde Mitre, and lots of refurbishments at the Samuel Pepys (all Central); lots of building work at the cottagey Case is Altered, the purchase of the pleasantly unpretentious Compton Arms by Greene King, the sale of the

Waterside Inn by Hoskins to Whitbreads, and a new licensee at the Flask (all North); new licensees at the Green Man (South), the Anglesea Arms and London Apprentice (West) and the Town of Ramsgate (East), while the Dickens Inn there is now tied to Courage. Some interesting newcomers include in Central London the lively Glassblower (with good real ales), in North London the White Lion of Mortimer (one of a new small chain mostly known as Wetherspoons – a refreshing new style of pub with several others suggested in the North london Lucky Dip at the end of the chapter), and in South London the engaging semi-continental yet thoroughly Youngsish Alma, and the spacious new Horni-man at the fine Hays Galleria development. The Lucky Dip section at the end of the chapter has some rich nuggets; in Central London we'd particularly note the Antelope, Nags Head, Red Lion (Duke of York Street; all these three are SW1) and Star (W1); in North London, the George IV (sold by Thwaites now, but still stocking their beers) and Island Queen (N1); in South London, the Crown and Greyhound (SE21), Fox & Grapes (SW19) and Boaters (Kingston); in West London, the Bell & Crown and Bulls Head (both W4), Scarsdale Arms (W8) and Hare & Hounds (Osterley); and in East London the Falcon & Firkin (E9 – particularly for its children's room) and the House They Left Behind (E14).

CENTRAL LONDON

Covering W1, W2, WC1, WC2, SW1, SW3, EC1, EC2, EC3 and EC4 postal districts

Parking throughout this area is metered during the day, and generally in short supply then; we mention difficulty only if evening parking is a problem too

Black Friar (City)   Map 13

174 Queen Victoria Street, EC4

Perhaps early evening is the best time to take in the fine Edwardian bronze and marble art-nouveau décor here – some say it's the best-preserved anywhere. Every inch of the walls and arched ceiling in the back inner room is full of inlaid Florentine marble, bronze reliefs of jolly monks, intricate nursery-rhyme scenes and so forth, as well as glittering mosaics and slender marble pillars. In the front room, see if you can spot the opium-smoking hints modelled into the fireplace. Good home-made food includes filled French bread (from £1.20), ploughman's (from £2), a varied cold buffet (from £2.75) and three daily hot specials such as beef in red wine, coq au vin or cranberry lamb stew (£2.90). Well kept Adnams, Bass, Boddingtons Bitter and Tetleys on handpump. There's a wide forecourt in front, by the approach to Blackfriars Bridge. *(Recommended by Chris Fluck, Nick Dowson, Alison Hayward, Nicolas Walter, William Meadon, Richard Steel, T E Cheshire)*

Nicholsons (Ind Coope)   Licensee David McKinstry   Real ale   Lunchtime meals (not Sat or Sun) and snacks (not Fri evening, not Sat or Sun)   Children in eating area of bar   Open 11.30–9 weekdays; closed weekends and bank hols

Cittie of Yorke (Holborn)   Map 13

22 High Holborn, WC1; find it by looking out for its big black and gold clock

The ceiling of the entrance hall in this very popular place – it gets packed at lunchtime and early evening, particularly with lawyers and judges – has medieval-style painted panels and plaster York roses. The bar counter in the main hall is the longest in Britain, with vast thousand-gallon wine vats (empty since prudently drained at the start of the Second World War) above the gantry, and a cat-walk running along the top of them. The most atmospheric place to sit is in one of the intimate old-fashioned and ornately carved cubicles, and there's an unusual big stove – uniquely triangular, with grates on all three sides; big bulbous lights hang from the extraordinarily high raftered roof. A smaller, comfortable wood-panelled room has lots of little prints of York and attractive brass lights. There's a lunchtime food counter in the main hall with more in the downstairs cellar bar: ploughman's, generously filled beef rolls, sausage and beans (£2.20), chilli con carne, vegetarian quiche, cider sausages or spicy beef pasta (all £2.65) and steak. Well kept Sam Smiths OB and Museum on handpump; efficient, friendly service; darts. *(Recommended by J S Evans, R Inns, Ian Phillips, Nigel Paine, Nick Dowson, Alison Hayward, Ted George)*

Sam Smiths   Licensee Allan Ramsay   Real ale   Meals and snacks (not Sat evening or Sun) Open 11–11 weekdays; 12–3, 5.30–11.30 Sat; closed Sun and bank hols

Cross Keys (Chelsea)   Map 12

Lawrence Street, SW3

This friendly Victorian pub is a popular and lively meeting-place in the evenings, quieter and more relaxing at lunchtime. The décor is old-fashioned, with a walk-round island serving-counter giving the effect of several interconnecting little rooms, military prints, a set of Cries of London prints and photographs of old London on the red or cream walls, high ceilings, and an open fire in winter. Good value food includes sandwiches, seven salads and home-made hot dishes like steak and kidney pie, beef bourguignonne or salt-beef (£2.50), and chicken Kiev (£2.75). Well kept Courage Best and Directors on handpump, good mulled wine, and quick and efficient service; shove-ha'penny, dominoes, cribbage and fruit machine. There are tables in a pretty little sunny back courtyard planted with creepers and tubs of brightly coloured flowers. *(Recommended by Patrick Stapley, Richard Gibbs)*

Courage   Licensee Arthur Goodall   Real ale   Meals and snacks (not Sun)   Open 11–4, 5.30–11 all year

Front Page ⊗ (Chelsea)   Map 12

Church Street, SW3

Restored a few years ago, this discreetly fashionable pub is in a quiet backstreet in an elegant part of Chelsea; it's light and airy, with a wood-strip floor, big navy ceiling-fans, pews and benches around the panelled walls, heavy wooden tables, huge windows with heavy navy curtains, and an open fire in one cosy area; lighting is virtually confined to brass picture-lights above small Edwardian monochrome pictures. Big blackboards at either end of the pub list the good value and nicely presented food: good soup of the day (£1.80), mushrooms and bacon in creamy sauce (£2.95), steak sandwich (£3.25), avocado, Mozzarella and tomato salad or pasta of the day (£3.50), lamb's liver and bacon (£3.95), stuffed chicken breast in various sauces (£4), rack of lamb or home-made salmon fishcakes (£5), and puddings like home-made treacle tart (£1.75). Well kept Ruddles Best and County and Websters Yorkshire on handpump; decent wines; quick, pleasant service even though the staff seem to change quite a lot. Fruit machine. Big copper gaslamps hang outside the pub, above pretty hanging baskets. *(Recommended by P Gillbe, S Matthews, L V Nutton, John Roué, Mrs A Fenwick, Jocelyn Bolton)*

Watneys   Licensees Christopher Phillips and Rupert Fowler   Real ale   Meals   Children in eating area of bar   Open 11–3, 5.30–11 all year, though they will stay open longer in afternoon if trade demands; closed 25 and 26 Dec

George (West End)   Map 13

55 Great Portland Street, W1

Recently refurbished, this solid place – popular with BBC regulars – has etched windows, deeply engraved mirrors, equestrian prints and heavy mahogany panelling, as well as comfortable red plush high chairs at the bar and captain's chairs around traditional cast-iron-framed tables on the new carpets. A good choice of well kept real ales on handpump might include Adnams Bitter, Greene King IPA and Abbot, Charles Wells Bombardier and Wilsons all on handpump. Bar food includes sandwiches (90p), ploughman's (from £1.50), hot salt-beef (£2) and home-made steak pie (£3.20). *(Recommended by Dr John Innes, Alan Mosley, P Denison, Michael Cooke, Louise Collins)*

Free house   Licensee T C Thomas   Real ale   Meals and snacks   Open 11–11 all year

Glassblower (Piccadilly Circus)   Map 13

42 Glasshouse Street, W1

Just off Piccadilly Circus, so it's busy and popular with tourists. The atmosphere is back-to-basics, but in a cultivated and deliberate way – the main bar has sawdust on gnarled floorboards, lots of untreated rough wooden beams with metal wheel-hoops hanging on them, and plain wooden settles and stools. An enormous copper and glass gaslight hangs from the centre of the ceiling, flickering gently, and there are more gaslight-style brackets around the walls, as well as lots of beer towels and framed sets of beer-mats. Some slates confront you with facetious questions, such as 'You've got too many beers here, don't you sell lager?'; which, given the range of real ales, has some relevance – on our visit they had, on handpump, Brakspears SB, Charles Wells, Courage Directors, Everards Tiger, Greene King Abbot, Greyhound Streatham Strong, Ringwood Old Thumper and Ruddles County (and they do sell lager). Food includes large sandwiches (from around £2), ploughman's or salads (£2.75) and a couple of hot dishes like turkey and ham pie or beef goulash (around £4); two fruit machines and piped music. The upstairs lounge (closed on Sundays) has more standard décor, with carpets and comfortable chairs. There are hanging flower baskets outside. *(Recommended by Ian Phillips, Dr and Mrs A V Clarke, Rob and Gill Weeks, John Branford)*

Free house   Licensee Alex Saville   Real ale   Meals and snacks   Children in upstairs lounge Open 11–11 all year

Grenadier (Belgravia)   Map 13

Wilton Row, SW1; the turning off Wilton Crescent looks prohibitive, but the barrier and watchman are there to keep out cars; walk straight past – the pub is just around the corner

The cramped front bar in this tucked-away little pub, crowded with a wide variety of customers, is a lively place, with well kept Ruddles Best and County and Websters Yorkshire on handpump from the rare pewter-topped bar counter. If you'd prefer it, the licensee or Tom the very long-standing head barman will shake you a most special Bloody Mary. A corner snack-counter serves very reasonably priced lunchtime food such as ploughman's (£2.20), and hot dishes like shepherd's pie, Somerset pork or lasagne (£2.95); in the evenings bar food is limited to giant sausages (60p). The pub is proud of its connection with Wellington, whose officers used to use it as their mess and had their horses stabled nearby; there's a grand painting of the Duke of Wellington presiding over a military banquet after Waterloo, smart prints of guardsmen through the ages and several weapons and powder horns. *(Recommended by Doug Kennedy, William Meadon, Richard Steel; more reports please)*

Watneys   Licensees Mr and Mrs Dodgson   Real ale   Lunchtime meals and snacks Intimate candlelit restaurant tel 01-235 3074   Open 11–3, 5.30–11 all year; closed 25 Dec

Henry J Bean's (Chelsea)   Map 13

195–197 King's Road, SW3

Absolutely not a pub (some readers feel it has no place in these pages – but we like it), this big, well run, busy bar is decorated in a 1950s American style (though the music is late-1970s). There's an interesting collection of old enamel advertising placards, photographs of Hollywood movie stars, snow-shoes and old skis. Spaced well apart on the polished wood-strip floor are good solid wooden tables with high stools – and up some low steps, a railed-off carpeted area with pale plum button-back banquettes and more tables. The long bar counter is manned by neat slicked-hair barmen, backed by tall mirrored shelves housing an excellent collection of whiskies. An interesting range of beers (no real ales and prices are high) includes several Americans, and you can have them served by the jug as well as with slugs of this and that in small or outsize glasses; there are American as well as good French house wines, and of course they do cocktails. You order food from the barman, and the till transmits the order to a grill area: a video screen shows your number when it's ready. The food includes deep-fried potato skins with sour cream or nachos, hot dog, salads or chilli con carne and burgers (£3.55). In summer the main attraction is the really big crazy-paved back courtyard – more spacious than that of any London pub we know of – reached through a cream-tiled area with bentwood chairs; there are sturdy seats and tables under plane and lime trees among well tended green pergolas and old street-lamps, a central fountain playing around a tall flame, and a children's play area. There's also a branch in Abingdon Road, W2, with a similar range of food and drink. *(Recommended by Dave Butler, Les Storey; more reports please)*

Watneys   Meals and snacks   Children in dining-room   Open 11.30–11.30 all year; closed 25 Dec, 1 Jan

Kings Arms (Mayfair) Map 13

2 Shepherd Market, W1

This lively busy pub – often with more space than other places nearby – has been given a stripped-down décor of bare timbers and the textured concrete that is the South Bank's hallmark, with a dimly lit galleried upper area. A good choice of well kept real ales includes Charles Wells Bombardier, Huntsman Royal Oak and Wethereds. Reasonably priced food includes steak and kidney pie, gammon steak, scampi, salads and dishes of the day such as savoury lamb cutlets. This busy little patch just north of Piccadilly has in the last few years become most attractive, and on a warm evening the narrow streets are filled with people overflowing from the bars and exotic restaurants that have come to roost here. *(Recommended by Quentin Williamson, Ian Phillips; more reports please)*

Clifton Inns (Watneys) – but run as free house   Real ale   Meals and snacks   Probably open 11–11 all year

Lamb ★ (Bloomsbury) Map 13

94 Lamb's Conduit Street, WC1

Named after the Kentish clothmaker William Lamb who brought fresh water to Holborn in 1577, this cosy and friendly pub has cut-glass swivelling 'snob-screens' all the way around the U-shaped bar counter, traditional cast-iron-framed tables with neat brass rails around the rim, and lots of sepia photographs on ochre panelling of 1890s actresses. Good bar food includes sandwiches, ploughman's and salads as well as lunchtime hot dishes such as home-made cottage pie or steak and kidney pie, and daily specials like stuffed hearts with vegetables or pork in cider casserole. Well kept Youngs Bitter and Special on handpump; prompt service, and a good mix of customers. There are slatted wooden seats in a little courtyard beyond the quiet room which is down a couple of steps at the back; dominoes, cribbage, chess, backgammon. *(Recommended by Brian Marsden, D J Cargill, Brian Jones, Dr and Mrs A K Clarke, Anne Morris)*

Youngs   Licensee Richard Whyte   Real ale   Meals and snacks   Children in courtyard weekend lunchtimes only   Open 11–3, 5.30–11, though 11–11 Fri and Sat for trial period – if successful, will open longer on other days too

Lamb & Flag (Covent Garden)   Map 13

Rose Street, WC2; off Garrick Street

In Regency days, the back room in this popular, friendly pub was known as the Bucket of Blood from the bare-knuckle prize-fights held here. It's still much as it was when Dickens described the Middle Temple lawyers who frequented it when he was working in nearby Catherine Street – low ceiling, high-backed black settles and an open fire. The upstairs Dryden Room tends to be less crowded. There's a choice of ten well kept cheeses and eight pâtés, served with hot bread or French bread (£2), as well as pasties (90p), quiche (£1), steak and kidney pie (£1.75), succulent roast beef baps (Monday to Friday), shepherd's pie, chilli con carne or curry (all £2.25). Well kept Courage Best and Directors and John Smiths on handpump. Darts in the small front public bar. Dryden was nearly beaten to death by hired thugs in the courtyard outside. *(Recommended by Peter Griffiths, Ian and James Phillips, Michael Bechley, Nick Dowson, Alison Hayward, William Meadon, Richard Steel, Nigel Paine, Marcus and Marcella Leith)*

Courage   Licensee Adrian Zimmerman   Real ale   Meals (lunchtime only, not Sun) and snacks (not Fri evening)   Open 11–11 all year; closed evenings 24 and 31 Dec, all day 25 and 26 Dec and 1 Jan

Museum Tavern (Bloomsbury)   Map 13

Museum Street, WC1

Decorated to emphasise its links with the days of Virginia Woolf, this friendly pub has old-fashioned high-backed benches around traditional cast-iron pub tables, old advertising mirrors between the wooden pillars behind the bar, and gas lamps above the tables outside. Karl Marx is fondly supposed to have had the odd glass here after the British Museum, opposite, had shut him out for the night. There's a range of bar food with sandwiches, ploughman's, home-made Scotch eggs, turkey and ham pie, with hot dishes such as steak and kidney or shepherd's pie, beef in ale or turkey in tarragon (all £3.50); food is served all day on Sunday. A good choice of real ales on handpump includes Brakspears, Everards, Greene King IPA and Abbot, Ruddles County and Websters Yorkshire, and there is a wide range of wines by the glass; piped music. *(Recommended by Prof A Barnett, Nick Dowson, Alison Hayward, Dr E Fellow-Smith, M White, Nicolas Walter)*

Free house   Licensee Michael Clarke   Real ale   Meals and snacks   Open 11–11; 12–10.30 Sun

Old Wine Shades (City)   Map 13

6 Martin Lane, EC4

Built in 1663, this building is one of the very few in the City to have escaped the Great Fire of 1666, and the heavy black beams and dark panelling are older than most things you'll see nearby. Subdued lighting, dignified alcoves, old prints, antique tables and old-fashioned high-backed settles underline the atmosphere, though it's a lively place at lunchtime. Bar lunches include sandwiches (from £1, roast beef £1.60, smoked salmon £2.70), various pies and quiche (from £1.60), baked potato filled with cheese (£1.80) and pâté or a choice of six cheeses with French bread (£2.10); they keep a good range of wines (under the same ownership as El Vino's). Make sure you're correctly dressed: collar, tie, jacket and trousers for men, and no jeans or jump-suits for women. *(Recommended by Quentin Williamson; more reports please)*

Free house   Licensee Victor Little   Snacks (lunchtime, Mon–Fri)   Restaurant   Open 11.30–3, 5–8; closed Sat and Sun and bank hols

If you know a pub's ever open all day now that the licensing laws have changed, please tell us.

Olde Cheshire Cheese (City) Map 13

Wine Office Court; off 145 Fleet Street, EC4

The bustling mixture of tourists, lawyers and journalists, squeezing up and down the panelled stairway or spilling out into the narrow courtyard, somehow suits this unpretentious pub very well. The small rooms, up and down stairs, have bare wooden benches built into the walls, sawdust on bare boards, and on the ground floor high beams, crackly old black varnish, Victorian paintings on the dark brown walls, and a big open fire in winter; the vaulted cellars survived the Great Fire of London. Snacks include filled rolls (50p); the steak, kidney, mushroom and game pie – £5.50 – in the busy little upstairs restaurant is something of an institution; Sam Smiths Old Brewery and Museum on handpump. Congreve, Pope, Voltaire, Thackeray, Dickens, Conan Doyle, Yeats and perhaps Dr Johnson used to eat and drink here. *(Recommended by Alison Hayward, Nick Dowson, Nicolas Walter, S J Edwards; more reports please)*

Sam Smiths   Licensee Gordon Garrity   Snacks (lunchtime, not Sat or Sun)   Restaurant tel 01-353 6170/4388   Children welcome   Open 11.30–11 all year; closed Sun evening

Ye Olde Mitre (City) Map 13

Ely Place, EC1; there's also an entrance beside 8 Hatton Garden

If redevelopment were allowed, the piece of land this engagingly countryfied little pub occupies would be worth millions. It carries the same name of an earlier inn built here in 1547 to serve the people working in the palace of the Bishop of Ely, who actually administered the law here. The dark panelled small rooms have antique settles and big vases of flowers. Good bar snacks include filled rolls (50p), Scotch eggs and pork pies (55p), a good selection of sandwiches such as ham, salmon and cucumber or egg mayonnaise (from 70p, toasties 5p extra), and ploughman's (90p); well kept Friary Meux, Ind Coope Burton and Tetleys on handpump, reasonably priced for the area. There are some seats with pot-plants and jasmine in the narrow yard between the pub and St Ethelreda's church. *(Recommended by John Roué, Quentin Williamson)*

Taylor-Walkers (Ind Coope)   Licensee Don O'Sullivan   Real ale   Snacks (not Sat or Sun) Open 11–11 all year; closed Sat, Sun and bank hols

Orange Brewery (Pimlico) Map 13

37 Pimlico Road, SW1

About three hundred gallons a week are brewed in the cellars of this friendly and lively pub: SW1, a stronger SW2, and Pimlico Light – and they usually have a couple of guest beers on handpump as well. The high ochre walls of the bar are decorated with sepia photographs, some decorative Victorian plates, and a stuffed fox above a nicely tiled fireplace, and there are solid armed seats, a chaise-longue, and one or two Chesterfields. This leads through to the cheery Pie and Ale Shop (open all day in summer) with lots more sepia photographs on the dark stained plank-panelling, plain wooden tables and chairs on pretty black and white tiles, and a shelf full of old flagons and jugs above the counter where they serve a range of home-made food, including sandwiches, ploughman's or pâté, salads and daily hot dishes, all in pie form. Fruit machine, piped music. There are seats outside facing a little concreted-over green beyond the quite busy street. *(Recommended by S R Holman, Quentin Williamson)*

Own brew (though tied to Clifton Inns, part of Watneys)   Real ale   Meals and snacks Children in eating area   Open 11–3, 5.30–11 all year

---

Though English and Welsh pubs have to stop serving bar drinks between 3 and 7 on Sundays, they are allowed to serve drinks with meals in a separate dining-room all afternoon.

Princess Louise (Holborn)   Map 13

208 High Holborn, WC1

There's a lively atmosphere in this grandiose Victorian pub with people clustered around the enormous island bar servery, eager for its wide range of well kept real ales on handpump. They serve at least ten, which change regularly, including Boddingtons, Brakspears, Darleys Best, Greene King IPA and Abbot, Vaux Samson, Wards Best and Kirby, and a beer brewed for the pub. As we went to press, they were serving, experimentally, Weizenbier from Wards – the first time a beer has been brewed from wheat rather than barley in this country for a century or more; quick, Antipodean staff in white shirts and red bow ties; fruit machine. The elaborate décor includes etched and gilt mirrors, brightly coloured and fruity-shaped tiles, and slender Portland stone columns soaring towards the lofty and deeply moulded crimson and gold plaster ceiling; the green plush seats and banquettes are comfortable; the magnificent gents is the subject of a separate preservation order. Food, from a separate serving-counter still supplied by the original dumb-waiter, includes rolls, sandwiches and hot snacks (from 95p). Upstairs they have a wider range of food such as salads and lunchtime hot dishes (from £1.50), and several wines by the glass – including champagne. (Recommended by G Cooper, Stephen R Holman, Ian Phillips, Tim Powell, Alan Mosley, Michael and Alison Sandy)

Free house   Licensee Ian Phillips   Real ale   Lunchtime meals and snacks (not Sat or Sun)
Jazz Sat evening   Open 11–3, 5.30–11 all year; opens 12 and 6 Sat

Red Lion (Mayfair)   Map 13

Waverton Street, W1

This stylish Mayfair pub has a little L-shaped bar with small winged settles on the partly carpeted scrubbed floorboards, old photographs of Sam Smiths' Tadcaster Brewery in the 1920s and London prints below the high shelf of china on its dark-panelled walls, and an atmosphere almost like that of a civilised country pub. Good food includes ploughman's, generous sandwiches, salads, and specials such as chicken bourguignonne, crab or salmon. Unusually for the area, food is served morning and evening seven days a week. Ruddles County and Websters Yorkshire on handpump. It can get crowded at lunchtime. Among the bay trees under its front awning there are cut-away barrel seats – unusually peaceful for London. (Recommended by Ian Phillips, Elaine Kellet, Quentin Williamson, George Little)

Watneys   Real ale   Meals and snacks   Children in restaurant   Restaurant tel 01-499 1307
Open 11–3, 5.30–11 all year

St George's Hotel (West End)   Map 13

Langham Place, W1; take express lift in far corner of hotel lobby

The first thing to say is that this is a hotel, not a pub. The civilised fourteenth-floor lounge has small armchairs, well spaced between the white marble walls, that look out of the great picture windows westwards over and far beyond London, and a pleasant and relaxed atmosphere. Uniformed and warmly friendly bar staff mix cocktails, bring your drinks to your low gilt and marble table, and make sure that your dishes of free nuts and little biscuits are always topped up. If you get there early enough they may give you little freshly grilled cocktail sausages wrapped in bacon, too. There should be a pianist at the grand piano (not Sunday), and always plenty of room; the atmosphere is at its most lively during the week. They don't expect you to pay until you leave: given the surroundings and service, you obviously can't expect normal pub prices. Bar food includes good sandwiches such as toasted chicken and cheese, open fish or cold meat, and steak, Parma ham and

---

Real ale to us means beer which has matured naturally in its cask – not pressurised or filtered.

melon salad, beef Stroganoff or spiced seafood, and dressed crab. *(Recommended by JMC, Ian Phillips, Wayne Brindle, Revd Ian Watson, TBB)*

Free house (THF) *Meals and snacks* *Children welcome* *Restaurant* *Open 11–11 all year*
Bedrooms tel 01-580 0111; £101.25B/£133.50B

Samuel Pepys (City) Map 13

High Timber Street, off 48 Upper Thames Street

Discreetly hidden away down a Thames-side alley, this was converted from part of a Victorian tea warehouse in around 1970. It's got two bars, each with its own river-view balcony, and a Toby grill restaurant on the floor between them. Since last year, there's been a lot of refurbishment – the top bar has new tables, chairs, high bar stools and carpets, lots of Pepysiana, prints of the river frontage over the past few centuries, and a vaulted brick ceiling. A few tables and chairs on the sheltered duckboarded upper balcony look beyond the river to the great mass of Bankside power station, with one or two attractive old houses surprisingly punctuating the vista of big blocks of flats and the Wilcox hose works. Home-made food served in the light-wood panelled and flagstoned lower bar (which is six feet below water level at high tide) includes quiche (£2.75), steak and kidney or cottage pie, lasagne or moussaka (all £3), popular chicken curry (£3.25), lots of fresh salads (50p each) and puddings (from £1.25); well produced piped music. Charrington IPA and Bass on handpump. *(Recommended by Heather Sharland; more reports please)*

Charringtons *Manager Roger Coulthard* *Real ale* *Lunchtime meals* *Restaurant tel 01-248 3048/489 9178; evenings only (not Sun), but do Sun lunch until 4* *Open 11–11 all year*

NORTH LONDON

Parking is not a special problem in this area, unless we say so

The Case is Altered (Harrow Weald) Map 12

Old Redding; off A409 at the Hare

It's the unspoilt country setting that is the special thing here: a big back terrace with its own outside serving-bar, weekend barbecues and white metal and plastic tables and chairs, then a great spread of sloping lawn, with sturdy log-framed swings, climbers and a slide – and peaceful views that somehow soften the sprawl of London in the distance. Inside – a lot of building work has been going on (with more decoration to come) and readers haven't been so keen on it during this phase – there are flagstones under the carpet, a low ochre ceiling, banquettes and wooden wall seats, and olde-worlde prints on the walls; some of the tables are in a big bay window down a couple of steps. Bar food includes sandwiches, burgers (from 90p), basket meals (£2.50), poached salmon trout (£4.50) and sixteen-ounce T-bone steak (£5.50). Well kept Benskins Best and Ind Coope Burton on handpump, fruit machine, rather obtrusive piped pop music, friendly efficient service. *(Recommended by S C Collett-Jones; more reports please, especially on the changes)*

Benskins (Ind Coope) *Real ale* *Meals (not Sat or Sun) and snacks (not Sun evening)* *Children welcome until 9* *Open 11–3, 5.30–11 all year*

Clifton ⊗ (St John's Wood) Map 12

96 Clifton Hill, NW8

Careful placing of wooden balustrades and one or two steps from one level to another keep the idea of small rooms in this spacious place, with its relaxed and countryfied atmosphere. There are bare-boarded floors, attractively stripped doors, panelling and other woodwork, high ceilings, Edwardian and Victorian engravings and 1920s comic prints on its elegant wallpaper, unusual art nouveau wall lamps, cast-iron tables, and fine brass and glass ceiling lights. Edward VII and Lily Langtree used to come here, and there are quite a few prints of both of them (one signed by the king and his son – who became George V). The glass conservatory in the back courtyard is a focus of St John's Wood social life. Bar food includes soup (£1.75), pâté (£1.75), creamcheese and smoked salmon roulade (£2.45), vegetarian lasagne (£4.25), salads (from £4.25), beef in ale pie (£4.75), and char-grilled chops (£5.75) or steaks (from £6.95); also, puddings (from £1.50) and daily specials like beef Stroganoff, with crisps, nuts and cheese on the bar on Sunday. Well kept Taylor-Walker and Ind Coope Burton and Tetleys on handpump; friendly staff; shove ha'penny, cribbage, fruit machine. A very leafy front terrace has attractive marble-topped tables. *(Recommended by L E May, GB, CH, Nick Dowson, Alison Hayward, Chris Cooke)*

Taylor-Walker   Licensee John Murtagh   Real ale   Meals and snacks   Restaurant   Children in restaurant   Open 11–3, 5.30–11 all year, though they will stay open longer in afternoons if trade demands

Compton Arms (Canonbury)   Map 12

4 Compton Avenue, off Canonbury Lane, N1

Hidden away up a mews, this villagey little pub has been gently refurbished this year; the small and cheerful rooms are simply furnished with wooden settles and assorted stools and chairs, there are low ceilings and little local pictures on the wall, and really friendly service. Well kept Greene King IPA and Abbot and Rayments BBA on handpump. Good bar food includes freshly cut sandwiches (from 85p, hot salt-beef and mustard £1.40), filled baked potatoes (from £1.35), ploughman's (from £1.50), salads or basket meals (from £1.75), and interesting daily specials like stuffed peppers (£1.95), mushroom curry (£2.10), tasty game pie (£2.20) or Caribbean cod with red beans (£2.25); dominoes, cribbage, chess. A quiet little crazy-paved back terrace has benches around cask tables under a big sycamore tree (though house-building opposite may spoil the tranquility for a while). *(Recommended by Peter Griffiths; more reports please)*

Greene King   Licensee G Burke   Real ale   Meals and snacks (not Sat or Sun)   Open 12–11 all year

Crockers ★ (Maida Vale)   Map 13

24 Aberdeen Place, NW8

Not far from Regent's Canal towpath, this imposing place has a ceiling in its main room more elaborately moulded than any we have seen in a London pub; also, marble pillars supporting arches inlaid with bronze reliefs, a sweeping marble bar counter, and a vast pillared marble fireplace with a log-effect gas fire. A row of great arched and glazed mahogany doors opens into a similarly ornate but more spacious room. Darts, bar billiards, fruit machine, space game, trivia and juke box are in a less opulent room; also piped music. The good range of real ales on handpump includes Arkells, Brakspears, Darleys Thorne, Greene King Abbot and Samson and Wards. As we went to press they were serving, experimentally, Weizenbier from Wards – the first time a beer has been brewed from wheat rather then barley in this country for a century or more. Bar food at lunchtime includes sandwiches, home-made Scotch eggs (£1.20), ploughman's (£1.40), steak and kidney pie and shepherd's pie (£2.85); in the evening they do grills such as burgers (£2.45) and rump steaks (£4.40). The pub's Victorian nickname – Crocker's Folly – came after it's builder miscalculated where the entrance to Marylebone Station would be; he built it hoping to cash in on floods of customers from the new railway

---

Please keep sending us reports. We rely on readers for news of new discoveries, and particularly for news of changes – however slight – at the fully described pubs. No stamp needed: *The Good Pub Guide*, FREEPOST, London SW10 0BR.

— missing them by half a mile or so. *(Recommended by Neil Barker, M C Howells, Gary Scott, Dr and Mrs A K Clarke, George Little)*

Vaux   Licensee Peter Cox   Real ale   Meals and snacks   Children in eating area Occasional piano player   Daytime parking-meters   Open 11–3, 5.30–11 weekdays; probably 11–11 Sat

Flask (Highgate)   Map 12

77 Highgate West Hill, N6

The small, partly panelled rooms in the lower, original part of this old inn have little wooden armchairs, a high-backed carved settle, an open fire, and a sash-windowed bar counter – so that you have to stoop below the sashes to see the barman; local historic pictures and prints are hung on the walls. Some steps lead up to the more spacious tile-floored extension, which has Windsor chairs, low settles, and tables for the home-made food: curried parsnip or tomato and lentil soup, sandwiches, filled baked potatoes, beef and Guinness or Welsh lamb pie, vegetable curry, and trout stuffed with almonds. Ind Coope Burton, Taylor-Walker Bitter and Tetleys on handpump; trivia. It gets very busy in the evenings and at weekends. It was here that one of Hogarth's rowdy friends clobbered a regular with his tankard, and Hogarth himself nearly got clobbered back for sketching the result. Outside, there are sturdy wooden tables – one or two protected by a wood-pillared porch decorated with hanging baskets of geraniums and petunias. *(Recommended by Alison Hayward, Ian Phillips, GB, Dave Butler, Lesley Storey)*

Taylor-Walker (Ind Coope)   Licensee Bernice Chamberlain   Real ale   Snacks and lunchtime meals (not Sun)   Children in eating area of bar, lunchtime only   Clog and morris dancers in summer   Open 11–11 all year

Holly Bush (Hampstead)   Map 12

Holly Mount, NW3

The back room in this modernised but old-fashioned pub is named after the painter George Romney: the present tavern was built in 1802 on the site of his stables. It has an embossed red ceiling, panelled and etched glass alcoves, ochre-painted brick walls covered with small prints and plates, and an intimate atmosphere. The front bar has hardly changed in the quarter-century we've known it: real gas lamps (which have been there for seventy years), a dark and sagging ceiling, brown and cream panelled walls (which are decorated with old advertisements and a few hanging plates), and cosy bays formed by partly glazed partitions. In between the two bars, a selection of hot and cold home-cooked food is served by the licensee: chilli con carne, pasta, pork in cider sauce or chicken casserole, and beef in Burton ale pie. Well kept Benskins and Ind Coope Burton and Tetleys on handpump, with draught cider; fruit machine. *(Recommended by Nicolas Walter; more reports please)*

Taylor-Walker (Ind Coope)   Real ale   Meals and snacks (not Mon, Sun evening)   Children in eating area   '60s music Weds and Thurs evening   Nearby parking sometimes quite a squeeze Open 11–3 (4 Sat), 5.30–11 all year

Olde White Bear (Hampstead)   Map 12

Well Road, NW3

The dimly lit main room in this neo-Victorian pub has wooden stools, cushioned captain's chairs, a couple of big tasseled armed chairs, and a flowery sofa (surrounded by the excrescences of an ornate Edwardian sideboard), as well as lots of Victorian prints and cartoons on the walls, and a tiled gas-effect log fire with a heavy wooden overmantel. A small central room – also dimly lit – has Lloyd Loom furniture, dried flower arrangements and signed photographs of actors and playwrights. The brighter end room has cushioned machine-tapestried ornate pews, marble-topped tables, a very worn butcher's table, dark brown paisley curtains and a food cabinet serving sandwiches, salads (from £2.50), seafood Mornay or lamb and mango curry with poppadums (£2.85) and moules marinière (£3); piped music. Well kept Adnams, Boddingtons, Ind Coope Burton, Marstons Pedigree and Tetleys on handpump, twenty-two malt whiskies and several wines. *(Recommended by Hazel and Denis Gildea, Jonathan Warner, Leo and Pam Cohen, George Little)*

Nicholsons (Ind Coope) – but run as free house   Licensees C Warry and T Polden   Real ale   Meals and snacks   Open 11–3, 5.30–11 weekdays; 11–11 Fri and Sat

Spaniards Inn (Hampstead) Map 12

Spaniards Lane, NW3

Named after the Spanish ambassador to the Court of James I (he is said to have lived here), this civilised and friendly old pub has genuinely antique winged settles, open fires and snug little alcoves in the low-ceilinged oak-panelled rooms; some redecoration is scheduled. The atmosphere is lively and busy, especially in the evenings (when it's lit by candle-shaped lamps in pink shades); the upstairs bar is quieter. The home-cooked good value food, that changes daily, includes plough-man's (from £1.95), quiche, vegetable curry (£2.75), vegetable moussaka (£2.95), chilli con carne (£3.25) and beef goulash (£3.50). Bass, Charrington IPA and Youngs Bitter on handpump; fruit machine. The attractive sheltered garden has slatted wooden tables and chairs on a crazy-paved terrace which opens on to a flagstoned walk around a small lawn, with roses, a side arbour of wistaria and clematis, and an aviary. *(Recommended by Tim Powell, Jon Wainwright, Col G D Stafford, GB)*

Charringtons   Licensee David Roper   Meals and snacks   Children anywhere alcohol is not served   Open 11–11 in summer; probably afternoon closing in winter

Waterside ⊗ (King's Cross) Map 13

82 York Way, N1

Sold by Hoskins to Whitbreads, this friendly, busy place seems to have changed little: latticed windows, stripped brickwork, genuinely old stripped timbers in white plaster, lots of dimly lit alcoves, spinning-wheels, milkmaid's yokes, horsebrasses and so on, with plenty of rustic tables and wooden benches. Outside, there's a spacious well kept terrace looking over Battlebridge Basin where daily barbecues are held (from around £2.85), and where the new barge restaurant has opened. Good bar food includes ploughman's (£2.25), lots of salads (from £3.50), and six daily hot dishes like pancakes, goulash, Stroganoff, pies and chilli con carne (from £3.75); on Sundays there are two roasts (£4.95). Well kept Adnams, Boddingtons, Brakspears and Greene King Abbot on handpump, as well as wines on draught. *(Recommended by Ian Phillips, Howard and Sue Gascoyne, NHB, Mrs Anne Simons, J R Grocott)*

Whitbreads   Licensee R Wren   Real ale   Meals and snacks   Restaurant on barge tel 01-837 7118   Open 11–11 in summer; probably afternoon closing in winter, according to demand by trade

White Lion of Mortimer (Finsbury Park) Map 12

Stroud Green Road, N4

This is one of a chain of North London pubs recently set up by Tim Martin as a reaction to the state of other establishments in the area – in his view, not enough real ale and too much loud piped music. The result is an atmosphere in all his pubs where it's possible to talk at ease over a well pulled pint. The White Lion is a particularly good example, with well kept Greene King Abbot, Marstons Pedigree, Youngers Scotch, maybe Wadworths 6X and a guest beer such as Brains SA on handpump. It was actually a garage showroom until 1986, when it was attractively renovated; it has a large etched front window, subdued gaslamp-style lighting throughout, and two full-size Victorian street-lamps just inside the entrance. The carved island servery runs the length of the spacious bar, which has carefully done cream tilework at the front, lion pictures on the partly panelled walls, and a medley of old tables, some of them marble with cast-iron legs. The cooking implements down the left-hand side contrast with the horse harness and farm tools on the right, which also has a public telephone with an old copper fireplace as its booth. Some alcoves have an old cast-iron fireplace and plush settees, and there's an attractive conservatory area at the back, with hanging ivy plants and a small fountain outside its door. Bar food includes sandwiches (from 90p), salads (from around £2.50), and hot dishes like curry and lasagne (£2.50); in the evenings they do only sandwiches. Two fruit machines, dominoes and cards; a relaxed, local atmosphere. There are some cast-iron tables on the pavement outside. Other Wetherspoons pubs include the Old Suffolk Punch on the Grand Parade and the Mortimer Arms in Green Lanes (both N4), and you'll find some mentioned in the North London Lucky Dip section at the end of the chapter. *(Recommended by Gavin May; more reports please)*

Free house   Managers Mr and Mrs Knipe   Real ale   Meals (lunchtime) and snacks   Open 11–11 all year

SOUTH LONDON

Parking is bad on weekday lunchtimes at the inner-city pubs here (SE1), and at the Orange Tree in Richmond, with a bit of a walk to the Rose & Crown in Wimbledon; it's ususally OK *everywhere in the evenings – you may again have a bit of a walk if a good band is on at the Bulls Head in Barnes, or at the Windmill on Clapham Common if it's a fine evening*

Alma (Battersea) Map 12

499 York Road, SW11

An enjoyable translation of the idea of a French cafe-bar into Battersea circumstances, this well run place has even got the details right – the pin-table and table footer, the barman's tight black waistcoat, the redundant wooden Frigidaire and of course the bentwood chairs around the cast-iron-framed tables. It all seems honest and straightforward, too, with a thriving local atmosphere (too thriving, some might say, on a busy night) and careful quick service. Besides Youngs Bitter and Special on handpump from the island bar counter, there are usually decent house wines, good coffee, tea or hot chocolate, newspapers out for customers, and bar food that might include onion soup (£1.45), eggs and bacon or kipper (£2.50), moules marinière (£2.65), a plate of cheeses (£2.20), salad niçoise (£2.45), dishes of the day such as pork ragout (£2.65) and steaks (£7). There's a lot of ochre and terracotta paintwork, gilded mosaics of the Battle of the Alma, an ornate mahogany chimney-piece and fireplace, bevelled mirrors in a pillared mahogany room divider, and in a side room a fine turn-of-the-century frieze of swirly nymphs. Good fun. *(Recommended by Richard Gibbs, RAB)*

Youngs   Real ale   Meals and snacks   Open 11–3, 5.30–11 all year

Anchor (South Bank) Map 12

Bankside, SE1; Southwark Bridge end

A series of separate rooms, up and down stairs, have creaky boards and beams, black panelling, and old-fashioned high-backed settles as well as sturdy leatherette chairs. Carefully restored in the 1960s and dating back to about 1750 (when it was rebuilt to replace the earlier tavern), this was probably where Pepys went to watch the Great Fire burning London: 'one entire arch of fire above a mile long, the churches, houses, and all on fire at once, a horrid noise the flames made, and the cracking of houses at their ruine'. It's still an atmospheric place (except when tourist coaches arrive). Bar food includes ploughman's with a good choice of cheeses, pies and cold meats with salads, as well as lunchtime hot dishes such as casseroles, curries, lasagne, cottage pie and steak and kidney pie. Well kept Courage Best and Directors on handpump; darts, fruit machine, space game and piped music. A terrace overlooks the river. *(Recommended by Nick Dowson, Alison Hayward, John Roué, John Branford)*

Courage   Real ale   Meals and snacks   Restaurant tel 01-407 1577; to stay open all afternoon Sun   Children welcome   Open 11.30–3, 5.30–11 all year; probably open all day Fri

Angel (Rotherhithe) Map 12

Bermondsey Wall East, SE16

Probably with the finest view of all the riverside pubs in London, this looks down to the Pool of London in one direction, though it's the upstream view which is exceptional. It centres on Tower Bridge in the classic perspective that is known throughout the world, but difficult to see from any other viewpoint. The open-plan bar is comfortably modernised, with bar food such as Scotch egg salad (£1.80), Cheddar ploughman's (£2), home-cooked ham or various pies and salad (£2.50), and at lunchtime a hot dish of the day such as chilli con carne or shepherd's pie or evening scampi (£2.95); well kept Courage Best and Directors on handpump; fruit machine. The bare-boarded balcony, on timber piles sunk into the river, is lit by lanterns at night. Pepys bought cherries for his wife at the jetty here. *(Recommended by Alun Palmer; more reports please)*

Courage   Licensee Nicholas Parker   Real ale   Meals and snacks   Restaurant tel 01-237 3608   Children in restaurant   Open 11–3, 5.30–11 all year

Bulls Head (Barnes) Map 12

373 Lonsdale Road, SW13

Top-class modern jazz groups every evening, and weekend lunchtime big band sessions (practice on Saturday, concert on Sunday) are the draw to this well run and solidly comfortable riverside pub. Though admission to the well equipped music room is £2 to £3, the sound is perfectly clear – if not authentically loud – in the adjoining lounge bar. Alcoves open off the main area around the efficient island servery, which has well kept Youngs Bitter and Special on handpump, reasonably priced for London. Bar lunches include soup with crusty bread, sandwiches, filled French bread, hot roast meat sandwiches, a pasta dish of the day, home-baked pies, and at lunchtime a carvery of home-roasted joints; darts, bar billiards, dominoes, cribbage, fruit machine and space game in the public bar. Across the road you can sit on the flood wall by the Thames. *(Recommended by Doug Kennedy, C J Cuss)*

Youngs   Licensee Daniel Fleming   Real ale   Meals and snacks   Restaurant (open noon–6 Sun) tel 01-876 5241   Children in eating area of bar and in restaurant   Jazz nightly and Sun lunchtime   Nearby parking may be difficult   Open 11–11 all year

George ★ (Southwark) Map 13 *[illustrated on page 751]*

Off 77 Borough High Street, SE1

Coming in from the busy high street through the great gates, you can hardly believe that this coaching-inn, with its tiers of open galleries looking down on the cobbled courtyard, has survived. It is the only one left in London, and is now carefully preserved by the National Trust. The row of ground-floor rooms and bars all have square-latticed windows, black beams, bare floorboards, some panelling, plain oak or elm tables, old-fashioned built-in settles, a 1797 Act of Parliament clock, dimpled glass lantern-lamps and so forth. It does of course attract quite a stream of tourists, and we'd recommend as the safest refuge from them the simple room nearest the street. This is where the well kept Brakspears, Flowers Original, Greene

King Abbot and Wethereds are served from an ancient beer engine looking like a cash register. Bar food, served at the far end, includes sausage and beans, quiche with three salads, and home-made steak and mushroom pie. A splendid central staircase goes up to a series of dining-rooms and to a gaslit balcony. The pub was noted as one of London's 'fair Inns for the receipt of travellers' in 1598, and rebuilt on its original plan after the great Southwark fire in 1676. In summer there may be morris men dancing in the courtyard; this is the revival of a very old tradition: jugglers, acrobats, conjurers, animal-trainers, musicians and even Shakespeare's strolling players used to perform here when Southwark was London's entertainment centre. This has been further revived by players from the nearby Globe Theatre performing in the courtyard at lunchtimes in spring. *(Recommended by Chris Cooke, R G Ollier, G S B G Dudley, Brian Jones, John Roué, Quentin Williamson, Rob and Gill Weeks, Alison Hayward, Nick Dowson, Philip Denison, John Branford)*

Whitbreads   Licensee John Hall   Real ale   Meals (not evening) and snacks   Restaurant tel 01-407 2056   Children in area by wine bar and restaurant   Nearby daytime parking difficult   Possibly the Globe Players in spring, morris dancers during summer   Open 11.30–3, 4.45–11 all year; closed 25 and 26 Dec

Green Man (Putney) Map 12

Wildcroft Road, SW15

Once the favourite hunting ground for footpads and highwaymen, this friendly old pub has small rooms and a lively, country atmosphere. The cosy green-carpeted main bar opens into a quiet sitting-room, and serves well kept Youngs Bitter and Special on handpump, reasonably priced for London. Good value bar food includes sandwiches, burgers, lasagne, chilli con carne or curry, plaice or scampi, and good value barbecues, weather permitting, with burgers, kebabs, ribs, one-pound Cumberland sausages, trout, steak and whole poussin. Ring the bull and dominoes as well as sensibly placed darts and a fruit machine. Outside, there's a new bar, lots of seats and a swing, slide and seesaw among the flowering shrubs and trees on the good-sized lawn behind, and there are also tables outside on sheltered colonnaded side terraces. The pub is on the edge of Putney Heath. *(Recommended by Doug Kennedy, Grahame and Brenda Blair, A D Jenkins, G Cooper)*

Youngs   Licensee Douglas Ord   Real ale   Meals and snacks   Licensees planning to open 11–11 but leaving before this edition is published – new licensees may not take the same view

Horniman (Southwark) Map 13

Hays Galleria, Battlebridge Lane, SE1

An ambitious adventure in pub design, this is part of a visually exciting development right on the Thames. The main concourse of the development has a soaring glass curved roof, several storeys high, supported by elegant thin cast-iron columns, and under this is an entertaining giant working (well, sometimes working) sculpture of a fantasy iron boat-fish or fish-boat, splashing about eccentrically in a pool. Various shops and boutiques open off, and down at the end, by the waterside, is the pub. It too is spacious, elegant and neatly kept; the area by the sweeping bar counter is a few steps down from the door, with squared black, red and white flooring-tiles, lots of polished wood, and efficiently served Adnams, Arkells, Boddingtons, Ind Coope Burton and Tetleys on handpump. Steps lead up from here to various comfortable carpeted areas, with the tables well spread so as to allow for a feeling of spacious relaxation at quiet times but give room for people standing in groups when it's busy. From some parts there are good views of the Thames, HMS *Belfast* and Tower Bridge, as there are from the picnic-table sets outside. There's a hundred-foot frieze showing the travels of the tea merchant whose firm formerly operated from this wharf; the set of clocks above the bar was made for his office, showing the time in various places around the world, and the former activities here are commemorated too by a tea-bar which also has coffee, chocolate and other hot drinks, and Danish pastries and so forth. Bar food includes filled baps and hot dishes such as steak and kidney pie (up to £3.85), and an upper carvery, within the same space, does full meals (around £13); in one place or another there's something to eat all day. Fruit machine, trivia machine, maybe piped music. *(Recommended by Richard Gibbs, Ian Phillips, David Fisher, Comus Elliott, Pete Storey)*

Nicholsons/Taylor-Walker (Ind Coope)   Licensee Colin Head   Real ale   Bar meals and snacks (lunchtime – and see above)   Children in eating area and restaurant   Open 11–11 all year

Market Porter (Southwark)   Map 13

9 Stoney Street, SE1

The main part of the long U-shaped bar in this lively, busy, recently redecorated pub has rough wooden ceiling-beams with beer barrels balanced on them, a heavy wooden bar counter with a beamed gantry, cushioned bar stools, an open fire with stuffed animals in glass cabinets on the mantelpiece, several mounted stags' heads, and '20s-style wall lamps. Green and brown cushioned captain's chairs sit on the patterned green and brown carpet, and at one end there is a glass cabinet for food, which includes sandwiches, steak and kidney pie (£2), wholemeal pasta (£2.50), chilli con carne (£2.60), and chicken Madras (£2.90); sometimes there are snacks such as prawns and mussels on the bar. As well as serving its well kept own-brew Market Bitter, there's Boddingtons, Greene King IPA and Abbot, and Marstons Pedigree on handpump; sensible darts, dominoes, fruit machine, pinball, trivia and piped music. A small partly panelled room has leaded-glass windows and a couple of tables. *(Recommended by Iain McNair, Nick Dowson, Alison Hayward, John Roué)*

Own brew   Licensee Peter Conlan   Real ale   Lunchtime meals and snacks (not Sun) Restaurant (not Sun evening) tel 01-407 2495   Children in restaurant   Occasional live music at weekends   Open 11–11 all year

Old Thameside (Southwark)   Map 13

St Mary Overy Wharf, off Clink Street; from junction of Southwark Street and Borough High Street follow signpost to Southwark Cathedral

There are picnic-table sets on the waterside terrace outside this exemplary new pub, by a 1900 West Country schooner docked in a waterlocked inlet, and narrow alleys lead away from the modern development past Southwark Cathedral and the ruined shell of St Mary's church to the old-fashioned warren of Borough Market. Inside, the main river-view bar has dark floorboards and bare yellow brickwork, high stools by narrow dividing elbow rests with just about enough room for a well balanced plate, dark brown kitchen chairs, barrel tables, and some hefty wooden baulks serving as props and beams. Swirly brass and glass lamps, and a rather plusher raised carpeted area, tone in more smartly with the neat young bankers who flock in from the stylish nearby ANZ building – but given a good coup they head anyway for the elegant adjoining champagne bar (the house brand is dry and well made). Black-waistcoated bar staff serve well kept Courage Best, Tetleys and Wethereds from handpump, and a food counter does filled French bread, good generously filled hot beef baps, pies and crab salad; there's a wider choice of food, with several hot dishes in the bigger but more intimate candlelit downstairs bar, all dark beams, pews and flagstones. The pub looks out over the Thames, between London and Blackfriars Bridges, to the Cityscape gloriously punctuated by the gilded sphere gleaming on top of the Monument. *(Recommended by GRE, AE, Heather Sharland, John Roué)*

Free house   Manager Mr Jones   Real ale   Meals and snacks   Restaurant (weekdays) tel 01-403 4253   Open 11–3, 5.30–11 all year

---

Most pubs in the *Guide* sell draught cider. We mention it specifically only if they have unusual farm-produced 'scrumpy' or even specialise in it.

Olde Windmill 🛏 (Clapham) Map 12

Clapham Common South Side, SW4

On the edge of Clapham Common, this large Victorian inn has courtyards at each end with picnic tables, and one has a colonnaded shelter and tubs of shrubs. The front room is dominated by the substantial and heavily manned bar counter, and the domed and spacious main room has big prints of Dutch windmill pictures on the flowery black and brown wallpaper, and clusters of orange leatherette seats, sofas and small armchairs around elegant black tables. Ploughman's, macaroni cheese, cottage pie, chilli con carne or ham salad, clam fries, curry and rice and lunchtime grills from the efficient food counter in this inner room; well kept Youngs Bitter, Special and John's London Lager on handpump, quite cheap; fruit machines. In summer it can get packed, when it seems to serve not just the pub but half the Common too. *(Recommended by Ian Phillips, Hazel Morgan, Len Beattie, G Cooper)*

Youngs   Licensee Mr Naylor   Real ale   Meals and snacks (not Sun)   Open 11–11 all year Bedrooms tel 01-673 4578; £27S/£32S

Orange Tree ⊗ (Richmond) Map 12

45 Kew Road

The embossed ceiling in the spacious main bar here has an unusual fruit and foliage pattern, and there are big coaching and Dickens prints, and the courtly paintings of the seven ages of man by Henry Stacy Marks – presented to the Green Room theatre club here in 1921; the upstairs fringe theatre carries on the long tradition. There are comfortable seats on the carpet that spreads around the efficient central servery. The cellar food bar, attractively lit and with the relaxed atmosphere of a spacious wine bar, has simple tables on a tiled floor and old stripped brickwork walls; it serves chilli con carne (£3.75), steak and kidney pie (£4.10), beef salad (£4.25), steaks (from £6.45) and fondues (from £9.50 for two). On the ground floor there's a full range of lunchtime sandwiches (from £1), ploughman's (£1.60), sausage and egg and scampi. Well kept Youngs Bitter and Special on handpump, relatively reasonably priced for London; fruit machine. *(Recommended by Raymond Palmer, Nigel Williamson)*

Youngs   Licensees Don and Chris Murphy   Real ale   Meals and snacks (not Sun evening) Restaurant tel 01-940 0944   Children in downstairs restaurant   Nearby parking difficult Open 11–11 all year; closed Sun evening

Phoenix & Firkin ★ (Denmark Hill) Map 12

5 Windsor Walk, SE5

This is a beautifully renovated, palatial Victorian building spanning the railway cutting – you feel it throb when trains pass underneath. The bar is a vast lofty pavilion, with a bar counter made from a single mahogany tree, solid wooden furniture on the stripped wooden floor, paintings of steam trains, old seaside posters, Bovril advertisements, old-fashioned station name-signs, plants, big revolving fans, and a huge double-faced station clock, originally from Llandudno Junction, hanging by chains from the incredibly high ceiling. At one end there's a gallery with similar furnishings reached by a spiral staircase, and at the other arches lead into a food room. In the evenings it can get packed with a good mixed crowd (often given a bit of fizz by young medics from the surrounding hospitals). The food includes big filled baps (£1.20), portion of pie (£1.40), bread with a selection of cheeses (£1.70), salads (from £2.10) and a daily hot dish. The beers include Phoenix, Rail and Dogbolter on handpump, as well as two changing guest beers kept under light blanket pressure. This was originally opened as a pub by David Bruce, who created a small chain of pubs brewing their own beers, all with the word Firkin in their name and all sharing a similar back-to-basics character. Another main entry is the Ferret & Firkin in West London, and many are mentioned in the Lucky Dip – the newer ones often having remarkably good children's facilities. In 1988 the chain was sold to Midsummer Inns, who run one of our top-rated pubs (the Fleece at Bretforton). They plan to run the Firkin pubs very much as before, and certainly by the time we went to press no change was evident. Piped music. Outside there are some tables and chairs with parasols, and the steps that follow the slope of the road are a popular place to sit. *(Recommended by Greg Parston, Peter Griffiths, Norman Foot, Michele and Andrew Wells, Margaret Drazin, Jilly Mills, Quentin Williamson, Alison Hayward, Nick Dowson, E G Parish, Heather Sharland)*

Own brew   Licensee Roger Howard   Real ale   Meals and snacks   Open 11–3, 5.30–11 all year; they are considering opening an hour earlier in the evening

Prince of Orange (Rotherhithe)   Map 12

118 Lower Road, SE16

East London's premier jazz spot, with different acts every night and weekend lunchtimes, this does very much focus on the music, with basic furnishings and simple (but good value) food such as nine- or fourteen-inch pizzas (from £2.75). Besides the main music bar, there are two smaller rooms, one with its walls completely covered with old photographs including some old 1930s jazz sessions at Abbey Road Studios. Ruddles Best and County, Trumans Best and Websters Yorkshire on handpump; fruit machine and piped music. *(More reports please)*

Trumans   Licensee Christopher French   Real ale   Evening snacks   Children in eating area of bar   Jazz every night   Open 7pm–midnight; 12–3, 7–10.30 Sun; closed 23 Dec–2 Jan

Ship ⊗ (Wandsworth)   Map 12

41 Jews Row, SW18

This year, the main bar here has been turned into more of a conservatory, with only a small part of the original ceiling, supported by two pillars, left. It's light and airy with a relaxed, chatty atmosphere, wooden tables (one a butcher's table), a medley of stools and old church chairs, and two comfortable leatherette Chesterfields on the wooden floorboards; one part has a Victorian fireplace, a huge clock surrounded by barge prints, and part of a milking machine on a table, and there's a rather battered harmonium, old-fashioned bagatelle, and jugs of flowers around the window sills. The simple public bar has plain wooden furniture, a black kitchen range in the fireplace and darts, pinball and a juke box; well kept Youngs Bitter and Special on handpump. Outside, the extensive riverside terrace, partly cobbled and partly concrete, is on two levels with picnic-table sets, pretty hanging baskets, brightly coloured flower beds and small trees; there's a bar here, and a charcoal barbecue counter (the reason for its food award): sausages (£3), fillet of mackerel (£3.20), burger (£3.50), chicken (£4), Mediterranean prawns (£5), lamb steak (£5.35), sirloin steak (£6.50) and Dover sole (£7.95); other food includes smoked salmon sandwich (£1.50), ploughman's (£2.35), moules marinière (£2.75), salads (£3.50, seafood £3.95), and poached trout with dill and cucumber (£4.95). A Thames barge is moored alongside and can be used for private parties, although she may sail along the East and South Coasts during the summer months. *(Recommended by Grahame and Brenda Blair, David Potter, Ian Howard, Jimmy Ellinas, Alan Docherty, Lindy May, Ian Phillips)*

Youngs   Licensee Charles Gotto   Real ale   Meals and snacks   You may have to park some way away   Open 11–11 all year

White Swan (Richmond)   Map 12

25/26 Old Palace Lane

The atmosphere in this very friendly and well kept little place is more like that of a cosy village local than a busy London pub. The open-plan bar has copper pots hanging from the dark beamed ceiling, old prints of London and china plates on the walls, captain's chairs, dark wood tables and plush banquettes on the green and terracotta patterned carpet, and an open brick fireplace. Good value bar food includes sandwiches (from 90p), quiche (£1.25), ploughman's (£1.90), salads (from £2.25), and fish or steak and kidney pie, chilli con carne or lasagne (all £2.50). Well kept Courage Best and Directors on handpump; quick, efficient service; fruit machine. There's a new conservatory with cane furniture, and a paved garden with climbing plants, flowering tubs, flower beds and wooden tables and benches. Summer evening barbecues on Tuesdays or Thursdays include sausage (£1.25), onion in a roll (90p), spare ribs (£3.25) and eight-ounce rump steak (£5.50). *(Recommended by Sheila Keene, Nigel Williamson, Grahame and Brenda Blair)*

Courage   Licensee Anthony Savage   Real ale   Snacks   Open 11–11 in summer; 11–3, 5.30–11 in winter

WEST LONDON

During weekday or Saturday daytime you may not be able to find a meter very close to the Anglesea Arms or the Windsor Castle, and parking very near in the evening may sometimes be tricky with both of these, but there shouldn't otherwise be problems in this area

Anglesea Arms (Chelsea)   Map 13

15 Selwood Terrace, SW7

The main bar in this popular pub has central elbow tables, leather Chesterfields, faded Turkey carpets on the bare wood-strip floor, wood panelling, and big windows with attractive swagged curtains; at one end several booths with partly glazed screens have cushioned pews and spindle-back chairs, and down some steps there's a small carpeted room with captain's chairs, high stools and a Victorian fireplace. The old-fashioned mood is heightened by some heavy portraits, prints of London, a big station clock, bits of brass and pottery, and large brass chandeliers; the atmosphere is relaxed and cheery. A good range of well kept ales on handpump includes Adnams, Boddingtons Bitter, Brakspears SB, Greene King Abbot, Huntsman Dorset and Dorchester, Theakstons Old Peculier and Youngs Special. Food, from a glass cabinet, includes Scotch eggs or jumbo sausages (from 80p), doorstep sandwiches (£1.50), ploughman's (£2.35) and salads, roast of the day or chicken Kiev (£3). It can get very busy in the evenings and at weekends – when even the outside terrace (which has seats and tables) tends to overflow into the quiet side street. *(Recommended by Ken Vostal, Howard and Sue Gascoyne, Alison Hayward, Nick Dowson)*

Free house   Licensee Patrick Timmons   Real ale   Meals and snacks (not Sat or Sun evening) Children under supervision at lunchtime only   Daytime parking metered   Open 11–11 in summer; 11–3, 5.30–11 in winter; closed 25 and 26 Dec

City Barge (Chiswick)   Map 12

27 Strand on the Green, W4

On warm summer evenings people tend to crowd along the towpath outside this ancient pub, many sitting on the low wall. In cooler weather the nicest places to head for are the two little low-ceilinged rooms of the cosy Old Bar: cushioned wooden seats built into the ochre walls, an ancient fireplace raised above the quarry-tiled floor as protection against floods, a really worn old overmantel, antique decorative mugs behind latticed glass and miniature bottles in a corner cupboard, and at least on weekday lunchtimes a relaxed local atmosphere. This original building in fact dates from 1484. A quite separate and very much more orthodox and carpeted New Bar has some tables, lots of standing room (as well as elbow rests around central pillars) and reproduction maritime painted signs and bird prints. A warm white-walled conservatory with cane bentwood chairs around cast-iron-framed tables, a few houseplants and plastic ferns leads off behind. Food in the New Bar includes nicely garnished beef sandwiches (£1.10), salads such as smoked mackerel, and hot dishes such as moussaka, lasagne or steak and kidney pie (around £2.50, good value even though without vegetables); well kept Courage Best and Directors; sensibly placed darts, fruit machine. The cosy restaurant opens off the Old Bar and matches it in style. *(Recommended by S C Collett-Jones, BKA, Doug Kennedy)*

Courage   Licensees T G Hitchings and C A Whately-Smith   Real ale   Meals and snacks Restaurant tel 01-994 2148   Open 11–11 in summer; 11–3, 5.30–11 in winter

Dove ★ ⊗ (Hammersmith) Map 12

19 Upper Mall, W6

By the entrance from the quiet alley, the main bar in this intimate and old-fashioned riverside pub has black wood panelling, red leatherette cushioned built-in wall settles and stools around dimpled copper tables, and old framed advertisements, photographs of the pub and a manuscript of 'Rule, Britannia!' on the walls: James Thomson, who wrote it, is said to have written the final part of his less well known 'The Seasons' in an upper room here, dying of a fever he had caught on a trip from here to Kew in bad weather. There's also a tiny front snug. Up some steps, a room with small settles and solid wooden furniture has a big, clean and efficiently served glass food cabinet: Cornish pasty (£1.85), sausage and beans (£1.95), ploughman's (from £1.95), pâté (£2.10), salads (from £2.95) and hot specials such as cauliflower cheese, home-made shepherd's or fish pie and lamb curry. From here, big glassless windows open out on to a smallish terrace with a large vine; the main flagstoned area, down some steps, has lots of teak tables and white metal and teak chairs looking over the low river wall to the Thames reach just above Hammersmith Bridge. Well kept Fullers London Pride and ESB on handpump. If this pub is really crowded (it's at its best at lunchtime when it's quiet and relaxed) you may find more room a short stroll up the river at the Old Ship (see Lucky Dip, W6). *(Recommended by M C Howells, Simon Collett-Jones, Doug Kennedy, Nick Dowson, Alison Hayward)*

Fullers   Licensee Brian Lovrey   Real ale   Meals and snacks (lunchtime)   Open 11–11 all year

Eel Pie (Twickenham) Map 12

9 Church Street

Popular with real-ale lovers, this lively, cheerful place has well kept Adnams Extra, Badger Best and Tanglefoot, Everards Tiger, Gales BBB, and Wadworths 6X and Farmers Glory (prices approach Central London levels) on handpump. The food is served upstairs, though you can take it down to the simply furnished bar and eat it there: toasted sandwiches (from £1), ploughman's (£1.80), salads (£2.50), cottage pie (£2.60), curry or goulash (£2.75) and steak, kidney and Guinness pie (£2.80). Darts, dominoes, cribbage and fruit machine, maybe piped music; a bench out on the pavement. *(Recommended by John Roué; more reports please)*

Badger   Licensee Brendan Mallon   Real ale   Lunchtime meals and snacks (not Sun) Children in eating area of bar   Open 11–11 all year

Ferret & Firkin (Fulham) Map 12

Lots Road, SW10

Another of the small chain of own-brew pubs started by David Bruce but sold by him in 1988 (see Phoenix & Firkin, South London), this determinedly basic pub has been enjoyed by many readers calling in on the *Good Pub Guide* offices – it's just around the corner. There are unsealed bare floorboards, traditional furnishings well made from good wood, slowly circulating colonial-style ceiling-fans, a log-effect gas fire, tall airy windows, and plenty of standing room in front of the long bar counter – which is curved, to match the front wall. There's an easy-going crowd of customers – most youngish but otherwise a very mixed bag indeed. A food counter serves heftily filled giant meat-and-salad rolls, pies, ploughman's, salads, spare ribs and chilli con carne. Well kept own-brew ales include Ferret, Stoat, the notoriously strong Dogbolter, and usually a Bruce's. With twenty-four hours' notice you can collect a bulk supply. There are also two or three guest beers from other breweries, and a couple of real ciders. There's usually a pianist or guitarist on duty in the evening, and there are seats out on the pavement. Sister pubs we'd recommend in London follow much the same pattern as this, so have not all been described in detail. *(Recommended by Ewan McCall, Roger Huggins, Tom McLean, Charles Gurney, John Roué, Ian Phillips, Len Beattie, Rob and Gill Weeks, Nick Dowson, Richard Coats)*

Own brew   Real ale   Meals (not evening) and snacks   Daytime parking metered   Open 11–3, 5.30–11 all year

London Apprentice (Isleworth) Map 12

Church Street

Dating back at least five hundred years, this picturesque riverside Chef & Brewer pub has a pretty terrace overlooking the river, with garden furniture and hanging baskets and tubs full of bright flowers. Inside, the spaciously comfortable L-shaped bar has tapestry-style covered benches and stools on the brown patterned carpet and lots of dark wood veneered tables. At one end there are darts, bar billiards and a fruit machine and at the other a separate room with partly panelled walls, wheel-back chairs and a glass food cabinet: a help-yourself selection of freshly made salads (£2.95), and a daily roast (£3.95). Ruddles Best and County, Trumans Best and Websters Yorkshire on handpump; fruit machine and piped music; young and friendly staff. As the pub is signposted from the main road it can get very crowded in summer and on winter weekends, especially with young people. *(Recommended by Hazel Morgan; more reports please)*

Watneys   Licensee Peter Wickham   Real ale   Meals and snacks   Restaurant (open all afternoon Sun) tel 01-560 1915   Children welcome   Occasional live music on terrace, summer evenings   Open 11–11 all year

Popes Grotto (Twickenham) Map 12

Cross Deep

The stroll-around main lounge in this well run, spacious and friendly modern pub (named after the poet Alexander Pope who had a villa nearby) is comfortably relaxed with lots of little round seats and armed chairs, and there's a quieter, more intimate fringe behind a balustrade at the back. Also, a snug and rather stylish bow-windowed front bar, and a public bar with darts, shove-ha'penny, dominoes, cribbage, fruit machine and trivia. Good bar food includes sandwiches (hot beef £2), salad bar with home-made pies and quiches (from £2), steak and kidney pie (£2.75), and a roast beef carvery (£4.25); well kept Youngs Bitter on handpump, and a good range of malt and other whiskies, three sherries and port from the wood. The back terraced garden has seats and tables under trees, with more on the front terrace. Public gardens opposite (closed at night) slope down to the Thames. *(Recommended by Adrian Kelly, John Roué)*

Youngs   Licensee Christopher Marley   Real ale   Meals and snacks   Children in eating area of bar   Open 11–3, 5.30–11 all year

---

Real ale to us means beer which has matured naturally in its cask – not pressurised or filtered. We name all real ales stocked. We usually name ales preserved under a light blanket of carbon dioxide too, though purists – pointing out that this stops the natural yeasts developing – would disagree (most people, including us, can't tell the difference!).

Sporting Page ⊗ (Chelsea) Map 12

6 Camera Place, SW10

In the same hands as the Front Page (see Central London section), this has an obvious family resemblance, with sturdy cleanly cut tables around the walls leaving plenty of room by the bar, an airy feel from big windows and light paintwork, and interesting decorations – here, firmly linked to famous sporting moments, and ranging from old prints of people playing polo, rugby football, cricket and so forth to big painted-tile-effect murals of similar scenes. There are picnic-table sets outside. Interesting bar food includes soup (£1.50), hot cheese salad (£3), steak sandwich (£3.35), smoked salmon and watercress terrine (£3.50), coulibiac (£4), chicken tikka or scrambled eggs with smoked salmon (£4.25) and smoked goose salad with quails' eggs (£4.50). Trumans Best, Ruddles Best and County and Websters Yorkshire on handpump; decent house wines, espresso coffee; civilised service. A fine Chelsea local which seems as if it's always been as it is – but was in fact completely redone when the Front Page people took it over in 1988. *(Recommended by RAB)*

Watneys   Licensees Christopher Phillips, Rupert Fowler and Michael Phillips   Real ale Meals and snacks (lunchtime)   Children in eating area   Open 11–3, 5.30–11 weekdays, 11–11 Sat, all year; closed 25 and 26 Dec

Windsor Castle ★ ⊗ (Holland Park/Kensington) Map 12

114 Campden Hill Road, W8

The series of little dark panelled rooms in this well kept old pub are delightfully old-fashioned with sturdy built-in elm benches, time-smoked ceilings and soft lighting; there's even a snug little pre-war-style dining-room opening off the bar – and no fruit machines or piped music. Bar food includes a good choice of sandwiches (from £1.10), ham and chips (£2.90), roast beef, steak and kidney or shepherd's pie (all £3.20), bacon, egg and black pudding (£3.40) and eight-ounce steak (£6.10); well kept Bass and Charrington IPA on handpump, reasonably priced by London standards. Usually fairly quiet at lunchtime, the pub is often packed in the evenings. A special summer feature is the big tree-shaded back terrace which has lots of sturdy teak seats and tables on flagstones, knee-high stone walls (eminently sittable-on) dividing them, high ivy-covered sheltering walls, and soft shade from the sweeping low branches of a plane tree, a lime and a flowering cherry. A bar counter serves the terrace directly, as does a separate food stall. Note that, unusually, no children are allowed there. *(Recommended by Louisa Salik, Ian Phillips, Nick Dowson, Alison Hayward)*

Charringtons   Licensee Anthony James Owen   Real ale   Meals and snacks (not Sun evening)   Daytime parking metered   Open 11–11 all year

EAST LONDON

Weekday daytime parking isn't too bad in this area, though you should expect quite a walk to the Dickens Inn; there should be no real problems in the evening or at weekends

Dickens Inn (Docklands) Map 12

St Katharine's Yacht Haven, off St Katharine's Way, E1

In the nicest, brightest part of the Docklands redevelopment, this unashamedly touristy pub draws a mixture of smartly dressed European tourists drinking tea or coffee, people from the nearby World Trade Centre or the Tower Hotel, and folk who like at least to imagine themselves messing about in boats. The big bar – looking down on the lively yacht harbour – has timber baulks for pillars and beams, stripped brickwork, worn floorboards, a very long polished brass bar counter, and a dim atmosphere emphasised by candles in bottles and by the partly glazed wooden partitions which separate it into smaller areas. There are doors out on to the verandah (a mass of window boxes), and steps down to the cobbled waterside terrace, though no food or drink can now be taken here – a great shame. Bar food includes hot beef with French bread or cold meat salad (£2.75), and hot dishes of the day (£3.50); Courage Best and Directors, John Smith and Dickens Own and Olivers, brewed especially for the pub just over the river in Tooley Street – drinks are at Central London prices. *(Recommended by Nick Dowson, GB, Ian Phillips, M J Masters)*

Courage   Licensee Adrian Hyde   Real ale   Meals and snacks   Restaurant tel 01-488 9936   Open 11–11 weekdays, 12–3, 7–10.30 Sat

Grapes (Limehouse)   Map 12

76 Narrow Street, E14

As it's off the tourist track, this long and narrow little pub has a quieter and more genuine atmosphere than many other river pubs, and the glass-roofed back balcony is one of the most sheltered places for a riverside drink. Inside, on the partly panelled walls of the bar, there are lots of prints, often of actors, and some elaborately etched windows. Fresh fish is a speciality of the bar food, which includes fish pasty (£1.95), seafood risotto (£2) and fish and chips or seafood Mornay (£3). Well kept Ind Coope Burton and Friary Meux and Taylor-Walker Bitter on handpump. Dickens used this pub as the basis of his 'Six Jolly Fellowship Porters' in *Our Mutual Friend* on the strength of its grim reputation for losing its best customers to the anatomists: when they were insensibly drunk, people would row them out into the Thames, tip them in, then fish them out as drowned and sell them as raw material for anatomy experiments. *(Recommended by NHB, Don Easton, Rob and Gill Weeks; more reports please)*

Taylor-Walker (Ind Coope)   Licensee Frank Johnson   Real ale   Meals and snacks (not Sat or Sun, not Mon evening)   Restaurant tel 01-987 4396   Children in restaurant   Open 11–11 for trial period

Hollands (Stepney)   Map 12

9 Exmouth Street, E1

Opened early in Queen Victoria's reign by the present landlord's great-grandfather, this friendly little pub has hardly changed since then, and all the decorations are original. There are swivelling etched and cut-glass snob screens on the heavy bar counter, antique mirrors, *Vanity Fair* pictures, Victorian cartoons and photographs, and a clutter of trumpets, glass and brass ornaments hanging from the ochre painted and panelled ceiling in the main bar. The lounge bar, on two levels and separated from the main bar by an arched doorway and heavy velvet curtains, has panelled and velveteen-cushioned bench seats, a red tiled floor, old sepia photographs, brass pots hanging from the ceiling and a big Victorian fireplace with large china ornaments on its mantelpiece. Bar food consists of freshly made sandwiches (95p); Wethereds on handpump; darts, cribbage. *(More reports please)*

Free house   Licensee J C Holland   Real ale   Lunchtime snacks (not Sat or Sun)   Open 11–11 as long as trade demands

Town of Ramsgate (Wapping)   Map 12

62 Wapping High St, E1

This old pub overlooks King Edward's Stairs, also known as Wapping Old Stairs, where the Ramsgate fishermen used to sell their catches. Inside, the dimly lit, long rather narrow bar is clean and well kept, with squared oak panelling, green plush button-back wall banquettes and sturdy captain's chairs. There are masses of old pots and pans, earthenware hot-water bottles, hop-bines, glass demijohns and bottles, charlotte moulds, pewter tankards, earthenware kegs and so on; the best features are the decorative plates, the criss-cross walking-canes on the ceiling, the old Limehouse prints, an enormous fine etched mirror showing Ramsgate harbour, and above all the interesting mixture of customers – true East London meeting the Porsche-driving entrepreneurs who've moved into nearby high-tech Docklands conversions. Bar food includes sausage or beef in French bread, ploughman's, vegetarian pie, salads and daily hot dishes; well kept Bass and Charrington IPA on handpump; cribbage, fruit machine and juke box. At the back, a floodlit flagstoned terrace and wooden platform (with pots of flowers and summer barbecues) looks out past the stairs and the high wall of Olivers Warehouse to the Thames. *(More reports please)*

Charringtons   Licensees G J Mangham and A Goodfellow   Real ale   Meals and snacks Open 11–11 all year

---

Lucky Dip

Besides the fully inspected pubs, you might like to try these Lucky Dips recommended to us and described by readers (if you do, please send us reports). We have split them into the main areas used for the full reports – Central, North, and so on. Within each area the Lucky Dips are listed by postal district, ending with Greater London suburbs on the edge of that area.

CENTRAL

EC1

[56 Farringdon Rd] *Betsey Trotwood*: Small recently redecorated pub popular with *Guardian* and *Morning Star* journalists and local printers *(Michael King)*

[88 Cowcross St] *Blue Posts*: Busy recently renovated open-plan bar, cheerful licensee, nice friendly mock-Tudor pub; Charringtons *(John Roué)*

[34 Cowcross St] *Castle*: Very relaxed atmosphere in large high-ceilinged corner pub, bright and cheerful with tall windows, friendly service *(John Roué)*

[115 Charterhouse St] *Fox & Anchor*: Victorian pub with good atmosphere even when empty, pleasant service, long narrow bar; Ind Coope *(John Roué)*

[1 Middle St] *Hand & Shears*: Traditional Smithfield sixteenth-century pub with small-roomed feel though in fact only one partition wall still survives – often crowded and lively, and one of London's least-spoilt pubs with marvellously mixed clientele; Courage real ales *(John Roué, LYM)*

[33 Seward St] *Leopard*: Out-of-the-way free house with changing choice of up to half a dozen real ales such as Greene King Abbot and Thwaites; solid-looking square-cut Georgian building with back garden, varied clientele, never crowded *(T J Maddison)*

☆ [166 Goswell Rd] *Pheasant & Firkin*: Good value ploughman's with Cheddar or Lymeswold, well kept own-brewed beers and guest beers such as Wadworths 6X; wooden stools, benches and tables on bare boards; popular with businessmen; changed hands 1988 *(LYM)*

[4 Leather Lane] *Sir Christopher Hatton*: Large and modern; bar food, real ales; a Charringtons Vintage Inn; named after Chancellor to Elizabeth I, who owned the area

[Carthusian St] *Sutton Arms*: Good, friendly atmosphere, real ales and hot and cold food both at lunchtime and in the evening; pleasant welcoming service *(Reginald Hawkins, John Roué)*

[66 Cowcross St] *Three Compasses*: Fairly new (though there has been a pub on this site since 1723), effective use of modern panelling to create Victorian/Edwardian atmosphere; jazz Tues evening; Watneys *(John Roué)*

EC2

[63 Charlotte Rd] *Bricklayers Arms*: Normally a dozen or more beers on tap including five real ales that change weekly – Adnams, Arkells, Greene King and so forth; very good lunchtime sandwiches and bar food *(Ken Vostal)*

[Foster Lane] *City Pipe*: Cellar ale-and-wine house with simple but good food from sandwiches to steaks, Davy's unusual good value wines and ports, and Old Wallop beer in pewter tankards or half-gallon copper jugs; tie required *(David Jones)*

[202 Bishopsgate] *Dirty Dicks*: Lively barrel-vaulted cellar with good loud pop music, traditional-style ground floor with good range of real ales and cheerfully served lunchtime food including fat sandwiches; upstairs wine bar *(LYM)*

EC3

[67 Fenchurch St] *East India Arms*: Basic

pub with super sandwiches, superb Youngs beers *(John Nice)*

[10 Leadenhall Market] *Lamb*: No-smoking bar; third floor nicely done up in dyed mahogany; Youngs real ales *(Gavin May)*

EC4

[Cousin Lane] *Banker*: New Fullers pub by River Thames and Cannon St Stn *(David Fisher)*

[Charterhouse St] *Fox & Anchor*: Archetypical meat-workers' haunt, opening early for breakfasts; long, narrow bar with corresponding tables, lunch includes some of the freshest, most tender meat imaginable *(Timothy Powell)*

[25 Old Bailey] *George*: Well kept pub with friendly staff and plenty of space (though it's very popular at lunchtime); good value food upstairs *(Ms A Findlay)*

[29 Watling St] *Olde Watling*: Well kept Bass and Charrington IPA in heavy-beamed and timbered pub built by Wren in 1662 as a site commissariat for his new St Paul's Cathedral; lunchtime bar food upstairs *(LYM)*

[Watling St] *Pavilion End*: Sky-blue ceiling with fluffy clouds and pavilion layout evokes summer cricket-match atmosphere – especially with Test broadcasts on TV; nice range of salads, often busy before noon with City dealers taking early lunches *(Tim Powell)*

[64 Queen Victoria St] *Sea Horse*: Small cosy City pub with very well kept Courage Best and Directors, limited range of food very well prepared and promptly served *(Chris Fluck, John Roué)*

[17 Paternoster Sq] *Sir Christopher Wren*: Lively City pub with unusually good wine by the glass, attractive atmosphere, hundreds of bottles along the walls of one very high-ceilinged room *(Mrs G Berneck)*

[Norwich St] *White Horse*: Quiet upstairs bar serving traditional hot food for eating in dining-room that evokes Anthony Powell novels; downstairs typical London businessman's pub *(Tim Powell)*

SW1

[Victoria St] *Albert*: Splendidly redecorated and commanding exterior, set off against bleak cliffs of modern glass; packed weekday lunchtimes, quiet otherwise; popular for bar food, a Scotland Yard local and used by some MPs and many civil servants *(BB)*

[22 Eaton Terrace] *Antelope*: Often enterprising lunchtime food in clubby old-fashioned local near Sloane Square, with upstairs wine bar; lots of sporting clippings, photographs and cartoons; well kept Benskins and Ind Coope Burton on handpump; once a haunt of Augustus John and Peter Warlock, and still has enough character to keep the yuppies in perspective *(Dr and Mrs A K Clarke, Lee Goulding, LYM)*

[104 Horseferry Rd] *Barley Mow*: Comfortable and well kept, handy for Royal Horticultural Society's Halls in Vincent Sq; Ind Coope, Ruddles and Websters on handpump, good value, extensive waitress-served food, a few pavement tables in side street; live entertainment Fri and Sat evening, Sun lunch *(John Booth, BB)*

[62 Petty France] *Buckingham Arms*: Massive helpings of food such as burger and chips, well kept Youngs, prices below Victoria average; staff predominantly Antipodean; close to Passport Office and Buckingham Palace; unusual long side corridor fitted out with elbow ledge for drinkers, only drawback crowds lunchtime and early evening *(D J Cargill, LYM)*

[23 Francis St] *Cardinal*: In the shadow of Westminster Cathedral, very restful and meditative outside peak times, off the beaten track; back wine bar, spacious saloon with some older Irish customers *(John Roué)*

[39 Palace St] *Cask & Glass*: A half-pint pub serving half pints of Watneys-related beers, sandwiches; one small room (which used to be divided into two), overflowing into street in summer – when it's a riot of colour; handy for Queen's Gallery *(Ian Phillips)*

[16 Duke St] *Chequers*: Need to get in by about noon to get a seat in this narrow bar just off Jermyn St; good atmosphere; collection of Prime Minister pictures and well kept Watneys-related beers with good basic rolls and sandwiches and cheap home-cooked hot dishes *(Ian Phillips)*

[53 Whitehall] *Clarence*: Troubadour in jester's costume plays lute among wooden tables and benches on sawdust-strewn floor, staff dressed as serving wenches and minstrels; well kept Arkells, Charles Wells Bombardier, Ruddles and weekly guest beers, food bar, summer tables on pavement; popular with Ministry of Defence and other Whitehall folk; close to Trafalgar Sq *(Ian Phillips, C D T Spooner, John Branford)*

[Oxendon St] *Comedy*: Lively and welcoming; interesting crowd constantly changing; food more imaginative than usual here, and prices very reasonable by West End standard; nice atmosphere, good service, well kept Marstons Pedigree and Ruddles County; spacious, with stuffed birds, playbills, old prints and books in profusion and not too hard to find a seat though always busy *(Ian Phillips, Sheila Keene)*

[63 Eaton Terr] *Duke of Wellington*: Friendly Whitbreads pub in elegant street not far from house where Mozart lived; real ales, very cheap snacks *(Quentin Williamson)*

[29 Passmore St] *Fox & Hounds*: Small and really unspoilt one-bar pub – doesn't even have a spirits licence; lively clientele, friendly staff *(Dr and Mrs A K Clarke)*

[25 King St] *Golden Lion*: Rather distinguished bow-fronted building, opp Christies auction rooms; large downstairs bar with seats out in side passage, upstairs bar, standard food

[Dolphin Sq] *Lighthouse Bar*: Good service, food and drinks, happy atmosphere and staff (*Lord and Lady Graves*)

[Millbank] *Morpeth Arms*: Lovely old pub said to be haunted, very clean, with polite staff, good beer and food; handy for the Tate Gallery (*P Garrad, Catherine Villals*)

☆ [53 Kinnerton St] *Nags Head*: Tiny old-fashioned and easy-going pub attractively placed in quiet mews; front area has low ceiling and old cooking-range; small back bar; Benskins and Ind Coope Burton on handpump; can get crowded (*Dr and Mrs A K Clarke, Heather McCarthy, LYM*)

☆ [Duke of York St] *Red Lion*: Architectural gem with magnificent Victorian mirrors, Edwardian lighting, chandeliers, windows and woodwork; quite small, gets very crowded early evening, usually spilling on to pavement; well kept Ind Coope Burton and Taylor-Walker, reasonably priced bar food, with quick and friendly service (*Ian Phillips, Marcus and Marcella Leith, J S Rutter, LYM*)

[23 Crown Passage, behind St James's St, off Pall Mall] *Red Lion*: A stone's throw from Christies auction rooms, small, with tiny lounge upstairs, very friendly though often very crowded; Watneys-related real ales and good value bar food (*Ian Phillips*)

[Parliament St] *St Stephens Tavern*: MPs' pub with elaborately old-fashioned high-ceilinged bar all etched glass and mahogany, basement food bar, upstairs restaurant (*LYM*)

☆ [Belgrave Mews West] *Star*: Virtually an institution – genuine locals' pub in heart of Belgravia, very busy and friendly; the Fullers beer is beyond reproach, and there may be queues for the good food, not as expensive as usual for the area; relaxed atmosphere (*Tony Ritson, LYM*)

[off Victoria Embankment] *Tattershall Castle*: Converted paddle steamer – great novelty value and marvellous vantage point for watching river traffic; canopied bar serveries, with barbecues and ice-creams too in summer, for both forward and aft decks with picnic-table sets; wardroom bar and nightclub below decks; keg beers, rather pricey (*Howard and Sue Gascoyne*)

[39 Dartmouth St] *Two Chairmen*: Packed at lunchtime for good freshly cut meat sandwiches and well kept Watneys real ale, refurbished in old-fashioned style, in pretty Georgian street near St James's Park (*BB*)

[9 Storeys Gate] *Westminster Arms*: Two-floor friendly pub with good choice of real ales, some food, and basement wine bar; can get crowded (*LYM*)

SW3

[17 Mossop St] *Admiral Codrington*: Good affluent atmosphere, well kept beer, pleasant conservatory seating area (*B J Collins*)

[207 Brompton Rd] *Bunch of Grapes*: Pleasant atmosphere, one of London's few pubs with signs of bar partitions still visible; free house (*John Roué*)

[298 King's Rd] *Cadogan Arms*: Rough timber baulks, red-bulbed lanterns, impression of intimacy, well kept Combes and Watneys Stag, friendly atmosphere, Chef & Brewer food in waitress-service area (*BB*)

[52 Fulham Rd] *Cranley*: Better than average for atmosphere (*John Roué*)

[43 Beauchamp Pl] *Grove*: Comfortable, smartly refurbished split-level bar with well kept Brakspears, Flowers and Wethereds, lovely brown baps good value (*Dr and Mrs A K Clarke and others*)

[50 Cheyne Walk] *Kings Head & Eight Bells*: Good location across gardens from Thames, quite a bit of atmosphere, good pub food (*Ian Phillips*)

[392 King's Rd] *Man in the Moon*: Roomy pub with interesting man-in-moon tile frieze, theatre downstairs (*LYM*)

[200 King's Rd] *Trafalgar*: Smart and spacious old-style renovation, well kept, good bar layout including food display, Charringtons (*BB*)

W1

[54 Old Compton St] *Admiral Duncan*: Simple but comfortable with bare brick and boards – clean and tidy, with plenty of room Sat lunchtime, good choice of good value food (*Michael and Alison Sandy*)

[37 Thayer St; bottom end of Marylebone High St] *Angel*: Well kept two-storey Sam Smiths pub, lively at lunchtime, quieter in the evening (*LYM*)

[18 Argyll St; opp Oxford Circus tube side exit] *Argyll Arms*: Busy tourist pub in good setting near Oxford Circus; wonderful Victorian décor of frosted windows, ornate ceilings and decorations, two bars downstairs and one up, attentive friendly staff, Boddingtons, Tetleys and Wadworths 6X on handpump, wide range of hot and cold food and sandwiches in separate food area; closed Sun (*Gary Scott, Dr and Mrs A K Clarke*)

☆ [41 Mount St] *Audley*: Spacious and very well kept Mayfair pub with heavily ornamented mahogany panelling, generous (if pricey) helpings of food; upstairs restaurant, basement wine bar; choice of well kept real ales; lots of people on the pavements (where there are some tables); sometimes very full but copes well (*Ian Phillips, LYM*)

[82 Duke St] *Barley Mow*: Externally eye-catching, and inside has genuine-seeming snugs rather like pine box-pews in a church, supported by iron hoops from wall; decent bar food including good ploughman's (except for wrapped butter), bright welcoming staff, unobtrusive background music, couple of machines, Ind Coope-related beers with guests such as Adnams (*Ian Phillips*)

[6 Rathbone Pl] *Black Horse*: Cheerful Charringtons pub, friendly young staff, literary associations including Dylan Thomas *(John Roué)*

[18 Kingly St; near back door of Regent St Boots] *Blue Posts*: Small corner pub in useful spot with friendly Australian staff, simply furnished to cope with standing diners; food such as steak sandwich, burgers, steak and kidney pie, scampi, Whitbreads-related real ale *(Ian Phillips)*

[Old Compton St] *Comptons*: Good basic pub, Bass real ale, simple good value food ideal for a quick lunch – a spacious place with swivelling stools with back rests around tall tables; *Gay News* on sale *(Anon)*

[21a Devonshire St] *Devonshire Arms*: Decorously friendly and comfortable Edwardian pub with bar food and upstairs dining-room, good coffee *(LYM)*

[21a Denman St] *Devonshire Arms*: Corner pub stripped bare, for basic wooden stools and tables, a few brasses and copper objects hanging from ceiling, reasonably priced Shepherd Neame, mosaic coat of arms behind food bar serving smoked salmon sandwiches, ploughman's, lasagne, moussaka and so forth *(IP)*

[18 Bateman St; corner of Frith St] *Dog & Duck*: Enchanting little real Soho pub, all wood, glass and superbly lively tiles, mosaic and mirrors, showing dogs and ducks; busy but not uncomfortable, well kept Taylor-Walkers *(T J Maddison, LYM)*

[43 Weymouth Mews] *Dover Castle*: Very nice pub with smartly dressed customers, good food in a small area set apart for diners (not a dining-room) *(John Roué)*

[77 Wardour St] *Duke of Wellington*: A good example of the chintzy little pubs which have been getting popular in London *(Dr and Mrs A K Clarke)*

[47 Rathbone St] *Duke of York*: Well kept Bass and Charrington IPA in old-fashioned welcoming local with popular and reasonably priced lunchtime home cooking *(LYM)*

[35 St James's Pl] *Dukes*: The bar of this comfortable and well run hotel is a wonderful retreat, with good choice of spirits, copious titbits, and excellent sandwiches; bedrooms – at a price, of course *(John Tyzack)*

[16 Charlotte St] *Fitzroy*: Historic pub, used in the past by writers and artists – pictures of Dylan Thomas, George Orwell and Augustus John, good friendly service, excellent Sam Smiths ale, good value food *(Mrs B Mallen, John Roué)*

[Dean St] *French House*: 1940s atmosphere – still have De Gaulle proclamation up on wall; popular with writers on the serious weeklies *(Martin Hamilton)*

[57 Berwick St] *Green Man*: Bass and Charrington IPA in large, comfortable and smartly furnished pub; service always good even if it's busy, polished brass round central island servery, woodwork and light fittings look newly redecorated *(Michael and Alison Sandy)*

[30 Bruton Pl] *Guinea*: Good no-nonsense pub; partly fifteenth-century, oak-panelled, well kept Youngs beer, smartly dressed customers overflow into the quiet mews – a long-standing part of traditional Mayfair; quickly served limited food including excellent steak and kidney pie; may be extremely busy *(S R Holman, LYM)*

[5–6 Argyll St; in Sutherland House] *Handsel*: Very good value food from cheerful Italian chef in spacious, clean and comfortable bar (quite separate from adjoining Beefeater restaurant); well kept Greene King IPA and Abbot and Flowers Original *(Michael and Alison Sandy)*

[Poland St] *Kings Arms*: Lots of character in gaslit pub with Everards Tiger and Old Bill, Well Bombardier and other beers, doorstep beef sandwich with salad, excellent Stilton ploughman's with lots of salad; full of American girls and tourists, sprinkling of businessmen; carved settle upstairs by window *(I M Phillips)*

[68 Gt Titchfield St] *Kings Arms*: Good reliable local with well kept Charrington IPA in long narrow bar, tables out on the corner with Riding House St; good fresh lunchtime food; where ITN staff come to escape the shop-talk in the Green Man; relaxed atmosphere *(Ian Phillips, LYM)*

[44 Glasshouse St] *Leicester*: Edwardian corner pub with seven real ales including Charles Wells Bombardier, Huntsman Royal Oak, Shepherd Neame and Websters Yorkshire, good choice of expensive bar food; busy bar with Turkey carpet, usual stools and small tables; light, airy and comfortable upstairs bar with blue plush settees, calm and quiet atmosphere *(Michael and Alison Sandy)*

[23 Rathbone St; corner Newman Passage] *Newman Arms*: Most attractive and friendly, very Naval atmosphere (model man-o'-war, prints, memorabilia); starts to get crowded about 12.45 *(John Roué)*

☆ [49 Beak St] *Old Coffee House*: Real jumble of stuffed foxes and fish, brass buckets, musical instruments, very good collection of 1914–18 recruiting posters, old banknotes, theatre and cinema handbills, even a nude in one corner; upstairs food room dripping with prints and pictures, well kept Ruddles; good atmosphere *(Dr and Mrs A K Clarke, R Kempen, Ian Phillips)*

[22 Portman Sq] *Portman*: Charming helpful staff inside pleasant uncrowded pub, within hotel; bar snacks, useful for meeting people *(Heather Sharland)*

[71 Marylebone High St] *Prince Regent*: Well kept Bass and Charrington IPA in friendly pub whose food area is festooned with cheese dishes, as is the lunchtime dining-room; interesting print collection *(Michael and Alison Sandy, John Roué)*

[15 Denman Street] *Queens Head*: One-room local beside Piccadilly Theatre, uncrowded at lunchtime with unusually good value though limited bar food and real ales such as Boddingtons, Tetleys and Wadworths; warm welcome *(Ian Phillips)*

[Kingly St] *Red Lion*: Warm and comfortable, smartly modernised and relaxing two-storey pub; full weekday lunchtime and evening but very nice Sat lunchtime, and good feel even when crowded; well kept Sam Smiths OB and Museum, lunchtime meals and big filled baguettes Mon–Sat *(Michael and Alison Sandy, LYM)*

[Duke of York St] *Red Lion*: Excellent value basic snacks including sandwiches, good mirrors, central location; stands out *(Ian Phillips)*

[5 Charles St] *Running Footman*: Small, crowded and friendly: its sign I Am The Only Running Footman was London's longest until the Ferret & Firkin In The Balloon Up The Creek took over *(John Roué)*

[50 Hertford St; Shepherd Mkt] *Shepherds Tavern*: Pleasant décor and well cooked well presented food in fine upstairs restaurant – not cheap but worth it *(FJK)*

[8 Woodstock St] *Spread Eagle*: Thorough and successful refurbishment, with lots of dark wood, old-fashioned lamps, brown and red décor in smallish but very comfortable upstairs bar; four well kept but distinctly pricey real ales *(Michael and Alison Sandy)*

☆ [Poland St] *Star & Garter*: Small but very lively and unspoilt, nicely served Courage, authentically smoky-coloured boards on walls and ceiling, basic food (enormous baps); continuous TV ads as not too obtrusive background; handy for Oxford St *(Dr and Mrs A K Clarke, Ian Phillips, LYM)*

[34 George St] *Westmorland Arms*: Deeply comfortable and welcoming, Tolly real ales, food bar *(LYM)*

W2

[Water Gdns, Norfolk Cr] *Heron*: Tastefully updated, comfortable and well kept *(Dr and Mrs A K Clarke)*

[132 Edgware Rd] *Old English Gentleman*: Real traditional pub feel, good friendly service, high standards, good food *(R Kempen)*

[66 Bayswater Rd] *Swan*: Courtyard with tree-shaded tables outside old pub looking across busy road to Kensington Gardens; well kept Watneys real ales, busy food bar *(LYM)*

☆ [Strathearn Pl] *Victoria*: Downstairs bar is attractive Dickensian tavern, including mock-up of Old Curiosity Shop; upstairs (not always open) has replica of bar from the Gaiety Theatre, all gilt and red velvet; Bass and Charrington IPA on handpump; picnic tables on pavement ; food includes winkles and cockles *(LYM)*

WC1

[31 University St] *Jeremy Bentham*: 'Welcome to Jeremy Bentham' picked out in seashells, with wax head of him and lots of captioned memorabilia – as well as pharmaceutical bottles and jars as reminder of UCH next door; discreet quietish clientele, cosy atmosphere, very friendly and obliging efficient staff; oasis for area, philosopher's-stone's-throw from UC which he founded *(Peter Griffiths)*

[245A Grays Inn Rd] *Lucas Arms*: Fairly typical late Victorian pub distinguished by its lively atmosphere – probably because it's just opposite NUJ HQ *(Dr and Mrs A K Clarke)*

[Queen Sq] *Queens Larder*: Friendly, with good value food such as Pig in the Poke, well kept Wethereds, charming upstairs dining-room overlooking square *(LYM)*

☆ [63 Lamb's Conduit St] *Sun*: Excellent choice of up to twenty or more real ales, at a price; can get very crowded with mixed clientele; bare boards, extremely attentive staff, beer taken really seriously (tours of temperature-controlled cellar bookable for groups – but they may let you go on one if you're there around 8pm); bar food lunchtime and evenings *(Robin Armstrong, Michael and Alison Sandy, Nick Dowson, Alison Hayward, Kevin Macey)*

[Cosmo Passage] *Swan*: Well kept Watneys real ales and good choice of lunchtime food in pub given old-fashioned refurbishment, seats outside in pedestrian alley *(LYM)*

WC2

[42 Wellington St] *Coach & Horses*: Nice small friendly pub with old-fashioned low copper-topped bar, lunchtime food, Watneys-related real ales a contrast to bustling commercialised pubs in the area *(T T Kelly)*

[91 Strand] *Coal Hole*: Spacious street-level bar with very high ceiling, painted panels and bas-relief on upper panels, two mounted caribou heads, bright mixed clientele; cave atmosphere in lower bar, relaxed in spite of piped music *(John Roué)*

[31 Endell St] *Cross Keys*: Very popular, good atmosphere, interesting memorabilia of well known people, beers normally well kept *(N R England)*

[Lisle St/Wardour St] *Falcon*: Quiet, comfortable oasis off Leicester Square, dark panelled bar with lots of mirrors and fireplaces at each end, steep stairs to lounge-buffet with brass-topped tables and more traditional back part with interesting cast-iron stove in old fireplace – homely and friendly; reasonably priced straightforward food, Watneys beers *(Ian Phillips)*

[Long Acre] *Freemasons Arms*: Pleasant relaxing atmosphere, nice staff and wide choice of good food in upstairs lounge, Sam Smiths OB and Museum ales, good ploughman's, generously garnished baked potato *(S R Holman)*

☆ [41 Maiden Lane] *Maple Leaf*: Noisy and really crowded at peak times, new décor with Canadian historical and political photographs, football and hockey pennants, cold beers, including interesting Molson beer from Canada *(John Roué, PLC)*

[10 James St] *Nags Head*: Plenty of seats in large lofty Edwardian-style pub with old ceramic spirit barrels and stone jars on high gantry, food reasonably priced for this tourist area, McMullens real ales, cheapish wine by the bottle *(Ian Phillips)*

[23 Catherine St] *Opera*: Busy two-floor pub with etched mirrors, lots of old playbills and other opera memorabilia, interesting filled rolls (muesli-style bread), baked potatoes and ploughman's; a Taylor-Walker (Ind Coope) pub *(Ian Phillips)*

[48 Charing Cross Rd] *Porcupine*: Good value food including excellent rare beef salad in firmly run upstairs bar, real personal table service ; downstairs bar basic *(Ian Phillips)*

[90 St Martins Lane] *Salisbury*: One of the best Victorian interiors in the West End – floridly decorated with red velvet, well preserved glass and mirrors, flamboyantly theatrical; good value food, close to theatres and antiquarian bookshops *(Marcus and Marcella Leith, S R Holman, BB, Patrick Young)*

[Strand] *Savoy*: The American Bar of this grand hotel has a good atmosphere, very superior service, not outrageous prices and some excellent canapés; a fine place for people-spotting; bedrooms, naturally *(J S Evans)*

[53 Carey St] *Seven Stars*: Small simple pub, packed with City gents at lunchtime; food *(T Nott, Nick Dowson, Alison Hayward)*

[10 Northumberland St; Craven Pl] *Sherlock Holmes*: Good choice of Whitbreads beers including Flowers and Samuel Whitbreads on handpump, pleasant and clean; lots of convincing Sherlock Holmes memorabilia, including a re-creation of the Baker St sitting-room; quick lunchtime food counter *(Nick Dowson, BB)*

[14 New Row] *White Swan*: Small pillared front bar crowded at lunchtime with publishing people, real public-bar atmosphere in roomier seventeenth-century panelled back part; closed Sun *(BB)*

NORTH

N1

[Highbury and Islington Tube], *Cock*: Mixed clientele, green plush stools and chairs, piped music; Arthur Mullard's local *(BB)*

[60 Copenhagen St] *George IV*: Thwaites the Lancashire brewers developed this as a friendly pastiche of a Northern pub, with lots of stripped woodwork, pine furniture and masses of old Burnley photographs; they've sold it now, but the pub still stocks their well kept beers; good chatty atmosphere, lunchtime bar food (not Sun), French windows to terrace and garden with play area, pleasant conservatory area; close to Regent's Canal towpath *(Alison Hayward, Nick Dowson, Wayne Brindle, Ian Phillips, Neil Baker, LYM)*

☆ [87 Noel Rd] *Island Queen*: Giant Alice-in-Wonderland characters floating above bar, big mirrors with applied jungle vegetation, good choice of freshly made and often unusual food, well kept Bass, Charrington IPA and Springfield, pool in back room, good juke box, tables in front; a real welcome for children, close to Camden Passage antiques area *(LYM)*

[Canonbury St; junction with Marquess Rd] *Marquess Tavern*: Large Youngs pub with comfortably plush domed back room, front bar with attractively stripped half-panelling, relaxed atmosphere, good value food including salads, toasted sandwiches and hot dish of day, well kept real ales *(BB)*

[Green Houses] *Robinson Crusoe*: Pleasant local with handpumped Bass *(Reginald Hawkins)*

[The Mall, Camden Pass] *Serendipity*: Brasserie/bar specialising in cocktails and wines; very good vegetarian moussaka, steak, meringue glacé, particularly imaginative soups, trendy décor, smart service, piped rock music *(Roger Farbey)*

☆ [Upper St] *Slug & Lettuce*: Generous helpings of excellent pub food, Ruddles County, Watneys Combes and Websters Yorkshire on handpump *(John Bennett)*

N6

[414 Archway Road] *Woodman*: Friendly pub with good fireplace and high-backed chairs, and outside beer garden with trees *(PS)*

N7

☆ [54 Holloway Rd] *Flounder & Firkin*: Typical of the Firkin chain; huge tropical aquarium; good children's adventure playroom; gets packed *(Michael Quine)*

[162 Tufnell Park Rd] *Tufnell Park Tavern*: Big roomy pub, efficient courteous staff, popular for jazz, especially on Sun for the Crouch End All Stars (with Wally Fawkes and Ian Christie – as well as this recommender, who founded the group) *(Graham Tayar)*

N10

☆ [Colney Hatch Lane] *Wetherspoons*: Cosy and friendly, four or five well kept real ales at remarkably low prices for London, wines too; the original pub of a growing chain of North London free houses under this name (see White Lion of Mortimer in main entries), though some have now been sold to Tollys *(Dave Kennard)*

N16

[Stoke Newington High St] *Tanners Hall*: Well kept Bass, many guest beers, country wines, interesting lagers in superbly decorated pub *(Angus Lindsay)*

N17

☆ [Lordship Lane] *Boar*: Long bar area leading to quite spacious and very comfortable library – nice to spend evening browsing through books; well kept ales; one of the best of the Weatherspoons chain *(Dave Kennard)*

N20

[1277 Whetstone High Rd] *Bull & Butcher*: Large friendly pub with chatty Irish landlady, good lunchtime food, Ind Coope Bitter and Burton and Tetleys real ales, separate games-room, occasional live Irish music *(Dave Kennard)*

[Totteridge Village] *Orange Tree*: Spacious pub by duck pond, plush décor, separate restaurant *(LYM)*

N21

[121 Hoppers Rd] *Salisbury Arms*: Friendly staff, well kept Bass on handpump, good atmosphere, splendid table d'hôte menu known as Salisbury Supper is excellent value; decent wine list *(J S B Vereker)*

NW1

[35 Chalk Farm Rd] *Lock*: Large downstairs bar with fruit machine, big cold food counter (also hot food), Bass and Charrington IPA, back terrace and smaller first-floor front roof-garden *(BB)*

☆ [Marylebone Rd; Baker St Underground Stn] *Moriartys*: This Underground station bar is a real surprise, with ten real ales and twenty whiskies – busy, as the regulars obviously know a good cellarman; lots of Holmesian decoration, most of it authentically Edwardian *(K A Topping, Michael Bechley)*

[Princess Rd] *Prince Albert*: Friendly, well run local, generous helpings of food, small well kept garden *(LYM)*

[49 Regent's Park Rd] *Queens*: Lots of mirrors downstairs, Victorian prints, stuffed birds, pictures of local personalities such as actor Robert Stephens, friendly staff, good view over Primrose Hill from balcony bar, decent food – the hot dishes are good value; stained glass in windows and outside lights, quietish clientele *(Peter Griffiths)*

[Marylebone Stn] *Victoria & Albert*: Huge range of real ales, wide choice of whiskies, attractively set out sandwiches in chill cabinet; immaculately kept plush chairs, reasonable prices *(Michael Bechley)*

[245 Baker St; by Regent's Park] *Volunteer*: Plush and black-panelled, popular with tourists, bar food, also restaurant and wine bar (good house wine); close to Regent's Park; pleasant ambience *(LYM)*

[Camden Rd; by Camden Town tube station] *Worlds End*: Good choice of ale, very good food, relaxed atmosphere *(C Fluck)*

NW3

[14 Flask Walk] *Flask*: Snug Hampstead local in the old part; well kept Youngs,

popular with actors and artists for 300 years, and still is *(BB)*

☆ [32 Downshire Hill] *Freemasons Arms*: Spacious, comfortable and friendly, with lots of tables out on terraces and among banks of roses by Hampstead Heath; cane-look chairs around well spaced tables in airy inner lounge, usually plenty of room in other bars too, food seven days a week including good choice of pies and quiches with salads, attractive steak and kidney pie; well kept Bass and Charrington IPA; skittle alley (one of only three in London) and unique lawn billiards court *(Michael and Alison Sandy, LYM)*

[79 Heath St] *Nags Head*: Recently refurbished open-plan bar with McMullens real ales and bar food ; popular with young *(Jonathan Warner)*

[North End Way] *Old Bull & Bush*: Lively and recently well refurbished pub on traffic-busy hill, interesting history – and the home of that famous song *(LYM)*

[30 Well Walk] *Wells*: Comfortable, friendly and well kept Hampstead local *(Gil Johnson)*

NW4

☆ [Church End] *Greyhound*: Pleasant free house with standard décor and good range of real ales including Brakspears, Flowers Original, Greene King Abbot, Wethereds and Whitbreads Castle Eden; nice atmosphere; pricey food servery *(Nick Dowson, Alison Hayward)*

NW5

[33 Dartmouth Park Hill] *Lord Palmerston*: Clean and tidy local, flowers on each table, good value doorstep sandwiches with weekday lunchtime hot food, licensees work hard raising funds for guide dogs and Gt Ormond St Children's Hospital *(Stuart Smith)*

NW6

[1 Kilburn High Rd] *Queens Arms*: Large, spacious, clean, very comfortable – with plenty of seats; Youngs pub, with nice atmosphere *(Michael and Alison Sandy)*

NW8

[11 Alma Sq; off Hill Rd] *Heroes of Alma*: Good value freshly cooked food and well kept Watneys real ales in friendly little Victorian pub with tables outside *(LYM)*

[St John's Wood Rd] *Lords Tavern*: Good food counter and well kept real ales in attractively mocked-up pubby interior, tables outside *(BB)*

☆ [St John's Wood] *Ordnance Arms*: Excellent fish and chips on Fri and Sat nights that a Yorkshireman would be proud of – 14 or 16oz fillets; lots of military paraphernalia (diagrams of guns and cannons, part of a heavy machinegun on the wall) and some leather Chesterfields; modern conservatory area and patio at back; well kept

Bass and Charrington IPA *(Stuart Smith, LYM)*

[23 Queens Grove] *Rossetti*: Fullers London Pride and ESB always well kept, cheap for area; nice Italian décor; service very friendly, good food such as delicious lasagne reasonably priced for London *(Richard Sanders, G Berneck, Nick Dowson, Alison Hayward)*

NW10

[Acton Lane] *Grand Junction*: By the Grand Union Canal, with some canalside tables; comfortable lounge, well kept Youngs real ales, good choice of bar food; rough-and-ready public bar *(Brian Jones)*

BARNET

[High St; opposite church] *Bat & Goldfish*: Atmospheric and busy pub with comfortable alcoves along long open bar; reasonable lunchtime food; part of the Wetherspoons chain *(Dave Kennard)*
[Barnet Road (A411); nr Hendon Wood Lane] *Gate at Arkley*: Delightful secluded garden perfect for children, good choice of food inc sandwiches, salads and hot dishes, good log fire in winter; attractive setting *(A J Silman, BB)*
[High St] *King George*: Deceptively quiet and peaceful local – one of the few pubs here with its own car park; well kept Charrington IPA *(ST)*
[High St] *Mitre*: Small-roomed friendly tavern with Dickens connections, well kept Benskins and Ind Coope Burton *(LYM)*

ENFIELD

[Gentlemans Row] *Coach & Horses*: Lots of atmosphere in warm and cheerful place with country-pub character, tucked away in a backwater; welcoming staff in L-shaped bar with garden extension, Flowers Original on handpump *(Gwen and Peter Andrews)*
[Bullsmoor Lane] *Pied Bull*: Three or four biggish low-ceilinged rooms, Wethereds on handpump; very busy but really efficient at lunchtime with good range of bar meals including an excellent ploughman's they call Crusty with either various meats or cheeses, very good value *(Ned Edwards)*

HARROW

[West St] *Castle*: Friendly Fullers pub; lounge leading into comfortable sitting-room with sofas, settees and tables, smaller front public bar, fresh filled rolls at lunchtime, well kept Fullers ales on electric pump; pleasant garden with chatty caged birds *(Denis Waters, Peter Edwards)*

PINNER

[High St] *Queens Head*: Nice old pub in attractive timbered building, with well kept Benskins and good atmosphere; friendly service, no piped music – just the pleasant murmur of conversation; fairly busy Sun lunchtime *(M C Howells, S C Collett-Jones)*

SOUTH

SE1

[Tower Bridge Rd] *Bridge House*: Up-market but not too pretentious, good house beers, friendly licensee *(Norman England)*
[48 Tooley St] *Cooperage*: Below London Bridge Stn, next to London Dungeon, entrance in Stainer St below railway; good atmosphere, original floor and ceiling, beer in pewter tankards, usual pub food *(Ian Phillips)*
☆ [Southwark] *Founders Arms*: Glass walls facing Thames give almost unobstructed view of St Paul's Cathedral; spacious bar divided into friendly sized areas by green plush banquettes and elbow-rest screens; Youngers Bitter and Special on handpump; large riverside terrace *(Elaine Kellet, Nick Dowson, Heather Sharland, LYM)*
[5 Mepham St] *Hole in the Wall*: Take-it-as-you-find-it pub with Waterloo suburban trains shaking its railway-arch ceiling, remarkable choice of well kept real ales at low prices, cheap bar food, basic furnishings *(LYM)*
[216 Blackfriars Rd] *Prince William Henry*: Comfortable modern estate pub with well kept Youngs beers and quick pleasant service *(BB)*
[320 Old Kent Rd] *St Thomas à Becket*: Very lively atmosphere in young people's pub with heavily emphasised boxing theme – from motif on carpet to boxing-ring stage for live bands; Henry Cooper, John Conteh, Alan Minter, Terry Downes have all used its upstairs gym; large ex-boxing bouncers make sure there's no trouble *(Tim Powell)*
[6 Stoney St] *Wheatsheaf*: Old London prints in cosy pub with very local clientele, mainly blue-collar *(John Roué)*

SE3

[1a Eliot Cottages] *Hare & Billet*: Nicely placed opposite pond, lovely views to South and East; recently refurbished by Whitbreads, with shelf of usual semi-antique props and old local photographs; Whitbreads-related and guest real ales, pleasant for a quiet weekday lunch; separate wine bar *(Anon)*

SE9

[86 Eltham High St; (opposite McDonalds)] *Greyhound*: Very big helpings of exceptionally good value food, nice atmosphere; lots of food awards on walls *(Neil Barker)*

SE10

[Lassell St] *Cutty Sark*: Particularly good position on interesting reach of the Thames with pleasant secluded area in front letting you watch sun set over Docklands; good atmosphere, good if somewhat pricey food, jazz some nights, occasional morris men *(Alan Franck)*

[56 Royal Hill] *Fox & Hounds*: Very welcoming and friendly local with old photographs of the area, stuffed fox, heroic Victorian fireman picture over mantelpiece, *Vanity Fair* prints in back bar; simple bar food, real ale *(Anon)*

[1 Crooms Hill; next to theatre] *Old Rose & Crown*: Nice cosy pub with pleasant service, friendly locals and theatre patrons, marvellous Victorian wrought-iron sign above lounge bar *(John Roué)*

[19 Park Vista] *Plume of Feathers*: Dimly lit front bar with cosy fire in winter, very efficient food area, tables under two shady trees in enclosed back garden, benches in side yard and under front awnings; barbecues Mon *(Ian Phillips)*

[52 Royal Hill] *Richard I*: Friendly and unpretentious, sound local reputation for well kept Youngs and good company; no music, handsome deep bay windows and echoing boarded floor, serviceable old tables in yard, marvellous cheese and onion rolls – long may it remain unmodernised *(Robert Gomme)*

[2 Blisset St] *Royal George*: Tiny, with sympathetic ambience, friendly staff and customers, Shepherd Neame, good bar food *(BRD)*

[Park Row] *Trafalgar*: Panoramic Thames views from unusual wood-floored free house with pianola, model ship built into window, Ruddles, reasonably priced restaurant, jazz on Thurs and antique fairs upstairs *(M J Masters)*

SE13

☆ [316 Lewisham High St] *Fox & Firkin*: Spacious and popular, no frills; good beer, straightforward good food inc remarkable huge baps with any two of four meats; parking may be difficult *(Peter Griffiths, C D T Spooner, LYM)*

SE16

[117 Rotherhithe St] *Mayflower*: Carefully restored eighteenth-century pub with old-fashioned main bar and side room recalling days when Pilgrim Fathers' ship sailed from here in 1611; well kept Bass and Charrington IPA, bar food (not Sat lunchtime or Sun evening), upstairs evening restaurant and wooden jetty overhanging Thames; only English pub licensed to sell UK and US postage stamps *(LYM)*

SE18

[Shooters Hill] *Bull*: Well kept Courage on handpump, friendly staff, very good value food, garden *(P Gillbe)*

[15 Thomas St] *Earl of Chatham*: Simple cheap food, excellent quick service even when busy, cheerful mixed clientele; refurbished inside, conservatory and terrace *(J B Simpson)*

SE19

☆ [262 Beulah Hill] *Conquering Hero*: Good, busy Courage pub, customers range from football teams to OAPs, solicitors to plumbers *(Michele and Andrew Wells)*

SE20

☆ [Ridsdale Rd] *Anerley Arms*: Very comfortably refurbished Victorian pub with lots of mahogany panelling, etched-glass windows and mirrors, red plush seats, tables with brass rails around their tops; interesting posters; well kept and reasonably priced Sam Smiths OB on handpump, good service, usual pub food nicely presented, including good value sandwiches; on site of old Anerley Tavern and by rustic little station – both part of the old Pleasure Gardens *(Ian Phillips, Philip Denison)*

SE21

[Park Hall Rd] *Alleyn Head*: Well managed pub in salubrious surroundings near Dulwich College, excellent service, comfortable bars, warm atmosphere, good Toby carvery (best to book at weekends – 01-670 6540) *(E G Parish, John Roué and others)*

☆ [73 Dulwich Village] *Crown & Greyhound*: Certainly the best sandwiches in this part of London, excellent service by experienced staff; popular with young at weekends under new licensees; good cider as well as well kept Benskins, décor has considerable character, and the big back garden, surrounded by beautiful mature trees, is a splendid feature in summer; reasonably priced food with four hot dishes – pork loin, beef curry, moussaka – with three veg, good range of pies including vegetarian, salads; restaurant food very good and not overpriced; a little parking on the premises if you get there early enough *(Michele and Andrew Wells, Alan Franck, Peter Griffiths, E G Parish)*

SE26

[39 Sydenham Hill] *Dulwich Wood House*: Comfortably refurbished suburban pub, well managed, with full range of Youngs real ales kept well, polite service, good value food *(E G Parish)*

SW4

[38 Old Town] *Prince of Wales*: Lots of excellent bric-à-brac including newspaper front pages of *Titanic* disaster and Munich crisis, excellent Flowers real ale; best visited early when not so crowded *(Michael Cooke, Louise Collins)*

SW11

[60 Battersea High St] *Woodman*: Not to be confused with the original Woodman next door, this busy pub has lots of prints and a stag's head in its little panelled front bar, with a long Turkey-carpeted room decorated with dried flowers, baskets, a boar's head and even an aged wheelbarrow; there are brocaded stools and chairs, some big casks, and log-effect gas fires; bar billiards, darts and trivia machine at one end, picnic-table sets on raised terrace with barbecue area; well kept Badger Best and Tanglefoot and Wadworths 6X on handpump *(RAB, Richard Gibbs)*

SW12

[39 Balham High Rd] *Duke of Devonshire*: Magnificent refurbished Victorian beer palace, good décor, comfortable, friendly efficient service, well kept Youngs *(David Fisher, Dave Kennard)*

SW13

[7 Church Rd] *Sun*: The last we heard this popular pondside pub was closed for renovation – more reports please

SW14

[42 Christ Church Rd] *Plough*: Plenty of room to sit outside country-style seventeenth-century pub not far from Sheen Gate of Richmond Park; good food, coffee, Whitbreads and Yorkshire on handpump; everyone welcome, whether in paint-covered dungarees or in riding habit; bedrooms *(Michael Dunne)*
[West Temple Sheen] *Victoria*: Popular place; good choice of well priced food *(J P Berryman)*

SW15

[8 Lower Richmond Rd] *Dukes Head*: Good atmosphere, super position, and more effort now going into food, with good freshly cooked choice at lunchtime; well kept *(Doug Kennedy)*

SW16

[151 Greyhound Lane] *Greyhound*: Homebrew pub associated with Watneys, piped music, large vaulted lounge and small bar (dedicated to Streatham Redskins ice-hockey team) with hockey photographs and memorabilia, rebuilt 1930, signs of recent Victorian-style refurbishment; can get very busy so beer garden useful; games-bar with pool-tables and children's area *(Gary Thomas, Allie Laing, Nick Dowson, John Roué)*
[498 Streatham High Rd] *Pied Bull*: Still one of the best: large, clean, bright and cheery Youngs pub, public, lounge and cocktail bars, reasonably priced food in buffet lounge; overlooking Streatham Common *(David Fisher, John Roué)*

SW18

[345 Trinity Rd] *County Arms*: Good Victorian décor, generally friendly service, good value filled rolls and other bar snacks; relaxed at weekday lunchtimes, crowded weekends; public grass area outside by dual carriageway is nice when it's sunny;

well kept Youngs real ales *(BB)*

SW19

[31 Wimbledon Hill Road] *Alexandra*: Very homely, nice pleasant clientele, good service *(Louisa Salik)*
☆ [Camp Rd] *Fox & Grapes*: Country pub in suburban London; well run, with huge beams in high ceiling of comfortable and spacious main bar, traditional dark wooden furniture on patterned carpet, leaded lights, good choice of fresh-cooked food, with big ploughman's and enjoyable seafood surprise – pasta; well kept Courage; easy parking – unusual around here *(Peter Griffiths, Doug Kennedy, Howard Pursey, Rodney Coe)*
☆ [6 Crooked Billet] *Hand in Hand*: Well kept Youngs real ale in busy cheerful pub on Wimbledon Common, with big horseshoe bar serving several small areas, some red-tiled, other carpeted; stripped brick walls; good atmosphere, plenty of choice of wines and spirits; separate darts room full of locals, bar food *(Doug Kennedy, G Cooper, P Griffiths)*
[25 Abbey Rd] *Princess Royal*: A local of some character – small but interestingly laid out lounge; good food *(Mike Muston)*
[14 Cawnpore St] *Railway Bell*: Small, bustling, very pleasant, with good local atmosphere and lots of locomotive and train pictures *(John Roué)*
☆ [55 High St, Wimbledon] *Rose & Crown*: Comfortably modernised ex-coaching-inn; set of Hogarth's proverb engravings above open fires, green plush seats in alcoves; well kept Youngs Bitter and Special on handpump; tables in courtyard and close to Wimbledon Common *(Adrian Kelly, LYM)*

BECKENHAM
[Chancery Lane] *Jolly Woodman*: Small and friendly place with cheap beer, seats out in nice cosy garden; popular with older people *(SJM)*

BEXLEY
[Vicarage Lane] *Rising Sun*: Pleasant, popular with young riders, honest very reasonably priced bar snacks, prompt service *(E G Parish)*
[North Cray Rd] *White Cross*: Busy friendly Green Belt pub with quick service; has kept some village atmosphere though on dual carriageway *(Dave Braisted)*

BROMLEY
[Widmore Rd] *Oak*: Pleasant friendly pub with good toasted sandwiches *(J S Rutter)*
[North Road] *Red Lion*: Very friendly, unpretentious pub serving Flowers, Fremlins and Wethereds; good balance of regulars and visitors *(Steve Ramsden)*
[High St] *Star & Garter*: Useful Edwardian pub nicely restored with miniature turret, balcony and beautiful sign; racing pictures in

the public bar, prints and cigarette cards in the lounge with comfortable seats around brass-topped tables; quick friendly service, straightforward pub food, plastic plants and so forth *(Anon)*

CHISLEHURST

[Royal Parade] *Bulls Head:* Airy and nicely furnished bars with very comfortable chairs and banquettes, well prepared and attractively presented bar food, very good polite service, very pleasant restaurant *(E G Parish)*
Queens Head: Super selection of comfortable easy chairs and settees as well as more straightforward furnishings in Georgian house with Victorian and later additions, with bay window overlooking large pond, ducks, weeping willow and so forth on edge of common; tables on front terrace, more on big back garden overlooking pond; fresh home-made food, Tetleys beer *(Ian Phillips)*
[just off Bickley Park Rd and Old Hill, by Summer Hill] *Ramblers Rest:* Most attractive tiled and weatherboarded cottage in excellent location by common, old-fashioned on right with big open-plan extension on lower level on left, Courage ale, food from noon; a couple of seats in front; said to have been built 1684 *(Ian Phillips, Anon)*

COULSDON

[Old Coulsdon] *Tudor Rose:* Spacious mock-medieval suburban pub with well kept Bass and Charrington IPA, good value lunchtime pub *(BB)*

CROYDON

[Laud St] *Bulls Head:* Very comfortable, in quiet area yet close to centre *(Neil Barker)*
[Park Lane; part of 1960s shopping complex] *Greyhound:* Enormous dark pub, a maze of mirrors and fairy lights, with good wholesome cafeteria-style lunchtime food including really tasty cottage pie, efficient friendly service, Courage ales, pianist; billiards upstairs, evening disco atmosphere *(Ian Phillips)*
[Olde Market] *Le Refuge:* This wine bar really has the feel of a pub – especially at weekends, when it may have loud music and get packed with young people; nice atmosphere, low ceilings, King & Barnes and Youngs Bitter and Special, nice beer garden *(Alasdair Knowles)*
[Church St, Old Town] *Rose & Crown:* Nice view from front of parish church and old surroundings; opens on to cul-de-sac, so little traffic; back garden *(NHB)*
[off Brighton Rd] *Woodman:* Great most evenings, especially Sat, always packed, excellent music, Watneys-related real ales, low ceiling *(A Knowles)*

CUDHAM

[Cudham Lane] *Blacksmiths Arms:* Great atmosphere in very popular country pub with summer barbecues in very pleasant garden, good reasonably priced food from ploughman's to steaks, well kept Courage *(Nick Dowson, Alison Hayward)*
Old Jail: Attractive country pub surrounded by fields, 1869 vintage; hard-working staff serve good sandwiches, salads and daily specials, puddings such as jam roly-poly or spotted dick; Friary Meux on handpump, coffee or tea, big garden with picnic-table sets *(E G Parish)*

DOWNE

[High St] *George & Dragon:* Most friendly service, with good furnishings, seats outside and well kept Bass and Charrington IPA on handpump; cosy village pub still relatively uninfected by London; good bar snacks; popular with CAMRA *(Dave Braisted, Anon)*
[High St] *Queens Head:* Most friendly obliging staff in snug and comfortable low-ceilinged pub with real ales and wide range of good bar food including most tasty sandwiches; comfortable chairs and seats, settles *(E G Parish)*

FOOTS CRAY

[High St] *Seven Stars:* Excellent real ale including Bass, run by a manager with the enthusiasm of a tenant, very clean; modernised seventeenth-century building with local atmosphere, juke box, space game, terrace; children in very nice food area *(Iain Johnson)*

KESTON

[Commonside] *Greyhound:* Spacious Courage pub with very good value bar food (especially hot-pot), Courage real ales, very friendly service, big garden with occasional barbecues and children's play area; handy for walks on common and in woods *(E G Parish)*

KEW

[Kew Green] *Coach & Horses:* Good pub, comfortable and very popular; bedrooms *(Doug Kennedy)*
[Pond Corner] *Greyhound:* Very friendly small pub with comfortable settles, very welcoming and charming barmaid, photographs of old Kew, red ceiling, reasonably priced food, easy parking *(Ian Phillips)*
[Sandycombe Rd; close to tube stn] *Kew Gardens:* Pleasant atmosphere, good choice of ale discussed knowledgeably by pleasant and helpful barmaid, huge helpings of food including delicious Cheddar ploughman's and pâté; roomy, attractive and relaxing *(Stephen R Holman)*

KINGSTON

[Eden St] *Applemarket:* Good crowd, very cheap beer and food excellent value, loudish music, no nearby parking, not too crowded *(Ian Phillips)*

[2 Bishops Hall; off Thames St] *Bishop out of Residence*: Popular place, beer always well kept, food good value, varied and tasty, fine Thames view from riverside tables overlooking Kingston Bridge; spacious and well furnished *(Adrian Kelly, Anon)*

☆ [Canbury Gdns; Lower Ham Rd] *Boaters*: Permission granted for this development only on condition that it would continue to provide teas, ice-creams and so forth for the people using the Gardens – but really qualifies as a pub, with Badger Tanglefoot, Courage, King & Barnes beers and quite a full fish menu in the evenings running to shark and salmon; lovely Thames views from riverside tables, modern but comfortable and friendly inside *(Ian Phillips, P Ashley)*

[88 London Rd] *Flamingo & Firkin*: Another in the chain of simple value own-brew pubs with similar names; children in family-room with adventure playground and view into brewery *(David Fisher)*

LEAVES GREEN
Crown: Excellent food such as poacher's pie, well kept Shepherd Neame ales, friendly staff and no-frills decoration with no juke box; summer barbecues *(R J Ambroziak)*

NEW MALDEN
[Coombe Rd] *Royal Oak*: Archetypal British pub with four areas including public bar with darts, cosy sitting-room with subdued lighting; Benskins and Tetleys real ales; good food, not overpriced considering quantity and quality *(Paul Finan, G T Rhys)*

RICHMOND
[The Green] *Cricketers*: Has new luxurious upstairs wine and food bar overlooking the Green, quite elaborate menu *(Nigel Williamson)*

[345 Petersham Rd; Ham Common] *New*: Excellent friendly free house, food impressive for quantity and price, service friendly, beer good – may include Brakspears; tables outside *(J P Berryman, P Gillbe, Doug Kennedy, Jenny and Brian Seller)*
Princes Head: Good food, excellent Fullers, clean and friendly; parking difficult *(P Gillbe)*
[Petersham Rd] *Rose of York*: Still a very good standard, one of the most pleasant places for drink or meal, gardens recently extended – hard to beat on sunny day, surrounded by views and flowering shrubs; excellent lunch even on Sun (but get there before 1) from carvery or extensive salad bar; service tends to be a bit impersonal, but efficient enough *(Doug Kennedy, Michael Bolam)*
[17 Parkshort; just tucked away from shopping centre] *Sun*: Warm and friendly recently refurbished pub, pleasant licensee, good lunchtime bar food, well kept Fullers ales; popular locally *(Comus Elliott)*
☆ [Cholmondeley Walk; riverside] *White*

Cross: Busy, friendly pub, well placed by the Thames, with good service, well kept beer, nice food and lots of character; mostly very busy *(Doug Kennedy, S C Collett-Jones)*

SIDCUP
[North Cray Rd] *White Cross*: Very good service, friendly, excellent food, well kept Courage *(P Gillbe)*

ST MARY CRAY
[Wellington Rd] *Beech Tree*: Considerable effort put into varied interesting bar food including sandwiches; Whitbreads-related real ale, warm atmosphere, unobtrusive piped jazz *(James Leigh)*
[Sevenoaks Way] *Broomwood*: Excellent bar food and reasonable prices, cheerful friendly staff, good atmosphere *(J S Quantill, J E Hillier)*

SURBITON
[1 Ewell Rd] *Railway*: Wide choice of consistently good real ales, excellent bar service; children have good facilities indoors *(Roy Goldsmith)*
[Victoria Rd] *Victoria*: Plenty of nooks and crannies in Youngs pub with pleasant ambience and decent restaurant *(D J Cargill)*

WEST WICKHAM
[Pickhurst Lane] *Pickhurst*: Large, busy suburban pub popular for lunch and dinner (two sittings) – especially spring and summer evenings; very good polite service, tasty well presented substantial bar food, well kept Watneys-related real ales, good coffee *(E G Parish)*

WEST

SW6
[235 New King's Rd] *Duke of Cumberland*: Big lavishly restored Edwardian lounge bar opposite Parsons Green, cheerful weekend lunchtimes, relaxed for weekday lunchtime food *(GRE, AE)*
[577 King's Rd] *Imperial Arms*: Spacious, welcoming and scrupulously clean, with imaginative food using first-class ingredients, Watneys-related real ales and excellent coffee including home-made biscuits *(Conrad Russell)*
[1 Parsons Green] *White Horse*: Busy place, especially at its Old Ale Festival around the last Sat in Nov, with up to 20 different Old and Winter Ales, morris dancing and jazz; varied choice of good food, good friendly service; brunch served from 11.15 on Sun (milk or fruit juice until noon) *(P Gillbe)*
[127 Gloucester Rd; opp Hereford Sq] *Hereford Arms*: Good range of beers including Charles Wells Bombardier and Huntsman Royal Oak, though the Antipodean staff may be a bit vague about them – very popular

with Australians in the evening; at Christmastime may have a wandering minstrel *(Nick Dowson, Alison Hayward)*
[44 Montpelier Sq] *King George IV*: Quiet Georgian pub, pleasant service, relaxing and comfortable inside, a few picnic-table sets out; well kept if pricey Flowers, attractive prints, competitively priced food including excellent sandwiches, ploughman's, filled baked potatoes, quiche, beef or ham salad; handy for Harrods *(Ian and Liz Phillips, John Roué)*
[Ashburn Pl; in Gloucester Hotel, 4 Harrington Gdns] *Merrie Go Down*: A few real ales and pleasant atmosphere in surprising little dark place *(Nick Dowson, Alison Hayward)*
[24 Montpelier Pl] *Nelson*: Excellent quite adventurous food with steak sandwiches a speciality, well kept Watneys-related real ales, masses of flowers and Nelson memorabilia in the cosy single room, iron tables and chairs outside *(Ian Phillips, John Roué)*
[30 Queens Gate Mews] *Queens Arms*: Victorian pub with period furniture, heavy plush seating, massive mahogany bookcases, lithographs (including two of the nearby Albert Hall); Charrington IPA on handpump, decent wine; in a delightful cobbled mews *(Gwen and Peter Andrews)*

SW10
[1 Billing Rd] *Fox & Pheasant*: Big fire in pleasant and quietly placed old-fashioned terrace pub with good atmosphere *(Jon Wainwright, BB)*
[190 Fulham Rd] *Kings Arms*: Very friendly staff and customers in old-fashioned pub with good buffet, free from pseuds and trendies *(Matt Buchan)*

W4
☆ [72 Strand on the Green] *Bell & Crown*: Cheap and cheerful food, including very wide range of good sandwiches, well kept Fullers, pleasant interesting prints and good atmosphere in eighteenth-century pub; Thames views from plant-filled conservatory and heavily panelled spacious main room, lots of dogs on a Saturday *(BKA, Jon Wainwright)*
☆ [15 Strand on the Green] *Bulls Head*: Little rambling rooms with black-panelled alcoves, simple traditional furnishings, well kept Watneys-related ales on handpump, reasonably priced lunchtime food from no-smoking food bar lunchtimes and Thurs–Sat evenings; back games-bar; right on Thames, with picnic-table sets by river; children allowed in Perspex-roofed back courtyard area *(Jon Wainwright, S C Collett-Jones, LYM)*
[corner Chiswick Lane S and Gt West Rd, by Fullers Brewery] *Mawson Arms*: Excellent Fullers ales and really friendly staff *(Richard Houghton)*
[145 Chiswick High Rd] *Packhorse & Talbot*: Excellent choice of beers such as

Brakspears, Everards Tiger and Felinfoel Double Dragon, with cheaper special; lunchtime food; very popular local in the evenings when it can get smoky; Weds folk club *(Doug Kennedy)*

W5
[Elm Grove Rd; by Warwick Dene] *Grange*: Cosy and comfortable, with pleasing décor in four drinking areas including small lounge, bar, bigger lounge on higher level and conservatory with own bar (leading to garden); Watneys-related real ales, tasty food *(Simon Collett-Jones)*
[33 Haven Lane] *Haven*: Lovely rambling old pub with good food at fair prices in conservatory buffet; friendly service, wide choice of beers and wines; parking a bit of a problem *(P J and S A Barrett)*
[South Ealing Rd (opp BBC Ealing Film Studios)] *Red Lion*: Small well kept one-bar Fullers pub with lunchtime food, excellent London Pride, Chiswick and ESB *(Peter Edwards)*

W6
☆ [2 South Black Lion Lane] *Black Lion*: Very comfortable and cosy Chef & Brewer pub with friendly staff, nice oil of A P Herbert over fireplace, photographs of Thames barges and so forth, tie collection over bar; excellent doorstep sandwiches, and hot dishes and Sun roasts; well kept Watneys-related beers; seats out on terrace *(Ian Phillips, Simon Collett-Jones, Nick Dowson, Alison Hayward, BB)*
[57 Black Lion Lane] *Cross Keys*: Well kept simple local with good friendly atmosphere, well kept Fullers ales, good bar food, not far from Thames; a village atmosphere in spite of W London location *(Nick Long, BB)*
[Hammersmith Rd] *Latymer*: Up-market new cocktail-bar style of pub opened here by Fullers spring 1988 – beer well kept, service prompt, food unusually good (licensee formerly with approval for this in Derby) *(C J Parsons)*
☆ [25 Upper Mall] *Old Ship*: Spacious riverside pub, comfortably modernised and filled with nautical bric-à-brac – model ships, navy lamps, hanging skiffs, dozens of oars as well as usual copper jugs and cast-iron cauldron, etc.; beams, panelling, Turkey carpet, banquettes, tables on big well kept terrace with view over Thames of St Paul's School playing-fields; good food – quiches pies, excellent roast beef, very good salads with real mayonnaise, hot dish of day, well kept Watneys-related real ales; can be very crowded weekends *(Patrick Young, G Cooper, LYM)*
☆ [13 Brook Green] *Queens Head*: Pleasantly placed Chef & Brewer, modernised but comfortable, decently kept beer, straightforward food, tasty and unusual Sun bar nibbles; piped music; what makes it worth knowing is the secluded and unusually spacious well

kept garden with tables under cocktail parasols, splendid for lunch on sunny days, and a real surprise in this area *(Jenny Woolf, S C Collett-Jones, Alison Hayward, Nick Dowson)*
[15 Lower Mall] *Rutland Ale House*: Comfortable, cheery and efficient, with carefully cultivated layer of 'designer dirt' – peeling paint, contrived 'damp' plaster, new 'old' bookcases and so forth, even a couple of old clinker sculling boats hanging from high rafters in front bar; plethora of bric-à-brac from stone bottles to aged lacrosse sticks, wide range of good food includes dishes cooked to order such as omelettes, Watneys-related real ale; benches on traffic-free mall, but high flood wall cuts off river view; lots of businessmen and serious rowing types from Amateur Rowing Association next door *(Ian Phillips)*

W7
[Green Lane, Hanwell] *Fox*: Pleasant and friendly traditional local in very quiet spot close to Grand Union Canal *(Neil Barker)*

W8
[1 Allen St; off Kensington High St] *Britannia*: Real haven of comfort and peace, good food, excellent Youngs *(Prof S Barnett)*
[9 Kensington Church St] *Churchill Arms*: Surprisingly light in spite of panelling, dark carpet, darkly comfortable furniture, spacious series of areas leading back to new conservatory; good range of food (evenings too), well kept Fullers beers, warm and friendly atmosphere *(Ian Phillips)*
[Notting Hill Gate] *Finches*: Recently given Victorian atmosphere by stained panelling, cut-glass windows and mirrors, good brass lamps, Victorian prints, kitchen chairs around cast-iron tables, lots of stoneware and glass bottles and huge plates on racks around walls and over bar; Bass, Courage, Youngs on handpump, pub food (soup good), soft piped music *(Patrick Young)*
[71 Palace Gdns Terr] *Gaiety*: Good pastiche of Edwardian pub with attractive posters, good range of food, comfortable well spaced seating; Whitbreads-related real ales, coal-effect gas fire *(Ian Phillips)*
☆ [23a Edwardes Sq] *Scarsdale Arms*: Well kept Watneys-related real ales in pub that's been done up as a Chef & Brewer but still keeps its bare boards, gas lighting, vases of fresh flowers and winter fires; decent food (not Sun), strong local following, pleasant small front terrace; children allowed in eating area *(Nick Dowson, LYM)*
[13 Uxbridge St] *Uxbridge Arms*: Pleasant up-market pub with simple plush décor, well kept real ales such as Brakspears, good lunchtime food, seats on pavement in summer; can be crowded in the evening, and parking would be a problem *(Nick Dowson, Alison Hayward, John Tyzack)*

W9
[30 Bristol Gdns] *Royal George*: Lovely relaxed atmosphere, bar staff very pleasant and always ready for a laugh, all age-groups, no poseurs – what pubs used to be like *(Mrs Y E M Betts)*
[6 Warwick Pl] *Warwick Castle*: Plenty of character, unspoilt atmosphere, in straightforward high-ceilinged Victorian pub with big old cast-iron fireplace, friendly service, seats on quiet pavement; guest beers such as Morrells as well as well kept Bass and Charrington IPA on handpump, reasonably priced bar lunches including good sandwiches; close to Little Venice *(Howard and Sue Gascoyne, LYM)*

W11
[100 Holland Park Ave] *Castle*: No airs and graces, but good and unusual lunchtime food and well kept Charrington IPA on handpump *(Patrick Young)*
[281 Westbourne Grove; corner Portobello Rd] *Earl of Lonsdale*: Almost circular bar in light and spacious pub with huge windows, banquettes and oak tables (bar oak-panelled too), decent weekday buffet, Sun roasts, popular with locals on weekdays, packed with market shoppers from Portobello Rd on Sat *(Patrick Young)*
[41 Tavistock Cres] *Frog & Firkin*: Usual Firkin standard, three home-brews and guest real ales, reasonable food including the big baps, enjoyable atmosphere with singalongs at weekends *(Michael Cooke, Louise Collins, Nick Dowson, Alison Hayward, LYM)*
☆ [54 Ladbroke Rd] *Ladbroke Arms*: Very cosy nicely decorated pub with Huntsman real ales, log-effect gas fire, nice friendly atmosphere *(Nick Dowson, Alison Hayward)*
☆ [95 Portobello Rd] *Portobello Gold*: Good value and often interesting home-made food and Watneys-related real ales, decent choice of wines, several Caribbean drinks, sliding-roof conservatory with Caribbean mural, cane chairs, tropical plants and so forth; excellent sound system in front bar (with videos), open fire, friendly atmosphere, pine furnishings; in Sat antiques market *(Bruce Woodhead, Patrick Young)*
[Ladbroke Grove; corner Holland Park Av] *Raj*: Theme pub with bamboo tables and chairs, electric pukka fans, old photographs of Viceroy, Poona, polo, etc.; good bar food including samosas and bhajis as well as lasagne, macaroni cheese, salads and roast beef; tables on street and in back garden with barbecues Fri and Sat evening and Sun lunch; Watneys-related real ales on handpump *(Patrick Young)*
[7 Portobello Rd] *Sun in Splendour*: Pleasant restored Victorian pub with red flock wallpaper and patterned carpet, red velvet banquettes, copper-topped tables and brass lamps; Bass and Charrington IPA on handpump, good straightforward pub food and

good barbecue on back terrace; gets packed on Sat *(Diane Duane, PTY)*

W14
[150 Warwick Rd] *Britannia Tap*: Simple lunchtime food, good beer (including Youngs Winter Warmer in season) and lots of interesting customers, in genuine local near Earls Court *(Dr and Mrs A K Clarke)*
[247 Warwick Rd] *Radnor Arms*: Small single-bar, quietly refurbished corner pub, good range of real ales, friendly staff *(Dr and Mrs A K Clarke)*
[253 North End Rd] *Seven Stars*: Excellent lunches, well kept Fullers and friendly service in small local *(C J Parsons)*
[171 North End Rd] *Three Kings*: Very large but still friendly, with something for everyone – including ten real ales on handpump; reasonable prices *(T E Cheshire)*

BRENTFORD
[3 High St] *O'Riordans*: Friendly and comfortable, with about ten real ales such as Adnams, Batemans, Brains, Brakspears, Wadworths 6X and Wiltshire Old Devil and Weedkiller; husband-and-wife team do good home-made food such as rolls oozing with salad, ham and eggs or scampi and chips; opposite organ and piano museum and steam museum, by riverside footpath to Kew Bridge *(Ian Phillips)*

EASTCOTE
[High Rd] *Case is Altered*: Well kept Benskins, quiet setting, seats outside – a useful pub to know in this area *(M C Howells)*

HAMPTON
[Uxbridge Rd] *Jolly Gardener*: Sadly made the Browns who made the garden of this Watneys pub really worthy of the name, and won firm approval from readers for friendly and considerate service, left at the end of 1987 *(Anon)*
[99 Higher Hampton Hill] *Valiant Knight*: Very spacious, well kept and well designed for its predominantly young customers, with lots of events – Sounds of the '60s one evening, barbecue in the small garden come rain or shine another, excellent atmosphere, well kept real ale, moderately priced wines, happy hour 6–7, bar food, jazz Sun *(Heather Sharland)*
[70 High St] *White Hart*: Big 1930sish mock-Tudor pub notable for its wide range of real ales such as Flowers, Hook Norton, King & Barnes and Wethereds, served from ceramic-handled pumps; it's popular and well kept, brightened up in winter by a big log fire and in spring with pots of daffodils; the atmosphere's best when it's busy – really jolly on a Sun morning *(Charles Owens, Heather Sharland, Ian Phillips)*

HATTON
[Green Man Lane; 30 yds from A30 crossroads at Bedfont] *Green Man*: Pretty little pub, now in the industrial area right under Heathrow Airport's main flight path but formerly a haunt of highwaymen on the Bath Rd and Hounslow Heath – there's still a hidden compartment behind the deep fireplace in the low-ceilinged and dimly lit bar; boarded ceiling and walls, cases of bottle-stoppers, labels and clay pipes found here, plenty of room in sympathetic extension, decent food, Watneys-related real ales *(Ian Phillips)*

ISLEWORTH
[183 London Rd] *Coach & Horses*: Very old Youngs pub recently thoughtfully refurbished, lunchtime bar food, well kept real ale, pleasant atmosphere, restaurant *(Stephen King)*
[Church St] *Red Lion*: Very attractive local, with friendly service and excellent Courage Best and Directors *(Raymond Lyons)*

NORTHWOOD
[Rickmansworth Rd] *True Lovers Knot*: Good helpings of very reasonably priced well presented food, very well run pub *(G R Heathcote)*

NORWOOD GREEN
☆ [Norwood Green Rd] *Plough*: Bright, cosy and attractive, well kept Fullers ales, with comparatively cheap country-style good value food from sandwiches to savoury omelettes and gammon and egg, and notable – given its outer London location – for its adjacent bowling-green; parts are said to go back to the fourteenth century *(Tom Evans)*

OSTERLEY
☆ [Windmill Lane; B454, off A4] *Hare & Hounds*: A rural island – mature garden with nooks and crannies to suit families of all ages, efficient service, good food in comfortable, busy but efficient pub with well kept Fullers ESB, London Pride and Chiswick; no music *(Neil and Elspeth Fearn, GRE, AE)*

TEDDINGTON
[Broom Rd/Ferry Rd; close to bridge at Teddington Lock] *Tide End Cottage*: Small friendly riverside local with real gas lamps, Watneys-related real ales, good bar food including home-made hot-pot and moussaka; can get very crowded at weekends *(Hazel Morgan)*

TWICKENHAM
[London Rd] *Cabbage Patch*: Open fire, good atmosphere and food, own parking – and near stn *(N L Westley)*
[Twickenham Green] *Prince Albert*: Good value lunchtime food including outstanding choice of sandwiches and ploughman's, well

kept Fullers ESB and London Pride, very hardworking licensees – like a country pub in town *(Stephen King)*

[Winchester Rd, St Margarets; behind roundabout on A316] *Turks Head*: Well kept Fullers, excellent food, very helpful landlord; avoid if there's a Rugby international at Twickenham (unless you're a regular you won't get in) *(Ian Phillips)*

☆ [Riverside] *White Swan*: A great favourite with many readers for its determined stand against modernity, with genuine food served at big country-style tables in an atmosphere that on weekday lunchtimes has been relatively quiet and relaxed, old-fashioned décor, well kept Watneys-related real ales and lovely riverside position (others have remarked on crowds at other times, slap-happy feeling, very slow service); for the last couple of years there's been talk of changes – more news please *(Charles Owens, Doug Kennedy, LYM)*

UXBRIDGE
Continental: Modern and noisy, but its excellent value sandwiches are a saving grace – really well filled in big slices of granary bread *(Rodney Coe)*

[High St; A4007] *Three Tuns*: Fairly recently refurbished, concentrating on good range of tasty food with section reserved for lunchers; Benskins, Ind Coope Burton, Taylor-Walker real ales, piped music not too loud *(Michael King)*

WEST HYDE
[Coppermill Lane] *Fisheries*: Open fires in comfortable and very newly refurbished canalside pub; standard bar food (notice says can't be served without accompanying purchase from the bar), seats on lawn with swings, slide and mechanical rides; notice requests clean smart casual wear only; waterside walks *(Lyn and Bill Capper)*

EAST

E1
☆ [269 Whitechapel Rd] *Grave Maurice*: Unexpectedly pleasant for the area; Sat evening bar meals (as well as in restaurant) most unusual in E London; popular with staff from London Hospital, quietly comfortable long lounge bar, well kept Trumans real ales *(Neil Barker, LYM)*

[285 Whitechapel Rd] *Lord Rodneys Head*: Friendly extrovert bar staff in unfussy but efficient pub with interesting fixtures and fittings, Banks & Taylors real ale in excellent condition; bar billiards and other traditional games; popular live music each night *(Judith Denwood, N R England)*

☆ [57 Wapping Wall] *Prospect of Whitby*: Rollicking pub done up old-style with cheerful evening live music, beams, panelling and

flagstones, well kept Watneys-related real ales, superb river views (much appreciated by the painter Turner) from flagstoned waterside courtyard; very touristy; has been a main entry for its very considerable entertainment value, but recent reports raise real doubts about food and service – more news please *(C Fluck, LYM)*

E2
[89 Dunbridge St] *Lord Hood*: Federation beers from the North in lively pub with free music hall Weds, Fri and Sat, lunchtime food, occasional morris dancing *(David Cook)*

[211 Old Ford Rd] *Royal Cricketers*: Pleasant canalside pub with terrace, good views of canal and Victoria Park – a rural oasis in the East End *(Neil Barker)*

E3
☆ [104 Empson St] *Beehive*: Charming local with interesting range of well kept real ales such as Flowers, Greene King Abbot, Pitfield Dark Star and Theakstons Old Peculier; open fire, warmly hospitable new licensees *(Andrew O'Doherty, Perry Board)*

[50 St Leonard St] *Imperial Crown*: Comfortable and friendly, interesting interior, close to walks along River Lee and Bow Back Rivers *(Neil Barker; reports on food please)*

E4
[Larkshall Rd] *Larkshall*: Comfortable pub with Victorian dining-room serving as saloon bar, old bar back salvaged from former Southwark Brewery; well kept Courage Best and Directors on handpump *(Robert Lester)*

[Mott St; off Sewardstone Rd – OS Sheet 177 reference 384983] *Plough*: Friendly roadside pub, with well kept McMullens, Christmas Ale in season, and good food including home-cooked daily specials and fresh vegetables; tables outside; in spite of its London address this is really out in Essex – perhaps the most extreme example of the eccentricity of Post Office addressing *(R P Hastings, Robert Lester)*

[219 Kings Head Hill] *Royal Oak*: Smartly decorated two-bar roadside pub with food lunchtime and evening, McMullens Country on handpump, and AK Mild *(Robert Lester)*

E9
☆ [274 Victoria Park Rd] *Falcon & Firkin*: Vast fun room for children in own-brew pub with bare boards, lots of falconry memorabilia, good value cheap food – big filled baps, quiche, ploughman's, Cumberland sausages and daily specials such as cheese and onion pie or chicken and bacon flan; brews include Falcon Ale and Hackney Bitter; garden *(Anon)*

E11
[24 Browning Rd] *North Star*: Genuine pub,

cosy and friendly, with well kept Bass and Charrington IPA, chippish food *(Simon Kleine)*

E14
☆ [27 Ropemakers Fields; off Narrow St, opp The Grapes] *House They Left Behind*: Recent attractive restoration of sole survivor of demolished 1857 terrace: long narrow bar, bare boards, a few good prints, interesting maps, paintings and clippings about Limehouse and the Basin; catches new Docklands feel (and customers) but has kept local base; friendly licensee, well kept Fullers; excellent food cooked before your eyes at very fair prices in open-plan area; one or two good tables for parties; convenient for end of Regent's Canal *(Judith Denwood, Ian Phillips, NHB, D J Wallington)*

E15
[9 Leytonstone Rd] *Bacchus Bin*: Good beers

and friendly bar staff, civilised customers *(Norman England)*

E17
[Hoe St] *Rose & Crown*: Good food, including curries on Weds; children in central eating area *(Rosemary Cladingbowl)*

COLLIER ROW
[St Johns Rd] *Pinewoods*: New free house with well kept beer, wide choice of excellent bar snacks and full meals, very attractive surroundings *(Anon)*

ROMFORD
Morland Arms: Unusually pleasant staff, extremely good bar food such as well filled ham salad roll; can get very busy *(R Coe)*

WOODFORD GREEN
Travellers Friend: Locally popular for well kept beer and good food *(R P Hastings)*

Scotland

Scotland

You should find that in this new edition the general standard of the Scottish main entries is higher than before. This is because the flow of readers' reports on Scotland in previous editions have been over-represented in the Guide – it's had more main entries than readers' favourable comments justified. So we have sifted through the Scottish entries more vigorously than before, raising what you might call our 'acceptance requirement' to bring them more closely into line with other main entries. This means that in the Lucky Dip section at the end of the chapter, you'll find many places with the identifying LYM initials among the recommenders; these are perfectly acceptable but do not perhaps justify a full entry. We have also found this year that few pubs in Scotland won firm approval from enough readers to justify editorial inspection – again, we have starred the Lucky Dip entries that at least look promising, and these are the ones on which we'd be particularly grateful for more reports. In this Lucky Dip section, places of special note include the Cawdor Inn at Cawdor, the Poolewe Hotel at Poolewe, the Grange at St Andrews, the Stein Inn at Stein on Skye (now re-opened but is likely to be more of a decorous hotel), the Wheatsheaf at Swinton, the Buccleuch & Queensberry and the Lion & Unicorn, Thornhill, the Towie at Turriff and the Ceilidh Place and the Ferry Boat, both at Ullapool. The Clifton in Nairn is a special case. Our top rated Scottish entry in previous editions, it has now emphasised even more its identity as a hotel rather than a pub, so reluctantly we have decided it is no longer appropriate as a main entry. But in our opinion it is still the nicest place in Scotland for a really civilised drink. Many of the pubs and inns included are in lovely positions. By the sea or on sea-lochs, as well as nice places to stay at, there are the comfortable Loch Melfort Hotel at Arduaine (looking out to sea, with a marvellous woodland garden, and good local seafood), the welcoming Ardvasar Hotel at Ardvasar (good, fresh food, and one of the bars

The Riverside, Canonbie

793

has been redecorated this year), the Crinan Hotel overlooking the entry to the Crinan Canal (good food and lovely views from its top-floor restaurant), the Crown & Anchor at Findhorn, the Steam Packet on the edge of the natural harbour of Isle of Whithorn, the cheerful Hotel Eilean Iarmain at Isle Ornsay (good food from Gaelic menus), the stylish Taychreggan at Kilchrenan (well kept gardens, a pretty courtyard and good food), the neat Udny Arms at Newburgh (new licensees), the delightful Crown on the harbour front at Portpatrick (the landlord catches much of the fish eaten here), and the elegant Creggans at Strachur (extensive grounds and good food). The Fisherman's Tavern at Broughty Ferry has good views of the Tay bridges, the Old Inn at Carbost is popular with walkers and climbers, the Cramond Inn at Cramond has new licensees who have been making several changes, the friendly little Ship is right on the harbour at Elie, the Plockton Hotel is on its quiet West Coast inlet among the palm trees, the Hawes at Queensferry is R L Stevenson's Kidnapped inn, and The Lookout is above the marina at Troon. Inland, the Loch Tummel Hotel (with new licensees) has views over its loch to the wooded mountains, the remote Tibbie Shiels Inn at St Mary's Loch has free fishing to residents and good value food, and the Letterfinlay Lodge near Spean Bridge has lovely views down to Loch Lochy – fishing and maybe deerstalking can be arranged, and there's popular lunchtime food, too. Other pubs include the ancient little George at Moniaive (good food and new licensees), the handsome Grant Arms in Monymusk, the Gordon Arms at Mountbenger (back as a main entry this year, with new licensees), and the Killiecrankie Hotel in its nice policies at Pitlochry. Pubs not yet mentioned that have good food are the civilised Riverside at Canonbie, the decorous Claret Jug and the spacious Jules (new licensees here), both in Edinburgh, the tranquil Tweeddale Arms at Gifford, the busy Bon Accord (new licensees) and the lively Babbity Bowster, both in Glasgow, the neatly kept Tormaukin at Glendevon, the Old Howgate Inn at Howgate (now a main entry again), the Dallam Tower Hotel at Loans (the new licensee is hoping to make it more of a country house), the very well run Burts Hotel at Melrose (totally refurbished bedrooms), the friendly Black Bull at Moffat, the nicely placed Skeabost House Hotel at Skeabost, the West Loch Hotel at Tarbert (the new licensees are placing more emphasis on Scottish cooking), the simple Tayvallich Inn at Tayvallich, and the Ailean Chraggan at Weem (reinstated as a main entry this year). Some other changes include new licensees at the Carbeth Inn at Blanefield, the Salmon Leap at Drymen (back as a main entry), Bennets Bar and Kay's Bar, both in Edinburgh, and the Buccleuch Arms at St Boswells (also back as a main entry this year).

ABERDEEN (Grampian)   NJ9305 Map 11

Ferryhill House Hotel

Bon Accord Street (bottom end)

The unusually wide choice of real ales and malt whiskies in this consistently well run place is always a draw, but in summer tables on the immaculate sheltered lawns are a big bonus. Inside, there are spacious and airy communicating bar areas with plenty of seating – more the atmosphere of a small hotel than a pub. Kept in immaculate condition, the real ales include Belhaven 80/-, Broughton Greenmantle and Merlin, Hartleys, McEwans 80/- and Youngers No 3, on handpump or electric pump. Wide-ranging bar food includes sandwiches (from 55p), baked potatoes and ploughman's (£1.80), with main courses from fried scampi (£3.85) and beef olives

(£4.10) to fillet steak (£7.40). Fruit machine and piped music. *(Recommended by Leith Stuart; more reports please)*

Free house Licensee Douglas Snowie Real ale Meals (not Fri evening or Sat or Sun) and snacks (not Fri or Sat evening or Sun) Restaurant Children in restaurant Open 11–11 all year Bedrooms tel Aberdeen (0224) 590867; £28B/£48B

Prince of Wales

7 St Nicholas Lane

As last year's *Guide* came out, this long-standing Aberdonian institution was at the centre of a row – the Next retailing chain planning its demolition for redevelopment, the locals fighting for its survival. As we write this we are keeping our fingers crossed for what is the longest bar counter in the city, with a cosy flagstoned area with a log-effect gas fire, and pews and other wooden furniture in screened booths, as well as its neatly refurbished main lounge. The staff are most friendly and welcoming. Popular good value lunchtime food includes soup, filled rolls and bridie-cakes, pies, three or four hot dishes and a vegetarian dish. Well kept Theakstons Best and Old Peculier on handpump, Caledonian 80/- and Youngers No 3 on air-pressure tall fount, and regular guest beers. Sensibly placed darts, dominoes, cribbage and fruit machine. It's reached down a Dickensianly narrow cobbled alley that twists right underneath Union Street. *(Recommended by Michael Cooke, Nigel Paine)*

Free house Licensee Peter Birnie Real ale Lunchtime meals and snacks (not Sun) No nearby parking Open 11–11 all year

ARDFERN (Strathclyde)   NM8004 Map 11

Galley of Lorne

B8002; village and inn signposted off A816 Lochgilphead–Oban

There's such a sense of community in this secluded waterside settlement that the friendly and informal character of this inn seems quite unaffected by changes of ownership. Of course what never changes is the lovely setting on Loch Craignish, with the views of the sea-loch and yacht anchorage. Inside, the main bar has big navigation lamps by the bar counter, old Highland dress prints and other pictures, and an easy-going assortment of chairs, little winged settles and rug-covered window seats on its lino tiles. Cheap bar food in generous helpings might include filled rolls, filled baked potatoes, rabbit stew, and braised steak or roast pork; a wide choice of whiskies; darts, piped pop music, space game and fruit machine. A spacious wine bar behind has a piano and dance floor, and a big pool-table, and there are easy chairs in the entrance lounge with windows looking out over the sheltered terrace; the pub is at the start of *Good Walks Guide* Walk 178. *(Recommended by Patrick Stapley, Richard Gibbs)*

Free house Meals and snacks Open 11–2.30, 5–11 all year; later closing Thurs–Sat evenings, open all day Sat Bedrooms tel Barbreck (085 25) 284; £16(£18B)/£32(£36B)

ARDUAINE (Strathclyde)   NM7911 Map 11

Loch Melfort Hotel ⊗ 🛏

By the big picture window in the light, modern bar of this comfortable hotel is a pair of powerful marine glasses through which you can search for birds and seals on the islets and on the coasts of the bigger islands beyond. It's especially popular in summer with yachtsmen (and windsurfers) and one wall is papered with nautical charts. Light oak tables are ringed by low dark brown fabric and wood easy chairs, and there's a free-standing wood-burning stove. At lunchtime the bar food includes home-made soup (90p), toasted sandwiches (£1.20), filled baked potatoes (£1.50), home-made pâté (£2.20), ploughman's (£3), a pint of prawns (£4), locally smoked salmon (£7.50), freshly caught langoustines (£8.50) and puddings (from £1.50); evening extras include pickled herring (£2), chicken fritters (£4), fried haddock (£4.25), and smoked whole trout (£4.50); helpful service; darts. Wooden seats on the front terrace are a step away from the rocky foreshore, backed by grass and wild flowers, and the neighbouring Arduaine woodland gardens, at their best from late April to early June, are magnificent. Some bedrooms are in a modern wing, some, older-fashioned, in the main house. (*Recommended by Mrs Sue Johnson, Neil and Angela Huxter, Mrs Nedelev*)

Free house   Licensees Colin and Jane Tindal   Meals and snacks   Restaurant   Children welcome   Open 11–2.30, 5–11.30; closed end Oct–Easter   Bedrooms tel Kilmelford (085 22) 233; £38B/£64B

ARDVASAR (Isle of Skye)   NG6203   Map 11
Ardvasar Hotel ⊗ 🛏

This is our southernmost entry on the island – a comfortably modernised and neatly kept eighteenth-century inn just past Armadale pier where the summer car ferries from Mallaig dock. Friendly and obliging young owners serve good fresh food in the dining-room, including local fish and shellfish, and the home-cooked bar food varies day by day. Typically, it might include tomato and orange soup (85p), sweet pickled herring platter (£1.30), home-made pâté (£1.45), potted crab or chilli con carne (£2.50), shoulder of lamb stuffed with apricots or cold home-cooked gammon with cheese and pineapple (£3.15), fried haddock fillet (£3.50), a vegetarian dish and puddings such as blackcurrant and lemon flan (£1.20). There's also a four-course set menu – which might include turbot, lobster or pheasant – at £13.50. The bars look out across the Sound of Sleat to the fierce Knoydart mountains: the newly refurbished cocktail bar has a red patterned carpet, Highland dress prints on the cream hessian and wood walls, crimson plush wall seats and stools, and dimpled copper coffee tables; the locally popular public bar has stripped pews and kitchen chairs. A room off the comfortable hotel lounge, which has armchairs around its open fire, has a huge TV. Near the Clan Donald centre; and the far side of the peninsula, by Tarskavaig, Tokavaig and Ord, has some of the most dramatic summer sunsets in Scotland – over the jagged Cuillin peaks, with the islands of Canna and Rhum off to your left. Well placed for exploring the Sleat peninsula. (*Recommended by Janet and John Pamment, Miles Walton, Rob and Gill Weeks, Mrs E Higson*)

Free house   Licensees Bill and Gretta Fowler   Meals and snacks   Restaurant   Children in eating area of bar   Impromptu fiddlers and Gaelic singing   Open 11–11 (12 Fri) June–Sept; 11–2.30, 5–11 Oct–May; closed 25 Dec, 1 and 2 Jan   Bedrooms tel Ardvasar (041 14) 223; £17(£20B)/£32(£38B)

BLANEFIELD (Central)   NS5579   Map 11
Carbeth Inn

West Carbeth; A809 Glasgow–Drymen, just S of junction with B821

The old-fashioned bar in this well kept, friendly country pub, below the Kilpatrick Hills, has a warm and cheerful atmosphere – helped by an open fire under the mounted stag's head at one end and the wood-burning stove at the other. There are heavy cast-iron-framed tables on the stone and tile floor, a high ceiling of brown planking, and cushioned booths built from the same wood under a high frieze of tartan curtain (with a big colour TV peeping out). The enthusiastic new licensees have put more emphasis on generous helpings of good value bar food: home-made soup (75p), sandwiches (from 90p, toasties from £1.20), filled baked potatoes (from £1.60), ploughman's (£1.90), burgers (from £2), salad with ham, prawns, cheese and egg or lasagne (£2.50), chicken and bacon or scampi (£2.75), gammon with pineapple (£2.95) and steaks (from £5.25); also, daily specials and children's

meals (from £1.30). Well kept Wethereds and Whitbreads Castle Eden on
handpump; sensibly placed darts, fruit machine, trivia and piped music. There's a
pleasant panelled family-room and the Ptarmigan – a rather smarter carpeted bar;
both have old stone walls, open fires and bric-à-brac. On the front terrace outside
there are lots of rustic benches and tables. *(Recommended by Nick Dowson and Alison
Hayward, Dr Iain McColl)*

*Whitbreads   Licensee Nigel Morrison   Real ale   Meals and snacks   Children in
family-room until 9   Singer Weds, band Fri   Open 11–11 Mon–Thurs; 11–midnight Fri and
Sat; 12.30–11 Sun   Bedrooms tel Blanefield (0360) 70382; £10/£20*

BROUGHTY FERRY (Tayside)   NO4630 Map 11
Fisherman's Tavern
12 Fort Street; turning off shore road

The cosy little snug in this small-roomed rambling pub has been recently redecorated with basket-weave wall panels, a new brown carpet, light pink, soft fabric
seating and beige lamps. As we went to press the back bar was also undergoing
redecoration which would include a Victorian fireplace, brass wall lights, a new bar
gantry and new carpets. The wide range of real ales includes Belhaven 80/-,
McEwans 70/- and 80/-, Maclays 80/-, Theakstons Best, Timothy Taylors Landlord, and two guest beers that change weekly on handpump, with Youngers No 3
on air-pressure tall fount; a goodish choice of whiskies, including distinguished
single malts, on the dispensing optics. Bar food includes sandwiches, and hot dishes
such as Finnan pie, beef olives, scampi, curry or lemon sole with prawns and
mushrooms (all £1.95); friendly and professional service. Darts, dominoes, cribbage, two fruit machines. The nearby seafront gives a good view of the two long,
low Tay bridges. *(Recommended by JAH, HLH)*

*Free house   Licensee Robert Paterson   Real ale   Snacks and lunchtime meals   Children in
snug bar until 6   Scottish folk music Mon   Open 11–midnight all year*

CANONBIE (Dumfries and Galloway)   NY3976 Map 9
Riverside ★ ★ ⊗ ⇐ [*illustrated on page 793*]
Village signposted from A7

We have about three times as many reader recommendations for this civilised and
friendly inn as for anywhere else north of the border. The comfortable and relaxing
communicating rooms of the bar have good, sensitively chosen chintzy furnishings,
open fires, stuffed wildlife and local pictures. The lunchtime bar food is exceptional
(as is the restaurant, noted for fresh fish). It includes home-made soups such as
Chinese-style mushroom (£1.20), poached duck egg with ham in port jelly (£1.75),
ploughman's with Cotherstone, Stilton and a green apple or home-made smoked
trout pâté (£2.65), Stilton quiche with wholemeal pastry (£3.55), cider-roast ham
or tandoori chicken (£3.95), casserole of duck with olives in Burgundy or six fresh
Loch Fyne oysters (£4.95), and fillet of fresh brill or freshly poached fillet of salmon
(£5.25). Puddings might include spiced brown-bread pudding, chocolate cream
meringue or nectarine split with fresh raspberry sauce (all £1.25). The food shows
lots of careful small touches, like virgin olive oil for salad dressings; breakfasts –
thoughtful as well as substantial – are special enough to lure you back for another
stay (the bedrooms are most attractive). Well kept Theakstons on handpump,
reasonably priced, with an interesting wine list; sympathetic service; friendly cat. In
summer – when it can get very busy – there are tables under the trees on the front
grass. Over the quiet road, a public playground runs down to the Border Esk (the
inn can arrange fishing permits). *(Recommended by J A H Townsend, Robert Olsen, John
Hanselman, T Nott, Robert and Vicky Tod, Mr and Mrs E J Smith, Dave Butler, Lesley Storey,*

Tony Pounder, Jon Dewhirst, Capt E P Gray, S V Bishop, SS, Jon Wainwright, Dr James
Haworth, Dr J R Hamilton, D H Nicholson, Eileen Broadbent, David and Ruth Hollands)

Free house   Licensee Robert Phillips   Real ale   Meals and snacks (lunchtime, not Sun, and
Sun evenings)   Children welcome   Restaurant (closed Sun)   Open 11–2.30, 6.30–11 all
year; closed Sun lunchtime, 25 and 26 Dec, 1 and 2 Jan, 2 weeks Feb, 2 weeks Nov   Bedrooms
tel Canonbie (054 15) 512 or 295; £36B/£46B

CARBOST (Isle of Skye)   NG3732 Map 11
Old Inn

This is the Carbost on the B8009, in the W of the central part of the island

Tucked down beside the sea-loch near the Talisker distillery, this cheerful old
white-painted stone inn has a simply furnished bar with red leatherette settles,
benches and seats and a peat fire. The popular bar meals – sandwiches, ploughman's, basket meals, pie and beans, haddock, scampi or a dish of the day – are
served in helpings robust enough for climbers down from the fiercely jagged peaks
of the Cuillin Hills; darts, dominoes, cribbage, piped traditional music and the
occasional ceilidh. There are guided tours around the distillery, with free samples,
most days in summer. *(Recommended by Rob and Gill Weeks; more reports please)*

Free house   Meals and snacks   Children welcome   Open 11–2.30, 5–11 all year   Bedrooms
tel Carbost (047 842) 205; £11/£22

CRAMOND (Lothian)   NT1876 Map 11
Cramond Inn

Cramond Glebe Road

In an attractively renovated fishing village by the Firth of Forth, this busy, friendly
old white pub has new owners who have put the bar back in its original place near
the main door, and re-opened the fireplace; there are ceiling-joists, brown
button-back wall banquettes, wheel-back chairs and little stools, and a long, white
clothed table set out for lunch. The bar menu changes daily and may include
home-made soup with soda bread (70p), home-made salmon mousse or ploughman's (£1.50), steak and kidney pie (£2.60), fresh haddock in beer batter (£2.75),
crayfish salad (£3.15), and home-made gateaux (95p). They've also installed five
tall founts dispensing Caledonian 80/-, Maclays 70/-, Marstons Pedigree, Timothy
Taylors Best, and guests such as Broughton Merlins or Thwaites – they travel down
to England to pick up beer from small independent breweries; reasonably priced
spirits are measured in quarter-gills; helpful service even when crowded. Darts,
dominoes, card games and piped music. The water is only a short walk away past
the smart, steep cottages, and the pub's car park has some fine views out over the
Forth; a small side terrace has seats and tables. *(Recommended by Roger Sherman,*
R P Taylor, Dr A V Lewis)

Free house   Licensees Tom Willis and Gordon Duncan   Real ale   Snacks and lunchtime
meals   Restaurant tel 031-336 2035   Children in eating area of bar (if 14 feet from
serving-counter) until 8   Open 11–2.30, 5–11 Mon–Thurs (midnight Fri); 11–midnight Sat;
closed 25 and 26 Dec, 1 Jan

CRINAN (Strathclyde)   NR7894 Map 11
Crinan Hotel ⊗ 🍴

The best view is from the smart top-floor restaurant (and associated evening bar,
where jacket and tie are needed) looking out to the islands and the sea; but
downstairs, from the ordinary mortals' bar, you can look down over the busy
entrance basin of the Crinan Canal, which is full of fishing-boats and yachts
wandering out towards the Hebrides. The décor includes sea drawings and

paintings, model boats in glass cases, and a nautical chest of drawers, and the latest coastal waters forecast is chalked on a blackboard; seats in the cosy carpeted back part and the tiled front part are comfortable. The simpler public bar has the same marvellous views, and there's a side terrace with seats outside. Good bar food includes Loch Crinan shellfish soup (£1.10), flan with salad (£2.95), mussels (£3.75), assorted, locally caught fresh fish, and a weekend buffet lunch. You can get sandwiches from their coffee shop or Lazy Jack's. (*Recommended by Michael Craig; more reports please*)

Free house   Licensee Nicholas Ryan   Lunchtime meals   Children welcome   Evening restaurant   Pianist in rooftop bar Fri, Sat, Sun evenings   Open 11–11 in summer; 11–2.30, 6–11 in winter   Bedrooms tel Crinan (054 683) 235; £37.50B/£68B

DALBEATTIE (Dumfries and Galloway)   NX8361 Map 9

Pheasant

1 Maxwell Street

This friendly inn serves food until 10 – late for the area – in the comfortable and relaxing upstairs lounge bar, which is now a lounge restaurant with piped music. The lively downstairs bar has darts, pool, dominoes, fruit machine, juke box, piped music and occasional disco. At lunchtime bar food includes soup (50p), pizza (£2), home-made burger (£2.25), salads (£2.50), breaded haddock (£2.75), roast Gallo-way beef (£2.80) and fresh Solway salmon (£3.80, when available); in the evenings there are omelettes (from £3.95), gammon and pineapple (£4.95) and charcoal grills (from £6.45). (*Recommended by J A V Rose; more reports please*)

Free house   Licensee Christine McGimpsey   Meals and snacks   Children welcome Restaurant   Open 11–midnight weekdays in summer, 11–1am Sat; 11–2.30, 5–11 in winter   Bedrooms tel Dalbeattie (0556) 610345; £12(£14B)/£24(£28B)

DRYMEN (Central)   NS4788 Map 11

Salmon Leap

The L-shaped public bar of this friendly and comfortable inn, established in 1759, has a pubbier atmosphere than many in the area, and quite a bit of character – with its harness on the walls, bric-à-brac hanging from the joists of the ceiling, and two good log fires. The plusher lounge, with stuffed fish and birds, also L-shaped, is, like the bar, partly panelled, and has a wood-burning stove. Bar food includes specialities such as a pint of prawns, home-made steak pie and poached salmon steaks, and there are barbecues in summer; piped music. (*Recommended by Mr and Mrs J H Adam, A Darroch Harkness, Hazel Morgan*)

Free house   Licensee A MacDonald   Real ales   Meals and snacks   Restaurant, open 12.30–midnight Sun   Children welcome   Monthly pipe band and ceilidhs   Open 11.30–1am Mon–Sat; 12.30–midnight Sun; closed 25 Dec, 1 Jan   Bedrooms tel Drymen (0360) 60357; £17.50B/£28.50B

DUMFRIES (Dumfries and Galloway)   NX9776 Map 9

Globe

High Street; up a narrow entry at S end of street, between Timpson Shoes and J Kerr Little (butcher), opposite Marks & Spencer

Down a flagstoned passage between high buildings, this old stone house hasn't changed much since it was one of Burns' favourite haunts. There's now a little museum devoted to him in the room that he used most often, and on the wall of the old-fashioned dark-panelled Snug Bar there's a facsimile of a letter (now in the J Pierpoint Morgan Library in New York): 'the Globe Tavern here... for these many years has been my Howff' (a Scots word meaning a regular haunt). McEwans 80/-

and Tennents 80/- from handpump and electric pump, very reasonably priced. A big plain public bar at the back has dominoes, a fruit machine, trivia and piped music. Good value simple bar food includes home-made soup or filled rolls (50p), quiche and salads, a three-course lunch at £2.75, and apple pie (50p). Upstairs, one bedroom has two window panes with verses scratched by diamond in Burns' handwriting (though not the touching verse he wrote for Anna Park, the barmaid here, who had his child). *(Recommended by C D T Spooner; more reports please)*

Free house   Licensee Mrs Maureen McKerrow   Real ale   Lunchtime meals and snacks (not Sun)   Restaurant tel Dumfries (0387) 52335   Children in eating area of bar   Nearby daytime parking difficult; car park 5 mins away   Open 11–11 Mon–Sat all year; closed 25 Dec, 2 Jan

EDINBURGH (Lothian)   NT2574   Map 11

The two main areas for finding good pubs here, both main entries and Lucky Dips, are around Rose Street (just behind Princes Street in the New Town) and along or just off the top part of the Royal Mile in the Old Town. In both areas parking can be difficult at lunchtime, but is not such a problem in the evening

Abbotsford

Rose Street; E end, beside South St David Street

There's a gently formal atmosphere and a remarkable mixture of customers in this long-standing Edinburgh institution. Dark-uniformed waitresses serve behind the heavily panelled Victorian island bar counter, there are leather-cushioned seats by the long deeply polished old tables and a handsome ceiling (a long way up – the elegantly panelled walls are tall). Good, reasonably priced food includes soup (50p), salads (from £2.20), grilled liver and bacon or haggis and neeps (£2.40), curried chicken or Lancashire hot-pot (£2.65), grilled gammon with pineapple (£2.70), scampi (£2.90), mixed grill (£3.95) and puddings such as rhubarb crumble (75p). Greenmantle and Tennents 80/- on air-pressure tall founts; fruit machine, tucked well away. Beware of the lunchtime crowds. *(Recommended by I R Hewitt, Mr and Mrs M D Jones, John Roué, TBB, Brian Marsden, Scott W Stucky)*

Free house   Licensee C J Grant   Real ale   Lunchtime meals and snacks (not Sun)   Restaurant tel 031-225 5276   Children in restaurant   Open 11–2.30, 5–11 all year; closed Sun

Athletic Arms

Angle Park Terrace; on corner of Kilmarnock Road (A71)

Quite unpretentious and a very busy pub known locally as 'The Diggers' because it was frequented by the gravediggers from the nearby graveyard. A team of red-jacketed barmen work hard at the gleaming row of air-pressure tall founts to keep the throng of mainly young and very thirsty customers supplied with McEwans 80/- in tip-top condition; good bar food. Opening off the central island servery there are some cubicles partitioned in glossy grey wood, and a side room is crowded with enthusiastic dominoes players. *(Recommended by J C Gould, AMcK, John Nice)*

Scottish & Newcastle   Real ale   Open 11–2.30, 5–11 all year

Bannermans Bar

212 Cowgate

Burrowing deep under some of the Old Town's tallest buildings, this warren of little rooms seems like one of its oldest corners: massive bare stone walls, flagstones, musty brick barrel-vaulted ceilings and old settles, pews and settees around barrels, red-painted tables and a long mahogany table. The front part has wood panelling and pillars, and rooms leading off have theatrical posters and handbills. A remarkably wide range of customers enjoy the well kept Arrols 70/- and 80/-, Caledonian 70/- and 80/- and Ind Coope Burton on handpump. There's an interesting choice of reasonably priced salads at lunchtime, and filled rolls in the evening (when it can get quite busy). The back area, open when busy, is no-smoking. *(Recommended by Michael Craig, Brian Marsden)*

Tennents (Ind Coope)   Real ale   Meals (lunchtime, not Sun) and snacks   Open 11–2.30, 5.30–11 all year

Bennets Bar

8 Leven Street; leaving centre southwards, follow Biggar, A702 signpost

An elaborate Victorian set-piece with arched and mahogany-pillared mirrors surrounded by tilework cherubs, Florentine-looking damsels and Roman warriors, red leather seats curving handsomely around the marble tables, and old brewery mirrors. The fancy dark maroon ceiling is supported by high elegantly moulded beams, and there are art nouveau stained-glass windows; the people here are often fun to watch, too, especially in the evening. The long bar counter serves the pub's own blend of whisky from the barrel as well as well kept McEwans 70/- and 80/- under air pressure. Bar food includes soup (60p), mince pie (£1.45), tuna and sweetcorn crumble or chilli con carne (£2.20), beef casserole, lamb and mushroom pie or fried fillet of haddock (£2.30), and puddings such as rhubarb tart (70p). *(Recommended by M C Howells)*

Free house   Licensee Peter Davidson   Real ale   Meals (lunchtime, not Sun) and snacks Open 11–11 Mon–Weds; 11–midnight Thurs–Fri; 11–11.45 Sat

Cafe Royal Circle Bar

West Register Street

The most striking feature in this sedate Victorian bar – originally a showroom for gas and plumbing fittings – was meant to show the craftsmanship of a leading sanitaryware manufacturer. This is a series of highly detailed Doulton tilework portraits of Watt, Faraday, Stephenson, Caxton, Benjamin Franklin and Robert Peel (in his day famous as the introducer of calico printing). The big island bar counter with hand-carved walnut gantry (a replica of the Victorian original) serves well kept McEwans 70/- and 80/-, Youngers No 3 and IPA from air-pressure tall founts; a good choice of whiskies. Simple bar food includes soup, filled rolls or pies (55p) and chilli con carne (£1.65); fruit machine and trivia machine. *(Recommended by Dewi and Linda Jones, AMcK, Dr Stewart Rae, Brian Marsden, R A Cavanagh)*

Free house   Real ale   Snacks (not Sun)   Restaurant tel 031-556 1884   Open 11–11 Mon–Thurs; 11–12 Fri–Sat; 7–12 Sun; all year

Claret Jug ⊗ 🛏

Basement of Howard Hotel, 32–36 Great King Street

L-shaped bar with russet velvet curtains, deep red, softly sprung leather Chester-fields and library chairs, wood-effect tables on the muted red patterned carpet, and prints of still lifes on the red-outlined panels of its walls – like the ceiling, very dark brown. A smaller side room is similar. A good choice of well kept real ales on electric pump includes Caledonian 80/-, Greenmantle, McEwans 80/- and Theakstons Best. The wide range of lunchtime bar food includes home-made soup (95p), home-made chicken liver pâté (£1.95), avocado pear with grapefruit segments and raspberry vinaigrette (£2.85), omelette of the day (£3.35), home-breaded haddock or roast of the day (£3.50), chicken pie with a creamy leek sauce (£3.75) and specials of the day (from £1.75); on Saturday they only do a cold buffet, and on Sunday only roast beef or fish and chips; service is efficient and

Food details, prices, timing, etc. refer to bar food – not to a separate restaurant if there is one.

friendly. The atmosphere at lunchtime is buoyantly clubby, though in the evenings it's peaceful and gently lit. *(Recommended by Scott W Stucky, Brian Marsden)*

Free house   Licensee Arthur Neil   Real ale   Lunchtime meals (not Sat or Sun) and snacks   Restaurant (not Sun lunchtime)   Children in eating area of bar   Open 10.30–2.30, 5–11 (midnight Fri, 11.45 Sat); 12.30–11 Sun; closed 25 and 26 Dec, 1 and 2 Jan   Bedrooms tel 031-557 3500; £45B/£65B

Guildford Arms

West Register Street

The chief glory of the main bar here – one reader was relieved to find that after a long absence and despite refurbishment, nothing had changed – is the remarkable Victorian ceiling: crusty plasterwork extending up from the walls, carefully painted in many colours. Other well preserved features include lots of mahogany, scrolly gilt wallpaper, big original advertising mirrors (and a lovely old mirror decorated with two tigers on the stairs down to the main bar), and heavy swagged velvet curtains for the arched windows. A cosy little gallery bar (closed on occasion) overlooks the main one, and under this is a cavern of little arched alcoves. But this is no museum-piece: the atmosphere is lively and welcoming, with the feeling that plenty is going on. Good basic pub food includes soup (40p), mince pie (£1.30), sausage, bacon, black pudding, egg and tomato (£1.70), and scampi (£2.30). Well kept Lorimers 80/- on handpump, and Lorimers 70/-, McEwans 80/- and Youngers No 3 on air-pressure tall founts; good service; lively piped music. *(Recommended by Dewi and Linda Jones, Ian Phillips, Michael Craig, Brian Marsden)*

Free house   Real ale   Meals (lunchtime, not Sun) and snacks (lunchtime)   Open 11–11 all year

Jolly Judge

James Court; by 495 Lawnmarket

In a courtyard just off the Royal Mile, this cosy tavern is part of one of the Old Town's original buildings. There are fruits and flowers painted on the low beam and board ceiling that are typical of sixteenth-century Scottish houses (a collection of foreign banknotes pinned to a beam near the bar has started), and a 1787 engraving commemorates Burns' triumphant stay in nearby Lady Stair's Close that January. The atmosphere is relaxed and cosy, with captain's chairs around the cast-iron-framed tables on the carpet, and quickly served small pies (60p–70p), sandwiches, pâtés, pizzas (£1.30), Scotch egg, ham or quiche salad and lasagne, cannelloni or enchiladas (all around £2.20); Ind Coope Burton on handpump; space game. *(Recommended by D H and M C Watkinson, Michael Craig, Brian Marsden)*

Free house   Licensee Mr De Vries   Real ale   Lunchtime snacks (not Sun)   Children in eating area of bar   Open 11–11 (11.45 Sat) all year

Jules

Waterloo Place (top end)

In a rather grand Georgian stone building, this airy, stylish bar has big orangery windows (with dusky pink swagged velvet curtains), masses of artificial plants, and a high oval-ended ceiling. It's broken up into various areas and levels by round or curved elbow-height rests for drinks and plates, stylish upturned deco lamps, theatrical lighting gantries and lots of maroon-stained woodwork. There are patchwork-pattern plush stools, chairs, settees and easy chairs, with carpet spreading throughout. Bar food includes filled rolls (50p), home-made soup (85p), ploughman's or home-made nut roast (£2.30), haggis and neeps (£2.40), salads with pies and cold meats (from £2.40) and pork in cream, apples and cider (£2.45);

If we know a pub has an outdoor play area for children, we mention it.

coffee is served all day; McEwans 80/- on air-pressure tall fount, fruit machine in lobby, piped pop music. *(Recommended by Quentin Williamson)*

Free house   Real ale   Meals and snacks (noon–7, not Sun)   Open 11–12 all year

Kay's Bar

39 Jamaica Street West; off India Street

A comfortable reproduction of a Victorian tavern, this cosy place has gas-type lamps, casks, vats and old wine and spirits merchants' notices, red plush wall banquettes and stools around cast-iron tables, and red pillars supporting a red ceiling. A quiet panelled back room leads off, with a narrow plank-panelled pitched ceiling. Simple bar food includes filled rolls (from 45p); well kept Belhaven 80/-, McEwans 70/- and 80/- and Youngers No 3 on handpump; dominoes and fruit machine. *(More reports please)*

Free house   Licensee Douglas Green   Real ale   Snacks (not Sun)   Children in small back room lunchtime only   Open 11–midnight all year; closed Sun

Peacock

Newhaven; Lindsay Road

It's not so long since this two-hundred-year-old place was a down-to-earth fishermen's pub, and interesting photographs on the wall give some idea of what Newhaven used to be like before the new development (named after the pub) and other modern changes set in here. The back room is well kept and cheerfully decorated with trellises and plants to seem like a conservatory (it leads out to a garden), and the main lounge is plushly comfortable, with lots of ply panelling and cosy seats. Bar food includes home-made soup or toasties (60p), quite a lot of fish such as haddock or lemon sole (£2.95) and a good value carvery (three courses £7.95). (Best to book for evening food – dishes are more expensive then – as it gets very crowded). Well kept McEwans 80/- under air pressure. *(Recommended by I R Hewitt, Dr Stewart Rae)*

Free house   Licensee Peter Carnie   Real ale   Meals and snacks   Children welcome Restaurant tel 031-552 5522   Open 11–11 all year

Sheep Heid

Duddingston; Causeway

The main room in this old-fashioned ex-coaching-inn has a warm welcome, a relaxing atmosphere and a good mix of people. Seats are built against the walls below Highland prints, there's some reproduction panelling, a fine rounded bar counter, turn-of-the-century Edinburgh photographs and a Turkey carpet; in a side room tables are given some privacy by elegant partly glazed screens dividing them. Bar food includes soup, soused herring salad, mince pie, ploughman's and sirloin steak. Tennents 80/- on handpump; dominoes, a fruit machine, TV and piped music. The garden behind is a pretty place, with hanging baskets and clematis on the sheltering stone walls of the house, a goldfish pond and fountain and a skittle alley – as far as we know, this is the only pub in Scotland that plays alley skittles; barbecues in fine weather – you can cook your own if you feel inclined. The little village is lovely, and getting to the pub is a pleasant expedition, past Holyrood-house, Arthur's Seat and the little nature reserve around Duddingston Loch. *(Recommended by R P Taylor, John Renwick, Rob Weeks, Gill Austin)*

Tennents (Bass)   Real ale   Snacks and meals (lunchtime, evenings Thurs–Sat)   Children welcome away from bar, lunchtime   Restaurant tel 031-661 1020   Open 11–11 all year

---

All main entries have been inspected anonymously by the Editor or Assistant Editor. We accept no payment for inclusion, no advertising, and no sponsorship from the drinks industry – or from anyone else.

ELIE (Fife)   NO4900 Map 11
Ship
Harbour

There are rumours that some locals want to modernise this small, friendly pub with it's lively nautical atmosphere. There are winged high-backed button-back leather seats against the partly panelled walls, beams in an ochre ceiling, and a cosy, carpeted back room; open fires in winter. Bar snacks include soup or filled rolls (45p). Well kept Belhaven 80/- on handpump; darts, dominoes, cribbage. Across the harbour lane, sturdy seats and timber-baulk benches have an attractive view over the low sea wall. There's the pier and the old stone fish granary on the left, the little town on the right, and a grassy headland opposite. At low tide the bay is mostly sand, with oystercatchers and gulls shrilling over the water's edge. *(Recommended by JAH, HCH, T and A D Kucharski, TBB)*

Free house   Licensee Robin Hendry   Real ale   Lunchtime snacks   Children in back room   Open 11–midnight

FINDHORN (Grampian)   NJ0464 Map 11
Crown & Anchor 🛏
Coming into Findhorn, keep left at signpost off to beach and car park

This attractively sited old stone inn, very close to the water where Highlanders would have stayed before taking ship for Edinburgh or even London, has a friendly and lively atmosphere. Also, several well kept beers – Brakspears PA, Courage Directors and a range of English guest beers that might include Adnams, Badger, Fullers London Pride and ESB, Marstons Pedigree, Ruddles, Sam Smiths OBB, Theakstons Old Peculier, Timothy Taylors Landlord and Best, and Wadworths 6X; they also have draught ciders (rare around here), and a good choice of spirits, including around a hundred malt whiskies. The lively public bar has old photographs of the area on the walls, and games (darts, dominoes, cribbage, fruit machine, trivia and juke box) and an unusually big arched fireplace; the comfortable lounge bar is decorated with lots of pictures. Bar food includes sandwiches, soup (60p), burger (90p), and haddock (£2.40), with specials such as stovies or cottage pie (£1.50), chilli con carne (£2.15), chicken curry (£2.50) and steak and kidney pie (£2.80). The water still plays a big part in life at the inn, and people staying have the use of its boats; sandy beaches are only a few moments' stroll away. *(Recommended by A Darroch Harkness, Vera Kelman, Leith Stuart, Brian and Anna Marsden)*

Free house   Licensees Roy and Peta Liddle   Real ale   Meals and snacks   Children in eating area of bar until 9   Folk, '60s and jazz Sun evening   Open 11–11 all year; closes 11.45 Fri and Sat; opens noon Sun   Bedrooms tel Findhorn (0309) 30243; £18.50B/£25B

GIFFORD (Lothian)   NT5368 Map 11
Tweeddale Arms ⊗ 🛏
High Street

In a quiet village just below the wooded slopes of the Border foothills, this civilised old inn faces the avenue to Yester House and a lovely long green with tall lime trees. The comfortable lounge has a relaxed atmosphere, modern tapestried settles and stools on its muted red patterned carpet, and brass lamps and big Impressionist prints on the apricot-coloured walls (there are matching curtains to divide the seats). A very wide choice of bar food that changes daily includes soup (70p), pear and cheese salad (£1.95), open sandwiches (from £2.50), omelettes (£2.80), lamb Madras (£2.95), steak and kidney pie, roast spring chicken and bacon or deep-fried haddock (£3), cold gammon salad (£3.50), scampi (£3.75), cold poached Tay salmon (£4) and home-made puddings like tropical fruit torte (from £1.25). The gracious dining-room has unusual antique wallpaper. McEwans 80/- on air-pressure tall founts; darts, pool, dominoes, cribbage, fruit machine, juke box and piped music. The tranquil hotel lounge is a lovely place to sit in over a long drink; there are antique tables and paintings, chinoiserie chairs and chintzy easy chairs, an oriental rug on one wall, a splendid corner sofa and magazines on a table. The B6355 southwards from here over the Lammermuirs, and its right fork through Longformacus, are both fine empty moors roads. *(Recommened by Eleanor Chandler, Dr R H M Stewart)*

Free house Licensee Chris Crook Meals and snacks (not Sat evening) Children welcome Restaurant Open 11–11 all year Bedrooms tel Gifford (062 081) 240; £35B/£48B

GLASGOW (Strathclyde)   NS5865 Map 11

Babbity Bowster ⊗

16–18 Blackfriars Street

On the pale grey walls of this unusual pub/hotel in a Robert Adam town house is a big ceramic of a kilted dancer and piper illustrating the folk song which gives the place its name – *Bab at the Bowster*; also, well lit photographs and big pen-and-wash drawings of Glasgow and its people and musicians. There are pierced-work stools and wall seats around dark grey tables on the stripped boards, an open fire and fine tall windows; piped Scottish music (and occasional good value musical dinners with folk like Dougie McLean). The atmosphere – and customers – have a stylish yet relaxed quality. Well kept Maclays 70/- on air-pressure tall fount, a remarkably sound collection of wines, and even good tea and coffee. Enterprising food, usefully available from 8am to 9pm, starts with good breakfasts, then, after 11am, includes soup (95p), filled baked potatoes (from £1.85), fresh mussels in wine or beer (£1.85), salads or vegetarian casseroles (from £2.95) and several dishes of the day such as haggis, neeps and tatties (£2.65), spicy chicken stovies (£3.25), and kolozsvari, a Hungarian dish of sausage with cabbage in sour cream and paprika (£3.25). Puddings range from hot cloutie dumpling (45p) to Bavarian apple strudel with cream (£1.65). A small terrace has tables under cocktail parasols – this is a quiet pedestrian-only street. *(Recommended by Ian Baillie)*

Free house Licensee Fraser Laurie Real ale Meals and snacks Restaurant (closed Sun) Children in restaurant Open 11–11 (and for breakfast) Bedrooms tel 041-552 5055; £22.50S/£40S

Bon Accord ⊗

153 North Street

The remarkably wide range of well kept real ales in this stylishly neat and simply refurbished place includes Belhaven 80/-, Greenmantle, Ind Coope Burton, Marstons Pedigree, Theakstons XB and Old Peculier, all on handpump, and Caledonian 70/- and 80/-, McEwans 70/- and Maclays 70/- and 80/- on air-pressure tall founts, and guest beers as well (on handpump) – there are eighteen founts in all. There are quite a few malt whiskies, too. A wide choice of bar food includes filled rolls (from 50p), home-made soup (95p), ploughman's, burgers (from £1.10), lasagne, seafood platter or beef stew in Belgian beer (£2.95) and mixed grill (£3.25). The floor is partly carpeted, partly new quarry tiles, the red hessian walls are decorated with beer-trays and there are padded leatherette seats and little rounded-back chairs; one side has quiet booth seating, with dominoes and cribbage, and there is a fruit machine and trivia game machine in a back lobby (a TV in the bar

---

Most pubs in this book sell wine by the glass. We mention wines only if they are a cut above the – generally low – average. Please let us know of any good pubs for wine.

may be on for sport). It can get very busy on weekend evenings, when the piano plays. *(Recommended by Alastair Campbell, Ian Baillie, John Nice)*

Free house   Licensee Duncan Campbell   Real ale   Children in restaurant   Restaurant tel 041-248 4427   Occasional live music   Daytime parking restricted   Open 11–midnight all year

Horseshoe

17–19 Drury Street

The horseshoe motif in this Victorian monument spreads from the horseshoe-shaped promontories of the enormous bar itself, through a horseshoe wall clock, to horseshoe-shaped fireplaces (most blocked by mirrors now); there's a mosaic tiled floor, a great deal of glistening mahogany and darkly varnished panelled dado, pictorial tile inserts of decorous ladies, lots of old photographs of Glasgow and its people, antique magazine colour plates, curly brass and glass wall lamps, and a lustrous pink and maroon ceiling. The bar counter, which still has pillared snob-screens, has old-fashioned brass water taps (and a house whisky blend); Tennents 80/- on handpump; fruit machine, TV. The upstairs bar is less special, though popular with young people. The three-course lunch, with a wide choice of main dishes, is a steal at £1.50 (not Sunday); evening hot dishes, served from 5pm, are £1.10. *(Recommended by Ian Baillie, BB)*

Tennents (Bass)   Real ale   Meals (not Sun lunch) and snacks   Live music every evening Open 11–midnight all year

Pot Still

154 Hope Street

The elegantly pillared and moulded bar gantry of this well run split-level pub is crammed with several hundred malt whiskies – helpfully documented – including several different versions of the great single malts in different ages and strengths, far more vatted malts than we knew of (these are blends, but malts only – no grain whisky), and a changing attractively priced malt-of-the-month. They sell by the bottle as well as the glass. It's attractively decorated, with comfortably upholstered banquettes in bays around heavy cast-iron-framed tables, photographs of old Glasgow on red baize walls, and slender pillars supporting the ornately coffered high dark maroon ceiling – with its two raj fans. Bar food includes home-made soup (60p), sandwiches (tuna or pâté with salad on toast £1.10), burgers (from £1.65), big ploughman's (£2.20), cold meat salads or lasagne (£2.35), lamb leg cutlet (£2.60) and a big grilled breakfast (£3.30). Maclays 70/- and 80/- and Tennents 80/- on air-pressure tall founts. No jeans allowed, and the white-shirted barmen wear black bow ties. *(Recommended by Mr and Mrs J H Adam, Ian Baillie)*

Free house   Real ale   Meals and snacks (not Sat evening, Sun)   Open 11–11 all year

GLENDEVON (Tayside)   NN9904 Map 11

Tormaukin ⊗ ⇔

A823

As we went to press, this welcoming and neatly kept inn was about to undergo some changes: the derelict coach-house was to be pulled down and four new bedrooms built, two rooms for eating were to be added off the back bar, the kitchen size doubled, and new lavatories added. The softly lit bar won't change, with plush seats against stripped stone and partly panelled walls, Ind Coope Burton on handpump, a good choice of wines (by the bottle or half-bottle) and malt whiskies, and gentle piped music. Very good bar good includes home-made soup (95p), rollmop herring in sherry (£1.50), home-made pâté (£1.75), home-made burger (£2.95), hand-made venison sausages with Cumberland sauce (£3.15), salads (from £3.15, salmon when available £6.50), grilled trout (£3.35), grilled bacon steak with apple sauce (£3.50), scampi (£3.85), steaks (from £4.50), daily specials or home-made pies, and puddings (from £1.35); they serve soup, cold meat and other salads and coffee throughout the day. This is perhaps the most attractive north–south route through this part of Scotland, and there are said to be ninety golf courses within an hour's drive. *(Recommended by Syd and Wyn Donald, J N Fiell, Ruby Porter)*

Free house   Licensee Marianne Worthy   Real ale   Meals   Children welcome until 7 Restaurant   Open 11–11 all year; closed 25 Dec, 1 Jan   Bedrooms tel Muckhart (025 981) 252; £29B/£42B

HOWGATE (Lothian)   NT2458   Map 11
Old Howgate Inn ⊗

Attractively presented and very tasty, the wide range of small Danish-style open sandwiches (they call them finger pieces) are the special thing in this civilised and interesting food pub. They include chicken liver pâté with mixed pickle (90p small, £1.80 large), Danish herring on rye bread or chicken with curry mayonnaise (£1.40 small, £2.80 large), prawn and lemon mayonnaise or a selection of each (£1.50 small, £3 large), gravadlax with dill mustard dressing (£1.85 small, £3.70 large) and lobster with lemon mayonnaise and asparagus (in season, £2.50 small, £5 large); they also do rib-eye steak sandwich (£3.60) and a pasta dish. The bar is airy and pretty, white panelled, with a stone fireplace, tiled floor, red plush window seats and nests of oak stools; Belhaven 80/-, McEwans 80/- and Theakstons Best on handpump as well as a weekly guest beer, and frozen akvavit. A couple of comfortable sitting-rooms have easy chairs and orange-red hessian walls. There are some slat wood tables on a small back lawn, edged with potentilla and herbaceous borders. The owners used also to own the Horseshoe at Eddleston (a popular main entry in previous editions), which they have recently sold to Scottish & Newcastle; the Horseshoe's former manager has now moved in here. *(Recommended by David and Ruth Hollands, Malcolm Ramsay)*

Free house   Licensees C A and M McIntosh Reid   Real ale   Snacks   Restaurant tel Penicuik (0968) 74244   Children in restaurant   Open 11–2.30, 5–11; closed 25 Dec, 1 Jan

INVERARAY (Strathclyde)   NN0908   Map 11
George

Main Street East

Comfortably modernised, this is in a central part of the little Georgian town that's stretched along the shores of Loch Fyne in front of Inveraray Castle. The quietly friendly cocktail bar has exposed joists, bared stone walls, old tiles and flagstones, modern winged settles as well as cushioned stone slabs along the walls, nicely grained wooden-topped cast-iron tables, lots of curling club and ships' badges, and a cosy log fire in winter. Evening bar food includes home-made soup (60p), quiche, locally smoked mackerel or lasagne (£2.60), gammon (£3.50), Scotch scampi (£3.60), poached salmon (£3.75), and entrecôte steak (£6.90) – in fact they serve some food from midday to 9pm; Tennents 80/- on handpump and a good choice of whiskies; helpful and efficient service from neatly aproned staff; darts, pool, dominoes, cribbage, fruit machine and juke box. The inn is well placed for the great Argyll woodland gardens – the rhododendrons are at their best in May and early June – and is near the start of *Good Walks Guide* Walk 180. *(Recommended by Mr and Mrs J H Adam, Ray Wainwright, John Roué)*

Free house   Licensee Donald Clark   Real ale   Meals and snacks   Restaurant (not Sun lunch)   Children welcome   Open 11–midnight (1am Fri and Sat)   Bedrooms tel Inveraray (0499) 2111; £12.50/£25(£33B)

INVERARNAN (Central)   NN3118 Map 11

Inverarnan Inn

A82 N of Loch Lomond

This early eighteenth-century house has the feeling of a small baronial hall: log fires burn in big fireplaces at each end of the long friendly room, there are stripped stone or butter-coloured plaster walls, small windows, red candles in Drambuie bottles if not candlesticks, and cupboards of pewter and china. The barman still wears the kilt, and there's piped Scottish traditional music as well as green tartan cushions and deerskins on the black winged settles, a stuffed golden eagle on the bar counter, a horsecollar and a gun among the Highland paintings on the walls, and bagpipes. Sandwiches, stags' broth (65p), pâté (£1.10), burger £1.95, cheese or ham salad (£2), herring with oatmeal (£2.50), gammon and pineapple (£3), grilled trout (£4.25) and fresh salmon steak (£5.50). McEwans 80/- and a range of good malts; peanuts 25p a handful. Lots of sporting trophies, horns and so forth hang on the high walls of the central hall where there's a full suit of armour. Outside, in a field beside the house (also on a small back terrace), there are tables and cocktail parasols; a stream runs behind. Worth knowing about, too, as a simple but decent place to stay at. *(Recommended by Nick Dowson, Alison Hayward, Roy Butler, Rob and Gill Weeks, Dr R Conrad, E J Alcock)*

Free house   Licensee Duncan McGregor   Meals and snacks   Restaurant   Children in restaurant   Impromptu live music   Open 11–11 all year   Bedrooms tel Inveruglas (030 14) 234; £13.50/£27

ISLE OF WHITHORN (Dumfries and Galloway)   NX4736 Map 9

Steam Packet 🛏

This comfortably modernised and friendly inn – in a lovely spot on the edge of a fine natural harbour – has picture windows looking out on the yachts and inshore fishing-boats. The low-ceilinged bar has two rooms: on the right, plush button-back banquettes, carpet and boat pictures; on the left, green leatherette stools around cast-iron-framed tables on big stone tiles, and an open fire in the bare stone wall. Good value bar food includes home-made soup (60p), filled rolls (from 65p), burger (£1.75), fried haddock (£2), salads (from £2.50), scampi (£2.75), grilled sole (£4.50) and a daily special such as steak pie or quiche (£2); there are evening extras such as chicken Kiev (£4.50) and steaks (from £5). It may be served in the lower beamed dining-room, which has a big model steam packet boat on the white walls, excellent colour wildlife photographs, rugs on its wooden floor, and a solid-fuel stove; pool and background music. The garden has new white tables and chairs. There are lots of boat trips (usually one and a half to four hours) from the harbour, and in the rocky grass by the harbour mouth are the remains of St Ninian's Kirk. *(Recommended by T Nott, Tony Pounder, J A V Rose, R M Williamson)*

Free house   Licensee John Scoular   Meals and snacks   Upstairs restaurant   Children in eating area of bar   Folk music alternate Weds evenings   Open 11–11 in summer; 12–11 Sun; 11–2.30, 5–11 weekdays in winter   Bedrooms tel Whithorn (098 85) 334; £15B/£30B

ISLE ORNSAY (Isle of Skye)   NG6912 Map 11

Hotel Eilean Iarmain ★ ⊗ 🛏

Signposted off A851 Broadford–Armadale

We've been getting lots of warm praise from the majority of readers for the welcome of the friendly staff and relaxed atmosphere in the big and cheerfully busy bar. There's a swooping stable-stall-like wooden divider that gives the bar a two-room feel; good tongue-and-groove panelling on the walls and ceiling, leatherette wall seats, brass lamps and a brass-mounted ceiling-fan, and a huge mirror over the open fire. The staff and many of the customers speak Gaelic, and even the drinks price list and menus are in Gaelic – with translations. Bar food includes sandwiches, home-made soup (60p), pâté (90p), haddock (£2.50), salmon steaks (£6.50), a hot daily special (£2), good local fish and interesting mushroom roast. Dinners are served in the pretty dining-room, which has a lovely sea view past the little island of Ornsay itself and the lighthouse on Sionnach (you can walk over the sands at low tide). Well kept McEwans 80/- on electric pump, local brands of blended and vatted malt whisky (including their own blended whisky called Te Bheag and a twelve-year vatted malt called Poit Dhubh), and a good wine list; darts, pool, dominoes and piped music. Some of the simple bedrooms are in a cottage opposite. This is an attractive part of Skye – less austere than the central mountains – where you will probably see red deer, and maybe otters and seals. *(Recommended by Vera Kelman, MJL, Mrs H Church, Colin Oliphant, AHNR, Rob and Gill Weeks)*

Free house   Licensee Sir Iain Noble   Real ale   Meals and snacks   Children welcome   Local folk or Scottish music Fri and Sat   Restaurant (not Sun lunch)   Open 11–11 in summer; 11–2.30, 5–11 in winter   Bedrooms tel Isle of Skye (047 13) 332; £20(£23B)/£40(£46B)

KILCHRENAN (Strathclyde)   NS5285   Map 11

Taychreggan ⊗ ⇌

B845 7 miles S of Taynuilt

The bar in this civilised lochside hotel has an unusually airy feel for Scotland, with arched French windows opening on to a cobbled inner courtyard which has slatted white seats and tables among bright hanging baskets, standard roses, and wistaria and clematis climbing the whitewashed walls. Inside, there are turquoise cloth easy chairs and banquettes around low glass-topped tables. The room is decorated with good locally made model boats, local photographs, stuffed birds, salmon flies and rods, and lots of stuffed locally caught fish – some of them real monsters. Talk is likely to be about fish, too (if not golf); the hotel has fishing, and hires boats on the loch (£8 a day – £16 with an outboard). Attractively served lunchtime bar food includes soup (£1), pâté or egg mayonnaise (£2), ploughman's (£2.25), delicious lightly smoked salmon sandwiches, quiche or hamburgers (£2.50), and lots of salads (from £3, smoked salmon or langoustine £4.50). Neatly dressed waiters; unobtrusive piped music. Some bedrooms overlook the loch. It's a beautiful spot, and well kept gardens run down to the water. *(Recommended by Heather Sharland, Clare Reynolds)*

Free house   Licensee John Taylor   Meals and snacks   Restaurant   Open 11–2.30, 5–11; closed mid-Oct–Easter   Bedrooms tel Kilchrenan (086 63) 211; £52B/£104B inc dinner

KILLEARN (Central)   NS5285   Map 11

Old Mill

A875

Quietly friendly old village pub with rustic cushioned built-in settles and wheel-back chairs around the dark tables on a brown patterned carpet, beams in the swirly white ceiling, and an open fire in the stone fireplace. A side room has a small bar servery, and there's a garden-room also served by this bar with a wood-burning stove in its stone fireplace. Bar food includes rolls (from 55p), home-made soup (80p), burgers or pizza (£1.65), quiche (£1.90), haddock (£2.45), scampi (£3.20), gammon with pineapple or half a chicken (£3.55); piped pop music; fruit machine in the lobby, and dominoes. There are fine views of the Campsie Fells from behind the pub – if it's not too cloudy. *(Recommended by T and A D Kucharski)*

Free house   Meals and snacks   Children in eating area and garden-room   Open 11–11; 11–2.30, 4.30–11 in winter

KILMARTIN (Strathclyde)   NR8398 Map 11
Kilmartin Hotel
A816 Lochgilphead–Oban

The two snug and softly lit rooms of this friendly and unassuming white-painted village inn have spindle-back armchairs, a settee and a variety of settles including some attractive carved ones; some are built into a stripped stone wall snugged under the lower part of the staircase. They are decorated with old Scottish landscape, field sport and genre pictures, and a fine pre-war Buchanan whisky advertisement of polo-players. Dog pictures, cartoons and show rosettes hint at the licensee's dog-breeding interests (she judges at Crufts, and still has a couple of deerhounds and a contrasting wire-haired dachshund). Bar food, served generously, includes sandwiches (from 65p), home-made soup (70p), breaded beef cutlet (£1.80), home-cooked gammon salad (£3.10), sole (£3.25) and minute steak (£3.45); sensibly placed darts, dominoes, maybe piped music. The inn is near the start of *Good Walks Guide* Walk 179. *(Recommended by Tim Locke; more reports please)*

Free house   Meals and snacks   Accordion and fiddle Fri evening   Evening candlelit restaurant   Children in eating area   Open 11–2.30, 5–12 all year   Bedrooms tel Kilmartin (054 65) 244; £14/£28(£32B), inc service charge

KILMELFORD (Strathclyde)   NM8412 Map 11
Cuilfail
A816 S of Oban

The pubby bar in this Virginia-creeper-covered stone-built hotel has little winged settles around sewing-machine treadle tables on the lino floor, stripped stone walls, even a stone bar counter with casks worked into it, foreign banknotes on the exposed joists, and a wood-burning stove (open in cold weather). An inner eating room has light wood furnishings, and the good choice of imaginative bar food includes soup (including a vegetarian one, 90p), sandwiches (£1.25), sweet-cured herring (£1.75), haddock (£2.85), mixed bean casserole (£2.95), home-made burger (£3.15), almond risotto with peanut sauce (£3.25) and steak and mushroom pie (£3.65), with good puddings (£1.10). Well kept Youngers No 3 on air-pressure tall fount (and served in jugs if you wish), and a good range of malt whiskies; darts, dominoes, cribbage and piped music. Across the road is a very pretty tree-sheltered garden, with picnic-table sets among pieris and rhododendrons (they serve afternoon tea here on request). Though dogs are welcome, the owners warn that Heidi their St Bernard is large and noisy – they also have a labrador. *(Recommended by Ray Wainwright, S J Robinson)*

Free house   Licensee James McFadyen   Real ale   Meals and snacks   Evening restaurant   Children welcome   Open 11–2.30 (may close earlier if not busy), 5–11 all year; closed Tues Nov–mid-Mar, closed last two weeks Jan, first week Feb   Bedrooms tel Kilmelford (085 22) 274; £15 (£18B)/£30 (£36B)

As we went to press the entry here
changed hands

LOCH TUMMEL (Tayside)   NN8460 Map 11

Loch Tummel Hotel

8019

The wooded mountains and Loch Tummel stretch away below this friendly, former coaching-inn. Its long bar has dark captain's chairs and small round tables, white-painted walls, a sturdy white beam supporting the black joists and creaky boards of the simple upstairs restaurant, and a big free-standing wood-burning stove; there's also an extractor fan. Bar food includes home-made soup (85p), ploughman's, steak pie (£3.60), steaks (£6.25) and trout (when available). McEwans 80/- on electric pump. A games-bar has pool, darts, dominoes, cribbage and a fruit machine. There are seats across the road looking down to the loch. (Recommended by S R Holman, Rob and Gill Weeks)

Scottish & Newcastle   Licensee John Saunders   Real ale   Meals and snacks Restaurant   Children in eating area of bar   Open 11–11(11.45 Fri and Sat); 12.30–11 Sun Bedrooms tel Tummel Bridge (088 24) 272; £17(£20B)/£34(£40B)

MELROSE (Borders)   NT5434 Map 9

Burts Hotel ⊗ 🛏

6091

If thou wouldst view fair Melrose aright,
Go visit it by the pale moonlight;
For the gay beams of the lightsome day
Gild, but to flout, the ruins grey.

Scott, in his 'Lay of the Last Minstrel', was talking about the abbey, and if you take his advice – it is lovely by moonlight – this well run, friendly inn would be an appropriate place to stay at. The comfortable L-shaped lounge bar has Windsor armchairs and cushioned wall seats on its Turkey carpet, and Scottish prints on the walls. A good range of waitress-served bar food includes soup (80p), two pâtés (£1.75), ploughman's (£2.50), double-decker prawn sandwich (£2.60), deep-fried breadcrumbed chicken (£3), scampi (£3.70), home-baked sugar ham and chicken breast salad (£3.80), sirloin steak (£6), and puddings like home-made apple pie (£1.20); also, specials such as corn fritters with cayenne sauce (£2), prawns, bacon and mushrooms in garlic butter (£2.40), sausage, kidney and black-eyed bean casserole (£3.90), venison burger or cold rare roast beef salad (£4). Belhaven 70/- and 80/- on air-pressure tall founts; snooker-room (residents only). The well tended garden has tables in summer. Melrose has perhaps the

---

We mention bottled beers and spirits only if there is something unusual about them – imported Belgian real ales, say, or dozens of malt whiskies; so do please let us know about them in your reports.

quietest and most villagey atmosphere of all the Scottish Border towns. *(Recommended by T Nott, Syd and Wyn Donald, John Spencely, F A Noble, Dr S G Donald)*

Free house   Licensee Graham Henderson   Real ale   Meals and snacks   Children welcome   Restaurant   Open 11–2.30, 5–11 all year   Bedrooms tel *Melrose (089 682) 2285; £26B/£40(£46B)*

MOFFAT (Dumfries and Galloway)   NT0905 Map 9

Black Bull ⊗

The bar across a small courtyard from the main building is more like an English pub than many in Scotland: red panelling covered with metal station plates and other railway memorabilia, built-in benches, and well kept McEwans 80/- and Youngers No 3 on air-pressure tall founts; a very good choice of malt whiskies. The softly lit cocktail bar is decidedly plusher and cosier, with plum-coloured walls, a pink ceiling and soft piped music. Lunchtime bar food includes soup (70p), pâté (£1.15), ploughman's (£2.20), salads (from £2.20) and good hot specials such as macaroni cheese or haggis (£2.40) and shepherd's or fish pie (£2.50); in the evening they have local trout (£3.30), gammon with pineapple (£3.55) and sirloin steak (£6.20); quick service. There's a side room with darts, dominoes, a fruit machine, space game, trivia and piped music. Burns scratched a witty verse about one of his girlfriends and her mother on a window here – but now the window, glass and all, is in a Moscow museum. *(Recommended by Mr and Mrs J H Adam, Jill Hadfield, Tony Gallagher, Neil and Angela Huxter, David Fisher, Heather Sharland, P J Bevan, Capt E P Gray, S V Bishop, Wayne Brindle, Rob and Gill Weeks, E J Alcock)*

Free house   Licensee Jim Hughes   Real ale   Meals and snacks (not Sun evenings in winter, not evenings Jan and Feb)   Children welcome until 9   Restaurant (not Sun evening)   Open 11–11 Sun–Weds, 11–midnight Thurs–Sat all year   Bedrooms tel *Moffat (0683) 20206; £16B/£28.50B*

MONIAIVE (Dumfries and Galloway)   NX7790 Map 9

George ⊗ 🛏

This seventeenth-century white stone Covenanters' inn has a delightful little flagstoned bar (with good antique Tam O'Shanter engravings on the butter-coloured timbered walls), a warm, friendly atmosphere and charming service. There are some small seats made from curious conical straight-sided kegs, high winged black settles upholstered with tartan carpet, open fires in winter, and dark butter-coloured ceiling-planks – it all adds up to something really rather special, worth quite a detour. A wide choice of good bar food includes tasty home-made soup (70p), good freshly cut sandwiches (from £1), home-made chicken liver pâté (£1.85), haggis (£2.25), haddock (£2.30), club sandwich or salads such as home-cooked tongue (£2.50), Solway salmon (£2.75), home-made steak and kidney pie (£3.25) and venison in red wine (£3.50). Darts, pool-table, dominoes, cribbage, fruit machine and juke box away in the public bar. The peaceful riverside village is surrounded by fine scenery. *(Recommended by Gethin Lewis, C D T Spooner, Tim Brierly)*

Free house   Licensees Mr and Mrs Price   Meals and snacks   Children welcome   Restaurant (Fri–Sun evenings; Sun lunch)   Open 11–11 (midnight Fri and Sat)   Bedrooms tel *Moniaive (084 82) 203; £13.50/£27*

MONYMUSK (Grampian)   NJ6815 Map 11

Grant Arms

Inn and village signposted from B993 SW of Kemnay

This handsome eighteenth-century stone inn has a log fire in the stub wall of the lounge bar, which divides it into two areas, some armchairs as well as other seats, a carpet of Grant hunting green and a high shelf of china above the dark panelling. Bar food includes soup (75p), fried lemon sole (£2.85), roast beef (£3.25), fresh crab (£3.75) and spicy crab claws (£3.95). The simpler public bar has darts, dominoes, cribbage, fruit machine, space game and piped music; Tennents 80/- on handpump. They have ten miles of trout and salmon fishing on the River Don. North of the village – spick and span in its estate colours of dark red woodwork and natural stone – the gently rolling wooded pastures soon give way to grander hills. *(Recommended by CMG, S V Bishop)*

Free house   Licensee Colin Hart   Real ale   Meals and snacks   Restaurant   Children welcome   Open 11–2.30, 5–11 (midnight Sat) all year   Bedrooms tel Monymusk (046 77) 226; £23(£29B)/£40(£42B)

MOUNTBENGER (Borders)   NT3125   Map 9
Gordon Arms
Junction of A708 and B709

The pub is a welcome sight from either of the two lonely moorland roads which cross here: both roads take you through attractive scenery, and the B-road in particular is very grand – indeed, it forms part of a splendid empty moorland route between the A74 and Edinburgh (from Lockerbie, B723/B709/B7062/A703/A6094). Good bar food includes home-made soup (80p), burgers (from £1.30), ploughman's or pâté (£1.75), a platter of cheese and meats (£1.95), salads (from £2.95), fresh Yarrow trout or home-made steak pie (£3.50) and grilled lamb cutlets (£3.75); very well kept Greenmantle on handpump (brewed in Broughton, near Peebles). A lounge bar serves high teas – a speciality here – and there's a games-room with darts, pool, dominoes, fruit machine and piped music. The cosy public bar has an interesting set of photographs of blackface rams from local hill farms, there's a fire in cold weather and a local 'shepherd song' is pinned on the wall; a hundred and fifty years ago another shepherd poet, James Hogg, the 'Ettrick Shepherd', recommended that this very inn should keep its licence, which Sir Walter Scott, in his capacity as a justice and who also knew the inn, subsequently granted. *(Recommended by Dave Butler, Lesley Storey)*

Free house   Licensees Mr and Mrs H M Mitchell   Real ale   Meals and snacks   Children in eating area and restaurant   Restaurant   Open 11–11 all year   Bedrooms tel Yarrow (0750) 82222; £13.50/£24

NEWBURGH (Grampian)   NJ9925   Map 11
Udny Arms ⊗ 🛏

A very far cry from your typical links-side small hotel, this attractively converted house has carefully chosen furniture in its lounge bar, including prettily cushioned stripped pine seats and wooden chairs around plain wooden tables on the grey carpet, and bird prints, salmon flies, and a pictorial map of the River Dee on the cream walls. Generous helpings of food in the new downstairs bar (open all day) includes green pea soup (75p), cold roast pork (£1.50), meat and potato pasties, sausage bake or lasagne (£1.75), and sticky toffee pudding (£1.25); in the lounge bar, lunchtime food includes sweet-cured herring (£1.95), ploughman's (£2.75), steak and game pie (£3.50), tagliatelle with mushrooms in lemon and thyme sauce (£2.95) and filled taco shells (£3.75). In the afternoon they serve tea and shortbread. Well kept Devanha XB on handpump, McEwans 80/-, and Youngers No 3 on air-pressure tall founts, house wines, a selection of bottled beers and espresso coffee; friendly, helpful service; dominoes, cribbage, piped music and pétanque. A sun lounge has green basket chairs around glass-topped wicker tables. On the sheltered back lawn of this well kept house there are lots of white tables, and from here a footbridge crosses the little Foveran Burn to the nine-hole golf links, the dunes and the sandy beach along the Ythan estuary. There are three good golf courses and Pitmedden Gardens nearby. *(Recommended by T and A D Kucharski, Chris France)*

Scottish & Newcastle   Licensee Alan Jappy   Real ale   Meals and snacks   Children welcome   Restaurant   Open 11–11.30 all year   Bedrooms tel Newburgh (Aberdeen) (035 86) 444; £32.34B/£44.48B

OBAN (Strathclyde)   NM8630   Map 11
Oban Inn
Stafford Street

The vibrant local atmosphere in this late eighteenth-century inn owes a lot to the fact that the owner is an ex-fishing skipper – harbour folk, fishermen and Navy divers rub shoulders with doctors and lawyers. The genuinely pubby bars have been carefully refurbished over the last few years; the downstairs beamed bar has small stools, pews and black winged modern settles on its uneven slate floor, blow-ups of old Oban postcards on its cream walls, and unusual brass-shaded wall lamps. A quieter and more decorous carpeted upstairs bar has some panelling, a coffered woodwork ceiling and button-back banquettes around cast-iron-framed tables; besides the real windows overlooking the harbour, it has little backlit arched false windows with heraldic roundels in seventeenth-century stained glass. Bar food, served all day (they are trying breakfasts from 7–11 in the summer months), includes soup (95p), fresh mussels (£1), home-made meat paste (£1.25), filled baked potatoes (£1.50), haggis and neeps, salads or steak and kidney pie (£2.95), and venison in red wine (£3.25); three-course children's menu (£1.95). Well kept McEwans 80/- and Youngers No 3 from tall founts, a large selection of whiskies, and hot toddies, served by bar staff in their own clan kilts; dominoes, piped pop music. *(Recommended by Roy Butler, Simon Holmes)*

Scottish & Newcastle   Licensee Michael Hewitt   Real ale   Meals (lunchtime) and snacks   Children in eating area if eating   Singer Sun evenings 9–midnight   Bedrooms under alteration as we went to press tel Oban (0631) 62484   Open 11–1am all year

nr PITLOCHRY (Tayside)   NN9458   Map 11
Killiecrankie Hotel ⊗ 🛏
Killiecrankie signposted from A9 N of Pitlochry

The bar in this comfortable and welcoming country hotel (which opens into a front sun-lounge extension) has light armchairs and dimpled copper tables, a red squirrel holding some nuts, lots of stuffed birds and good wildlife photographs. The very good food (available until 10pm – unusually late for the area) is strong on local cooking and at lunchtime includes soup (£1), sandwiches (from £1, rare Angus beef £1.50), home-made pâté (£1.35), sausages (£2.20), fresh salmon cocktail (£2.25), salads (from £2.30), smoked haddock flan (£2.80), steak pie (£3), game casserole (£3.50) and puddings such as banoffi pie (£1); there are evening main courses like a vegetarian dish (£3.55), fried West Coast scampi (£4.25) and Angus sirloin steak (£6.50). Reasonably priced wines and quick, charming service. The spacious grounds back on to the hills and include a putting-course and a croquet-lawn – sometimes there are roe deer and red squirrels. The views of the mountain pass are splendid. *(Recommended by RB, AHNR, Mr and Mrs Michael Daggett and family, Rob and Gill Weeks)*

Free house   Licensees Duncan and Jennifer Hattersley Smith   Meals and snacks   Children welcome; no infants in evenings   Restaurant   Open 12–2.30, 6–11; closed mid-Oct – Easter   Bedrooms tel Pitlochry (0796) 3220; £22.80(£25.30B)/£45.60(£50.60B)

Pubs with outstanding views are listed at the back of the book.

PLOCKTON (Highland)   NG8033 Map 11
Plockton Hotel
Village signposted from A87 near Kyle of Lochalsh

The inn is part of a long, low terrace of stone-built houses in this lovely National Trust village, strung out among palm trees along the seashore and looking across Loch Carron to rugged mountains. The partly panelled and partly bare stone lounge bar has window seats that look out to the boats on the water, and is comfortably furnished with green leatherette seats around neat Regency-style tables on a tartan carpet, an open fire and a model ship set into the woodwork. Bar food includes home-made soup (70p), filled rolls (from 65p, bacon 75p, fresh salmon 95p), sandwiches (from 75p, toasties 10p extra), home-made pâté or ploughman's (£1.95), vegetable pancake rolls (£2.50), fresh local prawns or smoked salmon quiche (£2.95), salads (from £2.95), with evening dishes like vegetable lasagne (£2.95), home-made steak and kidney pie (£3.25) and fresh cold salmon (£4.95); children's dishes (£1.25), good breakfasts and first-rate service. Tennents 80/- on air-pressure tall fount and a good collection of whiskies (this is one of the select handful of pubs which keep the Royal Household whisky). The separate public bar has darts, pool, shove-ha'penny, dominoes, cribbage and piped music; dogs welcome. *(Recommended by Paul King, Dr Q G Livingstone, Mr and Mrs R G Ing, Richard Gibbs, Dr and Mrs P J Morgan)*

Free house   Licensee Alasdair Bruce   Meals and snacks   Children welcome until 9   Open 11–2.30, 5–12 (11.30 Sat)   Bedrooms tel Plockton (059 984) 274; £14.50S/£29S (twin rooms only)

PORTPATRICK (Dumfries and Galloway)   NX0154 Map 9
Crown ★ ⊗ ⇔
On the harbourfront of this quiet village – perhaps at its most interesting on a Thursday, when the small fishing-fleet comes in – this delightful little pub is one of the nicest in Scotland: courteous friendly service, good bar food (especially fish, caught by the chef), and a really relaxing atmosphere. The rambling old-fashioned bar – full of atmosphere and bustle – has lots of little nooks, crannies and alcoves, and the partly panelled butter-coloured walls are decorated with old mirrors with landscapes painted in their side panels, shelves of old bottles above the bar counter and a stag's head over the coal fire; interesting furniture includes a carved settle with barking dogs as its arms and an antique wicker-backed armchair. Food includes sandwiches (from 75p, toasties 80p, Danish open prawn sandwich £2.75), home-made soup (80p), smoked mackerel (£1.45), ploughman's (£1.80), salads (from £2.45, fresh crab £4, prawn £5.10, lobster from £10), shellfish kebab (£2.75), cod fillet (£3.40), whole grilled jumbo prawns (from £3.95), scallops (£5.10), steak (from £5.95) and seafood platter (from £13.75); excellent breakfasts. Piped music; sensibly placed darts in the separate public bar; also dominoes, cribbage and a fruit machine. An airy and very attractively decorated 1930s-ish dining-room opens through a quiet and attractively planted conservatory area into a sheltered back garden. Seats outside in front – served by hatch in the front lobby – make the most of the evening sun. Unusually attractive bedrooms have individual touches such as uncommon Munch prints. *(Recommended by T Nott, NWN, J F Atherton, Marcus and Marcella Leith, Kevin Pearce, J A V Rose, Dr S G Donald)*

Free house   Licensee Miss Maureen Campbell   Meals and snacks   Restaurant   Children welcome   Open 11–11; 11–2.30, 5–11 in winter   Bedrooms tel Portpatrick (077 681) 261; £20B/£36B

Meal times are generally the normal times at which people eat in the region. But they tend to vary from day to day and with the season, depending on how busy the pub hopes to be. We don't specify them as our experience shows you can't rely on them.

QUEENSFERRY (Lothian)   NT1278 Map 11
Hawes

This waterside inn's spacious and comfortable lounge bar has a fine view of the
Forth stretching out between the massively practical railway bridge and the
elegantly supercilious road bridge. An efficient food counter serves soup (80p),
burgers (£2.55), chicken and corn pie, cold buffet with unusual salads, fried
haddock, braised lamb's liver, chillied beef with kidney beans (all £2.75) and
stir-fried ginger beef (£3.20). Well kept Arrols 70/- and Tennents 80/- are served on
handpump. In the quieter, older part, there's still something of the atmosphere that
made the inn so appealing to R L Stevenson – he used it as a setting in *Kidnapped*,
and may even have been moved to start writing the book while staying here. The
small public bar has darts, dominoes, fruit machine and piped music. Tables outside
overlook the Forth, and a back lawn with hedges and roses has white tables and a
children's play area. *(Recommended by Roger Huggins, R P Taylor)*

*Ind Coope   Meals and snacks   Children in family-room until 8   Restaurant (with pianist Sat
evenings)   Open 11–11   Bedrooms tel 031-331 1990; £28.50/£39.50*

ST ANDREWS (Fife)   NO5116 Map 11
Victoria Cafe

St Mary's Place; corner of Bell Street

Popular with students in term-time, this airy cafe has bentwood chairs around
marble-topped cast-iron tables on an oak floor, stripped panelling, tall green walls,
a darker green ceiling with a colonial fan, and brass lamps and potted plants;
maybe piped modern jazz. It opens on to a sunny roof terrace with three or four
tables. Bar food, served throughout the day, includes filled rolls (70p), soup (80p),
quiche (£2.95) and chicken (£3.20). McEwans 80/- from an air-pressure tall fount,
and good value fruit juices. A rather elegant oval room with waitress service is used
as a family-room. *(Recommended by Mrs A D Kucharski, Dr A V Lewis)*

*Maclays   Licensee Peter Dickson   Real ale   Meals and snacks   Summer restaurant tel St
Andrews (0334) 76964   Children in eating area and restaurant until 8   Occasional jazz Thurs
evening   Open 11–11; closes midnight Thurs, Fri and Sat*

ST BOSWELLS (Borders)   NT5931 Map 10
Buccleuch Arms

A68 just S of Newtown St Boswells

There's a quiet, genteel atmosphere in the bar of this Victorian sandstone inn as
well as pink plush seats, elegant banquettes, velvet curtains and reproduction
Georgian-style panelling; dishes of nuts and other nibbles on the bar; the public bar
is now a functions room. Imaginative bar food includes soup (85p), sandwiches
(from 85p), mushroom in Stilton and sweetcorn sauce (£1.25), chicken liver and
whisky pâté (£1.50), ploughman's (£1.85), cold meat platter with salad (£3.25),
daily specials like steak and kidney pie or spaghetti bolognese (around £3.50),
sugar-baked gammon with pineapple (£3.95), local trout (£4.50) and sirloin steak
(£6.25); they serve sandwiches all day, do afternoon teas, and occasional speciality
food nights such as Caribbean or Moroccan. The inn is near *Good Walks Guide*
Walk 162. *(Recommended by Robert and Vicky Tod, Syd and Wyn Donald, R H Sawyer)*

*Free house   Licensee Mrs Lucy Agnew   Meals and snacks   Restaurant   Children
welcome   Open 11–11 all year; closed 25 Dec   Bedrooms tel St Boswells (0835) 22243;
£22.50(£27.50B)/£40(£50B)*

If you have to cancel a reservation for a bedroom or restaurant, please telephone or write to
warn them. A small place – and its customers – will suffer if you don't.

ST MARY'S LOCH (Borders) NT2422 Map 9
Tibbie Shiels Inn

This unspoilt and remote old inn is named after a nineteenth-century landlady, wife of the local mole-catcher, who was a favourite character of Edinburgh literary society. In the original old stone part of the building, the cosy back bar has well cushioned black wall benches or leatherette armed chairs, and a photograph of Tibbie Shiels herself; there's a good mix of customers. Waitress-served, good value home-made food includes soup (60p), sandwiches (from 70p), ploughman's (£1.45), chilli con carne (£2), chicken curry (£2.25), haddock or vegetarian bulghur-wheat and walnut casserole (£2.55), local trout (£2.75), four-ounce rump steak (£2.95), and home-made puddings like cloutie dumpling and cream (75p); coffee (50p). Bar food is served from noon to 9pm, and there are home-baked scones, cakes and shortbread at high tea (from £3.50). Belhaven 60/- and 80/- on handpump. There's a no-smoking dining area off the main lounge; piped music. The Southern Upland Way – a long-distance footpath – passes close by, the Grey Mares Tail waterfall is just down the glen, and the loch is beautiful (with fishing free to residents); it's very peaceful – except when low-flying jets explode into your consciousness. (*Recommended by E J Alcock, Capt E P Gray, S V Bishop, SS, Eileen Broadbent, Rob and Gill Weeks, Brian and Anna Marsden*)

Free house   Licensees Shanks and Hildegard Fleming   Meals and snacks   Children in eating area of bar   Restaurant (open 12.30–9 Sun)   Open 11–11 in summer; 11–2.30, 6.30–11 in winter; 12.30–11 Sun; closed 25 Dec and Mon Nov–Mar   Bedrooms tel Selkirk (0750) 42231; £12/£24

SKEABOST (Isle of Skye) NG4148 Map 11
Skeabost House Hotel ★ ⊗ 🛏

A850 NW of Portree, 1½ miles past junction with A856

This very civilised small hotel has had such warm praise from readers this year for the very good food, friendly, happy service and lovely surroundings that we are awarding it a star. The high-ceilinged bar has red brocade seats on its thick red carpet and some in a big bay window which overlooks a terrace (with picnic-table sets) and the neatly kept lawn; this doubles as a putting-course and runs down to the loch, bright with bluebells on its far side. The spacious and airy no-smoking lounge has an attractively laid out buffet table with soup (75p), sandwiches (from £1.60), nineteen salads (vegetarian £2.55, meat £3.40, fresh salmon £3.95), a hot dish of the day and puddings (90p); coffee; note that service stops at 1.30. A fine panelled billiards room leads off the stately hall; darts, pool and juke box. The grounds around the hotel include a bog-and-water-garden under overhanging rocks and rhododendrons, a nine-hole golf course, and there is private fishing on the Snizort, perhaps Skye's best salmon river. The village post office here has particularly good value Harris wool sweaters, blankets, tweeds and wools. (*Recommended by Richard Whitehead, Guy Harris, Rob and Gill Weeks, Stephen R Holman, MJL, Mr and Mrs D E Milner, Mrs H Church, P J Bevan*)

Free house   Licensee Iain McNab   Meals and snacks (not Sun evening)   Evening restaurant   Children welcome   Open 11–2.30, 5–11; public bar closed Sun; closed end Oct–Easter   Bedrooms tel Skeabost Bridge (047 032) 202; £23(£28B)/£48(£58B)

nr SPEAN BRIDGE (Highland) NN2281 Map 11
Letterfinlay Lodge Hotel ⊗ 🛏

7 miles N of Spean Bridge on A82

A long glass wall in the big bar of this genteel family-run inn gives splendid views down to Loch Lochy and to the steep forests on the far side; comfortable brown plush seats cluster around dark tables, and there's a games area to one side with darts, pool, dominoes, cribbage, space game and backgammon. Good and popular lunchtime food is served buffet-style, and includes home-made soup (90p), sandwiches (£1.25, salmon when available £1.50), pâté with oatcakes (£1.60), salads such as fresh ox-tongue and roast local meats (£3.25), fresh fillet of haddock (£3.50), pork and pineapple curry or roast sirloin of Aberdeen Angus beef (£3.75), fresh Loch Ness salmon (£4.50) and puddings (£1.25); good, chilled wines and Kenco coffee (50p). Opening off one side of the main bar is an elegantly panelled small cocktail bar (with a black-bow-tied barman) furnished with button-back leather seats, old prints and a chart of the Caledonian Canal; piped music. A couple of white tables under cocktail umbrellas on the side gravel might be a good starting-point for a stroll down through the rhododendrons to the waterside. Fishing and perhaps deerstalking can be arranged; there are shower facilities for customers on boating holidays, and a small caravan club. *(Recommended by Richard Whitehead, D M Bednarowska, Rob and Gill Weeks, Stuart Fisher)*

Free house   Licensee Ian Forsyth   Lunchtime meals and snacks   Children welcome Restaurant (closed Sun lunch)   Open 11–1am weekdays; closes 12.45 am Sat; closed mid-Nov–Mar   Bedrooms tel Speanbridge (039 781) 622; £18(£22B)/£36(£40B)

STIRLING (Central)   NS7993 Map 11
Settle Inn

91 St Mary's Wynd; from Wallace Memorial in centre, go up Baker Street and keep right at the top

Stirling's oldest inn, built in 1733 and handsomely restored, has black beams and brown panelling, some stripped bare stone, Windsor chairs and wall benches and a great arched stone fireplace in its lower room (with two curling stones in front of the actual hearth). Up some steps, another room has a barrel-vaulted ceiling of big interlocking stone blocks and more of the simple furnishings, with old local landscape prints including a big Clark print of Stirling Castle (to compare with the aerial photograph downstairs). Bar food includes ready-filled rolls or pies. Belhaven 70/- and 80/- on handpump. Dominoes, cribbage, fruit machine and juke box, and a giant screen colour TV used for special sporting events and the like. *(Recommended by Mr J H Adam, John Renwick, Brian and Anna Marsden)*

Belhaven   Real ale   Snacks (until 7)   Open 11–11 all year; closes 11.30pm Fri and Sat; closed 25 Dec and 1–2 Jan

STRACHUR (Strathclyde)   NN0901 Map 11
Creggans ⊗ ⇌

A815 N of village

The view from the white tables in front of this elegant small hotel looks over the sea-loch to the hills on the far side; close by is the spot where Mary Queen of Scots landed in 1563. Inside, there's a similar view from the comfortable and attractively decorated tweedy lounge, with extra seats in a conservatory, and a public bar given more life by the locals who still use it – pool, darts, dominoes, a fruit machine and space game. Good bar food includes bacon roll (£1), home-made soup (£1.20), toasted sandwiches (from £1.40), a choice of home-made pâtés or terrines (£2.65), home-made burgers, including a venison one (£2.95), spiced beef open sandwiches (£3.80), local oysters (£4.75 the half-dozen), lamb cutlets (£5), Loch Fyne trout in oatmeal (£5.50), langoustines (£6.90), ten-ounce sirloin steak (£9.50) and specials like cold meat salads (£4.50) or smoked trout (£4.75). McEwans 80/- on handpump (actually rather cheap for the area), and a good selection of malt whiskies, including their own vatted malt. You can walk for hours on the owners' land; deerstalking as

---

well as fishing and pony-trekking may be arranged for residents. *(Recommended by Ian Clay; more reports please)*

Free house   Licensee Sir Fitzroy Maclean   Meals and snacks (lunchtime, though also available 5.45–6.30)   Children welcome   Restaurant   Open 11–midnight all year   Bedrooms tel Strachur (036 986) 279; £31(£35B)/£54(£68B)

TARBERT (Strathclyde)   NR8467   Map 11
West Loch Hotel ⊗ 🛏

A83 1 mile S

The new licensee has placed more emphasis on Scottish cooking in this quiet modernised country inn, which at lunchtime includes Scotch broth (90p), venison sausages (£2.95), black pudding and apple pancake (£3.50), tripe and onions or rabbit casserole (£3.75), good salads, filo parcels of leek and cheese (£4.10), excellent smoked salmon and scrambled duck eggs (£4.50), local seafood in a light curry mayonnaise (£4.60), grilled Argyll quail with orange wine butter (£4.95), and puddings (£1.75); set evening meals include local fish and game; good service. The cocktail bar has photographs of Tarbert, brown cloth upholstered easy chairs and little basket-weave chairs; it opens into a lounge with Liberty-print easy chairs, a log/peat fire and piped classical music. The small public bar has a wood-burning stove and old fishing photographs. *(Recommended by Christa Grosse, D M Bednarowska, D I Willey)*

Free house   Licensee Mrs Sandy Ferguson   Lunchtime meals and snacks   Restaurant Children welcome   Open 12–2.30, 5–11 all year   Bedrooms tel Tarbert (088 02) 283; £19/£38

TAYVALLICH (Strathclyde)   NR7386   Map 11
Tayvallich Inn ⊗

B8025, off A816 1 mile S of Kilmartin; or take B841 turn-off from A816 two miles N of Lochgilphead

This simple pub's small bar has exposed ceiling-joists, pale pine upright chairs, benches and tables on its quarry-tiled floor, cigarette cards and local nautical charts on brown hessian walls, and sliding glass doors opening on to a concrete terrace furnished with picnic-table sets. Both bar and terrace look over the lane and the muddy foreshore to the very sheltered yacht anchorage. Bar lunches include sandwiches (on request), home-made soup (90p), ploughman's (£1.95), salads (from £2.50), burger or haddock (£2.75), sweet-and-sour vegetables (£2.95), giant prawn salad (£5), sirloin steak (£6.50), lobster mayonnaise (£10.50, summer only) and home-made puddings (£1.30). The evening meals are very strong on local fish and, particularly, shellfish: mussels (£2.50), half a dozen deep-fried oysters with hot dip (£3.30), seafood platter or Loch Fyne smoked salmon (£4.50), and Sound of Jura clams (£7.50). Decent house wines; darts. *(More reports please)*

Free house   Licensee John Grafton   Meals and snacks   Restaurant   Children in restaurant   Open 11–1am (midnight Sat); 11–2, 5–11 in winter; closed Mon Nov–Mar, and 25 Dec   Bedrooms tel Tayvallich (054 67) 282; £9/£18

TROON (Strathclyde)   NS3230   Map 9
The Lookout ⊗

Troon Marina, Harbour Road; from centre, go into Temple Hill and keep bearing right

Big windows in the friendly, smart first-floor bar of this new blocky building (which looks like a yachting clubhouse but isn't) give a lovely view out over the crowded yachts of the marina to the sea and the coast beyond. There are comfortable grey-blue plush banquettes and wicker and bentwood chairs around low tables on a royal blue carpet, big colour yachting pictures on the grey walls and a high dark powder-blue ceiling. Good, reasonably priced food is served in a separate room away from the bar and includes soup (95p), home-made pâté (£2.10), lasagne or burgers (£3.95), steak (£7.25) and genuinely hot Mexican dishes. Well kept Greenmantle and Theakstons on electric pump, good espresso coffee; snooker-table, fruit machine, piped music. The wooden balcony-terrace outside (a bit breezy sometimes) has a do-it-yourself gas barbecue, and in the marina you can arrange sailing, windsurfing and waterskiing. *(Recommended by Dave Braisted, Harry Jackson)*

Free house   Licensee Yvonne Howie   Real ale   Meals and snacks   Restaurant tel *Troon (0292) 311523   Children welcome   Open 11–11; 11–2.30, 5–11 in winter; closes midnight Fri and Sat*

UDDINGSTON (Strathclyde)   NS6960   Map 11
Rowan Tree

60 Old Mill Road; in Uddingston High Street, turn into The Cut, which takes you into Old Mill Road with the pub almost opposite. A mile from M73 junction 6; leaving M73 from S, turn sharp right immediately at end of motorway, virtually doing a U-turn (permitted here) into A721, then following B7071 into village

Recently repainted, this old-fashioned town pub has tall tiers of mirrored shelves towering behind the high, heavily panelled serving-counter, gas-style chandeliers, interesting old brewery mirrors, Edwardian water fountains on the bar counter, and two coal fires. The bare benches built into the shinily panelled walls are divided by elegant wooden pillars which support an arch of panelling, which in turn curves into the embossed ceiling; there's also a lounge. Good, generously served, simple bar food includes soup (40p), filled rolls (60p, steak £1), egg mayonnaise (80p), lasagne or fried haddock (£2), and braised beef or golden scampi (£2.20); well kept Maclays 70/-, 80/- and Porter on air-pressure tall fount. Darts, dominoes, fruit machine and quiet piped music. *(Recommended by John Renwick, Rob and Gill Weeks)*

Maclays   Licensee George Tate   Real ale   Lunchtime meals and snacks (not Sun)   Disc jockey with Golden Oldies Thurs, Fri and Sat   Open 11–11 (11.45 Fri and Sat) all year

WEEM (Tayside)   NN8449   Map 11
Aileen Chraggan ⊗

B846

There are fine views of the mountains beyond the Tay Valley, sweeping up towards Ben Lawers (the highest in this part of Scotland) from the comfortable modern lounge of this friendly inn. It has long plump plum-coloured banquettes, with Bruce Bairnsfather First World War cartoons on the red and gold Regency-striped wallpaper. Bar food includes soup (95p), pâté (£1.95), lasagne (£2.65), omelettes (from £2.95), deep-fried plaice (£3.25), scampi or gammon and pineapple (£4.25), and good sirloin steak (£7.75), with specials such as Loch Etive mussels (£3.75), breast of duck salad (£5.75), fantastic Loch Etive prawns (£6.75) or wonderful Tay salmon. Winter darts, dominoes and piped music. There are tables on the large terrace outside. *(Recommended by Dr S G Donald, W A Low)*

Free house   Licensee Alistair Gillespie   Meals and snacks   Children welcome   Open 11–11 in summer; 11–2.30, 5–11 in winter   Bedrooms tel *Aberfeldy (0887) 20346; £19.50/£39*

Lucky Dip

Besides the fully inspected pubs, you might like to try these Lucky Dips recommended to us and described by readers (if you do, please send us reports).

☆ **Aberdeen**, Grampian [Dee St; NJ9305], *Gabriels*: Lofty converted chapel turned into showy bar without sparing expense; nightclub behind has most elaborate sound and lights system *(Michael Cooke, LYM)*

Aberdeen [Gallowgate], *Blue Lamp*: Small, dimly red-lit, mysterious; free juke box *(Michael Cooke)*; [6 Little Belmont St] *Camerons*: Solid stone building with many rooms and wide choice of well kept beers; open all day *(Michael Cooke, Michael Craig)*; [Docks, by Market St] *Drift*: Unpretentious and lively, popular with young people especially on Fri (witty live entertainment) and Sat (video disco) *(Michael Cooke)*; [Holborn St] *Hawthorne*: Lively bar popular with students and other young people, unpretentious and fun; good juke box, trivia machine, TV; open all day *(Michael Cooke)*; [Deemount Terr, nr Duthie Park] *Inn at the Park*: Comfortable pub with reasonable food, handy for carry-outs to Duthie Park *(Michael Cooke)*

Aberdour, Fife [A92 Inverkeithing–Kircaldy; NT1985], *Aberdour*: Attractive hotel in charming seaside village with harbour; quietly lit bar with wooden fittings, coal fire, darts and dominoes; good friendly service, Belhaven 70/- and 80/- on handpump and well priced tasty food from bar and separate restaurant; bedrooms *(N and M Gibbon)*

Aberlady, Lothian [A198 towards Edinburgh; NT4679], *Waggon*: Well run and friendly, view over the salt-flats and Firth to Fife from big windows in the airy high-ceilinged back extension, attractive front family-room, bar food on pricey side – especially considering the self-service arrangements, well kept McEwans 80/-; restaurant; nr GWG175 *(Dr Stewart Rae, LYM)*

Aboyne, Grampian [Charleston Rd; NO5298], *Boat*: Simple but friendly and comfortable inn, pleasantly refurbished after 1987 fire; good value bar food, real ale and restaurant; used to serve the Dee ferry; games in public bar; bedrooms *(H P K Hutton, LYM)*

Achnasheen, Highland [A832; NH2669], *Achnasheen*: It's the fantastic surroundings which focus attention on this isolated hotel served by single-track Inverness–Kyle of Lochalsh railway (and single-track road) – otherwise, it's very much the usual roadside establishment with simple modern furnishings in the bar, straightforward food, games on the public side and so forth; bedrooms *(Rob and Gill Weeks, GMP, LYM)*; [A890, just off A832] *Ledgowan Lodge*: Former shooting-lodge, now a country-house hotel in superb remote part of Highlands; enterprising bar food served in restaurant includes Scotch broth and tender well cooked lamb cutlets with a minted poached pear – smaller dishes too; also high teas and five-course dinners; bedrooms *(J D Cranston)*

Alyth, Tayside [Loyal Rd; NO2548], *Lands of Loyal*: Smart hotel – previously Lord Airlie's home – in own grounds; ancestral home atmosphere, but very warm welcome and cosy bar meals; good, imaginative reasonably priced food including absolutely fresh vegetables; restaurant; bedrooms *(Dr S G Donald)*

Anstruther, Fife [24 East Green; NO5704], *Cellar*: Cosy and attractive if simply decorated pub with low ceilings and remarkable value winter weekday three-course dinner *(Anon)*; *Dreel*: Historic site in very picturesque East Neuk fishing village with very friendly service and good value bar meals *(Pamela Milne)*; [High St] *Smugglers*: Good value straightforward bar food in friendly old inn with rambling and well kept attractive upstairs bar, noisier downstairs gamesbar, summer barbecues on pretty terrace; children in eating area; good value bedrooms *(Alastair Campbell, LYM)*; [East Shore] *Sun*: Snug harbourside tavern next door to Scottish Fisheries Museum, good local seafood, summer weekend live music, well kept McEwans real ales *(LYM)*

☆ **Ardentinny**, Strathclyde [NS1887], *Ardentinny*: Lovely views of Loch Long from well decorated waterside bars and garden, good choice of bar food, courtesy boat for guests; well placed for Younger Botanic Garden at Benmore; children in eating area; bedrooms; closed Jan/Feb *(LYM)*

Ardeonaig, Central [S side of Loch Tay; NN6635], *Ardeonaig*: Good food, wonderful lochside setting by a burn; keg McEwans; comfortable bedrooms *(Patrick Young)*

Arduaine, Strathclyde [NM7910], *Lord of the Isles*: Superb choice of food and huge log fire in comfortably furnished pub, well placed for view of Loch Melfort and the islands *(N F Doherty)*

Auchencairn, D&G [about 2½ miles off A711; NX7951], *Balcary Bay*: Bar and hotel with former smuggling affiliations, very pleasant; bedrooms *(T Nott)*

Auchentiber, Strathclyde [A736 Irvine–Glasgow; NS3647], *Blair*: Pleasant atmosphere and friendly, efficient staff; food above average – good value compared to pubs in South *(AJVB)*

Aultguish, Highland [NH3570], *Aultguish*: Isolated highland inn near Loch Glascarnoch, bar food; children welcome; bedrooms *(LYM)*

Aviemore, Highland [NH8912], *Macs*: Cheerful pub with good well filled rolls and well kept Tennents 80/- and Youngers No 3; lots of families *(Neil and Angela Huxter)*; *Red*

McGregors: Large lively open-plan pub, good value bar meals all day, free entertainment some evenings, very friendly staff; steak bar next door *(E J Alcock, Roger Huggins)*; *Winking Owl*: Upstairs Nest Bar a rather trendy mock-up of a Swiss chalet, Arrols 80/- and Ind Coope Burton on handpump, friendly, downstairs evening restaurant *(Anon)*

Badachro, Highland [B8056 by Gair Loch; NG7773], *Badachro*: Set in tranquil bay with small very relaxing garden and lots of pets; roaring fire in winter *(E J Alcock)*

Ballinluig, Tayside [NN9853], *Ballinluig*: Nice food (haggis) and friendly, efficient service, though atmosphere is a bit mixed; bedrooms *(Anon)*

Bargrennan, D&G (NX3576], *House O'Hill*: Good bar lunch in recently renovated and upgraded hotel at entrance to Glen Trool (Southern Upland Walkway passes here); fishing permits for River Cree and lochs; bedrooms *(Revd L W Kitchen)*

Beattock, D&G [NT0802], *Old Brig*: Interesting historical building, reasonable food; bar due for some refurbishment now *(T Nott)*

Belhaven, Lothian [NT6679], *Masons Arms*: Good value bar lunches in functional eating area; friendly atmosphere, very attentive staff *(M Wilkie)*

Bieldside, Grampian [North Deeside Rd; A93, W side of village; NJ8702], *Water Wheel*: Carefully restored watermill main bar and plusher cocktail bar which has had well kept McEwans 80/- and good value food *(LYM)*

Bothwell, Strathclyde [27 Hamilton Rd; NS7058], *Cricklewood*: Good food all day, well kept Whitbreads Castle Eden, well run pub *(John Renwick)*

Bower, Highland [B876 11m NW of Wick; ND2462], *Bower*: Strong submarine theme in atmospheric bars with Youngers No 3 and scrumpy on draught and good bar snacks; an oasis *(H P K Hutton)*

Braemar, Grampian [NO1491], *Fife Arms*: Good hot and cold buffet in refurbished lounge bar, friendly bar staff; nr start GWG166 *(John Roué)*

Bridge of Cally, Tayside (junction A93/ A924; NO1541], *Cally*: Reliably good stopping-place between Perth and Braemar or Pitlochry, and very popular with fishermen and painters; good food; bedrooms *(S V Bishop)*

Bridge of Don, Grampian [NJ1409], *Mill of Mundurno*: Good restaurant lunches, also bar food and more expensive evening menu; children in family-room *(Dr J M Jackson)*

Buckie, Grampian [High St; NJ4265], *Cluny*: Public bar and cafeteria with entrances separate from hotel, which has quickly and pleasantly served food in its two first-floor lounges; bedrooms *(S V Bishop)*

Cabrach, Grampian [A941; NJ3827],

Grouse: Family pub with souvenirs and cafeteria, open all day, handy stop on hill road from Braemar to Dufftown; remarkable stock of whiskies in full-sized bottles and in miniatures; bedrooms *(S V Bishop, LYM)*

Callander, Central [just outside; NN6208], *Lade*: Real ale and reasonably priced ably prepared food including good soup and fresh salmon; plus upholstery, flock wallpaper; nr start GWG164 *(Tim Locke)*

Calvine, Tayside [NN8066], *Bruar Falls*: Warm welcome, good value food in bar and restaurant, 70 malt whiskies in bar – and at least recently there's been a tame fox in the lounge; comfortable bedrooms *(K R and C E Watkins)*

Cardross, Strathclyde [NS3477], *Cardross*: Three bars, one with coal fire, another with snooker-table; glass conservatory serving good, home-cooked food at reasonable prices *(L Rowan)*

Carnock, Fife [A907 Dunfermline–Alloa; NT0489], *Old*: Polite and welcoming licensees; low-beamed ceiling in bar with pool-table well out of way, neat and tidy lounge with uniformly spaced tables; well kept Maclays 60/-, 70/-, 80/- and Porter, brass water-tap on bar, good value food quickly served; children welcome, with special food helpings *(Roger Huggins)*

Carnwath, Strathclyde [A721 E of Carstairs; NS9846], *Wee Bush*: Very hospitable landlady in comfortably refurbished old pub *(Dudley and Molly Woodget)*

Carsethorn, D&G [off A170; NX9959], *Steamboat*: Recommended chiefly for its position on the shores of the Solway Firth in a quiet backwater of a village which has just this pub and one wee shop; good bar lunches and pleasant English licensee with Scottish wife *(T A V Meikle)*

Castlecary, Central [NS7878], *Castlecary House*: Handily placed on Glasgow–Stirling route, cheerful main bar open all day (Sun afternoon high teas instead), good choice of well kept real ales, good value simple bar food, restaurant *(John Renwick, LYM)*

☆ **Cawdor**, Highland [OS Sheet 27 reference 848500; NH8450], *Cawdor Inn*: Very attractive little pub with plushly comfortable cosy lounge bar – the wooden panelling comes from nearby Cawdor Castle; well kept 80/- beer, exceptionally good range of malt whiskies, and for Scotland an unusually good choice of wines by the glass; real fire, gentle lighting, games and hunting prints, plates decorating panelled walls, fresh flowers and carved bar counter; connected games area; no evening food except by arrangement *(Dr John Innes, Brian and Anna Marsden, Rob and Gill Weeks)*

Chirnside, Borders [A6105 by church; NT8757], *Waterloo Arms*: Homely village inn with good value plain home cooking, well kept Belhaven 70/- and 80/-, entertaining pets; open all day summer weekends;

stables bar; bedrooms *(LYM)*

Inverness, Highland [Stoneyfield; outskirts, looks over towards Culloden], *Coach House:* Pleasant and friendly, food satisfactory, interesting comfortable bar with lots of beamery; in lovely location; children in restaurant; bedrooms *(Ruth Humphrey)*; [41 Haugh Rd] *Haugh:* Delightful find, just off centre by banks of River Ness; wood-panelled bar has huge collection of beermats on walls and ceiling, very friendly landlord, McEwans 80/- and Youngers No 3, good atmosphere, pleasant adjoining lounge bar; simple low-priced lunchtime food *(Ian Baillie, AJVB)*; [Academy St] *Phoenix:* Pleasant lounge at the back where food is served *(AJVB)*

Irvine, Strathclyde [NS3739], *Turf:* Imaginatively cooked, nicely presented and reasonably priced food; comfortable seating too *(AM)*

Isle of Whithorn, D&G [NX4736], *Queens Arms:* Partly sixteenth-century inn, friendly lounge with popular bar food, pool-room, public bar, just up street from harbour; open all day; bedrooms *(BB)*

Jedburgh, Borders [Abbey Dr; NT6521], *Carters Rest:* Friendly atmosphere, comfortable bars and restaurant; bar food lunchtime and evening *(A P Hudson)*

Kames, Strathclyde [NR9671], *Kames:* Very friendly service and good meals in comfortable bar; restaurant has lovely view of Kyles of Bute; bedrooms *(Clare Reynolds)*

Kelso, Borders [Bridge St (A699); NT7334], *Queens Head:* Very well kept Belhaven 70/- on handpump, big helpings of good food with very good waitress service, in welcoming eighteenth-century Georgian coaching-inn; bedrooms *(Mr and Mrs M D Jones, Mr and Mrs J H Adam)*

Kelso [signposted off A698 4 miles S], *Sunlaws House:* Elegant and expensive mansion-house hotel, beautifully furnished and decorated; by no means a pub (rather the sort of place where you speak in hushed tones), but included for its good range of lovely bar meals in panelled library with lots of interesting books; bedrooms *(Alan Bickley, AE)*; *Waggon:* Good town pub with large if sometimes crowded bar, decent food, well kept beer, pleasant efficient service *(Robert and Vicky Tod)*

Kenmore, Tayside [NN7745], *Kenmore:* Civilised and quietly old-fashioned small hotel with long landscape poem composed here written in Burns' own handwriting on residents' lounge wall, friendly back bar and lively separate barn bar; bar food, restaurant, Tayside gardens, good fishing; near start GWG185; bedrooms *(LYM)*

Kilberry, Strathclyde [NR7164], *Kilberry:* Very good home-cooked bar lunches and family atmosphere attract people from as far as Oban and Campbeltown; half-size helpings for children, high teas, good range of whiskies; no food winter Sun *(A H Doran)*

Kilfinnan, Highland [NN2795], *Kilfinnan:* Good bar food, delicious beer, friendly service and atmosphere; good fresh scallops and crème brûlée in restaurant; bedrooms *(Clare Reynolds)*

Kilmun, Strathclyde [NS1785], *Cot House:* Small, cosy lounge decorated with slabs of cedar, variety of pub dogs, well kept 80/-, good value bar food *(E J Alcock)*

Kingholm Quay, D&G [signposted off B725 Dumfries–Glencaple; NX9773], *Swan:* Busy well looked after little hotel on banks of River Nith, wide range of good bar food (restaurant open only at busiest times), well kept McEwans 80/-, staff very friendly in spite of being busy, garden with embryonic adventure playground; children welcome in lounge bar, open all day Sat and Sun; bedrooms *(G A Worthington)*

Kingussie, Highland [NH7501], *Osprey:* Charming pub, good food and wines, friendly licensees; comfortable bedrooms *(Jill and George Hadfield, T Gallagher)*; *Royal:* Good value food in cosy modernised pub with well over a hundred whiskies and free entertainment most nights; don't be put off by plain exterior; bedrooms *(E J Alcock)*

Kinlochard, Central [NN4502], *Altskeith:* Beautifully situated on banks of Loch Ard (3 miles west of Aberfoyle) near Loch Lomond and Trossachs; bar food and McEwans 80/- and Broughton Greenmantle real ales; open all day Sat; bedrooms *(David Fisher)*

Kinross, Tayside [The Muirs; NO1102], *Windlestrae:* Attractive hotel with bar and restaurant; bedrooms *(T Nott)*

Kippen, Central [NS6594], *Cross Keys:* Comfortably refurbished lounge with stuffed birds, McEwans 80/- and pleasantly served good bar food; militaria in public bar; one bedroom *(Mr and Mrs J H Adam, LYM)*

Kippford, D&G [NX8355], *Anchor:* Beautifully placed waterside inn facing quiet yacht anchorage, very popular main entry in previous editions but some serious problems during 1987; signs in early 1988 of uplift to former standards, under new management – more news please; bedrooms have enchanting outlook *(Stuart Murray, LYM)*; *Mariner:* Clean pub with 'ship' atmosphere, friendly staff, good value well presented food including provision for vegetarians *(Linda and Carl Worley)*

☆ **Kirkcudbright**, D&G [Old High St; NX6851], *Selkirk Arms:* Comfortable partly panelled hotel lounge bar, bar food, restaurant, evening steak bar, tables in spacious garden with summer live music; salmon and trout fishing; children in restaurant and lounge; good value bedrooms, good service *(John Wainwright, LYM)*

Kirkmichael, Strathclyde [NS3408], *Kirkmichael Arms:* Friendly and unpretentious, wide choice of good value food lunchtime and evening – cooked to order, so slight wait *(Linda and Carl Worley)*

Kylesku, Highland [A894; S side of former ferry crossing; NC2234], *Kylesku*: Quite good bar food in unsurpassed scenic surroundings – fresh fish, scallops, large prawns in garlic butter, sandwiches and soup; also restaurant; five bedrooms – a place which gives you time for contemplation *(JDC)*

nr Lairg, Highland [A838, 17 miles NW of Lairg along Loch Shin; NC4123], *Overscaig*: Welcoming with slightly basic facilities and substantial bar snacks; bedrooms, good full breakfasts *(H P K Hutton)*

Lauder, Borders [NT5347], *Black Bull*: Dachshund photographs on plank-panelled bar of pleasantly decorated seventeenth-century inn with wide choice of bar food; open all day; children welcome; bedrooms (breakfast from 8.15) *(Ruth Humphrey, LYM)*

☆ **Lewiston**, Highland [NH5029], *Lewiston Arms*: Comfortable well kept lounge, games in friendly public bar, Youngers No 3, good filling bar food, restaurant, attractive garden; handy for Loch Ness (near ruined Urquhart Castle) and Glen Coiltie, with nice drive up to Glen Affric and back; bedrooms *(H P K Hutton, LYM)*

Limekilns, Fife [NT0783], *Ship*: Small and welcoming, Belhaven on handpump, good value food, Englishmen from Rosyth *(Roger Huggins)*

Loans, Strathclyde [NS3431], *Bruce*: Big modernised lounge with dimpled copper tables, wooden lanterns, piped music; friendly and well kept, open all day; Fri singalong *(BB)*

☆ **Loch Eck**, Strathclyde [from A815 turn into Ardentinny lane by loch; NS1493], *Whistle-field*: Charmingly isolated seventeenth-century inn above loch, interesting bric-à-brac and log fire in cosy bar, unobtrusive piped music, well kept 80/-, good choice of bar food; children's room; bedrooms *(E J Alcock, LYM)*

Lochaline, Highland [NM6744], *Lochaline*: Friendly hotel in isolated village by Mull ferry landing; cheerful bar, good bar food; bedrooms *(HDC)*

Lochaweside, Strathclyde [B840; NN1227], *Portsonachan*: Beautifully placed lochside fishing-inn; the Trotters, who won it high marks in the 1988 edition both for service and for their imaginative food – including bar lunches in the old-fashioned Tartan Room overlooking the water and the far hills – have unfortunately left (we know not where) *(LYM)*

Lochearnhead, Central [NN3404], *Bog Haggis*: Small hotel with good bar meals, overlooking loch; bedrooms *(J V Dadswell)*

Longniddry, Lothian [NT4476], *Longniddry*: Long rambling building with two bars and a

restaurant which were all just crowded enough; well kept beer, pool-table *(Michael Craig)*

Luss, Strathclyde (A82 about 3 miles N; NS3593], *Inverbeg*: Handy for its position across road from Loch Lomond, lounge often crowded for waitress-served food (also restaurant), real ale, games in simple public bar; bedrooms *(F A Noble, Hazel Morgan, LYM)*

Moffat, D&G [signposted off A74; NT0905], *Auchen Castle*: Spectacular hill views from peaceful country house with trout loch in good-sized gardens; food good, especially soups; malt whiskies, very reasonably priced wines; bedrooms *(Alan Bickley)*; [High Street] *Moffat House*: Robert Adam mansion with a big, comfortably furnished and restfully decorated bar that's more like a club drawing-room; good reasonably priced food, Tennents 70/-, good stock of whiskies; ideal for those wanting a quiet restful atmosphere for a drink and snack; up-market ambience at mid-market prices; bedrooms *(S V Bishop)*

☆ **Nairn**, Highland [Viewfield St; NH8856], *Clifton Hotel*: Beautifully decorated, this charming and distinguished small hotel has in every preceding edition of this *Guide* been a main entry – and indeed our highest-rated main entry in Scotland; it's been the delightfully furnished and sumptuously decorated lounge bar which has earned this warm approval, and we continue to have the very highest regard for the Clifton – not just this lounge, but the restaurant, the garden and the bedrooms; there has always been a school of thought, though, which has held that despite the undeniable quality this is too unlike a pub to fit easily into these pages, and now Mr Macintyre, who has run it with such sympathetic flair for so long, is planning to take out the bar counter (which no one really uses anyway) and to turn that room into a sitting-room, changing the name of the establishment back to its prewar title of Clifton House; we feel that this is the proper moment to mark its retirement from the main entries – but this wonderfully civilised place will still welcome you for a delectable bar lunch made from the freshest and finest ingredients, for a glass of good wine or some interesting stronger drink, for a full meal, for a comfortable stay, or even just for a cup of coffee *(Leith Stuart, Vera Kelman, Wendy Arnold, GMG, LYM)*

Nairn, [Marine Rd; coming from Inverness on A96, turn left at central roundabout], *Royal Marine*: Marvellous meal-sized bar snacks; amazing views over the Moray Firth from welcoming cocktail bar, also terrace bar; bedrooms *(Peter Griffiths)*; [Harbour St] *Taste Bud*: Very friendly place with comfortable lounge bar, restaurant on one side and good bar snacks served at tables in wide corridor-like room on the other side of the bar; decent wine list in bar as well as restaurant; hardworking folk singer with extensive repertoire *(Peter Griffiths)*

Newton Stewart, D&G [Minnigaff; NX4166], *Creebridge House*: Friendly atmosphere, good bar lunches and well kept Broughton real ale in comfortable country-house hotel; good value bedrooms *(Mr and Mrs J H Adam, Tim Brierly)*

Newton Stewart, [Queen St; NX4165], *Black Horse*: Cheerful inn with food in simple main bar (where TV and juke box may be busy), cocktail bar (not always open), tables in sheltered courtyard, fishing and shooting for guests, open all day in summer; children welcome; bedrooms *(Tim Brierly, LYM)*

Oxton, Borders [NT5053], *Carfraemill*: Welcoming hotel converted from mill in eighteenth century, bar food served all day in beamed lounge, friendly service, games-room with darts, pool-table and juke box *(E R Thompson)*

Pathhead, Lothian [NT3964], *Foresters Arms*: Bright public bar with good range of whiskies and good food with home-made pies *(W A Wright)*

nr **Penicuik**, Lothian [Nine Mile Burn; off A702; NT1757], *Habbies Howe*: Attractively decorated lounge interestingly converted from stables, old-fashioned coaching-inn public bar; bedrooms *(LYM)*

Perth, Tayside [Canal Crescent; NO1123], *Granary*: Handsomely furnished comfortable saloon exuding hospitality and well-being, exceptional bar food – open sandwiches surrounded artfully by mounds of salads, relishes and chutneys, many other dishes; impeccable service; large helpings of good food in charming and comfortable upstairs restaurant *(Melvin D Buckner)*

Plockton, Highland [Innes St; NG8033], *Creag Nan Darach*: Small, homely hotel with friendly owners and good home-made food in generous helpings – decent bar meals, and in the dining-room good cooking with local prawns, game and salmon; efficient service, cosy bar with open fires, spacious extension with pool-table; bedrooms clean and comfortable, breakfast a feast; bedrooms very reasonable *(Peter Stratton, A Metherell, S Gruson)*

Polmont, Central [Gilston Crescent; under a mile from M9 junction 7; A803 towards Polmont, then left; NS9378], *Whyteside*: Friendly and well run Victorian hotel with extensive comfortably furnished open-plan bar – most notable for its 300-plus whiskies, dozens of other spirits, over 60 bottled beers and well kept Archibald Arrols 70/- and Ind Coope Burton on handpump; children in eating area (not after 7.30), restaurant; organ music Tues, Thurs; closed 1 Jan; bedrooms *(LYM)*

Poolewe, Highland [NB8580], *Poolewe Hotel*: Pleasant, typically Scottish eighteenth-century inn in lovely West Coast village, carefully refurbished under its fairly recent new ownership; generously served bar food (usually available all day, and may be served in restaurant) is good, especially haggis, mixed grill, and daily specials such as Dover sole, roast beef, venison – most dishes served with at least four decently done vegetables; good choice of ales; handy for the magnificent Inverewe Gardens (best May to early June); bedrooms *(Brian and Anna Marsden, E J Alcock, W A Rinaldi-Butcher)*

Poolewe, Highland [attached to Corriness Guest House], *Choppys*: Plain, clean and friendly modern bar with pool-table, useful for good plain food cooked to order including home-made soup and sandwiches as well as generous helpings of hot dishes; popular with mainly local people; bedrooms in guest-house behind *(W A White)*

Port Appin, Strathclyde [NM9045], *Airds*: Friendly and comfortable inn with lovely shoreside position, good food and charmingly attentive service; has been a main entry in previous editions but is now solely a hotel/restaurant – very much worth visiting for that, though; bedrooms *(Wendy Arnold, LYM)*

Portpatrick, D&G [NX0154], *Portpatrick Hotel*: Comfortable bar in big hotel with heated pool and tennis, in striking position on bluff overlooking harbour; bedrooms *(BB)*

☆ **Quothquan**, Strathclyde [E of village; marked as ancient monument on OS maps – OS Sheet 72 reference 005403; NS9939], *Shieldhill*: Originally twelfth-century keep of considerable architectural interest, in quiet countryside, with old spiral staircase in hall; comfortable oak-panelled lounge, quite good bar food, busier snack bar with games; bedrooms from £16 each *(Brian and Anna Marsden)*

☆ **Ratho**, Lothian [NT1370], *Bridge*: Popular pub by Caledonian Canal, good reasonably priced food, good choice of wine, open fires, interesting building; owners also run barge on canal with similar good food *(G L Archer)*

☆ **St Andrews**, Fife [Grange Rd, a mile S; NO5116], *Grange*: Good if perhaps somewhat restaurant-like atmosphere in fine old building; spotlessly clean, small bar with well kept beer, good bar food such as fresh haddock, roast beef, veal and pepper pie, cranachan with raspberries (double cream, crumbled oatcake, Drambuie) *(Dr Stewart Rae, J C Braidwood, Dr A V Lewis)*

Scone, Tayside [A94; NO1226], *Scone Arms*: Pleasant, comfortable surroundings; good, well presented bar food *(Mr and Mrs J H Adam)*

Scrabster, Highland [Harbourside; ND0970], *Upper Deck*: Good value food in a large upstairs room, looking out over Scrabster harbour *(Guy Harris)*

Selkirk, Borders [NT4728], *Queens Head*:
Open-plan beamed lounge bar with freshly
cooked food, Archibald Arrols 70/- on handpump, log fires; open all day (*LYM*)

Sherriff Muir, Central [NN8303], *Sherriff
Muir*: Isolated moorland inn with panoramic
views, simple wooden furniture and prints of
local scenes; good food with varied, reasonably priced menu (*Miss C Haworth*)

☆ **Shiel Bridge**, Highland [NG9318], *Kintail
Lodge*: Slightly up-market and formal but
with friendly atmosphere in the bar, very
good value bar meals lunchtime and evening
including good local salmon and children's
helpings; above-average ambience for West
Highlands; Theakstons Best under pressure,
good variety of malt scotches; bedrooms
large and comfortable (*H P K Hutton, Russell
Hafter*)

☆ **Shieldaig**, Highland [NG8154], *Tigh an
Eilean*: Charming country-house hotel with
warm Scottish welcome and terrific views
across Loch Torridon, help-yourself residents' bar; good value locally caught shellfish; friendly little pub part at side; bedrooms
attractive and good value (*David and Angela
Tindall*)

Springholm, D&G [A75 Crocketford–Castle
Douglas; NX8070], *Reoch*: Small, pleasant,
clean pub with friendly welcome; well kept
McEwans, good, plain bar food, tables outside, car park (*Col and Mrs J S Gratton*)

☆ **Stirling**, Central [Easter Cornton Rd, Cause-
wayhead; off A9 N of Stirling centre;
NS7993], *Birds & the Bees*: Interestingly furnished ex-byre, dimly lit and convivial, with
Arrols 70/- and 80/-, Harviestoun 80/-, Maclays 80/- and Youngers IPA on handpump,
food in bar and restaurant, live bands most
weekends, open all day until 1am – very
popular with young people, reliably well run;
children welcome (*Russell Hafter, LYM*)

Straiton, Strathclyde [NS3804], *Black Bull*:
Most attractive little eighteenth-century pub
doing good bar lunches, in very pretty village
(*Tim Brierly*)

☆ **Stranraer**, D&G [George St; NX0660],
George: Elegant and comfortable lounge bar
with friendly and welcoming staff, good
value bar food, log fire in huge fireplace,
cable TV; also wine bar/bistro with world-
wide choice of bottled beers; open all day;
children welcome; bedrooms most comfortable (*Michael Bechley, LYM*)

Stranraer, [Church St], *Arkhouse*: Small,
friendly local opposite old church with tiled
floor in side bar, more than 50 whiskies and
unusual Chinese and Japanese drinks such as
rice wine or saké (*Michael Bechley*)

☆ **Strathkinness**, Fife [Low Rd; NO4616],
Rufflets: Old-established country hotel with
wonderful gardens; food outstanding in
good value lunchtime buffet as well as set
lunch and à la carte meals; very peaceful,
service good; bedrooms comfortable
(*Dr S G Donald*)

Strathmiglo, Fife [NO2110], *Strathmiglo*:
Quiet, with plain décor and rather subdued
atmosphere, pleasant service, straightforward food very well cooked and presented
with three veg and potato, good helpings;
children welcome (*J C Braidwood, LYM*)

Struy, Highland [NH3939], *Struy Inn*:
Pleasant rural pub in peaceful unspoilt valley, has had well kept real ale on handpump,
light snacks such as sausage rolls and bridies,
TV and comfortable sofas in separate lounge;
bedrooms (*Brian and Anna Marsden*)

☆ **Swinton**, Borders [NT8448], *Wheatsheaf*:
Warm welcome from friendly staff, Greenmantle ale, superb and often imaginative
food in bar and restaurant, log fire – an oasis
(*Grahame Archer, Alan Hall*)

☆ **Tarbert**, Strathclyde [NR8467], *Tarbert
Hotel*: Atmospheric and very quaint hotel
with a lovely outlook over the harbour and
very good value evening meals; comfortable
bedrooms, fine breakfasts (*Pamela Milne*)

☆ **Thornhill**, D&G [NX8795], *Buccleuch &
Queensberry*: Comfortably refurbished yet
traditionally solid old red sandstone inn with
access to three miles of fishing on the River
Nith; sedate lounge bar, livelier public, usual
bar food, high teas, evening grills and restaurant; children welcome; bedrooms comfortable, breakfasts good (*John Spencely, S V
Bishop, LYM*)

☆ **Thornhill**, Central [A873 – note that this is a
completely different Thornhill, many miles
from the previous entry; NS6699], *Lion &
Unicorn*: Simple old-fashioned old inn with
own bowling-green, attractive, cosy bar with
very hot wood-burning stove; friendly service, well kept Maclays 80/- on handpump,
good range of spirits, decent bar lunches and
restaurant food; children in family lounge;
bedrooms (*Russell Hafter, FDB, LYM*)

Tighnabruaich, Strathclyde [NR9772], *Royal*:
Good home-made bar meals; bedrooms
(*Clare Reynolds*)

Tongue, Highland [NO5957], *Ben Loyal*:
Busy, pleasant bar with many malts, straightforward food; bedrooms (*H P K Hutton*)

Torrance, Strathclyde [Main St; NS6274],
Wheatsheaf: Well run pub with good food
from varied menu, good friendly service (*EC*)

☆ **Turriff**, Grampian [Auchterless; A947;
NJ7250], *Towie*: Short choice of lunchtime
food using fresh ingredients, well cooked,
including interesting vegetarian dishes;
friendly but quietly efficient service, no
smoking or music in dining area; more extensive choice for evening restaurant dinners,
similarly good value; stylish and up-market,
but a good friendly atmosphere; children
welcome; bedrooms (*A Graham Mackenzie,
Leith Stuart, Eileen Broadbent, A V Timmins*)

☆ **Tweedsmuir**, Borders [A701 a mile N of
village; NT0924], *Crook*: Convivial flagstoned back bar with well kept Greenmantle
on handpump (and bottled beer from Tra-
quair House), open fire, big airy 1920s-style

lounge, games-room; traditional bar food, attractive garden, seven miles of fishing on the River Tweed and two local lochs; a useful halt on this fine lonely road; children welcome; bedrooms *(LYM)*

Twynholm, D&G [Burn Brae; NX6654], *Burnbank*: Basic local village inn with cheerful licensees and cheap food; closed Mon lunchtimes; fine nearby coast and countryside; bedrooms *(LYM)*

Ullapool, Highland [West Argyle St; NH1294], *Ceilidh Place*: Small attractive bar in old converted boathouse laid out almost like a continental cafe/bar with wooden tables, plants, Venetian blinds, interesting paintings, unobtrusive piped folk and classical music and very friendly service; open all day; restaurant and coffee shop attached – food, including vegetarian dishes, a bit expensive but good, seats outside in charming surroundings; children welcome; bedrooms very reasonably priced *(Ian Baillie, A Darroch Harkness, Ruth Humphrey)*

Ullapool [Shire St], *Ferry Boat*: Small pub with character, well kept real ale, friendly landlord, big collection of banknotes and 1960s piped music, overlooking busy picturesque harbour; good set-price menu including fresh local fish in small restaurant – best to book *(S Braisted, J V Dadswell, E J Alcock)*

Ullapool [North Rd], *Morefield Motel*: Friendly modern place, clean and warm and popular with ships' officers; specialises in fresh seafood; supper dances Fri; bedrooms *(W A White)*

Wester Balgedie, Tayside [A911/B919 nr Milnathort; NO1604], *Balgedie Toll*: Old toll-house in lovely position with lovely bar meals; good restaurant too *(Pamela Milne)*

Wormit, Fife [Naughton Rd; NO4026], *Taybridge Halt*: Lounge overlooks Tay Bridge and estuary, tasteful décor has a railway theme (picking up the motif supplied by the smoke-blackened former tunnel which is now part of the car park); pleasant prompt service, wide choice of good value food, well kept Tennents 70/- and 80/-; very relaxing *(JAH, HCH)*

Yetts of Muckhart, Central [NO0101], *Yetts o' Muckhart Inn*: Very pleasant helpful staff, good food, no long waits; a relaxing place, spotless *(Mr and Mrs B Barnes)*

The Islands

GIGHA

Gigha, [NR6450], *Gigha Hotel*: Good bar lunches in this Hebridean hotel – ploughman's with home-made brown bread, oatcakes, masses of cheese and salad; good well filled sandwiches, delicious cheese and herb pâté with salad and hot toast; good puddings; bedrooms *(Mrs J Swanzy)*

ISLAY

Bowmore, [Shore St; NR3159], *Lochside*: Friendly efficient service, good food, good view from lounge; bedrooms *(Miles Walton)*

MULL

Craignure [NM7136], *Craignure Inn:* Good food in busy popular bar; bedrooms *(Miles Walton)*

Salen [Aros; NM5743], *Glenforsa*: Lovely setting, views of the Sound of Mull and the island grass air-strip outside; good food in bar and restaurant; bedrooms – a good place to stay at *(Ian Clay)*

ORKNEY

St Margarets Hope [Ronaldsway; ND4593], *Bellevue*: Good beer and other stronger liquids, very friendly staff and locals; on the edge of this small old village's harbour; bedrooms comfortable and inexpensive *(WFL)*

Stromness [HY2509], *Hannavou*: Remarkably warm welcome, delicious vegetable soup as snack, good interesting restaurant food *(Clare Reynolds)*

SEIL

☆ **Clachan Seil** [this island is linked to the mainland by bridge via B844, off A816 S of Oban; NM7718], *Tigh an Truish*: L-shaped panelled bar with log stove, prints and oil paintings, wheel-back chairs and stools, piano, tartan curtains, bay windows overlooking bridge and mainland; darts, well kept McEwans 80/- and Tennents 80/-, decent bar food including local giant prawns and crab as well as home-made burgers and so forth; restaurant; white chairs in small garden and at side; bedrooms *(Patrick Stapley)*

SHETLAND

Hillswick [HU2977], *Booth*: The oldest Shetland pub – very old indeed – and the closest to an authentic pub: low ceiling, flagstones, big peat fire, very friendly and amenable Lancastrian licensees; small lounge, darts and pool in plain back room overlooking St Magnus Bay (with seals); seats outside, terrific surroundings, good walks *(Denis Mann)*; *St Magnus Bay*: Pleasant bar and good food in hotel built from Norwegian wood – shipped piece by piece from Scandinavia; bedrooms *(Denis Mann)*

Lerwick [HU4741], *Lounge*: The folk music centre (everyone in Shetland seems to play the fiddle), with occasional legendary players Sat afternoon or Weds evening *(Denis Mann)*; [centre, by sea] *Queens*: The black back bar is where everyone in Lerwick seems to come for their dram; bedrooms *(Anon)*; [Docks]

Thule: On the docks, supported by hard-drinking fishermen, Russian pin-ups of Japanese girls on the walls, open 8am–11pm in the herring season *(Anon)*

Whiteness [Wormadale; HU4046], *Westings*: Splendid view over sheep pastures to Whiteness Voe and distant islands from plushly furnished and comfortably refurbished lounge bar; bedrooms comfortable and modern *(HKR)*

SKYE

Ardvasar [A851 towards Broadford; NG6203], *Clan Donald Centre*: Not a pub but worth knowing for its very good food such as local scallops, fresh haddock and crisp vegetables *(Mrs H Church)*

☆ **Dunvegan** [NG2548], *Misty Isle*: Hotel with good views from picture windows in lounge and dining-room of twin flat-topped mountains – McLeods Tables (not far from McLeod seat at Dunvegan Castle); collection of local clan and folk history on loan from island's folk museums, live entertainment or ceilidhs most weekends, open all day Apr–end Oct; bedrooms *(Rob and Gill Weeks)*

Sconser [NG5132], *Sconser Lodge*: The lovely view over to Raasay and the mainland is what distinguishes the basic locals' bar of this inn, handy for the Raasay ferry and the Red Hills; children in eating area and family-room *(LYM)*

☆ **Sligachan** [A850 Broadford–Portree;

junction with A863; NG4830], *Sligachan Hotel*: Marvellously placed walkers' and climbers' inn, remote in central Skye, with basic public bar and plusher more sedate hotel bar; spectacular setting overlooking the Cuillins, occasional folk band, ponytrekking from here in summer; generous helpings of simple reliable food in restaurant; closed Oct–mid May; bedrooms good value *(BB)*

☆ **Stein** [NG2556], *Stein Inn*: Marvellously situated above a quiet sea inlet, and previously the most popular of all the island's pubs with our readers, with heady atmosphere, good malt whiskies, lively entertainment and quite unspoiled away-from-it-all charm; but it closed down in early 1987 and only reopened fairly recently – though the building and setting are as delightful as ever, it may take a while to regain its former atmosphere; bedrooms *(SJAV, GCS, Mr and Mrs K N Offer, Dominic Cullearn, LYM – more reports please)*

Uig [NG3963], *Ferry*: Well run unpretentious inn with decent straightforward bar food in crowded but cosy and welcoming lounge with leatherette seats, dimpled copper tables, flock wallpaper; good value bedrooms overlook pier and loch *(Suzanne Gibbs, BB)*; *Bakur*: Good no-nonsense bar in building looking like a modern bungalow right by ferry, pleasant people, simple but well cooked bar food lunchtime and early evening, good choice of whisky, folk music Weds, pool, darts; sells Sunday papers *(Stephen R Holman, J P Ostle)*

Wales

Wales

A combination for which Wales's better pubs are often particularly notable are good food and attractive scenery. Pubs which stand out for this include the laid-back, family-run Druidstone at Broad Haven in its fabulous coastal position (a nice place to stay at), the friendly Welsh-speaking Sportmans Arms up on the moors near Bylchau, the idyllically placed Leyland Arms at Llanelidan (a neatly kept little farmyard pub), the stately Maenan Abbey Hotel at Llanrwst (charming gardens and a good place to stay at), and the George III by quiet waterside meadows at Penmaenpool (again, a fine place to stay at). Other Welsh pubs where food is a special factor are the ancient Olde Bulls Head at Beaumaris, the hospitable Ty Gwyn at Betws-y-Coed (a nice place to stay at, too), the Dinorben Arms at Bodfari (our highest-rated Welsh pub with lots of cleverly designs areas and a good value lunchtime smorgasbord buffet), the rather northern-flavoured Aleppo Merchant at Carno (new licensees this year), the Bear at Crickhowell (a civilised lounge, and a new back bedroom block), the Dolfor Inn up in the hills at Dolfor, the Blue Anchor at East Aberthaw (a good range of real ales), the spick-and-span St Brides Inn at Little Haven, the Italian-run Walnut Tree Inn at

Llandewi Skirrid (the food outclasses most restaurants), the straightforward Queens Head near Llandudno Junction, the picturesque White Swan at Llanfrynach, the Red Lion at Llangynidr (a nice place to stay at), the Crown at Llwyndafydd (a bustling country pub), the sporty Griffin at Llyswen (popular with fishermen), the Grapes at Maentwrog (they do spit-roasts, and it's a nice place to stay at), the friendly Pelican at Ogmore, and the pretty, shuttered Salusbury Arms at Tremeirchion. Pubs that owe part of their charm to their position include the Cresselly Arms facing the tidal creek at Cresswell Quay, the Sailors Safety under the dunes in its remote cove at Dinas Head, the Boat in an unsurpassed spot on the River Dee at Erbistock, the mountaineers' Pen-y-Gwryd in the heart of Snowdonia near Llanberis, the Abbey of Llanthony (part of a remote and glorious ruined Norman priory), and the friendly and old-fashioned Harp on its hill at Old Radnor (a nice place to stay at). Other places not yet mentioned that are nice to stay at include the neatly kept Bear in Cowbridge, the welcoming Harp at Glasbury (a real bargain), and the cheerful Trewern Arms at Nevern. New to the Guide *this year are the White Horse at Cilcain (simply furnished, with a homely atmosphere), the thatched Green Dragon at Llancadle (recently extended, with good food and an interesting range of drinks), the friendly Cerrigllwydion Arms at Llanynys (rambling rooms and good food), the ancient Old House at Llangynwyd (what is now its restaurant was the first Nonconformist chapel in the Valleys), the isolated and warmly welcoming Brynffynon at Llanwonno, and the successfully refurbished We Three Loggerheads at Mold. Back as main entries are the unpretentious Harbourmaster at Aberaeron and the fourteenth-century Pendre at Cilgerran (new licensees). There are also new licensees at the Joiners Arms at Bishopston (the best pub on the Gower Peninsula), the Swan at Little Haven (with its lovely view over the cove), the Red Lion in the Welsh-speaking village of Llansannan, and the lively Captain's Wife near Penarth. Lucky Dips worth a special mention are the White Horse at Capel Garmon, the Bridge End at Crickhowell, the Old Black Lion at Hay on Wye, the Hand and the West Arms, both at Llanarmon Dyffryn Ceiriog, the Glansevern Arms near Llangurig, the Radnor Arms at Llowes, the Ship at Porthmadog and the Royal at Usk; also, the Prince Llewelyn at Beddgelert, the Golden Cross at Cardiff, the Carew Inn at Carew, the Bluebell at Carmarthen, the Tyn-y-Groes at Ganllwyd, and the Llanerch at Llandrindod Wells.*

ABERAERON (Dyfed)   SN4462 Map 6

Harbourmaster

Quay Parade

Sitting on the harbour wall outside this friendly and unpretentious harbourside pub, you look across moored yachts and boats to a picture-book row of colourfully painted houses. Inside, the dark-panelled downstairs bar has good local sea photographs above its green button-back banquettes, and a fine atmosphere (especially when the skippers are in). Food includes a generous ploughman's (£1.75) and decent salads (from £3.25), though readers are most enthusiastic about the seafood – mussels in garlic butter, for instance (£2.50), or really fresh plaice (£2.95). Well kept Marstons Pedigree and Powells Bitter on handpump; efficient service. *(Recommended by Lord Evans of Claughton, D S Rusholme, Doug Kennedy, W S Mills and others)*

Free house   Licensee John Davies   Real ale   Meals and snacks (not Sun)   Upstairs restaurant (closed Sun)   Children welcome   Open 11.30–3, 5.30–11 (11–11 Sat) all year Bedrooms tel Aberaeron (0545) 570351; £12(£15B)/£20(£25B)

nr ABERYSTWYTH (Dyfed) SN5882 Map 6
Halfway Inn ★
Pisgah; on A4120 towards Devil's Bridge, 5¾ miles E of junction with A487

A warm and lively atmosphere, good no-nonsense food, sensible traditional furnishings, an attractive choice of wines in the communicating wine-bar area, charming Vale of Rheidol surroundings, and half a dozen well kept and often interesting changing real ales: what more could you want? Perhaps this fine pub's special bonus is the way you're trusted to pour your own beer, straight from the imposing row of casks, then leave the right money in the dish (they also pull pints by handpump for those who prefer to leave the task to the professionals). The bar has bare stone walls, stripped ceiling-beams, stripped deal tables and settles on its flagstones, and a heavily beamed dining area opening off; it can get very busy in summer, so arrive early if you want to eat. Bar food, genuinely no-chips, includes filled French bread, rich thick soup (98p), a good few vegetarian and vegan dishes (from £1.95), faggots (£2.20), quiche Lorraine (£2.40), giant Cornish pasty or chilli con carne (£2.60), good pies such as steak and kidney (£2.80), well made lasagne, pizzas (£2.95) and roasts (£3.10); Symonds farm cider or perry as well as the real ales – they rotate the choice of these among the fifty or sixty they can get delivered; darts, cribbage and dominoes, maybe loudish piped music; no dogs. Outside, picnic-tables sets under cocktail parasols have fine views of gentle pasture hills and forests; children's play area, free overnight camping for customers, a paddock for ponytrekkers, and even free parking and picnic space for visitors – whether or not they use the pub. They organise various special events such as sheep-shearing and vintage motor-cycle rallies. *(Recommended by Doug Kennedy, Peter Griffiths, W S Mills, Robert and Vicky Tod)*

Free house   Licensee Keith Mees   Real ale   Meals and snacks (not Sun)   Restaurant (closed Sun) tel *Capel Bangor (097 084) 631   Children in restaurant and eating area (not Sun) Occasional folk groups, open-air choirs, brass or silver bands as special events   Open 12–3, 6–11 all year; closed Sun*

BEAUMARIS (Anglesey) SH6076 Map 6
Olde Bulls Head ★ ⊗
Castle Street

Under the newish owners, the emphasis in this interesting partly fifteenth-century inn has shifted to food – particularly in the restaurant, where readers have recently been reporting imaginative cooking of good ingredients such as fresh halibut, sea-bass, salmon and local lobster or duck, pigeon and sirloin, interesting light sauces and attractive presentation. But the antique character of the rambling low-beamed bar stays much the same, with low-seated settles, leather-cushioned window seats and even the town's oak ducking-stool in a snug alcove at one end. It's decorated with copper and china jugs, masses of cutlasses, and a rare seventeenth-century brass water-clock over the open fire. Lunchtime bar food, changing daily, might include soup (90p), sandwiches (from £1.10), ploughman's (£1.95), fresh local seafood pancake with cheese sauce, fricassee of veal or home-made meatballs (£2.95) and poached salmon (£3.25); home-made puddings such as walnut and syrup tart and rhubarb crumble (£1.10); well kept Bass on handpump; cheerful service; dominoes. The entrance to the pretty courtyard is closed by the biggest single hinged door in Britain. *(Recommended by C J McFeeters, Lynne Farrell, KC, Gill and Neil Patrick)*

Free house   Licensee D I Robertson   Real ale   Meals and snacks (lunchtime, not Sun) Restaurant   Children in eating area and restaurant   Open 11–10.30 (11 Sat) all year Bedrooms tel *Beaumaris (0248) 810329; £28B/£47.50B*

BETWS-Y-COED (Gwynedd)   SH7956 Map 6
Ty Gwyn ⊗ 🛏

A5 just S of bridge to village

To enjoy this cottagey old place, you do have to eat – or stay. Connoisseurs of the unusual in inn furniture find that worth while, though: the bedrooms as well as the beamed lounge bar suggest an antique-shop rather than a pub. Indeed, the owners have one, next door. There's carpet on the oak parquet, comfortable chintz easy chairs, interesting antique prints and heavy-horse harness, and copper and brass pans brightening up the ancient black and brass range at one end. Bar food, all home made, includes very generous helpings of soup (£1.25), sandwiches, pâté or ploughman's (£2.25), Spanish omelette, lasagne, chicken, lamb's liver Strogonoff, crab claws in garlic butter or scampi (all £3.95), fresh plaice or gammon with pineapple (£4.50) and sirloin steak (£6.95); children's meals (£1.95). There's also a pretty two-roomed low-beamed dining-room. Well kept McEwans 80/- and Youngers Scotch Ale on handpump. *(Recommended by C F Walling, Wayne Brindle, John Innes; more reports please)*

Free house   Licensees Jim and Shelagh Ratcliffe   Real ale   Meals and snacks   Restaurant Children welcome   Open 12–3, 6.30–11 all year   Bedrooms tel Betws-y-Coed (069 02) 383; £15/£30(£37B)

BISHOPSTON (W Glam)   SS5789 Map 6
Joiners Arms

50 Bishopston Road; village signposted from B4436, on the Gower Peninsula

An unusually good atmosphere – like a warm-hearted local, but making strangers feel very at home – marks this neatly kept beamed pub, the best on the splendid Gower Peninsula. What you notice first in the attractively restored front bar is the unusual spiral staircase, the massive stove, and the copper-topped stone bar counter (serving well kept Bass and Worthington BB from handpump). There's a lot of stripped stone, with comfortable traditional furnishings (including some carved-oak fitted benches) on the quarry-tiled floor. The brighter white-painted lounge bar is full of local paintings. Good value simple home-made bar food includes filled rolls, chilli con carne (from £2), chicken curry (£2.50), chicken pie (£2.60) and steak and kidney pie (£2.75); children's meals from (£1.75); darts. *(Recommended by Mrs June Borrelli, Jenny and Brian Seller, Michael and Alison Sandy, Chris Perry)*

Free house   Licensees A H and G P Mort   Real ale   Meals and snacks   Children welcome Nearby parking can be difficult   Open 11–11; 11.30–3.30, 6–11 in winter

BODFARI (Clwyd)   SJ0970 Map 6
Dinorben Arms ★ ★ ⊗

From A541 in village, follow Tremeirchion 3 signpost

This is an object-lesson in how an old pub can move with the times (and cope efficiently with a great many diners) without losing its distinctive identity. It's been imaginatively extended, keeping old-fashioned settles and other seats, old beams with tankards and flagons hanging from them, tapestry-look wallpaper, high shelves of china, and open fires in the three rooms which open off its heart – the quick-service starters and puddings counter, by an ancient glassed-in well. Lunch-time bar food includes soup with unlimited French bread (80p), filled French bread, and a good value eat-as-much-as-you-like smorgasbord counter with three hot dishes as well as at least half a dozen cold meats, some ten fish dishes and a couple of dozen salads. Evening main courses include three-egg omelettes (from £2.75), plaice (£3.20), curries (from £3.55), scampi (£3.75), home-made steak and kidney pie or chicken, ham and mushroom pie (£3.75), salads (from £3.75, poached

sandwiches; a good choice of often original puddings such as lemon cream pie
(£1.50). Well kept Bass and Ruddles on handpump. There are seats on the sheltered
back lawn. The back bedrooms are the quieter, with readers keener on the new
block. *(Recommended by Angela Dewar, Gordon Theaker, Philip King, Nick Dowson,
Stephen R Holman, TBB, Janet and Gary Amos, Jon Wainwright, Dr Desmond Roberts,
John Milroy)*

*Free house   Licensee Mrs Judy Hindmarsh   Real ale   Meals and snacks   Restaurant (closed
Sun)   Children in eating area until 8.30   Open 11–11 all year   Bedrooms tel Crickhowell
(0873) 810408; £30/£30(£38B)*

CWM GWAUN (Dyfed)   SN0035 Map 6
Dyffryn Arms

Pontfaen; Cwm Gwaun and Pontfaen signposted from B4313 E of Fishguard

One of our favourite untouched-by-time pubs, this cottage has been run by the
same family for longer than any other we know of – since 1840. The cosy little bar
has deal settles and kitchen chairs on the red and black tiled floor, with well kept
Bass and Ind Coope Burton tapped from the cask into jugs and served through a
hatch. This little hamlet is tucked away in an idyllic oak wood valley (near start of
Good Walks Guide Walk 193) – well worth tracking down, and the pub's a
delightful place to spend a long evening; at the end, you might well imagine you've
time-warped back to about 1900. *(Recommended by Doug Kennedy; more reports please)*

*Free house   Licensee Bessie Davies   Real ale   Freshly cut sandwiches at lunchtimes
Children in separate room   Open 11–11 all year*

DINAS (Dyfed)   SN0139 Map 6
Sailors Safety [illustrated on page 835]

From A487 in Dinas Cross follow Bryn-henllan ½, Pwll Gwaelod 1 signpost

We first came across this pub after an exhilarating walk high above the waves
around windswept Dinas Head: huddled low behind the dunes of this isolated cove,
it's more or less survived the storms for four hundred years, though the garden
furniture clearly has a struggle. Inside, there are big scrubbed deal tables, fat whisky
kegs and pews on the sawdusted red tiles, with an engagingly yo-ho-ho décor of
nets, lobster-pots, seashells, sailing pictures and ships' wheels. There's a quieter
dimly lit back room, and a brighter side bar has darts, pool, dominoes, cribbage,
fruit machine, space game and video juke box. The atmosphere's really quite heady
and individualistic, even a bit like a private party in the evenings. Bar food includes
sandwiches (from 75p, fresh crab £1.25), Welsh cawl (£1.25), ploughman's
(£1.85), quiche (£2), salads (from £2 – fresh crab £3.50), home-made curry or lamb
kebabs (£3), Dover sole (£3.50), steaks (from £5.25) and fresh scallops (£5.75),
with children's dishes (£1). The elaborate brass-inlaid counter, carved for the pub in
1922, serves well kept Bass, Buckleys, Felinfoel Double Dragon and Ind Coope
Burton from handpump or straight from the cask; maybe piped music. *(Recommended by Mike and Alison Blank, Wayne Brindle, Doug Kennedy; more reports please)*

*Free house   Licensee Langley Forrest   Real ale   Meals (restricted Sat lunchtime) and snacks
Restaurant tel Dinas Cross (034 86) 207   Children welcome   Occasional summer folk
music weekends   Open 11–11; 11–3, 5.30–11 in winter*

DOLFOR (Powys)   SO1187 Map 6
Dolfor Inn ⊗ 🛏

Pub signposted up hill from A483 about 4 miles S of Newtown

Up an insignificant side road and really quite lost in the high hills, this simple
sixteenth-century country inn could easily have gone the way of so many others and

vanished. But it's been taken carefully in hand, and you can sense the energy that's gone into its modernisation from the obvious commitment of the friendly licensees – even ferrying readers to their cars under an umbrella. There are easy chairs, other comfortable seats and an open fire in the oak-beamed lounge, which opens into an eating area with red cloth banquettes around its well spaced dimpled copper tables; its white walls are decorated with reproduction advertising mirrors. Bar food includes filled rolls, fish (£3.30–£4.75), home-made lasagne (£3.50), salads (from £3.50), steak and kidney pie (£4.20), home-baked gammon and eggs (£4.95), steaks (from eight-ounce sirloin, £5.20) and home-made puddings (from £1); well kept Davenports and Tetleys on handpump, maybe piped music. The public bar has darts, bar billiards and dominoes. They ask for tidy dress, please. There are terrific views from the terrace. *(Recommended by P Grimshaw, Mr and Mrs John Robertson)*

Free house   Licensee Barry Wardle   Real ale   Meals and snacks   Restaurant   Well behaved children welcome   Open 10.45–2.30, 6–11 all year   Bedrooms tel Newtown (0686) 26531; £17/£30

EAST ABERTHAW (S Glam)   ST0367   Map 6
Blue Anchor ★ ⊗
B4265

In winter, the snug inglenook seats in the public bar are the prize spot – especially after around 2, when the low sun angles in on you from the small window. Beyond here, a real warren of little low-beamed rooms winds right around the pub, which dates from 1380. Ancient settles are worked into quaint alcoves, low doors take you through massive bare stone walls, and throughout there's an untroubled relaxed atmosphere, with plenty of open fires. Lunchtime bar food includes soup (55p), pasties or pie (55p), ploughman's (from £1.35), salads (from £1.90, fresh crab £2.50, fresh salmon £2.60), faggots or sausage and mash (£1.90), home-made cottage or steak and kidney pie (£2) and roasts (£2.50). They take a lot of trouble over their real ales, on handpump or tapped from the cask: Buckleys Best, Marstons Pedigree, Theakstons Old Peculier and Wadworths 6X and an interesting weekly guest beer such as Boddingtons or Butcombe; darts, dominoes and a sensibly isolated fruit machine. Rustic seats are set among tubs and troughs of flowers against the sunny front wall of the thatched and creeper-covered pub, with more stone tables on a newer terrace. From here a path leads to the shingly flats of the estuary. *(Recommended by Dr John Innes, Gwynne Harper, TBB, Lyn and Bill Capper; more reports please)*

Free house   Licensee W J G Coleman   Real ale   Lunchtime meals (not Sun) and snacks Children welcome until 8   Open 11–11; 11.30–3.30, 5.30–11 (11–11 Sat) in winter

ERBISTOCK (Clwyd)   SJ3542   Map 6
Boat
Village signposted from A539 W of Overton, then pub signposted

On the food side, the character of this sixteenth-century pub has become more that of a restaurant, and drinkers (most of them going on to eat) really have just the one small bar with oak tripod tables on crazy-paved flagstones, spindle-back chairs and a fire in an open-grate kitchen range. But you may still find customers in here playing dominoes or chess – and there are plenty of seats outside. Indeed, it's out here that the real charm of the place lies. Virtually alone by a country church, it looks out over the sleepy River Dee, with birds on the water and more singing in the steep woodland opposite. Old-fashioned seats by tables under cocktail parasols on a gravel terrace are surrounded by flowers and charming informal up-and-down lawns, with hanging baskets adorning the pub itself, and what amounts to a curtain of flowers on the low sandstone cliff behind it. Food includes soup (95p), sandwiches (from £1.25), ploughman's (£2.25), salads or lasagne (£3.25) and scampi or steak pie (£3.95); the puddings are enterprising (£1.10); children's meals (from £1.50). The comfortable beamed dining-room, with plush seats around antique oak tables, has small windows overlooking the river; a roomier annexe serves food from April to September; friendly service. *(Recommended by Gwynne Harper, Mr and Mrs J H Adam, AE, C F Walling, Jon Wainwright, J T Bridge, Ken and Barbara Turner)*

Free house   Licensee Mrs H G Mostyn   Real ale   Lunchtime meals and snacks   Restaurant (not Sun evening, nor Mon Oct–Apr) tel Bangor-on-Dee (0978) 780143   Children welcome   Open 11–3, 6–11 (11.30 Sat) all year

FISHGUARD (Dyfed)   SM9537 Map 6
Fishguard Arms
24 Main Street; A487 just E of central roundabout

Would that there were more town pubs like this unassuming yet idiosyncratic and warm-hearted little place, with its fine Felinfoel Double Dragon, Marstons Pedigree and Worthington BB tapped into a jug straight from the cask. The front bar is tiny, with some basic sturdy furnishings and an elbow-high serving-counter. Unless you're a rugby enthusiast (plenty of photographs for you), perhaps the most notable feature is the carefully lettered record, up on the ceiling, of how the price of beer here has changed since 1981. There are cheap snacks: baked potatoes, steak and kidney pies and pizza (around 55p–£1.10). The tiled entry corridor leads to a back room with a piano, coal fire and darts, shove-ha'penny, table skittles, dominoes and cribbage. *(Recommended by R A Corbett, Doug Kennedy, Dr and Mrs A K Clarke; more reports please)*

Free house   Licensee H C Phillips   Real ale   Snacks   No nearby daytime parking (but easy at night)   Impromptu piano and accordion music   Open 11–3, 6–11 all year; may open longer afternoons if trade demands

GLASBURY (Powys)   SO1739 Map 6
Harp 🛏
A438 just N of village turn-off

The lawn behind slopes down to the River Wye, with tables on a crazy-paved terrace; there are river views from big windows in the airy wood-floored games-bar, with its pine kitchen tables (and pool, shove-ha'penny, dominoes, cribbage, quoits, juke box and sitting space game). In winter the red-carpeted lounge has a log fire in its stripped-stone end wall; small red-cushioned Windsor chairs around dark tables, sensibly placed darts. Bar food includes filled rolls and sandwiches (from 70p), burger (85p), home-made soup (85p), filled baked potatoes (£1.20), steak and kidney or chicken and mushroom pie (£1.30), ploughman's (from £1.60), lasagne or chicken curry (£2.30), hot-pot (£2.40), scampi (£2.80) and a choice of vegetarian dishes; Flowers IPA and Original and Robinsons Best on handpump, Rombouts coffee; good service. At the price, the bedrooms are a real bargain. *(Recommended by Jonathan Rowe; more reports please)*

Free house   Licensees David and Lynda White   Real ale   Meals and snacks   Children welcome   Open 11–3, 6–11 all year; closed evening 25 Dec   Bedrooms tel Glasbury (049 74) 373; £10.50B/£20B

HAVERFORDWEST (Dyfed)   SM9515   Map 6
Bristol Trader
Old Quay, Quay Street; coming into town from A40 E, keep left after crossing river and take
first left turn

Ever since we've been hearing about it, readers have particularly enjoyed the warm
and friendly atmosphere here: it's had plenty of practice at looking after visitors,
catering to coasters from Bristol using the quay outside since 1360 (though the
trade ended in 1944). Popular home-made bar food includes sandwiches (from
60p), soup (£1.10, winter only), steak and kidney pie (£1.65), ploughman's (£1.75),
curries (£2.20), lasagne (£2.40), salads and chicken (£2.65), scampi (£3.10) and
gammon (£3.50); they grow some of the ingredients themselves. Comfortable seats
are set into the massive ancient walls, with green plush stools along the fine long bar
counter and around small round tables, and more tables up a couple of steps at one
quieter end. Well kept Ind Coope Burton on handpump; maybe piped pop music.
(Recommended by Wayne Brindle, Steve Dark; more reports please)

Free house   Licensee Michael Roach   Real ale   Meals (lunchtime, not Sun) and snacks
Open 11–3, 5.30–11 all year; all day Mon and Sat in summer; closed evening 25 Dec

KENFIG (Mid Glam)   SS8383   Map 6
Prince of Wales ★
2¼ miles from M4 junction 37; A4229 towards Porthcawl, then right when dual carriageway
narrows on bend, signposted Maudlam, Kenfig

Stripped back to ancient stone inside and now outside too, this is just about the only
survivor of the drifting dunes which by the early seventeenth century had buried
what was formerly an important medieval port. They still keep the alderman's mace
upstairs – and even hold Sunday school. The friendly main bar has heavy settles and
red leatherette seats around cast-iron-framed tables, closely set in a double row
(reminiscent of a bierkeller – and encouraging similar sociability). At remarkably
low prices, quickly served home-made food includes pasties, sandwiches and rolls
filled to order (from around 60p: the home-roasted meat is well done), lasagne,
cheese and potato pie or shepherd's pie (85p), steak and onion pie (90p) and faggots
(£1.05). There is a good range of well kept real ales: Bass, Marstons Pedigree,
Robinsons Old Tom, Theakstons Old Peculier and Wadworths 6X tapped from the
cask, and Worthington Dark Mild on handpump, with Worthington BB available
either way; dominoes, cribbage and card games; open fire. The pub is close to
Kenfig Nature Reserve, and sells fishing-permits during opening hours. *(Recommended by John and Joan Nash, TBB, Peter Griffiths, Tom Evans)*

Free house   Licensee Jeremy Evans   Real ale   Meals and snacks   Children in small lounge
(daytime only)   Spontaneous music in side room   Open 11.30–4, 6–11 all year

LITTLE HAVEN (Dyfed)   SM8512   Map 6
St Brides ⊗
Note: the inn is in the village itself, *not* at the hamlet of St Brides further W; park in village car
park opposite pub

Home-made bar food (spring and summer only) in this cottagey inn includes soup
served with home-baked bread (75p), sandwiches (from 80p, crab if available
£1.15), ploughman's (£1.50), crab pâté (£1.75), sausagemeat tart or mushroom
and cheese quiche (£2.25), smoked duck or ham salad (£2.75), sewin or salmon
(£3.50), fresh local crab (£3.75) and a daily special such as steak and kidney pie
(£2.75). The spick-and-span black-beamed bar is comfortably furnished, and its
decorations include unusually interesting variations on the brass theme: the
horsebrasses and harness include quite a few choice pieces, there are oriental wind

LLANDEWI SKIRRID (Gwent)   SO3416 Map 6
Walnut Tree Inn ★ ⊗
B4521

Food and service of the very highest order – by top restaurant standards, not just pub ones – lift this stylish Italian-run place right out of the ordinary. If our star ratings were for food quality (rather than for the earthier virtues of plain pubby appeal) the Walnut Tree would unquestionably have three. The remarkable choice of dishes runs to nearly twenty first courses, even more main dishes, and an almost endless range of splendidly eclectic puddings. Don't expect pub prices: the lightest starters now approach £5, and main dishes are commonly somewhat over £10. But all readers agree that the exceptional quality makes it worth every penny. Particular strengths include game, fresh fish and shellfish, home-cured meats, deftly fruity or herby sauces, and uncommon Welsh as well as Italian cheeses. The menu changes too often for us to predict particular dishes, but the sorts of things readers have liked most recently include fish terrine with a watercress coulis, salmon en croûte (the lightest filo pastry wrapping), and local lamb with a subtle sauce of orange, coriander and marsala, or with a beautifully dressed warm salad. Though people who do just make for the couple of token bar stools are treated kindly, this is decidedly a place to eat (the fact that they don't book tables except in the back restaurant lets us count the Walnut Tree as a pub – and they won't press you to have more than a first course if that's all you want). The small bar has some polished settles and country chairs around the tables on its flagstones, and pewter plates and advertising mirrors on the partly panelled white walls. It opens into an airy carpeted dining lounge with rush-seat Italianate chairs around gilt cast-iron-framed tables, and pictures on the walls. The atmosphere is pleasantly relaxed, and service efficient yet unrushing even at prodigiously busy holiday times. The wine list is excellent, especially in Italian wines (they import their own – as well as white truffles; the house wines by the glass are particularly good value); so is the coffee. There are a few white cast-iron tables outside in front. *(Recommended by Angela Dewar, Peter Griffiths, Philip King, Col G D Stafford, Rita Davis, M H Dickins)*

Free house   Licensees Franco and Ann Taruschio   Meals and snacks (not Sun, not Mon lunchtime)   Restaurant tel Abergavenny (0873) 2797   Children welcome   Open 12–3, 7–11 all year; closed Sun, 4 days at Christmas and 2 weeks Feb

nr LLANDUDNO JUNCTION (Gwynedd)   SH7883 Map 6
Queens Head ⊗
Glanwydden; heading towards Llandudno on A546 from Colwyn Bay, turn left into Llanrhos Road as you enter Penrhyn Bay speed limit; Glanwydden signposted as first left turn off this

Beautifully prepared home-made food, especially first-class local seafood, veget-ables, salads and puddings, brings what would otherwise be quite a straightforward village pub to the top of many holidaymakers' lists in summer. It's a welcoming and well kept place, too, with pleasant staff. The comfortable carpeted lounge bar has brown plush wall banquettes and Windsor chairs around neat black tables; it's given a slightly Spanish feel by the black wrought iron and arches in its white dividing wall. The food, in generous helpings, includes brown-bread sandwiches, soup (95p), quiche or lasagne (£3.25), steak and mushroom pie, Arbroath smokies with tomatoes and Parmesan cheese or sauté liver and smoked bacon (£3.75), lamb in tomatoes and ginger or fillets of fresh trout with anchovy and garlic butter (£3.95) and fresh salmon salad (£5.95); evening meals (when prices are slightly higher) have extras such as steaks (from £6.25) and seafood platter (£6.50). There are good puddings such as rum and raisin flan or cherry cheesecake (£1.40). The small public bar is quarry tiled; well kept Ind Coope and Burton and Tetleys or John Smiths on handpump, good coffee maybe served with a bowl of whipped cream; warm log fires in winter. There are some tables outside by the car park. *(Recommended by R M Sparkes, KC, David Millar, J R Smylie)*

Free house　Licensee Robert Cureton　Real ale　Meals and snacks　Open 11–3, 6.30–11 all year

LLANELIAN-YN-RHOS (Clwyd)　SH8676　Map 6
White Lion

Village signposted from A5830 (shown as B5383 on many maps) and B5381 S of Colwyn Bay

The carpeted front room of this cosy old pub has antique high-backed settles around its big winter log fire, one of them angled to screen off the door. Though the present building is only a few centuries old, there's been some sort of building here for 1200 years – the atmosphere has that assured welcoming depth that often seems to come to pubs with such a long pedigree. There are lots of toby jugs on the handsome beams, and a barometer among the pictorial plates on its butter-coloured walls. Beyond the flagstoned bar servery, a broad flight of steps leads up to a neatly spacious back dining area. Bar food includes good home-made soup (85p), sandwiches, big helpings of wholesome and well cooked straightforward hot dishes from chicken or pizza to steak, and salads; well kept Tetleys on handpump; genuinely friendly service, dominoes, cribbage, maybe piped music. Outside, rustic seats by tables under cocktail parasols look out to the hill pastures (there's good walking). This courtyard, sheltered between the pub and the church, is also used for parking. *(Recommended by Mr and Mrs J H Adam, M E A Horler, Laurence Manning; more reports please)*

Free house　Licensee Robert Doyle　Real ale　Meals and snacks　Children welcome lunchtimes and early evenings　Open 12–3, 7 (6.30 Sat)–11 all year

LLANELIDAN (Clwyd)　SJ1150　Map 6
Leyland Arms ★ ⊗

Village signposted from A494 S of Ruthin; pub on B5429 just E of village; OS Sheet 116 reference 110505

Rather elegant inside, with sophisticated food, this unusual and carefully run pub has a delightfully tranquil bucolic setting. It's part of a cluster of former farm buildings by a country church, separated by a stretch of quiet fields from the village itself. There are little bunches of flowers on the neat dark tables of the main room, with modern settles around dimpled copper tables in the smaller room by the servery, which has mugs hanging from its beams. Service is friendly, and the food might include soup (£1.20), sandwiches, chicken liver pâté (£1.75), lunchtime ploughman's (£1.95), good seafood pancakes, prawns in a light garlic sauce with chunks of home-made bread, various pies such as steak, mushroom and Guinness, rabbit or game (£4.25), pork, cider and walnut casserole (£4.95) and salmon with herb butter or halibut steaks (£6.95); pheasant, venison, partridge and sea-trout in season; Boddingtons Bitter on handpump, good coffee and cream; darts, dominoes. There are rustic seats on the grass outside, where the chatter of church-tower swallows vies with more distant poultry and farm-animal noises from the village. Booking would be wise if you want a meal. *(Recommended by Mr and Mrs J H Adam, J E Sharp, Cecil Eimerl, KL, Dewi and Linda Jones)*

Free house　Licensee Jenny Street　Real ale　Snacks (lunchtime) and meals　Restaurant Children in eating area　Open 11–3, 7–11 all year　Bedrooms tel Clawdd Newydd (082 45) 207;/£20

Sunday opening is 12–3 and 7–10.30 in Wales; but pubs in Ceredigion (Cardigan to the mouth of the Dovey) and the Lleyn Peninsula are not allowed to open at all that day.

LLANFRYNACH (Powys)   SO0725 Map 6

White Swan ⊗

Village signposted from B4558 just off A40 E of Brecon bypass

Considering it's so handy for a main tourist route into Wales, we're surprised we don't hear more of this attractive and well run food pub. It's sensibly laid out, with plenty of decently spaced tables by the front windows of the flagstoned lounge bar, which rambles back through the partly stripped stone walls into a series of softly lit alcoves; there's a big log fire. The wide choice includes soup (£1.10); light dishes from £2.10) such as ploughman's, lasagne or ratatouille au gratin; and more substantial dishes such as chicken curry (£3.80), haddock and prawn pie (£4.50), Welsh-style grilled trout with bacon or beef and mushroom pie (£6), scampi or baked crab (£6.50) and well hung steaks; they also do children's dishes (£1.70), and more egg cooking than most pubs. Though the friendly service is efficient, there may be longish waits at really busy times. Brains and Flowers IPA on handpump. It's a picturesque black and white building, facing the churchyard across a very quiet village lane; its secluded back courtyard is prettily divided into sections by roses and flowering shrubs, and overlooks peaceful paddocks. *(Recommended by Dr I J Thompson; more reports please)*

Free house   Licensee David Bell   Real ale   Meals and snacks (not Mon, exc bank hols) Children welcome   Open 12–3, 6.30 (6 Sat)–11 all year; open 7 in winter; closed Mon lunchtime (exc bank hols); closed lunchtime last three weeks Jan

LLANGYNIDR (Powys)   SO1519 Map 6

Red Lion ⊗ 🛏

Upper village, off B4558 (the quiet alternative to the A40 Crickhowell–Brecon)

The newish licensee's abundant energy has among other things gone into an unusually wide choice of well presented evening bar food. It includes nearly twenty starters, from home-made soup or mackerel pâté (£1.75) to curried prawns (£2.40), smoked haddock (£2.50) and prawns (£3.75). There are masses of main dishes such as home-boiled ham or home-made steak and kidney pie (£3.50), various vegetarian dishes such as chilli, curries, lasagne and wholemeal pies (£3.75), enterprisingly cooked rabbit (£4.25), lamb with rosemary and garlic (£4.50), grilled trout with almonds (£4.75) and steaks (from £5.75). The lunchtime choice has also been extended to include sandwiches (from 75p), ploughman's (£1.95) and salads (from £3.95). There are comfortable fox-brown leather armchairs and antique red-plush-cushioned settles in the old-fashioned bay-windowed bar, which leads into a simpler room with a wood-burning stove. Well kept Bass, Flowers Original and guest beers such as Greene King Abbot on handpump. Outside the creeper-covered sixteenth-century building is a neat sheltered garden. *(Recommended by Angela Dewar, Gordon Theaker; more reports please)*

Free house   Licensee Ellie Lloyd   Real ale   Snacks (lunchtime, not Sun) and meals (evening) Restaurant with midnight supper licence (closed Sun evening)   Children welcome Open 12–2, 6–11 all year   Bedrooms tel Bwlch (0874) 730223; £35(£40S) – terms for single occupancy by arrangement

LLANGYNWYD (Mid Glam)   SS8588 Map 6

Old House ⊗

Thatched and thick walled, this friendly pub known locally as Yr Hen Dy dates back in part to 1147, making it among the oldest in Wales; much more recently, what is now its restaurant was originally the first Nonconformist chapel in the valleys. The two rooms of the black-beamed bar have close-set gleaming copper tables, with a mixture of wheel-back chairs, old-fashioned but comfortably cushioned wooden wall benches and high-backed black built-in settles; there's quite a bit of china and brass (especially around the huge fireplace), and a relaxed but thriving local atmosphere. Perhaps the prize dish (even if it's not on the menu they'll usually do it for you) is well hung steak (sirloin £5.75), with other bar food including chicken or pork (£2.40), vegetarian lasagne or steak and kidney pie (£2.50), beef and ale pie (£3), gammon and eggs (£3.95) and fresh fish such as hake (£4.20); there are children's dishes (from 70p) and puddings such as raspberry charlotte (90p). Well kept Castle Eden, Flowers IPA and Original on handpump. The garden has a good play area. *(Recommended by John Nash, Alun and Eryl Davies, Julian Proudman)*

Whitbreads   Licensee Mrs W E David   Real ale   Meals and snacks   Children welcome   Restaurant tel Maesteg (0656) 733310   Open 11–11 all year

nr LLANRWST (Gwynedd)   SH8062   Map 6
Maenan Abbey Hotel ★ ⊗ ⇌

Maenan; A470 towards Colwyn Bay, 2½ miles N

Even in August this is the place for tranquillity. It's a steep-gabled early Victorian country house with a battlemented tower, set behind immaculate tree-sheltered lawns. Inside, a striking staircase and interesting settles in the hall make a good first impression, but the elegant back dining-lounge is even better, with its brocaded chairs around drop-leaf tables, lofty-pillared fireplace, landscape plates on a high Delft shelf above silky flowered wallpaper, and lots of potted plants in the tall windows. Everything's very well kept and solid. From the unusually wide choice of good bar food readers have picked out for value the original soups (95p), well garnished sandwiches (from 95p, crab £1.95), and asparagus wrapped in ham with cheese sauce (£2.95); other dishes include filled baked potatoes (from £1.75), ploughman's (from £1.95), pizzas (from £2.25), salads (from £2.45), beef curry with exotic fruit (£2.95), home-made lasagne (£3.25) and grilled local trout (£4.75). Besides interesting daily specials, you can choose from the restaurant menu, which includes a good value three-course lunch (£5.50). Vegetables are nicely cooked, and the puddings trolley wickedly toothsome. On a Saturday night there may be Welsh singing in the spacious front bar, which has Windsor chairs around the tables on its oak parquet floor, another log fire, and big stone-mullioned windows; well kept Bass on handpump, maybe unobtrusive piped music; friendly cats. Outside, there are plenty of tables on terraces and among topiary yews, with swings and a children's play-castle; fishing on the River Conwy and nearby lakes, and rough or clay-pigeon shooting. *(Recommended by KC, Rita Horridge, Mike Tucker, Eileen Broadbent, Cecil Eimerl, Ken and Barbara Turner)*

Free house   Licensee Richard Scott   Real ale   Meals and snacks   Restaurant with midnight supper licence   Children in coffee lounge   Welsh singing Sat evenings   Open 11–11; 11–2.30, 6–11 in winter   Bedrooms tel Dolgarrog (049 269) 247; £30(£45B)

LLANSANNAN (Clwyd)   SH9466   Map 6
Red Lion

A544 Abergele–Bylchau

The character of this traditional thirteenth-century inn continues much as ever since its recent change of tenant – especially in its highly traditional central parlour, with its grandfather clock, Victorian painting of a mother and her fractious child, shields and brasses on high beams, eighteenth-century oak armchair and great high-backed settle curving around the inglenook with its warm kitchen range. Bar food includes home-made soup (70p), sandwiches (60p), burgers (from £1.40), ploughman's (£2), steak and kidney pie or home-made cottage pie (£2.75) and salads (£3), with children's dishes (80p); cheap well kept Lees Bitter and Mild on handpump – or coffee, tea, hot chocolate. Other simpler bars have darts, pool, dominoes, cribbage, fruit machine, a juke box or maybe piped music; seats in the garden behind. The pub is set in a picturesque Welsh-speaking village where several lonely hill roads meet. *(Recommended by BKA; more reports on the new regime please)*

Lees   Licensee Mrs M Y Owen   Real ale   Meals and snacks   Children welcome   Open 11–3, 6–11 all year; considering longer afternoon opening in summer   Bedrooms tel Llansannan (074 577) 256; £9/£18

LLANTHONY (Gwent)   SO2928   Map 6
Abbey Hotel

Included for its unique setting which many readers adore, this is part of the prior's house of a graceful ruined Norman priory, founded in 1108. Steps up from the basic and simply furnished twin-vaulted crypt bar take you on to lawns among soaring broken arches, framing romantic views of the soft Welsh border hills. The pub is on the *Good Walks Guide* Walk 201. Both meaty and vegetarian burgers figure most strongly in readers' reports on the bar food, though puddings have come in for praise too; other snacks include soup (£1.10) and ploughman's (from £2.50); plastic plates and cutlery may be used in summer, when the friendly service may slow down. Well kept Brains Bitter, Flowers Original and IPA, and Ruddles County on handpump or tapped from the cask; also Welsh whisky. There are seats outside the front loggia. *(Recommended by Gordon and Daphne, Nancy Brien, Greg Parston, Mr and Mrs France, Julian Proudman; more reports please)*

Free house   Licensee I Prentice   Real ale   Meals and snacks (not Tues to Sat evenings) Restaurant (closed Sun)   Children welcome   Occasional live music   Open 11–5, 6–11; closed weekdays Dec–Mar   Bedrooms tel Crucorney (0873) 890487; £18/£30 (note that they get booked up many weekends ahead, when prices are £25/£35 instead)

LLANWONNO (Mid Glam)   ST0295   Map 6
Brynffynon

From B4277 Porth–Aberdare in Ferndale, turn off down into valley at S-bend by Commercial Hotel and Rhondda Independent Chapel; beyond the railway the road doubles so sharply back on itself that you have to go further up the dead-end and do a U-turn before you can continue uphill; also accessible from B4275 in Mountain Ash, and from Pontypridd via B4273 (keep straight on beyond Ynysybwl, bear left a mile later); OS Sheet 170 reference 028956

Alone by a church in the extensive mountain forest of St Gwynno, this unpretentious but well kept stone pub is truly welcoming (when we arrived at the end of a long wet walk, we were offered a towel to dry our hair). The main bar on the left can't have changed much since the last century, with its art nouveau mirrored coatstand, comfortably cushioned brown seat built right along one wall, high-backed upholstered settle, and round cast-iron-framed tables. Besides cheap pasties, filled baked potatoes and cheeseburgers, bar food very much depends on what happens to be in the larder; on our visit, light and fluffy home-made salmon rissoles with sturdy real chips (£2.25) or chicken (£2.50); other dishes could include curry (£3), lasagne or scampi (£3.60); well kept Flowers IPA on handpump; darts, TV, with a fruit machine in the hall and juke box in the spacious saloon on the right. Locals drop in with their dogs; Dino the little spaniel cross and the good-natured rottweiler seem to be fixtures. A fine place for walkers. *(Recommended by Julian Proudman, Dave Braisted)*

Whitbreads   Licensee R Williams   Real ale   Meals and snacks   Children welcome until 9 Occasional live music, quiz Weds in winter   Open 11.30–4, 6–11; 12.30–4, 6–11 in winter

Children welcome means the pub says it lets children inside without any special restriction. If it allows them in, but to restricted areas such as an eating area or family-room, we specify this. Places with separate restaurants usually let children use them; hotels usually let them into public areas such as lounges. Some pubs impose an evening time-limit – let us know if you find this.

LLANYNYS (Clwyd)   SJ1063 Map 6
Cerrigllwydion Arms ⊗

Village signposted from A525 by Drovers Arms just out of Ruthin, and by garage in Pentre
further towards Denbigh

One of those delightful places that looks quite small and even unremarkable outside
but turns out to ramble about unexpectedly once you get in, this has the additional
virtue of good bar food such as soup (£1), sandwiches (weekday lunchtimes), pâté
(£1.95), quiche (£3.50), steak and kidney pie (£3.95), fresh poached plaice with
lemon sauce (£4.20), chicken in white wine sauce (£4.50) and steaks (from sirloin
£7). The building dates back in part to around 1400, and without gimmicks (just a
few interesting knick-knacks) has a good deal of character – comfort too, with seats
ranging from green plush to older settles. Some walls are panelled, some stripped
back to old masonry, and the beams are clearly genuine. Well kept Buckleys Best,
Tetleys and Marstons Pedigree on handpump; darts, fruit machine, piped music; a
friendly and welcoming atmosphere. Teak tables on neat grass among fruit trees
across the quiet lane have a charming view up to low wooded hills; the church next
door is interesting. *(Recommended by Tim Locke, Mr and Mrs J H Adam, J A Jones)*

*Free house   Licensee Stephen Spicer   Real ale   Snacks (weekday lunchtimes, not Mon) and
meals (not Mon lunchtime)   Restaurant tel Llanysys (074 578) 247   Children in restaurant
Open 11.30–3, 7–11 all year; closed Mon lunchtime*

LLWYNDAFYDD (Clwyd)   SN3755 Map 6
Crown ⊗

Coming S from New Quay on A486, both the first two right turns eventually lead to the village;
the side roads N from A487 between junctions with B4321 and A486 also come within signpost
distance; OS Sheet 145 reference 371555

Now that they've settled in, the people who took over this country pub in 1987
have re-established the popularity of its honest bar food – sandwiches (from 70p),
soup (£1.10), ploughman's (£2.70), pizzas (from £3.20), salads including home-
made quiche (from £4), highly praised steak and kidney pie (£4.15), gammon
(£5.20) and steaks (from £6.60). The friendly bustling bar has red plush button-
back banquettes built against its partly stripped stone walls, copper-topped tables, a
big wood-burning stove, and a window seat looking down the prettily planted
tree-sheltered garden. It fills up very quickly on weekends, even out of season – get
there early if you want a table. Well kept Flowers IPA and Original and Sam
Whitbread, good cider; darts, dominoes and piped music in the bar, a fruit machine
in the back pool-room (winter only). A family-room has plenty of tables and
comfortable seats, and beyond it is a restaurant. Outside, there are picnic-table sets
on a terrace above a small pond among shrubs and flowers, and a play area has a
slide and rides. The side lane leads down to a cove with caves by National Trust
cliffs. *(Recommended by Wayne Brindle, D R Linnell, Denis Berry, Robert and Vicky Tod,
Dr R Hodgkinson)*

*Free house   Licensees D M Evans and K J Harper   Real ale   Meals and snacks (not Sun)
Restaurant tel New Quay (0545) 560396   Children in smoke-room   Open 11–3, 5.30–11
all year; closed Sun*

LLYSWEN (Powys)   SO1337 Map 6
Griffin ⊗

A470, village centre

Everyone who's told us of enjoying bar lunches in the comfortable and old-
fashioned Fishermen's Bar of this well kept inn has picked out the friendliness of the
landlord as a special reason for praise. The sandwiches can be relied on, and include
sugar-baked ham (£1.30), prawn (£1.80) and salmon, fresh or smoked (£2.15).

Indeed, with the River Wye just across the road, most days after Easter they serve brook-trout and salmon, caught by the family or by customers. Other bar food might include home-made Scotch eggs (£1.20), soup, moules marinière (£2.35), rabbit (£3.65), seasonal game such as roast pheasant (£4.95) and traditional home-made puddings like spotted dick. The heavy-beamed bar has comfortable upholstered stools, big Windsor armchairs and leatherette wall benches around its low tables, and a big stone fireplace with a good log fire. It's decorated with old fishing tackle and flies, horsebrasses and harness. The restaurant, which serves full meals in the evenings, gives extra seating space for the bar lunches. Well kept Brains Best and Flowers IPA on handpump, with a guest beer; quoits played, dogs allowed; Salmon and trout-fishing by arrangement. (*Recommended by L G and D L Smith, Anthony Land, Philip King, John Nicholson, Col G D Stafford*)

Free house Licensees Richard and Di Stockton Real ale Meals and snacks (not Sun evening) Restaurant (evening) Children welcome Open 11–3, 6–11 in summer; 12–2.30, 7–11 in winter Bedrooms tel Llyswen (087 485) 241; £16B/£30B

MAENTWROG (Gwynedd)   SH6741 Map 6
Grapes ★ ⊗ ⇌

A496; village signposted from A470

A shrine to stripped pine, this cheerful inn has settles, pews, panelling, pillars and carvings salvaged lovingly from one chapel or another. Even in winter, when the lively crowds have gone, there's a warm atmosphere – thanks to plenty of log fires (there may be spit-roasts in the great hearth of the silvery granite restaurant; more pine panelling here too, of course). For summer, there are seats on a good-sized verandah (with a shellfish counter at one end) overlooking the pleasant back terrace and walled garden, which has a fountain on the lawn. A wide choice of hearty home-made bar food includes filled baps (from 55p), salads (from £2.50) and ploughman's (from £1.80) – these three lunchtime only; jumbo sausage (£1.20), smoked bacon in French bread (£1.75), steak and kidney pie (£3.25), eight-ounce rump steak (£5.50) and a good many specials such as tandoori chicken (£3.85), local salmon (£5.95), or maybe lobster salad (£8.25). The restaurant now offers spit roasts, barbecues, fondues and other speciality evenings with a full à la carte menu over the weekend. Efficient and friendly service even at the busiest times, well kept Bass and Stones on handpump, piped music; darts, dominoes, cribbage and juke box in the public bar. (*Recommended by Gavin May, Anthony Land, G A Worthington, Steve Dark, KC, Chris and Liz Norman, Sue Cleasby, Mike Ledger, S V Bishop*)

Free house Licensee Brian Tarbox Real ale Meals and snacks Restaurant Children in dining-room and restaurant Open 11–11; 11–3, 6–11 in winter Bedrooms tel Maentwrog (076 685) 208; £17B/£34B

MOLD (Clwyd)   SJ1962 Map 7
We Three Loggerheads

Loggersheads; A494 3 miles towards Ruthin

For a long time this eighteenth-century roadside pub has been quite a sleepy local, but it's now had an expensive and very successful refurbishment. It's on two levels; most spacious up steps at the back, which has high rafters, pillars and a striking décor of deep greens and pinks, with heavy farm implements, carts and a stuffed rook up over a false ceiling, and green cloth banquettes set into stripped-wood stalls. Down below, a smaller area is more restrained but shares a similar style. There are attractive converted elaborate paraffin lamps, prints of owls and other country subjects, more stuffed birds and a stuffed fox; the atmosphere is quietly thriving. Bar food includes sandwiches (from 95p, with more elaborate double- and triple-deckers), samosas (£1.75), Greek sausage with pitta bread (£2.45), a choice of ploughman's (£2.95), home-made steak and kidney pie (£3.40) and chicken and mango curry (£3.95), with interesting daily specials, often charcoal-grilled such as fresh sardines (£2.25) or tandoori kebab (£6.95); well kept Bass on handpump, juke box; the tiled-floor locals' games-bar has pool, dominoes and cribbage. There are white tables and chairs on a side terrace. (*Recommended by Michele and Andrew Wells*)

Bass   Licensee G M Willard   Real ale   Meals and snacks (not Sun evening)   Children in eating area   Open probably 12–11 all year; closed evening 25 Dec

NEVERN (Dyfed)   SN0840 Map 6
Trewern Arms ★ 🏠

B4582 – a useful short-cut alternative to most of the A487 Newport–Cardigan

For a friendly evening in the bar, this is the first choice of a good many people living within a reasonable drive. It's an unusual room, with nets, ships' lamps, ancient farm and household equipment, shepherds' crooks and cauldrons strung from its high pitched rafters. Walls are stripped stone, floors slate (handy for one of the nearby River Nevern's rare floods), and there's a big log fire to warm the plush banquettes and pair of high-backed traditional settles. A back games-room has sensibly placed darts, pool and dominoes; beyond is a comfortable lounge. Reasonably priced bar food in generous helpings includes toasted sandwiches, ploughman's, cod or cold ham (£2.75), chicken (£2.90), plaice, lasagne or cottage pie (all £3), home-made steak and kidney pie (£3.15), scampi (£3.20), steaks (from £5.90) and children's dishes such as beefburger served with chips or waffles (£1.60); well kept Flowers IPA and Original on handpump. There are tables on the lawn among shrubs and small trees. Across the medieval bridge over the River Nyfer, the church has pre-Christian stones set into its windows, and a Celtic cross in the yew-shaded graveyard. (*Recommended by John Branford, Wayne Brindle, Steve Dark; more reports please*)

Free house   Licensee Molly Sanders   Real ale   Meals and snacks   Restaurant   Children welcome   Open 11–3, 5.30–11 all year   Bedrooms tel Newport (0239) 820395; £15B/£22.50B

OGMORE (Mid Glam)   SS8674 Map 6
Pelican ⊗

B4524

Just above the ruins of Ogmore Castle, this has a friendly and cosy carpeted bar with attractively upholstered built-in wall seats around the decent wooden tables in its snug alcoves, a shelf of decorative playes and polychrome mugs just below the ochre plank ceiling, swagged pink curtains, harmonising carpet, and curly wrought-iron wall lamps with pretty porcelain shades. Good value bar food changes from day to day; besides sandwiches (from £1), ploughman's (£1.65), salads (£3.25), soup in winter (£1) and the popular and well filled steak and mushroom toasted sandwich (£1.80), there might be fresh fish, home-made lasagne, curry or steak and kidney pie (£2.75) – help yourself to fresh vegetables. Stub walls with inset glass panels mark off a charming little carvery restaurant. Well kept Courage Best and Directors on handpump, unobtrusive fruit machine and piped music. A side terrace has picnic-table sets, with swings beside it. (*Recommended by Hugh O'Donnell, J P Berryman; more reports please*)

Courage   Licensee Owen Maund   Real ale   Meals and snacks   Open 11.30–4, 6.30–11; considering longer afternoon opening in summer

---

All *Guide* inspections are anonymous. Anyone claiming to be a *Good Pub Guide* inspector is a fraud, and should be reported to us with a name and description.

OLD RADNOR (Powys)   SO2559 Map 6

Harp ★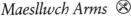

Village signposted from A44 Kington–New Radnor just W of B4362 junction

Readers have high praise for the licensees of this idyllically placed and meticulously kept hilltop inn. They've got the atmosphere and furnishings just right, and there are often interesting locals in the old-fashioned brownstone public bar, too; it has high-backed settles, an antique reader's chair and other elderly chairs around its log fire. There's another good fire in the lounge's fine inglenook, which still has its bread oven; furnishings in this cosy slate-floored room include a handsome curved antique settle, and it gives remarkable views out over the Radnor Forest and the Lugg Valley. Good simple bar food, changing from time to time, might include sandwiches (from 65p, toasties 85p), ploughman's with Stilton cut from the whole cheese (£1.65), baked potato with prawns (£2.50), faggots (£2.40), lasagne (£2.50), a good chicken curry (£3.50) and a hefty helping of gammon and egg (£3.60); children's meals (from £1.30); the dining-room, which has its own bar servery, is small and snug, with fresh flowers and lacy tablecloths – evening main dishes here mostly £6.50. Table quoits (matches on Mondays in winter, Tuesdays in summer), darts (Fridays) and tip-it. There's plenty of seating outside, under the big oak tree, on the green by the fifteenth-century turreted church, and on the side grass where there's a play area. *(Recommended by Alan Franck, Anne Morris, Colin and Caroline, M J Steward, Tim Locke, Mr and Mrs H G Bentley)*

Free house   Licensees Robert and Shirley Pritchard   Meals and snacks (not Tues lunchtime) Children welcome   Open 11.30–2.30, 7–11 all year (closed Tues lunchtime)   Bedrooms tel New Radnor (054 421) 655; £18B/£30B

PAINSCASTLE (Powys)   SO1646 Map 6

Maesllwch Arms ⊗

B4594

Run by two generations of the same family, this neatly kept inn is mentioned in Kilvert's *Diaries*. Good bar food – cooked by Mrs Gordon, the Joneses' daughter – includes soup (£1), ploughman's (£1.85), mussels in garlic (£1.95), cottage pie (£2.30), home-made steak and kidney or fish pie (£2.75), a couple of vegetarian dishes (£2.95), mixed grill (£4.95) and sirloin steak (£6) – all good, generous and well presented (proper salad dressing without being asked); puddings are uncommonly good. Quiet most lunchtimes, though often lively in the evenings, the simple little public bar has one stripped stone wall with a shelf of toby jugs, small settles around the three tables, a good wood-burning stove and sensibly placed darts. The airy lounge has big windows, plush bucket armchairs around coffee tables on the brown and green carpet, and a clean black and white look (black laths on the walls, black ceiling-joists); well kept Flowers Original and a guest beer tapped from the cask, good value house wines; dominoes, cribbage and piped music. There are one or two tables outside in front. At nine hundred feet up in the border hills, this remote village is surrounded by sheep pastures and higher moors criss-crossed with ancient tracks (useful now for the ponytrekkers). *(Recommended by J R Pye; more reports please)*

Free house   Licensees Mr R S Jones and Mrs W A Jones   Real ale   Meals and snacks Children welcome   Evening restaurant (though open for Sun lunch)   Open 11–2.30-ish, 7–11 all year   Bedrooms tel Painscastle (049 75) 279; £10/£20

Bedroom prices normally include full English breakfast, VAT and any inclusive service charge that we know of. Prices before the '/' are for single rooms, after for two people in double or twin (B includes a private bath, S a private shower). If there is no '/', the prices are only for twin or double rooms (as far as we know there are no singles).

nr PENARTH (S Glam)   ST1871 Map 6
Captains Wife ⊗

Beach Road, Swanbridge, which is signposted off B4267 at Penarth end of Sully

This entertaining seaside pub – opposite grassy Sully Island – has several areas that include snug booths with Liberty-print seats under a glossy red-plank ceiling, plush chairs and a high-backed traditional settle around an old tile-surrounded kitchen range in one low-ceilinged part, a high-backed curved settle and plush seats by an antique trestle table under high pitched rafters, and an upper gallery with a charcoal grill. There are exposed stone walls and Turkey rugs and carpets on broad bare boards. Well kept Brains Bitter, Flowers IPA and Original and a guest beer every two months on handpump from the good long bar counter, and lunchtime snacks. In summer you can eat at the heavy varnished tables on the flagstones of the pretty back courtyard, sheltered by low white former stable buildings. *(Recommended by Dr John Innes, TBB, Col G D Stafford, Michael Quine, Julian Proudman)*

Free house   Licensee Derfen Jones   Real ale   Lunchtime snacks (not Sun)   Two restaurants tel Penarth (0222) 530066; Grill open 7 days a week, Mariners open Tues–Sun lunchtime and Tues–Sat evening   Children in room set aside for them and in restaurant   Open 11–11 in summer; 11.30–3.30, 5.30–11 in winter

PENLLYN (S Glam)   SS9776 Map 6
Fox

Village signposted from A48

The smallish high-ceilinged bar here has plush seats and a biggish oriental rug on its dark flagstones, stylish dark tables, a coal fire, small prints on the white walls of the outer area, and stripped stone to go with the varnished beams of the inner part. Black and white uniformed waitresses serve the good bar food: sandwiches, home-made soup (£1.25), ploughman's (£2.25), tagliatelle (starter £2.75, main course £3.95), omelettes (from £2.95), home-baked ham (£3.50), pan-fried fresh plaice (£4.95), mixed grill (£5.45), king prawns (£6.95) and home-made puddings (£1.95). Well kept Flowers Original on handpump, good value house wines and decent malt whiskies; darts, dominoes, cribbage and piped music. There are neatly laid tables on a front terrace under a fairy-lit yew tree. *(Recommended by Barbara Symons; more reports please)*

Free house   Licensees Nigel and Sara Collett   Real ale   Meals and snacks (not Sat evening, not Sun)   Evening restaurant tel Cowbridge (044 63) 2352 (not Sun, though open Sun lunch) Children welcome   Open 11.30–4 (3 Sat), 6–11 all year; opens 7 in winter; closed Sun and 1 Jan

PENMAENPOOL (Gwynedd)   SH6918 Map 6
George III ★ ⊗ 🛏

Just off A493, near Dolgellau

This elegant seventeenth-century inn has a beamed and partly panelled upstairs bar with cushioned William Morris-style oak settles, more modern comfortable green cloth seats and older chairs around oak tripod tables, an antique salmon-rod and attractive local pictures on the walls, and a lovely view from its balconied bow windows to the forested hills on the far side of the Mawddach Estuary. Behind the bar, a cosy lounge has armchairs facing a big log fire in a stone inglenook, and there's an interesting collection of George III portraits. Home-made bar food includes soup (90p), pâté (£1.90), home-made steak and kidney pie (£2.95), roast spare rib of pork with barbecue sauce (£3), smoked trout (£3.60), Dublin Bay prawns (£5.45) and grilled Scotch sirloin steak (£7.25); maybe piped classical music. There's simpler summer food such as toasted sandwiches (from 95p), pizza

'1.50), and a self-service cold buffet (£2.75) in the cellar bar from Easter to
ctober; this has heavy beams, flagstones, long green leatherette seats around plain
rnished tables, stripped stone walls; darts, shove-ha'penny, dominoes and fruit
achine. The evening restaurant serves imaginative food, using good ingredients.
me bedrooms are in a very comfortable award-winning conversion of what used
be an adjacent station – the railway closed years ago; half the bedrooms in the
ain building have been redecorated, and the others will be completed at the end of
988. In competition with nearby otters, the hotel has estuary fishing just outside.
he waterside meadows are full of wildfowl, with a bird observation tower – you
ay even hear local rumours of ospreys kept secret from the RSPB, lest their reputed
st site up in the hills is inundated by birdwatchers. There are fine walks around
re, for example up the long ridge across the toll bridge. We have become so
customed to unanimous praise for this place that we have been pulled up short by
ne or two recent criticisms: surely there's been no real change? *(Recommended by
B Garside, D S Rusholme, Eileen Broadbent, Alan Franck, Gordon Mott, Gavin May,
oger and Judy Tame, Rita Horridge, Sue Cleasby, Mike Ledger, I J Clay, Rita Davis,
V Bishop)*

*ee house   Licensee Gail Hall   Lunchtime meals (not Sun) and summer snacks   Restaurant
losed Sun evening and May Day Mon)   Children in restaurant at lunchtime   Open 11–11 in
mmer; 10.30–3, 6–10.30 in winter; closed fortnight Christmas to New Year   Bedrooms tel
olgellau (0341) 422525; £38.50/£57.20B*

HIRENEWTON (Gwent)   ST4893   Map 6
Tredegar Arms ⊗

illage signposted off B4235 just W of Chepstow

his friendly village pub has a cosy carpeted main bar area with cushioned library
airs and Windsor chairs around wood-effect tables, and horsebrasses and etched
etal reproductions of brass-rubbings on the stripped stone walls. Good bar food
cludes pasties (95p), home-baked, filled French rolls (£1.20), pâté (£1.50),
oughman's (£2), scampi (£3), ham and egg, lasagne, chilli con carne and so forth
round £3–£3.25), home-made steak and Guinness pie (£3.50) and puddings such
chocolate-fudge sponge (£1.30); several dozen malt whiskies and well kept
ancocks PA, Smiles, Wadworths 6X and a guest beer on handpump. The public
ar has pool, sensibly placed darts, dominoes, fruit machine and juke box; open
re. There are seats in front and on a small and attractive sheltered back terrace,
ith pots of bright annuals. *(Recommended by Michael and Alison Sandy, E Kinnersly,
J E Phillips, AE)*

*ee house   Licensee Sidney Fell   Real ale   Meals and snacks   Children in eating area of
ar   Open 11–4, 6.30–11 all year*

ALGARTH (Powys)   SO1534   Map 6
Radnor Arms

oming from S take first turn-off into town, park in first car park and walk 50 yards up street

Vith so few pubs like this left today and, with news of the retirement of the present
censee, we have to keep our fingers crossed that it will retain its unique
nachronistic style. The kitchen parlour bar on the left is delightfully unspoilt – lots
f brass candlesticks and Bulmers' woodpeckers on the mantelpiece over the
oaring winter log fire in the gleaming black range, antique cream-painted settles in
ne polished flagstones, and beams in the dark ceiling. Well kept Whitbreads and
lowers Original are drawn into a jug at the glass-paned wooden servery, then your
rinks are brought to the table. There's a plainer room on the right. *(Recommended
y Roy and Pamela Wade, Simon Evans; more reports please)*

ee house   Real ale   Open 11.30–3, 5.30–11 all year; open all day Fri, second Sat of month

TREMEIRCHION (Clwyd)   SJ0873   Map 6
Salusbury Arms ⊗
Off B5429 up lane towards church

The beamed bar in this friendly, rural pub is on two levels – the lower part was originally the stables and dates from 1350, and some of the timbers came from St Asaph Cathedral. New carpets and furnishings in burgundy, cream and gold have been added, and there are oak beams, settles, brasses, log fires in winter, and a civilised and comfortable atmosphere. Bar food includes soup (85p), sandwiches (from £1.20), local sausages (£2.25), filled baked potatoes (from £2.25), ploughman's (£2.50), home-made curry, sweet-and-sour pork or steak and mushroom pie (£2.95), gammon with egg or pineapple (£4), steak (from £6), and daily seasonal specials such as moules marinière or game pie as well as occasional theme menus from Welsh to Chinese dishes; children's meals (£1.20). John Smiths on handpump, under light blanket pressure; dominoes, cribbage and trivia. The gardens are most attractive, with rustic furniture among neat flower and shrub borders, little waterfalls, and a pool with goldfish and Koi carp. When the weather's fine, you can see the coast. *(Recommended by KC, Dennis Royles, Mr and Mrs John Mathews, Mr and Mrs J H Adam)*

Free house   Licensees Iain and Catherine Craze   Real ale   Meals and snacks (not Mon lunchtime)   Restaurant tel Bodfari (074 575) 262   Children welcome   Open 12–3, 7–11 all year; closed Mon lunchtime (exc bank hols) and all day Mon Jan–Feb

WOLF'S CASTLE (Dyfed)   SM9526   Map 6
Wolfe ⊗
A40

Efficiently run and neatly kept, this busy food pub has a comfortable red-carpeted lounge, a garden-room or conservatory-restaurant, and a simpler tiled-floor public bar with darts, dominoes, fruit machine and piped music. Bar food includes sandwiches (from 70p), soup (95p), ploughman's (£1.85), a good choice of salads (from £2.25), smoked trout pâté (£2.35), locally smoked trout or ham off the bone (£2.85) and scampi (£3.95); you can also choose from the many restaurant dishes, including steaks (from £6.50). They're very good with children, and specialise in home-made puddings such as gateaux, syllabubs, roulades, meringues and profiteroles (£1.40). Felinfoel Double Dragon on handpump; brisk, friendly waitress service. Outside the slate-roofed stone house, white tables and chairs are sheltered by banks of shrubs, ash and sycamore trees, and surrounded by an arbour of roses and hanging baskets. *(Recommended by Wayne Brindle, D P and M E Cartwright; more reports please)*

Free house   Licensees Fritz and Judith Newmann   Real ale   Meals and snacks (not Sun evening, not Mon)   Restaurant (closed Sun evening)   Children in eating area and restaurant Pianist most Sat evenings   Open 11–11 in summer; 11–3, 6–11 in winter; closed 25–26 Dec, and Mon lunchtime Sept–Whitsun   One twin bedroom tel Haverfordwest (0437) 87662; £18S/£25S

Lucky Dip

Besides the fully inspected pubs, you might like to try these Lucky Dips recommended to us and described by readers (if you do, please send us reports):

Abercrave, Powys [SN8112], *Abercrave*: Very value good bar food at reasonable prices served quickly in atmospheric local with wide range of real ales; near Dan-yr-Ogof caves *(David Evans, J L and H M B Evans)*; [High St *Copper Beech*: A well laid-out free house with beams and dividers, friendly landlord and good atmosphere; comfortable benches and settles and a good range of beers such as Wadworths, Felinfoel, even Harveys; reasonable bar food, restaurant; bedrooms *(Mike Muston)*

Aberdare, Mid Glam [Heads of the Valley Rd; SO0002], *Baverstocks*: Hotel completely refurbished after extensive fire damage – spacious comfortably furnished lounge with one-price lunchtime buffet, serving hot dishes and salads; bedrooms *(Lyn and Bill Capper)*

Aberdovey, Gwynedd [SN6296], *Britannia*: Well kept Bass, good bar food and superb view over Dovey Estuary to mountains of N Cardigan, with balcony open in summer; hard to imagine a better situation *(A J Billingham, Mark Walpole, Melanie White)*

Aberdovey [opp Penhelig rly stn], *Penhelig Arms*: Attractive building overlooking sea with well kept Banks's Bitter and Mild, good bar snacks, warm atmosphere, privately owned, run with homely style; bedrooms good *(A J Billingham, J R Saunders)*

Abergavenny, Gwent [Flannel St; SO3014], *Hen & Chickens*: Seems to be getting increasingly busy at lunchtime and mercifully quieter at night; sandwiches first-class *(Pamela and Merlyn Horswell)*; [old A40, 2 miles E] *Horse & Jockey*: Clean and spacious pleasant pub with good value, freshly cooked bar food and good service *(K R Harris)*

Abergynolwyn, Gwynedd [SH6807], *Railway*: Old inn in tiny ex-mining village in beautiful countryside with exceptionally friendly landlord and staff, well kept Tetleys tapped from the cask; good home-prepared food including enormous club sandwiches *(Simon Gregory)*

Aberporth, Dyfed [SN2551], *Headland*: Good choice of Welsh Breweries beers, with Bass in summer; good reasonably priced pub food, well served; comfortable bedrooms *(C E Tyers)*

Abertridwr, Mid Glam [Eglwysilan; ST1289], *Rose & Crown*: Remote unspoilt hilltop pub above Pontypridd, surprisingly rural *(Julian Proudman)*

Aberystwyth, Dyfed [Queens Rd; 50 yds from N end of prom; SN5882], *Boars Head*: Cheerful back lounge and lively front pool-room, freshly cooked bar food, well kept Felinfoel, restaurant *(C D T Spooner, BB)*; [Corporation St] *Unicorn*: A fun pub with lots of knick-knacks and atmosphere; Bass on handpump *(Doug Kennedy)*

nr Aberystwyth, Dyfed [Llanbadarn Fawr; SN6080], *Black Lion*: Cheerful evening atmosphere in well run local with spacious back lounge, games area, well kept Banks's real ales, good value simple food and splendid play area in big sheltered garden with summer evening barbecues and well lit dance square *(LYM)*

Afon Wen, Clwyd [SJ1372], *Pwll Gwyn*: Attractive and cheery beamed Tudor pub, happy service, pleasant restaurant with good food, particularly steaks; flowers outside (tended daily by the chef) make it very pretty; name means White Pool (from marl clay behind inn); bedrooms *(Mr and Mrs P Jones, C M Phayre, Dr and Mrs A E Stubbs)*

Alltwalis, Dyfed [A485 about 7 miles N of Carmarthen; SN4431], *Masons Arms*: Good atmosphere, interesting varied décor, great range of local real ales, good-humoured licensee who takes a real interest in his customers – he and his wife dress in period costume; occasional dances *(Frank Cain, Patricia Deegan)*

Alltwen, W Glam [Alltwen Hill; SN7203], *Butchers Arms*: Nice view, good atmosphere, well kept Everards and Flowers, rustic décor with open fire and old settles; good reasonably priced home-made pies, separate dining-room *(Peter and Alison Davies)*

Bala, Gwynedd [High St; SH9336], *Olde Bulls Head*: Oldest inn in town – comfortably refurbished, with well kept Whitbreads, and straightforward bar food even in the evening when this area is a desert for food; bedrooms *(Eileen Broadbent, LYM)*; [High St] *Plas Coch*: Warm and friendly town-centre pub; bedrooms *(Wayne Brindle)*; [61 High St] *White Lion Royal*: New licensees doing well in eighteenth-century coaching-inn, beamed bar with inglenook fireplace, lots of character, Youngers No 3 on handpump, good bar meals, dinners and Sun lunches; bedrooms all with private bathroom *(Dougal Bannerman)*

Bangor, Gwynedd [High St; SH5973], *Harp*: Quite spacious softly lit converted 1740s coaching-inn, two welcoming open fires, Turkey carpet, beams, horsebrasses, high shelf of plates, well kept Marstons Pedigree, bar snacks; curious upstairs stone-floored pool-room, smaller TV room *(Jon Wainright)*

Barry, S Glam [Severn Ave; ST1168], *Cwm Talwg*: Comfortable new Brains estate pub, with good value food served in recently modernised upstairs restaurant, piped music *(Lyn and Bill Capper)*

Beaumaris, Gwynedd [SH6076], *Bishopsgate*: Well presented, good value food from a wide choice *(Mrs J Lloyd-Griffith)*; [Castle St] *Liverpool Arms*: Reasonably well modernised pub with lots of alcoves and a variety of bar snacks; bedrooms *(Mike Tucker)*

☆ **Beddgelert**, Gwynedd [SH5948], *Prince Llewelyn*: Civilised plush bar with raised dining area, simpler summer bar, rustic seats on verandah overlooking village stream and hills; new licensees doing decent choice of food at reasonable prices, well kept Robinsons, staff stay cheerful even when it's crowded; nr GWG206; bedrooms *(Drs G N and M G Yates, KC, BB)*

Beddgelert, Gwynedd [SH5948], *Tanronen*: Simply furnished main bar, separate lounge bar, well kept Robinsons real ale; nr GWG206; bedrooms simple but clean *(BB)*

Betws-y-coed, Gwynedd [A5 next to BP garage and Little Chef; SH7956], *Waterloo*: Modern and comfortable lounge bar used by locals and visitors with fine food from a wide selection of daily specials as well as a more standard menu, young enthusiastic staff; immaculate flower beds; comfortable bedrooms *(G Cotton)*

Bishopston, W Glam [Murton; off B4436 Bishopston–Swansea; SS5889], *Plough & Harrow*: Good choice of food in well run village pub with well kept real ales *(E J Knight)*

Bleddfa, Powys [A488; SO2168], *Hundred House*: Free house with good ales and good choice of reasonably priced, generously served food *(Joy Heatherley)*

Bonvilston, S Glam [ST0673], *Red Lion*: Friendly Brains pub with three areas in open-plan bar, decent bar food (not Sun), garden behind *(Lyn and Bill Capper)*

Bosherston, Dyfed [SR9694], *St Govans*: Straightforward decently run pub with Worthington on handpump, included for its value in this attractively bleak spot near the coast; piped music, bar billiards; nr start GWG190; bedrooms *(Neil and Elspeth Fearn, LYM)*

Brechfa, Dyfed [SN5230], *Forest Arms*: Big inglenook fireplace in main bar of simply furnished old stone inn popular with locals; restaurant; bedrooms *(BB)*

Broughton, W Glam [SS9170], *Plough & Arrow*: Attractive pub with real ale and first-class food *(Paul Watts)*

Bryncethin, Mid Glam [SS9184], *Masons Arms*: Good service, food, beer and atmosphere *(Paul Watts)*

☆ **Burton Meadows**, Clwyd [A483 Chester, right B5102 Rossett, right level-crossing, ¾m right T-junc – OS Sheet 117 reference 354587; SJ3559], *Golden Grove*: Half-timbered old pub with masses of carved beams, two open fires, settles and sofas, collection of plates, cosy corners though it's been knocked together; good atmosphere, efficient bar staff and Tetleys ales (recently taken over by them); also very smart restaurant *(Jon Wainwright)*

Bwlch, Powys [A40; SO1522], *Farmers*: A wide choice of good food – not cheap but often imaginative – in a smartly rejuvenated plush pub with big log fires and a good choice of real ales on handpump; primarily a dining place *(LYM)*; [A40] *Morning Star*: Unexpected range of snacks and meals – even frogs' legs – in very friendly eighteenth-century coaching-inn with Courage Best and Directors; closed Mon *(Gordon Smith)*

Caerleon, Gwent [Uskside; ST3490], *Hanbury Arms*: Pleasant old pub by the river with friendly licensee, Bass real ale, restaurant and bedrooms; cheap drinks during happy hour *(A C Lang)*;

Caerleon, Gwent [High St; ST3490], *Olde Bull*: Rather new olde-worlde surroundings which might quickly improve, especially if TV is removed; friendly staff, Ansells beer *(A C Lang)*

Caerphilly, Mid Glam [Cardiff Rd; ST1587], *Courthouse*: New pub with good range of food – including its own Caerphilly cheese; very friendly licensees and staff *(Paul and Rhian Hacker)*

nr Caerphilly, S Glam [Watford, off A469 just S of Caerphilly Common; quite near M4 junction 30 – OS Sheet 171 reference 144846; ST1487], *Black Cock*: Very popular well modernised country pub with well kept real ale, open fire and garden *(Tony Ritson)*

Caio, Dyfed [SN6739], *Brunant Arms*: Character, friendly atmosphere, good food at reasonable prices, licensees great fun *(Mrs M Ashwell)*

☆ **Capel Garmon**, Gwynedd [signposted from A470 just outside Betwys-y-coed, towards Llanrwst; SH8255], *White Horse*: Comfortable and cosy, with very friendly homely atmosphere, magnificent views, simple but good home-made food at good value prices, pleasant staff; in delightful countryside; bedrooms very reasonably priced and well equipped – marvellous breakfast *(Joy Heatherley, Cecil Eimerl, KC)*

☆ **Cardiff** [Custom House St; ST1877], *Golden Cross*: Renovated late Victorian pub, now a showpiece of conservation; much ornate tile-work, cast-iron tables and fireplace, and scrubbed floors; friendly licensees, Brains real ales and lunchtime bar food; has won first Prince of Wales award in Wales for conservation *(A J Ritson)*

Cardiff [St Mary St] *Albert*: Good atmosphere, lounge at back, well kept Brains Dark, Bitter and SA, bar food *(Alun Davies)*; [St Marys St] *Philharmonic*: Large theme pub with lots of atmospheric booths, a busy dark interior and huge chunks of good value various cheeses and bread at lunchtime; well kept Felinfoel and Websters *(A Cook)*; [West-gate St] *Queens Vaults*: Well run, Victorian-style pub, efficient friendly service, good value bar food, close to law courts and Cardiff Arms Park *(S Watkins)*

Cardigan, Dyfed [High St; SN1846], *Black Lion*: Well kept Flowers ale and quickly served bar food in spacious rambling lounge of seventeenth-century inn with stately Georgian façade; bedrooms *(Wayne Brindle, LYM)*

☆ **Carew**, Dyfed [A4075, just off A477; SN0403], *Carew Inn*: Simple welcome in traditionally furnished small country pub with well kept Worthington, snacks, pleasant seats outside and play area; attractive position near river, tidal watermill and ruined Norman castle *(Brian Jones, LYM)*

☆ **Carmarthen**, Dyfed [Cwmwyl Elfed, Llandeilo Rd; SN4102], *Bluebell*: Wholesome and extremely cheap home-made bar food in quaint old country pub with exceptional hospitality and friendliness, locals keep the atmosphere natural *(Alan Jones, S Watkins)*

Chepstow, Gwent [16 Bridge St; ST5394], *Castle View*: Perhaps a bit hotelish for this *Guide* but very efficiently run by charming welcoming people, well kept Marstons and John Smiths, outstanding good value food including vegetarian dishes, perfectly delightful garden; start GWG198; bedrooms well equipped and warm *(Joy Heatherley, SJC)*; [Moor St] *George*: Comfortable lounge bar in THF hotel: Bass and Websters Yorkshire, decent bar lunches; bedrooms *(Lyn and Bill Capper)*

Chirk, Clwyd [SJ2938], *Hand*: Plushly furnished connecting bars in spacious Georgian coaching-inn, food including children's dishes in buttery bar, Marstons Pedigree on handpump, games area in public bar; bedrooms *(Gordon Theaker, LYM)*

Cilycwm, Dyfed [SN7540], *Neuadd Fawr*: Welcoming Welsh-speaking village pub with home-made food, simple furnishings, cheerful atmosphere *(BB)*

Colwyn Bay, Clwyd [Chapel St, Mochdre; off link road between A470 and start of A55 dual carriageway – OS Sheet 116 reference 825785; SH8578], *Mountain View*: Well kept Burtonwood Best and Mild and fine choice of salads with other dishes from popular food counter, in neatly kept and spacious pub a bit like a comfortable modern clubhouse; pub games including pool *(Dr R Hodkinson, LYM)*

Colwyn Bay [Promenade], *Toad Hall*: Good food and accommodation (Balmoral Holiday Flatlets); spotlessly clean; in good position overlooking sea *(Mr R Mercer)*

Conwy, Gwynedd [Castle St; SH7878], *George & Dragon*: Recently restored old pub in attractive position, with garden backing on to town wall; superbly presented food, particularly puddings *(Wayne Brindle)*

Cosheston, Dyfed [SN0004], *Cosheston Brewery*: Good choice of real ales in attractive building with bistro-type food arrangements; locally popular *(Eric Stephens)*

Craig Penllyn, S Glam [SS9777], *Barley Mow*: Well kept Flowers IPA and Original, good bar meals, open fires in all three bars *(Paul Dennis)*

Crickhowell, Powys [New Rd; SO2118], *Bridge End*: New owners who formerly secured a main-entry place in this *Guide* for the Vine Tree at Llangattock have moved across the river to this delightful old pub in a splendid riverside setting; very busy, well kept beer and well served food, with lively, friendly atmosphere, pleasant décor and choice of Worthington real ales *(Pamela and Merlyn Horswell, Nick Dowson, Julian Proudman)*

Crickhowell, *Corn Exchange*: New owners have refurbished this pub and serve good, value-for-money food *(Pamela and Merlyn Horswell)*; [two or three miles NW, by junction A40/A479] *Nantyffin Cider Mill*: Popular food pub in attractive surroundings, lovely open fireplace with an original cider press, some cider-based food *(Mrs R Earle, John and Joan Wyatt)*; *Riverside*: Nice position on the River Usk, deservedly very popular for wide and imaginative choice of bar food including superb home-made

lasagne *(Tim Brierly)*

Cross Inn, Dyfed [B4337/B4577; SN5464], *Rhos yr Hafod*: Friendly and traditionally furnished Welsh-speaking country pub with well kept Flowers IPA; has had good value specials and smart upstairs restaurant, though no recent confirmation; NB not the Cross Inn near Newport *(LYM)*

Defynnog, Powys [SN9228], *Lion*: Carefully restored roadside pub with good value home cooking and real ales that may include ones rare for area, kept well; good atmosphere, enthusiastic and welcoming licensees – he's got a wicked wit *(Suzanne Thompson, LYM)*

Deganwy, Gwynedd [SH7880], *Deganwy Castle*: Plushly comfortable lounge with fine views, and pleasantly pubby rambling back bar with fat black beams, stripped stone, flagstones and lots of nooks and crannies; good choice of bar food, well kept Websters and Wilsons on handpump; bedrooms (this is a big hotel) *(LYM)*

Denbigh, Clwyd [SJ0666], *Bull*: Rambling bar with stylish Elizabethan staircase and old-fashioned furnishings, good robust range of bar food, real ale; bedrooms *(LYM)*

Dinas, Dyfed [A487; SN0139], *Freemasons Arms*: Cosy little pub, decently done up, part of a roadside terrace; bar food *(Wayne Brindle)*; *Ship Aground*: Several rooms opening off servery, sea pictures and ship's brassware, portholes and low pitched ceiling give boat feel to long side gallery, nice Nelson Jamaica Rum mirror over stone fireplace in softly lit back room; well kept Felinfoel Double Dragon on handpump, plain but good value bar food with children's helpings, good local atmosphere *(Mr and Mrs G D Amos, BB)*

Dinas Mawddwy, Gwynedd [SH8615], *Llew Coch*: Traditionally furnished village inn with hundreds of sparkling horse brasses, food including trout or salmon from River Dovey just behind (the dining area's very simple), well kept Bass, friendly local atmosphere and lively Sat evening music; surrounded by plunging fir forests *(S V Bishop, LYM)*

☆ **Dinas Powis**, S Glam [Station Rd; ST1571], *Star*: Good value Brains real ales and home-cooked pies and other food in attractively refurbished village pub with stripped stone walls or panelling and heavy Elizabethan beams *(Sheila Mackay, LYM)*

Dolgellau, Gwynedd [SH7318], *Unicorn*: Pleasant long room at two levels with fresh-cut sandwiches, hot snacks, Ansells Bitter and jazz on Weds; this is a busy concentrated small town with good facilities and an attractive centre from which to walk – Cader Idris–Fairbourne–Barmouth *(Peter Robinson)*

Eglwysbach, Gwynedd [SH8070], *Bee*: Handy for Bodnant Gardens, with simple bar food, Ansells real ales, lots of brass and copper, and goldfish; rustic seats outside *(LYM)*

Eglwyswrw, Dyfed [A487 Newport–Cardigan, at junction with B4332; SN1438], *Serjeants*: Antique high-backed settles in snug if basic bar with heavy black beams and capacious inglenook, Worthington BB on handpump, lounge and dining-room – and still a Petty Sessions court on the premises; bedrooms *(LYM)*

Fairbourne, Gwynedd [SH6213], *Fairbourne Inn*: Neatly kept and quite spacious bar that would be a credit to many big city suburbs, well kept Bass and McEwans real ale; grey stone hotel in holiday village near sea; bedrooms *(BB)*

Ffairfach, Dyfed [SN6221], *Torbay*: Wide choice of food, particularly reasonably priced seafood, in fairly straightforward oldish pub *(Mrs C Jennings)*

Fishguard, Dyfed [SM9537], *Ship*: Well kept Worthington real ales in nautically decorated and dimly lit fishermen's pub near old harbour *(LYM)*

☆ **Ganllwyd**, Gwynedd [SH7224], *Tyn-y-Groes*: Old Snowdonia inn owned by National Trust, fine forest views, salmon and sea-trout fishing, lots of malt whiskies, bar food and restaurant, sun lounge; bedrooms comfortable *(Peter Walker, LYM)*

Gladestry, Powys [SO2355], *Royal Oak*: Simple unpretentious and very friendly inn on Offa's Dyke, good simple home cooking at very reasonable prices, well kept Bass; children welcome; bedrooms *(Tim Locke)*

Graianrhyd, Clwyd [B5430; signposted off A494 and A5104; SJ2156], *Rose & Crown*: Small, bright, cosy country pub run by enthusiastic young licensee, good Marstons ale and good range of bar food including vegetarian dishes *(Mr and Mrs J H Adam)*

☆ **Grosmont**, Gwent [SO4024], *Angel*: Seventeenth-century village pub in attractive steep single street – nice to sit out, next to ancient market hall; welcoming atmosphere, reasonably priced simple home-cooked food (gammon and steak sandwich recommended), hospitable licensees who've been carefully modernising it, cheap Whitbreads real ale; bedrooms *(Julian Proudman, Lt Col R A Fell, Henry Outfin, David Ward Beecher, BB)*

☆ nr **Grosmont**, Gwent [B4347 N of Grosmont – OS Sheet 161 reference 408254; SO4024], *Cupids Hill*: Tiny homely pub, very basic and homely, alone on very steep hill in pretty countryside; friendly old landlord who doubles up as local undertaker (he was born here and took over from his father); main piece of furniture is sawn-off bagatelle table with plyboard top for standing the bottled beers (mainly Whitbreads) on; plain old settles by fire, low white ceiling; table skittles, dominoes, cribbage, friendly locals; of its type, a real prize *(Gordon and Daphne, MM, BB)*

Gwystre, Powys [A44 about 7 miles E of Rhayader – OS Sheet 136 reference 066657; SN0666], *Gwystre*: Friendly small free house

with good plain food, garden for children *(Dave Braisted)*

Hanmer, Clwyd [SJ4639], *Hanmer Arms*: Pubby atmosphere, good ales and food from sandwiches to steaks; very pretty village; bedrooms converted from stables, good value *(Keith Miller)*

Hawarden, Clwyd [SJ3266], *Blue Bell*: On the main street of a quiet town, this pub is warm, friendly and clean with good food and efficient service *(Mr R Davies)*

☆ **Hay-on-Wye**, Powys [26 Lion St; SO2342], *Old Black Lion*: Davenports on handpump and buffet food counter in comfortable low-beamed bar, handy for the antiquarian bookshops; under new owners and initially in a bit of a state of flux early in 1988, but as the year wore on readers were becoming enthusiastic about their refurbishments, and about well cooked food including good steaks; bedrooms comfortable and warm *(Mr and Mrs C M Metcalf, Mr and Mrs D Nicklin, Mrs P M Macaulay, LYM)*

Herbrandston, Dyfed [SM8707], *Sir Benfro*: Well kept inn with good food and comfortable good value bedrooms *(T P Lovesey)*

Higher Kinnerton, Clwyd [SJ3361], *Royal Oak*: Village pub with friendly bar and cosy lounge; Greenalls ales, good lunchtime and evening bar food at reasonable prices; small garden with aviary *(Peter Corris)*

Holywell, Clwyd [Greenfield Rd; SJ1876], *Royal Oak*: Good choice of well cooked food, presented nicely and served by waitress; massive choice of beers *(L Allen)*

Hundred House, Powys [SO1154], *Hundred House*: Low-beamed main bar and two further rooms, with wide range of food in huge helpings including imaginative daily specials such as chicken, vegetable and white wine pie or barbecued pork, very popular Sun lunch, children's dishes, even takeaways; well kept Welsh Bitter and HB, small choice of good value wines, charming efficient service, friendly locals, garden, marvellous countryside; closed Mon lunchtime, Tues; no food Mon evening *(Joy Heatherley)*

Kidwelly, Dyfed [SN4006], *Old Moat*: Old low stone building within ruined walls of splendid castle, tables on grass; concentration on somewhat pricey but popular food inside, good quickly served sandwiches, beers include Felinfoel, good log fire in old stone fireplace *(Anne Morris)*

Kittle, W Glam [SS5789], *Beaufort Arms*: Dates back to 1460 priory, run as pub for last hundred years; clean, popular and heavily refurbished (they've painted the heavy stone walls black with beige painted-in mortar); good food lunchtime and evening, a Buckleys pub, on Gower Peninsula *(Mr and Mrs R Batten, E J Knight)*

☆ **Landshipping**, Dyfed [SN0111], *Stanley Arms*: Attractive and surprisingly well appointed riverside pub with Worthington tapped from the cask and an imaginative choice of good value well served food that includes locally caught salmon and other fish; restaurant, ample parking (*E O Stephens, Canon G Hollis*)

Lawrenny, Dyfed [SN0107], *Lawrenny Arms*: Attractively situated, paved terrace (*Janet Williams*)

Letterston, Dyfed [SM9429], *Harp*: Good well renovated main-road pub with well kept beer and tables outside – most enjoyable (*Dr and Mrs A K Clarke*)

nr **Lisvane**, S Glam [follow Mill Rd into Graig Rd, then keep on; ST1883], *Ty Mawr Arms*: Country pub with sizeable garden, real ales such as Robinsons Best, Marstons Pedigree and Courage Directors on handpump, several comfortable rooms, lunchtime food (not Sun) (*LYM*)

☆ **Llanarmon D C**, Clwyd [SJ1633], *Hand*: Very civilised place to stay at, with atmosphere more reminiscent of a French country inn than a Welsh one, and good value food; it's a lovely village, too, and it's only a lack of readers' reports that keeps this – and indeed the next pub too – out of the main entries; bedrooms comfortable (*LYM*)

☆ **Llanarmon D C**, *West Arms*: Under same ownership as the Hand, and as civilised – though the back bar is a popular and often lively meeting-place for people from the surrounding hills; interesting lounge bar including elaborately carved confessional stall as well as sofas, antique settles and so forth; open fires, bar food, lawn running down to River Ceiriog (where residents of both places can fish free); children welcome in both inns, and this too has bedrooms (*LYM*)

Llanarmon Yn Ial, Clwyd [B5431; SJ1956], *Raven*: Basic take-it-as-you-find-it country inn with well kept Burtonwood Bitter and Dark Mild, simple bar food, friendly staff and locals, pleasant seats outside – this is an attractive village; bedrooms (*LYM*)

Llanarthney, Dyfed [B4300 (good fast alternative to A40); SN5320], *Golden Grove Arms*: Stylishly furnished and interestingly laid-out inn which has been popular for its unusually enterprising food, but was sold in July 1988 – just too late for us to get a clear idea of how it would turn out under its new owners; good value bedrooms (*Mike and Alison Blank, Frank and Jean Sherwood, Mr and Mrs N S L Smart, Prof A N Black, LYM*)

Llanbedr, Powys [nr Crickhowell; SO2420], *Red Lion*: Very friendly and attractively restored sixteenth-century pub, next to church in pleasant country village (*David Evans; reports on new management please*)

Llanbedr, Gwynedd [on A496; SH5827], *Victoria*: Pleasant riverside pub with attractive gardens; after extensive refurbishments this no longer has the wholly traditional bar that captivated people in the past – but it has at least kept its fine old-fashioned inglenook; well kept Robinsons, lounge bar food popular with holidaymakers; children's play area; bedrooms (*Tim and Lynne Crawford, LYM*)

Llanbedr Dyffryn Clwyd, Clwyd [SJ1359], *Griffin*: Pleasant comfortably furnished roadside pub with lounge looking out on small, attractive garden; Robinsons ale, good bar food, restaurant; bedrooms (*Mr and Mrs J H Adam*)

Llanbedrog, Gwynedd [Bryn-y-Gro; B4413; SH3332], *Ship*: Friendly local with well kept Burtonwood Mild and Best, lively family atmosphere in simple but comfortable lounge, good range of popular straightforward food; dry on Sun (*LYM*)

☆ **Llancarfan**, S Glam [signposted from A4226; can also be reached from A48 from Bonvilston or B4265 via Llancadle; ST0570], *Fox & Hounds*: Good attractively presented food and well kept Brains, Felinfoel Double Dragon, Wadworths 6X and a guest beer in rambling and comfortable bar, tables out on terrace in pretty surroundings; children in eating area (*TBB, Lyn and Bill Capper, LYM*)

Llandaff, S Glam [Cardiff Rd; A4119; ST1578], *Maltsters Arms*: Cheerful and spacious downstairs bar, easy chairs upstairs, well kept Brains real ales, quickly served food, separate darts room; pleasant and relaxing local atmosphere (*Jon Wainwright, LYM*)

Llanddarog, Dyfed [just off A48; SN5016], *Yr Hedd Gwyn*: Magnificent carved wood settles in simple but attractive bar with good range of spirits, snacks sometimes, keg beers; delightful building opposite church gate, real character, good company; the name means White Hart (*Tom Evans*)

☆ **Llandegla**, Clwyd [SJ1952], *Crown*: Very pleasant and friendly atmosphere, good choice of decent bar food, well kept Lees real ale; restaurant (*Mr and Mrs J H Adam, DE*)

Llandeilo, Dyfed [outside – A40 to Carmarthen; SN6222], *Cottage*: Food good and service friendly, though only keg beers; rather restaurantish; landlord Bernard Kindred set up Kindredson Publishing with local author Aeron Clements to publish his children's book about badgers, *The Cloud Moons*, rejected by other publishers; first printrun sold out in eight days, rights sold to Penguin for £140,000, and Mr Kindred gave up pub-keeping for publishing – the pub's now run by his brother-in-law and wife, Gerald and Ruth Chard (*Tom Evans*); [Carmarthen Rd] *White Hart*: Busy roadside pub with fairly extensive choice of food in bar, real ales, separate restaurant (*Derek Godfrey-Brown*)

Llandogo, Gwent [SO5204], *Sloop*: Beautiful Wye Valley setting, warmly welcoming, good-humoured landlord, real ale; bedrooms (*R A Hutson*)

☆ **Llandrindod Wells**, Powys [Waterloo Rd; SO0561], *Llanerch*: Very relaxed atmosphere in cheerful and friendly sixteenth-century inn with old-fashioned beamed and partitioned bar, two communicating lounges, plenty of room outside – including play area and summer bar; well kept Bass, Robinsons Best and Worthington BB, good bar food, separate pool-room; bedrooms (Mike Tucker, LYM)

☆ Llandudno, Gwynedd [Old St; SH7883], Kings Head: Friendly and spacious traditional pub, with good beer and huge range of good food including many dishes unusual for such an otherwise traditional pub; interesting position by Great Orme Tramway station (Paul and Margaret Baker, Dewi and Linda Jones)

☆ Llanferres, Clwyd [A494 Mold–Ruthin; SJ1961], Druid: Small soberly plush lounge with attractive view from bay window, some oak settles as well as plainer more modern furnishings in bigger saloon which also looks over to the hills; well run, with well kept Burtonwood Best, restaurant; bedrooms (Comus Elliott)

Llanfihangel Crucorney, Gwent [village signposted off A465; SO3321], Skirrid: Among the oldest pubs in Britain, with parts dating from 1110 – and formerly where sheepstealers were hanged; previously very popular with readers, but under a new regime the former interesting choice of real ales has narrowed to Courage, and the atmosphere has changed to 90 per cent restaurant (the food has changed too, but is said to be still quite good) (David Gwynne Harper, Gordon and Daphne, LYM)

Llanfihangel Nant Melan, Powys [A44 10 miles W of Kington; SO1858], Red Lion: Attractive, clean and well run pub with well above average food, in delightful countryside close to Elan Valley; comfortable bedrooms (Ivor Jarvis)

Llanfwrog, Clwyd [B5105 just outside Ruthin; SJ1158], Cross Keys: Great atmosphere, really friendly, with very good bar food and good beer; nice spot close to church (Wayne Brindle)

☆ Llangadfan, Powys [A458 Welshpool–Dolgellau; SJ0111], Cann Office: Spacious roadside hotel dating from 1310 and said to have been known to the early Tudors; lounge, cocktail and public bars, diningroom, children's room and garden; good value bar food including children's helpings, well kept Marstons Pedigree on handpump; bedrooms (G A Worthington, Dave Braisted)

Llangain, Dyfed [B4312 S of Carmarthen; SN3816], Pantydderwen: Comfortable pub with old settles and cushioned chairs; well kept Courage, good wines, good and varied bar food including lovely soups and local fish, friendly and attentive service (Pete Storey)

Llangammarch Wells, Powys [SN9347], Llangammarch Arms: Useful for the area – clean and well kept, pleasant staff, coal fire (Heather Sharland)

Llangattock, Powys [A4077; village sign-posted from Crickhowell; SO2117], Vine Tree: The former licensees have moved over the bridge to the Bridge End (listed under Crickhowell); here, with most of the space taken up for diners, people arriving for a casual drink or a sandwich may be disappointed – more reports please (LYM)

☆ Llangattock Lingoed, Gwent [SO3620], Hunters Moon: Thirteenth-century beamed and flagstoned pub near Offa's Dyke, well kept Tetleys, home-cooked bar food all week including good fish pie (H and P B, BB)

Llangeinor, Mid Glam [SS9187], Llangeinor Arms: Remote hill-top pub by church with good view of Bristol Channel from conservatory; two bars with fine collection of antique artefacts and porcelain; real fires and choice of real ales; good bar food (especially the chips) with an adjacent fifteenth-century restaurant (D Salt)

Llangenny, Powys [SO2417], Dragons Head: Pleasant and welcoming owners in busy and lively pub with good beer and reasonable food (Graham and Glenis Watkins)

Llangernyw, Clwyd [SH8767], Stag: Seventeenth-century pub with beams, open fire, small nooks and settles; two bars with interesting collection of pottery jugs and mugs, stag and fox heads, guns and other weapons; small TV on wall, Websters ale and good range of bar food; bedrooms (BKA)

Llangollen, Clwyd [Regent St; SJ2142], Wild Pheasant: Good value bar meals and very friendly licensees; must book restaurant for Sun lunch; nr start GWG187 (Mrs F J Hall)

☆ nr Llangollen, Clwyd [Horseshoe Pass; A542 N – extreme bottom right corner of OS Sheet 116 at junction with OS Sheet 117 reference 200454], Britannia: Fifteenth-century inn, modernised, extended (in character) and recently renovated, at foot of the famous pass – so good for walking; friendly licensees, good bar food, careful housekeeping, good views; good value bedrooms, spotless and well equipped (Mrs F J Hall, Mr and Mrs D F Fowler)

Llangranog, Dyfed [SN3054], Pentre: Old historic pub on seafront of breathtakingly beautiful fishing village; friendly landlord and family, Buckleys Best on handpump, good bar food, separate bistro (Lord Evans of Claughton)

Llangurig, Powys [SN9179], Blue Bell: Cheerfully basic country inn; bedrooms (LYM)

☆ nr Llangurig, Powys [Pant Mawr; A44 Aberystwyth rd, 4½ miles W of Llangurig – OS Sheet 135 reference 847824], Glansevern Arms: Very civilised, with cushioned antique settles and open fire in high-beamed bar, good value seven-course dinners (must book – bar snacks when available confined to home-made soup and sandwiches), well kept Bass and Worthington Dark Mild on handpump; in a smashing remote position over 1000 feet up, and comes into its own as a place to stay; only lack of recent readers' reports keeps it out of the main entries this year; bedrooms *(G T Jones, LYM)*

Llangwm, Gwent [B4235 S of Raglan; SO4200], *Bridge*: Varnished pews in bright and airy dining-bar with very wide choice of enterprising dishes – most around £5–£9; well kept Bass in separate pubbier bar with beams, nooks, crannies and traditional furnishings; some readers have found it very friendly, others not – more reports please; has been closed Sun evening and Mon lunchtime; children in restaurant *(Col G D Stafford, R Cussons, LYM)*

Llangyfelach, W Glam [B4489 just S of M4 junction 46; SS6498], *Plough & Harrow*: Smoothly comfortable modernised lounge bar with big helpings from food counter, very handy for M4 junctions 46 and 47 *(Tom Evans, LYM)*

Llangynidr, Powys [B4558; SO1519], *Coach & Horses*: Canalside lawn, safely fenced, a main attraction for families; spacious inside, with efficient food counter, Watneys-related real ales, open fire, pub games; children welcome *(LYM)*

Llanidloes, Powys [Long Bridge St; SN9584], *Red Lion*: Good choice of well cooked lunches at very reasonable price, very pleasant licensees *(F A and P J Sumner)*

Llanllwni, Dyfed [SN4741], *Talardd Arms*: Comfortable lounge bar and above-average food in well heated dining-room – vegetables properly cooked *(A R M Moate)*

Llannefydd, Clwyd [SH9871], *Hawk & Buckle*: Remarkable views from bedrooms of cleanly run and comfortably modernised hill-village inn *(LYM)*

Llanrhidian, W Glam [SS4992], *North Gower*: Spacious mock-timbered pub with reasonably priced food, Buckleys and Felinfoel real ales, good views, restaurant, garden *(LYM)*

Llanrhidian, W Glam [SS4992], *Welcome to Town*: Basic and very old-fashioned little pub with cheerful traditional bar, friendly landlady, well kept Marstons tapped from the cask; benches facing the green which looks down to the marshy foreshore of the Loughor Estuary and its endless cockle-sands *(LYM)*

Llansantffraid ym Mechain, Powys [SJ2221], *Station*: Old station house with old pictures and timetables, hats and lamps – a must for railway buffs; Sun lunch must be booked; bedrooms *(Mrs F J Hall)*

Llanteg, Dyfed [SN1810], *Llanteglos Hunting Lodge*: Very good Pembrokeshire Benfro ale brewed here; very attractive building with very good value food *(Nigel Winters)*

Llanthony, Gwent [SO2928], *Half Moon*: Charmingly placed country inn with lots of nearby ponytrekking centres and walks, bar meals, evening restaurant; bedrooms with mountain views *(Anon)*

Llantilio Crosseny, Gwent [SO3915], *Hostry*:

Until very recently this was quite untouched, like stepping back into the 1930s, but this year an extension and an extra door have changed the feel; service still good, reasonable food, old pictures and so forth; this quiet isolated hamlet is surrounded by lovely countryside *(Ian Campbell, Julian Proudman)*

Llantrisant, Gwent [ST3997], *Royal Oak*: Beautifully decorated superb pub/motel with lovely garden, in the Vale of Usk; good imaginative and reasonably priced food served in generous helpings; restaurant; bedrooms comfortable *(L J and C A Wood)*

Llanvihangel Gobion, Gwent [A40 on Usk turning, about 3½ miles from Abergavenny; SO3509], *Chart House*: Smoothly modernised with nautical memorabilia and soothing piped music, good food in bar and popular restaurant, distant hill views, Watneys-related ales *(Col G D Stafford, BB)*

Llanwnda, Gwynedd [A499 3½ miles SW of Caernarfon; SH4758], *Goat*: Good free house with well kept Bass and good lunchtime cold table but no evening bar meals; bedrooms good *(Ian Watson)*; *Stables*: Pleasant, welcoming atmosphere, good service and very good food *(Mrs J Lloyd-Griffith)*

☆ **Llanwnnen**, Dyfed [B4337 signposted Temple Bar from village, on A475 W of Lampeter; SN5346], *Fish & Anchor*: Snug bar with lots of stripped pine, well kept Bass and Buckleys on handpump, good collection of whiskies, decent food (not Sun), pretty little country dining-room, views from garden with good play area; has been closed Sun; children allowed until 9 if well behaved *(LYM)*

Llanwrtyd Wells, Powys [OS Sheet 147 reference 879467; SN8746], *Neuadd Arms*: Extremely friendly, with lots of lively events (from an autumn beer festival to a Bog Snorkling World Championship); well kept Felinfoel Double Dragon and Worthington, good walking and birdwatching (landlord knowledgeable about both); bedrooms *(G T Jones)*

☆ **Llowes**, Powys [A438 – OS Sheet 161 reference 192416; SO1941], *Radnor Arms*: Small, modest and very old, with log fire in bar and very prettily furnished quaint dining-room; particularly wide choice of food from beautifully filled big rye rolls or onion soup through stir-fried beef to veal with marsala sauce or wild duck in orange sauce – all these recently particularly recommended by readers, who say you should do your best (helpings are big) to leave room for one of their interesting puddings or ice-creams; most competent attractive service, well kept Felinfoel Double Dragon, spotless lavatories, pleasant garden looking out over fields *(Eileen Broadbent, PLC, B S Bourne, G B and E L Townend and others)*

Llyswen, Powys [B4350 towards Builth Wells; SO1337], *Boat*: Simple country pub with charming, spacious garden overlooking

River Wye tumbling through steep valley (*LYM*)

Machen, Gwent [ST2288], *Royal Oak*: Warm welcome, friendly landlord and staff, pleasant atmosphere, good reasonably priced bar food, separate restaurant (*Philippa Hawkins*)

Machynlleth, Powys [Maengwyn St; A489, nr junction with A487; SH7501], *Red Lion*: A marvellous local which is an experience on market days – Weds and Sat; decent bar food; bedrooms good value (*Roger Entwistle*)

Maerdy, Clwyd [A5 Corwen rd; SJ0344], *Goat*: Delightful setting beside river, friendly staff, very wide choice of good wholesome food including vegetarian; children's bar; bedrooms (*Michael Molineaux*)

Magor, Gwent [The Square; ST4287], *Golden Lion*: Good modernised pub in superb position (*Julian Proudman*); [a mile from M4 junction 23 – B4245] *Wheatsheaf*: Good choice of Whitbreads ales, good lunchtime snacks and pleasant atmosphere (*G C Gunning*)

Mamhilad, Gwent [SO3003], *Horseshoe*: Cheap, plentiful food and reasonable beer; busy at lunchtime as ICI and Health Authority nearby (*Pamela and Merlyn Horswell*)

Marcross, S Glam [SS9269], *Horseshoe*: Outstanding country pub, with friendly homely atmosphere; noted for jazz and folk music; on GWG195 (*Julian Proudman*)

Marianglas, Anglesey [SH5084], *Parciau Arms*: Attractive authentic surroundings and very friendly, pleasant staff; good standard and choice of food and a good, wide range of real ales such as Banks's, Bass, Marstons Pedigree and Youngers No 3; bedrooms (*Linda and Alex Christison*)

Marloes, Dyfed [OS Sheet 157 reference 793083; SM7908], *Lobster Pot*: Good food and well kept Hancocks HB on handpump; start GWG191 (*D P and M E Cartwright*)

Mawdlam, Mid Glam [nr M4 junction 37; SS8181], *Angel*: A good range of bar snacks and full-course meals at the restaurant – well presented and reasonably priced; good atmosphere (*T P Lovesey*)

Menai Bridge, Anglesey [Glyngarth; A545, half way towards Beaumaris; SH5572], *Gazelle*: Outstanding waterside situation looking across to Snowdonia, steep and aromatic sub-tropical garden behind, lively main bar and smaller rooms off, popular with yachtsmen, well kept Robinsons Best and Mild; children allowed away from serving-bar; bedrooms; a question-mark over food and management though (*Linda and Alex Christison, LYM*); *Liverpool Arms*: Friendly, good beer choice, interesting food well presented (*JRS*)

Milton, Dyfed [A477; SN0303], *Milton Brewery*: Comfortable stone-walled ex-brewery with seats outside has been popular for good choice of beers and good varied food, but for sale early 1988 (*E O Stephens; up-to-date reports please*)

☆ **Monknash**, S Glam [follow Marcross, Broughton signpost off B4265 St Brides Major–Llantwit Major and turn left at end of Water St; OS Sheet 170 reference 920706; SS9270], *Plough & Harrow*: Unspoilt and untouched isolated country pub, flagstones, old-fashioned stripped settles, logs burning in huge fireplace with cavernous side bread oven, good value plain food, Flowers IPA and Original on handpump; pool, juke box and fruit machine in room on left, picnic-table sets on grass outside the white cottage; nr start GWG195 (*Julian Proudman, BB*)

☆ **Monmouth**, Gwent [Agincourt Sq; SO5113], *Kings Head*: Lovely period building with open, inviting atmosphere, flowers everywhere, good food in up-market dining-room with attentive service; good game soup, cauliflower and Stilton soup, very tasty pigeon breast in port, good grouse, very good cheese choice including whole Stilton, decent wines; bedrooms comfortable (*DB, E J Knight*)

Monmouth [Dixton Gate], *Nags Head*: Attractive old pub built into old town gate (*Julian Proudman*); [coming on A466 or A4196, pub on right at T-junction] *Queens Head*: Good food, not expensive, no-smoking area (*Dr D M Forsyth*); [Cinderhill St] *Rising Sun*: Good service in family-owned modern pub – nothing too much trouble; biggish helpings of reasonably priced home-cooked bar food; bedrooms pleasant and well equipped (*L J and C A Ward*)

☆ **Montgomery**, Powys [SO2296], *Cottage*: Pleasant pub in shadow of Powis Castle looking over Vale of Severn and surrounding countryside; exceptionally clean with friendly, cheerful atmosphere, character, friendly welcome; Ansells beer, good range of well served and reasonably priced bar food, garden (*T Nott, D H W Davies*)

☆ **Montgomery**, Powys [The Square] *Dragon*: Friendly hotel lounge bar with enthusiastic new owners doing good food, also real ale; at top of steep, quiet town below ruined Norman castle; swimming-pool for residents; bedrooms very comfortable (*Mr and Mrs R H Martyn, LYM*)

Morfa Nefyn, Gwynedd [A497/B4412], *Bryncynan*: Quick service of above-average bar food including vegetarian dishes, well kept Ind Coope and Tetleys on handpump; this pew-furnished pub is a quiet local in winter, but lively with even a disco wing in summer; dry on Sun; well worth knowing for the area (*J and J A Pearson, Gavin May, LYM*)

Morganstown, S Glam [Ty Nant Rd; not far from M4 junction 32; ST1281], *Ty Nant*: Exceptionally well run and usually busy, pleasant interior with two rooms and pool-table; outside drinking area (*A J Ritson, Julian Proudman*)

Mumbles, W Glam [Newton Rd], *White Rose*: Recently extended using wood panelling from a ship; good food and beer;

popular at weekends *(M C Howells)*

Mynydd-y-Garreg, Dyfed [a mile or two NE of Kidwelly, follow signs to Industrial Museum; SN4308], *Gwenllian Court*: Useful for the area, pleasant situation, comfortable, with pleasantly and quickly served decent food; keg beer *(Prof A N Black)*

Narberth, Dyfed [High St; SN1114], *Angel*: Good home cooking and salad bar in friendly village inn in upper Wye Valley, well kept Flowers IPA, efficient service, spacious carpeted back lounge with button-back banquettes in big bays, good bookmatch collection in public bar with TV, snug Cabin Bar with cushioned wall benches, restaurant *(E J Knight, BB)*

Newcastle Emlyn, Dyfed [Sycamore St (A475); SN3040], *Pelican*: Seventeenth-century small-town inn with good choice of real ales, pews and panelling, and fireplace with bread oven still recognisable as the one where Rowlandson in 1797 sketched a dog driving the roasting-spit; local atmosphere, games area on left; bedrooms in adjoining cottage *(Wayne Brindle, LYM)*

Newgale, Dyfed [main road to St Davids; SM8422], *Duke of Edinburgh*: Simple pub included for its position just above splendid beach, lounge, public bar and pool-room; bedrooms *(BB)*

Newport, Dyfed [East St; A487 on E edge of Newport; SN0539], *Golden Lion*: Readers vary so much in their views of this interesting inn that it's hard to believe they're talking about the same place; there's agreement about the generous helpings of good value food, including very fresh fish and superb steak, but we'd like more reports on the bar itself and on service; children allowed in eating area and own bar; bedrooms comfortable for the price, breakfasts huge *(Philip King, PWB, LYM)*

Nottage, Mid Glam [SS8178], *Rose & Crown*: Smartly kept old inn handy for coast and M4 junction 37, neatly modernised; good value bar food, popular restaurant; comfortably refurbished bedrooms *(Mrs J Frost, A A Worthington, LYM)*

Old Church Stoke, Powys [SO2894], *Oak*: Welcoming sixteenth-century pub, well kept Powells Bitter and Sampsons Strong, good bar food attractively priced, small separate restaurant serving good Sun lunches *(David and Daphne Margetts)*

Oldwalls, W Glam [SS4891], *Greyhound*: Welcoming spacious comfortable lounge with good coal fire, good service despite lots of customers, reasonably priced straightforward bar food, attractive restaurant with lots of fresh locally caught fish *(A A Worthington, EGL)*

Overton Bridge, Clwyd [SJ3643], *Cross Foxes*: Old coaching-inn with fine elevated view of the Dee from the back; serves good reasonably priced food; no crowds *(A J Hill)*

Oystermouth, W Glam [SS6188], *White Rose*:

Very good reasonably priced bar food, well kept Bass and local beers, well run *(E J Knight)*

Pale, Gwynedd [B4401 nr Bala; SH9936], *Bryntirion Arms*: Very good beer and good value food, comfortable and friendly *(Alan Brooke)*

Parkmill, W Glam [SS5489], *Gower*: Popular and pleasant pub with good value carvery and well kept real ale *(Jenny and Brian Seller)*

Pelcomb Bridge, Dyfed [SM9317], *Rising Sun*: Outstanding appearance and welcome, food good for both quantity and quality; useful for the area *(W M Pinder)*

Pembroke, Dyfed [Main St; SM9801], *Old Kings Arms*: Good menu, modest prices, good service and real ale; bedrooms *(Canon G Hollis)*

Pembroke Dock, Dyfed [Melville St; SM9603], *Navy*: Food good, reasonable prices, welcome and atmosphere very friendly, good Worthington on handpump *(E O Stephens)*; [27 London Rd] *Welshmans Arms*: Good simple food, Websters Yorkshire on handpump, pleasant lounge, good bar with darts and pool, very pleasant staff; pub well renovated and recently extended; bedrooms good value – breakfasts good *(E O Stephens)*

☆ **Pembroke Ferry**, Dyfed [at foot of bridge over estuary; SM9603], *Ferry*: Good standard and range of food in bar (imaginative fish options), pleasant riverside setting, well kept Bass and Worthington on handpump; children welcome *(A J and M Thomasson, Janet Williams, CAJS)*

☆ **Penderyn**, Powys [off A4059 at Lamb to T-junc then up narrow hill – OS Sheet 160 reference 945085; SN9408], *Red Lion*: Old stone pub high in the hills, open fires, dark beams, stripped masonry, antique settles, unusually wide choice of well kept real ales, good atmosphere; opens 1pm and 7pm *(Gwynne Harper, LYM)*

Pendoylan, S Glam [2½ miles from M4 junction 34; ST0576], *Red Lion*: Friendly pub in pretty vale, Flowers IPA and Original on handpump, good bar food, separate restaurant *(Alun Davies)*

Penmark, S Glam [ST0568], *Six Bells*: Friendly Vale of Glamorgan pub, popular with young people *(Julian Proudman)*

Pentraeth, Anglesey [SH5278], *Panton Arms*: Large pub with comfortable bar and separate dining-room; real ale, helpful staff and big helpings of food including a choice of filled baked potatoes and children's dishes; fair-sized garden with play area *(Mike and Kay Wilson)*

Pont-ar-Gothi, Dyfed [SN5021], *Cothi Bridge*: Comfortable bow-windowed plush lounge included for its attractive position overlooking River Cothi; Courage ale, bar food, restaurant, riverside seats outside; bedrooms *(LYM)*

☆ nr **Ponterwyd**, Dyfed [A44 nearly two miles E of village; SN7581], *Dyffryn*

Castell: Good value bar food and well kept Marstons Pedigree, John Smiths and Worthington BB in unpretentious but comfortable inn dwarfed by the mountain slopes sweeping up from it – we're surprised we don't hear more of it from readers; bedrooms clean, comfortable and good value *(Mike Tucker, R H Griffiths, LYM)*

Pontneddfechan, Mid Glam [SN9007], *Old White Horse*: Small, comfortable, recently refurbished pub close to Ystradfellte Waterfalls; friendly welcome, good service, well kept Courage Best and Brains SA, bar food; can get busy at weekends *(Alun and Eryl Davies)*

☆**Pontypool**, Gwent [The Wern, Griffithstown; near Sebastopol; SO2901], *Open Hearth*: Canalside, real-ale oasis in an arid area; four to six beautifully kept real ales, mostly tapped from the cask, such as Courage, Davenports, Felinfoel, Hook Norton, Marstons, Robinsons, Wadworths 6X and Farmers Glory; friendly capable staff, unusually wide choice of promptly served good bar food with mountainous platefuls of Sun roasts; 300 different beer bottles decorate lounge which like saloon is by canal towpath; small restaurant down by canal embankment *(Dr R Fuller, Pamela and Merlyn Horswell)*

Pontypridd, Mid Glam [Eglwysilan; off A470 towards Rhydyfelin, then 'Superstore', then Eglwysilan; ST0690], *Rose & Crown*: Superbly atmospheric country pub perched above Taff and Rhymney valleys, up narrow lanes – spacious, with exposed beams, stone walls, good choice of beers, snacks; plenty of seats when quiet, great atmosphere at weekends when music brings pub alive *(P D Enderby)*

Porth Dinllaen, Gwynedd [SH2642], *Ty Coch*: Fantastic position right on the beach, haunt of seventeenth-century smugglers and pirates, well worth the walk over the golf course or along the beach from the nearest car park; interesting décor, quite good food; dry on Sun *(Dewi and Linda Jones)*

Porthcawl, S Glam [Newton; SS7277], *Jolly Sailor*: Friendly atmosphere in nautical-theme bar where the licensee is an expert on the genuine brass hardware which decorates it; well kept Brains beer *(P L Duncan)*

☆**Porthmadog**, Gwynedd [Lombard St; SH5639], *Ship*: Beautifully refurbished lounge bar with large, attractive fireplace; bustles with visitors at lunchtime; variety of appetising and well cooked bar meals, wide choice of well kept beers, decent house wines, wood-burning stoves, plenty of character, friendly staff; upstairs restaurant; Welsh-speaking locals (it's Y Llong to them) *(Dewi and Linda Jones, David Millar, David Lewis, Patrick Christine, Victoria Littlejohns)*

☆**Presteigne**, Powys [SO3265], *Radnorshire Arms*: Picturesque rambling timbered THF inn with decent food in panelled bar, Bass,

good service, well spaced tables on sheltered lawn *(Mrs Joan Harris, LYM)*

Raglan, Gwent [SO4108], *Beaufort Arms*: Comfortable and roomy, with piped music, well kept Courage and John Smiths, tables outside in summer, bar food; superb restaurant, friendly service; children welcome; bedrooms comfortably refurbished; it's changed hands, and the owners aren't so evident now *(Lyn and Bill Capper)*

Resolven, W Glam [A465, just S of junction with B4434; SN8202], *Farmers Arms*: Lounge bar like Victorian parlour with brass-topped tables, red plush seats, mock gas lighting, plants, walls adorned with plates and polished brass; lovely cosy atmosphere, wonderful staff, wide choice of good reasonably priced food *(Karen Bettesworth, Chris Down)*

Rhandirmwyn, Dyfed [SN7843], *Royal Oak*: Friendly staff and locals, usual pub food, very close to a number of Sites of Special Scientific Interest and the Dinas Hill RSPB reserve, among beautiful hills and valleys; bedrooms comfortable *(Steve Dark)*

☆**Rhosmaen**, Dyfed [SN6424], *Plough*: Comfortable and locally popular plush-seated dining pub with good value bar food – generously filled good ham sandwiches, sweet-and-sour pork and puddings have all been praised; service pleasant, picture-window views from lounge, tiled front bar, separate restaurant *(K Wood, Heather Sharland, LYM)*

Rhyd Ddu, Gwynedd [A4085 N of Beddgelert; SH5753], *Cwellyn Arms*: Fine stone pub just three miles from Snowdon's peak – visible from the bar; friendly staff, a welcome for walkers and children, open fires, good range of food including salad bar and vegetarian dishes; restaurant, garden with barbecue *(Gordon Theaker)*

Roath, S Glam [Newport Rd; ST1978], *Royal Oak*: Noisy, busy and boisterous Victorian local with original bar and fittings, full of period sporting mementoes; exceptionally well kept Brains SA tapped from the cask *(A J Ritson)*

Rosebush, Dyfed [SN0729], *Preseli*: Well kept beer tapped from cask into jug, in iron-clad building in interesting slate-quarry village *(TW)*

Rudry, Mid Glam [ST1986], *Maenllwyd*: Comfortably furnished traditional lounge in low-beamed Tudor pub with well kept Whitbreads, popular bar food, and spacious new restaurant with midnight supper licence *(Julian Proudman, LYM)*

Sigingstone, S Glam [SS9771], *Victoria*: Well managed pub with good value lunches, out of the way but very popular *(E J Knight, Mrs H March)*

Solva, Dyfed [not easy to find: park in free harbour car park, pub is opposite Nectarium – OS Sheet 157 reference 806245; SM8024], *Ship*: Unassuming exterior is deceptive –

good atmosphere, delicious real ale on hand-pump, pleasant licensee, real home cooking (same dishes in unpretentious restaurant, used by families); little garden has play area over stream *(Dr and Mrs C D E Morris, Alan Castle)*; *Harbour House*: Impressively placed by harbour, with good atmosphere and nice snacks *(Wayne Brindle)*

Southerndown, Mid Glam [SS8873], *Three Golden Cups*: Near an attractive stretch of the coast and locally popular for meals, views to Devon when it's clear; bedrooms *(LYM)*

St Asaph, Clwyd [SJ0475], *Red Lion*: Tetleys house with red lion statue on porch, white plaster walls inside, old prints, variety of teapots hung from beamed ceiling, piped music; wide choice of wines, bar food, good and friendly service, garden *(Gwynne Harper)*

St Clears, Dyfed [A477; SN2716], *Black Lion*: Well appointed village inn with very friendly staff, attractive décor and good home-cooked food – real fresh chips; bedrooms *(K R Harris)*

St Davids, Dyfed [on road to Porthclais harbour (and lifeboat); SM7525], *St Nons*: Hotel bar, but well worth a visit, with cheap but often imaginative food (especially puddings), good restaurant (especially fish), well kept Bass and lots of life; jazz Sat; bedrooms *(D Pearman)*

St Dogmaels, Dyfed [SN1645], *Ferry*: Popular waterside family pub, simply furnished *(LYM)*

St Hilary, S Glam [ST0173], *Bush*: Thatched village pub nestling behind church, old settles in traditional flagstoned public bar, comfortable low-beamed lounge, well kept Bass, Hancocks and Worthington, bar food including some Welsh dishes, restaurant *(Julian Proudman, LYM)*

Swansea, W Glam [SS6593], *Dragon*: Very reasonable value bar snacks in lively and popular place *(Anon)*; [Uplands Cres, Uplands] *Streets*: Unusual décor with shopfronts around the walls, central bar and integral Pizza Hut counter; good choice of reasonably priced beer; popular with students *(Bryan Drew)*; [seafront] *Woodman*: Popular pub with a good value carvery and Bass; need to book Sun lunch *(Jenny and Brian Seller)*

Taffs Well, Mid Glam [Cardiff Rd; nr M4 junction 32; ST1283], *Taffs Well*: Very good for this area *(Julian Proudman)*

Tal-y-Bont, Gwynedd [B5106 6 miles S of Conwy, towards Llanwrst; SH7669], *Y Bedol*: Well kept and reasonably comfortable pub in Vale of Conwy village, dark beams and winter open fire *(BB)*

Tal-y-Cafn, Gwynedd [SH7972], *Ferry*: Tasteful and unusual recent conversion, in beautiful setting; wide choice of good (if not cheap) bar food in comfortable lounge and big, big bar, well kept Whitbreads Castle Eden, lots of cocktails, interesting darts room

with 1920s nudes, happy atmosphere with young staff; river-view restaurant, attractive waterside gardens; newly converted and refurbished; bedrooms well equipped *(Cecil Eimerl, BKA)*

Tal-y-Cafn [A470 Conway–Llanwrst], *Tal-y-Cafn*: Handy for Bodnant Gardens, cheerful and comfortable lounge bar with big inglenook, simple bar meals, Greenalls on handpump, seats in spacious garden *(Anne Morris, Paul S McPherson, LYM)*

Talgarth, Powys [Bronllys Rd; SO1534], *Castle*: Good bar food tastefully garnished and presented in warm and cheerful free house with quick and efficient service *(Mr and Mrs A J Woodhouse, Mr and Mrs A Pickles)*

Talybont, Dyfed [the one nr Aberystwyth – SN6589], *Black Lion*: Seats in sheltered back garden behind substantial stone village inn with comfortably modernised back lounge, games in and off front public bar, bar food and restaurant, Bass real ale; bedrooms *(Wayne Brindle, LYM)*

☆ **Talybont-on-Usk**, Powys [B4558 – OS Sheet 161 reference 114226; SO1122], *Star*: A dozen or so well kept real ales, including unusual ones, are the reason for visiting this simple pub, with several plainly furnished rooms radiating from the central servery; bar food, seats outside; children welcome *(SC, LYM)*

Talycoed, Gwent [B4233 Monmouth–Abergavenny; SO4115], *Halfway House*: Has been popular for wonderfully inventive food (not Mon), good situation and view, and good range of well kept beers, but we've heard that it's changed hands and had no news yet of the new regime *(Anon)*

Talyllyn, Gwynedd [B4405, W end; SH7209], *Pen-y-Bont*: Fine lakeside position, imaginative salads in salad bar which with lounge is separate from hotel – first-class service and space for influx of summer tourists; picnic-table sets under trees by lake; hotel is one start for climb of Cader Idris; bedrooms reasonably priced *(S V Bishop)*

Tegryn, Dyfed [SN2233], *Butchers Arms*: Said to be Pembrokeshire's highest pub; picturesque view, good Buckleys bitter and bar snacks, small restaurant *(BB)*

☆ **Templeton**, Dyfed [A478; SN1111], *Boars Head*: Home-cooked reasonable value food (especially the baked potatoes) and well kept beer; an appealing family-run establishment, clean and tidy inside, neat out; good atmosphere; children at lunchtime *(D P and M E Cartwright, P Corris)*

Tenby, Dyfed [Upper Frog St; SN1300], *Coach & Horses*: Small town pub with well kept Marstons Pedigree and Worthington BB, cosy and clean, with good value chip-free food, comfortable lounge, public bar; parking can be very difficult *(Peter Robinson, P Corris)*; [The Paragon] *Imperial*: Substantial hotel on cliffs, with tasty food in PJs bar from filled baked potatoes and hot beef sandwiches to main dishes; reasonably priced beer, superb view of Caldy Island from terrace; comfortable bedrooms *(Wayne Brindle)*

Three Cocks, Powys [A438 Talgarth–Hay-on-Wye; SO1737], *Old Barn*: Long, spacious converted barn with choice of areas for games, quiet chats, drinking well kept Hancocks or eating generous helpings of simple bar food – though not exactly the atmosphere of a pub; seats outside with good play area and barbecues on fine Fri evenings *(LYM)*

Tintern, Gwent [Devauden Rd, off A446; SO5301], *Cherry Tree*: Beer and cider tapped from the cask in delightful old country pub where we have seen no change in 15 years *(H and P B)*; [A466 Chepstow–Monmouth] *Moon & Sixpence*: Good atmosphere, food, real ale, friendly service *(Dr R Fuller, Steve Dark)*

Trecastle, Powys [SN8729], *Castle*: Recently refurbished former coaching-inn with simple pleasant bar, tables outside; has had very wide choice of reasonably priced bar food, but we've had no news since it changed hands recently; bedrooms *(Anon)*

Tredunnock, Gwent [ST3896], *Newbridge*: Friendly and helpful licensees, well kept beer, good bar food, separate restaurant *(G L Carlisle)*

Trefriw, Gwynedd [B5106; SH7863], *Fairy Falls*: Pleasant free house, not too big, redecorated in old style; generous helpings of reasonably priced food, Ansells Mild, Banks's Bitter and Ind Coope Burton; live entertainment some nights *(Robert Scott)*

Trelleck, Gwent [B4293 6 miles S of Monmouth; SO5005], *Lion*: Good food in very pleasant bar-lounge of quiet and unpretentious backwater country pub – really worth knowing in the evening *(G W Tanner)*

Tremadog, Gwynedd [SH5640], *Golden Fleece*: Cheerful stone-built inn with simply furnished rambling beamed lounge bar, nice little snug, games in public bar, tables in sheltered inner courtyard under Perspex roof – even a solarium/sauna; wide choice of food from side food bar, well kept Marstons Pedigree tapped from the cask; children in bistro or small room off courtyard; closed Sun *(LYM)*; [The Square] *Union*: Old stone pub with friendly staff, above-average well presented bar food including reasonably authentic-tasting bouillabaisse, home-cooked rare beef in brown baps, vegetarian dishes, Ind Coope real ale *(Gordon Theaker, David Lewis)*

Treoes, S Glam [SS9478], *Star*: Friendly, relaxed village pub with tasteful interior, polished pine furniture and church pews; Crown beers and its own brewed on the premises; bar skittles and separate pool-room; good food which is sometimes served in evenings *(D Salt)*

Trevine, Dyfed [OS Sheet 157 reference 837325; SM8332], *Ship*: Very handy watering-hole on Coast Path, garden, rooms for hiding away the children, cheap pub food, keg beers *(Dr and Mrs C D E Morris)*

Troedyrhiw, Mid Glam [28 Bridge St; SO0702], *Green Meadow*: Friendly village local, recently renovated to show nineteenth-century open fireplace, good Brains real ale, superb mainly 1960s juke box (run by regulars), bar food, garden *(Richard Meredith)*

☆ **Tyn-y-Groes**, Gwynedd [B5106 N of village; SH7672], *Groes*: Rambling series of dimly lit low-beamed medieval rooms with miscellany of furnishings; food in bar and restaurant, roadside tables with view over River Conwy; has been closed weekday winter lunchtimes, but in summer 1988 warm reports on the helpful new owners started coming in, talking of good atmosphere and imaginative food; bedrooms lovely, overlooking valley *(Paul Yeoman, Alan Franck, LYM)*

☆ **Usk**, Gwent [New Market St; SO3801], *Royal*: Old crockery and pictures on the walls, old-fashioned fireplaces, comfortable wooden chairs and tables, nice civilised atmosphere and friendly service; well kept Bass, Felinfoel, Hancocks and Worthington, salads, hot dishes, choice of Sun roasts, more extensive evening menu *(Lyn and Bill Capper, Julian Proudman, Tony Ritson)*

Usk [town centre], *Cross Keys*: Good atmosphere and food – soup almost a meal in itself, hot dishes such as plaice and steak and kidney pie *(Alan Worthington)*; [The Square] *Nags Head*: Consistently good décor, service, beer and food *(Col G D Stafford)*

Velindre, Dyfed [A487 Newport–Cardigan; SN1039], *Olde Salutation*: Recently restored eighteenth-century roadside inn, with good value snacks and nice garden; in attractive spot, with fishing in nearby River Nevern; bedrooms *(Wayne Brindle)*

Welshpool, Powys [High St; SJ2207], *Mermaid*: Very friendly old-world fifteenth-century pub with dominoes played in cosy low-beamed little front bar (former cathedral glass in the windows), spacious pleasantly furnished back bar, well kept Banks's beer; very good atmosphere *(Pauline Watt, Stuart Smith)*; [Raven Sq] *Raven*: Generous helpings of consistently good bar food such as pâté, home-made steak and kidney pie or curry; handy for the narrow-gauge steam railway; functions room party buffets good value *(C M Whitehouse)*

Wrexham, Clwyd [Mold Rd, ½ mile from centre; SJ3450], *Turf*: Friendly atmosphere, efficient service, good Marstons Pedigree on handpump, good value home-cooked bar food *(John Rafferty)*

Ystradowen, S Glam [A4222 Llantrisant–Cowbridge; ST0177], *White Lion*: Pleasant village pub with open fire, pleasant service and good bar food *(A A Worthington)*

Channel Islands

Channel Islands

There's a remarkable diversity in the pubs of these islands. The only thing they have in common is a drinks price structure that fills mainlanders who discover it with wistful longing. On Jersey, beer, wine and spirits cost about half what they do in London. Guernsey and Sark, though not as cheap, are still a good deal cheaper than the mainland. Food prices are generally a welcome surprise too – specially with fish and seafood, often superb if it's fresh as opposed to frozen (always worth asking). On Jersey, we'd pick as the best places the the Old Court House overlooking the water at St Aubin (a charming place to stay at, with a magnificent seafood restaurant and a wonderfully pubby public bar, as well as its classier upstairs galleon bar), and the intriguing back locals' bar of Les Fontaines – genuinely unspoilt. On Guernsey, the top place to try is the civilised Hougue du Pommier, inland in Castel (a relaxed and comfortable place to stay at). A much higher proportion of the Lucky Dip entries here than on the mainland have been personally inspected by us, often proving a clear cut above the usual Lucky Dip run and on the borderline of deserving a full entry. We've described these more fully than usual – the BB initials signify which they are. As it's purely a hotel, we've no excuse for including it as a proper entry in this book, but we can firmly recommend La Frégate in St Peter Port, Guernsey, as a lovely place to stay at, with great food, a marvellous garden and views.

The OS numbers we give after placenames in Jersey (except in St Helier) are six-figure map references to the Ordnance Survey official leisure map of Jersey – the most useful island map we found. We should also mention a nice illustrated booklet, Jersey Pubs & Inns, *written by the licensee of the Old Smugglers Inn at Ouaisné on Jersey – one of the best pubs in the Lucky Dip section.*

BEAUMONT (Jersey)   OS613498 Map 1
Foresters Arms

Summer bar food in this delightful tiled house is served from a side servery and concentrates on a wide range of salads, from vegetarian or farmhouse pie to eight-ounce sirloin steak, with sandwiches, ploughman's and some simple hot dishes. In winter a wider range of hot dishes includes home-made soup, steak pudding and kebabs. The main bar is quarry-tiled, and has cushioned wheel-back chairs and black wooden seats built into bays, low black beams, small windows with heavy curtains in the thick walls, and, in winter, a log fire in the big stone fireplace; there's a good local atmosphere. The carpeted side lounge, with lots of shiny black woodwork, has blue plush stools and cushioned seats. It's just across the road from St Aubin's Bay, and its licence dates from 1717 – the oldest in Jersey. There are picnic-table sets on the front terrace, and the public bar has darts, dominoes, cribbage, space game and juke box.

Ann Street   Meals (not Sun lunchtime) and snacks   Children in lounge   Open 10–11 all year

CASTEL (Guernsey)   Map 1
Hougue du Pommier 🛏

Route de Hougue du Pommier, off Route de Carteret; just inland from Cobo Bay and Grandes Rocques

Dating from 1712, this comfortable hotel in a peaceful island setting was originally a cider farm – its name means 'Apple Tree Hill'. The bar is a spacious affair, and has red carpets, oak beams and wall timbers, old game and sporting prints, hare and stag heads, guns, a stuffed falcon, pewter platters on a high shelf, good brass candelabra, and a nice snug area by a big stone fireplace which has good log fires in cool weather. The oak bar counter is attractively carved, with some mellowed oak linenfold panelling. The generous bar food includes home-made soup (65p), ploughman's (from £1.25), open sandwiches (from £1.45), vegetarian mushroom dishes (from £2.20), salads (from £2.75) and hot dishes such as omelettes (£2.20), gammon and egg or steak and kidney pie (£2.90) and rump steak (£3.95), with several children's dishes (£1.25), a day's special such as lamb kleftico (£2.30) and a couple of carvery roasts (around £3.60); space game, piped music. The extensive grounds have leisure facilities such as a pitch-and-putt golf course (for visitors as well as residents), a swimming-pool in a sheltered walled garden (tables beside it for drinks or bar meals in summer), a tree-shaded courtyard with lots of flowers, and a neat lawn with white tables under fruit trees. *(Recommended by J S Rutter, Mr and Mrs G H Williams)*

Free house   Licensee J H Henke   Meals and snacks (lunchtime, not Sun)   Restaurant Children welcome   Folk groups Mon and Thurs   Open 11–2.30, 6–12 all year   Bedrooms tel Guernsey (0481) 565311; £23B/£46B

GOREY (Jersey)   OS714503 Map 1
Dolphin ⊗

For the view alone it's worth climbing the steep rise on the opposite side of the harbour here to Mont Orgueil Castle. The long and busily cheerful carpeted bar of this waterside pub has big bow windows overlooking the busy road, cushioned wheel-back and mate's chairs around the tables, and brown nets and the odd lobster-pot hung from its high black beams and woodwork. At lunchtime virtually everyone is eating (many of the high stools, with comfortable back rests, along the long bar counter are reserved for diners): the food is mainly simple fish, such as stuffed clams, moules marinière, rainbow trout or grilled sardines, local plaice, a dozen oysters or scallops poached in white wine. In the evening there may be a strolling minstrel. Rather loud piped pop music.

Free house   Meals and snacks   Open 10–11 all year

ROCQUAINE BAY (Guernsey)   Map 1
Rocquaine Bistro ⊗
On W of the island

The cool and quarry-tiled bar in this wine-barish pub has pale bentwood and cane chairs, red gingham tablecloths, a lazy brass fan in the dark green ceiling, and big antique engravings on its swirly cream plastered walls. As well as beer, there are decent wines by the glass, half-litre or bottle, bucks fizz, and coffee. There's a substantial range of fresh fish, now displayed prominently on crushed ice in the bar so that you can select exactly what you want; dishes include lobster soup (£1.25), grilled mackerel (£2.95), moules marinière (£2.95), king prawns with mayonnaise (£3.95), half a dozen oysters grilled with garlic (£3.50), Dublin Bay prawns (£3.95), whole plaice, lemon sole (£5.50), crab or king-prawn salad (£6.95) and lobster (£9.50), with plenty of non-fish dishes too, from omelette or spaghetti bolognese (£2.50). There are good views from the arched façade, with its enlarged terrace, to the sand-brightened sea in the bay, and to the low rocks beyond Fort Grey (now a maritime museum).

Free house   Licensee J R Tautscher   Meals and snacks   Restaurant (open 10.30–11.45 Mon–Sat; 12–2, 7–10.30 Sun) tel Guernsey (0481) 63149   Children welcome   Open 6–11.45 all year; closed Mon in winter

There are report forms at the back of the book.

SARK   Map 1
Stocks Hotel 🛏

Dixcart Lane

This comfortable hotel has stormy sailing-ship prints on the white rough stone walls of its snug carpeted bar, cushioned easy chairs and small settees as well as red leatherette button-back wall banquettes, and a low dark beam and plank ceiling. In summer there are rustic seats by an attractive fine-grit courtyard sheltered by the extensions of the granite house, with a lawn in the centre; the place keeps a fine balance between civility and liveliness. Food is efficiently served in a cheerful separate buffet and includes soup (£1), ploughman's (£2), burger (£2.75), vegetarian pasta or quiche (£3.25), chilli with natural yoghurt and tortilla chips or seafood provençale (£3.95), Sark shellfish (prices subject to availability), a daily special, steaks (from £3.75), and a good selection of salads from their new cold table. There's now a terrace outside the buffet, beside the swimming-pool, for which you can book a table.

Free house   Licensees the Armorgie family   Meals and snacks   Restaurant   Children welcome   Open 12–2.30, 6–9.30; closed Nov–Mar   Bedrooms tel Sark (048 183) 2001; £23(£25.50B)/£46(£51B)

ST AUBIN (Jersey)   OS607486 Map 1
Old Court House Inn ⊗ 🛏

A partly fifteenth-century inn, it's idyllically situated, with modern trappings and a warm and friendly atmosphere. The design of the elegant upstairs cocktail bar is clever – it's crafted as the aft cabin of a galleon, even to the mast kingpost at one end, the bowed varnished deckingplanks of the ceiling, and to the transom window looking out over the old harbour to the rocks of St Aubin's old fort (you can walk out over the sands at low tide) and right across the bay to St Helier. The main basement bar has cushioned pale wooden seats built against its stripped granite walls, low black beams and joists in a white ceiling, heavy marble-topped tables on a Turkey carpet, a dimly lantern-lit inner room with an internally lit rather brackish-looking deep well, and beyond that a spacious cellar room open in summer and at busy times. The front part of the building was originally a merchant's homestead, from the seventeenth-century storing privateers' plunder alongside more legitimate cargo. It's a lovely place to stay – not only because the bedrooms, each individually decorated and furnished and most with interesting sea views, are comfortable, but because you can then make the most of its fish restaurant, excellent even by Channel Islands standards. Bar meals include soup (£1), lasagne or pâté (£3.25), salads (from £2.50), moules marinière (£3.50), dish of the day (£3.50) and grilled prawns (£4.50). This is a fairly quiet corner of the island, though nearby parking can be difficult. *(Recommended by Roger Mallard, Miss J A Harvey, Simon Turner)*

Free house   Licensee Jonty Sharp   Meals and snacks (lunchtime, not Sun, and evenings, not Sun, Nov–Mar)   Restaurant   Children welcome   Open 11–11 all year   Bedrooms tel Jersey (0534) 46433; £30B/£60B

ST HELIER (Jersey)   Map 1
La Bourse

Charing Cross

This old-fashioned, small bar is at its best on a quiet afternoon, when the atmosphere is truly relaxing, with discreetly friendly service. It has nineteenth-century French coloured cartoons behind a plate of glass on one purple wall, framed junk bonds, and comfortably backed red leatherette tall stools at the bar counter and the ledge opposite it. Bar food includes onion soup (95p), sandwiches (from £1.20, steak £2), home-made pâté (£1.70), pizza, lasagne, escargots or half a dozen oysters (£3.20), avocado and prawns (£2.50) and king prawns (£4); decent juke box. It's placed between the main central multi-storey car park and the pedestrian-only bazaar territory of King Street, full of people hunting down their holiday duty-free bargains in electronics, cameras, alcohol, scent and, mainly, gold.

Free house   Licensee Sue Goodchild   Meals and snacks   Upstairs restaurant tel Jersey (0534) 77966   Open 10–11 all year

Lamplighter

Mulcaster Street

There's a carefully preserved atmosphere at this friendly local, from the old newspapers on the walls recording historic Jersey moments to the ornamental façade, with its elegantly arched windows and proudly carved Britannia on top. Inside, the grainy panelling, floorboards and lowered ceiling, captain's and kitchen chairs, pews and tables are all done out in stripped wood, and there are also heavy timber baulks, real gas lamps on swan's-neck brass fittings, photographs of old packet boats and so forth. Bar food includes sandwiches (from 70p), ploughman's (£1.40), home-made shepherd's pie (£1.70), liver and onions (£1.90), salads (from £2.20, beef or salmon £2.30) and scampi (£2.30); Bass on handpump; darts and piped music. *(Recommended by Simon Turner)*

Randalls   Licensee D Ellis   Real ale   Meals and snacks (lunchtime)   Open 10–11 all year

ST JOHN (Jersey)   OS620564 Map 1
Les Fontaines

Le Grand Mourier, Route du Nord

The main attraction in this country pub, set on the northernmost tip of the island, is the one marvellously unspoilt bar, tucked away unobtrusively, and nigh inaccessible to all but the most determined tourist. Either look for the worn and unmarked door at the side of the building, or as you go down the main entry lobby towards the bigger main bar slip through the tiny narrow unmarked door on your right. This is where the locals hide out, and where you'll hear the true Jersey patois. It has very heavy beams in its low dark ochre ceiling, stripped irregular red granite walls, old-fashioned red leatherette cushioned settles and solid black tables on the quarry-tiled floor, a massive fourteenth-century inglenook fireplace with a granite column supporting its great mantelstones (throwing out great waves of warmth from its winter log fire), and for decoration antique prints and Staffordshire china figurines and dogs. The main bar is clean and carpeted, and has plenty of wheel-back chairs around neat dark tables, and a spiral staircase up to a wooden gallery under the high pine-raftered plank ceiling. There are pool, bar billiards, pin-table, shove-ha'penny, three space games, juke box or piped music here, and darts, dominoes and cribbage in the original bar. Bar food includes soup (70p), sandwiches (£1), ploughman's (£2), burgers (from £1.80), steak and kidney or chicken and bacon pie (£2), trout (£2.70) and eight-ounce sirloin steak (£3.95); Bass on handpump (64p) and cheap house wine. *(Recommended by Brian Barefoot, Simon Turner)*

Randalls   Licensee Malcolm Shaw   Real ale   Meals and snacks (not Sun)   Children in eating area   Open 11–11 all year

---

Stars after the name of a pub show exceptional quality. One star means most people (after reading the report to see just why the star has been won) would think a special trip worth while. Two stars mean that the pub is really outstanding – one of just a handful in its region. The very very few with three stars are the real aristocrats – of their type, they could hardly be improved.